General, Organic, and Biological Chemistry

Structures of Life

Fifth Edition

Karen C. Timberlake

Contributions by
Laura Frost, Ph.D.
Director, Whitaker Center for STEM Education
Professor of Chemistry
Florida Gulf Coast University

PEARSON

Editor in Chief: Jeanne Zalesky
Senior Acquisitions Editor: Terry Haugen
Project Manager: Lisa Pierce
Program Manager: Coleen Morrison
Editorial Assistant: Caitlin Falco
Director of Development: Jennifer Hart
Product Marketing Manager: Will Moore
Field Marketing Manager: Chris Barker
Program Management Team Lead: Kristen Flathman
Project Management Team Lead: David Zielonka
Senior Project Manager: Jenna Vittorioso, Lumina Datamatics, Inc.
Copyeditor: Lumina Datamatics, Inc.
Compositor: Lumina Datamatics, Inc.
Art Coordinator: Wynne Au Yeung
Design Manager: Derek Bacchus
Interior Designer: Jerilyn Bockorick
Cover Designer: Jerilyn Bockorick
Illustrator: Imagineering
Text Permissions Manager: William Opaluch
Rights & Permissions Management: Rachel Youdelman
Photo Researchers: Steve Merland and Jennifer Simmons
Senior Specialist, Manufacturing: Maura Zaldivar-Garcia
Cover Photo Credit: ©Catalin Petolea/Shutterstock.com

Library of Congress Cataloging-in-Publication Data

Timberlake, Karen C., author.
  General, organic, and biological chemistry : structures of life / Karen C. Timberlake.—Fifth edition.
    pages cm
Includes bibliographical references and index.
  ISBN 978-0-321-96746-6 (alk. paper)—ISBN 0-321-96746-1 (alk. paper)
  1. Chemistry—Textbooks. I. Title.
  QD33.2.T56 2016
  540—dc23

                                            2014032010

ISBN-10: 0-321-96746-1; ISBN-13: 978-0-321-96746-6
Printed in the United States of America

2 3 4 5 6 7 8 9 10—V011—18 17 16 15

Atomic Masses of the Elements

Name	Symbol	Atomic Number	Atomic Mass[a]	Name	Symbol	Atomic Number	Atomic Mass[a]
Actinium	Ac	89	(227)[b]	Mendelevium	Md	101	(258)
Aluminum	Al	13	26.98	Mercury	Hg	80	200.6
Americium	Am	95	(243)	Molybdenum	Mo	42	95.94
Antimony	Sb	51	121.8	Neodymium	Nd	60	144.2
Argon	Ar	18	39.95	Neon	Ne	10	20.18
Arsenic	As	33	74.92	Neptunium	Np	93	(237)
Astatine	At	85	(210)	Nickel	Ni	28	58.69
Barium	Ba	56	137.3	Niobium	Nb	41	92.91
Berkelium	Bk	97	(247)	Nitrogen	N	7	14.01
Beryllium	Be	4	9.012	Nobelium	No	102	(259)
Bismuth	Bi	83	209.0	Osmium	Os	76	190.2
Bohrium	Bh	107	(264)	Oxygen	O	8	16.00
Boron	B	5	10.81	Palladium	Pd	46	106.4
Bromine	Br	35	79.90	Phosphorus	P	15	30.97
Cadmium	Cd	48	112.4	Platinum	Pt	78	195.1
Calcium	Ca	20	40.08	Plutonium	Pu	94	(244)
Californium	Cf	98	(251)	Polonium	Po	84	(209)
Carbon	C	6	12.01	Potassium	K	19	39.10
Cerium	Ce	58	140.1	Praseodymium	Pr	59	140.9
Cesium	Cs	55	132.9	Promethium	Pm	61	(145)
Chlorine	Cl	17	35.45	Protactinium	Pa	91	231.0
Chromium	Cr	24	52.00	Radium	Ra	88	(226)
Cobalt	Co	27	58.93	Radon	Rn	86	(222)
Copernicium	Cn	112	(285)	Rhenium	Re	75	186.2
Copper	Cu	29	63.55	Rhodium	Rh	45	102.9
Curium	Cm	96	(247)	Roentgenium	Rg	111	(272)
Darmstadtium	Ds	110	(271)	Rubidium	Rb	37	85.47
Dubnium	Db	105	(262)	Ruthenium	Ru	44	101.1
Dysprosium	Dy	66	162.5	Rutherfordium	Rf	104	(261)
Einsteinium	Es	99	(252)	Samarium	Sm	62	150.4
Erbium	Er	68	167.3	Scandium	Sc	21	44.96
Europium	Eu	63	152.0	Seaborgium	Sg	106	(266)
Fermium	Fm	100	(257)	Selenium	Se	34	78.96
Flerovium	Fl	114	(289)	Silicon	Si	14	28.09
Fluorine	F	9	19.00	Silver	Ag	47	107.9
Francium	Fr	87	(223)	Sodium	Na	11	22.99
Gadolinium	Gd	64	157.3	Strontium	Sr	38	87.62
Gallium	Ga	31	69.72	Sulfur	S	16	32.07
Germanium	Ge	32	72.64	Tantalum	Ta	73	180.9
Gold	Au	79	197.0	Technetium	Tc	43	(99)
Hafnium	Hf	72	178.5	Tellurium	Te	52	127.6
Hassium	Hs	108	(265)	Terbium	Tb	65	158.9
Helium	He	2	4.003	Thallium	Tl	81	204.4
Holmium	Ho	67	164.9	Thorium	Th	90	232.0
Hydrogen	H	1	1.008	Thulium	Tm	69	168.9
Indium	In	49	114.8	Tin	Sn	50	118.7
Iodine	I	53	126.9	Titanium	Ti	22	47.87
Iridium	Ir	77	192.2	Tungsten	W	74	183.8
Iron	Fe	26	55.85	Uranium	U	92	238.0
Krypton	Kr	36	83.80	Vanadium	V	23	50.94
Lanthanum	La	57	138.9	Xenon	Xe	54	131.3
Lawrencium	Lr	103	(262)	Ytterbium	Yb	70	173.0
Lead	Pb	82	207.2	Yttrium	Y	39	88.91
Lithium	Li	3	6.941	Zinc	Zn	30	65.41
Livermorium	Lv	116	(293)	Zirconium	Zr	40	91.22
Lutetium	Lu	71	175.0	—	—	113	(284)
Magnesium	Mg	12	24.31	—	—	115	(288)
Manganese	Mn	25	54.94	—	—	117	(293)
Meitnerium	Mt	109	(268)	—	—	118	(294)

[a]Values for atomic masses are given to four significant figures.
[b]Values in parentheses are the mass number of an important radioactive isotope.

Brief Contents

1 Chemistry in Our Lives 1

2 Chemistry and Measurements 25

3 Matter and Energy 62

4 Atoms 101

5 Nuclear Chemistry 151

6 Ionic and Molecular Compounds 183

7 Chemical Reactions and Quantities 235

8 Gases 288

9 Solutions 324

10 Reaction Rates and Chemical Equilibrium 370

11 Acids and Bases 399

12 Introduction to Organic Chemistry: Hydrocarbons 443

13 Alcohols, Phenols, Thiols, and Ethers 488

14 Aldehydes, Ketones, and Chiral Molecules 516

15 Carbohydrates 550

16 Carboxylic Acids and Esters 580

17 Lipids 608

18 Amines and Amides 649

19 Amino Acids and Proteins 688

20 Enzymes and Vitamins 722

21 Nucleic Acids and Protein Synthesis 753

22 Metabolic Pathways for Carbohydrates 797

23 Metabolism and Energy Production 836

24 Metabolic Pathways for Lipids and Amino Acids 861

Contents

1 Chemistry in Our Lives 1

CAREER: Forensic Scientist 1

1.1 Chemistry and Chemicals 2

1.2 Scientific Method: Thinking Like a Scientist 4

EXPLORE YOUR WORLD Nobel Prize Winners in Chemistry 4

CHEMISTRY LINK TO HEALTH Early Chemist: Paracelsus 5

1.3 Learning Chemistry: A Study Plan 6

1.4 Key Math Skills for Chemistry 9

GUIDE to Writing a Number in Scientific Notation 17

CLINICAL APPLICATIONS 4, 6, 19

CLINICAL UPDATE Forensic Evidence Solves the Murder 19

Concept Map 19
Chapter Review 20
Key Terms 20
Key Math Skills 20
Understanding the Concepts 22
Additional Questions and Problems 22
Challenge Questions 23
Answers 24

2 Chemistry and Measurements 25

CAREER: Registered Nurse 25

2.1 Units of Measurement 26

EXPLORE YOUR WORLD Units Listed on Labels 29

2.2 Measured Numbers and Significant Figures 30

2.3 Significant Figures in Calculations 32

2.4 Prefixes and Equalities 36

2.5 Writing Conversion Factors 39

EXPLORE YOUR WORLD SI and Metric Equalities on Product Labels 40

2.6 Problem Solving Using Unit Conversion 44

GUIDE to Problem Solving Using Conversion Factors 44

CHEMISTRY LINK TO HEALTH Toxicology and Risk–Benefit Assessment 47

2.7 Density 49

EXPLORE YOUR WORLD Sink or Float 50

CHEMISTRY LINK TO HEALTH Bone Density 51

GUIDE to Using Density 51

CLINICAL APPLICATIONS 29, 32, 44, 48, 53, 59

CLINICAL UPDATE Greg's Follow-Up Visit with His Doctor 53

Concept Map 54
Chapter Review 54
Key Terms 55
Key Math Skill 56
Core Chemistry Skills 56
Understanding the Concepts 57
Additional Questions and Problems 58
Challenge Questions 59
Answers 60

3 Matter and Energy 62

CAREER: Dietitian 62

3.1 Classification of Matter 63

CHEMISTRY LINK TO HEALTH Breathing Mixtures 66

3.2 States and Properties of Matter 67

3.3 Temperature 69

GUIDE to Calculating Temperature 71

CHEMISTRY LINK TO HEALTH Variation in Body Temperature 72

3.4 Energy 73

CHEMISTRY LINK TO THE ENVIRONMENT   Carbon Dioxide and Climate Change   75

3.5   **Energy and Nutrition**   76
GUIDE to Calculating the Energy from a Food   78
EXPLORE YOUR WORLD   Counting Calories   78
CHEMISTRY LINK TO HEALTH   Losing and Gaining Weight   78

3.6   **Specific Heat**   80
GUIDE to Calculations Using Specific Heat   81

3.7   **Changes of State**   81
GUIDE to Using a Heat Conversion Factor   83
CHEMISTRY LINK TO HEALTH   Steam Burns   86
CLINICAL APPLICATIONS   73, 79, 90, 95, 96
CLINICAL UPDATE   A Diet and Exercise Program for Charles   90

Concept Map   91
Chapter Review   91
Key Terms   92
Core Chemistry Skills   93
Understanding the Concepts   94
Additional Questions and Problems   95
Challenge Questions   97
Answers   97
Combining Ideas from Chapters 1 to 3   99
Answers   100

4
Atoms   101

CAREER: Farmer   101

4.1   **Elements and Symbols**   102
CHEMISTRY LINK TO HEALTH   Latin Names for Elements in Clinical Usage   104
CHEMISTRY LINK TO HEALTH   Toxicity of Mercury   104

4.2   **The Periodic Table**   105
CHEMISTRY LINK TO HEALTH   Elements Essential to Health   108

4.3   **The Atom**   110
EXPLORE YOUR WORLD   Repulsion and Attraction   113

4.4   **Atomic Number and Mass Number**   114
CHEMISTRY LINK TO THE ENVIRONMENT   Many Forms of Carbon   116

4.5   **Isotopes and Atomic Mass**   117
GUIDE to Calculating Atomic Mass   120

4.6   **Electron Energy Levels**   121
CHEMISTRY LINK TO HEALTH   Biological Reactions to UV Light   122

CHEMISTRY LINK TO THE ENVIRONMENT   Energy-Saving Fluorescent Bulbs   123

4.7   **Electron Configurations**   127
GUIDE to Drawing Orbital Diagrams   129
GUIDE to Writing Electron Configurations Using Sublevel Blocks   132

4.8   **Trends in Periodic Properties**   135
CLINICAL APPLICATIONS   104, 110, 117, 141
CLINICAL UPDATE   Improving Crop Production   141

Concept Map   142
Chapter Review   142
Key Terms   144
Core Chemistry Skills   145
Understanding the Concepts   146
Additional Questions and Problems   147
Challenge Questions   148
Answers   149

5
Nuclear Chemistry   151

CAREER: Nuclear Medicine Technologist   151

5.1   **Natural Radioactivity**   152

5.2   **Nuclear Reactions**   156
GUIDE to Completing a Nuclear Equation   157
CHEMISTRY LINK TO HEALTH   Radon in Our Homes   157

5.3   **Radiation Measurement**   162
CHEMISTRY LINK TO HEALTH   Radiation and Food   163

5.4   **Half-Life of a Radioisotope**   165
GUIDE to Using Half-Lives   166
CHEMISTRY LINK TO THE ENVIRONMENT   Dating Ancient Objects   167

5.5   **Medical Applications Using Radioactivity**   169
CHEMISTRY LINK TO HEALTH   Brachytherapy   171

5.6   **Nuclear Fission and Fusion**   172
CHEMISTRY LINK TO THE ENVIRONMENT   Nuclear Power Plants   175
CLINICAL APPLICATIONS   155, 165, 169, 172, 176, 180, 181
CLINICAL UPDATE   Cardiac Imaging Using a Radioisotope   176

Concept Map   176
Chapter Review   177
Key Terms   177

Core Chemistry Skills   178
Understanding the Concepts   178
Additional Questions and Problems   179
Challenge Questions   180
Answers   181

Understanding the Concepts   227
Additional Questions and Problems   228
Challenge Questions   229
Answers   230
Combining Ideas from Chapters 4 to 6   233
Answers   234

6
Ionic and Molecular Compounds   183

CAREER: Pharmacy Technician   183
6.1   Ions: Transfer of Electrons   184
      CHEMISTRY LINK TO HEALTH   Some Important Ions in the Body   188
6.2   Writing Formulas for Ionic Compounds   189
6.3   Naming and Writing Ionic Formulas   192
      GUIDE to Naming Ionic Compounds with Metals that Form a Single Ion   192
      GUIDE to Naming Ionic Compounds with Variable Charge Metals   194
      GUIDE to Writing Formulas from the Name of an Ionic Compound   195
6.4   Polyatomic Ions   196
      GUIDE to Writing Formulas with Polyatomic Ions   198
      GUIDE to Naming Ionic Compounds with Polyatomic Ions   199
6.5   Molecular Compounds: Sharing Electrons   200
      GUIDE to Naming Molecular Compounds   201
      GUIDE to Writing Formulas for Molecular Compounds   202
6.6   Lewis Structures for Molecules and Polyatomic Ions   204
      GUIDE to Drawing Lewis Structures   206
6.7   Electronegativity and Bond Polarity   209
6.8   Shapes and Polarity of Molecules   212
      GUIDE to Predicting Shape (VSEPR Theory)   215
      GUIDE to Determining the Polarity of a Molecule   217
6.9   Attractive Forces in Compounds   218
      CHEMISTRY LINK TO HEALTH   Attractive Forces in Biological Compounds   220
      CLINICAL APPLICATIONS   189, 196, 200, 204, 222
      CLINICAL UPDATE   Compounds at the Pharmacy   222

      Concept Map   223
      Chapter Review   223
      Key Terms   225
      Core Chemistry Skills   225

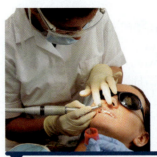

7
Chemical Reactions and Quantities   235

CAREER: Dental Hygienist   235
7.1   Equations for Chemical Reactions   236
      GUIDE to Balancing a Chemical Equation   240
7.2   Types of Reactions   243
      CHEMISTRY LINK TO HEALTH   Incomplete Combustion: Toxicity of Carbon Monoxide   247
7.3   Oxidation–Reduction Reactions   248
      EXPLORE YOUR WORLD   Oxidation of Fruits and Vegetables   250
7.4   The Mole   251
      GUIDE to Calculating the Atoms or Molecules of a Substance   253
      GUIDE to Calculating the Moles of an Element in a Compound   254
7.5   Molar Mass and Calculations   255
      GUIDE to Calculating Molar Mass   256
      EXPLORE YOUR WORLD   Calculating Moles in the Kitchen   256
      GUIDE to Calculating the Moles (or Grams) of a Substance from Grams (or Moles)   258
7.6   Mole Relationships in Chemical Equations   260
      GUIDE to Calculating the Quantities of Reactants and Products in a Chemical Reaction   262
7.7   Mass Calculations for Reactions   263
7.8   Limiting Reactants and Percent Yield   265
      GUIDE to Calculating the Moles of Product from a Limiting Reactant   266
      GUIDE to Calculating the Grams of Product from a Limiting Reactant   267
      GUIDE to Calculations for Percent Yield   269
7.9   Energy in Chemical Reactions   271
      GUIDE to Calculating Using the Heat of Reaction   273
      CHEMISTRY LINK TO HEALTH   Cold Packs and Hot Packs   273
      CLINICAL APPLICATIONS   243, 251, 255, 259, 265, 274, 275, 284
      CLINICAL UPDATE   Whitening of Tooth Enamel   275

Concept Map   276
Chapter Review   276
Key Terms   277
Core Chemistry Skills   278
Understanding the Concepts   280
Additional Questions and Problems   283
Challenge Questions   285
Answers   286

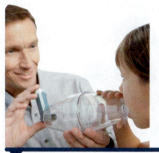

8
Gases 288

CAREER: Respiratory Therapist   288
8.1   Properties of Gases   289
EXPLORE YOUR WORLD   Forming a Gas   291
CHEMISTRY LINK TO HEALTH   Measuring Blood Pressure   294
8.2   Pressure and Volume (Boyle's Law)   295
GUIDE to Using the Gas Laws   296
CHEMISTRY LINK TO HEALTH   Pressure–Volume Relationship in Breathing   296
8.3   Temperature and Volume (Charles's Law)   298
8.4   Temperature and Pressure (Gay-Lussac's Law)   300
8.5   The Combined Gas Law   303
8.6   Volume and Moles (Avogadro's Law)   304
GUIDE to Using Molar Volume   307
8.7   The Ideal Gas Law   308
GUIDE to Using the Ideal Gas Law   309
CHEMISTRY LINK TO HEALTH   Hyperbaric Chambers   310
GUIDE to Using the Ideal Gas Law for Reactions   311
8.8   Partial Pressures (Dalton's Law)   312
GUIDE to Calculating Partial Pressure   313
CHEMISTRY LINK TO HEALTH   Blood Gases   314
CLINICAL APPLICATIONS   294, 297, 302, 312, 314, 315, 320
CLINICAL UPDATE   Exercise-Induced Asthma   315

Concept Map   315
Chapter Review   316
Key Terms   317
Core Chemistry Skills   317
Understanding the Concepts   318
Additional Questions and Problems   319
Challenge Questions   320
Answers   320
Combining Ideas from Chapters 7 and 8   322
Answers   323

9
Solutions 324

CAREER: Dialysis Nurse   324
9.1   Solutions   325
CHEMISTRY LINK TO HEALTH   Water in the Body   327
EXPLORE YOUR WORLD   Live Dissolves Like   328
9.2   Electrolytes and Nonelectrolytes   329
CHEMISTRY LINK TO HEALTH   Electrolytes in Body Fluids   331
9.3   Solubility   333
CHEMISTRY LINK TO HEALTH   Gout and Kidney Stones: A Problem of Saturation in Body Fluids   334
EXPLORE YOUR WORLD   Preparing Rock Candy   335
EXPLORE YOUR WORLD   Preparing Solutions   336
GUIDE to Writing an Equation for the Formation of an Insoluble Ionic Compound   338
9.4   Solution Concentrations and Reactions   339
GUIDE to Calculating Solution Concentration   340
GUIDE to Using Concentration to Calculate Mass or Volume   344
GUIDE to Calculations Involving Solutions in Chemical Reactions   345
9.5   Dilution of Solutions   349
GUIDE to Calculating Dilution Quantities   350
9.6   Properties of Solutions   352
CHEMISTRY LINK TO HEALTH   Colloids and Solutions in the Body   353
GUIDE to Calculating Freezing Point Lowering/Boiling Point Elevation   355
EXPLORE YOUR WORLD   Everyday Osmosis   356
GUIDE to Calculating Osmolarity   357
CHEMISTRY LINK TO HEALTH   Dialysis by the Kidneys and the Artificial Kidney   359
CLINICAL APPLICATIONS   329, 333, 348, 351, 361, 367, 368
CLINICAL UPDATE   Using Dialysis for Renal Failure   361

Concept Map   362
Chapter Review   362
Key Terms   363
Core Chemistry Skills   364
Understanding the Concepts   365
Additional Questions and Problems   366
Challenge Questions   367
Answers   368

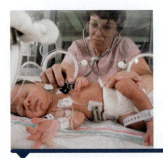

10
Reaction Rates and Chemical Equilibrium 370

CAREER: Neonatal Nurse   370

10.1 Rates of Reactions   372

CHEMISTRY LINK TO THE ENVIRONMENT   Catalytic Converters   375

10.2 Chemical Equilibrium   377

10.3 Equilibrium Constants   380

GUIDE to Writing the Equilibrium Constant Expression   381

GUIDE to Calculating the K_c Value   382

10.4 Using Equilibrium Constants   383

GUIDE to Using the Equilibrium Constant   385

10.5 Changing Equilibrium Conditions: Le Châtelier's Principle   387

CHEMISTRY LINK TO HEALTH   Oxygen–Hemoglobin Equilibrium and Hypoxia   389

CHEMISTRY LINK TO HEALTH   Homeostasis: Regulation of Body Temperature   392

CLINICAL APPLICATIONS   393

CLINICAL UPDATE   An Iron-Rich Diet for Children's Anemia   393

Concept Map   394
Chapter Review   394
Key Terms   395
Core Chemistry Skills   395
Understanding the Concepts   396
Additional Questions and Problems   396
Challenge Questions   397
Answers   398

11
Acids and Bases 399

CAREER: Clinical Laboratory Technician   399

11.1 Acids and Bases   400

11.2 Brønsted–Lowry Acids and Bases   403

GUIDE to Writing Conjugate Acid–Base Pairs   405

11.3 Strengths of Acids and Bases   406

11.4 Dissociation Constants for Acids and Bases   411

11.5 Dissociation of Water   413

GUIDE to Calculating $[H_3O^+]$ and $[OH^-]$ in Aqueous Solutions   415

11.6 The pH Scale   416

GUIDE to Calculating pH of an Aqueous Solution   419

GUIDE to Calculating $[H_3O^+]$ from pH   421

CHEMISTRY LINK TO HEALTH   Stomach Acid, HCl   422

11.7 Reactions of Acids and Bases   423

GUIDE to Balancing an Equation for Neutralization   424

CHEMISTRY LINK TO HEALTH   Antacids   424

11.8 Acid–Base Titration   425

GUIDE to Calculations for an Acid–Base Titration   426

11.9 Buffers   427

GUIDE to Calculating pH of a Buffer   429

CHEMISTRY LINK TO HEALTH   Buffers in the Blood Plasma   430

CLINICAL APPLICATIONS   416, 422, 432, 437, 438, 441

CLINICAL UPDATE   Acid Reflux Disease   432

Concept Map   433
Chapter Review   433
Key Terms   434
Key Math Skills   435
Core Chemistry Skills   435
Understanding the Concepts   436
Additional Questions and Problems   437
Challenge Questions   438
Answers   439
Combining Ideas from Chapters 9 to 11   441
Answers   442

12
Introduction to Organic Chemistry: Hydrocarbons 443

CAREER: Firefighter/Emergency Medical Technician   443

12.1 Organic Compounds   444

12.2 Alkanes   447

GUIDE to Drawing Structural Formulas for Alkanes   448

12.3 Alkanes with Substituents   451

GUIDE to Naming Alkanes with Substituents   454

GUIDE to Drawing Structural Formulas for Alkanes with Substituents   455

12.4 Properties of Alkanes 457
12.5 Alkenes and Alkynes 460
   EXPLORE YOUR WORLD Ripening Fruit 461
   GUIDE to Naming Alkenes and Alkynes 461
   CHEMISTRY LINK TO THE ENVIRONMENT Fragrant Alkenes 463
12.6 Cis–Trans Isomers 464
   EXPLORE YOUR WORLD Modeling Cis–Trans Isomers 465
   CHEMISTRY LINK TO THE ENVIRONMENT Pheromones in Insect Communication 466
   CHEMISTRY LINK TO HEALTH Cis-Trans Isomers for Night Vision 467
12.7 Addition Reactions for Alkenes 468
   EXPLORE YOUR WORLD Unsaturation in Fats and Oils 468
   CHEMISTRY LINK TO HEALTH Hydrogenation of Unsaturated Fats 469
   EXPLORE YOUR WORLD Polymers and Recycling Plastics 472
12.8 Aromatic Compounds 473
   CHEMISTRY LINK TO HEALTH Some Common Aromatic Compounds in Nature and Medicine 475
   CHEMISTRY LINK TO HEALTH Polycyclic Aromatic Hydrocarbons (PAHs) 477
   CLINICAL APPLICATIONS 477
   CLINICAL UPDATE Diane's Treatment in the Burn Unit 477

   Concept Map 478
   Chapter Review 479
   Summary of Naming 480
   Summary of Reactions 480
   Key Terms 481
   Core Chemistry Skills 481
   Understanding the Concepts 482
   Additional Questions and Problems 483
   Challenge Questions 485
   Answers 485

   CHEMISTRY LINK TO HEALTH Some Important Alcohols and Phenols 492
13.2 Ethers 495
   GUIDE to Writing IUPAC Names for Ethers 496
   CHEMISTRY LINK TO HEALTH Ethers as Anesthetics 496
13.3 Physical Properties of Alcohols, Phenols, and Ethers 497
   CHEMISTRY LINK TO HEALTH Hand Sanitizers and Ethanol 500
13.4 Reactions of Alcohols and Thiols 501
   CHEMISTRY LINK TO HEALTH Methanol Poisoning 503
   CHEMISTRY LINK TO HEALTH Oxidation of Alcohol in the Body 505
   CLINICAL APPLICATIONS 507, 512
   CLINICAL UPDATE Janet's New Diet Plan 507

   Concept Map 508
   Chapter Review 508
   Summary of Naming 509
   Summary of Reactions 509
   Key Terms 509
   Core Chemistry Skills 510
   Understanding the Concepts 510
   Additional Questions and Problems 511
   Challenge Questions 513
   Answers 513

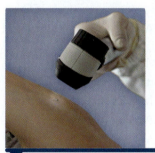

14
Aldehydes, Ketones, and Chiral Molecules 516

   CAREER: Dermatology Nurse 516
14.1 Aldehydes and Ketones 517
   GUIDE to Naming Aldehydes 518
   GUIDE to Naming Ketones 520
   CHEMISTRY LINK TO HEALTH Some Important Aldehydes and Ketones 521
14.2 Physical Properties of Aldehydes and Ketones 523
14.3 Oxidation and Reduction of Aldehydes and Ketones 525
14.4 Hemiacetals and Acetals 527
14.5 Chiral Molecules 531
   EXPLORE YOUR WORLD Using Gumdrops and Toothpicks to Model Chiral Objects 533

13
Alcohols, Phenols, Thiols, and Ethers 488

   CAREER: Nurse Anesthetist 488
13.1 Alcohols, Phenols, and Thiols 489
   GUIDE to Naming Alcohols and Phenols 491
   EXPLORE YOUR WORLD Alcohols in Household Products 491

CHEMISTRY LINK TO HEALTH   Enantiomers in Biological Systems   536
CLINICAL APPLICATIONS   522, 538, 539
CLINICAL UPDATE   Diana's Skin Protection Plan   539

Concept Map   539
Chapter Review   540
Summary of Naming   540
Summary of Reactions   541
Key Terms   541
Core Chemistry Skills   541
Understanding the Concepts   542
Additional Questions and Problems   543
Challenge Questions   545
Answers   545
Combining Ideas from Chapters 12 to 14   548
Answers   549

15
Carbohydrates   550

CAREER: Diabetes Nurse   550
15.1 Carbohydrates   551
15.2 Fischer Projections of Monosaccharides   554
GUIDE to Identifying D- or L-Monosaccharides   555
CHEMISTRY LINK TO HEALTH   Hyperglycemia and Hypoglycemia   557
15.3 Haworth Structures of Monosaccharides   558
GUIDE to Drawing Haworth Structures   560
15.4 Chemical Properties of Monosaccharides   561
CHEMISTRY LINK TO HEALTH   Testing for Glucose   563
15.5 Disaccharides   564
EXPLORE YOUR WORLD   Sugar and Sweeteners   565
CHEMISTRY LINK TO HEALTH   How Sweet Is My Sweetener?   566
CHEMISTRY LINK TO HEALTH   Blood Types and Carbohydrates   567
15.6 Polysaccharides   570
EXPLORE YOUR WORLD   Polysaccharides   572
CLINICAL APPLICATIONS   554, 558, 570, 572, 573
CLINICAL UPDATE   Kate's Program for Type 2 Diabetes   573

Concept Map   573
Chapter Review   574
Summary of Carbohydrates   574
Summary of Reactions   575
Key Terms   575
Core Chemistry Skills   576
Understanding the Concepts   576
Additional Questions and Problems   577
Challenge Questions   578
Answers   578

16
Carboxylic Acids and Esters   580

CAREER: Surgical Technician   580
16.1 Carboxylic Acids   581
GUIDE to Naming Carboxylic Acids   583
CHEMISTRY LINK TO HEALTH   Alpha Hydroxy Acids   583
16.2 Properties of Carboxylic Acids   585
CHEMISTRY LINK TO HEALTH   Carboxylic Acids in Metabolism   589
16.3 Esters   590
CHEMISTRY LINK TO HEALTH   Salicylic Acid from a Willow Tree   591
CHEMISTRY LINK TO THE ENVIRONMENT   Plastics   592
16.4 Naming Esters   593
GUIDE to Naming Esters   595
16.5 Properties of Esters   596
CLINICAL APPLICATIONS   599, 602
CLINICAL UPDATE   Liquid Bandages   599

Concept Map   599
Chapter Review   600
Summary of Naming   600
Summary of Reactions   601
Key Terms   601
Core Chemistry Skills   602
Understanding the Concepts   602
Additional Questions and Problems   602
Challenge Questions   604
Answers   605

17

Lipids 608

CAREER: Clinical Lipid Specialist 608

17.1 Lipids 609

17.2 Fatty Acids 610

EXPLORE YOUR WORLD Solubility of Fats and Oils 611

CHEMISTRY LINK TO HEALTH Omega-3 Fatty Acids in Fish Oils 615

17.3 Waxes and Triacylglycerols 617

GUIDE to Drawing Triacylglycerols 618

17.4 Chemical Properties of Triacylglycerols 621

CHEMISTRY LINK TO HEALTH Converting Unsaturated Fats to Saturated Fats: Hydrogenation and Interesterification 622

EXPLORE YOUR WORLD Types of Fats 624

CHEMISTRY LINK TO THE ENVIRONMENT Biodiesel as an Alternative Fuel 625

17.5 Phospholipids 627

CHEMISTRY LINK TO HEALTH Infant Respiratory Distress Syndrome (IRDS) 630

17.6 Steroids: Cholesterol, Bile Salts, and Steroid Hormones 632

CHEMISTRY LINK TO HEALTH Anabolic Steroids 636

17.7 Cell Membranes 638

CLINICAL APPLICATIONS 610, 616, 620, 631, 637, 640, 644

CLINICAL UPDATE Rebecca's Program to Lower Cholesterol in Familial Hypercholesterolemia (FH) 640

Concept Map 641
Chapter Review 641
Summary of Reactions 642
Key Terms 643
Core Chemistry Skills 643
Understanding the Concepts 644
Additional Questions and Problems 644
Challenge Questions 645
Answers 646

18

Amines and Amides 649

CAREER: Environmental Health Practitioner 649

18.1 Amines 650

GUIDE to IUPAC Naming of Amines 651

GUIDE to Naming Compounds with Two Functional Groups 653

18.2 Properties of Amines 656

18.3 Heterocyclic Amines 661

CHEMISTRY LINK TO HEALTH Synthesizing Drugs 663

18.4 Neurotransmitters 664

18.5 Amides 671

GUIDE to Naming Amides 673

CHEMISTRY LINK TO HEALTH Amides in Health and Medicine 674

18.6 Hydrolysis of Amides 676

CLINICAL APPLICATIONS 661, 664, 670, 678, 681, 683

CLINICAL UPDATE Testing Soil and Water Samples for Chemicals 678

Concept Map 678
Chapter Review 679
Summary of Naming 679
Summary of Reactions 680
Key Terms 680
Core Chemistry Skills 681
Understanding the Concepts 681
Additional Questions and Problems 682
Challenge Questions 683
Answers 684
Combining Ideas from Chapters 15 to 18 686
Answers 687

19

Amino Acids and Proteins 688

CAREER: Radiology Technician 688

19.1 Proteins and Amino Acids 689

CHEMISTRY LINK TO HEALTH Essential Amino Acids 693

19.2 Amino Acids as Acids and Bases 694

19.3 Formation of Peptides 697

GUIDE to Drawing a Peptide 698

CHEMISTRY LINK TO HEALTH Polypeptides in the Body 699

19.4 Protein Structure: Primary and Secondary Levels 701

CHEMISTRY LINK TO HEALTH Protein Sequencing 702

CHEMISTRY LINK TO HEALTH Protein Secondary Structures and Alzheimer's Disease 705

19.5 Protein Structure: Tertiary and Quaternary Levels 706

CHEMISTRY LINK TO HEALTH   Sickle Cell Anemia   710

19.6 Protein Hydrolysis and Denaturation   711

EXPLORE YOUR WORLD   Denaturation of Milk Protein   713

CLINICAL APPLICATIONS   694, 700, 706, 714, 718

CLINICAL UPDATE   Alzheimer's Diagnosis   714

Concept Map   715
Chapter Review   715
Key Terms   716
Core Chemistry Skills   717
Understanding the Concepts   717
Additional Questions and Problems   718
Challenge Questions   719
Answers   719

20
Enzymes and Vitamins   722

CAREER: Physician Assistant   722

20.1 Enzymes and Enzyme Action   723

20.2 Classification of Enzymes   726

CHEMISTRY LINK TO HEALTH   Isoenzymes As Diagnostic Tools   728

20.3 Factors Affecting Enzyme Activity   729

EXPLORE YOUR WORLD   Enzyme Activity   731

20.4 Regulation of Enzyme Activity   732

20.5 Enzyme Inhibition   735

GUIDE to Determining Type of Enzyme Inhibition   738

20.6 Enzyme Cofactors and Vitamins   739

CLINICAL APPLICATIONS   729, 732, 735, 739, 744, 745, 748, 749, 750

CLINICAL UPDATE   Noah's Diet for Lactose Intolerance   744

Concept Map   745
Chapter Review   746
Key Terms   747
Core Chemistry Skills   747
Understanding the Concepts   748
Additional Questions and Problems   749
Challenge Questions   750
Answers to Selected Questions and Problems   751

21
Nucleic Acids and Protein Synthesis   753

CAREER: Histology Technician   753

21.1 Components of Nucleic Acids   754

21.2 Primary Structure of Nucleic Acids   759

21.3 DNA Double Helix   761

21.4 DNA Replication   763

21.5 RNA and Transcription   766

21.6 The Genetic Code and Protein Synthesis   771

CHEMISTRY LINK TO HEALTH   Many Antibiotics Inhibit Protein Synthesis   774

21.7 Genetic Mutations   776

EXPLORE YOUR WORLD   A Model for DNA Replication and Mutation   776

21.8 Recombinant DNA   780

21.9 Viruses   782

CHEMISTRY LINK TO HEALTH   Cancer   785

CLINICAL APPLICATIONS   758, 775, 779, 786, 787, 791

CLINICAL UPDATE   Ellen's Medical Treatment Following Breast Cancer Surgery   786

Concept Map   788
Chapter Review   788
Key Terms   789
Core Chemistry Skills   790
Understanding the Concepts   790
Additional Questions and Problems   791
Challenge Questions   792
Answers   792
Combining Ideas from Chapters 19 to 21   795
Answers   796

22
Metabolic Pathways for Carbohydrates   797

CAREER: Hepatology Nurse   797

22.1 Metabolism and Energy   798

CHEMISTRY LINK TO HEALTH   ATP Energy and Ca^{2+} Needed to Contract Muscles   803

22.2 Important Coenzymes in Metabolic Pathways 804

22.3 Digestion of Carbohydrates 808

22.4 Glycolysis: Oxidation of Glucose 810

22.5 Pathways for Pyruvate 816

22.6 Glycogen Synthesis and Degradation 819

CHEMISTRY LINK TO HEALTH Glycogen Storage Diseases (GSDs) 822

22.7 Gluconeogenesis: Glucose Synthesis 824

CLINICAL APPLICATIONS 804, 816, 819, 824, 829, 833

CLINICAL UPDATE Philip's Diet for von Gierke's Disease 829

Concept Map 829
Chapter Review 830
Summary of Key Reactions 831
Key Terms 831
Core Chemistry Skills 832
Understanding the Concepts 832
Additional Questions and Problems 833
Challenge Questions 834
Answers 834

23
Metabolism and Energy Production 836

CAREER: Exercise Physiologist 836

23.1 The Citric Acid Cycle 837

23.2 Electron Transport and ATP 844

CHEMISTRY LINK TO HEALTH Toxins: Inhibitors of Electron Transport 847

CHEMISTRY LINK TO HEALTH Uncouplers of ATP Synthase 849

23.3 ATP Energy from Glucose 851

CHEMISTRY LINK TO HEALTH Efficiency of ATP Production 854

CLINICAL APPLICATIONS 844, 850, 855, 859

CLINICAL UPDATE Improving Natalie's Overall Fitness 855

Concept Map 855
Chapter Review 856
Summary of Key Reactions 856
Key Terms 856
Core Chemistry Skills 857
Understanding the Concepts 857
Additional Questions and Problems 858
Challenge Questions 859
Answers to Selected Questions and Problems 859

24
Metabolic Pathways for Lipids and Amino Acids 861

CAREER: Public Health Nurse (PHN) 861

24.1 Digestion of Triacylglycerols 862

EXPLORE YOUR WORLD Digestion of Fats 864

24.2 Oxidation of Fatty Acids 865

24.3 ATP and Fatty Acid Oxidation 870

CHEMISTRY LINK TO HEALTH Stored Fat and Obesity 871

EXPLORE YOUR WORLD Fat Storage and Blubber 872

24.4 Ketogenesis and Ketone Bodies 873

CHEMISTRY LINK TO HEALTH Diabetes and Ketone Bodies 875

24.5 Fatty Acid Synthesis 876

24.6 Degradation of Proteins and Amino Acids 880

24.7 Urea Cycle 884

24.8 Fates of the Carbon Atoms from Amino Acids 886

24.9 Synthesis of Amino Acids 888

CHEMISTRY LINK TO HEALTH Phenylketonuria (PKU) 890

CLINICAL APPLICATIONS 865, 873, 875, 880, 886, 892, 896

CLINICAL UPDATE Treatment of Luke's Hepatitis C 892

Concept Map 893
Chapter Review 893
Summary of Key Reactions 894
Key Terms 895
Core Chemistry Skills 895
Understanding the Concepts 896
Additional Questions and Problems 896
Challenge Questions 897
Answers 898
Combining Ideas from Chapters 22 to 24 900
Answers 900

Credits C-1
Glossary/Index I-1

About the Author

Karen at the Natural History Museum where she is a supporter of children's environmental programs.

KAREN TIMBERLAKE is Professor Emerita of chemistry at Los Angeles Valley College, where **she taught chemistry for allied health and preparatory chemistry for 36 years.** She received her bachelor's degree in chemistry from the University of Washington and her master's degree in biochemistry from the University of California at Los Angeles.

Professor Timberlake has been writing chemistry textbooks for 40 years. During that time, her name **has become associated with the strategic use of pedagogical tools that promote student success in chemistry and the application of chemistry to real-life situations.** More than one million students have learned chemistry using texts, laboratory manuals, and study guides written by Karen Timberlake. In addition to *General, Organic, and Biological Chemistry: Structures of Life,* fifth edition, she is also the author of *Chemistry: An Introduction to General, Organic, and Biological Chemistry,* twelfth edition, with the accompanying *Study Guide and Selected Solutions Manual,* and *Basic Chemistry,* fourth edition, with the accompanying *Study Guide and Selected Solutions Manual, Laboratory Manual,* and *Essentials Laboratory Manual.*

Professor Timberlake belongs to numerous scientific and educational organizations including the American Chemical Society (ACS) and the National Science Teachers Association (NSTA). She has been the Western Regional Winner of Excellence in College Chemistry Teaching Award given by the Chemical Manufacturers Association. She received the McGuffey Award in Physical Sciences from the Textbook Authors Association for her textbook *Chemistry: An Introduction to General, Organic, and Biological Chemistry,* eighth edition, which has demonstrated her excellence over time. She received the "Texty" Textbook Excellence Award from the Textbook Authors Association for the first edition of *Basic Chemistry.* She has participated in education grants for science teaching including the Los Angeles Collaborative for Teaching Excellence (LACTE) and a Title III grant at her college. She speaks at conferences and educational meetings on the use of student-centered teaching methods in chemistry to promote the learning success of students.

When Professor Timberlake is not writing textbooks, she and her husband relax by playing tennis, ballroom dancing, traveling, trying new restaurants, cooking, and taking care of their grandchildren, Daniel and Emily.

DEDICATION

I dedicate this book to

- My husband, Bill, for his patience, loving support, and preparation of late meals

- My son, John, daughter-in-law, Cindy, grandson, Daniel, and granddaughter, Emily, for the precious things in life

- The wonderful students over many years whose hard work and commitment always motivated me and put purpose in my writing

FAVORITE QUOTES

The whole art of teaching is only the art of awakening the natural curiosity of young minds.

—Anatole France

One must learn by doing the thing; though you think you know it, you have no certainty until you try.

—Sophocles

Discovery consists of seeing what everybody has seen and thinking what nobody has thought.

—Albert Szent-Györgyi

I never teach my pupils; I only attempt to provide the conditions in which they can learn.

—Albert Einstein

Preface

Welcome to the fifth edition of *General, Organic, and Biological Chemistry: Structures of Life*. This chemistry text was written and designed to help you prepare for a career in a health-related profession, such as nursing, dietetics, respiratory therapy, and environmental and agricultural science. This text assumes no prior knowledge of chemistry. My main objective in writing this text is to make the study of chemistry an engaging and a positive experience for you by relating the structure and behavior of matter to its role in health and the environment.

It is my goal to help you become a critical thinker by understanding scientific concepts that will form a basis for making important decisions about issues concerning health and the environment. Thus, I have utilized materials that

- help you to learn and enjoy chemistry
- relate chemistry to clinical stories and careers that interest you
- develop problem-solving skills that lead to your success in chemistry
- promote learning and success in chemistry

New for the Fifth Edition

This new edition introduces chemistry in a clinical environment beginning with the stories of patients in the Chapter Openers and Clinical Updates that follow the diagnosis and treatment for the patients. New problem-solving strategies include Key Math Skills; Core Chemistry Skills; new Analyze the Problem features; more Guides to Problem Solving; and new Clinical Applications throughout each chapter that add clinical relevance to the chemistry content.

- **NEW AND UPDATED! Chapter Openers** now provide engaging clinical stories in which a metabolic or genetic condition introduces the content of each chapter.
- **NEW! Clinical Careers** include lipidology nurse, exercise physiologist, hepatology nurse, and public health nurse.
- **NEW! Clinical Updates** give a follow up of the diagnosis and treatment for each patient in the Chapter Openers.
- **NEW! Clinical Applications** are added to Questions and Problems sets that show the relevance between the chemistry content and the clinical story.
- **NEW! Biochemistry Chapters 19 to 24** contain new and expanded material on recent topics in biochemistry including **CH 19** Alzheimer's and beta-amyloid proteins that form plaques in the brain, **CH 20** lactose intolerance and breath hydrogen test, **CH 21** transcription factors, the estrogen receptor, and the impact of altered genes BRAC1 and BRAC2 in breast cancer, **CH 22** enzyme deficiencies in glycogen storage diseases, and **CH 23** malate-aspartate

pathway added, ATP energy values updated to 2.5 ATP for NADH and 1.5 ATP for $FADH_2$, and **CH 24** updated beta-oxidation and synthesis of fatty acids.

- **NEW! Ribbon Models** of proteins have been added including lactase with amino acids in the active site, transaminase, trypsin, chymotrypsin, carboxypeptidase, alanine amino transferase, estrogen receptor, cytochrome c, and aspartate transaminase.
- **NEW AND UPDATED! Diagrams** are updated using current models for allosteric enzymes, covalent modification including phosphorylation, 2- and 3-dimensional models of tRNA, DNA transcription, transcription factors in the promoter region, the sites in electron transport blocked by toxins, and urea cycle showing transport between the mitochondrial matrix and the cytosol.
- **NEW AND UPDATED! New biochemistry problems** include action of viruses, transcription and the estrogen receptor, energy diagram for the hydrolysis of ATP, defective enzymes that block the degradation of glycogen, and current values for ATP energy from NADH and $FADH_2$.
- **NEW! Interactive Videos** give students the experience of step-by-step problem solving for problems from the text.
- **NEW! Chapter Readiness** sections at the beginning of each chapter list the Key Math Skills and Core Chemistry Skills from the previous chapters, which provide the foundation for learning new chemistry principles in the current chapter.
- **NEW! Key Math Skills** review basic math relevant to the chemistry you are learning throughout the text. A **Key Math Skill Review** at the end of each chapter summarizes and gives additional examples.
- **NEW! Core Chemistry Skills** identify the key chemical principles in each chapter that are required for successfully learning chemistry. A **Core Chemistry Skill Review** at the end of each chapter helps reinforce the material and gives additional examples.
- **UPDATED! Analyze the Problem** features included in the solutions of the Sample Problems strengthen critical-thinking skills and illustrate the breakdown of a word problem into the components required to solve it.
- **UPDATED! Questions and Problems, Sample Problems, and art** are directly related to nursing and health applications to better demonstrate the connection between the chemistry being discussed and how these skills will be needed in professional experience.
- **UPDATED! Combining Ideas** features offer sets of integrated problems that test students' understanding by integrating topics from two or more previous chapters.

Chapter Organization of the Fifth Edition

In each textbook I write, I consider it essential to relate every chemical concept to real-life issues of health and environment. Because a chemistry course may be taught in different time frames, it may be difficult to cover all the chapters in this text. However, each chapter is a complete package, which allows some chapters to be skipped or the order of presentation to be changed.

Chapter 1, Chemistry in our Lives, now discusses the Scientific Method in everyday terms, guides students in developing a study plan for learning chemistry, and now has a new section of Key Math Skills that review the basic math including scientific notation needed in chemistry calculations.

- A new chapter opener tells the story of a murder and features the work and career of a forensic scientist.
- A new Clinical Update feature follows up with forensic scientists that help solve the murder and includes Clinical Applications related to the story.
- A new section, "Scientific Method: Thinking Like a Scientist," has been added, which discusses the scientific method in everyday terms.
- A new section, "Key Math Skills," reviews basic math required in chemistry, such as Identifying Place Values (1.4A), Using Positive and Negative Numbers in Calculations (1.4B) including a new feature Calculator Operations, Calculating Percentages (1.4C), Solving Equations (1.4D), Interpreting Graphs (1.4E), and Writing Numbers in Scientific Notation (1.4 F).
- New sample problems with nursing applications are added. New Sample Problem 1.5 requires the interpretation of a graph to determine the decrease in a child's temperature when given Tylenol.
- New art includes a photo of a plastic strip thermometer placed on a baby's forehead to determine body temperature.

Chapter 2, Chemistry and Measurements, looks at measurement and emphasizes the need to understand numerical relationships of the metric system. Significant numbers are discussed in the determination of final answers. Prefixes from the metric system are used to write equalities and conversion factors for problem-solving strategies. Density is discussed and used as a conversion factor.

- A new chapter opener tells the story of a patient with high blood pressure and features the work and career of a registered nurse.
- A new Clinical Update describes the patient's follow-up visit with his doctor.
- New material is added that illustrates how to count significant figures in equalities and in conversion factors used in a problem setup.
- New abbreviation mcg for microgram is introduced as used in health and medicine.

- New Core Chemistry Skills are added: Counting Significant Figures (2.2), Using Significant Figures in Calculations (2.3), Using Prefixes (2.4), Writing Conversion Factors from Equalities (2.5), Using Conversion Factors (2.6), and Using Density as a Conversion Factor (2.7).
- New photos, including an endoscope, a urine dipstick, a pint of blood, Keflex capsules, and salmon for omega-3 fatty acids, are added to improve visual introduction to clinical applications of chemistry.
- Updated Guides to Problem Solving (GPS) use color blocks as visual guides through the solution pathway.
- Updated Sample Problems relate questions and problem solving to health-related topics such as the measurements that a nurse would make, blood volume, omega-3 fatty acids, radiological imaging, and medication orders.
- New Clinical Applications feature questions about health-related settings including measurements made by a nurse, daily values for minerals and vitamins, equalities and conversion factors for medications, and health questions related to the Clinical Update story.

Chapter 3, Matter and Energy, classifies matter and states of matter, describes temperature measurement, and discusses energy, specific heat, and energy in nutrition. Physical and chemical changes and physical and chemical properties are now discussed in more depth.

- A new chapter opener describes diet and exercise for an overweight child with type 2 diabetes and features the work and career of a dietitian. A new Clinical Update describes the new diet for weight loss.
- Chapter 3 has a new order of topics: 3.1 Classification of Matter, 3.2 States and Properties of Matter, 3.3 Temperature, 3.4 Energy, 3.5 Energy and Nutrition, 3.6 Specific Heat, and 3.7 Changes of State. Section 3.7 Changes of State now includes heat of fusion and vaporization, and combinations of energy calculations.
- New Core Chemistry Skills are added: Classifying Matter (3.1), Identifying Physical and Chemical Changes (3.2), Converting between Temperature Scales (3.3), Using Energy Units (3.4), and Using the Heat Equation (3.6).
- New Questions and Problems and Sample Problems now have more clinical applications to nursing and health, including Sample Problem 3.4, high temperatures used in cancer treatment; Sample Problem 3.5, the energy produced by a high-energy shock output of a defibrillator; Sample Problem 3.7, body temperature lowering using a cooling cap; and Sample Problem 3.8, ice bag therapy for muscle injury.
- The interchapter problem set, Combining Ideas from Chapters 1 to 3, completes the chapter.

Chapter 4, Atoms, introduces elements and atoms and the periodic table. The names and symbols of element 114, Flerovium, Fl, and 116, Livermorium, Lv, have been added to update the periodic table. Atomic numbers and mass number are determined for isotopes. Atomic mass is calculated using the masses of the naturally occurring isotopes and their abundances. Electron arrangements are written using orbital diagrams, electron configurations, and abbreviated electron configurations. Trends in the properties of elements are discussed, including atomic size, Lewis symbols, ionization energy, and metallic character.

- A new chapter opener features chemistry in agriculture and the career of a farmer.
- A new Clinical Update describes the improvement in crop production by the farmer.
- New Core Chemistry Skills are added: Counting Protons and Neutrons (4.4), Writing Atomic Symbols for Isotopes (4.5), Writing Electron Configurations (4.7), Using the Periodic Table to Write Electron Configurations (4.7), Identifying Trends in Periodic Properties (4.8), and Drawing Lewis Symbols (4.8).
- A new weighted average analogy uses 8-lb and 14-lb bowling balls and the percent abundance of each to calculate weighted average of a bowling ball.
- New nursing and clinical applications are added to Sample Problems/Questions and Problems.
- Updated Chemistry Link to Health, "Biological Reactions to UV Light," adds information on using light for neonatal jaundice.
- Updated photos and diagrams including a new diagram for the electromagnetic spectrum are added.

Chapter 5, Nuclear Chemistry,

looks at the types of radiation emitted from the nuclei of radioactive atoms. Nuclear equations are written and balanced for both naturally occurring radioactivity and artificially produced radioactivity. The half-lives of radioisotopes are discussed, and the amount of time for a sample to decay is calculated. Radioisotopes important in the field of nuclear medicine are described.

- A new chapter opener about the work and career of a nuclear medicine technologist is added.
- A new Clinical Update discusses cardiac imaging using the radioisotope Tl-201.
- New Core Chemistry Skills are added: Writing Nuclear Equations (5.2) and Using Half-Lives (5.4).
- New Sample Problems and Questions and Problems use nursing and clinical examples, including Sample Problem 5.3 that describe the radioisotope yttrium-90 use in cancer and arthritis treatments. Sample Problem 5.6 that uses phosphorus-32 for the treatment of leukemia and Sample Problem 5.9 that uses titanium seeds containing a radioactive isotope implanted in the body to treat cancer.
- Clinical applications include radioisotopes in nuclear medicine, activity, half-lives, and dosage of radioisotopes.

Chapter 6, Ionic and Molecular Compounds,

describes the formation of ionic and covalent bonds. Chemical formulas are written, and ionic compounds—including those with polyatomic ions—and molecular compounds are named. Section 6.2 is titled "Writing Formulas for Ionic Compounds," 6.5 is titled "Molecular Compounds: Sharing Electrons," and 6.6 is titled "Lewis Structure for Molecules and Polyatomic Ions."

- The chapter opener describes aspirin as a molecular compound and features the work and career of a pharmacy technician.
- A new Clinical Update describes several types of compounds at a pharmacy and includes Clinical Applications.
- "Ions: Transfer of Electrons" has been rewritten to emphasize the stability of the electron configuration of a noble gas.
- New Core Chemistry Skills are added: Writing Positive and Negative Ions (6.1), Writing Ionic Formulas (6.2), Naming Ionic Compounds (6.3), Writing the Names and Formulas for Molecular Compounds (6.5), Drawing Lewis Structures (6.6), Using Electronegativity (6.7), Predicting Shape (6.8), Identifying Polarity of Molecules (6.8), and Identifying Attractive Forces (6.9).
- A new art comparing the particles and bonding of ionic compounds and molecular compounds has been added.
- Bismuth was added to Table 6.5, Some Metals That Form More Than One Positive Ion.
- Analyze the Problem feature was updated for Sample Problems 6.4, 6.5, 6.6, 6.9, 6.10.
- The interchapter problem set, Combining Ideas from Chapters 4 to 6, completes the chapter.

Chapter 7, Chemical Reactions and Quantities,

introduces moles and molar masses of compounds, which are used in calculations to determine the mass or number of particles in a given quantity. Students learn to balance chemical equations and to recognize the types of chemical reactions: combination, decomposition, single replacement, double replacement, and combustion reactions. Section 7.3 discusses Oxidation–Reduction Reactions using real-life examples, including biological reactions. Section 7.6, Mole Relationships in Chemical Equations, and Section 7.7, Mass Calculations for Reactions, prepare students for the quantitative relationships of reactants and products in reactions. Section 7.8, Limiting Reactants and Percent Yield, identifies limiting reactants and calculates percent yield, and Section 7.9, Energy in Chemical Reactions, calculates the energy in exothermic and endothermic chemical reactions.

- A chapter opener describes the chemical reaction that is used to whiten teeth and features the work and career of a dental hygienist.
- Sample Problems and problem sets include Clinical Applications for nursing.
- New Core Chemistry Skills are added: Balancing a Chemical Equation (7.1), Classifying Types of Chemical Reactions (7.2), Identifying Oxidized and Reduced Substances (7.3), Converting Particles to Moles (7.4), Calculating Molar Mass (7.5), Using Molar Mass as a Conversion Factor (7.5), Using Mole–Mole Factors (7.6), Converting Grams to Grams (7.7), Calculating Quantity of Product from a Limiting Reactant (7.8), Calculating Percent Yield (7.8), and Using the Heat of Reaction (7.9).

Chapter 8, Gases, discusses the properties of gases and calculates changes in gases using the gas laws: Boyle's, Charles's, Gay-Lussac's, Avogadro's, Dalton's, and the Ideal Gas Law. Problem-solving strategies enhance the discussion and calculations with gas laws including chemical reactions using the ideal gas law.

- The chapter opener describes a child with asthma and her treatment with oxygen and features the work and career of a respiratory therapist is added. A new Clinical Update describes exercises to prevent exercise-induced asthma. Clinical Applications are related to lung volume and gas laws.
- New Sample Problems and Challenge Problems use nursing and medical examples, including Sample Problem 8.3, calculating the volume of oxygen gas delivered through a face mask during oxygen therapy; and Sample Problem 8.12, preparing a heliox breathing mixture for a scuba diver.
- New Core Chemistry Skills are added: Using the Gas Laws (8.2, 8.3, 8.4, 8.5, 8.6), Using the Ideal Gas Law (8.7), Calculating Mass or Volume of a Gas in a Chemical Reaction (8.7), and Calculating Partial Pressure (8.8).
- Clinical applications includes calculations of mass or pressure of oxygen in uses of hyperbaric chambers.
- The interchapter problem set, Combining Ideas from Chapters 7 and 8, completes the chapter.

Chapter 9, Solutions, describes solutions, electrolytes, saturation and solubility, insoluble salts, concentrations, and osmosis. New problem-solving strategies clarify the use of concentrations to determine volume or mass of solute. The volumes and concentrations of solutions are used in calculations of dilutions, reactions, and titrations. Properties of solutions, osmosis in the body, and dialysis are discussed.

- The chapter opener describes a patient with kidney failure and dialysis treatment and features the work and career of a dialysis nurse.
- New Core Chemistry Skills are added: Using Solubility Rules (9.3), Calculating Concentration (9.4), Using Concentration as a Conversion Factor (9.4), Calculating the Quantity of a Reactant or Product (9.4), and Calculating the Boiling Point/Freezing Point of a Solution (9.6).
- Table 9.6 Electrolytes in Blood Plasma and Selected Intravenous Solutions is updated. Table 9.7 Solubility Rules for Ionic Solids in Water is updated.
- Molality is removed.
- New clinical applications include saline solutions, mass of solution in a mannitol, a lactated Ringer's solution, and a Pedialyte solution, solutions of medications, electrolytes in dialysis, and reactions of antacids.

Chapter 10, Reaction Rates and Chemical Equilibrium, looks at the rates of reactions and the equilibrium condition when forward and reverse rates for a reaction become equal. Equilibrium expressions for reactions are written and equilibrium constants are calculated. Le Châtelier's principle is used to evaluate the impact on concentrations when stress is placed on the system.

- A new chapter opener describes the symptoms of *infant respiratory distress syndrome* (IRDS) and discusses the career of a neonatal nurse.
- The Clinical Update describes a child with anemia, hemoglobin-oxygen equilibrium, and a diet that is high in iron-containing foods.
- New Core Chemistry Skills are added: Writing the Equilibrium Constant (10.3), Calculating an Equilibrium Constant (10.3), Calculating Equilibrium Concentrations (10.4), and Using Le Châtelier's Principle (10.5).
- New problems that visually represent equilibrium situations are added.
- Clinical applications include hemoglobin equilibrium and anemia.
- A new diagram represents the transport of O_2 by hemoglobin from the lungs to the tissues and muscles.
- Updates of Analyze the Problem include Sample Problems 10.4 and 10.5.

Chapter 11, Acids and Bases, discusses acids and bases and their strengths, conjugate acid–base pairs. The dissociation of strong and weak acids and bases is related to their strengths as acids or bases. The dissociation of water leads to the water dissociation constant expression, K_w, the pH scale, and the calculation of pH. Chemical equations for acids in reactions are balanced and titration of an acid is illustrated. Buffers are discussed along with their role in the blood. The pH of a buffer is calculated.

- A new chapter opener describes a blood sample for an emergency room patient sent to the clinical laboratory for analysis of blood pH and CO_2 gas and features the work and career of a clinical laboratory technician.
- Section 11.2 is now a discussion of Brønsted–Lowry Acids and Bases.
- A new Clinical Update discusses the symptoms and treatment of acid reflux disease.
- Analyze the Problem was updated in Sample Problems 11.3, 11.6, 11.8, 11.10, 11.12, and 11.13.
- Key Math Skills are added: Calculating pH from $[H_3O^+]$ (11.6) and Calculating $[H_3O^+]$ from pH (11.6).
- New Core Chemistry Skills are added: Identifying Conjugate Acid–Base Pairs (11.2), Calculating $[H_3O^+]$ and $[OH^-]$ in Solutions (11.5), Writing Equations for Reactions of Acids and Bases (11.7), Calculating Molarity or Volume of an Acid or Base in a Titration (11.8), and Calculating the pH of a Buffer (11.9).
- A new Guide to Writing Conjugate Acid–Base Pairs has been added. Guide to Calculating pH of an Aqueous Solutions, Calculating $[H_3O^+]$ from pH, Calculations for an Acid-Base Titration, and Calculating pH of a Buffer were updated.
- Clinical applications include calculating $[OH^-]$ or $[H_3O^+]$ of body fluids, foods, blood plasma, pH of body fluids, grams of antacids to neutralize stomach acid, and buffers for stomach acid.
- New visuals include the ionization of the weak acid hydrofluoric acid, a new photo of calcium hydroxide and information about its use in the food industry and

dentistry, as well as a new photo of sodium bicarbonate reacting with acetic acid.
- The interchapter problem set, Combining Ideas from Chapters 9 to 11, completes the chapter.

Chapter 12, Introduction to Organic Chemistry: Hydrocarbons, combines Chapters 11 and 12 of GOB, fourth edition. This new chapter compares inorganic and organic compounds, and describes the structures and naming of alkanes, alkenes including cis–trans isomers, alkynes, and aromatic compounds.

- A new chapter opener describes a fire victim and the search for traces of accelerants and fuel at the arson scene and features the work and career of a firefighter/emergency medical technician.
- A Clinical Update describes treatment for a burn patient and the identification of the fuels at the arson scene.
- Chapter 12 has a new order of topics: 12.1 Organic Compounds, 12.2 Alkanes, 12.3 Alkanes with Substituents, 12.4 Properties of Alkanes, 12.5 Alkenes and Alkynes, 12.6 Cis–Trans Isomers, 12.7 Addition Reactions, and 12.8 Aromatic Compounds.
- The wedge-dash models of methane and ethane have been added.
- New Core Chemistry Skills are added: Naming and Drawing Alkanes (12.2) and Writing Equations for Hydrogenation, Hydration, and Polymerization Hydration, and Polymerization of Alkenes (12.7).
- Line-angle structural formulas were added to Table 12.2.
- Guides to Drawing Structural Formulas for Alkanes, and Naming Alkanes with Substituents have been added.
- The Chemistry Link to Industry *Crude Oil* has been removed.
- Polymerization was added to Table 12.8, Summary of Addition Reactions.
- The Analyze the Problem features were updated in Sample Problem 12.7, 12.9, and 12.10.

Chapter 13, Alcohols, Phenols, Thiols, and Ethers, describes the functional groups and names of alcohols, phenols, thiols, and ethers.

- The chapter opener describes regional anesthetics for child birth and features the work and career of a nurse anesthetist.
- A Clinical Update describes some foods added to a diet plan including a comparison of their functional groups.
- New Core Chemistry Skills are added: Identifying Alcohols, Phenols, and Thiols (13.1), Naming Alcohols and Phenols (13.1), Writing Equations for the Dehydration of Alcohols (13.4), and Writing Equations for the Oxidation of Alcohols (13.4).
- New Guides to Naming Alcohols, and Phenols, and Writing IUPAC Names for Ethers have been added.
- The classification of alcohols has been moved to Section 13.3 "Physical Properties of Alcohols, Phenols, and Ethers."

- New material on the use of phenol by Joseph Lister as the first surgical antiseptic is added.

Chapter 14, Aldehydes, Ketones, and Chiral Molecules, discusses the nomenclature, structures, and oxidation and reduction of aldehydes and ketones. The chapter discusses Fischer projections, chiral molecules, and mirror images to prepare students for the structures of carbohydrates in Chapter 15.

- A new chapter opener describes the risk factors for melanoma and discusses the career of a dermatology nurse.
- The Clinical Update discusses melanoma, skin protection, and functional groups of sunscreens.
- Line-angle structural formulas for aldehydes and ketones are added.
- New Core Chemistry Skills are added: Naming Aldehydes and Ketones (14.1), Identifying Chiral Molecules (14.5), and Identifying D- and L- Fischer Projections (14.5).
- New clinical applications include medicinal herbs, chiral carbon atoms in citronellol, alanine, amphetamine, and norepinephrine, and functional groups in sunscreens.
- The interchapter problem set, Combining Ideas from Chapters 12 to 14, completes the chapter.

Chapter 15, Carbohydrates, describes the carbohydrate molecules monosaccharides, disaccharides, and polysaccharides and their formation by photosynthesis. Monosaccharides are classified as aldo or keto pentoses or hexoses. Fischer projections and D and L notations are described. Carbohydrates used as sweeteners and carbohydrates used in blood typing are discussed. The formation of glycosidic bonds in disaccharides and polysaccharides is described.

- A new chapter opener describes a diabetes patient and her diet and the work and career of a diabetes nurse.
- New Core Chemistry Skills are added: Identifying D- and L-Fischer Projections (15.2) and Drawing Haworth Structures (15.3).
- Guide to Drawing Haworth Structures is updated.

Chapter 16, Carboxylic Acids and Esters, discusses the functional groups and naming of carboxylic acids and esters. Chemical reactions include esterification, amidation and acid and base hydrolysis of esters.

- A new chapter opener describes heart surgery and discusses the work and career of a surgical technician.
- A Clinical Update describes the use of liquid bandages.
- New Core Chemistry Skills are added: Naming Carboxylic Acids (16.1) and Hydrolyzing Esters (16.5).

Chapter 17, Lipids, discusses the alcohols and carboxylic acids found in fatty acids, and the formation of ester bonds in triacylglycerols and glycerophospholipids. Chemical properties of fatty acids and their melting points along with the hydrogenation of unsaturated triacylglycerols are discussed. Steroids, which are based on a group of connected multicyclic rings such as

cholesterol, bile salts, and steroid hormones, are described. Chemistry Links to Health include "Omega-3 Fatty Acids in Fish Oils," "Converting Unsaturated Fats to Saturated Fats: Hydrogenation and Interesterification," "Infant Respiratory Distress Syndrome (IRDS)," and "Anabolic Steroids." The role of phospholipids in the lipid bilayer of cell membranes is discussed as well as the lipids that function as steroid hormones.

- A new chapter opener describes a patient with symptoms of familial hypercholesterolemia and features the work and career of a clinical lipid specialist.
- The Clinical Update describes changes in diet and exercise along with medications for treating high LDL-cholesterol levels.
- New Core Chemistry Skills are added: Identifying Fatty Acids (17.2), Drawing Structures for Triacylglycerols (17.3), Drawing the Products for the Hydrogenation, Hydrolysis, and Saponification of a Triacylglycerol (17.4), and Identifying the Steroid Nucleus (17.6).
- New notation for number of carbon atoms and double bonds in a fatty acid is added.
- New color-block diagrams for triacylglycerols, glycerophospholipids, and sphingolipids are added.
- New lipid panel for cholesterol, triglycerides, HDL, LDL, and cholesterol/HDL ratio is added.
- New photos include jojoba plant, use of triacylglycerols to thicken creams and lotions, and poisonous snake with venom that hydrolyzes phospholipids in red blood cells.
- New clinical applications include omega-3 fatty acids in fish oils, prostaglandins, drawing condensed and line-angle structure formulas for triacylglycerols and phospholipids in the body, cholesterol, bile salts, steroid hormones, and cell membranes.

Chapter 18, Amines and Amides, emphasizes the nitrogen atom in their functional groups and their names. Alkaloids are discussed as the naturally occurring amines in plants. Section 18.4 is now Neurotransmitters. Chemical reactions include amidation, and acid and base hydrolysis of amides.

- The chapter opener describes pesticides and pharmaceuticals used on a ranch and discusses the career of an environmental health practitioner.
- The Clinical Update describes the collection of soil and water samples for testing of insecticides and antibiotics.
- New art includes hemlock for coniine, crack cocaine, sedamine, structures of dicyclanil and enrofloxacin, and a soil collection bag.
- More line-angle structure formulas are drawn in the text and problem sections.
- New clinical applications include novocaine, lidocaine, ritalin, niacin, serotonin, histamine, acetylcholine, dose calculations of pesticides and antibiotics, enrofloxacin, and volataren.
- New Core Chemistry Skills are added: Forming Amides (18.5) and Hydrolyzing Amides (18.6).

- The interchapter problem set, Combining Ideas from Chapters 15 to 18, completes the chapter.

Chapter 19, Amino Acids and Proteins, discusses amino acids, formation of peptide bonds and proteins, and structural levels of proteins. Amino acids are drawn as zwitterions in physiological solutions. Section 19.4 describes the primary and secondary levels of protein structure. Section 19.5 describes the tertiary and quaternary levels of proteins.

- A new chapter opener describe some symptoms of Alzheimer's disease and changes in brain proteins and discusses the career of a Radiology Technician.
- The Clinical Update describes a PET scan of the brain to determine the amount of plaque formation and cognitive decline, and the diagnosis and treatment for Alzheimer's disease.
- The terms N-terminus and C-terminus are now used and the repeat backbone of a peptide is introduced.
- The updated Chemistry Link to Health, "Essential Amino Acids," is moved to Section 19.1.
- Amino acids are drawn with the carboxyl or carboxylate groups showing single and double bonds to O atoms.
- Updates have been made in Analyze the Problem for Sample Problem 19.1, Sample Problem 19.3, and Sample Problem 19.4.
- New Core Chemical Skills are added: Drawing the Zwitterion for an Amino Acid (19.1) and Identifying the Primary, Secondary, Tertiary, and Quaternary Structures of Proteins (19.4, 19.5).
- New Chemistry Links to Health are added: "Protein Sequencing," and "Protein Secondary Structures and Alzheimer's Disease."
- The use of electrophoresis to diagnose sickle-cell anemia was added to Chemistry Link to Health: Sickle-Cell Anemia.
- New ribbon models of beta-amyloid proteins in normal brain and an Alzheimer's brain are added.
- A new diagram showing the separation of proteins by electrophoresis to diagnose sickle-cell anemia has been added.
- New clinical applications include essential amino acids, protein sequencing, proteins in Alzheimer's, drawing peptides, and identifying the C-terminus and the N-terminus of peptides in health.
- The material on mad cow disease has been removed.

Chapter 20, Enzymes and Vitamins, relates the importance of the three-dimensional shape of proteins to their function as enzymes. The shape of an enzyme and its substrate are factors in enzyme regulation. End products of an enzyme-catalyzed sequence can increase or decrease the rate of an enzyme-catalyzed reaction. Other regulatory processes include allosteric enzymes, covalent modification and phosphorylation, and zymogens. Proteins change shape and lose function when subjected to pH changes and high temperatures. The important role of water-soluble vitamins as coenzymes is related to enzyme function.

- A new chapter opener discusses the symptoms of lactose intolerance and describes the career of a physician assistant.
- The Clinical Update describes the hydrogen breath test to confirm lactose intolerance and a diet that is free of lactose and use of Lactaid.
- Regulation of Enzyme Activity is now Section 20.4 and includes new are for positive and negative allosteric enzyme regulation.
- New material on covalent modification including phosphorylation and new ribbon models of chymotrypsin are added to Section 20.4.
- A new art shows the quaternary ribbon model of lactase and the amino acid residues in the active site.
- Clinical applications include isoenzymes, activity of proteases, prothrombin, amoxicillin, vitamins, and lactose intolerance.
- New art added illustrates the hydrolysis of lactose by lactase.
- New Core Chemistry Skills are added: Describing Enzyme Action (20.1), Classifying Enzymes (20.2), Identifying Factors Affecting Enzyme Activity (20.3), and Describing the Role of Cofactors (20.6).

Chapter 21, Nucleic Acids and Protein Synthesis,

describes the nucleic acids and their importance as biomolecules that store and direct information for the synthesis of cellular components. The role of complementary base pairing is discussed in both DNA replication and the formation of mRNA during protein synthesis. The role of RNA is discussed in the relationship of the genetic code to the sequence of amino acids in a protein. Mutations describe ways in which the nucleotide sequences are altered in genetic diseases. We also look at how DNA or RNA in viruses utilizes host cells to produce more viruses.

- A new chapter opener describes a patient diagnosis and treatment of breast cancer and discusses the work and career of a histology technician.
- The Clinical Update describes estrogen positive tumors, the impact of the altered genes BRCA1 and BRCA2 on the estrogen receptor, and medications to suppress tumor growth.
- Nucleotides in RNA and DNA are now named by adding monophosphate such as adenosine monophosphate.
- The synthesis of the lagging strand now include primers and single-strand binding proteins in a new Figure 21.8 and Table 21.24.
- Clinical applications include mRNA segments for human insulin, mutations in sickle-cell anemia, estrogen receptors, and segments of BRCA1 and BRCA2 genes.
- Entry inhibitors are added in inhibitors of reverse transcription.
- The discussion of the lactose operon was omitted.
- New problems are added for DNA cleavage by restriction enzymes.
- Transcription factors that bind RNA polymerase to DNA are now discussed as part of the regulation of transcription.

- One-letter abbreviations for amino acids were added to Table 21.6 Codons in mRNA: The Genetic Code for Amino Acids.
- Mutations are now named as point mutations, deletion mutations, and insertion mutations.
- New Core Chemical Skills are added: Writing the Complementary DNA Strand (21.3), Writing the mRNA Segment for a DNA Template (21.5), and Writing the Amino Acid for an mRNA Codon (21.6).
- The interchapter problem set, Combining Ideas from Chapters 19 to 21, completes the chapter.

Chapter 22, Metabolic Pathways for Carbohydrates,

describes the stages of metabolism and the digestion of carbohydrates, our most important fuel. The breakdown of glucose to pyruvate is described using glycolysis, which is followed under aerobic conditions by the decarboxylation of pyruvate to acetyl CoA. The synthesis of glycogen and the synthesis of glucose from noncarbohydrate sources are discussed.

- A new chapter opener describes the symptoms of a glycogen storage disease and discusses the career of a hepatology nurse.
- The Clinical Update describes medical treatment of frequent feedings of glucose for *von Gierke's disease*, in which a child has a defective glucose-6-phosphatase and cannot break down glucose-6-phosphate to glucose.
- New or updated diagrams were prepared for hydrolysis of ATP, ATP and muscle contraction, glycolysis, entry of galactose and fructose into glycolysis pathway, pathways for pyruvate, summary of glycogenesis and glycogenolysis, summary of glycolysis and gluconeogenesis, and the Cori cycle.
- New to this edition is material describing the *pentose phosphate pathway* for the oxidation of glucose that produces NADPH and pentoses.
- Chemistry Links to Health include "ATP Energy and Ca^{2+} Needed to Contract Muscles," "Glycogen Storage Diseases (GSDs)".
- New tables are added to summarize enzymes and coenzymes in metabolic reactions: "Characteristics of Oxidation and Reduction in Metabolic Pathways" (Table 22.2) and "Enzymes and Coenzymes in Metabolic Reactions" (Table 22.3).
- New color-coded art was added for structures of NAD and FAD in Figures 22.5 and 22.6.
- New art in Figure 22.12 adds glucose structures for reactions for glycogenesis.
- New Core Chemical Skills are added: Identifying Important Coenzymes in Metabolism (22.2), Identifying the Compounds in Glycolysis (22.4), Identifying the Compounds and Enzymes in Glycogenesis and Glycogenolysis (22.6).

Chapter 23, Metabolism and Energy Production, looks

at the entry of acetyl CoA into the citric acid cycle and the production of reduced coenzymes for electron transport, oxidative phosphorylation, and the synthesis of ATP. The malate-aspartate pathway was added to describe the transport of NADH from the cytosol into the mitochondrial matrix. Many diagrams were added or updated, including catalysis of lactose, covalent modification, phosphorylation, formation of phospho-nucleotides, DNA replication, recombinant DNA, muscle contraction, glycolysis, and galactose and fructose in glycolysis.

- The chapter opener describes the symptoms of pulmonary emphysema and discusses the career of an exercise physiologist.
- Clinical applications include enzyme deficiencies in the citric acid cycle, inhibitors of electron transport, low levels of O_2 and NADH production, and basal metabolic rate, kilocalories, and kilograms of ATP.
- The Clinical Update describes the exercise stress test and normal values of oximeter readings, and the exercises used to improve fitness and blood O_2 saturation.
- A new diagram (Figure 23.7) illustrates the malate-aspartate shuttle, which transfers energy stored in NADH in the cytosol into the mitochondrial matrix by regenerating NADH.
- The citric acid cycle was updated with enzyme names, identification of acetyl carbon group, and removal of ATP from electron transport system.
- The diagram of electron transport was updated and a new diagram of the sites in electron transport that are blocked by inhibitors was added.
- The details of ATP production by ATP synthase and its protein subunits were removed.
- The values for ATP production were adjusted to 2.5 ATP for NADH and 1.5 ATP for $FADH_2$.
- A new diagram emphasizes a mitochondrion and the product of NADH and $FADH_2$ from the citric acid cycle, and the formation of ATP from electron transport.
- New Core Chemistry Skills are added: Describing the Reactions in the Citric Acid Cycle (23.1), and Calculating the ATP Produced from Glucose (23.4).

Chapter 24, Metabolic Pathways for Lipids and Amino Acids,

discusses the digestion of lipids and proteins and the metabolic pathways that convert fatty acids and amino acids into energy. Discussions include the conversion of excess carbohydrates to triacylglycerols in adipose tissue and how the intermediates of the citric acid cycle are converted to nonessential amino acids.

- A new chapter opener describes a liver profile with elevated levels of liver enzymes for a patient with chronic hepatitis C infection and discusses the career of a public health nurse.
- The Clinical Update describes interferon and ribavirin therapy for hepatitis C.
- The equations for the metabolism of glycerol were redrawn as two separate reactions.
- The diagram in Figure 24.3 was updated to include a transport region at the inner mitochondrial membrane for the transport of fatty acyl carnitine between the cytosol and the matrix.
- New ribbon model of aspartate transaminase is added to Sample Problem 24.8.
- Transport molecules are added to the urea cycle in Figure 24.9.
- New line-angle structural formulas replaced condensed structural formulas of fatty acyl CoA molecules.
- The Core Chemistry Skills are added: Calculating the ATP from Fatty Acid Oxidation (β Oxidation) (24.3), Describing How Ketone Bodies are Formed (24.4), and Distinguishing Anabolic and Catabolic Pathways (24.9).
- The interchapter problem set, Combining Ideas from Chapters 22 to 24, completes the chapter.

Acknowledgments

The preparation of a new text is a continuous effort of many people. I am thankful for the support, encouragement, and dedication of many people who put in hours of tireless effort to produce a high-quality book that provides an outstanding learning package. I am extremely grateful to Dr. Laura Frost, who provided new and expanded material on current topics in the Biochemistry Chapters 19–24. The editorial team at Pearson has done an exceptional job. I want to thank Jeanne Zalesky, Editor-in-Chief, and Terry Haugen, Senior Acquisitions Editor who supported our vision of this fifth edition.

I appreciate all the wonderful work of Lisa Pierce, project manager, who skillfully brought together reviews, art, web site materials, and all the things it takes to prepare a book for production. I appreciate the work of Meeta Pendharkar and Jenna Vittorioso, project managers, and of Lumina Datamatics, Inc., who brilliantly coordinated all phases of the manuscript to the final pages of a beautiful book. Thanks to Mark Quirie, manuscript and accuracy reviewer, and Lumina Datamatics copy editor and proofreaders, who precisely analyzed and edited the initial and final manuscripts and pages to make sure the words and problems were correct to help students learn chemistry. Their keen eyes and thoughtful comments were extremely helpful in the development of this text.

I am especially proud of the art program in this text, which lends beauty and understanding to chemistry. I would like to thank Wynne Au Yeung, art specialist; Derek Bacchus, Design Manager, and Jerilyn Bockorick, interior and cover designers, whose creative ideas provided the outstanding design for the cover and pages of the book. Stephen Merland and Jen Simmons, photo researchers, were outstanding in researching and selecting vivid photos for the text so that students can see the beauty of chemistry, and to William Opaluch, text permissions manager for clearing third party content. Thanks also to *Bio-Rad Laboratories* for their courtesy and use of *Know-ItAll ChemWindows*, drawing software that helped us produce chemical structures for the manuscript. The macro-to-micro illustrations designed by Imagineering give students visual impressions of the atomic and molecular organization of everyday things and are a fantastic learning tool. I also appreciate the hard work of Will Moore, Product Marketing Manager, and Chris Barker, Field Marketing Manager for their dedication in conveying the ideas of this revision through their marketing expertise.

I am extremely grateful to an incredible group of peers for their careful assessment of all the new ideas for the text; for their suggested additions, corrections, changes, and deletions; and for providing an incredible amount of feedback about improvements for the book. I admire and appreciate every one of you.

If you would like to share your experience with chemistry, or have questions and comments about this text, I would appreciate hearing from you.

Karen Timberlake
Email: khemist@aol.com

Students learn chemistry using real-world examples

Feature	Description	Benefit	Page
Chapter Opener 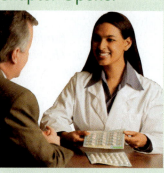	**Chapter Openers** begin with **Clinical Conditions** and discuss careers in fields such as nursing, agriculture, exercise physiology, and anesthesia.	Connects a clinical situation with the chemistry in the chapter and show you how health professionals use chemistry every day.	183
Chemistry Link to Health Chemistry Link to **Health** Losing and Gaining Weight The number of kilocalories or kilojoules needed in the daily diet of an adult depends on gender, age, and level of physical activity. Some typical levels of energy needs are given in Table 3.9. A person gains weight when food intake exceeds energy output.	**Chemistry Links to Health** apply chemical concepts to health and medicine such as weight loss and weight gain, trans fats, anabolic steroids, alcohol abuse, blood buffers, kidney dialysis, and cancer.	Provide you with connections that illustrate the importance of understanding chemistry in real-life health and medical situations.	78
Clinical Update Clinical Update A Diet and Exercise Program for Charles It has been two weeks since Charles met with Daniel, a dietitian, who provided Charles with a menu for weight loss. Charles and his mother are going back to see Daniel again with a chart of the food Charles has eaten. The following is what Charles ate in one day:	**Clinical Updates** give a follow-up to the medical condition and treatment discussed in the chapter opener and include Clinical Application questions.	Continue a clinical theme through the entire chapter utilizing the chemistry content of the chapter.	90
Macro-to-Micro Art Aspirin $C_9H_8O_4$	**Macro-to-Micro Art** utilizes photographs and drawings to illustrate the atomic structure of chemical phenomena.	Helps you connect the world of atoms and molecules to the macroscopic world.	253
Chemistry Link to the **Environment** Carbon Dioxide and Climate Change The Earth's climate is a product of interactions between sunlight, the atmosphere, and the oceans. The Sun provides us with energy in the form of solar radiation. Some of this radiation is reflected back into space. The rest is absorbed by the clouds, atmospheric gases including carbon dioxide, and the Earth's surface. For millions of	**Chemistry Links to the Environment** relate chemistry to environmental topics such as climate change, radon in our homes, and pheromones.	Helps you extend your understanding of the impact of chemistry on the environment	75

Engage students in the world of chemistry

Feature	Description	Benefit	Page
LEARNING GOAL Account for the ATP produced by the complete oxidation of glucose.	**Learning Goals** at the beginning and end of each section identify the key concepts for that section and provide a roadmap for your study.	Help you focus your studying by emphasizing what is most important in each section.	851
15.1 Carbohydrates **Carbohydrates** such as table sugar, lactose, and cellulose and oxygen. Simple sugars, which have formulas of C hydrates of carbon, thus the name *carbohydrate*. In a ser sis, energy from the Sun is used to combine the carbon	Timberlake's accessible **Writing Style** is based on careful development of chemical concepts suited to the skills and backgrounds of students in chemistry.	Helps you understand new terms and chemical concepts.	551
CONCEPT MAP METABOLISM AND ENERGY PRODUCTION Acetyl CoA enters the Citric Acid Cycle to yield GTP NADH FADH₂ CO₂ that enter Electron Transport	**Concept Maps** at the end of each chapter show how all the key concepts fit together.	Encourage learning by providing a visual guide to the interrelationship among all the concepts in each chapter.	859
KEY MATH SKILL Interpreting Graphs	**Key Math Skills** review the basic math required needed for chemistry. Instructors can also assign these through MasteringChemistry.	Help you master the basic quantitative skills to succeed in chemistry.	14
CORE CHEMISTRY SKILL Describing the Reactions in the Citric Acid Cycle	**Core Chemistry Skills** identify content crucial to problem-solving strategies related to chemistry. Instructors can also assign these through MasteringChemistry.	Help you master the basic problem-solving skills needed to succeed in chemistry.	837
FIGURE 15.3 ▶ Lactose, a disaccharid found in milk and milk products, contair galactose and glucose.	The **Art and Photo Program** is beautifully rendered, pedagogically effective, and includes questions with all the figures.	Helps you think critically using photos and illustrations.	565
CHAPTER REVIEW **19.1 Proteins and Amino Acids** **LEARNING GOAL** Classify proteins by their functions. Give the name and abbreviations for an amino acid, and draw its zwitterion. • Some proteins are enzymes or hormones, whereas others are important in structure, transport, protection, storage, and muscle contraction.	The **Chapter Reviews** include Learning Goals and visual thumbnails to summarize the key points in each section.	Help you determine your mastery of the chapter concepts and study for your tests.	715
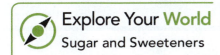 Explore Your World Sugar and Sweeteners	**Explore Your World** features are hands-on activities that use everyday materials to encourage you to explore selected chemistry topics.	Helps you interact with chemistry, learn scientific method, and support critical thinking.	580

Tools to engage students in chemistry and show them how to solve problems

Feature	Description	Benefit	Page
℞ Clinical Applications 3.19 a. A patient with hyperthermia has a temperature of 106 °F. What does this read on a Celsius thermometer? b. Because high fevers can cause convulsions in children, the doctor needs to be called if the child's temperature goes over 40.0 °C. Should the doctor be called if a child has a temperature of 103 °F?	Clinical Applications connect the chemistry in each section with health and clinical problems.	Shows you how the chemistry you are learning is related to health and medicine.	73
Guide to Problem Solving Using Conversion Factors STEP 1 State the given and needed quantities. STEP 2 Write a plan to convert the	**Guides to Problem Solving** (GPS) illustrate the steps needed to solve problems.	Visually guide you step-by-step through each problem-solving strategy.	44
ANALYZE THE PROBLEM — Given: 7.5 qt of blood, density of blood (1.06 g/mL) — Need: grams of blood	**Analyze the Problems** included in Sample Problem Solutions convert information in a word problem into components for problem solving.	Help you identify and utilize the components within a word problem to set up a solution strategy.	51
QUESTIONS AND PROBLEMS **15.1 Carbohydrates** **LEARNING GOAL** Classify a monosaccharide as an aldose or a ketose, and indicate the number of carbon atoms. 15.1 What reactants are needed for photosynthesis and respiration? 15.2 What is the relationship between photosynthesis and respiration?	**Questions and Problems** are placed at the end of each section. Problems are paired and the **Answers** to the odd-numbered problems are given at the end of each chapter.	Encourage you to become involved immediately in the process of problem solving.	554
▶ SAMPLE PROBLEM 2.9 Problem Solving Using Conversion Factors Greg's doctor has ordered a PET scan of his heart. In radiological imaging such as PET or CT scans, dosages of pharmaceuticals are based on body mass. If Greg weighs 144 lb, what is his body mass in kilograms? SOLUTION STEP 1 State the given and needed quantities. ANALYZE THE PROBLEM — Given: 144 lb — Need: kilograms STEP 2 Write a plan to convert the given unit to the needed unit. The conversion factor relates the given unit in the U.S. system of measurement and the needed unit in the metric system.	**Sample Problems** illustrate worked-out solutions with step-by-step explanations and required calculations. Study Checks associated with each Sample Problem allow you to check your problem solving strategies with the **Answer.**	Provide the intermediate steps to guide you successfully through each type of problem.	44
UNDERSTANDING THE CONCEPTS The chapter sections to review are shown in parentheses at the end of each question. 1.31 A "chemical-free" shampoo includes the following ingredients: water, cocoamide, glycerin, and citric acid. Is the shampoo truly "chemical-free"? (1.1) 1.32 A "chemical-free" sunscreen includes the following ingredients: 1.35 Classify each of the following statements as an observation (O) or a hypothesis (H): (1.2) a. A patient breaks out in hives after receiving penicillin. b. Dinosaurs became extinct when a large meteorite hit the Earth and caused a huge dust cloud that severely reduced the amount of light reaching the Earth. c. The 100-yd dash was run in 9.8 s.	**Understanding the Concepts** are questions with visual representations placed at the end of each chapter.	Build an understanding of newly learned chemical concepts.	22
ADDITIONAL QUESTIONS AND PROBLEMS 1.39 Identify each of the following as an observation (O), a hypothesis (H), an experiment (E), or a conclusion (C): (1.2) a. During an assessment in the emergency room, a nurse writes that the patient has a resting pulse of 30 beats/min. b. A nurse thinks that an incision from a recent surgery that is red and swollen is infected. c. Repeated studies show that lowering sodium in the diet leads to Nurses make 1.41 Select the correct phrase(s) to complete the following statement: If experimental results do not support your hypothesis, you should (1.2) a. pretend that the experimental results support your hypothesis b. modify your hypothesis c. do more experiments 1.42 Select the correct phrase(s) to complete the following statement: A conclusion confirms a hypothesis when (1.2) a. one experiment proves the hypothesis b. many experiments validate the hypothesis c. you think your hypothesis is correct	**Additional Questions and Problems** at the end of each chapter provide further study and application of the topics from the entire chapter. Problems are paired and the Answers to the odd-numbered problems are given at the end of each chapter.	Promote critical thinking.	22
CHALLENGE QUESTIONS The following groups of questions are related to the topics in this chapter. However, they do not all follow the chapter order, and they require you to combine concepts and skills from several sections. These questions will help you increase your critical thinking skills and prepare for your next exam. 1.51 Classify each of the following as an observation (O), a hypothesis (H), or an experiment (E): (1.2) a. The bicycle tire is flat. b. If I add air to the bicycle tire, it will expand to the proper size. c. When I added air to the bicycle tire, it was still flat. d. The bicycle tire must have a leak in it. 1.52 Classify each of the following as an observation (O), a hypothesis (H), or an experiment (E): (1.2) Use the following graph for problem — Solubility of Carbon Dioxide (Solubility (g CO₂/100 g water))	**Challenge Questions** at the end of each chapter provide complex questions.	Promote critical thinking, group work, and cooperative learning environments.	23
COMBINING IDEAS FROM Chapters 7 and 8 CI.13 In the following diagram, blue spheres represent the element A and yellow spheres represent the element B: (6.5, 7.1, 7.2) Reactants — Products Each capsule of Tamiflu. a. If black spheres are carbon atoms, white spheres are hydrogen atoms, and red spheres are oxygen atoms, what is the formula of shikimic acid? b. What is the molar mass of shikimic acid? c. How many moles of shikimic acid are in 130 g of shikimic acid? a. Write the formulas for each of the reactants and products. d. How many capsules containing 75 m	**Combining Ideas** are sets of integrated problems placed after every 2 to 4 chapters that are useful as Practice exams.	Test your understanding of the concepts from previous chapters by integrating topics.	322

Resources

General, Organic, and Biological Chemistry: Structures of Life, fifth edition, provides an integrated teaching and learning package of support material for both students and professors.

Name of Supplement	Available in Print	Available Online	Instructor or Student Supplement	Description
Study Guide and Selected Solutions Manual (ISBN 0133891917)	✓		Resource for Students	The *Study Guide and Selected Solutions Manual*, by Karen Timberlake and Mark Quirie, promotes active learning through a variety of exercises with answers as well as practice tests that are connected directly to the learning goals of the textbook. Complete solutions to odd-numbered problems are included.
MasteringChemistry® (www.masteringchemistry.com) (ISBN 0133858375)		✓	Resource for Students and Instructors	MasteringChemistry® from Pearson is the leading online teaching and learning system designed to improve results by engaging students before, during, and after class with powerful content. Ensure that students arrive ready to learn by assigning educationally effective content before class, and encourage critical thinking and retention with in-class resources such as Learning Catalytics. Students can further master concepts after class through traditional homework assignments that provide hints and answer-specific feedback. The Mastering gradebook records scores for all automatically graded assignments while diagnostic tools give instructors access to rich data to assess student understanding and misconceptions.
MasteringChemistry with Pearson eText (ISBN 0133899306)		✓	Resource for Students	The fifth edition of *General, Organic, and Biological Chemistry: Structures of Life* features a Pearson eText enhanced with media within Mastering. In conjunction with Mastering assessment capabilities, Interactive Videos and 3D animations will improve student engagement and knowledge retention. Each chapter will contain a balance of interactive animations, videos, sample calculations, and self-assessments/quizzes embedded directly in the eText. Additionally, the Pearson eText offers students the power to create notes, highlight text in different colors, create bookmarks, zoom, and view single or multiple pages.
Instructor's Solutions Manual–Download Only (ISBN 0133891909)		✓	Resource for Instructors	Prepared by Mark Quirie, the solutions manual highlights chapter topics, and includes answers and solutions for all questions and problems in the text.
Instructor Resource Materials–Download Only (ISBN 0133891887)		✓	Resource for Instructors	Includes all the art, photos, and tables from the book in JPEG format for use in classroom projection or when creating study materials and tests. In addition, the instructors can access modifiable PowerPoint™ lecture outlines. Also available are downloadable files of the Instructor's Solutions Manual and a set of "clicker questions" designed for use with classroom-response systems. Also visit the Pearson Education catalog page for Timberlake's *General, Organic, and Biological Chemistry: Structures of Life* fifth Edition, at www.pearsonhighered.com to download available instructor supplements.
TestGen Test Bank–Download Only (ISBN 0133891895)		✓	Resource for Instructors	Prepared by William Timberlake, this resource includes more than 2000 questions in multiple-choice, matching, true/false, and short-answer format.
Laboratory Manual by Karen Timberlake (ISBN 0321811852)	✓		Resource for Students	This best-selling lab manual coordinates 35 experiments with the topics in *General, Organic, and Biological Chemistry: Structures of Life* fifth edition, uses laboratory investigations to explore chemical concepts, develop skills of manipulating equipment, reporting data, solving problems, making calculations, and drawing conclusions.
Online Instructor Manual for Laboratory Manual (ISBN 0321812859)		✓	Resource for Instructors	This manual contains answers to report sheet pages for the *Laboratory Manual* and a list of the materials needed for each experiment with amounts given for 20 students working in pairs, available for download at www.pearsonhighered.com.

Highlighting Relevancy and Clinical Applications

Designed to prepare students for health-related careers, *General, Organic, and Biological Chemistry: Structures of Life* breaks chemical concepts and problem solving into clear, manageable pieces, ensuring students follow along and stay motivated throughout their first, and often only, chemistry course. Timberlake's friendly writing style, student focus, strong problems, and engaging health-related applications continue to help students make connections between chemistry and their future careers as they develop problem-solving skills they'll need beyond the classroom.

Clinical Conditions, Applications, and Updates

Clinical features throughout the chapter connect chemistry to real life. Each chapter begins with an image and details of a Clinical Condition being addressed in the field by professionals from nursing, agriculture, exercise physiology, and anesthesia. **Clinical Updates** throughout the chapter follow the medical condition and treatment discussed in the chapter opener. **Clinical Applications** within the chapter and end-of-chapter show students how the chemistry they are learning applies specifically to health and medicine.

---

1 Chemistry in Our Lives

A CALL CAME IN TO 911 FROM A MAN WHO FOUND

his wife lying on the floor of their home. When the police arrived at the home, they determined that the woman was dead. The husband said he had worked late, and just arrived at their home. The victim's body was lying on the floor of the living room. There was no blood at the scene, but the police did find a glass on the side table that contained a small amount of liquid. In an adjacent laundry room/garage, the police found a half-empty bottle of antifreeze. The bottle, glass, and liquid were bagged and sent to the forensic laboratory.

In another 911 call, a man was found lying on the grass outside his home. Blood was present on his body, and some bullet casings were found on the grass. Inside the victim's home, a weapon was recovered. The bullet casings and the weapon were bagged and sent to the forensic laboratory.

Sarah and Mark, forensic scientists, use scientific procedures and chemical tests to examine the evidence from law enforcement agencies. Sarah proceeds to analyze blood, stomach contents, and the unknown liquid from the first victim's home. She will look for the presence of drugs, poisons, and alcohol. Her lab partner Mark will analyze the fingerprints on the glass. He will also match the characteristics of the bullet casings to the weapon that was found at the second crime scene.

Evidence from a crime scene is sent to the forensic laboratory.

CAREER Forensic Scientist

Most forensic scientists work in crime laboratories that are part of city or county legal systems where they analyze bodily fluids and tissue samples collected by crime scene investigators. In analyzing these samples, forensic scientists identify the presence or absence of specific chemicals within the body to help solve the criminal case. Some of the chemicals they look for include alcohol, illegal or prescription drugs, poisons, arson debris, metals, and various gases such as carbon monoxide. In order to identify these substances, a variety of chemical instruments and highly specific methodologies are used. Forensic scientists also analyze samples from criminal suspects, athletes, and potential employees. They also work on cases involving environmental contamination and animal samples for wildlife crimes. Forensic scientists usually have a bachelor's degree that includes courses in math, chemistry, and biology.

1

Clinical Update

Forensic Evidence Solves the Murder

Using a variety of laboratory tests, Sarah finds ethylene glycol in the victim's blood. The quantitative tests indicate that the victim had ingested 125 g of ethylene glycol. Sarah determines that the liquid in the glass found at the crime scene was ethylene glycol that had been added to an alcoholic beverage. Ethylene glycol is a clear, sweet-tasting, thick liquid that is odorless and mixes with water. It is easy to obtain since it is used as antifreeze in automobiles and in brake fluid. Because the initial symptoms of ethylene glycol poisoning are similar to being intoxicated, the victim is often unaware of its presence.

If ingestion of ethylene glycol occurs, it can cause depression of the central nervous system, cardiovascular damage, and kidney failure. If discovered quickly, hemodialysis may be used to remove ethylene glycol from the blood. A toxic amount of ethylene glycol is 1.5 g of ethylene glycol/kg of body mass. Thus, 75 g could be fatal for a 50-kg (110 lb) person.

Mark determines that a fingerprint on the glass found in the victim's home is a match to the victim's husband. This evidence along with the container of antifreeze found in the home led to the arrest and conviction of the husband for poisoning his wife.

Clinical Applications

1.29 A container was found in the home of the victim that contained 120 g of ethylene glycol in 450 g of liquid. What was the percentage of ethylene glycol? Express your answer to the ones place.

1.30 How many drinks, each containing 100 g of the liquid in problem 1.29, would a 50-kg victim need to consume to reach a toxic level of ethylene glycol?

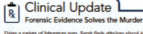

xxviii

Interactive Videos

Interactive videos and demonstrations help students through some of the more challenging topics by showing how chemistry works in real life and introducing a bit of humor into chemical problem solving and demonstrations. Topics include Using Conversion Factors, Balancing Nuclear Equations, Chemical v. Physical Change, and Dehydration of Sucrose.

Sample Calculations walk students through the most challenging chemistry problems and provide a fresh perspective on how to approach individual problems and reach their solutions. Topics include Using Conversion Factors, Mass Calculations for Reactions, and Concentration of Solutions.

 Green play button icons appear in the margins throughout the text. In the eText, the icons link to new interactive videos that the student can use to clarify and reinforce important concepts. All Interactive Videos are available in web and mobile-friendly formats through the eText, and are assignable activities in MasteringChemistry.

To obtain T_C by itself, we divide both sides by 1.8.

$$\frac{T_F - 32}{1.8} = \frac{1.8(T_C)}{1.8} = T_C$$

SAMPLE PROBLEM 1.4 Solving Equations

Solve the following equation for V_2:

$$P_1 V_1 = P_2 V_2$$

SOLUTION

$$P_1 V_1 = P_2 V_2$$

To solve for V_2, divide both sides by the symbol P_2.

$$\frac{P_1 V_1}{P_2} = \frac{P_2 V_2}{P_2}$$

$$V_2 = \frac{P_1 V_1}{P_2}$$

Interactive Video

Solving Equations

MasteringChemistry®

MasteringChemistry® from Pearson is the leading online teaching and learning system designed to improve results by engaging students before, during, and after class with powerful content. Ensure that students arrive ready to learn by assigning educationally effective content before class, and encourage critical thinking and retention with in-class resources such as Learning Catalytics. Students can further master concepts after class through traditional homework assignments that provide hints and answer-specific feedback. The Mastering gradebook records scores for all automatically graded assignments while diagnostic tools give instructors access to rich data to assess student understanding and misconceptions.

Mastering brings learning full circle by continuously adapting to each student and making learning more personal than ever—before, during, and after class.

Before Class

Dynamic Study Modules

Help students quickly learn chemistry!

Now assignable, Dynamic Study Modules (DSMs) enable your students to study on their own and be better prepared with the basic math and chemistry skills needed to succeed in the GOB course. The mobile app is available for iOS and Android devices for study on the go and results can be tracked in the MasteringChemistry gradebook.

Reading Quizzes

Reading Quizzes give instructors the opportunity to assign reading and test students on their comprehension of chapter content.

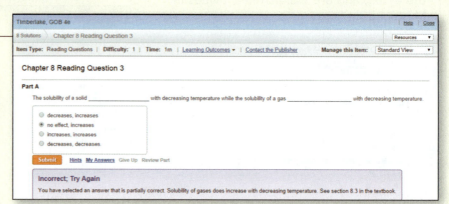

During Class

▶ Learning Catalytics

Learning Catalytics is a "bring your own device" student engagement, assessment, and classroom intelligence system. With Learning Catalytics you can:

- Assess students in real time, using open-ended tasks to probe student understanding.
- Understand immediately where students are and adjust your lecture accordingly.
- Manage student interactions with intelligent grouping and timing.

After Class

Tutorials and Coaching

Students learn chemistry by practicing chemistry.

Tutorials, featuring specific wrong-answer feedback, hints, and a wide variety of educationally effective content, guide your students through the toughest topics in General, Organic, and Biological chemistry.

▶ Adaptive Follow-Ups

Mastering continuously adapts to each student, making learning more personal than ever.

Adaptive Follow-Ups are personalized assignments that pair Mastering's powerful content with Knewton's adaptive learning engine to provide personalized help to students before misconceptions take hold. These assignments are based on each student's performance on homework assignments and on all work in the course to date, including core prerequisite topics.

1

Chemistry in Our Lives

A CALL CAME IN TO 911 FROM A MAN WHO FOUND

his wife lying on the floor of their home. When the police arrived at the home, they determined that the woman was dead. The husband said he had worked late, and just arrived at their home. The victim's body was lying on the floor of the living room. There was no blood at the scene, but the police did find a glass on the side table that contained a small amount of liquid. In an adjacent laundry room/garage, the police found a half-empty bottle of antifreeze. The bottle, glass, and liquid were bagged and sent to the forensic laboratory.

In another 911 call, a man was found lying on the grass outside his home. Blood was present on his body, and some bullet casings were found on the grass. Inside the victim's home, a weapon was recovered. The bullet casings and the weapon were bagged and sent to the forensic laboratory.

Sarah and Mark, forensic scientists, use scientific procedures and chemical tests to examine the evidence from law enforcement agencies. Sarah proceeds to analyze blood, stomach contents, and the unknown liquid from the first victim's home. She will look for the presence of drugs, poisons, and alcohol. Her lab partner Mark will analyze the fingerprints on the glass. He will also match the characteristics of the bullet casings to the weapon that was found at the second crime scene.

Evidence from a crime scene is sent to the forensic laboratory.

CAREER Forensic Scientist

Most forensic scientists work in crime laboratories that are part of city or county legal systems where they analyze bodily fluids and tissue samples collected by crime scene investigators. In analyzing these samples, forensic scientists identify the presence or absence of specific chemicals within the body to help solve the criminal case. Some of the chemicals they look for include alcohol, illegal or prescription drugs, poisons, arson debris, metals, and various gases such as carbon monoxide. In order to identify these substances, a variety of chemical instruments and highly specific methodologies are used. Forensic scientists also analyze samples from criminal suspects, athletes, and potential employees. They also work on cases involving environmental contamination and animal samples for wildlife crimes. Forensic scientists usually have a bachelor's degree that includes courses in math, chemistry, and biology.

LOOKING AHEAD

1.1 Chemistry and Chemicals 2

1.2 Scientific Method: Thinking Like a Scientist 4

 Chemistry Link to Health
Early Chemist: Paracelsus 5

1.3 Learning Chemistry: A Study Plan 6

1.4 Key Math Skills for Chemistry 9
   A. Identifying Place Values
   B. Using Positive and Negative Numbers in Calculations
   C. Calculating Percentages
   D. Solving Equations
   E. Interpreting Graphs
   F. Writing Numbers in Scientific Notation

℞ **Clinical Applications** 4, 6, 19

℞ **Clinical Update** *Forensic Evidence Solves the Murder* 19

Chemists working in research laboratories test new products and develop new pharmaceuticals.

LEARNING GOAL

Define the term chemistry and identify substances as chemicals.

Now that you are in a chemistry class, you may be wondering what you will be learning. What questions in science have you been curious about? Perhaps you are interested in what hemoglobin does in the body or how aspirin relieves a headache. Just like you, chemists are curious about the world we live in.

▶ What does hemoglobin do in the body? Hemoglobin consists of four polypeptide chains, each containing a heme group with an iron atom that binds to oxygen (O_2) in the lungs. From the lungs, hemoglobin transports oxygen to the tissues of the body where it is used to provide energy. Once the oxygen is released, hemoglobin binds to carbon dioxide (CO_2) for transport to the lungs where it is released.

Heme group

Hemoglobin transports oxygen to the tissues and carbon dioxide to the lungs.

▶ Why does aspirin relieve a headache? When a part of the body is injured, substances called prostaglandins are produced, which cause inflammation and pain. Aspirin acts to block the production of prostaglandins, thereby reducing inflammation, pain, and fever.

Chemists in the medical field develop new treatments for diabetes, genetic defects, cancer, AIDS, and other diseases. Researchers in the environmental field study the ways in which human development impacts the environment and develop processes that help reduce environmental degradation. For the chemist in the forensic laboratory, the nurse in the dialysis unit, the dietitian, or the agricultural scientist, chemistry plays a central role in understanding problems, assessing possible solutions, and making important decisions.

1.1 Chemistry and Chemicals

Chemistry is the study of the composition, structure, properties, and reactions of matter. *Matter* is another word for all the substances that make up our world. Perhaps you imagine that chemistry takes place only in a laboratory where a chemist is working in a white coat and goggles. Actually, chemistry happens all around you every day and has an impact on everything you use and do. You are doing chemistry when you cook food, add bleach to your laundry, or start your car. A chemical reaction has taken place when silver tarnishes or an antacid tablet fizzes when dropped into water. Plants grow because chemical reactions convert carbon dioxide, water, and energy to carbohydrates. Chemical reactions take place when you digest food and break it down into substances that you need for energy and health.

Antacid tablets undergo a chemical reaction when dropped into water.

Chemicals

A **chemical** is a substance that always has the same composition and properties wherever it is found. All the things you see around you are composed of one or more chemicals. Chemical processes take place in chemistry laboratories, manufacturing plants, and pharmaceutical labs as well as every day in nature and in our bodies. Often the terms *chemical* and *substance* are used interchangeably to describe a specific type of matter.

Every day, you use products containing substances that were developed and prepared by chemists. Soaps and shampoos contain chemicals that remove oils on your skin and scalp. When you brush your teeth, the substances in toothpaste clean your teeth, prevent plaque formation, and stop tooth decay. Some of the chemicals used to make toothpaste are listed in Table 1.1.

In cosmetics and lotions, chemicals are used to moisturize, prevent deterioration of the product, fight bacteria, and thicken the product. Your clothes may be made of natural materials such as cotton or synthetic substances such as nylon or polyester. Perhaps you wear a ring or watch made of gold, silver, or platinum. Your breakfast cereal is probably fortified with iron, calcium, and phosphorus, whereas the milk you drink is enriched with vitamins A and D. Antioxidants are chemicals added to food to prevent it from spoiling. Some of the chemicals you may encounter when you cook in the kitchen are shown in Figure 1.1.

Toothpaste is a combination of many chemicals.

TABLE 1.1 Chemicals Commonly Used in Toothpaste

Chemical	Function
Calcium carbonate	Used as an abrasive to remove plaque
Sorbitol	Prevents loss of water and hardening of toothpaste
Sodium lauryl sulfate	Used to loosen plaque
Titanium dioxide	Makes toothpaste white and opaque
Triclosan	Inhibits bacteria that cause plaque and gum disease
Sodium fluorophosphate	Prevents formation of cavities by strengthening tooth enamel with fluoride
Methyl salicylate	Gives toothpaste a pleasant wintergreen flavor

Silicon dioxide (glass)

Chemically treated water

Metal alloy

Natural polymers

Natural gas

Fruits grown with fertilizers and pesticides

FIGURE 1.1 ▶ Many of the items found in a kitchen are chemicals or products of chemical reactions.

Q What are some other chemicals found in a kitchen?

QUESTIONS AND PROBLEMS

1.1 Chemistry and Chemicals

LEARNING GOAL Define the term chemistry and identify substances as chemicals.

In every chapter, odd-numbered exercises in the *Questions and Problems* are paired with even-numbered exercises. The answers for the magenta, odd-numbered *Questions and Problems* are given at the end of each chapter. The complete solutions to the odd-numbered *Questions and Problems* are in the *Student Solutions Manual*.

1.1 Write a one-sentence definition for each of the following:
   a. chemistry
   b. chemical

1.2 Ask two of your friends (not in this class) to define the terms in problem 1.1. Do their answers agree with the definitions you provided?

1.3 Obtain a bottle of multivitamins and read the list of ingredients. What are four chemicals from the list?

1.4 Obtain a box of breakfast cereal and read the list of ingredients. What are four chemicals from the list?

℞ Clinical Applications

1.5 Read the labels on some items found in your medicine cabinet. What are the names of some chemicals contained in those items?

1.6 Read the labels on products used to wash your dishes. What are the names of some chemicals contained in those products?

Describe the activities that are part of the scientific method.

Linus Pauling won the Nobel Prize in Chemistry in 1954.

Explore Your World

Nobel Prize Winners in Chemistry

Use the Internet to find information about each of the following:

1. Who won the latest Nobel Prize in Chemistry?
2. What was the area of research for question **1**?

1.2 Scientific Method: Thinking Like a Scientist

When you were very young, you explored the things around you by touching and tasting. As you grew, you asked questions about the world in which you live. What is lightning? Where does a rainbow come from? Why is water blue? As an adult, you may have wondered how antibiotics work or why vitamins are important to your health. Every day, you ask questions and seek answers to organize and make sense of the world around you.

When the late Nobel Laureate Linus Pauling described his student life in Oregon, he recalled that he read many books on chemistry, mineralogy, and physics. "I mulled over the properties of materials: why are some substances colored and others not, why are some minerals or inorganic compounds hard and others soft?" He said, "I was building up this tremendous background of empirical knowledge and at the same time asking a great number of questions." Linus Pauling won two Nobel Prizes: the first, in 1954, was in chemistry for his work on the nature of chemical bonds and the determination of the structures of complex substances; the second, in 1962, was the Peace Prize.

Scientific Method

Although the process of trying to understand nature is unique to each scientist, a set of general principles, called the **scientific method**, helps to describe how a scientist thinks.

1. **Observations** The first step in the scientific method is to make *observations* about nature and ask questions about what you observe.
2. **Hypothesis** Propose a *hypothesis*, which states a possible explanation of the observations. The hypothesis must be stated in such a way that it can be tested by experiments.
3. **Experiments** Several *experiments* may be done to test the hypothesis.
4. **Conclusion** When the results of the experiments are analyzed, a *conclusion* is made as to whether the hypothesis is *true* or *false*. When experiments give consistent results, the hypothesis may be confirmed. Even then, a hypothesis continues to be tested and, based on new experimental results, may need to be modified or replaced.

Chemistry Link to **Health**

Early Chemist: Paracelsus

Paracelsus (1493–1541) was a physician and an alchemist who thought that alchemy should be about preparing new medicines. Using observation and experimentation, he proposed that a healthy body was regulated by a series of chemical processes that could be unbalanced by certain chemical compounds and rebalanced by using minerals and medicines. For example, he determined that inhaled dust, not underground spirits, caused lung disease in miners. He also thought that goiter was a problem caused by contaminated water, and he treated syphilis with compounds of mercury. His opinion of medicines was that the right dose makes the difference between a poison and a cure. Paracelsus changed alchemy in ways that helped to establish modern medicine and chemistry.

Swiss physician and alchemist Paracelsus (1493–1541) believed that chemicals and minerals could be used as medicines.

Using the Scientific Method in Everyday Life

You may be surprised to realize that you use the scientific method in your everyday life. Suppose you visit a friend in her home. Soon after you arrive, your eyes start to itch and you begin to sneeze. Then you observe that your friend has a new cat. Perhaps you ask yourself why you are sneezing and you form the hypothesis that you are allergic to cats. To test your hypothesis, you leave your friend's home. If the sneezing stops, perhaps your hypothesis is correct. You test your hypothesis further by visiting another friend who also has a cat. If you start to sneeze again, your experimental results support your hypothesis and you come to the conclusion that you are allergic to cats. However, if you continue sneezing after you leave your friend's home, your hypothesis is not supported. Now you need to form a new hypothesis, which could be that you have a cold.

Scientific Method

Observations

Hypothesis — The hypothesis is modified if the results of the experiments do not support it.

Experiments

Conclusion

The scientific method develops conclusions using observations, hypotheses, and experiments.

Through observation you may determine that you are allergic to cat hair and dander.

QUESTIONS AND PROBLEMS

1.2 Scientific Method: Thinking Like a Scientist

LEARNING GOAL Describe the activities that are part of the scientific method.

1.7 Identify each activity, **a** to **f**, as an observation (O), a hypothesis (H), an experiment (E), or a conclusion (C).
At a popular restaurant, where Chang is the head chef, the following occurred:
   a. Chang determined that sales of the house salad had dropped.
   b. Chang decided that the house salad needed a new dressing.
   c. In a taste test, Chang prepared four bowls of lettuce, each with a new dressing: sesame seed, olive oil and balsamic vinegar, creamy Italian, and blue cheese.
   d. The tasters rated the sesame seed salad dressing as the favorite.
   e. After two weeks, Chang noted that the orders for the house salad with the new sesame seed dressing had doubled.
   f. Chang decided that the sesame seed dressing improved the sales of the house salad because the sesame seed dressing enhanced the taste.

1.8 Identify each activity, **a** to **f**, as an observation (O), a hypothesis (H), an experiment (E), or a conclusion (C).
Lucia wants to develop a process for dyeing shirts so that the color will not fade when the shirt is washed. She proceeds with the following activities:

Customers rated the sesame seed dressing as the best.

   a. Lucia notices that the dye in a design fades when the shirt is washed.
   b. Lucia decides that the dye needs something to help it combine with the fabric.
   c. She places a spot of dye on each of four shirts and then places each one separately in water, salt water, vinegar, and baking soda and water.
   d. After one hour, all the shirts are removed and washed with a detergent.
   e. Lucia notices that the dye has faded on the shirts in water, salt water, and baking soda, whereas the dye did not fade on the shirt soaked in vinegar.
   f. Lucia thinks that the vinegar binds with the dye so it does not fade when the shirt is washed.

Clinical Applications

1.9 Identify each of the following as an observation (O), a hypothesis (H), an experiment (E), or a conclusion (C):
   a. One hour after drinking a glass of regular milk, Jim experienced stomach cramps.
   b. Jim thinks he may be lactose intolerant.
   c. Jim drinks a glass of lactose-free milk and does not have any stomach cramps.
   d. Jim drinks a glass of regular milk to which he has added lactase, an enzyme that breaks down lactose, and has no stomach cramps.

1.10 Identify each of the following as an observation (O), a hypothesis (H), an experiment (E), or a conclusion (C):
   a. Sally thinks she may be allergic to shrimp.
   b. Yesterday, one hour after Sally ate a shrimp salad, she broke out in hives.
   c. Today, Sally had some soup that contained shrimp, but she did not break out in hives.
   d. Sally realizes that she does not have an allergy to shrimp.

KEY MATH SKILL

CORE CHEMISTRY SKILL

1.3 Learning Chemistry: A Study Plan

Here you are taking chemistry, perhaps for the first time. Whatever your reasons for choosing to study chemistry, you can look forward to learning many new and exciting ideas.

Features in This Text Help You Study Chemistry

This text has been designed with study features to complement your individual learning style. On the inside of the front cover is a periodic table of the elements. On the inside of the back cover are tables that summarize useful information needed throughout your study of chemistry. Each chapter begins with *Looking Ahead*, which outlines the topics in the chapter. At the end of the text, there is a comprehensive *Glossary and Index*, which lists and defines key terms used in the text. *Key Math Skills* and *Core Chemistry Skills* that are critical to learning chemistry are indicated by icons in the margin, and summarized at the end of each chapter. In the *Chapter Readiness* list at the beginning of every chapter, the *Key Math Skills* and *Core Chemistry Skills* from previous chapters related to the current chapter concepts are highlighted for your review.

Before you begin reading, obtain an overview of a chapter by reviewing the topics in *Looking Ahead*. As you prepare to read a section of the chapter, look at the section title and turn it into a question. For example, for section 1.1, "Chemistry and Chemicals," you could ask, "What is chemistry?" or "What are chemicals?" When you come to a *Sample Problem*, take the time to work it through and compare your solution to the one provided. Then try the associated *Study Check*. Many *Sample Problems* are accompanied by a *Guide to Problem Solving*, which gives the steps needed to work the problem. In some *Sample Problems*, an *Analyze the Problem* feature shows how to organize the data in the word problem to obtain a solution. At the end of each chapter section, you will find a set of *Questions and Problems* that allows you to apply problem solving immediately to the new concepts.

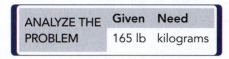

ANALYZE THE PROBLEM	Given	Need
	165 lb	kilograms

Throughout each chapter, boxes titled "Chemistry Link to Health" and "Chemistry Link to the Environment" help you connect the chemical concepts you are learning to real-life situations. Many of the figures and diagrams use macro-to-micro illustrations to depict the atomic level of organization of ordinary objects. These visual models illustrate the concepts described in the text and allow you to "see" the world in a microscopic way. The *Explore Your World* features investigate concepts with materials found at home.

At the end of each chapter, you will find several study aids that complete the chapter. *Chapter Reviews* provide a summary in easy-to-read bullet points and *Concept Maps* visually show the connections between important topics. The *Key Terms*, which are in boldface type within the chapter, are listed with their definitions. *Understanding the Concepts*, a set of questions that use art and models, helps you visualize concepts. *Additional Questions and Problems* and *Challenge Problems* provide additional exercises to test your understanding of the topics in the chapter. The problems are paired, which means that each of the odd-numbered problems is matched to the following even-numbered problem. *Clinical Applications* are groups of problems that apply section content to health-related topics. The answers to all the *Study Checks* are included with the Sample Problems and the answers to all the odd-numbered problems are provided at the end of the chapter. If the answers provided match your answers, you most likely understand the topic; if not, you need to study the section again.

After some chapters, problem sets called *Combining Ideas* test your ability to solve problems containing material from more than one chapter.

Using Active Learning

A student who is an active learner continually interacts with the chemical ideas while reading the text, working problems, and attending lectures. Let's see how this is done.

As you read and practice problem solving, you remain actively involved in studying, which enhances the learning process. In this way, you learn small bits of information at a time and establish the necessary foundation for understanding the next section. You may also note questions you have about the reading to discuss with your professor or laboratory instructor. Table 1.2 summarizes these steps for active learning. The time you spend in a lecture is also a useful learning time. By keeping track of the class schedule and reading the assigned material before a lecture, you become aware of the new terms and concepts you need to learn. Some questions that occur during your reading may be answered during the lecture. If not, you can ask your professor for further clarification.

Many students find that studying with a group can be beneficial to learning. In a group, students motivate each other to study, fill in gaps, and correct misunderstandings by teaching and learning together. Studying alone does not allow the process of peer correction. In a group, you can cover the ideas more thoroughly as you discuss the reading and problem solve with other students. You may find that it is easier to retain new material and new ideas if you study in short sessions throughout the week rather than all at once. Waiting to study until the night before an exam does not give you time to understand concepts and practice problem solving.

Studying in a group can be beneficial to learning.

TABLE 1.2 Steps in Active Learning

1. Read each *Learning Goal* for an overview of the material.

2. Form a question from the title of the section you are going to read.

3. Read the section, looking for answers to your question.

4. Self-test by working *Sample Problems* and *Study Checks*.

5. Complete the *Questions and Problems* that follow that section, and check the answers for the magenta odd-numbered problems.

6. Proceed to the next section and repeat the steps.

Making a Study Plan

As you embark on your journey into the world of chemistry, think about your approach to studying and learning chemistry. You might consider some of the ideas in the following list. Check those ideas that will help you successfully learn chemistry. Commit to them now. *Your* success depends on *you*.

My study plan for learning chemistry will include the following:

_____ reading the chapter before lecture

_____ going to lecture

_____ reviewing the *Learning Goals*

_____ keeping a problem notebook

_____ reading the text as an active learner

_____ working the *Questions and Problems* following each section and checking answers at the end of the chapter

_____ being an active learner in lecture

_____ organizing a study group

_____ seeing the professor during office hours

_____ reviewing *Key Math Skills* and *Core Chemistry Skills*

_____ attending review sessions

_____ organizing my own review sessions

_____ studying as often as I can

Students discuss a chemistry problem with their professor during office hours.

▶ SAMPLE PROBLEM 1.1   A Study Plan for Learning Chemistry

Which of the following activities would you include in your study plan for learning chemistry successfully?

a. skipping lecture
b. going to the professor's office hours
c. keeping a problem notebook
d. waiting to study until the night before the exam
e. becoming an active learner

SOLUTION

Your success in chemistry can be improved by

b. going to the professor's office hours
c. keeping a problem notebook
e. becoming an active learner

STUDY CHECK 1.1

Which of the following will help you learn chemistry?

a. skipping review sessions
b. working assigned problems
c. staying up all night before an exam
d. reading the assignment before a lecture

ANSWER

b and **d**

QUESTIONS AND PROBLEMS

1.3 Learning Chemistry: A Study Plan

LEARNING GOAL Develop a study plan for learning chemistry.

1.11 What are four things you can do to help yourself to succeed in chemistry?

1.12 What are four things that would make it difficult for you to learn chemistry?

1.13 A student in your class asks you for advice on learning chemistry. Which of the following might you suggest?
 a. forming a study group
 b. skipping a lecture
 c. visiting the professor during office hours
 d. waiting until the night before an exam to study
 e. being an active learner

1.14 A student in your class asks you for advice on learning chemistry. Which of the following might you suggest?
 a. doing the assigned problems
 b. not reading the text; it's never on the test
 c. attending review sessions
 d. reading the assignment before a lecture
 e. keeping a problem notebook

1.4 Key Math Skills for Chemistry

During your study of chemistry, you will work many problems that involve numbers. You will need various math skills and operations. We will review some of the key math skills that are particularly important for chemistry. As we move through the chapters, we will also reference the key math skills as they apply.

A. Identifying Place Values

For any number, we can identify the *place value* for each of the digits in that number. These place values have names such as the ones place (first place to the left of the decimal point) or the tens place (second place to the left of the decimal point). A premature baby has a mass of 2518 g. We can indicate the place values for the number 2518 as follows:

Digit	Place Value
2	thousands
5	hundreds
1	tens
8	ones

We also identify place values such as the tenths place (first place to the right of the decimal point) and the hundredths place (second place to the right of the decimal place). A silver coin has a mass of 6.407 g. We can indicate the place values for the number 6.407 as follows:

Digit	Place Value
6	ones
4	ten**ths**
0	hundred**ths**
7	thousand**ths**

Note that place values ending with the suffix *ths* refer to the decimal places to the right of the decimal point.

SAMPLE PROBLEM 1.2 **Identifying Place Values**

A bullet found at a crime scene has a mass of 15.24 g. What are the place values for the digits in the mass of the bullet?

SOLUTION

Digit	Place Value
1	tens
5	ones
2	tenths
4	hundredths

STUDY CHECK 1.2

A bullet found at a crime scene contains 0.925 g of lead. What are the place values for the digits in the mass of the lead?

ANSWER

Digit	Place Value
9	tenths
2	hundredths
5	thousandths

KEY MATH SKILL

Using Positive and Negative Numbers in Calculations

B. Using Positive and Negative Numbers in Calculations

A *positive number* is any number that is greater than zero and has a positive sign $(+)$. Often the positive sign is understood and not written in front of the number. For example, the number $+8$ can also be written as 8. A *negative number* is any number that is less than zero and is written with a negative sign $(-)$. For example, a negative eight is written as -8.

Multiplication and Division of Positive and Negative Numbers
When two positive numbers or two negative numbers are multiplied, the answer is positive $(+)$.

$$2 \times 3 = +6$$
$$(-2) \times (-3) = +6$$

When a positive number and a negative number are multiplied, the answer is negative $(-)$.

$$2 \times (-3) = -6$$
$$(-2) \times 3 = -6$$

The rules for the division of positive and negative numbers are the same as the rules for multiplication. When two positive numbers or two negative numbers are divided, the answer is positive $(+)$.

$$\frac{6}{3} = 2 \qquad \frac{-6}{-3} = 2$$

When a positive number and a negative number are divided, the answer is negative $(-)$.

$$\frac{-6}{3} = -2 \qquad \frac{6}{-3} = -2$$

Addition of Positive and Negative Numbers

When positive numbers are added, the sign of the answer is positive.

$3 + 4 = 7$ The $+$ sign $(+7)$ is understood.

When negative numbers are added, the sign of the answer is negative.

$(-3) + (-4) = -7$

When a positive number and a negative number are added, the smaller number is subtracted from the larger number, and the result has the same sign as the larger number.

$12 + (-15) = -3$

Subtraction of Positive and Negative Numbers

When two numbers are subtracted, change the sign of the number to be subtracted and follow the rules for addition shown above.

$$12 - (\mathbf{+5}) \ \ = 12 - \mathbf{5} \ \ = 7$$
$$12 - (\mathbf{-5}) \ \ = 12 + \mathbf{5} \ \ = 17$$
$$-12 - (\mathbf{-5}) = -12 + \mathbf{5} = -7$$
$$-12 - (\mathbf{+5}) = -12 - \mathbf{5} = -17$$

Calculator Operations

On your calculator, there are four keys that are used for basic mathematical operations. The change sign $\boxed{+/-}$ key is used to change the sign of a number.

To practice these basic calculations on the calculator, work through the problem going from the left to the right doing the operations in the order they occur. If your calculator has a change sign $\boxed{+/-}$ key, a negative number is entered by pressing the number and then pressing the change sign $\boxed{+/-}$ key. At the end, press the equals $\boxed{=}$ key or ANS or ENTER.

Change sign   Addition

Multiplication
Division
Subtraction
Equals

Addition and Subtraction

Example 1: $15 - 8 + 2 =$

Solution: $15 \ \boxed{-} \ 8 \ \boxed{+} \ 2 \ \boxed{=} \ 9$

Example 2: $4 + (-10) - 5 =$

Solution: $4 \ \boxed{+} \ 10 \ \boxed{+/-} \ \boxed{-} \ 5 \ \boxed{=} \ -11$

Multiplication and Division

Example 3: $2 \times (-3) =$

Solution: $2 \ \boxed{\times} \ 3 \ \boxed{+/-} \ \boxed{=} \ -6$

Example 4: $\dfrac{8 \times 3}{4} =$

Solution: $8 \ \boxed{\times} \ 3 \ \boxed{\div} \ 4 \ \boxed{=} \ 6$

📱 **KEY MATH SKILL**

Calculating Percentages

C. Calculating Percentages

To determine a percentage, divide the parts by the total (whole) and multiply by 100%. For example, if an aspirin tablet contains 325 mg of aspirin (active ingredient) and the tablet has a mass of 545 mg, what is the percentage of aspirin in the tablet?

$$\frac{325 \text{ mg aspirin}}{545 \text{ mg tablet}} \times 100\% = 59.6\% \text{ aspirin}$$

When a value is described as a percentage (%), it represents the number of parts of an item in 100 of those items. If the percentage of red balls is 5, it means there are 5 red balls in every 100 balls. If the percentage of green balls is 50, there are 50 green balls in every 100 balls.

$$5\% \text{ red balls} = \frac{5 \text{ red balls}}{100 \text{ balls}} \qquad 50\% \text{ green balls} = \frac{50 \text{ green balls}}{100 \text{ balls}}$$

▶ **SAMPLE PROBLEM 1.3** Calculating a Percentage

In the forensic laboratory, a bullet found at a crime scene may be used as evidence in a trial if the percentage of three metals, usually lead, tin, and antimony, is a match to the composition of metals in a bullet from the suspect's ammunition. If a bullet found at the crime scene contains 13.9 g of lead, 0.3 g of tin, and 0.9 g of antimony, what is the percentage of each metal in the bullet? Express your answers to the ones place.

SOLUTION

Total mass = 13.9 g + 0.3 g + 0.9 g = 15.1 g

Percentage of lead

$$\frac{13.9 \text{ g}}{15.1 \text{ g}} \times 100\% = 92\% \text{ lead}$$

Percentage of tin

$$\frac{0.3 \text{ g}}{15.1 \text{ g}} \times 100\% = 2\% \text{ tin}$$

Percentage of antimony

$$\frac{0.9 \text{ g}}{15.1 \text{ g}} \times 100\% = 6\% \text{ antimony}$$

STUDY CHECK 1.3

A bullet seized from the suspect's ammunition has a composition of lead 11.6 g, tin 0.5 g, and antimony 0.4 g.

a. What is the percentage of each metal in the bullet? Express your answers to the ones place.
b. Could the bullet removed from the suspect's ammunition be considered as evidence that the suspect was at the crime scene?

ANSWER

a. The bullet from the suspect's ammunition is lead 93%, tin 4%, and antimony 3%.
b. The bullet in part **a** does not match the bullet from the crime scene and cannot be used as evidence.

A bullet casing at a crime scene is marked as evidence.

📱 **KEY MATH SKILL**

Solving Equations

D. Solving Equations

In chemistry, we use equations that express the relationship between certain variables. Let's look at how we would solve for x in the following equation:

$$2x + 8 = 14$$

Our overall goal is to rearrange the items in the equation to obtain x on one side.

1. *Place all like terms on one side.* The numbers 8 and 14 are like terms. To remove the 8 from the left side of the equation, we subtract 8. To keep a balance, we need to subtract 8 from the 14 on the other side.

$$2x + 8 - 8 = 14 - 8$$
$$2x = 6$$

2. *Isolate the variable you need to solve for.* In this problem, we obtain x by dividing both sides of the equation by 2. The value of x is the result when 6 is divided by 2.

$$\frac{2x}{2} = \frac{6}{2}$$
$$x = 3$$

3. *Check your answer.* Check your answer by substituting your value for x back into the original equation.

$$2(3) + 8 = 14$$
$$6 + 8 = 14$$
$$14 = 14 \quad \text{Your answer } x = 3 \text{ is correct.}$$

Summary: To solve an equation for a particular variable, be sure you perform the same mathematical operations on *both* sides of the equation.

If you eliminate a symbol or number by subtracting, you need to subtract that same symbol or number on the opposite side.

If you eliminate a symbol or number by adding, you need to add that same symbol or number on the opposite side.

If you cancel a symbol or number by dividing, you need to divide both sides by that same symbol or number.

If you cancel a symbol or number by multiplying, you need to multiply both sides by that same symbol or number.

When we work with temperature, we may need to convert between degrees Celsius and degrees Fahrenheit using the following equation:

$$T_F = 1.8(T_C) + 32$$

To obtain the equation for converting degrees Fahrenheit to degrees Celsius, we subtract 32 from both sides.

$$T_F = 1.8(T_C) + 32$$
$$T_F - 32 = 1.8(T_C) + 32 - 32$$
$$T_F - 32 = 1.8(T_C)$$

To obtain T_C by itself, we divide both sides by 1.8.

$$\frac{T_F - 32}{1.8} = \frac{1.8(T_C)}{1.8} = T_C$$

A plastic strip thermometer changes color to indicate body temperature.

▶ **SAMPLE PROBLEM 1.4** Solving Equations

Solve the following equation for V_2:

$$P_1V_1 = P_2V_2$$

SOLUTION

$$P_1V_1 = P_2V_2$$

To solve for V_2, divide both sides by the symbol P_2.

$$\frac{P_1V_1}{P_2} = \frac{P_2V_2}{P_2}$$
$$V_2 = \frac{P_1V_1}{P_2}$$

Interactive Video

Solving Equations

STUDY CHECK 1.4

Solve the following equation for *m*:

heat = $m \times \Delta T \times SH$

ANSWER

$$m = \frac{\text{heat}}{\Delta T \times SH}$$

📱 **KEY MATH SKILL**

Interpreting Graphs

E. Interpreting Graphs

A graph represents the relationship between two variables. These quantities are plotted along two perpendicular axes, which are the *x* axis (horizontal) and *y* axis (vertical).

Example

In the following graph, the volume of a gas in a balloon is plotted against its temperature.

Title

Look at the title. What does it tell us about the graph? The title indicates that the volume of a balloon was measured at different temperatures.

Vertical Axis

Look at the label and the numbers on the vertical (*y*) axis. The label indicates that the volume of the balloon was measured in liters (L). The numbers, which are chosen to include the low and high measurements of the volume of the gas, are evenly spaced from 22.0 L to 30.0 L.

Horizontal Axis

The label on the horizontal (*x*) axis indicates that the temperature of the balloon was measured in degrees Celsius (°C). The numbers are measurements of the Celsius temperature, which are evenly spaced from 0. °C to 100. °C.

Points on the Graph

Each point on the graph represents a volume in liters that was measured at a specific temperature. When these points are connected, a straight line is obtained.

Interpreting the Graph

From the graph, we see that the volume of the gas increases as the temperature of the gas increases. This is called a *direct relationship*. Now we use the graph to determine the volume at various temperatures. For example, suppose we want to know the volume of the gas at 50. °C. We would start by finding 50. °C on the *x* axis and then drawing a line up to the plotted line. From there, we would draw a horizontal line that intersects the *y* axis and read the volume value where the line crosses the *y* axis.

▶ **SAMPLE PROBLEM 1.5** Interpreting a Graph

A nurse administers Tylenol to lower a child's fever. The graph shows the body temperature of the child plotted against time.

a. What is measured on the vertical axis?
b. What is the range of values on the vertical axis?
c. What is measured on the horizontal axis?
d. What is the range of values on the horizontal axis?

SOLUTION

a. temperature in degrees Celsius
b. 37.0 °C to 39.4 °C
c. time, in minutes, after Tylenol was given
d. 0 min to 30 min

STUDY CHECK 1.5

a. Using the graph in Sample Problem 1.5, what was the child's temperature 15 min after Tylenol was given?
b. How many minutes elapsed before the temperature decreased to 38.0 °C?

ANSWER

a. 37.6 °C   **b.** 8 min

F. Writing Numbers in Scientific Notation

In chemistry, we use numbers that are very large and very small. We might measure something as tiny as the width of a human hair, which is about 0.000 008 m. Or perhaps we want to count the number of hairs on the average human scalp, which is about 100 000 hairs. In this text, we add spaces between sets of three digits when it helps make the places easier to count. However, we will see that it is more convenient to write large and small numbers in *scientific notation*.

🖩 **KEY MATH SKILL**

Writing Numbers in Scientific Notation

1×10^5 hairs 8×10^{-6} m

Humans have an average of 1×10^5 hairs on their scalps. Each hair is about 8×10^{-6} m wide.

Standard Number	Scientific Notation
0.000 008 m	8×10^{-6} m
100 000 hairs	1×10^5 hairs

A number written in **scientific notation** has two parts: a coefficient and a power of 10. For example, the number 2400 is written in scientific notation as 2.4×10^3. The coefficient, 2.4, is obtained by moving the decimal point to the left to give a number that is at least 1 but less than 10. Because we moved the decimal point three places to the left, the power of 10 is a positive 3, which is written as 10^3. When a number greater than 1 is converted to scientific notation, the power of 10 is positive.

$$2400. \quad = \quad 2.4 \quad \times \quad 10^3$$
$$\leftarrow \text{3 places} \qquad \text{Coefficient} \qquad \text{Power of 10}$$

In another example, a number smaller than 1, 0.000 86, is written in scientific notation as 8.6×10^{-4}. The coefficient, 8.6, is obtained by moving the decimal point to the right. Because the decimal point is moved four places to the right, the power of 10 is a negative 4, written as 10^{-4}. When a number less than 1 is written in scientific notation, the power of 10 is negative.

$$0.00086 \quad = \quad 8.6 \quad \times \quad 10^{-4}$$
$$\text{4 places} \rightarrow \qquad \text{Coefficient} \qquad \text{Power of 10}$$

Table 1.3 gives some examples of numbers written as positive and negative powers of 10. The powers of 10 are a way of keeping track of the decimal point in the number. Table 1.4 gives several examples of writing measurements in scientific notation.

TABLE 1.3 Some Powers of 10

Number	Multiples of 10	Scientific Notation	
10 000	$10 \times 10 \times 10 \times 10$	1×10^4	
1 000	$10 \times 10 \times 10$	1×10^3	
100	10×10	1×10^2	Some positive powers of 10
10	10	1×10^1	
1	0	1×10^0	
0.1	$\dfrac{1}{10}$	1×10^{-1}	
0.01	$\dfrac{1}{10} \times \dfrac{1}{10} = \dfrac{1}{100}$	1×10^{-2}	Some negative powers of 10
0.001	$\dfrac{1}{10} \times \dfrac{1}{10} \times \dfrac{1}{10} = \dfrac{1}{1\,000}$	1×10^{-3}	
0.0001	$\dfrac{1}{10} \times \dfrac{1}{10} \times \dfrac{1}{10} \times \dfrac{1}{10} = \dfrac{1}{10\,000}$	1×10^{-4}	

A chickenpox virus has a diameter of 3×10^{-7} m.

TABLE 1.4 Some Measurements Written in Scientific Notation

Measured Quantity	Standard Number	Scientific Notation
Volume of gasoline used in the United States each year	550 000 000 000 L	5.5×10^{11} L
Diameter of the Earth	12 800 000 m	1.28×10^7 m
Average volume of blood pumped in 1 day	8500 L	8.5×10^3 L
Time for light to travel from the Sun to the Earth	500 s	5×10^2 s
Mass of a typical human	68 kg	6.8×10^1 kg
Mass of stirrup bone in ear	0.003 g	3×10^{-3} g
Diameter of a chickenpox (*Varicella zoster*) virus	0.000 000 3 m	3×10^{-7} m
Mass of bacterium (mycoplasma)	0.000 000 000 000 000 000 1 kg	1×10^{-19} kg

Scientific Notation and Calculators

You can enter a number in scientific notation on many calculators using the [EE or EXP] key. After you enter the coefficient, press the [EE or EXP] key and enter only the power of 10, because the [EE or EXP] key already includes the $\times 10$ value. To enter a negative power of 10, press the [+/-] key or the [-] key, depending on your calculator.

Number to Enter	Procedure	Calculator Display
4×10^6	4 [EE or EXP] 6	*4 06* or *4⁰⁶* or *4E06*
2.5×10^{-4}	2.5 [EE or EXP] [+/-] 4	*2.5-04* or *2.5⁻⁰⁴* or *2.5E-04*

When a calculator display appears in scientific notation, it is shown as a number between 1 and 10 followed by a space and the power of 10. To express this display in scientific notation, write the coefficient value, write $\times 10$, and use the power of 10 as an exponent.

Calculator Display	Expressed in Scientific Notation
7.52 04 or *7.52⁰⁴* or *7.52E04*	7.52×10^4
5.8-02 or *5.8⁻⁰²* or *5.8E-02*	5.8×10^{-2}

On many scientific calculators, a number is converted into scientific notation using the appropriate keys. For example, the number 0.000 52 is entered, followed by pressing the 2nd or 3rd function key and the SCI key. The scientific notation appears in the calculator display as a coefficient and the power of 10.

0.000 52 [2ⁿᵈ or 3ʳᵈ function key] [SCI] $=$ *5.2-04* or *5.2⁻⁰⁴* or *5.2E-04* $= 5.2 \times 10^{-4}$

Calculator display

▶ **SAMPLE PROBLEM 1.6 Scientific Notation**

Write each of the following in scientific notation:

a. 3500   **b.** 0.000 016

SOLUTION

a. 3500

STEP 1 Move the decimal point to obtain a coefficient that is at least 1 but less than 10. For a number greater than 1, the decimal point is moved to the left three places to give a coefficient of 3.5.

STEP 2 Express the number of places moved as a power of 10. Moving the decimal point three places to the left gives a power of 3, written as 10^3.

STEP 3 Write the product of the coefficient multiplied by the power of 10.
3.5×10^3

b. 0.000 016

STEP 1 Move the decimal point to obtain a coefficient that is at least 1 but less than 10. For a number less than one, the decimal point is moved to the right five places to give a coefficient of 1.6.

STEP 2 Express the number of places moved as a power of 10. Moving the decimal point five places to the right gives a power of negative 5, written as 10^{-5}.

STEP 3 Write the product of the coefficient multiplied by the power of 10.
1.6×10^{-5}

Guide to Writing a Number in Scientific Notation

STEP 1
Move the decimal point to obtain a coefficient that is at least 1 but less than 10.

STEP 2
Express the number of places moved as a power of 10.

STEP 3
Write the product of the coefficient multiplied by the power of 10.

STUDY CHECK 1.6

Write each of the following in scientific notation:

a. 425 000   **b.** 0.000 000 86

ANSWER

a. 4.25×10^5 **b.** 8.6×10^{-7}

QUESTIONS AND PROBLEMS

1.4 Key Math Skills in Chemistry

LEARNING GOAL Review math concepts used in chemistry: place values, positive and negative numbers, percentages, solving equations, interpreting graphs, and writing numbers in scientific notation.

1.15 What is the place value for the bold digit?
 a. 7.32**8**8
 b. 16.1**2**34
 c. **4**675.99

1.16 What is the place value for the bold digit?
 a. 97.**5**689
 b. 375.8**8**
 c. 46.1**0**00

1.17 Evaluate each of the following:
 a. $15 - (-8) = $ _____
 b. $-8 + (-22) = $ _____
 c. $4 \times (-2) + 6 = $ _____

1.18 Evaluate each of the following:
 a. $-11 - (-9) = $ _____
 b. $34 + (-55) = $ _____
 c. $\dfrac{-56}{8} = $ _____

1.19 **a.** A clinic had 25 patients on Friday morning. If 21 patients were given flu shots, what percentage of the patients received flu shots? Express your answer to the ones place.
 b. An alloy contains 56 g of pure silver and 22 g of pure copper. What is the percentage of silver in the alloy? Express your answer to the ones place.
 c. A collection of coins contains 11 nickels, 5 quarters, and 7 dimes. What is the percentage of dimes in the collection? Express your answer to the ones place.

1.20 **a.** At a local hospital, 35 babies were born. If 22 were boys, what percentage of the newborns were boys? Express your answer to the ones place.
 b. An alloy contains 67 g of pure gold and 35 g of pure zinc. What is the percentage of zinc in the alloy? Express your answer to the ones place.
 c. A collection of coins contains 15 pennies, 14 dimes, and 6 quarters. What is the percentage of pennies in the collection? Express your answer to the ones place.

1.21 Solve each of the following for a:
 a. $4a + 4 = 40$ **b.** $\dfrac{a}{6} = 7$

1.22 Solve each of the following for b:
 a. $2b + 7 = b + 10$ **b.** $3b - 4 = 24 - b$

Use the following graph for questions 1.23 and 1.24:

Time for Cooling of Tea Versus Temperature

1.23 **a.** What does the title indicate about the graph?
 b. What is measured on the vertical axis?
 c. What is the range of values on the vertical axis?
 d. Does the temperature increase or decrease with an increase in time?

1.24 **a.** What is measured on the horizontal axis?
 b. What is the range of values on the horizontal axis?
 c. What is the temperature of the tea after 20 min?
 d. How many minutes were needed to reach a temperature of 45 °C?

1.25 Write each of the following in scientific notation:
 a. 55 000   **b.** 480
 c. 0.000 005   **d.** 0.000 14
 e. 0.0072   **f.** 670 000

1.26 Write each of the following in scientific notation:
 a. 180 000 000   **b.** 0.000 06
 c. 750   **d.** 0.15
 e. 0.024   **f.** 1500

1.27 Which number in each of the following pairs is larger?
 a. 7.2×10^3 or 8.2×10^2 **b.** 4.5×10^{-4} or 3.2×10^{-2}
 c. 1×10^4 or 1×10^{-4} **d.** 0.000 52 or 6.8×10^{-2}

1.28 Which number in each of the following pairs is smaller?
 a. 4.9×10^{-3} or 5.5×10^{-9} **b.** 1250 or 3.4×10^2
 c. 0.000 000 4 or 5.0×10^2 **d.** 2.50×10^2 or 4×10^5

℞ Clinical Update
Forensic Evidence Solves the Murder

Using a variety of laboratory tests, Sarah finds ethylene glycol in the victim's blood. The quantitative tests indicate that the victim had ingested 125 g of ethylene glycol. Sarah determines that the liquid in the glass found at the crime scene was ethylene glycol that had been added to an alcoholic beverage. Ethylene glycol is a clear, sweet-tasting, thick liquid that is odorless and mixes with water. It is easy to obtain since it is used as antifreeze in automobiles and in brake fluid. Because the initial symptoms of ethylene glycol poisoning are similar to being intoxicated, the victim is often unaware of its presence.

If ingestion of ethylene glycol occurs, it can cause depression of the central nervous system, cardiovascular damage, and kidney failure. If discovered quickly, hemodialysis may be used to remove ethylene glycol from the blood. A toxic amount of ethylene glycol is 1.5 g of ethylene glycol/kg of body mass. Thus, 75 g could be fatal for a 50-kg (110 lb) person.

Mark determines that a fingerprint on the glass found in the victim's home is match to the victim's husband. This evidence along with the container of antifreeze found in the home led to the arrest and conviction of the husband for poisoning his wife.

℞ Clinical Applications

1.29 A container was found in the home of the victim that contained 120 g of ethylene glycol in 450 g of liquid. What was the percentage of ethylene glycol? Express your answer to the ones place.

1.30 If the toxic quantity is 1.5 g per 1000 g of body mass, what percentage of ethylene glycol is fatal?

CONCEPT MAP

CHEMISTRY IN OUR LIVES

deals with	uses the	is learned by	uses key math skills
Substances	**Scientific Method**	**Reading the Text**	**Identifying Place Values**
called	*starting with*	**Practicing Problem Solving**	**Using Positive and Negative Numbers**
Chemicals	**Observations**	**Self-Testing**	**Calculating Percentages**
	that lead to	**Working with a Group**	**Solving Equations**
	Hypothesis		**Interpreting Graphs**
	Experiments		**Writing Numbers in Scientific Notation**
	Conclusion		

CHAPTER REVIEW

1.1 Chemistry and Chemicals
LEARNING GOAL Define the term chemistry and identify substances as chemicals.

- Chemistry is the study of the composition, structure, properties, and reactions of matter.
- A chemical is any substance that always has the same composition and properties wherever it is found.

1.2 Scientific Method: Thinking Like a Scientist
LEARNING GOAL Describe the activities that are part of the scientific method.

- The scientific method is a process of explaining natural phenomena beginning with making observations, forming a hypothesis, and performing experiments.
- After repeated experiments, a conclusion may be reached as to whether the hypothesis is true or not.

1.3 Learning Chemistry: A Study Plan
LEARNING GOAL Develop a study plan for learning chemistry.

- A study plan for learning chemistry utilizes the features in the text and develops an active learning approach to study.
- By using the *Learning Goals* in the chapter and working the *Sample Problems*, *Study Checks*, and the *Questions and Problems* at the end of each section, you can successfully learn the concepts of chemistry.

1.4 Key Math Skills for Chemistry
LEARNING GOAL Review math concepts used in chemistry: place values, positive and negative numbers, percentages, solving equations, interpreting graphs, and writing numbers in scientific notation.

1×10^5 hairs 8×10^{-6} m

- Solving chemistry problems involves a number of math skills: identifying place values, using positive and negative numbers, calculating percentages, solving equations, interpreting graphs, and writing numbers in scientific notation.

KEY TERMS

chemical A substance that has the same composition and properties wherever it is found.

chemistry The study of the composition, structure, properties, and reactions of matter.

conclusion An explanation of an observation that has been validated by repeated experiments that support a hypothesis.

experiment A procedure that tests the validity of a hypothesis.

hypothesis An unverified explanation of a natural phenomenon.

observation Information determined by noting and recording a natural phenomenon.

scientific method The process of making observations, proposing a hypothesis, testing the hypothesis, and making a conclusion as to the validity of the hypothesis.

scientific notation A form of writing large and small numbers using a coefficient that is at least 1 but less than 10, followed by a power of 10.

KEY MATH SKILLS

The chapter section containing each Key Math Skill is shown in parentheses at the end of each heading.

Identifying Place Values (1.4A)

- The place value identifies the numerical value of each digit in a number.

Example: Identify the place value for each of the digits in the number 456.78.

Answer:

Digit	Place Value
4	hundreds
5	tens
6	ones
7	tenths
8	hundredths

Using Positive and Negative Numbers in Calculations (1.4B)

- A *positive number* is any number that is greater than zero and has a positive sign $(+)$. A *negative number* is any number that is less than zero and is written with a negative sign $(-)$.
- When two positive numbers are added, multiplied, or divided, the answer is positive.
- When two negative numbers are multiplied or divided, the answer is positive. When two negative numbers are added, the answer is negative.
- When a positive and a negative number are multiplied or divided, the answer is negative.
- When a positive and a negative number are added, the smaller number is subtracted from the larger number and the result has the same sign as the larger number.
- When two numbers are subtracted, change the sign of the number to be subtracted then follow the rules for addition.

Example: Evaluate each of the following:
   a. $-8 - 14 = $ _____
   b. $6 \times (-3) = $ _____
Answer: **a.** $-8 - 14 = -22$
   b. $6 \times (-3) = -18$

Calculating Percentages (1.4C)

- A percentage is the part divided by the total (whole) multiplied by 100%.

Example: A drawer contains 6 white socks and 18 black socks. What is the percentage of white socks?

Answer: $\dfrac{6 \text{ white socks}}{24 \text{ total socks}} \times 100\% = 25\% \text{ white socks}$

Solving Equations (1.4D)

An equation in chemistry often contains an unknown. To rearrange an equation to obtain the unknown factor by itself, you keep it balanced by performing matching mathematical operations on both sides of the equation.

- If you eliminate a number or symbol by subtracting, subtract that same number or symbol on the opposite side.
- If you eliminate a number or symbol by adding, add that same number or symbol on the opposite side.
- If you cancel a number or symbol by dividing, divide both sides by that same number or symbol.
- If you cancel a number or symbol by multiplying, multiply both sides by that same number or symbol.

Example: Solve the equation for a: $3a - 8 = 28$
Answer: *Add 8 to both sides* $3a - 8 + 8 = 28 + 8$
                                             $3a = 36$

Divide both sides by 3 $\dfrac{3a}{3} = \dfrac{36}{3}$

                                             $a = 12$

Check: $3(12) - 8 = 28$
                                   $36 - 8 = 28$
                                        $28 = 28$

Your answer $a = 12$ is correct.

Interpreting Graphs (1.4E)

A graph represents the relationship between two variables. These quantities are plotted along two perpendicular axes, which are the x axis (horizontal) and y axis (vertical). The title indicates the components of the x and y axes. Numbers on the x and y axes show the range of values of the variables. The graph shows the relationship between the component on the y axis and that on the x axis.

Example:

Solubility of Sugar in Water Versus Temperature

a. Does the amount of sugar that dissolves in 100 mL of water increase or decrease when the temperature increases?
b. How many grams of sugar dissolve in 100 mL of water at 70 °C?
c. At what temperature (°C) will 275 g of sugar dissolve in 100 mL of water?

Answer: **a.** increase
   b. 320 g
   c. 55 °C

Writing Numbers in Scientific Notation (1.4F)

A number is written in scientific notation by:

- Moving the decimal point to obtain a coefficient that is at least 1 but less than 10.
- Expressing the number of places moved as a power of 10. The power of 10 is positive if the decimal point is moved to the left, negative if the decimal point is moved to the right.
- A number written in scientific notation consists of a coefficient and a power of 10.

Example: Write the number 28 000 in scientific notation.
Answer: Moving the decimal point four places to the left gives a coefficient of 2.8 and a positive power of 10, 10^4. The number 28 000 written in scientific notation is 2.8×10^4.
Example: Write the number 0.000 056 in scientific notation.
Answer: Moving the decimal point five places to the right gives a coefficient of 5.6 and a negative power of 10, 10^{-5}. The number 0.000 056 written in scientific notation is 5.6×10^{-5}.

UNDERSTANDING THE CONCEPTS

The chapter sections to review are shown in parentheses at the end of each question.

1.31 A "chemical-free" shampoo includes the following ingredients: water, cocomide, glycerin, and citric acid. Is the shampoo truly "chemical-free"? (1.1)

1.32 A "chemical-free" sunscreen includes the following ingredients: titanium dioxide, vitamin E, and vitamin C. Is the sunscreen truly "chemical-free"? (1.1)

1.33 According to Sherlock Holmes, "One must follow the rules of scientific inquiry, gathering, observing, and testing data, then formulating, modifying, and rejecting hypotheses, until only one remains." Did Holmes use the scientific method? Why or why not? (1.2)

1.34 In *A Scandal in Bohemia*, Sherlock Holmes receives a mysterious note. He states, "I have no data yet. It is a capital mistake to theorize before one has data. Insensibly one begins to twist facts to suit theories, instead of theories to suit facts." What do you think Holmes meant? (1.2)

Sherlock Holmes is a fictional detective in novels written by Arthur Conan Doyle.

1.35 Classify each of the following statements as an observation (O) or a hypothesis (H): (1.2)
a. A patient breaks out in hives after receiving penicillin.
b. Dinosaurs became extinct when a large meteorite struck the Earth and caused a huge dust cloud that severely decreased the amount of light reaching the Earth.
c. The 100-yd dash was run in 9.8 s.

1.36 Classify each of the following statements as an observation (O) or a hypothesis (H): (1.2)
a. Analysis of 10 ceramic dishes showed that four dishes contained lead levels that exceeded federal safety standards.
b. Marble statues undergo corrosion in acid rain.
c. A child with a high fever and a rash may have chicken pox.

1.37 For each of the following, indicate if the answer has a positive or negative sign: (1.4)
a. Two negative numbers are added.
b. A positive and negative number are multiplied.

1.38 For each of the following, indicate if the answer has a positive or negative sign: (1.4)
a. A negative number is subtracted from a positive number.
b. Two negative numbers are divided.

ADDITIONAL QUESTIONS AND PROBLEMS

1.39 Identify each of the following as an observation (O), a hypothesis (H), an experiment (E), or a conclusion (C): (1.2)
a. During an assessment in the emergency room, a nurse writes that the patient has a resting pulse of 30 beats/min.
b. A nurse thinks that an incision from a recent surgery that is red and swollen is infected.
c. Repeated studies show that lowering sodium in the diet leads to a decrease in blood pressure.

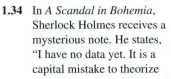

Nurses make observations in the hospital.

1.40 Identify each of the following as an observation (O), a hypothesis (H), an experiment (E), or a conclusion (C): (1.2)
a. Drinking coffee at night keeps me awake.
b. If I stop drinking coffee in the afternoon, I will be able to sleep at night.
c. I will try drinking coffee only in the morning.

1.41 Select the correct phrase(s) to complete the following statement: If experimental results do not support your hypothesis, you should (1.2)
a. pretend that the experimental results support your hypothesis
b. modify your hypothesis
c. do more experiments

1.42 Select the correct phrase(s) to complete the following statement: A conclusion confirms a hypothesis when (1.2)
a. one experiment proves the hypothesis
b. many experiments validate the hypothesis
c. you think your hypothesis is correct

1.43 Which of the following will help you develop a successful study plan? (1.3)
a. skipping lecture and just reading the text
b. working the *Sample Problems* as you go through a chapter
c. going to your professor's office hours
d. reading through the chapter, but working the problems later

1.44 Which of the following will help you develop a successful study plan? (1.3)
a. studying all night before the exam
b. forming a study group and discussing the problems together
c. working problems in a notebook for easy reference
d. copying the homework answers from a friend

1.45 Evaluate each of the following: (1.4)
a. $4 \times (-8) =$ _____
b. $-12 - 48 =$ _____
c. $\dfrac{-168}{-4} =$ _____

1.46 Evaluate each of the following: (1.4)
a. $-95 - (-11) =$ _____
b. $\dfrac{152}{-19} =$ _____
c. $4 - 56 =$ _____

1.47 A bag of gumdrops contains 16 orange gumdrops, 8 yellow gumdrops, and 16 black gumdrops. (1.4)
a. What is the percentage of yellow gumdrops? Express your answer to the ones place.
b. What is the percentage of black gumdrops? Express your answer to the ones place.

1.48 On the first chemistry test, 12 students got As, 18 students got Bs, and 20 students got Cs. (1.4)
a. What is the percentage of students who received Bs? Express your answer to the ones place.
b. What is the percentage of students who received Cs? Express your answer to the ones place.

1.49 Express each of the following numbers in scientific notation: (1.4)
a. 120 000
b. 0.000 000 34
c. 0.066
d. 2700

1.50 Express each of the following numbers in scientific notation: (1.4)
a. 0.0042
b. 310
c. 890 000 000
d. 0.000 000 056

CHALLENGE QUESTIONS

The following groups of questions are related to the topics in this chapter. However, they do not all follow the chapter order, and they require you to combine concepts and skills from several sections. These questions will help you increase your critical thinking skills and prepare for your next exam.

1.51 Classify each of the following as an observation (O), a hypothesis (H), or an experiment (E): (1.2)
a. The bicycle tire is flat.
b. If I add air to the bicycle tire, it will expand to the proper size.
c. When I added air to the bicycle tire, it was still flat.
d. The bicycle tire must have a leak in it.

1.52 Classify each of the following as an observation (O), a hypothesis (H), or an experiment (E): (1.2)
a. A big log in the fire does not burn well.
b. If I chop the log into smaller wood pieces, it will burn better.
c. The small wood pieces burn brighter and make a hotter fire.
d. The small wood pieces are used up faster than burning the big log.

1.53 Solve each of the following for x: (1.4)
a. $2x + 5 = 41$
b. $\dfrac{5x}{3} = 40$

1.54 Solve each of the following for z: (1.4)
a. $3z - (-6) = 12$
b. $\dfrac{4z}{-12} = -8$

Use the following graph for problems 1.55 and 1.56:

Solubility of Carbon Dioxide in Water Versus Temperature

1.55 a. What does the title indicate about the graph? (1.4)
b. What is measured on the vertical axis?
c. What is the range of values on the vertical axis?
d. Does the solubility of carbon dioxide increase or decrease with an increase in temperature?

1.56 a. What is measured on the horizontal axis? (1.4)
b. What is the range of values on the horizontal axis?
c. What is the solubility of carbon dioxide in water at 25 °C?
d. At what temperature does carbon dioxide have a solubility of 0.20 g/100 g water?

ANSWERS

Answers to Selected Questions and Problems

1.1 a. Chemistry is the study of the composition, structure, properties, and reactions of matter.
b. A chemical is a substance that has the same composition and properties wherever it is found.

1.3 Many chemicals are listed on a vitamin bottle such as vitamin A, vitamin B_3, vitamin B_{12}, vitamin C, and folic acid.

1.5 Typical items found in a medicine cabinet and some of the chemicals they contain are as follows:

Antacid tablets: calcium carbonate, cellulose, starch, stearic acid, silicon dioxide

Mouthwash: water, alcohol, thymol, glycerol, sodium benzoate, benzoic acid

Cough suppressant: menthol, beta-carotene, sucrose, glucose

1.7 a. observation (O)   **b.** hypothesis (H)
c. experiment (E)   **d.** observation (O)
e. observation (O)   **f.** conclusion (C)

1.9 a. observation (O)   **b.** hypothesis (H)
c. experiment (E)   **d.** experiment (E)

1.11 There are several things you can do that will help you successfully learn chemistry: forming a study group, going to lecture, working *Sample Problems* and *Study Checks*, working *Questions and Problems* and checking answers, reading the assignment ahead of class, and keeping a problem notebook.

1.13 a, c, and **e**

1.15 a. thousandths   **b.** ones   **c.** hundreds

1.17 a. 23   **b.** -30 **c.** -2

1.19 a. 84%   **b.** 72%   **c.** 30%

1.21 a. 9   **b.** 42

1.23 a. The graph shows the relationship between the temperature of a cup of tea and time.
b. temperature, in °C
c. 20 °C to 80 °C
d. decrease

1.25 a. 5.5×10^4 **b.** 4.8×10^2
c. 5×10^{-6} **d.** 1.4×10^{-4}
e. 7.2×10^{-3} **f.** 6.7×10^5

1.27 a. 7.2×10^3 **b.** 3.2×10^{-2}
c. 1×10^4 **d.** 6.8×10^{-2}

1.29 27% ethylene glycol

1.31 No. All of the ingredients are chemicals.

1.33 Yes. Sherlock's investigation includes making observations (gathering data), formulating a hypothesis, testing the hypothesis, and modifying it until one of the hypotheses is validated.

1.35 a. observation (O)   **b.** hypothesis (H)
c. observation (O)

1.37 a. negative   **b.** negative

1.39 a. observation (O)   **b.** hypothesis (H)
c. conclusion (C)

1.41 b

1.43 b and **c**

1.45 a. -32 **b.** -60 **c.** 42

1.47 a. 20%   **b.** 40%

1.49 a. 1.2×10^5 **b.** 3.4×10^{-7}
c. 6.6×10^{-2} **d.** 2.7×10^3

1.51 a. observation (O)   **b.** hypothesis (H)
c. experiment (E)   **d.** hypothesis (H)

1.53 a. 18   **b.** 24

1.55 a. The graph shows the relationship between the solubility of carbon dioxide in water and temperature.
b. solubility of carbon dioxide (g CO_2/100 g water)
c. 0 to 0.35 g of CO_2/100 g of water
d. decrease

2

Chemistry and Measurements

DURING THE PAST FEW MONTHS, GREG HAS BEEN experiencing an increased number of headaches, and frequently feels dizzy and nauseous. He goes to his doctor's office where, Sandra, the registered nurse completes the initial part of the exam by recording several measurements: weight 65.5 kg, height 171 cm, temperature 37.2 °C, and blood pressure 155/95. Normal blood pressure is 120/80 or below.

When Greg sees his doctor, he is diagnosed as having high blood pressure (hypertension). The doctor prescribes 80. mg of Inderal (propranolol). Inderal is a beta blocker, which relaxes the muscles of the heart. It is used to treat hypertension, angina (chest pain), arrhythmia, and migraine headaches.

Two weeks later, Greg visits his doctor again, who determines that Greg's blood pressure is now 152/90. The doctor increases the dosage of Inderal to 160 mg. The registered nurse, Sandra, informs Greg that he needs to increase his daily dosage from two tablets to four tablets.

CAREER Registered Nurse

In addition to assisting physicians, registered nurses work to promote patient health, and prevent and treat disease. They provide patient care and help patients cope with illness. They take measurements such as a patient's weight, height, temperature, and blood pressure; make conversions; and calculate drug dosage rates. Registered nurses also maintain detailed medical records of patient symptoms and prescribed medications.

LOOKING AHEAD

2.1 Units of Measurement 26

2.2 Measured Numbers and Significant Figures 30

2.3 Significant Figures in Calculations 32

2.4 Prefixes and Equalities 36

2.5 Writing Conversion Factors 39

2.6 Problem Solving Using Unit Conversion 44

💗 **Chemistry Link to Health** *Toxicology and Risk–Benefit Assessment* 47

2.7 Density 49

💗 **Chemistry Link to Health** *Bone Density* 51

℞ **Clinical Applications** 29, 32, 44, 48, 53, 59

℞ **Clinical Update** *Greg's Follow-Up Visit with His Doctor* 53

Chemistry and measurements are an important part of our everyday lives. Levels of toxic materials in the air, soil, and water are discussed in our newspapers. We read about radon gas in our homes, holes in the ozone layer, trans fatty acids, and climate change. Understanding chemistry and measurement helps us make proper choices about our world.

Think about your day. You probably took some measurements. Perhaps you checked your weight by stepping on a bathroom scale. If you made some rice for dinner, you added two cups of water to one cup of rice. If you did not feel well, you may have taken your temperature. Whenever you take a measurement, you use a measuring device such as a balance, a measuring cup, or a thermometer. Over the years, you have learned to read the markings on each device to take a correct measurement.

Your weight on a bathroom scale is a measurement.

Measurement is an essential part of health careers such as nursing, dental hygiene, respiratory therapy, nutrition, and veterinary technology. The temperature, height, and weight of a patient are measured and recorded. Samples of blood and urine are collected and sent to a laboratory where glucose, pH, urea, and protein are measured by the clinical technicians. By learning about measurement, you develop skills for solving problems and working with numbers.

CHAPTER READINESS*

🖩 KEY MATH SKILLS

- Identifying Place Values (1.4A)
- Using Positive and Negative Numbers in Calculations (1.4B)
- Calculating Percentages (1.4C)
- Writing Numbers in Scientific Notation (1.4F)

*These Key Math Skills from the previous chapter are listed here for your review as you proceed to the new material in this chapter.

LEARNING GOAL

Write the names and abbreviations for the metric or SI units used in measurements of length, volume, mass, temperature, and time.

2.1 Units of Measurement

Scientists and health professionals throughout the world use the **metric system** of measurement. It is also the common measuring system in all but a few countries in the world. The **International System of Units (SI)**, or Système International, is the official system of measurement throughout the world except for the United States. In chemistry, we use metric units and SI units for length, volume, mass, temperature, and time, as listed in Table 2.1.

Suppose you walked 1.3 mi to campus today, carrying a backpack that weighs 26 lb. The temperature was 72 °F. Perhaps you weigh 128 lb and your height is 65 in. These measurements and units may seem familiar to you because they are stated in the U.S.

TABLE 2.1 Units of Measurement and Their Abbreviations

Measurement	Metric	SI
Length	meter (m)	meter (m)
Volume	liter (L)	cubic meter (m^3)
Mass	gram (g)	kilogram (kg)
Temperature	degree Celsius (°C)	kelvin (K)
Time	second (s)	second (s)

system of measurement. However, in chemistry, we use the *metric system* in making our measurements. Using the metric system, you walked 2.1 km to campus, carrying a backpack that has a mass of 12 kg, when the temperature was 22 °C. You have a mass of 58.2 kg and a height of 1.65 m.

8:30 A.M.

1.65 m (65 in.)

22 °C (72 °F)

58.2 kg (128 lb)

12 kg (26 lb)

2.1 km (1.3 mi)

There are many measurements in everyday life.

Length

The metric and SI unit of length is the **meter (m)**. A meter is 39.4 inches (in.), which makes it slightly longer than a yard (yd). The **centimeter (cm)**, a smaller unit of length, is commonly used in chemistry and is about equal to the width of your little finger. For comparison, there are 2.54 cm in 1 in. (see Figure 2.1). Some relationships between units for length are

$$1 \text{ m} = 100 \text{ cm}$$
$$1 \text{ m} = 39.4 \text{ in.}$$
$$1 \text{ m} = 1.09 \text{ yd}$$
$$2.54 \text{ cm} = 1 \text{ in.}$$

Meterstick

1 m = 39.4 in.

Centimeters
1   2   3   4   5

1 in. = 2.54 cm

Yardstick

Inches   1

1 ft   2 ft   3 ft

FIGURE 2.1 ▶ Length in the metric (SI) system is based on the meter, which is slightly longer than a yard.

🔍 How many centimeters are in a length of 1 inch?

Volume

Volume is the amount of space a substance occupies. A **liter (L)** is slightly larger than a quart (qt), (1 L = 1.06 qt). In a laboratory or a hospital, chemists work with metric units of volume that are smaller and more convenient, such as the **milliliter (mL)**. There are 1000 mL in 1 L. A comparison of metric and U.S. units for volume appears in Figure 2.2. Some relationships between units for volume are

$$1 \text{ L} = 1000 \text{ mL}$$
$$1 \text{ L} = 1.06 \text{ qt}$$
$$946 \text{ mL} = 1 \text{ qt}$$

1 L = 1.06 qt

946 mL = 1 qt

FIGURE 2.2 ▶ Volume is the space occupied by a substance. In the metric system, volume is based on the liter, which is slightly larger than a quart.

🔍 How many milliliters are in 1 quart?

Mass

The **mass** of an object is a measure of the quantity of material it contains. The SI unit of mass, the **kilogram (kg)**, is used for larger masses such as body mass. In the metric system, the unit for mass is the **gram (g)**, which is used for smaller masses. There are 1000 g in 1 kg. It takes 2.20 lb to make 1 kg, and 454 g is equal to 1 lb. Some relationships between units for mass are

$$1 \text{ kg} = 1000 \text{ g}$$
$$1 \text{ kg} = 2.20 \text{ lb}$$
$$454 \text{ g} = 1 \text{ lb}$$

You may be more familiar with the term *weight* than with mass. *Weight* is a measure of the gravitational pull on an object. On the Earth, an astronaut with a mass of 75.0 kg has a weight of 165 lb. On the Moon where the gravitational pull is one-sixth that of the Earth, the astronaut has a weight of 27.5 lb. However, the mass of the astronaut is the same as on Earth, 75.0 kg. Scientists measure mass rather than weight because mass does not depend on gravity.

In a chemistry laboratory, an electronic balance is used to measure the mass in grams of a substance (see Figure 2.3).

The standard kilogram for the United States is stored at the National Institute of Standards and Technology (NIST).

FIGURE 2.3 ▶ On an electronic balance, the digital readout gives the mass of a nickel, which is 5.01 g.

Q What is the mass of 10 nickels?

Temperature

Temperature tells us how hot something is, how cold it is outside, or helps us determine if we have a fever (see Figure 2.4). In the metric system, temperature is measured using Celsius temperature. On the **Celsius (°C) temperature scale**, water freezes at 0 °C and boils at 100 °C, whereas on the Fahrenheit (°F) scale, water freezes at 32 °F and boils at 212 °F. In the SI system, temperature is measured using the **Kelvin (K) temperature scale** on which the lowest possible temperature is 0 K. A unit on the Kelvin scale is called a kelvin (K) and is not written with a degree sign.

FIGURE 2.4 ▶ A thermometer is used to determine temperature.

Q What kinds of temperature readings have you made today?

Time

We typically measure time in units such as years (yr), days, hours (h), minutes (min), or seconds (s). Of these, the SI and metric unit of time is the **second (s)**. The standard now used to determine a second is an atomic clock.

A stopwatch is used to measure the time of a race.

▶ SAMPLE PROBLEM 2.1 **Units of Measurement**

On a typical day, a nurse encounters several situations involving measurement. State the name and type of measurement indicated by the units in each of the following:

a. A patient has a temperature of 38.5 °C.
b. A physician orders 1.5 g of Cefuroxime for injection.
c. A physician orders 1 L of a sodium chloride solution to be given intravenously.
d. A medication is to be given to a patient every 4 h.

SOLUTION

a. Degrees Celsius is a unit of temperature.
b. A gram is a unit of mass.
c. A liter is a unit of volume.
d. An hour is a unit of time.

STUDY CHECK 2.1

State the name and type of measurement indicated by an infant that is 32.5 cm long.

ANSWER

A centimeter is a unit of length.

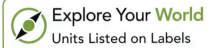

Explore Your World
Units Listed on Labels

Read the labels on a variety of products such as sugar, salt, soft drinks, vitamins, and dental floss.

Questions

1. What metric or SI units of measurement are listed?
2. What type of measurement (mass, volume, etc.) does each indicate?
3. Write each quantity as a number and a metric or SI unit.

QUESTIONS AND PROBLEMS

2.1 Units of Measurement

LEARNING GOAL Write the names and abbreviations for the metric or SI units used in measurements of length, volume, mass, temperature, and time.

2.1 State the type of measurement in each of the following statements:
  a. I put 12 L of gasoline in my gas tank.
  b. My friend is 170 cm tall.
  c. We are 385 000 km away from the Moon.
  d. The horse won the race by 1.2 s.

2.2 State the type of measurement in each of the following statements:
  a. I rode my bicycle 15 km today.
  b. My dog weighs 12 kg.
  c. It is hot today. It is 30 °C.
  d. I added 2 L of water to my fish tank.

2.3 State the name of the unit and the type of measurement indicated for each of the following quantities:
  a. 4.8 m   **b.** 325 g   **c.** 1.5 mL
  d. 4.8×10^2 s   **e.** 28 °C

2.4 State the name of the unit and the type of measurement indicated for each of the following quantities:
  a. 0.8 L   **b.** 3.6 cm   **c.** 4 kg
  d. 3.5 h   **e.** 373 K

℞ Clinical Applications

2.5 On a typical day, a nurse encounters several situations involving measurement. State the name and type of measurement indicated by the units in each of the following:
  a. The prothrombin time (clotting time) for a blood sample is 12 s.
  b. A premature baby weighs 2.0 kg.

  c. An antacid tablet contains 1.0 g of calcium carbonate.
  d. An infant has a temperature 39.2 °C.

2.6 On a typical day, a nurse encounters several situations involving measurement. State the name and type of measurement indicated by the units in each of the following:
  a. During open-heart surgery, the temperature of a patient is lowered to 29 °C.
  b. The circulation time of a red blood cell through the body is 20 s.
  c. A patient with a persistent cough is given 10. mL of cough syrup.
  d. The amount of iron in the red blood cells of the body is 2.5 g.

A volume of 10. mL of cough syrup is measured for a patient.

(a)

(b)

(c)

FIGURE 2.5 ▶ The lengths of the rectangular objects are measured as **(a)** 4.5 cm and **(b)** 4.55 cm.

Q What is the length of the object in **(c)**?

2.2 Measured Numbers and Significant Figures

When you make a measurement, you use some type of measuring device. For example, you may use a meterstick to measure your height, a scale to check your weight, or a thermometer to take your temperature.

Measured Numbers

Measured numbers are the numbers you obtain when you measure a quantity such as your height, weight, or temperature. Suppose you are going to measure the lengths of the objects in Figure 2.5. The metric ruler that you use may have lines marked in 1-cm divisions or perhaps in divisions of 0.1 cm. To report the length of the object, you observe the numerical values of the marked lines at the end of the object. Then you can *estimate* by visually dividing the space between the marked lines. This estimated value is the final digit in a measured number.

For example, in Figure 2.5a, the end of the object is between the marks of 4 cm and 5 cm, which means that the length is more than 4 cm but less than 5 cm. This is written as 4 cm plus an estimated digit. If you estimate that the end of the object is halfway between 4 cm and 5 cm, you would report its length as 4.5 cm. The last digit in a measured number may differ because people do not always estimate in the same way. Thus, someone else might report the length of the same object as 4.4 cm.

The metric ruler shown in Figure 2.5b is marked at every 0.1 cm. With this ruler, you can estimate to the hundredths place (0.01 cm). Now you can determine that the end of the object is between 4.5 cm and 4.6 cm. Perhaps you report its length as 4.55 cm, whereas another student reports its length as 4.56 cm. Both results are acceptable.

In Figure 2.5c, the end of the object appears to line up with the 3-cm mark. Because the divisions are marked in units of 1 cm, the length of the object is between 3 cm and 4 cm. Because the end of the object is on the 3-cm mark, the estimated digit is 0, which means the measurement is reported as 3.0 cm.

Significant Figures

In a measured number, the **significant figures (SFs)** are all the digits including the estimated digit. Nonzero numbers are always counted as significant figures. However, a zero may or may not be a significant figure depending on its position in a number. Table 2.2 gives the rules and examples of counting significant figures.

TABLE 2.2 Significant Figures in Measured Numbers

Rule	Measured Number	Number of Significant Figures
1. A number is a *significant figure* if it is		
a. not a zero	4.5 g	2
	122.35 m	5
b. a zero between nonzero digits	205 m	3
	5.008 kg	4
c. a zero at the end of a decimal number	50. L	2
	25.0 °C	3
	16.00 g	4
d. in the coefficient of a number written in scientific notation	4.8×10^{5} m	2
	5.70×10^{-3} g	3
2. A zero is *not significant* if it is		
a. at the beginning of a decimal number	0.0004 s	1
	0.075 cm	2
b. used as a placeholder in a large number without a decimal point	850 000 m	2
	1 250 000 g	3

Significant Zeros and Scientific Notation

When one or more zeros in a large number are significant, they are shown clearly by writing the number in scientific notation. For example, if the first zero in the measurement 300 m is significant, but the second zero is not, the measurement is written as 3.0×10^2 m. *In this text, we will place a decimal point after a significant zero at the end of a number.* For example, if a measurement is written as 500. g, the decimal point after the second zero indicates that *both zeros* are significant. To show this more clearly, we can write it as 5.00×10^2 g. We will assume that zeros at the end of large standard numbers without a decimal point are not significant. Therefore, we write 400 000 g as 4×10^5 g, which has only one significant figure.

> ▶ **SAMPLE PROBLEM 2.2 Significant Zeros**
>
> Identify the significant zeros in each of the following measured numbers:
>
> **a.** 0.000 250 m   **b.** 70.040 g   **c.** 1 020 000 L
>
> **SOLUTION**
>
> **a.** The zero in the last decimal place following the 5 is significant. The zeros preceding the 2 are not significant.
> **b.** Zeros between nonzero digits or at the end of decimal numbers are significant. All the zeros in 70.040 g are significant.
> **c.** Zeros between nonzero digits are significant. Zeros at the end of a large number with no decimal point are placeholders but not significant. The zero between 1 and 2 is significant, but the four zeros following the 2 are not significant.
>
> **STUDY CHECK 2.2**
>
> Identify the significant zeros in each of the following measured numbers:
>
> **a.** 0.04008 m   **b.** 6.00×10^3 g
>
> **ANSWER**
>
> **a.** The zeros between 4 and 8 are significant. The zeros preceding the first nonzero digit 4 are not significant.
> **b.** All zeros in the coefficient of a number written in scientific notation are significant.

Exact Numbers

Exact numbers *are those numbers obtained by counting items or using a definition that compares two units in the same measuring system.* Suppose a friend asks you how many classes you are taking. You would answer by counting the number of classes in your schedule. It would not use any measuring tool. Suppose you are asked to state the number of seconds in one minute. Without using any measuring device, you would give the definition: There are 60 s in 1 min. *Exact numbers are not measured, do not have a limited number of significant figures, and do not affect the number of significant figures in a calculated answer.* For more examples of exact numbers, see Table 2.3.

TABLE 2.3 Examples of Some Exact Numbers

Counted Numbers	Defined Equalities	
Items	Metric System	U.S. System
8 doughnuts	1 L = 1000 mL	1 ft = 12 in.
2 baseballs	1 m = 100 cm	1 qt = 4 cups
5 capsules	1 kg = 1000 g	1 lb = 16 oz

For example, a mass of 42.2 g and a length of 5.0×10^{-3} cm are measured numbers because they are obtained using measuring tools. There are three SFs in 42.2 g because all nonzero digits are always significant. There are two SFs in 5.0×10^{-3} cm because all the digits in the coefficient of a number written in scientific notation are significant. However, a quantity of three eggs is an exact number that is obtained by counting the eggs. In the equality 1 kg = 1000 g, the masses of 1 kg and 1000 g are both exact numbers because this equality is a definition in the metric system of measurement.

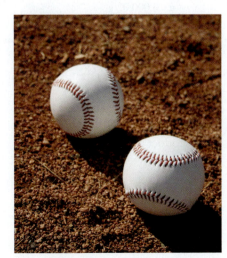

The number of baseballs is counted, which means 2 is an exact number.

QUESTIONS AND PROBLEMS

2.2 Measured Numbers and Significant Figures

LEARNING GOAL Identify a number as measured or exact; determine the number of significant figures in a measured number.

2.7 Identify the numbers in each of the following statements as measured or exact:
   a. A patient has a mass of 67.5 kg.
   b. A patient is given 2 tablets of medication.
   c. In the metric system, 1 L is equal to 1000 mL.
   d. The distance from Denver, Colorado, to Houston, Texas, is 1720 km.

2.8 Identify the numbers in each of the following statements as measured or exact:
   a. There are 31 students in the laboratory.
   b. The oldest known flower lived 1.20×10^8 yr ago.
   c. The largest gem ever found, an aquamarine, has a mass of 104 kg.
   d. A laboratory test shows a blood cholesterol level of 184 mg/dL.

2.9 Identify the measured number(s), if any, in each of the following pairs of numbers:
   a. 3 hamburgers and 6 oz of hamburger
   b. 1 table and 4 chairs
   c. 0.75 lb of grapes and 350 g of butter
   d. 60 s = 1 min

2.10 Identify the exact number(s), if any, in each of the following pairs of numbers:
   a. 5 pizzas and 50.0 g of cheese
   b. 6 nickels and 16 g of nickel
   c. 3 onions and 3 lb of onions
   d. 5 miles and 5 cars

2.11 Indicate if the zeros are significant in each of the following measurements:
   a. 0.0038 m   **b.** 5.04 cm
   c. 800. L   **d.** 3.0×10^{-3} kg
   e. 85 000 g

2.12 Indicate if the zeros are significant in each of the following measurements:
   a. 20.05 °C   **b.** 5.00 m
   c. 0.000 02 g   **d.** 120 000 yr
   e. 8.05×10^2 L

2.13 How many significant figures are in each of the following?
   a. 11.005 g
   b. 0.000 32 m
   c. 36 000 000 km
   d. 1.80×10^4 kg
   e. 0.8250 L
   f. 30.0 °C

2.14 How many significant figures are in each of the following?
   a. 20.60 mL
   b. 1036.48 kg
   c. 4.00 m
   d. 20.8 °C
   e. 60 800 000 g
   f. 5.0×10^{-3} L

2.15 In which of the following pairs do both numbers contain the same number of significant figures?
   a. 11.0 m and 11.00 m
   b. 0.0250 m and 0.205 m
   c. 0.000 12 s and 12 000 s
   d. 250.0 L and 2.5×10^{-2} L

2.16 In which of the following pairs do both numbers contain the same number of significant figures?
   a. 0.005 75 g and 5.75×10^{-3} g
   b. 405 K and 405.0 K
   c. 150 000 s and 1.50×10^4 s
   d. 3.8×10^{-2} L and 3.0×10^5 L

℞ Clinical Applications

2.17 Identify the number of significant figures in each of the following:
   a. The mass of a neonate is 1.607 kg.
   b. The Daily Value (DV) for iodine for an infant is 130 mcg.
   c. There are 4.02×10^6 red blood cells in a blood sample.

2.18 Identify the number of significant figures in each of the following:
   a. An adult with the flu has a temperature of 103.5 °F.
   b. A brain contains 1.20×10^{10} neurons.
   c. The time for a nerve impulse to travel from the feet to the brain is 0.46 s.

LEARNING GOAL

Adjust calculated answers to give the correct number of significant figures.

2.3 Significant Figures in Calculations

In the sciences, we measure many things: the length of a bacterium, the volume of a gas sample, the temperature of a reaction mixture, or the mass of iron in a sample. The numbers obtained from these types of measurements are often used in calculations. The number of significant figures in the measured numbers determines the number of significant figures in the calculated answer.

Using a calculator will help you perform calculations faster. However, calculators cannot think for you. It is up to you to enter the numbers correctly, press the correct function keys, and give an answer with the correct number of significant figures.

Rounding Off

Suppose you decide to buy carpeting for a room that measures 5.52 m by 3.58 m. Each of these measurements has three significant figures because the measuring tape limits your estimated place to 0.01 m. To determine how much carpeting you need, you would calculate the area of the room by multiplying 5.52 times 3.58 on your calculator. The calculator shows the number 19.7616 in its display. However, this is not the correct final answer because there are too many digits, which is the result of the multiplication process. Because each of the original measurements has only three significant figures, the displayed number (19.7616) must be *rounded off* to three significant figures, 19.8. Therefore, you can order carpeting that will cover an area of 19.8 m^2.

Each time you use a calculator, it is important to look at the original measurements and determine the number of significant figures that can be used for the answer. You can use the following rules to round off the numbers shown in a calculator display.

Rules for Rounding Off

1. If the first digit to be dropped is *4 or less*, then it and all following digits are simply dropped from the number.
2. If the first digit to be dropped is *5 or greater*, then the last retained digit of the number is increased by 1.

Number to Round Off	Three Significant Figures	Two Significant Figures
8.4234	8.42 (drop 34)	8.4 (drop 234)
14.780	14.8 (drop 80, increase the last retained digit by 1)	15 (drop 780, increase the last retained digit by 1)
3256	3260* (drop 6, increase the last retained digit by 1, add 0) (3.26×10^3)	3300* (drop 56, increase the last retained digit by 1, add 00) (3.3×10^3)

*The value of a large number is retained by using placeholder zeros to replace dropped digits.

KEY MATH SKILL

Rounding Off

A technician uses a calculator in the laboratory.

> **SAMPLE PROBLEM 2.3 Rounding Off**

Round off each of the following numbers to three significant figures:

a. 35.7823 m
b. 0.002 621 7 L
c. 3.8268×10^3 g

SOLUTION

a. To round off 35.7823 m to three significant figures, drop 823 and increase the last retained digit by 1 to give 35.8 m.
b. To round off 0.002 621 7 L to three significant figures, drop 17 to give 0.002 62 L.
c. To round off 3.8268×10^3 g to three significant figures, drop 68 and increase the last retained digit by 1 to give 3.83×10^3 g.

STUDY CHECK 2.3

Round off each of the numbers in Sample Problem 2.3 to two significant figures.

ANSWER

a. 36 m
b. 0.0026 L
c. 3.8×10^3 g

A calculator is helpful in working problems and doing calculations faster.

Multiplication and Division with Measured Numbers

In multiplication or division, the final answer is written so that it has the same number of significant figures (SFs) as the measurement with the fewest SFs. An example of rounding off a calculator display follows:

Perform the following operations with measured numbers:

$$\frac{2.8 \times 67.40}{34.8} =$$

When the problem has multiple steps, the numbers in the numerator are multiplied and then divided by each of the numbers in the denominator.

2.8	⊠	67.40	÷	34.8	=	5.422988506	=	5.4
Two SFs		Four SFs		Three SFs		Calculator display		Answer, rounded off to two SFs

Because the calculator display has more digits than the significant figures in the measured numbers allow, we need to round off. Using the measured number that has the fewest number (two) of significant figures, 2.8, we round off the calculator display to the answer with two SFs.

Adding Significant Zeros

Sometimes, a calculator display gives a small whole number. Then we add one or more significant zeros to the calculator display to obtain the correct number of significant figures. For example, suppose the calculator display is 4, but you used measurements that have three significant numbers. Then two significant zeros are *added* to give 4.00 as the correct answer.

Three SFs
$$\frac{8.00}{2.00} = \qquad 4. \qquad = \qquad 4.00$$

Three SFs	Calculator display	Final answer, two zeros added to give three SFs

---

SAMPLE PROBLEM 2.4 Significant Figures in Multiplication and Division

Perform the following calculations of measured numbers. Round off the calculator display or add zeros to give each answer with the correct number of significant figures.

a. 56.8×0.37 **b.** $\dfrac{(2.075)(0.585)}{(8.42)(0.0045)}$ **c.** $\dfrac{25.0}{5.00}$

SOLUTION

a. 21 **b.** 32 **c.** 5.00 (add two significant zeros)

STUDY CHECK 2.4

Perform the following calculations of measured numbers and give the answers with the correct number of significant figures:

a. $45.26 \times 0.010\,88$ **b.** $2.6 \div 324$ **c.** $\dfrac{4.0 \times 8.00}{16}$

ANSWER

a. 0.4924 **b.** 0.0080 or 8.0×10^{-3} **c.** 2.0

Addition and Subtraction with Measured Numbers

In addition or subtraction, the final answer is written so that it has the same number of decimal places as the measurement having the fewest decimal places.

2.045	Thousandths place
+ 34.1	Tenths place
36.145	Calculator display
36.1	Answer, rounded off to the tenths place

When numbers are added or subtracted to give an answer ending in zero, the zero does not appear after the decimal point in the calculator display. For example, 14.5 g − 2.5 g = 12.0 g. However, if you do the subtraction on your calculator, the display shows 12. To write the correct answer, a significant zero is written after the decimal point.

▶**SAMPLE PROBLEM 2.5** **Significant Figures in Addition and Subtraction**

Perform the following calculations and round off the calculator display or add zeros to give each answer with the correct number of decimal places:

a. 104.45 mL + 0.838 mL + 46 mL   **b.** 153.247 g − 14.82 g

SOLUTION

a.   104.45 mL   Hundredths place
           0.838 mL   Thousandths place
     + 46 mL   Ones place
     ───────────
        151 mL   Answer, rounded off to the ones place

b.   153.247 g   Thousandths place
     − 14.82 g   Hundredths place
     ───────────
        138.43 g   Answer, rounded off to the hundredths place

STUDY CHECK 2.5

Perform the following calculations and give the answers with the correct number of decimal places:

a. 82.45 mg + 1.245 mg + 0.000 56 mg   **b.** 4.259 L − 3.8 L

ANSWER

a. 83.70 mg   **b.** 0.5 L

QUESTIONS AND PROBLEMS

2.3 Significant Figures in Calculations

LEARNING GOAL Adjust calculated answers to give the correct number of significant figures.

2.19 Why do we usually need to round off calculations that use measured numbers?

2.20 Why do we sometimes add a zero to a number in a calculator display?

2.21 Round off each of the following measurements to three significant figures:
  a. 1.854 kg   **b.** 88.2038 L
  c. 0.004 738 265 cm **d.** 8807 m
  e. 1.832×10^5 s

2.22 Round off each of the measurements in problem 2.21 to two significant figures.

2.23 Round off to three significant figures and express in scientific notation.
  a. 5080 L   **b.** 37 400 g
  c. 104 720 m   **d.** 0.000 250 82 s

2.24 Round off to three significant figures and express in scientific notation.
  a. 5 100 000 L   **b.** 26 711 s
  c. 0.003 378 m   **d.** 56.982 g

2.25 Perform each of the following calculations, and give an answer with the correct number of significant figures:
  a. 45.7×0.034 **b.** $0.002\ 78 \times 5$
  c. $\dfrac{34.56}{1.25}$ **d.** $\dfrac{(0.2465)(25)}{1.78}$

2.26 Perform each of the following calculations, and give an answer with the correct number of significant figures:
  a. 400×185
  b. $\dfrac{2.40}{(4)(125)}$
  c. $0.825 \times 3.6 \times 5.1$
  d. $\dfrac{3.5 \times 0.261}{8.24 \times 20.0}$

2.27 Perform each of the following calculations, and give an answer with the correct number of decimal places:
  a. 45.48 cm + 8.057 cm
  b. 23.45 g + 104.1 g + 0.025 g
  c. 145.675 mL − 24.2 mL
  d. 1.08 L − 0.585 L

2.28 Perform each of the following calculations, and give an answer with the correct number of decimal places:
  a. 5.08 g + 25.1 g
  b. 85.66 cm + 104.10 cm + 0.025 cm
  c. 24.568 mL − 14.25 mL
  d. 0.2654 L − 0.2585 L

Use the numerical values of prefixes to write a metric equality.

TABLE 2.5 Daily Values for Selected Nutrients

Nutrient	Amount Recommended
Protein	50 g
Vitamin C	60 mg
Vitamin B$_{12}$	6 μg (6 mcg)
Calcium	1000 mg
Copper	2 mg
Iodine	150 μg (150 mcg)
Iron	18 mg
Magnesium	400 mg
Niacin	20 mg
Potassium	3500 mg
Selenium	70 μg (70 mcg)
Sodium	2400 mg
Zinc	15 mg

⚛ **CORE CHEMISTRY SKILL**

Using Prefixes

2.4 Prefixes and Equalities

The special feature of the SI as well as the metric system is that a **prefix** can be placed in front of any unit to increase or decrease its size by some factor of 10. For example, the prefixes *milli* and *micro* are used to make the smaller units, milligram (mg) and microgram (μg). Table 2.4 lists some of the metric prefixes, their symbols, and their numerical values.

The prefix *centi* is like cents in a dollar. One cent would be a "centidollar" or 0.01 of a dollar. That also means that one dollar is the same as 100 cents. The prefix *deci* is like dimes in a dollar. One dime would be a "decidollar" or 0.1 of a dollar. That also means that one dollar is the same as 10 dimes.

The U.S. Food and Drug Administration has determined the Daily Values (DV) for nutrients for adults and children aged 4 or older. Examples of these recommended Daily Values, some of which use prefixes, are listed in Table 2.5.

The relationship of a prefix to a unit can be expressed by replacing the prefix with its numerical value. For example, when the prefix *kilo* in kilometer is replaced with its value of 1000, we find that a kilometer is equal to 1000 m. Other examples follow:

1 **kilo**meter (1 km) = **1000** meters (1000 m = 10^3 m)
1 **kilo**liter (1 kL) = **1000** liters (1000 L = 10^3 L)
1 **kilo**gram (1 kg) = **1000** grams (1000 g = 10^3 g)

TABLE 2.4 Metric and SI Prefixes

Prefix	Symbol	Numerical Value	Scientific Notation	Equality
Prefixes That Increase the Size of the Unit				
peta	P	1 000 000 000 000 000	10^{15}	1 Pg = 1 × 10^{15} g 1 g = 1 × 10^{-15} Pg
tera	T	1 000 000 000 000	10^{12}	1 Ts = 1 × 10^{12} s 1 s = 1 × 10^{-12} Ts
giga	G	1 000 000 000	10^{9}	1 Gm = 1 × 10^{9} m 1 m = 1 × 10^{-9} Gm
mega	M	1 000 000	10^{6}	1 Mg = 1 × 10^{6} g 1 g = 1 × 10^{-6} Mg
kilo	k	1 000	10^{3}	1 km = 1 × 10^{3} m 1 m = 1 × 10^{-3} km
Prefixes That Decrease the Size of the Unit				
deci	d	0.1	10^{-1}	1 dL = 1 × 10^{-1} L 1 L = 10 dL
centi	c	0.01	10^{-2}	1 cm = 1 × 10^{-2} m 1 m = 100 cm
milli	m	0.001	10^{-3}	1 ms = 1 × 10^{-3} s 1 s = 1 × 10^{3} ms
micro	μ*	0.000 001	10^{-6}	1 μg = 1 × 10^{-6} g 1 g = 1 × 10^{6} μg
nano	n	0.000 000 001	10^{-9}	1 nm = 1 × 10^{-9} m 1 m = 1 × 10^{9} nm
pico	p	0.000 000 000 001	10^{-12}	1 ps = 1 × 10^{-12} s 1 s = 1 × 10^{12} ps
femto	f	0.000 000 000 000 001	10^{-15}	1 fs = 1 × 10^{-15} s 1 s = 1 × 10^{15} fs

*In medicine and nursing, the abbreviation mc for the prefix micro is used because the symbol μ may be misread, which could result in a medication error. Thus, 1 μg would be written as 1 mcg.

▶ **SAMPLE PROBLEM 2.6** **Prefixes and Equalities**

An endoscopic camera has a width of 1 mm. Complete each of the following equalities involving millimeters:

a. 1 m = _____ mm

b. 1 cm = _____ mm

SOLUTION

a. 1 m = 1000 mm

b. 1 cm = 10 mm

STUDY CHECK 2.6

What is the relationship between millimeters and micrometers?

ANSWER

1 mm = 1000 μm (mcm)

An endoscope, used to see inside the body, has a tiny video camera with a width of 1 mm attached to the end of a long, thin cable.

Measuring Length

An ophthalmologist may measure the diameter of the retina of an eye in centimeters (cm), whereas a surgeon may need to know the length of a nerve in millimeters (mm). When the prefix *centi* is used with the unit meter, it becomes *centimeter*, a length that is one-hundredth of a meter (0.01 m). When the prefix *milli* is used with the unit meter, it becomes *millimeter*, a length that is one-thousandth of a meter (0.001 m). There are 100 cm and 1000 mm in a meter.

If we compare the lengths of a millimeter and a centimeter, we find that 1 mm is 0.1 cm; there are 10 mm in 1 cm. These comparisons are examples of **equalities**, which show the relationship between two units that measure the same quantity. In every equality, each quantity has both a number and a unit. Examples of equalities between different metric units of length follow:

1 m = 100 cm = 1×10^2 cm
1 m = 1000 mm = 1×10^3 mm
1 cm = 10 mm   = 1×10^1 mm

Some metric units for length are compared in Figure 2.6.

Using a retinal camera, an ophthal-mologist photographs the retina of an eye.

First quantity		Second quantity	
1	m	100	cm
Number + unit		Number + unit	

This example of an equality shows the relationship between meters and centimeters.

FIGURE 2.6 ▶ The metric length of 1 m is the same length as 10 dm, 100 cm, or 1000 mm.
How many millimeters (mm) are in 1 centimeter (cm)?

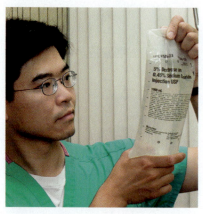

FIGURE 2.7 ▶ A plastic intravenous fluid container contains 1000 mL.

Q How many liters of solution are in the intravenous fluid container?

Measuring Volume

Volumes of 1 L or smaller are common in the health sciences. When a liter is divided into 10 equal portions, each portion is a deciliter (dL). There are 10 dL in 1 L. Laboratory results for blood work are often reported in mass per deciliter. Table 2.6 lists typical laboratory test values for some substances in the blood.

TABLE 2.6 Some Typical Laboratory Test Values

Substance in Blood	Typical Range
Albumin	3.5–5.0 g/dL
Ammonia	20–150 mcg/dL
Calcium	8.5–10.5 mg/dL
Cholesterol	105–250 mg/dL
Iron (male)	80–160 mcg/dL
Protein (total)	6.0–8.0 g/dL

When a liter is divided into a thousand parts, each of the smaller volumes is called a milliliter (mL). In a 1-L container of physiological saline, there are 1000 mL of solution (see Figure 2.7). Examples of equalities between different metric units of volume follow:

$$1\,L\ =\ 10\,dL\ \ \ =\ 1 \times 10^1\,dL$$
$$1\,L\ =\ 1000\,mL\ =\ 1 \times 10^3\,mL$$
$$1\,dL\ =\ 100\,mL\ \ =\ 1 \times 10^2\,mL$$

The **cubic centimeter** (abbreviated as **cm³** or **cc**) is the volume of a cube whose dimensions are 1 cm on each side. A cubic centimeter has the same volume as a milliliter, and the units are often used interchangeably.

$$1\,cm^3\ =\ 1\,cc\ =\ 1\,mL$$

When you see *1 cm*, you are reading about length; when you see *1 cm³* or *1 cc* or *1 mL*, you are reading about volume. A comparison of units of volume is illustrated in Figure 2.8.

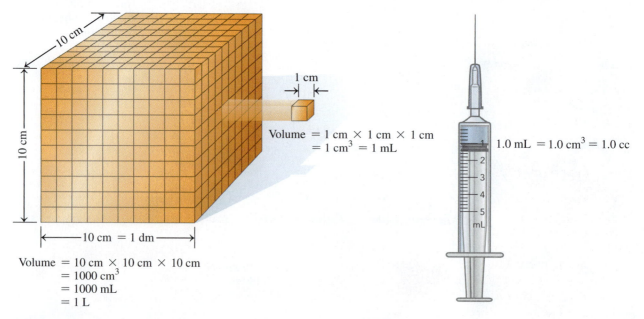

Volume = 10 cm × 10 cm × 10 cm
= 1000 cm³
= 1000 mL
= 1 L

Volume = 1 cm × 1 cm × 1 cm
= 1 cm³ = 1 mL

10 cm = 1 dm

1.0 mL = 1.0 cm³ = 1.0 cc

FIGURE 2.8 ▶ A cube measuring 10 cm on each side has a volume of 1000 cm³, or 1 L; a cube measuring 1 cm on each side has a volume of 1 cm³ (cc) or 1 mL.

Q What is the relationship between a milliliter (mL) and a cubic centimeter (cm³)?

Measuring Mass

When you go to the doctor for a physical examination, your mass is recorded in kilograms, whereas the results of your laboratory tests are reported in grams, milligrams (mg), or micrograms (μg or mcg). A kilogram is equal to 1000 g. One gram represents the same mass as 1000 mg, and one mg equals 1000 μg (or 1000 mcg). Examples of equalities between different metric units of mass follow:

$$1 \text{ kg} = 1000 \text{ g} \qquad\qquad = 1 \times 10^3 \text{ g}$$
$$1 \text{ g} = 1000 \text{ mg} \qquad\qquad = 1 \times 10^3 \text{ mg}$$
$$1 \text{ mg} = 1000\ \mu\text{g (or 1000 mcg)} = 1 \times 10^3\ \mu\text{g (or } 1 \times 10^3 \text{ mcg)}$$

QUESTIONS AND PROBLEMS

2.4 Prefixes and Equalities

LEARNING GOAL Use the numerical values of prefixes to write a metric equality.

2.29 The speedometer is marked in both km/h and mi/h, or mph. What is the meaning of each abbreviation?

2.30 In a French car, the odometer reads 22269. What units would this be? What units would it be if this were an odometer in a car made for the United States?

2.31 Write the abbreviation for each of the following units:
   a. milligram   **b.** deciliter
   c. kilometer   **d.** femtogram

2.32 Write the abbreviation for each of the following units:
   a. gigagram   **b.** megameter
   c. microliter   **d.** nanosecond

2.33 Write the complete name for each of the following units:
   a. cL   **b.** kg   **c.** ms   **d.** Gm

2.34 Write the complete name for each of the following units:
   a. dL   **b.** Ts   **c.** mcg   **d.** pm

2.35 Write the numerical value for each of the following prefixes:
   a. centi   **b.** tera   **c.** milli   **d.** deci

2.36 Write the numerical value for each of the following prefixes:
   a. giga   **b.** micro   **c.** mega   **d.** nano

2.37 Use a prefix to write the name for each of the following:
   a. 0.1 g   **b.** 10^{-6} g   **c.** 1000 g   **d.** 0.01 g

2.38 Use a prefix to write the name for each of the following:
   a. 10^9 m   **b.** 10^6 m   **c.** 0.001 m   **d.** 10^{-15} m

2.39 Complete each of the following metric relationships:
   a. 1 m = _____ cm   **b.** 1 m = _____ nm
   c. 1 mm = _____ m   **d.** 1 L = _____ mL

2.40 Complete each of the following metric relationships:
   a. 1 Mg = _____ g   **b.** 1 mL = _____ μL
   c. 1 g = _____ kg   **d.** 1 g = _____ mg

2.41 For each of the following pairs, which is the larger unit?
   a. milligram or kilogram   **b.** milliliter or microliter
   c. m or km   **d.** kL or dL
   e. nanometer or picometer

2.42 For each of the following pairs, which is the smaller unit?
   a. mg or g   **b.** centimeter or nanometer
   c. millimeter or micrometer **d.** mL or dL
   e. centigram or megagram

2.5 Writing Conversion Factors

LEARNING GOAL

Write a conversion factor for two units that describe the same quantity.

Many problems in chemistry and the health sciences require you to change from one unit to another unit. You make changes in units every day. For example, suppose you worked 2.0 hours (h) on your homework, and someone asked you how many minutes that was. You would answer 120 minutes (min). You must have multiplied 2.0 h × 60 min/h because you knew the equality (1 h = 60 min) that related the two units. When you expressed 2.0 h as 120 min, you did not change the amount of time you spent studying. You changed only the unit of measurement used to express the time. *Any equality can be written as fractions called* **conversion factors** *with one of the quantities in the numerator and the other quantity in the denominator.* Be sure to include the units when you write the conversion factors. Two conversion factors are always possible from any equality.

Explore Your World

SI and Metric Equalities on Product Labels

Read the labels on some food products on your kitchen shelves and in your refrigerator, or refer to the labels in Figure 2.9. List the amount of product given in different units. Write a relationship for two of the amounts for the same product and container. Look for measurements of grams and pounds or quarts and milliliters.

Questions

1. Use the stated measurement to derive a metric–U.S. conversion factor.
2. How do your results compare with the conversion factors we have described in this text?

TABLE 2.7 Some Common Equalities

Quantity	Metric (SI)	U.S.	Metric–U.S.
Length	1 km = 1000 m	1 ft = 12 in.	2.54 cm = 1 in. (exact)
	1 m = 1000 mm	1 yd = 3 ft	1 m = 39.4 in.
	1 cm = 10 mm	1 mi = 5280 ft	1 km = 0.621 mi
Volume	1 L = 1000 mL	1 qt = 4 cups	946 mL = 1 qt
	1 dL = 100 mL	1 qt = 2 pt	1 L = 1.06 qt
	1 mL = 1 cm³	1 gal = 4 qt	473 mL = 1 pt
	1 mL = 1 cc*		1 mL = 15 drops*
			5 mL = 1 tsp*
			15 mL = 1 T (tbsp)*
Mass	1 kg = 1000 g	1 lb = 16 oz	1 kg = 2.20 lb
	1 g = 1000 mg		454 g = 1 lb
	1 mg = 1000 mcg*		
Time	1 h = 60 min	1 h = 60 min	
	1 min = 60 s	1 min = 60 s	

*Used in nursing and medicine.

Two Conversion Factors for the Equality: 60 min = 1 h

$$\frac{\text{Numerator} \longrightarrow}{\text{Denominator} \longrightarrow} \quad \frac{60 \text{ min}}{1 \text{ h}} \quad \text{and} \quad \frac{1 \text{ h}}{60 \text{ min}}$$

These factors are read as "60 minutes per 1 hour" and "1 hour per 60 minutes." The term *per* means "divide." Some common relationships are given in Table 2.7. It is important that the equality you select to form a conversion factor is a *true* relationship.

The numbers in any equality between two metric units or between two U.S. system units are obtained by definition. Because numbers in a definition are exact, they are not used to determine significant figures. For example, the equality of 1 g = 1000 mg is defined, which means that both of the numbers 1 and 1000 are exact. *However, when an equality consists of a metric unit and a U.S. unit, one of the numbers in the equality is obtained by measurement and counts toward the significant figures in the answer.* For example, the equality of 1 lb = 454 g is obtained by measuring the grams in exactly 1 lb. In this equality, the measured quantity 454 g has three significant figures, whereas the 1 is exact. An exception is the relationship of 1 in. = 2.54 cm where 2.54 has been defined as exact.

Metric Conversion Factors

We can write metric conversion factors for any of the metric relationships. For example, from the equality for meters and centimeters, we can write the following factors:

Metric Equality	Conversion Factors		
1 m = 100 cm	$\dfrac{100 \text{ cm}}{1 \text{ m}}$	and	$\dfrac{1 \text{ m}}{100 \text{ cm}}$

Both are proper conversion factors for the relationship; one is just the inverse of the other. *The usefulness of conversion factors is enhanced by the fact that we can turn a conversion factor over and use its inverse.* The number 100 and 1 in this equality and its conversion factors are both *exact* numbers.

Metric–U.S. System Conversion Factors

Suppose you need to convert from pounds, a unit in the U.S. system, to kilograms in the metric (or SI) system. A relationship you could use is

1 kg = 2.20 lb

The corresponding conversion factors would be

$$\frac{2.20 \text{ lb}}{1 \text{ kg}} \quad \text{and} \quad \frac{1 \text{ kg}}{2.20 \text{ lb}}$$

Figure 2.9 illustrates the contents of some packaged foods in both U.S. and metric units.

▶ **SAMPLE PROBLEM 2.7 Writing Conversion Factors**

Identify the correct conversion factor(s) for the equality: 1 pt of blood contains 473 mL of blood.

a. $\dfrac{473 \text{ pt}}{1 \text{ mL}}$ **b.** $\dfrac{1 \text{ pt}}{473 \text{ mL}}$

c. $\dfrac{473 \text{ mL}}{1 \text{ pt}}$ **d.** $\dfrac{1 \text{ mL}}{473 \text{ pt}}$

SOLUTION

The equality for pints and milliliters is 1 pt = 473 mL. Answers **b** and **c** are correctly written conversion factors for the equality.

STUDY CHECK 2.7

What are the two correctly written conversion factors for the equality: 1000 mm = 1 m?

ANSWER

$$\frac{1000 \text{ mm}}{1 \text{ m}} \quad \text{and} \quad \frac{1 \text{ m}}{1000 \text{ mm}}$$

1 pt of blood contains 473 mL.

Equalities and Conversion Factors Stated Within a Problem

An equality may also be stated within a problem that applies only to that problem. For example, the speed of a car in kilometers per hour or the milligrams of vitamin C in a tablet would be specific relationships for that problem only. However, it is possible to identify these relationships within a problem and to write corresponding conversion factors.

From each of the following statements, we can write an equality, and its conversion factors, and identify each number as exact or give its significant figures.

The car was traveling at a speed of 85 km/h.

Equality	Conversion Factors	Significant Figures or Exact
85 km = 1 h	$\dfrac{85 \text{ km}}{1 \text{ h}}$ and $\dfrac{1 \text{ h}}{85 \text{ km}}$	The 85 km is measured: It has two significant figures. The 1 h is exact.

One tablet contains 500 mg of vitamin C.

Equality	Conversion Factors	Significant Figures or Exact
1 tablet = 500 mg of vitamin C	$\dfrac{500 \text{ mg vitamin C}}{1 \text{ tablet}}$ and $\dfrac{1 \text{ tablet}}{500 \text{ mg vitamin C}}$	The 500 mg is measured: It has one significant figure. The 1 tablet is exact.

Vitamin C, an antioxidant needed by the body, is found in fruits such as lemons.

Keflex (Cephalexin), used to treat respiratory infections, is available in 250-mg capsules.

The thickness of the skin fold at the abdomen is used to determine the percentage of body fat.

Conversion Factors from Dosage Problems

Equalities stated within dosage problems for medications can also be written as conversion factors. For example, Keflex (Cephalexin), an antibiotic used for respiratory and ear infections, is available in 250-mg capsules. The quantity of Keflex in a capsule can be written as an equality from which two conversion factors are possible.

Equality	Conversion Factors	Significant Figures or Exact
1 capsule = 250 mg of Keflex	$\dfrac{250 \text{ mg Keflex}}{1 \text{ capsule}}$ and $\dfrac{1 \text{ capsule}}{250 \text{ mg Keflex}}$	The 250 mg is measured: It has two significant figures. The 1 capsule is exact.

Conversion Factors from a Percentage, ppm, and ppb

A percentage (%) is written as a conversion factor by choosing a unit and expressing the numerical relationship of the parts of this unit to 100 parts of the whole. For example, a person might have 18% body fat by mass. The percentage quantity can be written as 18 mass units of body fat in every 100 mass units of body mass. Different mass units such as grams (g), kilograms (kg), or pounds (lb) can be used, but both units in the factor must be the same.

Equality	Conversion Factors	Significant Figures or Exact
18 kg of body fat = 100 kg of body mass	$\dfrac{18 \text{ kg body fat}}{100 \text{ kg body mass}}$ and $\dfrac{100 \text{ kg body mass}}{18 \text{ kg body fat}}$	The 18 kg is measured: It has two significant figures. The 100 kg is exact.

When scientists want to indicate very small ratios, they use numerical relationships called *parts per million* (ppm) or *parts per billion* (ppb). The ratio of parts per million is the same as the milligrams of a substance per kilogram (mg/kg). The ratio of parts per billion equals the micrograms per kilogram (μg/kg, mcg/kg).

Ratio	Units
parts per million (ppm)	milligrams per kilogram (mg/kg)
parts per billion (ppb)	micrograms per kilogram (μg/kg, mcg/kg)

For example, the maximum amount of lead that is allowed by the Food and Drug Administration (FDA) in glazed pottery bowls is 2 ppm, which is 2 mg/kg.

Equality	Conversion Factors	Significant Figures or Exact
2 mg of lead = 1 kg of glaze	$\dfrac{2 \text{ mg lead}}{1 \text{ kg glaze}}$ and $\dfrac{1 \text{ kg glaze}}{2 \text{ mg lead}}$	The 2 mg is measured: It has one significant figure. The 1 kg is exact.

▶ **SAMPLE PROBLEM 2.8** Equalities and Conversion Factors Stated in a Problem

Write the equality and conversion factors, and identify each number as exact or give the number of significant figures for each of the following:

a. The medication that Greg takes for his high blood pressure contains 40. mg of propranolol in 1 tablet.

b. Cold water fish such as salmon contains 1.9% omega-3 fatty acids by mass.

c. The U.S. Environmental Protection Agency (EPA) has set the maximum level for mercury in tuna at 0.5 ppm.

SOLUTION

a. There are 40. mg of propranolol in 1 tablet.

Equality	Conversion Factors	Significant Figures or Exact
1 tablet = 40. mg of propranolol	$\dfrac{40.\text{ mg propranolol}}{1\text{ tablet}}$ and $\dfrac{1\text{ tablet}}{40.\text{ mg propranolol}}$	The 40. mg is measured: It has two significant figures. The 1 tablet is exact.

Propranolol is used to lower high blood pressure.

b. Cold water fish such as salmon contains 1.9% omega-3 fatty acids by mass.

Equality	Conversion Factors	Significant Figures or Exact
1.9 g of omega-3 fatty acids = 100 g of salmon	$\dfrac{1.9\text{ g omega-3 fatty acids}}{100\text{ g salmon}}$ and $\dfrac{100\text{ g salmon}}{1.9\text{ g omega-3 fatty acids}}$	The 1.9 g is measured: It has two significant figures. The 100 g is exact.

Salmon contains high levels of omega-3 fatty acids.

c. The EPA has set the maximum level for mercury in tuna at 0.5 ppm.

Equality	Conversion Factors	Significant Figures or Exact
0.5 mg of mercury = 1 kg of tuna	$\dfrac{0.5\text{ mg mercury}}{1\text{ kg tuna}}$ and $\dfrac{1\text{ kg tuna}}{0.5\text{ mg mercury}}$	The 0.5 mg is measured: It has one significant figure. The 1 kg is exact.

STUDY CHECK 2.8

Levsin (hyoscyamine), used to treat stomach and bladder problems, is available as drops with 0.125 mg Levsin per 1 mL of solution. Write the equality and its corresponding conversion factors, and identify each number as exact or give the number of significant figures.

The maximum amount of mercury allowed in tuna is 0.5 ppm.

ANSWER

0.125 mg of Levsin = 1 mL of solution

$\dfrac{0.125\text{ mg Levsin}}{1\text{ mL solution}}$ and $\dfrac{1\text{ mL solution}}{0.125\text{ mg Levsin}}$

The 0.125 mg is measured: It has three SFs. The 1 mL is exact.

QUESTIONS AND PROBLEMS

2.5 Writing Conversion Factors

LEARNING GOAL Write a conversion factor for two units that describe the same quantity.

2.43 Write the equality and conversion factors for each of the following pairs of units:
    a. centimeters and meters
    b. milligrams and grams
    c. liters and milliliters
    d. deciliters and milliliters

2.44 Write the equality and conversion factors for each of the following pairs of units:
    a. centimeters and inches
    b. pounds and kilograms
    c. pounds and grams
    d. quarts and liters

2.45 Write the equality and conversion factors, and identify the numbers as exact or give the number of significant figures for each of the following:
    a. One yard is 3 ft.
    b. One kilogram is 2.20 lb.
    c. One minute is 60 s.
    d. A car goes 27 mi on 1 gal of gas.
    e. Sterling silver is 93% silver by mass.

2.46 Write the equality and conversion factors, and identify the numbers as exact or give the number of significant figures for each of the following:
   a. One liter is 1.06 qt.
   b. At the store, oranges are $1.29 per lb.
   c. There are 7 days in 1 week.
   d. One deciliter contains 100 mL.
   e. An 18-carat gold ring contains 75% gold by mass.

2.47 Write the equality and conversion factors, and identify the numbers as exact or give the number of significant figures for each of the following:
   a. A bee flies at an average speed of 3.5 m per second.
   b. The Daily Value (DV) for potassium is 4700 mg.
   c. An automobile traveled 46.0 km on 1 gal of gasoline.
   d. The pesticide level in plums was 29 ppb.

2.48 Write the equality and conversion factors, and identify the numbers as exact or give the number of significant figures for each of the following:
   a. The Daily Value (DV) for iodine is 150 mcg.
   b. The nitrate level in well water was 32 ppm.
   c. Gold jewelry contains 58% gold by mass.
   d. The price of a liter of milk is $1.65.

℞ Clinical Applications

2.49 Write the equality and conversion factors, and identify the numbers as exact or give the number of significant figures for each of the following:
   a. A calcium supplement contains 630 mg of calcium per tablet.
   b. The Daily Value (DV) for vitamin C is 60 mg.

   c. The label on a bottle reads 50 mg of atenolol per tablet.
   d. A low-dose aspirin contains 81 mg of aspirin per tablet.

2.50 Write the equality and conversion factors, and identify the numbers as exact or give the number of significant figures for each of the following:
   a. The label on a bottle reads 10 mg of furosemide per 1 mL.
   b. The Daily Value (DV) for selenium is 70. mcg.
   c. An IV of normal saline solution has a flow rate of 85 mL per hour.
   d. One capsule of fish oil contains 360 mg of omega-3 fatty acids.

2.51 Write an equality and two conversion factors for each of the following medications in stock:
   a. 10 mg of Atarax per 5 mL of Atarax syrup
   b. 0.25 g of Lanoxin per 1 tablet of Lanoxin
   c. 300 mg of Motrin per 1 tablet of Motrin

2.52 Write an equality and two conversion factors for each of the following medications in stock:
   a. 2.5 mg of Coumadin per 1 tablet of Coumadin
   b. 100 mg of Clozapine per 1 tablet of Clozapine
   c. 1.5 g of Cefuroxime per 1 mL of Cefuroxime

LEARNING GOAL

Use conversion factors to change from one unit to another.

2.6 Problem Solving Using Unit Conversion

The process of problem solving in chemistry often requires one or more conversion factors to change a given unit to the needed unit. For the problem, the unit of the given quantity and the unit of the needed quantity are identified. From there, the problem is set up with one or more conversion factors used to convert the given unit to the needed unit as seen in the following Sample Problem.

Given unit × one or more conversion factors = needed unit

SAMPLE PROBLEM 2.9 Problem Solving Using Conversion Factors

Greg's doctor has ordered a PET scan of his heart. In radiological imaging such as PET or CT scans, dosages of pharmaceuticals are based on body mass. If Greg weighs 144 lb, what is his body mass in kilograms?

Guide to Problem Solving Using Conversion Factors

STEP 1
State the given and needed quantities.

STEP 2
Write a plan to convert the given unit to the needed unit.

STEP 3
State the equalities and conversion factors.

STEP 4
Set up the problem to cancel units and calculate the answer.

SOLUTION

STEP 1 State the given and needed quantities.

ANALYZE THE PROBLEM	Given	Need
	144 lb	kilograms

STEP 2 Write a plan to convert the given unit to the needed unit. The conversion factor relates the given unit in the U.S. system of measurement and the needed unit in the metric system.

pounds → U.S.–Metric factor → kilograms

STEP 3   State the equalities and conversion factors.

$$1 \text{ kg} = 2.20 \text{ lb}$$
$$\frac{2.20 \text{ lb}}{1 \text{ kg}} \quad \text{and} \quad \frac{1 \text{ kg}}{2.20 \text{ lb}}$$

STEP 4   Set up the problem to cancel units and calculate the answer. Write the given, 144 lb, and multiply by the conversion factor that has the unit lb in the denominator (bottom number) to cancel out the given unit (lb) in the numerator.

Unit for answer goes here

$$144 \text{ l\!b} \quad \times \quad \frac{1 \text{ kg}}{2.20 \text{ l\!b}} \quad = \quad 65.5 \text{ kg}$$

Given   Conversion factor   Answer

Look at how the units cancel. The given unit lb cancels out and the needed unit kg is in the numerator. *The unit you want in the final answer is the one that remains after all the other units have canceled out.* This is a helpful way to check that you set up a problem properly.

$$\text{l\!b} \times \frac{\text{kg}}{\text{l\!b}} = \text{kg} \quad \text{Unit needed for answer}$$

The calculator display gives the numerical answer, which is adjusted to give a final answer with the proper number of significant figures (SFs).

Exact

$$144 \quad \times \quad \frac{1}{2.20} \quad = \quad 144 \div 2.20 \quad = \quad \boxed{65.45454545} \quad = \quad 65.5$$

Three SFs   Three SFs   Calculator   Three SFs
                                           display   (rounded off)

The value of 65.5 combined with the unit, kg, gives the final answer of 65.5 kg. With few exceptions, answers to numerical problems contain a number and a unit.

STUDY CHECK 2.9

A total of 2500 mL of a boric acid antiseptic solution is prepared from boric acid concentrate. How many quarts of boric acid has been prepared?

ANSWER

2.6 qt

Interactive Video

Conversion Factors

Using Two or More Conversion Factors

In problem solving, two or more conversion factors are often needed to complete the change of units. In setting up these problems, one factor follows the other. Each factor is arranged to cancel the preceding unit until the needed unit is obtained. Once the problem is set up to cancel units properly, the calculations can be done without writing intermediate results. The process is worth practicing until you understand unit cancelation, the steps on the calculator, and rounding off to give a final answer. In this text, when two or more conversion factors are required, the final answer will be based on obtaining a final calculator display and rounding off (or adding zeros) to give the correct number of significant figures.

⊛ **CORE CHEMISTRY SKILL**

Using Conversion Factors

SAMPLE PROBLEM 2.10 Using Two or More Conversion Factors

A doctor's order for 0.50 g of Keflex is available as 250-mg tablets. How many tablets of Keflex are needed? In the following setup, fill in the missing parts of the conversion factors, show the canceled units, and give the correct answer:

$$0.50 \text{ g Keflex} \times \frac{\_\_\_ \text{ mg Keflex}}{1 \text{ g Keflex}} \times \frac{1 \text{ tablet}}{\_\_\_ \text{ mg Keflex}} =$$

SOLUTION

$$0.50 \text{ g Keflex} \times \frac{1000 \text{ mg Keflex}}{1 \text{ g Keflex}} \times \frac{1 \text{ tablet}}{250 \text{ mg Keflex}} = 2 \text{ tablets}$$

STUDY CHECK 2.10

A newborn has a length of 450 mm. In the following setup that calculates the baby's length in inches, fill in the missing parts of the conversion factors, show the canceled units, and give the correct answer:

$$450 \text{ mm} \times \frac{1 \text{ cm}}{\_\_\_ \text{ mm}} \times \frac{1 \text{ in.}}{\_\_\_ \text{ cm}} =$$

ANSWER

$$450 \text{ mm} \times \frac{1 \text{ cm}}{10 \text{ mm}} \times \frac{1 \text{ in.}}{2.54 \text{ cm}} = 18 \text{ in.}$$

SAMPLE PROBLEM 2.11 Problem Solving Using Two Conversion Factors

Synthroid is used as a replacement or supplemental therapy for diminished thyroid function. A doctor's order prescribes a dosage of 0.150 mg of Synthroid. If tablets in stock contain 75 mcg of Synthroid, how many tablets are required to provide the prescribed medication?

SOLUTION

STEP 1 State the given and needed quantities.

ANALYZE THE PROBLEM	Given	Need
	0.150 mg of Synthroid	number of tablets

STEP 2 Write a plan to convert the given unit to the needed unit.

milligrams → Metric factor → micrograms → Clinical factor → number of tablets

STEP 3 State the equalities and conversion factors.

1 mg = 1000 mcg	1 tablet = 75 mcg of Synthroid
$\frac{1 \text{ mg}}{1000 \text{ mcg}}$ and $\frac{1000 \text{ mcg}}{1 \text{ mg}}$	$\frac{1 \text{ tablet}}{75 \text{ mcg Synthroid}}$ and $\frac{75 \text{ mcg Synthroid}}{1 \text{ tablet}}$

STEP 4 Set up the problem to cancel units and calculate the answer. The problem can be set up using the metric factor to cancel milligrams, and then the clinical factor to obtain the number of tablets as the final unit.

$$0.150 \text{ mg Synthroid} \times \frac{1000 \text{ mcg}}{1 \text{ mg}} \times \frac{1 \text{ tablet}}{75 \text{ mcg Synthroid}} = 2 \text{ tablets}$$

Three SFs   Exact   Exact   Two SFs

STUDY CHECK 2.11

A bottle contains 120 mL of cough syrup. If one teaspoon (5 mL) is given four times a day, how many days will elapse before a refill is needed?

ANSWER

6 days

SAMPLE PROBLEM 2.12 Using a Percentage as a Conversion Factor

A person who exercises regularly has 16% body fat by mass. If this person weighs 155 lb, what is the mass, in kilograms, of body fat?

SOLUTION

STEP 1 State the given and needed quantities.

ANALYZE THE PROBLEM	Given	Need
	155 lb body weight, 16% body fat	kilograms of body fat

STEP 2 Write a plan to convert the given unit to the needed unit.

pounds of body weight → U.S.–Metric factor → kilograms of body mass → Percentage factor → kilograms of body fat

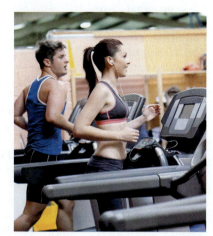

Exercising regularly helps reduce body fat.

STEP 3 State the equalities and conversion factors.

1 kg of body mass = 2.20 lb of body weight

$$\frac{2.20 \text{ lb body weight}}{1 \text{ kg body mass}} \text{ and } \frac{1 \text{ kg body mass}}{2.20 \text{ lb body weight}}$$

16 kg of body fat = 100 kg of body mass

$$\frac{16 \text{ kg body fat}}{100 \text{ kg body mass}} \text{ and } \frac{100 \text{ kg body mass}}{16 \text{ kg body fat}}$$

STEP 4 Set up the problem to cancel units and calculate the answer. We set up the problem using conversion factors to cancel each unit, starting with lb of body weight, until we obtain the final unit, kg of body fat, in the numerator.

$$155 \text{ lb body weight} \times \frac{1 \text{ kg body mass}}{2.20 \text{ lb body weight}} \times \frac{16 \text{ kg body fat}}{100 \text{ kg body mass}} = 11 \text{ kg of body fat}$$

Three SFs — Exact / Three SFs — Two SFs / Exact — Two SFs

STUDY CHECK 2.12

Uncooked lean ground beef can contain up to 22% fat by mass. How many grams of fat would be contained in 0.25 lb of the ground beef?

ANSWER

25 g of fat

Chemistry Link to **Health**
Toxicology and Risk–Benefit Assessment

Each day, we make choices about what we do or what we eat, often without thinking about the risks associated with these choices. We are aware of the risks of cancer from smoking or the risks of lead poisoning, and we know there is a greater risk of having an accident if we cross a street where there is no light or crosswalk.

A basic concept of toxicology is the statement of Paracelsus that the dose is the difference between a poison and a cure. To evaluate the level of danger from various substances, natural or synthetic, a risk assessment is made by exposing laboratory animals to the substances and monitoring the health effects. Often, doses very much greater than humans might ordinarily encounter are given to the test animals.

Many hazardous chemicals or substances have been identified by these tests. One measure of toxicity is the LD_{50}, or lethal dose, which is the concentration of the substance that causes death in

The LD_{50} of caffeine is 192 mg/kg.

50% of the test animals. A dosage is typically measured in milligrams per kilogram (mg/kg) of body mass or micrograms per kilogram (mcg/kg) of body mass.

Other evaluations need to be made, but it is easy to compare LD_{50} values. Parathion, a pesticide, with an LD_{50} of 3 mg/kg, would be highly toxic. This means that 3 mg of parathion per kg of body mass would be fatal to half the test animals. Table salt (sodium chloride) with an LD_{50} of 3000 mg/kg would have a much lower toxicity. You would need to ingest a huge amount of salt before any toxic effect would be observed. Although the risk to animals can be evaluated in the laboratory, it is more difficult to determine the impact in the environment since there is also a difference between continued exposure and a single, large dose of the substance.

Table 2.8 lists some LD_{50} values and compares substances in order of increasing toxicity.

TABLE 2.8 Some LD_{50} Values for Substances Tested in Rats

Substance	LD_{50} (mg/kg)
Table sugar	29 700
Boric acid	5140
Baking soda	4220
Table salt	3300
Ethanol	2080
Aspirin	1100
Codeine	800
Oxycodone	480
Caffeine	192
DDT	113
Cocaine (injected)	95
Dichlorvos (pesticide strips)	56
Ricin	30
Sodium cyanide	6
Parathion	3

QUESTIONS AND PROBLEMS

2.6 Problem Solving Using Unit Conversion

LEARNING GOAL Use conversion factors to change from one unit to another.

2.53   Use metric conversion factors to solve each of the following problems:
   a. The height of a student is 175 cm. How tall is the student in meters?
   b. A cooler has a volume of 5500 mL. What is the capacity of the cooler in liters?
   c. A Bee Hummingbird has a mass of 0.0018 kg. What is the mass of the hummingbird in grams?

2.54   Use metric conversion factors to solve each of the following problems:
   a. The Daily Value (DV) for phosphorus is 800 mg. How many grams of phosphorus are recommended?
   b. A glass of orange juice contains 0.85 dL of juice. How many milliliters of orange juice is that?
   c. A package of chocolate instant pudding contains 2840 mg of sodium. How many grams of sodium is that?

2.55   Solve each of the following problems using one or more conversion factors:
   a. A container holds 0.500 qt of liquid. How many milliliters of lemonade will it hold?
   b. What is the mass, in kilograms, of a person who weighs 175 lb?
   c. An athlete has 15% body fat by mass. What is the weight of fat, in pounds, of a 74-kg athlete?
   d. A plant fertilizer contains 15% nitrogen (N) by mass. In a container of soluble plant food, there are 10.0 oz of fertilizer. How many grams of nitrogen are in the container?

Agricultural fertilizers applied to a field provide nitrogen for plant growth.

2.56   Solve each of the following problems using one or more conversion factors:
   a. Wine is 12% alcohol by volume. How many milliliters of alcohol are in a 0.750-L bottle of wine?
   b. Blueberry high-fiber muffins contain 51% dietary fiber by mass. If a package with a net weight of 12 oz contains six muffins, how many grams of fiber are in each muffin?
   c. A jar of crunchy peanut butter contains 1.43 kg of peanut butter. If you use 8.0% of the peanut butter for a sandwich, how many ounces of peanut butter did you take out of the container?
   d. In a candy factory, the nutty chocolate bars contain 22.0% pecans by mass. If 5.0 kg of pecans were used for candy last Tuesday, how many pounds of nutty chocolate bars were made?

℞ Clinical Applications

2.57   Using conversion factors, solve each of the following clinical problems:
   a. You have used 250 L of distilled water for a dialysis patient. How many gallons of water is that?
   b. A patient needs 0.024 g of a sulfa drug. There are 8-mg tablets in stock. How many tablets should be given?

c. The daily dose of ampicillin for the treatment of an ear infection is 115 mg/kg of body weight. What is the daily dose for a 34-lb child?

d. You need 4.0 oz of a steroid ointment. If there are 16 oz in 1 lb, how many grams of ointment does the pharmacist need to prepare?

2.58 Using conversion factors, solve each of the following clinical problems:

a. The physician has ordered 1.0 g of tetracycline to be given every six hours to a patient. If your stock on hand is 500-mg tablets, how many will you need for one day's treatment?

b. An intramuscular medication is given at 5.00 mg/kg of body weight. What is the dose for a 180-lb patient?

c. A physician has ordered 0.50 mg of atropine, intramuscularly. If atropine were available as 0.10 mg/mL of solution, how many milliliters would you need to give?

d. During surgery, a patient receives 5.0 pt of plasma. How many milliliters of plasma were given?

2.59 Using conversion factors, solve each of the following clinical problems:

a. A nurse practitioner prepares 500. mL of an IV of normal saline solution to be delivered at a rate of 80. mL/h. What is the infusion time, in hours, to deliver 500. mL?

b. A nurse practitioner orders Medrol to be given 1.5 mg/kg of body weight. Medrol is an anti-inflammatory administered as an intramuscular injection. If a child weighs 72.6 lb and the available stock of Medrol is 20. mg/mL, how many milliliters does the nurse administer to the child?

2.60 Using conversion factors, solve each of the following clinical problems:

a. A nurse practitioner prepares an injection of promethazine, an antihistamine used to treat allergic rhinitis. If the stock bottle is labeled 25 mg/mL and the order is a dose of 12.5 mg, how many milliliters will the nurse draw up in the syringe?

b. You are to give ampicillin 25 mg/kg to a child with a mass of 28 kg. If stock on hand is 250 mg/capsule, how many capsules should be given?

2.61 Using Table 2.8, calculate the number of grams that would provide the LD_{50} for a 175-lb person for each of the following:
a. table salt   b. sodium cyanide   c. aspirin

2.62 Using Table 2.8, calculate the number of grams that would provide the LD_{50} for a 148-lb person for each of the following:
a. ethanol   b. ricin   c. baking soda

2.7 Density

The mass and volume of any object can be measured. If we compare the mass of the object to its volume, we obtain a relationship called **density**.

$$\text{Density} = \frac{\text{mass of substance}}{\text{volume of substance}}$$

Every substance has a unique density, which distinguishes it from other substances. For example, lead has a density of 11.3 g/mL, whereas cork has a density of 0.26 g/mL. From these densities, we can predict if these substances will sink or float in water. *If an object is less dense than a liquid, the object floats when placed in the liquid.* If a substance, such as cork, is less dense than water, it will float. However, a lead object sinks because its density is greater than that of water (see Figure 2.10).

LEARNING GOAL

Calculate the density of a substance; use the density to calculate the mass or volume of a substance.

Cork (D = 0.26 g/mL)
Ice (D = 0.92 g/mL)
Water (D = 1.00 g/mL)
Aluminum (D = 2.70 g/mL)
Lead (D = 11.3 g/mL)

FIGURE 2.10 ▶ Objects that sink in water are more dense than water; objects that float are less dense.

Q Why does an ice cube float and a piece of aluminum sink?

Metals such as gold and lead tend to have higher densities, whereas gases have low densities. In the metric system, the densities of solids and liquids are usually expressed as grams per cubic centimeter (g/cm^3) or grams per milliliter (g/mL). The densities of gases are usually stated as grams per liter (g/L). Table 2.9 gives the densities of some common substances.

TABLE 2.9 Densities of Some Common Substances

Solids (at 25 °C)	Density (g/mL)	Liquids (at 25 °C)	Density (g/mL)	Gases (at 0 °C)	Density (g/L)
Cork	0.26	Gasoline	0.74	Hydrogen	0.090
Body fat	0.909	Ethanol	0.79	Helium	0.179
Ice (at 0 °C)	0.92	Olive oil	0.92	Methane	0.714
Muscle	1.06	Water (at 4 °C)	1.00	Neon	0.902
Sugar	1.59	Urine	1.012–1.030	Nitrogen	1.25
Bone	1.80	Plasma (blood)	1.03	Air (dry)	1.29
Salt (NaCl)	2.16	Milk	1.04	Oxygen	1.43
Aluminum	2.70	Blood	1.06	Carbon dioxide	1.96
Iron	7.86	Mercury	13.6		
Copper	8.92				
Silver	10.5				
Lead	11.3				
Gold	19.3				

Calculating Density

We can calculate the density of a substance from its mass and volume. High-density lipoprotein (HDL) is a type of cholesterol, sometimes called "good cholesterol," that is measured in a routine blood test. If we have a 0.258-g sample of HDL with a volume of 0.22 mL, we can calculate the density of the HDL as follows:

$$\text{Density} = \frac{\text{mass of HDL sample}}{\text{volume of HDL sample}} = \frac{\overset{\text{Three SFs}}{0.258 \text{ g}}}{\underset{\text{Two SFs}}{0.22 \text{ mL}}} = \underset{\text{Two SFs}}{1.2 \text{ g/mL}}$$

Density of Solids

The volume of a solid can be determined by volume displacement. When a solid is completely submerged in water, it displaces a volume that is equal to the volume of the solid. In Figure 2.11, the water level rises from 35.5 mL to 45.0 mL after the zinc object is added. This means that 9.5 mL of water is displaced and that the volume of the object is 9.5 mL. The density of the zinc is calculated using volume displacement as follows:

$$\text{Density} = \frac{\overset{\text{Four SFs}}{68.60 \text{ g zinc}}}{\underset{\text{Two SFs}}{9.5 \text{ mL}}} = \underset{\text{Two SFs}}{7.2 \text{ g/mL}}$$

Mass of zinc object   Submerged zinc object

Volume increase
45.0 mL
35.5 mL

FIGURE 2.11 ▶ The density of a solid can be determined by volume displacement because a submerged object displaces a volume of water equal to its own volume.

 How is the volume of the zinc object determined?

Chemistry Link to **Health**
Bone Density

The density of our bones determines their health and strength. Our bones are constantly gaining and losing minerals such as calcium, magnesium, and phosphate. In childhood, bones form at a faster rate than they break down. As we age, the breakdown of bone occurs more rapidly than new bone forms. As the loss of bone minerals increases, bones begin to thin, causing a decrease in mass and density. Thinner bones lack strength, which increases the risk of fracture. Hormonal changes, disease, and certain medications can also contribute to the thinning of bone. Eventually, a condition of severe thinning of bone known as *osteoporosis* may occur. *Scanning electron micrographs* (SEMs) show **(a)** normal bone and **(b)** bone with osteoporosis due to loss of bone minerals.

Bone density is often determined by passing low-dose X-rays through the narrow part at the top of the femur (hip) and the spine **(c)**. These locations are where fractures are more likely to occur, especially as we age. Bones with high density will block more of the X-rays compared to bones that are less dense. The results of a bone density test are compared to a healthy young adult as well as to other people of the same age.

Recommendations to improve bone strength include supplements of calcium and vitamin D. Weight-bearing exercise such as walking and lifting weights can also improve muscle strength, which in turn increases bone strength.

(a) Normal bone

(b) Bone with osteoporosis

(c) Viewing a low-dose X-ray of the spine

Problem Solving Using Density

Density can be used as a conversion factor. For example, if the volume and the density of a sample are known, the mass in grams of the sample can be calculated as shown in the following Sample Problem.

⚛ CORE CHEMISTRY SKILL

Using Density as a Conversion Factor

▶ **SAMPLE PROBLEM 2.13 Problem Solving with Density**

Ken, a 195-lb male patient, has a blood volume of 7.5 qt. If the density of blood is 1.06 g/mL, what is the mass, in grams, of Ken's blood?

SOLUTION

STEP 1 State the given and needed quantities.

ANALYZE THE PROBLEM	Given	Need
	7.5 qt of blood, density of blood (1.06 g/mL)	grams of blood

STEP 2 Write a plan to calculate the needed quantity.

quarts → [U.S.–Metric factor] → milliliters → [Density factor] → grams

Guide to Using Density

STEP 1
State the given and needed quantities.

STEP 2
Write a plan to calculate the needed quantity.

STEP 3
Write the equalities and their conversion factors including density.

STEP 4
Set up the problem to calculate the needed quantity.

FIGURE 2.12 ▶ A hydrometer is used to measure the specific gravity of urine, which, for adults, is 1.012 to 1.030.

Q If the hydrometer reading is 1.006, what is the density of the urine?

A dipstick is used to measure the specific gravity of a urine sample.

STEP 3 Write the equalities and their conversion factors including density.

1 qt = 946 mL		1 mL of blood = 1.06 g of blood	
$\dfrac{946 \text{ mL}}{1 \text{ qt}}$	and $\dfrac{1 \text{ qt}}{946 \text{ mL}}$	$\dfrac{1 \text{ mL}}{1.06 \text{ g blood}}$	and $\dfrac{1.06 \text{ g blood}}{1 \text{ mL}}$

STEP 4 Set up the problem to calculate the needed quantity.

$$7.5 \text{ qt blood} \times \underset{\text{Exact}}{\underbrace{\frac{946 \text{ mL}}{1 \text{ qt}}}_{\text{Three SFs}}} \times \underset{\text{Exact}}{\underbrace{\frac{1.06 \text{ g blood}}{1 \text{ mL}}}_{\text{Three SFs}}} = \underset{\text{Two SFs}}{7500 \text{ g of blood}}$$

Two SFs

STUDY CHECK 2.13

During surgery, a patient receives 3.0 pt of blood. How many kilograms of blood (density = 1.06 g/mL) were needed for the transfusion?

ANSWER

1.5 kg of blood

Specific Gravity

Specific gravity (sp gr) is a relationship between the density of a substance and the density of water. Specific gravity is calculated by dividing the density of a sample by the density of water, which is 1.00 g/mL at 4 °C. A substance with a specific gravity of 1.00 has the same density as water (1.00 g/mL).

$$\text{Specific gravity} = \frac{\text{density of sample}}{\text{density of water}}$$

Specific gravity is one of the few unitless values you will encounter in chemistry. An instrument called a hydrometer is often used to measure the specific gravity of fluids such as wine or a sample of urine. The specific gravity of the urine helps to evaluate the water balance in the body and the substances in the urine. In Figure 2.12, a hydrometer is used to measure the specific gravity of urine. The normal range of specific gravity for urine is 1.012 to 1.030. The specific gravity can decrease with *type 2 diabetes* and kidney disease. Increased specific gravity may occur with dehydration, kidney infection, and liver disease. In a clinic or hospital, a dipstick containing chemical pads is used to evaluate specific gravity.

QUESTIONS AND PROBLEMS

2.7 Density

LEARNING GOAL Calculate the density of a substance; use the density to calculate the mass or volume of a substance.

2.63 What is the density (g/mL) of each of the following samples?

Lightweight heads on golf clubs are made of titanium.

a. A solid object with a mass of 1.65 lb and a volume of 170 mL.
b. A gem has a mass of 4.50 g. When the gem is placed in a graduated cylinder containing 20.00 mL of water, the water level rises to 21.45 mL.
c. A lightweight head on the driver of a golf club is made of titanium. The volume of a sample of titanium is 114 cm³ and the mass is 514.1 g.

2.64 What is the density (g/mL) of each of the following samples?
   a. A medication, if 3.00 mL has a mass of 3.85 g.
   b. The fluid in a car battery, if it has a volume of 125 mL and a mass of 155 g.
   c. A syrup is added to an empty container with a mass of 115.25 g. When 0.100 pt of syrup is added, the total mass of the container and syrup is 182.48 g.

115.25 g   **182.48 g**

2.65 Solve the following problems:
   a. What is the mass, in grams, of 150 mL of a liquid with a density of 1.4 g/mL?
   b. What is the mass of a glucose solution that fills a 0.500-L intravenous bottle if the density of the glucose solution is 1.15 g/mL?
   c. A sculptor has prepared a mold for casting a bronze figure. The figure has a volume of 225 mL. If bronze has a density of 7.8 g/mL, how many ounces of bronze are needed in the preparation of the bronze figure?

2.66 Use Table 2.9 to solve the following problems:
   a. A graduated cylinder contains 18.0 mL of water. What is the new water level after 35.6 g of silver metal with a density of 10.5 g/mL is submerged in the water?
   b. A thermometer containing 8.3 g of mercury has broken. If mercury has a density of 13.6 g/mL, what volume, in milliliters, spilled?

   c. A fish tank holds 35 gal of water. Using the density of 1.00 g/mL for water, determine the number of pounds of water in the fish tank.

℞ Clinical Applications

2.67 Solve each of the following problems:
   a. A urine sample has a density of 1.030 g/mL. What is the specific gravity of the sample?
   b. A 20.0-mL sample of a glucose IV solution that has a mass of 20.6 g. What is the density of the glucose solution?
   c. The specific gravity of a vegetable oil is 0.85. What is its density?
   d. A 0.200-mL sample of high-density lipoprotein (HDL) has a mass of 0.230 g. What is the density of the HDL?

2.68 Solve each of the following problems:
   a. A glucose solution has a density of 1.02 g/mL. What is its specific gravity?
   b. A bottle containing 325 g of cleaning solution is used to clean hospital equipment. If the cleaning solution has a specific gravity of 0.850, what volume, in milliliters, of solution was used?
   c. Butter has a specific gravity of 0.86. What is the mass, in grams, of 2.15 L of butter?
   d. A 5.000-mL urine sample has a mass of 5.025 g. If the normal range for the specific gravity of urine is 1.012 to 1.030, would the specific gravity of this urine sample indicate that the patient could have type 2 diabetes?

℞ Clinical Update

Greg's Follow-Up Visit with His Doctor

On Greg's last visit to his doctor, he complained of feeling tired. His doctor orders a blood test for iron. Sandra, the registered nurse, does a venipuncture and withdraws 8.0 mL of blood. About 70% of the iron in the body is used to form hemoglobin, which is a protein in the red blood cells that carries oxygen to the cells of the body. About 30% is stored in ferritin, bone marrow, and the liver. When the iron level is low, a person may have fatigue and decreased immunity.

The normal range for serum iron in men is 80 to 160 mcg/dL. Greg's iron test showed a blood serum iron level of 42 mcg/dL, which indicates that Greg has iron deficiency anemia. His doctor orders an iron supplement to be taken twice daily (b.i.d.). One tablet of the iron supplement contains 65 mg of iron.

℞ Clinical Applications

2.69 **a.** Write an equality and two conversion factors for Greg's serum iron level.
   b. How many micrograms of iron were in the 8.0 mL sample of Greg's blood?

2.70 **a.** Write an equality and two conversion factors for one tablet of the iron supplement.
   b. How many grams of iron will Greg consume in one week?

Each tablet contains 65 mg of iron, which is given for iron supplementation.

CONCEPT MAP

CHEMISTRY AND MEASUREMENTS

Measurements

in chemistry involve

Metric Units — for measuring — **Length (m)**, **Mass (g)**, **Volume (L)**, **Temperature (°C)**, **Time (s)**

give **Density** and **Specific Gravity**

Measured Numbers — have — **Significant Figures** — that require — **Rounding Off Answers** — or — **Adding Zeros**

Prefixes — that change the size of — **Metric Units** — to give — **Equalities** — used for — **Conversion Factors** — to change units in — **Problem Solving**

CHAPTER REVIEW

2.1 Units of Measurement
LEARNING GOAL Write the names and abbreviations for the metric or SI units used in measurements of length, volume, mass, temperature, and time.

- In science, physical quantities are described in units of the metric or International System of Units (SI).
- Some important units are meter (m) for length, liter (L) for volume, gram (g) and kilogram (kg) for mass, degree Celsius (°C) and Kelvin (K) for temperature, and second (s) for time.

2.2 Measured Numbers and Significant Figures
LEARNING GOAL Identify a number as measured or exact; determine the number of significant figures in a measured number.

- A measured number is any number obtained by using a measuring device.
- An exact number is obtained by counting items or from a definition; no measuring device is needed.
- Significant figures are the numbers reported in a measurement including the estimated digit.
- Zeros in front of a decimal number or at the end of a nondecimal number are not significant.

2.3 Significant Figures in Calculations
LEARNING GOAL Adjust calculated answers to give the correct number of significant figures.

- In multiplication and division, the final answer is written so that it has the same number of significant figures as the measurement with the fewest significant figures.
- In addition and subtraction, the final answer is written so that it has the same number of decimal places as the measurement with the fewest decimal places.

2.4 Prefixes and Equalities

LEARNING GOAL Use the numerical values of prefixes to write a metric equality.

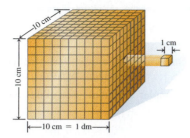

- A prefix placed in front of a metric or SI unit changes the size of the unit by factors of 10.
- Prefixes such as *centi*, *milli*, and *micro* provide smaller units; prefixes such as *kilo*, *mega*, and *tera* provide larger units.
- An equality shows the relationship between two units that measure the same quantity of length, volume, mass, or time.
- Examples of metric equalities are 1 m = 100 cm, 1 L = 1000 mL, 1 kg = 1000 g, and 1 min = 60 s.

2.5 Writing Conversion Factors

LEARNING GOAL Write a conversion factor for two units that describe the same quantity.

- Conversion factors are used to express a relationship in the form of a fraction.
- Two conversion factors can be written for any relationship in the metric or U.S. system.
- A percentage is written as a conversion factor by expressing matching units as the parts in 100 parts of the whole.

2.6 Problem Solving Using Unit Conversion

LEARNING GOAL Use conversion factors to change from one unit to another.

- Conversion factors are useful when changing a quantity expressed in one unit to a quantity expressed in another unit.
- In the problem-solving process, a given unit is multiplied by one or more conversion factors that cancel units until the needed answer is obtained.

2.7 Density

LEARNING GOAL Calculate the density of a substance; use the density to calculate the mass or volume of a substance.

- The density of a substance is a ratio of its mass to its volume, usually g/mL or g/cm^3.
- The units of density can be used to write conversion factors that convert between the mass and volume of a substance.
- Specific gravity (sp gr) compares the density of a substance to the density of water, 1.00 g/mL.

KEY TERMS

Celsius (°C) temperature scale A temperature scale on which water has a freezing point of 0 °C and a boiling point of 100 °C.

centimeter (cm) A unit of length in the metric system; there are 2.54 cm in 1 in.

conversion factor A ratio in which the numerator and denominator are quantities from an equality or given relationship. For example, the conversion factors for the relationship 1 kg = 2.20 lb are written as

$$\frac{2.20\ \text{lb}}{1\ \text{kg}} \quad \text{and} \quad \frac{1\ \text{kg}}{2.20\ \text{lb}}$$

cubic centimeter (cm³, cc) The volume of a cube that has 1-cm sides; 1 cm³ is equal to 1 mL.

density The relationship of the mass of an object to its volume expressed as grams per cubic centimeter (g/cm^3), grams per milliliter (g/mL), or grams per liter (g/L).

equality A relationship between two units that measure the same quantity.

exact number A number obtained by counting or by definition.

gram (g) The metric unit used in measurements of mass.

International System of Units (SI) An international system of units that modifies the metric system.

Kelvin (K) temperature scale A temperature scale on which the lowest possible temperature is 0 K.

kilogram (kg) A metric mass of 1000 g, equal to 2.20 lb. The kilogram is the SI standard unit of mass.

liter (L) The metric unit for volume that is slightly larger than a quart.

mass A measure of the quantity of material in an object.

measured number A number obtained when a quantity is determined by using a measuring device.

meter (m) The metric unit for length that is slightly longer than a yard. The meter is the SI standard unit of length.

metric system A system of measurement used by scientists and in most countries of the world.

milliliter (mL) A metric unit of volume equal to one-thousandth of a liter (0.001 L).

prefix The part of the name of a metric unit that precedes the base unit and specifies the size of the measurement. All prefixes are related on a decimal scale.

second (s) A unit of time used in both the SI and metric systems.

significant figures (SFs) The numbers recorded in a measurement.

specific gravity (sp gr) A relationship between the density of a substance and the density of water:

$$\text{sp gr} = \frac{\text{density of sample}}{\text{density of water}}$$

temperature An indicator of the hotness or coldness of an object.

volume The amount of space occupied by a substance.

🖩 KEY MATH SKILL

The chapter section containing each Key Math Skill is shown in parentheses at the end of each heading.

Rounding Off (2.3)

Calculator displays are rounded off to give the correct number of significant figures.

- If the first digit to be dropped is *4 or less*, then it and all following digits are simply dropped from the number.
- If the first digit to be dropped is *5 or greater*, then the last retained digit of the number is increased by 1.

One or more significant zeros are added when the calculator display has fewer digits than the needed number of significant figures.

Example: Round off each of the following to three significant figures:

3.608 92 L	**Answer:** 3.61 L
0.003 870 298 m	0.003 87 m
6 g	6.00 g

⚛ CORE CHEMISTRY SKILLS

The chapter section containing each Core Chemistry Skill is shown in parentheses at the end of each heading.

Counting Significant Figures (2.2)

The significant figures are all the *measured* numbers including the last, estimated digit:

- All nonzero digits
- Zeros between nonzero digits
- Zeros within a decimal number
- All digits in a coefficient of a number written in scientific notation

An *exact* number is obtained from counting or a definition and has no effect on the number of significant figures in the final answer.

Example: State the number of significant figures in each of the following:

0.003 045 mm	**Answer:**	four SFs
15 000 m		two SFs
45.067 kg		five SFs
5.30×10^3 g		three SFs
2 cans of soda		exact

Using Significant Figures in Calculations (2.3)

- In multiplication or division, the final answer is written so that it has the same number of significant figures as the measurement with the fewest significant figures (SFs).
- In addition or subtraction, the final answer is written so that it has the same number of decimal places as the measurement having the fewest decimal places.

Perform the following calculations using measured numbers and give answers with the correct number of SFs:

Example: $4.05 \text{ m} \times 0.6078 \text{ m}$

Answer: 2.461 59 rounded off to 2.46 m² (three SFs)

Example: $\dfrac{4.50 \text{ g}}{3.27 \text{ mL}}$

Answer: 1.376 146 789 rounded off to 1.38 g/mL (three SFs)

Example: 0.758 g + 3.10 g

Answer: 3.858 rounded off to 3.86 g (hundredths place)

Example: 13.538 km − 8.6 km

Answer: 4.938 rounded off to 4.9 km (tenths place)

Using Prefixes (2.4)

- In the metric and SI systems of units, a prefix attached to any unit increases or decreases its size by some factor of 10.
- When the prefix *centi* is used with the unit meter, it becomes centimeter, a length that is one-hundredth of a meter (0.01 m).
- When the prefix *milli* is used with the unit meter, it becomes millimeter, a length that is one-thousandth of a meter (0.001 m).

Example: Complete the following statements with the correct prefix symbol:

a. 1000 m = 1 _____ m   **b.** 0.01 g = 1 _____ g

Answer: **a.** 1000 m = 1 km   **b.** 0.01 g = 1 cg

Writing Conversion Factors from Equalities (2.5)

- A conversion factor allows you to change from one unit to another.
- Two conversion factors can be written for any equality in the metric, U.S., or metric–U.S. systems of measurement.
- Two conversion factors can be written for a relationship stated within a problem.

Example: Write two conversion factors for the equality: 1 L = 1000 mL.

Answer: $\dfrac{1000 \text{ mL}}{1 \text{ L}}$ and $\dfrac{1 \text{ L}}{1000 \text{ mL}}$

Using Conversion Factors (2.6)

In problem solving, conversion factors are used to cancel the given unit and to provide the needed unit for the answer.

- State the given and needed quantities.
- Write a plan to convert the given unit to the needed unit.
- State the equalities and conversion factors.
- Set up the problem to cancel units and calculate the answer.

Example: A computer chip has a width of 0.75 in. What is that distance in millimeters?

Every day, we see a variety of materials with many different shapes and forms. To a scientist, all of this material is *matter*. Matter is everywhere around us: the orange juice we had for breakfast, the water we put in the coffee maker, the plastic bag we put our sandwich in, our toothbrush and toothpaste, the oxygen we inhale, and the carbon dioxide we exhale.

When we look around, we see that matter takes the physical form of a solid, a liquid, or a gas. Water is a familiar example that we routinely observe in all three states. In the solid state, water can be an ice cube or a snowflake. It is a liquid when it comes out of a faucet or fills a pool. Water forms a gas, or vapor, when it evaporates from wet clothes or boils in a pan. In these examples, water changes its state by gaining or losing energy. For example, energy is added to melt ice cubes and to boil water in a teakettle. Conversely, energy is removed to freeze liquid water in an ice cube tray and to condense water vapor to liquid droplets.

Almost everything we do involves energy. We use energy when we heat water, cook food, turn on lights, walk, study, use a washing machine, or drive our cars. Of course, that energy has to come from something. In our bodies, the food we eat provides us with energy. Energy from burning fossil fuels or the Sun is used to heat a home or water for a pool.

LOOKING AHEAD

3.1 Classification of Matter 63
Chemistry Link to Health
Breathing Mixtures 66

3.2 States and Properties of Matter 67

3.3 Temperature 69
Chemistry Link to Health
Variation in Body Temperature 72

3.4 Energy 73

3.5 Energy and Nutrition 76
Chemistry Link to Health
Losing and Gaining Weight 78

3.6 Specific Heat 80

3.7 Changes of State 81
Chemistry Link to Health
Steam Burns 86

℞ Clinical Applications 73, 79, 90, 95, 96

℞ Clinical Update *A Diet and Exercise Program for Charles* 90

3.1 Classification of Matter

Matter is anything that has mass and occupies space. Matter makes up all the things we use such as water, wood, plates, plastic bags, clothes, and shoes. The different types of matter are classified by their composition.

Pure Substances: Elements and Compounds

A **pure substance** is matter that has a fixed or definite composition. There are two kinds of pure substances: elements and compounds. An **element**, the simplest type of a pure substance, is composed of only one type of material such as silver, iron, or aluminum. Every element is composed of *atoms*, which are extremely tiny particles that make up each type of matter. Silver is composed of silver atoms, iron of iron atoms, and aluminum of aluminum atoms. A full list of the elements is found on the inside front cover of this text.

An aluminum can consists of many atoms of aluminum.

A molecule of water, H_2O, consists of two atoms of hydrogen (white) for one atom of oxygen (red).

A **compound** is also a pure substance, but it consists of atoms of two or more elements always chemically combined in the same proportion. In compounds, the atoms are held together by attractions called *bonds*, which form small groups of atoms called *molecules*. For example, a molecule of the compound water has two hydrogen atoms for every one oxygen atom and is represented by the formula H_2O. This means that water found anywhere always has the same composition of H_2O. Another compound that consists of a chemical combination of hydrogen and oxygen is hydrogen peroxide. It has two hydrogen atoms for every two oxygen atoms, and is represented by the formula H_2O_2. Thus, water (H_2O) and hydrogen peroxide (H_2O_2) are different compounds that have different properties.

Pure substances that are compounds can be broken down by chemical processes into their elements. They cannot be broken down through physical methods such as boiling or sifting. For example, ordinary table salt consists of the compound NaCl, which can be separated by chemical processes into sodium metal and chlorine gas, as seen in Figure 3.1. Elements cannot be broken down further.

A molecule of hydrogen peroxide, H_2O_2, consists of two atoms of hydrogen (white) for every two atoms of oxygen (red).

Sodium chloride

Chemical process

Sodium metal   and   Chlorine gas

FIGURE 3.1 ▶ The decomposition of salt, NaCl, produces the elements sodium and chlorine.

Ⓠ How do elements and compounds differ?

Mixtures

In a **mixture**, two or more different substances are physically mixed, but not chemically combined. Much of the matter in our everyday lives consists of mixtures. The air we breathe is a mixture of mostly oxygen and nitrogen gases. The steel in buildings and railroad tracks is a mixture of iron, nickel, carbon, and chromium. The brass in doorknobs and fixtures is a mixture of zinc and copper (see Figure 3.2). Tea, coffee, and ocean water are mixtures too. Unlike compounds, the proportions of the substances in a mixture are not consistent but can vary. For example, two sugar–water mixtures may look the same, but the one with the higher ratio of sugar to water would taste sweeter.

Physical processes can be used to separate mixtures because there are no chemical interactions between the components. For example, different coins, such as nickels, dimes, and

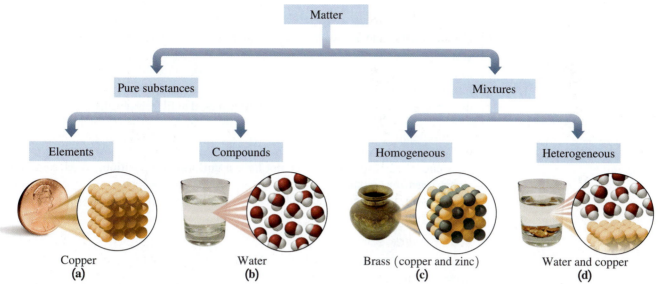

FIGURE 3.2 ▶ Matter is organized by its components: elements, compounds, and mixtures. **(a)** The element copper consists of copper atoms. **(b)** The compound water consists of H_2O molecules. **(c)** Brass is a homogeneous mixture of copper and zinc atoms. **(d)** Copper metal in water is a heterogeneous mixture of copper atoms and H_2O molecules.

 Why are copper and water pure substances, but brass is a mixture?

quarters, can be separated by size; iron particles mixed with sand can be picked up with a magnet; and water is separated from cooked spaghetti by using a strainer (see Figure 3.3).

Types of Mixtures

Mixtures are classified further as homogeneous or heterogeneous. In a *homogeneous mixture*, also called a *solution*, the composition is uniform throughout the sample. Familiar examples of homogeneous mixtures are air, which contains oxygen and nitrogen gases, and seawater, a solution of salt and water.

In a *heterogeneous mixture*, the components do not have a uniform composition throughout the sample. For example, a mixture of oil and water is heterogeneous because the oil floats on the surface of the water. Other examples of heterogeneous mixtures are a cookie with raisins and pulp in orange juice.

In the chemistry laboratory, mixtures are separated by various methods. Solids are separated from liquids by *filtration*, which involves pouring a mixture through a filter paper set in a funnel. In *chromatography*, different components of a liquid mixture separate as they move at different rates up the surface of a piece of chromatography paper.

FIGURE 3.3 ▶ A mixture of spaghetti and water is separated using a strainer, a physical method of separation.

 Why can physical methods be used to separate mixtures but not compounds?

(a) A mixture of a liquid and a solid is separated by filtration. **(b)** Different substances are separated as they travel at different rates up the surface of chromatography paper.

> **SAMPLE PROBLEM 3.1** **Classifying Mixtures**
>
> Classify each of the following as a pure substance (element or compound) or a mixture (homogeneous or heterogeneous):
>
> **a.** copper in copper wire
> **b.** a chocolate-chip cookie
> **c.** nitrox, a combination of oxygen and nitrogen used to fill scuba tanks
>
> **SOLUTION**
>
> **a.** Copper is an element, which is a pure substance.
> **b.** A chocolate-chip cookie does not have a uniform composition, which makes it a heterogeneous mixture.
> **c.** The gases oxygen and nitrogen have a uniform composition in nitrox, which makes it a homogeneous mixture.
>
> **STUDY CHECK 3.1**
>
> A salad dressing is prepared with oil, vinegar, and chunks of blue cheese. Is this a homogeneous or heterogeneous mixture?
>
> **ANSWER**
>
> heterogeneous

Chemistry Link to **Health**
Breathing Mixtures

The air we breathe is composed mostly of the gases oxygen (21%) and nitrogen (79%). The homogeneous breathing mixtures used by scuba divers differ from the air we breathe depending on the depth of the dive. Nitrox is a mixture of oxygen and nitrogen, but with more oxygen gas (up to 32%) and less nitrogen gas (68%) than air. A breathing mixture with less nitrogen gas decreases the risk of *nitrogen narcosis* associated with breathing regular air while diving. Heliox contains oxygen and helium, which is typically used for diving to more than 200 ft. By replacing nitrogen with helium, nitrogen narcosis does not occur. However, at dive depths over 300 ft, helium is associated with severe shaking and body temperature drop.

A breathing mixture used for dives over 400 ft is trimix, which contains oxygen, helium, and some nitrogen. The addition of some nitrogen lessens the problem of shaking that comes with breathing high levels of helium. Heliox and trimix are used only by professional, military, or other highly trained divers.

In hospitals, heliox may be used as a treatment for respiratory disorders and lung constriction in adults and premature infants. Heliox is less dense than air, which reduces the effort of breathing, and helps distribute the oxygen gas to the tissues.

A nitrox mixture is used to fill scuba tanks.

QUESTIONS AND PROBLEMS

3.1 Classification of Matter

LEARNING GOAL Classify examples of matter as pure substances or mixtures.

3.1 Classify each of the following as a pure substance or a mixture:
   a. baking soda ($NaHCO_3$)   **b.** a blueberry muffin
   c. ice (H_2O)   **d.** zinc (Zn)
   e. trimix (oxygen, nitrogen, and helium) in a scuba tank

3.2 Classify each of the following as a pure substance or a mixture:
   a. a soft drink   **b.** propane (C_3H_8)
   c. a cheese sandwich   **d.** an iron (Fe) nail
   e. salt substitute (KCl)

3.3 Classify each of the following pure substances as an element or a compound:
   a. a silicon (Si) chip   **b.** hydrogen peroxide (H_2O_2)
   c. oxygen (O_2)   **d.** rust (Fe_2O_3)
   e. methane (CH_4) in natural gas

3.4 Classify each of the following pure substances as an element or a compound:
   a. helium gas (He)   **b.** mercury (Hg) in a thermometer
   c. sugar ($C_{12}H_{22}O_{11}$)   **d.** sulfur (S)
   e. lye (NaOH)

3.5 Classify each of the following mixtures as homogeneous or heterogeneous:
   a. vegetable soup   **b.** seawater
   c. tea   **d.** tea with ice and lemon slices
   e. fruit salad

3.6 Classify each of the following mixtures as homogeneous or heterogeneous:
   a. nonfat milk   **b.** chocolate-chip ice cream
   c. gasoline   **d.** peanut butter sandwich
   e. cranberry juice

3.2 States and Properties of Matter

On Earth, matter exists in one of three *physical forms* called the **states of matter**: solids, liquids, and gases. A **solid**, such as a pebble or a baseball, has a definite shape and volume. You can probably recognize several solids within your reach right now such as books, pencils, or a computer mouse. In a solid, strong attractive forces hold the particles such as atoms or molecules close together. The particles in a solid are arranged in such a rigid pattern, their only movement is to vibrate slowly in fixed positions. For many solids, this rigid structure produces a crystal such as that seen in amethyst.

A **liquid** has a definite volume, but not a definite shape. In a liquid, the particles move in random directions but are sufficiently attracted to each other to maintain a definite volume, although not a rigid structure. Thus, when water, oil, or vinegar is poured from one container to another, the liquid maintains its own volume but takes the shape of the new container.

A **gas** does not have a definite shape or volume. In a gas, the particles are far apart, have little attraction to each other, and move at high speeds, taking the shape and volume of their container. When you inflate a bicycle tire, the air, which is a gas, fills the entire volume of the tire. The propane gas in a tank fills the entire volume of the tank. Table 3.1 compares the three states of matter.

LEARNING GOAL

Identify the states and the physical and chemical properties of matter.

Amethyst, a solid, is a purple form of quartz (SiO_2).

Water as a liquid takes the shape of its container.

A gas takes the shape and volume of its container.

TABLE 3.1 A Comparison of Solids, Liquids, and Gases

Characteristic	Solid	Liquid	Gas
Shape	Has a definite shape	Takes the shape of the container	Takes the shape of the container
Volume	Has a definite volume	Has a definite volume	Fills the volume of the container
Arrangement of Particles	Fixed, very close	Random, close	Random, far apart
Interaction between Particles	Very strong	Strong	Essentially none
Movement of Particles	Very slow	Moderate	Very fast
Examples	Ice, salt, iron	Water, oil, vinegar	Water vapor, helium, air

Physical Properties and Physical Changes

One way to describe matter is to observe its properties. For example, if you were asked to describe yourself, you might list your characteristics such as the color of your eyes and skin or the length, color, and texture of your hair.

Physical properties are those characteristics that can be observed or measured without affecting the identity of a substance. In chemistry, typical physical properties include the shape, color, melting point, boiling point, and physical state of a substance. For example, a penny has the physical properties of a round shape, an orange-red color, solid state, and a shiny luster. Table 3.2 gives more examples of physical properties of copper found in pennies, electrical wiring, and copper pans.

Water is a substance that is commonly found in all three states: solid, liquid, and gas. When matter undergoes a **physical change**, its state, size, or its appearance will change, but its composition remains the same. The solid state of water, snow or ice, has a different appearance than its liquid or gaseous state, but all three states are water.

TABLE 3.2 Some Physical Properties of Copper

State at 25 °C	Solid
Color	Orange-red
Odor	Odorless
Melting Point	1083 °C
Boiling Point	2567 °C
Luster	Shiny
Conduction of Electricity	Excellent
Conduction of Heat	Excellent

The evaporation of water from seawater gives white, solid crystals of salt (sodium chloride).

Copper, used in cookware, is a good conductor of heat.

The physical appearance of a substance can change in other ways too. Suppose that you dissolve some salt in water. The appearance of the salt changes, but you could re-form the salt crystals by evaporating the water. Thus in a physical change of state, no new substances are produced. Table 3.3 gives more examples of physical changes.

Flan has a topping of caramelized sugar.

Chemical Properties and Chemical Changes

Chemical properties are those that describe the ability of a substance to change into a new substance. When a **chemical change** takes place, the original substance is converted into one or more new substances, which have different physical and chemical properties. For example, the rusting or corrosion of a metal such as iron is a chemical property. In the rain, an iron (Fe) nail undergoes a chemical change when it reacts with oxygen (O_2) to form rust (Fe_2O_3). A chemical change has taken place: Rust is a new substance with new physical and chemical properties. Table 3.4 gives examples of some chemical changes.

TABLE 3.3 Examples of Some Physical Changes

Water boils to form water vapor.
Sugar dissolves in water to form a solution.
Copper is drawn into thin copper wires.
Paper is cut into tiny pieces of confetti.
Pepper is ground into flakes.

TABLE 3.4 Examples of Some Chemical Changes

Shiny, silver metal reacts in air to give a black, grainy coating.
A piece of wood burns with a bright flame and produces heat, ashes, carbon dioxide, and water vapor.
Heating white, granular sugar forms a smooth, caramel-colored substance.
Iron, which is gray and shiny, combines with oxygen to form orange-red rust.

A gold ingot is hammered to form gold leaf.

Interactive Video

▶

Chemical vs. Physical Changes

▶ **SAMPLE PROBLEM 3.2** **Physical and Chemical Changes**

Classify each of the following as a physical or chemical change:

a. A gold ingot is hammered to form gold leaf.
b. Gasoline burns in air.
c. Garlic is chopped into small pieces.

SOLUTION

a. A physical change occurs when the gold ingot changes shape.
b. A chemical change occurs when gasoline burns and forms different substances with new properties.
c. A physical change occurs when the size of the garlic pieces changes.

STUDY CHECK 3.2

Classify each of the following as a physical or chemical change:

a. Water freezes on a pond.
b. Gas bubbles form when baking powder is placed in vinegar.
c. A log is cut for firewood.

ANSWER

a. physical change   **b.** chemical change   **c.** physical change

QUESTIONS AND PROBLEMS

3.2 States and Properties of Matter

LEARNING GOAL Identify the states and the physical and chemical properties of matter.

3.7 Indicate whether each of the following describes a gas, a liquid, or a solid:
  a. The gaseous breathing mixture in a scuba tank has no definite volume or shape.
  b. The neon atoms in a lighting display do not interact with each other.
  c. The particles in an ice cube are held in a rigid structure.

3.8 Indicate whether each of the following describes a gas, a liquid, or a solid:
  a. Lemonade has a definite volume but takes the shape of its container.
  b. The particles in a tank of oxygen are very far apart.
  c. Helium occupies the entire volume of a balloon.

3.9 Describe each of the following as a physical or chemical property:
  a. Chromium is a steel-gray solid.
  b. Hydrogen reacts readily with oxygen.
  c. A patient has a temperature of 40.2 °C.
  d. Milk will sour when left in a warm room.
  e. Butane gas in an igniter burns in oxygen.

3.10 Describe each of the following as a physical or chemical property:
  a. Neon is a colorless gas at room temperature.
  b. Apple slices turn brown when they are exposed to air.
  c. Phosphorus will ignite when exposed to air.
  d. At room temperature, mercury is a liquid.
  e. Propane gas is compressed to a liquid for placement in a small cylinder.

3.11 What type of change, physical or chemical, takes place in each of the following?
  a. Water vapor condenses to form rain.
  b. Cesium metal reacts explosively with water.
  c. Gold melts at 1064 °C.
  d. A puzzle is cut into 1000 pieces.
  e. Cheese is grated.

3.12 What type of change, physical or chemical, takes place in each of the following?
  a. Pie dough is rolled into thin pieces for a crust.
  b. A silver pin tarnishes in the air.
  c. A tree is cut into boards at a saw mill.
  d. Food is digested.
  e. A chocolate bar melts.

3.13 Describe each property of the element fluorine as physical or chemical.
  a. is highly reactive
  b. is a gas at room temperature
  c. has a pale, yellow color
  d. will explode in the presence of hydrogen
  e. has a melting point of −220 °C

3.14 Describe each property of the element zirconium as physical or chemical.
  a. melts at 1852 °C
  b. is resistant to corrosion
  c. has a grayish white color
  d. ignites spontaneously in air when finely divided
  e. is a shiny metal

3.3 Temperature

Temperatures in science are measured and reported in *Celsius* (°C) units. On the Celsius scale, the reference points are the freezing point of water, defined as 0 °C, and the boiling point, 100 °C. In the United States, everyday temperatures are commonly reported in *Fahrenheit* (°F) units. On the Fahrenheit scale, water freezes at exactly 32 °F and boils at 212 °F. A typical room temperature of 22 °C would be the same as 72 °F. Normal human body temperature is 37.0 °C, which is the same temperature as 98.6 °C.

On the Celsius and Fahrenheit temperature scales, the temperature difference between freezing and boiling is divided into smaller units called *degrees*. On the Celsius scale, there are 100 degrees Celsius between the freezing and boiling points of water, whereas the Fahrenheit scale has 180 degrees Fahrenheit between the freezing and boiling points of water. That makes a degree Celsius almost twice the size of a degree Fahrenheit: 1 °C = 1.8 °F (see Figure 3.4).

$$180 \text{ degrees Fahrenheit} = 100 \text{ degrees Celsius}$$

$$\frac{180 \text{ degrees Fahrenheit}}{100 \text{ degrees Celsius}} = \frac{1.8 \text{ °F}}{1 \text{ °C}}$$

We can write a temperature equation that relates a Fahrenheit temperature and its corresponding Celsius temperature.

$$T_F = 1.8(T_C) + 32$$

Changes   Adjusts   Temperature equation to obtain
°C to °F   freezing   degrees Fahrenheit
           point

A digital ear thermometer is used to measure body temperature.

FIGURE 3.4 ▶ A comparison of the Fahrenheit, Celsius, and Kelvin temperature scales between the freezing and boiling points of water.

🔍 What is the difference in the freezing points of water on the Celsius and Fahrenheit temperature scales?

In this equation, the Celsius temperature is multiplied by 1.8 to change °C to °F; then 32 is added to adjust the freezing point from 0 °C to the Fahrenheit freezing point, 32 °F. The values, 1.8 and 32, used in the temperature equation are exact numbers and are not used to determine significant figures in the answer.

To convert from degrees Fahrenheit to degrees Celsius, the temperature equation is rearranged to solve for T_C. First, we subtract 32 from both sides since we must apply the same operation to both sides of the equation.

$$T_F - 32 = 1.8(T_C) + \cancel{32} - \cancel{32}$$
$$T_F - 32 = 1.8(T_C)$$

Second, we solve the equation for T_C by dividing both sides by 1.8.

$$\frac{T_F - 32}{1.8} = \frac{\cancel{1.8}(T_C)}{\cancel{1.8}}$$

$$\frac{T_F - 32}{1.8} = T_C \qquad \text{Temperature equation to obtain degrees Celsius}$$

TABLE 3.5 A Comparison of Temperatures

Example	Fahrenheit (°F)	Celsius (°C)	Kelvin (K)
Sun	9937	5503	5776
A hot oven	450	232	505
A desert	120	49	322
A high fever	104	40	313
Normal body temperature	98.6	37.0	310
Room temperature	70	21	294
Water freezes	32	0	273
A northern winter	−66	−54	219
Nitrogen liquefies	−346	−210	63
Helium boils	−452	−269	4
Absolute zero	−459	−273	0

Scientists have learned that the coldest temperature possible is −273 °C (more precisely, −273.15 °C). On the *Kelvin* scale, this temperature, called *absolute zero*, has the value of 0 K. Units on the Kelvin scale are called kelvins (K); *no degree symbol is used.* Because there are no lower temperatures, the Kelvin scale has no negative temperature values. Between the freezing point of water, 273 K, and the boiling point, 373 K, there are 100 kelvins, which makes a kelvin equal in size to a degree Celsius.

$$1 \text{ K} = 1 \text{ °C}$$

We can write an equation that relates a Celsius temperature to its corresponding Kelvin temperature by adding 273 to the Celsius temperature. Table 3.5 gives a comparison of some temperatures on the three scales.

$T_K = T_C + 273$ Temperature equation to obtain kelvins

Suppose that a dermatologist uses liquid nitrogen at $-196\,°C$ to remove skin lesions and some skin cancer. We can calculate the temperature of the liquid nitrogen in kelvins by adding 273 to the temperature in degrees Celsius.

$T_K = -196 + 273 = 77\text{ K}$

▶ **SAMPLE PROBLEM 3.3** **Converting from Degrees Celsius to Degrees Fahrenheit**

The typical temperature in a hospital room is set at $21\,°C$. What is that temperature in degrees Fahrenheit?

SOLUTION

STEP 1 State the given and needed quantities.

ANALYZE THE PROBLEM	Given	Need
	$21\,°C$	T in degrees Fahrenheit

STEP 2 Write a temperature equation.

$T_F = 1.8(T_C) + 32$

STEP 3 Substitute in the known values and calculate the new temperature.

$T_F = 1.8(21) + 32$ 1.8 is exact; 32 is exact
Two SFs

$T_F = 38 + 32$
$= 70.\,°F$ Answer to the ones place

In the equation, *the values of 1.8 and 32 are exact numbers*, which do not affect the number of SFs used in the answer.

STUDY CHECK 3.3

In the process of making ice cream, rock salt is added to crushed ice to chill the ice cream mixture. If the temperature drops to $-11\,°C$, what is it in degrees Fahrenheit?

ANSWER
$12\,°F$

▶ **SAMPLE PROBLEM 3.4** **Converting from Degrees Fahrenheit to Degrees Celsius**

In a type of cancer treatment called *thermotherapy*, temperatures as high as $113\,°F$ are used to destroy cancer cells or make them more sensitive to radiation. What is that temperature in degrees Celsius?

SOLUTION

STEP 1 State the given and needed quantities.

ANALYZE THE PROBLEM	Given	Need
	$113\,°F$	T in degrees Celsius

STEP 2 Write a temperature equation.

$T_C = \dfrac{T_F - 32}{1.8}$

Guide to Calculating Temperature

STEP 1 State the given and needed quantities.

STEP 2 Write a temperature equation.

STEP 3 Substitute in the known values and calculate the new temperature.

STEP **3**   Substitute in the known values and calculate the new temperature.

$$T_C = \frac{(113 - 32)}{1.8}$$ 32 is exact; 1.8 is exact

$$= \frac{81}{1.8} = 45\ ^\circ C$$ Answer to the ones place

STUDY CHECK 3.4

A child has a temperature of 103.6 °F. What is this temperature on a Celsius thermometer?

ANSWER

39.8 °C

Chemistry Link to **Health**
Variation in Body Temperature

Normal body temperature is considered to be 37.0 °C, although it varies throughout the day and from person to person. Oral temperatures of 36.1 °C are common in the morning and climb to a high of 37.2 °C between 6 P.M. and 10 P.M. Temperatures above 37.2 °C for a person at rest are usually an indication of illness. Individuals who are involved in prolonged exercise may also experience elevated temperatures. Body temperatures of marathon runners can range from 39 °C to 41 °C as heat production during exercise exceeds the body's ability to lose heat.

Changes of more than 3.5 °C from the normal body temperature begin to interfere with bodily functions. Body temperatures above 41 °C, *hyperthermia*, can lead to convulsions, particularly in children, which may cause permanent brain damage. Heatstroke occurs above 41.1 °C. Sweat production stops, and the skin becomes hot and dry. The pulse rate is elevated, and respiration becomes weak and rapid. The person can become lethargic and lapse into a coma. Damage to internal organs is a major concern, and treatment, which must be immediate, may include immersing the person in an ice-water bath.

At the low temperature extreme of *hypothermia*, body temperature can drop as low as 28.5 °C. The person may appear cold and pale and have an irregular heartbeat. Unconsciousness can occur if the body temperature drops below 26.7 °C. Respiration becomes slow and shallow, and oxygenation of the tissues decreases. Treatment involves providing oxygen and increasing blood volume with glucose and saline fluids. Injecting warm fluids (37.0 °C) into the peritoneal cavity may restore the internal temperature.

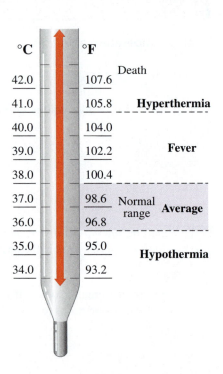

QUESTIONS AND PROBLEMS

3.3 Temperature

LEARNING GOAL Given a temperature, calculate a corresponding temperature on another scale.

3.15 Your friend who is visiting from Canada just took her temperature. When she reads 99.8 °F, she becomes concerned that she is quite ill. How would you explain this temperature to your friend?

3.16 You have a friend who is using a recipe for flan from a Mexican cookbook. You notice that he set your oven temperature at 175 °F. What would you advise him to do?

3.17 Calculate the unknown temperature in each of the following:
a. 37.0 °C = _____ °F   b. 65.3 °F = _____ °C
c. −27 °C = _____ K   d. 62 °C = _____ K
e. 114 °F = _____ °C

3.18 Calculate the unknown temperature in each of the following:
a. 25 °C = _____ °F   b. 155 °C = _____ °F
c. −25 °F = _____ °C   d. 224 K = _____ °C
e. 145 °C = _____ K

R Clinical Applications

3.19 **a.** A patient with hyperthermia has a temperature of 106 °F. What does this read on a Celsius thermometer?

   b. Because high fevers can cause convulsions in children, the doctor needs to be called if the child's temperature goes over 40.0 °C. Should the doctor be called if a child has a temperature of 103 °F?

3.20 **a.** Hot compresses for a patient are prepared with water heated to 145 °F. What is the temperature of the hot water in degrees Celsius?

   b. During extreme hypothermia, a boy's temperature dropped to 20.6 °C. What was his temperature in degrees Fahrenheit?

3.4 Energy

When you are running, walking, dancing, or thinking, you are using energy to do *work*, any activity that requires energy. In fact, **energy** is defined as the ability to do work. Suppose you are climbing a steep hill and you become too tired to go on. At that moment, you do not have the energy to do any more work. Now suppose you sit down and have lunch. In a while, you will have obtained some energy from the food, and you will be able to do more work and complete the climb.

Kinetic and Potential Energy

Energy can be classified as kinetic energy or potential energy. **Kinetic energy** is the energy of motion. Any object that is moving has kinetic energy. **Potential energy** is determined by the position of an object or by the chemical composition of a substance. A boulder resting on top of a mountain has potential energy because of its location. If the boulder rolls down the mountain, the potential energy becomes kinetic energy. Water stored in a reservoir has potential energy. When the water goes over the dam and falls to the stream below, its potential energy is converted to kinetic energy. Foods and fossil fuels have potential energy in their molecules. When you digest food or burn gasoline in your car, potential energy is converted to kinetic energy to do work.

Heat and Energy

Heat is the energy associated with the motion of particles. An ice cube feels cold because heat flows from your hand into the ice cube. The faster the particles move, the greater the heat or thermal energy of the substance. In the ice cube, the particles are moving very slowly. As heat is added, the motion of the particles in the ice cube increases. Eventually, the particles have enough energy to make the ice cube melt as it changes from a solid to a liquid.

Units of Energy

The SI unit of energy and work is the **joule (J)** (pronounced "jewel"). The joule is a small amount of energy, so scientists often use the kilojoule (kJ), 1000 joules. To heat water for one cup of tea, you need about 75 000 J or 75 kJ of heat. Table 3.6 shows a comparison of energy in joules for several energy sources.

You may be more familiar with the unit **calorie (cal)**, from the Latin *caloric*, meaning "heat." The calorie was originally defined as the amount of energy (heat) needed to raise the temperature of 1 g of water by 1 °C. Now one calorie is defined as exactly 4.184 J. This equality can be written as two conversion factors:

$$1 \text{ cal} = 4.184 \text{ J (exact)} \qquad \frac{4.184 \text{ J}}{1 \text{ cal}} \quad \text{and} \quad \frac{1 \text{ cal}}{4.184 \text{ J}}$$

One *kilocalorie* (kcal) is equal to 1000 calories, and one *kilojoule* (kJ) is equal to 1000 joules. The equalities and conversion factors follow:

$$1 \text{ kcal} = 1000 \text{ cal} \qquad \frac{1000 \text{ cal}}{1 \text{ kcal}} \quad \text{and} \quad \frac{1 \text{ kcal}}{1000 \text{ cal}}$$

$$1 \text{ kJ} = 1000 \text{ J} \qquad \frac{1000 \text{ J}}{1 \text{ kJ}} \quad \text{and} \quad \frac{1 \text{ kJ}}{1000 \text{ J}}$$

LEARNING GOAL

Identify energy as potential or kinetic; convert between units of energy.

Water at the top of the dam stores potential energy. When the water flows over the dam, potential energy is converted to kinetic energy.

⚛ **CORE CHEMISTRY SKILL**

Using Energy Units

TABLE 3.6 A Comparison of Energy for Various Resources

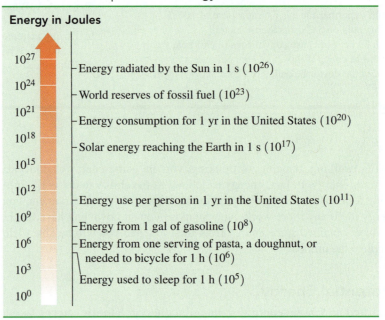

Energy in Joules

10^{27}	
	Energy radiated by the Sun in 1 s (10^{26})
10^{24}	
	World reserves of fossil fuel (10^{23})
10^{21}	
	Energy consumption for 1 yr in the United States (10^{20})
10^{18}	
	Solar energy reaching the Earth in 1 s (10^{17})
10^{15}	
10^{12}	
	Energy use per person in 1 yr in the United States (10^{11})
10^{9}	
	Energy from 1 gal of gasoline (10^{8})
10^{6}	Energy from one serving of pasta, a doughnut, or needed to bicycle for 1 h (10^{6})
10^{3}	
	Energy used to sleep for 1 h (10^{5})
10^{0}	

A defibrillator provides electrical energy to heart muscle to re-establish normal rhythm.

▶ **SAMPLE PROBLEM 3.5** Energy Units

A defibrillator gives a high-energy-shock output of 360 J. What is this quantity of energy in calories?

SOLUTION

STEP 1 State the given and needed quantities.

ANALYZE THE PROBLEM	Given	Need
	360 J	calories

STEP 2 Write a plan to convert the given unit to the needed unit.

joules → Energy factor → calories

STEP 3 State the equalities and conversion factors.

$$1 \text{ cal} = 4.184 \text{ J}$$

$$\frac{4.184 \text{ J}}{1 \text{ cal}} \quad \text{and} \quad \frac{1 \text{ cal}}{4.184 \text{ J}}$$

STEP 4 Set up the problem to calculate the needed quantity.

$$360 \text{ J} \times \frac{1 \text{ cal}}{4.184 \text{ J}} = 86 \text{ cal}$$

Two SFs   Exact   Exact   Two SFs

STUDY CHECK 3.5

When 1.0 g of glucose is metabolized in the body, it produces 3.8 kcal. How many kilojoules are produced?

ANSWER

16 kJ

QUESTIONS AND PROBLEMS

3.4 Energy

LEARNING GOAL Identify energy as potential or kinetic; convert between units of energy.

3.21 Discuss the changes in the potential and kinetic energy of a roller-coaster ride as the roller-coaster car climbs to the top and goes down the other side.

3.22 Discuss the changes in the potential and kinetic energy of a ski jumper taking the elevator to the top of the jump and going down the ramp.

3.23 Indicate whether each of the following statements describes potential or kinetic energy:
  a. water at the top of a waterfall
  b. kicking a ball
  c. the energy in a lump of coal
  d. a skier at the top of a hill

3.24 Indicate whether each of the following statements describes potential or kinetic energy:
  a. the energy in your food
  b. a tightly wound spring
  c. an earthquake
  d. a car speeding down the freeway

3.25 The energy needed to keep a 75-watt light bulb burning for 1.0 h is 270 kJ. Calculate the energy required to keep the light bulb burning for 3.0 h in each of the following energy units:
  a. joules
  b. kilocalories

3.26 A person uses 750 kcal on a long walk. Calculate the energy used for the walk in each of the following energy units:
  a. joules
  b. kilojoules

 Chemistry Link to the **Environment**

Carbon Dioxide and Climate Change

The Earth's climate is a product of interactions between sunlight, the atmosphere, and the oceans. The Sun provides us with energy in the form of solar radiation. Some of this radiation is reflected back into space. The rest is absorbed by the clouds, atmospheric gases including carbon dioxide, and the Earth's surface. For millions of years, concentrations of carbon dioxide (CO_2) have fluctuated. However in the last 100 years, the amount of carbon dioxide (CO_2) gas in our atmosphere has increased significantly. From the years 1000 to 1800, the atmospheric carbon dioxide averaged 280 ppm. The concentration of ppm indicates the parts per million by volume, which for gases is the same as mL of CO_2 per kL of air. But since the beginning of the Industrial Revolution in 1800 up until 2005, the level of atmospheric carbon dioxide has risen from about 280 ppm to about 394 ppm in 2013, a 40% increase.

As the atmospheric CO_2 level increases, more solar radiation is trapped by the atmospheric gases, which raises the temperature at the surface of the Earth. Some scientists have estimated that if the carbon dioxide level doubles from its level before the Industrial Revolution, the average global temperature could increase by 2.0 to 4.4 °C. Although this seems to be a small temperature change, it could have dramatic impact worldwide. Even now, glaciers and snow cover in much of the world have diminished. Ice sheets in Antarctica and Greenland are melting faster and breaking apart. Although no one knows for sure how rapidly the ice in the polar regions is melting, this accelerating change will contribute to a rise in sea level. In the twenti-

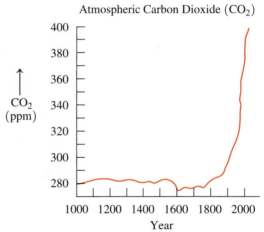

Atmospheric carbon dioxide levels are shown for the years from 1000 C.E. to 2010 C.E.

eth century, the sea level rose by 15 to 23 cm. Some scientists predict the sea level will rise by 1 m in this century. Such an increase will have a major impact on coastal areas.

Until recently, the carbon dioxide level was maintained as algae in the oceans and the trees in the forests utilized the carbon dioxide. However, the ability of these and other forms of plant life to absorb carbon dioxide is not keeping up with the increase in carbon dioxide. Most scientists agree that the primary source of the increase of carbon dioxide is the burning of fossil fuels such as gasoline, coal, and natural gas. The cutting and burning of trees in the rainforests (deforestation) also reduces the amount of carbon dioxide removed from the atmosphere.

Worldwide efforts are being made to reduce the carbon dioxide produced by burning fossil fuels that heat our homes, run our cars, and provide energy for industries. Scientists are exploring ways to provide alternative energy sources and to reduce the effects of deforestation. Meanwhile, we can reduce energy use in our homes by using appliances that are more energy efficient such as replacing incandescent light bulbs with fluorescent lights. Such an effort worldwide will reduce the possible impact of climate change and at the same time save our fuel resources.

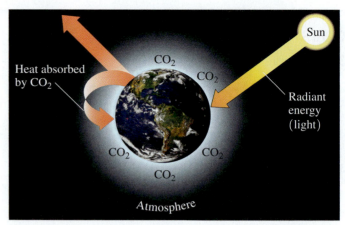

Heat from the Sun is trapped by the CO_2 layer in the atmosphere.

LEARNING GOAL

Use the energy values to calculate the kilocalories (kcal) or kilojoules (kJ) for a food.

3.5 Energy and Nutrition

The food we eat provides energy to do work in the body, which includes the growth and repair of cells. Carbohydrates are the primary fuel for the body, but if the carbohydrate reserves are exhausted, fats and then proteins are used for energy.

For many years in the field of nutrition, the energy from food was measured as Calories or kilocalories. The nutritional unit *Calorie*, *Cal* (with an uppercase C), is the same as 1000 cal, or 1 kcal. The international unit, kilojoule (kJ), is becoming more prevalent. For example, a baked potato has an energy value of 100 Calories, which is 100 kcal or 440 kJ. A typical diet that provides 2100 Cal (kcal) is the same as an 8800 kJ diet.

$$1 \text{ Cal} = 1 \text{ kcal} = 1000 \text{ cal}$$
$$1 \text{ Cal} = 4.184 \text{ kJ} = 4184 \text{ J}$$

In the nutrition laboratory, foods are burned in a *calorimeter* to determine their *energy value* (kcal/g or kJ/g) (see Figure 3.5). A sample of food is placed in a steel container called a calorimeter filled with oxygen. A measured amount of water is added to fill the area surrounding the combustion chamber. The food sample is ignited, releasing heat that increases the temperature of the water. From the known mass of the food and water as well as the measured temperature increase, the energy value for the food is calculated. We will assume that the energy absorbed by the calorimeter is negligible.

FIGURE 3.5 ▶ Heat released from burning a food sample in a calorimeter is used to determine the energy value for the food.

Q What happens to the temperature of water in a calorimeter during the combustion of a food sample?

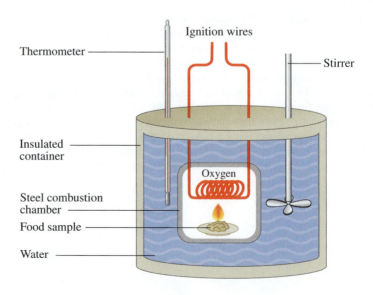

Energy Values for Foods

The **energy values** for food are the kilocalories or kilojoules obtained from burning 1 g of carbohydrate, fat, or protein, which are listed in Table 3.7.

Using these energy values, we can calculate the total energy for a food if the mass of each food type is known.

$$\text{kilocalories} = \cancel{g} \times \frac{\text{kcal}}{\cancel{g}} \qquad\qquad \text{kilojoules} = \cancel{g} \times \frac{\text{kJ}}{\cancel{g}}$$

On packaged food, the energy content is listed on the Nutrition Facts label, usually in terms of the number of Calories or kilojoules for one serving. The general composition and energy content for some foods are given in Table 3.8. The total energy, in kilocalories, for each food type was calculated using energy values in kilocalories. Total energy, in kilojoules, was calculated using energy values in kilojoules. The energy for each food type was rounded off to the tens place.

TABLE 3.7 Typical Energy Values for the Three Food Types

Food Type	kcal/g	kJ/g
Carbohydrate	4	17
Fat	9	38
Protein	4	17

TABLE 3.8 General Composition and Energy Content for Some Foods

Food	Carbohydrate (g)	Fat (g)	Protein (g)	Energy
Apple, 1 medium	15	0	0	60 kcal (260 kJ)
Banana, 1 medium	26	0	1	110 kcal (460 kJ)
Beef, ground, 3 oz	0	14	22	220 kcal (900 kJ)
Broccoli, 3 oz	4	0	3	30 kcal (120 kJ)
Carrots, 1 cup	11	0	2	50 kcal (220 kJ)
Chicken, no skin, 3 oz	0	3	20	110 kcal (450 kJ)
Egg, 1 large	0	6	6	70 kcal (330 kJ)
Milk, nonfat, 1 cup	12	0	9	90 kcal (350 kJ)
Potato, baked	23	0	3	100 kcal (440 kJ)
Salmon, 3 oz	0	5	16	110 kcal (460 kJ)
Steak, 3 oz	0	27	19	320 kcal (1350 kJ)

▶ **SAMPLE PROBLEM 3.6** Energy Content for a Food Using Nutrition Facts

The Nutrition Facts label for crackers states that 1 serving contains 19 g of carbohydrate, 4 g of fat, and 2 g of protein. What is the energy from each food type and the total energy, in kilocalories, for one serving of crackers? Round off the kilocalories for each food type to the tens place.

SOLUTION

STEP **1** State the given and needed quantities.

	Given	Need
ANALYZE THE PROBLEM	carbohydrate, 19 g fat, 4 g protein, 2 g	kilocalories for each food type, total number of kilocalories

The Nutrition Facts include the total Calories and kilojoules, and the grams of carbohydrate, fat, and protein per serving.

Guide to Calculating the Energy from a Food

STEP 1
State the given and needed quantities.

STEP 2
Use the energy value for each food type and calculate the kcal or kJ rounded off to the tens place.

STEP 3
Add the energy for each food type to give the total energy from the food.

Explore Your World
Counting Calories

Obtain a food item that has a Nutrition Facts label. From the information on the label, determine the number of grams of carbohydrate, fat, and protein in one serving. Using the energy values for each food type, calculate the total Calories (kilocalories) for one serving. (For most products, the kilocalories for each food type are rounded off to the tens place.)

Question

How does your total for the Calories (kilocalories) in one serving compare to the Calories (kilocalories) stated on the label for a single serving?

STEP 2 Use the energy value for each food type and calculate the kcal rounded off to the tens place. Using the energy values for carbohydrate, fat, and protein (see Table 3.7), we can calculate the energy for each type of food.

Food Type	Mass		Energy Value		Energy
Carbohydrate	19 g	×	$\dfrac{4\ \text{kcal}}{1\ \text{g}}$	=	80 kcal
Fat	4 g	×	$\dfrac{9\ \text{kcal}}{1\ \text{g}}$	=	40 kcal
Protein	2 g	×	$\dfrac{4\ \text{kcal}}{1\ \text{g}}$	=	10 kcal

STEP 3 Add the energy for each food type to give the total energy from the food.

Total energy = 80 kcal + 40 kcal + 10 kcal = 130 kcal

STUDY CHECK 3.6

a. Using the nutrition values for one serving of crackers in Sample Problem 3.6, calculate the energy, in kilojoules, for each food type. Round off the kilojoules for each food type to the tens place.
b. What is the total energy, in kilojoules, for one serving of crackers?

ANSWER

a. carbohydrate, 320 kJ; fat, 150 kJ; protein, 30 kJ
b. 500 kJ

Chemistry Link to **Health**
Losing and Gaining Weight

The number of kilocalories or kilojoules needed in the daily diet of an adult depends on gender, age, and level of physical activity. Some typical levels of energy needs are given in Table 3.9.

A person gains weight when food intake exceeds energy output. The amount of food a person eats is regulated by the hunger center in the hypothalamus, which is located in the brain. Food intake is normally proportional to the nutrient stores in the body. If these nutrient stores are low, you feel hungry; if they are high, you do not feel like eating.

TABLE 3.9 Typical Energy Requirements for Adults

Gender	Age	Moderately Active kcal (kJ)	Highly Active kcal (kJ)
Female	19–30	2100 (8800)	2400 (10 000)
	31–50	2000 (8400)	2200 (9200)
Male	19–30	2700 (11 300)	3000 (12 600)
	31–50	2500 (10 500)	2900 (12 100)

A person loses weight when food intake is less than energy output. Many diet products contain cellulose, which has no nutritive value but provides bulk and makes you feel full. Some diet drugs depress the hunger center and must be used with caution, because they excite the nervous system and can elevate blood pressure. Because muscular exercise is an important way to expend energy, an increase in daily exercise aids weight loss. Table 3.10 lists some activities and the amount of energy they require.

TABLE 3.10 Energy Expended by a 70.0-kg (154-lb) Adult

Activity	Energy (kcal/h)	Energy (kJ/h)
Sleeping	60	250
Sitting	100	420
Walking	200	840
Swimming	500	2100
Running	750	3100

One hour of swimming uses 2100 kJ of energy.

QUESTIONS AND PROBLEMS

3.5 Energy and Nutrition

LEARNING GOAL Use the energy values to calculate the kilocalories (kcal) or kilojoules (kJ) for a food.

3.27 Calculate the kilocalories for each of the following:
  a. one stalk of celery that produces 125 kJ when burned in a calorimeter
  b. a waffle that produces 870. kJ when burned in a calorimeter

3.28 Calculate the kilocalories for each of the following:
  a. one cup of popcorn that produces 131 kJ when burned in a calorimeter
  b. a sample of butter that produces 23.4 kJ when burned in a calorimeter

3.29 Using the energy values for foods (see Table 3.7), determine each of the following (round off the answers in kilocalories or kilojoules to the tens place):
  a. the total kilojoules for one cup of orange juice that contains 26 g of carbohydrate, no fat, and 2 g of protein
  b. the grams of carbohydrate in one apple if the apple has no fat and no protein and provides 72 kcal of energy
  c. the kilocalories in one tablespoon of vegetable oil, which contains 14 g of fat and no carbohydrate or protein
  d. the grams of fat in one avocado that has 405 kcal, 13 g of carbohydrate, and 5 g of protein

3.30 Using the energy values for foods (see Table 3.7), determine each of the following (round off the answers in kilocalories or kilojoules to the tens place):
  a. the total kilojoules in two tablespoons of crunchy peanut butter that contains 6 g of carbohydrate, 16 g of fat, and 7 g of protein

  b. the grams of protein in one cup of soup that has 110 kcal with 9 g of carbohydrate and 6 g of fat
  c. the kilocalories in one can of cola if it has 40. g of carbohydrate and no fat or protein
  d. the total kilocalories for a diet that consists of 68 g of carbohydrate, 9 g of fat, and 150 g of protein

3.31 One cup of clam chowder contains 16 g of carbohydrate, 12 g of fat, and 9 g of protein. How much energy, in kilocalories and kilojoules, is in the clam chowder? (Round off the kilocalories and kilojoules to the tens place.)

3.32 A high-protein diet contains 70.0 g of carbohydrate, 5.0 g of fat, and 150 g of protein. How much energy, in kilocalories and kilojoules, does this diet provide? (Round off the kilocalories and kilojoules to the tens place.)

℞ Clinical Applications

3.33 A patient receives 3.2 L of glucose solution intravenously (IV). If 100. mL of the solution contains 5.0 g of glucose (carbohydrate), how many kilocalories did the patient obtain from the glucose solution?

3.34 For lunch, a patient consumed 3 oz of skinless chicken, 3 oz of broccoli, 1 medium apple, and 1 cup of nonfat milk (see Table 3.8). How many kilocalories did the patient obtain from the lunch?

Use specific heat to calculate heat loss or gain.

3.6 Specific Heat

Every substance has its own characteristic ability to absorb heat. When you bake a potato, you place it in a hot oven. If you are cooking pasta, you add the pasta to boiling water. You already know that adding heat to water increases its temperature until it boils. Certain substances must absorb more heat than others to reach a certain temperature.

The energy requirements for different substances are described in terms of a physical property called *specific heat*. The **specific heat (SH)** for a substance is defined as the amount of heat needed to raise the temperature of exactly 1 g of a substance by exactly 1 °C. This temperature change is written as ΔT (*delta T*), where the delta symbol means "change in."

TABLE 3.11 Specific Heats for Some Substances

Substance	cal/g °C	J/g °C
Elements		
Aluminum, Al(s)	0.214	0.897
Copper, Cu(s)	0.0920	0.385
Gold, Au(s)	0.0308	0.129
Iron, Fe(s)	0.108	0.452
Silver, Ag(s)	0.0562	0.235
Titanium, Ti(s)	0.125	0.523
Compounds		
Ammonia, NH$_3$(g)	0.488	2.04
Ethanol, C$_2$H$_5$OH(l)	0.588	2.46
Sodium chloride, NaCl(s)	0.207	0.864
Water, H$_2$O(l)	1.00	4.184
Water, H$_2$O(s)	0.485	2.03

$$\text{Specific heat } (SH) = \frac{\text{heat}}{\text{grams} \times \Delta T} = \frac{\text{cal (or J)}}{\text{g °C}}$$

The specific heat for water is written using our definition of the calorie and joule.

$$SH \text{ for } H_2O(l) = \frac{1.00 \text{ cal}}{\text{g °C}} = \frac{4.184 \text{ J}}{\text{g °C}}$$

If we look at Table 3.11, we see that 1 g of water requires 1.00 cal or 4.184 J to increase its temperature by 1 °C. Water has a large specific heat that is about five times the specific heat of aluminum. Aluminum has a specific heat that is about twice that of copper. However, adding the same amount of heat (1.00 cal or 4.184 J) will raise the temperature of 1 g of aluminum by about 5 °C and 1 g of copper by about 10 °C. The low specific heats of aluminum and copper mean they transfer heat efficiently, which makes them useful in cookware.

The high specific heat of water has a major impact on the temperatures in a coastal city compared to an inland city. A large mass of water near a coastal city can absorb or release five times the energy absorbed or released by the same mass of rock near an inland city. This means that in the summer a body of water absorbs large quantities of heat, which cools a coastal city, and then in the winter that same body of water releases large quantities of heat, which provides warmer temperatures. A similar effect happens with our bodies, which contain 70% water by mass. Water in the body absorbs or releases large quantities of heat to maintain an almost constant body temperature.

The high specific heat of water keeps temperatures more moderate in summer and winter.

CORE CHEMISTRY SKILL

Using the Heat Equation

A cooling cap lowers the body temperature to reduce the oxygen required by the tissues.

Calculations Using Specific Heat

When we know the specific heat of a substance, we can calculate the heat lost or gained by measuring the mass of the substance and the initial and final temperature. We can substitute these measurements into the specific heat expression that is rearranged to solve for heat, which we call the *heat equation*.

$$\text{Heat} = \text{mass} \times \text{temperature change} \times \text{specific heat}$$

Heat	=	m	×	ΔT	×	SH
cal	=	g	×	°C	×	$\dfrac{\text{cal}}{\text{g °C}}$
J	=	g	×	°C	×	$\dfrac{\text{J}}{\text{g °C}}$

SAMPLE PROBLEM 3.7   Calculating Heat Loss

During surgery or when a patient has suffered a cardiac arrest or stroke, lowering the body temperature will reduce the amount of oxygen needed by the body. Some methods used to lower body temperature include cooled saline solution, cool water blankets, or cooling caps worn on the head. How many kilojoules are lost when the body temperature of a surgery patient with a blood volume of 5500 mL is cooled from 38.5 °C to 33.2 °C? (Assume that the specific heat and density of blood is the same as for water.)

SOLUTION

STEP 1 State the given and needed quantities.

	Given	Need
ANALYZE THE PROBLEM	5500 mL of blood = 5500 g of blood, cooled from 38.5 °C to 33.2 °C	kilojoules removed

STEP 2 Calculate the temperature change (ΔT).

$\Delta T = 38.5\,°C - 33.2\,°C = 5.3\,°C$

STEP 3 Write the heat equation and needed conversion factors.

$\text{Heat} = m \times \Delta T \times SH$

$$SH_{water} = \frac{4.184\,J}{g\,°C}$$

$$\frac{4.184\,J}{g\,°C} \quad \text{and} \quad \frac{g\,°C}{4.184\,J}$$

$$1\,kJ = 1000\,J$$

$$\frac{1000\,J}{1\,kJ} \quad \text{and} \quad \frac{1\,kJ}{1000\,J}$$

STEP 4 Substitute in the given values and calculate the heat, making sure units cancel.

$$\text{Heat} = 5500\,\cancel{g} \times 5.3\,\cancel{°C} \times \frac{4.184\,\cancel{J}}{\cancel{g}\,\cancel{°C}} \times \frac{1\,kJ}{1000\,\cancel{J}} = 120\,kJ$$

Exact   Exact

Two SFs   Two SFs   Exact   Two SFs

STUDY CHECK 3.7

How many kilocalories are lost when 560 g of water cools from 67 °C to 22 °C?

ANSWER

25 kcal

Guide to Calculations Using Specific Heat

STEP 1
State the given and needed quantities.

STEP 2
Calculate the temperature change (ΔT).

STEP 3
Write the heat equation and needed conversion factors.

STEP 4
Substitute in the given values and calculate the heat, making sure units cancel.

QUESTIONS AND PROBLEMS

3.6 Specific Heat

LEARNING GOAL Use specific heat to calculate heat loss or gain.

3.35 If the same amount of heat is supplied to samples of 10.0 g each of aluminum, iron, and copper all at 15.0 °C, which sample would reach the highest temperature (see Table 3.11)?

3.36 Substances **A** and **B** are the same mass and at the same initial temperature. When they are heated, the final temperature of **A** is 55 °C higher than the temperature of **B**. What does this tell you about the specific heats of **A** and **B**?

3.37 Use the heat equation to calculate the energy for each of the following (see Table 3.11):
  a. calories to heat 8.5 g of water from 15 °C to 36 °C
  b. 2600 joules lost when 25 g of water cools from 86 °C to 61 °C
  c. 9.3 kilocalories to heat 150 g of water from 15 °C to 77 °C
  d. kilojoules to heat 175 g of copper from 28 °C to 188 °C

3.38 Use the heat equation to calculate the energy for each of the following (see Table 3.11):

  a. calories lost when 85 g of water cools from 45 °C to 25 °C
  b. joules to heat 75 g of water from 22 °C to 66 °C
  c. kilocalories to heat 5.0 kg of water from 22 °C to 28 °C
  d. kilojoules to heat 224 g of gold from 18 °C to 185 °C

3.39 Use the heat equation to calculate the energy, in joules and calories, for each of the following (see Table 3.11):
  a. to heat 25.0 g of water from 12.5 °C to 25.7 °C
  b. to heat 38.0 g of copper from 122 °C to 246 °C
  c. lost when 15.0 g of ethanol, C_2H_5OH, cools from 60.5 °C to −42.0 °C
  d. lost when 125 g of iron cools from 118 °C to 55 °C

3.40 Use the heat equation to calculate the energy, in joules and calories, for each of the following (see Table 3.11):
  a. to heat 5.25 g of water from 5.5 °C to 64.8 °C
  b. lost when 75.0 g of water cools from 86.4 °C to 2.1 °C
  c. to heat 10.0 g of silver from 112 °C to 275 °C
  d. lost when 18.0 g of gold cools from 224 °C to 118 °C

3.7 Changes of State

Matter undergoes a **change of state** when it is converted from one state to another state (see Figure 3.6).

LEARNING GOAL

Describe the changes of state between solids, liquids, and gases; calculate the energy involved.

Heat absorbed

Heat released

FIGURE 3.6 ▶ Changes of state include melting and freezing, vaporization and condensation, sublimation and deposition.

Q Is heat added or released when liquid water freezes?

Melting and freezing are reversible processes.

Melting and Freezing

When heat is added to a solid, the particles move faster. At a temperature called the **melting point (mp)**, the particles of a solid gain sufficient energy to overcome the attractive forces that hold them together. The particles in the solid separate and move about in random patterns. The substance is **melting**, changing from a solid to a liquid.

If the temperature of a liquid is lowered, the reverse process takes place. Kinetic energy is lost, the particles slow down, and attractive forces pull the particles close together. The substance is **freezing**. A liquid changes to a solid at the **freezing point (fp)**, which is the same temperature as its melting point. Every substance has its own freezing (melting) point: Solid water (ice) melts at 0 °C when heat is added, and freezes at 0 °C when heat is removed. Gold melts at 1064 °C when heat is added, and freezes at 1064 °C when heat is removed.

During a change of state, the temperature of a substance remains constant. Suppose we have a glass containing ice and water. The ice melts when heat is added at 0 °C, forming more liquid. When heat is removed at 0 °C, the liquid water freezes, forming more solid. The process of melting requires heat; the process of freezing releases heat. Melting and freezing are reversible at 0 °C.

Heat of Fusion

During melting, the **heat of fusion** is the energy that must be added to convert exactly 1 g of solid to liquid at the melting point. For example, 80. cal (334 J) of heat is needed to melt exactly 1 g of ice at its melting point (0 °C).

$$H_2O(s) + 80. \text{ cal/g (or 334 J/g)} \longrightarrow H_2O(l)$$

Heat of Fusion for Water

$$\frac{80. \text{ cal}}{1 \text{ g } H_2O} \quad \text{and} \quad \frac{1 \text{ g } H_2O}{80. \text{ cal}} \qquad\qquad \frac{334 \text{ J}}{1 \text{ g } H_2O} \quad \text{and} \quad \frac{1 \text{ g } H_2O}{334 \text{ J}}$$

The heat of fusion (80. cal/g or 334 J/g) is also the quantity of heat that must be removed to freeze exactly 1 g of water at its freezing point (0 °C).

Water is sometimes sprayed in fruit orchards during subfreezing weather. If the air temperature drops to 0 °C, the water begins to freeze. Because heat is released as the water molecules form solid ice, the air warms above 0 °C and protects the fruit.

$$H_2O(l) \longrightarrow H_2O(s) + 80. \text{ cal/g (or 334 J/g)}$$

The heat of fusion can be used as a conversion factor in calculations. For example, to determine the heat needed to melt a sample of ice, the mass of ice, in grams, is multiplied by the heat of fusion. Because the temperature remains constant as long as the ice is melting, there is no temperature change given in the calculation, as shown in Sample Problem 3.8.

Calculating Heat to Melt (or Freeze) Water

Heat = mass × heat of fusion

$$\text{cal} = \cancel{g} \times \frac{80. \text{ cal}}{\cancel{g}} \qquad \text{J} = \cancel{g} \times \frac{334 \text{ J}}{\cancel{g}}$$

▸SAMPLE PROBLEM 3.8 Heat of Fusion

Ice bag therapy is used by sports trainers to treat muscle injuries. If 260. g of ice are placed in an ice bag, how much heat, in joules, will be absorbed to melt all the ice at 0 °C?

An ice bag is used to treat a sports injury.

SOLUTION

STEP 1 State the given and needed quantities.

ANALYZE THE PROBLEM	Given	Need
	260. g of ice at 0 °C, heat of fusion = 334 J/g	joules to melt ice at 0 °C

STEP 2 Write a plan to convert the given quantity to the needed quantity.

grams of ice → Heat of fusion → joules

STEP 3 Write the heat conversion factor and any metric factor.

$$1 \text{ g of } H_2O(s \rightarrow l) = 334 \text{ J}$$

$$\frac{334 \text{ J}}{1 \text{ g } H_2O} \quad \text{and} \quad \frac{1 \text{ g } H_2O}{334 \text{ J}}$$

STEP 4 Set up the problem and calculate the needed quantity.

Three SFs

$$260. \ \cancel{g \ H_2O} \times \frac{334 \text{ J}}{1 \ \cancel{g \ H_2O}} = 86\ 800 \text{ J } (8.68 \times 10^4 \text{ J})$$

Three SFs   Exact   Three SFs

STUDY CHECK 3.8

In a freezer, 150 g of water at 0 °C is placed in an ice cube tray. How much heat, in kilocalories, must be removed to form ice cubes at 0 °C?

ANSWER

12 kcal

Guide to Using a Heat Conversion Factor

STEP 1
State the given and needed quantities.

STEP 2
Write a plan to convert the given quantity to the needed quantity.

STEP 3
Write the heat conversion factor and any metric factor.

STEP 4
Set up the problem and calculate the needed quantity.

Liquid   + Heat   Gas

Vaporization

Condensation

– Heat

Vaporization and condensation are reversible processes.

Evaporation, Boiling, and Condensation

Water in a mud puddle disappears, unwrapped food dries out, and clothes hung on a line dry. **Evaporation** is taking place as water molecules with sufficient energy escape from the liquid surface and enter the gas phase (see Figure 3.7a). The loss of the "hot" water molecules removes heat, which cools the remaining liquid water. As heat is added, more and more water molecules gain sufficient energy to evaporate. At the **boiling point (bp)**, the molecules within a liquid have enough energy to overcome their attractive forces and become a gas. We observe the **boiling** of a liquid such as water as gas bubbles form throughout the liquid, rise to the surface, and escape (see Figure 3.7b).

When heat is removed, a reverse process takes place. In **condensation**, water vapor is converted back to liquid as the water molecules lose kinetic energy and slow down. Condensation occurs at the same temperature as boiling but differs because heat is removed. You may have noticed that condensation occurs when you take a hot shower and the water vapor forms water droplets on a mirror. Because a substance loses heat as it condenses, its surroundings become warmer. That is why, when a rainstorm is approaching, you may notice a warming of the air as gaseous water molecules condense to rain.

FIGURE 3.7 ▶ (a) Evaporation occurs at the surface of a liquid. **(b)** Boiling occurs as bubbles of gas form throughout the liquid.

🔵 Why does water evaporate faster at 85 °C than at 15 °C?

— 50 °C

100 °C: the boiling point of water

(a)

(b)

Sublimation

In a process called **sublimation**, the particles on the surface of a solid change directly to a gas with no temperature change and without going through the liquid state. In the reverse process called **deposition**, gas particles change directly to a solid. For example, dry ice, which is solid carbon dioxide, sublimes at $-78\ ^\circ C$. It is called "dry" because it does not form a liquid as it warms. In extremely cold areas, snow does not melt but sublimes directly to water vapor.

Dry ice sublimes at $-78\ ^\circ C$.

Solid   + Heat   Gas

Sublimation

Deposition

– Heat

Sublimation and deposition are reversible processes.

When frozen foods are left in the freezer for a long time, so much water sublimes that foods, especially meats, become dry and shrunken, a condition called *freezer burn*. Deposition occurs in a freezer when water vapor forms ice crystals on the surface of freezer bags and frozen food.

Freeze-dried foods prepared by sublimation are convenient for long-term storage and for camping and hiking. A food that has been frozen is placed in a vacuum chamber where it dries as the ice sublimes. The dried food retains all of its nutritional value and needs only water to be edible. A food that is freeze-dried does not need refrigeration because bacteria cannot grow without moisture.

Water vapor will change to solid on contact with a cold surface.

Heat of Vaporization

The **heat of vaporization** is the energy that must be added to convert exactly 1 g of liquid to gas at its boiling point. For water, 540 cal (2260 J) is needed to convert 1 g of water to vapor at 100 °C.

$$H_2O(l) + 540 \text{ cal/g (or 2260 J/g)} \longrightarrow H_2O(g)$$

This same amount of heat is released when 1 g of water vapor (gas) changes to liquid at 100 °C.

$$H_2O(g) \longrightarrow H_2O(l) + 540 \text{ cal/g (or 2260 J/g)}$$

Therefore, 2260 J/g or 540 cal/g is also the *heat of condensation* of water.

Freeze-dried foods have a long shelf life because they contain no water.

Heat of Vaporization for Water

$$\frac{540 \text{ cal}}{1 \text{ g } H_2O} \quad \text{and} \quad \frac{1 \text{ g } H_2O}{540 \text{ cal}} \qquad \frac{2260 \text{ J}}{1 \text{ g } H_2O} \quad \text{and} \quad \frac{1 \text{ g } H_2O}{2260 \text{ J}}$$

To determine the heat needed to boil a sample of water, the mass, in grams, is multiplied by the heat of vaporization. Because the temperature remains constant as long as the water is boiling, there is no temperature change given in the calculation, as shown in Sample Problem 3.9.

Calculating Heat to Vaporize (or Condense) Water

Heat = mass × heat of vaporization

$$\text{cal} = \cancel{g} \times \frac{540 \text{ cal}}{\cancel{g}} \qquad\qquad \text{J} = \cancel{g} \times \frac{2260 \text{ J}}{\cancel{g}}$$

▶ **SAMPLE PROBLEM 3.9 Using Heat of Vaporization**

In a sauna, 122 g of water is converted to steam at 100 °C. How many kilojoules of heat are needed?

SOLUTION

STEP 1 State the given and needed quantities.

ANALYZE THE PROBLEM	Given	Need
	122 g of water at 100 °C, heat of vaporization = 2260 J/g	kilojoules to convert to steam at 100 °C

STEP 2 Write a plan to convert the given quantity to the needed quantity.

grams of water → Heat of vaporization → joules → Metric factor → kilojoules

STEP 3 Write the heat conversion factor and any metric factor.

1 g of $H_2O(l \rightarrow g)$ = 2260 J

$$\frac{2260 \text{ J}}{1 \text{ g } H_2O} \quad \text{and} \quad \frac{1 \text{ g } H_2O}{2260 \text{ J}}$$

1 kJ = 1000 J

$$\frac{1000 \text{ J}}{1 \text{ kJ}} \quad \text{and} \quad \frac{1 \text{ kJ}}{1000 \text{ J}}$$

STEP **4**   Set up the problem and calculate the needed quantity.

$$122 \; \cancel{g \; H_2O} \times \underset{\text{Exact}}{\boxed{\frac{\overset{\text{Three SFs}}{2260 \; \cancel{J}}}{1 \; \cancel{g \; H_2O}}}} \times \underset{\text{Exact}}{\boxed{\frac{\overset{\text{Exact}}{1 \; kJ}}{1000 \; \cancel{J}}}} = \underset{\text{Three SFs}}{276 \; kJ}$$

STUDY CHECK 3.9

When steam from a pan of boiling water reaches a cool window, it condenses. How much heat, in kilojoules, is released when 25.0 g of steam condenses at 100 °C?

ANSWER

56.5 kJ released

Chemistry Link to **Health**

Steam Burns

Hot water at 100 °C will cause burns and damage to the skin. However, getting steam on the skin is even more dangerous. If 25 g of hot water at 100 °C falls on a person's skin, the temperature of the water will drop to body temperature, 37 °C. The heat released during cooling can cause severe burns. The amount of heat can be calculated from the mass, the temperature change, 100 °C − 37 °C = 63 °C, and the specific heat of water, 4.184 J/g °C.

$$25 \; \cancel{g} \times 63 \; \cancel{°C} \times \frac{4.184 \; J}{\cancel{g} \; \cancel{°C}} = 6600 \; J \text{ of heat released when}$$
water cools

However, getting steam on the skin is even more damaging. The condensation of the same quantity of steam to liquid at 100 °C releases much more heat—almost ten times as much. This amount of heat can be calculated using the heat of vaporization, which is 2260 J/g for water at 100 °C.

$$25 \; \cancel{g} \times \frac{2260 \; J}{1 \; \cancel{g}} = 57\,000 \; J \text{ released when water (gas)}$$
condenses to water (liquid) at 100 °C

The total heat released is calculated by combining the heat from the condensation at 100 °C and the heat from cooling of the steam from 100 °C to 37 °C (body temperature). We can see that most of the heat is from the condensation of steam. This large amount of heat released on the skin is what causes damage from steam burns.

Condensation (100 °C)	= 57 000 J
Cooling (100 °C to 37 °C) =	6 600 J
Heat released	= 64 000 J (rounded off)

The amount of heat released from steam is almost ten times greater than the heat from the same amount of hot water.

When 1 g of steam condenses, 2260 J is released.

Heating and Cooling Curves

All the changes of state during the heating or cooling of a substance can be illustrated visually. On a **heating curve** or **cooling curve**, the temperature is shown on the vertical axis and the loss or gain of heat is shown on the horizontal axis.

Steps on a Heating Curve

The first diagonal line indicates a warming of a solid as heat is added. When the melting temperature is reached, a horizontal line, or plateau, indicates that the solid is melting. As melting takes place, the solid is changing to liquid without any change in temperature (see Figure 3.8).

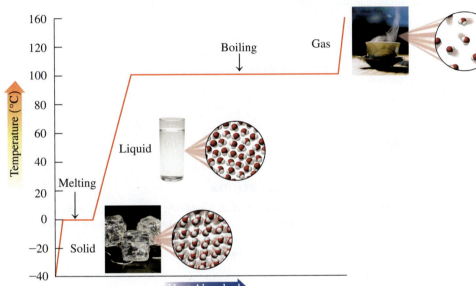

FIGURE 3.8 ▶ A heating curve diagrams the temperature increases and changes of state as heat is added.

Q What does the plateau at 100 °C represent on the heating curve for water?

Once all the particles are in the liquid state, heat that is added will increase the temperature of the liquid. This increase is drawn as a diagonal line from the melting point temperature to the boiling point temperature. Once the liquid reaches its boiling point, a horizontal line indicates that the temperature is constant as liquid changes to gas. Because the heat of vaporization is greater than the heat of fusion, the horizontal line at the boiling point is longer than the line at the melting point. Once all the liquid becomes gas, adding more heat increases the temperature of the gas.

Steps on a Cooling Curve

A cooling curve is a diagram of the cooling process in which the temperature decreases as heat is removed. Initially, a diagonal line to the boiling (condensation) point is drawn to show that heat is removed from a gas until it begins to condense. At the boiling (condensation) point, a horizontal line is drawn that indicates a change of state as gas condenses to form a liquid. After all the gas has changed into liquid, further cooling lowers the temperature. The decrease in temperature is shown as a diagonal line from the condensation temperature to the freezing temperature. At the freezing point, another horizontal line indicates that liquid is changing to solid at the freezing point temperature. Once all the substance is frozen, the removal of more heat decreases the temperature of the solid below its freezing point, which is shown as a diagonal line below its freezing point.

A cooling curve for water illustrates the change in temperature and changes of state as heat is removed.

> ▶ SAMPLE PROBLEM 3.10 Using a Cooling Curve
>
> Using the cooling curve for water, identify the state or change of state for water as solid, liquid, gas, condensation, or freezing.
>
> **a.** at 120 °C   **b.** at 100 °C   **c.** at 40 °C
>
> **SOLUTION**
>
> **a.** A temperature of 120 °C occurs on the diagonal line above the boiling (condensation) point, which indicates that water is a gas.
> **b.** A temperature of 100 °C, shown as a horizontal line, indicates that the water vapor is changing to liquid water, or condensing.
> **c.** A temperature of 40 °C occurs on the diagonal line below the boiling point but above the freezing point, which indicates that the water is in the liquid state.
>
> **STUDY CHECK 3.10**
>
> Using the cooling curve for water, identify the state or change of state for water as solid, liquid, gas, condensation, or freezing.
>
> **a.** at 0 °C   **b.** at −20 °C
>
> **ANSWER**
>
> **a.** freezing   **b.** solid

Combining Energy Calculations

Up to now, we have calculated one step in a heating or cooling curve. However, many problems require a combination of steps that include a temperature change as well as a change of state. The heat is calculated for each step separately and then added together to find the total energy, as seen in Sample Problem 3.11.

> ▶ SAMPLE PROBLEM 3.11 Combining Heat Calculations
>
> Charles has increased his activity by doing more exercise. After a session of using small weights, he has a sore arm. An ice bag is filled with 125 g of ice at 0.0 °C. The heat of fusion for ice is 334 J/g. How much heat, in kilojoules, is absorbed to melt the ice, and to raise the temperature of the water to body temperature, 37.0 °C?
>
> **SOLUTION**
>
> **STEP 1** State the given and needed quantities.
>
> | | Given | Need |
> |---|---|---|
> | ANALYZE THE PROBLEM | 125 g of ice at 0.0 °C, heat of fusion of ice = 334 J/g | total kilojoules to melt ice at 0.0 °C and to raise temperature of water to 37.0 °C |
>
> **STEP 2** Write a plan to convert the given quantity to the needed quantity.
>
> Total heat = kilojoules needed to melt the ice and heat the water from 0.0 °C (freezing point) to 37.0 °C
>
> **STEP 3** Write the heat conversion factor and any metric factor.
>
> $$1 \text{ g of } H_2O(s \rightarrow l) = 334 \text{ J} \qquad SH_{water} = \frac{4.184 \text{ J}}{\text{g °C}} \qquad 1 \text{ kJ} = 1000 \text{ J}$$
>
> $$\frac{334 \text{ J}}{1 \text{ g } H_2O} \text{ and } \frac{1 \text{ g } H_2O}{334 \text{ J}} \qquad \frac{4.184 \text{ J}}{\text{g °C}} \text{ and } \frac{\text{g °C}}{4.184 \text{ J}} \qquad \frac{1000 \text{ J}}{1 \text{ kJ}} \text{ and } \frac{1 \text{ kJ}}{1000 \text{ J}}$$

STEP 4 Set up the problem and calculate the needed quantity.

$$\Delta T = 37.0\,°C - 0.0\,°C = 37.0\,°C$$

Heat needed to change ice (solid) to water (liquid) at 0.0 °C:

Three SFs   Exact

$$125 \; \text{g ice} \;\times\; \frac{334 \text{ J}}{1 \text{ g ice}} \;\times\; \frac{1 \text{ kJ}}{1000 \text{ J}} \;=\; 41.8 \text{ kJ}$$

Three SFs   Exact   Exact   Three SFs

Heat needed to warm water (liquid) from 0.0 °C to water (liquid) at 37.0 °C:

Exact   Exact

$$125 \text{ g} \;\times\; 37.0\,°C \;\times\; \frac{4.184 \text{ J}}{\text{g}\,°C} \;\times\; \frac{1 \text{ kJ}}{1000 \text{ J}} \;=\; 19.4 \text{ kJ}$$

Three SFs   Three SFs   Exact   Three SFs

Calculate the total heat:

Melting ice at 0.0 °C	41.8 kJ
Heating water (0.0 °C to 37.0 °C)	19.4 kJ
Total heat needed	61.2 kJ

STUDY CHECK 3.11

How many kilojoules are released when 75.0 g of steam at 100 °C condenses, cools to 0 °C, and freezes at 0 °C? (*Hint*: The solution will require three energy calculations.)

ANSWER

226 kJ

QUESTIONS AND PROBLEMS

3.7 Changes of State

LEARNING GOAL Describe the changes of state between solids, liquids, and gases; calculate the energy involved.

3.41 Identify each of the following changes of state as melting, freezing, sublimation, or deposition:
  a. The solid structure of a substance breaks down as liquid forms.
  b. Coffee is freeze-dried.
  c. Water on the street turns to ice during a cold wintry night.
  d. Ice crystals form on a package of frozen corn.

3.42 Identify each of the following changes of state as melting, freezing, sublimation, or deposition:
  a. Dry ice in an ice-cream cart disappears.
  b. Snow on the ground turns to liquid water.
  c. Heat is removed from 125 g of liquid water at 0 °C.
  d. Frost (ice) forms on the walls of a freezer unit of a refrigerator.

3.43 Calculate the heat change at 0 °C for each of the following, and indicate whether heat was absorbed or released:
  a. calories to melt 65 g of ice
  b. joules to melt 17.0 g of ice
  c. kilocalories to freeze 225 g of water
  d. kilojoules to freeze 50.0 g of water

3.44 Calculate the heat change at 0 °C for each of the following, and indicate whether heat was absorbed or released:
  a. calories to freeze 35 g of water
  b. joules to freeze 275 g of water
  c. kilocalories to melt 140 g of ice
  d. kilojoules to melt 5.00 g of ice

3.45 Identify each of the following changes of state as evaporation, boiling, or condensation:
  a. The water vapor in the clouds changes to rain.
  b. Wet clothes dry on a clothesline.
  c. Lava flows into the ocean and steam forms.
  d. After a hot shower, your bathroom mirror is covered with water.

3.46 Identify each of the following changes of state as evaporation, boiling, or condensation:
  a. At 100 °C, the water in a pan changes to steam.
  b. On a cool morning, the windows in your car fog up.
  c. A shallow pond dries up in the summer.
  d. Your teakettle whistles when the water is ready for tea.

3.47 Calculate the heat change at 100 °C for each of the following, and indicate whether heat was absorbed or released:
  a. calories to vaporize 10.0 g of water
  b. joules to vaporize 5.00 g of water
  c. kilocalories to condense 8.0 kg of steam
  d. kilojoules to condense 175 g of steam

3.48 Calculate the heat change at 100 °C for each of the following, and indicate whether heat was absorbed or released:
  a. calories to condense 10.0 g of steam
  b. joules to condense 7.60 g of steam
  c. kilocalories to vaporize 44 g of water
  d. kilojoules to vaporize 5.00 kg of water

3.49 Draw a heating curve for a sample of ice that is heated from −20 °C to 150 °C. Indicate the segment of the graph that corresponds to each of the following:
   a. solid   **b.** melting   **c.** liquid
   d. boiling   **e.** gas

3.50 Draw a cooling curve for a sample of steam that cools from 110 °C to −10 °C. Indicate the segment of the graph that corresponds to each of the following:
   a. solid   **b.** freezing   **c.** liquid
   d. condensation   **e.** gas

3.51 Using the values for the heat of fusion, specific heat of water, and/or heat of vaporization, calculate the amount of heat energy in each of the following:
   a. joules needed to melt 50.0 g of ice at 0 °C and to warm the liquid to 65.0 °C
   b. kilocalories released when 15.0 g of steam condenses at 100 °C and the liquid cools to 0 °C
   c. kilojoules needed to melt 24.0 g of ice at 0 °C, warm the liquid to 100 °C, and change it to steam at 100 °C

3.52 Using the values for the heat of fusion, specific heat of water, and/or heat of vaporization, calculate the amount of heat energy in each of the following:
   a. joules released when 125 g of steam at 100 °C condenses and cools to liquid at 15.0 °C
   b. kilocalories needed to melt a 525-g ice sculpture at 0 °C and to warm the liquid to 15.0 °C
   c. kilojoules released when 85.0 g of steam condenses at 100 °C, cools, and freezes at 0 °C

℞ Clinical Applications

3.53 A patient arrives in the emergency room with a burn caused by steam. Calculate the heat, in kilocalories, that is released when 18.0 g of steam at 100. °C hits the skin, condenses, and cools to body temperature of 37.0 °C.

3.54 A sports trainer applies an ice bag to the back of an injured athlete. Calculate the heat, in kilocalories, that is absorbed if 145 g of ice at 0.0 °C is placed in an ice bag, melts, and rises to body temperature of 37.0 °C.

Clinical Update
A Diet and Exercise Program for Charles

It has been two weeks since Charles met with Daniel, a dietitian, who provided Charles with a menu for weight loss. Charles and his mother are going back to see Daniel again with a chart of the food Charles has eaten. The following is what Charles ate in one day:

Breakfast
1 banana, 1 cup of nonfat milk, 1 egg

Lunch
1 cup of carrots, 3 oz of ground beef, 1 apple, 1 cup of nonfat milk

Dinner
6 oz of skinless chicken, 1 baked potato, 3 oz of broccoli, 1 cup of nonfat milk

℞ Clinical Applications

3.55 Using energy values from Table 3.8, determine each of the following:
   a. the total kilocalories for each meal
   b. the total kilocalories for one day
   c. If Charles consumes 1800 kcal per day, he will maintain his weight. Would he lose weight on his new diet?
   d. If the loss of 3500 kcal is equal to a loss of 1.0 lb, how many days will it take Charles to lose 5.0 lb?

3.56 **a.** During one week, Charles swam for a total of 2.5 h and walked for a total of 8.0 h. If Charles expends 340 kcal/h swimming and 160 kcal/h walking, how many total kilocalories did he expend for one week?
   b. For the amount of exercise that Charles did for one week in part **a**, how much weight, in pounds, did he lose?
   c. How many hours would Charles have to walk to lose 1.0 lb?
   d. How many hours would Charles have to swim to lose 1.0 lb?

MATTER AND ENERGY

Matter — **Energy**

Matter *has states of*:

Solid   **Liquid**   **Gas**

Energy *affects*:

Particle Motion

Solid / Liquid *can be*:

Pure Substances   **Mixtures**

Gas *undergo*:

Changes of State

Particle Motion *as*:

Heat

Pure Substances *that are*:

Elements

or

Compounds

Mixtures *that are*:

Homogeneous

or

Heterogeneous

Changes of State *gain/loss of heat during*:

Melting or Freezing

Boiling or Condensation

Heat *measured in*:

Calories or Joules

using

Temperature Change

Specific Heat

Mass

Boiling or Condensation *require*:

Heat of Fusion

Heat of Vaporization

are drawn as a

Heating or Cooling Curve

CHAPTER REVIEW

3.1 Classification of Matter

LEARNING GOAL Classify examples of matter as pure substances or mixtures.

- Matter is anything that has mass and occupies space.
- Matter is classified as pure substances or mixtures.
- Pure substances, which are elements or compounds, have fixed compositions, and mixtures have variable compositions.
- The substances in mixtures can be separated using physical methods.

3.2 States and Properties of Matter

LEARNING GOAL Identify the states and the physical and chemical properties of matter.

- The three states of matter are solid, liquid, and gas.
- A physical property is a characteristic of a substance in that it can be observed or measured without affecting the identity of the substance.
- A physical change occurs when physical properties change, but not the composition of the substance.
- A chemical property indicates the ability of a substance to change into another substance.
- A chemical change occurs when one or more substances react to form a substance with new physical and chemical properties.

3.3 Temperature
LEARNING GOAL Given a temperature, calculate a corresponding temperature on another scale.

- In science, temperature is measured in degrees Celsius (°C) or kelvins (K).
- On the Celsius scale, there are 100 units between the freezing point (0 °C) and the boiling point (100 °C) of water.
- On the Fahrenheit scale, there are 180 units between the freezing point (32 °F) and the boiling point (212 °F) of water. A Fahrenheit temperature is related to its Celsius temperature by the equation $T_F = 1.8(T_C) + 32$.
- The SI unit, kelvin, is related to the Celsius temperature by the equation $T_K = T_C + 273$.

3.4 Energy
LEARNING GOAL Identify energy as potential or kinetic; convert between units of energy.

- Energy is the ability to do work.
- Potential energy is stored energy; kinetic energy is the energy of motion.
- Common units of energy are the calorie (cal), kilocalorie (kcal), joule (J), and kilojoule (kJ).
- One calorie is equal to 4.184 J.

3.5 Energy and Nutrition
LEARNING GOAL Use the energy values to calculate the kilocalories (kcal) or kilojoules (kJ) for a food.

- The nutritional Calorie is the same amount of energy as 1 kcal or 1000 calories.
- The energy of a food is the sum of kilocalories or kilojoules from carbohydrate, fat, and protein.

Nutrition Facts
Serving Size 14 crackers (31g)
Servings Per Container About 7

Amount Per Serving

Calories 130   Calories from Fat 40
Kilojoules 500   kJ from Fat   150

3.6 Specific Heat
LEARNING GOAL Use specific heat to calculate heat loss or gain.

- Specific heat is the amount of energy required to raise the temperature of exactly 1 g of a substance by exactly 1 °C.
- The heat lost or gained by a substance is determined by multiplying its mass, the temperature change, and its specific heat.

3.7 Changes of State
LEARNING GOAL Describe the changes of state between solids, liquids, and gases; calculate the energy involved.

- Melting occurs when the particles in a solid absorb enough energy to break apart and form a liquid.
- The amount of energy required to convert exactly 1 g of solid to liquid is called the heat of fusion.
- For water, 80. cal (334 J) is needed to melt 1 g of ice or must be removed to freeze 1 g of water.
- Evaporation occurs when particles in a liquid state absorb enough energy to break apart and form gaseous particles.
- Boiling is the vaporization of liquid at its boiling point. The heat of vaporization is the amount of heat needed to convert exactly 1 g of liquid to vapor.
- For water, 540 cal (2260 J) is needed to vaporize 1 g of water or must be removed to condense 1 g of steam.
- A heating or cooling curve illustrates the changes in temperature and state as heat is added to or removed from a substance. Plateaus on the graph indicate changes of state.
- The total heat absorbed or removed from a substance undergoing temperature changes and changes of state is the sum of energy calculations for change(s) of state and change(s) in temperature.
- Sublimation is a process whereby a solid changes directly to a gas.

KEY TERMS

boiling The formation of bubbles of gas throughout a liquid.

boiling point (bp) The temperature at which a liquid changes to gas (boils) and gas changes to liquid (condenses).

calorie (cal) The amount of heat energy that raises the temperature of exactly 1 g of water by exactly 1 °C.

change of state The transformation of one state of matter to another; for example, solid to liquid, liquid to solid, liquid to gas.

chemical change A change during which the original substance is converted into a new substance that has a different composition and new physical and chemical properties.

chemical properties The properties that indicate the ability of a substance to change into a new substance.

compound A pure substance consisting of two or more elements, with a definite composition, that can be broken down into simpler substances only by chemical methods.

condensation The change of state from a gas to a liquid.

cooling curve A diagram that illustrates temperature changes and changes of state for a substance as heat is removed.

deposition The change of a gas directly into a solid; the reverse of sublimation.

element A pure substance containing only one type of matter, which cannot be broken down by chemical methods.

energy The ability to do work.

energy value The kilocalories (or kilojoules) obtained per gram of the food types: carbohydrate, fat, and protein.

evaporation The formation of a gas (vapor) by the escape of high-energy molecules from the surface of a liquid.

freezing The change of state from liquid to solid.

freezing point (fp) The temperature at which a liquid changes to a solid (freezes), a solid changes to a liquid (melts).

gas A state of matter that does not have a definite shape or volume.

heat The energy associated with the motion of particles in a substance.

heat of fusion The energy required to melt exactly 1 g of a substance at its melting point. For water, 80. cal (334 J) is needed to melt 1 g of ice; 80. cal (334 J) is released when 1 g of water freezes.

heat of vaporization The energy required to vaporize exactly 1 g of a substance at its boiling point. For water, 540 cal (2260 J) is needed to vaporize 1 g of liquid; 1 g of steam gives off 540 cal (2260 J) when it condenses.

heating curve A diagram that illustrates the temperature changes and changes of state of a substance as it is heated.

joule (J) The SI unit of heat energy; 4.184 J = 1 cal.

kinetic energy The energy of moving particles.

liquid A state of matter that takes the shape of its container but has a definite volume.

matter The material that makes up a substance and has mass and occupies space.

melting The change of state from a solid to a liquid.

melting point (mp) The temperature at which a solid becomes a liquid (melts). It is the same temperature as the freezing point.

mixture The physical combination of two or more substances that does not change the identities of the mixed substances.

physical change A change in which the physical properties of a substance change but its identity stays the same.

physical properties The properties that can be observed or measured without affecting the identity of a substance.

potential energy A type of energy related to position or composition of a substance.

pure substance A type of matter that has a definite composition.

solid A state of matter that has its own shape and volume.

specific heat (SH) A quantity of heat that changes the temperature of exactly 1 g of a substance by exactly 1 °C.

states of matter Three forms of matter: solid, liquid, and gas.

sublimation The change of state in which a solid is transformed directly to a gas without forming a liquid first.

⚛ CORE CHEMISTRY SKILLS

The chapter section containing each Core Chemistry Skill is shown in parentheses at the end of each heading.

Classifying Matter (3.1)

- A pure substance is matter that has a fixed or constant composition.
- An element, the simplest type of a pure substance, is composed of only one type of matter, such as silver, iron, or aluminum.
- A compound is also a pure substance, but it consists of two or more elements chemically combined in the same proportion.
- In a *homogeneous mixture*, also called a *solution*, the composition of the substances in the mixture is uniform.
- In a *heterogeneous mixture*, the components are visible and do not have a uniform composition throughout the sample.

Example: Classify each of the following as a pure substance (element or compound) or a mixture (homogeneous or heterogeneous):
  a. iron in a nail
  b. black coffee
  c. carbon dioxide, a greenhouse gas

Answer: **a.** Iron is a pure substance, which is an element.
  b. Black coffee contains different substances with uniform composition, which makes it a homogeneous mixture.
  c. The gas carbon dioxide, which is a pure substance that contains two elements chemically combined, is a compound.

Identifying Physical and Chemical Changes (3.2)

- When matter undergoes a physical change, its state or its appearance changes, but its composition remains the same.
- When a chemical change takes place, the original substance is converted into a new substance, which has different physical and chemical properties.

Example: Classify each of the following as a physical or chemical property:
  a. Helium in a balloon is a gas.
  b. Methane, in natural gas, burns.
  c. Hydrogen sulfide smells like rotten eggs.

Answer: **a.** A gas is a state of matter, which makes it a physical property.

  b. When methane burns, it changes to different substances with new properties, which is a chemical property.
  c. The odor of hydrogen sulfide is a physical property.

Converting between Temperature Scales (3.3)

- The temperature equation $T_F = 1.8(T_C) + 32$ is used to convert from Celsius to Fahrenheit and can be rearranged to convert from Fahrenheit to Celsius.
- The temperature equation $T_K = T_C + 273$ is used to convert from Celsius to Kelvin and can be rearranged to convert from Kelvin to Celsius.

Example: Convert 75.0 °C to degrees Fahrenheit.

Answer: $T_F = 1.8(T_C) + 32$
  $T_F = 1.8(75.0) + 32 = 135 + 32$
  $= 167 °F$

Example: Convert 355 K to degrees Celsius.

Answer: $T_K = T_C + 273$
  To solve the equation for T_C, subtract 273 from both sides.
  $T_K - 273 = T_C + 273 - 273$
  $T_C = T_K - 273$
  $T_C = 355 - 273$
  $= 82 °C$

Using Energy Units (3.4)

- Equalities for energy units include 1 cal = 4.184 J, 1 kcal = 1000 cal, and 1 kJ = 1000 J.
- Each equality for energy units can be written as two conversion factors:

$$\frac{4.184 \text{ J}}{1 \text{ cal}} \text{ and } \frac{1 \text{ cal}}{4.184 \text{ J}} \quad \frac{1000 \text{ cal}}{1 \text{ kcal}} \text{ and } \frac{1 \text{ kcal}}{1000 \text{ cal}} \quad \frac{1000 \text{ J}}{1 \text{ kJ}} \text{ and } \frac{1 \text{ kJ}}{1000 \text{ J}}$$

- The energy unit conversion factors are used to cancel given units of energy and to obtain the needed unit of energy.

Example: Convert 45 000 J to kilocalories.

Answer: Using the conversion factors above, we start with the given 45 000 J and convert it to kilocalories.

$$45\,000 \text{ J} \times \frac{1 \text{ cal}}{4.184 \text{ J}} \times \frac{1 \text{ kcal}}{1000 \text{ cal}} = 11 \text{ kcal}$$

Using the Heat Equation (3.6)

- The quantity of heat absorbed or lost by a substance is calculated using the heat equation.

  Heat = $m \times \Delta T \times SH$

- Heat, in joules, is obtained when the specific heat of a substance in J/g °C is used.
- To cancel, the unit grams is used for mass, and the unit °C is used for temperature change.

Example: How many joules are required to heat 5.25 g of titanium from 85.5 °C to 132.5 °C?

Answer: $m = 5.25$ g, $\Delta T = 132.5\,°C - 85.5\,°C = 47.0\,°C$
SH for titanium $= 0.523$ J/g °C

The known values are substituted into the heat equation making sure units cancel.

$$\text{Heat} = m \times \Delta T \times SH = 5.25\ \cancel{g}\ \times 47.0\ \cancel{°C} \times \frac{0.523\ \text{J}}{\cancel{g}\ \cancel{°C}}$$

$$= 129\ \text{J}$$

UNDERSTANDING THE CONCEPTS

The chapter sections to review are shown in parentheses at the end of each question.

3.57 Identify each of the following as an element, a compound, or a mixture. Explain your choice. (3.1)

a.   **b.**

c.

3.58 Identify each of the following as a homogeneous or heterogeneous mixture. Explain your choice. (3.1)

a.   **b.**

c.

3.59 Classify each of the following as a homogeneous or heterogeneous mixture: (3.1)
a. lemon-flavored water
b. stuffed mushrooms
c. eye drops

3.60 Classify each of the following as a homogeneous or heterogeneous mixture: (3.1)
a. ketchup   **b.** hard-boiled egg   **c.** tortilla soup

3.61 State the temperature on the Celsius thermometer and convert to Fahrenheit. (3.3)

3.62 State the temperature on the Celsius thermometer and convert to Fahrenheit. (3.3)

3.63 Compost can be made at home from grass clippings, some kitchen scraps, and dry leaves. As microbes break down organic matter, heat is generated and the compost can reach a temperature of 155 °F, which kills most pathogens. What is this temperature in degrees Celsius? In kelvins? (3.3)

Compost produced from decayed plant material is used to enrich the soil.

3.64 After a week, biochemical reactions in compost slow, and the temperature drops to 45 °C. The dark brown organic-rich mixture is ready for use in the garden. What is this temperature in degrees Fahrenheit? In kelvins? (3.3)

3.65 Calculate the energy to heat two cubes (gold and aluminum) each with a volume of 10.0 cm³ from 15 °C to 25 °C. Refer to Tables 2.9 and 3.11. (3.6)

3.66 Calculate the energy to heat two cubes (silver and copper), each with a volume of 10.0 cm³ from 15 °C to 25 °C. Refer to Tables 2.9 and 3.11. (3.6)

℞ Clinical Applications

3.67 A 70.0-kg person had a quarter-pound cheeseburger, french fries, and a chocolate shake. (3.5)

Item	Carbohydrate (g)	Fat (g)	Protein (g)
Cheeseburger	46	40.	47
French fries	47	16	4
Chocolate shake	76	10.	10.

a. Using Table 3.7, calculate the total kilocalories for each food type in this meal (round off the kilocalories to the tens place).

b. Determine the total kilocalories for the meal (round off to the tens place).

c. Using Table 3.10, determine the number of hours of sleep needed to burn off the kilocalories in this meal.

d. Using Table 3.10, determine the number of hours of running needed to burn off the kilocalories in this meal.

3.68 Your friend, who has a mass of 70.0 kg, has a slice of pizza, a cola soft drink, and ice cream. (3.5)

Item	Carbohydrate (g)	Fat (g)	Protein (g)
Pizza	29	10.	13
Cola	51	0	0
Ice cream	44	28	8

a. Using Table 3.7, calculate the total kilocalories for each food type in this meal (round off the kilocalories to the tens place).

b. Determine the total kilocalories for the meal (round off to the tens place).

c. Using Table 3.10, determine the number of hours of sitting needed to burn off the kilocalories in this meal.

d. Using Table 3.10, determine the number of hours of swimming needed to burn off the kilocalories in this meal.

ADDITIONAL QUESTIONS AND PROBLEMS

3.69 Classify each of the following as an element, a compound, or a mixture: (3.1)
a. carbon in pencils
b. carbon monoxide (CO) in automobile exhaust
c. orange juice

3.70 Classify each of the following as an element, a compound, or a mixture: (3.1)
a. neon gas in lights
b. a salad dressing of oil and vinegar
c. sodium hypochlorite (NaOCl) in bleach

3.71 Classify each of the following mixtures as homogeneous or heterogeneous: (3.1)
a. hot fudge sundae **b.** herbal tea **c.** vegetable oil

3.72 Classify each of the following mixtures as homogeneous or heterogeneous: (3.1)
a. water and sand **b.** mustard **c.** blue ink

3.73 Identify each of the following as solid, liquid, or gas: (3.2)
a. vitamin tablets in a bottle **b.** helium in a balloon
c. milk in a bottle **d.** the air you breathe
e. charcoal briquettes on a barbecue

3.74 Identify each of the following as solid, liquid, or gas: (3.2)
a. popcorn in a bag **b.** water in a garden hose
c. a computer mouse **d.** air in a tire
e. hot tea in a teacup

3.75 Identify each of the following as a physical or chemical property: (3.2)
a. Gold is shiny.
b. Gold melts at 1064 °C.
c. Gold is a good conductor of electricity.
d. When gold reacts with yellow sulfur, a black sulfide compound forms.

3.76 Identify each of the following as a physical or chemical property: (3.2)
a. A candle is 10 in. high and 2 in. in diameter.
b. A candle burns.
c. The wax of a candle softens on a hot day.
d. A candle is blue.

3.77 Identify each of the following as a physical or chemical change: (3.2)
a. A plant grows a new leaf.
b. Chocolate is melted for a dessert.
c. Wood is chopped for the fireplace.
d. Wood burns in a woodstove.

3.78 Identify each of the following as a physical or chemical change: (3.2)
a. Aspirin tablets are broken in half.
b. Carrots are grated for use in a salad.
c. Malt undergoes fermentation to make beer.
d. A copper pipe reacts with air and turns green.

3.79 Calculate each of the following temperatures in degrees Celsius and kelvins: (3.3)

    a. The highest recorded temperature in the continental United States was 134 °F in Death Valley, California, on July 10, 1913.

    b. The lowest recorded temperature in the continental United States was −69.7 °F in Rodgers Pass, Montana, on January 20, 1954.

3.80 Calculate each of the following temperatures in kelvins and degrees Fahrenheit: (3.3)

    a. The highest recorded temperature in the world was 58.0 °C in El Azizia, Libya, on September 13, 1922.

    b. The lowest recorded temperature in the world was −89.2 °C in Vostok, Antarctica, on July 21, 1983.

3.81 What is −15 °F in degrees Celsius and in kelvins? (3.3)

3.82 On a hot sunny day, you get out of the swimming pool and sit in a metal chair, which is very hot. Would you predict that the specific heat of the metal is higher or lower than that of water? Explain. (3.6)

3.83 On a hot day, the beach sand gets hot but the water stays cool. Would you predict that the specific heat of sand is higher or lower than that of water? Explain. (3.6)

On a sunny day, the sand gets hot but the water stays cool.

3.84 A large bottle containing 883 g of water at 4 °C is removed from the refrigerator. How many kilojoules are absorbed to warm the water to room temperature of 22 °C? (3.6)

3.85 A 0.50-g sample of vegetable oil is placed in a calorimeter. When the sample is burned, 18.9 kJ is given off. What is the energy value (kcal/g) for the oil? (3.5)

3.86 A 1.3-g sample of rice is placed in a calorimeter. When the sample is burned, 22 kJ is given off. What is the energy value (kcal/g) for the rice? (3.5)

3.87 The following graph is a heating curve for chloroform, a solvent for fats, oils, and waxes: (3.7)

    a. What is the approximate melting point of chloroform?

    b. What is the approximate boiling point of chloroform?

    c. On the heating curve, identify the segments **A**, **B**, **C**, **D**, and **E** as solid, liquid, gas, melting, or boiling.

    d. At the following temperatures, is chloroform a solid, liquid, or gas?

$$-80\ °C;\ -40\ °C;\ 25\ °C;\ 80\ °C$$

3.88 Associate the contents of the beakers (**1** to **5**) with segments (**A** to **E**) on the following heating curve for water: (3.7)

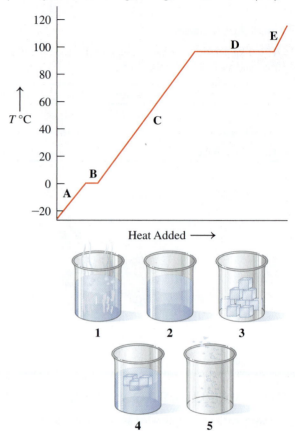

3.89 The melting point of dibromomethane is −53 °C and its boiling point is 97 °C. Sketch a heating curve for dibromomethane from −100 °C to 120 °C. (3.7)

    a. What is the state of dibromomethane at −75 °C?

    b. What happens on the curve at −53 °C?

    c. What is the state of dibromomethane at −18 °C?

    d. What is the state of dibromomethane at 110 °C?

    e. At what temperature will both solid and liquid be present?

3.90 The melting point of benzene is 5.5 °C and its boiling point is 80.1 °C. Sketch a heating curve for benzene from 0 °C to 100 °C. (3.7)

    a. What is the state of benzene at 15 °C?

    b. What happens on the curve at 5.5 °C?

    c. What is the state of benzene at 63 °C?

    d. What is the state of benzene at 98 °C?

    e. At what temperature will both liquid and gas be present?

℞ Clinical Applications

3.91 If you want to lose 1 lb of "body fat," which is 15% water, how many kilocalories do you need to expend? (3.5)

3.92 The highest recorded body temperature that a person has survived is 46.5 °C. Calculate that temperature in degrees Fahrenheit and in kelvins. (3.3)

3.93 A hot-water bottle for a patient contains 725 g of water at 65 °C. If the water cools to body temperature (37 °C), how many kilojoules of heat could be transferred to sore muscles? (3.6)

3.94 A young patient drinks whole milk as part of her diet. Calculate the total kilocalories if the glass of milk contains 12 g of carbohydrate, 9 g of fat, and 9 g of protein. (Round off answers for each food type to the tens place.) (3.5)

CHALLENGE QUESTIONS

The following groups of questions are related to the topics in this chapter. However, they do not all follow the chapter order, and they require you to combine concepts and skills from several sections. These questions will help you increase your critical thinking skills and prepare for your next exam.

3.95 When a 0.66-g sample of olive oil is burned in a calorimeter, the heat released increases the temperature of 370 g of water from 22.7 °C to 38.8 °C. What is the energy value for the olive oil in kcal/g? (3.5, 3.6)

3.96 A 45-g piece of ice at 0.0 °C is added to a sample of water at 8.0 °C. All of the ice melts and the temperature of the water decreases to 0.0 °C. How many grams of water were in the sample? (3.6, 3.7)

3.97 In a large building, oil is used in a steam boiler heating system. The combustion of 1.0 lb of oil provides 2.4×10^7 J. (3.4, 3.6)
 a. How many kilograms of oil are needed to heat 150 kg of water from 22 °C to 100 °C?
 b. How many kilograms of oil are needed to change 150 kg of water to steam at 100 °C?

3.98 When 1.0 g of gasoline burns, it releases 11 kcal of heat. The density of gasoline is 0.74 g/mL. (3.4, 3.6)
 a. How many megajoules are released when 1.0 gal of gasoline burns?
 b. If a television requires 150 kJ/h to run, how many hours can the television run on the energy provided by 1.0 gal of gasoline?

3.99 An ice bag containing 275 g of ice at 0 °C was used to treat sore muscles. When the bag was removed, the ice had melted and the liquid water had a temperature of 24.0 °C. How many kilojoules of heat were absorbed? (3.6, 3.7)

3.100 A 115-g sample of steam at 100 °C is emitted from a volcano. It condenses, cools, and falls as snow at 0 °C. How many kilojoules of heat were released? (3.6, 3.7)

3.101 A 70.0-g piece of copper metal at 54.0 °C is placed in 50.0 g of water at 26.0 °C. If the final temperature of the water and metal is 29.2 °C, what is the specific heat (J/g °C) of copper? (3.6)

3.102 A 125-g piece of metal is heated to 288 °C and dropped into 85.0 g of water at 12.0 °C. The metal and water come to the same temperature of 24.0 °C. What is the specific heat, in J/g °C, of the metal? (3.6)

3.103 A metal is thought to be titanium or aluminum. When 4.7 g of the metal absorbs 11 J, its temperature rises by 4.5 °C. (3.6)
 a. What is the specific heat (J/g °C) of the metal?
 b. Would you identify the metal as titanium or aluminum (see Table 3.11)?

3.104 A metal is thought to be copper or gold. When 18 g of the metal absorbs 58 cal, its temperature rises by 35 °C. (3.6)
 a. What is the specific heat, in cal/g °C, of the metal?
 b. Would you identify the metal as copper or gold (see Table 3.11)?

ANSWERS

Answers to Selected Questions and Problems

3.1 a. pure substance **b.** mixture
 c. pure substance **d.** pure substance
 e. mixture

3.3 a. element **b.** compound
 c. element **d.** compound
 e. compound

3.5 a. heterogeneous **b.** homogeneous
 c. homogeneous **d.** heterogeneous
 e. heterogeneous

3.7 a. gas **b.** gas
 c. solid

3.9 a. physical **b.** chemical
 c. physical **d.** chemical
 e. chemical

3.11 a. physical **b.** chemical
 c. physical **d.** physical
 e. physical

3.13 a. chemical **b.** physical
 c. physical **d.** chemical
 e. physical

3.15 In the United States, we still use the Fahrenheit temperature scale. In °F, normal body temperature is 98.6. On the Celsius scale, her temperature would be 37.7 °C, a mild fever.

3.17 a. 98.6 °F **b.** 18.5 °C
 c. 246 K **d.** 335 K
 e. 46 °C

3.19 a. 41 °C
 b. No. The temperature is equivalent to 39 °C.

3.21 When the roller-coaster car is at the top of the ramp, it has its maximum potential energy. As it descends, potential energy changes to kinetic energy. At the bottom, all the energy is kinetic.

3.23 a. potential **b.** kinetic
 c. potential **d.** potential

3.25 a. 8.1×10^5 J **b.** 190 kcal

3.27 a. 29.9 kcal   **b.** 208 kcal

3.29 a. 470 kJ   **b.** 18 g
     c. 130 kcal   **d.** 37 g

3.31 210 kcal, 880 kJ

3.33 640 kcal

3.35 Copper has the lowest specific heat of the samples and will reach the highest temperature.

3.37 a. 180 cal   **b.** 14 000 J
     c. 2600 J   **d.** 10.8 kJ

3.39 a. 1380 J, 330. cal   **b.** 1810 J, 434 cal
     c. 3780 J, 904 cal   **d.** 3600 J, 850 cal

3.41 a. melting   **b.** sublimation
     c. freezing   **d.** deposition

3.43 a. 5200 cal absorbed   **b.** 5680 J absorbed
     c. 18 kcal released   **d.** 16.7 kJ released

3.45 a. condensation   **b.** evaporation
     c. boiling   **d.** condensation

3.47 a. 5400 cal absorbed   **b.** 11 300 J absorbed
     c. 4300 kcal released   **d.** 396 kJ released

3.49

3.51 a. 30 300 J   **b.** 9.6 kcal
     c. 72.2 kJ

3.53 11 kcal

3.55 a. Breakfast 270 kcal; Lunch 420 kcal; Dinner 440 kcal
     b. 1130 kcal total
     c. Yes. Charles should be losing weight.
     d. 26 days

3.57 a. compound, the molecules have a definite 2:1 ratio of atoms
     b. mixture, has two different kinds of atoms and molecules
     c. element, has a single kind of atom

3.59 a. homogeneous   **b.** heterogeneous
     c. homogeneous

3.61 61.4 °C, 143 °F

3.63 68.3 °C, 341 K

3.65 gold, 250 J or 60.0 cal; aluminum, 240 J or 58 cal

3.67 a. carbohydrate, 680 kcal; fat, 590 kcal; protein, 240 kcal
     b. 1510 kcal
     c. 25 h
     d. 2.0 h

3.69 a. element   **b.** compound
     c. mixture

3.71 a. heterogeneous   **b.** homogeneous
     c. homogeneous

3.73 a. solid   **b.** gas
     c. liquid   **d.** gas
     e. solid

3.75 a. physical   **b.** physical
     c. physical   **d.** chemical

3.77 a. chemical   **b.** physical
     c. physical   **d.** chemical

3.79 a. 56.7 °C, 330. K   **b.** −56.5 °C, 217 K

3.81 −26 °C, 247 K

3.83 The same amount of heat causes a greater temperature change in the sand than in the water; thus the sand must have a lower specific heat than that of water.

3.85 9.0 kcal/g

3.87 a. about −60 °C
     b. about 60 °C
     c. The diagonal line A represents the solid state as temperature increases. The horizontal line B represents the change from solid to liquid or melting of the substance. The diagonal line C represents the liquid state as temperature increases. The horizontal line D represents the change from liquid to gas or boiling of the liquid. The diagonal line E represents the gas state as temperature increases.
     d. At −80 °C, solid; at −40 °C, liquid; at 25 °C, liquid; at 80 °C, gas

3.89

     a. solid   **b.** solid dibromomethane melts
     c. liquid   **d.** gas
     e. −53 °C

3.91 3500 kcal

3.93 85 kJ

3.95 9.0 kcal/g

3.97 a. 0.93 kg   **b.** 6.4 kg

3.99 119.5 kJ

3.101 Specific heat = 0.385 J/g °C

3.103 a. 0.52 J/g °C   **b.** titanium

CI.1 Gold, one of the most sought-after metals in the world, has a density of 19.3 g/cm³, a melting point of 1064 °C, a specific heat of 0.129 J/g °C, and a heat of fusion of 63.6 J/g. A gold nugget found in Alaska in 1998 weighs 20.17 lb. (2.4, 2.6, 2.7, 3.3, 3.6, 3.7)

Gold nuggets, also called native gold, can be found in streams and mines.

a. How many significant figures are in the measurement of the weight of the nugget?
b. Which is the mass of the nugget in kilograms?
c. If the nugget were pure gold, what would its volume be in cm³?
d. What is the melting point of gold in degrees Fahrenheit and kelvins?
e. How many kilocalories are required to raise the temperature of the nugget from 500. °C to 1064 °C and melt all the gold to liquid at 1064 °C?
f. If the price of gold is $45.98 per gram, what is the nugget worth, in dollars?

CI.2 The mileage for a motorcycle with a fuel-tank capacity of 22 L is 35 mi/gal. (2.5, 2.6, 2.7, 3.4)

a. How long a trip, in kilometers, can be made on one full tank of gasoline?
b. If the price of gasoline is $3.82 per gallon, what would be the cost of fuel for the trip?
c. If the average speed during the trip is 44 mi/h, how many hours will it take to reach the destination?

When 1.00 g of gasoline burns, 47 kJ of energy are released.

d. If the density of gasoline is 0.74 g/mL, what is the mass, in grams, of the fuel in the tank?
e. When 1.00 g of gasoline burns, 47 kJ of energy is released. How many kilojoules are produced when the fuel in one full tank is burned?

CI.3 Answer the following questions for the water samples **A** and **B** shown in the diagrams: (3.1, 3.2, 3.6)

a. In which sample (**A** or **B**) does the water have its own shape?
b. Which diagram (**1** or **2** or **3**) represents the arrangement of particles in water sample **A**?
c. Which diagram (**1** or **2** or **3**) represents the arrangement of particles in water sample **B**?

Answer the following for diagrams **1**, **2**, and **3**: (3.2, 3.3)
d. The state of matter indicated in diagram **1** is a _____; in diagram **2**, it is a _____; and in diagram **3**, it is a _____.
e. The motion of the particles is slowest in diagram _____.
f. The arrangement of particles is farthest apart in diagram _____.
g. The particles fill the volume of the container in diagram _____.
h. If the water in diagram **2** has a mass of 19 g and a temperature of 45 °C, how much heat, in kilojoules, is removed to cool the liquid to 0 °C?

CI.4 The label of a black cherry almond energy bar with a mass of 68 g lists the nutrition facts as 39 g of carbohydrate, 5 g of fat, and 10. g of protein. (2.5, 2.6, 3.4, 3.5)

a. Using the energy values for carbohydrates, fats, and proteins (see Table 3.7), what are the total kilocalories (Calories) listed for a black cherry almond bar? (Round off answers for each food type to the tens place.)
b. What are the kilojoules for the black cherry almond bar? (Round off answers for each food type to the tens place.)

An energy bar contains carbohydrate, fat, and protein.

c. If you obtain 160 kJ, how many grams of the black cherry almond bar did you eat?
d. If you are walking and using energy at a rate of 840 kJ/h, how many minutes will you need to walk to expend the energy from two black cherry almond bars?

CI.5 In one box of nails, there are 75 iron nails weighing 0.250 lb. The density of iron is 7.86 g/cm³. The specific heat of iron is 0.452 J/g °C. The melting point of iron is 1535 °C. The heat of fusion for iron is 272 J/g. (2.5, 2.6, 2.7, 3.4, 3.6, 3.7)

Nails made of iron have a density of 7.86 g/cm³.

a. What is the volume, in cm³, of the iron nails in the box?
b. If 30 nails are added to a graduated cylinder containing 17.6 mL of water, what is the new level of water, in milliliters, in the cylinder?
c. How much heat, in joules, must be added to the nails in the box to raise their temperature from 16 °C to 125 °C?
d. How much heat, in joules, is required to heat one nail from 25 °C to its melting point and change it to liquid iron?

CI.6 A hot tub is filled with 450 gal of water. (2.5, 2.6, 2.7, 3.3, 3.4, 3.6)

A hot tub filled with water is heated to 105 °F.

a. What is the volume of water, in liters, in the tub?
b. What is the mass, in kilograms, of water in the tub?
c. How many kilocalories are needed to heat the water from 62 °F to 105 °F?
d. If the hot-tub heater provides 5900 kJ/min, how long, in minutes, will it take to heat the water in the hot tub from 62 °F to 105 °F?

ANSWERS

CI.1 a. 4 significant figures
b. 9.17 kg
c. 475 cm³
d. 1947 °F; 1337 K
e. 298 kcal
f. $422 000

CI.3 a. B
b. A is represented by diagram **2**.
c. B is represented by diagram **1**.
d. solid; liquid; gas

e. diagram **1**
f. diagram **3**
g. diagram **3**
h. 3.6 kJ

CI.5 a. 14.4 cm³
b. 23.4 mL
c. 5590 J
d. 1440 J

4

Atoms

JOHN IS PREPARING FOR THE NEXT GROWING

season as he decides how much of each crop should be planted and their location on his farm. Part of this decision is determined by the quality of the soil including the pH, the amount of moisture, and the nutrient content in the soil. He begins by sampling the soil and performing a few chemical tests on the soil. John determines that several of his fields need additional fertilizer before the crops can be planted. John considers several different types of fertilizers as each supplies different nutrients to the soil to help increase crop production. Plants need three basic elements for growth. These elements are potassium, nitrogen, and phosphorus. Potassium (K on the periodic table) is a metal, whereas nitrogen (N) and phosphorus (P) are nonmetals. Fertilizers may also contain several other elements including calcium (Ca), magnesium (Mg), and sulfur (S). John applies a fertilizer containing a mixture of all of these elements to his soil and plans to re-check the soil nutrient content in a few days.

CAREER Farmer

Farming involves much more than growing crops and raising animals. Farmers must understand how to perform chemical tests and how to apply fertilizer to soil and pesticides or herbicides to crops. Pesticides are chemicals used to kill insects that could destroy the crop, whereas herbicides are chemicals used to kill weeds that would compete for the crop's water and nutrient supply. This requires knowledge of how these chemicals work, their safety, effectiveness, and their storage. In using this information, farmers are able to grow crops that produce a higher yield, greater nutritional value, and better taste.

LOOKING AHEAD

4.1 Elements and Symbols 102

♥ **Chemistry Link to Health** *Latin Names for Elements in Clinical Usage* 104

♥ **Chemistry Link to Health** *Toxicity of Mercury* 104

4.2 The Periodic Table 105

♥ **Chemistry Link to Health** *Elements Essential to Health* 108

4.3 The Atom 110

4.4 Atomic Number and Mass Number 114

4.5 Isotopes and Atomic Mass 117

4.6 Electron Energy Levels 121

♥ **Chemistry Link to Health** *Biological Reactions to UV Light* 122

4.7 Electron Configurations 127

4.8 Trends in Periodic Properties 135

℞ **Clinical Applications** 104, 110, 117, 141

℞ **Clinical Update** *Improving Crop Production* 141

LEARNING GOAL

Given the name of an element, write its correct symbol; from the symbol, write the correct name.

All matter is composed of *elements*, of which there are 118 different kinds. Of these, 88 elements occur naturally and make up all the substances in our world. Many elements are already familiar to you. Perhaps you use aluminum in the form of foil or drink soft drinks from aluminum cans. You may have a ring or necklace made of gold, silver, or perhaps platinum. If you play tennis or golf, then you may have noticed that your racket or clubs may be made from the elements titanium or carbon. In our bodies, calcium and phosphorus form the structure of bones and teeth, iron and copper are needed in the formation of red blood cells, and iodine is required for the proper functioning of the thyroid.

The correct amounts of certain elements are crucial to the proper growth and function of the body. Low levels of iron can lead to anemia, whereas lack of iodine can cause hypothyroidism and goiter. Some elements known as microminerals, such as chromium, cobalt, and selenium, are needed in our bodies in very small amounts. Laboratory tests are used to confirm that these elements are within normal ranges in our bodies.

CHAPTER READINESS*

📟 KEY MATH SKILLS
- Using Positive and Negative Numbers in Calculations (1.4B)
- Calculating Percentages (1.4C)
- Rounding Off (2.3)

⚛ CORE CHEMISTRY SKILLS
- Counting Significant Figures (2.2)
- Using Significant Figures in Calculations (2.3)

*These Key Math Skills and Core Chemistry Skills from previous chapters are listed here for your review as you proceed to the new material in this chapter.

4.1 Elements and Symbols

Elements are pure substances from which all other things are built. Elements cannot be broken down into simpler substances. Over the centuries, elements have been named for planets, mythological figures, colors, minerals, geographic locations, and famous people. Some sources of names of elements are listed in Table 4.1. A complete list of all the elements and their symbols are found on the inside front cover of this text.

Chemical Symbols

Chemical symbols are one- or two-letter abbreviations for the names of the elements. Only the first letter of an element's symbol is capitalized. If the symbol has a second letter, it is lowercase so that we know when a different element is indicated. If two letters are

TABLE 4.1 Some Elements, Symbols, and Source of Names

Element	Symbol	Source of Name
Uranium	U	The planet Uranus
Titanium	Ti	Titans (mythology)
Chlorine	Cl	*Chloros*: "greenish yellow" (Greek)
Iodine	I	*Ioeides*: "violet" (Greek)
Magnesium	Mg	Magnesia, a mineral
Californium	Cf	California
Curium	Cm	Marie and Pierre Curie
Copernicium	Cn	Nicolaus Copernicus

One-Letter Symbols		Two-Letter Symbols	
C	Carbon	Co	Cobalt
S	Sulfur	Si	Silicon
N	Nitrogen	Ne	Neon
I	Iodine	Ni	Nickel

capitalized, they represent the symbols of two different elements. For example, the element cobalt has the symbol Co. However, the two capital letters CO specify two elements, carbon (C) and oxygen (O).

Although most of the symbols use letters from the current names, some are derived from their ancient names. For example, Na, the symbol for sodium, comes from the Latin word *natrium*. The symbol for iron, Fe, is derived from the Latin name *ferrum*. Table 4.2 lists the names and symbols of some common elements. Learning their names and symbols will greatly help your learning of chemistry.

TABLE 4.2 Names and Symbols of Some Common Elements

Name*	Symbol	Name*	Symbol	Name*	Symbol
Aluminum	Al	Gallium	Ga	Oxygen	O
Argon	Ar	Gold (*aurum*)	Au	Phosphorus	P
Arsenic	As	Helium	He	Platinum	Pt
Barium	Ba	Hydrogen	H	Potassium (*kalium*)	K
Boron	B	Iodine	I	Radium	Ra
Bromine	Br	Iron (*ferrum*)	Fe	Silicon	Si
Cadmium	Cd	Lead (*plumbum*)	Pb	Silver (*argentum*)	Ag
Calcium	Ca	Lithium	Li	Sodium (*natrium*)	Na
Carbon	C	Magnesium	Mg	Strontium	Sr
Chlorine	Cl	Manganese	Mn	Sulfur	S
Chromium	Cr	Mercury (*hydrargyrum*)	Hg	Tin (*stannum*)	Sn
Cobalt	Co	Neon	Ne	Titanium	Ti
Copper (*cuprum*)	Cu	Nickel	Ni	Uranium	U
Fluorine	F	Nitrogen	N	Zinc	Zn

*Names given in parentheses are ancient Latin or Greek words from which the symbols are derived.

SAMPLE PROBLEM 4.1 Names and Symbols of Chemical Elements

Complete the following table with the correct symbol or name of each element:

Name	Symbol
nickel	___
nitrogen	___
___	Zn
___	K
iron	___

SOLUTION

Name	Symbol
nickel	Ni
nitrogen	N
zinc	Zn
potassium	K
iron	Fe

STUDY CHECK 4.1

Write the chemical symbols for the elements silicon, sulfur, and silver.

ANSWER

Si, S, and Ag

Aluminum

Carbon

Gold

Silver

Sulfur

Chemistry Link to **Health**
Latin Names for Elements in Clinical Usage

In medicine, the Latin name *natrium* is often used for sodium, an important electrolyte in body fluids and cells. An increase in serum sodium, a condition called *hypernatremia*, may occur when water is lost because of profuse sweating, severe diarrhea, or vomiting, or when there is inadequate water intake. A decrease in sodium, a condition called *hyponatremia*, may occur when a person takes in a large amount of water or fluid-replacement solutions. Conditions that occur in cardiac failure, liver failure, and malnutrition can also cause hyponatremia.

The Latin name *kalium* is often used for potassium, the most common electrolyte inside the cells. Potassium regulates osmotic pressure,

acid–base balance, nerve and muscle excitability, and the function of cellular enzymes. Serum potassium measures potassium outside the cells, which amounts to only 2% of total body potassium. An increase in serum potassium (*hyperkalemia* or *hyperpotassemia*) may occur when cells are severely injured, in renal failure when potassium is not properly excreted, and in Addison's disease. A severe loss of potassium (*hypokalemia* or *hypopotassemia*) may occur during excessive vomiting, diarrhea, renal tubular defects, and glucose or insulin therapy.

Chemistry Link to **Health**
Toxicity of Mercury

Mercury is a silvery, shiny element that is a liquid at room temperature. Mercury can enter the body through inhaled mercury vapor, contact with the skin, or ingestion of foods or water contaminated with mercury. In the body, mercury destroys proteins and disrupts cell function. Long-term exposure to mercury can damage the brain and kidneys, cause mental retardation, and decrease physical development. Blood, urine, and hair samples are used to test for mercury.

In both freshwater and seawater, bacteria convert mercury into toxic methylmercury, which attacks the central nervous system. Because fish absorb methylmercury, we are exposed to mercury by consuming mercury-contaminated fish. As levels of mercury ingested from fish became a concern, the Food and Drug Administration set a maximum level of one part mercury per million parts seafood (1 ppm), which is the same as 1 mg of mercury in every kilogram of seafood. Fish higher in the food chain, such as swordfish and shark, can have such high levels of mercury that the Environmental Protection Agency recommends they be consumed no more than once a week.

One of the worst incidents of mercury poisoning occurred in Minamata and Niigata, Japan, in 1950. At that time, the ocean was polluted with high levels of mercury from industrial wastes. Because fish were a major food in the diet, more than 2000 people were affected with mercury poisoning and died or developed neural damage. In the United States between 1988 and 1997, the use of mercury decreased by 75%

when the use of mercury was banned in paint and pesticides, and regulated in batteries and other products. Certain batteries and compact fluorescent light bulbs (CFL) contain mercury, and instructions for their safe disposal should be followed.

The element mercury is a silvery, shiny liquid at room temperature.

QUESTIONS AND PROBLEMS

4.1 Elements and Symbols

LEARNING GOAL Given the name of an element, write its correct symbol; from the symbol, write the correct name.

4.1 Write the symbols for the following elements:
  a. copper **b.** platinum **c.** calcium **d.** manganese
  e. iron **f.** barium **g.** lead **h.** strontium

4.2 Write the symbols for the following elements:
  a. oxygen **b.** lithium **c.** uranium **d.** titanium
  e. hydrogen **f.** chromium **g.** tin **h.** gold

℞ Clinical Applications

4.3 Write the name for the symbol of each of the following elements essential in the body:
  a. C **b.** Cl **c.** I **d.** Se
  e. N **f.** S **g.** Zn **h.** Co

4.4 Write the name for the symbol of each of the following elements essential in the body:
  a. V **b.** P **c.** Na **d.** As
  e. Ca **f.** Mo **g.** Mg **h.** Si

4.5   Write the names for the elements in each of the following formulas of compounds used in health and medicine:
a.   table salt, NaCl
b.   plaster casts, $CaSO_4$
c.   Demerol, $C_{15}H_{22}ClNO_2$
d.   treatment of bipolar disorder, Li_2CO_3

4.6   Write the names for the elements in each of the following formulas of compounds used in health and medicine:
a.   salt substitute, KCl
b.   dental cement, $Zn_3(PO_4)_2$
c.   antacid, $Mg(OH)_2$
d.   contrast agent for X-ray, $BaSO_4$

4.2 The Periodic Table

As more elements were discovered, it became necessary to organize them into some type of classification system. By the late 1800s, scientists recognized that certain elements looked alike and behaved much the same way. In 1872, a Russian chemist, Dmitri Mendeleev, arranged the 60 elements known at that time into groups with similar properties and placed them in order of increasing atomic masses. Today, this arrangement of 118 elements is known as the **periodic table** (see Figure 4.1).

LEARNING GOAL

Use the periodic table to identify the group and the period of an element; identify the element as a metal, a nonmetal, or a metalloid.

Periodic Table of Elements

FIGURE 4.1 ▶ On the periodic table, groups are the elements arranged as vertical columns, and periods are the elements in each horizontal row.

◉ What is the symbol of the alkali metal in Period 3?

Periods and Groups

Each horizontal row in the periodic table is a **period** (see Figure 4.2). The periods are counted from the top of the table as Periods 1 to 7. The first period contains two elements: hydrogen (H) and helium (He). The second period contains eight elements: lithium (Li), beryllium (Be), boron (B), carbon (C), nitrogen (N), oxygen (O), fluorine (F), and neon (Ne). The third period also contains eight elements beginning with sodium (Na) and ending with argon (Ar). The fourth period, which begins with potassium (K), and the fifth period, which begins with rubidium (Rb), have 18 elements each. The sixth period, which begins with cesium (Cs), has 32 elements. The seventh period, as of today, contains 32 elements, for a total of 118 elements.

Each vertical column on the periodic table contains a **group** (or family) of elements that have similar properties. A **group number** is written at the top of each vertical column (group) in the periodic table. For many years, the **representative elements** have had group numbers 1A to 8A. In the center of the periodic table is a block of elements known as the **transition**

elements, which have had group numbers followed by the letter "B." A newer system assigns numbers of 1 to 18 to all of the groups going left to right across the periodic table. Because both systems are currently in use, they are both shown on the periodic table in this text and are included in our discussions of elements and group numbers. The two rows of 14 elements called the *lanthanides* and *actinides* (or the inner transition elements), which are part of Periods 6 and 7, are placed at the bottom of the periodic table to allow it to fit on a page.

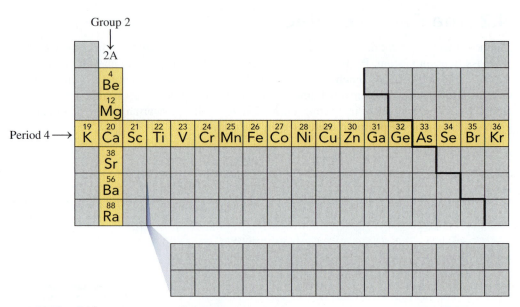

FIGURE 4.2 ▶ On the periodic table, each vertical column represents a group of elements and each horizontal row of elements represents a period.

🅠 Are the elements Si, P, and S part of a group or a period?

Names of Groups

Several groups in the periodic table have special names (see Figure 4.3). Group 1A (1) elements—lithium (Li), sodium (Na), potassium (K), rubidium (Rb), cesium (Cs), and francium (Fr)—are a family of elements known as the **alkali metals** (see Figure 4.4). The elements within this group are soft, shiny metals that are good conductors of heat and electricity and have relatively low melting points. Alkali metals react vigorously with water and form white products when they combine with oxygen.

Lithium (Li)

Sodium (Na)

Potassium (K)

FIGURE 4.4 ▶ Lithium (Li), sodium (Na), and potassium (K) are some alkali metals from Group 1A (1).

🅠 What physical properties do these alkali metals have in common?

FIGURE 4.3 ▶ Certain groups on the periodic table have common names.

🅠 What is the common name for the group of elements that includes helium and argon?

Major elements in the human body   Macrominerals   Microminerals (trace elements)

TABLE 4.4 Typical Amounts of Essential Elements in a 60.-kg Adult

Element	Quantity	Function
Major Elements		
Oxygen (O)	39 kg	Building block of biomolecules and water (H_2O)
Carbon (C)	11 kg	Building block of organic and biomolecules
Hydrogen (H)	6 kg	Component of biomolecules, water (H_2O), and pH of body fluids, stomach acid (HCl)
Nitrogen (N)	1.5 kg	Component of proteins and nucleic acids
Macrominerals		
Calcium (Ca)	1000 g	Needed for bones and teeth, muscle contraction, nerve impulses
Phosphorus (P)	600 g	Needed for bones and teeth, nucleic acids
Potassium (K)	120 g	Most prevalent positive ion (K^+) in cells, muscle contraction, nerve impulses
Chlorine (Cl)	100 g	Most prevalent negative ion (Cl^-) in fluids outside cells, stomach acid (HCl)
Sulfur (S)	86 g	Component of proteins, liver, vitamin B_1, insulin
Sodium (Na)	60 g	Most prevalent positive ion (Na^+) in fluids outside cells, water balance, muscle contraction, nerve impulses
Magnesium (Mg)	36 g	Component of bones, required for metabolic reactions
Microminerals (trace elements)		
Iron (Fe)	3600 mg	Component of oxygen carrier hemoglobin
Silicon (Si)	3000 mg	Needed for growth and maintenance of bones and teeth, tendons and ligaments, hair and skin
Zinc (Zn)	2000 mg	Used in metabolic reactions in cells, DNA synthesis, growth of bones, teeth, connective tissue, immune system
Copper (Cu)	240 mg	Needed for blood vessels, blood pressure, immune system
Manganese (Mn)	60 mg	Needed for growth of bones, blood clotting, necessary for metabolic reactions
Iodine (I)	20 mg	Needed for proper thyroid function
Molybdenum (Mo)	12 mg	Needed to process Fe and N from food
Arsenic (As)	3 mg	Needed for growth and reproduction
Chromium (Cr)	3 mg	Needed for maintenance of blood sugar levels, synthesis of biomolecules
Cobalt (Co)	3 mg	Component of vitamin B_{12}, red blood cells
Selenium (Se)	2 mg	Used in the immune system, health of heart and pancreas
Vanadium (V)	2 mg	Needed in the formation of bones and teeth, energy from food

QUESTIONS AND PROBLEMS

4.2 The Periodic Table

LEARNING GOAL Use the periodic table to identify the group and the period of an element; identify the element as a metal, a nonmetal, or a metalloid.

4.7 Identify the group or period number described by each of the following:
   a. contains the elements C, N, and O
   b. begins with helium
   c. contains the alkali metals
   d. ends with neon

4.8 Identify the group or period number described by each of the following:
   a. contains Na, K, and Rb
   b. begins with Li
   c. contains the noble gases
   d. contains F, Cl, Br, and I

4.9 Give the symbol of the element described by each of the following:
   a. Group 4A (14), Period 2
   b. a noble gas in Period 1
   c. an alkali metal in Period 3
   d. Group 2A (2), Period 4
   e. Group 3A (13), Period 3

4.10 Give the symbol of the element described by each of the following:
   a. an alkaline earth metal in Period 2
   b. Group 5A (15), Period 3
   c. a noble gas in Period 4
   d. a halogen in Period 5
   e. Group 4A (14), Period 4

4.11 Identify each of the following elements as a metal, a nonmetal, or a metalloid:
   a. calcium
   b. sulfur
   c. a shiny element
   d. an element that is a gas at room temperature
   e. located in Group 8A (18)
   f. bromine

   g. boron
   h. silver

4.12 Identify each of the following elements as a metal, a nonmetal, or a metalloid:
   a. located in Group 2A (2)
   b. a good conductor of electricity
   c. chlorine
   d. arsenic
   e. an element that is not shiny
   f. oxygen
   g. nitrogen
   h. tin

℞ Clinical Applications

4.13 Using Table 4.4, identify the function of each of the following in the body and classify each as an alkali metal, an alkaline earth metal, a transition element, or a halogen:
   a. Ca   **b.** Fe   **c.** K   **d.** Cl

4.14 Using Table 4.4, identify the function of each of the following in the body and classify each as an alkali metal, an alkaline earth metal, a transition element, or a halogen:
   a. Mg   **b.** Cu   **c.** I   **d.** Na

4.15 Using the Chemistry Link to Health: Elements Essential to Health, answer each of the following:
   a. What is a macromineral?
   b. What is the role of sulfur in the human body?
   c. How many grams of sulfur would be a typical amount in a 60.-kg adult?

4.16 Using the Chemistry Link to Health: Elements Essential to Health, answer each of the following:
   a. What is a micromineral?
   b. What is the role of iodine in the human body?
   c. How many milligrams of iodine would be a typical amount in a 60.-kg adult?

LEARNING GOAL

Describe the electrical charge and location in an atom for a proton, a neutron, and an electron.

4.3 The Atom

All the elements listed on the periodic table are made up of atoms. An **atom** is the smallest particle of an element that retains the characteristics of that element. Imagine that you are tearing a piece of aluminum foil into smaller and smaller pieces. Now imagine that you have a microscopic piece so small that it cannot be divided any further. Then you would have a single atom of aluminum.

The concept of the atom is relatively recent. Although the Greek philosophers in 500 B.C.E. reasoned that everything must contain minute particles they called *atomos*, the idea of atoms did not become a scientific theory until 1808. Then John Dalton (1766–1844) developed an atomic theory that proposed that atoms were responsible for the combinations of elements found in compounds.

Dalton's Atomic Theory

1. All matter is made up of tiny particles called atoms.
2. All atoms of a given element are similar to one another and different from atoms of other elements.
3. Atoms of two or more different elements combine to form compounds. A particular compound is always made up of the same kinds of atoms and always has the same number of each kind of atom.
4. A chemical reaction involves the rearrangement, separation, or combination of atoms. Atoms are neither created nor destroyed during a chemical reaction.

Dalton's atomic theory formed the basis of current atomic theory, although we have modified some of Dalton's statements. We now know that atoms of the same element are not completely identical to each other and consist of even smaller particles. However, an atom is still the smallest particle that retains the properties of an element.

Although atoms are the building blocks of everything we see around us, we cannot see an atom or even a billion atoms with the naked eye. However, when billions and billions of atoms are packed together, the characteristics of each atom are added to those of the next until we can see the characteristics we associate with the element. For example, a small piece of the shiny element nickel consists of many, many nickel atoms. A special kind of microscope called a *scanning tunneling microscope* (STM) produces images of individual atoms (see Figure 4.7).

Electrical Charges in an Atom

By the end of the 1800s, experiments with electricity showed that atoms were not solid spheres but were composed of even smaller bits of matter called **subatomic particles**, three of which are the *proton*, *neutron*, and *electron*. Two of these subatomic particles were discovered because they have electrical charges.

An electrical charge can be positive or negative. Experiments show that like charges repel or push away from each other. When you brush your hair on a dry day, electrical charges that are alike build up on the brush and in your hair. As a result, your hair flies away from the brush. However, opposite or unlike charges attract. The crackle of clothes taken from the clothes dryer indicates the presence of electrical charges. The clinginess of the clothing results from the attraction of opposite, unlike charges (see Figure 4.8).

Structure of the Atom

In 1897, J. J. Thomson, an English physicist, applied electricity to a glass tube, which produced streams of small particles called *cathode rays*. Because these rays were attracted to a positively charged electrode, Thomson realized that the particles in the rays must be negatively charged. In further experiments, these particles called **electrons** were found to be much smaller than the atom and to have extremely small masses. Because atoms are neutral, scientists soon discovered that atoms contained positively charged particles called **protons** that were much heavier than the electrons.

Aluminum foil consists of atoms of aluminum.

FIGURE 4.7 ▶ Images of nickel atoms are produced when nickel is magnified millions of times by a scanning tunneling microscope (STM).

Q Why is a microscope with extremely high magnification needed to see these atoms?

Positive charges repel

Negative charges repel

Unlike charges attract

FIGURE 4.8 ▶ Like charges repel and unlike charges attract.

Q Why are the electrons attracted to the protons in the nucleus of an atom?

Positive electrode
Electron beam
Cathode ray tube
Negatively charged cathode rays (electrons) are attracted to the positive electrode.

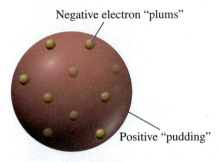

Negative electron "plums"

Positive "pudding"

Thomson's "plum-pudding" model had protons and electrons scattered throughout the atom.

Thomson proposed a "plum-pudding" model for the atom in which the electrons and protons were randomly distributed in a positively charged cloud like "plums in a pudding" or "chocolate chips in a cookie." In 1911, Ernest Rutherford worked with Thomson to test this model. In Rutherford's experiment, positively charged particles were aimed at a thin sheet of gold foil (see Figure 4.9). If the Thomson model were correct, the particles would travel in straight paths through the gold foil. Rutherford was greatly surprised to find that some of the particles were deflected as they passed through the gold foil, and a few particles were deflected so much that they went back in the opposite direction. According to Rutherford, it was as though he had shot a cannonball at a piece of tissue paper, and it bounced back at him.

From his gold-foil experiments, Rutherford realized that the protons must be contained in a small, positively charged region at the center of the atom, which he called the **nucleus**. He proposed that the electrons in the atom occupy the space surrounding the nucleus through which most of the particles traveled undisturbed. Only the particles that came near this dense, positive center were deflected. If an atom were the size of a football stadium, the nucleus would be about the size of a golf ball placed in the center of the field.

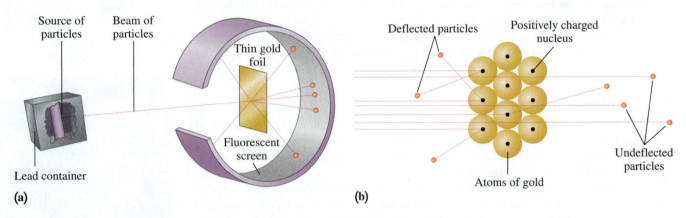

(a) Source of particles / Lead container / Beam of particles / Thin gold foil / Fluorescent screen

(b) Deflected particles / Positively charged nucleus / Undeflected particles / Atoms of gold

FIGURE 4.9 ▶ **(a)** Positive particles are aimed at a piece of gold foil. **(b)** Particles that come close to the atomic nuclei are deflected from their straight path.

Ⓠ Why are some particles deflected whereas most pass through the gold foil undeflected?

Interactive Video

Rutherford Gold-Foil Experiment

Scientists knew that the nucleus was heavier than the mass of the protons, so they looked for another subatomic particle. Eventually, they discovered that the nucleus also contained a particle that is neutral, which they called a **neutron**. Thus, the masses of the protons and neutrons in the nucleus determine the mass of an atom (see Figure 4.10).

Atomic diameter ~ 10^{-10} m

Electrons (−)

Nucleus (+)

Nuclear diameter ~ 10^{-15} m

Lithium metal   Lithium atoms

Proton ●   Neutron ●   Electron •

FIGURE 4.10 ▶ In an atom, the protons and neutrons that make up almost all the mass are packed into the tiny volume of the nucleus. The rapidly moving electrons (negative charge) surround the nucleus and account for the large volume of the atom.

Ⓠ Why can we say that the atom is mostly empty space?

Mass of the Atom

All the subatomic particles are extremely small compared with the things you see around you. One proton has a mass of 1.67×10^{-24} g, and the neutron is about the same. However, the electron has a mass 9.11×10^{-28} g, which is much less than the mass of either a proton or neutron. Because the masses of subatomic particles are so small, chemists use a very small unit of mass called an **atomic mass unit (amu)**. An amu is defined as one-twelfth of the mass of a carbon atom, which has a nucleus containing six protons and six neutrons. In biology, the atomic mass unit is called a *Dalton* (Da) in honor of John Dalton. On the amu scale, the proton and neutron each have a mass of about 1 amu. Because the electron mass is so small, it is usually ignored in atomic mass calculations. Table 4.5 summarizes some information about the subatomic particles in an atom.

TABLE 4.5 Subatomic Particles in the Atom

Particle	Symbol	Charge	Mass (amu)	Location in Atom
Proton	p or p^+	1+	1.007	Nucleus
Neutron	n or n^0	0	1.008	Nucleus
Electron	e^-	1−	0.000 55	Outside nucleus

▶ **SAMPLE PROBLEM 4.3** Subatomic Particles

Indicate whether each of the following is *true* or *false*:

a. A proton is heavier than an electron.
b. An electron is attracted to a neutron.
c. The nucleus contains all the protons and neutrons of an atom.

SOLUTION

a. True
b. False; an electron is attracted to a proton.
c. True

STUDY CHECK 4.3

Is the following statement *true* or *false*?
The nucleus occupies a large volume in an atom.

ANSWER

False, most of the volume of the atom is outside the nucleus.

Explore Your World
Repulsion and Attraction

Tear a small piece of paper into bits. Brush your hair several times, and place the brush just above the bits of paper. Use your knowledge of electrical charges to give an explanation for your observations. Try the same experiment with a comb.

Questions

1. What happens when objects with like charges are placed close together?
2. What happens when objects with unlike charges are placed close together?

QUESTIONS AND PROBLEMS

4.3 The Atom

LEARNING GOAL Describe the electrical charge and location in an atom for a proton, a neutron, and an electron.

4.17 Identify each of the following as describing either a proton, a neutron, or an electron:
 a. has the smallest mass
 b. has a 1+ charge
 c. is found outside the nucleus
 d. is electrically neutral

4.18 Identify each of the following as describing either a proton, a neutron, or an electron:
 a. has a mass about the same as a proton
 b. is found in the nucleus
 c. is attracted to the protons
 d. has a 1− charge

4.19 What did Rutherford determine about the structure of the atom from his gold-foil experiment?

4.20 How did Thomson determine that the electrons have a negative charge?

4.21 Is each of the following statements *true* or *false*?
 a. A proton and an electron have opposite charges.
 b. The nucleus contains most of the mass of an atom.
 c. Electrons repel each other.
 d. A proton is attracted to a neutron.

4.22 Is each of the following statements *true* or *false*?
 a. A proton is attracted to an electron.
 b. A neutron has twice the mass of a proton.
 c. Neutrons repel each other.
 d. Electrons and neutrons have opposite charges.

4.23 On a dry day, your hair flies apart when you brush it. How would you explain this?

4.24 Sometimes clothes cling together when removed from a dryer. What kinds of charges are on the clothes?

LEARNING GOAL

Given the atomic number and the mass number of an atom, state the number of protons, neutrons, and electrons.

CORE CHEMISTRY SKILL

Counting Protons and Neutrons

4.4 Atomic Number and Mass Number

All the atoms of the same element always have the same number of protons. This feature distinguishes atoms of one element from atoms of all the other elements.

Atomic Number

The **atomic number** of an element is equal to the number of protons in every atom of that element. The atomic number is the whole number that appears above the symbol of each element on the periodic table.

Atomic number = number of protons in an atom

The periodic table on the inside front cover of this text shows the elements in order of atomic number from 1 to 118. We can use an atomic number to identify the number of protons in an atom of any element. For example, a lithium atom, with atomic number 3, has 3 protons. Every lithium atom has 3 and only 3 protons. Any atom with 3 protons is always a lithium atom. In the same way, we determine that a carbon atom, with atomic number 6, has 6 protons. Every carbon atom has 6 protons, and any atom with 6 protons is carbon; every copper atom, with atomic number 29, has 29 protons and any atom with 29 protons is copper.

An atom is electrically neutral. That means that the number of protons in an atom is equal to the number of electrons, which gives every atom an overall charge of zero. Thus, for every atom, the atomic number also gives the number of electrons.

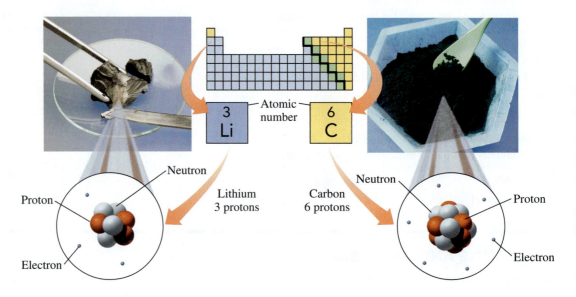

All atoms of lithium (left) contain three protons, and all atoms of carbon (right) contain six protons.

Mass Number

We now know that the protons and neutrons determine the mass of the nucleus. Thus, for a single atom, we assign a **mass number**, which is the total number of protons and neutrons in its nucleus. However, the mass number does not appear on the periodic table because it applies to single atoms only.

Mass number = number of protons + number of neutrons

For example, the nucleus of a single oxygen atom that contains 8 protons and 8 neutrons has a mass number of 16. An atom of iron that contains 26 protons and 32 neutrons has a mass number of 58.

If we are given the mass number of an atom and its atomic number, we can calculate the number of neutrons in its nucleus.

Number of neutrons in a nucleus = mass number − number of protons

For example, if we are given a mass number of 37 for an atom of chlorine (atomic number 17), we can calculate the number of neutrons in its nucleus.

Number of neutrons = 37 (mass number) − 17 (protons) = 20 neutrons

Table 4.6 illustrates these relationships between atomic number, mass number, and the number of protons, neutrons, and electrons in examples of single atoms for different elements.

TABLE 4.6 Composition of Some Atoms of Different Elements

Element	Symbol	Atomic Number	Mass Number	Number of Protons	Number of Neutrons	Number of Electrons
Hydrogen	H	1	1	1	0	1
Nitrogen	N	7	14	7	7	7
Oxygen	O	8	16	8	8	8
Chlorine	Cl	17	37	17	20	17
Potassium	K	19	39	19	20	19
Iron	Fe	26	58	26	32	26
Gold	Au	79	197	79	118	79

▶ **SAMPLE PROBLEM 4.4** Calculating Numbers of Protons, Neutrons, and Electrons

Zinc, a micromineral, is needed for metabolic reactions in cells, DNA synthesis, the growth of bones, teeth, and connective tissue, and the proper functioning of the immune system. For an atom of zinc that has a mass number of 68, determine the following:

a. the number of protons   **b.** the number of neutrons   **c.** the number of electrons

SOLUTION

	Given	Need
ANALYZE THE PROBLEM	zinc (Zn), mass number 68	number of protons, number of neutrons, number of electrons

a. Zinc (Zn), with an atomic number of 30, has 30 protons.
b. The number of neutrons in this atom is found by subtracting number of protons (atomic number) from the mass number.

Mass number − atomic number = number of neutrons
68 − 30 = 38

c. Because the zinc atom is neutral, the number of electrons is equal to the number of protons. A zinc atom has 30 electrons.

STUDY CHECK 4.4

How many neutrons are in the nucleus of a bromine atom that has a mass number of 80?

ANSWER
45

Chemistry Link to the **Environment**
Many Forms of Carbon

Carbon has the symbol C. However, its atoms can be arranged in different ways to give several different substances. Two forms of carbon—diamond and graphite—have been known since prehistoric times. In diamond, carbon atoms are arranged in a rigid structure. A diamond is transparent and harder than any other substance, whereas graphite is black and soft. In graphite, carbon atoms are arranged in sheets that slide over each other. Graphite is used as pencil lead, as lubricants, and as carbon fibers for the manufacture of lightweight golf clubs and tennis rackets.

Two other forms of carbon have been discovered more recently. In the form called *Buckminsterfullerene* or *buckyball* (named after R. Buckminster Fuller, who popularized the geodesic dome), 60 carbon atoms are arranged as rings of five and six atoms to give a spherical, cage-like structure. When a fullerene structure is stretched out, it produces a cylinder with a diameter of only a few nanometers called a *nanotube*. Practical uses for buckyballs and nanotubes are not yet developed, but they are expected to find use in lightweight structural materials, heat conductors, computer parts, and medicine. Recent research has shown that carbon nanotubes (CNTs) can carry many drug molecules that can be released once the CNTs enter the targeted cells.

Graphite

Diamond

Buckminsterfullerene

Nanotubes

Carbon atoms can form different types of structures.

QUESTIONS AND PROBLEMS

4.4 Atomic Number and Mass Number

LEARNING GOAL Given the atomic number and the mass number of an atom, state the number of protons, neutrons, and electrons.

4.25 Would you use the atomic number, mass number, or both to determine each of the following?
   a. number of protons in an atom
   b. number of neutrons in an atom
   c. number of particles in the nucleus
   d. number of electrons in a neutral atom

4.26 Identify the type of subatomic particles described by each of the following:
   a. atomic number
   b. mass number
   c. mass number − atomic number
   d. mass number + atomic number

4.27 Write the names and symbols for the elements with the following atomic numbers:
   a. 3   **b.** 9   **c.** 20   **d.** 30
   e. 10   **f.** 14   **g.** 53   **h.** 8

4.28 Write the names and symbols for the elements with the following atomic numbers:
   a. 1   **b.** 11   **c.** 19   **d.** 82
   e. 35   **f.** 47   **g.** 15   **h.** 2

4.29 How many protons and electrons are there in a neutral atom of each of the following elements?
   a. argon   **b.** manganese
   c. iodine   **d.** cadmium

4.30 How many protons and electrons are there in a neutral atom of each of the following elements?
   a. carbon   **b.** fluorine
   c. tin   **d.** nickel

℞ Clinical Applications

4.31 Complete the following table for atoms of essential elements in the body:

Name of the Element	Symbol	Atomic Number	Mass Number	Number of Protons	Number of Neutrons	Number of Electrons
	Zn		66			
		12			12	
Potassium					20	
				16	15	
			56			26

4.32 Complete the following table for atoms of essential elements in the body:

Name of the Element	Symbol	Atomic Number	Mass Number	Number of Protons	Number of Neutrons	Number of Electrons
	N		15			
Calcium			42			
				53	72	
			14		16	
		29	65			

4.5 Isotopes and Atomic Mass

We have seen that all atoms of the same element have the same number of protons and electrons. However, the atoms of any one element are not entirely identical because the atoms of most elements have different numbers of neutrons. When a sample of an element consists of two or more atoms with differing numbers of neutrons, those atoms are called *isotopes*.

Atoms and Isotopes

Isotopes are atoms of the same element that have the same atomic number but different numbers of neutrons. For example, all atoms of the element magnesium (Mg) have an atomic number of 12. Thus every magnesium atom always has 12 protons. However, some naturally occurring magnesium atoms have 12 neutrons, others have 13 neutrons, and still others have 14 neutrons. The different numbers of neutrons give the magnesium atoms different mass numbers but do not change their chemical behavior. The three isotopes of magnesium have the same atomic number but different mass numbers.

To distinguish between the different isotopes of an element, we write an **atomic symbol** for a particular isotope that indicates the mass number in the upper left corner and the atomic number in the lower left corner.

An isotope may be referred to by its name or symbol, followed by its mass number, such as magnesium-24 or Mg-24. Magnesium has three naturally occurring isotopes, as

Mass number ⟶
Atomic number ⟶ $^{24}_{12}\text{Mg}$ ⟵ Symbol of element

Atomic symbol for an isotope of magnesium, Mg-24.

shown in Table 4.7. In a large sample of naturally occurring magnesium atoms, each type of isotope can be present as a low percentage or a high percentage. For example, the Mg-24 isotope makes up almost 80% of the total sample, whereas Mg-25 and Mg-26 each make up only about 10% of the total number of magnesium atoms.

TABLE 4.7 Isotopes of Magnesium

Atomic Symbol	$^{24}_{12}\text{Mg}$	$^{25}_{12}\text{Mg}$	$^{26}_{12}\text{Mg}$
Name	Mg-24	Mg-25	Mg-26
Number of Protons	12	12	12
Number of Electrons	12	12	12
Mass Number	24	25	26
Number of Neutrons	12	13	14
Mass of Isotope (amu)	23.99	24.99	25.98
Percent Abundance	78.70	10.13	11.17

LEARNING GOAL

Determine the number of protons, neutrons, and electrons in one or more of the isotopes of an element; calculate the atomic mass of an element using the percent abundance and mass of its naturally occurring isotopes.

⚛ CORE CHEMISTRY SKILL

Writing Atomic Symbols for Isotopes

Atoms of Mg

Isotopes of Mg

$^{24}_{12}\text{Mg}$ $^{25}_{12}\text{Mg}$ $^{26}_{12}\text{Mg}$

The nuclei of three naturally occurring magnesium isotopes have the same number of protons but different numbers of neutrons.

▶ **SAMPLE PROBLEM 4.5** Identifying Protons and Neutrons in Isotopes

Chromium, a micromineral needed for maintenance of blood sugar levels, has four naturally occurring isotopes:

a. $^{50}_{24}Cr$ **b.** $^{52}_{24}Cr$ **c.** $^{53}_{24}Cr$ **d.** $^{54}_{24}Cr$

Determine the number of protons and number of neutrons in each of these isotopes.

SOLUTION

ANALYZE THE PROBLEM	Given	Need
	atomic symbols for Cr isotopes	number of protons, number of neutrons

In the atomic symbol, the mass number is shown in the upper left corner of the symbol, and the atomic number is shown in the lower left corner of the symbol. Thus, each isotope of Cr, atomic number 24, has 24 protons. The number of neutrons is found by subtracting the number of protons (24) from the mass number of each isotope.

Atomic Symbol	Atomic Number	Mass Number	Number of Protons	Number of Neutrons
a. $^{50}_{24}Cr$	24	50	24	26 (50 − 24)
b. $^{52}_{24}Cr$	24	52	24	28 (52 − 24)
c. $^{53}_{24}Cr$	24	53	24	29 (53 − 24)
d. $^{54}_{24}Cr$	24	53	24	30 (54 − 24)

STUDY CHECK 4.5

Vanadium is a micromineral needed in the formation of bones and teeth. Write the atomic symbol for the single naturally occurring isotope of vanadium, which has 27 neutrons.

ANSWER

$^{50}_{23}V$

Vanadium along with calcium is important in forming strong bones and preventing osteoporosis.

Atomic Mass

In laboratory work, a chemist generally uses samples with many atoms that contain all the different atoms or isotopes of an element. Because each isotope has a different mass, chemists have calculated an **atomic mass** for an "average atom," which is a *weighted average* of the masses of all the naturally occurring isotopes of that element. On the periodic table, the atomic mass is the number including decimal places that is given below the symbol of each element. Most elements consist of two or more isotopes, which is one reason that the atomic masses on the periodic table are seldom whole numbers.

Weighted Average Analogy

To understand how the atomic mass as a weighted average for a group of isotopes is calculated, we will use an analogy of bowling balls with different weights. Suppose that a bowling alley has ordered 5 bowling balls that weigh 8 lb each and 20 bowling balls that weigh 14 lb each. In this group of bowling balls, there are more 14-lb balls than 8-lb balls. The abundance of the 14-lb balls is 80.% (20/25), and the abundance of the 8-lb balls is 20.% (5/25). Now we can calculate a weighted average for the "average" bowling ball using the weight and percent abundance of the two types of bowling balls.

The weighted average of 8-lb and 14-lb bowling balls is calculated using their percent abundance.

	Weight		Percent Abundance		Weight from Each Type
14-lb bowling balls	14 lb	×	$\frac{80.}{100}$	=	11.2 lb
8-lb bowling balls	8 lb	×	$\frac{20.}{100}$	=	1.6 lb
	Weighted average of a bowling ball			=	12.8 lb
	"Atomic mass" of a bowling ball			=	12.8 lb

Calculating Atomic Mass

To calculate the atomic mass of an element, we need to know the percentage abundance and the mass of each isotope, which must be determined experimentally. For example, a large sample of naturally occurring chlorine atoms consists of 75.76% of $^{35}_{17}Cl$ atoms and 24.24% of $^{37}_{17}Cl$ atoms. The $^{35}_{17}Cl$ isotope has a mass of 34.97 amu and the $^{37}_{17}Cl$ isotope has a mass of 36.97 amu.

$$\text{Atomic mass of Cl} = \text{mass of } ^{35}_{17}Cl \times \frac{^{35}_{17}Cl\%}{100\%} + \text{mass of } ^{37}_{17}Cl \times \frac{^{37}_{17}Cl\%}{100\%}$$

amu from $^{35}_{17}Cl$ amu from $^{37}_{17}Cl$

Atomic Symbol	Mass (amu)	×	Abundance (%)	=	Contribution to Average Cl Atom
$^{35}_{17}Cl$	34.97	×	$\frac{75.76}{100}$	=	26.49 amu
$^{37}_{17}Cl$	36.97	×	$\frac{24.24}{100}$	=	8.962 amu
			Atomic mass of Cl	=	35.45 amu (weighted average mass)

The atomic mass of 35.45 amu is the weighted average mass of a sample of Cl atoms, although no individual Cl atom actually has this mass. An atomic mass of 35.45, which is closer to the mass number of Cl-35, also indicates there is a higher percentage of $^{35}_{17}Cl$ atoms in the chlorine sample. In fact, there are about three atoms of $^{35}_{17}Cl$ for every one atom of $^{37}_{17}Cl$ in a sample of chlorine atoms.

Table 4.8 lists the naturally occurring isotopes of some selected elements and their atomic masses along with their most prevalent isotopes.

TABLE 4.8 The Atomic Mass of Some Elements

Element	Atomic Symbols	Atomic Mass (weighted average)	Most Prevalent Isotope
Lithium	$^6_3Li, ^7_3Li$	6.941 amu	^7_3Li
Carbon	$^{12}_6C, ^{13}_6C, ^{14}_6C$	12.01 amu	$^{12}_6C$
Oxygen	$^{16}_8O, ^{17}_8O, ^{18}_8O$	16.00 amu	$^{16}_8O$
Fluorine	$^{19}_9F$	19.00 amu	$^{19}_9F$
Sulfur	$^{32}_{16}S, ^{33}_{16}S, ^{34}_{16}S, ^{36}_{16}S$	32.07 amu	$^{32}_{16}S$
Potassium	$^{39}_{19}K, ^{40}_{19}K, ^{41}_{19}K$	39.10 amu	$^{39}_{19}K$
Copper	$^{63}_{29}Cu, ^{65}_{29}Cu$	63.55 amu	$^{63}_{29}Cu$

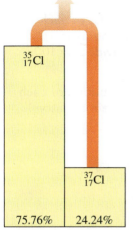

Chlorine, with two naturally occurring isotopes, has an atomic mass of 35.45 amu.

Magnesium, with three naturally occurring isotopes, has an atomic mass of 24.31 amu.

▶**SAMPLE PROBLEM 4.6** Calculating Atomic Mass

Magnesium is a macromineral needed in the contraction of muscles and metabolic reactions. Using Table 4.7, calculate the atomic mass for magnesium using the weighted average mass method.

SOLUTION

STEP 1 Multiply the mass of each isotope by its percent abundance divided by 100.

Atomic Symbol	Mass (amu)		Abundance (%)		Contribution to the Atomic Mass
$^{24}_{12}Mg$	23.99	×	$\frac{78.70}{100}$	=	18.88 amu
$^{25}_{12}Mg$	24.99	×	$\frac{10.13}{100}$	=	2.531 amu
$^{26}_{12}Mg$	25.98	×	$\frac{11.17}{100}$	=	2.902 amu

STEP 2 Add the contribution of each isotope to obtain the atomic mass. Add the contribution of each isotope to give the weighted average mass, which is the atomic mass.

Atomic mass of Mg = 18.88 amu + 2.531 amu + 2.902 amu
= 24.31 amu (weighted average mass)

STUDY CHECK 4.6

There are two naturally occurring isotopes of boron. The isotope $^{10}_{5}B$ has a mass of 10.01 amu with an abundance of 19.80%, and the isotope $^{11}_{5}B$ has a mass of 11.01 amu with an abundance of 80.20%. Calculate the atomic mass for boron using the weighted average mass method.

ANSWER

10.81 amu

Guide to Calculating Atomic Mass

STEP 1
Multiply the mass of each isotope by its percent abundance divided by 100.

STEP 2
Add the contribution of each isotope to obtain the atomic mass.

QUESTIONS AND PROBLEMS

4.5 Isotopes and Atomic Mass

LEARNING GOAL Determine the number of protons, neutrons, and electrons in one or more of the isotopes of an element; calculate the atomic mass of an element using the percent abundance and mass of its naturally occurring isotopes.

4.33 What are the number of protons, neutrons, and electrons in the following isotopes?
   a. $^{89}_{38}Sr$ **b.** $^{52}_{24}Cr$
   c. $^{34}_{16}S$ **d.** $^{81}_{35}Br$

4.34 What are the number of protons, neutrons, and electrons in the following isotopes?
   a. $^{2}_{1}H$ **b.** $^{14}_{7}N$
   c. $^{26}_{14}Si$ **d.** $^{70}_{30}Zn$

4.35 Write the atomic symbol for the isotope with each of the following characteristics:
   a. 15 protons and 16 neutrons
   b. 35 protons and 45 neutrons
   c. 50 electrons and 72 neutrons
   d. a chlorine atom with 18 neutrons
   e. a mercury atom with 122 neutrons

4.36 Write the atomic symbol for the isotope with each of the following characteristics:
   a. an oxygen atom with 10 neutrons
   b. 4 protons and 5 neutrons
   c. 25 electrons and 28 neutrons
   d. a mass number of 24 and 13 neutrons
   e. a nickel atom with 32 neutrons

4.37 Argon has three naturally occurring isotopes, with mass numbers 36, 38, and 40.
  a. Write the atomic symbol for each of these atoms.
  b. How are these isotopes alike?
  c. How are they different?
  d. Why is the atomic mass of argon listed on the periodic table not a whole number?
  e. Which isotope is the most prevalent in a sample of argon?

4.38 Strontium has four naturally occurring isotopes, with mass numbers 84, 86, 87, and 88.
  a. Write the atomic symbol for each of these atoms.
  b. How are these isotopes alike?
  c. How are they different?
  d. Why is the atomic mass of strontium listed on the periodic table not a whole number?
  e. Which isotope is the most prevalent in a sample of strontium?

4.39 Two isotopes of gallium are naturally occurring, with $^{69}_{31}Ga$ at 60.11% (68.93 amu) and $^{71}_{31}Ga$ at 39.89% (70.92 amu). Calculate the atomic mass for gallium using the weighted average mass method.

4.40 Two isotopes of rubidium occur naturally, with $^{85}_{37}Rb$ at 72.17% (84.91 amu) and $^{87}_{37}Rb$ at 27.83% (86.91 amu). Calculate the atomic mass for rubidium using the weighted average mass method.

4.6 Electron Energy Levels

LEARNING GOAL

Describe the energy levels, sublevels, and orbitals for the electrons in an atom.

When we listen to a radio, use a microwave oven, turn on a light, see the colors of a rainbow, or have an X-ray taken, we are experiencing various forms of *electromagnetic radiation*. Light and other electromagnetic radiation consist of energy particles that move as waves of energy. In a wave, just like the waves in an ocean, the distance between the peaks is called the *wavelength*. All forms of electromagnetic radiation travel in space at the speed of light, 3.0×10^8 m/s, but differ in energy and wavelength. High-energy radiation has short wavelengths compared to low-energy radiation, which has longer wavelengths. The *electromagnetic spectrum* shows the arrangement of different types of electromagnetic radiation in order of increasing energy (see Figure 4.11).

When the light from the Sun passes through a prism, the light separates into a continuous color spectrum, which consists of the colors we see in a rainbow. In contrast, when light from a heated element passes through a prism, it separates into distinct lines of color separated by dark areas called an *atomic spectrum*. Each element has its own unique atomic spectrum.

A rainbow forms when light passes through water droplets.

Light passes through a slit   Prism   Film

Barium light spectrum

In an atomic spectrum, light from a heated element separates into distinct lines.

Electron Energy Levels

Scientists have now determined that the lines in the atomic spectra of elements are associated with changes in the energies of the electrons. In an atom, each electron has a specific energy known as its **energy level**, which is assigned values called *principal quantum numbers* (n), $(n = 1, n = 2, \ldots)$. Generally, electrons in the lower energy levels are closer to the nucleus, whereas electrons in the higher energy levels are farther away. The energy of an electron is *quantized*, which means that the energy of an electron can only have specific energy values, but cannot have values between them.

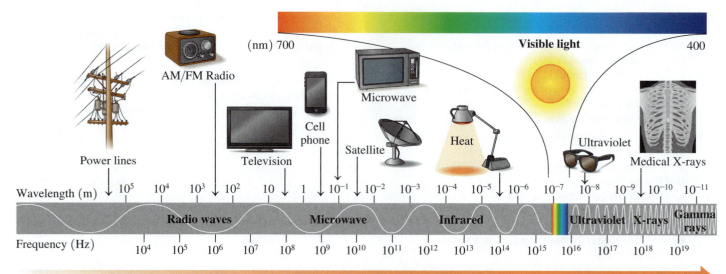

Wavelength (m) 10^5 10^4 10^3 10^2 10 1 10^{-1} 10^{-2} 10^{-3} 10^{-4} 10^{-5} 10^{-6} 10^{-7} 10^{-8} 10^{-9} 10^{-10} 10^{-11}

Radio waves   Microwave   Infrared   Ultraviolet   X-rays   Gamma rays

Frequency (Hz) 10^4 10^5 10^6 10^7 10^8 10^9 10^{10} 10^{11} 10^{12} 10^{13} 10^{14} 10^{15} 10^{16} 10^{17} 10^{18} 10^{19}

Energy Increases

Low energy   High energy

FIGURE 4.11 ▶ The electromagnetic spectrum shows the arrangement of wavelengths of electromagnetic radiation. The visible portion consists of wavelengths from 700 nm to 400 nm.

Q How does the wavelength of ultraviolet light compare to that of a microwave?

Order of Increasing Energy of Levels

$$1 < 2 < 3 < 4 < 5 < 6 < 7$$

Lowest   ⟶   Highest
energy   energy

All the electrons with the same energy are grouped in the same energy level. As an analogy, we can think of the energy levels of an atom as similar to the shelves in a bookcase. The first shelf is the lowest energy level; the second shelf is the second energy level,

---

Chemistry Link to **Health**
Biological Reactions to UV Light

Our everyday life depends on sunlight, but exposure to sunlight can have damaging effects on living cells, and too much exposure can even cause their death. The light energy, especially ultraviolet (UV), excites electrons and may lead to unwanted chemical reactions. The list of damaging effects of sunlight includes sunburn; wrinkling; premature aging of the skin; changes in the DNA of the cells, which can lead to skin cancers; inflammation of the eyes; and perhaps cataracts. Some drugs, like the acne medications Accutane and Retin-A, as well as antibiotics, diuretics, sulfonamides, and estrogen, make the skin extremely sensitive to light.

However, medicine does take advantage of the beneficial effect of sunlight. *Phototherapy* can be used to treat certain skin conditions, including psoriasis, eczema, and dermatitis. In the treatment of psoriasis, for example, oral drugs are given to make the skin more photosensitive; exposure to UV follows. Low-energy light is used to break down bilirubin in neonatal jaundice. Sunlight is also a factor in stimulating the immune system.

Babies with neonatal jaundice are treated with UV light.

In a disorder called *seasonal affective disorder* or SAD, people experience mood swings and depression during the winter. Some research suggests that SAD is the result of a decrease of serotonin, or an increase in melatonin, when there are fewer hours of sunlight. One treatment for SAD is therapy using bright light provided by a lamp called a light box. A daily exposure to intense light for 30 to 60 min seems to reduce symptoms of SAD.

and so on. If we are arranging books on the shelves, it would take less energy to fill the bottom shelf first, and then the second shelf, and so on. However, we could never get any book to stay in the space between any of the shelves. Similarly, the energy of an electron must be at specific energy levels, and not between.

Unlike standard bookcases, however, there is a large difference between the energy of the first and second levels, but then the higher energy levels are closer together. Another difference is that the lower electron energy levels hold fewer electrons than the higher energy levels.

Changes in Electron Energy Level

An electron can change from one energy level to a higher level only if it absorbs the energy equal to the difference in energy levels. When an electron changes to a lower energy level, it emits energy equal to the difference between the two levels (see Figure 4.12). If the energy emitted is in the visible range, we see one of the colors of visible light. The yellow color of sodium streetlights and the red color of neon lights are examples of electrons emitting energy in the visible color range.

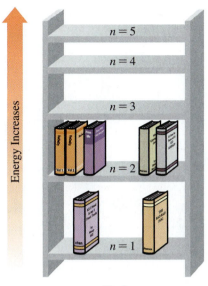

An electron can have only the energy of one of the energy levels in an atom.

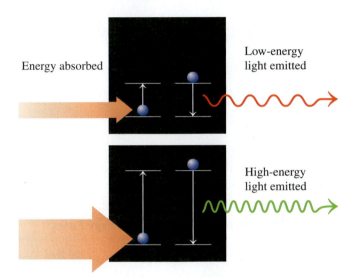

FIGURE 4.12 ▶ Electrons absorb a specific amount of energy to move to a higher energy level. When electrons lose energy, a specific quantity of energy is emitted.

Q What causes electrons to move to higher energy levels?

Chemistry Link to the **Environment**

Energy-Saving Fluorescent Bulbs

Compact fluorescent lights (CFL) are replacing the standard light bulb we use in our homes and workplaces. Compared to a standard light bulb, the CFL has a longer life and uses less electricity. Within about 20 days of use, the CFL saves enough money in electricity costs to pay for its higher initial cost.

A standard incandescent light bulb has a thin tungsten filament inside a sealed glass bulb. When the light is switched on, electricity flows through this filament, and electrical energy is converted to heat energy. When the filament reaches a temperature around 2300 °C, we see white light.

A fluorescent bulb produces light in a different way. When the switch is turned on, electrons move between two electrodes and collide with mercury atoms in a mixture of mercury and argon gas inside the light. When the electrons in the mercury atoms absorb energy from the collisions, they are raised to higher energy levels. As electrons fall to lower energy levels emitting ultraviolet radiation, they strike the phosphor coating inside the tube, and fluorescence occurs as visible light is emitted.

The production of light in a fluorescent bulb is more efficient than in an incandescent light bulb. A 75-watt incandescent bulb can be replaced by a 20-watt CFL that gives the same amount of light, providing a 70% reduction in electricity costs. A typical incandescent light bulb lasts for one to two months, whereas a CFL lasts from 1 to 2 yr. One drawback of the CFL is that each contains about 4 mg of mercury. As long as the bulb stays intact, no mercury is released. However, used CFL bulbs should not be disposed of in household trash but rather should be taken to a recycling center.

A compact fluorescent light (CFL) uses up to 70% less energy.

Sublevels

We have seen that the protons and neutrons are contained in the small, dense nucleus of an atom. However, it is the electrons within the atoms that determine the physical and chemical properties of the elements. Therefore, we will look at the arrangement of electrons within the large volume of space surrounding the nucleus.

Each of the energy levels consists of one or more **sublevels**, in which electrons with identical energy are found. The sublevels are identified by the letters s, p, d, and f. The number of sublevels within an energy level is equal to the principal quantum number, n. For example, the first energy level ($n = 1$) has only one sublevel, $1s$. The second energy level ($n = 2$) has two sublevels, $2s$ and $2p$. The third energy level ($n = 3$) has three sublevels, $3s$, $3p$, and $3d$. The fourth energy level ($n = 4$) has four sublevels, $4s$, $4p$, $4d$, and $4f$. Energy levels $n = 5$, $n = 6$, and $n = 7$ also have as many sublevels as the value of n, but only s, p, d, and f sublevels are needed to hold the electrons in atoms of the 118 known elements (see Figure 4.13).

Energy Level	Number of Sublevels	Types of Sublevels			
		s	p	d	f
$n = 4$	4	▢	▢▢▢	▢▢▢▢▢	▢▢▢▢▢▢▢
$n = 3$	3	▢	▢▢▢	▢▢▢▢▢	
$n = 2$	2	▢	▢▢▢		
$n = 1$	1	▢			

FIGURE 4.13 ▶ The number of sublevels in an energy level is the same as the principal quantum number, n.

Q How many sublevels are in the $n = 5$ energy level?

Within each energy level, the s sublevel has the lowest energy. If there are additional sublevels, the p sublevel has the next lowest energy, then the d sublevel, and finally the f sublevel.

Order of Increasing Energy of Sublevels in an Energy Level

$$s < p < d < f$$

Lowest energy $\longrightarrow$ Highest energy

Orbitals

There is no way to know the exact location of an electron in an atom. Instead, scientists describe the location of an electron in terms of probability. The **orbital** is the three-dimensional volume in which electrons have the highest probability of being found.

As an analogy, imagine that you could draw a circle with a 100-m radius around your chemistry classroom. There is a high probability of finding you within that circle when your chemistry class is in session. But once in a while, you may be outside that circle because you were sick or your car did not start.

3s

2s

1s

s orbitals

(a)   **(b)**

FIGURE 4.14 ▶ **(a)** The electron cloud of an s orbital represents the highest probability of finding an s electron. **(b)** The s orbitals are shown as spheres. The sizes of the s orbitals increase because they contain electrons at higher energy levels.

Q Is the probability high or low of finding an s electron outside an s orbital?

Shapes of Orbitals

Each type of orbital has a unique three-dimensional shape. Electrons in an s orbital are most likely found in a region with a spherical shape. Imagine that you take a picture of the location of an electron in an s orbital every second for an hour. When all these pictures are overlaid, the result, called a *probability density*, would look like the electron cloud shown in Figure 4.14a. For convenience, we draw this electron cloud as a sphere called an s orbital. There is one s orbital for every energy level starting with $n = 1$. For example, in the first, second, and third energy levels there are s orbitals designated as $1s$, $2s$, and $3s$. As the principal quantum number increases, there is an increase in the size of the s orbitals, although the shape is the same (see Figure 4.14b).

The orbitals occupied by *p*, *d*, and *f* electrons have three-dimensional shapes different from those of the *s* electrons. There are three *p* orbitals, starting with $n = 2$. Each *p* orbital has two lobes like a balloon tied in the middle. The three *p* orbitals are arranged in three perpendicular directions, along the *x*, *y*, and *z* axes around the nucleus (see Figure 4.15). As with *s* orbitals, the shape of *p* orbitals is the same, but the volume increases at higher energy levels.

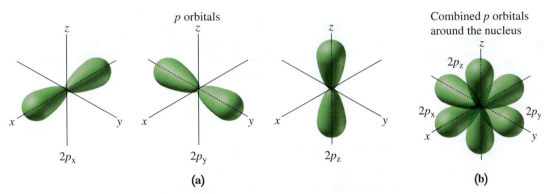

FIGURE 4.15 ▶ A *p* orbital has two regions of high probability, which gives a "dumbbell" shape. **(a)** Each *p* orbital is aligned along a different axis from the other *p* orbitals. **(b)** All three *p* orbitals are shown around the nucleus.

 What are some similarities and differences of the *p* orbitals in the $n = 3$ energy level?

In summary, the $n = 2$ energy level, which has 2*s* and 2*p* sublevels, consists of one *s* orbital and three *p* orbitals.

Energy level $n = 2$ consists of one 2*s* orbital and three 2*p* orbitals.

Energy level $n = 3$ consists of three sublevels *s*, *p*, and *d*. The *d* sublevels contain five *d* orbitals (see Figure 4.16).

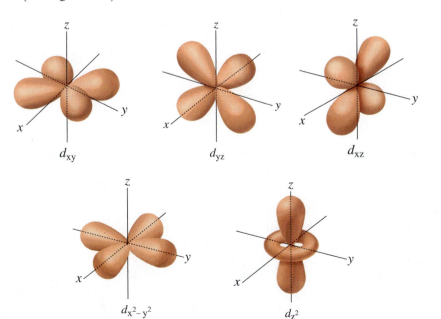

FIGURE 4.16 ▶ Four of the five *d* orbitals consist of four lobes that are aligned along or between different axes. One *d* orbital consists of two lobes and a doughnut-shaped ring around its center.

 How many orbitals are there in the 5*d* sublevel?

Energy level $n = 4$ consists of four sublevels s, p, d, and f. In the f sublevel, there are seven f orbitals. The shapes of f orbitals are complex and so we have not included them in this text.

Orbital Capacity and Electron Spin

The *Pauli exclusion principle* states that each orbital can hold a maximum of two electrons. According to a useful model for electron behavior, an electron is seen as spinning on its axis, which generates a magnetic field. When two electrons are in the same orbital, they will repel each other unless their magnetic fields cancel. This happens only when the two electrons spin in opposite directions. We can represent the spins of the electrons in the same orbital with one arrow pointing up and the other pointing down.

Electron spinning   Electron spinning
counterclockwise   clockwise

Opposite spins of
electrons in an orbital

An orbital can hold up to two
electrons with opposite spins.

Number of Electrons in Sublevels

There is a maximum number of electrons that can occupy each sublevel. An s sublevel holds one or two electrons. Because each p orbital can hold up to two electrons, the three p orbitals in a p sublevel can accommodate six electrons. A d sublevel with five d orbitals can hold a maximum of 10 electrons. With seven f orbitals, an f sublevel can hold up to 14 electrons.

As mentioned earlier, higher energy levels such as $n = 5, 6$, and 7 would have 5, 6, and 7 sublevels, but those beyond sublevel f are not utilized by the atoms of the elements known today. The total number of electrons in all the sublevels adds up to give the electrons allowed in an energy level. The number of sublevels, the number of orbitals, and the maximum number of electrons for energy levels 1 to 4 are shown in Table 4.9.

TABLE 4.9 Electron Capacity in Sublevels for Energy Levels 1 to 4

Energy Level (n)	Number of Sublevels	Type of Sublevel	Number of Orbitals	Maximum Number of Electrons	Total Electrons
4	4	4f	7	14	
		4d	5	10	
		4p	3	6	32
		4s	1	2	
3	3	3d	5	10	
		3p	3	6	18
		3s	1	2	
2	2	2p	3	6	
		2s	1	2	8
1	1	1s	1	2	2

QUESTIONS AND PROBLEMS

4.6 Electron Energy Levels

LEARNING GOAL Describe the energy levels, sublevels, and orbitals for the electrons in an atom.

4.41 Describe the shape of each of the following orbitals:
  a. 1s **b.** 2p **c.** 5s

4.42 Describe the shape of each of the following orbitals:
  a. 3p **b.** 6s **c.** 4p

4.43 Match statements **1** to **3** with **a** to **d**:
  1. They have the same shape.
  2. The maximum number of electrons is the same.
  3. They are in the same energy level.

  a. 1s and 2s orbitals   **b.** 3s and 3p sublevels
  c. 3p and 4p sublevels   **d.** three 3p orbitals

4.44 Match statements **1** to **3** with **a** to **d**:
1. They have the same shape.
2. The maximum number of electrons is the same.
3. They are in the same energy level.

   a. 5s and 6s orbitals   **b.** 3p and 4p orbitals
   c. 3s and 4s sublevels   **d.** 2s and 2p orbitals

4.45 Indicate the number of each in the following:
   a. orbitals in the 3d sublevel
   b. sublevels in the $n = 1$ energy level
   c. orbitals in the 6s sublevel
   d. orbitals in the $n = 3$ energy level

4.46 Indicate the number of each in the following:
   a. orbitals in the $n = 2$ energy level
   b. sublevels in the $n = 4$ energy level
   c. orbitals in the 5f sublevel
   d. orbitals in the 6p sublevel

4.47 Indicate the maximum number of electrons in the following:
   a. 2p orbital   **b.** 3p sublevel
   c. $n = 4$ energy level   **d.** 5d sublevel

4.48 Indicate the maximum number of electrons in the following:
   a. 3s sublevel   **b.** 4p orbital
   c. $n = 3$ energy level   **d.** 4f sublevel

4.7 Electron Configurations

We can now look at how electrons are arranged in the orbitals within an atom. An **orbital diagram** shows the placement of the electrons in the orbitals in order of increasing energy (Figure 4.17). In this energy diagram, we see that the electrons in the 1s orbital have the lowest energy level. The energy level is higher for the 2s orbital and is even higher for the 2p orbitals.

LEARNING GOAL

Draw the orbital diagram and write the electron configuration for an element.

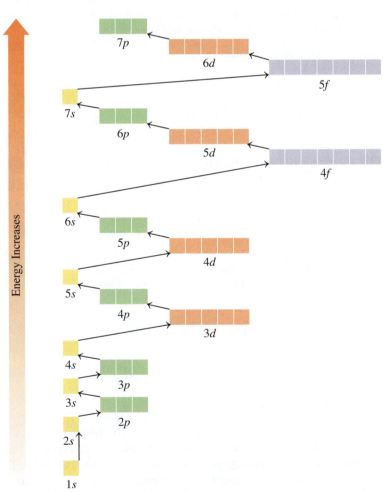

FIGURE 4.17 ▶ The orbitals in an atom fill in order of increasing energy beginning with 1s.

Q Why do 3d orbitals fill after the 4s orbital?

We begin our discussion of electron configuration by using orbital diagrams in which boxes represent the orbitals. Any orbital can have a maximum of two electrons.

To draw an orbital diagram, the lowest energy orbitals are filled first. For example, we can draw the orbital diagram for carbon. The atomic number of carbon is 6, which means that a carbon atom has six electrons. The first two electrons go into the $1s$ orbital; the next two electrons go into the $2s$ orbital. In the orbital diagram, the two electrons in the $1s$ and $2s$ orbitals are shown with opposite spins; the first arrow is up and the second is down. The last two electrons in carbon begin to fill the $2p$ sublevel, which has the next lowest energy. However, there are three $2p$ orbitals of equal energy. Because the negatively charged electrons repel each other, they are placed in separate $2p$ orbitals. With few exceptions (which will be noted later in this chapter) lower energy sublevels are filled first, and then the "building" of electrons continues to the next lowest energy sublevel that is available until all the electrons are placed.

Electron Configurations

Chemists use a notation called the **electron configuration** to indicate the placement of the electrons of an atom in order of increasing energy. The electron configuration is written with the lowest energy sublevel first, followed by the next lowest energy sublevel. The number of electrons in each sublevel is shown as a superscript.

Electron Configuration for Carbon

Period 1: Hydrogen and Helium

We will draw orbital diagrams and write electron configurations for the elements H and He in Period 1. The $1s$ orbital (which is the $1s$ sublevel) is written first because it has the lowest energy. Hydrogen has one electron in the $1s$ sublevel; helium has two. In the orbital diagram, the electrons for helium are shown as arrows pointing in opposite directions.

Element	Atomic Number	Orbital Diagram	Electron Configuration
		$1s$	
H	1	↑	$1s^1$
He	2	↑↓	$1s^2$

Period 2: Lithium to Neon

Period 2 begins with lithium, which has three electrons. The first two electrons fill the $1s$ orbital, whereas the third electron goes into the $2s$ orbital, the sublevel with the next lowest energy. In beryllium, another electron is added to complete the $2s$ orbital. The next six electrons are used to fill the $2p$ orbitals. The electrons are added one at a time from boron to nitrogen, which gives three half-filled $2p$ orbitals.

From oxygen to neon, the remaining three electrons are paired up using opposite spins to complete the $2p$ sublevel. In writing the electron configurations for the elements in Period 2, begin with the $1s$ orbital followed by the $2s$ and then the $2p$ orbitals.

An electron configuration can also be written in an *abbreviated configuration*. The electron configuration of the preceding noble gas is replaced by writing its element symbol inside square brackets. For example, the electron configuration for lithium, $1s^2 2s^1$, can be abbreviated as $[He]2s^1$ where $[He]$ replaces $1s^2$.

Element	Atomic Number	Orbital Diagram	Electron Configuration	Abbreviated Electron Configuration
Li	3		$1s^2 2s^1$	$[He]2s^1$
Be	4		$1s^2 2s^2$	$[He]2s^2$
B	5		$1s^2 2s^2 2p^1$	$[He]2s^2 2p^1$
C	6		$1s^2 2s^2 2p^2$	$[He]2s^2 2p^2$
N	7		$1s^2 2s^2 2p^3$	$[He]2s^2 2p^3$
O	8		$1s^2 2s^2 2p^4$	$[He]2s^2 2p^4$
F	9		$1s^2 2s^2 2p^5$	$[He]2s^2 2p^5$
Ne	10		$1s^2 2s^2 2p^6$	$[He]2s^2 2p^6$

Unpaired electrons

►SAMPLE PROBLEM 4.7 Drawing Orbital Diagrams

Nitrogen is an element that is used in the formation of amino acids, proteins, and nucleic acids. Draw the orbital diagram for nitrogen.

SOLUTION

STEP 1 **Draw boxes to represent the occupied orbitals.** Nitrogen has atomic number 7, which means it has seven electrons. For the orbital diagram, we draw boxes to represent the $1s$, $2s$, and $2p$ orbitals.

$1s$ $2s$ $2p$

STEP 2 **Place a pair of electrons with opposite spins in each filled orbital.** First, we place a pair of electrons with opposite spins in both the $1s$ and $2s$ orbitals.

$1s$ $2s$ $2p$

STEP 3 **Place the remaining electrons in the last occupied sublevel in separate orbitals.** Then we place the three remaining electrons in three separate $2p$ orbitals with arrows drawn in the same direction.

$1s$ $2s$ $2p$

Orbital diagram for nitrogen (N)

Guide to Drawing Orbital Diagrams

STEP 1
Draw boxes to represent the occupied orbitals.

STEP 2
Place a pair of electrons with opposite spins in each filled orbital.

STEP 3
Place the remaining electrons in the last occupied sublevel in separate orbitals.

STUDY CHECK 4.7

Draw the orbital diagram for fluorine.

ANSWER

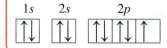

1s   2s   2p

Period 3: Sodium to Argon

In Period 3, electrons enter the orbitals of the $3s$ and $3p$ sublevels, but not the $3d$ sublevel. We notice that the elements sodium to argon, which are directly below the elements lithium to neon in Period 2, have a similar pattern of filling their s and p orbitals. In sodium and magnesium, one and two electrons go into the $3s$ orbital. The electrons for aluminum, silicon, and phosphorus go into separate $3p$ orbitals. The remaining electrons in sulfur, chlorine, and argon are paired up (opposite spins) with the electrons already in the $3p$ orbitals. For the abbreviated electron configurations of Period 3, the symbol [Ne] replaces $1s^2 2s^2 2p^6$.

Element	Atomic Number	Orbital Diagram (3s and 3p orbitals only)		Electron Configuration	Abbreviated Electron Configuration
		3s	3p		
Na	11	[Ne] ↑		$1s^2 2s^2 2p^6 3s^1$	$[Ne]3s^1$
Mg	12	[Ne] ↑↓		$1s^2 2s^2 2p^6 3s^2$	$[Ne]3s^2$
Al	13	[Ne] ↑↓	↑	$1s^2 2s^2 2p^6 3s^2 3p^1$	$[Ne]3s^2 3p^1$
Si	14	[Ne] ↑↓	↑ ↑	$1s^2 2s^2 2p^6 3s^2 3p^2$	$[Ne]3s^2 3p^2$
P	15	[Ne] ↑↓	↑ ↑ ↑	$1s^2 2s^2 2p^6 3s^2 3p^3$	$[Ne]3s^2 3p^3$
S	16	[Ne] ↑↓	↑↓ ↑ ↑	$1s^2 2s^2 2p^6 3s^2 3p^4$	$[Ne]3s^2 3p^4$
Cl	17	[Ne] ↑↓	↑↓ ↑↓ ↑	$1s^2 2s^2 2p^6 3s^2 3p^5$	$[Ne]3s^2 3p^5$
Ar	18	[Ne] ↑↓	↑↓ ↑↓ ↑↓	$1s^2 2s^2 2p^6 3s^2 3p^6$	$[Ne]3s^2 3p^6$

▶**SAMPLE PROBLEM 4.8** Orbital Diagrams and Electron Configurations

Silicon is a micromineral needed for the growth of bones, tendons, and ligaments. Draw or write each of the following for silicon:

a. orbital diagram
b. abbreviated orbital diagram
c. electron configuration
d. abbreviated electron configuration

SOLUTION

	Given	Need
ANALYZE THE PROBLEM	silicon (Si)	orbital diagram, abbreviated orbital diagram, electron configuration, abbreviated electron configuration

a. Place two electrons in each orbital, and single electrons in the highest energy level.

Complete orbital diagram for Si

b. Write the symbol for the preceding noble gas followed by the orbitals for the remaining electrons.

Abbreviated orbital diagram for Si

c. List the sublevels in order of filling and add the number of electrons.

$1s^2 2s^2 2p^6 3s^2 3p^2$ Electron configuration for Si

d. Write the symbol for the preceding noble gas followed by the configuration for the remaining electrons.

$[\text{Ne}]3s^2 3p^2$ Abbreviated electron configuration for Si

STUDY CHECK 4.8

Write the complete and abbreviated electron configurations for sulfur, which is a macromineral in proteins, vitamin B_1, and insulin.

ANSWER

$1s^2 2s^2 2p^6 3s^2 3p^4$, $[\text{Ne}]3s^2 3p^4$

Electron Configurations and the Periodic Table

The electron configurations of the elements are also related to their position on the periodic table. Different sections or blocks within the periodic table correspond to the *s*, *p*, *d*, and *f* sublevels (see Figure 4.18).

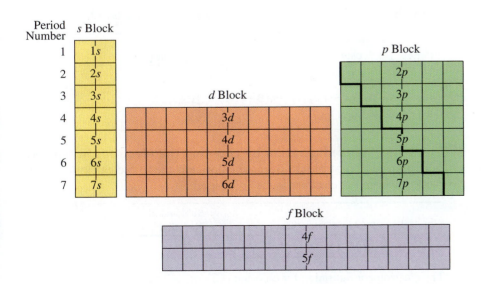

FIGURE 4.18 ▶ Electron configurations follow the order of occupied sublevels on the periodic table.

◉ If neon is in Group 8A (18), Period 2, how many electrons are in the 1s, 2s, and 2p sublevels of neon?

⚛ **CORE CHEMISTRY SKILL**

Using the Periodic Table to Write
Electron Configurations

Blocks on the Periodic Table

1. The *s* **block** includes hydrogen and helium as well as the elements in Group 1A (1) and Group 2A (2). This means that the final one or two electrons in the elements of the *s* block are located in an *s* orbital. The period number indicates the particular *s* orbital that is filling: 1*s*, 2*s*, and so on.

2. The *p* **block** consists of the elements in Group 3A (13) to Group 8A (18). There are six *p* block elements in each period because three *p* orbitals can hold up to six electrons. The period number indicates the particular *p* sublevel that is filling: 2*p*, 3*p*, and so on.

3. The *d* **block**, containing the transition elements, first appears after calcium (atomic number 20). There are 10 elements in each period of the *d* block because five *d* orbitals can hold up to 10 electrons. The particular *d* sublevel is one less $(n - 1)$ than the period number. For example, in Period 4, the *d* block is the 3*d* sublevel. In Period 5, the *d* block is the 4*d* sublevel.

4. The *f* **block**, the inner transition elements, are the two rows at the bottom of the periodic table. There are 14 elements in each *f* block because seven *f* orbitals can hold up to 14 electrons. Elements that have atomic numbers higher than 57 (La) have electrons in the 4*f* block. The particular *f* sublevel is two less $(n - 2)$ than the period number. For example, in Period 6, the *f* block is the 4*f* sublevel. In Period 7, the *f* block is the 5*f* sublevel.

Writing Electron Configurations Using Sublevel Blocks

Now we can write electron configurations using the sublevel blocks on the periodic table. As before, each configuration begins at H. But now we move across the table from left to right, writing down each sublevel block we come to until we reach the element for which we are writing an electron configuration. We show how to write the electron configuration for chlorine (atomic number 17) using the sublevel blocks on the periodic table in Sample Problem 4.9.

> **▸SAMPLE PROBLEM 4.9** **Using Sublevel Blocks to Write Electron Configurations**

Chlorine is a macromineral that is prevalent in extracellular fluids and stomach acid. Use the sublevel blocks on the periodic table to write the electron configuration for chlorine.

SOLUTION

Guide to Writing Electron Configurations Using Sublevel Blocks

STEP 1
Locate the element on the periodic table.

STEP 2
Write the filled sublevels in order, going across each period.

STEP 3
Complete the configuration by counting the electrons in the last occupied sublevel block.

STEP 1 Locate the element on the periodic table. Chlorine (atomic number 17) is in Group 7A (17) and Period 3.

STEP 2 Write the filled sublevels in order, going across each period.

Period	Sublevel Block Filling	Sublevel Block Notation (filled)
1	1*s* (H → He)	$1s^2$
2	2*s* (Li → Be) and 2*p* (B → Ne)	$2s^2 2p^6$
3	3*s* (Na → Mg)	$3s^2$

STEP 3 Complete the configuration by counting the electrons in the last occupied sublevel block. Because chlorine is the fifth element in the 3*p* block, there are five electrons in the 3*p* sublevel.

Period	Sublevel Block Filling	Sublevel Block Notation
3	3*p* (Al → Cl)	$3p^5$

The electron configuration for chlorine (Cl) is: $1s^2 2s^2 2p^6 3s^2 3p^5$.

STUDY CHECK 4.9

Use the sublevel blocks on the periodic table to write the electron configuration for magnesium, a macromineral needed to form bones and required for metabolic reactions.

ANSWER

$1s^2 2s^2 2p^6 3s^2$

Electron Configurations for Period 4 and Above

Up to Period 4, the filling of the sublevels has progressed in order. However, if we look at the sublevel blocks in Period 4, we see that the $4s$ sublevel fills before the $3d$ sublevel. This occurs because the electrons in the $4s$ sublevel have slightly lower energy than the electrons in the $3d$ sublevel. This order occurs again in Period 5 when the $5s$ sublevel fills before the $4d$ sublevel and again in Period 6 when the $6s$ fills before the $5d$.

At the beginning of Period 4, the electrons in potassium (19) and calcium (20) go into the $4s$ sublevel. In scandium, the next electron added goes into the $3d$ block, which continues to fill until it is complete with 10 electrons at zinc (30). Once the $3d$ block is complete, the next six electrons, gallium to krypton, go into the $4p$ block.

Element	Atomic Number	Electron Configuration	Abbreviated Electron Configuration	
4s Block				
K	19	$1s^2 2s^2 2p^6 3s^2 3p^6 4s^1$	$[Ar]4s^1$	
Ca	20	$1s^2 2s^2 2p^6 3s^2 3p^6 4s^2$	$[Ar]4s^2$	
3d Block				
Sc	21	$1s^2 2s^2 2p^6 3s^2 3p^6 4s^2 3d^1$	$[Ar]4s^2 3d^1$	
Ti	22	$1s^2 2s^2 2p^6 3s^2 3p^6 4s^2 3d^2$	$[Ar]4s^2 3d^2$	
V	23	$1s^2 2s^2 2p^6 3s^2 3p^6 4s^2 3d^3$	$[Ar]4s^2 3d^3$	
Cr*	24	$1s^2 2s^2 2p^6 3s^2 3p^6 4s^1 3d^5$	$[Ar]4s^1 3d^5$	(half-filled d sublevel is stable)
Mn	25	$1s^2 2s^2 2p^6 3s^2 3p^6 4s^2 3d^5$	$[Ar]4s^2 3d^5$	
Fe	26	$1s^2 2s^2 2p^6 3s^2 3p^6 4s^2 3d^6$	$[Ar]4s^2 3d^6$	
Co	27	$1s^2 2s^2 2p^6 3s^2 3p^6 4s^2 3d^7$	$[Ar]4s^2 3d^7$	
Ni	28	$1s^2 2s^2 2p^6 3s^2 3p^6 4s^2 3d^8$	$[Ar]4s^2 3d^8$	
Cu*	29	$1s^2 2s^2 2p^6 3s^2 3p^6 4s^1 3d^{10}$	$[Ar]4s^1 3d^{10}$	(filled d sublevel is stable)
Zn	30	$1s^2 2s^2 2p^6 3s^2 3p^6 4s^2 3d^{10}$	$[Ar]4s^2 3d^{10}$	
4p Block				
Ga	31	$1s^2 2s^2 2p^6 3s^2 3p^6 4s^2 3d^{10} 4p^1$	$[Ar]4s^2 3d^{10} 4p^1$	
Ge	32	$1s^2 2s^2 2p^6 3s^2 3p^6 4s^2 3d^{10} 4p^2$	$[Ar]4s^2 3d^{10} 4p^2$	
As	33	$1s^2 2s^2 2p^6 3s^2 3p^6 4s^2 3d^{10} 4p^3$	$[Ar]4s^2 3d^{10} 4p^3$	
Se	34	$1s^2 2s^2 2p^6 3s^2 3p^6 4s^2 3d^{10} 4p^4$	$[Ar]4s^2 3d^{10} 4p^4$	
Br	35	$1s^2 2s^2 2p^6 3s^2 3p^6 4s^2 3d^{10} 4p^5$	$[Ar]4s^2 3d^{10} 4p^5$	
Kr	36	$1s^2 2s^2 2p^6 3s^2 3p^6 4s^2 3d^{10} 4p^6$	$[Ar]4s^2 3d^{10} 4p^6$	

*Exceptions to the order of filling

▶ **SAMPLE PROBLEM 4.10** **Using Sublevel Blocks to Write Electron Configurations**

Selenium is a micromineral used in the immune system and cardiac health. Use the sublevel blocks on the periodic table to write the electron configuration for selenium.

SOLUTION

STEP 1 Locate the element on the periodic table. Selenium is in Period 4 and Group 6A (16).

STEP 2 Write the filled sublevels in order, going across each period.

Period	Sublevel Block Filling	Sublevel Block Notation (filled)
1	$1s$ (H → He)	$1s^2$
2	$2s$ (Li → Be) and $2p$ (B → Ne)	$2s^2 2p^6$
3	$3s$ (Na → Mg) and $3p$ (Al → Ar)	$3s^2 3p^6$
4	$4s$ (K → Ca) and $3d$ (Sc → Zn)	$4s^2 3d^{10}$

STEP 3 Complete the configuration by counting the electrons in the last occupied sublevel block. Because selenium is the fourth element in the $4p$ block, there are four electrons to place in the $4p$ sublevel.

Period	Sublevel Block Filling	Sublevel Block Notation
4	$4p$ (Ga → Se)	$4p^4$

The electron configuration for selenium (Se) is: $1s^2 2s^2 2p^6 3s^2 3p^6 4s^2 3d^{10} 4p^4$.

STUDY CHECK 4.10

Use the sublevel blocks on the periodic table to write the electron configuration for iodine, a micromineral needed for thyroid function.

ANSWER

$1s^2 2s^2 2p^6 3s^2 3p^6 4s^2 3d^{10} 4p^6 5s^2 4d^{10} 5p^5$

Some Exceptions in Sublevel Block Order

Within the filling of the $3d$ sublevel, exceptions occur for chromium and copper. In Cr and Cu, the $3d$ sublevel is close to being a half-filled or filled sublevel, which is particularly stable. Thus, the electron configuration for chromium has only one electron in the $4s$ and five electrons in the $3d$ sublevel to give the added stability of a half-filled d sublevel. This is shown in the abbreviated orbital diagram for chromium:

Abbreviated orbital diagram for chromium

A similar exception occurs when copper achieves a stable, filled $3d$ sublevel with 10 electrons and only one electron in the $4s$ orbital. This is shown in the abbreviated orbital diagram for copper:

Abbreviated orbital diagram for copper

After the $4s$ and $3d$ sublevels are completed, the $4p$ sublevel fills as expected from gallium to krypton, the noble gas that completes Period 4. There are also exceptions in filling for the higher d and f electron sublevels, some caused by the added stability of half-filled shells and others where the cause is not known.

QUESTIONS AND PROBLEMS

4.7 Electron Configurations

LEARNING GOAL Draw the orbital diagram and write the electron configuration for an element.

4.49 Compare the terms *electron configuration* and *abbreviated electron configuration*.

4.50 Compare the terms *orbital diagram* and *electron configuration*.

4.51 Draw the orbital diagram for each of the following:
a. boron   **b.** aluminum
c. phosphorus   **d.** argon

4.52 Draw the orbital diagram for each of the following:
a. fluorine   **b.** sulfur
c. magnesium   **d.** beryllium

4.53 Write a complete electron configuration for each of the following:
a. boron   **b.** sodium
c. lithium   **d.** magnesium

4.54 Write a complete electron configuration for each of the following:
a. nitrogen   **b.** chlorine
c. oxygen   **d.** neon

4.55 Write an abbreviated electron configuration for each of the following:
a. carbon   **b.** silicon
c. phosphorus   **d.** fluorine

4.56 Write an abbreviated electron configuration for each of the following:
a. magnesium   **b.** oxygen
c. sulfur   **d.** nitrogen

4.57 Give the symbol of the element with each of the following electron or abbreviated electron configurations:
a. $1s^2 2s^1$ **b.** $1s^2 2s^2 2p^6 3s^2 3p^4$
c. $[Ne]3s^2 3p^2$ **d.** $[He]2s^2 2p^5$

4.58 Give the symbol of the element with each of the following electron or abbreviated electron configurations:
a. $1s^2 2s^2 2p^4$ **b.** $[Ne]3s^2$
c. $1s^2 2s^2 2p^6 3s^2 3p^6$ **d.** $[Ne]3s^2 3p^1$

4.59 Give the symbol of the element that meets the following conditions:
a. has three electrons in the $n = 3$ energy level
b. has two $2p$ electrons

c. completes the $3p$ sublevel
d. completes the $2s$ sublevel

4.60 Give the symbol of the element that meets the following conditions:
a. has five electrons in the $3p$ sublevel
b. has four $2p$ electrons
c. completes the $3s$ sublevel
d. has one electron in the $3s$ sublevel

4.61 Use the sublevel blocks on the periodic table to write a complete electron configuration and abbreviated electron configuration for an atom of each of the following:
a. arsenic   **b.** iron
c. indium   **d.** iodine
e. titanium

4.62 Use the sublevel blocks on the periodic table to write a complete electron configuration and abbreviated electron configuration for an atom of each of the following:
a. calcium   **b.** cobalt
c. gallium   **d.** cadmium
e. tin

4.63 Use the periodic table to give the symbol of the element that meets the following conditions:
a. has three electrons in the $n = 4$ energy level
b. has three $2p$ electrons
c. completes the $5p$ sublevel
d. has two electrons in the $4d$ sublevel

4.64 Use the periodic table to give the symbol of the element that meets the following conditions:
a. has five electrons in the $n = 3$ energy level
b. has one electron in the $6p$ sublevel
c. completes the $7s$ sublevel
d. has four $5p$ electrons

4.65 Use the periodic table to give the number of electrons in the indicated sublevels for the following:
a. $3d$ in zinc   **b.** $2p$ in sodium
c. $4p$ in arsenic   **d.** $5s$ in rubidium

4.66 Use the periodic table to give the number of electrons in the indicated sublevels for the following:
a. $3d$ in manganese   **b.** $5p$ in antimony
c. $6p$ in lead   **d.** $3s$ in magnesium

4.8 Trends in Periodic Properties

LEARNING GOAL

Use the electron configurations of elements to explain the trends in periodic properties.

The electron configurations of atoms are an important factor in the physical and chemical properties of the elements and in the properties of the compounds that they form. In this section, we will look at the *valence electrons* in atoms, the trends in *atomic size, ionization energy*, and *metallic character*. Going across a period, there is a pattern of regular change in these properties from one group to the next. Known as *periodic properties*, each property increases or decreases across a period, and then the trend is repeated in each successive period. We can use the seasonal changes in temperatures as an analogy for periodic properties. In the winter, temperatures are cold and become warmer in the spring. By summer, the outdoor temperatures are hot but begin to cool in the fall. By winter, we expect cold temperatures again as the pattern of decreasing and increasing temperatures repeats for another year.

Group Number and Valence Electrons

The chemical properties of representative elements are mostly due to the **valence electrons**, which are the electrons in the outermost energy level. These valence electrons occupy the s and p sublevels with the highest principal quantum number n. The group numbers indicate the number of valence (outer) electrons for the elements in each vertical column. For example, the elements in Group 1A (1), such as lithium, sodium, and potassium, all have one electron in an s orbital. Looking at the sublevel block, we can represent the valence electron in the alkali metals of Group 1A (1) as ns^1. All the elements in Group 2A (2), the alkaline earth metals, have two valence electrons, ns^2. The halogens in Group 7A (17) have seven valence electrons, ns^2np^5.

We can see the repetition of the outermost s and p electrons for the representative elements for Periods 1 to 4 in Table 4.10. Helium is included in Group 8A (18) because it is a noble gas, but it has only two electrons in its complete energy level.

TABLE 4.10 Valence Electron Configuration for Representative Elements in Periods 1 to 4

1A (1)	2A (2)	3A (13)	4A (14)	5A (15)	6A (16)	7A (17)	8A (18)
1 H $1s^1$							2 He $1s^2$
3 Li $2s^1$	4 Be $2s^2$	5 B $2s^22p^1$	6 C $2s^22p^2$	7 N $2s^22p^3$	8 O $2s^22p^4$	9 F $2s^22p^5$	10 Ne $2s^22p^6$
11 Na $3s^1$	12 Mg $3s^2$	13 Al $3s^23p^1$	14 Si $3s^23p^2$	15 P $3s^23p^3$	16 S $3s^23p^4$	17 Cl $3s^23p^5$	18 Ar $3s^23p^6$
19 K $4s^1$	20 Ca $4s^2$	31 Ga $4s^24p^1$	32 Ge $4s^24p^2$	33 As $4s^24p^3$	34 Se $4s^24p^4$	35 Br $4s^24p^5$	36 Kr $4s^24p^6$

▶ **SAMPLE PROBLEM 4.11   Using Group Numbers**

Using the periodic table, write the group number, the period, and the valence electron configuration for the following:

a. calcium   **b.** iodine   **c.** lead

SOLUTION

The valence electrons are the outermost s and p electrons. Although there may be electrons in the d or f sublevels, they are not valence electrons.

a. Calcium is in Group 2A (2), Period 4. It has a valence electron configuration of $4s^2$.
b. Iodine is in Group 7A (17), Period 5. It has a valence electron configuration of $5s^25p^5$.
c. Lead is in Group 4A (14), Period 6. It has a valence electron configuration of $6s^26p^2$.

STUDY CHECK 4.11

What are the group numbers, the periods, and the valence electron configurations for sulfur and strontium?

ANSWER

Sulfur is in Group 6A (16), Period 3, and has a $3s^23p^4$ valence electron configuration. Strontium is in Group 2A (2), Period 5, and has a $5s^2$ valence electron configuration.

Lewis Symbols

A **Lewis symbol** is a convenient way to represent the valence electrons, which are shown as dots placed on the sides, top, or bottom of the symbol for the element. One to four valence electrons are arranged as single dots. When there are five to eight electrons, one or more electrons are paired. Any of the following would be an acceptable Lewis symbol for magnesium, which has two valence electrons:

⚛ **CORE CHEMISTRY SKILL**

Drawing Lewis Symbols

Lewis Symbols for Magnesium

Ṁg· Mg̈ ·Ṁg ·Mg· Mg· ·Mg

Lewis symbols for selected elements are given in Table 4.11.

Number of Valence Electrons Increases ➡

TABLE 4.11 Lewis Symbols for Selected Elements in Periods 1 to 4

	Group Number							
	IA (1)	2A (2)	3A (13)	4A (14)	5A (15)	6A (16)	7A (17)	8A (18)
Number of Valence Electrons	1	2	3	4	5	6	7	8*
Lewis Symbol	H·							He: *
	Li·	Be·	·B·	·C·	·N:	·O:	·F:	:Ne:
	Na·	Mg·	·Al·	·Si·	·P·	·S:	·Cl:	:Ar:
	K·	Ca·	·Ga·	·Ge·	·As·	·Se:	·Br:	:Kr:

*Helium (He) is stable with two valence electrons.

▶ SAMPLE PROBLEM 4.12 Drawing Lewis Symbols

Draw the Lewis symbol for each of the following:

a. bromine
b. aluminum

SOLUTION

a. The Lewis symbol for bromine, which is in Group 7A (17), has seven valence electrons. Thus, three pairs of dots and one single dot are drawn on the sides of the Br symbol.

·Br:

b. The Lewis symbol for aluminum, which is in Group 3A (13), has three valence electrons drawn as single dots on the sides of the Al symbol.

·Al·

STUDY CHECK 4.12

Draw the Lewis symbol for phosphorus, a macromineral needed for bones and teeth.

ANSWER

·P·

Atomic Size

The **atomic size** of an atom is determined by the distance of the valence electrons from the nucleus. For each group of representative elements, the atomic size *increases* going from the top to the bottom because the outermost electrons in each energy level are farther from the nucleus. For example, in Group 1A (1), Li has a valence electron in energy level 2; Na has a valence electron in energy level 3; and K has a valence electron in energy level 4. This means that the K atom is larger than the Na atom, and the Na atom is larger than the Li atom (see Figure 4.19).

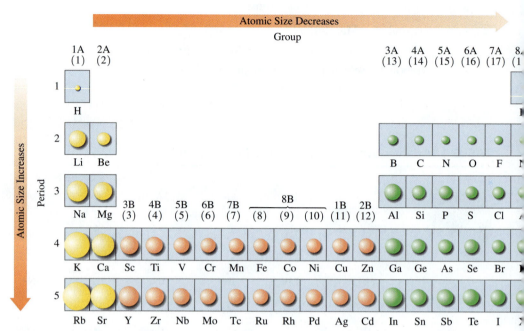

FIGURE 4.19 ▶ The atomic size increases going down a group but decreases going from left to right across a period.

Q Why does the atomic size increase going down a group?

The atomic size of representative elements is affected by the attractive forces of the protons in the nucleus on the electrons in the outermost level. For the elements going across a period, the increase in the number of protons in the nucleus increases the positive charge of the nucleus. As a result, the electrons are pulled closer to the nucleus, which means that the atomic size of representative elements decreases going from left to right across a period.

The size of atoms of transition elements within the same period changes only slightly because electrons are filling *d* orbitals rather than the outermost energy level. Because the increase in nuclear charge is canceled by an increase in *d* electrons, the attraction of the valence electrons by the nucleus remains about the same. Because there is little change in the nuclear attraction for the valence electrons, the atomic size remains relatively constant for the transition elements.

▶**SAMPLE PROBLEM 4.13** Size of Atoms

Identify the smaller atom in each of the following pairs:

a. N or F   **b.** K or Kr   **c.** Ca and Sr

SOLUTION

a. The F atom has a greater positive charge on the nucleus, which pulls electrons closer, and makes the F atom smaller than the N atom. Atomic size decreases going from left to right across a period.

b. The Kr atom has a greater positive charge on the nucleus, which pulls electrons closer, and makes the Kr atom smaller than the K atom. Atomic size decreases going from left to right across a period.

c. The outer electrons in the Ca atom are closer to the nucleus than in the Sr atom, which makes the Ca atom smaller than the Sr atom. Atomic size increases going down a group.

STUDY CHECK 4.13

Which atom has the largest atomic size, P, As, or Se?

ANSWER

As

Ionization Energy

In an atom, negatively charged electrons are attracted to the positive charge of the protons in the nucleus. Therefore, energy is required to remove an electron from an atom. The **ionization energy** is the energy needed to remove one electron from an atom in the gaseous (g) state. When an electron is removed from a neutral atom, a cation with a 1+ charge is formed.

$$Na(g) + \text{energy (ionization)} \longrightarrow Na^+(g) + e^-$$

The attraction of a nucleus for the outermost electrons decreases as those electrons are farther from the nucleus. Thus the ionization energy decreases going down a group (see Figure 4.20). However, going across a period from left to right, the positive charge of the nucleus increases because there is an increase in the number of protons. Thus the ionization energy increases going from left to right across the periodic table.

In summary, the ionization energy is low for the metals and high for the nonmetals. The high ionization energies of the noble gases indicate that their electron configurations are especially stable.

▶ **SAMPLE PROBLEM 4.14 Ionization Energy**

Indicate the element in each group that has the higher ionization energy and explain your choice.

a. K or Na   **b.** Mg or Cl   **c.** F, N, or C

SOLUTION

a. Na. In Na, an electron is removed from an energy level closer to the nucleus, which requires a higher ionization energy for Na compared to K.
b. Cl. The increased nuclear charge of Cl increases the attraction for the valence electrons, which requires a higher ionization energy for Cl compared to Mg.
c. F. The increased nuclear charge of F increases the attraction for the valence electrons, which requires a higher ionization energy for F compared to C or N.

STUDY CHECK 4.14

Arrange Sn, Sr, and I in order of increasing ionization energy.

ANSWER

Ionization energy increases going from left to right across a period: Sr, Sn, I.

FIGURE 4.20 ▶ As the distance from the nucleus to the valence electron in Li, Na, and K atoms increases in Group 1A (1), the ionization energy decreases and less energy is required to remove the valence electron.

Q Why would Cs have a lower ionization energy than K?

Ionization energy decreases going down a group and increases going from left to right across a period.

Metallic character increases going down a group and decreases going from left to right across a period.

Metallic Character

An element that has **metallic character** is an element that loses valence electrons easily. Metallic character is more prevalent in the elements (metals) on the left side of the periodic table and decreases going from left to right across a period. The elements (nonmetals) on the right side of the periodic table do not easily lose electrons, which means they are less metallic. Most of the metalloids between the metals and nonmetals tend to lose electrons, but not as easily as the metals. Thus, in Period 3, sodium, which loses electrons most easily, would be the most metallic. Going across from left to right in Period 3, metallic character decreases to argon, which has the least metallic character.

For elements in the same group of representative elements, metallic character increases going from top to bottom. Atoms at the bottom of any group have more electron levels, which makes it easier to lose electrons. Thus, the elements at the bottom of a group on the periodic table have lower ionization energy and are more metallic compared to the elements at the top.

A summary of the trends in periodic properties we have discussed is given in Table 4.12.

TABLE 4.12 Summary of Trends in Periodic Properties of Representative Elements

Periodic Property	Top to Bottom within a Group	Left to Right across a Period
Valence Electrons	Remains the same	Increases
Atomic Size	Increases because of the increase in the number of energy levels	Decreases as the number of protons increases, which strengthens the attraction of the nucleus for the valence electrons, and pulls them closer to the nucleus
Ionization Energy	Decreases because the valence electrons are easier to remove when they are farther from the nucleus	Increases as the increase in the number of protons strengthens the attraction of the nucleus for the valence electrons, and more energy is required to remove an electron
Metallic Character	Increases because the valence electrons are easier to remove when they are farther from the nucleus	Decreases as the number of protons increases, which strengthens the attraction of the nucleus for the valence electrons, and makes it more difficult to remove a valence electron

QUESTIONS AND PROBLEMS

4.8 Trends in Periodic Properties

LEARNING GOAL Use the electron configurations of elements to explain the trends in periodic properties.

4.67 Indicate the number of valence electrons in each of the following:
   a. aluminum   **b.** Group 5A
   c. barium   **d.** F, Cl, Br, and I

4.68 Indicate the number of valence electrons in each of the following:
   a. Li, Na, K, Rb, and Cs   **b.** Se
   c. C, Si, Ge, Sn, and Pb   **d.** Group 8A

4.69 Write the group number and Lewis symbol for each of the following elements:
   a. sulfur   **b.** nitrogen
   c. calcium   **d.** sodium
   e. gallium

4.70 Write the group number and Lewis symbol for each of the following elements:
   a. carbon   **b.** oxygen
   c. argon   **d.** lithium
   e. chlorine

4.71 Select the larger atom in each pair.
   a. Na or Cl   **b.** Na or Rb
   c. Na or Mg   **d.** Rb or I

4.72 Select the larger atom in each pair.
   a. S or Ar   **b.** S or O
   c. S or K   **d.** S or Mg

4.73 Arrange each set of elements in order of decreasing atomic size.
   a. Al, Si, Mg   **b.** Cl, I, Br
   c. Sb, Sr, I   **d.** P, Si, Na

4.74 Arrange each set of elements in order of decreasing atomic size.
  a. Cl, S, P
  b. Ge, Si, C
  c. Ba, Ca, Sr
  d. S, O, Se

4.75 Select the element in each pair with the higher ionization energy.
  a. Br or I
  b. Mg or Sr
  c. Si or P
  d. I or Xe

4.76 Select the element in each pair with the higher ionization energy.
  a. O or Ne
  b. K or Br
  c. Ca or Ba
  d. N or Ne

4.77 Arrange each set of elements in order of increasing ionization energy.
  a. F, Cl, Br
  b. Na, Cl, Al
  c. Na, K, Cs
  d. As, Ca, Br

4.78 Arrange each set of elements in order of increasing ionization energy.
  a. O, N, C
  b. S, P, Cl
  c. P, As, N
  d. Al, Si, P

4.79 Arrange the following in order of decreasing metallic character:

  Br, Ge, Ca, Ga

4.80 Arrange the following in order of increasing metallic character:

  Na, P, Al, Ar

4.81 Fill in each of the following blanks using *higher* or *lower*, *more* or *less*: Sr has a _____ ionization energy and _____ metallic character than Sb.

4.82 Fill in each of the following blanks using *higher* or *lower*, *more* or *less*: N has a _____ ionization energy and _____ metallic character than As.

4.83 Complete each of the following statements **a** to **d** using **1**, **2**, or **3**:
  1. decreases **2.** increases **3.** remains the same

  Going down Group 6A (16),
  a. the ionization energy _____
  b. the atomic size _____
  c. the metallic character _____
  d. the number of valence electrons _____

4.84 Complete each of the following statements **a** to **d** using **1**, **2**, or **3**:
  1. decreases **2.** increases **3.** remains the same

  Going from left to right across Period 3,
  a. the ionization energy _____
  b. the atomic size _____
  c. the metallic character _____
  d. the number of valence electrons _____

4.85 Which statements completed with **a** to **e** will be *true* and which will be *false*?

  An atom of N compared to an atom of Li has a larger (greater)
  a. atomic size
  b. ionization energy
  c. number of protons
  d. metallic character
  e. number of valence electrons

4.86 Which statements completed with **a** to **e** will be *true* and which will be *false*?

  An atom of C compared to an atom of Sn has a larger (greater)
  a. atomic size
  b. ionization energy
  c. number of protons
  d. metallic character
  e. number of valence electrons

Clinical Update
Improving Crop Production

In plants, potassium is needed for metabolic processes including the regulation of plant growth. Potassium (K) is required by plants for protein synthesis, photosynthesis, enzymes, and ionic balance. Potassium-deficient potato plants may show purple or brown spots and plant, root, and seed growth is reduced. John has noticed that the leaves of his recent crop of potatoes had brown spots, the potatoes were undersized, and the crop yield was low.

Tests on soil samples indicated that the potassium levels were below 100 ppm, which indicated that supplemental potassium was needed. John applied a fertilizer containing potassium chloride (KCl). To apply the correct amount of potassium, John needs to apply 170 kg of fertilizer per hectare.

Clinical Applications

4.87 **a.** What is the group number and name of the group that contains potassium?
  b. Is potassium a metal, a nonmetal, or a metalloid?
  c. How many protons are in an atom of potassium?
  d. What is the most prevalent isotope of potassium (see Table 4.8)?
  e. Potassium has three naturally occurring isotopes. They are K-39 (93.26%, 38.964 amu), K-40 (0.0117%, 39.964 amu),

and K-41 (6.73%, 40.962 amu). Calculate the atomic mass of potassium from the naturally occurring isotopes and their abundance using the weighted average mass method.

4.88 **a.** How many neutrons are in K-41?
  b. Write the electron configuration for potassium.
  c. Which is the larger atom, K or Cs?
  d. Which is the smallest atom, K, As, or Br?
  e. If John's potato farm has an area of 34.5 hectares, how many pounds of fertilizer does John need to use?

A mineral deficiency of potassium causes brown spots on potato leaves.

CONCEPT MAP

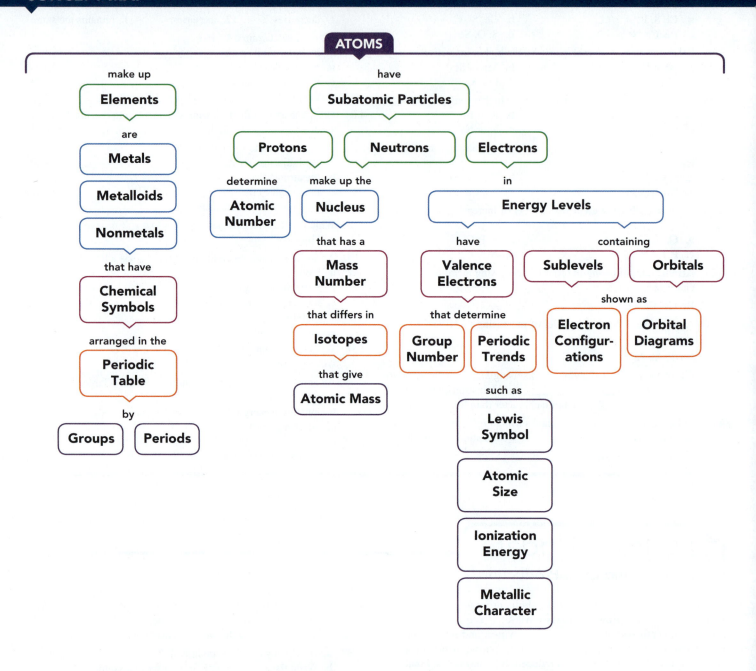

ATOMS

- make up → **Elements**
  - are → **Metals**, **Metalloids**, **Nonmetals**
  - that have → **Chemical Symbols**
  - arranged in the → **Periodic Table**
  - by → **Groups**, **Periods**

- have → **Subatomic Particles**
  - **Protons**, **Neutrons**, **Electrons**
  - Protons determine → **Atomic Number**
  - Neutrons make up the → **Nucleus**
    - that has a → **Mass Number**
    - that differs in → **Isotopes**
    - that give → **Atomic Mass**
  - Electrons in → **Energy Levels**
    - have → **Valence Electrons**
      - that determine → **Group Number**, **Periodic Trends**
        - such as → **Lewis Symbol**, **Atomic Size**, **Ionization Energy**, **Metallic Character**
    - containing → **Sublevels**, **Orbitals**
      - shown as → **Electron Configurations**, **Orbital Diagrams**

CHAPTER REVIEW

4.1 Elements and Symbols
LEARNING GOAL Given the name of an element, write its correct symbol; from the symbol, write the correct name.

- Elements are the primary substances of matter.
- Chemical symbols are one- or two-letter abbreviations of the names of the elements.

4.2 The Periodic Table
LEARNING GOAL Use the periodic table to identify the group and the period of an element; identify the element as a metal, a nonmetal, or a metalloid.

- The periodic table is an arrangement of the elements by increasing atomic number.

- A horizontal row is called a *period*.
  A vertical column on the periodic table containing elements with similar properties is called a *group*.
- Elements in Group 1A (1) are called the *alkali metals*; Group 2A (2), the *alkaline earth metals*; Group 7A (17), the *halogens*; and Group 8A (18), the *noble gases*.
- On the periodic table, *metals* are located on the left of the heavy zigzag line, and *nonmetals* are to the right of the heavy zigzag line.
- Except for aluminum, elements located along the heavy zigzag line are called *metalloids*.

4.3 The Atom
LEARNING GOAL Describe the electrical charge and location in an atom for a proton, a neutron, and an electron.

- An atom is the smallest particle that retains the characteristics of an element.
- Atoms are composed of three types of subatomic particles.
- Protons have a positive charge $(+)$, electrons carry a negative charge $(-)$, and neutrons are electrically neutral.
- The protons and neutrons are found in the tiny, dense nucleus; electrons are located outside the nucleus.

4.4 Atomic Number and Mass Number
LEARNING GOAL Given the atomic number and the mass number of an atom, state the number of protons, neutrons, and electrons.

- The atomic number gives the number of protons in all the atoms of the same element.
- In a neutral atom, the number of protons and electrons is equal.
- The mass number is the total number of protons and neutrons in an atom.

4.5 Isotopes and Atomic Mass
LEARNING GOAL Determine the number of protons, neutrons, and electrons in one or more of the isotopes of an element; calculate the atomic mass of an element using the percent abundance and mass of its naturally occurring isotopes.

- Atoms that have the same number of protons but different numbers of neutrons are called *isotopes*.
- The atomic mass of an element is the weighted average mass of all the isotopes in a naturally occurring sample of that element.

4.6 Electron Energy Levels
LEARNING GOAL Describe the energy levels, sublevels, and orbitals for the electrons in an atom.

- Electromagnetic radiation such as radio waves and visible light is energy that travels at the speed of light.
- Each particular type of radiation has a specific wavelength and frequency.
- Long-wavelength radiation has low frequencies, whereas short-wavelength radiation has high frequencies.

- Radiation with a high frequency has high energy.
- The atomic spectra of elements are related to the specific energy levels occupied by electrons.
- When an electron absorbs energy, it attains a higher energy level. When an electron drops to a lower energy level, energy is emitted.
- An orbital is a region around the nucleus where an electron with a specific energy is most likely to be found.
- Each orbital holds a maximum of two electrons, which must have opposite spins.
- In each energy level (n), electrons occupy orbitals of identical energy within sublevels.
- An *s* sublevel contains one *s* orbital, a *p* sublevel contains three *p* orbitals, a *d* sublevel contains five *d* orbitals, and an *f* sublevel contains seven *f* orbitals.

4.7 Electron Configurations
LEARNING GOAL Draw the orbital diagram and write the electron configuration for an element.

- Within a sublevel, electrons enter orbitals in the same energy level one at a time until all the orbitals are half-filled.
- Additional electrons enter with opposite spins until the orbitals in that sublevel are filled with two electrons each.
- The orbital diagram for an element such as silicon shows the orbitals that are occupied by paired and unpaired electrons:

- The electron configuration for an element such as silicon shows the number of electrons in each sublevel: $1s^2 2s^2 2p^6 3s^2 3p^2$.
- An abbreviated electron configuration for an element such as silicon places the symbol of a noble gas in brackets to represent the filled sublevels: $[\text{Ne}]3s^2 3p^2$.
- The periodic table consists of *s*, *p*, *d*, and *f* sublevel blocks.
- An electron configuration can be written following the order of the sublevel blocks on the periodic table.
- Beginning with $1s$, an electron configuration is obtained by writing the sublevel blocks in order going across each period on the periodic table until the element is reached.

4.8 Trends in Periodic Properties
LEARNING GOAL Use the electron configurations of elements to explain the trends in periodic properties.

- The properties of elements are related to the valence electrons of the atoms.
- With only a few exceptions, each group of elements has the same arrangement of valence electrons differing only in the energy level.
- Valence electrons are represented as dots around the symbol of the element.
- The size of an atom increases going down a group and decreases going from left to right across a period.
- The energy required to remove a valence electron is the ionization energy, which decreases going down a group, and generally increases going from left to right across a period.
- The metallic character of an element increases going down a group and decreases going from left to right across a period.

KEY TERMS

alkali metal An element in Group 1A (1), except hydrogen, that is a soft, shiny metal with one electron in its outermost energy level.

alkaline earth metal An element in Group 2A (2) that has two electrons in its outermost energy level.

atom The smallest particle of an element that retains the characteristics of the element.

atomic mass The weighted average mass of all the naturally occurring isotopes of an element.

atomic mass unit (amu) A small mass unit used to describe the mass of extremely small particles such as atoms and subatomic particles; 1 amu is equal to one-twelfth the mass of a $^{12}_{6}C$ atom.

atomic number A number that is equal to the number of protons in an atom.

atomic size The distance between the outermost electrons and the nucleus.

atomic symbol An abbreviation used to indicate the mass number and atomic number of an isotope.

chemical symbol An abbreviation that represents the name of an element.

d block The block of ten elements from Groups 3B (3) to 2B (12) in which electrons fill the five d orbitals in the d sublevels.

electron A negatively charged subatomic particle having a minute mass that is usually ignored in mass calculations; its symbol is e^-.

electron configuration A list of the number of electrons in each sublevel within an atom, arranged by increasing energy.

energy level A group of electrons with similar energy.

f block The block of 14 elements in the rows at the bottom of the periodic table in which electrons fill the seven f orbitals in the $4f$ and $5f$ sublevels.

group A vertical column in the periodic table that contains elements having similar physical and chemical properties.

group number A number that appears at the top of each vertical column (group) in the periodic table and indicates the number of electrons in the outermost energy level.

halogen An element in Group 7A (17)—fluorine, chlorine, bromine, iodine, and astatine—that has seven electrons in its outermost energy level.

ionization energy The energy needed to remove the least tightly bound electron from the outermost energy level of an atom.

isotope An atom that differs only in mass number from another atom of the same element. Isotopes have the same atomic number (number of protons), but different numbers of neutrons.

Lewis symbol The representation of an atom that shows valence electrons as dots around the symbol of the element.

mass number The total number of protons and neutrons in the nucleus of an atom.

metal An element that is shiny, malleable, ductile, and a good conductor of heat and electricity. The metals are located to the left of the heavy zigzag line on the periodic table.

metallic character A measure of how easily an element loses a valence electron.

metalloid Elements with properties of both metals and nonmetals located along the heavy zigzag line on the periodic table.

neutron A neutral subatomic particle having a mass of about 1 amu and found in the nucleus of an atom; its symbol is n or n^0.

noble gas An element in Group 8A (18) of the periodic table, generally unreactive and seldom found in combination with other elements, that has eight electrons (helium has two electrons) in its outermost energy level.

nonmetal An element with little or no luster that is a poor conductor of heat and electricity. The nonmetals are located to the right of the heavy zigzag line on the periodic table.

nucleus The compact, extremely dense center of an atom, containing the protons and neutrons of the atom.

orbital The region around the nucleus where electrons of a certain energy are more likely to be found. The s orbitals are spherical; the p orbitals have two lobes.

orbital diagram A diagram that shows the distribution of electrons in the orbitals of the energy levels.

p block The elements in Groups 3A (13) to 8A (18) in which electrons fill the p orbitals in the p sublevels.

period A horizontal row of elements in the periodic table.

periodic table An arrangement of elements by increasing atomic number such that elements having similar chemical behavior are grouped in vertical columns.

proton A positively charged subatomic particle having a mass of about 1 amu and found in the nucleus of an atom; its symbol is p or p^+.

representative element An element in the first two columns on the left of the periodic table and the last six columns on the right that has a group number of 1A through 8A or 1, 2, and 13 through 18.

s block The elements in Groups 1A (1) and 2A (2) in which electrons fill the s orbitals.

subatomic particle A particle within an atom; protons, neutrons, and electrons are subatomic particles.

sublevel A group of orbitals of equal energy within an energy level. The number of sublevels in each energy level is the same as the principal quantum number (n).

transition element An element in the center of the periodic table that is designated with the letter "B" or the group number of 3 through 12.

valence electrons Electrons in the highest energy level of an atom.

⚛ CORE CHEMISTRY SKILLS

The chapter section containing each Core Chemistry Skill is shown in parentheses at the end of each heading.

Counting Protons and Neutrons (4.4)

- The atomic number of an element is equal to the number of protons in every atom of that element. The atomic number is the whole number that appears above the symbol of each element on the periodic table.

  Atomic number = number of protons in an atom

- Because atoms are neutral, the number of electrons is equal to the number of protons. Thus, the atomic number gives the number of electrons.
- The mass number is the total number of protons and neutrons in the nucleus of an atom.

  Mass number = number of protons + number of neutrons

- The number of neutrons is calculated from the mass number and atomic number.

  Number of neutrons = mass number − number of protons

Example: Calculate the number of protons, neutrons, and electrons in a krypton atom with a mass number of 80.

Answer:

Element	Atomic Number	Mass Number	Number of Protons	Number of Neutrons	Number of Electrons
Kr	36	80	equal to atomic number (36)	equal to mass number − number of protons 80 − 36 = 44	equal to number of protons (36)

Writing Atomic Symbols for Isotopes (4.5)

- Isotopes are atoms of the same element that have the same atomic number but different numbers of neutrons.
- An atomic symbol is written for a particular isotope, with its mass number (protons and neutrons) shown in the upper left corner and its atomic number (protons) shown in the lower left corner.

Mass number ⟶ $^{24}_{12}\text{Mg}$ ⟵ Symbol of element
Atomic number ⟶

Example: Calculate the number of protons and neutrons in the cadmium isotope $^{112}_{48}\text{Cd}$.

Answer:

Atomic Symbol	Atomic Number	Mass Number	Number of Protons	Number of Neutrons
$^{112}_{48}\text{Cd}$	number (48) in lower left corner	number (112) in upper left corner	equal to atomic number (48)	equal to mass number−number of protons 112 − 48 = 64

Writing Electron Configurations (4.7)

- The electron configuration for an atom specifies the energy levels and sublevels occupied by the electrons of an atom.

- An electron configuration is written starting with the lowest energy sublevel, followed by the next lowest energy sublevel.
- The number of electrons in each sublevel is shown as a superscript.

Example: Write the electron configuration for palladium.

Answer: Palladium has atomic number 46, which means it has 46 protons and 46 electrons.

$$1s^2 2s^2 2p^6 3s^2 3p^6 4s^2 3d^{10} 4p^6 5s^2 4d^8$$

Using the Periodic Table to Write Electron Configurations (4.7)

- An electron configuration corresponds to the location of an element on the periodic table, where different blocks within the periodic table are identified as the *s*, *p*, *d*, and *f* sublevels.

Example: Use the periodic table to write the electron configuration for sulfur.

Answer: Sulfur (atomic number 16) is in Group 6A (16) and Period 3.

Period	Sublevel Block Filling	Sublevel Block Notation (filled)
1	1s (H → He)	$1s^2$
2	2s (Li → Be) and 2p (B → Ne)	$2s^2 2p^6$
3	3s (Na → Mg)	$3s^2$
	3p (Al → S)	$3p^4$

The electron configuration for sulfur (S) is: $1s^2 2s^2 2p^6 3s^2 3p^4$.

Identifying Trends in Periodic Properties (4.8)

- The size of an atom increases going down a group and decreases going from left to right across a period.
- The ionization energy decreases going down a group and increases going from left to right across a period.
- The metallic character of an element increases going down a group and decreases going from left to right across a period.

Example: For Mg, P, and Cl, identify which has the

  a. largest atomic size
  b. highest ionization energy
  c. most metallic character

Answer: **a.** Mg **b.** Cl **c.** Mg

Drawing Lewis Symbols (4.8)

- The valence electrons are the electrons in the outermost energy level.
- The number of valence electrons is the same as the group number for the representative elements.
- A Lewis symbol represents the number of valence electrons shown as dots placed around the symbol for the element.

Example: Give the group number and number of valence electrons, and draw the Lewis symbol for each of the following:

  a. Rb **b.** Se **c.** Xe

Answer: **a.** Group 1A (1), one valence electron, Rb ·

  b. Group 6A (16), six valence electrons, ·S̈e:

  c. Group 8A (18), eight valence electrons, :Ẍe:

UNDERSTANDING THE CONCEPTS

The chapter sections to review are shown in parentheses at the end of each question.

4.89 According to Dalton's atomic theory, which of the following are *true* or *false*? If false, correct the statement to make it true. (4.3)
   a. Atoms of an element are identical to atoms of other elements.
   b. Every element is made of atoms.
   c. Atoms of different elements combine to form compounds.
   d. In a chemical reaction, some atoms disappear and new atoms appear.

4.90 Use Rutherford's gold-foil experiment to answer each of the following: (4.3)
   a. What did Rutherford expect to happen when he aimed particles at the gold foil?
   b. How did the results differ from what he expected?
   c. How did he use the results to propose a model of the atom?

4.91 Match the subatomic particles (**1** to **3**) to each of the descriptions below: (4.4)
   1. protons   **2.** neutrons   **3.** electrons

   a. atomic mass
   b. atomic number
   c. positive charge
   d. negative charge
   e. mass number – atomic number

4.92 Match the subatomic particles (**1** to **3**) to each of the descriptions below: (4.4)
   1. protons   **2.** neutrons   **3.** electrons

   a. mass number
   b. surround the nucleus
   c. in the nucleus
   d. charge of 0
   e. equal to number of electrons

4.93 Consider the following atoms in which X represents the chemical symbol of the element: (4.4, 4.5)

   $^{16}_{8}X$ $^{16}_{9}X$ $^{18}_{10}X$ $^{17}_{8}X$ $^{18}_{8}X$

   a. What atoms have the same number of protons?
   b. Which atoms are isotopes? Of what element?
   c. Which atoms have the same mass number?

4.94 Consider the following atoms in which X represents the chemical symbol of the element: (4.4, 4.5)

   $^{124}_{47}X$ $^{116}_{49}X$ $^{116}_{50}X$ $^{124}_{50}X$ $^{116}_{48}X$

   a. What atoms have the same number of protons?
   b. Which atoms are isotopes? Of what element?
   c. Which atoms have the same mass number?

4.95 Complete the following table for three of the naturally occurring isotopes of germanium, which is a metalloid used in semiconductors: (4.4, 4.5)

	Atomic Symbol		
	$^{70}_{32}Ge$	$^{73}_{32}Ge$	$^{76}_{32}Ge$
Atomic Number			
Mass Number			
Number of Protons			
Number of Neutrons			
Number of Electrons			

4.96 Complete the following table for the three naturally occurring isotopes of silicon, the major component in computer chips: (4.4, 4.5)

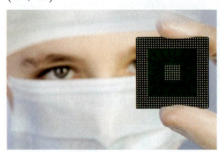

Computer chips consist primarily of the element silicon.

	Atomic Symbol		
	$^{28}_{14}Si$	$^{29}_{14}Si$	$^{30}_{14}Si$
Atomic Number			
Mass Number			
Number of Protons			
Number of Neutrons			
Number of Electrons			

4.97 For each representation of a nucleus **A** through **E**, write the atomic symbol, and identify which are isotopes. (4.4, 4.5)

Proton ●
Neutron ●

   A   B   C   D   E

4.98 Identify the element represented by each nucleus **A** through **E** in problem 4.97 as a metal, a nonmetal, or a metalloid. (4.3)

4.99 Indicate whether or not the following orbital diagrams are possible and explain. When possible, indicate the element it represents. (4.7)

a.

1s   2s   2p   3s

b.

1s   2s   2p   3s

4.100 Indicate whether or not the following abbreviated orbital diagrams are possible and explain. When possible, indicate the element it represents. (4.7)

a.
[He]
2s   2p

b.
[Ar]
4s   3d

4.101 Match the spheres **A** through **D** with atoms of Li, Na, K, and Rb. (4.8)

A   B   C   D

4.102 Match the spheres **A** through **D** with atoms of K, Ge, Ca, and Kr. (4.8)

A   B   C   D

4.103 Of the elements Na, Mg, Si, S, Cl, and Ar, identify one that fits each of the following: (4.2, 4.6, 4.7, 4.8)
a. largest atomic size
b. a halogen
c. electron configuration $1s^2 2s^2 2p^6 3s^2 3p^2$
d. highest ionization energy
e. in Group 6A (16)
f. most metallic character
g. two valence electrons

4.104 Of the elements Sn, Xe, Te, Sr, I, and Rb, identify one that fits each of the following: (4.2, 4.6, 4.7, 4.8)
a. smallest atomic size
b. an alkaline earth metal
c. a metalloid
d. lowest ionization energy
e. in Group 4A (14)
f. least metallic character
g. seven valence electrons

ADDITIONAL QUESTIONS AND PROBLEMS

4.105 Give the group and period number for each of the following elements: (4.2)
a. bromine   **b.** argon
c. lithium   **d.** radium

4.106 Give the group and period number for each of the following elements: (4.2)
a. radon   **b.** tin
c. carbon   **d.** magnesium

4.107 The following trace elements have been found to be crucial to the functions of the body. Indicate each as a metal, a nonmetal, or a metalloid. (4.2)
a. zinc   **b.** cobalt
c. manganese   **d.** iodine

4.108 The following trace elements have been found to be crucial to the functions of the body. Indicate each as a metal, a nonmetal, or a metalloid. (4.2)
a. copper   **b.** selenium
c. arsenic   **d.** chromium

4.109 Indicate if each of the following statements is *true* or *false*: (4.3)
a. The proton is a negatively charged particle.
b. The neutron is 2000 times as heavy as a proton.
c. The atomic mass unit is based on a carbon atom with 6 protons and 6 neutrons.

d. The nucleus is the largest part of the atom.
e. The electrons are located outside the nucleus.

4.110 Indicate if each of the following statements is *true* or *false*: (4.3)
a. The neutron is electrically neutral.
b. Most of the mass of an atom is because of the protons and neutrons.
c. The charge of an electron is equal, but opposite, to the charge of a neutron.
d. The proton and the electron have about the same mass.
e. The mass number is the number of protons.

4.111 For the following atoms, give the number of protons, neutrons, and electrons: (4.3)
a. $^{114}_{48}\text{Cd}$ **b.** $^{98}_{43}\text{Tc}$ **c.** $^{199}_{79}\text{Au}$
d. $^{222}_{86}\text{Rn}$ **e.** $^{136}_{54}\text{Xe}$

4.112 For the following atoms, give the number of protons, neutrons, and electrons: (4.3)
a. $^{202}_{80}\text{Hg}$ **b.** $^{127}_{53}\text{I}$ **c.** $^{75}_{35}\text{Br}$
d. $^{133}_{55}\text{Cs}$ **e.** $^{195}_{78}\text{Pt}$

4.113 Complete the following table: (4.3)

Name of the Element	Atomic Symbol	Number of Protons	Number of Neutrons	Number of Electrons
	$^{80}_{34}\text{Se}$			
		28	34	
Magnesium			14	
	$^{228}_{88}\text{Ra}$			

4.114 Complete the following table: (4.3)

Name of the Element	Atomic Symbol	Number of Protons	Number of Neutrons	Number of Electrons
Potassium			22	
	$^{51}_{23}\text{V}$			
		48	64	
Barium			82	

4.115 a. What electron sublevel starts to fill after completion of the 3s sublevel? (4.7)
   b. What electron sublevel starts to fill after completion of the 4p sublevel?
   c. What electron sublevel starts to fill after completion of the 3d sublevel?
   d. What electron sublevel starts to fill after completion of the 3p sublevel?

4.116 a. What electron sublevel starts to fill after completion of the 5s sublevel? (4.7)
   b. What electron sublevel starts to fill after completion of the 4d sublevel?
   c. What electron sublevel starts to fill after completion of the 4f sublevel?
   d. What electron sublevel starts to fill after completion of the 5p sublevel?

4.117 a. How many 3d electrons are in Fe? (4.7)
   b. How many 5p electrons are in Ba?
   c. How many 4d electrons are in I?
   d. How many 7s electrons are in Ra?

4.118 a. How many 4d electrons are in Cd? (4.7)
   b. How many 4p electrons are in Br?
   c. How many 6p electrons are in Bi?
   d. How many 5s electrons are in Zn?

4.119 Name the element that corresponds to each of the following: (4.7, 4.8)
   a. $1s^22s^22p^63s^23p^3$
   b. alkali metal with the smallest atomic size
   c. $[\text{Kr}]5s^24d^{10}$
   d. Group 5A (15) element with the highest ionization energy
   e. Period 3 element with the largest atomic size

4.120 Name the element that corresponds to each of the following: (4.7, 4.8)
   a. $1s^22s^22p^63s^23p^64s^13d^5$
   b. $[\text{Xe}]6s^24f^{14}5d^{10}6p^5$
   c. halogen with the highest ionization energy
   d. Group 2A (2) element with the smallest ionization energy
   e. Period 4 element with the smallest atomic size

4.121 Of the elements Na, P, Cl, and F, which (4.2, 4.7, 4.8)
   a. is a metal?
   b. is in Group 5A (15)?
   c. has the highest ionization energy?
   d. loses an electron most easily?
   e. is found in Group 7A (17), Period 3?

4.122 Of the elements K, Ca, Br, and Kr, which (4.2, 4.7, 4.8)
   a. is a halogen?
   b. has the smallest atomic size?
   c. has the lowest ionization energy?
   d. requires the most energy to remove an electron?
   e. is found in Group 2A (2), Period 4?

CHALLENGE QUESTIONS

The following groups of questions are related to the topics in this chapter. However, they do not all follow the chapter order, and they require you to combine concepts and skills from several sections. These questions will help you increase your critical thinking skills and prepare for you next exam.

4.123 The most abundant isotope of lead is $^{208}_{82}\text{Pb}$. (4.4)
   a. How many protons, neutrons, and electrons are in $^{208}_{82}\text{Pb}$?
   b. What is the atomic symbol of another isotope of lead with 132 neutrons?
   c. What is the name and symbol of an atom with the same mass number as in part **b** and 131 neutrons?

4.124 The most abundant isotope of silver is $^{107}_{47}\text{Ag}$. (4.4)
   a. How many protons, neutrons, and electrons are in $^{107}_{47}\text{Ag}$?
   b. What is the symbol of another isotope of silver with 62 neutrons?
   c. What is the name and symbol of an atom with the same mass number as in part **b** and 61 neutrons?

4.125 Give the symbol of the element that has the (4.8)
   a. smallest atomic size in Group 6A (16)
   b. smallest atomic size in Period 3

   c. highest ionization energy in Group 4A (14)
   d. lowest ionization energy in Period 3
   e. most metallic character in Group 2A (2)

4.126 Give the symbol of the element that has the (4.8)
   a. largest atomic size in Group 1A (1)
   b. largest atomic size in Period 4
   c. highest ionization energy in Group 2A (2)
   d. lowest ionization energy in Group 7A (17)
   e. least metallic character in Group 4A (14)

4.127 Silicon has three naturally occurring isotopes: Si-28 that has a percent abundance of 92.23% and a mass of 27.977 amu, Si-29 that has a 4.68% abundance and a mass of 28.976 amu, and Si-30 that has a percent abundance of 3.09% and a mass of 29.974 amu. Calculate the atomic mass for silicon using the weighted average mass method. (4.5)

4.128 Antimony (Sb) has two naturally occurring isotopes: Sb-121 that has a percent abundance of 57.21% and a mass of 120.90 amu, and Sb-123 that has a percent abundance of 42.79% and a mass of 122.90 amu. Calculate the atomic mass for antimony using the weighted average mass method. (4.5)

4.129 Consider three elements with the following abbreviated electron configurations: (4.2, 4.7, 4.8)

$$X = [Ar]4s^2 \qquad Y = [Ne]3s^23p^4$$
$$Z = [Ar]4s^23d^{10}4p^4$$

a. Identify each element as a metal, a nonmetal, or a metalloid.
b. Which element has the largest atomic size?
c. Which elements have similar properties?
d. Which element has the highest ionization energy?
e. Which element has the smallest atomic size?

4.130 Consider three elements with the following abbreviated electron configurations: (4.2, 4.7, 4.8)

$$X = [Ar]4s^23d^5 \qquad Y = [Ar]4s^23d^{10}4p^1$$
$$Z = [Ar]4s^23d^{10}4p^6$$

a. Identify each element as a metal, a nonmetal, or a metalloid.
b. Which element has the smallest atomic size?
c. Which elements have similar properties?
d. Which element has the highest ionization energy?
e. Which element has a half-filled sublevel?

ANSWERS

Answers to Selected Questions and Problems

4.1 a. Cu b. Pt c. Ca d. Mn
e. Fe f. Ba g. Pb h. Sr

4.3 a. carbon b. chlorine c. iodine d. selenium
e. nitrogen f. sulfur g. zinc h. cobalt

4.5 a. sodium, chlorine
b. calcium, sulfur, oxygen
c. carbon, hydrogen, chlorine, nitrogen, oxygen
d. lithium, carbon, oxygen

4.7 a. Period 2 b. Group 8A (18)
c. Group 1A (1) d. Period 2

4.9 a. C b. He c. Na
d. Ca e. Al

4.11 a. metal b. nonmetal c. metal d. nonmetal
e. nonmetal f. nonmetal g. metalloid h. metal

4.13 a. needed for bones and teeth, muscle contraction, nerve impulses; alkaline earth metal
b. component of hemoglobin; transition element
c. muscle contraction, nerve impulses; alkali metal
d. found in fluids outside cells; halogen

4.15 a. A macromineral is an element essential to health, which is present in the body in amounts from 5 to 1000 g.
b. Sulfur is a component of proteins, liver, vitamin B_1, and insulin.
c. 86 g

4.17 a. electron b. proton
c. electron d. neutron

4.19 Rutherford determined that an atom contains a small, compact nucleus that is positively charged.

4.21 a. True b. True
c. True d. False; a proton is attracted to an electron

4.23 In the process of brushing hair, strands of hair become charged with like charges that repel each other.

4.25 a. atomic number b. both
c. mass number d. atomic number

4.27 a. lithium, Li b. fluorine, F
c. calcium, Ca d. zinc, Zn
e. neon, Ne f. silicon, Si
g. iodine, I h. oxygen, O

4.29 a. 18 protons and 18 electrons
b. 25 protons and 25 electrons
c. 53 protons and 53 electrons
d. 48 protons and 48 electrons

4.31

Name of the Element	Symbol	Atomic Number	Mass Number	Number of Protons	Number of Neutrons	Number of Electrons
Zinc	Zn	30	66	30	36	30
Magnesium	Mg	12	24	12	12	12
Potassium	K	19	39	19	20	19
Sulfur	S	16	31	16	15	16
Iron	Fe	26	56	26	30	26

4.33 a. 38 protons, 51 neutrons, 38 electrons
b. 24 protons, 28 neutrons, 24 electrons
c. 16 protons, 18 neutrons, 16 electrons
d. 35 protons, 46 neutrons, 35 electrons

4.35 a. $^{31}_{15}P$ b. $^{80}_{35}Br$ c. $^{122}_{50}Sn$
d. $^{35}_{17}Cl$ e. $^{202}_{80}Hg$

4.37 a. $^{36}_{18}Ar$ $^{38}_{18}Ar$ $^{40}_{18}Ar$
b. They all have the same number of protons and electrons.
c. They have different numbers of neutrons, which gives them different mass numbers.
d. The atomic mass of Ar listed on the periodic table is the weighted average atomic mass of all the naturally occurring isotopes.
e. The isotope Ar-40 is most prevalent because its mass is closest to the atomic mass of Ar on the periodic table.

4.39 69.72 amu

4.41 a. spherical b. two lobes c. spherical

4.43 a. 1 and 2 b. 3
c. 1 and 2 d. 1, 2, and 3

4.45 a. There are five orbitals in the $3d$ sublevel.
b. There is one sublevel in the $n = 1$ energy level.
c. There is one orbital in the $6s$ sublevel.
d. There are nine orbitals in the $n = 3$ energy level.

4.47 a. There is a maximum of two electrons in a $2p$ orbital.
b. There is a maximum of six electrons in the $3p$ sublevel.
c. There is a maximum of 32 electrons in the $n = 4$ energy level.
d. There is a maximum of 10 electrons in the $5d$ sublevel.

4.49 The electron configuration shows the number of electrons in each sublevel of an atom. The abbreviated electron configuration uses the symbol of the preceding noble gas to show completed sublevels.

4.51 a.

1s 2s 2p

b.

1s 2s 2p 3s 3p

c.

1s 2s 2p 3s 3p

d.

1s 2s 2p 3s 3p

4.53 a. $1s^2 2s^2 2p^1$
b. $1s^2 2s^2 2p^6 3s^1$
c. $1s^2 2s^1$
d. $1s^2 2s^2 2p^6 3s^2$

4.55 a. $[He]2s^2 2p^2$ **b.** $[Ne]3s^2 3p^2$
c. $[Ne]3s^2 3p^3$ **d.** $[He]2s^2 2p^5$

4.57 a. Li   **b.** S   **c.** Si   **d.** F

4.59 a. Al   **b.** C   **c.** Ar   **d.** Be

4.61 a. $1s^2 2s^2 2p^6 3s^2 3p^6 4s^2 3d^{10} 4p^3$, $[Ar]4s^2 3d^{10} 4p^3$
b. $1s^2 2s^2 2p^6 3s^2 3p^6 4s^2 3d^6$, $[Ar]4s^2 3d^6$
c. $1s^2 2s^2 2p^6 3s^2 3p^6 4s^2 3d^{10} 4p^6 5s^2 4d^{10} 5p^1$, $[Kr]5s^2 4d^{10} 5p^1$
d. $1s^2 2s^2 2p^6 3s^2 3p^6 4s^2 3d^{10} 4p^6 5s^2 4d^{10} 5p^5$, $[Kr]5s^2 4d^{10} 5p^5$
e. $1s^2 2s^2 2p^6 3s^2 3p^6 4s^2 3d^2$, $[Ar]4s^2 3d^2$

4.63 a. Ga   **b.** N   **c.** Xe   **d.** Zr

4.65 a. 10   **b.** 6   **c.** 3   **d.** 1

4.67 a. 3   **b.** 5   **c.** 2   **d.** 7

4.69 a. Sulfur is in Group 6A (16); ·S̈:
b. Nitrogen is in Group 5A (15); ·N̈·
c. Calcium is in Group 2A (2); Ca·
d. Sodium is in Group 1A (1); Na·
e. Gallium is in Group 3A (13); ·Ga·

4.71 a. Na   **b.** Rb   **c.** Na   **d.** Rb

4.73 a. Mg, Al, Si   **b.** I, Br, Cl
c. Sr, Sb, I   **d.** Na, Si, P

4.75 a. Br   **b.** Mg   **c.** P   **d.** Xe

4.77 a. Br, Cl, F   **b.** Na, Al, Cl
c. Cs, K, Na   **d.** Ca, As, Br

4.79 Ca, Ga, Ge, Br

4.81 lower, more

4.83 a. 1. decreases   **b. 2.** increases
c. 2. increases   **d. 3.** remains the same

4.85 a. false   **b.** true   **c.** true   **d.** false   **e.** true

4.87 a. Group 1A (1), alkali metals   **b.** metal
c. 19 protons   **d.** K-39
e. 39.10 amu

4.89 a. False; All atoms of a given element are different from atoms of other elements.
b. True
c. True
d. False; In a chemical reaction, atoms are neither created nor destroyed.

4.91 a. 1 + 2   **b.** 1   **c.** 1
d. 3   **e.** 2

4.93 a. $^{16}_8 X$, $^{17}_8 X$, $^{18}_8 X$ all have eight protons.
b. $^{16}_8 X$, $^{17}_8 X$, $^{18}_8 X$ are all isotopes of oxygen.

c. $^{16}_8 X$ and $^{16}_9 X$ have mass numbers of 16, and $^{18}_{10} X$ and $^{18}_8 X$ have mass numbers of 18.

4.95

	Atomic Symbol		
	$^{70}_{32}$Ge	$^{73}_{32}$Ge	$^{76}_{32}$Ge
Atomic Number	32	32	32
Mass Number	70	73	76
Number of Protons	32	32	32
Number of Neutrons	38	41	44
Number of Electrons	32	32	32

4.97 a. $^9_4$Be   **b.** $^{11}_5$B   **c.** $^{13}_6$C   **d.** $^{10}_5$B   **e.** $^{12}_6$C

Representations **B** and **D** are isotopes of boron; **C** and **E** are isotopes of carbon.

4.99 a. This is possible. This element is magnesium.
b. Not possible. The 2p sublevel would fill before the 3s, and only two electrons are allowed in an s orbital.

4.101 Li is **D**, Na is **A**, K is **C**, and Rb is **B**.

4.103 a. Na   **b.** Cl   **c.** Si   **d.** Ar
e. S   **f.** Na   **g.** Mg

4.105 a. Group 7A (17), Period 4
b. Group 8A (18), Period 3
c. Group 1A (1), Period 2
d. Group 2A (2), Period 7

4.107 a. metal   **b.** metal
c. metal   **d.** nonmetal

4.109 a. false   **b.** false   **c.** true
d. false   **e.** true

4.111 a. 48 protons, 66 neutrons, 48 electrons
b. 43 protons, 55 neutrons, 43 electrons
c. 79 protons, 120 neutrons, 79 electrons
d. 86 protons, 136 neutrons, 86 electrons
e. 54 protons, 82 neutrons, 54 electrons

4.113

Name of the Element	Atomic Symbol	Number of Protons	Number of Neutrons	Number of Electrons
Selenium	$^{80}_{34}$Se	34	46	34
Nickel	$^{62}_{28}$Ni	28	34	28
Magnesium	$^{26}_{12}$Mg	12	14	12
Radium	$^{228}_{88}$Ra	88	140	88

4.115 a. 3p   **b.** 5s   **c.** 4p   **d.** 4s

4.117 a. 6   **b.** 6   **c.** 10   **d.** 2

4.119 a. phosphorus   **b.** lithium (H is a nonmetal.)
c. cadmium   **d.** nitrogen
e. sodium

4.121 a. Na   **b.** P   **c.** F   **d.** Na   **e.** Cl

4.123 a. 82 protons, 126 neutrons, 82 electrons
b. $^{214}_{82}$Pb
c. $^{214}_{83}$Bi

4.125 a. O   **b.** Ar   **c.** C   **d.** Na   **e.** Ra

4.127 28.09 amu

4.129 a. X is a metal; Y and Z are nonmetals.
b. X has the largest atomic size.
c. Y and Z have six valence electrons and are in Group 6A (16).
d. Y has the highest ionization energy.
e. Y has the smallest atomic size.

5

Nuclear Chemistry

SIMONE'S DOCTOR IS CONCERNED ABOUT HER

elevated cholesterol, which could lead to coronary heart disease and a heart attack. He sends her to a nuclear medicine center to undergo a cardiac stress test. Paul, the nuclear medicine technician, explains to Simone that a nuclear stress test measures the blood flow to her heart muscle at rest and then during stress. The test is performed in a similar way as a routine exercise stress test, but images are produced that show areas of low blood flow through the heart and areas of damaged heart muscle. It involves taking two sets of images of her heart, one when the heart is at rest, and one when she is exercising on a treadmill.

Paul tells Simone that he will inject thallium-201 into her bloodstream. He explains that Tl-201 is a radioactive isotope that has a half-life of 3.0 days. Simone is curious about the term "half-life." Paul explains that a half-life is the amount of time it takes for one-half of a radioactive sample to break down. He assures her that after four half-lives, the radiation emitted will be almost zero. Paul tells Simone that Tl-201 decays to Hg-201 and emits energy similar to X-rays and gamma rays. When the Tl-201 reaches any areas within her heart with restricted blood supply, small amounts of the radioisotope will accumulate.

CAREER Nuclear Medicine Technologist

A nuclear medicine technologist works in a hospital or imaging center where nuclear medicine is used to diagnose and treat a variety of medical conditions. Typically, a nuclear medicine technologist prepares radioisotopes, which are given to patients for diagnostic or therapeutic procedures. In a diagnostic test, the nuclear medicine technologist uses a scanner, which converts radiation from various parts of the body into images. The images are evaluated to determine any abnormalities in the body. A nuclear medicine technologist operates the instrumentation and computers associated with nuclear medicine such as Computed Tomography (CT), Magnetic Resonance Imaging (MRI), and Positron Emission Tomography (PET). A nuclear medicine technologist must know how to handle radioisotopes safely, use the necessary type of shielding, and give radioactive isotopes to patients. In addition, they must physically and mentally prepare patients for imaging by explaining the procedure to them.

LOOKING AHEAD

5.1 Natural Radioactivity 152

5.2 Nuclear Reactions 156

♥ **Chemistry Link to Health**
Radon in Our Homes 157

5.3 Radiation Measurement 162

♥ **Chemistry Link to Health**
Radiation and Food 163

5.4 Half-Life of a
Radioisotope 165

5.5 Medical Applications Using
Radioactivity 169

♥ **Chemistry Link to Health**
Brachytherapy 171

5.6 Nuclear Fission and
Fusion 172

℞ **Clinical Applications** 155,
165, 169, 172, 176, 180, 181

℞ **Clinical Update** *Cardiac
Imaging Using a
Radioisotope* 176

With the production of artificial radioactive substances in 1934, the field of nuclear medicine was established. In 1937, the first radioactive isotope was used to treat a person with leukemia at the University of California at Berkeley. Major strides in the use of radioactivity in medicine occurred in 1946, when a radioactive iodine isotope was successfully used to diagnose thyroid function and to treat hyperthyroidism and thyroid cancer. Radioactive substances are now used to produce images of organs, such as liver, spleen, thyroid gland, kidneys, and the brain, and to detect heart disease. Today, procedures in nuclear medicine provide information about the function and structure of every organ in the body, which allows the nuclear physician to diagnose and treat diseases early.

CHAPTER READINESS*

📱 KEY MATH SKILLS

- Using Positive and Negative Numbers in Calculations (1.4B)
- Solving Equations (1.4D)
- Interpreting a Graph (1.4E)

⚛ CORE CHEMISTRY SKILLS

- Using Conversion Factors (2.6)
- Counting Protons and Neutrons (4.4)
- Writing Atomic Symbols for Isotopes (4.5)

*These Key Math Skills and Core Chemistry Skills from previous chapters are listed here for your review as you proceed to the new material in this chapter.

LEARNING GOAL

Describe alpha, beta, positron, and gamma radiation.

5.1 Natural Radioactivity

Most naturally occurring isotopes of elements up to atomic number 19 have stable nuclei. Elements with atomic numbers 20 and higher usually have one or more isotopes that have unstable nuclei in which the nuclear forces cannot offset the repulsions between the protons. An unstable nucleus is *radioactive*, which means that it spontaneously emits small particles of energy called **radiation** to become more stable. Radiation may take the form of alpha (α) and beta (β) particles, positrons (β^+), or pure energy such as gamma (γ) rays. An isotope of an element that emits radiation is called a **radioisotope**. For most types of radiation, there is a change in the number of protons in the nucleus, which means that an atom is converted into an atom of a different element. This kind of nuclear change was not evident to Dalton when he made his predictions about atoms. Elements with atomic numbers of 93 and higher are produced artificially in nuclear laboratories and consist only of radioactive isotopes.

The atomic symbols for the different isotopes are written with the mass number in the upper left corner and the atomic number in the lower left corner. The mass number is the sum of the number of protons and neutrons in the nucleus, and the atomic number is equal to the number of protons. For example, a radioactive isotope of iodine used in the diagnosis and treatment of thyroid conditions has a mass number of 131 and an atomic number of 53.

Mass number (protons and neutrons) ⟶ $^{131}_{53}\text{I}$ ⟵ Symbol of element

Atomic number (protons) ⟶

Radioactive isotopes are identified by writing the mass number after the element's name or symbol. Thus, in this example, the isotope is called iodine-131 or I-131. Table 5.1 compares some stable, nonradioactive isotopes with some radioactive isotopes.

TABLE 5.1 Stable and Radioactive Isotopes of Some Elements

Magnesium	Iodine	Uranium
Stable Isotopes		
$^{24}_{12}\text{Mg}$	$^{127}_{53}\text{I}$	None
Magnesium-24	Iodine-127	
Radioactive Isotopes		
$^{23}_{12}\text{Mg}$	$^{125}_{53}\text{I}$	$^{235}_{92}\text{U}$
Magnesium-23	Iodine-125	Uranium-235
$^{27}_{12}\text{Mg}$	$^{131}_{53}\text{I}$	$^{238}_{92}\text{U}$
Magnesium-27	Iodine-131	Uranium-238

Types of Radiation

By emitting radiation, an unstable nucleus forms a more stable, lower energy nucleus. One type of radiation consists of *alpha particles*. An **alpha particle** is identical to a helium (He) nucleus, which has two protons and two neutrons. An alpha particle has a mass number of 4, an atomic number of 2, and a charge of 2+. The symbol for an alpha particle is the Greek letter alpha (α) or the symbol of a helium nucleus except that the 2+ charge is omitted.

Another type of radiation occurs when a radioisotope emits a *beta particle*. A **beta particle**, which is a high-energy electron, has a charge of 1−, and because its mass is so much less than the mass of a proton, it has a mass number of 0. It is represented by the Greek letter beta (β) or by the symbol for the electron including the mass number and the charge ($^{0}_{-1}e$). A beta particle is formed when a neutron in an unstable nucleus changes into a proton.

A **positron**, similar to a beta particle, has a positive (1+) charge with a mass number of 0. It is represented by the Greek letter beta with a 1+ charge, β^+, or by the symbol of an electron, which includes the mass number and the charge ($^{0}_{+1}e$). A positron is produced by an unstable nucleus when a proton is transformed into a neutron and a positron.

A positron is an example of *antimatter*, a term physicists use to describe a particle that is the opposite of another particle, in this case, an electron. When an electron and a positron collide, their minute masses are completely converted to energy in the form of *gamma rays*.

$$^{0}_{-1}e + {}^{0}_{+1}e \longrightarrow 2\,{}^{0}_{0}\gamma$$

Gamma rays are high-energy radiation, released when an unstable nucleus undergoes a rearrangement of its particles to give a more stable, lower energy nucleus. Gamma rays are often emitted along with other types of radiation. A gamma ray is written as the Greek letter gamma ($^{0}_{0}\gamma$). Because gamma rays are energy only, zeros are used to show that a gamma ray has no mass or charge.

Table 5.2 summarizes the types of radiation we will use in nuclear equations.

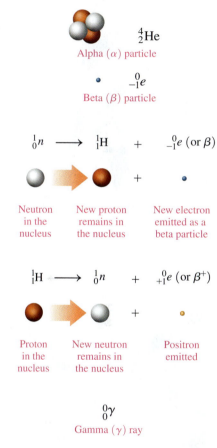

$^{4}_{2}\text{He}$
Alpha (α) particle

$^{0}_{-1}e$
Beta (β) particle

$^{1}_{0}n \longrightarrow {}^{1}_{1}\text{H} + {}^{0}_{-1}e$ (or β)

| Neutron in the nucleus | New proton remains in the nucleus | New electron emitted as a beta particle |

$^{1}_{1}\text{H} \longrightarrow {}^{1}_{0}n + {}^{0}_{+1}e$ (or β^+)

| Proton in the nucleus | New neutron remains in the nucleus | Positron emitted |

$^{0}_{0}\gamma$
Gamma (γ) ray

TABLE 5.2 Some Forms of Radiation

Type of Radiation	Symbol		Change in Nucleus	Mass Number	Charge
Alpha Particle	α	$^{4}_{2}\text{He}$	Two protons and two neutrons are emitted as an alpha particle.	4	2+
Beta Particle	β	$^{0}_{-1}e$	A neutron changes to a proton and an electron is emitted.	0	1−
Positron	β^+	$^{0}_{+1}e$	A proton changes to a neutron and a positron is emitted.	0	1+
Gamma Ray	γ	$^{0}_{0}\gamma$	Energy is lost to stabilize the nucleus.	0	0
Proton	p	$^{1}_{1}\text{H}$	A proton is emitted.	1	1+
Neutron	n	$^{1}_{0}n$	A neutron is emitted.	1	0

Different types of radiation penetrate the body to different depths.

FIGURE 5.1 ▶ In a nuclear pharmacy, a person working with radioisotopes wears protective clothing and gloves and uses a lead glass shield on a syringe.

🔍 What types of radiation does a lead shield block?

> ▶ **SAMPLE PROBLEM 5.1** Radiation Particles
>
> Identify and write the symbol for each of the following types of radiation:
>
> **a.** contains two protons and two neutrons
> **b.** has a mass number of 0 and a 1− charge
>
> **SOLUTION**
>
> **a.** An alpha (α) particle, $_2^4$He, has two protons and two neutrons.
> **b.** A beta (β) particle, $_{-1}^0e$, is like an electron with a mass number of 0 and a 1− charge.
>
> **STUDY CHECK 5.1**
>
> Identify and write the symbol for the type of radiation that has a mass number of zero and a 1+ charge.
>
> **ANSWER**
>
> A positron, $_{+1}^0e$, has a mass number of 0 and a 1+ charge.

Biological Effects of Radiation

When radiation strikes molecules in its path, electrons may be knocked away, forming unstable ions. If this *ionizing radiation* passes through the human body, it may interact with water molecules, removing electrons and producing H_2O^+, which can cause undesirable chemical reactions.

The cells most sensitive to radiation are the ones undergoing rapid division—those of the bone marrow, skin, reproductive organs, and intestinal lining, as well as all cells of growing children. Damaged cells may lose their ability to produce necessary materials. For example, if radiation damages cells of the bone marrow, red blood cells may no longer be produced. If sperm cells, ova, or the cells of a fetus are damaged, birth defects may result. In contrast, cells of the nerves, muscles, liver, and adult bones are much less sensitive to radiation because they undergo little or no cellular division.

Cancer cells are another example of rapidly dividing cells. Because cancer cells are highly sensitive to radiation, large doses of radiation are used to destroy them. The normal tissue that surrounds cancer cells divides at a slower rate and suffers less damage from radiation. However, radiation may cause malignant tumors, leukemia, anemia, and genetic mutations.

Radiation Protection

Nuclear medicine technologists, chemists, doctors, and nurses who work with radioactive isotopes must use proper radiation protection. Proper *shielding* is necessary to prevent exposure. Alpha particles, which have the largest mass and charge of the radiation particles, travel only a few centimeters in the air before they collide with air molecules, acquire electrons, and become helium atoms. A piece of paper, clothing, and our skin are protection against alpha particles. Lab coats and gloves will also provide sufficient shielding. However, if alpha emitters are ingested or inhaled, the alpha particles they give off can cause serious internal damage.

Beta particles have a very small mass and move much faster and farther than alpha particles, traveling as much as several meters through air. They can pass through paper and penetrate as far as 4 to 5 mm into body tissue. External exposure to beta particles can burn the surface of the skin, but they do not travel far enough to reach the internal organs. Heavy clothing such as lab coats and gloves are needed to protect the skin from beta particles.

Gamma rays travel great distances through the air and pass through many materials, including body tissues. Because gamma rays penetrate so deeply, exposure to gamma rays can be extremely hazardous. Only very dense shielding, such as lead or concrete, will stop them. Syringes used for injections of radioactive materials use shielding made of lead or heavy-weight materials such as tungsten and plastic composites.

When working with radioactive materials, medical personnel wear protective clothing and gloves and stand behind a shield (see Figure 5.1). Long tongs may be used to pick up vials of radioactive material, keeping them away from the hands and body. Table 5.3 summarizes the shielding materials required for the various types of radiation.

TABLE 5.3 Properties of Radiation and Shielding Required

Property	Alpha (α) Particle	Beta (β) Particle	Gamma (γ) Ray
Travel Distance in Air	2 to 4 cm	200 to 300 cm	500 m
Tissue Depth	0.05 mm	4 to 5 mm	50 cm or more
Shielding	Paper, clothing	Heavy clothing, lab coats, gloves	Lead, thick concrete
Typical Source	Radium-226	Carbon-14	Technetium-99m

If you work in an environment where radioactive materials are present, such as a nuclear medicine facility, try to keep the time you spend in a radioactive area to a minimum. Remaining in a radioactive area twice as long exposes you to twice as much radiation.

Keep your distance! The greater the distance from the radioactive source, the lower the intensity of radiation received. By doubling your distance from the radiation source, the intensity of radiation drops to $\left(\frac{1}{2}\right)^2$, or one-fourth of its previous value.

QUESTIONS AND PROBLEMS

5.1 Natural Radioactivity

LEARNING GOAL Describe alpha, beta, positron, and gamma radiation.

5.1 Identify the type of particle or radiation for each of the following:
   a. ^4_2He **b.** $^0_{+1}e$ **c.** $^0_0\gamma$

5.2 Identify the type of particle or radiation for each of the following:
   a. $^0_{-1}e$ **b.** ^1_1H **c.** ^1_0n

5.3 Naturally occurring potassium consists of three isotopes: potassium-39, potassium-40, and potassium-41.
   a. Write the atomic symbol for each isotope.
   b. In what ways are the isotopes similar, and in what ways do they differ?

5.4 Naturally occurring iodine is iodine-127. Medically, radioactive isotopes of iodine-125 and iodine-131 are used.
   a. Write the atomic symbol for each isotope.
   b. In what ways are the isotopes similar, and in what ways do they differ?

5.5 Identify each of the following:
   a. $^0_{-1}\text{X}$ **b.** ^4_2X **c.** ^1_0X
   d. $^{38}_{18}\text{X}$ **e.** $^{14}_6\text{X}$

5.6 Identify each of the following:
   a. ^1_1X **b.** $^{81}_{35}\text{X}$ **c.** ^0_0X
   d. $^{59}_{26}\text{X}$ **e.** $^0_{+1}\text{X}$

℞ Clinical Applications

5.7 Write the symbol for each of the following isotopes used in nuclear medicine:
   a. copper-64   **b.** selenium-75
   c. sodium-24   **d.** nitrogen-15

5.8 Write the symbol for each of the following isotopes used in nuclear medicine:
   a. indium-111   **b.** palladium-103
   c. barium-131   **d.** rubidium-82

5.9 Supply the missing information in the following table:

Medical Use	Atomic Symbol	Mass Number	Number of Protons	Number of Neutrons
Heart imaging	$^{201}_{81}\text{Tl}$			
Radiation therapy			60	27
Abdominal scan			31	36
Hyperthyroidism	$^{131}_{53}\text{I}$			
Leukemia treatment		32		17

5.10 Supply the missing information in the following table:

Medical Use	Atomic Symbol	Mass Number	Number of Protons	Number of Neutrons
Cancer treatment	$^{131}_{55}\text{Cs}$			
Brain scan			43	56
Blood flow		141	58	
Bone scan		85		47
Lung function	$^{133}_{54}\text{Xe}$			

5.11 Match the type of radiation (**1** to **3**) with each of the following statements:
   1. alpha particle
   2. beta particle
   3. gamma radiation

   a. does not penetrate skin
   b. shielding protection includes lead or thick concrete
   c. can be very harmful if ingested

5.12 Match the type of radiation (**1** to **3**) with each of the following statements:
   1. alpha particle
   2. beta particle
   3. gamma radiation

   a. penetrates farthest into skin and body tissues
   b. shielding protection includes lab coats and gloves
   c. travels only a short distance in air

Write a balanced nuclear equation showing mass numbers and atomic numbers for radioactive decay.

⊗ CORE CHEMISTRY SKILL

Writing Nuclear Equations

5.2 Nuclear Reactions

In a process called **radioactive decay**, a nucleus spontaneously breaks down by emitting radiation. This process is shown by writing a *nuclear equation* with the atomic symbols of the original radioactive nucleus on the left, an arrow, and the new nucleus and the type of radiation emitted on the right.

$$\text{Radioactive nucleus} \longrightarrow \text{new nucleus} + \text{radiation } (\alpha, \beta, \beta^+, \gamma)$$

In a nuclear equation, the sum of the mass numbers and the sum of the atomic numbers on one side of the arrow must equal the sum of the mass numbers and the sum of the atomic numbers on the other side.

Alpha Decay

An unstable nucleus may emit an alpha particle, which consists of two protons and two neutrons. Thus, the mass number of the radioactive nucleus decreases by 4, and its atomic number decreases by 2. For example, when uranium-238 emits an alpha particle, the new nucleus that forms has a mass number of 234. Compared to uranium with 92 protons, the new nucleus has 90 protons, which is thorium.

Radioactive uranium nucleus

Alpha particle

Radiation

$^{4}_{2}\text{He}$

Thorium-234 nucleus

New nucleus

$^{238}_{92}\text{U}$

○ Neutron

● Proton

$^{234}_{90}\text{Th}$

146 neutrons
92 protons

$^{238}_{92}\text{U}$

Radioactive nucleus

144 neutrons
90 protons

2 neutrons
2 protons

$$^{238}_{92}\text{U} \longrightarrow {}^{234}_{90}\text{Th} + {}^{4}_{2}\text{He}$$

New nucleus

Alpha particle

In the nuclear equation for alpha decay, the mass number of the new nucleus decreases by 4 and its atomic number decreases by 2.

We can look at writing a balanced nuclear equation for americium-241, which undergoes alpha decay as shown in Sample Problem 5.2.

▶ SAMPLE PROBLEM 5.2 Writing an Equation for Alpha Decay

Smoke detectors that are used in homes and apartments contain americium-241, which undergoes alpha decay. When alpha particles collide with air molecules, charged particles are produced that generate an electrical current. If smoke particles enter the detector, they interfere with the formation of charged particles in the air, and the electrical current is interrupted. This causes the alarm to sound and warns the occupants of the danger of fire. Write the balanced nuclear equation for the decay of americium-241.

SOLUTION

ANALYZE THE PROBLEM	Given	Need
	Am-241, alpha decay	balanced nuclear equation

A smoke detector sounds an alarm when smoke enters its ionization chamber.

STEP 1 Write the incomplete nuclear equation.

$$^{241}_{95}\text{Am} \longrightarrow ? + ^{4}_{2}\text{He}$$

STEP 2 Determine the missing mass number. In the equation, the mass number of the americium, 241, is equal to the sum of the mass numbers of the new nucleus and the alpha particle.

$$241 \qquad = ? + 4$$
$$241 - 4 = ?$$
$$241 - 4 = 237 \text{ (mass number of new nucleus)}$$

STEP 3 Determine the missing atomic number. The atomic number of americium, 95, must equal the sum of the atomic numbers of the new nucleus and the alpha particle.

$$95 \qquad = ? + 2$$
$$95 - 2 = ?$$
$$95 - 2 = 93 \text{ (atomic number of new nucleus)}$$

STEP 4 Determine the symbol of the new nucleus. On the periodic table, the element that has atomic number 93 is neptunium, Np. The nucleus of this isotope of Np is written as $^{237}_{93}\text{Np}$.

STEP 5 Complete the nuclear equation.

$$^{241}_{95}\text{Am} \longrightarrow ^{237}_{93}\text{Np} + ^{4}_{2}\text{He}$$

STUDY CHECK 5.2

Write the balanced nuclear equation for the alpha decay of Po-214.

ANSWER

$$^{214}_{84}\text{Po} \longrightarrow ^{210}_{82}\text{Pb} + ^{4}_{2}\text{He}$$

> **Guide to Completing a Nuclear Equation**
>
> **STEP 1**
> Write the incomplete nuclear equation.
>
> **STEP 2**
> Determine the missing mass number.
>
> **STEP 3**
> Determine the missing atomic number.
>
> **STEP 4**
> Determine the symbol of the new nucleus.
>
> **STEP 5**
> Complete the nuclear equation.

$^{4}_{2}\text{He}$

$^{237}_{93}\text{Np}$ | Pu | $^{241}_{95}\text{Am}$

Chemistry Link to **Health**

Radon in Our Homes

The presence of radon gas has become a much publicized environmental and health issue because of the radiation danger it poses. Radioactive isotopes such as radium-226 are naturally present in many types of rocks and soils. Radium-226 emits an alpha particle and is converted into radon gas, which diffuses out of the rocks and soil.

$$^{226}_{88}\text{Ra} \longrightarrow ^{222}_{86}\text{Rn} + ^{4}_{2}\text{He}$$

Outdoors, radon gas poses little danger because it disperses in the air. However, if the radioactive source is under a house or building, the radon gas can enter the house through cracks in the foundation or other openings. Those who live or work there may inhale the radon. Inside the lungs, radon-222 emits alpha particles to form polonium-218, which is known to cause lung cancer.

$$^{222}_{86}\text{Rn} \longrightarrow ^{218}_{84}\text{Po} + ^{4}_{2}\text{He}$$

The Environmental Protection Agency (EPA) recommends that the maximum level of radon not exceed 4 picocuries (pCi) per liter of air in a home. One picocurie (pCi) is equal to 10^{-12} curies (Ci); curies are described in section 5.3. In California, 1% of all the houses surveyed exceeded the EPA's recommended maximum radon level.

A radon gas detector is used to determine radon levels in buildings.

Beta Decay

The formation of a beta particle is the result of the breakdown of a neutron into a proton and an electron (beta particle). Because the proton remains in the nucleus, the number of protons increases by one, whereas the number of neutrons decreases by one. Thus, in a nuclear equation for beta decay, the mass number of the radioactive nucleus and the mass number of the new nucleus are the same. However, the atomic number of the new nucleus increases by one, which makes it a nucleus of a different element (*transmutation*). For example, the beta decay of a carbon-14 nucleus produces a nitrogen-14 nucleus.

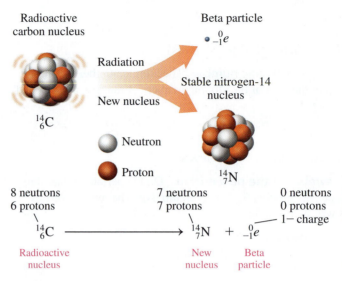

$$^{14}_{6}\text{C} \longrightarrow ^{14}_{7}\text{N} + ^{0}_{-1}e$$

Radioactive   New   Beta
nucleus   nucleus   particle

In the nuclear equation for beta decay, the mass number of the new nucleus remains the same and its atomic number increases by 1.

A radioisotope is injected into joint of the hand to relieve the pain caused by arthritis.

▶ **SAMPLE PROBLEM 5.3** **Writing a Nuclear Equation for Beta Decay**

The radioactive isotope yttrium-90, a beta emitter, is used in cancer treatment and as a colloidal injection into large joints to relieve the pain caused by arthritis. Write the balanced nuclear equation for the beta decay of yttrium-90.

SOLUTION

ANALYZE THE PROBLEM	Given	Need
	Y-90, beta decay	balanced nuclear equation

STEP 1 Write the incomplete nuclear equation.

$$^{90}_{39}\text{Y} \longrightarrow ? + ^{0}_{-1}e$$

STEP 2 Determine the missing mass number. In the equation, the mass number of the yttrium, 90, is equal to the sum of the mass numbers of the new nucleus and the beta particle.

$$90 = ? + 0$$
$$90 - 0 = ?$$
$$90 - 0 = 90 \text{ (mass number of new nucleus)}$$

STEP 3 Determine the missing atomic number. The atomic number of yttrium, 39, must equal the sum of the atomic numbers of the new nucleus and the beta particle.

$$39 = ? - 1$$
$$39 + 1 = ?$$
$$39 + 1 = 40 \text{ (atomic number of new nucleus)}$$

STEP 4 Determine the symbol of the new nucleus. On the periodic table, the element that has atomic number 40 is zirconium, Zr. The nucleus of this isotope of Zr is written as $^{90}_{40}\text{Zr}$.

STEP 5 Complete the nuclear equation.

$$^{90}_{39}\text{Y} \longrightarrow ^{90}_{40}\text{Zr} + ^{0}_{-1}e$$

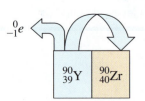

STUDY CHECK 5.3

Write the balanced nuclear equation for the beta decay of chromium-51.

ANSWER

$^{51}_{24}\text{Cr} \longrightarrow \, ^{51}_{25}\text{Mn} + \, ^{0}_{-1}e$

Positron Emission

In positron emission, a proton in an unstable nucleus is converted to a neutron and a positron. The neutron remains in the nucleus, but the positron is emitted from the nucleus. In a nuclear equation for positron emission, the mass number of the radioactive nucleus and the mass number of the new nucleus are the same. However, the atomic number of the new nucleus decreases by one, indicating a change of one element into another. For example, an aluminum-24 nucleus undergoes positron emission to produce a magnesium-24 nucleus. The atomic number of magnesium (12) and the charge of the positron (1+) give the atomic number of aluminum (13).

$^{24}_{13}\text{Al} \longrightarrow \, ^{24}_{12}\text{Mg} + \, ^{0}_{+1}e$

▶ **SAMPLE PROBLEM 5.4** Writing a Nuclear Equation for Positron Emission

Write the balanced nuclear equation for manganese-49, which decays by emitting a positron.

SOLUTION

ANALYZE THE PROBLEM	Given	Need
	Mn-49, positron emission	balanced nuclear equation

STEP 1 Write the incomplete nuclear equation.

$^{49}_{25}\text{Mn} \longrightarrow \, ? + \, ^{0}_{+1}e$

STEP 2 Determine the missing mass number. In the equation, the mass number of the manganese, 49, is equal to the sum of the mass numbers of the new nucleus and the positron.

$49 \quad\;\; = ? + 0$
$49 - 0 = ?$
$49 - 0 = 49 \text{ (mass number of new nucleus)}$

STEP 3 Determine the missing atomic number. The atomic number of manganese, 25, must equal the sum of the atomic numbers of the new nucleus and the positron.

$25 \quad\;\; = ? + 1$
$25 - 1 = ?$
$25 - 1 = 24 \text{ (atomic number of new nucleus)}$

STEP 4 Determine the symbol of the new nucleus. On the periodic table, the element that has atomic number 24 is chromium (Cr). The nucleus of this isotope of Cr is written as $^{49}_{24}\text{Cr}$.

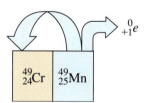

STEP 5 Complete the nuclear equation.

$^{49}_{25}\text{Mn} \longrightarrow \, ^{49}_{24}\text{Cr} + \, ^{0}_{+1}e$

STUDY CHECK 5.4

Write the balanced nuclear equation for xenon-118, which undergoes positron emission.

ANSWER

$^{118}_{54}\text{Xe} \longrightarrow \, ^{118}_{53}\text{I} + \, ^{0}_{+1}e$

Radiation Source **Radiation** **New Nucleus**

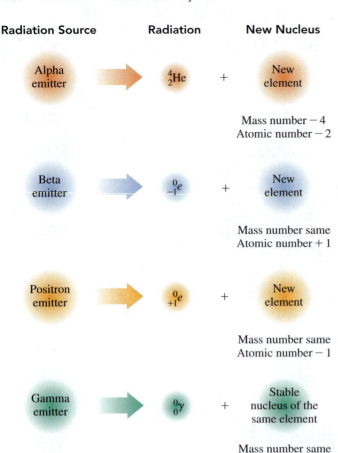

Mass number − 4
Atomic number − 2

Mass number same
Atomic number + 1

Mass number same
Atomic number − 1

Mass number same
Atomic number same

Gamma Emission

Pure gamma emitters are rare, although gamma radiation accompanies most alpha and beta radiation. In radiology, one of the most commonly used gamma emitters is technetium (Tc). The unstable isotope of technetium is written as the *metastable* (symbol m) isotope technetium-99m, Tc-99m, or $^{99m}_{43}$Tc. By emitting energy in the form of gamma rays, the nucleus becomes more stable.

$$^{99m}_{43}\text{Tc} \longrightarrow {}^{99}_{43}\text{Tc} + {}^{0}_{0}\gamma$$

Figure 5.2 summarizes the changes in the nucleus for alpha, beta, positron, and gamma radiation.

Producing Radioactive Isotopes

Today, many radioisotopes are produced in small amounts by bombarding stable, nonradioactive isotopes with high-speed particles such as alpha particles, protons, neutrons, and small nuclei. When one of these particles is absorbed, the stable nucleus is converted to a radioactive isotope and usually some type of radiation particle.

FIGURE 5.2 ▶ When the nuclei of alpha, beta, positron, and gamma emitters emit radiation, new, more stable nuclei are produced.

Q What changes occur in the number of protons and neutrons when an alpha emitter gives off radiation?

$$^{4}_{2}\text{He} \quad + \quad {}^{10}_{5}\text{B} \longrightarrow {}^{13}_{7}\text{N} \quad + \quad {}^{1}_{0}n$$

Bombarding particle   Stable nucleus   New radioactive nucleus   Neutron

When nonradioactive B-10 is bombarded by an alpha particle, the products are radioactive N-13 and a neutron.

All elements that have an atomic number greater than 92 have been produced by bombardment. Most have been produced in only small amounts and exist for only a short time, making it difficult to study their properties. For example, when californium-249 is bombarded with nitrogen-15, the radioactive element dubnium-260 and four neutrons are produced.

$$^{15}_{7}\text{N} + {}^{249}_{98}\text{Cf} \longrightarrow {}^{260}_{105}\text{Db} + 4{}^{1}_{0}n$$

Technetium-99m is a radioisotope used in nuclear medicine for several diagnostic procedures, including the detection of brain tumors and examinations of the liver and spleen. The source of technetium-99m is molybdenum-99, which is produced in a nuclear reactor by neutron bombardment of molybdenum-98.

$$^{1}_{0}n + {}^{98}_{42}\text{Mo} \longrightarrow {}^{99}_{42}\text{Mo}$$

Many radiology laboratories have small generators containing molybdenum-99, which decays to the technetium-99m radioisotope.

$$^{99}_{42}\text{Mo} \longrightarrow \,^{99m}_{43}\text{Tc} + \,^{0}_{-1}e$$

The technetium-99m radioisotope decays by emitting gamma rays. Gamma emission is desirable for diagnostic work because the gamma rays pass through the body to the detection equipment.

$$^{99m}_{43}\text{Tc} \longrightarrow \,^{99}_{43}\text{Tc} + \,^{0}_{0}\gamma$$

A generator is used to prepare technetium-99m.

▶ **SAMPLE PROBLEM 5.5** Writing an Equation for an Isotope Produced by Bombardment

Write the balanced nuclear equation for the bombardment of nickel-58 by a proton, $^{1}_{1}\text{H}$, which produces a radioactive isotope and an alpha particle.

SOLUTION

ANALYZE THE PROBLEM	Given	Need
	proton bombardment of Ni-58	balanced nuclear equation

STEP 1 Write the incomplete nuclear equation.

$$^{1}_{1}\text{H} + \,^{58}_{28}\text{Ni} \longrightarrow \,? + \,^{4}_{2}\text{He}$$

STEP 2 Determine the missing mass number. In the equation, the sum of the mass numbers of the proton, 1, and the nickel, 58, must equal the sum of the mass numbers of the new nucleus and the alpha particle.

$1 + 58 = ? + 4$
$59 - 4 = ?$
$59 - 4 = 55$ (mass number of new nucleus)

STEP 3 Determine the missing atomic number. The sum of the atomic numbers of the proton, 1, and nickel, 28, must equal the sum of the atomic numbers of the new nucleus and the alpha particle.

$1 + 28 = ? + 2$
$29 - 2 = ?$
$29 - 2 = 27$ (atomic number of new nucleus)

STEP 4 Determine the symbol of the new nucleus. On the periodic table, the element that has atomic number 27 is cobalt, Co. The nucleus of this isotope of Co is written as $^{55}_{27}\text{Co}$.

STEP 5 Complete the nuclear equation.

$$^{1}_{1}\text{H} + \,^{58}_{28}\text{Ni} \longrightarrow \,^{55}_{27}\text{Co} + \,^{4}_{2}\text{He}$$

STUDY CHECK 5.5

The first radioactive isotope was produced in 1934 by the bombardment of aluminum-27 by an alpha particle to produce a radioactive isotope and one neutron. Write the balanced nuclear equation for this bombardment.

Interactive Video

Writing Equations for an Isotope Produced by Bombardment

ANSWER

$$^{4}_{2}\text{He} + \,^{27}_{13}\text{Al} \longrightarrow \,^{30}_{15}\text{P} + \,^{1}_{0}n$$

QUESTIONS AND PROBLEMS

5.2 Nuclear Reactions

LEARNING GOAL Write a balanced nuclear equation showing mass numbers and atomic numbers for radioactive decay.

5.13 Write a balanced nuclear equation for the alpha decay of each of the following radioactive isotopes:
a. $^{208}_{84}Po$ b. $^{232}_{90}Th$
c. $^{251}_{102}No$ d. radon-220

5.14 Write a balanced nuclear equation for the alpha decay of each of the following radioactive isotopes:
a. curium-243   b. $^{252}_{99}Es$
c. $^{251}_{98}Cf$ d. $^{261}_{107}Bh$

5.15 Write a balanced nuclear equation for the beta decay of each of the following radioactive isotopes:
a. $^{25}_{11}Na$ b. $^{20}_{8}O$
c. strontium-92   d. iron-60

5.16 Write a balanced nuclear equation for the beta decay of each of the following radioactive isotopes:
a. $^{44}_{19}K$ b. iron-59
c. potassium-42   d. $^{141}_{56}Ba$

5.17 Write a balanced nuclear equation for the positron emission of each of the following radioactive isotopes:
a. silicon-26   b. cobalt-54
c. $^{77}_{37}Rb$ d. $^{93}_{45}Rh$

5.18 Write a balanced nuclear equation for the positron emission of each of the following radioactive isotopes:
a. boron-8   b. $^{15}_{8}O$
c. $^{40}_{19}K$ d. nitrogen-13

5.19 Complete each of the following nuclear equations and describe the type of radiation:
a. $^{28}_{13}Al \longrightarrow ? + ^{0}_{-1}e$ b. $^{180m}_{73}Ta \longrightarrow ^{180}_{73}Ta + ?$
c. $^{66}_{29}Cu \longrightarrow ^{66}_{30}Zn + ?$ d. $? \longrightarrow ^{234}_{90}Th + ^{4}_{2}He$
e. $^{188}_{80}Hg \longrightarrow ? + ^{0}_{+1}e$

5.20 Complete each of the following nuclear equations and describe the type of radiation:
a. $^{11}_{6}C \longrightarrow ^{11}_{5}B + ?$ b. $^{35}_{16}S \longrightarrow ? + ^{0}_{-1}e$
c. $? \longrightarrow ^{90}_{39}Y + ^{0}_{-1}e$ d. $^{210}_{83}Bi \longrightarrow ? + ^{4}_{2}He$
e. $? \longrightarrow ^{89}_{39}Y + ^{0}_{+1}e$

5.21 Complete each of the following bombardment reactions:
a. $^{1}_{0}n + ^{9}_{4}Be \longrightarrow ?$
b. $^{1}_{0}n + ^{131}_{52}Te \longrightarrow ? + ^{0}_{-1}e$
c. $^{1}_{0}n + ? \longrightarrow ^{24}_{11}Na + ^{4}_{2}He$
d. $^{4}_{2}He + ^{14}_{7}N \longrightarrow ? + ^{1}_{1}H$

5.22 Complete each of the following bombardment reactions:
a. $? + ^{40}_{18}Ar \longrightarrow ^{43}_{19}K + ^{1}_{1}H$
b. $^{1}_{0}n + ^{238}_{92}U \longrightarrow ?$
c. $^{1}_{0}n + ? \longrightarrow ^{14}_{6}C + ^{1}_{1}H$
d. $? + ^{64}_{28}Ni \longrightarrow ^{272}_{111}Rg + ^{1}_{0}n$

5.3 Radiation Measurement

One of the most common instruments for detecting beta and gamma radiation is the Geiger counter. It consists of a metal tube filled with a gas such as argon. When radiation enters a window on the end of the tube, it forms charged particles in the gas, which produce an electrical current. Each burst of current is amplified to give a click and a reading on a meter.

$$Ar + radiation \longrightarrow Ar^{+} + e^{-}$$

Measuring Radiation

Radiation is measured in several different ways. When a radiology laboratory obtains a radioisotope, the *activity* of the sample is measured in terms of the number of nuclear disintegrations per second. The **curie (Ci)**, the original unit of activity, was defined as the

A radiation counter is used to determine radiation levels in workers at the Fukushima Daiichi nuclear power plant.

number of disintegrations that occur in 1 s for 1 g of radium, which is equal to 3.7×10^{10} disintegrations/s. The unit was named for the Polish scientist Marie Curie, who along with her husband, Pierre, discovered the radioactive elements radium and polonium. The SI unit of radiation activity is the **becquerel (Bq)**, which is 1 disintegration/s.

The **rad (radiation absorbed dose)** is a unit that measures the amount of radiation absorbed by a gram of material such as body tissue. The SI unit for absorbed dose is the **gray (Gy)**, which is defined as the joules of energy absorbed by 1 kg of body tissue. The gray is equal to 100 rad.

The **rem (radiation equivalent in humans)** is a unit that measures the biological effects of different kinds of radiation. Although alpha particles do not penetrate the skin, if they should enter the body by some other route, they can cause extensive damage within a short distance in tissue. High-energy radiation, such as beta particles, high-energy protons, and neutrons that travel into tissue, causes more damage. Gamma rays are damaging because they travel a long way through body tissue.

To determine the **equivalent dose** or rem dose, the absorbed dose (rad) is multiplied by a factor that adjusts for biological damage caused by a particular form of radiation. For beta and gamma radiation the factor is 1, so the biological damage in rems is the same as the absorbed radiation (rad). For high-energy protons and neutrons, the factor is about 10, and for alpha particles it is 20.

Biological damage (rem) = Absorbed dose (rad) × Factor

Often, the measurement for an equivalent dose will be in units of millirems (mrem). One rem is equal to 1000 mrem. The SI unit is the **sievert (Sv)**. One sievert is equal to 100 rem. Table 5.4 summarizes the units used to measure radiation.

Chemistry Link to **Health**
Radiation and Food

Foodborne illnesses caused by pathogenic bacteria such as *Salmonella*, *Listeria*, and *Escherichia coli* have become a major health concern in the United States. The Centers for Disease Control and Prevention estimates that each year, *E. coli* in contaminated foods infects 20 000 people in the United States and that 500 people die. *E. coli* has been responsible for outbreaks of illness from contaminated ground beef, fruit juices, lettuce, and alfalfa sprouts.

The U.S. Food and Drug Administration (FDA) has approved the use of 0.3 kGy to 1 kGy of radiation produced by cobalt-60 or cesium-137 for the treatment of foods. The irradiation technology is much like that used to sterilize medical supplies. Cobalt pellets are placed in stainless steel tubes, which are arranged in racks. When food moves through the series of racks, the gamma rays pass through the food and kill the bacteria.

It is important for consumers to understand that when food is irradiated, it never comes in contact with the radioactive source. The gamma rays pass through the food to kill bacteria, but that does not make the food radioactive. The radiation kills bacteria because it stops their ability to divide and grow. We cook or heat food thoroughly for the same purpose. Radiation, as well as heat, has little effect on the food itself because its cells are no longer dividing or growing. Thus irradiated food is not harmed, although a small amount of vitamin B_1 and C may be lost.

Currently, tomatoes, blueberries, strawberries, and mushrooms are being irradiated to allow them to be harvested when completely ripe and extend their shelf life (see Figure 5.3). The FDA has also approved the irradiation of pork, poultry, and beef to decrease potential infections and to extend shelf life. Currently, irradiated vegetable and meat products are available in retail markets in more than 40 countries. In the United States, irradiated foods such as tropical fruits, spinach, and ground meats are found in some stores. *Apollo 17* astronauts ate irradiated foods on the Moon, and some U.S. hospitals and nursing homes now use irradiated poultry to reduce the possibility of salmonella infections among residents. The extended shelf life of irradiated food also makes it useful for campers and military personnel. Soon, consumers concerned about food safety will have a choice of irradiated meats, fruits, and vegetables at the market.

(a)

(b)

FIGURE 5.3 ▶ **(a)** The FDA requires this symbol to appear on irradiated retail foods. **(b)** After two weeks, the irradiated strawberries on the right show no spoilage. Mold is growing on the nonirradiated ones on the left.

🔵 Why are irradiated foods used on spaceships and in nursing homes?

A dosimeter measures radiation exposure.

TABLE 5.5 Average Annual Radiation Received by a Person in the United States

Source	Dose (mrem)
Natural	
Ground	20
Air, water, food	30
Cosmic rays	40
Wood, concrete, brick	50
Medical	
Chest X-ray	20
Dental X-ray	20
Mammogram	40
Hip X-ray	60
Lumbar spine X-ray	70
Upper gastrointestinal tract X-ray	200
Other	
Nuclear power plants	0.1
Television	20
Air travel	10
Radon	200*

*Varies widely.

TABLE 5.6 Lethal Doses of Radiation for Some Life Forms

Life Form	LD_{50} (rem)
Insect	100 000
Bacterium	50 000
Rat	800
Human	500
Dog	300

TABLE 5.4 Units of Radiation Measurement

Measurement	Common Unit	SI Unit	Relationship
Activity	curie (Ci) $1\ Ci = 3.7 \times 10^{10}$ disintegrations/s	becquerel (Bq) $1\ Bq = 1$ disintegration/s	$1\ Ci = 3.7 \times 10^{10}\ Bq$
Absorbed Dose	rad	gray (Gy) $1\ Gy = 1\ J/kg$ of tissue	$1\ Gy = 100\ rad$
Biological Damage	rem	sievert (Sv)	$1\ Sv = 100\ rem$

People who work in radiology laboratories wear dosimeters attached to their clothing to determine any exposure to radiation such as X-rays, gamma rays, or beta particles. A dosimeter can be thermoluminescent (TLD), optically stimulated luminescence (OSL), or electronic personal (EPD). Dosimeters provide real time radiation levels measured by monitors in the work area.

> **SAMPLE PROBLEM 5.6** Radiation Measurement
>
> One treatment for bone pain involves intravenous administration of the radioisotope phosphorus-32, which is incorporated into bone. A typical dose of 7 mCi can produce up to 450 rad in the bone. What is the difference between the units of mCi and rad?
>
> **SOLUTION**
>
> The millicuries (mCi) indicate the activity of the P-32 in terms of nuclei that break down in 1 s. The radiation absorbed dose (rad) is a measure of amount of radiation absorbed by the bone.
>
> **STUDY CHECK 5.6**
>
> For Sample Problem 5.6, what is the absorbed dose of radiation in grays (Gy)?
>
> **ANSWER**
>
> 4.5 Gy

Exposure to Radiation

Every day, we are exposed to low levels of radiation from naturally occurring radioactive isotopes in the buildings where we live and work, in our food and water, and in the air we breathe. For example, potassium-40, a naturally occurring radioactive isotope, is present in any potassium-containing food. Other naturally occurring radioisotopes in air and food are carbon-14, radon-222, strontium-90, and iodine-131. The average person in the United States is exposed to about 360 mrem of radiation annually. Medical sources of radiation, including dental, hip, spine, and chest X-rays and mammograms, add to our radiation exposure. Table 5.5 lists some common sources of radiation.

Another source of background radiation is cosmic radiation produced in space by the Sun. People who live at high altitudes or travel by airplane receive a greater amount of cosmic radiation because there are fewer molecules in the atmosphere to absorb the radiation. For example, a person living in Denver receives about twice the cosmic radiation as a person living in Los Angeles. A person living close to a nuclear power plant normally does not receive much additional radiation, perhaps 0.1 mrem in 1 yr. (One rem equals 1000 mrem.) However, in the accident at the Chernobyl nuclear power plant in 1986 in Ukraine, it is estimated that people in a nearby town received as much as 1 rem/h.

Radiation Sickness

The larger the dose of radiation received at one time, the greater the effect on the body. Exposure to radiation of less than 25 rem usually cannot be detected. Whole-body exposure of 100 rem produces a temporary decrease in the number of white blood cells. If the exposure to radiation is greater than 100 rem, a person may suffer the symptoms of radiation sickness: nausea, vomiting, fatigue, and a reduction in white-cell count. A whole-body dosage greater than

300 rem can decrease the white-cell count to zero. The person suffers diarrhea, hair loss, and infection. Exposure to radiation of 500 rem is expected to cause death in 50% of the people receiving that dose. This amount of radiation to the whole body is called the *lethal dose for one-half the population*, or the LD_{50}. The LD_{50} varies for different life forms, as Table 5.6 shows. Whole-body radiation of 600 rem or greater would be fatal to all humans within a few weeks.

QUESTIONS AND PROBLEMS

5.3 Radiation Measurement

LEARNING GOAL Describe the detection and measurement of radiation.

5.23 Match each property (**1** to **3**) with its unit of measurement.
  1. activity
  2. absorbed dose
  3. biological damage

  a. rad   **b.** mrem
  c. mCi   **d.** Gy

5.24 Match each property (**1** to **3**) with its unit of measurement.
  1. activity
  2. absorbed dose
  3. biological damage

  a. mrad   **b.** gray
  c. becquerel   **d.** Sv

Rx Clinical Applications

5.25 Two technicians in a nuclear laboratory were accidentally exposed to radiation. If one was exposed to 8 mGy and the other to 5 rad, which technician received more radiation?

5.26 Two samples of a radioisotope were spilled in a nuclear laboratory. The activity of one sample was 8 kBq and the other 15 mCi. Which sample produced the higher amount of radiation?

5.27 a. The recommended dosage of iodine-131 is 4.20 μCi/kg of body mass. How many microcuries of iodine-131 are needed for a 70.0-kg person with hyperthyroidism?
  b. A person receives 50 rad of gamma radiation. What is that amount in grays?

5.28 a. The dosage of technetium-99m for a lung scan is 20. μCi/kg of body mass. How many millicuries of technetium-99m should be given to a 50.0-kg person (1 mCi = 1000 μCi)?
  b. Suppose a person absorbed 50 mrad of alpha radiation. What would be the equivalent dose in millirems?

5.4 Half-Life of a Radioisotope

LEARNING GOAL

Given the half-life of a radioisotope, calculate the amount of radio-isotope remaining after one or more half-lives.

The **half-life** of a radioisotope is the amount of time it takes for one-half of a sample to decay. For example, $^{131}_{53}I$ has a half-life of 8.0 days. As $^{131}_{53}I$ decays, it produces the non-radioactive isotope $^{131}_{54}Xe$ and a beta particle.

$$^{131}_{53}I \longrightarrow {}^{131}_{54}Xe + {}^{0}_{-1}e$$

Suppose we have a sample that initially contains 20. mg of $^{131}_{53}I$. In 8.0 days, one-half (10. mg) of all the I-131 nuclei in the sample will decay, which leaves 10. mg of I-131. After 16 days (two half-lives), 5.0 mg of the remaining I-131 decays, which leaves 5.0 mg of I-131. After 24 days (three half-lives), 2.5 mg of the remaining I-131 decays, which leaves 2.5 mg of I-131 nuclei still capable of producing radiation.

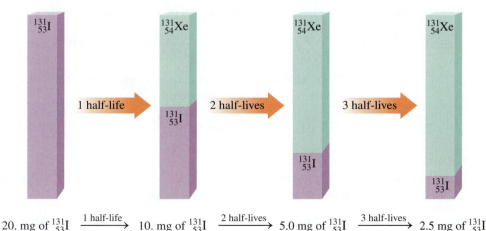

$$20.\ mg\ of\ ^{131}_{53}I \xrightarrow{\ 1\ half\text{-}life\ } 10.\ mg\ of\ ^{131}_{53}I \xrightarrow{\ 2\ half\text{-}lives\ } 5.0\ mg\ of\ ^{131}_{53}I \xrightarrow{\ 3\ half\text{-}lives\ } 2.5\ mg\ of\ ^{131}_{53}I$$

A **decay curve** is a diagram of the decay of a radioactive isotope. Figure 5.4 shows such a curve for the $^{131}_{53}I$ we have discussed.

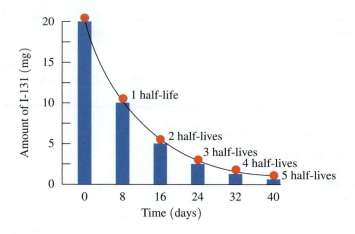

FIGURE 5.4 ▶ The decay curve for iodine-131 shows that one-half of the radioactive sample decays and one-half remains radioactive after each half-life of 8.0 days.

Q How many milligrams of the 20.-mg sample remain radioactive after two half-lives?

⚛ **CORE CHEMISTRY SKILL**

Using Half-Lives

Guide to Using Half-Lives

STEP 1
State the given and needed quantities.

STEP 2
Write a plan to calculate the unknown quantity.

STEP 3
Write the half-life equality and conversion factors.

STEP 4
Set up the problem to calculate the needed quantity.

▶ **SAMPLE PROBLEM 5.7** Using Half-Lives of a Radioisotope

Phosphorus-32, a radioisotope used in the treatment of leukemia, has a half-life of 14.3 days. If a sample contains 8.0 mg of phosphorus-32, how many milligrams of phosphorus-32 remain after 42.9 days?

SOLUTION

STEP 1 State the given and needed quantities.

	Given	Need
ANALYZE THE PROBLEM	8.0 mg of P-32, 42.9 days elapsed, half-life = 14.3 days	milligrams of P-32 remaining

STEP 2 Write a plan to calculate the unknown quantity.

days $\boxed{\text{Half-life}}$ number of half-lives

milligrams of $^{32}_{15}P$ $\boxed{\begin{array}{c}\text{Number of}\\\text{half-lives}\end{array}}$ milligrams of $^{32}_{15}P$ remaining

STEP 3 Write the half-life equality and conversion factors.

$$1 \text{ half-life} = 14.3 \text{ days}$$

$$\frac{14.3 \text{ days}}{1 \text{ half-life}} \quad \text{and} \quad \frac{1 \text{ half-life}}{14.3 \text{ days}}$$

STEP 4 Set up the problem to calculate the needed quantity. First, we determine the number of half-lives in the amount of time that has elapsed.

$$\text{number of half-lives} = 42.9 \text{ days} \times \frac{1 \text{ half-life}}{14.3 \text{ days}} = 3.00 \text{ half-lives}$$

Now we can determine how much of the sample decays in three half-lives and how many grams of the phosphorus remain.

$$8.0 \text{ mg of } ^{32}_{15}P \xrightarrow{1 \text{ half-life}} 4.0 \text{ mg of } ^{32}_{15}P \xrightarrow{2 \text{ half-lives}} 2.0 \text{ mg of } ^{32}_{15}P \xrightarrow{3 \text{ half-lives}} 1.0 \text{ mg of } ^{32}_{15}P$$

Interactive Video

Half-Lives

STUDY CHECK 5.7

Iron-59 has a half-life of 44 days. If a nuclear laboratory receives a sample of 8.0 μg of iron-59, how many micrograms of iron-59 are still active after 176 days?

ANSWER

0.50 μg of iron-59

TABLE 5.7 Half-Lives of Some Radioisotopes

Element	Radioisotope	Half-Life	Type of Radiation
Naturally Occurring Radioisotopes			
Carbon-14	$^{14}_{6}C$	5730 yr	Beta
Potassium-40	$^{40}_{19}K$	1.3×10^9 yr	Beta, gamma
Radium-226	$^{226}_{88}Ra$	1600 yr	Alpha
Strontium-90	$^{90}_{38}Sr$	38.1 yr	Alpha
Uranium-238	$^{238}_{92}U$	4.5×10^9 yr	Alpha
Some Medical Radioisotopes			
Carbon-11	$^{11}_{6}C$	20 min	Positron
Chromium-51	$^{51}_{24}Cr$	28 days	Gamma
Iodine-131	$^{131}_{53}I$	8.0 days	Gamma
Oxygen-15	$^{15}_{8}O$	2.0 min	Positron
Iron-59	$^{59}_{26}Fe$	44 days	Beta, gamma
Radon-222	$^{222}_{86}Rn$	3.8 days	Alpha
Technetium-99m	$^{99m}_{43}Tc$	6.0 h	Beta, gamma

Naturally occurring isotopes of the elements usually have long half-lives, as shown in Table 5.7. They disintegrate slowly and produce radiation over a long period of time, even hundreds or millions of years. In contrast, the radioisotopes used in nuclear medicine have much shorter half-lives. They disintegrate rapidly and produce almost all their radiation in a short period of time. For example, technetium-99m emits half of its radiation in the first 6 h. This means that a small amount of the radioisotope given to a patient is essentially gone within two days. The decay products of technetium-99m are totally eliminated by the body.

Chemistry Link to the **Environment**

Dating Ancient Objects

Radiological dating is a technique used by geologists, archaeologists, and historians to determine the age of ancient objects. The age of an object derived from plants or animals (such as wood, fiber, natural pigments, bone, and cotton or woolen clothing) is determined by measuring the amount of carbon-14, a naturally occurring radioactive form of carbon. In 1960, Willard Libby received the Nobel Prize for the work he did developing carbon-14 dating techniques during the 1940s. Carbon-14 is produced in the upper atmosphere by the bombardment of $^{14}_{7}N$ by high-energy neutrons from cosmic rays.

$$^{1}_{0}n \quad + \quad ^{14}_{7}N \quad \longrightarrow \quad ^{14}_{6}C \quad + \quad ^{1}_{1}H$$

Neutron from cosmic rays   Nitrogen in atmosphere   Radioactive carbon-14   Proton

The carbon-14 reacts with oxygen to form radioactive carbon dioxide, $^{14}_{6}CO_2$. Living plants continuously absorb carbon dioxide, which incorporates carbon-14 into the plant material. The uptake of carbon-14 stops when the plant dies.

$$^{14}_{6}C \longrightarrow ^{14}_{7}N + ^{0}_{-1}e$$

As the carbon-14 decays, the amount of radioactive carbon-14 in the plant material steadily decreases. In a process called *carbon dating*, scientists use the half-life of carbon-14 (5730 yr) to calculate the length of time since the plant died. For example, a wooden beam found in an ancient dwelling might have one-half of the carbon-14 found in living plants today. Because one half-life of carbon-14 is 5730 yr, the dwelling was constructed about 5730 yr ago. Carbon-14 dating was used to determine that the Dead Sea Scrolls are about 2000 yr old.

The age of the Dead Sea Scrolls was determined using carbon-14.

A radiological dating method used for determining the age of much older items is based on the radioisotope uranium-238, which decays through a series of reactions to lead-206. The uranium-238 isotope has an incredibly long half-life, about 4×10^9 (4 billion) yr. Measurements of the amounts of uranium-238 and lead-206 enable geologists to determine the age of rock samples. The older rocks will have a higher percentage of lead-206 because more of the uranium-238 has decayed. The age of rocks brought back from the Moon by the *Apollo* missions, for example, was determined using uranium-238. They were found to be about 4×10^9 yr old, approximately the same age calculated for the Earth.

The age of a bone sample from a skeleton can be determined by carbon dating.

▶ **SAMPLE PROBLEM 5.8** Dating Using Half-Lives

Carbon material in the bones of humans and animals assimilates carbon until death. Using radiocarbon dating, the number of half-lives of carbon-14 from a bone sample determines the age of the bone. Suppose a sample is obtained from a prehistoric animal and used for radiocarbon dating. We can calculate the age of the bone or the years elapsed since the animal died by using the half-life of carbon-14, which is 5730 yr. If the sample shows that four half-lives have passed, how much time has elapsed since the animal died?

SOLUTION

STEP 1 State the given and needed quantities.

ANALYZE THE PROBLEM	Given	Need
	1 half-life of C-14 = 5730 yr, 4 half-lives elapsed	years elapsed

STEP 2 Write a plan to calculate the unknown quantity.

4 half-lives [Half-life] years elapsed

STEP 3 Write the half-life equality and conversion factors.

$$1 \text{ half-life} = 5730 \text{ yr}$$

$$\frac{5730 \text{ yr}}{1 \text{ half-life}} \quad \text{and} \quad \frac{1 \text{ half-life}}{5730 \text{ yr}}$$

STEP 4 Set up the problem to calculate the needed quantity.

$$\text{Years elapsed} = 4.0 \text{ half-lives} \times \frac{5730 \text{ yr}}{1 \text{ half-life}} = 23\,000 \text{ yr}$$

We would estimate that the animal lived 23 000 yr ago.

STUDY CHECK 5.8

Suppose that a piece of wood found in a tomb had one-eighth of its original carbon-14 activity. About how many years ago was the wood part of a living tree?

ANSWER

17 200 yr

QUESTIONS AND PROBLEMS

5.4 Half-Life of a Radioisotope

LEARNING GOAL Given the half-life of a radioisotope, calculate the amount of radioisotope remaining after one or more half-lives.

5.29 For each of the following, indicate if the number of half-lives elapsed is:
  1. one half-life
  2. two half-lives
  3. three half-lives

  a. a sample of Pd-103 with a half-life of 17 days after 34 days
  b. a sample of C-11 with a half-life of 20 min after 20 min
  c. a sample of At-211 with a half-life of 7 h after 21 h

5.30 For each of the following, indicate if the number of half-lives elapsed is:
  1. one half-life
  2. two half-lives
  3. three half-lives

  a. a sample of Ce-141 with a half-life of 32.5 days after 32.5 days
  b. a sample of F-18 with a half-life of 110 min after 330 min
  c. a sample of Au-198 with a half-life of 2.7 days after 5.4 days

5.31 Technetium-99m is an ideal radioisotope for scanning organs because it has a half-life of 6.0 h and is a pure gamma emitter. Suppose that 80.0 mg were prepared in the technetium generator this morning. How many milligrams of technetium-99m would remain after each of the following intervals?
   a. one half-life   **b.** two half-lives
   c. 18 h   **d.** 24 h

5.32 A sample of sodium-24 with an activity of 12 mCi is used to study the rate of blood flow in the circulatory system. If sodium-24 has a half-life of 15 h, what is the activity after each of the following intervals?
   a. one half-life   **b.** 30 h
   c. three half-lives   **d.** 2.5 days

5.33 Strontium-85, used for bone scans, has a half-life of 65 days.
   a. How long will it take for the radiation level of strontium-85 to drop to one-fourth of its original level?
   b. How long will it take for the radiation level of strontium-85 to drop to one-eighth of its original level?

5.34 Fluorine-18, which has a half-life of 110 min, is used in PET scans.
   a. If 100. mg of fluorine-18 is shipped at 8:00 A.M., how many milligrams of the radioisotope are still active after 110 min?
   b. If 100. mg of fluorine-18 is shipped at 8:00 A.M., how many milligrams of the radioisotope are still active when the sample arrives at the radiology laboratory at 1:30 P.M.?

5.5 Medical Applications Using Radioactivity

To determine the condition of an organ in the body, a nuclear medicine technologist may use a radioisotope that concentrates in that organ. The cells in the body do not differentiate between a nonradioactive atom and a radioactive one, so these radioisotopes are easily incorporated. Then the radioactive atoms are detected because they emit radiation. Some radioisotopes used in nuclear medicine are listed in Table 5.8.

TABLE 5.8 Medical Applications of Radioisotopes

Isotope	Half-Life	Radiation	Medical Application
Au-198	2.7 days	Beta	Liver imaging; treatment of abdominal carcinoma
Ce-141	32.5 days	Beta	Gastrointestinal tract diagnosis; measuring blood flow to the heart
Cs-131	9.7 days	Gamma	Prostate brachytherapy
F-18	110 min	Positron	Positron emission tomography (PET)
Ga-67	78 h	Gamma	Abdominal imaging; tumor detection
Ga-68	68 min	Gamma	Detection of pancreatic cancer
I-123	13.2 h	Gamma	Treatment of thyroid, brain, and prostate cancer
I-131	8.0 days	Beta	Treatment of Graves' disease, goiter, hyperthyroidism, thyroid and prostate cancer
Ir-192	74 days	Gamma	Treatment of breast and prostate cancer
P-32	14.3 days	Beta	Treatment of leukemia, excess red blood cells, and pancreatic cancer
Pd-103	17 days	Gamma	Prostate brachytherapy
Sr-85	65 days	Gamma	Detection of bone lesions; brain scans
Tc-99m	6.0 h	Gamma	Imaging of skeleton and heart muscle, brain, liver, heart, lungs, bone, spleen, kidney, and thyroid; most widely used radioisotope in nuclear medicine
Y-90	2.7 days	Beta	Treatment of liver cancer

▶ **SAMPLE PROBLEM 5.9** Medical Applications of Radioactivity

In the treatment of abdominal carcinoma, a person is treated with "seeds" of gold-198, which is a beta emitter. Write the balanced nuclear equation for the beta decay of gold-198.

SOLUTION

ANALYZE THE PROBLEM	Given	Need
	gold-198, beta decay	balanced nuclear equation

Titanium "seeds" filled with a radioactive isotope are implanted in the body to treat cancer.

We can write the incomplete nuclear equation starting with gold-198.

$$^{198}_{79}\text{Au} \longrightarrow \text{?} + ^{0}_{-1}e$$

In beta decay, the mass number, 198, does not change, but the atomic number of the new nucleus increases by one. The new atomic number is 80, which is mercury, Hg.

$$^{198}_{79}\text{Au} \longrightarrow ^{198}_{80}\text{Hg} + ^{0}_{-1}e$$

STUDY CHECK 5.9

In an experimental treatment, a person is given boron-10, which is taken up by malignant tumors. When bombarded with neutrons, boron-10 decays by emitting alpha particles that destroy the surrounding tumor cells. Write the balanced nuclear equation for the reaction for this experimental procedure.

ANSWER

$$^{1}_{0}n + ^{10}_{5}\text{B} \longrightarrow ^{7}_{3}\text{Li} + ^{4}_{2}\text{He}$$

Scans with Radioisotopes

After a person receives a radioisotope, the radiologist determines the level and location of radioactivity emitted by the radioisotope. An apparatus called a *scanner* is used to produce an image of the organ. The scanner moves slowly across the body above the region where the organ containing the radioisotope is located. The gamma rays emitted from the radioisotope in the organ can be used to expose a photographic plate, producing a *scan* of the organ. On a scan, an area of decreased or increased radiation can indicate conditions such as a disease of the organ, a tumor, a blood clot, or edema.

A common method of determining thyroid function is the use of *radioactive iodine uptake*. Taken orally, the radioisotope iodine-131 mixes with the iodine already present in the thyroid. Twenty-four hours later, the amount of iodine taken up by the thyroid is determined. A detection tube held up to the area of the thyroid gland detects the radiation coming from the iodine-131 that has located there (see Figure 5.5).

A person with a hyperactive thyroid will have a higher than normal level of radioactive iodine, whereas a person with a hypoactive thyroid will have lower values. If a person has hyperthyroidism, treatment is begun to lower the activity of the thyroid. One treatment involves giving a therapeutic dosage of radioactive iodine, which has a higher radiation level than the diagnostic dose. The radioactive iodine goes to the thyroid where its radiation destroys some of the thyroid cells. The thyroid produces less thyroid hormone, bringing the hyperthyroid condition under control.

Positron Emission Tomography

Positron emitters with short half-lives such as carbon-11, oxygen-15, nitrogen-13, and fluorine-18 are used in an imaging method called *positron emission tomography* (PET). A positron-emitting isotope such as fluorine-18 combined with substances in the body such as glucose is used to study brain function, metabolism, and blood flow.

$$^{18}_{9}\text{F} \longrightarrow ^{18}_{8}\text{O} + ^{0}_{+1}e$$

As positrons are emitted, they combine with electrons to produce gamma rays that are detected by computerized equipment to create a three-dimensional image of the organ (see Figure 5.6).

(a)

(b)

FIGURE 5.5 ▶ **(a)** A scanner detects radiation from a radioisotope in an organ. **(b)** A scan shows radioactive iodine-131 in the thyroid.

🅠 What type of radiation would move through body tissues to create a scan?

FIGURE 5.6 ▶ These PET scans of the brain show a normal brain on the left and a brain affected by Alzheimer's disease on the right.

🅠 When positrons collide with electrons, what type of radiation is produced that gives an image of an organ?

Computed Tomography

Another imaging method used to scan organs such as the brain, lungs, and heart is *computed tomography* (CT). A computer monitors the absorption of 30 000 X-ray beams directed at successive layers of the target organ. Based on the densities of the tissues and fluids in the organ, the differences in absorption of the X-rays provide a series of images of the organ. This technique is successful in the identification of hemorrhages, tumors, and atrophy.

Magnetic Resonance Imaging

Magnetic resonance imaging (MRI) is a powerful imaging technique that does not involve X-ray radiation. It is the least invasive imaging method available. MRI is based on the absorption of energy when the protons in hydrogen atoms are excited by a strong magnetic field. Hydrogen atoms make up 63% of all the atoms in the body. In the hydrogen nuclei, the protons act like tiny bar magnets. With no external field, the protons have random orientations. However, when placed within a strong magnetic field, the protons align with the field. A proton aligned with the field has a lower energy than one that is aligned against the field. As the MRI scan proceeds, radiofrequency pulses of energy are applied and the hydrogen nuclei resonate at a certain frequency. Then the radio waves are quickly turned off, and the protons slowly return to their natural alignment within the magnetic field and resonate at a different frequency. They release the energy absorbed from the radio wave pulses. The difference in energy between the two states is released, which produces the electromagnetic signal that the scanner detects. These signals are sent to a computer system, where a color image of the body is generated. Because hydrogen atoms in the body are in different chemical environments, different energies are absorbed. MRI is particularly useful in obtaining images of soft tissues, which contain large amounts of hydrogen atoms in the form of water.

A CT scan shows a tumor (yellow) in the brain.

An MRI scan provides images of the heart and lungs.

Chemistry Link to **Health**
Brachytherapy

The process called *brachytherapy*, or seed implantation, is an internal form of radiation therapy. The prefix *brachy* is from the Greek word for short distance. With internal radiation, a high dose of radiation is delivered to a cancerous area, whereas normal tissue sustains minimal damage. Because higher doses are used, fewer treatments of shorter duration are needed. Conventional external treatment delivers a lower dose per treatment, but requires six to eight weeks of treatment.

Permanent Brachytherapy

One of the most common forms of cancer in males is prostate cancer. In addition to surgery and chemotherapy, one treatment option is to place 40 or more titanium capsules, or "seeds," in the malignant area. Each seed, which is the size of a grain of rice, contains radioactive iodine-125, palladium-103, or cesium-131, which decay by gamma emission. The radiation from the seeds destroys the cancer by interfering with the reproduction of cancer cells with minimal damage to adjacent normal tissues. Ninety percent (90%) of the radioisotopes decay within a few months because they have short half-lives.

Isotope	I-125	Pd-103	Cs-131
Radiation	Gamma	Gamma	Gamma
Half-Life	60 days	17 days	10 days
Time Required to Deliver 90% of Radiation	7 months	2 months	1 month

Almost no radiation passes out of the patient's body. The amount of radiation received by a family member is no greater than that received on a long plane flight. Because the radioisotopes decay to products that are not radioactive, the inert titanium capsules can be left in the body.

Temporary Brachytherapy

In another type of treatment for prostate cancer, long needles containing iridium-192 are placed in the tumor. However, the needles are removed after 5 to 10 min, depending on the activity of the iridium isotope. Compared to permanent brachytherapy, temporary brachytherapy can deliver a higher dose of radiation over a shorter time. The procedure may be repeated in a few days.

Brachytherapy is also used following breast cancer lumpectomy. An iridium-192 isotope is inserted into the catheter implanted in the space left by the removal of the tumor. The isotope is removed after 5 to 10 min, depending on the activity of the iridium source. Radiation is delivered primarily to the tissue surrounding the cavity that contained the tumor and where the cancer is most likely to recur. The procedure is repeated twice a day for five days to give an absorbed dose of 34 Gy (3400 rad). The catheter is removed, and no radioactive material remains in the body.

In conventional external beam therapy for breast cancer, a patient is given 2 Gy once a day for six to seven weeks, which gives a total absorbed dose of about 80 Gy or 8000 rad. The external beam therapy irradiates the entire breast, including the tumor cavity.

A catheter placed temporarily in the breast for radiation from Ir-192.

QUESTIONS AND PROBLEMS

5.5 Medical Applications Using Radioactivity

LEARNING GOAL Describe the use of radioisotopes in medicine.

℞ Clinical Applications

5.35 Bone and bony structures contain calcium and phosphorus.
  a. Why would the radioisotopes calcium-47 and phosphorus-32 be used in the diagnosis and treatment of bone diseases?
  b. During nuclear tests, scientists were concerned that strontium-85, a radioactive product, would be harmful to the growth of bone in children. Explain.

5.36 **a.** Technetium-99m emits only gamma radiation. Why would this type of radiation be used in diagnostic imaging rather than an isotope that also emits beta or alpha radiation?

  b. A person with *polycythemia vera* (excess production of red blood cells) receives radioactive phosphorus-32. Why would this treatment reduce the production of red blood cells in the bone marrow of the patient?

5.37 In a diagnostic test for leukemia, a person receives 4.0 mL of a solution containing selenium-75. If the activity of the selenium-75 is 45 μCi/mL, what dose, in microcuries, does the patient receive?

5.38 A vial contains radioactive iodine-131 with an activity of 2.0 mCi/mL. If a thyroid test requires 3.0 mCi in an "atomic cocktail," how many milliliters are used to prepare the iodine-131 solution?

LEARNING GOAL

Describe the processes of nuclear fission and fusion.

5.6 Nuclear Fission and Fusion

During the 1930s, scientists bombarding uranium-235 with neutrons discovered that the U-235 nucleus splits into two smaller nuclei and produces a great amount of energy. This was the discovery of nuclear **fission**. The energy generated by splitting the atom was called *atomic energy*. A typical equation for nuclear fission is:

$$\ce{^{1}_{0}n} + \ce{^{235}_{92}U} \longrightarrow \ce{^{236}_{92}U} \longrightarrow \ce{^{91}_{36}Kr} + \ce{^{142}_{56}Ba} + 3\,\ce{^{1}_{0}n} + \text{energy}$$

If we could determine the mass of the products krypton, barium, and three neutrons, with great accuracy, we would find that their total mass is slightly less than the mass of the starting materials. The missing mass has been converted into an enormous amount of energy, consistent with the famous equation derived by Albert Einstein.

$$E = mc^2$$

where E is the energy released, m is the mass lost, and c is the speed of light, 3×10^8 m/s. Even though the mass loss is very small, when it is multiplied by the speed of light squared, the result is a large value for the energy released. The fission of 1 g of uranium-235 produces about as much energy as the burning of 3 tons of coal.

Chain Reaction

Fission begins when a neutron collides with the nucleus of a uranium atom. The resulting nucleus is unstable and splits into smaller nuclei. This fission process also releases several neutrons and large amounts of gamma radiation and energy. The neutrons emitted have high energies and bombard other uranium-235 nuclei. In a **chain reaction**, there is a rapid increase in the number of high-energy neutrons available to react with more uranium. To sustain a nuclear chain reaction, sufficient quantities of uranium-235 must be brought together to provide a *critical mass* in which almost all the neutrons immediately collide with more uranium-235 nuclei. So much heat and energy build up that an atomic explosion can occur (see Figure 5.7).

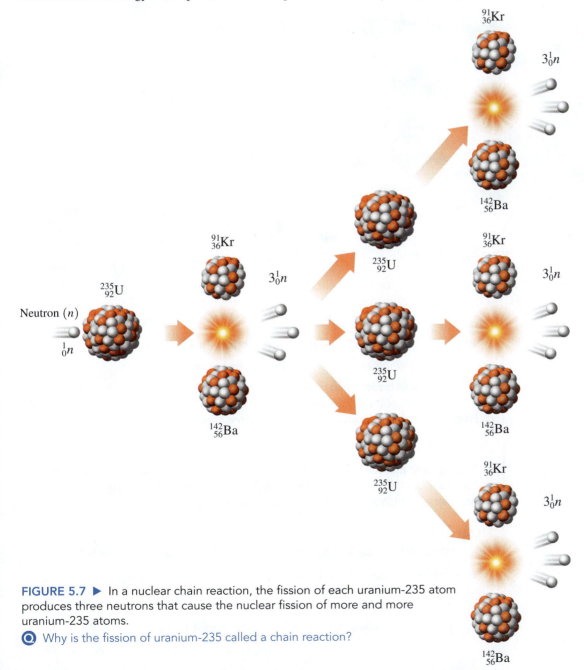

FIGURE 5.7 ▶ In a nuclear chain reaction, the fission of each uranium-235 atom produces three neutrons that cause the nuclear fission of more and more uranium-235 atoms.

🔘 Why is the fission of uranium-235 called a chain reaction?

Nuclear Fusion

In **fusion**, two small nuclei combine to form a larger nucleus. Mass is lost, and a tremendous amount of energy is released, even more than the energy released from nuclear fission. However, a fusion reaction requires a temperature of 100 000 000 °C to overcome the repulsion of the hydrogen nuclei and cause them to undergo fusion. Fusion reactions occur continuously in the Sun and other stars, providing us with heat and light. The huge amounts of energy produced by our sun come from the fusion of 6×10^{11} kg of hydrogen every second. In a fusion reaction, isotopes of hydrogen combine to form helium and large amounts of energy.

Scientists expect less radioactive waste with shorter half-lives from fusion reactors. However, fusion is still in the experimental stage because the extremely high temperatures needed have been difficult to reach and even more difficult to maintain. Research groups around the world are attempting to develop the technology needed to make the harnessing of the fusion reaction for energy a reality in our lifetime.

$$^3_1\text{H} + \,^2_1\text{H} \longrightarrow \,^4_2\text{He} + \,^1_0n + \text{energy}$$

In a fusion reactor, high temperatures are needed to combine hydrogen atoms.

SAMPLE PROBLEM 5.10 Identifying Fission and Fusion

Classify the following as pertaining to fission, fusion, or both:

a. A large nucleus breaks apart to produce smaller nuclei.
b. Large amounts of energy are released.
c. Extremely high temperatures are needed for reaction.

SOLUTION

a. When a large nucleus breaks apart to produce smaller nuclei, the process is fission.
b. Large amounts of energy are generated in both the fusion and fission processes.
c. An extremely high temperature is required for fusion.

STUDY CHECK 5.10

Classify the following nuclear equation as pertaining to fission, fusion, or both:

$$^3_1\text{H} + \,^2_1\text{H} \longrightarrow \,^4_2\text{He} + \,^1_0n + \text{energy}$$

ANSWER

When small nuclei combine to release energy, the process is fusion.

QUESTIONS AND PROBLEMS

5.6 Nuclear Fission and Fusion

LEARNING GOAL Describe the processes of nuclear fission and fusion.

5.39 What is nuclear fission?

5.40 How does a chain reaction occur in nuclear fission?

5.41 Complete the following fission reaction:

$$^{1}_{0}n + ^{235}_{92}U \longrightarrow ^{131}_{50}Sn + ? + 2^{1}_{0}n + \text{energy}$$

5.42 In another fission reaction, uranium-235 bombarded with a neutron produces strontium-94, another small nucleus, and three neutrons. Write the balanced nuclear equation for the fission reaction.

5.43 Indicate whether each of the following is characteristic of the fission or fusion process, or both:
  a. Neutrons bombard a nucleus.
  b. The nuclear process occurs in the Sun.
  c. A large nucleus splits into smaller nuclei.
  d. Small nuclei combine to form larger nuclei.

5.44 Indicate whether each of the following is characteristic of the fission or fusion process, or both:
  a. Very high temperatures are required to initiate the reaction.
  b. Less radioactive waste is produced.
  c. Hydrogen nuclei are the reactants.
  d. Large amounts of energy are released when the nuclear reaction occurs.

Chemistry Link to the **Environment**

Nuclear Power Plants

In a nuclear power plant, the quantity of uranium-235 is held below a critical mass, so it cannot sustain a chain reaction. The fission reactions are slowed by placing control rods, which absorb some of the fast-moving neutrons, among the uranium samples. In this way, less fission occurs, and there is a slower, controlled production of energy. The heat from the controlled fission is used to produce steam. The steam drives a generator, which produces electricity. Approximately 10% of the electrical energy produced in the United States is generated in nuclear power plants.

Although nuclear power plants help meet some of our energy needs, there are some problems associated with nuclear power. One of the most serious problems is the production of radioactive byproducts that have very long half-lives, such as plutonium-239 with a half-life of 24 000 yr. It is essential that these waste products be stored safely in a place where they do not contaminate the environment. Several countries are now in the process of selecting areas where nuclear waste can be placed in caverns 1000 m below the surface of the Earth. In the United States, a current proposed repository site for nuclear waste is Yucca Mountain, Nevada.

Nuclear power plants supply about 10% of electricity in the United States.

Heat from nuclear fission is used to generate electricity.

Clinical Update
Cardiac Imaging Using a Radioisotope

As part of her nuclear stress test, Simone starts to walk on the treadmill. When she reaches the maximum level, Paul injects a radioactive dye with Tl-201 with an activity of 74 MBq. The radiation emitted from areas of heart is detected by a scanner and produces images of her heart muscle. After Simone rests for 3 h, Paul injects more dye with Tl-201 and she is placed under the scanner again. A second set of images of her heart muscle at rest are taken. When Simone's doctor reviews her scans, he assures her that she had normal blood flow to her heart muscle, both at rest and under stress.

℞ Clinical Applications

5.45 What is the activity of the radioactive dye injection for Simone
    a. in curies?
    b. in millicuries?

5.46 If the half-life of Tl-201 is 3.0 days, what is its activity, in megabecquerels
    a. after 3.0 days?
    b. after 6.0 days?

5.47 How many days will it take until the activity of the Tl-201 in Simone's body is one-eighth of the initial activity?

5.48 Radiation from Tl-201 to Simone's kidneys can be 24 mGy. What is this amount of radiation in rads?

CONCEPT MAP

NUCLEAR CHEMISTRY

Radioisotopes

emit → **Radiation and Energy**

are measured by their → **Activity** — measured in → **Becquerel**, **Curie**

decay by one-half in one → **Half-Life**

Radiation and Energy from the nucleus as → **Alpha**, **Beta**, **Positron**, **Gamma**

Activity or → **Biological Effect**

Half-Life and are used in → **Nuclear Medicine**

Alpha, **Beta**, **Positron**, **Gamma** as shown in → **Nuclear Equations**

Biological Effect as absorbed → **Rad**, **Gray**; as exposure → **Rem**, **Sievert**

Nuclear Medicine and in → **Fission**, **Fusion**

CHAPTER REVIEW

5.1 Natural Radioactivity
LEARNING GOAL Describe alpha, beta, positron, and gamma radiation.

$^{4}_{2}$He
Alpha (α) particle

- Radioactive isotopes have unstable nuclei that break down (decay), spontaneously emitting alpha (α), beta (β), positron (β^{+}), and gamma (γ) radiation.
- Because radiation can damage the cells in the body, proper protection must be used: shielding, limiting the time of exposure, and distance.

5.2 Nuclear Reactions
LEARNING GOAL Write a balanced nuclear equation showing mass numbers and atomic numbers for radioactive decay.

Radioactive carbon nucleus
Radiation
New nucleus
$^{14}_{6}$C
Beta particle
$^{0}_{-1}e$
Stable nitrogen-14 nucleus
$^{14}_{7}$N

- A balanced nuclear equation is used to represent the changes that take place in the nuclei of the reactants and products.
- The new isotopes and the type of radiation emitted can be determined from the symbols that show the mass numbers and atomic numbers of the isotopes in the nuclear equation.
- A radioisotope is produced artificially when a nonradioactive isotope is bombarded by a small particle.

5.3 Radiation Measurement
LEARNING GOAL Describe the detection and measurement of radiation.

- In a Geiger counter, radiation produces charged particles in the gas contained in a tube, which generates an electrical current.
- The curie (Ci) and the becquerel (Bq) measure the activity, which is the number of nuclear transformations per second.
- The amount of radiation absorbed by a substance is measured in rads or the gray (Gy).
- The rem and the sievert (Sv) are units used to determine the biological damage from the different types of radiation.

5.4 Half-Life of a Radioisotope
LEARNING GOAL Given the half-life of a radioisotope, calculate the amount of radioisotope remaining after one or more half-lives.

- Every radioisotope has its own rate of emitting radiation.
- The time it takes for one-half of a radioactive sample to decay is called its half-life.
- For many medical radioisotopes, such as Tc-99m and I-131, half-lives are short.
- For other isotopes, usually naturally occurring ones such as C-14, Ra-226, and U-238, half-lives are extremely long.

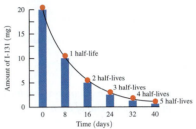

5.5 Medical Applications Using Radioactivity
LEARNING GOAL Describe the use of radioisotopes in medicine.

- In nuclear medicine, radioisotopes that go to specific sites in the body are given to the patient.
- By detecting the radiation they emit, an evaluation can be made about the location and extent of an injury, disease, tumor, or the level of function of a particular organ.
- Higher levels of radiation are used to treat or destroy tumors.

5.6 Nuclear Fission and Fusion
LEARNING GOAL
Describe the processes of nuclear fission and fusion.

$^{235}_{92}$U
$^{1}_{0}n$
$^{91}_{36}$Kr
$3^{1}_{0}n$
$^{142}_{56}$Ba

- In fission, the bombardment of a large nucleus breaks it apart into smaller nuclei, releasing one or more types of radiation and a great amount of energy.
- In fusion, small nuclei combine to form larger nuclei while great amounts of energy are released.

KEY TERMS

alpha particle A nuclear particle identical to a helium nucleus, symbol α or $^{4}_{2}$He.

becquerel (Bq) A unit of activity of a radioactive sample equal to one disintegration per second.

beta particle A particle identical to an electron, symbol $^{0}_{-1}e$ or β, that forms in the nucleus when a neutron changes to a proton and an electron.

chain reaction A fission reaction that will continue once it has been initiated by a high-energy neutron bombarding a heavy nucleus such as uranium-235.

curie (Ci) A unit of activity of a radioactive sample equal to 3.7×10^{10} disintegrations/s.

decay curve A diagram of the decay of a radioactive element.

equivalent dose The measure of biological damage from an absorbed dose that has been adjusted for the type of radiation.

fission A process in which large nuclei are split into smaller pieces, releasing large amounts of energy.

fusion A reaction in which large amounts of energy are released when small nuclei combine to form larger nuclei.

gamma ray High-energy radiation, symbol $^{0}_{0}\gamma$, emitted by an unstable nucleus.

gray (Gy) A unit of absorbed dose equal to 100 rad.

half-life The length of time it takes for one-half of a radioactive sample to decay.

positron A particle of radiation with no mass and a positive charge, symbol β^+ or $_{+1}^{0}e$, produced when a proton is transformed into a neutron and a positron.

rad (radiation absorbed dose) A measure of an amount of radiation absorbed by the body.

radiation Energy or particles released by radioactive atoms.

radioactive decay The process by which an unstable nucleus breaks down with the release of high-energy radiation.

radioisotope A radioactive atom of an element.

rem (radiation equivalent in humans) A measure of the biological damage caused by the various kinds of radiation (rad × radiation biological factor).

sievert (Sv) A unit of biological damage (equivalent dose) equal to 100 rem.

⚛ CORE CHEMISTRY SKILLS

The chapter section containing each Core Chemistry Skill is shown in parentheses at the end of each heading.

Writing Nuclear Equations (5.2)

- A nuclear equation is written with the atomic symbols of the original radioactive nucleus on the left, an arrow, and the new nucleus and the type of radiation emitted on the right.
- The sum of the mass numbers and the sum of the atomic numbers on one side of the arrow must equal the sum of the mass numbers and the sum of the atomic numbers on the other side.
- When an alpha particle is emitted, the mass number of the new nucleus decreases by 4, and its atomic number decreases by 2.
- When a beta particle is emitted, there is no change in the mass number of the new nucleus, but its atomic number increases by one.
- When a positron is emitted, there is no change in the mass number of the new nucleus, but its atomic number decreases by one.
- In gamma emission, there is no change in the mass number or the atomic number of the new nucleus.

Example: a. Write a balanced nuclear equation for the alpha decay of Po-210.

b. Write a balanced nuclear equation for the beta decay of Co-60.

Answer: a. When an alpha particle is emitted, we calculate the decrease of 4 in the mass number (210) of the polonium, and a decrease of 2 in its atomic number.

$$_{84}^{210}\text{Po} \longrightarrow _{82}^{206}? + _{2}^{4}\text{He}$$

Because lead has atomic number 82, the new nucleus must be an isotope of lead.

$$_{84}^{210}\text{Po} \longrightarrow _{82}^{206}\text{Pb} + _{2}^{4}\text{He}$$

b. When a beta particle is emitted, there is no change in the mass number (60) of the cobalt, but there is an increase of 1 in its atomic number.

$$_{27}^{60}\text{Co} \longrightarrow _{28}^{60}? + _{-1}^{0}e$$

Because nickel has atomic number 28, the new nucleus must be an isotope of nickel.

$$_{27}^{60}\text{Co} \longrightarrow _{28}^{60}\text{Ni} + _{-1}^{0}e$$

Using Half-Lives (5.4)

- The half-life of a radioisotope is the amount of time it takes for one-half of a sample to decay.
- The remaining amount of a radioisotope is calculated by dividing its quantity or activity by one-half for each half-life that has elapsed.

Example: Co-60 has a half-life of 5.3 yr. If the initial sample of Co-60 has an activity of 1200 Ci, what is its activity after 15.9 yr?

Answer:

Years	Number of Half-Lives	Co-60 (Activity)
0	0	1200 Ci
5.3	1	600 Ci
10.6	2	300 Ci
15.9	3	150 Ci

In 15.9 yr, three half-lives have passed. Thus, the activity was reduced from 1200 Ci to 150 Ci.

$$1200 \text{ Ci} \xrightarrow{\text{1 half-life}} 600 \text{ Ci} \xrightarrow{\text{2 half-lives}} 300 \text{ Ci} \xrightarrow{\text{3 half-lives}} 150 \text{ Ci}$$

UNDERSTANDING THE CONCEPTS

The chapter sections to review are shown in parentheses at the end of each question.

In problems 5.49 to 5.52, a nucleus is shown with protons and neutrons.

5.49 Draw the new nucleus when this isotope emits a positron to complete the following figure: (5.2)

5.50 Draw the nucleus that emits a beta particle to complete the following figure: (5.2)

+ •

beta particle

5.51 Draw the nucleus of the isotope that is bombarded in the following figure: (5.2)

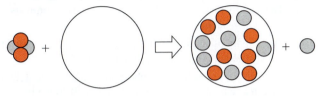

5.52 Complete the following bombardment reaction by drawing the nucleus of the new isotope that is produced in the following figure: (5.2)

5.53 Carbon dating of small bits of charcoal used in cave paintings has determined that some of the paintings are from 10 000 to 30 000 yr old. Carbon-14 has a half-life of 5730 yr. In a 1 μg-sample of carbon from a live tree, the activity of carbon-14 is 6.4 μCi. If researchers determine that 1 μg of charcoal from a prehistoric cave painting in France has an activity of 0.80 μCi, what is the age of the painting? (5.4)

The technique of carbon dating is used to determine the age of ancient cave paintings.

5.54 Use the following decay curve for iodine-131 to answer questions **a** to **c**: (5.4)

a. Complete the values for the mass of radioactive iodine-131 on the vertical axis.
b. Complete the number of days on the horizontal axis.
c. What is the half-life, in days, of iodine-131?

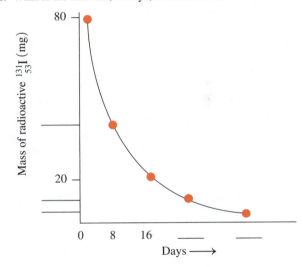

ADDITIONAL QUESTIONS AND PROBLEMS

5.55 Determine the number of protons and number of neutrons in the nucleus of each of the following: (5.1)
a. sodium-25
b. nickel-61
c. rubidium-84
d. silver-110

5.56 Determine the number of protons and number of neutrons in the nucleus of each of the following: (5.1)
a. boron-10
b. zinc-72
c. iron-59
d. gold-198

5.57 Identify each of the following as alpha decay, beta decay, positron emission, or gamma emission: (5.1, 5.2)
a. $^{27m}_{13}\text{Al} \longrightarrow ^{27}_{13}\text{Al} + ^{0}_{0}\gamma$
b. $^{8}_{5}\text{B} \longrightarrow ^{8}_{4}\text{Be} + ^{0}_{+1}e$
c. $^{220}_{86}\text{Rn} \longrightarrow ^{216}_{84}\text{Po} + ^{4}_{2}\text{He}$

5.58 Identify each of the following as alpha decay, beta decay, positron emission, or gamma emission: (5.1, 5.2)
a. $^{127}_{55}\text{Cs} \longrightarrow ^{127}_{54}\text{Xe} + ^{0}_{+1}e$
b. $^{90}_{38}\text{Sr} \longrightarrow ^{90}_{39}\text{Y} + ^{0}_{-1}e$
c. $^{218}_{85}\text{At} \longrightarrow ^{214}_{83}\text{Bi} + ^{4}_{2}\text{He}$

5.59 Write the balanced nuclear equation for each of the following: (5.1, 5.2)
a. Th-225 (α decay)
b. Bi-210 (α decay)
c. cesium-137 (β decay)
d. tin-126 (β decay)
e. F-18 (β⁺ emission)

5.60 Write the balanced nuclear equation for each of the following: (5.1, 5.2)
a. potassium-40 (β decay)
b. sulfur-35 (β decay)
c. platinum-190 (α decay)
d. Ra-210 (α decay)
e. In-113m (γ emission)

5.61 Complete each of the following nuclear equations: (5.2)

a. $^{4}_{2}He + ^{14}_{7}N \longrightarrow ? + ^{1}_{1}H$

b. $^{4}_{2}He + ^{27}_{13}Al \longrightarrow ^{30}_{14}Si + ?$

c. $^{1}_{0}n + ^{235}_{92}U \longrightarrow ^{90}_{38}Sr + 3^{1}_{0}n + ?$

d. $^{23m}_{12}Mg \longrightarrow ? + ^{0}_{0}\gamma$

5.62 Complete each of the following nuclear equations: (5.2)

a. $? + ^{59}_{27}Co \longrightarrow ^{56}_{25}Mn + ^{4}_{2}He$

b. $? \longrightarrow ^{14}_{7}N + ^{0}_{-1}e$

c. $^{0}_{-1}e + ^{76}_{36}Kr \longrightarrow ?$

d. $^{4}_{2}He + ^{241}_{95}Am \longrightarrow ? + 2^{1}_{0}n$

5.63 Write the balanced nuclear equation for each of the following: (5.2)

a. When two oxygen-16 atoms collide, one of the products is an alpha particle.

b. When californium-249 is bombarded by oxygen-18, a new element, seaborgium-263, and four neutrons are produced.

c. Radon-222 undergoes alpha decay.

d. An atom of strontium-80 emits a positron.

5.64 Write the balanced nuclear equation for each of the following: (5.2)

a. Polonium-210 decays to give lead-206.

b. Bismuth-211 emits an alpha particle.

c. A radioisotope emits a positron to form titanium-48.

d. An atom of germanium-69 emits a positron.

5.65 A 120-mg sample of technetium-99m is used for a diagnostic test. If technetium-99m has a half-life of 6.0 h, how many milligrams of the technetium-99m sample remains active 24 h after the test? (5.4)

5.66 The half-life of oxygen-15 is 124 s. If a sample of oxygen-15 has an activity of 4000 Bq, how many minutes will elapse before it has an activity of 500 Bq? (5.4)

5.67 What is the difference between fission and fusion? (5.6)

5.68 a. What are the products in the fission of uranium-235 that make possible a nuclear chain reaction? (5.6)

b. What is the purpose of placing control rods among uranium samples in a nuclear reactor?

5.69 Where does fusion occur naturally? (5.6)

5.70 Why are scientists continuing to try to build a fusion reactor even though the very high temperatures it requires have been difficult to reach and maintain? (5.6)

℞ Clinical Applications

5.71 The activity of K-40 in a 70.-kg human body is estimated to be 120 nCi. What is this activity in becquerels? (5.3)

5.72 The activity of C-14 in a 70.-kg human body is estimated to be 3.7 kBq. What is this activity in microcuries? (5.3)

5.73 If the amount of radioactive phosphorus-32, used to treat leukemia, in a sample decreases from 1.2 mg to 0.30 mg in 28.6 days, what is the half-life of phosphorus-32? (5.4)

5.74 If the amount of radioactive iodine-123, used to treat thyroid cancer, in a sample decreases from 0.4 mg to 0.1 mg in 26.4 h, what is the half-life of iodine-123? (5.4)

5.75 Calcium-47, used to evaluate bone metabolism, has a half-life of 4.5 days. (5.2, 5.4)

a. Write the balanced nuclear equation for the beta decay of calcium-47.

b. How many milligrams of a 16-mg sample of calcium-47 remain after 18 days?

c. How many days have passed if 4.8 mg of calcium-47 decayed to 1.2 mg of calcium-47?

5.76 Cesium-137, used in cancer treatment, has a half-life of 30 yr. (5.2, 5.4)

a. Write the balanced nuclear equation for the beta decay of cesium-137.

b. How many milligrams of a 16-mg sample of cesium-137 remain after 90 yr?

c. How many years are required for 28 mg of cesium-137 to decay to 3.5 mg of cesium-137?

CHALLENGE QUESTIONS

The following groups of questions are related to the topics in this chapter. However, they do not all follow the chapter order, and they require you to combine concepts and skills from several sections. These questions will help you increase your critical thinking skills and prepare for your next exam.

5.77 Write the balanced nuclear equation for each of the following radioactive emissions: (5.2)

a. an alpha particle from Hg-180

b. a beta particle from Au-198

c. a positron from Rb-82

5.78 Write the balanced nuclear equation for each of the following radioactive emissions: (5.2)

a. an alpha particle from Gd-148

b. a beta particle from Sr-90

c. a positron from Al-25

5.79 All the elements beyond uranium, the transuranium elements, have been prepared by bombardment and are not naturally occurring elements. The first transuranium element neptunium, Np, was prepared by bombarding U-238 with neutrons to form a neptunium atom and a beta particle. Complete the following equation: (5.2)

$^{1}_{0}n + ^{238}_{92}U \longrightarrow ? + ?$

5.80 One of the most recent transuranium elements ununoctium-294 (Uuo-294), atomic number 118, was prepared by bombarding californium-249 with another isotope. Complete the following equation for the preparation of this new element: (5.2)

$? + ^{249}_{98}Cf \longrightarrow ^{294}_{118}Uuo + 3^{1}_{0}n$

5.81 A 64-μCi sample of Tl-201 decays to 4.0 μCi in 12 days. What is the half-life, in days, of Tl-201? (5.3, 5.4)

5.82 A wooden object from the site of an ancient temple has a carbon-14 activity of 10 counts/min compared with a reference piece of wood cut today that has an activity of 40 counts/min. If the half-life for carbon-14 is 5730 yr, what is the age of the ancient wood object? (5.3, 5.4)

5.83 The half-life for the radioactive decay of calcium-47 is 4.5 days. If a sample has an activity of 1.0 μCi after 27 days, what was the initial activity, in microcuries, of the sample? (5.3, 5.4)

5.84 The half-life for the radioactive decay of Ce-141 is 32.5 days. If a sample has an activity of 4.0 μCi after 130 days have elapsed, what was the initial activity, in microcuries, of the sample? (5.3, 5.4)

5.85 Element 114 was recently named flerovium, symbol Fl. The reaction for its synthesis involves bombarding Pu-244 with Ca-48. Write the balanced nuclear equation for the synthesis of flerovium. (5.2)

5.86 Element 116 was recently named livermorium, symbol Lv. The reaction for its synthesis involves bombarding Cm-248 with Ca-48. Write the balanced nuclear equation for the synthesis of livermorium. (5.2)

℞ Clinical Applications

5.87 A nuclear technician was accidentally exposed to potassium-42 while doing brain scans for possible tumors. The error was not discovered until 36 h later when the activity of the potassium-42 sample was 2.0 μCi. If potassium-42 has a half-life of 12 h, what was the activity of the sample at the time the technician was exposed? (5.3, 5.4)

5.88 The radioisotope sodium-24 is used to determine the levels of electrolytes in the body. A 16-μg sample of sodium-24 decays to 2.0 μg in 45 h. What is the half-life, in hours, of sodium-24? (5.4)

ANSWERS

Answers to Selected Questions and Problems

5.1 a. alpha particle
b. positron
c. gamma radiation

5.3 a. $^{39}_{19}K$, $^{40}_{19}K$, $^{41}_{19}K$
b. They all have 19 protons and 19 electrons, but they differ in the number of neutrons.

5.5 a. β or $^{0}_{-1}e$
b. α or $^{4}_{2}He$
c. n or $^{1}_{0}n$
d. $^{38}_{18}Ar$
e. $^{14}_{6}C$

5.7 a. $^{64}_{29}Cu$
b. $^{75}_{34}Se$
c. $^{24}_{11}Na$
d. $^{15}_{7}N$

5.9

Medical Use	Atomic Symbol	Mass Number	Number of Protons	Number of Neutrons
Heart imaging	$^{201}_{81}Tl$	201	81	120
Radiation therapy	$^{60}_{27}Co$	60	27	33
Abdominal scan	$^{67}_{31}Ga$	67	31	36
Hyperthyroidism	$^{131}_{53}I$	131	53	78
Leukemia treatment	$^{32}_{15}P$	32	15	17

5.11 a. 1. alpha particle
b. 3. gamma radiation
c. 1. alpha particle

5.13 a. $^{208}_{84}Po \longrightarrow ^{204}_{82}Pb + ^{4}_{2}He$
b. $^{232}_{90}Th \longrightarrow ^{228}_{88}Ra + ^{4}_{2}He$
c. $^{251}_{102}No \longrightarrow ^{247}_{100}Fm + ^{4}_{2}He$
d. $^{220}_{86}Rn \longrightarrow ^{216}_{84}Po + ^{4}_{2}He$

5.15 a. $^{25}_{11}Na \longrightarrow ^{25}_{12}Mg + ^{0}_{-1}e$
b. $^{20}_{8}O \longrightarrow ^{20}_{9}F + ^{0}_{-1}e$
c. $^{92}_{38}Sr \longrightarrow ^{92}_{39}Y + ^{0}_{-1}e$
d. $^{60}_{26}Fe \longrightarrow ^{60}_{27}Co + ^{0}_{-1}e$

5.17 a. $^{26}_{14}Si \longrightarrow ^{26}_{13}Al + ^{0}_{+1}e$
b. $^{54}_{27}Co \longrightarrow ^{54}_{26}Fe + ^{0}_{+1}e$
c. $^{77}_{37}Rb \longrightarrow ^{77}_{36}Kr + ^{0}_{+1}e$
d. $^{93}_{45}Rh \longrightarrow ^{93}_{44}Ru + ^{0}_{+1}e$

5.19 a. $^{28}_{14}Si$, beta decay
b. $^{0}_{0}\gamma$, gamma emission
c. $^{0}_{-1}e$, beta decay
d. $^{238}_{92}U$, alpha decay
e. $^{188}_{79}Au$, positron emission

5.21 a. $^{10}_{4}Be$
b. $^{132}_{53}I$
c. $^{27}_{13}Al$
d. $^{17}_{8}O$

5.23 a. 2. absorbed dose
b. 3. biological damage
c. 1. activity
d. 2. absorbed dose

5.25 The technician exposed to 5 rad received the higher amount of radiation.

5.27 a. 294 μCi
b. 0.5 Gy

5.29 a. two half-lives
b. one half-life
c. three half-lives

5.31 a. 40.0 mg
b. 20.0 mg
c. 10.0 mg
d. 5.00 mg

5.33 a. 130 days
b. 195 days

5.35 a. Because the elements Ca and P are part of the bone, the radioactive isotopes of Ca and P will become part of the bony structures of the body, where their radiation can be used to diagnose or treat bone diseases.
b. Strontium (Sr) acts much like calcium (Ca) because both are Group 2A (2) elements. The body will accumulate radioactive strontium in bones in the same way that it incorporates calcium. Radioactive strontium is harmful to children because the radiation it produces causes more damage in cells that are dividing rapidly.

5.37 180 μCi

5.39 Nuclear fission is the splitting of a large atom into smaller fragments with the release of large amounts of energy.

5.41 $^{103}_{42}\text{Mo}$

5.43 a. fission
 b. fusion
 c. fission
 d. fusion

5.45 a. 2.0×10^{-3} Ci
 b. 2.0 mCi

5.47 9.0 days

5.49

5.51

5.53 17 200 yr old

5.55 a. 11 protons and 14 neutrons
 b. 28 protons and 33 neutrons
 c. 37 protons and 47 neutrons
 d. 47 protons and 63 neutrons

5.57 a. gamma emission
 b. positron emission
 c. alpha decay

5.59 a. $^{225}_{90}\text{Th} \longrightarrow {}^{221}_{88}\text{Ra} + {}^{4}_{2}\text{He}$
 b. $^{210}_{83}\text{Bi} \longrightarrow {}^{206}_{81}\text{Tl} + {}^{4}_{2}\text{He}$
 c. $^{137}_{55}\text{Cs} \longrightarrow {}^{137}_{56}\text{Ba} + {}^{0}_{-1}e$
 d. $^{126}_{50}\text{Sn} \longrightarrow {}^{126}_{51}\text{Sb} + {}^{0}_{-1}e$
 e. $^{18}_{9}\text{F} \longrightarrow {}^{18}_{8}\text{O} + {}^{0}_{+1}e$

5.61 a. $^{17}_{8}\text{O}$
 b. $^{1}_{1}\text{H}$
 c. $^{143}_{54}\text{Xe}$
 d. $^{23}_{12}\text{Mg}$

5.63 a. $^{16}_{8}\text{O} + {}^{16}_{8}\text{O} \longrightarrow {}^{28}_{14}\text{Si} + {}^{4}_{2}\text{He}$
 b. $^{18}_{8}\text{O} + {}^{249}_{98}\text{Cf} \longrightarrow {}^{263}_{106}\text{Sg} + 4{}^{1}_{0}n$
 c. $^{222}_{86}\text{Rn} \longrightarrow {}^{218}_{84}\text{Po} + {}^{4}_{2}\text{He}$
 d. $^{80}_{38}\text{Sr} \longrightarrow {}^{80}_{37}\text{Rb} + {}^{0}_{+1}e$

5.65 7.5 mg of Tc-99m

5.67 In the fission process, an atom splits into smaller nuclei. In fusion, small nuclei combine (fuse) to form a larger nucleus.

5.69 Fusion occurs naturally in the Sun and other stars.

5.71 4.4×10^3 Bq

5.73 14.3 days

5.75 a. $^{47}_{20}\text{Ca} \longrightarrow {}^{47}_{21}\text{Sc} + {}^{0}_{-1}e$
 b. 1.0 mg of Ca-47
 c. 9.0 days

5.77 a. $^{180}_{80}\text{Hg} \longrightarrow {}^{176}_{78}\text{Pt} + {}^{4}_{2}\text{He}$
 b. $^{198}_{79}\text{Au} \longrightarrow {}^{198}_{80}\text{Hg} + {}^{0}_{-1}e$
 c. $^{82}_{37}\text{Rb} \longrightarrow {}^{82}_{36}\text{Kr} + {}^{0}_{+1}e$

5.79 $^{1}_{0}n + {}^{238}_{92}\text{U} \longrightarrow {}^{239}_{93}\text{Np} + {}^{0}_{-1}e$

5.81 3.0 days

5.83 64 μCi

5.85 $^{48}_{20}\text{Ca} + {}^{244}_{94}\text{Pu} \longrightarrow {}^{292}_{114}\text{Fl}$

5.87 16 μCi

6

Ionic and Molecular Compounds

RICHARD'S DOCTOR HAS RECOMMENDED THAT

he take a low-dose aspirin (81 mg) every day to prevent a heart attack or stroke. Richard is concerned about taking aspirin and asks Sarah, a pharmacy technician working at a local pharmacy, about the effects of aspirin. Sarah explains to Richard that aspirin is acetylsalicylic acid, and has the chemical formula $C_9H_8O_4$. Aspirin is a molecular compound, often referred to as an organic molecule because it contains the nonmetals carbon (C), hydrogen (H), and oxygen (O). Sarah explains to Richard that aspirin is used to relieve minor pains, to reduce inflammation and fever, and to slow blood clotting. Aspirin is one of several nonsteroidal anti-inflammatory drugs (NSAIDs) that reduce pain and fever by blocking the formation of prostaglandins, which are chemical messengers that transmit pain signals to the brain and cause fever. Some potential side effects of aspirin may include heartburn, upset stomach, nausea, and an increased risk of a stomach ulcer.

CAREER Pharmacy Technician

Pharmacy technicians work under the supervision of a pharmacist, and their main responsibility is to fill prescriptions by preparing pharmaceutical medications. They obtain the proper medication, calculate, measure, and label the patient's medication, which is then approved by the pharmacist. After the prescription is filled, the technician prices and files the prescription. Pharmacy technicians also provide customer service by receiving prescription requests, interacting with customers, and answering any questions they may have about the drugs and their health condition. Pharmacy technicians also prepare insurance claims, and create and maintain patient profiles.

LOOKING AHEAD

6.1 Ions: Transfer of Electrons 184

♥ **Chemistry Link to Health**
Some Important Ions in the Body 188

6.2 Writing Formulas for Ionic Compounds 189

6.3 Naming and Writing Ionic Formulas 192

6.4 Polyatomic Ions 196

6.5 Molecular Compounds: Sharing Electrons 200

6.6 Lewis Structures for Molecules and Polyatomic Ions 204

6.7 Electronegativity and Bond Polarity 209

6.8 Shapes and Polarity of Molecules 212

6.9 Attractive Forces in Compounds 218

♥ **Chemistry Link to Health**
Attractive Forces in Biological Compounds 220

℞ **Clinical Applications** 189, 196, 200, 204, 222

℞ **Clinical Update** *Compounds at the Pharmacy* 222

The ionic formulas of gemstones contain metallic ions that produce their different colors.

In nature, atoms of almost all the elements on the periodic table are found in combination with other atoms. Only the atoms of the noble gases—He, Ne, Ar, Kr, Xe, and Rn—do not combine in nature with other atoms. A *compound* is composed of two or more elements, with a definite composition.

Compounds may be ionic or molecular. In an *ionic compound*, one or more electrons are transferred from metals to nonmetals, which form positive and negative ions. The attraction between these ions is called an *ionic bond*.

We utilize ionic compounds every day, including salt, NaCl, and baking soda, $NaHCO_3$. Milk of magnesia, $Mg(OH)_2$, or calcium carbonate, $CaCO_3$, may be taken to settle an upset stomach. In a mineral supplement, iron may be present as iron(II) sulfate, $FeSO_4$, iodine as potassium iodide, KI, and manganese as manganese(II) sulfate, $MnSO_4$. Some sunscreens contain zinc oxide, ZnO, and tin(II) fluoride, SnF_2, in toothpaste provides fluoride to help prevent tooth decay. Precious and semiprecious gemstones are examples of ionic compounds called minerals that are cut and polished to make jewelry. For example, sapphires and rubies are made of aluminum oxide, Al_2O_3. Impurities of chromium ions make rubies red, and iron and titanium ions make sapphires blue.

A *molecular compound* consists of two or more nonmetals that share one or more valence electrons. The resulting molecules are held together by *covalent bonds*. There are many more molecular compounds than there are ionic ones. For example, water (H_2O) and carbon dioxide (CO_2) are both molecular compounds. Molecular compounds consist of molecules, which are discrete groups of atoms in a definite proportion. A molecule of water (H_2O) consists of two atoms of hydrogen and one atom of oxygen. When you have iced tea, perhaps you add molecules of sugar ($C_{12}H_{22}O_{11}$), which is a molecular compound. Other molecular compounds include propane (C_3H_8), alcohol (C_2H_6O), the antibiotic amoxicillin ($C_{16}H_{19}N_3O_5S$), and the antidepressant Prozac ($C_{17}H_{18}F_3NO$).

CHAPTER READINESS*

🔢 KEY MATH SKILLS
- Using Positive and Negative Numbers in Calculations (1.4B)
- Solving Equations (1.4D)

⚛ CORE CHEMISTRY SKILLS
- Writing Electron Configurations (4.7)
- Drawing Lewis Symbols (4.8)

*These Key Math Skills and Core Chemistry Skills from previous chapters are listed here for your review as you proceed to the new material in this chapter.

LEARNING GOAL

Write the symbols for the simple ions of the representative elements.

6.1 Ions: Transfer of Electrons

Most of the elements, except the noble gases, are found in nature combined as compounds. The noble gases are so stable that they form compounds only under extreme conditions. One explanation for the stability of noble gases is that they have a filled valence electron energy level.

Compounds form when electrons are transferred or shared to give stable electron configuration to the atoms. In the formation of either an *ionic bond* or a *covalent bond*, atoms lose, gain, or share valence electrons to acquire an **octet** of eight valence electrons. This tendency of atoms to attain a stable electron configuration is known as the **octet rule** and provides a key to our understanding of the ways in which atoms bond and form compounds.

A few elements achieve the stability of helium with two valence electrons. However, we do not use the octet rule with transition elements.

Ionic bonds occur when the valence electrons of atoms of a metal are transferred to atoms of nonmetals. For example, sodium atoms lose electrons and chlorine atoms gain electrons to form the ionic compound NaCl. *Covalent bonds* form when atoms of nonmetals share valence electrons. In the molecular compounds H_2O and C_3H_8, atoms share electrons.

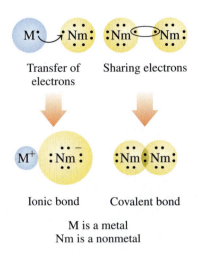

Transfer of electrons   Sharing electrons

Ionic bond   Covalent bond

M is a metal
Nm is a nonmetal

Type	Ionic Compounds	Molecular Compounds	
Particles	Ions	Molecules	
Bonding	Ionic bonds	Covalent bonds	
Examples			
	$Na^+ Cl^-$ ions	H_2O molecules	C_3H_8 molecules

Positive Ions: Loss of Electrons

In ionic bonding, **ions**, which have electrical charges, form when atoms lose or gain electrons to form a stable electron configuration. Because the ionization energies of metals of Groups 1A (1), 2A (2), and 3A (13) are low, metal atoms readily lose their valence electrons. In doing so, they form ions with positive charges. A metal atom obtains the same electron configuration as its nearest noble gas (usually eight valence electrons). For example, when a sodium atom loses its single valence electron, the remaining electrons have a stable electron configuration. By losing an electron, sodium has 10 negatively charged electrons instead of 11. Because there are still 11 positively charged protons in its nucleus, the atom is no longer neutral. It is now a sodium ion with a positive electrical charge, called an **ionic charge**, of 1+. In the Lewis symbol for the sodium ion, the ionic charge of 1+ is written in the upper right-hand corner, Na^+, where the 1 is understood. The sodium ion is smaller than the sodium atom because the ion has lost its outermost electron from the third energy level. The positively charged ions of metals are called **cations** (pronounced *cat-eye-uns*) and use the name of the element.

Ionic charge = Charge of protons + Charge of electrons
$$1+ = (11+) \quad\quad + (10-)$$

Name	Sodium atom		Sodium ion
Lewis Symbol	$Na\bullet$		Na^+
		Loss of valence electron	
Protons	$11\,p^+$		$11\,p^+$
Electrons	$11\,e^-$		$10\,e^-$
Electron Configuration	$1s^2 2s^2 2p^6 3s^1$		$1s^2 2s^2 2p^6$

Magnesium, a metal in Group 2A (2), obtains a stable electron configuration by losing two valence electrons to form a magnesium ion with a 2+ ionic charge, Mg^{2+}. A metal ion is named by its element name. Thus, Mg^{2+} is named the *magnesium ion*. The magnesium ion is smaller than the magnesium atom because the outermost electrons in the third energy level were removed. The octet in the magnesium ion is made up of electrons that fill its second energy level.

	Name	Magnesium atom		Magnesium ion
	Lewis Symbol	$\dot{\text{Mg}}\bullet$		Mg^{2+}
Protons		$12\,p^+$	Loss of two valence electrons	$12\,p^+$
Electrons		$12\,e^-$		$10\,e^-$
Electron Configuration		$1s^2 2s^2 2p^6 3s^2$		$1s^2 2s^2 2p^6$

⚛ **CORE CHEMISTRY SKILL**

Writing Positive and Negative Ions

Negative Ions: Gain of Electrons

The ionization energy of a nonmetal atom in Groups 5A (15), 6A (16), or 7A (17) is high. In an ionic compound, a nonmetal atom gains one or more valence electrons to obtain a stable electron configuration. By gaining electrons, a nonmetal atom forms a negatively charged ion. For example, an atom of chlorine with seven valence electrons gains one electron to form an octet. Because it now has 18 electrons and 17 protons in its nucleus, the chlorine atom is no longer neutral. It is a *chloride ion* with an ionic charge of 1−, which is written as Cl^-, with the 1 understood. A negatively charged ion, called an **anion** (pronounced *an-eye-un*), is named by using the first syllable of its element name followed by *ide*. The chloride ion is larger than the chlorine atom because the ion has an additional electron, which completes its outermost energy level.

$$\text{Ionic charge} = \text{Charge of protons} + \text{Charge of electrons}$$
$$1- = (17+) \qquad + (18-)$$

	Name	Chlorine atom		Chloride ion
	Lewis Symbol	$:\ddot{\text{Cl}}\bullet$		$[:\ddot{\text{Cl}}:]^-$
Protons		$17\,p^+$	Gain of one valence electron	$17\,p^+$
Electrons		$17\,e^-$		$18\,e^-$
Electron Configuration		$1s^2 2s^2 2p^6 3s^2 3p^5$		$1s^2 2s^2 2p^6 3s^2 3p^6$

Table 6.1 lists the names of some important metal and nonmetal ions.

TABLE 6.1 Formulas and Names of Some Common Ions

Metals			Nonmetals		
Group Number	Cation	Name of Cation	Group Number	Anion	Name of Anion
1A (1)	Li^+	Lithium	5A (15)	N^{3-}	Nitride
	Na^+	Sodium		P^{3-}	Phosphide
	K^+	Potassium	6A (16)	O^{2-}	Oxide
2A (2)	Mg^{2+}	Magnesium		S^{2-}	Sulfide
	Ca^{2+}	Calcium	7A (17)	F^-	Fluoride
	Ba^{2+}	Barium		Cl^-	Chloride
3A (13)	Al^{3+}	Aluminum		Br^-	Bromide
				I^-	Iodide

▶ **SAMPLE PROBLEM 6.1 Ions**

a. Write the symbol and name for the ion that has 7 protons and 10 electrons.
b. Write the symbol and name for the ion that has 20 protons and 18 electrons.

SOLUTION

a. The element with seven protons is nitrogen. In an ion of nitrogen with 10 electrons, the ionic charge would be 3−, $[(7+) + (10-) = 3-]$. The ion, written as N^{3-}, is the *nitride* ion.
b. The element with 20 protons is calcium. In an ion of calcium with 18 electrons, the ionic charge would be 2+, $[(20+) + (18-) = 2+]$. The ion, written as Ca^{2+}, is the *calcium* ion.

STUDY CHECK 6.1

How many protons and electrons are in each of the following ions?

a. S^{2-} **b.** Al^{3+}

ANSWER

a. 16 protons, 18 electrons   **b.** 13 protons, 10 electrons

Ionic Charges from Group Numbers

In ionic compounds, representative elements usually lose or gain electrons to give eight valence electrons like their nearest noble gas (or two for helium). We can use the group numbers in the periodic table to determine the charges for the ions of the representative elements. The elements in Group 1A (1) lose one electron to form ions with a 1+ charge. The elements in Group 2A (2) lose two electrons to form ions with a 2+ charge. The elements in Group 3A (13) lose three electrons to form ions with a 3+ charge. In this text, we do not use the group numbers of the transition elements to determine their ionic charges.

In ionic compounds, the elements in Group 7A (17) gain one electron to form ions with a 1− charge. The elements in Group 6A (16) gain two electrons to form ions with a 2− charge. The elements in Group 5A (15) gain three electrons to form ions with a 3− charge.

The nonmetals of Group 4A (14) do not typically form ions. However, the metals Sn and Pb in Group 4A (14) lose electrons to form positive ions. Table 6.2 lists the ionic charges for some common monatomic ions of representative elements.

TABLE 6.2 Examples of Monatomic Ions and Their Nearest Noble Gases

Noble Gases		Metals Lose Valence Electrons			Nonmetals Gain Valence Electrons				Noble Gases
		1A (1)	2A (2)	3A (13)	5A (15)	6A (16)	7A (17)		
He	⇐	Li^+							
Ne	⇐	Na^+	Mg^{2+}	Al^{3+}	N^{3-}	O^{2-}	F^-	⇒	Ne
Ar	⇐	K^+	Ca^{2+}		P^{3-}	S^{2-}	Cl^-	⇒	Ar
Kr	⇐	Rb^+	Sr^{2+}				Br^-	⇒	Kr
Xe	⇐	Cs^+	Ba^{2+}				I^-	⇒	Xe

SAMPLE PROBLEM 6.2 Writing Symbols for Ions

Consider the elements aluminum and oxygen.

a. Identify each as a metal or a nonmetal.
b. State the number of valence electrons for each.
c. State the number of electrons that must be lost or gained for each to achieve an octet.
d. Write the symbol, including its ionic charge, and name for each resulting ion.

SOLUTION

Aluminum	Oxygen
a. metal	nonmetal
b. three valence electrons	six valence electrons
c. loses $3\ e^-$	gains $2\ e^-$
d. Al^{3+}, $[(13+) + (10-) = 3+]$, aluminum ion	O^{2-}, $[(8+) + (10-) = 2-]$, oxide ion

STUDY CHECK 6.2

Write the symbols for the ions formed by potassium and sulfur.

ANSWER

K^+ and S^{2-}

Chemistry Link to **Health**

Some Important Ions in the Body

Several ions in body fluids have important physiological and metabolic functions. Some are listed in Table 6.3.

Foods such as bananas, milk, cheese, and potatoes provide the body with ions that are important in regulating body functions.

Milk, cheese, bananas, cereal, and potatoes provide ions for the body.

TABLE 6.3 Ions in the Body

Ion	Occurrence	Function	Source	Result of Too Little	Result of Too Much
Na^+	Principal cation outside the cell	Regulation and control of body fluids	Salt, cheese, pickles	Hyponatremia, anxiety, diarrhea, circulatory failure, decrease in body fluid	Hypernatremia, little urine, thirst, edema
K^+	Principal cation inside the cell	Regulation of body fluids and cellular functions	Bananas, orange juice, milk, prunes, potatoes	Hypokalemia (hypopotassemia), lethargy, muscle weakness, failure of neurological impulses	Hyperkalemia (hyperpotassemia), irritability, nausea, little urine, cardiac arrest
Ca^{2+}	Cation outside the cell; 90% of calcium in the body in bones as $Ca_3(PO_4)_2$ or $CaCO_3$	Major cation of bones; needed for muscle contraction	Milk, yogurt, cheese, greens, spinach	Hypocalcemia, tingling fingertips, muscle cramps, osteoporosis	Hypercalcemia, relaxed muscles, kidney stones, deep bone pain
Mg^{2+}	Cation outside the cell; 50% of magnesium in the body in bone structure	Essential for certain enzymes, muscles, nerve control	Widely distributed (part of chlorophyll of all green plants), nuts, whole grains	Disorientation, hypertension, tremors, slow pulse	Drowsiness
Cl^-	Principal anion outside the cell	Gastric juice, regulation of body fluids	Salt	Same as for Na^+	Same as for Na^+

QUESTIONS AND PROBLEMS

6.1 Ions: Transfer of Electrons

LEARNING GOAL Write the symbols for the simple ions of the representative elements.

6.1 State the number of electrons that must be lost by atoms of each of the following to achieve a stable electron configuration:
   a. Li   **b.** Ca   **c.** Ga   **d.** Cs   **e.** Ba

6.2 State the number of electrons that must be gained by atoms of each of the following to achieve a stable electron configuration:
   a. Cl   **b.** Se   **c.** N   **d.** I   **e.** S

6.3 State the number of electrons lost or gained when the following elements form ions:
   a. Sr   **b.** P   **c.** Group 7A (17)
   d. Na   **e.** Br

6.4 State the number of electrons lost or gained when the following elements form ions:
   a. O   **b.** Group 2A (2)   **c.** F
   d. K   **e.** Rb

6.5 Write the symbols for the ions with the following number of protons and electrons:
   a. 3 protons, 2 electrons   **b.** 9 protons, 10 electrons
   c. 12 protons, 10 electrons   **d.** 26 protons, 23 electrons

6.6 Write the symbols for the ions with the following number of protons and electrons:
   a. 8 protons, 10 electrons   **b.** 19 protons, 18 electrons
   c. 35 protons, 36 electrons   **d.** 50 protons, 46 electrons

6.7 Write the symbol for the ion of each of the following:
   a. chlorine   **b.** cesium
   c. nitrogen   **d.** radium

6.8 Write the symbol for the ion of each of the following:
   a. fluorine   **b.** calcium
   c. sodium   **d.** iodine

℞ Clinical Applications

6.9 State the number of protons and electrons in each of the following ions:
   a. O^{2-}, used to build biomolecules and water
   b. K^+, most prevalent positive ion in cells, needed for muscle contraction, nerve impulses
   c. I^-, needed for thyroid function
   d. Na^+, most prevalent positive ion in extracellular fluid

6.10 State the number of protons and electrons in each of the following ions:
   a. P^{3-}, needed for bones and teeth
   b. F^-, used to strengthen tooth enamel
   c. Mg^{2+}, needed for bones and teeth
   d. Ca^{2+}, needed for bones and teeth

6.2 Writing Formulas for Ionic Compounds

LEARNING GOAL

Using charge balance, write the correct formula for an ionic compound.

Ionic compounds consist of positive and negative ions. The ions are held together by strong electrical attractions between the oppositely charged ions, called *ionic bonds*. The positive ions are formed by *metals* losing electrons, and the negative ions are formed when *nonmetals* gain electrons. Even though noble gases are nonmetals, they already have stable electron configurations and do not form compounds.

Properties of Ionic Compounds

The physical and chemical properties of an ionic compound such as NaCl are very different from those of the original elements. For example, the original elements of NaCl were sodium, which is a soft, shiny metal, and chlorine, which is a yellow-green poisonous gas. However, when they react and form positive and negative ions, they produce NaCl, which is ordinary table salt, a hard, white, crystalline substance that is important in our diet.

In a crystal of NaCl, the larger Cl^- ions are arranged in a three-dimensional structure in which the smaller Na^+ ions occupy the spaces between the Cl^- ions (see Figure 6.1). In this crystal, every Na^+ ion is surrounded by six Cl^- ions, and every Cl^- ion is surrounded by six Na^+ ions. Thus, there are many strong attractions between the positive and negative ions, which account for the high melting points of ionic compounds. For example, the melting point of NaCl is 801 °C. At room temperature, ionic compounds are solids.

Chemical Formulas of Ionic Compounds

The **chemical formula** of a compound represents the symbols and subscripts in the lowest whole-number ratio of the atoms or ions. In the formula of an ionic compound, the sum of the ionic charges in the formula is always zero. *Thus, the total amount of positive charge is equal to the total amount of negative charge.* For example, to achieve a stable electron configuration, one Na atom (metal) loses its one valence electron to form Na^+, and one Cl

Sodium metal   and   Chlorine gas

— Na⁺
— Cl⁻

Sodium chloride

FIGURE 6.1 ▶ The elements sodium and chlorine react to form the ionic compound sodium chloride, the compound that makes up table salt. The magnification of NaCl crystals shows the arrangement of Na⁺ and Cl⁻ ions.

Q What is the type of bonding between Na⁺ and Cl⁻ ions in NaCl?

atom (nonmetal) gains one electron to form a Cl⁻ ion. The formula NaCl indicates that the compound has charge balance because there is one sodium ion, Na⁺, for every chloride ion, Cl⁻. Although the ions are positively or negatively charged, they are not shown in the formula of the compound.

Loses 1 e^- Gains 1 e^-

Na⁺   Cl⁻
$1(1+) + 1(1-) = 0$
NaCl, sodium chloride

Subscripts in Formulas

Consider a compound of magnesium and chlorine. To achieve a stable electron configuration, one Mg atom (metal) loses its two valence electrons to form Mg^{2+}. Two Cl atoms (nonmetals) each gain one electron to form two Cl⁻ ions. The two Cl⁻ ions are needed to balance the positive charge of Mg^{2+}. This gives the formula $MgCl_2$, magnesium chloride, in which the subscript 2 shows that two Cl⁻ ions are needed for charge balance.

Loses 2 e^- Each gains 1 e^-

Mg^{2+} 2Cl⁻
$1(2+) + 2(1-) = 0$
$MgCl_2$, magnesium chloride

Writing Ionic Formulas from Ionic Charges

⊛ **CORE CHEMISTRY SKILL**

Writing Ionic Formulas

The subscripts in the formula of an ionic compound represent the number of positive and negative ions that give an overall charge of zero. Thus, we can now write a formula directly from the ionic charges of the positive and negative ions. Suppose we wish to write the formula for the ionic compound containing Na^+ and S^{2-} ions. To balance the ionic charge of the S^{2-} ion, we will need to place two Na^+ ions in the formula. This gives the formula Na_2S, which has an overall charge of zero. In the formula of an ionic compound, the cation is written first followed by the anion. Appropriate subscripts are used to show the number of each of the ions. This formula, which is the lowest ratio of the ions in an ionic compound, is called a *formula unit*.

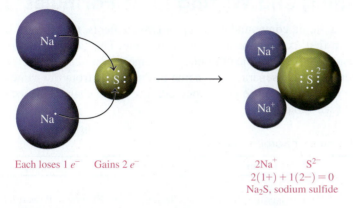

Each loses $1\ e^-$ Gains $2\ e^-$

$2Na^+$ S^{2-}
$2(1+) + 1(2-) = 0$
Na_2S, sodium sulfide

▶ **SAMPLE PROBLEM 6.3 Writing Formulas from Ionic Charges**

Write the symbols for the ions, and the correct formula for the ionic compound formed when lithium and nitrogen react.

SOLUTION

Lithium, which is a metal in Group 1A (1), forms Li^+; nitrogen, which is a nonmetal in Group 5A (15), forms N^{3-}. The charge of 3− is balanced by three Li^+ ions.

$$3(1+) + 1(3-) = 0$$

Writing the cation (positive ion) first and the anion (negative ion) second gives the formula Li_3N.

STUDY CHECK 6.3

Write the symbols for the ions, and the correct formula for the ionic compound that would form when calcium and oxygen react.

ANSWER

Ca^{2+}, O^{2-}, CaO

QUESTIONS AND PROBLEMS

6.2 Writing Formulas for Ionic Compounds

LEARNING GOAL Using charge balance, write the correct formula for an ionic compound.

6.11 Which of the following pairs of elements are likely to form an ionic compound?
  a. lithium and chlorine
  b. oxygen and bromine
  c. potassium and oxygen
  d. sodium and neon
  e. cesium and magnesium
  f. nitrogen and fluorine

6.12 Which of the following pairs of elements are likely to form an ionic compound?
  a. helium and oxygen
  b. magnesium and chlorine
  c. chlorine and bromine
  d. potassium and sulfur
  e. sodium and potassium
  f. nitrogen and iodine

6.13 Write the correct ionic formula for the compound formed between each of the following pairs of ions:
  a. Na^+ and O^{2-}
  b. Al^{3+} and Br^-
  c. Ba^{2+} and N^{3-}
  d. Mg^{2+} and F^-
  e. Al^{3+} and S^{2-}

6.14 Write the correct ionic formula for the compound formed between each of the following pairs of ions:
   a. Al^{3+} and Cl^- **b.** Ca^{2+} and S^{2-} **c.** Li^+ and S^{2-}
   d. Rb^+ and P^{3-} **e.** Cs^+ and I^-

6.15 Write the symbols for the ions, and the correct formula for the ionic compound formed by each of the following:
   a. potassium and sulfur   **b.** sodium and nitrogen
   c. aluminum and iodine   **d.** gallium and oxygen

6.16 Write the symbols for the ions, and the correct formula for the ionic compound formed by each of the following:
   a. calcium and chlorine   **b.** rubidium and bromine
   c. sodium and phosphorus   **d.** magnesium and oxygen

LEARNING GOAL

Given the formula of an ionic compound, write the correct name; given the name of an ionic compound, write the correct formula.

⚛ CORE CHEMISTRY SKILL

Naming Ionic Compounds

Iodized salt contains KI to prevent iodine deficiency.

6.3 Naming and Writing Ionic Formulas

In the name of an ionic compound made up of two elements, the name of the metal ion, which is written first, is the same as its element name. The name of the nonmetal ion is obtained by using the first syllable of its element name followed by *ide*. In the name of any ionic compound, a space separates the name of the cation from the name of the anion. Subscripts are not used; they are understood because of the charge balance of the ions in the compound (see Table 6.4).

TABLE 6.4 Names of Some Ionic Compounds

Compound	Metal Ion	Nonmetal Ion	Name
KI	K^+ Potassium	I^- Iodide	Potassium iodide
$MgBr_2$	Mg^{2+} Magnesium	Br^- Bromide	Magnesium bromide
Al_2O_3	Al^{3+} Aluminum	O^{2-} Oxide	Aluminum oxide

▶ **SAMPLE PROBLEM 6.4** Naming Ionic Compounds

Write the name for the ionic compound Mg_3N_2.

SOLUTION

ANALYZE THE PROBLEM	Given	Ions	Need
	Mg_3N_2	cation, Mg^{2+} anion, N^{3-}	name of compound

Guide to Naming Ionic Compounds with Metals That Form a Single Ion

STEP 1
Identify the cation and anion.

STEP 2
Name the cation by its element name.

STEP 3
Name the anion by using the first syllable of its element name followed by *ide*.

STEP 4
Write the name for the cation first and the name for the anion second.

STEP 1 Identify the cation and anion. The cation, Mg^{2+}, is from Group 2A (2), and the anion, N^{3-}, is from Group 5A (15).

STEP 2 Name the cation by its element name. The cation Mg^{2+} is magnesium.

STEP 3 Name the anion by using the first syllable of its element name followed by *ide*. The anion N^{3-} is nitride.

STEP 4 Write the name for the cation first and the name for the anion second.
Mg_3N_2 magnesium nitride

STUDY CHECK 6.4

Name the compound Ga_2S_3.

ANSWER

gallium sulfide

Metals with Variable Charges

We have seen that the charge of an ion of a representative element can be obtained from its group number. However, we cannot determine the charge of a transition element because it typically forms two or more positive ions. The transition elements lose electrons, but they are lost from the highest energy level and sometimes from a lower energy level as well. This is also true for metals of representative elements in Groups 4A (14) and 5A (15), such as Pb, Sn, and Bi.

In some ionic compounds, iron is in the Fe^{2+} form, but in other compounds, it has the Fe^{3+} form. Copper also forms two different ions, Cu^+ and Cu^{2+}. When a metal can form two or more types of ions, it has *variable charge*. Then we cannot predict the ionic charge from the group number.

For metals that form two or more ions, a naming system is used to identify the particular cation. To do this, a Roman numeral that is equal to the ionic charge is placed in parentheses immediately after the name of the metal. For example, Fe^{2+} is iron(II), and Fe^{3+} is iron(III). Table 6.5 lists the ions of some metals that produce more than one ion.

Figure 6.2 shows some ions and their location on the periodic table. The transition elements form more than one positive ion except for zinc (Zn^{2+}), cadmium (Cd^{2+}), and silver (Ag^+), which form only one ion. Thus, no Roman numerals are used with zinc, cadmium, and silver when naming their cations in ionic compounds. Metals in Groups 4A (14) and 5A (15) also form more than one type of positive ion. For example, lead and tin in Group 4A (14) form cations with charges of 2+ and 4+, and bismuth in Group 5A (15) forms cations with charges of 3+ and 5+.

Determination of Variable Charge

When you name an ionic compound, you need to determine if the metal is a representative element or a transition element. If it is a transition element, except for zinc, cadmium, or silver, you will need to use its ionic charge as a Roman numeral as part of its name. The calculation of ionic charge depends on the negative charge of the anions in the formula. For example, we use charge balance to determine the charge of a copper cation in the ionic compound $CuCl_2$. Because there are two chloride ions, each with a 1− charge, the total negative charge is 2−. To balance this 2− charge, the copper ion must have a charge of 2+, or Cu^{2+}:

$CuCl_2$

Cu charge + 2 Cl^- charge = 0
?   + 2(1−)   = 0
2+   + 2−   = 0

To indicate the 2+ charge for the copper ion Cu^{2+}, we place the Roman numeral (II) immediately after copper when naming this compound: copper(II) chloride.

TABLE 6.5 Some Metals That Form More Than One Positive Ion

Element	Possible Ions	Name of Ion
Bismuth	Bi^{3+}	Bismuth(III)
	Bi^{5+}	Bismuth(V)
Chromium	Cr^{2+}	Chromium(II)
	Cr^{3+}	Chromium(III)
Cobalt	Co^{2+}	Cobalt(II)
	Co^{3+}	Cobalt(III)
Copper	Cu^+	Copper(I)
	Cu^{2+}	Copper(II)
Gold	Au^+	Gold(I)
	Au^{3+}	Gold(III)
Iron	Fe^{2+}	Iron(II)
	Fe^{3+}	Iron(III)
Lead	Pb^{2+}	Lead(II)
	Pb^{4+}	Lead(IV)
Manganese	Mn^{2+}	Manganese(II)
	Mn^{3+}	Manganese(III)
Mercury	Hg_2^{2+}	Mercury(I)*
	Hg^{2+}	Mercury(II)
Nickel	Ni^{2+}	Nickel(II)
	Ni^{3+}	Nickel(III)
Tin	Sn^{2+}	Tin(II)
	Sn^{4+}	Tin(IV)

*Mercury(I) ions form an ion pair with a 2+ charge.

																	18 Group 8A
1 Group 1A																	
H^+	2 Group 2A											13 Group 3A	14 Group 4A	15 Group 5A	16 Group 6A	17 Group 7A	
Li^+														N^{3-}	O^{2-}	F^-	
Na^+	Mg^{2+}	3 3B	4 4B	5 5B	6 6B	7 7B	8	9 -8B-	10	11 1B	12 2B	Al^{3+}		P^{3-}	S^{2-}	Cl^-	
K^+	Ca^{2+}				Cr^{2+} Cr^{3+}	Mn^{2+} Mn^{3+}	Fe^{2+} Fe^{3+}	Co^{2+} Co^{3+}	Ni^{2+} Ni^{3+}	Cu^+ Cu^{2+}	Zn^{2+}					Br^-	
Rb^+	Sr^{2+}									Ag^+	Cd^{2+}	Sn^{2+} Sn^{4+}				I^-	
Cs^+	Ba^{2+}									Au^+ Au^{3+}	Hg_2^{2+} Hg^{2+}	Pb^{2+} Pb^{4+}	Bi^{3+} Bi^{5+}				

☐ Metals   ☐ Metalloids   ☐ Nonmetals

FIGURE 6.2 ▶ In ionic compounds, metals form positive ions, and nonmetals form negative ions.
◉ What are the typical ions of calcium, copper, and oxygen in ionic compounds?

The growth of barnacles is prevented by using a paint with Cu_2O on the bottom of a boat.

Guide to Naming Ionic Compounds with Variable Charge Metals

STEP 1
Determine the charge of the cation from the anion.

STEP 2
Name the cation by its element name and use a Roman numeral in parentheses for the charge.

STEP 3
Name the anion by using the first syllable of its element name followed by *ide*.

STEP 4
Write the name for the cation first and the name for the anion second.

TABLE 6.6 Some Ionic Compounds of Metals That Form Two Kinds of Positive Ions

Compound	Systematic Name
$FeCl_2$	Iron(II) chloride
Fe_2O_3	Iron(III) oxide
Cu_3P	Copper(I) phosphide
$CrBr_2$	Chromium(II) bromide
$SnCl_2$	Tin(II) chloride
PbS_2	Lead(IV) sulfide
BiF_3	Bismuth(III) fluoride

▶ SAMPLE PROBLEM 6.5 Naming Ionic Compounds with Variable Charge Metal Ions

Antifouling paint contains Cu_2O, which prevents the growth of barnacles and algae on the bottoms of boats. What is the name of Cu_2O?

SOLUTION

ANALYZE THE PROBLEM	Given	Need
	Cu_2O	name

STEP 1 Determine the charge of the cation from the anion.

		Metal	Nonmetal
Elements		copper (Cu)	oxygen (O)
Groups		transition element	6A (16)
Ions		Cu?	O^{2-}
Charge Balance		$2Cu?$ $+$	$2- = 0$
		$\dfrac{2Cu?}{2} = \dfrac{2+}{2} = 1+$	
Ions		Cu^+	O^{2-}

STEP 2 Name the cation by its element name and use a Roman numeral in parentheses for the charge. copper(I)

STEP 3 Name the anion by using the first syllable of its element name followed by *ide*. oxide

STEP 4 Write the name for the cation first and the name for the anion second. copper(I) oxide

STUDY CHECK 6.5

Write the name for the compound with the formula Mn_2S_3.

ANSWER

manganese(III) sulfide

Table 6.6 lists the names of some ionic compounds in which the transition elements and metals from Groups 4A (14) and 5A (15) have more than one positive ion.

Writing Formulas from the Name of an Ionic Compound

The formula for an ionic compound is written from the first part of the name that describes the metal ion, including its charge, and the second part of the name that specifies the non-metal ion. Subscripts are added, as needed, to balance the charge. The steps for writing a formula from the name of an ionic compound are shown in Sample Problem 6.6.

▶ SAMPLE PROBLEM 6.6 Writing Formulas for Ionic Compounds

Write the correct formula for iron(III) chloride.

SOLUTION

ANALYZE THE PROBLEM	Given	Need
	iron(III) chloride	ionic formula

STEP 1 Identify the cation and anion. Iron(III) chloride consists of a metal and a nonmetal, which means that it is an ionic compound.

Type of Ion	Cation	Anion
Name	iron(III)	chloride
Group	transition element	7A (17)
Symbol of Ion	Fe^{3+}	Cl^-

STEP 2 Balance the charges.

Fe^{3+} Cl^-

Cl^-

Cl^-

_____

$1(3+) + 3(1-) = 0$

↑

Becomes a subscript in the formula

STEP 3 Write the formula, cation first, using subscripts from the charge balance. $FeCl_3$

STUDY CHECK 6.6

Write the correct formula for chromium(III) oxide.

ANSWER

Cr_2O_3

The pigment chrome oxide green contains chromium(III) oxide.

QUESTIONS AND PROBLEMS

6.3 Naming and Writing Ionic Formulas

LEARNING GOAL Given the formula of an ionic compound, write the correct name; given the name of an ionic compound, write the correct formula.

6.17 Write the name for each of the following ionic compounds:
  a. Al_2O_3 **b.** $CaCl_2$ **c.** Na_2O
  d. Mg_3P_2 **e.** KI   **f.** BaF_2

6.18 Write the name for each of the following ionic compounds:
  a. $MgCl_2$ **b.** K_3P **c.** Li_2S
  d. CsF   **e.** MgO   **f.** $SrBr_2$

6.19 Write the name for each of the following ions (include the Roman numeral when necessary):
  a. Fe^{2+} **b.** Cu^{2+} **c.** Zn^{2+}
  d. Pb^{4+} **e.** Cr^{3+} **f.** Mn^{2+}

6.20 Write the name for each of the following ions (include the Roman numeral when necessary):
  a. Ag^+ **b.** Cu^+ **c.** Bi^{3+}
  d. Sn^{2+} **e.** Au^{3+} **f.** Ni^{2+}

6.21 Write the name for each of the following ionic compounds:
  a. $SnCl_2$ **b.** FeO   **c.** Cu_2S
  d. CuS   **e.** $CdBr_2$ **f.** $HgCl_2$

6.22 Write the name for each of the following ionic compounds:
  a. Ag_3P **b.** PbS   **c.** SnO_2
  d. $MnCl_3$ **e.** Bi_2O_3 **f.** $CoCl_2$

6.23 Write the symbol for the cation in each of the following ionic compounds:
  a. $AuCl_3$ **b.** Fe_2O_3 **c.** PbI_4 **d.** $SnCl_2$

6.24 Write the symbol for the cation in each of the following ionic compounds:
  a. $FeCl_2$ **b.** CrO   **c.** Ni_2S_3 **d.** AlP

6.25 Write the formula for each of the following ionic compounds:
  a. magnesium chloride   **b.** sodium sulfide
  c. copper(I) oxide   **d.** zinc phosphide
  e. gold(III) nitride   **f.** cobalt(III) fluoride

6.26 Write the formula for each of the following ionic compounds:
  a. nickel(III) oxide   **b.** barium fluoride
  c. tin(IV) chloride   **d.** silver sulfide
  e. bismuth(V) chloride   **f.** potassium nitride

6.27 Write the formula for each of the following ionic compounds:
  a. cobalt(III) chloride   **b.** lead(IV) oxide
  c. silver iodide   **d.** calcium nitride
  e. copper(I) phosphide   **f.** chromium(II) chloride

6.28 Write the formula for each of the following ionic compounds:
  a. zinc bromide   **b.** iron(III) sulfide
  c. manganese(IV) oxide   **d.** chromium(III) iodide
  e. lithium nitride   **f.** gold(I) oxide

℞ Clinical Applications

6.29 The following compounds contain ions that are required in small amounts by the body. Write the formula for each:
   a. potassium phosphide   **b.** copper(II) chloride
   c. iron(III) bromide   **d.** magnesium oxide

6.30 The following compounds contain ions that are required in small amounts by the body. Write the formula for each:
   a. calcium chloride   **b.** nickel(II) iodide
   c. manganese(II) oxide   **d.** zinc nitride

Vitamins and minerals are substances required in small amounts by the body for growth and activity.

LEARNING GOAL

Write the name and formula for an ionic compound containing a polyatomic ion.

6.4 Polyatomic Ions

An ionic compound may also contain a *polyatomic ion* as one of its cations or anions. A **polyatomic ion** is a group of covalently bonded atoms that has an overall ionic charge. Most polyatomic ions consist of a nonmetal such as phosphorus, sulfur, carbon, or nitrogen covalently bonded to oxygen atoms.

Almost all the polyatomic ions are anions with charges $1-, 2-,$ or $3-$. Only one common polyatomic ion, NH_4^+, has a positive charge. Some models of common polyatomic ions are shown in Figure 6.3.

Plaster cast
$CaSO_4$

Fertilizer
NH_4NO_3

Ca^{2+} SO_4^{2-} NH_4^+ NO_3^-
              Sulfate ion   Ammonium ion   Nitrate ion

FIGURE 6.3 ▶ Many products contain polyatomic ions, which are groups of atoms that have an ionic charge.

Q What is the charge of a sulfate ion?

Names of Polyatomic Ions

The names of the most common polyatomic ions end in *ate*, such as nitrate and sulfate. When a related ion has one less oxygen atom, the *ite* ending is used for its name such as nitrite and sulfite. Recognizing these endings will help you identify polyatomic ions in the name of a compound. The hydroxide ion (OH^-) and cyanide ion (CN^-) are exceptions to this naming pattern.

By learning the formulas, charges, and names of the polyatomic ions shown in bold type in Table 6.7, you can derive the related ions. Note that both the *ate* ion and *ite* ion of a particular nonmetal have the same ionic charge. For example, the sulfate ion is SO_4^{2-}, and the sulfite ion, which has one less oxygen atom, is SO_3^{2-}. Phosphate and phosphite ions

TABLE 6.7 Names and Formulas of Some Common Polyatomic Ions

Nonmetal	Formula of Ion*	Name of Ion
Hydrogen	OH^-	Hydroxide
Nitrogen	NH_4^+	Ammonium
	NO_3^-	**Nitrate**
	NO_2^-	Nitrite
Chlorine	ClO_4^-	Perchlorate
	ClO_3^-	**Chlorate**
	ClO_2^-	Chlorite
	ClO^-	Hypochlorite
Carbon	CO_3^{2-}	**Carbonate**
	HCO_3^-	Hydrogen carbonate (or bicarbonate)
	CN^-	Cyanide
	$C_2H_3O_2^-$	Acetate
Sulfur	SO_4^{2-}	**Sulfate**
	HSO_4^-	Hydrogen sulfate (or bisulfate)
	SO_3^{2-}	Sulfite
	HSO_3^-	Hydrogen sulfite (or bisulfite)
Phosphorus	PO_4^{3-}	**Phosphate**
	HPO_4^{2-}	Hydrogen phosphate
	$H_2PO_4^-$	Dihydrogen phosphate
	PO_3^{3-}	Phosphite

*Formulas and names in bold type indicate the most common polyatomic ion for that element.

each have a 3− charge; nitrate and nitrite each have a 1− charge; and perchlorate, chlorate, chlorite, and hypochlorite all have a 1− charge. The halogens form four different polyatomic ions with oxygen.

The formula of hydrogen carbonate, or *bicarbonate*, is written by placing a hydrogen in front of the polyatomic ion formula for carbonate (CO_3^{2-}), and the charge is decreased from 2− to 1− to give HCO_3^-.

$$H^+ + CO_3^{2-} = HCO_3^-$$

Writing Formulas for Compounds Containing Polyatomic Ions

No polyatomic ion exists by itself. Like any ion, a polyatomic ion must be associated with ions of opposite charge. The bonding between polyatomic ions and other ions is one of electrical attraction. For example, the compound sodium chlorite consists of sodium ions (Na^+) and chlorite ions (ClO_2^-) held together by ionic bonds.

To write correct formulas for compounds containing polyatomic ions, we follow the same rules of charge balance that we used for writing the formulas for simple ionic compounds. The total negative and positive charges must equal zero. For example, consider the formula for a compound containing sodium ions and chlorite ions. The ions are written as

$$Na^+ \quad ClO_2^-$$

Sodium ion   Chlorite ion

Ionic charge: $(1+) + (1-) = 0$

Because one ion of each balances the charge, the formula is written as

$NaClO_2$

Sodium chlorite

When more than one polyatomic ion is needed for charge balance, parentheses are used to enclose the formula of the ion. A subscript is written outside the right parenthesis

Sodium chlorite is used in the processing and bleaching of pulp from wood fibers and recycled cardboard.

of the polyatomic ion to indicate the number needed for charge balance. Consider the formula for magnesium nitrate. The ions in this compound are the magnesium ion and the nitrate ion, a polyatomic ion.

$$Mg^{2+} \qquad NO_3^-$$

Magnesium ion   Nitrate ion

To balance the positive charge of 2+ on the magnesium ion, two nitrate ions are needed. In the formula of the compound, parentheses are placed around the nitrate ion, and the subscript 2 is written outside the right parenthesis.

$$NO_3^-$$
$$Mg^{2+}$$
$$NO_3^-$$
$$(2+) + 2(1-) = 0$$

Magnesium nitrate
$$Mg(NO_3)_2$$

Parentheses enclose the formula of the nitrate ion   Subscript outside the parenthesis indicates the use of two nitrate ions

Aluminum hydroxide is an antacid used to treat acid indigestion.

Guide to Writing Formulas with Polyatomic Ions

STEP 1
Identify the cation and polyatomic ion (anion).

STEP 2
Balance the charges.

STEP 3
Write the formula, cation first, using the subscripts from charge balance.

▶**SAMPLE PROBLEM 6.7 Writing Formulas Containing Polyatomic Ions**

An antacid called Amphojel contains aluminum hydroxide, which treats acid indigestion and heartburn. Write the formula for aluminum hydroxide.

SOLUTION

STEP 1   Identify the cation and polyatomic ion (anion).

Cation	Polyatomic Ion (anion)
aluminum	hydroxide
Al^{3+}	OH^-

STEP 2   Balance the charges.

$$Al^{3+} \qquad\qquad OH^-$$
$$OH^-$$
$$OH^-$$
$$\overline{}$$
$$\mathbf{1}(3+) \;+\; \mathbf{3}(1-) = 0$$
$$\uparrow$$

Becomes a subscript in the formula

STEP 3   Write the formula, cation first, using the subscripts from charge balance. The formula for the compound is written by enclosing the formula of the hydroxide ion, OH^-, in parentheses and writing the subscript 3 outside the right parenthesis.

$$Al(OH)_3$$

STUDY CHECK 6.7

Write the formula for a compound containing ammonium ions and phosphate ions.

ANSWER

$$(NH_4)_3PO_4$$

Naming Ionic Compounds Containing Polyatomic Ions

When naming ionic compounds containing polyatomic ions, we first write the positive ion, usually a metal, and then we write the name for the polyatomic ion. It is important that you learn to recognize the polyatomic ion in the formula and name it correctly. As with other ionic compounds, no prefixes are used.

Na_2SO_4 $\qquad$ $FePO_4$ $\qquad$ $Al_2(CO_3)_3$

$Na_2\boxed{SO_4}$ $\qquad$ $Fe\boxed{PO_4}$ $\qquad$ $Al_2(\boxed{CO_3})_3$

Sodium sulfate $\quad$ Iron(III) phosphate $\quad$ Aluminum carbonate

Table 6.8 lists the formulas and names of some ionic compounds that include polyatomic ions and also gives their uses in medicine and industry.

TABLE 6.8 Some Ionic Compounds That Contain Polyatomic Ions

Formula	Name	Medical Use
$BaSO_4$	Barium sulfate	Contrast medium for X-rays
$CaCO_3$	Calcium carbonate	Antacid, calcium supplement
$Ca_3(PO_4)_2$	Calcium phosphate	Calcium dietary supplement
$CaSO_4$	Calcium sulfate	Plaster casts
$AgNO_3$	Silver nitrate	Topical anti-infective
$NaHCO_3$	Sodium bicarbonate or sodium hydrogen carbonate	Antacid
$Zn_3(PO_4)_2$	Zinc phosphate	Dental cement
K_2CO_3	Potassium carbonate	Alkalizer, diuretic
$Al_2(SO_4)_3$	Aluminum sulfate	Antiperspirant, anti-infective
$AlPO_4$	Aluminum phosphate	Antacid
$MgSO_4$	Magnesium sulfate	Cathartic, Epsom salts

A solution of Epsom salts, magnesium sulfate, $MgSO_4$, may be used to soothe sore muscles.

▶ **SAMPLE PROBLEM 6.8** Naming Compounds Containing Polyatomic Ions

Name the following ionic compounds:

a. $Cu(NO_2)_2$ $\qquad\qquad\qquad$ **b.** $KClO_3$

SOLUTION

	STEP 1		STEP 2	STEP 3	STEP 4
Formula	Cation	Anion	Name of Cation	Name of Anion	Name of Compound
a. $Cu(NO_2)_2$	Cu^{2+}	NO_2^-	Copper(II) ion	Nitrite ion	Copper(II) nitrite
b. $KClO_3$	K^+	ClO_3^-	Potassium ion	Chlorate ion	Potassium chlorate

STUDY CHECK 6.8

What is the name of $Co_3(PO_4)_2$?

ANSWER

cobalt(II) phosphate

Guide to Naming Ionic Compounds with Polyatomic Ions

STEP 1
Identify the cation and polyatomic ion (anion).

STEP 2
Name the cation using a Roman numeral, if needed.

STEP 3
Name the polyatomic ion.

STEP 4
Write the name for the compound, cation first and the polyatomic ion second.

QUESTIONS AND PROBLEMS

6.4 Polyatomic Ions

LEARNING GOAL Write the name and formula for an ionic compound containing a polyatomic ion.

6.31 Write the formula including the charge for each of the following polyatomic ions:
   a. hydrogen carbonate (bicarbonate)   **b.** ammonium
   c. phosphite   **d.** chlorate

6.32 Write the formula including the charge for each of the following polyatomic ions:
   a. nitrite   **b.** sulfite
   c. hydroxide **d.** acetate

6.33 Name the following polyatomic ions:
   a. SO_4^{2-} **b.** CO_3^{2-} **c.** HSO_3^- **d.** NO_3^-

6.34 Name the following polyatomic ions:
   a. OH^- **b.** PO_4^{3-} **c.** CN^- **d.** NO_2^-

6.35 Complete the following table with the formula and name of the compound that forms between each pair of ions:

	NO_2^-	CO_3^{2-}	HSO_4^-	PO_4^{3-}
Li^+				
Cu^{2+}				
Ba^{2+}				

6.36 Complete the following table with the formula and name of the compound that forms between each pair of ions:

	NO_3^-	HCO_3^-	SO_3^{2-}	HPO_4^{2-}
NH_4^+				
Al^{3+}				
Pb^{4+}				

6.37 Write the correct formula for the following ionic compounds:
   a. barium hydroxide   **b.** sodium hydrogen sulfate
   c. iron(II) nitrite   **d.** zinc phosphate
   e. iron(III) carbonate

6.38 Write the correct formula for the following ionic compounds:
   a. aluminum chlorate   **b.** ammonium oxide
   c. magnesium bicarbonate **d.** sodium nitrite
   e. copper(I) sulfate

6.39 Write the formula for the polyatomic ion and name each of the following compounds:
   a. Na_2CO_3 **b.** $(NH_4)_2S$
   c. $Ba_3(PO_4)_2$ **d.** $Sn(NO_2)_2$

6.40 Write the formula for the polyatomic ion and name each of the following compounds:
   a. $MnCO_3$ **b.** Au_2SO_4
   c. $Mg_3(PO_4)_2$ **d.** $Fe(HCO_3)_3$

℞ Clinical Applications

6.41 Name each of the following ionic compounds:
   a. $Zn(C_2H_3O_2)_2$, cold remedy
   b. $Mg_3(PO_4)_2$, antacid
   c. NH_4Cl, expectorant
   d. $NaHCO_3$, corrects pH imbalance

6.42 Name each of the following ionic compounds:
   a. Li_2CO_3, antidepressant
   b. $MgSO_4$, Epsom salts
   c. $NaClO$, disinfectant
   d. Na_3PO_4, laxative

LEARNING GOAL

Given the formula of a molecular compound, write its correct name; given the name of a molecular compound, write its formula.

⚛ CORE CHEMISTRY SKILL

Writing the Names and Formulas for Molecular Compounds

6.5 Molecular Compounds: Sharing Electrons

A **molecular compound** contains two or more nonmetals that form *covalent bonds*. Because nonmetals have high ionization energies, valence electrons are shared by non-metal atoms to achieve stability. When atoms share electrons, the bond is a **covalent bond**. When two or more atoms share electrons, they form a **molecule**.

Names and Formulas of Molecular Compounds

When naming a molecular compound, the first nonmetal in the formula is named by its element name; the second nonmetal is named using the first syllable of its element name, followed by *ide*. When a subscript indicates two or more atoms of an element, a prefix is shown in front of its name. Table 6.9 lists prefixes used in naming molecular compounds.

The names of molecular compounds need prefixes because several different compounds can be formed from the same two nonmetals. For example, carbon and oxygen can form two different compounds, carbon monoxide, CO, and carbon dioxide, CO_2, in which the number of atoms of oxygen in each compound is indicated by the prefixes *mono* or *di* in their names.

When the vowels *o* and *o* or *a* and *o* appear together, the first vowel is omitted, as in carbon monoxide. In the name of a molecular compound, the prefix *mono* is usually omitted, as in NO, nitrogen oxide. Traditionally, however, CO is named carbon monoxide. Table 6.10 lists the formulas, names, and commercial uses of some molecular compounds.

TABLE 6.9 Prefixes Used in Naming Molecular Compounds

1 mono	6 hexa
2 di	7 hepta
3 tri	8 octa
4 tetra	9 nona
5 penta	10 deca

TABLE 6.10 Some Common Molecular Compounds

Formula	Name	Commercial Uses
CS_2	Carbon disulfide	Manufacture of rayon
CO_2	Carbon dioxide	Fire extinguishers, dry ice, propellant in aerosols, carbonation of beverages
NO	Nitrogen oxide	Stabilizer, biochemical messenger in cells
N_2O	Dinitrogen oxide	Inhalation anesthetic, "laughing gas"
SO_2	Sulfur dioxide	Preserving fruits, vegetables; disinfectant in breweries; bleaching textiles
SO_3	Sulfur trioxide	Manufacture of explosives
SF_6	Sulfur hexafluoride	Electrical circuits

▶ **SAMPLE PROBLEM 6.9** Naming Molecular Compounds

Name the molecular compound NCl_3.

SOLUTION

ANALYZE THE PROBLEM	Given	Need
	NCl_3	name

STEP 1 Name the first nonmetal by its element name. In NCl_3, the first nonmetal (N) is nitrogen.

Symbol of Element	N	Cl
Name	nitrogen	chloride
Subscript	1	3
Prefix	none	tri

STEP 2 Name the second nonmetal by using the first syllable of its element name followed by *ide*. The second nonmetal (Cl) is named chloride.

STEP 3 Add prefixes to indicate the number of atoms (subscripts). Because there is one nitrogen atom, no prefix is needed. The subscript 3 for the Cl atoms is shown as the prefix *tri*. The name of NCl_3 is nitrogen trichloride.

Guide to Naming Molecular Compounds

STEP 1 Name the first nonmetal by its element name.

STEP 2 Name the second nonmetal by using the first syllable of its element name followed by *ide*.

STEP 3 Add prefixes to indicate the number of atoms (subscripts).

STUDY CHECK 6.9

Write the name for each of the following molecular compounds:

a. $SiBr_4$

b. Br_2O

ANSWER

a. silicon tetrabromide

b. dibromine oxide

Writing Formulas from the Names of Molecular Compounds

In the name of a molecular compound, the names of two nonmetals are given along with prefixes for the number of atoms of each. To write the formula from the name, we use the symbol for each element and a subscript if a prefix indicates two or more atoms.

> **SAMPLE PROBLEM 6.10** Writing Formulas for Molecular Compounds
>
> Write the formula for the molecular compound diboron trioxide.
>
> **SOLUTION**

Guide to Writing Formulas for Molecular Compounds

STEP 1
Write the symbols in the order of the elements in the name.

STEP 2
Write any prefixes as subscripts.

ANALYZE THE PROBLEM	Given	Need
	diboron trioxide	formula

STEP 1 Write the symbols in the order of the elements in the name.

Name of Element	boron	oxygen
Symbol of Element	B	O
Subscript	2 (di)	3 (tri)

STEP 2 Write any prefixes as subscripts. The prefix *di* in *di*boron indicates that there are two atoms of boron, shown as a subscript 2 in the formula. The prefix *tri* in *tri*oxide indicates that there are three atoms of oxygen, shown as a subscript 3 in the formula.

B_2O_3

STUDY CHECK 6.10

Write the formula for the molecular compound iodine pentafluoride.

ANSWER

IF_5

Summary of Naming Ionic and Molecular Compounds

We have now examined strategies for naming ionic and molecular compounds. In general, compounds having two elements are named by stating the first element name followed by the name of the second element with an *ide* ending. If the first element is a metal, the compound is usually ionic; if the first element is a nonmetal, the compound is usually molecular. For ionic compounds, it is necessary to determine whether the metal can form more than one type of positive ion; if so, a Roman numeral following the name of the metal indicates the particular ionic charge. One exception is the ammonium ion, NH_4^+, which is also written first as a positively charged polyatomic ion. Ionic compounds having three or more elements include some type of polyatomic ion. They are named by ionic rules but have an *ate* or *ite* ending when the polyatomic ion has a negative charge.

In naming molecular compounds having two elements, prefixes are necessary to indicate two or more atoms of each nonmetal as shown in that particular formula (see Figure 6.4).

> **SAMPLE PROBLEM 6.11** Naming Ionic and Molecular Compounds
>
> Identify each of the following compounds as ionic or molecular and give its name:
>
> **a.** K_3P **b.** $NiSO_4$ **c.** SO_3
>
> **SOLUTION**
>
> **a.** K_3P, consisting of a metal and a nonmetal, is an ionic compound. As a representative element in Group 1A (1), K forms the potassium ion, K^+. Phosphorus, as a representative element in Group 5A (15), forms a phosphide ion, P^{3-}. Writing the name of the cation followed by the name of the anion gives the name potassium phosphide.

b. $NiSO_4$, consisting of a cation of a transition element and a polyatomic ion SO_4^{2-}, is an ionic compound. As a transition element, Ni forms more than one type of ion. In this formula, the 2− charge of SO_4^{2-} is balanced by one nickel ion, Ni^{2+}. In the name, a Roman numeral written after the metal name, nickel(II), specifies the 2+ charge. The anion SO_4^{2-} is a polyatomic ion named sulfate. The compound is named nickel(II) sulfate.

c. SO_3 consists of two nonmetals, which indicates that it is a molecular compound. The first element S is sulfur (no prefix is needed). The second element O, oxide, has subscript 3, which requires a prefix *tri* in the name. The compound is named sulfur trioxide.

STUDY CHECK 6.11

What is the name of $Fe(NO_3)_3$?

ANSWER

iron(III) nitrate

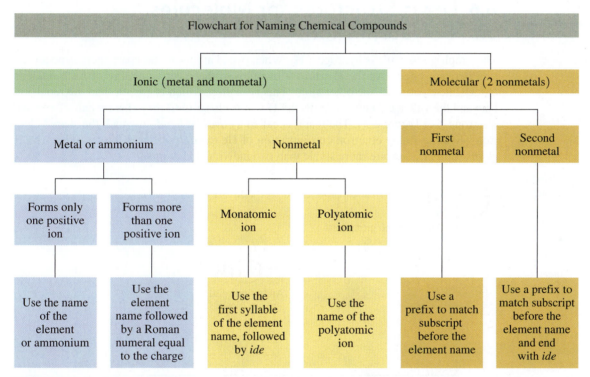

FIGURE 6.4 ▶ A flowchart illustrates naming for ionic and molecular compounds.

Q Why are the names of some metal ions followed by a Roman numeral in the name of a compound?

QUESTIONS AND PROBLEMS

6.5 Molecular Compounds: Sharing Electrons

LEARNING GOAL Given the formula of a molecular compound, write its correct name; given the name of a molecular compound, write its formula.

6.43 Name each of the following molecular compounds:
    a. PBr_3 **b.** Cl_2O **c.** CBr_4 **d.** HF   **e.** NF_3

6.44 Name each of the following molecular compounds:
    a. CS_2 **b.** P_2O_5 **c.** SiO_2 **d.** PCl_3 **e.** CO

6.45 Name each of the following molecular compounds:
    a. N_2O_3 **b.** Si_2Br_6 **c.** P_4S_3 **d.** PCl_5 **e.** SeF_6

6.46 Name each of the following molecular compounds:
    a. SiF_4 **b.** IBr_3 **c.** CO_2 **d.** N_2F_2 **e.** N_2S_3

6.47 Write the formula for each of the following molecular compounds:
    a. carbon tetrachloride   **b.** carbon monoxide
    c. phosphorus trichloride   **d.** dinitrogen tetroxide

6.48 Write the formula for each of the following molecular compounds:
  a. sulfur dioxide
  b. silicon tetrachloride
  c. iodine trifluoride
  d. dinitrogen oxide

6.49 Write the formula for each of the following molecular compounds:
  a. oxygen difluoride
  b. boron trichloride
  c. dinitrogen trioxide
  d. sulfur hexafluoride

6.50 Write the formula for each of the following molecular compounds:
  a. sulfur dibromide
  b. carbon disulfide
  c. tetraphosphorus hexoxide
  d. dinitrogen pentoxide

℞ Clinical Applications

6.51 Name each of the following ionic or molecular compounds:
  a. $Al_2(SO_4)_3$, antiperspirant
  b. $CaCO_3$, antacid
  c. N_2O, "laughing gas," inhaled anesthetic
  d. $Mg(OH)_2$, laxative

6.52 Name each of the following ionic or molecular compounds:
  a. $Al(OH)_3$, antacid
  b. $FeSO_4$, iron supplement in vitamins
  c. NO, vasodilator
  d. $Cu(OH)_2$, fungicide

LEARNING GOAL

Draw the Lewis structures for molecular compounds or polyatomic ions.

6.6 Lewis Structures for Molecules and Polyatomic Ions

The simplest molecule is hydrogen, H_2. When two H atoms are far apart, there is no attraction between them. As the H atoms move closer, the positive charge of each nucleus attracts the electron of the other atom. This attraction, which is greater than the repulsion between the valence electrons, pulls the H atoms closer until they share a pair of valence electrons (see Figure 6.5). The result is called a *covalent bond*, in which the shared electrons give the stable electron configuration of He to *each* of the H atoms. When the H atoms form H_2, they are more stable than two individual H atoms.

FIGURE 6.5 ▶ A covalent bond forms as H atoms move close together to share electrons.

Q What determines the attraction between two H atoms?

The elements hydrogen, nitrogen, oxygen, fluorine, chlorine, bromine, and iodine exist as diatomic molecules.

Lewis Structures for Molecular Compounds

A molecule is represented by a **Lewis structure** in which the valence electrons of all the atoms are arranged to give octets except two electrons for hydrogen. The shared electrons, or *bonding pairs*, are shown as two dots or a single line between atoms. The nonbonding pairs of electrons, or *lone pairs*, are placed on the outside. For example, a fluorine molecule, F_2, consists of two fluorine atoms, which are in Group 7A (17), each with seven valence electrons. In the Lewis structure of the F_2 molecule, each F atom achieves an octet by sharing its unpaired valence electron.

Hydrogen (H_2) and fluorine (F_2) are examples of nonmetal elements whose natural state is diatomic; that is, they contain two like atoms. The elements that exist as diatomic molecules are listed in Table 6.11.

Sharing Electrons Between Atoms of Different Elements

The number of electrons that a nonmetal atom shares and the number of covalent bonds it forms are usually equal to the number of electrons it needs to achieve a stable electron configuration. Table 6.12 gives the most typical bonding patterns for some nonmetals.

TABLE 6.12 Typical Bonding Patterns of Some Nonmetals

1A (1)	3A (13)	4A (14)	5A (15)	6A (16)	7A (17)
*H 1 bond					
	*B 3 bonds	C 4 bonds	N 3 bonds	O 2 bonds	F 1 bond
		Si 4 bonds	P 3 bonds	S 2 bonds	Cl, Br, I 1 bond

*H and B do not form octets. H atoms share one electron pair; B atoms share three electron pairs for a set of six electrons.

Drawing Lewis Structures

To draw the Lewis structure for CH_4, we first draw the Lewis symbols for carbon and hydrogen.

$$\cdot \overset{\textstyle\cdot}{\underset{\textstyle\cdot}{C}} \cdot \qquad \cdot H$$

Then we can determine the number of valence electrons needed for carbon and hydrogen. When a carbon atom shares its four electrons with four hydrogen atoms, carbon obtains an octet and each hydrogen atom is complete with two shared electrons. The Lewis structure is drawn with the carbon atom as the central atom, with the hydrogen atoms on each of the sides. The bonding pairs of electrons, which are single covalent bonds, may also be shown as single lines between the carbon atom and each of the hydrogen atoms.

$$H : \overset{\textstyle H}{\underset{\textstyle H}{\overset{..}{\underset{..}{C}}}} : H \qquad\qquad H - \overset{\textstyle H}{\underset{\textstyle H}{C}} - H$$

Table 6.13 gives the formulas and three-dimensional models of some molecules.

When we draw a Lewis structure for a molecule or polyatomic ion, we show the sequence of atoms, the bonding pairs of electrons shared between atoms, and the nonbonding or *lone pairs* of electrons. From the formula, we identify the central atom, which is the element that has the fewer atoms. Then, the central atom is bonded to the other atoms, as shown in Sample Problem 6.12.

TABLE 6.11 Elements That Exist as Diatomic Molecules

Diatomic Molecule	Name
H_2	Hydrogen
N_2	Nitrogen
O_2	Oxygen
F_2	Fluorine
Cl_2	Chlorine
Br_2	Bromine
I_2	Iodine

Examples: CH_4, PCl_3, SF_2, HBr

The number of covalent bonds that a nonmetal atom forms is usually equal to the number of electrons it needs to achieve a stable electron configuration.

⚛ CORE CHEMISTRY SKILL

Drawing Lewis Structures

TABLE 6.13 Lewis Structures for Some Molecular Compounds

CH_4	NH_3	H_2O
Lewis Structures		
$H : \overset{H}{\underset{H}{\overset{..}{\underset{..}{C}}}} : H$	$H : \overset{..}{\underset{H}{N}} : H$	$: \overset{..}{\underset{..}{O}} : H$
Formulas Using Bonds and Electron Dots		
$H - \overset{H}{\underset{H}{C}} - H$	$H - \overset{..}{\underset{H}{N}} - H$	$: \overset{..}{\underset{..}{O}} - H$
Molecular Models		

Methane molecule   Ammonia molecule   Water molecule

Guide to Drawing Lewis Structures

STEP 1
Determine the arrangement of atoms.

STEP 2
Determine the total number of valence electrons.

STEP 3
Attach each bonded atom to the central atom with a pair of electrons.

STEP 4
Place the remaining electrons using single or multiple bonds to complete octets (two for H).

The ball-and-stick model of PCl_3 consists of P and Cl atoms connected by single bonds.

SAMPLE PROBLEM 6.12 Drawing Lewis Structures

Draw the Lewis structure for PCl_3, phosphorus trichloride, used commercially to prepare insecticides and flame retardants.

SOLUTION

STEP 1 Determine the arrangement of atoms. In PCl_3, the central atom is P because there is only one P atom.

$$Cl \quad P \quad Cl$$
$$Cl$$

STEP 2 Determine the total number of valence electrons. We use the group number to determine the number of valence electrons for each of the atoms in the molecule.

Element	Group	Atoms		Valence Electrons	=	Total
P	5A (15)	1 P	×	$5\,e^-$	=	$5\,e^-$
Cl	7A (17)	3 Cl	×	$7\,e^-$	=	$21\,e^-$
		Total valence electrons for PCl_3			=	$26\,e^-$

STEP 3 Attach each bonded atom to the central atom with a pair of electrons. Each bonding pair can also be represented by a bond line.

$$Cl\!:\!P\!:\!Cl \quad\quad or \quad\quad Cl\!-\!P\!-\!Cl$$
$$\quad\;\; Cl \quad\quad\quad\quad\quad\quad\quad Cl$$

STEP 4 Place the remaining electrons using single or multiple bonds to complete the octets. Six electrons ($3 \times 2\,e^-$) are used to bond the central P atom to three Cl atoms. Twenty valence electrons are left.

$$26 \text{ valence } e^- - 6 \text{ bonding } e^- = 20\,e^- \text{ remaining}$$

We use the remaining 20 electrons as lone pairs, which are placed around the outer Cl atoms and on the P atom, such that all the atoms have octets.

$$:\!\ddot{C}\!l\!:\!\ddot{P}\!:\!\ddot{C}\!l\!: \quad\quad or \quad\quad :\!\ddot{C}\!l\!-\!\ddot{P}\!-\!\ddot{C}\!l\!:$$
$$\quad\;\;\; :\!\ddot{C}\!l\!: \quad\quad\quad\quad\quad\quad\quad\quad\quad\;\; :\!\ddot{C}\!l\!:$$

STUDY CHECK 6.12

Draw the Lewis structure for Cl_2O.

ANSWER

$$:\!\ddot{C}\!l\!:\!\ddot{O}\!:\!\ddot{C}\!l\!: \quad or \quad :\!\ddot{C}\!l\!-\!\ddot{O}\!-\!\ddot{C}\!l\!:$$

SAMPLE PROBLEM 6.13 Drawing Lewis Structures for Polyatomic Ions

Sodium chlorite, $NaClO_2$, is a component of mouthwashes, toothpastes, and contact lens cleaning solutions. Draw the Lewis structure for the chlorite ion, ClO_2^-.

SOLUTION

STEP 1 Determine the arrangement of atoms. For the polyatomic ion ClO_2^-, the central atom is Cl because there is only one Cl atom. For a polyatomic ion, the atoms and electrons are placed in brackets, and the charge is written outside to the upper right.

$$[O \quad Cl \quad O]^-$$

STEP 2 Determine the total number of valence electrons. We use the group numbers to determine the number of valence electrons for each of the atoms in the ion. Because the ion has a negative charge, one more electron is added to the valence electrons.

Element	Group	Atoms		Valence Electrons	=	Total
O	6A (16)	2 O	×	$6\,e^-$	=	$12\,e^-$
Cl	7A (17)	1 Cl	×	$7\,e^-$	=	$7\,e^-$
Ionic charge (negative) add				$1\,e^-$	=	$1\,e^-$
		Total valence electrons for ClO_2^-			=	$20\,e^-$

STEP 3 Attach each bonded atom to the central atom with a pair of electrons. Each bonding pair can also be represented by a line, which indicates a single bond.

$$[O:Cl:O]^- \quad \text{or} \quad [O-Cl-O]^-$$

STEP 4 Place the remaining electrons using single or multiple bonds to complete the octets. Four electrons are used to bond the O atoms to the central Cl atom, which leaves 16 valence electrons. Of these, 12 electrons are drawn as lone pairs to complete the octets of the O atoms.

$$\left[:\ddot{O}:Cl:\ddot{O}:\right]^- \quad \text{or} \quad \left[:\ddot{O}-Cl-\ddot{O}:\right]^-$$

The remaining four electrons are placed as two lone pairs on the central Cl atom.

$$\left[:\ddot{O}:\ddot{Cl}:\ddot{O}:\right]^- \quad \text{or} \quad \left[:\ddot{O}-\ddot{Cl}-\ddot{O}:\right]^-$$

In ClO_2^-, the central Cl atom is bonded to two O atoms.

STUDY CHECK 6.13

Draw the Lewis structure for the polyatomic ion NH_2^-.

ANSWER

$$\left[H:\ddot{N}:H\right]^- \quad \text{or} \quad \left[H-\ddot{N}-H\right]^-$$

Double and Triple Bonds

Up to now, we have looked at bonding in molecules having only single bonds. In many molecular compounds, atoms share two or three pairs of electrons to complete their octets.

Double and triple bonds form when the number of valence electrons is not enough to complete the octets of all the atoms in the molecule. Then one or more lone pairs of electrons from the atoms attached to the central atom are shared with the central atom. A **double bond** occurs when two pairs of electrons are shared; in a **triple bond**, three pairs of electrons are shared. Atoms of carbon, oxygen, nitrogen, and sulfur are most likely to form multiple bonds.

Atoms of hydrogen and the halogens do not form double or triple bonds. The process of drawing a Lewis structure with multiple bonds is shown in Sample Problem 6.14.

▶**SAMPLE PROBLEM 6.14** **Drawing Lewis Structures with Multiple Bonds**

Draw the Lewis structure for carbon dioxide, CO_2, in which the central atom is C.

SOLUTION

STEP 1 Determine the arrangement of atoms. O C O

STEP 2 Determine the total number of valence electrons. Using the group number to determine valence electrons, the carbon atom has four valence electrons, and each oxygen atom has six valence electrons, which gives a total of 16 valence electrons.

Element	Group	Atoms	Valence Electrons	=	Total
C	4A (14)	1 C	$\times$ 4 e^-	=	4 e^-
O	6A (16)	2 O	$\times$ 6 e^-	=	12 e^-
		Total valence electrons for CO_2		=	16 e^-

STEP 3 Attach each bonded atom to the central atom with a pair of electrons.

O:C:O   or   O—C—O

STEP 4 Place the remaining electrons to complete octets. Because we used four valence electrons to attach the C atom to two O atoms, there are 12 valence electrons remaining.

$$16 \text{ valence } e^- - 4 \text{ bonding } e^- = 12 \text{ } e^- \text{ remaining}$$

The 12 remaining electrons are placed as six lone pairs of electrons on the outside O atoms. However, this does not complete the octet of the C atom.

:Ö:C:Ö: or   :Ö—C—Ö:

To obtain an octet, the C atom must share lone pairs of electrons from each of the O atoms. When two bonding pairs occur between atoms, it is known as a double bond.

Lone pairs converted to bonding pairs

Double bonds   Double bonds   Molecule of carbon dioxide

:O::C::O: or   :O=C=O:

STUDY CHECK 6.14

Draw the Lewis structure for HCN, which has a triple bond.

ANSWER

H:C:::N: or   H—C≡N:

Exceptions to the Octet Rule

Although the octet rule is useful for bonding in many compounds, there are exceptions. We have already seen that a hydrogen (H_2) molecule requires just two electrons or a single bond. Usually the nonmetals form octets. However, in BCl_3, the B atom has only three valence electrons to share. Boron compounds typically have six valence electrons on the central B atoms and form just three bonds. Although we will generally see compounds of P, S, Cl, Br, and I with octets, they can form molecules in which they share more of their valence electrons. This expands their valence electrons to 10, 12, or even 14 electrons. For example, we have seen that the P atom in PCl_3 has an octet, but in PCl_5, the P atom has five bonds with 10 valence electrons. In H_2S, the S atom has an octet, but in SF_6, there are six bonds to sulfur with 12 valence electrons.

In BCl_3, the central B atom is bonded to three Cl atoms.

In SF_6, the central S atom is bonded to six F atoms.

QUESTIONS AND PROBLEMS

6.6 Lewis Structures for Molecules and Polyatomic Ions

LEARNING GOAL Draw the Lewis structures for molecular compounds or polyatomic ions.

6.53 Determine the total number of valence electrons for each of the following:
    a. H_2S **b.** I_2 **c.** CCl_4 **d.** OH^-

6.54 Determine the total number of valence electrons for each of the following:
    a. SBr_2 **b.** NBr_3 **c.** CH_3OH **d.** NH_4^+

6.55 Draw the Lewis structure for each of the following molecules or ions:
    a. HF   **b.** SF_2 **c.** NBr_3 **d.** BH_4^-

6.56 Draw the Lewis structure for each of the following molecules or ions:
    a. H_2O **b.** CCl_4 **c.** H_3O^+ **d.** SiF_4

6.57 When is it necessary to draw a multiple bond in a Lewis structure?

6.58 If the available number of valence electrons for a molecule or polyatomic ion does not complete all of the octets in a Lewis structure, what should you do?

6.59 Draw the Lewis structure for each of the following molecules or ions:
    a. CO
    b. NO_3^- (N is the central atom)
    c. H_2CO (C is the central atom)

6.60 Draw the Lewis structure for each of the following molecules or ions:
    a. HCCH (ethyne)
    b. CS_2
    c. NO^+

6.7 Electronegativity and Bond Polarity

We can learn more about the chemistry of compounds by looking at how bonding electrons are shared between atoms. The bonding electrons are shared equally in a bond between identical nonmetal atoms. However, when a bond is between atoms of different elements, the electron pairs are usually shared unequally. Then the shared pairs of electrons are attracted to one atom in the bond more than the other.

The **electronegativity** of an atom is its ability to attract the shared electrons in a chemical bond. Nonmetals have higher electronegativities than do metals, because nonmetals have a greater attraction for electrons than metals. On the electronegativity scale, fluorine was assigned a value of 4.0, and the electronegativities for all other elements were determined relative to the attraction of fluorine for shared electrons. The nonmetal fluorine, which has the highest electronegativity (4.0), is located in the upper right corner of the periodic table. The metal cesium, which has the lowest electronegativity (0.7), is located in the lower left corner of the periodic table. The electronegativities for the representative elements are shown in Figure 6.6. Note that there are no electronegativity values for the noble gases because they do not typically form bonds. The electronegativity values for transition elements are also low, but we have not included them in our discussion.

LEARNING GOAL

Use electronegativity to determine the polarity of a bond.

⊗ CORE CHEMISTRY SKILL

Using Electronegativity

FIGURE 6.6 ▶ The electronegativity values of representative elements in Group 1A (1) to Group 7A (17), which indicate the ability of atoms to attract shared electrons, increase going across a period from left to right and decrease going down a group.

Q What element on the periodic table has the strongest attraction for shared electrons?

Electronegativity Increases →

Electronegativity Decreases ↓

	H 2.1									18 Group 8A

1 Group 1A	2 Group 2A		13 Group 3A	14 Group 4A	15 Group 5A	16 Group 6A	17 Group 7A	
Li 1.0	Be 1.5		B 2.0	C 2.5	N 3.0	O 3.5	F 4.0	
Na 0.9	Mg 1.2		Al 1.5	Si 1.8	P 2.1	S 2.5	Cl 3.0	
K 0.8	Ca 1.0		Ga 1.6	Ge 1.8	As 2.0	Se 2.4	Br 2.8	
Rb 0.8	Sr 1.0		In 1.7	Sn 1.8	Sb 1.9	Te 2.1	I 2.5	
Cs 0.7	Ba 0.9		Tl 1.8	Pb 1.9	Bi 1.9	Po 2.0	At 2.1	

Polarity of Bonds

The difference in the electronegativity values of two atoms can be used to predict the type of chemical bond, ionic or covalent, that forms. For the H—H bond, the electronegativity difference is zero $(2.1 - 2.1 = 0)$, which means the bonding electrons are shared equally. A bond between atoms with identical or very similar electronegativity values is a **nonpolar covalent bond**. However, when bonds are between atoms with different electronegativity values, the electrons are shared unequally; the bond is a **polar covalent bond**. For the H—Cl bond, there is an electronegativity difference of $3.0 \, (\text{Cl}) - 2.1(\text{H}) = 0.9$, which means that the H—Cl bond is polar covalent (see Figure 6.7).

FIGURE 6.7 ▶ In the nonpolar covalent bond of H_2, electrons are shared equally. In the polar covalent bond of HCl, electrons are shared unequally.

Q H_2 has a nonpolar covalent bond, but HCl has a polar covalent bond. Explain.

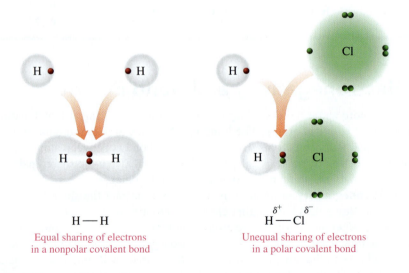

H —— H
Equal sharing of electrons
in a nonpolar covalent bond

$\overset{\delta^+}{\text{H}} —— \overset{\delta^-}{\text{Cl}}$
Unequal sharing of electrons
in a polar covalent bond

Dipoles and Bond Polarity

The **polarity** of a bond depends on the difference in the electronegativity values of its atoms. In a polar covalent bond, the shared electrons are attracted to the more electronegative atom, which makes it partially negative, because of the negatively charged electrons around that atom. At the other end of the bond, the atom with the lower electronegativity becomes partially positive because of the lack of electrons at that atom.

A bond becomes more *polar* as the electronegativity difference increases. A polar covalent bond that has a separation of charges is called a **dipole**. The positive and negative ends of the dipole are indicated by the lowercase Greek letter delta with a positive or negative sign, δ^+ and δ^-. Sometimes we use an arrow that points from the positive charge to the negative charge $\longmapsto$ to indicate the dipole.

Examples of Dipoles in Polar Covalent Bonds

$$\overset{\delta^+}{C}-\overset{\delta^-}{O} \qquad \overset{\delta^+}{N}-\overset{\delta^-}{O} \qquad \overset{\delta^+}{Cl}-\overset{\delta^-}{F}$$
$$\longmapsto \qquad\qquad \longmapsto \qquad\qquad \longmapsto$$

Variations in Bonding

The variations in bonding are continuous; there is no definite point at which one type of bond stops and the next starts. When the electronegativity difference is between 0.0 and 0.4, the electrons are considered to be shared equally in a *nonpolar covalent bond*. For example, the C—C bond (2.5 − 2.5 = 0.0) and the C—H bond (2.5 − 2.1 = 0.4) are classified as nonpolar covalent bonds. As the electronegativity difference increases, the shared electrons are attracted more strongly to the more electronegative atom, which increases the polarity of the bond. When the electronegativity difference is from 0.5 to 1.8, the bond is a *polar covalent bond*. For example, the O—H bond (3.5 − 2.1 = 1.4) is classified as a polar covalent bond (see Table 6.14).

TABLE 6.14 Electronegativity Differences and Types of Bonds

Electronegativity Difference	0	0.4	1.8	3.3
Bond Type	Nonpolar covalent	Polar covalent	Ionic	
Electron Bonding	Electrons shared equally	Electrons shared unequally	Electrons transferred	

When the electronegativity difference is greater than 1.8, electrons are transferred from one atom to another, which results in an *ionic bond*. For example, the electronegativity difference for the ionic compound NaCl is 3.0 − 0.9 = 2.1. Thus, for large differences in electronegativity, we would predict an ionic bond (see Table 6.15).

TABLE 6.15 Predicting Bond Type from Electronegativity Differences

Molecule	Bond	Type of Electron Sharing	Electronegativity Difference*	Type of Bond	Reason
H_2	H—H	Shared equally	2.1 − 2.1 = 0.0	Nonpolar covalent	Between 0.0 and 0.4
BrCl	Br—Cl	Shared about equally	3.0 − 2.8 = 0.2	Nonpolar covalent	Between 0.0 and 0.4
HBr	$\overset{\delta^+}{H}-\overset{\delta^-}{Br}$	Shared unequally	2.8 − 2.1 = 0.7	Polar covalent	Greater than 0.4, but less than 1.8
HCl	$\overset{\delta^+}{H}-\overset{\delta^-}{Cl}$	Shared unequally	3.0 − 2.1 = 0.9	Polar covalent	Greater than 0.4, but less than 1.8
NaCl	Na^+Cl^-	Electron transfer	3.0 − 0.9 = 2.1	Ionic	Greater than 1.8
MgO	$Mg^{2+}O^{2-}$	Electron transfer	3.5 − 1.2 = 2.3	Ionic	Greater than 1.8

*Values are taken from Figure 6.6.

▶ **SAMPLE PROBLEM 6.15** Bond Polarity

Using electronegativity values, classify each of the following bonds as nonpolar covalent, polar covalent, or ionic:

O—K,   Cl—As,   N—N,   P—Br

SOLUTION

For each bond, we obtain the electronegativity values and calculate the difference in electronegativity.

Bond	Electronegativity Difference	Type of Bond
O—K	$3.5 - 0.8 = 2.7$	Ionic
Cl—As	$3.0 - 2.0 = 1.0$	Polar covalent
N—N	$3.0 - 3.0 = 0.0$	Nonpolar covalent
P—Br	$2.8 - 2.1 = 0.7$	Polar covalent

STUDY CHECK 6.15

Using electronegativity values, classify each of the following bonds as nonpolar covalent, polar covalent, or ionic:

a. P—Cl   **b.** Br—Br   **c.** Na—O

ANSWER

a. polar covalent (0.9)   **b.** nonpolar covalent (0.0)   **c.** ionic (2.6)

QUESTIONS AND PROBLEMS

6.7 Electronegativity and Bond Polarity

LEARNING GOAL Use electronegativity to determine the polarity of a bond.

6.61 Describe the trend in electronegativity as *increases* or *decreases* for each of the following:
  a. from B to F   **b.** from Mg to Ba   **c.** from F to I

6.62 Describe the trend in electronegativity as *increases* or *decreases* for each of the following:
  a. from Al to Cl   **b.** from Br to K   **c.** from Li to Cs

6.63 Using the periodic table, arrange the atoms in each of the following sets in order of increasing electronegativity:
  a. Li, Na, K   **b.** Na, Cl, P   **c.** Se, Ca, O

6.64 Using the periodic table, arrange the atoms in each of the following sets in order of increasing electronegativity:
  a. Cl, F, Br   **b.** B, O, N   **c.** Mg, F, S

6.65 Predict whether each of the following bonds is nonpolar covalent, polar covalent, or ionic:
  a. Si—Br   **b.** Li—F   **c.** Br—F
  d. I—I   **e.** N—P   **f.** C—P

6.66 Predict whether each of the following bonds is nonpolar covalent, polar covalent, or ionic:
  a. Si—O   **b.** K—Cl   **c.** S—F
  d. P—Br   **e.** Li—O   **f.** N—S

6.67 For each of the following bonds, indicate the positive end with δ^+ and the negative end with δ^-. Draw an arrow to show the dipole for each.
  a. N—F   **b.** Si—Br   **c.** C—O
  d. P—Br   **e.** N—P

6.68 For each of the following bonds, indicate the positive end with δ^+ and the negative end with δ^-. Draw an arrow to show the dipole for each.
  a. P—Cl   **b.** Se—F   **c.** Br—F
  d. N—H   **e.** B—Cl

LEARNING GOAL

Predict the three-dimensional structure of a molecule, and classify it as polar or nonpolar.

6.8 Shapes and Polarity of Molecules

Using the Lewis structures, we can predict the three-dimensional shapes of many molecules. The shape is important in our understanding of how molecules interact with enzymes or certain antibiotics or produce our sense of taste and smell.

The three-dimensional shape of a molecule is determined by drawing its Lewis structure and identifying the number of electron groups (one or more electron pairs) around the central atom. We count lone pairs of electrons, single, double, or triple bonds as *one* electron group. In the **valence shell electron-pair repulsion (VSEPR) theory**, the electron groups are arranged as far apart as possible around the central atom to minimize the repulsion between their negative charges. Once we have counted the number of electron groups surrounding the central atom, we can determine its specific shape from the number of atoms bonded to the central atom.

Central Atoms with Two Electron Groups

In the Lewis structure for CO_2, there are two electron groups (two double bonds) attached to the central atom. According to VSEPR theory, minimal repulsion occurs when two electron groups are on opposite sides of the central C atom. This gives the CO_2 molecule a *linear* electron-group geometry and a *linear shape* with a bond angle of 180°.

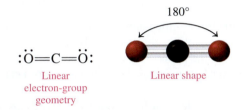

Linear
electron-group
geometry

Linear shape

Central Atoms with Three Electron Groups

In the Lewis structure for formaldehyde, H_2CO, the central atom C is attached to two H atoms by single bonds and to the O atom by a double bond. Minimal repulsion occurs when three electron groups are as far apart as possible around the central C atom, which gives 120° bond angles. This type of electron-group geometry is *trigonal planar* and gives a shape for H_2CO called *trigonal planar*.

Lewis
structure

Trigonal planar
electron-group
geometry

Trigonal planar shape

In the Lewis structure for SO_2, there are also three electron groups around the central S atom: a single bond to an O atom, a double bond to another O atom, and a lone pair of electrons. As in H_2CO, three electron groups have minimal repulsion when they form trigonal planar electron-group geometry. However, in SO_2 one of the electron groups is a lone pair of electrons. Therefore, the shape of the SO_2 molecule is determined by the two O atoms bonded to the central S atom, which gives the SO_2 molecule a *bent shape* with a bond angle of 120°. When there are one or more lone pairs on the central atom, the shape has a different name than that of the electron-group geometry.

Lewis
structure

Trigonal planar
electron-group
geometry

Bent shape

Central Atom with Four Electron Groups

In a molecule of methane, CH_4, the central C atom is bonded to four H atoms. From the Lewis structure, you may think that CH_4 is planar with 90° bond angles. However, the best geometry for minimal repulsion is *tetrahedral*, giving bond angles of 109°. When there are four atoms attached to four electron groups, the shape of the molecule is *tetrahedral*.

Lewis structure · Tetrahedral electron-group geometry · Tetrahedral shape · Tetrahedral wedge–dash notation

A way to represent the three-dimensional structure of methane is to use the wedge–dash notation. In this representation, the two bonds connecting carbon to hydrogen by solid lines are in the plane of the paper. The wedge represents a carbon-to-hydrogen bond coming out of the page toward us, whereas the dash represents a carbon-to-hydrogen bond going into the page away from us.

Now we can look at molecules that have four electron groups, of which one or more are lone pairs of electrons. Then the central atom is attached to only two or three atoms. For example, in the Lewis structure for ammonia, NH_3, four electron groups have a tetrahedral electron-group geometry. However, in NH_3 one of the electron groups is a lone pair of electrons. Therefore, the shape of NH_3 is determined by the three H atoms bonded to the central N atom. Therefore, the shape of the NH_3 molecule is *trigonal pyramidal*, with a bond angle of 109°. The wedge–dash notation can also represent this three-dimensional structure of ammonia with one N—H bond in the plane, one N—H bond coming toward us, and one N—H bond going away from us.

Lone pair of electrons

Lewis structure · Tetrahedral electron-group geometry · Trigonal pyramidal shape · Trigonal pyramidal wedge–dash notation

In the Lewis structure for water, H_2O, there are also four electron groups, which have minimal repulsion when the electron-group geometry is tetrahedral. However, in H_2O, two of the electron groups are lone pairs of electrons. Because the shape of H_2O is determined by the two H atoms bonded to the central O atom, the H_2O molecule has a *bent shape* with a bond angle of 109°. Table 6.16 gives the shapes of molecules with two, three, or four bonded atoms.

Two lone pairs of electrons

Lewis structure · Tetrahedral electron-group geometry · Bent shape · Bent wedge–dash notation

TABLE 6.16 Molecular Shapes for a Central Atom with Two, Three, and Four Bonded Atoms

Electron Groups	Electron-Group Geometry	Bonded Atoms	Lone Pairs	Bond Angle*	Molecular Shape	Example	Three-Dimensional Model
2	Linear	2	0	180°	Linear	CO_2	
3	Trigonal planar	3	0	120°	Trigonal planar	H_2CO	
3	Trigonal planar	2	1	120°	Bent	SO_2	
4	Tetrahedral	4	0	109°	Tetrahedral	CH_4	
4	Tetrahedral	3	1	109°	Trigonal pyramidal	NH_3	
4	Tetrahedral	2	2	109°	Bent	H_2O	

*The bond angles in actual molecules may vary slightly.

▶ **SAMPLE PROBLEM 6.16 Shapes of Molecules**

Predict the shape of a molecule of $SiCl_4$.

SOLUTION

ANALYZE THE PROBLEM	Given	Need
	$SiCl_4$	shape

STEP 1   Draw the Lewis structure. Using $32\ e^-$, we draw the bonds and lone pairs for the Lewis structure of $SiCl_4$.

Name of Element	Silicon	Chlorine
Symbol of Element	Si	Cl
Atoms of Element	1	4
Valence Electrons	$4\ e^-$	$7\ e^-$
Total Electrons	$1(4\ e^-)$ +	$4(7\ e^-) = 32\ e^-$

STEP 2   Arrange the electron groups around the central atom to minimize repulsion. To minimize repulsion, the electron-group geometry would be tetrahedral.

STEP 3   Use the atoms bonded to the central atom to determine the shape. Because the central Si atom has four bonded pairs and no lone pairs of electrons, the $SiCl_4$ molecule has a tetrahedral shape.

Guide to Predicting Shape (VSEPR Theory)

STEP 1
Draw the Lewis structure.

STEP 2
Arrange the electron groups around the central atom to minimize repulsion.

STEP 3
Use the atoms bonded to the central atom to determine the shape.

STUDY CHECK 6.16

Predict the shape of SCl_2.

ANSWER

The central atom S has four electron groups: two bonded atoms and two lone pairs of electrons. The shape of SCl_2 is bent, 109°.

SAMPLE PROBLEM 6.17 Predicting Shape of an Ion

Use VSEPR theory to predict the shape of the polyatomic ion NO_3^-.

SOLUTION

STEP **1** Draw the Lewis structure. The polyatomic ion, NO_3^-, contains three electron groups (two single bonds between the central N atom and O atoms, and one double bond between N and O). Note that the double bond can be drawn to any of the O atoms.

$$\left[\ddot{\underset{..}{O}} - N = \ddot{O}: \atop \underset{\displaystyle :\underset{..}{O}:}{|} \right]^-$$

STEP **2** Arrange the electron groups around the central atom to minimize repulsion. To minimize repulsion, three electron groups would have a trigonal planar geometry.

STEP **3** Use the atoms bonded to the central atom to determine the shape. Because NO_3^- has three bonded atoms, it has a trigonal planar shape.

STUDY CHECK 6.17

Use VSEPR theory to predict the shape of ClO_2^-.

ANSWER

With two bonded atoms and two lone pairs of electrons, the shape of ClO_2^- is bent with a bond angle of 109°.

⚛ CORE CHEMISTRY SKILL

Identifying Polarity of Molecules

Polarity of Molecules

We have seen that covalent bonds in molecules can be polar or nonpolar. Now we will look at how the bonds in a molecule and its shape determine whether that molecule is classified as polar or nonpolar.

Nonpolar Molecules

In a **nonpolar molecule**, all the bonds are nonpolar or the polar bonds cancel each other out. Molecules such as H_2, Cl_2, and CH_4 are nonpolar because they contain only nonpolar covalent bonds.

$$H - H \qquad Cl - Cl \qquad H - \overset{\displaystyle H}{\underset{\displaystyle H}{\overset{|}{\underset{|}{C}}}} - H$$

Nonpolar molecules

A *nonpolar molecule* also occurs when polar bonds (dipoles) cancel each other because they are in a symmetrical arrangement. For example, CO_2, a linear molecule, contains two equal polar covalent bonds whose dipoles point in opposite directions. As a result, the dipoles cancel out, which makes a CO_2 molecule nonpolar.

$$O = C = O$$

Dipoles cancel

CO_2 is a nonpolar molecule.

Another example of a nonpolar molecule is the CCl_4 molecule, which has four polar bonds symmetrically arranged around the central C atom. Each of the C—Cl bonds has the same polarity, but because they have a tetrahedral arrangement, their opposing dipoles cancel out. As a result, a molecule of CCl_4 is nonpolar.

The four C—Cl dipoles cancel out.

Polar Molecules

In a **polar molecule**, one end of the molecule is more negatively charged than the other end. Polarity in a molecule occurs when the dipoles from the individual polar bonds do not cancel each other. For example, HCl is a polar molecule because it has one covalent bond that is polar.

In molecules with two or more electron groups, the shape, such as bent or trigonal pyramidal, determines whether the dipoles cancel. For example, we have seen that H_2O has a bent shape. Thus, a water molecule is polar because the individual dipoles do not cancel.

A single dipole does not cancel.

More negative end of molecule

More positive end of molecule

H_2O is a polar molecule because its dipoles do not cancel.

The NH_3 molecule has a tetrahedral electron-group geometry with three bonded atoms, which gives it a trigonal pyramidal shape. Thus, the NH_3 molecule is polar because the individual N—H dipoles do not cancel.

More negative end of molecule

More positive end of molecule

NH_3 is a polar molecule because its dipoles do not cancel.

In the molecule CH_3F, the C—F bond is polar covalent, but the three C—H bonds are nonpolar covalent. Because there is only one dipole in CH_3F, which does not cancel, CH_3F is a polar molecule.

CH_3F is a polar molecule.

> ## SAMPLE PROBLEM 6.18 Polarity of Molecules
>
> Determine whether a molecule of OF_2 is polar or nonpolar.
>
> ### SOLUTION
>
> **STEP 1** Determine if the bonds are polar covalent or nonpolar covalent. From Figure 6.6, F and O have an electronegativity difference of 0.5 ($4.0 - 3.5 = 0.5$), which makes each of the O—F bonds polar covalent.
>
> **STEP 2** If the bonds are polar covalent, draw the Lewis structure and determine if the dipoles cancel. The Lewis structure for OF_2 has four electron groups and two bonded atoms. The molecule has a bent shape in which the dipoles of the O—F bonds do not cancel. The OF_2 molecule would be polar.

> ### Guide to Determining the Polarity of a Molecule
>
> **STEP 1**
> Determine if the bonds are polar covalent or nonpolar covalent.
>
> **STEP 2**
> If the bonds are polar covalent, draw the Lewis structure and determine if the dipoles cancel.

OF_2 is a polar molecule.

STUDY CHECK 6.18

Would a PCl_3 molecule be polar or nonpolar?

ANSWER

polar

QUESTIONS AND PROBLEMS

6.8 Shapes and Polarity of Molecules

LEARNING GOAL Predict the three-dimensional structure of a molecule, and classify it as polar or nonpolar.

6.69 Choose the shape (**1** to **6**) that matches each of the following descriptions (**a** to **c**):

    1. linear   **2.** bent (109°)   **3.** trigonal planar
    4. bent (120°)   **5.** trigonal pyramidal   **6.** tetrahedral

    a. a molecule with a central atom that has four electron groups and four bonded atoms
    b. a molecule with a central atom that has four electron groups and three bonded atoms
    c. a molecule with a central atom that has three electron groups and three bonded atoms

6.70 Choose the shape (**1** to **6**) that matches each of the following descriptions (**a** to **c**):

    1. linear   **2.** bent (109°)   **3.** trigonal planar
    4. bent (120°)   **5.** trigonal pyramidal   **6.** tetrahedral

    a. a molecule with a central atom that has four electron groups and two bonded atoms
    b. a molecule with a central atom that has two electron groups and two bonded atoms
    c. a molecule with a central atom that has three electron groups and two bonded atoms

6.71 Complete each of the following statements for a molecule of SeO_3:

    a. There are _____ electron groups around the central Se atom.
    b. The electron-group geometry is _____.
    c. The number of atoms attached to the central Se atom is _____.
    d. The shape of the molecule is _____.

6.72 Complete each of the following statements for a molecule of H_2S:

    a. There are _____ electron groups around the central S atom.
    b. The electron-group geometry is _____.
    c. The number of atoms attached to the central S atom is _____.
    d. The shape of the molecule is _____.

6.73 Compare the Lewis structures of PH_3 and NH_3. Why do these molecules have the same shape?

6.74 Compare the Lewis structures of CH_4 and H_2O. Why do these molecules have approximately the same bond angles but different molecular shapes?

6.75 Use VSEPR theory to predict the shape of each of the following:
    a. $SeBr_2$ **b.** CCl_4 **c.** OBr_2

6.76 Use VSEPR theory to predict the shape of each of the following:
    a. NCl_3 **b.** SeO_2 **c.** SiF_2Cl_2

6.77 The molecule Cl_2 is nonpolar, but HCl is polar. Explain.

6.78 The molecules CH_4 and CH_3Cl both contain four bonds. Why is CH_4 nonpolar whereas CH_3Cl is polar?

6.79 Identify each of the following molecules as polar or nonpolar:
    a. HBr   **b.** NF_3 **c.** CHF_3

6.80 Identify each of the following molecules as polar or nonpolar:
    a. SeF_2 **b.** PBr_3 **c.** $SiCl_4$

LEARNING GOAL

Describe the attractive forces between ions, polar covalent molecules, and nonpolar covalent molecules.

⊗ **CORE CHEMISTRY SKILL**

Identifying Attractive Forces

Dipole–dipole attraction

Hydrogen bond

6.9 Attractive Forces in Compounds

In gases, the interactions between particles are minimal, which allows gas molecules to move far apart from each other. In solids and liquids, there are sufficient interactions between the particles to hold them close together, although some solids have low melting points whereas others have very high melting points. Such differences in properties are explained by looking at the various kinds of attractive forces between particles including *dipole–dipole attractions, hydrogen bonding, dispersion forces*, as well as *ionic bonds*.

Ionic compounds have high melting points. For example, solid NaCl melts at 801 °C. Large amounts of energy are needed to overcome the strong attractive forces between positive and negative ions. In solids containing molecules with covalent bonds, there are attractive forces too, but they are weaker than those of an ionic compound.

Dipole–Dipole Attractions

For polar molecules, attractive forces called **dipole–dipole attractions** occur between the positive end of one molecule and the negative end of another. For a polar molecule with a dipole such as HCl, the partially positive H atom of one HCl molecule attracts the partially negative Cl atom in another HCl molecule.

Hydrogen Bonds

Polar molecules containing hydrogen atoms bonded to highly electronegative atoms of nitrogen, oxygen, or fluorine form especially strong dipole–dipole attractions. This type of attraction, called a **hydrogen bond**, occurs between the partially positive hydrogen atom in one molecule and the partially negative fluorine, oxygen, or nitrogen atom in another molecule. Hydrogen bonds are the strongest type of attractive forces between polar covalent molecules. They are a major factor in the formation and structure of biological molecules such as proteins and DNA.

Dispersion Forces

Nonpolar compounds do form solids, but at low temperatures. Very weak attractions called **dispersion forces** occur between nonpolar molecules. Usually, the electrons in a nonpolar covalent molecule are distributed symmetrically. However, electrons may accumulate more in one part of the molecule than another, which forms a *temporary dipole*. Although dispersion forces are very weak, they make it possible for nonpolar molecules to form liquids and solids.

Hydrogen bond

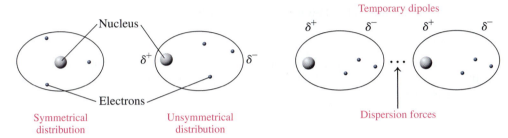

Nonpolar covalent molecules have weak attractions when they form temporary dipoles.

The melting points of substances are related to the strength of the attractive forces. Compounds with weak attractive forces, such as dispersion forces, have low melting points because only a small amount of energy is needed to separate the molecules and form a liquid. Compounds with hydrogen bonds and dipole–dipole attractions require more energy to break the attractive forces between the molecules. The highest melting points are seen with ionic compounds that have very strong attractions between ions. Table 6.17 compares the melting points of some substances with various kinds of attractive forces. The various types of attractions between particles in solids and liquids are summarized in Table 6.18.

TABLE 6.17 Melting Points of Selected Substances

Substance	Melting Point (°C)
Ionic Bonds	
MgF_2	1248
NaCl	801
Hydrogen Bonds	
H_2O	0
NH_3	−78
Dipole–Dipole Attractions	
HBr	−89
HCl	−115
Dispersion Forces	
Cl_2	−101
F_2	−220

TABLE 6.18 Comparison of Bonding and Attractive Forces

Type of Force	Particle Arrangement	Example	Strength
Between Atoms or Ions			Strong
Ionic bond		Na^+Cl^-	
Covalent bond (X = nonmetal)	X:X	Cl—Cl	
Between Molecules			
Hydrogen bond (X = F, O, or N)	$H\ X \cdots H\ X$	$H^{\delta+}—F^{\delta-}\cdots H^{\delta+}—F^{\delta-}$	
Dipole–dipole attractions (X and Y = nonmetals)	$Y\ X \cdots Y\ X$	$Br^{\delta+}—Cl^{\delta-}\cdots Br^{\delta+}—Cl^{\delta-}$	
Dispersion forces (temporary shift of electrons in nonpolar bonds)	$X:X \cdots X:X$ (temporary dipoles)	$F^{\delta+}—F^{\delta-}\cdots F^{\delta+}—F^{\delta-}$	Weak

> **SAMPLE PROBLEM 6.19** **Attractive Forces Between Particles**
>
> Indicate the major type of molecular interaction—dipole–dipole attractions, hydrogen bonding, or dispersion forces—expected of each of the following:
>
> **a.** HF **b.** Br_2 **c.** PCl_3
>
> **SOLUTION**
>
> **a.** HF is a polar molecule that interacts with other HF molecules by hydrogen bonding.
> **b.** Br_2 is nonpolar; only dispersion forces provide attractive forces.
> **c.** The polarity of the PCl_3 molecules provides dipole–dipole attractions.
>
> **STUDY CHECK 6.19**
>
> Why is the melting point of H_2S lower than that of H_2O?
>
> **ANSWER**
>
> The attractive forces between H_2S molecules are dipole–dipole attractions, whereas the attractive forces between H_2O molecules are hydrogen bonds, which are stronger and require more energy to break.

Chemistry Link to **Health**

Attractive Forces in Biological Compounds

The proteins in our bodies are biological molecules that have many different functions. They are needed for structural components such as cartilage, muscles, hair, and nails, and for the formation of enzymes that regulate biological reactions. Other proteins, such as hemoglobin and myoglobin, transport oxygen in the blood and muscle.

Proteins are composed of building blocks called *amino acids*. Every amino acid has a central carbon atom bonded to $-NH_3^+$ from an amine, a $-COO^-$ from a carboxylic acid, an H atom, and a side chain called an R group, which is unique for each amino acid. For example, the R group for the amino acid alanine is a methyl group ($-CH_3$).

The ionized form of alanine contains $-NH_3^+$, $-COO^-$, H, and a $-CH_3$ group.

Several of the amino acids have side chains that contain groups such as hydroxyl $-OH$, amide $-CONH_2$, amine $-NH_2$, which is ionized as ammonium $-NH_3^+$, and carboxyl $-COOH$, which is ionized as carboxylate $-COO^-$.

Serine

Asparagine

Lysine

Aspartate

In the primary structure of proteins, amino acids are linked together by peptide bonds, which are amide bonds that form between the —COO⁻ group of one amino acid and the —NH₃⁺ group of the next amino acid. When there are more than 50 amino acids in a chain, it is called a protein. Every protein in our body has a unique sequence of amino acids in a primary structure that determines its biological function. In addition, proteins have higher levels of structure. In an *alpha helix*, hydrogen bonds form between the hydrogen atom of the N—H groups and the oxygen atom of a C=O group in the next turn. Because many hydrogen bonds form, the backbone of a protein takes a helical shape similar to a corkscrew or a spiral staircase.

Shapes of Biologically Active Proteins

Many proteins have compact, spherical shapes because sections of the chain fold over on top of other sections of the chain. This shape is stabilized by attractive forces between functional groups of side chains (R groups), causing the protein to twist and bend into a specific three-dimensional shape.

Hydrogen bonds form between the side chains within the protein. For example, a hydrogen bond can occur between the —OH groups on two serines or between the —OH of a serine and the —NH₂ of asparagine. Hydrogen bonding also occurs between the polar side chains of the amino acids on the outer surface of the protein and —OH or —H of polar water molecules in the external aqueous environment.

Ionic bonds can form between the positively and negatively charged R groups of acidic and basic amino acids. For example, an ionic bond can form between the —NH₃⁺ in the R group of lysine and the —COO⁻ of aspartate.

The shape of an alpha helix is stabilized by hydrogen bonds.

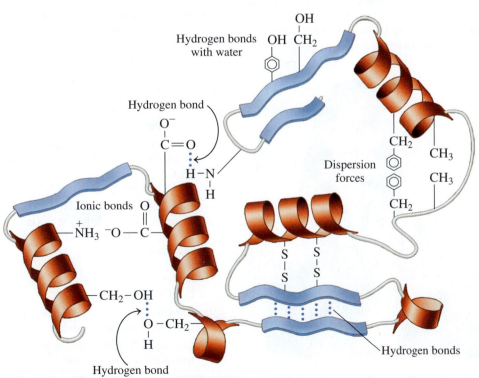

Attractive forces hold the protein in a specific shape.

QUESTIONS AND PROBLEMS

6.9 Attractive Forces in Compounds

LEARNING GOAL Describe the attractive forces between ions, polar covalent molecules, and nonpolar covalent molecules.

6.81 Identify the major type of attractive force between the particles of each of the following:
   a. BrF   **b.** KCl   **c.** NF_3 **d.** Cl_2

6.82 Identify the major type of attractive force between the particles of each of the following:
   a. HCl   **b.** MgF_2 **c.** PBr_3 **d.** NH_3

6.83 Identify the strongest attractive forces between the particles of each of the following:
   a. CH_3OH **b.** CO
   c. CF_4 **d.** CH_3-CH_3

6.84 Identify the strongest attractive forces between the particles of each of the following:
   a. O_2 **b.** SiH_4
   c. CH_3Cl **d.** H_2O_2

6.85 Identify the substance in each of the following pairs that would have the higher boiling point and explain your choice:
   a. HF or HBr   **b.** HF or NaF
   c. $MgBr_2$ or PBr_3 **d.** CH_4 or CH_3OH

6.86 Identify the substance in each of the following pairs that would have the higher boiling point and explain your choice:
   a. NaCl or HCl   **b.** H_2O or H_2Se
   c. NH_3 or PH_3 **d.** F_2 or HF

Clinical Update
Compounds at the Pharmacy

A few days ago, Richard went back to the pharmacy to pick up aspirin, $C_9H_8O_4$, and acetaminophen, $C_8H_9NO_2$. He also wanted to talk to Sarah about a way to treat his sore toe. Sarah recommended soaking his foot in a solution of Epsom salts, which is magnesium sulfate. Richard also asked Sarah to recommend an antacid for his upset stomach and an iron supplement. Sarah suggested an antacid that contains calcium carbonate, aluminum hydroxide, and iron(II) sulfate as an iron supplement. Richard also picked up toothpaste containing tin(II) fluoride, and carbonated water, which contains carbon dioxide.

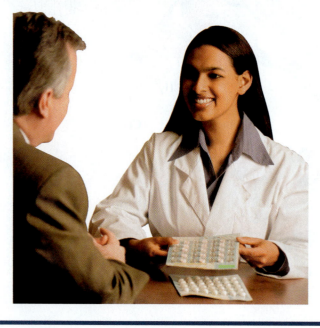

Ⓡ Clinical Applications

6.87 Write the chemical formula for each of the following:
   a. magnesium sulfate
   b. calcium carbonate
   c. aluminum hydroxide

6.88 Write the chemical formula for each of the following:
   a. tin(II) fluoride
   b. carbon dioxide
   c. iron(II) sulfate

6.89 Identify each of the compounds in problem 6.87 as ionic or molecular.

6.90 Identify each of the compounds in problem 6.88 as ionic or molecular.

6.91 Using the electronegativity values in Figure 6.6, calculate the electronegativity difference for the following bonds present in aspirin:
   a. C—C
   b. C—H
   c. C—O

6.92 Using the electronegativity values in Figure 6.6, calculate the electronegativity difference for the following bonds present in acetaminophen:
   a. C—N
   b. N—H
   c. H—O

6.93 Classify each of the bonds in problem 6.91 as nonpolar covalent, polar covalent, or ionic.

6.94 Classify each of the bonds in problem 6.92 as nonpolar covalent, polar covalent, or ionic.

CONCEPT MAP

IONIC AND MOLECULAR COMPOUNDS

Ionic Compounds
contain
Ionic Bonds
between

Metals — that form — **Positive Ions**
Nonmetals — that form — **Negative Ions**
use
Charge Balance
to write subscripts for the
Chemical Formula

Molecular Compounds
contain
Covalent Bonds
between
Nonmetals
can be
Polar | **Nonpolar**
are drawn as
Lewis Structures
use
VSEPR Theory | **Electronegativity**
to determine
Shape | **Polarity**

have
Attractive Forces
called
Dipole–Dipole Attractions, Hydrogen Bonds, or Dispersion Forces

---

CHAPTER REVIEW

6.1 Ions: Transfer of Electrons
LEARNING GOAL Write the symbols for the simple ions of the representative elements.

- The stability of the noble gases is associated with a stable electron configuration in the outermost energy level.
- With the exception of helium, which has two electrons, noble gases have eight valence electrons, which is an octet.
- Atoms of elements in Groups 1A–7A (1, 2, 13–17) achieve stability by losing, gaining, or sharing their valence electrons in the formation of compounds.
- Metals of the representative elements lose valence electrons to form positively charged ions (cations): Group 1A (1), 1+, Group 2A (2), 2+, and Group 3A (13), 3+.
- When reacting with metals, nonmetals gain electrons to form octets and form negatively charged ions (anions): Groups 5A (15), 3−, 6A (16), 2−, and 7A (17), 1−.

Transfer of electrons

Ionic bond

6.2 Writing Formulas for Ionic Compounds
LEARNING GOAL Using charge balance, write the correct formula for an ionic compound.

- The total positive and negative ionic charge is balanced in the formula of an ionic compound.
- Charge balance in a formula is achieved by using subscripts after each symbol so that the overall charge is zero.

Na⁺
Cl⁻
Sodium chloride

6.3 Naming and Writing Ionic Formulas
LEARNING GOAL Given the formula of an ionic compound, write the correct name; given the name of an ionic compound, write the correct formula.

- In naming ionic compounds, the positive ion is given first followed by the name of the negative ion.
- The names of ionic compounds containing two elements end with *ide*.
- Except for Ag, Cd, and Zn, transition elements form cations with two or more ionic charges.
- The charge of the cation is determined from the total negative charge in the formula and included as a Roman numeral immediately following the name of the metal that has a variable charge.

6.4 Polyatomic Ions

LEARNING GOAL Write the name and formula for an ionic compound containing a polyatomic ion.

Plaster cast $CaSO_4$

Ca^{2+} SO_4^{2-}
Sulfate ion

- A polyatomic ion is a covalently bonded group of atoms with an electrical charge; for example, the carbonate ion has the formula CO_3^{2-}.
- Most polyatomic ions have names that end with *ate* or *ite*.
- Most polyatomic ions contain a nonmetal and one or more oxygen atoms.
- The ammonium ion, NH_4^+, is a positive polyatomic ion.
- When more than one polyatomic ion is used for charge balance, parentheses enclose the formula of the polyatomic ion.

6.5 Molecular Compounds: Sharing Electrons

LEARNING GOAL Given the formula of a molecular compound, write its correct name; given the name of a molecular compound, write its formula.

1	mono
2	di
3	tri
4	tetra
5	penta

- In a covalent bond, atoms of nonmetals share valence electrons such that each atom has a stable electron configuration.
- The first nonmetal in a molecular compound uses its element name; the second nonmetal uses the first syllable of its element name followed by *ide*.
- The name of a molecular compound with two different atoms uses prefixes to indicate the subscripts in the formula.

6.6 Lewis Structures for Molecules and Polyatomic Ions

LEARNING GOAL Draw the Lewis structures for molecular compounds or polyatomic ions.

- The total number of valence electrons is determined for all the atoms in the molecule or polyatomic ion.
- Any negative charge is added to the total valence electrons, whereas any positive charge is subtracted.
- In the Lewis structure, a bonding pair of electrons is placed between the central atom and each of the attached atoms.
- Any remaining valence electrons are used as lone pairs to complete the octets of the surrounding atoms and then the central atom.
- If octets are not completed, one or more lone pairs of electrons are placed as bonding pairs forming double or triple bonds.

6.7 Electronegativity and Bond Polarity

LEARNING GOAL Use electronegativity to determine the polarity of a bond.

$$\overset{\delta^+}{H}\!-\!\overset{\delta^-}{Cl}$$

Unequal sharing of electrons in a polar covalent bond

- Electronegativity is the ability of an atom to attract the electrons it shares with another atom. In general, the electronegativities of metals are low, whereas nonmetals have high electronegativities.
- In a nonpolar covalent bond, atoms share electrons equally.
- In a polar covalent bond, the electrons are unequally shared because they are attracted to the more electronegative atom.
- The atom in a polar bond with the lower electronegativity is partially positive (δ^+), and the atom with the higher electronegativity is partially negative (δ^-).
- Atoms that form ionic bonds have large differences in electronegativities.

6.8 Shapes and Polarity of Molecules

LEARNING GOAL Predict the three-dimensional structure of a molecule, and classify it as polar or nonpolar.

- The shape of a molecule is determined from the Lewis structure, the electron-group geometry, and the number of bonded atoms.
- The electron-group geometry around a central atom with two electron groups is linear; with three electron groups, the geometry is trigonal planar; and with four electron groups, the geometry is tetrahedral.
- When all the electron groups are bonded to atoms, the shape has the same name as the electron arrangement.
- A central atom with three electron groups and two bonded atoms has a bent shape, 120°.
- A central atom with four electron groups and three bonded atoms has a trigonal pyramidal shape.
- A central atom with four electron groups and two bonded atoms has a bent shape, 109°.
- Nonpolar molecules contain nonpolar covalent bonds or have an arrangement of bonded atoms that causes the dipoles to cancel out.
- In polar molecules, the dipoles do not cancel.

6.9 Attractive Forces in Compounds

LEARNING GOAL Describe the attractive forces between ions, polar covalent molecules, and nonpolar covalent molecules.

Dipole–dipole attraction

- In ionic solids, oppositely charged ions are held in a rigid structure by ionic bonds.
- Attractive forces called dipole–dipole attractions and hydrogen bonds hold the solid and liquid states of polar molecular compounds together.
- Nonpolar compounds form solids and liquids by weak attractions between temporary dipoles called dispersion forces.

KEY TERMS

anion A negatively charged ion such as Cl^-, O^{2-}, or SO_4^{2-}.
cation A positively charged ion such as Na^+, Mg^{2+}, Al^{3+}, or NH_4^+.
chemical formula The group of symbols and subscripts that represents the atoms or ions in a compound.
covalent bond A sharing of valence electrons by atoms.
dipole The separation of positive and negative charges in a polar bond indicated by an arrow that is drawn from the more positive atom to the more negative atom.
dipole–dipole attractions Attractive forces between oppositely charged ends of polar molecules.
dispersion forces Weak dipole bonding that results from a momentary polarization of nonpolar molecules.
double bond A sharing of two pairs of electrons by two atoms.
electronegativity The relative ability of an element to attract electrons in a bond.
hydrogen bond The attraction between a partially positive H atom and a strongly electronegative atom of F, O, or N.
ion An atom or group of atoms having an electrical charge because of a loss or gain of electrons.
ionic charge The difference between the number of protons (positive) and the number of electrons (negative) written in the upper right corner of the symbol for the element or polyatomic ion.
ionic compound A compound of positive and negative ions held together by ionic bonds.
Lewis structure A representation of a molecule or ion that shows the valence electrons.

molecular compound A combination of atoms in which stable electron configurations are attained by sharing electrons.
molecule The smallest unit of two or more atoms held together by covalent bonds.
nonpolar covalent bond A covalent bond in which the electrons are shared equally between atoms.
nonpolar molecule A molecule that has only nonpolar bonds or in which the bond dipoles cancel.
octet A set of eight valence electrons.
octet rule Elements in Groups 1A–7A (1, 2, 13–17) react with other elements by forming ionic or covalent bonds to produce a stable electron configuration, usually eight electrons in the outer shell.
polar covalent bond A covalent bond in which the electrons are shared unequally between atoms.
polar molecule A molecule containing bond dipoles that do not cancel.
polarity A measure of the unequal sharing of electrons indicated by the difference in electronegativities.
polyatomic ion A group of covalently bonded nonmetal atoms that has an overall electrical charge.
triple bond A sharing of three pairs of electrons by two atoms.
valence shell electron-pair repulsion (VSEPR) theory A theory that predicts the shape of a molecule by placing the electron pairs on a central atom as far apart as possible to minimize the mutual repulsion of the electrons.

⚛ CORE CHEMISTRY SKILLS

The chapter section containing each Core Chemistry Skill is shown in parentheses at the end of each heading.

Writing Positive and Negative Ions (6.1)

- In the formation of an ionic bond, atoms of a metal lose and atoms of a nonmetal gain valence electrons to acquire a stable electron configuration, usually eight valence electrons.
- This tendency of atoms to attain a stable electron configuration is known as the octet rule.

Example: State the number of electrons lost or gained by atoms and the ion formed for each of the following to obtain a stable electron configuration:

    a. Br   **b.** Ca   **c.** S

Answer: **a.** Br atoms gain one electron to achieve a stable electron configuration, Br^-.
    b. Ca atoms lose two electrons to achieve a stable electron configuration, Ca^{2+}.
    c. S atoms gain two electrons to achieve a stable electron configuration, S^{2-}.

Writing Ionic Formulas (6.2)

- The chemical formula of a compound represents the lowest whole-number ratio of the atoms or ions.
- In the chemical formula of an ionic compound, the sum of the positive and negative charges is always zero.
- Thus, in a chemical formula of an ionic compound, the total positive charge is equal to the total negative charge.

Example: Write the formula for magnesium phosphate.

Answer: Magnesium phosphate is an ionic compound that contains the ions Mg^{2+} and PO_4^{3-}.
Using charge balance, we determine the number(s) of each type of ion.

$$3(2+) + 2(3-) = 0$$

$3Mg^{2+}$ and $2PO_4^{3-}$ give the formula $Mg_3(PO_4)_2$.

Naming Ionic Compounds (6.3)

- In the name of an ionic compound made up of two elements, the name of the metal ion, which is written first, is the same as its element name.
- For metals that form two or more different ions, a Roman numeral that is equal to the ionic charge is placed in parentheses immediately after the name of the metal.
- The name of a nonmetal ion is obtained by using the first syllable of its element name followed by *ide*.
- The name of a polyatomic ion usually ends in *ate* or *ite*.

Example: What is the name of $PbSO_4$?

Answer: This compound contains the polyatomic ion SO_4^{2-}, which is sulfate with a 2− charge.
For charge balance, the positive ion must have a charge of 2+.

$$Pb? + (2-) = 0; \quad Pb = 2+$$

Because lead can form two different positive ions, a Roman numeral (II) is used in the name of the compound: lead(II) sulfate.

Writing the Names and Formulas for Molecular Compounds (6.5)

- When naming a molecular compound, the first nonmetal in the formula is named by its element name; the second nonmetal is named using the first syllable of its element name followed by *ide*.

Example: Name the molecular compound BrF_5.

Answer: Two nonmetals share electrons and form a molecular compound. Br (first nonmetal) is bromine; F (second nonmetal) is fluoride. In the name for a molecular compound, prefixes indicate the subscripts in the formulas. The subscript 1 is understood for Br. The subscript 5 for fluoride is written with the prefix *penta*. The name is bromine pentafluoride.

Drawing Lewis Structures (6.6)

- The Lewis structure for a molecule shows the sequence of atoms, the bonding pairs of electrons shared between atoms, and the nonbonding or *lone pairs* of electrons.
- Double or triple bonds result when a second or third electron pair is shared between the same atoms to complete octets.

Example: Draw the Lewis structure for CS_2.

Answer: The central atom in the atom arrangement is C.

S   C   S

Determine the total number of valence electrons.

$$1\,C \times 4\,e^- = 4\,e^-$$
$$2\,S \times 6\,e^- = 12\,e^-$$
$$\text{Total} = 16\,e^-$$

Attach each bonded atom to the central atom using a pair of electrons. Two bonding pairs use four electrons.

S:C:S

Place the 12 remaining electrons as lone pairs around the S atoms.

:S̈:C:S̈:

To complete the octet for C, a lone pair of electrons from each of the S atoms is shared with C, which forms two double bonds.

:S̈::C::S̈:   or   :S̈=C=S̈:

Using Electronegativity (6.7)

- The electronegativity values indicate the ability of atoms to attract shared electrons.
- Electronegativity values increase going across a period from left to right, and decrease going down a group.
- A nonpolar covalent bond occurs between atoms with identical or very similar electronegativity values such that the electronegativity difference is 0.0 to 0.4.
- A polar covalent bond occurs when electrons are shared unequally between atoms with electronegativity differences from 0.5 to 1.8.
- An ionic bond typically occurs when the difference in electronegativity for two atoms is greater than 1.8.

Example: Use electronegativity values to classify each of the following bonds as nonpolar covalent, polar covalent, or ionic:

a. Sr—Cl   b. C—S   c. O—Br

Answer:
a. An electronegativity difference of 2.0 (Cl 3.0 − Sr 1.0) makes this an ionic bond.
b. An electronegativity difference of 0.0 (C 2.5 − S 2.5) makes this a nonpolar covalent bond.
c. An electronegativity difference of 0.7 (O 3.5 − Br 2.8) makes this a polar covalent bond.

Predicting Shape (6.8)

- The three-dimensional shape of a molecule or polyatomic ion is determined by drawing a Lewis structure and identifying the number of electron groups (one or more electron pairs) around the central atom and the number of bonded atoms.
- In the valence shell electron-pair repulsion (VSEPR) theory, the electron groups are arranged as far apart as possible around a central atom to minimize the repulsion.
- A central atom with two electron groups bonded to two atoms is linear. A central atom with three electron groups bonded to three atoms is trigonal planar, and to two atoms is bent (120°). A central atom with four electron groups bonded to four atoms is tetrahedral, to three atoms is trigonal pyramidal, and to two atoms is bent (109°).

Identifying Polarity of Molecules (6.8)

- A molecule is nonpolar if all of its bonds are nonpolar or it has polar bonds that cancel out. CCl_4 is a nonpolar molecule that consists of four polar bonds that cancel out.

- A molecule is polar if it contains polar bonds that do not cancel out. H_2O is a polar molecule that consists of polar bonds that do not cancel out.

O
H   H

Example: Predict whether $AsCl_3$ is polar or nonpolar.

Answer: From its Lewis structure, we see that $AsCl_3$ has four electron groups with three bonded atoms.

:C̈l:Äs:C̈l:
:C̈l:

The shape of a molecule of $AsCl_3$ would be trigonal pyramidal with three polar bonds (As—Cl = 3.0 − 2.0 = 1.0) that do not cancel. Thus, it is a polar molecule.

Äs
Cl   Cl
Cl

Identifying Attractive Forces (6.9)

- Dipole–dipole attractions occur between the dipoles in polar compounds because the positively charged end of one molecule is attracted to the negatively charged end of another molecule.

$$\delta^+ \quad \delta^- \qquad \delta^+ \quad \delta^-$$

$$\text{H} \quad \text{Cl} \cdots \cdots \text{H} \quad \text{Cl}$$

Dipole–dipole
attraction

- Strong dipole–dipole attractions called hydrogen bonds occur in compounds in which H is bonded to F, O, or N. The partially positive H atom in one molecule has a strong attraction to the partially negative F, O, or N in another molecule.

- Dispersion forces are very weak attractive forces between nonpolar molecules that occur when *temporary dipoles* form as electrons are unequally distributed.

Example: Identify the strongest type of attractive forces in each of the following:

    a. HF   **b.** F_2 **c.** NF_3

Answer: **a.** HF molecules, which are polar with H bonded to F, have hydrogen bonding.
      b. Nonpolar F_2 molecules have only dispersion forces.
      c. NF_3 molecules, which are polar, have dipole–dipole attractions.

UNDERSTANDING THE CONCEPTS

The chapter sections to review are shown in parentheses at the end of each question.

6.95 **a.** How does the octet rule explain the formation of a magnesium ion? (6.1)
     b. What noble gas has the same electron configuration as the magnesium ion?
     c. Why are Group 1A (1) and Group 2A (2) elements found in many compounds, but not Group 8A (18) elements?

6.96 **a.** How does the octet rule explain the formation of a chloride ion? (6.1)
     b. What noble gas has the same electron configuration as the chloride ion?
     c. Why are Group 7A (17) elements found in many compounds, but not Group 8A (18) elements?

6.97 Identify each of the following atoms or ions: (6.1)

$18\,e^-$	$8\,e^-$	$28\,e^-$	$23\,e^-$
$15\,p^+$	$8\,p^+$	$30\,p^+$	$26\,p^+$
$16\,n$	$8\,n$	$35\,n$	$28\,n$
A	**B**	**C**	**D**

6.98 Identify each of the following atoms or ions: (6.1)

$2\,e^-$	$0\,e^-$	$3\,e^-$	$10\,e^-$
$3\,p^+$	$1\,p^+$	$3\,p^+$	$7\,p^+$
$4\,n$		$4\,n$	$8\,n$
A	**B**	**C**	**D**

6.99 Consider the following Lewis symbols for elements X and Y: (6.1, 6.2, 6.5)

$$\dot{\text{X}} \qquad \cdot \ddot{\text{Y}} \cdot$$

    a. What are the group numbers of X and Y?
    b. Will a compound of X and Y be ionic or molecular?

    c. What ions would be formed by X and Y?
    d. What would be the formula of a compound of X and Y?
    e. What would be the formula of a compound of X and sulfur?
    f. What would be the formula of a compound of Y and chlorine?
    g. Is the compound in part **f** ionic or molecular?

6.100 Consider the following Lewis symbols for elements X and Y: (6.1, 6.5)

$$\dot{\text{X}} \cdot \qquad \cdot \ddot{\text{Y}} \cdot$$

    a. What are the group numbers of X and Y?
    b. Will a compound of X and Y be ionic or molecular?
    c. What ions would be formed by X and Y?
    d. What would be the formula of a compound of X and Y?
    e. What would be the formula of a compound of X and sulfur?
    f. What would be the formula of a compound of Y and chlorine?
    g. Is the compound in part **f** ionic or molecular?

6.101 Match each of the Lewis structures (**a** to **c**) with the correct diagram (**1** to **3**) of its shape, and name the shape; indicate if each molecule is polar or nonpolar. (Assume X and Y are nonmetals and all bonds are polar covalent.) (6.8)

1   2   3

a. $\text{X}-\overset{\displaystyle \text{X}}{\underset{}{\text{Y}}}-\text{X}$ **b.** $:\ddot{\text{Y}}-\text{X}$ **c.** $\text{X}-\overset{\displaystyle \text{X}}{\underset{\displaystyle \text{X}}{\text{Y}}}-\text{X}$

6.102 Match each of the formulas (**a** to **c**) with the correct diagram (**1** to **3**) of its shape, and name the shape; indicate if each molecule is polar or nonpolar. (6.8)

1   **2**   **3**

a. PBr_3 **b.** $SiCl_4$ **c.** OF_2

6.103 Using each of the following electron configurations, give the formulas of the cation and anion that form, the formula for the compound they form, and its name. (6.2, 6.3)

Electron Configurations		Cation	Anion	Formula of Compound	Name of Compound
$1s^2 2s^2 2p^6 3s^2$	$1s^2 2s^2 2p^3$				
$1s^2 2s^2 2p^6 3s^2 3p^6 4s^1$	$1s^2 2s^2 2p^4$				
$1s^2 2s^2 2p^6 3s^2 3p^1$	$1s^2 2s^2 2p^6 3s^2 3p^5$				

6.104 Using each of the following electron configurations, give the formulas of the cation and anion that form, the formula of the compound they form, and its name. (6.2, 6.3)

Electron Configurations		Cation	Anion	Formula of Compound	Name of Compound
$1s^2 2s^2 2p^6 3s^1$	$1s^2 2s^2 2p^5$				
$1s^2 2s^2 2p^6 3s^2 3p^6 4s^2$	$1s^2 2s^2 2p^6 3s^2 3p^4$				
$1s^2 2s^2 2p^6 3s^2 3p^1$	$1s^2 2s^2 2p^6 3s^2 3p^3$				

6.105 State the number of valence electrons, bonding pairs, and lone pairs in each of the following Lewis structures: (6.5)

    a. H:H   **b.** H:B̈r̈:   **c.** :B̈r:B̈r:

6.106 State the number of valence electrons, bonding pairs, and lone pairs in each of the following Lewis structures: (6.5)

        H
    a. H:Ö: **b.** H:N̈:H   **c.** :B̈r:Ö:B̈r:
                   H

ADDITIONAL QUESTIONS AND PROBLEMS

6.107 Write the electron configuration for the following: (6.1)
    a. N^{3-} **b.** Mg^{2+} **c.** P^{3-} **d.** Al^{3+} **e.** Li^+

6.108 Write the electron configuration for the following: (6.1)
    a. K^+ **b.** Na^+ **c.** S^{2-} **d.** Cl^- **e.** Ca^{2+}

6.109 Consider an ion with the symbol X^{2+} formed from a representative element. (6.1, 6.2, 6.3)
    a. What is the group number of the element?
    b. What is the Lewis symbol of the element?
    c. If X is in Period 3, what is the element?
    d. What is the formula of the compound formed from X and the nitride ion?

6.110 Consider an ion with the symbol Y^{3-} formed from a representative element. (6.1, 6.2, 6.3)
    a. What is the group number of the element?
    b. What is the Lewis symbol of the element?
    c. If Y is in Period 3, what is the element?
    d. What is the formula of the compound formed from the barium ion and Y?

6.111 One of the ions of tin is tin(IV). (6.1, 6.2, 6.3, 6.4)
    a. What is the symbol for this ion?
    b. How many protons and electrons are in the ion?
    c. What is the formula of tin(IV) oxide?
    d. What is the formula of tin(IV) phosphate?

6.112 One of the ions of gold is gold(III). (6.1, 6.2, 6.3, 6.4)
    a. What is the symbol for this ion?
    b. How many protons and electrons are in the ion?
    c. What is the formula of gold(III) sulfate?
    d. What is the formula of gold(III) nitrate?

6.113 Write the formula for each of the following ionic compounds: (6.2, 6.3)
    a. tin(II) sulfide   **b.** lead(IV) oxide
    c. silver chloride   **d.** calcium nitride
    e. copper(I) phosphide   **f.** chromium(II) bromide

6.114 Write the formula for each of the following ionic compounds: (6.2, 6.3)
    a. nickel(III) oxide   **b.** iron(III) sulfide
    c. lead(II) sulfate   **d.** chromium(III) iodide
    e. lithium nitride   **f.** gold(I) oxide

6.115 Name each of the following molecular compounds: (6.5)
    a. NCl_3 **b.** N_2S_3 **c.** N_2O
    d. IF **e.** BF_3 **f.** P_2O_5

6.116 Name each of the following molecular compounds: (6.5)
    a. CBr_4 **b.** SF_6 **c.** $BrCl$
    d. N_2O_4 **e.** SO_2 **f.** CS_2

6.117 Write the formula for each of the following molecular compounds: (6.5)
    a. carbon sulfide   **b.** diphosphorus pentoxide
    c. dihydrogen sulfide   **d.** sulfur dichloride

6.118 Write the formula for each of the following molecular compounds: (6.5)
    a. silicon dioxide   **b.** carbon tetrabromide
    c. diphosphorus tetraiodide **d.** dinitrogen trioxide

6.119 Classify each of the following as ionic or molecular, and give its name: (6.3, 6.5)
    a. $FeCl_3$ **b.** Na_2SO_4 **c.** NO_2
    d. N_2 **e.** PF_5 **f.** CF_4

6.120 Classify each of the following as ionic or molecular, and give its name: (6.3, 6.5)
    a. $Al_2(CO_3)_3$ **b.** ClF_5 **c.** H_2
    d. Mg_3N_2 **e.** ClO_2 **f.** $CrPO_4$

6.121 Write the formula for each of the following: (6.3, 6.4, 6.5)
    a. tin(II) carbonate   **b.** lithium phosphide
    c. silicon tetrachloride   **d.** manganese(III) oxide
    e. bromine   **f.** calcium bromide

6.122 Write the formula for each of the following: (6.3, 6.4, 6.5)
- **a.** sodium carbonate
- **b.** nitrogen dioxide
- **c.** aluminum nitrate
- **d.** copper(I) nitride
- **e.** potassium phosphate
- **f.** cobalt(III) sulfate

6.123 Draw the Lewis structure for each of the following: (6.6)
- **a.** BF_4^-
- **b.** Cl_2O
- **c.** H_2NOH (N is the central atom)
- **d.** H_2CCCl_2

6.124 Draw the Lewis structure for each of the following: (6.6)
- **a.** H_3COCH_3 (the atoms are in the order C O C)
- **b.** HNO_2 (the atoms are in the order HONO)
- **c.** ClO_2^-
- **d.** BrO^-

6.125 Draw the Lewis structure for each of the following: (6.6)
- **a.** N_3^-
- **b.** NO_2^+
- **c.** CNS^-

6.126 Draw the Lewis structure for each of the following: (6.6)
- **a.** NO_3^-
- **b.** CO_3^{2-}
- **c.** SCN^-

6.127 Select the more polar bond in each of the following pairs: (6.7)
- **a.** C—N or C—O
- **b.** N—F or N—Br
- **c.** Br—Cl or S—Cl
- **d.** Br—Cl or Br—I
- **e.** N—F or N—O

6.128 Select the more polar bond in each of the following pairs: (6.7)
- **a.** C—C or C—O
- **b.** P—Cl or P—Br
- **c.** Si—S or Si—Cl
- **d.** F—Cl or F—Br
- **e.** P—O or P—S

6.129 Calculate the electronegativity difference and classify each of the following bonds as nonpolar covalent, polar covalent, or ionic: (6.7)
- **a.** Si—Cl
- **b.** C—C
- **c.** Na—Cl
- **d.** C—H
- **e.** F—F

6.130 Calculate the electronegativity difference and classify each of the following bonds as nonpolar covalent, polar covalent, or ionic: (6.7)
- **a.** C—N
- **b.** Cl—Cl
- **c.** K—Br
- **d.** H—H
- **e.** N—F

6.131 Predict the shape and polarity of each of the following molecules: (6.8)
- **a.** A central atom with three identical bonded atoms and one lone pair.
- **b.** A central atom with two bonded atoms and two lone pairs.

6.132 Predict the shape and polarity of each of the following molecules: (6.8)
- **a.** A central atom with four identical bonded atoms and no lone pairs.
- **b.** A central atom with four bonded atoms that are not identical and no lone pairs.

6.133 Classify the following molecules as polar or nonpolar: (6.8)
- **a.** NH_3
- **b.** CH_3Cl
- **c.** SiF_4

6.134 Classify the following molecules as polar or nonpolar: (6.8)
- **a.** GeH_4
- **b.** SeO_2
- **c.** SCl_2

6.135 Predict the shape and polarity of each of the following molecules: (6.8)
- **a.** SI_2
- **b.** PF_3

6.136 Predict the shape and polarity of each of the following molecules: (6.8)
- **a.** H_2O
- **b.** CF_4

6.137 Indicate the major type of attractive force—(1) ionic bonds, (2) dipole–dipole attractions, (3) hydrogen bonds, (4) dispersion forces—that occurs between particles of the following substances: (6.9)
- **a.** NH_3
- **b.** HI
- **c.** I_2
- **d.** Cs_2O

6.138 Indicate the major type of attractive force—(1) ionic bonds, (2) dipole–dipole attractions, (3) hydrogen bonds, (4) dispersion forces—that occurs between particles of the following substances: (6.9)
- **a.** CHF_3
- **b.** H_2O
- **c.** LiCl
- **d.** N_2

CHALLENGE QUESTIONS

The following groups of questions are related to the topics in this chapter. However, they do not all follow the chapter order, and they require you to combine concepts and skills from several sections. These questions will help you increase your critical thinking skills and prepare for your next exam.

6.139 Complete the following table for atoms or ions: (6.1)

Atom or Ion	Number of Protons	Number of Electrons	Electrons Lost/ Gained
K^+			
	$12\,p^+$	$10\,e^-$	
	$8\,p^+$		$2\,e^-$ gained
		$10\,e^-$	$3\,e^-$ lost

6.140 Complete the following table for atoms or ions: (6.1)

Atom or Ion	Number of Protons	Number of Electrons	Electrons Lost/ Gained
	$30\,p^+$		$2\,e^-$ lost
	$36\,p^+$	$36\,e^-$	
	$16\,p^+$		$2\,e^-$ gained
		$46\,e^-$	$4\,e^-$ lost

6.141 Identify the group number in the periodic table of X, a representative element, in each of the following ionic compounds: (6.2)
- **a.** XCl_3
- **b.** Al_2X_3
- **c.** XCO_3

6.142 Identify the group number in the periodic table of X, a representative element, in each of the following ionic compounds: (6.2)
- **a.** X_2O_3
- **b.** X_2SO_3
- **c.** Na_3X

6.143 Classify each of the following as ionic or molecular, and name each: (6.2, 6.3, 6.4, 6.5)

a. Li_2HPO_4 b. $Cr(NO_2)_2$ c. $Mg(ClO_2)_2$
d. NF_3 e. $Ca(HSO_4)_2$ f. $KClO_4$
g. $Au_2(SO_3)_3$ h. I_2

6.144 Classify each of the following as ionic or molecular, and name each: (6.2, 6.3, 6.4, 6.5)

a. $FePO_3$ b. Cl_2O_7 c. Br_2
d. $Ca_3(PO_4)_2$ e. PCl_3 f. $Al(ClO_2)_3$
g. $Pb(C_2H_3O_2)_2$ h. $MgCO_3$

ANSWERS

Answers to Selected Questions and Problems

6.1 a. 1 **b.** 2 **c.** 3 **d.** 1 **e.** 2

6.3 a. $2\ e^-$ lost **b.** $3\ e^-$ gained **c.** $1\ e^-$ gained
d. $1\ e^-$ lost **e.** $1\ e^-$ gained

6.5 a. Li^+ **b.** F^- **c.** Mg^{2+} **d.** Fe^{3+}

6.7 a. Cl^- **b.** Cs^+ **c.** N^{3-} **d.** Ra^{2+}

6.9 a. 8 protons, 10 electrons **b.** 19 protons, 18 electrons
c. 53 protons, 54 electrons **d.** 11 protons, 10 electrons

6.11 a and c

6.13 a. Na_2O **b.** $AlBr_3$ **c.** Ba_3N_2
d. MgF_2 **e.** Al_2S_3

6.15 a. K^+ and S^{2-}, K_2S **b.** Na^+ and N^{3-}, Na_3N
c. Al^{3+} and I^-, AlI_3 **d.** Ga^{3+} and O^{2-}, Ga_2O_3

6.17 a. aluminum oxide **b.** calcium chloride
c. sodium oxide **d.** magnesium phosphide
e. potassium iodide **f.** barium fluoride

6.19 a. iron(II) **b.** copper(II)
c. zinc **d.** lead(IV)
e. chromium(III) **f.** manganese(II)

6.21 a. tin(II) chloride **b.** iron(II) oxide
c. copper(I) sulfide **d.** copper(II) sulfide
e. cadmium bromide **f.** mercury(II) chloride

6.23 a. Au^{3+} **b.** Fe^{3+} **c.** Pb^{4+} **d.** Sn^{2+}

6.25 a. $MgCl_2$ **b.** Na_2S **c.** Cu_2O **d.** Zn_3P_2
e. AuN **f.** CoF_3

6.27 a. $CoCl_3$ **b.** PbO_2 **c.** AgI **d.** Ca_3N_2
e. Cu_3P **f.** $CrCl_2$

6.29 a. K_3P **b.** $CuCl_2$ **c.** $FeBr_3$ **d.** MgO

6.31 a. HCO_3^- **b.** NH_4^+ **c.** PO_3^{3-} **d.** ClO_3^-

6.33 a. sulfate **b.** carbonate
c. hydrogen sulfite (bisulfite) **d.** nitrate

6.35

	NO_2^-	CO_3^{2-}	HSO_4^-	PO_4^{3-}
Li^+	$LiNO_2$ Lithium nitrite	Li_2CO_3 Lithium carbonate	$LiHSO_4$ Lithium hydrogen sulfate	Li_3PO_4 Lithium phosphate
Cu^{2+}	$Cu(NO_2)_2$ Copper(II) nitrite	$CuCO_3$ Copper(II) carbonate	$Cu(HSO_4)_2$ Copper(II) hydrogen sulfate	$Cu_3(PO_4)_2$ Copper(II) phosphate
Ba^{2+}	$Ba(NO_2)_2$ Barium nitrite	$BaCO_3$ Barium carbonate	$Ba(HSO_4)_2$ Barium hydrogen sulfate	$Ba_3(PO_4)_2$ Barium phosphate

6.37 a. $Ba(OH)_2$ **b.** $NaHSO_4$ **c.** $Fe(NO_2)_2$
d. $Zn_3(PO_4)_2$ **e.** $Fe_2(CO_3)_3$

6.39 a. CO_3^{2-}, sodium carbonate **b.** NH_4^+, ammonium sulfide
c. PO_4^{3-}, barium phosphate **d.** NO_2^-, tin(II) nitrite

6.41 a. zinc acetate **b.** magnesium phosphate
c. ammonium chloride
d. sodium bicarbonate or sodium hydrogen bicarbonate

6.43 a. phosphorus tribromide **b.** dichlorine oxide
c. carbon tetrabromide **d.** hydrogen fluoride
e. nitrogen trifluoride

6.45 a. dinitrogen trioxide **b.** disilicon hexabromide
c. tetraphosphorus trisulfide **d.** phosphorus pentachloride
e. selenium hexafluoride

6.47 a. CCl_4 **b.** CO **c.** PCl_3 **d.** N_2O_4

6.49 a. OF_2 **b.** BCl_3 **c.** N_2O_3 **d.** SF_6

6.51 a. aluminum sulfate **b.** calcium carbonate
c. dinitrogen oxide **d.** magnesium hydroxide

6.53 a. 8 valence electrons **b.** 14 valence electrons
c. 32 valence electrons **d.** 8 valence electrons

6.55 a. HF $(8\ e^-)$ $H\!:\!\ddot{F}\!:$ or $H\!-\!\ddot{\underset{..}{F}}\!:$

b. SF_2 $(20\ e^-)$ $:\!\ddot{F}\!:\!\ddot{S}\!:\!\ddot{F}\!:$ or $:\!\ddot{F}\!-\!\ddot{S}\!-\!\ddot{F}\!:$

c. NBr_3 $(26\ e^-)$ $:\!\ddot{Br}\!:\!\ddot{N}\!:\!\ddot{Br}\!:$ or $:\!\ddot{Br}\!-\!\underset{..}{\overset{:\ddot{Br}:}{N}}\!-\!\ddot{Br}\!:$

d. BH_4^- $(8\ e^-)$ $\left[\,H\!:\!\underset{H}{\overset{H}{B}}\!:\!H\,\right]^-$ or $\left[\,H\!-\!\underset{H}{\overset{H}{\underset{|}{\overset{|}{B}}}}\!-\!H\,\right]^-$

6.57 If complete octets cannot be formed by using all the valence electrons, it is necessary to draw multiple bonds.

6.59 a. CO $(10\ e^-)$ $:\!C\!:\!:\!O\!:$ or $:\!C\!\equiv\!O\!:$

b. NO_3^- $(24\ e^-)$ $\left[\,:\!\ddot{O}\!:\!\overset{:\ddot{O}:}{N}\!:\!\ddot{O}\!:\,\right]^-$ or $\left[\,:\!\ddot{O}\!-\!\overset{\overset{:\ddot{O}:}{\|}}{N}\!-\!\ddot{O}\!:\,\right]^-$

c. H_2CO $(12\ e^-)$ $H\!:\!\overset{:\ddot{O}:}{C}\!:\!H$ or $H\!-\!\overset{\overset{:\ddot{O}:}{\|}}{C}\!-\!H$

6.61 a. increases **b.** decreases **c.** decreases

6.63 a. K, Na, Li **b.** Na, P, Cl **c.** Ca, Se, O

6.65 a. polar covalent **b.** ionic
c. polar covalent **d.** nonpolar covalent
e. polar covalent **f.** nonpolar covalent

6.67 a. $\overset{\delta^+}{N}\text{—}\overset{\delta^-}{F}$ →

b. $\overset{\delta^+}{Si}\text{—}\overset{\delta^-}{Br}$ →

c. $\overset{\delta^+}{C}\text{—}\overset{\delta^-}{O}$ →

d. $\overset{\delta^+}{P}\text{—}\overset{\delta^-}{Br}$ →

e. $\overset{\delta^-}{N}\text{—}\overset{\delta^+}{P}$ ←

6.69 a. 6. tetrahedral   **b. 5.** trigonal pyramidal
c. 3. trigonal planar

6.71 a. three   **b.** trigonal planar
c. three   **d.** trigonal planar

6.73 In both PH_3 and NH_3, there are three bonded atoms and one lone pair of electrons on the central atoms. The shapes of both are trigonal pyramidal.

6.75 a. bent, 109°   **b.** tetrahedral   **c.** bent, 109°

6.77 Cl_2 is a nonpolar molecule because there is a nonpolar covalent bond between Cl atoms, which have identical electronegativity values. In HCl, the bond is a polar bond, which makes HCl a polar molecule.

6.79 a. polar   **b.** polar   **c.** polar

6.81 a. dipole–dipole attractions   **b.** ionic bonds
c. dipole–dipole attractions   **d.** dispersion forces

6.83 a. hydrogen bonds   **b.** dipole–dipole attractions
c. dispersion forces   **d.** dispersion forces

6.85 a. HF; hydrogen bonds are stronger than the dipole–dipole attractions in HBr.
b. NaF; ionic bonds are stronger than the hydrogen bonds in HF.
c. $MgBr_2$; ionic bonds are stronger than the dipole–dipole attractions in PBr_3.
d. CH_3OH; hydrogen bonds are stronger than the dispersion forces in CH_4.

6.87 a. $MgSO_4$ **b.** $CaCO_3$ **c.** $Al(OH)_3$

6.89 a. ionic   **b.** ionic   **c.** ionic

6.91 a. 0.0   **b.** 0.4   **c.** 1.0

6.93 a. nonpolar covalent   **b.** nonpolar covalent
c. polar covalent

6.95 a. By losing two valence electrons from the third energy level, magnesium achieves an octet in the second energy level.
b. The magnesium ion Mg^{2+} has the same electron configuration as Ne $(1s^22s^22p^6)$.
c. Group 1A (1) and 2A (2) elements achieve octets by losing electrons to form compounds. Group 8A (18) elements are stable with octets (or two electrons for helium).

6.97 a. P^{3-} ion   **b.** O atom
c. Zn^{2+} ion   **d.** Fe^{3+} ion

6.99 a. X = Group 1A (1), Y = Group 6A (16)
b. ionic   **c.** X^+ and Y^{2-} **d.** X_2Y
e. X_2S **f.** YCl_2 **g.** molecular

6.101 a. 2. trigonal pyramidal, polar
b. 1. bent, 109°, polar
c. 3. tetrahedral, nonpolar

6.103

Electron Configurations		Cation	Anion	Formula of Compound	Name of Compound
$1s^22s^22p^63s^2$	$1s^22s^22p^3$	Mg^{2+}	N^{3-}	Mg_3N_2	Magnesium nitride
$1s^22s^22p^63s^23p^64s^1$	$1s^22s^22p^4$	K^+	O^{2-}	K_2O	Potassium oxide
$1s^22s^22p^63s^23p^1$	$1s^22s^22p^63s^23p^5$	Al^{3+}	Cl^-	$AlCl_3$	Aluminum chloride

6.105 a. two valence electrons, one bonding pair, no lone pairs
b. eight valence electrons, one bonding pair, three lone pairs
c. 14 valence electrons, one bonding pair, six lone pairs

6.107 a. $1s^22s^22p^6$ **b.** $1s^22s^22p^6$ **c.** $1s^22s^22p^63s^23p^6$
d. $1s^22s^22p^6$ **e.** $1s^2$

6.109 a. 2A (2)   **b.** $\dot{\text{X}}\cdot$ **c.** Mg   **d.** X_3N_2

6.111 a. Sn^{4+}
b. 50 protons and 46 electrons
c. SnO_2
d. $Sn_3(PO_4)_4$

6.113 a. SnS   **b.** PbO_2 **c.** AgCl
d. Ca_3N_2 **e.** Cu_3P **f.** $CrBr_2$

6.115 a. nitrogen trichloride   **b.** dinitrogen trisulfide
c. dinitrogen oxide   **d.** iodine fluoride
e. boron trifluoride   **f.** diphosphorus pentoxide

6.117 a. CS   **b.** P_2O_5 **c.** H_2S **d.** SCl_2

6.119 a. ionic, iron(III) chloride
b. ionic, sodium sulfate
c. molecular, nitrogen dioxide
d. molecular, nitrogen
e. molecular, phosphorus pentafluoride
f. molecular, carbon tetrafluoride

6.121 a. $SnCO_3$ **b.** Li_3P **c.** $SiCl_4$
d. Mn_2O_3 **e.** Br_2 **f.** $CaBr_2$

6.123 a. BF_4^- $(32\ e^-)$
$$\left[\begin{array}{c} :\ddot{F}: \\ :\ddot{F}:B:\ddot{F}: \\ :\ddot{F}: \end{array}\right]^- \quad \text{or} \quad \left[\begin{array}{c} :\ddot{F}: \\ | \\ :\ddot{F}\text{—}B\text{—}\ddot{F}: \\ | \\ :\ddot{F}: \end{array}\right]^-$$

b. Cl_2O $(20\ e^-)$ $:\ddot{C}l:\ddot{O}:\ddot{C}l:$ or $:\ddot{C}l\text{—}\ddot{O}\text{—}\ddot{C}l:$

c. H_2NOH $(14\ e^-)$
$\begin{array}{c} H \ \ \ \ \ddot{} \\ H:\ddot{N}:\ddot{O}:H \end{array}$ or $\begin{array}{c} H \\ | \\ H\text{—}N\text{—}\ddot{O}\text{—}H \\ \ \ \ \ \ \ \ddot{} \end{array}$

d. H_2CCCl_2 $(24\ e^-)$
$\begin{array}{c} H\ :\ddot{C}l: \\ H:C::C:\ddot{C}l: \end{array}$ or

$$\begin{array}{c} H\ \ \ :\ddot{C}l: \\ |\ \ \ \ \ | \\ H\text{—}C\text{=}C\text{—}\ddot{C}l: \end{array}$$

6.125

a. 16 valence electrons $\left[:\ddot{N}::N::\ddot{N}:\right]^-$ or $\left[:\ddot{N}\text{=}N\text{=}\ddot{N}:\right]^-$

b. 16 valence electrons $\left[:\ddot{O}::N::\ddot{O}:\right]^+$ or $\left[:\ddot{O}\text{=}N\text{=}\ddot{O}:\right]^+$

c. 16 valence electrons $\left[:C::N:\ddot{S}:\right]^-$ or $\left[:C\text{≡}N\text{—}\ddot{S}:\right]^-$

6.127 a. C—O   **b.** N—F   **c.** S—Cl
     d. Br—I   **e.** N—F

6.129 a. polar covalent (Cl 3.0 − Si 1.8 = 1.2)
     b. nonpolar covalent (C 2.5 − C 2.5 = 0.0)
     c. ionic (Cl 3.0 − Na 0.9 = 2.1)
     d. nonpolar covalent (C 2.5 − H 2.1 = 0.4)
     e. nonpolar covalent (F 4.0 − F 4.0 = 0.0)

6.131 a. trigonal pyramidal, polar
     b. bent 109°, polar

6.133 a. polar   **b.** polar   **c.** nonpolar

6.135 a. bent 109°, nonpolar
     b. trigonal pyramidal, polar

6.137 a. (3) hydrogen bonds   **b.** (2) dipole–dipole attractions
     c. (4) dispersion forces   **d.** (1) ionic bonds

6.139

Atom or Ion	Number of Protons	Number of Electrons	Electrons Lost/ Gained
K^+	$19\,p^+$	$18\,e^-$	$1\,e^-$ lost
Mg^{2+}	$12\,p^+$	$10\,e^-$	$2\,e^-$ lost
O^{2-}	$8\,p^+$	$10\,e^-$	$2\,e^-$ gained
Al^{3+}	$13\,p^+$	$10\,e^-$	$3\,e^-$ lost

6.141 a. Group 3A (13)   **b.** Group 6A (16)   **c.** Group 2A (2)

6.143 a. ionic, lithium hydrogen phosphate
     b. ionic, chromium(II) nitrite
     c. ionic, magnesium chlorite
     d. molecular, nitrogen trifluoride
     e. ionic, calcium bisulfate or calcium hydrogen sulfate
     f. ionic, potassium perchlorate
     g. ionic, gold(III) sulfite
     h. molecular, iodine

CI.7 For parts **a** to **f**, consider the loss of electrons by atoms of the element X, and a gain of electrons by atoms of the element Y, if X is in Group 2A (2), Period 3, and Y is in Group 7A (17), Period 3. (4.6, 6.1, 6.2, 6.3, 6.7)

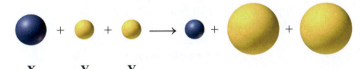

X   Y   Y

    a. Which reactant has the higher electronegativity?
    b. What are the ionic charges of **X** and **Y** in the product?
    c. Write the electron configurations for the atoms **X** and **Y**.
    d. Write the electron configurations for the ions of **X** and **Y**.
    e. Give the names for the noble gases with the same electron configurations as each of these ions.
    f. Write the formula and name for the ionic compound formed by the ions of **X** and **Y**.

CI.8 A sterling silver bracelet, which is 92.5% silver by mass, has a volume of 25.6 cm^3 and a density of 10.2 g/cm^3. (2.7, 4.5, 5.2, 5.4)

Sterling silver is 92.5% silver by mass.

    a. What is the mass, in kilograms, of the bracelet?
    b. Determine the number of protons and neutrons in each of the two stable isotopes of silver:

$$^{107}_{47}\text{Ag} \qquad ^{109}_{47}\text{Ag}$$

    c. Silver (Ag) has two naturally occurring isotopes: Ag-107 (106.905 amu) with an abundance of 51.84% and Ag-109 (108.905 amu) with an abundance of 48.16%. Calculate the atomic mass for silver using the weighted average mass method.
    d. Ag-112 decays by beta emission. Write the balanced nuclear equation for the decay of Ag-112.
    e. A 64.0-μCi sample of Ag-112 decays to 8.00 μCi in 9.3 h. What is the half-life of Ag-112?

CI.9 Some of the isotopes of silicon are listed in the following table: (4.5, 4.6, 5.2, 5.4, 6.7, 6.8)

Isotope	% Natural Abundance	Atomic Mass	Half-Life (radioactive)	Radiation
$^{27}_{14}$Si		26.987	4.9 s	Positron
$^{28}_{14}$Si	92.23	27.977	Stable	None
$^{29}_{14}$Si	4.683	28.976	Stable	None
$^{30}_{14}$Si	3.087	29.974	Stable	None
$^{31}_{14}$Si		30.975	2.6 h	Beta

    a. In the following table, indicate the number of protons, neutrons, and electrons for each isotope listed:

Isotope	Number of Protons	Number of Neutrons	Number of Electrons
$^{27}_{14}$Si			
$^{28}_{14}$Si			
$^{29}_{14}$Si			
$^{30}_{14}$Si			
$^{31}_{14}$Si			

    b. What is the electron configuration of silicon?
    c. Calculate the atomic mass for silicon using the weighted average mass method.
    d. Write the balanced nuclear equations for the positron emission of Si-27 and the beta decay of Si-31.
    e. Draw the Lewis structure and predict the shape of $SiCl_4$.
    f. How many hours are needed for a sample of Si-31 with an activity of 16 μCi to decay to 2.0 μCi?

CI.10 The iceman known as Ötzi was discovered in a high mountain pass on the Austrian–Italian border. Samples of his hair and bones had carbon-14 activity that was 50% of that present in new hair or bone. Carbon-14 undergoes beta decay and has a half-life of 5730 yr. (5.2, 5.4)

The mummified remains of Ötzi were discovered in 1991.

    a. How long ago did Ötzi live?
    b. Write a balanced nuclear equation for the decay of carbon-14.

CI.11 K$^+$ is an electrolyte required by the human body and is found in many foods as well as salt substitutes. One of the isotopes of potassium is potassium-40, which has a natural abundance of 0.012% and a half-life of 1.30×10^9 yr. The isotope potassium-40 decays to calcium-40 or to argon-40. A typical activity for potassium-40 is 7.0 μCi per gram. (5.2, 5.3, 5.4)

Potassium chloride is used as a salt substitute.

    a. Write a balanced nuclear equation for each type of decay and identify the particle emitted.
    b. A shaker of salt substitute contains 1.6 oz of K. What is the activity, in millicuries and becquerels, of the potassium in the shaker?

CI.12 Of much concern to environmentalists is radon-222, which is a radioactive noble gas that can seep from the ground into basements of homes and buildings. Radon-222 is a product of the decay of radium-226 that occurs naturally in rocks and soil in much of the United States. Radon-222, which has a half-life of 3.8 days, decays by emitting an alpha particle. Radon-222, which is a gas, can be inhaled into the lungs where it is can cause lung cancer. Radon levels in a home can be measured with a home radon-detection kit. Environmental agencies have set the maximum level of radon-222 in a home at 4 picocuries per liter (pCi/L) of air. (5.2, 5.3, 5.4)

A home detection kit is used to measure the level of radon-222.

a. Write the balanced nuclear equation for the decay of Ra-226.
b. Write the balanced nuclear equation for the decay of Rn-222.
c. If a room contains 24 000 atoms of radon-222, how many atoms of radon-222 remain after 15.2 days?
d. Suppose a room has a volume of 72 000 L (7.2×10^4 L). If the radon level is the maximum allowed (4 pCi/L), how many alpha particles are emitted from Rn-222 in 1 day? (1 Ci = 3.7×10^{10} disintegrations/s)

ANSWERS

CI.7
a. Y has the higher electronegativity.
b. X^{2+}, Y^{-}
c. $X = 1s^2 2s^2 2p^6 3s^2$ $Y = 1s^2 2s^2 2p^6 3s^2 3p^5$
d. $X^{2+} = 1s^2 2s^2 2p^6$ $Y^{-} = 1s^2 2s^2 2p^6 3s^2 3p^6$
e. X^{2+} has the same electron configuration as Ne. Y^{-} has the same electron configuration as Ar.
f. $MgCl_2$, magnesium chloride

CI.9 a.

Isotope	Number of Protons	Number of Neutrons	Number of Electrons
$^{27}_{14}Si$	14	13	14
$^{28}_{14}Si$	14	14	14
$^{29}_{14}Si$	14	15	14
$^{30}_{14}Si$	14	16	14
$^{31}_{14}Si$	14	17	14

b. $1s^2 2s^2 2p^6 3s^2 3p^2$
c. 28.09 amu
d. $^{27}_{14}Si \longrightarrow {}^{27}_{13}Al + {}^{0}_{+1}e$
    $^{31}_{14}Si \longrightarrow {}^{31}_{15}P + {}^{0}_{-1}e$

e.

$$\overset{\displaystyle :\ddot{C}l:}{\underset{\displaystyle :\ddot{C}l:}{:\ddot{C}l-Si-\ddot{C}l:}} \qquad \text{Tetrahedral}$$

f. 7.8 h

CI.11 a. $^{40}_{19}K \longrightarrow {}^{40}_{20}Ca + {}^{0}_{-1}e$ Beta particle
      $^{40}_{19}K \longrightarrow {}^{40}_{18}Ar + {}^{0}_{+1}e$ Positron
b. 3.8×10^{-5} mCi; 1.4×10^3 Bq

7

Chemical Reactions and Quantities

JANE'S TEETH HAVE BECOME BADLY STAINED

because of drinking excessive amounts of coffee. Dark colored compounds in coffee, tea, fruit juices, wine, and smoke cause discoloration of the teeth when they penetrate the hydroxyapatite, which is a porous compound in the enamel layer. Jane makes an appointment with Kimberly, her dental hygienist, to have her teeth whitened. After Kimberly cleans Jane's teeth, she begins the process of whitening by placing a gel composed of 15 to 35% hydrogen peroxide (H_2O_2) on the surface of Jane's teeth. The hydrogen peroxide penetrates the enamel of Jane's teeth where it causes a chemical reaction occurs that produces oxygen (O_2). As the O_2 reacts with the discoloration in the enamel, the teeth are whitened.

CAREER Dental Hygienist

A visit to the dentist frequently begins with a dental hygienist who cleans and polishes the patient's teeth by removing tartar, stains, and plaque. This requires the hygienist to use a variety of tools, including hand and rotary instruments, as well as ultrasonic equipment. The hygienist also discusses the proper technique for brushing and flossing with each patient. The dental hygienist may also take X-rays of a patient's teeth to detect any abnormalities. A dental hygienist must be knowledgeable about the proper safety procedures for taking X-rays and how to protect themselves from disease transmission by wearing the proper safety attire like safety glasses, surgical masks, and gloves.

LOOKING AHEAD

7.1 Equations for Chemical Reactions 236

7.2 Types of Reactions 243

♡ **Chemistry Link to Health**
Incomplete Combustion: Toxicity of Carbon Monoxide 247

7.3 Oxidation–Reduction Reactions 248

7.4 The Mole 251

7.5 Molar Mass and Calculations 255

7.6 Mole Relationships in Chemical Equations 260

7.7 Mass Calculations for Reactions 263

7.8 Limiting Reactants and Percent Yield 265

7.9 Energy in Chemical Reactions 271

♡ **Chemistry Link to Health**
Cold Packs and Hot Packs 273

℞ **Clinical Applications** 243, 251, 255, 259, 265, 274, 275, 284

℞ **Clinical Update** *Whitening of Tooth Enamel* 275

C hemical reactions occur everywhere. The fuel in our cars burns with oxygen to make the car move and run the air conditioner. When we cook our food or bleach our hair, chemical reactions take place. In our bodies, chemical reactions convert food into molecules that build muscles and move them. In the leaves of trees and plants, carbon dioxide and water are converted into carbohydrates.

Some chemical reactions are simple, whereas others are quite complex. However, they can all be written with chemical equations that chemists use to describe chemical reactions. In every chemical reaction, the atoms in the reacting substances, called *reactants*, are rearranged to give new substances called *products*.

In chemistry, you calculate and measure the amounts of substances to use in lab. Actually, measuring the amount of a substance is something you do every day. When you cook, you measure out the proper amounts of ingredients so you don't have too much of one or too little of another. At the gas station, you pump a certain amount of fuel into your gas tank. If you paint the walls of a room, you measure the area and purchase the amount of paint that will cover the walls. In the lab, the chemical formula of a substance tells you the number and kinds of atoms it has, which you then use to determine the mass of the substance to use in an experiment.

You do the same thing at home when you use a recipe to make cookies. At the automotive repair shop, a mechanic goes through a similar process when adjusting the fuel system of an engine to allow for the correct amounts of fuel and oxygen. In the body, a certain amount of O_2 must reach the tissues for efficient metabolic reactions. If the oxygenation of the blood is low, the respiratory therapist will oxygenate the patient and recheck the blood levels.

CHAPTER READINESS*

🖩 KEY MATH SKILLS
- Calculating Percentages (1.4C)
- Solving Equations (1.4D)
- Writing Numbers in Scientific Notation (1.4F)

⚛ CORE CHEMISTRY SKILLS
- Counting Significant Figures (2.2)
- Using Significant Figures in Calculations (2.3)

- Writing Conversion Factors from Equalities (2.5)
- Using Conversion Factors (2.6)
- Using Energy Units (3.4)
- Writing Ionic Formulas (6.2)
- Naming Ionic Compounds (6.3)
- Writing the Names and Formulas for Molecular Compounds (6.5)

*These Key Math Skills and Core Chemistry Skills from previous chapters are listed here for your review as you proceed to the new material in this chapter.

LEARNING GOAL

Write a balanced chemical equation from the formulas of the reactants and products for a reaction; determine the number of atoms in the reactants and products.

7.1 Equations for Chemical Reactions

A *chemical change* occurs when a substance is converted into one or more new substances that have different formulas and different properties. For example, when silver tarnishes, the shiny silver metal (Ag) reacts with sulfur (S) to become the dull, black substance we call tarnish (Ag_2S) (see Figure 7.1).

A chemical change:
the tarnishing of silver

Ag   Ag₂S

FIGURE 7.1 ▶ A chemical change produces new substances with new properties.

Q Why is the formation of tarnish a chemical change?

Fe   Fe₂O₃

FIGURE 7.2 ▶ Chemical reactions involve chemical changes. When iron (Fe) reacts with oxygen (O_2), the product is rust (Fe_2O_3).

Q What is the evidence for chemical change in this chemical reaction?

A *chemical reaction* always involves chemical change because atoms of the reacting substances form new combinations with new properties. For example, a chemical reaction takes place when a piece of iron (Fe) combines with oxygen (O_2) in the air to produce a new substance, rust (Fe_2O_3), which has a reddish-brown color (see Figure 7.2). During a chemical change, new properties become visible, which are an indication that a chemical reaction has taken place (see Table 7.1).

When you build a model airplane, prepare a new recipe, or mix a medication, you follow a set of directions. These directions tell you what materials to use and the products you will obtain. In chemistry, a *chemical equation* tells us the materials we need and the products that will form.

TABLE 7.1 Types of Visible Evidence of a Chemical Reaction

1. Change in color
2. Formation of a gas (bubbles)
3. Formation of a solid (precipitate)
4. Heat (or a flame) produced or heat absorbed

Writing a Chemical Equation

Suppose you work in a bicycle shop, assembling wheels and frames into bicycles. You could represent this process by a simple equation:

Equation: 2 Wheels + 1 Frame ⟶ 1 Bicycle

Reactants   Product

When you burn charcoal in a grill, the carbon in the charcoal combines with oxygen to form carbon dioxide. We can represent this reaction by a chemical equation.

Equation: $C(s) + O_2(g) \xrightarrow{\Delta} CO_2(g)$

TABLE 7.2 Some Symbols Used in Writing Equations

Symbol	Meaning
+	Separates two or more formulas
$\longrightarrow$	Reacts to form products
$\xrightarrow{\Delta}$	Reactants are heated
(s)	Solid
(l)	Liquid
(g)	Gas
(aq)	Aqueous

In a **chemical equation**, the formulas of the **reactants** are written on the left of the arrow and the formulas of the **products** on the right. When there are two or more formulas on the same side, they are separated by plus $(+)$ signs. The delta sign (Δ) indicates that heat was used to start the reaction.

Generally, each formula in an equation is followed by an abbreviation, in parentheses, that gives the physical state of the substance: solid (s), liquid (l), or gas (g). If a substance is dissolved in water, it is an aqueous (aq) solution. Table 7.2 summarizes some of the symbols used in equations.

Identifying a Balanced Chemical Equation

When a chemical reaction takes place, the bonds between the atoms of the reactants are broken and new bonds are formed to give the products. All atoms are conserved, which means that atoms cannot be gained, lost, or changed into other types of atoms during a chemical reaction. Every chemical reaction must be written as a **balanced equation**, which shows the same number of atoms for each element in the reactants as well as in the products. For example, the chemical equation we wrote previously for burning carbon is balanced because there is one carbon atom and two oxygen atoms in both the reactants and the products:

$$C(s) + O_2(g) \xrightarrow{\Delta} CO_2(g)$$

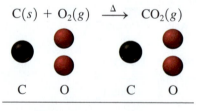

| C | O | | C | O |

Reactant atoms   =   Product atoms

Now consider the reaction in which hydrogen reacts with oxygen to form water written as follows:

$$H_2(g) + O_2(g) \longrightarrow H_2O(g) \qquad \text{Unbalanced}$$

In the *balanced* equation, there are whole numbers called **coefficients** in front of the formulas. On the reactant side, the coefficient of 2 in front of the H_2 formula represents two molecules of hydrogen, which is 4 atoms of H. A coefficient of 1 is understood for O_2,

$$2H_2(g) + O_2(g) \longrightarrow 2H_2O(g)$$

Balanced

which gives 2 atoms of O. On the product side, the coefficient of 2 in front of the H_2O formula represents 2 molecules of water. Because the coefficient of 2 multiplies all the atoms in H_2O, there are 4 hydrogen atoms and 2 oxygen atoms in the products. Because there are the same number of hydrogen atoms and oxygen atoms in the reactants as in the products, we know that the equation is *balanced*. This illustrates the *Law of Conservation of Matter*, which states that matter cannot be created or destroyed during a chemical reaction.

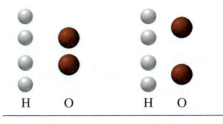

Reactant atoms = Product atoms

▶ **SAMPLE PROBLEM 7.1 Number of Atoms in Balanced Chemical Equations**

Indicate the number of each type of atom in the following balanced chemical equation:

$$Fe_2S_3(s) + 6HCl(aq) \longrightarrow 2FeCl_3(aq) + 3H_2S(g)$$

	Reactants	Products
Fe		
S		
H		
Cl		

SOLUTION

The total number of atoms in each formula is obtained by multiplying the coefficient by each subscript in a chemical formula.

	Reactants	Products
Fe	$2\,(1 \times 2)$	$2\,(2 \times 1)$
S	$3\,(1 \times 3)$	$3\,(3 \times 1)$
H	$6\,(6 \times 1)$	$6\,(3 \times 2)$
Cl	$6\,(6 \times 1)$	$6\,(2 \times 3)$

STUDY CHECK 7.1

When ethane, C_2H_6, burns in oxygen, the products are carbon dioxide and water. The balanced chemical equation is written as

$$2C_2H_6(g) + 7O_2(g) \xrightarrow{\Delta} 4CO_2(g) + 6H_2O(g)$$

Calculate the number of each type of atom in the reactants and in the products.

ANSWER

In both the reactants and products, there are 4 C atoms, 12 H atoms, and 14 O atoms.

Balancing a Chemical Equation

The chemical reaction that occurs in the flame of a gas burner you use in the laboratory or a gas cooktop is the reaction of methane gas, CH_4, and oxygen to produce carbon dioxide and water. We now show the process of balancing a chemical equation in Sample Problem 7.2.

⚛ **CORE CHEMISTRY SKILL**

Balancing a Chemical Equation

▶ **SAMPLE PROBLEM 7.2 Balancing a Chemical Equation**

The chemical reaction of methane, CH_4, and oxygen gas, O_2, produces carbon dioxide (CO_2) and water (H_2O). Write a balanced chemical equation for this reaction.

Guide to Balancing a Chemical Equation

STEP 1
Write an equation using the correct formulas for the reactants and products.

STEP 2
Count the atoms of each element in the reactants and products.

STEP 3
Use coefficients to balance each element.

STEP 4
Check the final equation to confirm it is balanced.

SOLUTION

STEP 1 Write an equation using the correct formulas for the reactants and products.

$$CH_4(g) + O_2(g) \xrightarrow{\Delta} CO_2(g) + H_2O(g)$$

CH_4 O_2 CO_2 H_2O

STEP 2 Count the atoms of each element in the reactants and products. When we compare the atoms on the reactant side and the atoms on the product side, we see that there are more H atoms in the reactants and more O atoms in the products.

$$CH_4(g) + O_2(g) \xrightarrow{\Delta} CO_2(g) + H_2O(g)$$

Reactants	Products	
1 C atom	1 C atom	Balanced
4 H atoms	2 H atoms	Not balanced
2 O atoms	3 O atoms	Not balanced

STEP 3 Use coefficients to balance each element. We will start by balancing the H atoms in CH_4 because it has the most atoms. By placing a coefficient of 2 in front of the formula for H_2O, a total of 4 H atoms in the products is obtained. *Only use coefficients to balance an equation. Do not change any of the subscripts: This would alter the chemical formula of a reactant or product.*

$$CH_4(g) + O_2(g) \xrightarrow{\Delta} CO_2(g) + 2H_2O(g)$$

Reactants	Products	
1 C atom	1 C atom	Balanced
4 H atoms	4 H atoms	Balanced
2 O atoms	4 O atoms	Not balanced

We can balance the O atoms on the reactant side by placing a coefficient of 2 in front of the formula O_2. There are now 4 O atoms in both the reactants and products.

$$CH_4(g) + 2O_2(g) \xrightarrow{\Delta} CO_2(g) + 2H_2O(g) \quad \text{Balanced}$$

STEP 4 Check the final equation to confirm it is balanced. In the final equation, the numbers of atoms of C, H, and O are the same in both the reactants and the products. The equation is balanced.

$$CH_4(g) + 2O_2(g) \xrightarrow{\Delta} CO_2(g) + 2H_2O(g)$$

Reactants	Products	
1 C atom	1 C atom	Balanced
4 H atoms	4 H atoms	Balanced
4 O atoms	4 O atoms	Balanced

In a balanced chemical equation, the coefficients must be the *lowest possible whole numbers*. Suppose you had obtained the following for the balanced equation:

$$2CH_4(g) + 4O_2(g) \xrightarrow{\Delta} 2CO_2(g) + 4H_2O(g) \quad \text{Incorrect}$$

Although there are equal numbers of atoms on both sides of the equation, this is not written correctly. To obtain coefficients that are the lowest whole numbers, we divide all the coefficients by 2.

STUDY CHECK 7.2

Balance the following chemical equation:

$$Al(s) + Cl_2(g) \longrightarrow AlCl_3(s)$$

ANSWER

$$2Al(s) + 3Cl_2(g) \longrightarrow 2AlCl_3(s)$$

▶ **SAMPLE PROBLEM 7.3 Balancing Chemical Equations with Polyatomic Ions**

Balance the following chemical equation:

$$Na_3PO_4(aq) + MgCl_2(aq) \longrightarrow Mg_3(PO_4)_2(s) + NaCl(aq)$$

SOLUTION

STEP 1 Write an equation using the correct formulas for the reactants and products.

$$Na_3PO_4(aq) + MgCl_2(aq) \longrightarrow Mg_3(PO_4)_2(s) + NaCl(aq) \quad \text{Unbalanced}$$

STEP 2 Count the atoms of each element in the reactants and products. When we compare the number of ions in the reactants and products, we find that the equation is not balanced. In this equation, we can balance the phosphate ion as a group of atoms because it appears on both sides of the equation.

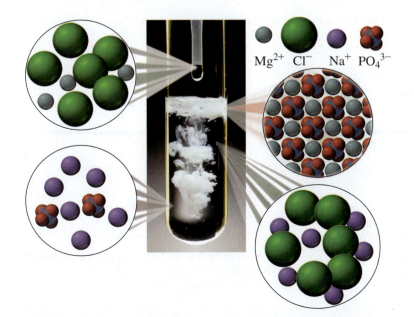

Mg^{2+} Cl^- Na^+ $PO_4{}^{3-}$

$$Na_3PO_4(aq) + MgCl_2(aq) \longrightarrow Mg_3(PO_4)_2(s) + NaCl(aq)$$

Reactants	Products	
3 Na^+	1 Na^+	Not balanced
1 PO_4^{3-}	2 PO_4^{3-}	Not balanced
1 Mg^{2+}	3 Mg^{2+}	Not balanced
2 Cl^-	1 Cl^-	Not balanced

STEP 3 **Use coefficients to balance each element.** We begin with the formula that has the highest subscript values, which in this equation is $Mg_3(PO_4)_2$. The subscript 3 in $Mg_3(PO_4)_2$ is used as a coefficient for $MgCl_2$ to balance magnesium. The subscript 2 in $Mg_3(PO_4)_2$ is used as a coefficient for Na_3PO_4 to balance the phosphate ion.

$$2Na_3PO_4(aq) + 3MgCl_2(aq) \longrightarrow Mg_3(PO_4)_2(s) + NaCl(aq)$$

Reactants	Products	
6 Na^+	1 Na^+	Not balanced
2 PO_4^{3-}	2 PO_4^{3-}	Balanced
3 Mg^{2+}	3 Mg^{2+}	Balanced
6 Cl^-	1 Cl^-	Not balanced

In the reactants and products, we see that the sodium and chloride ions are not yet balanced. A coefficient of 6 is placed in front of the NaCl to balance the equation.

$$2Na_3PO_4(aq) + 3MgCl_2(aq) \longrightarrow Mg_3(PO_4)_2(s) + 6NaCl(aq)$$

STEP 4 **Check the final equation to confirm it is balanced.** A check of the total number of ions confirms the equation is balanced. A coefficient of 1 is understood and not usually written.

$$2Na_3PO_4(aq) + 3MgCl_2(aq) \longrightarrow Mg_3(PO_4)_2(s) + 6NaCl(aq) \quad \text{Balanced}$$

Reactants	Products	
6 Na^+	6 Na^+	Balanced
2 PO_4^{3-}	2 PO_4^{3-}	Balanced
3 Mg^{2+}	3 Mg^{2+}	Balanced
6 Cl^-	6 Cl^-	Balanced

STUDY CHECK 7.3

Balance the following chemical equation:

$$Pb(NO_3)_2(aq) + AlBr_3(aq) \longrightarrow PbBr_2(s) + Al(NO_3)_3(aq)$$

ANSWER

$$3Pb(NO_3)_2(aq) + 2AlBr_3(aq) \longrightarrow 3PbBr_2(s) + 2Al(NO_3)_3(aq)$$

QUESTIONS AND PROBLEMS

7.1 Equations for Chemical Reactions

LEARNING GOAL Write a balanced chemical equation from the formulas of the reactants and products for a reaction; determine the number of atoms in the reactants and products.

7.1 Balance each of the following chemical equations:
  a. $N_2(g) + O_2(g) \longrightarrow NO(g)$
  b. $HgO(s) \longrightarrow Hg(l) + O_2(g)$

  c. $Fe(s) + O_2(g) \longrightarrow Fe_2O_3(s)$
  d. $Na(s) + Cl_2(g) \longrightarrow NaCl(s)$
  e. $Cu_2O(s) + O_2(g) \longrightarrow CuO(s)$

7.2 Balance each of the following chemical equations:
  a. $Ca(s) + Br_2(l) \longrightarrow CaBr_2(s)$
  b. $P_4(s) + O_2(g) \longrightarrow P_4O_{10}(s)$

c. $C_4H_8(g) + O_2(g) \xrightarrow{\Delta} CO_2(g) + H_2O(g)$
d. $Ca(OH)_2(aq) + HNO_3(aq) \longrightarrow$
$$Ca(NO_3)_2(aq) + H_2O(l)$$
e. $Fe_2O_3(s) + C(s) \longrightarrow Fe(s) + CO(g)$

7.3 Balance each of the following chemical equations:
a. $Mg(s) + AgNO_3(aq) \longrightarrow Mg(NO_3)_2(aq) + Ag(s)$
b. $CuCO_3(s) \longrightarrow CuO(s) + CO_2(g)$
c. $Al(s) + CuSO_4(aq) \longrightarrow Cu(s) + Al_2(SO_4)_3(aq)$
d. $Pb(NO_3)_2(aq) + NaCl(aq) \longrightarrow PbCl_2(s) + NaNO_3(aq)$
e. $Al(s) + HCl(aq) \longrightarrow AlCl_3(aq) + H_2(g)$

7.4 Balance each of the following chemical equations:
a. $Zn(s) + HNO_3(aq) \longrightarrow Zn(NO_3)_2(aq) + H_2(g)$
b. $Al(s) + H_2SO_4(aq) \longrightarrow Al_2(SO_4)_3(aq) + H_2(g)$
c. $K_2SO_4(aq) + BaCl_2(aq) \longrightarrow BaSO_4(s) + KCl(aq)$
d. $CaCO_3(s) \longrightarrow CaO(s) + CO_2(g)$
e. $AlCl_3(aq) + KOH(aq) \longrightarrow Al(OH)_3(s) + KCl(aq)$

7.5 Balance each of the following chemical equations:
a. $Fe_2O_3(s) + CO(g) \longrightarrow Fe(s) + CO_2(g)$
b. $Li_3N(s) \longrightarrow Li(s) + N_2(g)$
c. $Al(s) + HBr(aq) \longrightarrow AlBr_3(aq) + H_2(g)$
d. $Ba(OH)_2(aq) + Na_3PO_4(aq) \longrightarrow$
$$Ba_3(PO_4)_2(s) + NaOH(aq)$$
e. $As_4S_6(s) + O_2(g) \longrightarrow As_4O_6(s) + SO_2(g)$

7.6 Balance each of the following chemical equations:
a. $K(s) + H_2O(l) \longrightarrow KOH(aq) + H_2(g)$
b. $Cr(s) + S_8(s) \longrightarrow Cr_2S_3(s)$
c. $BCl_3(s) + H_2O(l) \longrightarrow H_3BO_3(aq) + HCl(aq)$
d. $Fe(OH)_3(s) + H_2SO_4(aq) \longrightarrow Fe_2(SO_4)_3(aq) + H_2O(l)$
e. $BaCl_2(aq) + Na_3PO_4(aq) \longrightarrow$
$$Ba_3(PO_4)_2(s) + NaCl(aq)$$

7.7 Write a balanced equation using the correct formulas and include conditions ($s, l, g,$ or aq) for each of the following chemical reactions:
a. Lithium metal reacts with liquid water to form hydrogen gas and aqueous lithium hydroxide.
b. Solid phosphorus reacts with chlorine gas to form solid phosphorus pentachloride.

c. Solid iron(II) oxide reacts with carbon monoxide gas to form solid iron and carbon dioxide gas.
d. Liquid pentene (C_5H_{10}) burns in oxygen gas to form carbon dioxide gas and water vapor.
e. Hydrogen sulfide gas and solid iron(III) chloride react to form solid iron(III) sulfide and hydrogen chloride gas.

7.8 Write a balanced equation using the correct formulas and include conditions ($s, l, g,$ or aq) for each of the following chemical reactions:
a. Solid sodium carbonate decomposes to produce solid sodium oxide and carbon dioxide gas.
b. Nitrogen oxide gas reacts with carbon monoxide gas to produce nitrogen gas and carbon dioxide gas.
c. Iron metal reacts with solid sulfur to produce solid iron(III) sulfide.
d. Solid calcium reacts with nitrogen gas to produce solid calcium nitride.
e. In the *Apollo* lunar module, hydrazine gas, N_2H_4, reacts with dinitrogen tetroxide gas to produce gaseous nitrogen and water vapor.

℞ Clinical Applications

7.9 Dinitrogen oxide, also known as laughing gas, is a sweet-tasting gas used in dentistry. When solid ammonium nitrate is heated, the products are gaseous water and gaseous dinitrogen oxide. Write the balanced chemical equation for the reaction.

7.10 When ethanol $C_2H_6O(aq)$ is consumed, it reacts with O_2 gas in the body to produce gaseous carbon dioxide and liquid water. Write the balanced chemical equation for the reaction.

7.11 In the body, the amino acid alanine $C_3H_7NO_2(aq)$ reacts with O_2 gas to produce gaseous carbon dioxide, liquid water, and urea, $CH_4N_2O(aq)$. Write the balanced chemical equation for the reaction.

7.12 In the body, the amino acid asparagine $C_4H_8N_2O_3(aq)$ reacts with O_2 gas in the body to produce gaseous carbon dioxide, liquid water, and urea, $CH_4N_2O(aq)$. Write the balanced chemical equation for the reaction.

7.2 Types of Reactions

A great number of reactions occur in nature, in biological systems, and in the laboratory. However, there are some general patterns among all reactions that help us classify reactions. Some reactions may fit into more than one reaction type.

Combination Reactions

In a **combination reaction**, two or more elements or compounds bond to form one product. For example, sulfur and oxygen combine to form the product sulfur dioxide.

$$S(s) + O_2(g) \longrightarrow SO_2(g)$$

In Figure 7.3, the elements magnesium and oxygen combine to form a single product, which is the ionic compound magnesium oxide formed from Mg^{2+} and O^{2-} ions.

$$2Mg(s) + O_2(g) \longrightarrow 2MgO(s)$$

LEARNING GOAL

Identify a reaction as a combination, decomposition, single replacement, double replacement, or combustion.

Combination

Two or more reactants   combine to yield   a single product

  + $\longrightarrow$

⚛ CORE CHEMISTRY SKILL

Classifying Types of Chemical Reactions

In other examples of combination reactions, elements or compounds combine to form a single product.

$$N_2(g) + 3H_2(g) \longrightarrow 2NH_3(g)$$
Ammonia

$$Cu(s) + S(s) \longrightarrow CuS(s)$$

$$MgO(s) + CO_2(g) \longrightarrow MgCO_3(s)$$

| $2Mg(s)$ | + | $O_2(g)$ | $\xrightarrow{\Delta}$ | $2MgO(s)$ |
| Magnesium | | Oxygen | | Magnesium oxide |

FIGURE 7.3 ▶ In a combination reaction, two or more substances combine to form one substance as product.

Q What happens to the atoms in the reactants in a combination reaction?

Decomposition Reactions

In a **decomposition reaction**, a reactant splits into two or more simpler products. For example, when mercury(II) oxide is heated, the compound breaks apart into mercury atoms and oxygen (see Figure 7.4).

$$2HgO(s) \xrightarrow{\Delta} 2Hg(l) + O_2(g)$$

In another example of a decomposition reaction, calcium carbonate breaks apart into simpler compounds of calcium oxide and carbon dioxide.

$$CaCO_3(s) \xrightarrow{\Delta} CaO(s) + CO_2(g)$$

Replacement Reactions

In a replacement reaction, elements in a compound are replaced by other elements. In a **single replacement reaction**, a reacting element switches place with an element in the other reacting compound.

Single replacement

One element   replaces   another element

 + $\longrightarrow$

In the single replacement reaction shown in Figure 7.5, zinc replaces hydrogen in hydrochloric acid, $HCl(aq)$.

$$Zn(s) + 2HCl(aq) \longrightarrow H_2(g) + ZnCl_2(aq)$$

Decomposition

A   splits   two or more
reactant   into   products

  $\longrightarrow$ +

In another single replacement reaction, chlorine replaces bromine in the compound potassium bromide.

$$Cl_2(g) + 2KBr(s) \longrightarrow 2KCl(s) + Br_2(l)$$

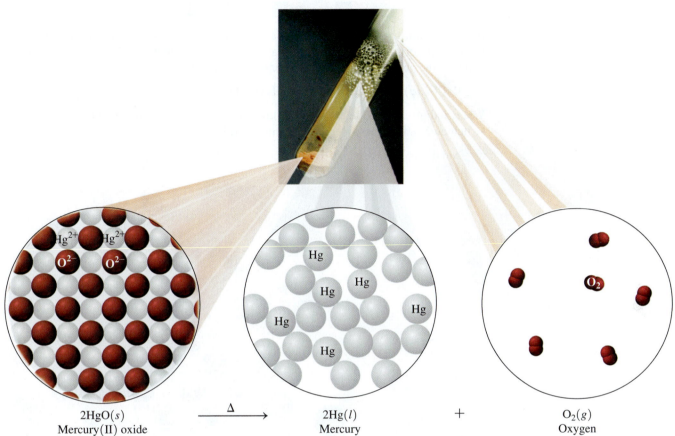

$$2HgO(s) \xrightarrow{\Delta} 2Hg(l) + O_2(g)$$

Mercury(II) oxide   Mercury   Oxygen

FIGURE 7.4 ▶ In a decomposition reaction, one reactant breaks down into two or more products.

🅠 How do the differences in the reactant and products classify this as a decomposition reaction?

Zn   Cl⁻
H₂   H⁺
Zn²⁺

$$Zn(s) + 2HCl(aq) \longrightarrow ZnCl_2(aq) + H_2(g)$$

Zinc   Hydrochloric acid   Zinc chloride   Hydrogen

FIGURE 7.5 ▶ In a single replacement reaction, an atom or ion replaces an atom or ion in a compound.

🅠 What changes in the formulas of the reactants identify this equation as a single replacement?

In a **double replacement reaction**, the positive ions in the reacting compounds switch places.

Double replacement

Two elements   replace   each other

$$\boxed{A}\,\boxed{B} + \boxed{C}\,\boxed{D} \longrightarrow \boxed{A}\,\boxed{D} + \boxed{C}\,\boxed{B}$$

In the reaction shown in Figure 7.6, barium ions change places with sodium ions in the reactants to form sodium chloride and a white solid precipitate of barium sulfate. The formulas of the products depend on the charges of the ions.

$$BaCl_2(aq) + Na_2SO_4(aq) \longrightarrow BaSO_4(s) + 2NaCl(aq)$$

When sodium hydroxide and hydrochloric acid (HCl) react, sodium and hydrogen ions switch places, forming water and sodium chloride.

$$NaOH(aq) + HCl(aq) \longrightarrow H_2O(l) + NaCl(aq)$$

SO_4^{2-} Ba^{2+}

Na^+ Cl^-

| $Na_2SO_4(aq)$ | + | $BaCl_2(aq)$ | $\longrightarrow$ | $BaSO_4(s)$ | + | $2NaCl(aq)$ |
| Sodium sulfate | | Barium chloride | | Barium sulfate | | Sodium chloride |

FIGURE 7.6 ▶ In a double replacement reaction, the positive ions in the reactants replace each other.

🔍 How do the changes in the formulas of the reactants identify this equation as a double replacement reaction?

Combustion Reactions

The burning of a candle and the burning of fuel in the engine of a car are examples of combustion reactions. In a **combustion reaction**, a carbon-containing compound, usually a fuel, burns in oxygen from the air to produce carbon dioxide (CO_2), water (H_2O), and energy in the form of heat or a flame. For example, methane gas (CH_4) undergoes combustion when used to cook our food on a gas cooktop and to heat our homes. In the equation for the combustion of methane, each element in the fuel (CH_4) forms a compound with oxygen.

$$CH_4(g) + 2O_2(g) \xrightarrow{\Delta} CO_2(g) + 2H_2O(g) + \text{energy}$$

Methane

The balanced equation for the combustion of propane (C_3H_8) is

$$C_3H_8(g) + 5O_2(g) \xrightarrow{\Delta} 3CO_2(g) + 4H_2O(g) + \text{energy}$$

In a combustion reaction, a candle burns using the oxygen in the air.

Propane is the fuel used in portable heaters and gas barbecues. Gasoline, a mixture of liquid hydrocarbons, is the fuel that powers our cars, lawn mowers, and snow blowers.

Table 7.3 summarizes the reaction types and gives examples.

TABLE 7.3 Summary of Reaction Types

Reaction Type	Example
Combination	
$A + B \longrightarrow AB$	$Ca(s) + Cl_2(g) \longrightarrow CaCl_2(s)$
Decomposition	
$AB \longrightarrow A + B$	$Fe_2S_3(s) \longrightarrow 2Fe(s) + 3S(s)$
Single Replacement	
$A + BC \longrightarrow AC + B$	$Cu(s) + 2AgNO_3(aq) \longrightarrow Cu(NO_3)_2(aq) + 2Ag(s)$
Double Replacement	
$AB + CD \longrightarrow AD + CB$	$BaCl_2(aq) + K_2SO_4(aq) \longrightarrow BaSO_4(s) + 2KCl(aq)$
Combustion	
$C_XH_Y + ZO_2(g) \xrightarrow{\Delta} XCO_2(g) + \frac{Y}{2}H_2O(g) + \text{energy}$	$CH_4(g) + 2O_2(g) \xrightarrow{\Delta} CO_2(g) + 2H_2O(g) + \text{energy}$

▶**SAMPLE PROBLEM 7.4** Identifying Reactions and Predicting Products

Classify each of the following as a combination, decomposition, single replacement, double replacement, or combustion reaction:

a. $2Fe_2O_3(s) + 3C(s) \longrightarrow 3CO_2(g) + 4Fe(s)$
b. $2KClO_3(s) \xrightarrow{\Delta} 2KCl(s) + 3O_2(g)$
c. $C_2H_4(g) + 3O_2(g) \xrightarrow{\Delta} 2CO_2(g) + 2H_2O(g) + \text{energy}$

SOLUTION

a. In this single replacement reaction, a C atom replaces Fe in Fe_2O_3 to form the compound CO_2 and Fe atoms.
b. When one reactant breaks down to produce two products, the reaction is decomposition.
c. The reaction of a carbon compound with oxygen to produce carbon dioxide, water, and energy makes this a combustion reaction.

STUDY CHECK 7.4

Nitrogen gas (N_2) and oxygen gas (O_2) react to form nitrogen dioxide gas. Write the balanced chemical equation using the correct chemical formulas of the reactants and product, and identify the reaction type.

ANSWER

$N_2(g) + 2O_2(g) \longrightarrow 2NO_2(g)$ combination

Chemistry Link to **Health**
Incomplete Combustion: Toxicity of Carbon Monoxide

When a propane heater, fireplace, or woodstove is used in a closed room, there must be adequate ventilation. If the supply of oxygen is limited, incomplete combustion from burning gas, oil, or wood produces carbon monoxide. The incomplete combustion of methane in natural gas is written

$$2CH_4(g) + 3O_2(g) \xrightarrow{\Delta} 2CO(g) + 4H_2O(g) + \text{heat}$$

(Limited oxygen supply / Carbon monoxide)

Carbon monoxide (CO) is a colorless, odorless, poisonous gas. When inhaled, CO passes into the bloodstream, where it attaches to hemoglobin, which reduces the amount of oxygen (O_2) reaching the cells.

As a result, a person can experience a reduction in exercise capability, visual perception, and manual dexterity.

Hemoglobin is the protein that transports O_2 in the blood. When the amount of hemoglobin bound to CO (COHb) is about 10%, a person may experience shortness of breath, mild headache, and drowsiness. Heavy smokers can have levels of COHb in their blood as high as 9%. When as much as 30% of the hemoglobin is bound to CO, a person may experience more severe symptoms, including dizziness, mental confusion, severe headache, and nausea. If 50% or more of the hemoglobin is bound to CO, a person could become unconscious and die if not treated immediately with oxygen.

QUESTIONS AND PROBLEMS

7.2 Types of Reactions

LEARNING GOAL Identify a reaction as a combination, decomposition, single replacement, double replacement, or combustion.

7.13 Classify each of the following as a combination, decomposition, single replacement, double replacement, or combustion reaction:
a. $2Al_2O_3(s) \xrightarrow{\Delta} 4Al(s) + 3O_2(g)$
b. $Br_2(g) + BaI_2(s) \longrightarrow BaBr_2(s) + I_2(g)$
c. $2C_2H_2(g) + 5O_2(g) \xrightarrow{\Delta} 4CO_2(g) + 2H_2O(g)$
d. $BaCl_2(aq) + K_2CO_3(aq) \longrightarrow BaCO_3(s) + 2KCl(aq)$
e. $Pb(s) + O_2(g) \longrightarrow PbO_2(s)$

7.14 Classify each of the following as a combination, decomposition, single replacement, double replacement, or combustion reaction:
a. $H_2(g) + Br_2(g) \longrightarrow 2HBr(g)$
b. $AgNO_3(aq) + NaCl(aq) \longrightarrow AgCl(s) + NaNO_3(aq)$
c. $2H_2O_2(aq) \longrightarrow 2H_2O(l) + O_2(g)$
d. $Zn(s) + CuCl_2(aq) \xrightarrow{\Delta} Cu(s) + ZnCl_2(aq)$
e. $C_5H_8(g) + 7O_2(g) \xrightarrow{\Delta} 5CO_2(g) + 4H_2O(g)$

7.15 Classify each of the following as a combination, decomposition, single replacement, double replacement, or combustion reaction:
a. $4Fe(s) + 3O_2(g) \longrightarrow 2Fe_2O_3(s)$
b. $Mg(s) + 2AgNO_3(aq) \longrightarrow Mg(NO_3)_2(aq) + 2Ag(s)$
c. $CuCO_3(s) \xrightarrow{\Delta} CuO(s) + CO_2(g)$

d. $Al_2(SO_4)_3(aq) + 6KOH(aq) \longrightarrow$
$$2Al(OH)_3(s) + 3K_2SO_4(aq)$$
e. $C_4H_8(g) + 6O_2(g) \xrightarrow{\Delta} 4CO_2(g) + 4H_2O(g)$

7.16 Classify each of the following as a combination, decomposition, single replacement, double replacement, or combustion reaction:
a. $CuO(s) + 2HCl(aq) \longrightarrow CuCl_2(aq) + H_2O(l)$
b. $2Al(s) + 3Br_2(g) \longrightarrow 2AlBr_3(s)$
c. $2C_2H_2(g) + 5O_2(g) \xrightarrow{\Delta} 4CO_2(g) + 2H_2O(g)$
d. $Fe_2O_3(s) + 3C(s) \longrightarrow 2Fe(s) + 3CO(g)$
e. $C_6H_{12}O_6(aq) \longrightarrow 2C_2H_6O(aq) + 2CO_2(g)$

7.17 Using Table 7.3, predict the products that would result from each of the following reactions and balance:
a. combination: $Mg(s) + Cl_2(g) \longrightarrow$
b. decomposition: $HBr(g) \longrightarrow$
c. single replacement: $Mg(s) + Zn(NO_3)_2(aq) \longrightarrow$
d. double replacement: $K_2S(aq) + Pb(NO_3)_2(aq) \longrightarrow$
e. combustion: $C_2H_6(g) + O_2(g) \xrightarrow{\Delta}$

7.18 Using Table 7.3, predict the products that would result from each of the following reactions and balance:
a. combination: $Ca(s) + O_2(g) \longrightarrow$
b. combustion: $C_6H_6(g) + O_2(g) \xrightarrow{\Delta}$
c. decomposition: $PbO_2(s) \xrightarrow{\Delta}$
d. single replacement: $KI(s) + Cl_2(g) \longrightarrow$
e. double replacement: $CuCl_2(aq) + Na_2S(aq) \longrightarrow$

LEARNING GOAL

Define the terms oxidation and reduction; identify the reactants oxidized and reduced.

Rust forms when the oxygen in the air reacts with iron.

7.3 Oxidation–Reduction Reactions

Perhaps you have never heard of an oxidation and reduction reaction. However, this type of reaction has many important applications in your everyday life. When you see a rusty nail, tarnish on a silver spoon, or corrosion on metal, you are observing oxidation.

$$4Fe(s) + 3O_2(g) \longrightarrow 2Fe_2O_3(s) \quad \text{Fe is oxidized}$$
Rust

When we turn the lights on in our automobiles, an oxidation–reduction reaction within the car battery provides the electricity. On a cold, wintry day, we might build a fire. As the wood burns, oxygen combines with carbon and hydrogen to produce carbon dioxide, water, and heat. In the previous section, we called this a combustion reaction, but it is also an *oxidation–reduction reaction*. When we eat foods with starches in them, the starches break down to give glucose, which is oxidized in our cells to give us energy along with carbon dioxide and water. Every breath we take provides oxygen to carry out oxidation in our cells.

$$C_6H_{12}O_6(aq) + 6O_2(g) \longrightarrow 6CO_2(g) + 6H_2O(l) + \text{energy}$$
Glucose

Oxidation–Reduction Reactions

In an **oxidation–reduction reaction** (*redox*), electrons are transferred from one substance to another. If one substance loses electrons, another substance must gain electrons. **Oxidation** is defined as the *loss* of electrons; **reduction** is the *gain* of electrons.

One way to remember these definitions is to use the following acronym:

OIL RIG

Oxidation **I**s **L**oss of electrons
Reduction **I**s **G**ain of electrons

Oxidation–Reduction

In general, atoms of metals lose electrons to form positive ions, whereas nonmetals gain electrons to form negative ions. Now we can say that metals are oxidized and nonmetals are reduced.

The green color that appears on copper surfaces from weathering, known as *patina*, is a mixture of $CuCO_3$ and CuO. We can now look at the oxidation and reduction reactions that take place when copper metal reacts with oxygen in the air to produce copper(II) oxide.

$$2Cu(s) + O_2(g) \longrightarrow 2CuO(s)$$

The element Cu in the reactants has a charge of 0, but in the CuO product, it is present as Cu^{2+}, which has a 2+ charge. Because the Cu atom lost two electrons, the charge is more positive. This means that Cu was oxidized in the reaction.

$$Cu^0(s) \longrightarrow Cu^{2+}(s) + 2\,e^- \quad \text{Oxidation: loss of electrons by Cu}$$

At the same time, the element O in the reactants has a charge of 0, but in the CuO product, it is present as O^{2-}, which has a 2− charge. Because the O atom has gained two electrons, the charge is more negative. This means that O was reduced in the reaction.

$$O_2^0(g) + 4\,e^- \longrightarrow 2O^{2-}(s) \quad \text{Reduction: gain of electrons by O}$$

Thus, the overall equation for the formation of CuO involves an oxidation and a reduction that occur simultaneously. In every oxidation and reduction, the number of electrons lost must be equal to the number of electrons gained. Therefore, we multiply the oxidation reaction of Cu by 2. Canceling the $4\,e^-$ on each side, we obtain the overall oxidation–reduction equation for the formation of CuO.

$$2Cu(s) \longrightarrow 2Cu^{2+}(s) + \cancel{4\,e^-} \quad \text{Oxidation}$$
$$O_2(g) + \cancel{4\,e^-} \longrightarrow 2O^{2-}(s) \quad \text{Reduction}$$
$$\overline{2Cu(s) + O_2(g) \longrightarrow 2CuO(s)} \quad \text{Oxidation–reduction equation}$$

As we see in the next reaction between zinc and copper(II) sulfate, there is always an oxidation with every reduction (see Figure 7.7).

$$Zn(s) + CuSO_4(aq) \longrightarrow ZnSO_4(aq) + Cu(s)$$

We rewrite the equation to show the atoms and ions.

$$\mathbf{Zn}(s) + \mathbf{Cu^{2+}}(aq) + SO_4{}^{2-}(aq) \longrightarrow Zn^{2+}(aq) + SO_4{}^{2-}(aq) + \mathbf{Cu}(s)$$

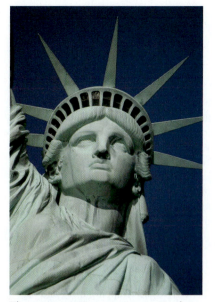

The green patina on copper is due to oxidation.

Reduced		Oxidized
Na	Oxidation: Lose e^- →	$Na^+ + e^-$
Ca		$Ca^{2+} + 2\,e^-$
$2Br^-$		$Br_2 + 2\,e^-$
Fe^{2+}	← Reduction: Gain e^-	$Fe^{3+} + e^-$

Oxidation is a loss of electrons; reduction is a gain of electrons.

⊗ CORE CHEMISTRY SKILL

Identifying Oxidized and Reduced Substances

Solution of Cu^{2+} and $SO_4{}^{2-}$

Zn strip

Cu^{2+} ion

Zn^0

$Zn^0 \longrightarrow Zn^{2+}$

$2\,e^-$

$Cu^{2+} \longrightarrow Cu^0$

Zn^0

Zn^{2+} ion

Cu^0

Zn^0

$Cu(s)$

FIGURE 7.7 ▶ In this single replacement reaction, Zn(s) is oxidized to $Zn^{2+}(aq)$ when it provides two electrons to reduce $Cu^{2+}(aq)$ to Cu(s):

$$Zn(s) + Cu^{2+}(aq) \longrightarrow Cu(s) + Zn^{2+}(aq)$$

 In the oxidation, does Zn(s) lose or gain electrons?

Explore Your World

Oxidation of Fruits and Vegetables

Freshly cut surfaces of fruits and vegetables discolor when exposed to oxygen in the air. Cut three slices of a fruit or vegetable such as apple, potato, avocado, or banana. Leave one piece on the kitchen counter (uncovered). Wrap one piece in plastic wrap and leave it on the kitchen counter. Dip one piece in lemon juice and leave it uncovered.

Questions

1. What changes take place in each sample after 1 to 2 h?
2. Why would wrapping fruits and vegetables slow the rate of discoloration?
3. If lemon juice contains vitamin C (an antioxidant), why would dipping a fruit or vegetable in lemon juice affect the oxidation reaction on the surface of the fruit or vegetable?
4. Other kinds of antioxidants are vitamin E, citric acid, and BHT. Look for these antioxidants on the labels of cereals, potato chips, and other foods in your kitchen. Why are antioxidants added to food products that will be stored on our kitchen shelves?

In this reaction, Zn atoms lose two electrons to form Zn^{2+}. The increase in positive charge indicates that Zn is oxidized. At the same time, Cu^{2+} gains two electrons. The decrease in charge indicates that Cu is reduced. The SO_4^{2-} ions are *spectator ions*, which are present in both the reactants and products and do not change.

$$Zn(s) \longrightarrow Zn^{2+}(aq) + 2\,e^- \quad \text{Oxidation of Zn}$$

$$Cu^{2+}(aq) + 2\,e^- \longrightarrow Cu(s) \quad \text{Reduction of } Cu^{2+}$$

In this single replacement reaction, zinc was oxidized and copper(II) ion was reduced.

Oxidation and Reduction in Biological Systems

Oxidation may also involve the addition of oxygen or the loss of hydrogen, and reduction may involve the loss of oxygen or the gain of hydrogen. In the cells of the body, oxidation of organic (carbon) compounds involves the transfer of hydrogen atoms (H), which are composed of electrons and protons. For example, the oxidation of a typical biochemical molecule can involve the transfer of two hydrogen atoms (or $2H^+$ and $2\,e^-$) to a hydrogen ion acceptor such as the coenzyme FAD (flavin adenine dinucleotide). The coenzyme is reduced to $FADH_2$.

In many biochemical oxidation–reduction reactions, the transfer of hydrogen atoms is necessary for the production of energy in the cells. For example, methyl alcohol (CH_3OH), a poisonous substance, is metabolized in the body by the following reactions:

$$CH_3OH \longrightarrow H_2CO + 2H \quad \text{Oxidation: loss of H atoms}$$
Methyl alcohol   Formaldehyde

The formaldehyde can be oxidized further, this time by the addition of oxygen, to produce formic acid.

$$2H_2CO + O_2 \longrightarrow 2H_2CO_2 \quad \text{Oxidation: addition of O atoms}$$
Formaldehyde   Formic acid

Finally, formic acid is oxidized to carbon dioxide and water.

$$2H_2CO_2 + O_2 \longrightarrow 2CO_2 + 2H_2O \quad \text{Oxidation: addition of O atoms}$$
Formic acid

The intermediate products of the oxidation of methyl alcohol are quite toxic, causing blindness and possibly death as they interfere with key reactions in the cells of the body.

In summary, we find that the particular definition of oxidation and reduction we use depends on the process that occurs in the reaction. All these definitions are summarized in Table 7.4. Oxidation always involves a loss of electrons, but it may also be seen as an addition of oxygen or the loss of hydrogen atoms. A reduction always involves a gain of electrons and may also be seen as the loss of oxygen or the gain of hydrogen.

TABLE 7.4 Characteristics of Oxidation and Reduction

Always Involves	May Involve
Oxidation	
Loss of electrons	Addition of oxygen
	Loss of hydrogen
Reduction	
Gain of electrons	Loss of oxygen
	Gain of hydrogen

QUESTIONS AND PROBLEMS

7.3 Oxidation–Reduction Reactions

LEARNING GOAL Define the terms oxidation and reduction; identify the reactants oxidized and reduced.

7.19 Identify each of the following as an oxidation or a reduction:
a. $Na^+(aq) + e^- \longrightarrow Na(s)$
b. $Ni(s) \longrightarrow Ni^{2+}(aq) + 2\,e^-$
c. $Cr^{3+}(aq) + 3\,e^- \longrightarrow Cr(s)$
d. $2H^+(aq) + 2\,e^- \longrightarrow H_2(g)$

7.20 Identify each of the following as an oxidation or a reduction:
a. $O_2(g) + 4\,e^- \longrightarrow 2O^{2-}(aq)$
b. $Ag(s) \longrightarrow Ag^+(aq) + e^-$
c. $Fe^{3+}(aq) + e^- \longrightarrow Fe^{2+}(aq)$
d. $2Br^-(aq) \longrightarrow Br_2(l) + 2\,e^-$

7.21 In each of the following reactions, identify the reactant that is oxidized and the reactant that is reduced:
a. $Zn(s) + Cl_2(g) \longrightarrow ZnCl_2(s)$
b. $Cl_2(g) + 2NaBr(aq) \longrightarrow 2NaCl(aq) + Br_2(l)$
c. $2PbO(s) \longrightarrow 2Pb(s) + O_2(g)$
d. $2Fe^{3+}(aq) + Sn^{2+}(aq) \longrightarrow 2Fe^{2+}(aq) + Sn^{4+}(aq)$

7.22 In each of the following reactions, identify the reactant that is oxidized and the reactant that is reduced:
a. $2Li(s) + F_2(g) \longrightarrow 2LiF(s)$
b. $Cl_2(g) + 2KI(aq) \longrightarrow 2KCl(aq) + I_2(s)$
c. $2Al(s) + 3Sn^{2+}(aq) \longrightarrow 2Al^{3+}(aq) + 3Sn(s)$
d. $Fe(s) + CuSO_4(aq) \longrightarrow FeSO_4(aq) + Cu(s)$

Rx Clinical Applications

7.23 In the mitochondria of human cells, energy is provided by the oxidation and reduction reactions of the iron ions in the cytochromes in electron transport. Identify each of the following reactions as an oxidation or reduction:
a. $Fe^{3+} + e^- \longrightarrow Fe^{2+}$ **b.** $Fe^{2+} \longrightarrow Fe^{3+} + e^-$

7.24 Chlorine (Cl_2) is a strong germicide used to disinfect drinking water and to kill microbes in swimming pools. If the product is Cl^-, was the elemental chlorine oxidized or reduced?

7.25 When linoleic acid, an unsaturated fatty acid, reacts with hydrogen, it forms a saturated fatty acid. Is linoleic acid oxidized or reduced in the hydrogenation reaction?
$$C_{18}H_{32}O_2 + 2H_2 \longrightarrow C_{18}H_{36}O_2$$
Linoleic acid

7.26 In one of the reactions in the citric acid cycle, which provides energy, succinic acid is converted to fumaric acid.
$$C_4H_6O_4 \longrightarrow C_4H_4O_4 + 2H$$
Succinic acid   Fumaric acid

The reaction is accompanied by a coenzyme, flavin adenine dinucleotide (FAD).
$$FAD + 2H \longrightarrow FADH_2$$
a. Is succinic acid oxidized or reduced?
b. Is FAD oxidized or reduced?
c. Why would the two reactions occur together?

7.4 The Mole

At the grocery store, you buy eggs by the dozen or soda by the case. In an office-supply store, pencils are ordered by the gross and paper by the ream. The terms *dozen*, *case*, *gross*, and *ream* are used to count the number of items present. For example, when you buy a dozen eggs, you know that there will be 12 eggs in the carton.

LEARNING GOAL

Use Avogadro's number to determine the number of particles in a given number of moles.

24 cans = 1 case

144 pencils = 1 gross

500 sheets = 1 ream

12 eggs = 1 dozen

Collections of items include dozen, case, gross, and ream.

Avogadro's Number

In chemistry, particles such as atoms, molecules, and ions are counted by the **mole**, which contains 6.02×10^{23} items. This value, known as **Avogadro's number**, is a very big number because atoms are so small that it takes an extremely large number of atoms to provide a sufficient amount to weigh and use in chemical reactions. Avogadro's number is named for Amedeo Avogadro (1776–1856), an Italian physicist.

⚛ CORE CHEMISTRY SKILL

Converting Particles to Moles

One mole of sulfur contains 6.02×10^{23} sulfur atoms.

Avogadro's number

$$602\ 000\ 000\ 000\ 000\ 000\ 000\ 000\ 000 = 6.02 \times 10^{23}$$

One mole of any element always contains Avogadro's number of atoms. For example, 1 mole of carbon contains 6.02×10^{23} carbon atoms; 1 mole of aluminum contains 6.02×10^{23} aluminum atoms; 1 mole of sulfur contains 6.02×10^{23} sulfur atoms.

$$1 \text{ mole of an element} = 6.02 \times 10^{23} \text{ atoms of that element}$$

Avogadro's number tells us that one mole of a compound contains 6.02×10^{23} of the particular type of particles that make up that compound. One mole of a molecular compound contains Avogadro's number of molecules. For example, 1 mole of CO_2 contains 6.02×10^{23} molecules of CO_2. One mole of an ionic compound contains Avogadro's number of **formula units**, which are the groups of ions represented by the formula of an ionic compound. One mole of NaCl contains 6.02×10^{23} formula units of NaCl (Na^+, Cl^-). Table 7.5 gives examples of the number of particles in some 1-mole quantities.

TABLE 7.5 Number of Particles in 1-Mole Samples

Substance	Number and Type of Particles
1 mole of Al	6.02×10^{23} atoms of Al
1 mole of S	6.02×10^{23} atoms of S
1 mole of water (H_2O)	6.02×10^{23} molecules of H_2O
1 mole of vitamin C ($C_6H_8O_6$)	6.02×10^{23} molecules of vitamin C
1 mole of NaCl	6.02×10^{23} formula units of NaCl

We use Avogadro's number as a conversion factor to convert between the moles of a substance and the number of particles it contains.

$$\frac{6.02 \times 10^{23} \text{ particles}}{1 \text{ mole}} \quad \text{and} \quad \frac{1 \text{ mole}}{6.02 \times 10^{23} \text{ particles}}$$

For example, we use Avogadro's number to convert 4.00 moles of sulfur to atoms of sulfur.

$$4.00 \text{ moles S} \times \frac{6.02 \times 10^{23} \text{ atoms S}}{1 \text{ mole S}} = 2.41 \times 10^{24} \text{ atoms of S}$$
Avogadro's number as a conversion factor

We also use Avogadro's number to convert 3.01×10^{24} molecules of CO_2 to moles of CO_2.

$$3.01 \times 10^{24} \text{ molecules } CO_2 \times \frac{1 \text{ mole } CO_2}{6.02 \times 10^{23} \text{ molecules } CO_2} = 5.00 \text{ moles of } CO_2$$
Avogadro's number as a conversion factor

In calculations that convert between moles and particles, the number of moles will be a small number compared to the number of atoms or molecules, which will be large.

SAMPLE PROBLEM 7.5 Calculating the Number of Molecules

How many molecules are present in 1.75 moles of carbon dioxide, CO_2?

CO₂ molecules

The solid form of carbon dioxide is known as "dry ice."

SOLUTION

STEP **1** State the given and needed quantities.

ANALYZE THE PROBLEM	Given	Need
	1.75 moles of CO_2	molecules of CO_2

STEP **2** Write a plan to convert moles to atoms or molecules.

moles of CO_2 — Avogadro's number — molecules of CO_2

STEP **3** Use Avogadro's number to write conversion factors.

$$1 \text{ mole of } CO_2 = 6.02 \times 10^{23} \text{ molecules of } CO_2$$

$$\frac{6.02 \times 10^{23} \text{ molecules } CO_2}{1 \text{ mole } CO_2} \quad \text{and} \quad \frac{1 \text{ mole } CO_2}{6.02 \times 10^{23} \text{ molecules } CO_2}$$

STEP **4** Set up the problem to calculate the number of particles.

$$1.75 \text{ moles } CO_2 \times \frac{6.02 \times 10^{23} \text{ molecules } CO_2}{1 \text{ mole } CO_2} = 1.05 \times 10^{24} \text{ molecules of } CO_2$$

STUDY CHECK 7.5

How many moles of water, H_2O, contain 2.60×10^{23} molecules of water?

ANSWER

0.432 mole of H_2O

Guide to Calculating the Atoms or Molecules of a Substance

STEP **1** State the given and needed quantities.

STEP **2** Write a plan to convert moles to atoms or molecules.

STEP **3** Use Avogadro's number to write conversion factors.

STEP **4** Set up the problem to calculate the number of particles.

Moles of Elements in a Chemical Formula

We have seen that the subscripts in the chemical formula of a compound indicate the number of atoms of each type of element in the compound. For example, aspirin, $C_9H_8O_4$, is a drug used to reduce pain and inflammation in the body. Using the subscripts in the chemical formula of aspirin shows that there are 9 carbon atoms, 8 hydrogen atoms, and 4 oxygen atoms in each molecule of aspirin. The subscripts also tell us the number of moles of each element in 1 mole of aspirin: 9 moles of C atoms, 8 moles of H atoms, and 4 moles of O atoms.

Aspirin $C_9H_8O_4$

Number of atoms in 1 molecule
Carbon (C)   Hydrogen (H)   Oxygen (O)

The chemical formula subscripts specify the $C_9H_8O_4$

	Carbon	Hydrogen	Oxygen
Atoms in 1 molecule	9 atoms of C	8 atoms of H	4 atoms of O
Moles of each element in 1 mole	9 moles of C	8 moles of H	4 moles of O

Using the subscripts from the formula, $C_9H_8O_4$, we can write the conversion factors for each of the elements in 1 mole of aspirin.

$$\frac{9 \text{ moles C}}{1 \text{ mole } C_9H_8O_4} \qquad \frac{8 \text{ moles H}}{1 \text{ mole } C_9H_8O_4} \qquad \frac{4 \text{ moles O}}{1 \text{ mole } C_9H_8O_4}$$

$$\frac{1 \text{ mole } C_9H_8O_4}{9 \text{ moles C}} \qquad \frac{1 \text{ mole } C_9H_8O_4}{8 \text{ moles H}} \qquad \frac{1 \text{ mole } C_9H_8O_4}{4 \text{ moles O}}$$

Guide to Calculating the Moles of an Element in a Compound

STEP 1
State the given and needed quantities.

STEP 2
Write a plan to convert moles of compound to moles of an element.

STEP 3
Write equalities and conversion factors using subscripts.

STEP 4
Set up the problem to calculate the moles of an element.

The compound propyl acetate provides the odor and taste of pears.

SAMPLE PROBLEM 7.6 Calculating the Moles of an Element in a Compound

Propyl acetate, $C_5H_{10}O_2$, gives the odor and taste to pears. How many moles of C are present in 1.50 moles of propyl acetate?

SOLUTION

STEP 1 State the given and needed quantities.

ANALYZE THE PROBLEM	Given	Need
	1.50 moles of propyl acetate, chemical formula $C_5H_{10}O_2$	moles of C

STEP 2 Write a plan to convert moles of compound to moles of an element.

moles of $C_5H_{10}O_2$ →Subscript→ moles of C atoms

STEP 3 Write equalities and conversion factors using subscripts.

$$1 \text{ mole of } C_5H_{10}O_2 = 5 \text{ moles of C}$$

$$\frac{5 \text{ moles C}}{1 \text{ mole } C_5H_{10}O_2} \quad \text{and} \quad \frac{1 \text{ mole } C_5H_{10}O_2}{5 \text{ moles C}}$$

STEP 4 Set up the problem to calculate the moles of an element.

$$1.50 \text{ moles } C_5H_{10}O_2 \times \frac{5 \text{ moles C}}{1 \text{ mole } C_5H_{10}O_2} = 7.50 \text{ moles of C}$$

STUDY CHECK 7.6

How many moles of propyl acetate, $C_5H_{10}O_2$, contain 0.480 mole of O?

ANSWER

0.240 mole of propyl acetate

QUESTIONS AND PROBLEMS

7.4 The Mole

LEARNING GOAL Use Avogadro's number to determine the number of particles in a given number of moles.

7.27 What is a mole?

7.28 What is Avogadro's number?

7.29 Calculate each of the following:
    a. number of C atoms in 0.500 mole of C
    b. number of SO_2 molecules in 1.28 moles of SO_2
    c. moles of Fe in 5.22×10^{22} atoms of Fe
    d. moles of C_2H_6O in 8.50×10^{24} molecules of C_2H_6O

7.30 Calculate each of the following:
    a. number of Li atoms in 4.5 moles of Li
    b. number of CO_2 molecules in 0.0180 mole of CO_2
    c. moles of Cu in 7.8×10^{21} atoms of Cu
    d. moles of C_2H_6 in 3.75×10^{23} molecules of C_2H_6

7.31 Calculate each of the following quantities in 2.00 moles of H_3PO_4:
    a. moles of H   **b.** moles of O
    c. atoms of P   **d.** atoms of O

7.32 Calculate each of the following quantities in 0.185 mole of $C_6H_{14}O$:
   a. moles of C
   b. moles of O
   c. atoms of H
   d. atoms of C

Rx Clinical Applications

7.33 Quinine, $C_{20}H_{24}N_2O_2$, is a component of tonic water and bitter lemon.
   a. How many moles of H are in 1.0 mole of quinine?
   b. How many moles of C are in 5.0 moles of quinine?
   c. How many moles of N are in 0.020 mole of quinine?

7.34 Aluminum sulfate, $Al_2(SO_4)_3$, is used in some antiperspirants.
   a. How many moles of S are present in 3.0 moles of $Al_2(SO_4)_3$?
   b. How many moles of aluminum ions (Al^{3+}) are present in 0.40 mole of $Al_2(SO_4)_3$?
   c. How many moles of sulfate ions (SO_4^{2-}) are present in 1.5 moles of $Al_2(SO_4)_3$?

7.35 Naproxen is used to treat the pain and inflammation caused by arthritis. Naproxen has a formula of $C_{14}H_{14}O_3$.
   a. How many moles of C are present in 2.30 moles of naproxen?
   b. How many moles of H are present in 0.444 mole of naproxen?

c. How many moles of O are present in 0.0765 mole of naproxen?

Naproxen is used to treat pain and inflammation caused by arthritis.

7.36 Benadryl is an over-the-counter drug used to treat allergy symptoms. The formula of benadryl is $C_{17}H_{21}NO$.
   a. How many moles of C are present in 0.733 mole of benadryl?
   b. How many moles of H are present in 2.20 moles of benadryl?
   c. How many moles of N are present in 1.54 moles of benadryl?

7.5 Molar Mass and Calculations

LEARNING GOAL

Calculate the molar mass for a substance given its chemical formula; use molar mass to convert between grams and moles.

A single atom or molecule is much too small to weigh, even on the most accurate balance. In fact, it takes a huge number of atoms or molecules to make enough of a substance for you to see. An amount of water that contains Avogadro's number of water molecules is only a few sips. In the laboratory, we can use a balance to weigh out Avogadro's number of particles or 1 mole of a substance.

For any element, the quantity called **molar mass** is the quantity in grams that equals the atomic mass of that element. We are counting 6.02×10^{23} atoms of an element when we weigh out the number of grams equal to its molar mass. For example, carbon has an atomic mass of 12.01 on the periodic table. This means 1 mole of carbon atoms has a mass of 12.01 g. Then to obtain 1 mole of carbon atoms, we would weigh out 12.01 g of carbon. The molar mass of carbon is found by looking at its atomic mass on the periodic table.

6.02×10^{23} atoms of C

1 mole of C atoms

12.01 g of C atoms

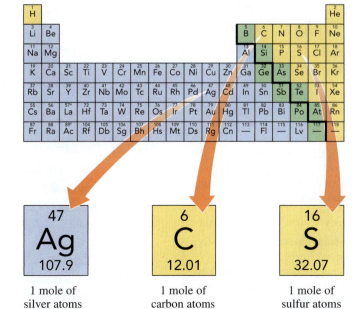

1 mole of silver atoms has a mass of 107.9 g

1 mole of carbon atoms has a mass of 12.01 g

1 mole of sulfur atoms has a mass of 32.07 g

Calculating Molar Mass

Lithium carbonate is used to treat bipolar disorder.

Guide to Calculating Molar Mass

STEP 1
Obtain the molar mass of each element.

STEP 2
Multiply each molar mass by the number of moles (subscript) in the formula.

STEP 3
Calculate the molar mass by adding the masses of the elements.

 Explore Your World

Calculating Moles in the Kitchen

The labels on food products list the components in grams and milligrams. It is possible to convert those values to moles, which is also interesting. Read the labels of some products in the kitchen and convert the amounts given in grams or milligrams to moles using molar mass. Here are some examples.

Questions

1. How many moles of NaCl are in a box of salt?
2. How many moles of sugar are contained in a 5-lb bag of sugar if sugar has the formula $C_{12}H_{22}O_{11}$?
3. A serving of cereal contains 90 mg of potassium. If there are 11 servings of cereal in the box, how many moles of K^+ are present in the cereal in the box?

The molar mass of an element is useful to convert moles of an element to grams, or grams to moles. For example, 1 mole of sulfur has a mass of 32.07 g. We can express the molar mass of sulfur as an equality

$$1 \text{ mole of S} = 32.07 \text{ g of S}$$

From this equality, two conversion factors can be written as

$$\frac{32.07 \text{ g S}}{1 \text{ mole S}} \quad \text{and} \quad \frac{1 \text{ mole S}}{32.07 \text{ g S}}$$

Molar Mass of a Compound

To calculate the molar mass for a compound, we multiply the molar mass of each element by its subscript in the formula, and add the results as shown in Sample Problem 7.7.

▶ **SAMPLE PROBLEM 7.7   Calculating the Molar Mass for a Compound**

Calculate the molar mass for lithium carbonate, Li_2CO_3, used to treat bipolar disorder.

SOLUTION

ANALYZE THE PROBLEM	Given	Need
	formula Li_2CO_3	molar mass of Li_2CO_3

STEP 1 Obtain the molar mass of each element.

$\dfrac{6.941 \text{ g Li}}{1 \text{ mole Li}}$	$\dfrac{12.01 \text{ g C}}{1 \text{ mole C}}$	$\dfrac{16.00 \text{ g O}}{1 \text{ mole O}}$

STEP 2 Multiply each molar mass by the number of moles (subscript) in the formula.

Grams from 2 moles of Li:

$$2 \text{ moles Li} \times \frac{6.941 \text{ g Li}}{1 \text{ mole Li}} = 13.88 \text{ g of Li}$$

Grams from 1 mole of C:

$$1 \text{ mole C} \times \frac{12.01 \text{ g C}}{1 \text{ mole C}} = 12.01 \text{ g of C}$$

Grams from 3 moles of O:

$$3 \text{ moles O} \times \frac{16.00 \text{ g O}}{1 \text{ mole O}} = 48.00 \text{ g of O}$$

STEP 3 Calculate the molar mass by adding the masses of the elements.

2 moles of Li	=	13.88 g of Li
1 mole of C	=	12.01 g of C
3 moles of O	=	+48.00 g of O
Molar mass of Li_2CO_3	=	73.89 g

STUDY CHECK 7.7

Calculate the molar mass for salicylic acid, $C_7H_6O_3$, used to treat skin conditions such as acne, psoriasis, and dandruff.

ANSWER

138.12 g

Figure 7.8 shows some 1-mole quantities of substances. Table 7.6 lists the molar mass for several 1-mole samples.

1-Mole Quantities

| S | Fe | NaCl | $K_2Cr_2O_7$ | $C_{12}H_{22}O_{11}$ |

FIGURE 7.8 ▶ 1-mole samples: sulfur, S (32.07 g); iron, Fe (55.85 g); salt, NaCl (58.44 g); potassium dichromate, $K_2Cr_2O_7$ (294.2 g); and sucrose, $C_{12}H_{22}O_{11}$ (342.3 g).

🅠 How is the molar mass for $K_2Cr_2O_7$ obtained?

Calculations Using Molar Mass

We can now change from moles to grams, or grams to moles, using the conversion factors derived from the molar mass as shown in Sample Problem 7.8. (Remember, you must determine the molar mass of the substance first.)

▶**SAMPLE PROBLEM 7.8** Converting Moles of an Element to Grams

Silver metal is used in the manufacture of tableware, mirrors, jewelry, and dental alloys. If the design for a piece of jewelry requires 0.750 mole of silver, how many grams of silver are needed?

SOLUTION

STEP 1 State the given and needed quantities.

ANALYZE THE PROBLEM	Given	Need
	0.750 mole of Ag	grams of Ag

STEP 2 Write a plan to convert moles to grams.

moles of Ag │ Molar mass factor ⟩ grams of Ag

STEP 3 Determine the molar mass and write conversion factors.

$$1 \text{ mole of Ag } = 107.9 \text{ g of Ag}$$
$$\frac{107.9 \text{ g Ag}}{1 \text{ mole Ag}} \quad \text{and} \quad \frac{1 \text{ mole Ag}}{107.9 \text{ g Ag}}$$

TABLE 7.6 The Molar Mass of Selected Elements and Compounds

Substance	Molar Mass
1 mole of C	12.01 g
1 mole of Na	22.99 g
1 mole of Fe	55.85 g
1 mole of NaF	41.99 g
1 mole of $C_6H_{12}O_6$ (glucose)	180.16 g
1 mole of $C_8H_{10}N_4O_2$ (caffeine)	194.20 g

⚛ **CORE CHEMISTRY SKILL**

Using Molar Mass as a Conversion Factor

Silver metal is used to make jewelry.

Guide to Calculating the Moles (or Grams) of a Substance from Grams (or Moles)

STEP 1
State the given and needed quantities.

STEP 2
Write a plan to convert moles to grams (or grams to moles).

STEP 3
Determine the molar mass and write conversion factors.

STEP 4
Set up the problem to convert moles to grams (or grams to moles).

STEP 4 Set up the problem to convert moles to grams. Calculate the grams of silver using the molar mass factor that cancels mole Ag.

$$0.750 \text{ mole Ag} \times \frac{107.9 \text{ g Ag}}{1 \text{ mole Ag}} = 80.9 \text{ g of Ag}$$

STUDY CHECK 7.8

A dentist orders gold to prepare dental crowns and fillings. Calculate the number of grams of gold (Au) present in 0.124 mole of gold.

ANSWER

24.4 g of Au

The conversion factors for a compound are also written from the molar mass. For example, the molar mass of the compound H_2O is written

1 mole of H_2O = 18.02 g of H_2O

From this equality, conversion factors for the molar mass of H_2O are written as

$$\frac{18.02 \text{ g } H_2O}{1 \text{ mole } H_2O} \quad \text{and} \quad \frac{1 \text{ mole } H_2O}{18.02 \text{ g } H_2O}$$

Table salt is sodium chloride, NaCl.

▶ **SAMPLE PROBLEM 7.9** Converting the Mass of a Compound to Moles

A box of salt contains 737 g of NaCl. How many moles of NaCl are present?

SOLUTION

STEP 1 State the given and needed quantities.

ANALYZE THE PROBLEM	Given	Need
	737 g of NaCl	moles of NaCl

STEP 2 Write a plan to convert grams to moles.

grams of NaCl → Molar mass factor → moles of NaCl

STEP 3 Determine the molar mass and write conversion factors.

$(1 \times 22.99) + (1 \times 35.45) = 58.44$ g/mole

$$1 \text{ mole of NaCl} = 58.44 \text{ g of NaCl}$$
$$\frac{58.44 \text{ g NaCl}}{1 \text{ mole NaCl}} \quad \text{and} \quad \frac{1 \text{ mole NaCl}}{58.44 \text{ g NaCl}}$$

STEP 4 Set up the problem to convert grams to moles.

$$737 \text{ g NaCl} \times \frac{1 \text{ mole NaCl}}{58.44 \text{ g NaCl}} = 12.6 \text{ moles of NaCl}$$

STUDY CHECK 7.9

One tablet of an antacid contains 680. mg of $CaCO_3$. How many moles of $CaCO_3$ are present?

ANSWER

0.00679 mole of $CaCO_3$

We can summarize the calculations to show the connections between the moles of a compound, its mass in grams, number of molecules (or formula units if ionic), and the moles and atoms of each element in that compound in the following flowchart:

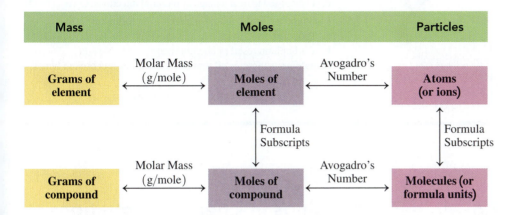

QUESTIONS AND PROBLEMS

7.5 Molar Mass and Calculations

LEARNING GOAL Calculate the molar mass for a substance given its chemical formula; use molar mass to convert between grams and moles.

7.37 Calculate the molar mass for each of the following:
 a. $KC_4H_5O_6$ (cream of tartar)
 b. Fe_2O_3 (rust)
 c. $Al_2(SO_4)_3$ (antiperspirant)
 d. $Mg(OH)_2$ (antacid)

7.38 Calculate the molar mass for each of the following:
 a. $FeSO_4$ (iron supplement)
 b. Al_2O_3 (absorbent and abrasive)
 c. $C_7H_5NO_3S$ (saccharin)
 d. $(NH_4)_2CO_3$ (baking powder)

7.39 Calculate the molar mass for each of the following:
 a. Cl_2 b. $C_3H_6O_3$
 c. $Mg_3(PO_4)_2$ d. AlF_3

7.40 Calculate the molar mass for each of the following:
 a. O_2 b. KH_2PO_4
 c. $Fe(ClO_4)_3$ d. $C_4H_8O_4$

7.41 Calculate the mass, in grams, for each of the following:
 a. 2.00 moles of Na   b. 2.80 moles of Ca
 c. 0.125 mole of Sn   d. 1.76 moles of Cu

7.42 Calculate the mass, in grams, for each of the following:
 a. 1.50 moles of K   b. 2.5 moles of C
 c. 0.25 mole of P   d. 12.5 moles of He

7.43 Calculate the number of grams in each of the following:
 a. 0.500 mole of NaCl   b. 1.75 moles of Na_2O
 c. 0.225 mole of H_2O d. 4.42 moles of CO_2

7.44 Calculate the number of grams in each of the following:
 a. 2.0 moles of $MgCl_2$ b. 3.5 moles of C_6H_6
 c. 5.00 moles of C_2H_6O d. 0.488 mole of $C_3H_6O_3$

7.45 How many moles are contained in each of the following?
 a. 50.0 g of Ag   b. 0.200 g of C
 c. 15.0 g of NH_3 d. 75.0 g of SO_2

7.46 How many moles are contained in each of the following?
 a. 25.0 g of Ca   b. 5.00 g of S
 c. 40.0 g of H_2O d. 100.0 g of O_2

7.47 Calculate the number of moles in 25.0 g of each of the following:
 a. Ne   b. O_2
 c. $Al(OH)_3$ d. Ga_2S_3

7.48 Calculate the number of moles in 4.00 g of each of the following:
 a. He   b. SnO_2
 c. $Cr(OH)_3$ d. Ca_3N_2

7.49 How many moles of S are in each of the following quantities?
 a. 25 g of S   b. 125 g of SO_2 c. 2.0 moles of Al_2S_3

7.50 How many moles of C are in each of the following quantities?
 a. 75 g of C   b. 0.25 mole of C_2H_6 c. 88 g of CO_2

℞ Clinical Applications

7.51 a. The compound $MgSO_4$, Epsom salts, is used to soothe sore feet and muscles. How many grams will you need to prepare a bath containing 5.00 moles of Epsom salts?
 b. Potassium iodide, KI, is used as an expectorant. How many grams of KI are in 0.450 mole of KI?

7.52 a. Cyclopropane, C_3H_6, is an anesthetic given by inhalation. How many grams are in 0.25 mole of cyclopropane?
 b. The sedative Demerol hydrochloride has the formula $C_{15}H_{22}ClNO_2$. How many grams are in 0.025 mole of Demerol hydrochloride?

7.53 Dinitrogen oxide (or nitrous oxide), N_2O, also known as laughing gas, is widely used as an anesthetic in dentistry.
 a. How many grams of the compound are in 1.50 moles of N_2O?
 b. How many moles of the compound are in 34.0 g of N_2O?
 c. How many grams of N are in 34.0 g of N_2O?

7.54 Allyl sulfide, $C_6H_{10}S$, is the substance that gives garlic, onions, and leeks their characteristic odor. Some studies indicate that garlic may be beneficial for the heart and in lowering cholesterol.
a. How many moles of H are in 0.75 mole of $C_6H_{10}S$?
b. How many moles of S are in 23.2 g of $C_6H_{10}S$?
c. How many grams of C are in 44.0 g of $C_6H_{10}S$?

The characteristic odor of garlic is a sulfur-containing compound.

7.55 Calculate the molar mass for each of the following:
a. Paxil, an antidepressant, $C_{19}H_{20}FNO_3$
b. calcium citrate, a calcium supplement, $Ca_3C_{12}H_{10}O_{14}$
c. rubbing alcohol, C_3H_8O
d. Cipro, used to treat a range of bacterial infections, $C_{17}H_{18}FN_3O_3$

7.56 Calculate the molar mass for each of the following:
a. Propofol, used to induce anesthesia during surgery, $C_{12}H_{18}O$
b. Carboplatin, used in chemotherapy, $C_6H_{12}N_2O_4Pt$
c. calcium sulfate, used to make casts to protect broken bones, $CaSO_4$
d. Amoxicillin, an antibiotic, $C_{16}H_{19}N_3O_5S$

Given a quantity in moles of reactant or product, use a mole–mole factor from the balanced chemical equation to calculate the number of moles of another substance in the reaction.

7.6 Mole Relationships in Chemical Equations

In any chemical reaction, the total amount of matter in the reactants is equal to the total amount of matter in the products. Thus, the total mass of all the reactants must be equal to the total mass of all the products. This is known as the *law of conservation of mass*, which states that there is no change in the total mass of the substances reacting in a chemical reaction. Thus, no material is lost or gained as original substances are changed to new substances.

For example, tarnish (Ag_2S) forms when silver reacts with sulfur to form silver sulfide.

$$2Ag(s) + S(s) \longrightarrow Ag_2S(s)$$

$$2Ag(s) \qquad + \qquad S(s) \qquad \longrightarrow \qquad Ag_2S(s)$$

Mass of reactants $\qquad = \qquad$ Mass of product

In the chemical reaction of Ag and S, the mass of the reactants is the same as the mass of the product, Ag_2S.

In this reaction, the number of silver atoms that reacts is twice the number of sulfur atoms. When 200 silver atoms react, 100 sulfur atoms are required. However, in the actual chemical reaction, many more atoms of both silver and sulfur would react. If we are dealing with moles of silver and sulfur, then the coefficients in the equation can be interpreted in terms of moles. Thus, 2 moles of silver react with 1 mole of sulfur to form 1 mole of Ag_2S. Because the molar mass of each can be determined, the moles of Ag, S, and Ag_2S can also be stated in terms of mass in grams of each. Thus, 215.8 g of Ag and 32.1 g of S react to form 247.9 g of Ag_2S. The total mass of the reactants (247.9 g) is equal to the mass of product (247.9 g). The various ways in which a chemical equation can be interpreted are seen in Table 7.7.

TABLE 7.7 Information Available from a Balanced Equation

	Reactants		Products
Equation	$2Ag(s)$	$+ S(s)$	$\longrightarrow Ag_2S(s)$
Atoms	2 Ag atoms	+ 1 S atom	$\longrightarrow$ 1 Ag₂S formula unit
	200 Ag atoms	+ 100 S atoms	$\longrightarrow$ 100 Ag₂S formula units
Avogadro's Number of Atoms	$2(6.02 \times 10^{23})$ Ag atoms	$+ 1(6.02 \times 10^{23})$ S atoms	$\longrightarrow 1(6.02 \times 10^{23})$ Ag₂S formula units
Moles	2 moles of Ag	+ 1 mole of S	$\longrightarrow$ 1 mole of Ag₂S
Mass (g)	$2(107.9 \text{ g})$ of Ag	$+ 1(32.07 \text{ g})$ of S	$\longrightarrow 1(247.9 \text{ g})$ of Ag₂S
Total Mass (g)	247.9 g		$\longrightarrow$ 247.9 g

Mole–Mole Factors from an Equation

When iron reacts with sulfur, the product is iron(III) sulfide.

$$2Fe(s) + 3S(s) \longrightarrow Fe_2S_3(s)$$

Iron (Fe)   Sulfur (S)   Iron(III) sulfide (Fe₂S₃)
$2Fe(s)$ $+$ $3S(s)$ $\longrightarrow$ $Fe_2S_3(s)$

In the chemical reaction of Fe and S, the mass of the reactants is the same as the mass of the product, Fe₂S₃.

From the balanced chemical equation, we see that 2 moles of iron reacts with 3 moles of sulfur to form 1 mole of iron(III) sulfide. Actually, any amount of iron or sulfur may be used, but the *ratio* of iron reacting with sulfur will always be the same. From the coefficients, we can write **mole–mole factors** between reactants and between reactants and products. The coefficients used in the mole–mole factors are *exact* numbers; they do not limit the number of significant figures.

Fe and S: $\dfrac{2 \text{ moles Fe}}{3 \text{ moles S}}$ and $\dfrac{3 \text{ moles S}}{2 \text{ moles Fe}}$

Fe and Fe₂S₃: $\dfrac{2 \text{ moles Fe}}{1 \text{ mole Fe}_2\text{S}_3}$ and $\dfrac{1 \text{ mole Fe}_2\text{S}_3}{2 \text{ moles Fe}}$

S and Fe₂S₃: $\dfrac{3 \text{ moles S}}{1 \text{ mole Fe}_2\text{S}_3}$ and $\dfrac{1 \text{ mole Fe}_2\text{S}_3}{3 \text{ moles S}}$

Using Mole–Mole Factors in Calculations

Whenever you prepare a recipe, adjust an engine for the proper mixture of fuel and air, or prepare medicines in a pharmaceutical laboratory, you need to know the proper amounts of reactants to use and how much of the product will form. Now that we have written all the possible conversion factors for the balanced equation $2Fe(s) + 3S(s) \longrightarrow Fe_2S_3(s)$, we will use those mole–mole factors in a chemical calculation in Sample Problem 7.10.

 CORE CHEMISTRY SKILL

Using Mole–Mole Factors

SAMPLE PROBLEM 7.10 Calculating Moles of a Reactant

In the chemical reaction of iron and sulfur, how many moles of sulfur are needed to react with 1.42 moles of iron?

$$2Fe(s) + 3S(s) \longrightarrow Fe_2S_3(s)$$

SOLUTION

STEP 1 State the given and needed quantities (moles).

ANALYZE THE PROBLEM	Given	Need
	1.42 moles of Fe	moles of S
	Equation	
	$2Fe(s) + 3S(s) \longrightarrow Fe_2S_3(s)$	

STEP 2 Write a plan to convert the given to the needed quantity (moles).

moles of Fe → Mole–mole factor → moles of S

STEP 3 Use coefficients to write mole–mole factors.

2 moles of Fe = 3 moles of S

$$\frac{2 \text{ moles Fe}}{3 \text{ moles S}} \quad \text{and} \quad \frac{3 \text{ moles S}}{2 \text{ moles Fe}}$$

STEP 4 Set up the problem to give the needed quantity (moles).

$$1.42 \text{ moles Fe} \times \frac{3 \text{ moles S}}{2 \text{ moles Fe}} = 2.13 \text{ moles of S}$$

Three SFs   Exact   Three SFs

STUDY CHECK 7.10

Using the equation in Sample Problem 7.10, calculate the number of moles of iron needed to react with 2.75 moles of sulfur.

ANSWER

1.83 moles of iron

Guide to Calculating the Quantities of Reactants and Products in a Chemical Reaction

STEP 1 State the given and needed quantities (moles or grams).

STEP 2 Write a plan to convert the given to the needed quantity (moles or grams).

STEP 3 Use coefficients to write mole–mole factors; write molar mass factors if needed.

STEP 4 Set up the problem to give the needed quantity (moles or grams).

QUESTIONS AND PROBLEMS

7.6 Mole Relationships in Chemical Equations

LEARNING GOAL Given a quantity in moles of reactant or product, use a mole–mole factor from the balanced chemical equation to calculate the number of moles of another substance in the reaction.

7.57 Write all the mole–mole factors for each of the following chemical equations:
a. $2SO_2(g) + O_2(g) \longrightarrow 2SO_3(g)$
b. $4P(s) + 5O_2(g) \longrightarrow 2P_2O_5(s)$

7.58 Write all the mole–mole factors for each of the following chemical equations:
a. $2Al(s) + 3Cl_2(g) \longrightarrow 2AlCl_3(s)$
b. $4HCl(g) + O_2(g) \longrightarrow 2Cl_2(g) + 2H_2O(g)$

7.59 The chemical reaction of hydrogen with oxygen produces water.
$$2H_2(g) + O_2(g) \longrightarrow 2H_2O(g)$$
a. How many moles of O_2 are required to react with 2.0 moles of H_2?
b. How many moles of H_2 are needed to react with 5.0 moles of O_2?
c. How many moles of H_2O form when 2.5 moles of O_2 reacts?

7.60 Ammonia is produced by the chemical reaction of nitrogen and hydrogen.

$$N_2(g) + 3H_2(g) \longrightarrow 2NH_3(g)$$
Ammonia

a. How many moles of H_2 are needed to react with 1.0 mole of N_2?
b. How many moles of N_2 reacted if 0.60 mole of NH_3 is produced?
c. How many moles of NH_3 are produced when 1.4 moles of H_2 reacts?

7.61 Carbon disulfide and carbon monoxide are produced when carbon is heated with sulfur dioxide.

$$5C(s) + 2SO_2(g) \xrightarrow{\Delta} CS_2(l) + 4CO(g)$$

a. How many moles of C are needed to react with 0.500 mole of SO_2?
b. How many moles of CO are produced when 1.2 moles of C reacts?

c. How many moles of SO_2 are needed to produce 0.50 mole of CS_2?
d. How many moles of CS_2 are produced when 2.5 moles of C reacts?

7.62 In the acetylene torch, acetylene gas (C_2H_2) burns in oxygen to produce carbon dioxide and water.

$$2C_2H_2(g) + 5O_2(g) \xrightarrow{\Delta} 4CO_2(g) + 2H_2O(g)$$

a. How many moles of O_2 are needed to react with 2.00 moles of C_2H_2?
b. How many moles of CO_2 are produced when 3.5 moles of C_2H_2 reacts?
c. How many moles of C_2H_2 are needed to produce 0.50 mole of H_2O?
d. How many moles of CO_2 are produced from 0.100 mole of O_2?

7.7 Mass Calculations for Reactions

When we have the balanced chemical equation for a reaction, we can use the mass of one of the substances (A) in the reaction to calculate the mass of another substance (B) in the reaction. However, the calculations require us to convert the mass of A to moles of A using the molar mass factor for A. Then we use the mole–mole factor that links substance A to substance B, which we obtain from the coefficients in the balanced equation. This mole–mole factor (B/A) will convert the moles of A to moles of B. Then the molar mass factor of B is used to calculate the grams of substance B.

LEARNING GOAL

Given the mass in grams of a substance in a reaction, calculate the mass in grams of another substance in the reaction.

⊛ **CORE CHEMISTRY SKILL**

Converting Grams to Grams

Substance A   **Substance B**

grams of A | Molar mass factor A | moles of A | Mole–mole factor B/A | moles of B | Molar mass factor B | grams of B

▶ **SAMPLE PROBLEM 7.11 Mass of Product**

When acetylene, C_2H_2, burns in oxygen, high temperatures are produced that are used for welding metals.

$$2C_2H_2(g) + 5O_2(g) \xrightarrow{\Delta} 4CO_2(g) + 2H_2O(g)$$

How many grams of CO_2 are produced when 54.6 g of C_2H_2 is burned?

SOLUTION

STEP 1 State the given and needed quantities (grams).

	Given	Need
ANALYZE THE PROBLEM	54.6 g of C_2H_2	grams of CO_2
	Equation	
	$2C_2H_2(g) + 5O_2(g) \xrightarrow{\Delta} 4CO_2(g) + 2H_2O(g) + energy$	

STEP 2 Write a plan to convert the given to the needed quantity (grams).

grams of C_2H_2 | Molar mass | moles of C_2H_2 | Mole–mole factor | moles of CO_2 | Molar mass | grams of CO_2

A mixture of acetylene and oxygen undergoes combustion during the welding of metals.

STEP 3 Use coefficients to write mole–mole factors; write molar mass factors if needed.

$$1 \text{ mole of } C_2H_2 = 26.04 \text{ g of } C_2H_2$$

$$\frac{26.04 \text{ g } C_2H_2}{1 \text{ mole } C_2H_2} \quad \text{and} \quad \frac{1 \text{ mole } C_2H_2}{26.04 \text{ g } C_2H_2}$$

$$2 \text{ moles of } C_2H_2 = 4 \text{ moles of } CO_2$$

$$\frac{2 \text{ moles } C_2H_2}{4 \text{ moles } CO_2} \quad \text{and} \quad \frac{4 \text{ moles } CO_2}{2 \text{ moles } C_2H_2}$$

$$1 \text{ mole of } CO_2 = 44.01 \text{ g of } CO_2$$

$$\frac{44.01 \text{ g } CO_2}{1 \text{ mole } CO_2} \quad \text{and} \quad \frac{1 \text{ mole } CO_2}{44.01 \text{ g } CO_2}$$

STEP 4 Set up the problem to give the needed quantity (grams).

$$\underset{\text{Three SFs}}{54.6 \text{ g } C_2H_2} \times \underset{\text{Four SFs}}{\overset{\text{Exact}}{\frac{1 \text{ mole } C_2H_2}{26.04 \text{ g } C_2H_2}}} \times \underset{\text{Exact}}{\overset{\text{Exact}}{\frac{4 \text{ moles } CO_2}{2 \text{ moles } C_2H_2}}} \times \underset{\text{Exact}}{\overset{\text{Four SFs}}{\frac{44.01 \text{ g } CO_2}{1 \text{ mole } CO_2}}} = \underset{\text{Three SFs}}{185 \text{ g of } CO_2}$$

STUDY CHECK 7.11

Using the equation in Sample Problem 7.11, calculate the grams of CO_2 that can be produced when 25.0 g of O_2 reacts.

ANSWER

27.5 g of CO_2

QUESTIONS AND PROBLEMS

7.7 Mass Calculations for Reactions

LEARNING GOAL Given the mass in grams of a substance in a reaction, calculate the mass in grams of another substance in the reaction.

7.63 Sodium reacts with oxygen to produce sodium oxide.

$$4Na(s) + O_2(g) \longrightarrow 2Na_2O(s)$$

   a. How many grams of Na_2O are produced when 57.5 g of Na reacts?
   b. If you have 18.0 g of Na, how many grams of O_2 are needed for the reaction?
   c. How many grams of O_2 are needed in a reaction that produces 75.0 g of Na_2O?

7.64 Nitrogen gas reacts with hydrogen gas to produce ammonia.

$$N_2(g) + 3H_2(g) \longrightarrow 2NH_3(g)$$

   a. If you have 3.64 g of H_2, how many grams of NH_3 can be produced?
   b. How many grams of H_2 are needed to react with 2.80 g of N_2?
   c. How many grams of NH_3 can be produced from 12.0 g of H_2?

7.65 Ammonia and oxygen react to form nitrogen and water.

$$4NH_3(g) + 3O_2(g) \longrightarrow 2N_2(g) + 6H_2O(g)$$

   a. How many grams of O_2 are needed to react with 13.6 g of NH_3?
   b. How many grams of N_2 can be produced when 6.50 g of O_2 reacts?
   c. How many grams of H_2O are formed from the reaction of 34.0 g of NH_3?

7.66 Iron(III) oxide reacts with carbon to give iron and carbon monoxide.

$$Fe_2O_3(s) + 3C(s) \longrightarrow 2Fe(s) + 3CO(g)$$

   a. How many grams of C are required to react with 16.5 g of Fe_2O_3?
   b. How many grams of CO are produced when 36.0 g of C reacts?
   c. How many grams of Fe can be produced when 6.00 g of Fe_2O_3 reacts?

7.67 Nitrogen dioxide and water react to produce nitric acid, HNO_3, and nitrogen oxide.

$$3NO_2(g) + H_2O(l) \longrightarrow 2HNO_3(aq) + NO(g)$$

   a. How many grams of H_2O are needed to react with 28.0 g of NO_2?
   b. How many grams of NO are produced from 15.8 g of NO_2?
   c. How many grams of HNO_3 are produced from 8.25 g of NO_2?

7.68 Calcium cyanamide reacts with water to form calcium carbonate and ammonia.

$$CaCN_2(s) + 3H_2O(l) \longrightarrow CaCO_3(s) + 2NH_3(g)$$

   a. How many grams of H_2O are needed to react with 75.0 g of $CaCN_2$?
   b. How many grams of NH_3 are produced from 5.24 g of $CaCN_2$?
   c. How many grams of $CaCO_3$ form if 155 g of H_2O reacts?

7.69 When solid lead(II) sulfide ore burns in oxygen gas, the products are solid lead(II) oxide and sulfur dioxide gas.
  a. Write the balanced chemical equation for the reaction.
  b. How many grams of oxygen are required to react with 30.0 g of lead(II) sulfide?
  c. How many grams of sulfur dioxide can be produced when 65.0 g of lead(II) sulfide reacts?
  d. How many grams of lead(II) sulfide are used to produce 128 g of lead(II) oxide?

7.70 When the gases dihydrogen sulfide and oxygen react, they form the gases sulfur dioxide and water vapor.
  a. Write the balanced chemical equation for the reaction.
  b. How many grams of oxygen are needed to react with 2.50 g of dihydrogen sulfide?
  c. How many grams of sulfur dioxide can be produced when 38.5 g of oxygen reacts?
  d. How many grams of oxygen are needed to produce 55.8 g of water vapor?

Interactive Video

Stoichiometry

℞ Clinical Applications

7.71 In the body, the amino acid glycine, $C_2H_5NO_2$, reacts according to the following equation:

$$2C_2H_5NO_2(aq) + 3O_2(g) \longrightarrow$$
Glycine $\qquad 3CO_2(g) + 3H_2O(l) + CH_4N_2O(aq)$
$\qquad\qquad\qquad\qquad\qquad\qquad\qquad\qquad$ Urea

  a. How many grams of O_2 are needed to react with 15.0 g of glycine?
  b. How many grams of urea are produced from 15.0 g of glycine?
  c. How many grams of CO_2 are produced from 15.0 g of glycine?

7.72 In the body, ethanol, C_2H_6O, reacts according to the following equation:

$$C_2H_6O(aq) + 3O_2(g) \longrightarrow 2CO_2(g) + 3H_2O(l)$$
Ethanol

  a. How many grams of O_2 are needed to react with 8.40 g of ethanol?
  b. How many grams of H_2O are produced from 8.40 g of ethanol?
  c. How many grams of CO_2 are produced from 8.40 g of ethanol?

7.8 Limiting Reactants and Percent Yield

When you make peanut butter sandwiches for lunch, you need 2 slices of bread and 1 tablespoon of peanut butter for each sandwich. As an equation, we could write:

2 slices of bread + 1 tablespoon of peanut butter $\longrightarrow$ 1 peanut butter sandwich

If you have 8 slices of bread and a full jar of peanut butter, you will run out of bread after you make 4 peanut butter sandwiches. You cannot make any more sandwiches once the bread is used up, even though there is a lot of peanut butter left in the jar. The number of slices of bread has limited the number of sandwiches you can make.

On a different day, you might have 8 slices of bread but only a tablespoon of peanut butter left in the peanut butter jar. You will run out of peanut butter after you make just 1 peanut butter sandwich and have 6 slices of bread left over. The small amount of peanut butter available has limited the number of sandwiches you can make.

LEARNING GOAL

Identify a limiting reactant and calculate the amount of product formed from the limiting reactant. Given the actual quantity of product, determine the percent yield for a reaction.

8 slices of bread + 1 jar of peanut butter make 4 peanut butter sandwiches + peanut butter left over

8 slices of bread + 1 tablespoon of peanut butter make 1 peanut butter sandwich + 6 slices of bread left over

The reactant that is completely used up is the **limiting reactant**. The reactant that does not completely react and is left over is called the *excess reactant*.

Bread	Peanut Butter	Sandwiches	Limiting Reactant	Excess Reactant
1 loaf (20 slices)	1 tablespoon	1	Peanut butter	Bread
4 slices	1 full jar	2	Bread	Peanut butter
8 slices	1 full jar	4	Bread	Peanut butter

Calculating Moles of Product from a Limiting Reactant

In a similar way, the reactants in a chemical reaction do not always combine in quantities that allow each to be used up at exactly the same time. In many reactions, there is a limiting reactant that determines the amount of product that can be formed. When we know the quantities of the reactants of a chemical reaction, we calculate the amount of product that is possible from each reactant if it were completely consumed. We are looking for the *limiting reactant*, which is the one that runs out first, producing the smaller amount of product.

▶ **SAMPLE PROBLEM 7.12** Moles of Product from Limiting Reactant

The chemical reaction of carbon monoxide and hydrogen is used to produce methanol, CH_3OH.

$$CO(g) + 2H_2(g) \longrightarrow CH_3OH(g)$$

If 3.00 moles of CO and 5.00 moles of H_2 are the initial reactants, what is the limiting reactant and how many moles of methanol can be produced?

SOLUTION

STEP **1** State the given and needed moles.

ANALYZE THE PROBLEM	Given	Need
	3.00 moles of CO, 5.00 moles of H_2	moles of CH_3OH produced, limiting reactant
	Equation	
	$CO(g) + 2H_2(g) \longrightarrow CH_3OH(g)$	

STEP **2** Write a plan to convert the moles of each reactant to moles of product.

moles of CO → Mole–mole factor → moles of CH_3OH

moles of H_2 → Mole–mole factor → moles of CH_3OH

STEP **3** Write the mole–mole factors from the equation.

1 mole of CO = 1 mole of CH_3OH
$$\frac{1 \text{ mole CO}}{1 \text{ mole CH}_3\text{OH}} \text{ and } \frac{1 \text{ mole CH}_3\text{OH}}{1 \text{ mole CO}}$$

2 moles of H_2 = 1 mole of CH_3OH
$$\frac{2 \text{ moles H}_2}{1 \text{ mole CH}_3\text{OH}} \text{ and } \frac{1 \text{ mole CH}_3\text{OH}}{2 \text{ moles H}_2}$$

Guide to Calculating the Moles of Product from a Limiting Reactant

STEP **1**
State the given and needed moles.

STEP **2**
Write a plan to convert the moles of each reactant to moles of product.

STEP **3**
Write the mole–mole factors from the equation.

STEP **4**
Calculate the number of moles of product from each reactant and select the smaller number of moles as the amount of product from the limiting reactant.

STEP 4 Calculate the number of moles of product from each reactant and select the smaller number of moles as the amount of product from the limiting reactant.

Moles of CH_3OH (product) from CO:

$$3.00 \text{ moles CO} \times \underbrace{\frac{1 \text{ mole } CH_3OH}{1 \text{ mole CO}}}_{\text{Exact}} = 3.00 \text{ moles of } CH_3OH$$

Three SFs · Exact · Three SFs

Moles of CH_3OH (product) from H_2:

$$5.00 \text{ moles } H_2 \times \underbrace{\frac{1 \text{ mole } CH_3OH}{2 \text{ moles } H_2}}_{\text{Exact}} = 2.50 \text{ moles of } CH_3OH$$

Three SFs · Exact

Limiting reactant · Exact · Three SFs · Smaller amount of product

The smaller amount, 2.50 moles of CH_3OH, is the maximum amount of methanol that can be produced from the limiting reactant, H_2, when it is completely consumed.

STUDY CHECK 7.12

If the initial mixture of reactants for Sample Problem 7.12 contains 4.00 moles of CO and 4.00 moles of H_2, what is the limiting reactant and how many moles of methanol can be produced?

ANSWER

H_2 is the limiting reactant; 2.00 moles of methanol can be produced.

Calculating Mass of Product from a Limiting Reactant

The quantities of the reactants can also be given in grams. The calculations to identify the limiting reactant are the same as before, but the grams of each reactant must first be converted to moles, then to moles of product, and finally to grams of product. Then select the smaller mass of product, which is from complete use of the limiting reactant. This calculation is shown in Sample Problem 7.13.

A ceramic brake disc in a sports car withstands temperatures of 1400 °C.

SAMPLE PROBLEM 7.13 Mass of Product from a Limiting Reactant

When silicon dioxide (sand) and carbon are heated, the products are silicon carbide, SiC, and carbon monoxide. Silicon carbide is a ceramic material that tolerates extreme temperatures and is used as an abrasive and in the brake discs of sports cars. How many grams of CO are formed from 70.0 g of SiO_2 and 50.0 g of C?

$$SiO_2(s) + 3C(s) \xrightarrow{\text{Heat}} SiC(s) + 2CO(g)$$

SOLUTION

STEP 1 State the given and needed grams.

	Given	Need
ANALYZE THE PROBLEM	70.0 g of SiO_2, 50.0 g of C	grams of CO from limiting reactant
	Equation	
	$SiO_2(s) + 3C(s) \xrightarrow{\text{Heat}} SiC(s) + 2CO(g)$	

Guide to Calculating the Grams of Product from a Limiting Reactant

STEP 1
State the given and needed grams.

STEP 2
Write a plan to convert the grams of each reactant to grams of product.

STEP 3
Write the molar mass factors and the mole–mole factors from the equation.

STEP 4
Calculate the number of grams of product from each reactant and select the smaller number of grams as the amount of product from the limiting reactant.

STEP 2 Write a plan to convert the grams of each reactant to grams of product.

grams of SiO_2 → | Molar mass | → moles of SiO_2 → | Mole–mole factor | → moles of CO → | Molar mass | → grams of CO

grams of C → | Molar mass | → moles of C → | Mole–mole factor | → moles of CO → | Molar mass | → grams of CO

STEP 3 Write the molar mass factors and mole–mole factors from the equation.

Molar mass factors:

1 mole of SiO_2 = 60.09 g of SiO_2

$$\frac{1 \text{ mole } SiO_2}{60.09 \text{ g } SiO_2} \quad \text{and} \quad \frac{60.09 \text{ g } SiO_2}{1 \text{ mole } SiO_2}$$

1 mole of C = 12.01 g of C

$$\frac{1 \text{ mole C}}{12.01 \text{ g C}} \quad \text{and} \quad \frac{12.01 \text{ g C}}{1 \text{ mole C}}$$

1 mole of CO = 28.01 g of CO

$$\frac{1 \text{ mole CO}}{28.01 \text{ g CO}} \quad \text{and} \quad \frac{28.01 \text{ g CO}}{1 \text{ mole CO}}$$

Mole–mole factors:

2 moles of CO = 1 mole of SiO_2

$$\frac{2 \text{ moles CO}}{1 \text{ mole } SiO_2} \quad \text{and} \quad \frac{1 \text{ mole } SiO_2}{2 \text{ moles CO}}$$

2 moles of CO = 3 moles of C

$$\frac{2 \text{ moles CO}}{3 \text{ moles C}} \quad \text{and} \quad \frac{3 \text{ moles C}}{2 \text{ moles CO}}$$

STEP 4 Calculate the number of grams of product from each reactant and select the smaller number of grams as the amount of product from the limiting reactant.

Grams of CO (product) from SiO_2:

Three SFs   Exact   Exact   Four SFs   Three SFs

$$70.0 \text{ g } SiO_2 \times \frac{1 \text{ mole } SiO_2}{60.09 \text{ g } SiO_2} \times \frac{2 \text{ moles CO}}{1 \text{ mole } SiO_2} \times \frac{28.01 \text{ g CO}}{1 \text{ mole CO}} = 65.3 \text{ g of CO}$$

Limiting reactant   Four SFs   Exact   Exact   Smaller amount of product

Grams of CO (product) from C:

Three SFs   Exact   Exact   Four SFs   Three SFs

$$50.0 \text{ g C} \times \frac{1 \text{ mole C}}{12.01 \text{ g C}} \times \frac{2 \text{ moles CO}}{3 \text{ moles C}} \times \frac{28.01 \text{ g CO}}{1 \text{ mole CO}} = 77.7 \text{ g of CO}$$

Four SFs   Exact   Exact

The smaller amount, 65.3 g of CO, is the most CO that can be produced.

STUDY CHECK 7.13

Hydrogen sulfide burns with oxygen to give sulfur dioxide and water. How many grams of sulfur dioxide are formed from the reaction of 8.52 g of H_2S and 9.60 g of O_2?

$$2H_2S(g) + 3O_2(g) \xrightarrow{\Delta} 2SO_2(g) + 2H_2O(g)$$

ANSWER

12.8 g of SO_2

Percent Yield

In our problems up to now, we assumed that all of the reactants changed completely to product. Thus, we have calculated the amount of product as the maximum quantity possible, or 100%. While this would be an ideal situation, it does not usually happen. As we carry out a reaction and transfer products from one container to another, some product is usually lost. In the lab as well as commercially, the starting materials may not be completely pure, and side reactions may use some of the reactants to give unwanted products. Thus, 100% of the desired product is not actually obtained.

When we do a chemical reaction in the laboratory, we measure out specific quantities of the reactants. We calculate the **theoretical yield** for the reaction, which is the amount of product (100%) we would expect if all the reactants were converted to the desired product. When the reaction ends, we collect and measure the mass of the product, which is the **actual yield** for the product. Because some product is usually lost, the actual yield is less than the theoretical yield. Using the actual yield and the theoretical yield for a product, we can calculate the **percent yield**.

$$\text{Percent yield (\%)} = \frac{\text{actual yield}}{\text{theoretical yield}} \times 100\%$$

CORE CHEMISTRY SKILL

Calculating Percent Yield

▶ SAMPLE PROBLEM 7.14 Calculating Percent Yield

On a space shuttle, LiOH is used to absorb exhaled CO_2 from breathing air to form $LiHCO_3$.

$$LiOH(s) + CO_2(g) \longrightarrow LiHCO_3(s)$$

What is the percent yield of $LiHCO_3$ for the reaction if 50.0 g of LiOH gives 72.8 g of $LiHCO_3$?

SOLUTION

STEP 1 State the given and needed quantities.

ANALYZE THE PROBLEM	Given	Need
	50.0 g of LiOH (reactant), 72.8 g of $LiHCO_3$ (actual product)	theoretical yield of $LiHCO_3$, percent yield of $LiHCO_3$
	Equation	
	$LiOH(s) + CO_2(g) \longrightarrow LiHCO_3(s)$	

STEP 2 Write a plan to calculate the theoretical yield and the percent yield.

Calculation of theoretical yield:

grams of LiOH → [Molar mass] → moles of LiOH → [Mole–mole factor] → moles of $LiHCO_3$ → [Molar mass] → grams of $LiHCO_3$
Theoretical yield

Calculation of percent yield:

$$\text{Percent yield (\%)} = \frac{\text{actual yield of LiHCO}_3}{\text{theoretical yield of LiHCO}_3} \times 100\%$$

STEP 3 Write the molar mass factors and the mole–mole factor from the balanced equation.

Molar mass factors:

1 mole of LiOH = 23.95 g of LiOH   1 mole of $LiHCO_3$ = 67.96 g of $LiHCO_3$

$\dfrac{1 \text{ mole LiOH}}{23.95 \text{ g LiOH}}$ and $\dfrac{23.95 \text{ g LiOH}}{1 \text{ mole LiOH}}$ $\dfrac{1 \text{ mole LiHCO}_3}{67.96 \text{ g LiHCO}_3}$ and $\dfrac{67.96 \text{ g LiHCO}_3}{1 \text{ mole LiHCO}_3}$

Mole–mole factors:

1 mole of $LiHCO_3$ = 1 mole of LiOH

$\dfrac{1 \text{ mole LiHCO}_3}{1 \text{ mole LiOH}}$ and $\dfrac{1 \text{ mole LiOH}}{1 \text{ mole LiHCO}_3}$

Guide to Calculations for Percent Yield

STEP 1
State the given and needed quantities.

STEP 2
Write a plan to calculate the theoretical yield and the percent yield.

STEP 3
Write the molar mass factors and the mole–mole factors from the balanced equation.

STEP 4
Calculate the percent yield by dividing the actual yield (given) by the theoretical yield and multiplying the result by 100%.

On a space shuttle, the LiOH in the canisters removes CO_2 from the air.

STEP 4 Calculate the percent yield by dividing the actual yield (given) by the theoretical yield and multiplying the result by 100%.

Calculation of theoretical yield:

$$50.0 \text{ g LiOH} \times \underbrace{\frac{1 \text{ mole LiOH}}{23.95 \text{ g LiOH}}}_{\text{Exact}} \times \underbrace{\frac{1 \text{ mole LiHCO}_3}{1 \text{ mole LiOH}}}_{\text{Exact}} \times \underbrace{\frac{67.96 \text{ g LiHCO}_3}{1 \text{ mole LiHCO}_3}}_{\text{Four SFs}}$$

Three SFs — Four SFs — Exact — Exact

$$= 142 \text{ g of LiHCO}_3$$
Three SFs

Calculation of percent yield:

$$\frac{\text{actual yield (given)}}{\text{theoretical yield (calculated)}} \times 100\% = \frac{72.8 \text{ g LiHCO}_3 \text{ (Three SFs)}}{142 \text{ g LiHCO}_3 \text{ (Three SFs)}} \times 100\% = 51.3\% \text{ (Three SFs)}$$

A percent yield of 51.3% means that 72.8 g of the theoretical amount of 142 g of LiHCO$_3$ was actually produced by the reaction.

STUDY CHECK 7.14

For the reaction in Sample Problem 7.14, what is the percent yield of LiHCO$_3$ if 8.00 g of CO$_2$ produces 10.5 g of LiHCO$_3$?

ANSWER

84.7%

QUESTIONS AND PROBLEMS

7.8 Limiting Reactants and Percent Yield

LEARNING GOAL Identify a limiting reactant and calculate the amount of product formed from the limiting reactant. Given the actual quantity of product, determine the percent yield for a reaction.

7.73 A taxi company has 10 taxis.
   a. On a certain day, only eight taxi drivers show up for work. How many taxis can be used to pick up passengers?
   b. On another day, 10 taxi drivers show up for work but three taxis are in the repair shop. How many taxis can be driven?

7.74 A clock maker has 15 clock faces. Each clock requires one face and two hands.
   a. If the clock maker has 42 hands, how many clocks can be produced?
   b. If the clock maker has only eight hands, how many clocks can be produced?

7.75 Nitrogen and hydrogen react to form ammonia.

$$N_2(g) + 3H_2(g) \longrightarrow 2NH_3(g)$$

Determine the limiting reactant in each of the following mixtures of reactants:
   a. 3.0 moles of N$_2$ and 5.0 moles of H$_2$
   b. 8.0 moles of N$_2$ and 4.0 moles of H$_2$
   c. 3.0 moles of N$_2$ and 12.0 moles of H$_2$

7.76 Iron and oxygen react to form iron(III) oxide.

$$4Fe(s) + 3O_2(g) \longrightarrow 2Fe_2O_3(s)$$

Determine the limiting reactant in each of the following mixtures of reactants:
   a. 2.0 moles of Fe and 6.0 moles of O$_2$

   b. 5.0 moles of Fe and 4.0 moles of O$_2$
   c. 16.0 moles of Fe and 20.0 moles of O$_2$

7.77 For each of the following reactions, 20.0 g of each reactant is present initially. Determine the limiting reactant, and calculate the grams of product in parentheses that would be produced.
   a. $2Al(s) + 3Cl_2(g) \longrightarrow 2AlCl_3(s)$ (AlCl$_3$)
   b. $4NH_3(g) + 5O_2(g) \longrightarrow 4NO(g) + 6H_2O(g)$ (H$_2$O)
   c. $CS_2(g) + 3O_2(g) \xrightarrow{\Delta} CO_2(g) + 2SO_2(g)$ (SO$_2$)

7.78 For each of the following reactions, 20.0 g of each reactant is present initially. Determine the limiting reactant, and calculate the grams of product in parentheses that would be produced.
   a. $4Al(s) + 3O_2(g) \longrightarrow 2Al_2O_3(s)$ (Al$_2$O$_3$)
   b. $3NO_2(g) + H_2O(l) \longrightarrow 2HNO_3(aq) + NO(g)$ (HNO$_3$)
   c. $C_2H_5OH(l) + 3O_2(g) \xrightarrow{\Delta} 2CO_2(g) + 3H_2O(g)$ (H$_2$O)

7.79 For each of the following reactions, calculate the grams of indicated product when 25.0 g of the first reactant and 40.0 g of the second reactant is used:
   a. $2SO_2(g) + O_2(g) \longrightarrow 2SO_3(g)$ (SO$_3$)
   b. $3Fe(s) + 4H_2O(l) \longrightarrow Fe_3O_4(s) + 4H_2(g)$ (Fe$_3$O$_4$)
   c. $C_7H_{16}(g) + 11O_2(g) \xrightarrow{\Delta} 7CO_2(g) + 8H_2O(g)$ (CO$_2$)

7.80 For each of the following reactions, calculate the grams of indicated product when 15.0 g of the first reactant and 10.0 g of the second reactant is used:
   a. $4Li(s) + O_2(g) \longrightarrow 2Li_2O(s)$ (Li$_2$O)
   b. $Fe_2O_3(s) + 3H_2(g) \longrightarrow 2Fe(s) + 3H_2O(l)$ (Fe)
   c. $Al_2S_3(s) + 6H_2O(l) \longrightarrow$
      $2Al(OH)_3(aq) + 3H_2S(g)$ (H$_2$S)

7.81 Carbon disulfide is produced by the reaction of carbon and sulfur dioxide.

$$5C(s) + 2SO_2(g) \longrightarrow CS_2(g) + 4CO(g)$$

a. What is the percent yield of carbon disulfide if the reaction of 40.0 g of carbon produces 36.0 g of carbon disulfide?

b. What is the percent yield of carbon disulfide if the reaction of 32.0 g of sulfur dioxide produces 12.0 g of carbon disulfide?

7.82 Iron(III) oxide reacts with carbon monoxide to produce iron and carbon dioxide.

$$Fe_2O_3(s) + 3CO(g) \longrightarrow 2Fe(s) + 3CO_2(g)$$

a. What is the percent yield of iron if the reaction of 65.0 g of iron(III) oxide produces 15.0 g of iron?

b. What is the percent yield of carbon dioxide if the reaction of 75.0 g of carbon monoxide produces 85.0 g of carbon dioxide?

7.83 Aluminum reacts with oxygen to produce aluminum oxide.

$$4Al(s) + 3O_2(g) \longrightarrow 2Al_2O_3(s)$$

Calculate the mass of Al_2O_3 that can be produced if the reaction of 50.0 g of aluminum and sufficient oxygen has a 75.0% yield.

7.84 Propane (C_3H_8) burns in oxygen to produce carbon dioxide and water.

$$C_3H_8(g) + 5O_2(g) \xrightarrow{\Delta} 3CO_2(g) + 4H_2O(g)$$

Calculate the mass of CO_2 that can be produced if the reaction of 45.0 g of propane and sufficient oxygen has a 60.0% yield.

7.85 When 30.0 g of carbon is heated with silicon dioxide, 28.2 g of carbon monoxide is produced. What is the percent yield of carbon monoxide for this reaction?

$$SiO_2(s) + 3C(s) \longrightarrow SiC(s) + 2CO(g)$$

7.86 When 56.6 g of calcium is reacted with nitrogen gas, 32.4 g of calcium nitride is produced. What is the percent yield of calcium nitride for this reaction?

$$3Ca(s) + N_2(g) \longrightarrow Ca_3N_2(s)$$

7.9 Energy in Chemical Reactions

LEARNING GOAL

Given the heat of reaction, calculate the loss or gain of heat for an exothermic or endothermic reaction.

Almost every chemical reaction involves a loss or gain of energy. To discuss energy change for a reaction, we look at the energy of the reactants before the reaction and the energy of the products after the reaction.

Energy Units for Chemical Reactions

The SI unit for energy is the *joule* (J). Often, the unit of *kilojoules* (kJ) is used to show the energy change in a reaction.

1 kilojoule (kJ) = 1000 joules (J)

Heat of Reaction

The **heat of reaction** is the amount of heat absorbed or released during a reaction that takes place at constant pressure. A change of energy occurs as reactants interact, bonds break apart, and products form. We determine a heat of reaction or *enthalpy change*, symbol ΔH, as the difference in the energy of the products and the reactants.

$$\Delta H = H_{products} - H_{reactants}$$

Exothermic Reactions

In an **exothermic reaction** (*exo* means "out"), the energy of the products is lower than that of the reactants. This means that heat is released along with the products that form. Let us look at the equation for the exothermic reaction in which 185 kJ of heat is released when 1 mole of hydrogen and 1 mole of chlorine react to form 2 moles of hydrogen chloride. For an exothermic reaction, the heat of reaction can be written as one of the products. It can also be written as a ΔH value with a negative sign ($-$).

Exothermic, Heat Released	Heat Is a Product
$H_2(g) + Cl_2(g) \longrightarrow 2HCl(g) + 185 \text{ kJ}$	$\Delta H = -185 \text{ kJ}$ Negative sign

Endothermic Reactions

In an **endothermic reaction** (*endo* means "within"), the energy of the products is higher than that of the reactants. Heat is required to convert the reactants to products. Let us look at the equation for the endothermic reaction in which 180 kJ of heat is needed to convert 1 mole of nitrogen and 1 mole of oxygen to 2 moles of nitrogen oxide. For an endothermic reaction, the heat of reaction can be written as one of the reactants. It can also be written as a ΔH value with a positive sign ($+$).

Endothermic, Heat Absorbed	Heat Is a Reactant
$N_2(g) + O_2(g) + 180 \text{ kJ} \longrightarrow 2NO(g)$	$\Delta H = +180 \text{ kJ}$ Positive sign

Reaction	Energy Change	Heat in the Equation	Sign of ΔH
Endothermic	Heat absorbed	Reactant side	Positive sign ($+$)
Exothermic	Heat released	Product side	Negative sign ($-$)

Calculations of Heat in Reactions

The value of ΔH refers to the heat change for each substance in the balanced equation. Consider the following decomposition reaction:

$$2H_2O(l) \longrightarrow 2H_2(g) + O_2(g) \quad \Delta H = +572 \text{ kJ}$$
$$2H_2O(l) + 572 \text{ kJ} \longrightarrow 2H_2(g) + O_2(g)$$

For this reaction, 572 kJ are absorbed by 2 moles of H_2O to produce 2 moles of H_2 and 1 mole of O_2. We can write heat conversion factors for each substance in this reaction as follows:

$$\frac{+572 \text{ kJ}}{2 \text{ moles } H_2O} \quad \frac{+572 \text{ kJ}}{2 \text{ moles } H_2} \quad \frac{+572 \text{ kJ}}{1 \text{ mole } O_2}$$

Suppose in this reaction that 9.00 g of H_2O undergoes reaction. We can calculate the amount of heat absorbed as

$$9.00 \text{ g } H_2O \times \frac{1 \text{ mole } H_2O}{18.02 \text{ g } H_2O} \times \frac{+572 \text{ kJ}}{2 \text{ moles } H_2O} = +143 \text{ kJ}$$

SAMPLE PROBLEM 7.15 Calculating Heat in a Reaction

How much heat, in kilojoules, is released when nitrogen and hydrogen react to form 50.0 g of ammonia?

$$N_2(g) + 3H_2(g) \longrightarrow 2NH_3(g) \qquad \Delta H = -92.2 \text{ kJ}$$

⊗ **CORE CHEMISTRY SKILL**

Using the Heat of Reaction

SOLUTION

STEP 1 State the given and needed quantities.

ANALYZE THE PROBLEM	Given	Need
	50.0 g of NH_3, $\Delta H = -92.2$ kJ	heat released, in kilojoules
	Equation	
	$N_2(g) + 3H_2(g) \longrightarrow 2NH_3(g)$	

STEP 2 Write a plan using the heat of reaction and any molar mass needed.

grams of NH_3 → [Molar mass] → moles of NH_3 → [Heat of reaction] → kilojoules

STEP 3 Write the conversion factors including heat of reaction.

$$1 \text{ mole of } NH_3 = 17.03 \text{ g of } NH_3$$
$$\frac{17.03 \text{ g } NH_3}{1 \text{ mole } NH_3} \text{ and } \frac{1 \text{ mole } NH_3}{17.03 \text{ g } NH_3}$$

$$2 \text{ moles of } NH_3 = -92.2 \text{ kJ}$$
$$\frac{-92.2 \text{ kJ}}{2 \text{ moles } NH_3} \text{ and } \frac{2 \text{ moles } NH_3}{-92.2 \text{ kJ}}$$

STEP 4 Set up the problem to calculate the heat.

$$50.0 \text{ g } NH_3 \times \underset{\text{Four SFs}}{\frac{\overset{\text{Exact}}{1 \text{ mole } NH_3}}{17.03 \text{ g } NH_3}} \times \underset{\text{Exact}}{\frac{\overset{\text{Three SFs}}{-92.2 \text{ kJ}}}{2 \text{ moles } NH_3}} = \underset{\text{Three SFs}}{-135 \text{ kJ}}$$

(Three SFs)

Guide to Calculations Using the Heat of Reaction

STEP 1
State the given and needed quantities.

STEP 2
Write a plan using the heat of reaction and any molar mass needed.

STEP 3
Write the conversion factors including heat of reaction.

STEP 4
Set up the problem to calculate the heat.

STUDY CHECK 7.15

Mercury(II) oxide decomposes to mercury and oxygen.

$$2HgO(s) \longrightarrow 2Hg(l) + O_2(g) \quad \Delta H = +182 \text{ kJ}$$

a. Is the reaction exothermic or endothermic?
b. How many kilojoules are needed to react 25.0 g of mercury(II) oxide?

ANSWER

a. endothermic **b.** 20.5 kJ

 # Chemistry Link to **Health**
Cold Packs and Hot Packs

In a hospital, at a first-aid station, or at an athletic event, an instant *cold pack* may be used to reduce swelling from an injury, remove heat from inflammation, or decrease capillary size to lessen the effect of hemorrhaging. Inside the plastic container of a cold pack, there is a compartment containing solid ammonium nitrate

(NH_4NO_3) that is separated from a compartment containing water. The pack is activated when it is hit or squeezed hard enough to break the walls between the compartments and cause the ammonium nitrate to mix with the water (shown as H_2O over the reaction arrow). In an endothermic process, 1 mole of NH_4NO_3 that dissolves absorbs

26 kJ of heat. The temperature drops to about 4 to 5 °C to give a cold pack that is ready to use.

Endothermic Reaction in a Cold Pack

$$NH_4NO_3(s) + 26 \text{ kJ} \xrightarrow{H_2O} NH_4NO_3(aq)$$

Hot packs are used to relax muscles, lessen aches and cramps, and increase circulation by expanding capillary size. Constructed in the same way as cold packs, a hot pack contains a salt such as $CaCl_2$. When 1 mole of $CaCl_2$ dissolves in water, 82 kJ are released as heat. The temperature increases as much as 66 °C to give a hot pack that is ready to use.

Exothermic Reaction in a Hot Pack

$$CaCl_2(s) \xrightarrow{H_2O} CaCl_2(aq) + 82 \text{ kJ}$$

Cold packs use an endothermic reaction.

QUESTIONS AND PROBLEMS

7.9 Energy in Chemical Reactions

LEARNING GOAL Given the heat of reaction, calculate the loss or gain of heat for an exothermic or endothermic reaction.

7.87 In an exothermic reaction, is the energy of the products higher or lower than that of the reactants?

7.88 In an endothermic reaction, is the energy of the products higher or lower than that of the reactants?

7.89 Classify each of the following as exothermic or endothermic:
  a. A reaction releases 550 kJ.
  b. The energy level of the products is higher than that of the reactants.
  c. The metabolism of glucose in the body provides energy.

7.90 Classify each of the following as exothermic or endothermic:
  a. The energy level of the products is lower than that of the reactants.
  b. In the body, the synthesis of proteins requires energy.
  c. A reaction absorbs 125 kJ.

7.91 Classify each of the following as exothermic or endothermic and give the ΔH for each:
  a. $CH_4(g) + 2O_2(g) \xrightarrow{\Delta} CO_2(g) + 2H_2O(g) + 802 \text{ kJ}$
  b. $Ca(OH)_2(s) + 65.3 \text{ kJ} \longrightarrow CaO(s) + H_2O(l)$
  c. $2Al(s) + Fe_2O_3(s) \longrightarrow Al_2O_3(s) + 2Fe(l) + 850 \text{ kJ}$

The thermite reaction of aluminum and iron(III) oxide produces very high temperatures used to cut or weld railroad tracks.

7.92 Classify each of the following as exothermic or endothermic and give the ΔH for each:
  a. $C_3H_8(g) + 5O_2(g) \xrightarrow{\Delta} 3CO_2(g) + 4H_2O(g) + 2220 \text{ kJ}$
  b. $2Na(s) + Cl_2(g) \longrightarrow 2NaCl(s) + 819 \text{ kJ}$
  c. $PCl_5(g) + 67 \text{ kJ} \longrightarrow PCl_3(g) + Cl_2(g)$

7.93 **a.** How many kilojoules are released when 125 g of Cl_2 reacts with silicon?

$$Si(s) + 2Cl_2(g) \longrightarrow SiCl_4(g) \quad \Delta H = -657 \text{ kJ}$$

  b. How many kilojoules are absorbed when 278 g of PCl_5 reacts?

$$PCl_5(g) \longrightarrow PCl_3(g) + Cl_2(g) \quad \Delta H = +67 \text{ kJ}$$

7.94 **a.** How many kilojoules are released when 75.0 g of methanol reacts?

$$2CH_3OH(l) + 3O_2(g) \xrightarrow{\Delta} 2CO_2(g) + 4H_2O(l)$$
$$\Delta H = -726 \text{ kJ}$$

  b. How many kilojoules are absorbed when 315 g of $Ca(OH)_2$ reacts?

$$Ca(OH)_2(s) \longrightarrow CaO(s) + H_2O(l) \quad \Delta H = +65.3 \text{ kJ}$$

℞ Clinical Applications

7.95 In photosynthesis, glucose, $C_6H_{12}O_6$, and O_2 are produced from CO_2 and H_2O. Glucose from starches is the major fuel for the body.

$$6CO_2(g) + 6H_2O(l) + 680 \text{ kcal} \longrightarrow C_6H_{12}O_6(aq) + 6O_2(g)$$
Glucose

  a. Is the reaction endothermic or exothermic?
  b. How many grams of glucose are produced from 18.0 g of CO_2?
  c. How much heat, in kilojoules, is needed to produce 25.0 g of $C_6H_{12}O_6$?

7.96 Ethanol, C_2H_6O, reacts in the body using the following equation:

$$C_2H_6O(aq) + 3O_2(g) \longrightarrow 2CO_2(g) + 3H_2O(l) + 327 \text{ kcal}$$
Ethanol

  a. Is the reaction endothermic or exothermic?
  b. How much heat, in kilocalories, is produced when 5.00 g of ethanol reacts with O_2 gas?
  c. How many grams of ethanol react if 1250 kJ are produced?

Clinical Update
Whitening of Tooth Enamel

The reaction of hydrogen peroxide, $H_2O_2(aq)$, placed on Jane's teeth produces water, $H_2O(l)$, and oxygen gas. After Jane had her teeth cleaned and whitened, Kimberly recommended that she use a toothpaste with tin(II) fluoride when she brushes her teeth. Most toothpastes and mouthwashes contain fluoride ions. Tooth enamel, which is composed of hydroxyapatite, $Ca_5(PO_4)_3OH$, is strengthened when it reacts with fluoride ions to form fluoroapatite, $Ca_5(PO_4)_3F$.

℞ Clinical Applications

7.97 The hydroxyapatite that makes up the enamel of teeth has the formula $Ca_5(PO_4)_3OH$.

  a. How many moles of phosphorus (P) are in 0.0500 mole of hydroxyapatite?

  b. How many calcium ions (Ca^{2+}) are in 0.250 mole of hydroxyapatite?

  c. How many moles of hydroxyapatite contain 8.5×10^{23} atoms of hydrogen (H)?

  d. What is the molar mass of hydroxyapatite?

7.98 The fluoroapatite that makes up the enamel of teeth has the formula $Ca_5(PO_4)_3F$.

  a. How many moles of oxygen (O) are in 0.0500 mole of fluoroapatite?

  b. How many calcium ions (Ca^{2+}) are in 0.460 mole of fluoroapatite?

  c. How many moles of fluoroapatite contain 7.2×10^{23} fluoride (F^-) ions?

  d. What is the molar mass of fluoroapatite?

7.99 **a.** Write the balanced chemical equation for the reaction when aqueous hydrogen peroxide, H_2O_2, reacts to form liquid water and O_2 gas.

  b. Classify the reaction in part **a** as a combination, decomposition, single replacement, double replacement, or combustion reaction.

Use your balanced chemical equation in part **a** to make the following calculations:

  c. the moles of O_2 that can be produced from 1.65 moles of H_2O_2

  d. the grams of H_2O_2 that react to produce 4.28 g of O_2

  e. If 3.0 g of a gel, which is 25% H_2O_2 by mass, is applied to Jane's teeth, how many grams of O_2 are produced?

  f. What is the percent yield for the reaction if 8.00 g of H_2O_2 gives 2.33 g of O_2?

7.100 **a.** Write the balanced chemical equation for the reaction of solid tin(II) oxide with aqueous hydrogen fluoride to produce aqueous tin(II) fluoride and water.

  b. Classify the reaction in part **a** as a combination, decomposition, single replacement, double replacement, or combustion reaction.

Use your balanced chemical equation in part **a** to make the following calculations:

  c. the moles of HF needed to react with 0.725 mole of SnO

  d. the grams of HF that need to react to produce 4.28 g of SnF_2

  e. If 5.00 g of HF completely reacts, what is the theoretical yield of SnF_2?

  f. What is the percent yield for the reaction in part **e** if 16.2 g of SnF_2 are produced?

CONCEPT MAP

CHEMICAL REACTIONS AND QUANTITIES

CHAPTER REVIEW

7.1 Equations for Chemical Reactions

LEARNING GOAL Write a balanced chemical equation from the formulas of the reactants and products for a reaction; determine the number of atoms in the reactants and products.

$$2H_2(g) + O_2(g) \longrightarrow 2H_2O(g)$$
Balanced

- A chemical change occurs when the atoms of the initial substances rearrange to form new substances.
- A chemical equation shows the formulas of the substances that react on the left side of a reaction arrow and the products that form on the right side of the reaction arrow.
- A chemical equation is balanced by writing coefficients, small whole numbers, in front of formulas to equalize the atoms of each of the elements in the reactants and the products.

7.2 Types of Reactions

LEARNING GOAL Identify a reaction as a combination, decomposition, single replacement, double replacement, or combustion.

Single replacement

One element replaces another element

 +

- Many chemical reactions can be organized by reaction type: combination, decomposition, single replacement, double replacement, or combustion.

7.3 Oxidation–Reduction Reactions

LEARNING GOAL Define the terms oxidation and reduction; identify the reactants oxidized and reduced.

Oxidation (loss of electron)

Reduction (gain of electron)

- When electrons are transferred in a reaction, it is an oxidation–reduction reaction.
- One reactant loses electrons, and another reactant gains electrons.
- Overall, the number of electrons lost and gained is equal.

7.4 The Mole

LEARNING GOAL Use Avogadro's number to determine the number of particles in a given number of moles.

- One mole of an element contains 6.02×10^{23} atoms.
- One mole of a compound contains 6.02×10^{23} molecules or formula units.

7.5 Molar Mass and Calculations
LEARNING GOAL Calculate the molar mass for a substance given its chemical formula; use molar mass to convert between grams and moles.

- The molar mass (g/mole) of any substance is the mass in grams equal numerically to its atomic mass, or the sum of the atomic masses, which have been multiplied by their subscripts in a formula.
- The molar mass is used as a conversion factor to change a quantity in grams to moles or to change a given number of moles to grams.

7.6 Mole Relationships in Chemical Equations
LEARNING GOAL Given a quantity in moles of reactant or product, use a mole–mole factor from the balanced chemical equation to calculate the number of moles of another substance in the reaction.

$2Ag(s)$ + $S(s)$ ⟶ $Ag_2S(s)$

Mass of reactants = Mass of product

- In a balanced equation, the total mass of the reactants is equal to the total mass of the products.
- The coefficients in an equation describing the relationship between the moles of any two components are used to write mole–mole factors.
- When the number of moles for one substance is known, a mole–mole factor is used to find the moles of a different substance in the reaction.

7.7 Mass Calculations for Reactions
LEARNING GOAL Given the mass in grams of a substance in a reaction, calculate the mass in grams of another substance in the reaction.

- In calculations using equations, the molar masses of the substances and their mole–mole factors are used to change the number of grams of one substance to the corresponding grams of a different substance.

7.8 Limiting Reactants and Percent Yield
LEARNING GOAL Identify a limiting reactant and calculate the amount of product formed from the limiting reactant. Given the actual quantity of product, determine the percent yield for a reaction.

- A limiting reactant is the reactant that produces the smaller amount of product while the other reactant is left over.
- When the masses of two reactants are given, the mass of a product is calculated from the limiting reactant.
- The percent yield for a reaction indicates the percent of product actually produced during a reaction.
- The percent yield is calculated by dividing the actual yield in grams of a product by the theoretical yield in grams and multiplying by 100%.

7.9 Energy in Chemical Reactions
LEARNING GOAL Given the heat of reaction, calculate the loss or gain of heat for an exothermic or endothermic reaction.

- In chemical reactions, the heat of reaction (ΔH) is the energy difference between the products and the reactants.
- In an exothermic reaction, the energy of the products is lower than that of the reactants. Heat is released, and ΔH is negative.
- In an endothermic reaction, the energy of the products is higher than that of the reactants; heat is absorbed, and ΔH is positive.

KEY TERMS

actual yield The actual amount of product produced by a reaction.

Avogadro's number The number of items in a mole, equal to 6.02×10^{23}.

balanced equation The final form of a chemical equation that shows the same number of atoms of each element in the reactants and products.

chemical equation A shorthand way to represent a chemical reaction using chemical formulas to indicate the reactants and products and coefficients to show reacting ratios.

coefficients Whole numbers placed in front of the formulas to balance the number of atoms or moles of atoms of each element on both sides of an equation.

combination reaction A chemical reaction in which reactants combine to form a single product.

combustion reaction A chemical reaction in which a fuel containing carbon and hydrogen reacts with oxygen to produce CO_2, H_2O, and energy.

decomposition reaction A reaction in which a single reactant splits into two or more simpler substances.

double replacement reaction A reaction in which parts of two different reactants exchange places.

endothermic reaction A reaction that requires heat; the energy of the products is higher than the energy of the reactants.

exothermic reaction A reaction that releases heat; the energy of the products is lower than the energy of the reactants.

formula unit The group of ions represented by the formula of an ionic compound.

heat of reaction The heat (symbol ΔH) absorbed or released when a reaction takes place at constant pressure.

limiting reactant The reactant used up during a chemical reaction, which limits the amount of product that can form.

molar mass The mass in grams of 1 mole of an element equal numerically to its atomic mass. The molar mass of a compound is equal to the sum of the masses of the elements multiplied by their subscripts in the formula.

mole A group of atoms, molecules, or formula units that contains 6.02×10^{23} of these items.

mole–mole factor A conversion factor that relates the number of moles of two compounds derived from the coefficients in an equation.

oxidation The loss of electrons by a substance. Biological oxidation may involve the addition of oxygen or the loss of hydrogen.

oxidation–reduction reaction A reaction in which the oxidation of one reactant is always accompanied by the reduction of another reactant.

percent yield The ratio of the actual yield for a reaction to the theoretical yield possible for the reaction.

products The substances formed as a result of a chemical reaction.

reactants The initial substances that undergo change in a chemical reaction.

reduction The gain of electrons by a substance. Biological reduction may involve the loss of oxygen or the gain of hydrogen.

single replacement reaction A reaction in which an element replaces a different element in a compound.

theoretical yield The maximum amount of product that a reaction can produce from a given amount of reactant.

⚛ CORE CHEMISTRY SKILLS

The chapter section containing each Core Chemistry Skill is shown in parentheses at the end of each heading.

Balancing a Chemical Equation (7.1)

- In a *balanced* equation, whole numbers called coefficients multiply each of the atoms in the chemical formulas so that the number of each type of atom in the reactants is equal to the number of the same type of atom in the products.

Example: Balance the following chemical equation:

$SnCl_4(s) + H_2O(l) \longrightarrow Sn(OH)_4(s) + HCl(aq)$ Unbalanced

Answer: When we compare the atoms on the reactant side and the product side, we see that there are more Cl atoms in the reactants and more O and H atoms in the products.

To balance the equation, we need to use coefficients in front of the formulas containing the Cl atoms, H atoms, and O atoms.

- Place a 4 in front of the formula HCl to give 8 H atoms and 4 Cl atoms in the products.

$SnCl_4(s) + H_2O(l) \longrightarrow Sn(OH)_4(s) + 4HCl(aq)$

- Place a 4 in front of the formula H_2O to give 8 H atoms and 4 O atoms in the reactants.

$SnCl_4(s) + 4H_2O(l) \longrightarrow Sn(OH)_4(s) + 4HCl(aq)$

- The total number of Sn (1), Cl (4), H (8), and O (4) atoms is now equal on both sides of the equation.

$SnCl_4(s) + 4H_2O(l) \longrightarrow Sn(OH)_4(s) + 4HCl(aq)$ Balanced

Classifying Types of Chemical Reactions (7.2)

- Chemical reactions are classified by identifying general patterns in their equations.
- In a combination reaction, two or more elements or compounds bond to form one product.
- In a decomposition reaction, a single reactant splits into two or more products.
- In a single replacement reaction, an uncombined element takes the place of an element in a compound.
- In a double replacement reaction, the positive ions in the reacting compounds switch places.

- In combustion reaction, a carbon-containing compound that is the fuel burns in oxygen from the air to produce carbon dioxide (CO_2), water (H_2O), and energy.

Example: Classify the type of the following reaction:

$$2Al(s) + Fe_2O_3(s) \xrightarrow{\Delta} Al_2O_3(s) + 2Fe(l)$$

Answer: The iron in iron(III) oxide is replaced by aluminum, which makes this a single replacement reaction.

Identifying Oxidized and Reduced Substances (7.3)

- In an oxidation–reduction reaction (abbreviated *redox*), one reactant is oxidized when it loses electrons, and another reactant is reduced when it gains electrons.
- Oxidation is the *loss* of electrons; reduction is the *gain* of electrons.

Example: For the following redox reaction, identify the reactant that is oxidized, and the reactant that is reduced:

$$Fe(s) + Cu^{2+}(aq) \longrightarrow Fe^{2+}(aq) + Cu(s)$$

Answer: $Fe^0(s) \longrightarrow Fe^{2+}(aq) + 2\,e^-$

Fe loses electrons; it is oxidized.

$Cu^{2+}(aq) + 2\,e^- \longrightarrow Cu^0(s)$

Cu^{2+} gains electrons; it is reduced.

Converting Particles to Moles (7.4)

- In chemistry, atoms, molecules, and ions are counted by the mole, a unit that contains 6.02×10^{23} items, which is Avogadro's number.
- For example, 1 mole of carbon contains 6.02×10^{23} atoms of carbon and 1 mole of H_2O contains 6.02×10^{23} molecules of H_2O.
- Avogadro's number is used to convert between particles and moles.

Example: How many moles of nickel contain 2.45×10^{24} Ni atoms?

Answer: 2.45×10^{24} Ni atoms $\times \dfrac{\overset{\text{Exact}}{1 \text{ mole Ni}}}{\underset{\text{Three SFs}}{6.02 \times 10^{23} \text{ Ni atoms}}}$

Three SFs

$= 4.07$ moles of Ni

Three SFs

Calculating Molar Mass (7.5)

- The molar mass of a compound is the sum of the molar mass of each element in its chemical formula multiplied by its subscript in the formula.

Example: Pinene, $C_{10}H_{16}$, which is found in pine tree sap and essential oils, has anti-inflammatory properties. Calculate the molar mass for pinene.

Pinene is a component of pine sap.

Answer:

$$10 \text{ moles C} \times \frac{12.01 \text{ g C}}{1 \text{ mole C}} = 120.1 \text{ g of C}$$

$$16 \text{ moles H} \times \frac{1.008 \text{ g H}}{1 \text{ mole H}} = 16.13 \text{ g of H}$$

Molar mass of $C_{10}H_{16} = 136.2$ g

Using Molar Mass as a Conversion Factor (7.5)

- The molar mass of an element is its mass in grams equal numerically to its atomic mass.
- The molar mass of a compound is its mass in grams equal numerically to the sum of the masses of its elements.
- Molar mass is used as a conversion factor to convert between the moles and grams of a substance.

Some bicycles have aluminum frames.

Equality: 1 mole of Al = 26.98 g of Al

Conversion Factors: $\dfrac{26.98 \text{ g Al}}{1 \text{ mole Al}}$ and $\dfrac{1 \text{ mole Al}}{26.98 \text{ g Al}}$

Example: The frame of a bicycle contains 6500 g of aluminum. How many moles of aluminum are in the bicycle frame?

Answer:
$$6500 \text{ g Al} \times \frac{1 \text{ mole Al}}{26.98 \text{ g Al}} = 240 \text{ moles of Al}$$

Two SFs — Four SFs — Two SFs

Using Mole–Mole Factors (7.6)

Consider the balanced chemical equation

$$4Na(s) + O_2(g) \longrightarrow 2Na_2O(s)$$

- The coefficients in a balanced chemical equation represent the moles of reactants and the moles of products. Thus, 4 moles of Na react with 1 mole of O_2 to form 2 moles of Na_2O.
- From the coefficients, mole–mole factors can be written for any two substances as follows:

Na and O_2 $\dfrac{4 \text{ moles Na}}{1 \text{ mole } O_2}$ and $\dfrac{1 \text{ mole } O_2}{4 \text{ moles Na}}$

Na and Na_2O $\dfrac{4 \text{ moles Na}}{2 \text{ moles } Na_2O}$ and $\dfrac{2 \text{ moles } Na_2O}{4 \text{ moles Na}}$

O_2 and Na_2O $\dfrac{1 \text{ mole } O_2}{2 \text{ moles } Na_2O}$ and $\dfrac{2 \text{ moles } Na_2O}{1 \text{ mole } O_2}$

- A mole–mole factor is used to convert the number of moles of one substance in the reaction to the number of moles of another substance in the reaction.

Example: How many moles of sodium are needed to produce 3.5 moles of sodium oxide?

Answer: Given: 3.5 moles of Na_2O **Need:** moles of Na

$$3.5 \text{ moles } Na_2O \times \frac{4 \text{ moles Na}}{2 \text{ moles } Na_2O} = 7.0 \text{ moles of Na}$$

Two SFs — Exact — Two SFs

Converting Grams to Grams (7.7)

- When we have the balanced chemical equation for a reaction, we can use the mass of substance A and then calculate the mass of substance B.

$$A \longrightarrow B$$

- The process is as follows:

(1) Use the molar mass factor of A to convert the mass, in grams, of A to moles of A.
(2) Use the mole–mole factor that converts moles of A to moles of B.
(3) Use the molar mass factor of B to calculate the mass, in grams, of B.

grams of A $\xrightarrow{\text{molar mass A}}$ moles of A $\xrightarrow{\text{mole–mole factor}}$ moles of B $\xrightarrow{\text{molar mass B}}$ grams of B

Example: How many grams of O_2 are needed to completely react with 14.6 g of Na?

$$4Na(s) + O_2(g) \longrightarrow 2Na_2O(s)$$

Answer:
$$14.6 \text{ g Na} \times \frac{1 \text{ mole Na}}{22.99 \text{ g Na}} \times \frac{1 \text{ mole } O_2}{4 \text{ moles Na}} \times \frac{32.00 \text{ g } O_2}{1 \text{ mole } O_2} = 5.08 \text{ g of } O_2$$

Three SFs — Four SFs — Exact — Exact — Three SFs

Calculating Quantity of Product from a Limiting Reactant (7.8)

Often in reactions, the reactants are not consumed at exactly the same time. Then one of the reactants, called the *limiting reactant*, determines the maximum amount of product that can form.

- To determine the limiting reactant, we calculate the amount of product that is possible from each reactant.
- The limiting reactant is the one that produces the smaller amount of product.

Example: If 12.5 g of S reacts with 17.2 g of O_2, what is the limiting reactant and the mass, in grams, of SO_3 produced?

$$2S(s) + 3O_2(g) \longrightarrow 2SO_3(g)$$

Answer:

Mass of SO_3 from S:

$$12.5 \text{ g S} \times \frac{1 \text{ mole S}}{32.07 \text{ g S}} \times \frac{2 \text{ moles } SO_3}{2 \text{ moles S}} \times \frac{80.07 \text{ g } SO_3}{1 \text{ mole } SO_3} = 31.2 \text{ g of } SO_3$$

Three SFs — Four SFs — Exact — Exact — Three SFs

Mass of SO_3 from O_2:

$$17.2 \text{ g } O_2 \times \frac{1 \text{ mole } O_2}{32.00 \text{ g } O_2} \times \frac{2 \text{ moles } SO_3}{3 \text{ moles } O_2} \times \frac{80.07 \text{ g } SO_3}{1 \text{ mole } SO_3}$$

Three SFs — Four SFs — Exact — Exact

Limiting reactant = 28.7 g of SO_3 Smaller amount of SO_3

Three SFs

Calculating Percent Yield (7.8)

- The *theoretical yield* for a reaction is the amount of product (100%) formed if all the reactants were converted to desired product.
- The *actual yield* for the reaction is the mass, in grams, of the product obtained at the end of the experiment. Because some product is usually lost, the actual yield is less than the theoretical yield.
- The *percent yield* is calculated from the actual yield divided by the theoretical yield and multiplied by 100%.

$$\text{Percent yield }(\%) = \frac{\text{actual yield}}{\text{theoretical yield}} \times 100\%$$

Example: If 22.6 g of Al reacts completely with O_2, and 37.8 g of Al_2O_3 is obtained, what is the percent yield of Al_2O_3 for the reaction?

$$4Al(s) + 3O_2(g) \longrightarrow 2Al_2O_3(s)$$

Answer:

Calculation of theoretical yield:

Three SFs   Exact   Exact   Five SFs

$$22.6 \text{ g Al} \times \frac{1 \text{ mole Al}}{26.98 \text{ g Al}} \times \frac{2 \text{ moles Al}_2O_3}{4 \text{ moles Al}} \times \frac{101.96 \text{ g Al}_2O_3}{1 \text{ mole Al}_2O_3}$$

Four SFs   Exact   Exact

$= 42.7$ g of Al_2O_3 Theoretical yield

Three SFs

Calculation of percent yield:

$$\frac{\text{actual yield (given)}}{\text{theoretical yield (calculated)}} \times 100\% = \frac{37.8 \text{ g Al}_2O_3}{42.7 \text{ g Al}_2O_3} \times 100\%$$

Three SFs

Three SFs

$= 88.5\%$

Three SFs

Using the Heat of Reaction (7.9)

- The heat of reaction is the amount of heat, in kJ or kcal, that is absorbed or released during a reaction.
- The heat of reaction, symbol ΔH, is the difference in the energy of the products and the reactants.

$$\Delta H = H_{products} - H_{reactants}$$

- In an exothermic reaction (*exo* means "out"), the energy of the products is lower than that of the reactants. This means that heat is released along with the products that form. Then the sign for the heat of reaction, ΔH, is negative.
- In an endothermic reaction (*endo* means "within"), the energy of the products is higher than that of the reactants. The heat is required to convert the reactants to products. Then the sign for the heat of reaction, ΔH, is positive.

Example: How many kilojoules are released when 3.50 g of CH_4 undergoes combustion?

$$CH_4(g) + 2O_2(g) \xrightarrow{\Delta} CO_2(g) + 2H_2O(g) \quad \Delta H = -802 \text{ kJ}$$

Exact   Three SFs

Answer: $3.50 \text{ g CH}_4 \times \dfrac{1 \text{ mole CH}_4}{16.04 \text{ g CH}_4} \times \dfrac{-802 \text{ kJ}}{1 \text{ mole CH}_4} = -175 \text{ kJ}$

Three SFs   Four SFs   Exact   Three SFs

UNDERSTANDING THE CONCEPTS

The chapter sections to review are shown in parentheses at the end of each question.

7.101 Balance each of the following by adding coefficients, and identify the type of reaction for each: (7.1, 7.2)

a.

b.

7.102 Balance each of the following by adding coefficients, and identify the type of reaction for each: (7.1, 7.2)

a.

b.

7.103 If red spheres represent oxygen atoms, blue spheres represent nitrogen atoms, and all the molecules are gases, (7.1, 7.2)

Reactants   Products

a. write the formula for each of the reactants and products.
b. write a balanced equation for the reaction.
c. indicate the type of reaction as combination, decomposition, single replacement, double replacement, or combustion.

7.104 If purple spheres represent iodine atoms, white spheres represent hydrogen atoms, and all the molecules are gases, (7.1, 7.2)

Reactants   Products

a. write the formula for each of the reactants and products.
b. write a balanced equation for the reaction.
c. indicate the type of reaction as combination, decomposition, single replacement, double replacement, or combustion.

7.105 If blue spheres represent nitrogen atoms, purple spheres represent iodine atoms, the reacting molecules are solid, and the products are gases, (7.1, 7.2)

Reactants   **Products**

a. write the formula for each of the reactants and products.
b. write a balanced equation for the reaction.
c. indicate the type of reaction as combination, decomposition, single replacement, double replacement, or combustion.

7.106 If green spheres represent chlorine atoms, yellow-green spheres represent fluorine atoms, white spheres represent hydrogen atoms, and all the molecules are gases, (7.1, 7.2)

Reactants   **Products**

a. write the formula for each of the reactants and products.
b. write a balanced equation for the reaction.
c. indicate the type of reaction as combination, decomposition, single replacement, double replacement, or combustion.

7.107 If green spheres represent chlorine atoms, red spheres represent oxygen atoms, and all the molecules are gases, (7.1, 7.2)

Reactants   **Products**

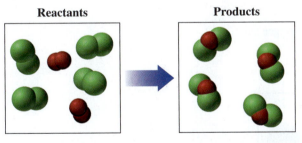

a. write the formula for each of the reactants and products.
b. write a balanced equation for the reaction.
c. indicate the type of reaction as combination, decomposition, single replacement, double replacement, or combustion.

7.108 If blue spheres represent nitrogen atoms, purple spheres represent iodine atoms, the reacting molecules are gases, and the products are solid, (7.1, 7.2)

Reactants   **Products**

a. write the formula for each of the reactants and products.
b. write a balanced equation for the reaction.

c. indicate the type of reaction as combination, decomposition, single replacement, double replacement, or combustion.

7.109 Using the models of the molecules (black = C, white = H, yellow = S, green = Cl), determine each of the following for models of compounds **1** and **2**: (7.4, 7.5)

1.   **2.**

a. molecular formula   **b.** molar mass
c. number of moles in 10.0 g

7.110 Using the models of the molecules (black = C, white = H, yellow = S, red = O), determine each of the following for models of compounds **1** and **2**: (7.4, 7.5)

1.   **2.**

a. molecular formula
b. molar mass
c. number of moles in 10.0 g

7.111 A dandruff shampoo contains dipyrithione, $C_{10}H_8N_2O_2S_2$, which acts as an antibacterial and antifungal agent. (7.4, 7.5)
a. What is the molar mass of dipyrithione?
b. How many moles of dipyrithione are in 25.0 g?
c. How many moles of C are in 25.0 g of dipyrithione?
d. How many moles of dipyrithione contain 8.2×10^{24} atoms of N?

Dandruff shampoo contains dipyrithione.

7.112 Ibuprofen, an anti-inflammatory, has the formula $C_{13}H_{18}O_2$. (7.4, 7.5)

Ibuprofen is an anti-inflammatory.

a. What is the molar mass of ibuprofen?
b. How many grams of ibuprofen are in 0.525 mole?
c. How many moles of C are in 12.0 g of ibuprofen?
d. How many moles of ibuprofen contain 1.22×10^{23} atoms of C?

7.113 If red spheres represent oxygen atoms and blue spheres represent nitrogen atoms, (7.1, 7.8)

Reactants   **Products**

a. write a balanced equation for the reaction.
b. identify the limiting reactant.

7.114 If green spheres represent chlorine atoms, yellow-green spheres represent fluorine atoms, and white spheres represent hydrogen atoms, (7.1, 7.8)

Reactants   **Products**

a. write a balanced equation for the reaction.
b. identify the limiting reactant.

7.115 If blue spheres represent nitrogen atoms and white spheres represent hydrogen atoms, (7.1, 7.8)

Reactants

Products

A   B

or

a. write a balanced equation for the reaction.
b. identify the diagram that shows the products.

7.116 If purple spheres represent iodine atoms and white spheres represent hydrogen atoms, (7.1, 7.8)
a. write a balanced equation for the reaction.
b. identify the diagram that shows the products.

Reactants

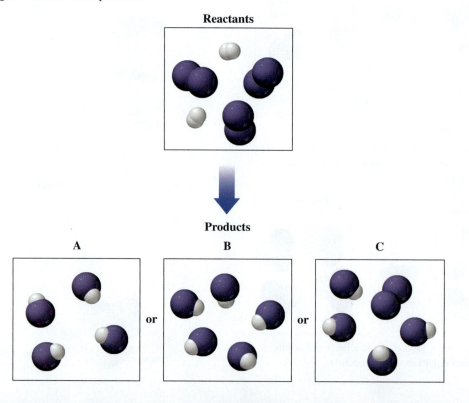

Products

A   B   C

or   or

7.117 If blue spheres represent nitrogen atoms and purple spheres represent iodine atoms, (7.1, 7.8)

Reactants	Actual products

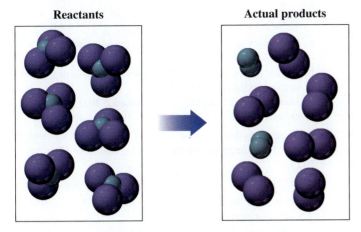

a. write a balanced equation for the reaction.
b. from the diagram of the actual products that result, calculate the percent yield for the reaction.

7.118 If green spheres represent chlorine atoms and red spheres represent oxygen atoms, (7.1, 7.8)

Reactants	Actual products

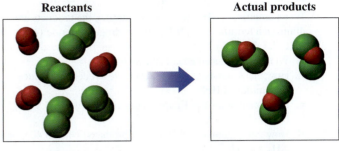

a. write a balanced equation for the reaction.
b. identify the limiting reactant.
c. from the diagram of the actual products that result, calculate the percent yield for the reaction.

ADDITIONAL QUESTIONS AND PROBLEMS

7.119 Identify the type of reaction for each of the following as combination, decomposition, single replacement, double replacement, or combustion: (7.2)
a. A metal and a nonmetal form an ionic compound.
b. A compound of hydrogen and carbon reacts with oxygen to produce carbon dioxide and water.
c. Heating calcium carbonate produces calcium oxide and carbon dioxide.
d. Zinc replaces copper in $Cu(NO_3)_2$.

7.120 Identify the type of reaction for each of the following as combination, decomposition, single replacement, double replacement, or combustion: (7.2)
a. A compound breaks apart into its elements.
b. Copper and bromine form copper(II) bromide.
c. Iron(II) sulfite breaks down to iron(II) oxide and sulfur dioxide.
d. Silver ion from $AgNO_3(aq)$ forms a solid with bromide ion from $KBr(aq)$.

7.121 Balance each of the following chemical equations, and identify the type of reaction: (7.1, 7.2)
a. $NH_3(g) + HCl(g) \longrightarrow NH_4Cl(s)$
b. $C_4H_8(g) + O_2(g) \xrightarrow{\Delta} CO_2(g) + H_2O(g)$
c. $Sb(s) + Cl_2(g) \longrightarrow SbCl_3(s)$
d. $NI_3(s) \longrightarrow N_2(g) + I_2(g)$
e. $KBr(aq) + Cl_2(aq) \longrightarrow KCl(aq) + Br_2(l)$
f. $Fe(s) + H_2SO_4(aq) \longrightarrow Fe_2(SO_4)_3(aq) + H_2(g)$
g. $Al_2(SO_4)_3(aq) + NaOH(aq) \longrightarrow$
$\qquad\qquad\qquad Na_2SO_4(aq) + Al(OH)_3(s)$

7.122 Balance each of the following chemical equations, and identify the type of reaction: (7.1, 7.2)
a. $Si_3N_4(s) \longrightarrow Si(s) + N_2(g)$
b. $Mg(s) + N_2(g) \longrightarrow Mg_3N_2(s)$
c. $Al(s) + H_3PO_4(aq) \longrightarrow AlPO_4(aq) + H_2(g)$
d. $C_3H_4(g) + O_2(g) \xrightarrow{\Delta} CO_2(g) + H_2O(g)$
e. $Cr_2O_3(s) + H_2(g) \longrightarrow Cr(s) + H_2O(g)$
f. $Al(s) + Cl_2(g) \longrightarrow AlCl_3(s)$
g. $MgCl_2(aq) + AgNO_3(aq) \longrightarrow$
$\qquad\qquad\qquad Mg(NO_3)_2(aq) + AgCl(s)$

7.123 Predict the products and write a balanced equation for each of the following: (7.1, 7.2)
a. single replacement:
$Zn(s) + HCl(aq) \longrightarrow \underline{\qquad} + \underline{\qquad}$
b. decomposition: $BaCO_3(s) \xrightarrow{\Delta} \underline{\qquad} + \underline{\qquad}$
c. double replacement:
$NaOH(aq) + HCl(aq) \longrightarrow \underline{\qquad} + \underline{\qquad}$
d. combination: $Al(s) + F_2(g) \longrightarrow \underline{\qquad}$

7.124 Predict the products and write a balanced equation for each of the following: (7.1, 7.2)
a. decomposition: $NaCl(s) \xrightarrow{\text{Electricity}} \underline{\qquad} + \underline{\qquad}$
b. combination: $Ca(s) + Br_2(g) \longrightarrow \underline{\qquad}$
c. combustion:
$C_2H_4(g) + O_2(g) \xrightarrow{\Delta} \underline{\qquad} + \underline{\qquad}$
d. double replacement:
$NiCl_2(aq) + NaOH(aq) \longrightarrow \underline{\qquad} + \underline{\qquad}$

7.125 Calculate the molar mass for each of the following: (7.5)
a. $ZnSO_4$, zinc sulfate, zinc supplement
b. $Ca(IO_3)_2$, calcium iodate, iodine source in table salt
c. $C_5H_8NNaO_4$, monosodium glutamate, flavor enhancer
d. $C_6H_{12}O_2$, isoamyl formate, used to make artificial fruit syrups

7.126 Calculate the molar mass for each of the following: (7.5)
a. $MgCO_3$, magnesium carbonate, used in antacids
b. $Au(OH)_3$, gold(III) hydroxide, used in gold plating
c. $C_{18}H_{34}O_2$, oleic acid, from olive oil
d. $C_{21}H_{26}O_5$, prednisone, anti-inflammatory

7.127 How many grams are in 0.150 mole of each of the following? (7.5)
a. K   **b.** Cl_2 **c.** Na_2CO_3

7.128 How many grams are in 2.25 moles of each of the following? (7.5)
a. N_2 **b.** NaBr   **c.** C_6H_{14}

7.129 How many moles are in 25.0 g of each of the following compounds? (7.5)
a. CO_2 **b.** Al_2O_3 **c.** $MgCl_2$

7.130 How many moles are in 4.00 g of each of the following compounds? (7.5)
    a. NH_3 **b.** $Ca(NO_3)_2$ **c.** SO_3

7.131 When ammonia (NH_3) reacts with fluorine, the products are dinitrogen tetrafluoride (N_2F_4) and hydrogen fluoride (HF). (7.1, 7.5, 7.6, 7.7)
    a. Write the balanced chemical equation.
    b. How many moles of each reactant are needed to produce 4.00 moles of HF?
    c. How many grams of F_2 are needed to react with 25.5 g of NH_3?
    d. How many grams of N_2F_4 can be produced when 3.40 g of NH_3 reacts?

7.132 When nitrogen dioxide (NO_2) from car exhaust combines with water in the air, it forms nitric acid (HNO_3), which causes acid rain, and nitrogen oxide. (7.1, 7.5, 7.6, 7.7)
    a. Write the balanced chemical equation.
    b. How many moles of each product are produced from 0.250 mole of H_2O?
    c. How many grams of HNO_3 are produced when 60.0 g of NO_2 completely reacts?
    d. How many grams of NO_2 are needed to form 75.0 g of HNO_3?

7.133 When hydrogen peroxide (H_2O_2) is used in rocket fuels, it produces water and oxygen (O_2). (7.5, 7.6, 7.7)
$$2H_2O_2(l) \longrightarrow 2H_2O(l) + O_2(g)$$
    a. How many moles of H_2O_2 are needed to produce 3.00 moles of H_2O?
    b. How many grams of H_2O_2 are required to produce 36.5 g of O_2?
    c. How many grams of H_2O can be produced when 12.2 g of H_2O_2 reacts?

7.134 Propane gas (C_3H_8) reacts with oxygen to produce carbon dioxide and water. (7.5, 7.6, 7.7)
$$C_3H_8(g) + 5O_2(g) \xrightarrow{\Delta} 3CO_2(g) + 4H_2O(l)$$
    a. How many moles of H_2O form when 5.00 moles of C_3H_8 completely reacts?
    b. How many grams of CO_2 are produced from 18.5 g of oxygen gas?
    c. How many grams of H_2O can be produced when 46.3 g of C_3H_8 reacts?

7.135 When 12.8 g of Na and 10.2 g of Cl_2 react, what is the mass, in grams, of NaCl that is produced? (7.5, 7.6, 7.7)
$$2Na(s) + Cl_2(g) \longrightarrow 2NaCl(s)$$

7.136 If 35.8 g of CH_4 and 75.5 g of S react, how many grams of H_2S are produced? (7.5, 7.6, 7.7)
$$CH_4(g) + 4S(g) \longrightarrow CS_2(g) + 2H_2S(g)$$

7.137 Pentane gas (C_5H_{12}) reacts with oxygen to produce carbon dioxide and water. (7.5, 7.6, 7.7)
$$C_5H_{12}(g) + 8O_2(g) \xrightarrow{\Delta} 5CO_2(g) + 6H_2O(g)$$
    a. How many moles of C_5H_{12} must react to produce 4.00 moles of water?
    b. How many grams of CO_2 are produced from 32.0 g of O_2?
    c. How many grams of CO_2 are formed if 44.5 g of C_5H_{12} is mixed with 108 g of O_2?

7.138 Gasohol is a fuel that contains ethanol (C_2H_6O) that burns in oxygen (O_2) to give carbon dioxide and water. (7.5, 7.6, 7.7, 7.8)
$$C_2H_6O(g) + 3O_2(g) \xrightarrow{\Delta} 2CO_2(g) + 3H_2O(g)$$
    a. How many moles of O_2 are needed to completely react with 4.0 moles of C_2H_6O?
    b. If a car produces 88 g of CO_2, how many grams of O_2 are used up in the reaction?
    c. How many grams of CO_2 are produced if 50.0 g of C_2H_6O are mixed with 75.0 g of O_2?

7.139 The gaseous hydrocarbon acetylene (C_2H_2) used in welders' torches, burns according to the following equation: (7.5, 7.6, 7.7, 7.8)
$$2C_2H_2(g) + 5O_2(g) \xrightarrow{\Delta} 4CO_2(g) + 2H_2O(g)$$
    a. What is the theoretical yield, in grams, of CO_2, if 22.0 g of C_2H_2 completely reacts?
    b. If the actual yield in part **a** is 64.0 g of CO_2, what is the percent yield of CO_2 for the reaction?

7.140 The equation for the decomposition of potassium chlorate is written as (7.5, 7.6, 7.7, 7.8)
$$2KClO_3(s) \xrightarrow{\Delta} 2KCl(s) + 3O_2(g)$$
    a. When 46.0 g of $KClO_3$ is completely decomposed, what is the theoretical yield, in grams, of O_2?
    b. If 12.1 g of O_2 is produced, what is the percent yield of O_2?

7.141 When 28.0 g of acetylene reacts with hydrogen, 24.5 g of ethane is produced. What is the percent yield of C_2H_6 for the reaction? (7.5, 7.6, 7.7, 7.8)
$$C_2H_2(g) + 2H_2(g) \xrightarrow{Pt} C_2H_6(g)$$

7.142 When 50.0 g of iron(III) oxide reacts with carbon monoxide, 32.8 g of iron is produced. What is the percent yield of Fe for the reaction? (7.5, 7.6, 7.7, 7.8)
$$Fe_2O_3(s) + 3CO(g) \longrightarrow 2Fe(s) + 3CO_2(g)$$

7.143 The equation for the reaction of nitrogen and oxygen to form nitrogen oxide is written as (7.5, 7.6, 7.7, 7.9)
$$N_2(g) + O_2(g) \longrightarrow 2NO(g) \qquad \Delta H = +90.2 \text{ kJ}$$
    a. How many kilojoules are required to form 3.00 g of NO?
    b. What is the complete equation (including heat) for the decomposition of NO?
    c. How many kilojoules are released when 5.00 g of NO decomposes to N_2 and O_2?

7.144 The equation for the reaction of iron and oxygen gas to form rust (Fe_2O_3) is written as (7.5, 7.6, 7.7, 7.9)
$$4Fe(s) + 3O_2(g) \longrightarrow 2Fe_2O_3(s) \quad \Delta H = -1.7 \times 10^3 \text{ kJ}$$
    a. How many kilojoules are released when 2.00 g of Fe reacts?
    b. How many grams of rust form when 150 kJ are released?

℞ Clinical Applications

7.145 Each of the following is a reaction that occurs in the cells of the body. Identify which is exothermic and endothermic. (7.9)
    a. Succinyl CoA + H_2O $\longrightarrow$ succinate + CoA + 8.9 kcal
    b. GDP + P_i + 34 kJ $\longrightarrow$ GTP + H_2O

7.146 Each of the following is a reaction that is needed by the cells of the body. Identify which is exothermic and endothermic. (7.9)
    a. Phosphocreatine + H_2O $\longrightarrow$ creatine + P_i + 10.2 kcal
    b. Fructose-6-phosphate + P_i + 16 kJ $\longrightarrow$
                                   fructose-1,6-bisphosphate

CHALLENGE QUESTIONS

The following groups of questions are related to the topics in this chapter. However, they do not all follow the chapter order, and they require you to combine concepts and skills from several sections. These questions will help you increase your critical thinking skills and prepare for your next exam.

7.147 At a winery, glucose ($C_6H_{12}O_6$) in grapes undergoes fermentation to produce ethanol (C_2H_6O) and carbon dioxide. (7.6, 7.7)

$$C_6H_{12}O_6 \longrightarrow 2C_2H_6O + 2CO_2$$

Glucose   Ethanol

Glucose in grapes ferments to produce ethanol.

   a. How many grams of glucose are required to form 124 g of ethanol?
   b. How many grams of ethanol would be formed from the reaction of 0.240 kg of glucose?

7.148 Gasohol is a fuel containing ethanol (C_2H_6O) that burns in oxygen (O_2) to give carbon dioxide and water. (7.1, 7.6, 7.7)
   a. Write the balanced chemical equation.
   b. How many moles of O_2 are needed to completely react with 8.0 moles of C_2H_6O?
   c. If a car produces 4.4 g of CO_2, how many grams of O_2 are used up in the reaction?
   d. If you burn 125 g of C_2H_6O, how many grams of CO_2 and H_2O can be produced?

7.149 Consider the following *unbalanced* equation: (7.1, 7.2, 7.6, 7.7)

$$Al(s) + O_2(g) \longrightarrow Al_2O_3(s)$$

   a. Write the balanced chemical equation.
   b. Identify the type of reaction.
   c. How many moles of O_2 are needed to react with 4.50 moles of Al?
   d. How many grams of Al_2O_3 are produced when 50.2 g of Al reacts?
   e. When Al is reacted in a closed container with 8.00 g of O_2, how many grams of Al_2O_3 can form?

7.150 A toothpaste contains 0.240% by mass sodium fluoride used to prevent dental caries and 0.30% by mass triclosan $C_{12}H_7Cl_3O_2$, an antigingivitis agent. One tube contains 119 g of toothpaste. (7.4, 7.5)

Components in toothpaste include triclosan and NaF.

   a. How many moles of NaF are in the tube of toothpaste?
   b. How many fluoride ions, F^-, are in the tube of toothpaste?
   c. How many grams of sodium ion, Na^+, are in 1.50 g of toothpaste?
   d. How many molecules of triclosan are in the tube of toothpaste?

7.151 Chromium and oxygen combine to form chromium(III) oxide. (7.6, 7.7, 7.8)

$$4Cr(s) + 3O_2(g) \longrightarrow 2Cr_2O_3(s)$$

   a. How many moles of O_2 react with 4.50 moles of Cr?
   b. How many grams of Cr_2O_3 are produced when 24.8 g of Cr reacts?
   c. When 26.0 g of Cr reacts with 8.00 g of O_2, how many grams of Cr_2O_3 can form?
   d. If 74.0 g of Cr and 62.0 g of O_2 are mixed, and 87.3 g of Cr_2O_3 is actually obtained, what is the percent yield of Cr_2O_3 for the reaction?

7.152 Aluminum and chlorine combine to form aluminum chloride. (7.6, 7.7, 7.8)

$$2Al(s) + 3Cl_2(g) \longrightarrow 2AlCl_3(s)$$

   a. How many moles of Cl_2 are needed to react with 2.50 moles of Al?
   b. How many grams of $AlCl_3$ are produced when 37.7 g of Al reacts?
   c. When 13.5 g of Al reacts with 8.00 g of Cl_2, how many grams of $AlCl_3$ can form?
   d. If 45.0 g of Al and 62.0 g of Cl_2 are mixed, and 66.5 g of $AlCl_3$ is actually obtained, what is the percent yield of $AlCl_3$ for the reaction?

7.153 The combustion of propyne (C_3H_4) releases heat when it burns according to the following equation: (7.6, 7.7, 7.8)

$$C_3H_4(g) + 4O_2(g) \xrightarrow{\Delta} 3CO_2(g) + 2H_2O(g)$$

   a. How many moles of O_2 are needed to react completely with 0.225 mole of C_3H_4?
   b. How many grams of water are produced from the complete reaction of 64.0 g of O_2?
   c. How many grams of CO_2 are produced from the complete reaction of 78.0 g of C_3H_4?
   d. If the reaction in part **c** produces 186 g of CO_2, what is the percent yield of CO_2 for the reaction?

7.154 The gaseous hydrocarbon butane (C_4H_{10}) burns according to the following equation: (7.6, 7.7, 7.8)

$$2C_4H_{10}(g) + 13O_2(g) \xrightarrow{\Delta} 8CO_2(g) + 10H_2O(g)$$

   a. How many moles of H_2O are produced from the complete reaction of 2.50 moles of C_4H_{10}?
   b. How many grams of O_2 are needed to react completely with 22.5 g of C_4H_{10}?
   c. How many grams of CO_2 are produced from the complete reaction of 55.0 g of C_4H_{10}?
   d. If the reaction in part **c** produces 145 g of CO_2, what is the percent yield of CO_2 for the reaction?

7.155 Sulfur trioxide decomposes to sulfur and oxygen. (7.6, 7.7, 7.9)

$$2SO_3(g) \longrightarrow 2S(s) + 3O_2(g) \quad \Delta H = +790 \, kJ$$

    a. Is the reaction endothermic or exothermic?
    b. How many kilojoules are required when 1.5 moles of SO_3 reacts?
    c. How many kilojoules are required when 150 g of O_2 is formed?

7.156 When hydrogen peroxide (H_2O_2) is used in rocket fuels, it produces water, oxygen, and heat. (7.6, 7.7, 7.9)

$$2H_2O_2(l) \longrightarrow 2H_2O(l) + O_2(g) \quad \Delta H = -196 \, kJ$$

    a. Is the reaction endothermic or exothermic?
    b. How many kilojoules are released when 2.50 moles of H_2O_2 reacts?
    c. How many kilojoules are released when 275 g of O_2 is produced?

ANSWERS

Answers to Selected Questions and Problems

7.1 a. $N_2(g) + O_2(g) \longrightarrow 2NO(g)$
    b. $2HgO(s) \longrightarrow 2Hg(l) + O_2(g)$
    c. $4Fe(s) + 3O_2(g) \longrightarrow 2Fe_2O_3(s)$
    d. $2Na(s) + Cl_2(g) \longrightarrow 2NaCl(s)$
    e. $2Cu_2O(s) + O_2(g) \longrightarrow 4CuO(s)$

7.3 a. $Mg(s) + 2AgNO_3(aq) \longrightarrow Mg(NO_3)_2(aq) + 2Ag(s)$
    b. $CuCO_3(s) \longrightarrow CuO(s) + CO_2(g)$
    c. $2Al(s) + 3CuSO_4(aq) \longrightarrow 3Cu(s) + Al_2(SO_4)_3(aq)$
    d. $Pb(NO_3)_2(aq) + 2NaCl(aq) \longrightarrow$
                       $PbCl_2(s) + 2NaNO_3(aq)$
    e. $2Al(s) + 6HCl(aq) \longrightarrow 2AlCl_3(aq) + 3H_2(g)$

7.5 a. $Fe_2O_3(s) + 3CO(g) \longrightarrow 2Fe(s) + 3CO_2(g)$
    b. $2Li_3N(s) \longrightarrow 6Li(s) + N_2(g)$
    c. $2Al(s) + 6HBr(aq) \longrightarrow 2AlBr_3(aq) + 3H_2(g)$
    d. $3Ba(OH)_2(aq) + 2Na_3PO_4(aq) \longrightarrow$
                       $Ba_3(PO_4)_2(s) + 6NaOH(aq)$
    e. $As_4S_6(s) + 9O_2(g) \longrightarrow As_4O_6(s) + 6SO_2(g)$

7.7 a. $2Li(s) + 2H_2O(l) \longrightarrow H_2(g) + 2LiOH(aq)$
    b. $2P(s) + 5Cl_2(g) \longrightarrow 2PCl_5(s)$
    c. $FeO(s) + CO(g) \longrightarrow Fe(s) + CO_2(g)$
    d. $2C_5H_{10}(l) + 15O_2(g) \xrightarrow{\Delta} 10CO_2(g) + 10H_2O(g)$
    e. $3H_2S(g) + 2FeCl_3(s) \longrightarrow Fe_2S_3(s) + 6HCl(g)$

7.9 $NH_4NO_3(s) \xrightarrow{\Delta} 2H_2O(g) + N_2O(g)$

7.11 $2C_3H_7NO_2(aq) + 6O_2(g) \longrightarrow$
             $5CO_2(g) + 5H_2O(l) + CH_4N_2O(aq)$

7.13 a. decomposition   **b.** single replacement
    c. combustion   **d.** double replacement
    e. combination

7.15 a. combination   **b.** single replacement
    c. decomposition   **d.** double replacement
    e. combustion

7.17 a. $Mg(s) + Cl_2(g) \longrightarrow MgCl_2(s)$
    b. $2HBr(g) \longrightarrow H_2(g) + Br_2(g)$
    c. $Mg(s) + Zn(NO_3)_2(aq) \longrightarrow Zn(s) + Mg(NO_3)_2(aq)$
    d. $K_2S(aq) + Pb(NO_3)_2(aq) \longrightarrow 2KNO_3(aq) + PbS(s)$
    e. $2C_2H_6(g) + 7O_2(g) \xrightarrow{\Delta} 4CO_2(g) + 6H_2O(g)$

7.19 a. reduction   **b.** oxidation
    c. reduction   **d.** reduction

7.21 a. Zn is oxidized, Cl_2 is reduced.
    b. The Br^- in NaBr is oxidized, Cl_2 is reduced.
    c. The O^{2-} in PbO is oxidized, the Pb^{2+} in PbO is reduced.
    d. Sn^{2+} is oxidized, Fe^{3+} is reduced.

7.23 a. reduction   **b.** oxidation

7.25 Linoleic acid gains hydrogen atoms and is reduced.

7.27 One mole contains 6.02×10^{23} atoms of an element, molecules of a molecular substance, or formula units of an ionic substance.

7.29 a. 3.01×10^{23} atoms of C
    b. 7.71×10^{23} molecules of SO_2
    c. 0.0867 mole of Fe
    d. 14.1 moles of C_2H_6O

7.31 a. 6.00 moles of H
    b. 8.00 moles of O
    c. 1.20×10^{24} atoms of P
    d. 4.82×10^{24} atoms of O

7.33 a. 24 moles of H   **b.** 1.0×10^2 moles of C
    c. 0.040 mole of N

7.35 a. 32.2 moles of C   **b.** 6.22 moles of H
    c. 0.230 mole of O

7.37 a. 188.18 g   **b.** 159.7 g
    c. 342.2 g   **d.** 58.33 g

7.39 a. 70.90 g   **b.** 90.08 g   **c.** 262.9 g   **d.** 83.98 g

7.41 a. 46.0 g   **b.** 112 g   **c.** 14.8 g   **d.** 112 g

7.43 a. 29.2 g   **b.** 108 g   **c.** 4.05 g   **d.** 195 g

7.45 a. 0.463 mole of Ag   **b.** 0.0167 mole of C
    c. 0.881 mole of NH_3 **d.** 1.17 moles of SO_2

7.47 a. 1.24 moles of Ne   **b.** 0.781 mole of O_2
    c. 0.321 mole of $Al(OH)_3$ **d.** 0.106 mole of Ga_2S_3

7.49 a. 0.78 mole of S   **b.** 1.95 moles of S
    c. 6.0 moles of S

7.51 a. 602 g   **b.** 74.7 g

7.53 a. 66.0 g of N_2O **b.** 0.772 mole of N_2O
    c. 21.6 g of N

7.55 a. 329.4 g   **b.** 498.4 g
    c. 60.09 g   **d.** 331.4 g

7.57 a. $\dfrac{2 \text{ moles } SO_2}{1 \text{ mole } O_2}$ and $\dfrac{1 \text{ mole } O_2}{2 \text{ moles } SO_2}$

       $\dfrac{2 \text{ moles } SO_2}{2 \text{ moles } SO_3}$ and $\dfrac{2 \text{ moles } SO_3}{2 \text{ moles } SO_2}$

       $\dfrac{2 \text{ moles } SO_3}{1 \text{ mole } O_2}$ and $\dfrac{1 \text{ mole } O_2}{2 \text{ moles } SO_3}$

    b. $\dfrac{4 \text{ moles } P}{5 \text{ moles } O_2}$ and $\dfrac{5 \text{ moles } O_2}{4 \text{ moles } P}$

       $\dfrac{4 \text{ moles } P}{2 \text{ moles } P_2O_5}$ and $\dfrac{2 \text{ moles } P_2O_5}{4 \text{ moles } P}$

       $\dfrac{5 \text{ moles } O_2}{2 \text{ moles } P_2O_5}$ and $\dfrac{2 \text{ moles } P_2O_5}{5 \text{ moles } O_2}$

7.59 a. 1.0 mole of O_2 **b.** 10. moles of H_2
   c. 5.0 moles of H_2O

7.61 a. 1.25 moles of C   **b.** 0.96 mole of CO
   c. 1.0 mole of SO_2 **d.** 0.50 mole of CS_2

7.63 a. 77.5 g of Na_2O **b.** 6.26 g of O_2
   c. 19.4 g of O_2

7.65 a. 19.2 g of O_2 **b.** 3.79 g of N_2
   c. 54.0 g of H_2O

7.67 a. 3.66 g of H_2O **b.** 3.44 g of NO
   c. 7.53 g of HNO_3

7.69 a. $2PbS(s) + 3O_2(g) \longrightarrow 2PbO(s) + 2SO_2(g)$
   b. 6.02 g of O_2
   c. 17.4 g of SO_2
   d. 137 g of PbS

7.71 a. 9.59 g of O_2 **b.** 6.00 g of urea
   c. 13.2 g of CO_2

7.73 a. Eight taxis can be used to pick up passengers.
   b. Seven taxis can be driven.

7.75 a. 5.0 moles of H_2 **b.** 4.0 moles of H_2
   c. 3.0 moles of N_2

7.77 a. 25.1 g of $AlCl_3$ **b.** 13.5 g of H_2O
   c. 26.7 g of SO_2

7.79 a. 31.2 g of SO_3 **b.** 34.6 g of Fe_3O_4
   c. 35.0 g of CO_2

7.81 a. 71.0%   **b.** 63.2%

7.83 70.9 g of Al_2O_3

7.85 60.5%

7.87 In exothermic reactions, the energy of the products is lower than that of the reactants.

7.89 a. exothermic   **b.** endothermic
   c. exothermic

7.91 a. Heat is released, exothermic, $\Delta H = -802$ kJ
   b. Heat is absorbed, endothermic, $\Delta H = +65.3$ kJ
   c. Heat is released, exothermic, $\Delta H = -850$ kJ

7.93 a. 579 kJ   **b.** 89 kJ

7.95 a. endothermic   **b.** 12.3 g of glucose
   c. 390 kJ

7.97 a. 0.150 mole of P   **b.** 7.53×10^{23} Ca^{2+} ions
   c. 1.41 moles of hydroxyapatite   **d.** 502.3 g/mole

7.99 a. $2H_2O_2(aq) \longrightarrow 2H_2O(l) + O_2(g)$
   b. decomposition   **c.** 0.825 mole of O_2
   d. 9.10 g of H_2O_2 **e.** 0.35 g of O_2
   f. 62.0% yield

7.101 a. 1,1,2 combination   **b.** 2,2,1 decomposition

7.103 a. reactants NO and O_2; product NO_2
   b. $2NO(g) + O_2(g) \longrightarrow 2NO_2(g)$
   c. combination

7.105 a. reactant NI_3; product N_2 and I_2
   b. $2NI_3(s) \longrightarrow N_2(g) + 3I_2(g)$
   c. decomposition

7.107 a. reactants Cl_2 and O_2; product OCl_2
   b. $2Cl_2(g) + O_2(g) \longrightarrow 2OCl_2(g)$
   c. combination

7.109 1. a. S_2Cl_2 **b.** 135.04 g/mole
   c. 0.0741 mole

   2. a. C_6H_6 **b.** 78.11 g/mole
   c. 0.128 mole

7.111 a. 252.3 g/mole
   b. 0.0991 mole of dipyrithione
   c. 0.991 mole of C
   d. 6.8 moles of dipyrithione

7.113 a. $2NO + O_2 \longrightarrow 2NO_2$
   b. NO is the limiting reactant.

7.115 a. $N_2 + 3H_2 \longrightarrow 2NH_3$ **b.** A

7.117 a. $2NI_3 \longrightarrow N_2 + 3I_2$ **b.** 67%

7.119 a. combination   **b.** combustion
   c. decomposition   **d.** single replacement

7.121 a. $NH_3(g) + HCl(g) \longrightarrow NH_4Cl(s)$ combination
   b. $C_4H_8(g) + 6O_2(g) \xrightarrow{\Delta}$
                  $4CO_2(g) + 4H_2O(g)$ combustion
   c. $2Sb(s) + 3Cl_2(g) \longrightarrow 2SbCl_3(s)$ combination
   d. $2NI_3(s) \longrightarrow N_2(g) + 3I_2(g)$ decomposition
   e. $2KBr(aq) + Cl_2(aq) \longrightarrow$
                  $2KCl(aq) + Br_2(l)$ single replacement
   f. $2Fe(s) + 3H_2SO_4(aq) \longrightarrow$
                  $Fe_2(SO_4)_3(aq) + 3H_2(g)$ single replacement
   g. $Al_2(SO_4)_3(aq) + 6NaOH(aq) \longrightarrow$
                  $3Na_2SO_4(aq) + 2Al(OH)_3(s)$ double replacement

7.123 a. $Zn(s) + 2HCl(aq) \longrightarrow ZnCl_2(aq) + H_2(g)$
   b. $BaCO_3(s) \xrightarrow{\Delta} BaO(s) + CO_2(g)$
   c. $NaOH(aq) + HCl(aq) \longrightarrow NaCl(aq) + H_2O(l)$
   d. $2Al(s) + 3F_2(g) \longrightarrow 2AlF_3(s)$

7.125 a. 161.48 g/mole   **b.** 389.9 g/mole
   c. 169.11 g/mole   **d.** 116.16 g/mole

7.127 a. 5.87 g   **b.** 10.6 g   **c.** 15.9 g

7.129 a. 0.568 mole   **b.** 0.245 mole   **c.** 0.263 mole

7.131 a. $2NH_3(g) + 5F_2(g) \longrightarrow N_2F_4(g) + 6HF(g)$
   b. 1.33 moles of NH_3 and 3.33 moles of F_2
   c. 142 g of F_2
   d. 10.4 g of N_2F_4

7.133 a. 3.00 moles of H_2O_2 **b.** 77.6 g of H_2O_2
   c. 6.46 g of H_2O

7.135 16.8 g of NaCl

7.137 a. 0.667 mole of C_5H_{12} **b.** 27.5 g of CO_2
   c. 92.8 g of CO_2

7.139 a. 74.4 g of CO_2 **b.** 86.0%

7.141 75.9%

7.143 a. 4.51 kJ
   b. $2NO(g) \longrightarrow N_2(g) + O_2(g) + 90.2$ kJ
   c. 7.51 kJ

7.145 a. exothermic   **b.** endothermic

7.147 a. 242 g of glucose   **b.** 123 g of ethanol

7.149 a. $4Al(s) + 3O_2(g) \longrightarrow 2Al_2O_3(s)$
   b. combination   **c.** 3.38 moles of oxygen
   d. 94.9 g of Al_2O_3 **e.** 17.0 g of Al_2O_3

7.151 a. 3.38 moles of oxygen
   b. 36.2 g of chromium(III) oxide
   c. 25.3 g of chromium(III) oxide
   d. 80.8%

7.153 a. 0.900 mole of oxygen
   b. 18.0 g of water
   c. 257 g of carbon dioxide
   d. 72.4%

7.155 a. endothermic   **b.** 590 kJ
   c. 1200 kJ

8

Gases

AFTER SOCCER PRACTICE, WHITNEY COMPLAINED

that she was having difficulty breathing. Her father took her to the emergency room where she was seen by Sam, a respiratory therapist, who listened to Whitney's chest and then tested her breathing capacity. Based on her limited breathing capacity and the wheezing noise in her chest, Whitney was diagnosed as having asthma.

Sam gave Whitney a nebulizer containing a bronchodilator that opens the airways and allows more air to go into the lungs. During the breathing treatment, he measured the amount of oxygen (O_2) in her blood and explained to Whitney and her father that air is a mixture of gases containing 78% nitrogen (N_2) gas and 21% oxygen (O_2) gas. Because Whitney had difficulty obtaining sufficient oxygen breathing air, Sam gave her supplemental oxygen through an oxygen mask. Within a short period of time, Whitney's breathing returned to normal. The therapist then explained that the lungs work according to Boyle's law: The volume of the lungs increases upon inhalation, and the pressure decreases to make air flow in. However, during an asthma attack, the airways become restricted, and it becomes more difficult to expand the volume of the lungs.

CAREER Respiratory Therapist

Respiratory therapists assess and treat a range of patients, including premature infants whose lungs have not developed and asthmatics or patients with emphysema or cystic fibrosis. In assessing patients, they perform a variety of diagnostic tests including breathing capacity, concentrations of oxygen and carbon dioxide in a patient's blood, as well as blood pH.

In order to treat patients, therapists provide oxygen or aerosol medications to the patient, as well as chest physiotherapy to remove mucus from their lungs. Respiratory therapists also educate patients on how to correctly use their inhalers.

We all live at the bottom of a sea of gases called the atmosphere. The most important of these gases is oxygen, which constitutes about 21% of the atmosphere. Without oxygen, life on this planet would be impossible: Oxygen is vital to all life processes of plants and animals. Ozone (O_3), formed in the upper atmosphere by the interaction of oxygen with ultraviolet light, absorbs some of the harmful radiation before it can strike the Earth's surface. The other gases in the atmosphere include nitrogen (78% of the atmosphere), argon, carbon dioxide (CO_2), and water vapor. Carbon dioxide gas, a product of combustion and metabolism, is used by plants in photosynthesis, a process that produces the oxygen that is essential for humans and animals.

The atmosphere has become a dumping ground for other gases, such as methane, chlorofluorocarbons, and nitrogen oxides as well as volatile organic compounds (VOCs), which are gases from paints, paint thinners, and cleaning supplies. The chemical reactions of these gases with sunlight and oxygen in the air are contributing to air pollution, ozone depletion, climate change, and acid rain. Such chemical changes can seriously affect our health and our lifestyle. An understanding of gases and some of the laws that govern gas behavior can help us understand the nature of matter and allow us to make decisions concerning important environmental and health issues.

LOOKING AHEAD

8.1 Properties of Gases 289

♡ **Chemistry Link to Health** *Measuring Blood Pressure* 294

8.2 Pressure and Volume (Boyle's Law) 295

♡ **Chemistry Link to Health** *Pressure–Volume Relationship in Breathing* 296

8.3 Temperature and Volume (Charles's Law) 298

8.4 Temperature and Pressure (Gay-Lussac's Law) 300

8.5 The Combined Gas Law 303

8.6 Volume and Moles (Avogadro's Law) 304

8.7 The Ideal Gas Law 308

♡ **Chemistry Link to Health** *Hyperbaric Chambers* 310

8.8 Partial Pressures (Dalton's Law) 312

♡ **Chemistry Link to Health** *Blood Gases* 314

℞ **Clinical Applications** 294, 297, 302, 312, 314, 315, 320

℞ **Clinical Update** *Exercise-Induced Asthma* 315

CHAPTER READINESS*

🖩 KEY MATH SKILL
- Solving Equations (1.4D)

⚛ CORE CHEMISTRY SKILLS
- Using Significant Figures in Calculations (2.3)

- Writing Conversion Factors from Equalities (2.5)
- Using Conversion Factors (2.6)
- Using Molar Mass as a Conversion Factor (7.5)
- Using Mole–Mole Factors (7.6)

*These Key Math Skills and Core Chemistry Skills from previous chapters are listed here for your review as you proceed to the new material in this chapter.

8.1 Properties of Gases

We are surrounded by gases, but are not often aware of their presence. Of the elements on the periodic table, only a handful exist as gases at room temperature: H_2, N_2, O_2, F_2, Cl_2, and the noble gases. Another group of gases includes the oxides of the nonmetals on the upper right corner of the periodic table, such as CO, CO_2, NO, NO_2, SO_2, and SO_3. Generally molecules that are gases at room temperature have fewer than five atoms from the first or second period.

The behavior of gases is quite different from that of liquids and solids. Gas particles are far apart, whereas particles of both liquids and solids are held close together. A gas has no definite shape or volume and will completely fill any container. Because there are great distances between gas particles, a gas is less dense than a solid or liquid, and easy to compress. A model for the behavior of a gas, called the **kinetic molecular theory of gases**, helps us understand gas behavior.

LEARNING GOAL

Describe the kinetic molecular theory of gases and the units of measurement used for gases.

Interactive Video

Kinetic Molecular Theory

Kinetic Molecular Theory of Gases

1. **A gas consists of small particles (atoms or molecules) that move randomly with high velocities.** Gas molecules moving in random directions at high speeds cause a gas to fill the entire volume of a container.

2. **The attractive forces between the particles of a gas are usually very small.** Gas particles are far apart and fill a container of any size and shape.

3. **The actual volume occupied by gas molecules is extremely small compared with the volume that the gas occupies.** The volume of the gas is considered equal to the volume of the container. Most of the volume of a gas is empty space, which allows gases to be easily compressed.

4. **Gas particles are in constant motion, moving rapidly in straight paths.** When gas particles collide, they rebound and travel in new directions. Every time they hit the walls of the container, they exert pressure. An increase in the number or force of collisions against the walls of the container causes an increase in the pressure of the gas.

5. **The average kinetic energy of gas molecules is proportional to the Kelvin temperature.** Gas particles move faster as the temperature increases. At higher temperatures, gas particles hit the walls of the container more often and with more force, producing higher pressures.

The kinetic molecular theory helps explain some of the characteristics of gases. For example, we can quickly smell perfume when a bottle is opened on the other side of a room, because its particles move rapidly in all directions. At room temperature, the molecules in the air are moving at about 450 m/s, which is 1000 mi/h. They move faster at higher temperatures and more slowly at lower temperatures. Sometimes tires or gas-filled containers explode when temperatures are too high. From the kinetic molecular theory, we know that gas particles move faster when heated, hit the walls of a container with more force, and cause a buildup of pressure inside a container.

When we talk about a gas, we describe it in terms of four properties: pressure, volume, temperature, and the amount of gas.

Pressure (P)

Gas particles are extremely small and move rapidly. When they hit the walls of a container, they exert **pressure** (see Figure 8.1). If we heat the container, the molecules move faster and smash into the walls more often and with increased force, thus increasing the pressure. The gas particles in the air, mostly oxygen and nitrogen, exert a pressure on us called **atmospheric pressure** (see Figure 8.2). As you go to higher altitudes, the atmospheric pressure is less because there are fewer particles in the air. The most common units used for gas pressure measurement are the *atmosphere* (atm) and *millimeters of mercury* (mmHg). On the TV weather report, you may hear or see the atmospheric pressure given in inches of mercury, or kilopascals in countries other than the United States. In a hospital, the unit torr or psi (pounds per square inch) may be used.

Volume (V)

The volume of gas equals the size of the container in which the gas is placed. When you inflate a tire or a basketball, you are adding more gas particles. The increase in the number of particles hitting the walls of the tire or basketball increases the volume. Sometimes, on a cold morning, a tire looks flat. The volume of the tire has decreased because a lower temperature decreases the speed of the molecules, which in turn reduces the force of their impacts on the walls of the tire. The most common units for volume measurement are liters (L) and milliliters (mL).

Temperature (T)

The temperature of a gas is related to the kinetic energy of its particles. For example, if we have a gas at 200 K in a rigid container and heat it to a temperature of 400 K, the gas particles will have twice the kinetic energy that they did at 200 K. This also means that the gas at 400 K exerts twice the pressure of the gas at 200 K. Although you measure gas

FIGURE 8.1 ▶ Gas particles which move in straight lines within a container, exert pressure when they collide with the walls of the container.

◉ Why does heating the container increase the pressure of the gas within it?

Molecules in air

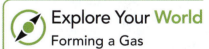

O$_2$ N$_2$ Other gases

21%   78%   ~1%

FIGURE 8.2 ▶ A column of air extending from the upper atmosphere to the surface of the Earth produces a pressure on each of us of about 1 atm. While there is a lot of pressure on the body, it is balanced by the pressure inside the body.

Q Why is there less atmospheric pressure at higher altitudes?

temperature using a Celsius thermometer, all comparisons of gas behavior and all calculations related to temperature must use the Kelvin temperature scale. No one has quite created the conditions for absolute zero (0 K), but we predict that the particles will have zero kinetic energy and the gas will exert zero pressure at absolute zero.

Amount of Gas (*n*)

When you add air to a bicycle tire, you increase the amount of gas, which results in a higher pressure in the tire. Usually we measure the amount of gas by its mass in grams. In gas law calculations, we need to change the grams of gas to moles.

A summary of the four properties of a gas are given in Table 8.1.

TABLE 8.1 Properties That Describe a Gas

Property	Description	Units of Measurement
Pressure (*P*)	The force exerted by a gas against the walls of the container	atmosphere (atm); millimeters of mercury (mmHg); torr (Torr); pascal (Pa)
Volume (*V*)	The space occupied by a gas	liter (L); milliliter (mL)
Temperature (*T*)	The determining factor of the kinetic energy and rate of motion of gas particles	degree Celsius (°C); Kelvin (K) *is required in calculations*
Amount (*n*)	The quantity of gas present in a container	grams (g); moles (*n*) *is required in calculations*

Explore Your World
Forming a Gas

Obtain baking soda and a jar or a plastic bottle. You will also need an elastic glove that fits over the mouth of the jar or a balloon that fits snugly over the top of the plastic bottle. Place a cup of vinegar in the jar or bottle. Sprinkle some baking soda into the fingertips of the glove or into the balloon. Carefully fit the glove or balloon over the top of the jar or bottle. Slowly lift the fingers of the glove or the balloon so that the baking soda falls into the vinegar. Watch what happens. Squeeze the glove or balloon.

Questions

1. Describe the properties of gas that you observe as the reaction takes place between vinegar and baking soda.
2. How do you know that a gas was formed?

SAMPLE PROBLEM 8.1 Properties of Gases

Identify the property of a gas that is described by each of the following:

a. increases the kinetic energy of gas particles
b. the force of the gas particles hitting the walls of the container
c. the space that is occupied by a gas

SOLUTION

a. temperature
b. pressure
c. volume

STUDY CHECK 8.1

As more helium gas is added to a balloon, the number of grams of helium increases. What property of a gas is described?

ANSWER

The mass, in grams, gives the amount of gas.

Vacuum (no air particles)

Gases of the atmosphere at 1 atm

760 mmHg

Liquid mercury

FIGURE 8.3 ▶ A barometer: The pressure exerted by the gases in the atmosphere is equal to the downward pressure of a mercury column in a closed glass tube. The height of the mercury column measured in mmHg is called atmospheric pressure.

Q Why does the height of the mercury column change from day to day?

Measurement of Gas Pressure

When billions and billions of gas particles hit against the walls of a container, they exert *pressure*, which is defined as a force acting on a certain area.

$$\text{Pressure } (P) = \frac{\text{force}}{\text{area}}$$

The atmospheric pressure can be measured using a barometer (see Figure 8.3). At a pressure of exactly 1 atmosphere (atm), a mercury column in an inverted tube would be *exactly* 760 mm high. One **atmosphere (atm)** is defined as *exactly* 760 mmHg (millimeters of mercury). One atmosphere is also 760 Torr, a pressure unit named to honor Evangelista Torricelli, the inventor of the barometer. Because the units of torr and mmHg are equal, they are used interchangeably. One atmosphere is also equivalent to 29.9 in. of mercury (inHg).

1 atm = 760 mmHg = 760 Torr (exact)
1 atm = 29.9 inHg
1 mmHg = 1 Torr (exact)

In SI units, pressure is measured in pascals (Pa); 1 atm is equal to 101 325 Pa. Because a pascal is a very small unit, pressures are usually reported in kilopascals.

1 atm = 1.01325×10^5 Pa = 101.325 kPa

The U.S. equivalent of 1 atm is 14.7 lb/in.^{2} (psi). When you use a pressure gauge to check the air pressure in the tires of a car, it may read 30 to 35 psi. This measurement is actually 30 to 35 psi above the pressure that the atmosphere exerts on the outside of the tire.

1 atm = 14.7 lb/in.^{2}

Table 8.2 summarizes the various units and their symbols used in the measurement of pressure.

TABLE 8.2 Units for Measuring Pressure

Unit	Abbreviation	Unit Equivalent to 1 atm
atmosphere	atm	1 atm (exact)
millimeters of Hg	mmHg	760 mmHg (exact)
torr	Torr	760 Torr (exact)
inches of Hg	inHg	29.9 inHg
pounds per square inch	lb/in.^{2} (psi)	14.7 lb/in.^{2}
pascal	Pa	101 325 Pa
kilopascal	kPa	101.325 kPa

Atmospheric pressure changes with variations in weather and altitude. On a hot, sunny day, a column of air has more particles, which increases the pressure on the mercury surface. The mercury column rises, indicating a higher atmospheric pressure. On a rainy day, the atmosphere exerts less pressure, which causes the mercury column to fall. In the weather report, this type of weather is called a *low-pressure system*. Above sea level, the density of the gases in the air decreases, which causes lower atmospheric pressures; the atmospheric pressure is greater than 760 mmHg at the Dead Sea because it is below sea level (see Table 8.3).

$P = 0.70$ atm (530 mmHg) $P = 1.0$ atm (760 mmHg)

TABLE 8.3 Altitude and Atmospheric Pressure

Location	Altitude (km)	Atmospheric Pressure (mmHg)
Dead Sea	−0.40	800
Sea level	0.00	760
Los Angeles	0.09	752
Las Vegas	0.70	700
Denver	1.60	630
Mount Whitney	4.50	440
Mount Everest	8.90	253

The atmospheric pressure decreases as the altitude increases.

Divers must be concerned about increasing pressures on their ears and lungs when they dive below the surface of the ocean. Because water is more dense than air, the pressure on a diver increases rapidly as the diver descends. At a depth of 33 ft below the surface of the ocean, an additional 1 atm of pressure is exerted by the water on a diver, for a total of 2 atm. At 100 ft, there is a total pressure of 4 atm on a diver. The regulator that a diver uses continuously adjusts the pressure of the breathing mixture to match the increase in pressure.

SAMPLE PROBLEM 8.2 Units of Pressure

The oxygen in a tank in the hospital respiratory unit has a pressure of 4820 mmHg. Calculate the pressure, in atmospheres, of the oxygen gas (see Table 8.2).

SOLUTION

The equality 1 atm = 760 mmHg can be written as two conversion factors:

$$\frac{760 \text{ mmHg}}{1 \text{ atm}} \quad \text{and} \quad \frac{1 \text{ atm}}{760 \text{ mmHg}}$$

Using the conversion factor that cancels mmHg and gives atm, we can set up the problem as

$$4820 \text{ mmHg} \times \frac{\overset{\text{Exact}}{1 \text{ atm}}}{760 \text{ mmHg}} = 6.34 \text{ atm}$$

Three SFs   Exact   Three SFs

A patient with severe COPD obtains oxygen from an oxygen tank.

STUDY CHECK 8.2

A tank of nitrous oxide (N_2O) used as an anesthetic has a pressure of 48 psi. What is that pressure in atmospheres (see Table 8.2)?

ANSWER

3.3 atm

The anesthetic N_2O gas is used for pain relief.

Chemistry Link to **Health**
Measuring Blood Pressure

Your blood pressure is one of the vital signs a doctor or nurse checks during a physical examination. It actually consists of two separate measurements. Acting like a pump, the heart contracts to create the pressure that pushes blood through the circulatory system. During contraction, the blood pressure is at its highest; this is your *systolic* pressure. When the heart muscles relax, the blood pressure falls; this is your *diastolic* pressure. The normal range for systolic pressure is 100 to 120 mmHg. For diastolic pressure, it is 60 to 80 mmHg. These two measurements are usually expressed as a ratio such as 100/80. These values are somewhat higher in older people. When blood pressures are elevated, such as 140/90, there is a greater risk of stroke, heart attack, or kidney damage. Low blood pressure prevents the brain from receiving adequate oxygen, causing dizziness and fainting.

The blood pressures are measured by a sphygmomanometer, an instrument consisting of a stethoscope and an inflatable cuff connected to a tube of mercury called a manometer. After the cuff is wrapped around the upper arm, it is pumped up with air until it cuts off the flow of blood through the arm. With the stethoscope over the artery, the air is slowly released from the cuff, decreasing the pressure on the artery. When the blood flow first starts again in the artery, a noise can be heard through the stethoscope signifying the systolic blood pressure as the pressure shown on the manometer. As air continues to be released, the cuff deflates until no sound is heard in the artery. A second pressure reading is taken at the moment of silence and denotes the diastolic pressure, the pressure when the heart is not contracting.

The use of digital blood pressure monitors is becoming more common. However, they have not been validated for use in all situations and can sometimes give inaccurate readings.

The measurement of blood pressure is part of a routine physical exam.

QUESTIONS AND PROBLEMS

8.1 Properties of Gases

LEARNING GOAL Describe the kinetic molecular theory of gases and the units of measurement used for gases.

8.1 Use the kinetic molecular theory of gases to explain each of the following:
a. Gases move faster at higher temperatures.
b. Gases can be compressed much more than liquids or solids.
c. Gases have low densities.

8.2 Use the kinetic molecular theory of gases to explain each of the following:
a. A container of nonstick cooking spray explodes when thrown into a fire.
b. The air in a hot-air balloon is heated to make the balloon rise.
c. You can smell the odor of cooking onions from far away.

8.3 Identify the property of a gas that is measured in each of the following:
a. 350 K
b. 125 mL
c. 2.00 g of O_2
d. 755 mmHg

8.4 Identify the property of a gas that is measured in each of the following:
a. 425 K
b. 1.0 atm
c. 10.0 L
d. 0.50 mole of He

8.5 Which of the following statement(s) describes the pressure of a gas?
a. the force of the gas particles on the walls of the container
b. the number of gas particles in a container
c. 4.5 L of helium gas
d. 750 Torr
e. 28.8 lb/in.^{2}

8.6 Which of the following statement(s) describes the pressure of a gas?
a. the temperature of the gas
b. the volume of the container
c. 3.00 atm
d. 0.25 mole of O_2
e. 101 kPa

℞ Clinical Applications

8.7 A tank contains oxygen (O_2) at a pressure of 2.00 atm. What is the pressure in the tank in terms of the following units?
a. torr
b. mmHg

8.8 On a climb up Mt. Whitney, the atmospheric pressure drops to 467 mmHg. What is the pressure in terms of the following units?
a. atm
b. torr

8.2 Pressure and Volume (Boyle's Law)

Imagine that you can see air particles hitting the walls inside a bicycle tire pump. What happens to the pressure inside the pump as you push down on the handle? As the volume decreases, there is a decrease in the surface area of the container. The air particles are crowded together, more collisions occur, and the pressure increases within the container.

When a change in one property (in this case, volume) causes a change in another property (in this case, pressure), the properties are related. If the changes occur in opposite directions, the properties have an *inverse relationship*. The inverse relationship between the pressure and volume of a gas is known as **Boyle's law**. The law states that the volume (V) of a sample of gas changes inversely with the pressure (P) of the gas as long as there is no change in the temperature (T) or amount of gas (n) (see Figure 8.4).

If the volume or pressure of a gas sample changes without any change in the temperature or in the amount of the gas, then the final volume will give the same PV product as the initial pressure and volume. Then we can set the initial and final PV products equal to each other.

Boyle's Law

$$P_1 V_1 = P_2 V_2 \qquad \text{No change in number of moles and temperature}$$

> **SAMPLE PROBLEM 8.3** Calculating Volume When Pressure Changes

When Whitney had her asthma attack, oxygen was delivered through a face mask. The gauge on a 12-L tank of compressed oxygen reads 3800 mmHg. How many liters would this same gas occupy at a pressure of 0.75 atm when temperature and amount of gas do not change?

SOLUTION

STEP 1 **Organize the data in a table of initial and final conditions.** To match the units for the initial and final pressures, we can convert either atm to mmHg or mmHg to atm.

$$0.75 \ \cancel{\text{atm}} \times \frac{760 \ \text{mmHg}}{1 \ \cancel{\text{atm}}} = 570 \ \text{mmHg}$$

or

$$3800 \ \cancel{\text{mmHg}} \times \frac{1 \ \text{atm}}{760 \ \cancel{\text{mmHg}}} = 5.0 \ \text{atm}$$

We place the gas data using units of mmHg for pressure and liters for volume in a table. (We could have both pressures in units of atm as well.) The properties that do not change, which are temperature and amount of gas, are shown below the table. We know that pressure decreases, and can predict that the volume increases.

	Conditions 1	Conditions 2	Know	Predict
ANALYZE THE PROBLEM	$P_1 = 3800$ mmHg (5.0 atm)	$P_2 = 570$ mmHg (0.75 atm)	P decreases	
	$V_1 = 12$ L	$V_2 = ?$ L		V increases

Factors that remain constant: T and n

STEP 2 **Rearrange the gas law equation to solve for the unknown quantity.** For a PV relationship, we use Boyle's law and solve for V_2 by dividing both sides by P_2. According to Boyle's law, a decrease in the pressure will cause an increase in the volume when T and n remain constant.

$$P_1 V_1 = P_2 V_2$$
$$\frac{P_1 V_1}{P_2} = \frac{P_2 V_2}{P_2}$$
$$V_2 = V_1 \times \frac{P_1}{P_2}$$

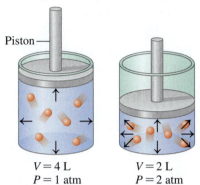

$V = 4$ L
$P = 1$ atm

$V = 2$ L
$P = 2$ atm

FIGURE 8.4 ▶ Boyle's law: As volume decreases, gas molecules become more crowded, which causes the pressure to increase. Pressure and volume are inversely related.

Q If the volume of a gas increases, what will happen to its pressure?

Oxygen therapy increases the oxygen available to the tissues of the body.

⚛ CORE CHEMISTRY SKILL

Using the Gas Laws

Guide to Using the Gas Laws

STEP 1
Organize the data in a table of initial and final conditions.

STEP 2
Rearrange the gas law equation to solve for the unknown quantity.

STEP 3
Substitute values into the gas law equation and calculate.

STEP 3 Substitute values into the gas law equation and calculate. When we substitute in the values with pressures in units of mmHg or atm, the ratio of pressures (pressure factor) is greater than 1, which increases the volume as predicted in Step 1.

$$V_2 = 12\text{ L} \times \frac{3800\text{ mmHg}}{570\text{ mmHg}} = 80.\text{ L}$$

Pressure factor increases volume

or

$$V_2 = 12\text{ L} \times \frac{5.0\text{ atm}}{0.75\text{ atm}} = 80.\text{ L}$$

Pressure factor increases volume

STUDY CHECK 8.3

In an underground natural gas reserve, a bubble of methane gas, CH_4, has a volume of 45.0 mL at 1.60 atm. What volume, in milliliters, will the gas bubble occupy when it reaches the surface where the atmospheric pressure is 744 mmHg, if there is no change in the temperature or amount of gas?

ANSWER

73.5 mL

Chemistry Link to **Health**

Pressure–Volume Relationship in Breathing

The importance of Boyle's law becomes more apparent when you consider the mechanics of breathing. Our lungs are elastic, balloon-like structures contained within an airtight chamber called the thoracic cavity. The diaphragm, a muscle, forms the flexible floor of the cavity.

Inspiration

The process of taking a breath of air begins when the diaphragm contracts and the rib cage expands, causing an increase in the volume of the thoracic cavity. The elasticity of the lungs allows them to expand when the thoracic cavity expands. According to Boyle's law, the pressure inside the lungs decreases when their volume increases, causing the pressure inside the lungs to fall below the pressure of the atmosphere. This difference in pressures produces a *pressure gradient* between the lungs and the atmosphere. In a pressure gradient, molecules flow from an area of higher pressure to an area of lower pressure. During the inhalation phase of breathing, air flows into the lungs (*inspiration*), until the pressure within the lungs becomes equal to the pressure of the atmosphere.

Expiration

Expiration, or the exhalation phase of breathing, occurs when the diaphragm relaxes and moves back up into the thoracic cavity to its

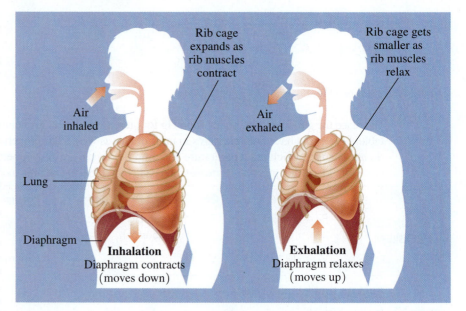

resting position. The volume of the thoracic cavity decreases, which squeezes the lungs and decreases their volume. Now the pressure in the lungs is higher than the pressure of the atmosphere, so air flows out of the lungs. Thus, breathing is a process in which pressure gradients are continuously created between the lungs and the environment because of the changes in the volume and pressure.

QUESTIONS AND PROBLEMS

8.2 Pressure and Volume (Boyle's Law)

LEARNING GOAL Use the pressure–volume relationship (Boyle's law) to determine the final pressure or volume when the temperature and amount of gas are constant.

8.9 Why do scuba divers need to exhale air when they ascend to the surface of the water?

8.10 Why does a sealed bag of chips expand when you take it to a higher altitude?

8.11 The air in a cylinder with a piston has a volume of 220 mL and a pressure of 650 mmHg.

    a. To obtain a higher pressure inside the cylinder at constant temperature and amount of gas, would the cylinder change as shown in **A** or **B**? Explain your choice.

Initial ⟶ **A**   or   **B**

    b. If the pressure inside the cylinder increases to 1.2 atm, what is the final volume, in milliliters, of the cylinder? Complete the following data table:

Property	Conditions 1	Conditions 2	Know	Predict
Pressure (P)				
Volume (V)				

8.12 A balloon is filled with helium gas. When each of the following changes are made at constant temperature, which of the following diagrams (**A**, **B**, or **C**) shows the final volume of the balloon?

Initial volume   **A**   **B**   **C**

    a. The balloon floats to a higher altitude where the outside pressure is lower.

    b. The balloon is taken inside the house, but the atmospheric pressure does not change.

    c. The balloon is put in a hyperbaric chamber in which the pressure is increased.

8.13 A gas with a volume of 4.0 L is in a closed container. Indicate the changes (*increases*, *decreases*, *does not change*) in pressure when the volume undergoes the following changes at constant temperature and amount of gas:

    a. The volume is compressed to 2.0 L.

    b. The volume expands to 12 L.

    c. The volume is compressed to 0.40 L.

8.14 A gas at a pressure of 2.0 atm is in a closed container. Indicate the changes (*increases*, *decreases*, *does not change*) in its volume when the pressure undergoes the following changes at constant temperature and amount of gas:

    a. The pressure increases to 6.0 atm.

    b. The pressure remains at 2.0 atm.

    c. The pressure drops to 0.40 atm.

8.15 A 10.0-L balloon contains helium gas at a pressure of 655 mmHg. What is the final pressure, in millimeters of mercury, of the helium gas at each of the following volumes, if there is no change in temperature and amount of gas?

    a. 20.0 L   **b.** 2.50 L

    c. 13 800 mL   **d.** 1250 mL

8.16 The air in a 5.00-L tank has a pressure of 1.20 atm. What is the final pressure, in atmospheres, when the air is placed in tanks that have the following volumes, if there is no change in temperature and amount of gas?

    a. 1.00 L   **b.** 2500. mL

    c. 750. mL   **d.** 8.00 L

8.17 A sample of nitrogen (N_2) has a volume of 50.0 L at a pressure of 760. mmHg. What is the final volume, in liters, of the gas at each of the following pressures, if there is no change in temperature and amount of gas?

    a. 725 mmHg   **b.** 2.0 atm

    c. 0.500 atm   **d.** 850 Torr

8.18 A sample of methane (CH_4) has a volume of 25 mL at a pressure of 0.80 atm. What is the final volume, in milliliters, of the gas at each of the following pressures, if there is no change in temperature and amount of gas?

    a. 0.40 atm   **b.** 2.00 atm

    c. 2500 mmHg   **d.** 80.0 Torr

℞ Clinical Applications

8.19 Cyclopropane, C_3H_6, is a general anesthetic. A 5.0-L sample has a pressure of 5.0 atm. What is the volume, in liters, of the anesthetic given to a patient at a pressure of 1.0 atm with no change in temperature and amount of gas?

8.20 The volume of air in a person's lungs is 615 mL at a pressure of 760. mmHg. Inhalation occurs as the pressure in the lungs drops to 752 mmHg with no change in temperature and amount of gas. To what volume, in milliliters, did the lungs expand?

8.21 Use the word *inspiration* or *expiration* to describe the part of the breathing cycle that occurs as a result of each of the following:

    a. The diaphragm contracts (flattens out).

    b. The volume of the lungs decreases.

    c. The pressure within the lungs is less than that of the atmosphere.

8.22 Use the word *inspiration* or *expiration* to describe the part of the breathing cycle that occurs as a result of each of the following:

    a. The diaphragm relaxes, moving up into the thoracic cavity.

    b. The volume of the lungs expands.

    c. The pressure within the lungs is greater than that of the atmosphere.

LEARNING GOAL

Use the temperature–volume relationship (Charles's law) to determine the final temperature or volume when the pressure and amount of gas are constant.

As the gas in a hot-air balloon is heated, it expands.

$T = 200$ K $T = 400$ K
$V = 1$ L $V = 2$ L

FIGURE 8.5 ▶ **Charles's law:** The Kelvin temperature of a gas is directly related to the volume of the gas when there is no change in the pressure and amount. When the temperature increases, making the molecules move faster, the volume must increase to maintain constant pressure.

❓ If the temperature of a gas decreases at constant pressure and amount of gas, how will the volume change?

8.3 Temperature and Volume (Charles's Law)

Suppose that you are going to take a ride in a hot-air balloon. The captain turns on a propane burner to heat the air inside the balloon. As the air is heated, it expands and becomes less dense than the air outside, causing the balloon and its passengers to lift off. In 1787, Jacques Charles, a balloonist as well as a physicist, proposed that the volume of a gas is related to the temperature. This became **Charles's law**, which states that the volume (V) of a gas is directly related to the temperature (T) when there is no change in the pressure (P) or amount (n) of gas. A *direct relationship* is one in which the related properties increase or decrease together. For two conditions, initial and final, we can write Charles's law as follows:

Charles's Law

$$\frac{V_1}{T_1} = \frac{V_2}{T_2} \qquad \text{No change in number of moles and pressure}$$

All temperatures used in gas law calculations must be converted to their corresponding Kelvin (K) temperatures.

To determine the effect of changing temperature on the volume of a gas, the pressure and the amount of gas are kept constant. If we increase the temperature of a gas sample, we know from the kinetic molecular theory that the motion (kinetic energy) of the gas particles will also increase. To keep the pressure constant, the volume of the container must increase (see Figure 8.5). If the temperature of the gas decreases, the volume of the container must decrease to maintain the same pressure when the amount of gas is constant.

▶ **SAMPLE PROBLEM 8.4** Calculating Volume When Temperature Changes

Helium gas is used to inflate the abdomen during laparoscopic surgery. A sample of helium gas has a volume of 5.40 L and a temperature of 15 °C. What is the final volume, in liters, of the gas if the temperature has been increased to 42 °C at constant pressure and amount of gas?

SOLUTION

STEP 1 Organize the data in a table of initial and final conditions. The properties that change, which are the temperature and volume, are listed in the following table. The properties that do not change, which are pressure and amount of gas, are shown below the table. When the temperature is given in degrees Celsius, it must be changed to kelvins. Because we know the initial and final temperatures of the gas, we know that the temperature increases. Thus, we can predict that the volume increases.

$$T_1 = 15\,°C + 273 = 288\ K$$
$$T_2 = 42\,°C + 273 = 315\ K$$

	Conditions 1	Conditions 2	Know	Predict
ANALYZE THE PROBLEM	$T_1 = 288$ K	$T_2 = 315$ K	T increases	
	$V_1 = 5.40$ L	$V_2 = ?$ L		V increases

Factors that remain constant: P and n

STEP 2 Rearrange the gas law equation to solve for the unknown quantity. In this problem, we want to know the final volume (V_2) when the temperature increases. Using Charles's law, we solve for V_2 by multiplying both sides by T_2.

$$\frac{V_1}{T_1} = \frac{V_2}{T_2}$$

$$\frac{V_1}{T_1} \times T_2 = \frac{V_2}{\cancel{T_2}} \times \cancel{T_2}$$

$$V_2 = V_1 \times \frac{T_2}{T_1}$$

STEP 3 Substitute values into the gas law equation and calculate. From the table, we see that the temperature has increased. Because temperature is directly related to volume, the volume must increase. When we substitute in the values, we see that the ratio of the temperatures (temperature factor) is greater than 1, which increases the volume as predicted in Step 1.

$$V_2 = 5.40 \text{ L} \times \frac{315 \text{ K}}{288 \text{ K}} = 5.91 \text{ L}$$

Temperature factor increases volume

STUDY CHECK 8.4

A mountain climber with a body temperature of 37 °C inhales 486 mL of air at a temperature of −8 °C. What volume, in milliliters, will the air occupy in the lungs, if the pressure and amount of gas do not change?

ANSWER

569 mL

QUESTIONS AND PROBLEMS

8.3 Temperature and Volume (Charles's Law)

LEARNING GOAL Use the temperature–volume relationship (Charles's law) to determine the final temperature or volume when the pressure and amount of gas are constant.

8.23 Select the diagram that shows the final volume of a balloon when the following changes are made at constant pressure and amount of gas:

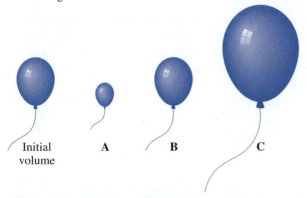

Initial volume   A   B   C

a. The temperature changes from 100 K to 300 K.
b. The balloon is placed in a freezer.
c. The balloon is first warmed and then returned to its starting temperature.

8.24 Indicate whether the final volume of gas in each of the following is the *same*, *larger*, or *smaller* than the initial volume, if pressure and amount of gas do not change:
   a. A volume of 505 mL of air on a cold winter day at −15 °C is breathed into the lungs, where body temperature is 37 °C.
   b. The heater used to heat the air in a hot-air balloon is turned off.
   c. A balloon filled with helium at the amusement park is left in a car on a hot day.

8.25 A sample of neon initially has a volume of 2.50 L at 15 °C. What final temperature, in degrees Celsius, is needed to change the volume of the gas to each of the following, if n and P do not change?
   a. 5.00 L   b. 1250 mL
   c. 7.50 L   d. 3550 mL

8.26 A gas has a volume of 4.00 L at 0 °C. What final temperature, in degrees Celsius, is needed to change the volume of the gas to each of the following, if n and P do not change?
   a. 1.50 L   b. 1200 mL
   c. 10.0 L   d. 50.0 mL

8.27 A balloon contains 2500 mL of helium gas at 75 °C. What is the final volume, in milliliters, of the gas when the temperature changes to each of the following, if *n* and *P* do not change?
a. 55 °C
b. 680. K
c. −25 °C
d. 240. K

8.28 An air bubble has a volume of 0.500 L at 18 °C. What is the final volume, in liters, of the gas when the temperature changes to each of the following, if *n* and *P* do not change?
a. 0 °C
b. 425 K
c. −12 °C
d. 575 K

Use the temperature–pressure relationship (Gay-Lussac's law) to determine the final temperature or pressure when the volume and amount of gas are constant.

$T = 200$ K $T = 400$ K
$P = 1$ atm $P = 2$ atm

FIGURE 8.6 ▶ Gay-Lussac's law: When the Kelvin temperature of a gas doubles at constant volume and amount of gas, the pressure also doubles.

Q How does a decrease in the temperature of a gas affect its pressure at constant volume and amount of gas?

8.4 Temperature and Pressure (Gay-Lussac's Law)

If we could observe the molecules of a gas as the temperature rises, we would notice that they move faster and hit the sides of the container more often and with greater force. If we maintain a constant volume and amount of gas, the pressure will increase. In the temperature–pressure relationship known as **Gay-Lussac's law**, the pressure of a gas is directly related to its Kelvin temperature. This means that an increase in temperature increases the pressure of a gas and a decrease in temperature decreases the pressure of the gas, as long as the volume and amount of gas do not change (see Figure 8.6).

Gay-Lussac's Law

$$\frac{P_1}{T_1} = \frac{P_2}{T_2} \qquad \text{No change in number of moles and volume}$$

All temperatures used in gas law calculations must be converted to their corresponding Kelvin (K) temperatures.

▶ SAMPLE PROBLEM 8.5 Calculating Pressure When Temperature Changes

Home oxygen tanks, which provide an oxygen-rich environment, can be dangerous if they are heated, because they can explode. Suppose an oxygen tank has a pressure of 120 atm at a room temperature of 25 °C. If a fire in the room causes the temperature of the gas inside the oxygen tank to reach 402 °C, what will be its pressure in atmospheres? The oxygen tank may rupture if the pressure inside exceeds 180 atm. Would you expect it to rupture?

SOLUTION

STEP 1 **Organize the data in a table of initial and final conditions.** We list the properties that change, which are the pressure and temperature, in a table. The properties that do not change, which are volume and amount of gas, are shown below the table. The temperatures given in degrees Celsius must be changed to kelvins. Because we know the initial and final temperatures of the gas, we know that the temperature increases. Thus, we can predict that the pressure increases.

$$T_1 = 25\,°C + 273 = 298\ K$$
$$T_2 = 402\,°C + 273 = 675\ K$$

ANALYZE THE PROBLEM	Conditions 1	Conditions 2	Know	Predict
	$P_1 = 120$ atm	$P_2 = \ ?$ atm		*P* increases
	$T_1 = 298$ K	$T_2 = 675$ K	*T* increases	

Factors that remain constant: *V* and *n*

STEP 2 Rearrange the gas law equation to solve for the unknown quantity. Using Gay-Lussac's law, we can solve for P_2 by multiplying both sides by T_2.

$$\frac{P_1}{T_1} = \frac{P_2}{T_2}$$

$$\frac{P_1}{T_1} \times T_2 = \frac{P_2}{\cancel{T_2}} \times \cancel{T_2}$$

$$P_2 = P_1 \times \frac{T_2}{T_1}$$

STEP 3 Substitute values into the gas law equation and calculate. When we substitute in the values, we see that the ratio of the temperatures (temperature factor), is greater than 1, which increases pressure as predicted in Step 1.

$$P_2 = 120 \text{ atm} \times \underbrace{\frac{675 \text{ K}}{298 \text{ K}}}_{\substack{\text{Temperature factor} \\ \text{increases pressure}}} = 270 \text{ atm}$$

Because the calculated pressure of 270 atm of the gas exceeds the limit of 180 atm, we would expect the oxygen tank to rupture.

STUDY CHECK 8.5

In a storage area of a hospital where the temperature has reached 55 °C, the pressure of oxygen gas in a 15.0-L steel cylinder is 965 Torr. To what temperature, in degrees Celsius, would the gas have to be cooled to reduce the pressure to 850. Torr when the volume and amount of the gas do not change?

ANSWER

16 °C

Vapor Pressure and Boiling Point

When liquid molecules with sufficient kinetic energy break away from the surface, they become gas particles or vapor. In an open container, all the liquid will eventually evaporate. In a closed container, the vapor accumulates and creates pressure called **vapor pressure**. Each liquid exerts its own vapor pressure at a given temperature. As temperature increases, more vapor forms, and vapor pressure increases. Table 8.4 lists the vapor pressure of water at various temperatures.

A liquid reaches its boiling point when its vapor pressure becomes equal to the external pressure. As boiling occurs, bubbles of the gas form within the liquid and quickly rise to the surface. For example, at an atmospheric pressure of 760 mmHg, water will boil at 100 °C, the temperature at which its vapor pressure reaches 760 mmHg (see Table 8.4).

At high altitudes, where atmospheric pressures are lower than 760 mmHg, the boiling point of water is lower than 100 °C. For example, a typical atmospheric pressure in Denver is 630 mmHg. This means that water in Denver boils when the vapor pressure is 630 mmHg. From Table 8.5, we see that water has a vapor pressure of 630 mmHg at 95 °C, which means that water boils at 95 °C in Denver.

In a closed container such as a pressure cooker, a pressure greater than 1 atm can be obtained, which means that water boils at a temperature higher than 100 °C. Laboratories and hospitals use closed containers called *autoclaves* to sterilize laboratory and surgical equipment. Table 8.5 shows how the boiling point of water increases as pressure increases.

TABLE 8.4 Vapor Pressure of Water

Temperature (°C)	Vapor Pressure (mmHg)
0	5
10	9
20	18
30	32
37*	47
40	55
50	93
60	149
70	234
80	355
90	528
100	760

*At body temperature

TABLE 8.5 Pressure and the Boiling Point of Water

Pressure (mmHg)	Boiling Point (°C)
270	70
467	87
630	95
752	99
760	100
800	100.4
1075	110
1520 (2 atm)	120
3800 (5 atm)	160
7600 (10 atm)	180

100 °C

Atmospheric
pressure
760 mmHg

760 mmHg

Vapor pressure in
the bubble equals
the atmospheric
pressure

An autoclave used to sterilize equipment attains
a temperature higher than 100 °C.

QUESTIONS AND PROBLEMS

8.4 Temperature and Pressure (Gay-Lussac's Law)

LEARNING GOAL Use the temperature–pressure relationship (Gay-Lussac's law) to determine the final temperature or pressure when the volume and amount of gas are constant.

8.29 Calculate the final pressure, in millimeters of mercury, for each of the following, if n and V do not change:
  a. A gas with an initial pressure of 1200 Torr at 155 °C is cooled to 0 °C.
  b. A gas in an aerosol can at an initial pressure of 1.40 atm at 12 °C is heated to 35 °C.

8.30 Calculate the final pressure, in atmospheres, for each of the following, if n and V do not change:
  a. A gas with an initial pressure of 1.20 atm at 75 °C is cooled to −32 °C.
  b. A sample of N_2 with an initial pressure of 780. mmHg at −75 °C is heated to 28 °C.

8.31 Calculate the final temperature, in degrees Celsius for each of the following, if n and V do not change:
  a. A sample of xenon gas at 25 °C and 740. mmHg is cooled to give a pressure of 620. mmHg.

b. A tank of argon gas with a pressure of 0.950 atm at −18 °C is heated to give a pressure of 1250 Torr.

8.32 Calculate the final temperature, in degrees Celsius, for each of the following, if n and V do not change:
  a. A sample of helium gas with a pressure of 250 Torr at 0 °C is heated to give a pressure of 1500 Torr.
  b. A sample of air at 40 °C and 740. mmHg is cooled to give a pressure of 680. mmHg.

℞ Clinical Applications

8.33 A tank contains isoflurane, an inhaled anesthetic, at a pressure of 1.8 atm and 5 °C. What is the pressure, in atmospheres, if the gas is warmed to a temperature of 22 °C, if n and V do not change?

8.34 Bacteria and viruses are inactivated by temperatures above 135 °C in an autoclave. An autoclave contains steam at 1.00 atm and 100 °C. At what pressure, in atmospheres, will the temperature of the steam in the autoclave reach 135 °C, if n and V do not change?

8.5 The Combined Gas Law

LEARNING GOAL

Use the combined gas law to calculate the final pressure, volume, or temperature of a gas when changes in two of these properties are given and the amount of gas is constant.

All of the pressure–volume–temperature relationships for gases that we have studied may be combined into a single relationship called the **combined gas law**. This expression is useful for studying the effect of changes in two of these variables on the third as long as the amount of gas (number of moles) remains constant.

Combined Gas Law

$$\frac{P_1 V_1}{T_1} = \frac{P_2 V_2}{T_2} \qquad \text{No change in number of moles of gas}$$

By using the combined gas law, we can derive any of the gas laws by omitting those properties that do not change as seen in Table 8.6.

TABLE 8.6 Summary of Gas Laws

Combined Gas Law	Properties Held Constant	Relationship	Name of Gas Law
$\frac{P_1 V_1}{\cancel{T_1}} = \frac{P_2 V_2}{\cancel{T_2}}$	T, n	$P_1 V_1 = P_2 V_2$	Boyle's law
$\frac{\cancel{P_1} V_1}{T_1} = \frac{\cancel{P_2} V_2}{T_2}$	P, n	$\frac{V_1}{T_1} = \frac{V_2}{T_2}$	Charles's law
$\frac{P_1 \cancel{V_1}}{T_1} = \frac{P_2 \cancel{V_2}}{T_2}$	V, n	$\frac{P_1}{T_1} = \frac{P_2}{T_2}$	Gay-Lussac's law

---

▶ **SAMPLE PROBLEM 8.6 Using the Combined Gas Law**

A 25.0-mL bubble is released from a diver's air tank at a pressure of 4.00 atm and a temperature of 11 °C. What is the volume, in milliliters, of the bubble when it reaches the ocean surface, where the pressure is 1.00 atm and the temperature is 18 °C? (Assume the amount of gas in the bubble does not change.)

SOLUTION

STEP 1 Organize the data in a table of initial and final conditions. We list the properties that change, which are the pressure, volume, and temperature, in a table. The property that remains constant, which is the amount of gas, is shown below the table. The temperatures in degrees Celsius must be changed to kelvins.

$$T_1 = 11\,°\text{C} + 273 = 284\ \text{K}$$
$$T_2 = 18\,°\text{C} + 273 = 291\ \text{K}$$

ANALYZE THE PROBLEM	Conditions 1	Conditions 2
	$P_1 = 4.00$ atm	$P_2 = 1.00$ atm
	$V_1 = 25.0$ mL	$V_2 = ?$ mL
	$T_1 = 284$ K	$T_2 = 291$ K

Factor that remains constant: n

STEP 2 Rearrange the gas law equation to solve for the unknown quantity.

$$\frac{P_1 V_1}{T_1} = \frac{P_2 V_2}{T_2}$$

$$\frac{P_1 V_1}{T_1} \times \frac{T_2}{P_2} = \frac{\cancel{P_2} V_2}{\cancel{T_2}} \times \frac{\cancel{T_2}}{\cancel{P_2}}$$

$$V_2 = V_1 \times \frac{P_1}{P_2} \times \frac{T_2}{T_1}$$

Under water, the pressure on a diver is greater than the atmospheric pressure.

STEP **3** Substitute values into the gas law equation and calculate. From the data table, we determine that both the pressure decrease and the temperature increase will increase the volume.

$$V_2 = 25.0 \text{ mL} \times \frac{4.00 \text{ atm}}{1.00 \text{ atm}} \times \frac{291 \text{ K}}{284 \text{ K}} = 102 \text{ mL}$$

Pressure factor increases volume   Temperature factor increases volume

However, when the unknown value is decreased by one change but increased by the second change, it is difficult to predict the overall change for the unknown.

STUDY CHECK 8.6

A weather balloon is filled with 15.0 L of helium at a temperature of 25 °C and a pressure of 685 mmHg. What is the pressure, in millimeters of mercury, of the helium in the balloon in the upper atmosphere when the temperature is −35 °C and the final volume becomes 34.0 L, if the amount of He does not change?

ANSWER
241 mmHg

QUESTIONS AND PROBLEMS

8.5 The Combined Gas Law

LEARNING GOAL Use the combined gas law to calculate the final pressure, volume, or temperature of a gas when changes in two of these properties are given and the amount of gas is constant.

8.35 A sample of helium gas has a volume of 6.50 L at a pressure of 845 mmHg and a temperature of 25 °C. What is the final pressure of the gas, in atmospheres, when the volume and temperature of the gas sample are changed to the following, if the amount of gas does not change?
a. 1850 mL and 325 K
b. 2.25 L and 12 °C
c. 12.8 L and 47 °C

8.36 A sample of argon gas has a volume of 735 mL at a pressure of 1.20 atm and a temperature of 112 °C. What is the final volume of the gas, in milliliters, when the pressure and temperature of the gas sample are changed to the following, if the amount of gas does not change?
a. 658 mmHg and 281 K
b. 0.55 atm and 75 °C
c. 15.4 atm and −15 °C

8.37 A 124-mL bubble of hot gases at 212 °C and 1.80 atm is emitted from an active volcano. What is the final temperature, in degrees Celsius, of the gas in the bubble outside the volcano if the final volume of the bubble is 138 mL and the pressure is 0.800 atm, if the amount of gas does not change?

8.38 A scuba diver 60 ft below the ocean surface inhales 50.0 mL of compressed air from a scuba tank at a pressure of 3.00 atm and a temperature of 8 °C. What is the final pressure of air, in atmospheres, in the lungs when the gas expands to 150.0 mL at a body temperature of 37 °C, if the amount of gas does not change?

8.6 Volume and Moles (Avogadro's Law)

LEARNING GOAL

Use Avogadro's law to calculate the amount or volume of a gas when the pressure and temperature are constant.

In our study of the gas laws, we have looked at changes in properties for a specified amount (n) of gas. Now we will consider how the properties of a gas change when there is a change in the number of moles or grams of the gas.

When you blow up a balloon, its volume increases because you add more air molecules. If the balloon has a hole in it, air leaks out, causing its volume to decrease. In 1811, Amedeo Avogadro formulated **Avogadro's law**, which states that the volume of a gas is directly related to the number of moles of a gas when temperature and pressure do not change. For example, if the number of moles of a gas is doubled, then the volume will also double as long as we do not change the pressure or the temperature (see Figure 8.7). At constant pressure and temperature, we can write Avogadro's law:

Avogadro's Law

$$\frac{V_1}{n_1} = \frac{V_2}{n_2} \qquad \text{No change in pressure and temperature}$$

▶SAMPLE PROBLEM 8.7 Calculating Volume for a Change in Moles

A weather balloon with a volume of 44 L is filled with 2.0 moles of helium. What is the final volume, in liters, if 3.0 moles of helium gas are added, to give a total of 5.0 moles of helium gas, if the pressure and temperature do not change?

$n = 1$ mole $n = 2$ moles
$V = 1$ L $V = 2$ L

FIGURE 8.7 ▶ **Avogadro's law:** The volume of a gas is directly related to the number of moles of the gas. If the number of moles is doubled, the volume must double at constant temperature and pressure.

SOLUTION

STEP 1 Organize the data in a table of initial and final conditions. We list those properties that change, which are volume and amount (moles) of gas, in a table. The properties that do not change, which are pressure and temperature, are shown below the table. Because there is an increase in the number of moles of gas, we can predict that the volume increases.

Q If a balloon has a leak, what happens to its volume?

ANALYZE THE PROBLEM	Conditions 1	Conditions 2	Know	Predict
	$V_1 = 44$ L	$V_2 = ?$ L		V increases
	$n_1 = 2.0$ moles	$n_2 = 5.0$ moles	n increases	

Factors that remain constant: P and T

STEP 2 Rearrange the gas law equation to solve for the unknown quantity. Using Avogadro's law, we can solve for V_2 by multiplying both sides by n_2.

$$\frac{V_1}{n_1} = \frac{V_2}{n_2}$$

$$\frac{V_1}{n_1} \times n_2 = \frac{V_2}{\cancel{n_2}} \times \cancel{n_2}$$

$$V_2 = V_1 \times \frac{n_2}{n_1}$$

STEP 3 Substitute values into the gas law equation and calculate. When we substitute in the values, we see that the ratio of the moles (mole factor) is greater than 1, which increases the volume as predicted in Step 1.

$$V_2 = 44 \text{ L} \times \frac{5.0 \text{ moles}}{2.0 \text{ moles}} = 110 \text{ L}$$

Mole factor
increases volume

STUDY CHECK 8.7

A sample containing 8.00 g of oxygen gas has a volume of 5.00 L. What is the final volume, in liters, after 4.00 g of oxygen gas is added to the 8.00 g of oxygen in the balloon, if the temperature and pressure do not change?

ANSWER

7.50 L

STP and Molar Volume

Using Avogadro's law, we can say that any two gases will have equal volumes if they contain the same number of moles of gas at the same temperature and pressure. To help us make comparisons between different gases, arbitrary conditions called *standard temperature* (273 K) and *standard pressure* (1 atm) together abbreviated **STP**, were selected by scientists:

STP Conditions

Standard temperature is *exactly* 0 °C (273 K).

Standard pressure is *exactly* 1 atm (760 mmHg).

At STP, one mole of any gas occupies a volume of 22.4 L, which is about the same as the volume of three basketballs. This volume, 22.4 L, of any gas at STP is called its **molar volume** (see Figure 8.8).

When a gas is at STP conditions (0 °C and 1 atm), its molar volume can be used to write conversion factors between the number of moles of gas and its volume, in liters.

The molar volume of a gas at STP is about the same as the volume of three basketballs.

Molar Volume Conversion Factors

$$1 \text{ mole of gas} = 22.4 \text{ L of gas (STP)}$$

$$\frac{1 \text{ mole gas}}{22.4 \text{ L gas (STP)}} \quad \text{and} \quad \frac{22.4 \text{ L gas (STP)}}{1 \text{ mole gas}}$$

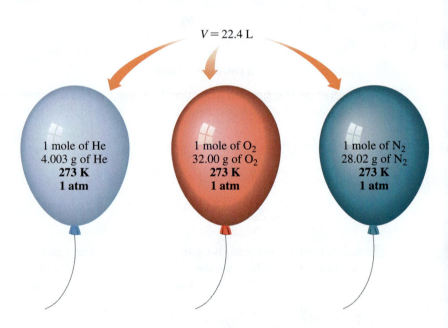

$V = 22.4$ L

1 mole of He
4.003 g of He
273 K
1 atm

1 mole of O_2
32.00 g of O_2
273 K
1 atm

1 mole of N_2
28.02 g of N_2
273 K
1 atm

FIGURE 8.8 ▶ Avogadro's law indicates that 1 mole of any gas at STP has a volume of 22.4 L.

◉ What volume of gas, in liters, is occupied by 16.0 g of methane gas, CH_4, at STP?

▶**SAMPLE PROBLEM 8.8   Using Molar Volume to Find Volume at STP**

What is the volume, in liters, of 64.0 g of O_2 gas at STP?

SOLUTION

STEP 1   State the given and needed quantities.

ANALYZE THE PROBLEM	Given	Need
	64.0 g of $O_2(g)$ at STP	liters of O_2 gas at STP

STEP 2 Write a plan to calculate the needed quantity. The grams of O_2 are converted to moles using molar mass. Then a molar volume conversion factor is used to convert the number of moles to volume (L).

grams of O_2 [Molar mass] moles of O_2 [Molar volume] liters of O_2

STEP 3 Write the equalities and conversion factors including 22.4 L/mole at STP.

1 mole of O_2 = 32.00 g of O_2

$$\frac{32.00 \text{ g } O_2}{1 \text{ mole } O_2} \quad \text{and} \quad \frac{1 \text{ mole } O_2}{32.00 \text{ g } O_2}$$

1 mole of O_2 = 22.4 L of O_2 (STP)

$$\frac{22.4 \text{ L } O_2 \text{ (STP)}}{1 \text{ mole } O_2} \quad \text{and} \quad \frac{1 \text{ mole } O_2}{22.4 \text{ L } O_2 \text{ (STP)}}$$

STEP 4 Set up the problem with factors to cancel units.

$$64.0 \text{ g } O_2 \times \frac{1 \text{ mole } O_2}{32.00 \text{ g } O_2} \times \frac{22.4 \text{ L } O_2 \text{ (STP)}}{1 \text{ mole } O_2} = 44.8 \text{ L of } O_2 \text{ (STP)}$$

> **Guide to Using Molar Volume**
>
> **STEP 1**
> State the given and needed quantities.
>
> **STEP 2**
> Write a plan to calculate the needed quantity.
>
> **STEP 3**
> Write the equalities and conversion factors including 22.4 L/mole at STP.
>
> **STEP 4**
> Set up the problem with factors to cancel units.

STUDY CHECK 8.8

How many grams of $N_2(g)$ are in 5.6 L of $N_2(g)$ at STP?

ANSWER

7.0 g of N_2

QUESTIONS AND PROBLEMS

8.6 Volume and Moles (Avogadro's Law)

LEARNING GOAL Use Avogadro's law to calculate the amount or volume of a gas when the pressure and temperature are constant.

8.39 What happens to the volume of a bicycle tire or a basketball when you use an air pump to add air?

8.40 Sometimes when you blow up a balloon and release it, it flies around the room. What is happening to the air that was in the balloon and its volume?

8.41 A sample containing 1.50 moles of Ne gas has an initial volume of 8.00 L. What is the final volume of the gas, in liters, when each of the following changes occurs in the quantity of the gas at constant pressure and temperature?
a. A leak allows one-half of the Ne atoms to escape.
b. A sample of 3.50 moles of Ne is added to the 1.50 moles of Ne gas in the container.
c. A sample of 25.0 g of Ne is added to the 1.50 moles of Ne gas in the container.

8.42 A sample containing 4.80 g of O_2 gas has an initial volume of 15.0 L. What is the final volume, in liters, when each of the following changes occurs in the quantity of the gas at constant pressure and temperature?
a. A sample of 0.500 mole of O_2 is added to the 4.80 g of O_2 in the container.
b. A sample of 2.00 g of O_2 is removed.
c. A sample of 4.00 g of O_2 is added to the 4.80 g of O_2 gas in the container.

8.43 Use molar volume to calculate each of the following at STP:
a. the number of moles of O_2 in 44.8 L of O_2 gas
b. the volume, in liters, occupied by 0.420 mole of He gas

8.44 Use molar volume to calculate each of the following at STP:
a. the volume, in liters, occupied by 2.50 moles of N_2 gas
b. the number of moles of CO_2 in 4.00 L of CO_2 gas

8.45 Use molar volume to calculate each of the following at STP:
a. the volume, in liters, occupied by 6.40 g of O_2 gas
b. the number of grams of H_2 in 1620 mL of H_2 gas

8.46 Use molar volume to calculate each of the following at STP:
a. the number of grams of Ne in 11.2 L of Ne gas
b. the volume, in liters, occupied by 50.0 g of Ar gas

Use the ideal gas law equation to solve for P, V, T, or n of a gas when given three of the four values in the ideal gas law equation. Calculate mass or volume of a gas in a chemical reaction.

8.7 The Ideal Gas Law

The **ideal gas law** is the combination of the four properties used in the measurement of a gas—pressure (P), volume (V), temperature (T), and amount of a gas (n)—to give a single expression, which is written as

Ideal Gas Law

$$PV = nRT$$

Rearranging the ideal gas law equation shows that the four gas properties equal the gas law constant, R.

$$\frac{PV}{nT} = R$$

To calculate the value of R, we substitute the STP conditions for molar volume into the expression: 1.00 mole of any gas occupies 22.4 L at STP (273 K and 1.00 atm).

$$R = \frac{(1.00 \text{ atm})(22.4 \text{ L})}{(1.00 \text{ mole})(273 \text{ K})} = \frac{0.0821 \text{ L} \cdot \text{atm}}{\text{mole} \cdot \text{K}}$$

The value for the **ideal gas constant, R**, is 0.0821 L · atm per mole · K. If we use 760. mmHg for the pressure, we obtain another useful value for R of 62.4 L · mmHg per mole · K.

$$R = \frac{(760. \text{ mmHg})(22.4 \text{ L})}{(1.00 \text{ mole})(273 \text{ K})} = \frac{62.4 \text{ L} \cdot \text{mmHg}}{\text{mole} \cdot \text{K}}$$

The ideal gas law is a useful expression when you are given the quantities for any three of the four properties of a gas. Although real gases show some deviations in behavior, the ideal gas law closely approximates the behavior of real gases at typical conditions. In working problems using the ideal gas law, the units of each variable must match the units in the R you select.

Ideal Gas Constant (R)	$\dfrac{0.0821 \text{ L} \cdot \text{atm}}{\text{mole} \cdot \text{K}}$	$\dfrac{62.4 \text{ L} \cdot \text{mmHg}}{\text{mole} \cdot \text{K}}$
Pressure (P)	atm	mmHg
Volume (V)	L	L
Amount (n)	mole	mole
Temperature (T)	K	K

⚛ CORE CHEMISTRY SKILL

Using the Ideal Gas Law

Dinitrogen oxide is used as an anesthetic in dentistry.

▶ **SAMPLE PROBLEM 8.9 Using the Ideal Gas Law**

Dinitrogen oxide, N_2O, which is used in dentistry, is an anesthetic also called laughing gas. What is the pressure, in atmospheres, of 0.350 mole of N_2O at 22 °C in a 5.00-L container?

SOLUTION

STEP **1** **State the given and needed quantities.** When three of the four quantities (P, V, n, and T) are known, we use the ideal gas law equation to solve for the unknown quantity. It is helpful to organize the data in a table. The temperature is converted from degrees Celsius to kelvins so that the units of V, n, and T match the unit of the gas constant R.

		P	V	n	R	T
ANALYZE THE PROBLEM	Given		5.00 L	0.350 mole	$\dfrac{0.0821 \text{ L} \cdot \text{atm}}{\text{mole} \cdot \text{K}}$	22 °C + 273 = 295 K
	Need	atm				

STEP 2 Rearrange the ideal gas law equation to solve for the needed quantity. By dividing both sides of the ideal gas law equation by V, we solve for pressure, P.

$$PV = nRT \quad \text{Ideal gas law equation}$$

$$\frac{P\cancel{V}}{\cancel{V}} = \frac{nRT}{V}$$

$$P = \frac{nRT}{V}$$

STEP 3 Substitute the gas data into the equation and calculate the needed quantity.

$$P = \frac{0.350 \text{ mole} \times \dfrac{0.0821 \text{ } \cancel{L} \cdot \text{atm}}{\text{mole} \cdot \text{K}} \times 295 \text{ K}}{5.00 \text{ } \cancel{L}} = 1.70 \text{ atm}$$

STUDY CHECK 8.9

Chlorine gas, Cl_2, is used to purify water. How many moles of chlorine gas are in a 7.00-L tank if the gas has a pressure of 865 mmHg and a temperature of 24 °C?

ANSWER

0.327 mole of Cl_2

> ### Guide to Using the Ideal Gas Law
>
> **STEP 1**
> State the given and needed quantities.
>
> **STEP 2**
> Rearrange the ideal gas law equation to solve for the needed quantity.
>
> **STEP 3**
> Substitute the gas data into the equation and calculate the needed quantity.

Many times we need to know the amount of gas, in grams, involved in a reaction. Then the ideal gas law equation can be rearranged to solve for the amount (n) of gas, which is converted to mass in grams using its molar mass as shown in Sample Problem 8.10.

▶ **SAMPLE PROBLEM 8.10** Calculating Mass Using the Ideal Gas Law

Butane, C_4H_{10}, is used as a fuel for camping stoves. If you have 108 mL of butane gas at 715 mmHg and 25 °C, what is the mass, in grams, of butane?

SOLUTION

STEP 1 State the given and needed quantities. When three of the quantities (P, V, and T) are known, we use the ideal gas law equation to solve for the unknown quantity, moles (n). Because the pressure is given in mmHg, we will use R in mmHg. The volume given in milliliters (mL) is converted to a volume in liters (L). The temperature is converted from degrees Celsius to kelvins.

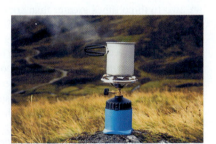

When camping, butane is used as a fuel for a portable stove.

		P	V	n	R	T
ANALYZE THE PROBLEM	**Given**	715 mmHg	108 mL (0.108 L)		$\dfrac{62.4 \text{ L} \cdot \text{mmHg}}{\text{mole} \cdot \text{K}}$	25 °C + 273 = 298 K
	Need			g of C_4H_{10} (mole of C_4H_{10})		

STEP 2 Rearrange the ideal gas law equation to solve for the needed quantity. By dividing both sides of the ideal gas law equation by RT, we solve for moles, n.

$$PV = nRT \quad \text{Ideal gas law equation}$$

$$\frac{PV}{RT} = \frac{n\cancel{RT}}{\cancel{RT}}$$

$$n = \frac{PV}{RT}$$

STEP **3** Substitute the gas data into the equation and calculate the needed quantity.

$$n = \frac{715 \; \text{mmHg} \times 0.108 \; L}{\dfrac{62.4 \; L \cdot \text{mmHg}}{\text{mole} \cdot K} \times 298 \; K} = 0.00415 \; \text{mole} \; (4.15 \times 10^{-3} \; \text{mole})$$

Now we can convert the moles of butane to grams using its molar mass of 58.12 g/mole:

$$0.00415 \; \text{mole} \; C_4H_{10} \times \frac{58.12 \; \text{g} \; C_4H_{10}}{1 \; \text{mole} \; C_4H_{10}} = 0.241 \; \text{g of} \; C_4H_{10}$$

STUDY CHECK 8.10

What is the volume, in liters, of 1.20 g of carbon monoxide at 8 °C if it has a pressure of 724 mmHg?

ANSWER

1.04 L

Chemistry Link to **Health**
Hyperbaric Chambers

A burn patient may undergo treatment for burns and infections in a hyperbaric chamber, a device in which pressures can be obtained that are two to three times greater than atmospheric pressure. A greater oxygen pressure increases the level of dissolved oxygen in the blood and tissues, where it fights bacterial infections. High levels of oxygen are toxic to many strains of bacteria. The hyperbaric chamber may also be used during surgery, to help counteract carbon monoxide (CO) poisoning, and to treat some cancers.

The blood is normally capable of dissolving up to 95% of the oxygen. Thus, if the partial pressure of the oxygen in the hyperbaric chamber is 2280 mmHg (3 atm), about 2170 mmHg of oxygen can dissolve in the blood where it saturates the tissues. In the treatment for carbon monoxide poisoning, oxygen at high pressure is used to displace the CO from the hemoglobin faster than breathing pure oxygen at 1 atm.

A patient undergoing treatment in a hyperbaric chamber must also undergo decompression (reduction of pressure) at a rate that slowly reduces the concentration of dissolved oxygen in the blood. If decompression is too rapid, the oxygen dissolved in the blood may form gas bubbles in the circulatory system.

Similarly, if a scuba diver does not decompress slowly, a condition called the "bends" may occur. While below the surface of the ocean, a

A hyperbaric chamber is used in the treatment of certain diseases.

diver uses a breathing mixture with a higher pressure. If there is nitrogen in the mixture, higher quantities of nitrogen gas will dissolve in the blood. If the diver ascends to the surface too quickly, the dissolved nitrogen forms gas bubbles that can block a blood vessel and cut off the flow of blood in the joints and tissues of the body and be quite painful. A diver suffering from the bends is placed immediately into a hyperbaric chamber where pressure is first increased and then slowly decreased. The dissolved nitrogen can then diffuse through the lungs until atmospheric pressure is reached.

⚛ CORE CHEMISTRY SKILL

Calculating Mass or Volume of a Gas in a Chemical Reaction

Gas Laws and Chemical Reactions

Gases are involved as reactants and products in many chemical reactions. Typically, the information given for a gas in a reaction is its pressure (P), volume (V), and temperature (T). Then we can use the ideal gas law equation to determine the moles of a gas in a reaction. If we know the number of moles for one of the gases in a reaction, we can use mole–mole factors to determine the moles of any other substance.

▶SAMPLE PROBLEM 8.11 Gases in Chemical Reactions

Calcium carbonate, $CaCO_3$, in antacids reacts with HCl in the stomach to reduce acid reflux.

$$CaCO_3(s) + 2HCl(aq) \longrightarrow CO_2(g) + H_2O(l) + CaCl_2(aq)$$

How many liters of CO_2 are produced at 752 mmHg and 24 °C from a 25.0-g sample of calcium carbonate?

SOLUTION

STEP 1 State the given and needed quantities.

ANALYZE THE PROBLEM	Given	Need
	reactant: 25.0 g of $CaCO_3$	liters of $CO_2(g)$
	product: $CO_2(g)$ at 752 mmHg, 24 °C (24 °C + 273 = 297 K)	
	Equation	
	$CaCO_3(s) + 2HCl(aq) \longrightarrow CO_2(g) + H_2O(l) + CaCl_2(aq)$	

STEP 2 Write a plan to convert the given quantity to the needed moles.

grams of $CaCO_3$ | Molar mass | moles of $CaCO_3$ | Mole–mole factor | moles of CO_2

STEP 3 Write the equalities and conversion factors for molar mass and mole–mole factors.

$$1 \text{ mole of } CaCO_3 = 100.09 \text{ g of } CaCO_3$$
$$\frac{100.09 \text{ g } CaCO_3}{1 \text{ mole } CaCO_3} \quad \text{and} \quad \frac{1 \text{ mole } CaCO_3}{100.09 \text{ g } CaCO_3}$$

$$1 \text{ mole of } CaCO_3 = 1 \text{ mole of } CO_2$$
$$\frac{1 \text{ mole } CaCO_3}{1 \text{ mole } CO_2} \quad \text{and} \quad \frac{1 \text{ mole } CO_2}{1 \text{ mole } CaCO_3}$$

STEP 4 Set up the problem to calculate moles of needed quantity.

$$25.0 \text{ g } CaCO_3 \times \frac{1 \text{ mole } CaCO_3}{100.09 \text{ g } CaCO_3} \times \frac{1 \text{ mole } CO_2}{1 \text{ mole } CaCO_3} = 0.250 \text{ mole of } CO_2$$

STEP 5 Convert the moles of needed quantity to mass or volume using the molar mass or the ideal gas law equation.

$$V = \frac{nRT}{P}$$

$$V = \frac{0.250 \text{ mole} \times \dfrac{62.4 \text{ L} \cdot \text{mmHg}}{\text{mole} \cdot \text{K}} \times 297 \text{ K}}{752 \text{ mmHg}} = 6.16 \text{ L of } CO_2$$

STUDY CHECK 8.11

If 12.8 g of aluminum reacts with HCl, how many liters of H_2 would be formed at 715 mmHg and 19 °C?

$$2Al(s) + 6HCl(aq) \longrightarrow 3H_2(g) + 2AlCl_3(aq)$$

ANSWER

18.1 L of H_2

Guide to Using the Ideal Gas Law for Reactions

STEP 1
State the given and needed quantities.

STEP 2
Write a plan to convert the given quantity to the needed moles.

STEP 3
Write the equalities and conversion factors for molar mass and mole–mole factors.

STEP 4
Set up the problem to calculate moles of needed quantity.

STEP 5
Convert the moles of needed quantity to mass or volume using the molar mass or the ideal gas law equation.

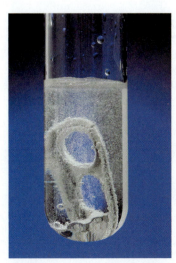

When aluminum reacts with HCl, bubbles of H_2 gas form.

QUESTIONS AND PROBLEMS

8.7 The Ideal Gas Law

LEARNING GOAL Use the ideal gas law equation to solve for P, V, T, or n of a gas when given three of the four values in the ideal gas law equation. Calculate mass or volume of a gas in a chemical reaction.

8.47 Calculate the pressure, in atmospheres, of 2.00 moles of helium gas in a 10.0-L container at 27 °C.

8.48 What is the volume, in liters, of 4.00 moles of methane gas, CH_4, at 18 °C and 1.40 atm?

8.49 An oxygen gas container has a volume of 20.0 L. How many grams of oxygen are in the container if the gas has a pressure of 845 mmHg at 22 °C?

8.50 A 10.0-g sample of krypton has a temperature of 25 °C at 575 mmHg. What is the volume, in milliliters, of the krypton gas?

8.51 A 25.0-g sample of nitrogen, N_2, has a volume of 50.0 L and a pressure of 630. mmHg. What is the temperature, in kelvins and degrees Celsius, of the gas?

8.52 A 0.226-g sample of carbon dioxide, CO_2, has a volume of 525 mL and a pressure of 455 mmHg. What is the temperature, in kelvins and degrees Celsius, of the gas?

8.53 Mg metal reacts with HCl to produce hydrogen gas.

$$Mg(s) + 2HCl(aq) \longrightarrow H_2(g) + MgCl_2(aq)$$

   a. What volume, in liters, of hydrogen at 0 °C and 1.00 atm (STP) is released when 8.25 g of Mg reacts?

   b. How many grams of magnesium are needed to prepare 5.00 L of H_2 at 735 mmHg and 18 °C?

8.54 When heated to 350 °C at 0.950 atm, ammonium nitrate decomposes to produce nitrogen, water, and oxygen gases.

$$2NH_4NO_3(s) \xrightarrow{\Delta} 2N_2(g) + 4H_2O(g) + O_2(g)$$

   a. How many liters of water vapor are produced when 25.8 g of NH_4NO_3 decomposes?

   b. How many grams of NH_4NO_3 are needed to produce 10.0 L of oxygen?

8.55 Butane undergoes combustion when it reacts with oxygen to produce carbon dioxide and water. What volume, in liters, of oxygen is needed to react with 55.2 g of butane at 0.850 atm and 25 °C?

$$2C_4H_{10}(g) + 13O_2(g) \xrightarrow{\Delta} 8CO_2(g) + 10H_2O(g)$$

8.56 Potassium nitrate decomposes to potassium nitrite and oxygen. What volume, in liters, of O_2 can be produced from the decomposition of 50.0 g of KNO_3 at 35 °C and 1.19 atm?

$$2KNO_3(s) \longrightarrow 2KNO_2(s) + O_2(g)$$

8.57 Aluminum and oxygen react to form aluminum oxide. How many liters of oxygen at 0 °C and 760 mmHg (STP) are required to completely react with 5.4 g of aluminum?

$$4Al(s) + 3O_2(g) \longrightarrow 2Al_2O_3(s)$$

8.58 Nitrogen dioxide reacts with water to produce oxygen and ammonia. How many grams of NH_3 can be produced when 4.00 L of NO_2 reacts at 415 °C and 725 mmHg?

$$4NO_2(g) + 6H_2O(g) \longrightarrow 7O_2(g) + 4NH_3(g)$$

℞ Clinical Applications

8.59 A single-patient hyperbaric chamber has a volume of 640 L. At a temperature of 24 °C, how many grams of oxygen are needed to give a pressure of 1.6 atm?

8.60 A multipatient hyperbaric chamber has a volume of 3400 L. At a temperature of 22 °C, how many grams of oxygen are needed to give a pressure of 2.4 atm?

LEARNING GOAL

Use Dalton's law of partial pressures to calculate the total pressure of a mixture of gases.

8.8 Partial Pressures (Dalton's Law)

Many gas samples are a mixture of gases. For example, the air you breathe is a mixture of mostly oxygen and nitrogen gases. In gas mixtures, scientists observed that all gas particles behave in the same way. Therefore, the total pressure of the gases in a mixture is a result of the collisions of the gas particles regardless of what type of gas they are.

In a gas mixture, each gas exerts its **partial pressure**, which is the pressure it would exert if it were the only gas in the container. **Dalton's law** states that the total pressure of a gas mixture is the sum of the partial pressures of the gases in the mixture.

Dalton's Law

$$P_{total} = P_1 + P_2 + P_3 + \cdots$$

Total pressure = Sum of the partial pressures
of a gas mixture   of the gases in the mixture

⚛ **CORE CHEMISTRY SKILL**

Calculating Partial Pressure

Suppose we have two separate tanks, one filled with helium at 2.0 atm and the other filled with argon at 4.0 atm. When the gases are combined in a single tank at the same volume and temperature, the number of gas molecules, not the type of gas, determines the pressure in a container. Then the pressure of the gases in the gas mixture would be 6.0 atm, which is the sum of their individual or partial pressures.

$$P_{total} = P_{He} + P_{Ar}$$
$$= 2.0 \text{ atm} + 4.0 \text{ atm}$$
$$= 6.0 \text{ atm}$$

$$P_{He} = 2.0 \text{ atm} \qquad P_{Ar} = 4.0 \text{ atm}$$

The total pressure of two gases is the sum of their partial pressures.

SAMPLE PROBLEM 8.12 Partial Pressure of a Gas in a Mixture

A heliox breathing mixture of oxygen and helium is prepared for a patient with COPD (chronic obstructive pulmonary disease). The gas mixture has a total pressure of 7.00 atm. If the partial pressure of the oxygen in the tank is 1140 mmHg, what is the partial pressure, in atmospheres, of the helium in the breathing mixture?

SOLUTION

STEP 1 Write the equation for the sum of the partial pressures.

$$P_{total} = P_{O_2} + P_{He}$$

STEP 2 Rearrange the equation to solve for the unknown pressure. To solve for the partial pressure of helium (P_{He}), we rearrange the equation to give the following:

$$P_{He} = P_{total} - P_{O_2}$$

Convert units to match.

$$P_{O_2} = 1140 \text{ mmHg} \times \frac{1 \text{ atm}}{760 \text{ mmHg}} = 1.50 \text{ atm}$$

STEP 3 Substitute known pressures into the equation and calculate the unknown partial pressure.

$$P_{He} = P_{total} - P_{O_2}$$
$$P_{He} = 7.00 \text{ atm} - 1.50 \text{ atm} = 5.50 \text{ atm}$$

STUDY CHECK 8.12

An anesthetic consists of a mixture of cyclopropane gas, C_3H_6, and oxygen gas, O_2. If the mixture has a total pressure of 1.09 atm, and the partial pressure of the cyclopropane is 73 mmHg, what is the partial pressure, in millimeters of mercury, of the oxygen in the anesthetic?

ANSWER

755 mmHg

Guide to Calculating Partial Pressure

STEP 1
Write the equation for the sum of the partial pressures.

STEP 2
Rearrange the equation to solve for the unknown pressure.

STEP 3
Substitute known pressures into the equation and calculate the unknown partial pressure.

Chemistry Link to Health

Blood Gases

Our cells continuously use oxygen and produce carbon dioxide. Both gases move in and out of the lungs through the membranes of the alveoli, the tiny air sacs at the ends of the airways in the lungs. An exchange of gases occurs in which oxygen from the air diffuses into the lungs and into the blood, while carbon dioxide produced in the cells is carried to the lungs to be exhaled. In Table 8.7, partial pressures are given for the gases in air that we inhale (inspired air), air in the alveoli, and air that we exhale (expired air).

At sea level, oxygen normally has a partial pressure of 100 mmHg in the alveoli of the lungs. Because the partial pressure of oxygen in venous blood is 40 mmHg, oxygen diffuses from the alveoli into the

bloodstream. The oxygen combines with hemoglobin, which carries it to the tissues of the body where the partial pressure of oxygen can be very low, less than 30 mmHg. Oxygen diffuses from the blood, where the partial pressure of O_2 is high, into the tissues where O_2 pressure is low.

As oxygen is used in the cells of the body during metabolic processes, carbon dioxide is produced, so the partial pressure of CO_2 may be as high as 50 mmHg or more. Carbon dioxide diffuses from the tissues into the bloodstream and is carried to the lungs. There it diffuses out of the blood, where CO_2 has a partial pressure of 46 mmHg, into the alveoli, where the CO_2 is at 40 mmHg and is exhaled. Table 8.8 gives the partial pressures of blood gases in the tissues and in oxygenated and deoxygenated blood.

TABLE 8.7 Partial Pressures of Gases During Breathing

Gas	Partial Pressure (mmHg)		
	Inspired Air	Alveolar Air	Expired Air
Nitrogen, N_2	594	573	569
Oxygen, O_2	160.	100.	116
Carbon dioxide, CO_2	0.3	40.	28
Water vapor, H_2O	5.7	47	47
Total	760.	760.	760.

TABLE 8.8 Partial Pressures of Oxygen and Carbon Dioxide in Blood and Tissues

Gas	Partial Pressure (mmHg)		
	Oxygenated Blood	Deoxygenated Blood	Tissues
O_2	100	40	30 or less
CO_2	40	46	50 or greater

QUESTIONS AND PROBLEMS

8.8 Partial Pressures (Dalton's Law)

LEARNING GOAL Use Dalton's law of partial pressures to calculate the total pressure of a mixture of gases.

8.61 In a gas mixture, the partial pressures are nitrogen 425 Torr, oxygen 115 Torr, and helium 225 Torr. What is the total pressure, in torr, exerted by the gas mixture?

8.62 In a gas mixture, the partial pressures are argon 415 mmHg, neon 75 mmHg, and nitrogen 125 mmHg. What is the total pressure, in millimeters of mercury, exerted by the gas mixture?

8.63 A gas mixture containing oxygen, nitrogen, and helium exerts a total pressure of 925 Torr. If the partial pressures are oxygen

425 Torr and helium 75 Torr, what is the partial pressure, in torr, of the nitrogen in the mixture?

8.64 A gas mixture containing oxygen, nitrogen, and neon exerts a total pressure of 1.20 atm. If helium added to the mixture increases the pressure to 1.50 atm, what is the partial pressure, in atmospheres, of the helium?

Rx Clinical Applications

8.65 In certain lung ailments such as emphysema, there is a decrease in the ability of oxygen to diffuse into the blood.

a. How would the partial pressure of oxygen in the blood change?

b. Why does a person with severe emphysema sometimes use a portable oxygen tank?

8.66 An accident to the head can affect the ability of a person to ventilate (breathe in and out).

   a. What would happen to the partial pressures of oxygen and carbon dioxide in the blood if a person cannot properly ventilate?

   b. When a person who cannot breathe properly is placed on a ventilator, an air mixture is delivered at pressures that are alternately above the air pressure in the person's lung, and

then below. How will this move oxygen gas into the lungs, and carbon dioxide out?

8.67 An air sample in the lungs contains oxygen at 93 mmHg, nitrogen at 565 mmHg, carbon dioxide at 38 mmHg, and water vapor at 47 mmHg. What is the total pressure, in atmospheres, exerted by the gas mixture?

8.68 A nitrox II gas mixture for scuba diving contains oxygen gas at 53 atm and nitrogen gas at 94 atm. What is the total pressure, in torr, of the scuba gas mixture?

Clinical Update
Exercise-Induced Asthma

Vigorous exercise with high levels of physical activity can induce asthma particularly in children. When Whitney had her asthma attack, her breathing became more rapid, the temperature within her airways increased, and the muscles around the bronchi contracted causing a narrowing of the airways. Whitney's symptoms, which may occur within 5 to 20 min after the start of vigorous exercise, include shortness of breath, wheezing, and coughing.

Whitney now does several things to prevent exercise-induced asthma. She uses a pre-exercise inhaled medication before she starts her activity. The medication relaxes the muscles that surround the

airways and opens up the airways. Then she does a warm-up set of exercises. If pollen counts are high, she avoids exercising outdoors.

Clinical Applications

8.69 Whitney's lung capacity was measured as 3.2 L at a body temperature of 37 °C and a pressure of 745 mmHg. How many moles of oxygen is in her lungs if air contains 21% oxygen?

8.70 Whitney's tidal volume, which is the volume of air that she inhales and exhales, was 0.54 L. Her tidal volume was measured at a body temperature of 37 °C and a pressure of 745 mmHg. How many moles of nitrogen does she inhale in one breath if air contains 78% nitrogen?

CONCEPT MAP

GASES

are described by — **Kinetic Molecular Theory of Gases**
states that gas particles — **Are Far Apart**, **Move Fast** and **Exert Pressure**

behave according to — **Gas Laws**
that relate — **P and V Boyle's Law**, **V and T Charles's Law**, **P and T Gay-Lussac's Law**, **P, V, and T Combined Gas Law**, **PV = nRT Ideal Gas Law**

volume and moles are related by — **V and n Avogadro's Law**
at STP gives — **Molar Volume**
for a gas or — **Gas Mixture** where gases exert — **Partial Pressures**
used to find — **Moles or Volume of Gases** in — **Reactions of Gases**

CHAPTER REVIEW

8.1 Properties of Gases

LEARNING GOAL Describe the kinetic molecular theory of gases and the units of measurement used for gases.

- In a gas, particles are so far apart and moving so fast that their attractions are negligible.
- A gas is described by the physical properties of pressure (P), volume (V), temperature (T) in kelvins (K), and the amount in moles (n).
- A gas exerts pressure, the force of the gas particles striking the walls of a container.
- Gas pressure is measured in units such as torr, mmHg, atm, and Pa.

8.2 Pressure and Volume (Boyle's Law)

LEARNING GOAL Use the pressure–volume relationship (Boyle's law) to determine the final pressure or volume when the temperature and amount of gas are constant.

- The volume (V) of a gas changes inversely with the pressure (P) of the gas if there is no change in the temperature and the amount of gas.

$$P_1V_1 = P_2V_2$$

- The pressure increases if volume decreases; pressure decreases if volume increases.

8.3 Temperature and Volume (Charles's Law)

LEARNING GOAL Use the temperature–volume relationship (Charles's law) to determine the final temperature or volume when the pressure and amount of gas are constant.

- The volume (V) of a gas is directly related to its Kelvin temperature (T) when there is no change in the pressure and amount of the gas.

$$\frac{V_1}{T_1} = \frac{V_2}{T_2}$$

- As temperature of a gas increases, its volume increases; if its temperature decreases, volume decreases.

8.4 Temperature and Pressure (Gay-Lussac's Law)

LEARNING GOAL Use the temperature–pressure relationship (Gay-Lussac's law) to determine the final temperature or pressure when the volume and amount of gas are constant.

- The pressure (P) of a gas is directly related to its Kelvin temperature (T) when there is no change in the volume and amount of the gas.

$$\frac{P_1}{T_1} = \frac{P_2}{T_2}$$

- As temperature of a gas increases, its pressure increases; if its temperature decreases, pressure decreases.
- Vapor pressure is the pressure of the gas that forms when a liquid evaporates.
- At the boiling point of a liquid, the vapor pressure equals the external pressure.

8.5 The Combined Gas Law

LEARNING GOAL Use the combined gas law to calculate the final pressure, volume, or temperature of a gas when changes in two of these properties are given and the amount of gas is constant.

- The combined gas law is the relationship of pressure (P), volume (V), and temperature (T) for a constant amount (n) of gas.

$$\frac{P_1V_1}{T_1} = \frac{P_2V_2}{T_2}$$

- The combined gas law is used to determine the effect of changes in two of the variables on the third.

8.6 Volume and Moles (Avogadro's Law)

LEARNING GOAL Use Avogadro's law to calculate the amount or volume of a gas when the pressure and temperature are constant.

- The volume (V) of a gas is directly related to the number of moles (n) of the gas when the pressure and temperature of the gas do not change.

$$\frac{V_1}{n_1} = \frac{V_2}{n_2}$$

- If the moles of gas are increased, the volume must increase; if the moles of gas are decreased, the volume must decrease.
- At standard temperature (273 K) and standard pressure (1 atm), abbreviated STP, one mole of any gas has a volume of 22.4 L.

8.7 The Ideal Gas Law

LEARNING GOAL Use the ideal gas law equation to solve for P, V, T, or n of a gas when given three of the four values in the ideal gas law equation. Calculate mass or volume of a gas in a chemical reaction.

- The ideal gas law gives the relationship of the quantities P, V, n, and T that describe and measure a gas.

$$PV = nRT$$

- Any of the four variables can be calculated if the values of the other three are known.
- The ideal gas law equation is used to convert the quantities (P, V, and T) of gases to moles in a chemical reaction.
- The moles of gases can be used to determine the number of moles or grams of other substances in the reaction.

8.8 Partial Pressures (Dalton's Law)

LEARNING GOAL Use Dalton's law of partial pressures to calculate the total pressure of a mixture of gases.

- In a mixture of two or more gases, the total pressure is the sum of the partial pressures of the individual gases.

$$P_{\text{total}} = P_1 + P_2 + P_3 + \cdots$$

- The partial pressure of a gas in a mixture is the pressure it would exert if it were the only gas in the container.

KEY TERMS

atmosphere (atm) A unit equal to pressure exerted by a column of mercury 760 mm high.

atmospheric pressure The pressure exerted by the atmosphere.

Avogadro's law A gas law stating that the volume of a gas is directly related to the number of moles of gas when pressure and temperature do not change.

Boyle's law A gas law stating that the pressure of a gas is inversely related to the volume when temperature and moles of the gas do not change.

Charles's law A gas law stating that the volume of a gas changes directly with a change in Kelvin temperature when pressure and moles of the gas do not change.

combined gas law A relationship that combines several gas laws relating pressure, volume, and temperature when the amount of gas does not change.

$$\frac{P_1 V_1}{T_1} = \frac{P_2 V_2}{T_2}$$

Dalton's law A gas law stating that the total pressure exerted by a mixture of gases in a container is the sum of the partial pressures that each gas would exert alone.

Gay-Lussac's law A gas law stating that the pressure of a gas changes directly with a change in the Kelvin temperature when the number of moles of a gas and its volume do not change.

ideal gas constant, R A numerical value that relates the quantities P, V, n, and T in the ideal gas law, $PV = nRT$.

ideal gas law A law that combines the four measured properties of a gas.

$$PV = nRT$$

kinetic molecular theory of gases A model used to explain the behavior of gases.

molar volume A volume of 22.4 L occupied by 1 mole of a gas at STP conditions of 0 °C (273 K) and 1 atm.

partial pressure The pressure exerted by a single gas in a gas mixture.

pressure The force exerted by gas particles that hit the walls of a container.

STP Standard conditions of exactly 0 °C (273 K) temperature and 1 atm pressure used for the comparison of gases.

vapor pressure The pressure exerted by the particles of vapor above a liquid.

⚛ CORE CHEMISTRY SKILLS

The chapter section containing each Core Chemistry Skill is shown in parentheses at the end of each heading.

Using the Gas Laws (8.2, 8.3, 8.4, 8.5, 8.6)

- Boyle's, Charles's, Gay-Lussac's, and Avogadro's laws show the relationships between two properties of a gas.

$$P_1 V_1 = P_2 V_2 \quad \text{Boyle's law}$$
$$\frac{V_1}{T_1} = \frac{V_2}{T_2} \quad \text{Charles's law}$$
$$\frac{P_1}{T_1} = \frac{P_2}{T_2} \quad \text{Gay-Lussac's law}$$
$$\frac{V_1}{n_1} = \frac{V_2}{n_2} \quad \text{Avogadro's law}$$

- The combined gas law shows the relationship between P, V, and T for a gas.

$$\frac{P_1 V_1}{T_1} = \frac{P_2 V_2}{T_2}$$

- When two properties of a gas vary and the other two are constant, we list the initial and final conditions of each property in a table.

Example: A sample of helium gas (He) has a volume of 6.8 L and a pressure of 2.5 atm. What is the final volume, in liters, if it has a final pressure of 1.2 atm with no change in temperature and amount of gas?

Answer:

ANALYZE THE PROBLEM	Conditions 1	Conditions 2	Know	Predict
	$P_1 = 2.5$ atm	$P_2 = 1.2$ atm	P decreases	
	$V_1 = 6.8$ L	$V_2 = ?$ L		V increases

Factors that remain constant: T and n

Using Boyle's law, we can write the relationship for V_2, which we predict will increase.

$$V_2 = V_1 \times \frac{P_1}{P_2}$$
$$V_2 = 6.8\text{ L} \times \frac{2.5 \text{ atm}}{1.2 \text{ atm}} = 14\text{ L}$$

Using the Ideal Gas Law (8.7)

- The ideal gas law equation combines the relationships of the four properties of a gas into one equation.

$$PV = nRT$$

- When three of the four properties are given, we rearrange the ideal gas law equation for the needed quantity.

Example: What is the volume, in liters, of 0.750 mole of CO_2 at a pressure of 1340 mmHg and a temperature of 295 K?

Answer: $V = \dfrac{nRT}{P}$

$$= \frac{0.750 \text{ mole} \times \dfrac{62.4\text{ L} \cdot \text{mmHg}}{\text{mole} \cdot \text{K}} \times 295\text{ K}}{1340 \text{ mmHg}} = 10.3\text{ L}$$

Calculating Mass or Volume of a Gas in a Chemical Reaction (8.7)

- The ideal gas law equation is used to calculate the pressure, volume, moles (or grams) of a gas in a chemical reaction.

Example: What is the volume, in liters, of N_2 required to react with 18.5 g of magnesium at a pressure of 1.20 atm and a temperature of 303 K?

$$3Mg(s) + N_2(g) \longrightarrow Mg_3N_2(s)$$

Answer: Initially, we convert the grams of Mg to moles and use a mole–mole factor from the balanced equation to calculate the moles of N_2 gas.

$$18.5 \text{ g Mg} \times \frac{1 \text{ mole Mg}}{24.31 \text{ g Mg}} \times \frac{1 \text{ mole } N_2}{3 \text{ moles Mg}} = 0.254 \text{ mole of } N_2$$

Now, we use the moles of N_2 in the ideal gas law equation and solve for liters, the needed quantity.

$$V = \frac{nRT}{P} = \frac{0.254 \text{ mole } N_2 \times \dfrac{0.0821 \text{ L} \cdot \text{atm}}{\text{mole} \cdot \text{K}} \times 303 \text{ K}}{1.20 \text{ atm}} = 5.27 \text{ L}$$

Calculating Partial Pressure (8.8)

- In a gas mixture, each gas exerts its partial pressure, which is the pressure it would exert if it were the only gas in the container.
- Dalton's law states that the total pressure of a gas mixture is the sum of the partial pressures of the gases in the mixture.

$$P_{total} = P_1 + P_2 + P_3 + \cdots$$

Example: A gas mixture with a total pressure of 1.18 atm contains helium gas at a partial pressure of 465 mmHg and nitrogen gas. What is the partial pressure, in atmospheres, of the nitrogen gas?

Answer: Initially, we convert the partial pressure of helium gas from mmHg to atm.

$$465 \text{ mmHg} \times \frac{1 \text{ atm}}{760 \text{ mmHg}} = 0.612 \text{ atm of He gas}$$

Using Dalton's law, we solve for the needed quantity, P_{N_2} in atm.

$$P_{total} = P_{N_2} + P_{He}$$
$$P_{N_2} = P_{total} - P_{He}$$
$$P_{N_2} = 1.18 \text{ atm} - 0.612 \text{ atm} = 0.57 \text{ atm}$$

UNDERSTANDING THE CONCEPTS

The chapter sections to review are shown in parentheses at the end of each question.

8.71 Two flasks of equal volume and at the same temperature contain different gases. One flask contains 10.0 g of Ne, and the other flask contains 10.0 g of He. Is each of the following statements *true* or *false*? Explain. (8.1)
  a. The flask that contains He has a higher pressure than the flask that contains Ne.
  b. The densities of the gases are the same.

8.72 Two flasks of equal volume and at the same temperature contain different gases. One flask contains 5.0 g of O_2, and the other flask contains 5.0 g of H_2. Is each of the following statements *true* or *false*? Explain. (8.1)
  a. Both flasks contain the same number of molecules.
  b. The pressures in the flasks are the same.

8.73 At 100 °C, which of the following diagrams (**1, 2,** or **3**) represents a gas sample that exerts the (8.1)
  a. lowest pressure?   **b.** highest pressure?

8.74 Indicate which diagram (**1, 2,** or **3**) represents the volume of the gas sample in a flexible container when each of the following changes (**a** to **e**) takes place: (8.2, 8.3, 8.4)

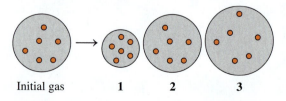

Initial gas   1   2   3

  a. Temperature increases at constant pressure.
  b. Temperature decreases at constant pressure.
  c. Atmospheric pressure increases at constant temperature.
  d. Atmospheric pressure decreases at constant temperature.
  e. Doubling the atmospheric pressure and doubling the Kelvin temperature.

8.75 A balloon is filled with helium gas with a partial pressure of 1.00 atm and neon gas with a partial pressure of 0.50 atm. For each of the following changes of the initial balloon, select the diagram (**A**, **B**, or **C**) that shows the final volume of the balloon: (8.2, 8.3, 8.4, 8.6)

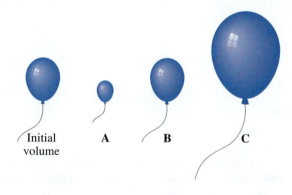

Initial   A   B   C
volume

  a. The balloon is put in a cold storage unit (*P* and *n* constant).
  b. The balloon floats to a higher altitude where the pressure is less (*n* and *T* constant).
  c. All of the neon gas is removed (*T* and *P* constant).
  d. The Kelvin temperature doubles and half of the gas atoms leak out (*P* constant).
  e. 2.0 moles of O_2 gas is added (*T* and *P* constant).

8.76 Indicate if pressure *increases*, *decreases*, or *stays the same* in each of the following: (8.2, 8.4, 8.6)

a.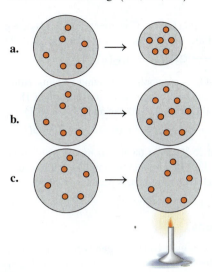

b.

c.

8.77 At a restaurant, a customer chokes on a piece of food. You put your arms around the person's waist and use your fists to push up on the person's abdomen, an action called the Heimlich maneuver. (8.2)
   a. How would this action change the volume of the chest and lungs?
   b. Why does it cause the person to expel the food item from the airway?

8.78 An airplane is pressurized with air to 650. mmHg. (8.8)
   a. If air is 21% oxygen, what is the partial pressure of oxygen on the plane?
   b. If the partial pressure of oxygen drops below 100. mmHg, passengers become drowsy. If this happens, oxygen masks are released. What is the total cabin pressure at which oxygen masks are dropped?

ADDITIONAL QUESTIONS AND PROBLEMS

8.79 A sample of hydrogen (H_2) gas at 127 °C has a pressure of 2.00 atm. At what final temperature, in degrees Celsius, will the pressure of the H_2 decrease to 0.25 atm, if V and n are constant? (8.4)

8.80 A fire extinguisher has a pressure of 10. atm at 25 °C. What is the final pressure, in atmospheres, when the fire extinguisher is used at a temperature of 75 °C, if V and n are constant? (8.4)

8.81 In 1783, Jacques Charles launched his first balloon filled with hydrogen gas (H_2), which he chose because it was lighter than air. The balloon had a volume of 31 000 L at a pressure of 755 mmHg and a temperature of 22 °C. When the balloon reached an altitude of 1000 m, the pressure was 658 mmHg and the temperature was −8 °C. What was the volume, in liters, of the balloon at these conditions, if the amount of hydrogen remains the same? (8.5)

Jacques Charles used hydrogen to launch his balloon in 1783.

8.82 During laparoscopic surgery, carbon dioxide gas is used to expand the abdomen to help create a larger working space. If 4.80 L of CO_2 gas at 18 °C at 785 mmHg is used, what is the final volume, in liters, of the gas at 37 °C and a pressure of 745 mmHg, if the amount of CO_2 remains the same? (8.5)

8.83 A 2.00-L container is filled with methane gas, CH_4, at a pressure of 2500. mmHg and a temperature of 18 °C. How many grams of methane are in the container? (8.7)

8.84 A steel cylinder with a volume of 15.0 L is filled with 50.0 g of nitrogen gas at 25 °C. What is the pressure, in atmospheres, of the N_2 gas in the cylinder? (8.7)

8.85 How many grams of CO_2 are in 35.0 L of $CO_2(g)$ at 1.20 atm and 5 °C? (8.7)

8.86 A container is filled with 0.644 g of O_2 at 5 °C and 845 mmHg. What is the volume, in milliliters, of the container? (8.7)

8.87 How many liters of H_2 gas can be produced at 0 °C and 1.00 atm (STP) from 25.0 g of Zn? (8.7)

$$Zn(s) + 2HCl(aq) \longrightarrow H_2(g) + ZnCl_2(aq)$$

8.88 In the formation of smog, nitrogen and oxygen gas react to form nitrogen dioxide. How many grams of NO_2 will be produced when 2.0 L of nitrogen at 840 mmHg and 24 °C are completely reacted? (8.7)

$$N_2(g) + 2O_2(g) \longrightarrow 2NO_2(g)$$

8.89 Nitrogen dioxide reacts with water to produce oxygen and ammonia. A 5.00-L sample of $H_2O(g)$ reacts at a temperature of 375 °C and a pressure of 725 mmHg. How many grams of NH_3 can be produced? (8.7)

$$4NO_2(g) + 6H_2O(g) \longrightarrow 7O_2(g) + 4NH_3(g)$$

8.90 Hydrogen gas can be produced in the laboratory through the reaction of magnesium metal with hydrochloric acid. When 12.0 g of Mg reacts, what volume, in liters, of H_2 gas is produced at 24 °C and 835 mmHg? (8.7)

$$Mg(s) + 2HCl(aq) \longrightarrow H_2(g) + MgCl_2(aq)$$

8.91 A gas mixture contains oxygen and argon at partial pressures of 0.60 atm and 425 mmHg. If nitrogen gas added to the sample increases the total pressure to 1250 Torr, what is the partial pressure, in torr, of the nitrogen added? (8.8)

8.92 What is the total pressure, in millimeters of mercury, of a gas mixture containing argon gas at 0.25 atm, helium gas at 350 mmHg, and nitrogen gas at 360 Torr? (8.8)

CHALLENGE QUESTIONS

The following groups of questions are related to the topics in this chapter. However, they do not all follow the chapter order, and they require you to combine concepts and skills from several sections. These questions will help you increase your critical thinking skills and prepare for your next exam.

8.93 Your spaceship has docked at a space station above Mars. The temperature inside the space station is a carefully controlled 24 °C at a pressure of 745 mmHg. A balloon with a volume of 425 mL drifts into the airlock where the temperature is −95 °C and the pressure is 0.115 atm. What is the final volume, in milliliters, of the balloon if n remains constant and the balloon is very elastic? (8.5)

8.94 You are doing research on planet X. The temperature inside the space station is a carefully controlled 24 °C and the pressure is 755 mmHg. Suppose that a balloon, which has a volume of 850. mL inside the space station, is placed into the airlock, and floats out to planet X. If planet X has an atmospheric pressure of 0.150 atm and the volume of the balloon changes to 3.22 L, what is the temperature, in degrees Celsius, on planet X (n does not change)? (8.5)

8.95 A gas sample has a volume of 4250 mL at 15 °C and 745 mmHg. What is the final temperature, in degrees Celsius, after the sample is transferred to a different container with a volume of 2.50 L and a pressure of 1.20 atm when n is constant? (8.5)

8.96 In the fermentation of glucose (wine making), 780 mL of CO_2 gas was produced at 37 °C and 1.00 atm. What is the final volume, in liters, of the gas when measured at 22 °C and 675 mmHg, when n is constant? (8.5)

8.97 The propane, C_3H_8, in a fuel cylinder, undergoes combustion with oxygen in the air. How many liters of CO_2 are produced at STP if the cylinder contains 881 g of propane? (8.7)

$$C_3H_8(g) + 5O_2(g) \xrightarrow{\Delta} 3CO_2(g) + 4H_2O(g)$$

8.98 When sensors in a car detect a collision, they cause the reaction of sodium azide, NaN_3, which generates nitrogen gas to fill the airbags within 0.03 s. How many liters of N_2 are produced at STP if the airbag contains 132 g of NaN_3? (8.7)

$$2NaN_3(s) \longrightarrow 2Na(s) + 3N_2(g)$$

8.99 Glucose, $C_6H_{12}O_6$, is metabolized in living systems. How many grams of water can be produced from the reaction of 18.0 g of glucose and 7.50 L of O_2 at 1.00 atm and 37 °C? (8.7)

$$C_6H_{12}O_6(s) + 6O_2(g) \longrightarrow 6CO_2(g) + 6H_2O(l)$$

8.100 2.00 L of N_2, at 25 °C and 1.08 atm, is mixed with 4.00 L of O_2, at 25 °C and 0.118 atm, and the mixture is allowed to react. How much NO, in grams, is produced? (8.7)

$$N_2(g) + O_2(g) \longrightarrow 2NO(g)$$

℞ Clinical Applications

8.101 Hyperbaric therapy uses 100% oxygen at pressure to help heal wounds and infections, and to treat carbon monoxide poisoning. If the pressure inside a hyperbaric chamber is 3.0 atm, what is the volume, in liters, of the chamber containing 2400 g of O_2 at 28 °C? (8.7)

8.102 A hyperbaric chamber has a volume of 1510 L. How many kilograms of O_2 gas are needed to give an oxygen pressure of 2.04 atm at 25 °C? (8.7)

8.103 Laparoscopic surgery involves inflating the abdomen with carbon dioxide gas to separate the internal organs and the abdominal wall. If the CO_2 injected into the abdomen produces a pressure of 20. mmHg and a volume of 4.00 L at 32 °C, how many grams of CO_2 were used? (8.7)

8.104 In another laparoscopic surgery, helium is used to inflate the abdomen to separate the internal organs and the abdominal wall. If the He injected into the abdomen produces a pressure of 15 mmHg and a volume of 3.1 L at 28 °C, how many grams of He were used? (8.7)

ANSWERS

Answers to Selected Questions and Problems

8.1 a. At a higher temperature, gas particles have greater kinetic energy, which makes them move faster.
b. Because there are great distances between the particles of a gas, they can be pushed closer together and still remain a gas.
c. Gas particles are very far apart, which means that the mass of a gas in a certain volume is very small, resulting in a low density.

8.3 a. temperature **b.** volume
c. amount **d.** pressure

8.5 a, d, and **e** describe the pressure of a gas.

8.7 a. 1520 Torr **b.** 1520 mmHg

8.9 As a diver ascends to the surface, external pressure decreases. If the air in the lungs were not exhaled, its volume would expand and severely damage the lungs. The pressure in the lungs must adjust to changes in the external pressure.

8.11 a. The pressure is greater in cylinder **A**. According to Boyle's law, a decrease in volume pushes the gas particles closer together, which will cause an increase in the pressure.
b.

Property	Conditions 1	Conditions 2	Know	Predict
Pressure (P)	650 mmHg	1.2 atm (910 mmHg)	P increases	
Volume (V)	220 mL	160 mL		V decreases

8.13 a. increases **b.** decreases **c.** increases

8.15 a. 328 mmHg **b.** 2620 mmHg
c. 475 mmHg **d.** 5240 mmHg

8.17 a. 52.4 L **b.** 25 L
c. 100. L **d.** 45 L

8.19 25 L of cyclopropane

8.21 **a.** inspiration   **b.** expiration   **c.** inspiration

8.23 **a.** C   **b.** A   **c.** B

8.25 **a.** 303 °C   **b.** −129 °C
      c. 591 °C   **d.** 136 °C

8.27 **a.** 2400 mL   **b.** 4900 mL
      c. 1800 mL   **d.** 1700 mL

8.29 **a.** 770 mmHg   **b.** 1150 mmHg

8.31 **a.** −23 °C   **b.** 168 °C

8.33 1.9 atm

8.35 **a.** 4.26 atm   **b.** 3.07 atm   **c.** 0.606 atm

8.37 −33 °C

8.39 The volume increases because the number of gas particles is increased.

8.41 **a.** 4.00 L   **b.** 26.7 L   **c.** 14.6 L

8.43 **a.** 2.00 moles of O_2 **b.** 9.41 L of He

8.45 **a.** 4.48 L of O_2 **b.** 0.146 g of H_2

8.47 4.93 atm

8.49 29.4 g of O_2

8.51 566 K (293 °C)

8.53 **a.** 7.60 L of H_2 **b.** 4.92 g of Mg

8.55 178 L of O_2

8.57 3.4 L of O_2

8.59 1300 g of O_2

8.61 765 Torr

8.63 425 Torr

8.65 **a.** The partial pressure of oxygen will be lower than normal.
      b. Breathing a higher concentration of oxygen will help to increase the supply of oxygen in the lungs and blood and raise the partial pressure of oxygen in the blood.

8.67 0.978 atm

8.69 0.025 mole of O_2

8.71 **a.** True. The flask containing helium has more moles of helium and thus more helium atoms.
      b. True. The mass and volume of each are the same, which means the mass/volume ratio or density is the same in both flasks.

8.73 **a.** 2   **b.** 1

8.75 **a.** A   **b.** C
      c. A   **d.** B
      e. C

8.77 **a.** The volume of the chest and lungs is decreased.
      b. The decrease in volume increases the pressure, which can dislodge the food in the trachea.

8.79 −223 °C

8.81 32 000 L

8.83 4.41 g of CH_4

8.85 81.0 g of CO_2

8.87 8.56 L of H_2

8.89 1.02 g of NH_3

8.91 370 Torr

8.93 2170 mL

8.95 −66 °C

8.97 1340 L of CO_2

8.99 5.31 g of water

8.101 620 L

8.103 0.18 g of CO_2

CI.13 In the following diagram, blue spheres represent the element **A** and yellow spheres represent the element **B**: (6.5, 7.1, 7.2)

Reactants   **Products**

a. Write the formulas for each of the reactants and products.
b. Write a balanced chemical equation for the reaction.
c. Indicate the type of reaction as combination, decomposition, single replacement, double replacement, or combustion.

CI.14 The active ingredient in Tums is calcium carbonate. One Tums tablet contains 500. mg of calcium carbonate. (6.3, 6.4, 7.4, 7.5)

The active ingredient in Tums neutralizes excess stomach acid.

a. What is the formula of calcium carbonate?
b. What is the molar mass of calcium carbonate?
c. How many moles of calcium carbonate are in one roll of Tums that contains 12 tablets?
d. If a person takes two Tums tablets, how many grams of calcium are obtained?
e. If the daily recommended quantity of Ca^{2+} to maintain bone strength in older women is 1500 mg, how many Tums tablets are needed each day to supply the needed calcium?

CI.15 Tamiflu (Oseltamivir), $C_{16}H_{28}N_2O_4$, is an antiviral drug used to treat influenza. The preparation of Tamiflu begins with the extraction of shikimic acid from the seedpods of star anise. From 2.6 g of star anise, 0.13 g of shikimic acid can be obtained and used to produce one capsule containing 75 mg of Tamiflu. The usual adult dosage for treatment of influenza is two capsules of Tamiflu daily for 5 days. (7.4, 7.5)

Shikimic acid is the basis for the antiviral drug in Tamiflu.

The spice called star anise is a plant source of shikimic acid.

Each capsule contains 75 mg of Tamiflu.

a. If black spheres are carbon atoms, white spheres are hydrogen atoms, and red spheres are oxygen atoms, what is the formula of shikimic acid?
b. What is the molar mass of shikimic acid?
c. How many moles of shikimic acid are contained in 130 g of shikimic acid?
d. How many capsules containing 75 mg of Tamiflu could be produced from 155 g of star anise?
e. What is the molar mass of Tamiflu?
f. How many kilograms of Tamiflu would be needed to treat all the people in a city with a population of 500 000 if each person consumes two Tamiflu capsules a day for 5 days?

CI.16 The compound butyric acid gives rancid butter its characteristic odor. (6.7, 7.4, 7.5)

Butyric acid produces the characteristic odor of rancid butter.

a. If black spheres are carbon atoms, white spheres are hydrogen atoms, and red spheres are oxygen atoms, what is the molecular formula of butyric acid?
b. What is the molar mass of butyric acid?
c. How many grams of butyric acid contain 3.28×10^{23} atoms of oxygen?
d. How many grams of carbon are in 5.28 g of butyric acid?
e. Butyric acid has a density of 0.959 g/mL at 20 °C. How many moles of butyric acid are contained in 1.56 mL of butyric acid?
f. Identify the bonds C—C, C—H, and C—O in a molecule of butyric acid as polar covalent or nonpolar covalent.

CI.17 Methane is a major component of purified natural gas used for heating and cooking. When 1.0 mole of methane gas burns with oxygen to produce carbon dioxide and water, 883 kJ is produced. Methane gas has a density of 0.715 g/L at STP. For transport, the natural gas is cooled to −163 °C to form liquefied natural gas (LNG) with a density of 0.45 g/mL. A tank on a ship can hold 7.0 million gallons of LNG. (2.7, 6.6, 7.1, 7.5, 7.7, 7.9, 8.6)

An LNG carrier transports liquefied natural gas.

a. Draw the Lewis structure formula for methane, which has the formula CH_4.

b. What is the mass, in kilograms, of LNG (assume that LNG is all methane) transported in one tank on a ship?

c. What is the volume, in liters, of LNG (methane) from one tank when the LNG is converted to gas at STP?

d. Write a balanced chemical equation for the combustion of methane in a gas burner, including the heat of reaction.

Methane is the fuel burned in a gas cooktop.

e. How many kilograms of oxygen are needed to react with all of the methane provided by one tank of LNG?

f. How much heat, in kilojoules, is released from burning all of the methane in one tank of LNG?

CI.18 Automobile exhaust is a major cause of air pollution. One pollutant is nitrogen oxide, which forms from nitrogen and oxygen gases in the air at the high temperatures in an automobile engine. Once emitted into the air, nitrogen oxide reacts with oxygen to produce nitrogen dioxide, a reddish brown gas with a sharp, pungent odor that makes up smog. One component of gasoline is heptane, C_7H_{16}, which has a density of 0.684 g/mL. In one year, a typical automobile uses 550 gal of gasoline and produces 41 lb of nitrogen oxide. (7.1, 7.5, 7.7, 8.6)

Two gases found in automobile exhaust are carbon dioxide and nitrogen oxide.

a. Write a balanced chemical equations for the production of nitrogen oxide and nitrogen dioxide.

b. If all the nitrogen oxide emitted by one automobile is converted to nitrogen dioxide in the atmosphere, how many kilograms of nitrogen dioxide are produced in one year by a single automobile?

c. Write a balanced chemical equation for the combustion of heptane.

d. How many moles of CO_2 are produced from the gasoline used by the typical automobile in one year, assuming the gasoline is all heptane?

e. How many liters of carbon dioxide at STP are produced in one year from the gasoline used by the typical automobile?

ANSWERS

CI.13 a. Reactants: A and B_2; Products: AB_3
    b. $2A + 3B_2 \longrightarrow 2AB_3$
    c. combination

CI.15 a. $C_7H_{10}O_5$ **b.** 174.15 g/mole
    c. 0.75 mole   **d.** 59 capsules
    e. 312.4 g/mole   **f.** 400 kg

CI.17 a.
$$H\!:\!\overset{\displaystyle ..}{\underset{\displaystyle ..}{C}}\!:\!H \quad \text{or} \quad H\!-\!\overset{\textstyle H}{\underset{\textstyle H}{\overset{|}{\underset{|}{C}}}}\!-\!H$$

    b. 1.2×10^7 kg of LNG (methane)
    c. 1.7×10^{10} L of LNG (methane) at STP
    d. $CH_4(g) + 2O_2(g) \xrightarrow{\Delta} CO_2(g) + 2H_2O(g) + 883$ kJ
    e. 4.8×10^7 kg of O_2
    f. 6.6×10^{11} kJ

9 Solutions

OUR KIDNEYS PRODUCE URINE, WHICH CARRIES WASTE

products and excess fluid from the body. They also reabsorb electrolytes such as potassium and produce hormones that regulate blood pressure and calcium blood levels. Diseases such as diabetes and high blood pressure can cause a decrease in kidney function. Symptoms of kidney malfunction include protein in the urine, an abnormal level of urea nitrogen in the blood, frequent urination, and swollen feet. If kidney failure occurs, it may be treated with dialysis or transplantation.

Michelle has been suffering from kidney disease because of severe strep throat as a child. When her kidneys stopped functioning, Michelle was placed on dialysis three times a week. As she enters the dialysis unit, her dialysis nurse, Amanda, asks Michelle how she is feeling. Michelle indicates that she feels tired today and has considerable swelling around her ankles. The dialysis nurse informs her that these side effects occur because of her body's inability to regulate the amount of water in her cells. Amanda explains that the amount of water is regulated by the concentration of electrolytes in her body fluids and the rate at which waste products are removed from her body. Amanda explains that although water is essential for the many chemical reactions that occur in the body, the amount of water can become too high or too low because of various diseases and conditions. Because Michelle's kidneys no longer perform dialysis, she cannot regulate the amount of electrolytes or waste in her body fluids. As a result, she has an electrolyte imbalance and a buildup of waste products, so her body is retaining water. Amanda then explains that the dialysis machine does the work of her kidneys to reduce the high levels of electrolytes and waste products.

CAREER Dialysis Nurse

A dialysis nurse specializes in assisting patients with kidney disease undergoing dialysis. This requires monitoring the patient before, during, and after dialysis for any complications such as a drop in blood pressure or cramping. The dialysis nurse connects the patient to the dialysis unit via a dialysis catheter that is inserted into the neck or chest, which must be kept clean to prevent infection. A dialysis nurse must have considerable knowledge about how the dialysis machine functions to ensure that it is operating correctly at all times.

9.1   Solutions 325

Chemistry Link to Health
Water in the Body 327

9.2   Electrolytes and
Nonelectrolytes 329

Chemistry Link to Health
Electrolytes in Body
Fluids 331

9.3   Solubility 333

Chemistry Link to Health
Gout and Kidney Stones:
A Problem of Saturation in
Body Fluids 334

9.4   Solution Concentrations
and Reactions 339

9.5   Dilution of Solutions 349

9.6   Properties of Solutions 352

Chemistry Link to Health
Colloids and Solutions in the
Body 353

Chemistry Link to Health
Dialysis by the Kidneys and
the Artificial Kidney 359

℞   Clinical Applications 329,
333, 348, 351, 361, 367, 368

℞   Clinical Update Using
Dialysis for Renal Failure 361

olutions are everywhere around us. Most of the gases, liquids, and solids we see are mixtures of at least one substance dissolved in another. There are different types of solutions. The air we breathe is a solution that is primarily oxygen and nitrogen gases. Carbon dioxide gas dissolved in water makes carbonated drinks. When we make solutions of coffee or tea, we use hot water to dissolve substances from coffee beans or tea leaves. The ocean is also a solution, consisting of many ionic compounds such as sodium chloride dissolved in water. In your medicine cabinet, the antiseptic tincture of iodine is a solution of iodine dissolved in ethanol.

Our body fluids contain water and dissolved substances such as glucose and urea and electrolytes such as K^+, Na^+, Cl^-, Mg^{2+}, HCO_3^-, and HPO_4^{2-}. Proper amounts of each of these dissolved substances and water must be maintained in the body fluids. Small changes in electrolyte levels can seriously disrupt cellular processes and endanger our health. Solutions can be described by their concentration, which is the amount of solute in a specific amount of that solution. These relationships, which include mass % (m/m), volume % (v/v), mass /volume % (m/v), and molarity (M), can be used to convert between the amount of a solute and the quantity of its solution. Solutions are also diluted by adding a specific amount of solvent to a solution.

In the processes of osmosis and dialysis, water, essential nutrients, and waste products enter and leave the cells of the body. The kidneys utilize osmosis and dialysis to regulate the amount of water and electrolytes that are excreted.

CHAPTER READINESS*

🖩 KEY MATH SKILLS
- Calculating a Percentage (1.4C)
- Solving Equations (1.4D)
- Interpreting a Graph (1.4E)

⚛ CORE CHEMISTRY SKILLS
- Writing Conversion Factors from Equalities (2.5)
- Using Conversion Factors (2.6)
- Identifying Attractive Forces (6.9)
- Using Mole–Mole Factors (7.6)

*These Key Math Skills and Core Chemistry Skills from previous chapters are listed here for your review as you proceed to the new material in this chapter.

9.1 Solutions

A **solution** is a homogeneous mixture in which one substance, called the **solute**, is uniformly dispersed in another substance called the **solvent**. Because the solute and the solvent do not react with each other, they can be mixed in varying proportions. A solution of a little salt dissolved in water tastes slightly salty. When a large amount of salt is dissolved in water, the solution tastes very salty. Usually, the solute (in this case, salt) is the substance present in the lesser amount, whereas the solvent (in this case, water) is present in the greater amount. For example, in a solution composed of 5.0 g of salt and 50. g of water, salt is the solute and water is the solvent. In a solution, the particles of the solute are evenly dispersed among the molecules within the solvent (see Figure 9.1).

A solution has at least one solute dispersed in a solvent.

LEARNING GOAL

Identify the solute and solvent in a solution; describe the formation of a solution.

Solute: The substance present in lesser amount

Salt

Water

Solvent: The substance present in greater amount

FIGURE 9.1 ▶ A solution of copper(II) sulfate ($CuSO_4$) forms as particles of solute dissolve, move away from the crystal, and become evenly dispersed among the solvent (water) molecules.

Q What does the uniform blue color in the graduated cylinder on the right indicate?

Types of Solutes and Solvents

Solutes and solvents may be solids, liquids, or gases. The solution that forms has the same physical state as the solvent. When sugar crystals are dissolved in water, the resulting sugar solution is liquid. Sugar is the solute, and water is the solvent. Soda water and soft drinks are prepared by dissolving carbon dioxide gas in water. The carbon dioxide gas is the solute, and water is the solvent. Table 9.1 lists some solutes and solvents and their solutions.

TABLE 9.1 Some Examples of Solutions

Type	Example	Primary Solute	Solvent
Gas Solutions			
Gas in a gas	Air	$O_2(g)$	$N_2(g)$
Liquid Solutions			
Gas in a liquid	Soda water	$CO_2(g)$	$H_2O(l)$
	Household ammonia	$NH_3(g)$	$H_2O(l)$
Liquid in a liquid	Vinegar	$HC_2H_3O_2(l)$	$H_2O(l)$
Solid in a liquid	Seawater	$NaCl(s)$	$H_2O(l)$
	Tincture of iodine	$I_2(s)$	$C_2H_5OH(l)$
Solid Solutions			
Solid in a solid	Brass	$Zn(s)$	$Cu(s)$
	Steel	$C(s)$	$Fe(s)$

Water as a Solvent

Water is one of the most common solvents in nature. In the H_2O molecule, an oxygen atom shares electrons with two hydrogen atoms. Because oxygen is much more electronegative than hydrogen, the O—H bonds are polar. In each polar bond, the oxygen atom has a partial negative (δ^-) charge and the hydrogen atom has a partial positive (δ^+) charge. Because the shape of a water molecule is bent, not linear, its dipoles do not cancel out. Thus, water is polar, and is a *polar solvent*.

Attractive forces known as *hydrogen bonds* occur between molecules where partially positive hydrogen atoms are attracted to the partially negative atoms F, O, or N. As seen in the diagram, the hydrogen bonds are shown as a series of dots. Although hydrogen bonds are much weaker than covalent or ionic bonds, there are many of them linking water molecules together. Hydrogen bonds are important in the properties of biological compounds such as proteins, carbohydrates, and DNA.

In water, hydrogen bonds form between an oxygen atom in one water molecule and the hydrogen atom in another.

 # Chemistry Link to **Health**
Water in the Body

The average adult is about 60% water by mass, and the average infant about 75%. About 60% of the body's water is contained within the cells as intracellular fluids; the other 40% makes up extracellular fluids, which include the interstitial fluid in tissue and the plasma in the blood. These external fluids carry nutrients and waste materials between the cells and the circulatory system.

Typical water gain and loss during 24 hours

Water Gain	
Liquid	1000 mL
Food	1200 mL
Metabolism	300 mL
Total	2500 mL

Water Loss	
Urine	1500 mL
Perspiration	300 mL
Breath	600 mL
Feces	100 mL
Total	2500 mL

The water lost from the body is replaced by the intake of fluids.

Every day you lose between 1500 and 3000 mL of water from the kidneys as urine, from the skin as perspiration, from the lungs as you exhale, and from the gastrointestinal tract. Serious dehydration can occur in an adult if there is a 10% net loss in total body fluid; a 20% loss of fluid can be fatal. An infant suffers severe dehydration with only a 5 to 10% loss in body fluid.

Water loss is continually replaced by the liquids and foods in the diet and from metabolic processes that produce water in the cells of the body. Table 9.2 lists the percentage by mass of water contained in some foods.

TABLE 9.2 Percentage of Water in Some Foods

Food	Water (% by mass)	Food	Water (% by mass)
Vegetables		**Meats/Fish**	
Carrot	88	Chicken, cooked	71
Celery	94	Hamburger, broiled	60
Cucumber	96	Salmon	71
Tomato	94		
Fruits		**Milk Products**	
Apple	85	Cottage cheese	78
Cantaloupe	91	Milk, whole	87
Orange	86	Yogurt	88
Strawberry	90		
Watermelon	93		

Formation of Solutions

The interactions between solute and solvent will determine whether a solution will form. Initially, energy is needed to separate the particles in the solute and the solvent particles. Then energy is released as solute particles move between the solvent particles to form a solution. However, there must be attractions between the solute and the solvent particles to provide the energy for the initial separation. These attractions occur when the solute and the solvent have similar polarities. The expression "like dissolves like" is a way of saying that the polarities of a solute and a solvent must be similar in order for a solution to form (see Figure 9.2). In the absence of attractions between a solute and a solvent, there is insufficient energy to form a solution (see Table 9.3).

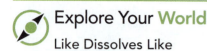

Explore Your World

Like Dissolves Like

Obtain small samples of vegetable oil, water, vinegar, salt, and sugar. Then combine and mix the substances as listed in **a** through **e**.

a. oil and water
b. water and vinegar
c. salt and water
d. sugar and water
e. salt and oil

Questions

1. Which of the mixtures formed a solution?
2. Which of the mixtures did not form a solution?
3. Why do some mixtures form solutions, but others do not?

FIGURE 9.2 ▶ Like dissolves like. In each test tube, the lower layer is CH_2Cl_2 (more dense), and the upper layer is water (less dense).
(a) CH_2Cl_2 is nonpolar and water is polar; the two layers do not mix. **(b)** The nonpolar solute I_2 (purple) is soluble in the nonpolar solvent CH_2Cl_2. **(c)** The ionic solute $Ni(NO_3)_2$ (green) is soluble in the polar solvent water.

🔵 In which layer would polar molecules of sucrose $(C_{12}H_{22}O_{11})$ be soluble?

(a)   (b)   (c)

TABLE 9.3 Possible Combinations of Solutes and Solvents

Solutions Will Form		Solutions Will Not Form	
Solute	Solvent	Solute	Solvent
Polar	Polar	Polar	Nonpolar
Nonpolar	Nonpolar	Nonpolar	Polar

Solutions with Ionic and Polar Solutes

In ionic solutes such as sodium chloride, NaCl, there are strong ionic bonds between positively charged Na^+ ions and negatively charged Cl^- ions. In water, a polar solvent, the hydrogen bonds provide strong solvent–solvent attractions. When NaCl crystals are placed in water, partially negative oxygen atoms in water molecules attract positive Na^+ ions, and the partially positive hydrogen atoms in other water molecules attract negative Cl^- ions (see Figure 9.3). As soon as the Na^+ ions and the Cl^- ions form a solution, they undergo **hydration** as water molecules surround each ion. Hydration of the ions diminishes their attraction to other ions and keeps them in solution.

In the equation for the formation of the NaCl solution, the solid and aqueous NaCl are shown with the formula H_2O over the arrow, which indicates that water is needed for the dissociation process but is not a reactant.

$$NaCl(s) \xrightarrow[\text{Dissociation}]{H_2O} Na^+(aq) + Cl^-(aq)$$

In another example, we find that a polar molecular compound such as methanol, CH_3—OH, is soluble in water because methanol has a polar —OH group that forms hydrogen bonds with water (see Figure 9.4). Polar solutes require polar solvents for a solution to form.

FIGURE 9.3 ▶ Ions on the surface of a crystal of NaCl dissolve in water as they are attracted to the polar water molecules that pull the ions into solution and surround them.

🔵 What helps keep Na^+ and Cl^- ions in solution?

Solutions with Nonpolar Solutes

Compounds containing nonpolar molecules, such as iodine (I_2), oil, or grease, do not dissolve in water because there are essentially no attractions between the particles of a nonpolar solute and the polar solvent. Nonpolar solutes require nonpolar solvents for a solution to form.

Methanol (CH_3 — OH) solute   Water solvent   Methanol–water solution with hydrogen bonding

FIGURE 9.4 ▶ Molecules of methanol, CH_3—OH, form hydrogen bonds with polar water molecules to form a methanol–water solution.

🔵 Why are there attractions between the solute methanol and the solvent water?

QUESTIONS AND PROBLEMS

9.1 Solutions

LEARNING GOAL Identify the solute and solvent in a solution; describe the formation of a solution.

9.1 Identify the solute and the solvent in each solution composed of the following:
 a. 10.0 g of NaCl and 100.0 g of H_2O
 b. 50.0 mL of ethanol, C_2H_5OH, and 10.0 mL of H_2O
 c. 0.20 L of O_2 and 0.80 L of N_2

9.2 Identify the solute and the solvent in each solution composed of the following:
 a. 10.0 mL of acetic acid and 200. mL of water
 b. 100.0 mL of water and 5.0 g of sugar
 c. 1.0 g of Br_2 and 50.0 mL of methylene chloride(l)

9.3 Describe the formation of an aqueous KI solution, when solid KI dissolves in water.

9.4 Describe the formation of an aqueous LiBr solution, when solid LiBr dissolves in water.

℞ Clinical Applications

9.5 Water is a polar solvent and carbon tetrachloride (CCl_4) is a nonpolar solvent. In which solvent is each of the following, which is found or used in the body, more likely to be soluble?
 a. $CaCO_3$ (calcium supplement), ionic
 b. retinol (vitamin A), nonpolar
 c. sucrose (table sugar), polar
 d. cholesterol (lipid), nonpolar

9.6 Water is a polar solvent and hexane is a nonpolar solvent. In which solvent is each of the following, which is found or used in the body, more likely to be soluble?
 a. vegetable oil, nonpolar
 b. oleic acid (lipid), nonpolar
 c. niacin (vitamin B_3), polar
 d. $FeSO_4$ (iron supplement), ionic

9.2 Electrolytes and Nonelectrolytes

Solutes can be classified by their ability to conduct an electrical current. When **electrolytes** dissolve in water, the process of *dissociation* separates them into ions forming solutions that conduct electricity. When **nonelectrolytes** dissolve in water, they do not separate into ions and their solutions do not conduct electricity.

To test solutions for the presence of ions, we can use an apparatus that consists of a battery and a pair of electrodes connected by wires to a light bulb. The light bulb glows when electricity can flow, which can only happen when electrolytes provide ions that move between the electrodes to complete the circuit.

Types of Electrolytes

Electrolytes can be further classified as *strong electrolytes* or *weak electrolytes*. For a **strong electrolyte**, such as sodium chloride (NaCl), there is 100% dissociation of the solute into ions. When the electrodes from the light bulb apparatus are placed in the NaCl solution, the light bulb glows very brightly.

In an equation for dissociation of a compound in water, the charges must balance. For example, magnesium nitrate dissociates to give one magnesium ion for every two nitrate ions. However, only the ionic bonds between Mg^{2+} and NO_3^- are broken, not the covalent bonds within the polyatomic ion. The equation for the dissociation of $Mg(NO_3)_2$ is written as follows:

$$Mg(NO_3)_2(s) \xrightarrow[\text{Dissociation}]{H_2O} Mg^{2+}(aq) + 2NO_3^-(aq)$$

A **weak electrolyte** is a compound that dissolves in water mostly as molecules. Only a few of the dissolved solute molecules undergo *dissociation*, producing a small number of ions in solution. Thus solutions of weak electrolytes do not conduct electrical current as well as solutions of strong electrolytes. When the electrodes are placed in a solution of a weak electrolyte, the glow of the light bulb is very dim. In an aqueous solution of the weak electrolyte HF, a few HF molecules dissociate to produce H^+ and F^- ions. As more H^+ and F^- ions form, some recombine to give HF molecules. These forward and reverse reactions of molecules to ions and back again are indicated by two arrows between reactant and products that point in opposite directions:

$$HF(aq) \xrightleftharpoons[\text{Recombination}]{\text{Dissociation}} H^+(aq) + F^-(aq)$$

LEARNING GOAL

Identify solutes as electrolytes or nonelectrolytes.

(a) Strong electrolyte

(b) Weak electrolyte

TABLE 9.4 Classification of Solutes in Aqueous Solutions

Type of Solute	In Solution	Type(s) of Particles in Solution	Conducts Electricity?	Examples
Strong electrolyte	Dissociates completely	Ions only	Yes	Ionic compounds such as NaCl, KBr, MgCl$_2$, NaNO$_3$; bases such as NaOH, KOH; acids such as HCl, HBr, HI, HNO$_3$, HClO$_4$, H$_2$SO$_4$
Weak electrolyte	Ionizes partially	Mostly molecules and a few ions	Weakly	HF, H$_2$O, NH$_3$, HC$_2$H$_3$O$_2$ (acetic acid)
Nonelectrolyte	No ionization	Molecules only	No	Carbon compounds such as CH$_3$OH (methanol), C$_2$H$_5$OH (ethanol), C$_{12}$H$_{22}$O$_{11}$ (sucrose), CH$_4$N$_2$O (urea)

(c) Nonelectrolyte

A nonelectrolyte such as methanol (CH$_3$OH) dissolves in water only as molecules, which do not ionize. When electrodes of the light bulb apparatus are placed in a solution of a nonelectrolyte, the light bulb does not glow, because the solution does not contain ions and cannot conduct electricity.

$$CH_3OH(l) \xrightarrow{H_2O} CH_3OH(aq)$$

Table 9.4 summarizes the classification of solutes in aqueous solutions.

▶ **SAMPLE PROBLEM 9.1** **Solutions of Electrolytes and Nonelectrolytes**

Indicate whether solutions of each of the following contain only ions, only molecules, or mostly molecules and a few ions. Write the equation for the formation of a solution for each of the following:

a. Na$_2$SO$_4$(s), a strong electrolyte
b. sucrose, C$_{12}$H$_{22}$O$_{11}$(s), a nonelectrolyte
c. acetic acid, HC$_2$H$_3$O$_2$(l), a weak electrolyte

SOLUTION

a. An aqueous solution of Na$_2$SO$_4$(s) contains only the ions Na$^+$ and SO$_4^{2-}$.

$$Na_2SO_4(s) \xrightarrow{H_2O} 2Na^+(aq) + SO_4^{2-}(aq)$$

b. A nonelectrolyte such as sucrose, C$_{12}$H$_{22}$O$_{11}$(s), produces only molecules when it dissolves in water.

$$C_{12}H_{22}O_{11}(s) \xrightarrow{H_2O} C_{12}H_{22}O_{11}(aq)$$

c. A weak electrolyte such as HC$_2$H$_3$O$_2$(l) produces mostly molecules and a few ions when it dissolves in water.

$$HC_2H_3O_2(l) \xrightleftharpoons{H_2O} H^+(aq) + C_2H_3O_2^-(aq)$$

STUDY CHECK 9.1

Boric acid, H$_3$BO$_3$(s), is a weak electrolyte. Would you expect a boric acid solution to contain only ions, only molecules, or mostly molecules and a few ions?

ANSWER

A solution of a weak electrolyte would contain mostly molecules and a few ions.

Equivalents

Body fluids and intravenous (IV) solutions contain a mixture of electrolytes, such as Na$^+$, Cl$^-$, K$^+$, and Ca^{2+}. We measure each individual ion in terms of an **equivalent (Eq)**, which is the amount of that ion equal to 1 mole of positive or negative electrical charge. For example, 1 mole of Na$^+$ ions and 1 mole of Cl$^-$ ions are each 1 equivalent because they each contain 1 mole of charge. For an ion with a charge of 2+ or 2−, there are 2 equivalents for each mole. Some examples of ions and equivalents are shown in Table 9.5.

TABLE 9.5 Equivalents of Electrolytes in Clinical Intravenous (IV) Solutions

Ion	Ionic Charge	Number of Equivalents in 1 Mole
Na^+, K^+, Li^+, NH_4^+	1+	1 Eq
Ca^{2+}, Mg^{2+}	2+	2 Eq
Fe^{3+}	3+	3 Eq
Cl^-, $C_2H_3O_2^-$ (acetate), $H_2PO_4^-$, $C_3H_5O_3^-$ (lactate)	1−	1 Eq
CO_3^{2-}, HPO_4^{2-}	2−	2 Eq
PO_4^{3-}, $C_6H_5O_7^{3-}$ (citrate)	3−	3 Eq

In any solution, the charge of the positive ions is always balanced by the charge of the negative ions. The concentrations of electrolytes in intravenous fluids are expressed in milliequivalents per liter (mEq/L); 1 Eq = 1000 mEq. For example, a solution containing 25 mEq/L of Na^+ and 4 mEq/L of K^+ has a total positive charge of 29 mEq/L. If Cl^- is the only anion, its concentration must be 29 mEq/L.

SAMPLE PROBLEM 9.2 Electrolyte Concentration

The laboratory tests for a patient indicate a blood calcium level of 8.8 mEq/L.

a. How many moles of calcium ion are in 0.50 L of blood?
b. If chloride ion is the only other ion present, what is its concentration in mEq/L?

SOLUTION

a. Using the volume and the electrolyte concentration in mEq/L, we can find the number of equivalents in 0.50 L of blood.

$$0.50 \ \cancel{L} \times \frac{8.8 \ \text{mEq} \ \cancel{Ca^{2+}}}{1 \ \cancel{L}} \times \frac{1 \ \text{Eq} \ Ca^{2+}}{1000 \ \text{mEq} \ \cancel{Ca^{2+}}} = 0.0044 \ \text{Eq of} \ Ca^{2+}$$

We can then convert equivalents to moles (for Ca^{2+} there are 2 Eq per mole).

$$0.0044 \ \text{Eq} \ \cancel{Ca^{2+}} \times \frac{1 \ \text{mole} \ Ca^{2+}}{2 \ \text{Eq} \ \cancel{Ca^{2+}}} = 0.0022 \ \text{mole of} \ Ca^{2+}$$

b. If the concentration of Ca^{2+} is 8.8 mEq/L, then the concentration of Cl^- must be 8.8 mEq/L to balance the charge.

STUDY CHECK 9.2

A lactated Ringer's solution for intravenous fluid replacement contains 109 mEq of Cl^- per liter of solution. If a patient received 1250 mL of Ringer's solution, how many moles of chloride ion were given?

ANSWER

0.136 mole of Cl^-

Chemistry Link to **Health**
Electrolytes in Body Fluids

Electrolytes in the body play an important role in maintaining the proper function of the cells and organs in the body. Typically, the electrolytes sodium, potassium, chloride, and bicarbonate are measured in a blood test. Sodium ions regulate the water content in the body and are important in carrying electrical impulses through the nervous system. Potassium ions are also involved in the transmission of electrical impulses and play a role in the maintenance of a regular heartbeat. Chloride ions balance the charges of the positive ions and also control the balance of fluids in the body. Bicarbonate is important in maintaining the proper pH of the blood. Sometimes when vomiting, diarrhea, or sweating is excessive, the concentrations of certain electrolytes may decrease. Then fluids such as Pedialyte may be given to return electrolyte levels to normal.

An intravenous solution is used to replace electrolytes in the body.

The concentrations of electrolytes present in body fluids and in intravenous fluids given to a patient are often expressed in milliequivalents per liter (mEq/L) of solution. For example, one liter of Pedialyte contains the following electrolytes: Na^+ 45 mEq, Cl^- 35 mEq, K^+ 20 mEq, and $citrate^{3-}$ 30 mEq.

Table 9.6 gives the concentrations of some typical electrolytes in blood plasma and various types of solutions. There is a charge balance because the total number of positive charges is equal to the total number of negative charges. The use of a specific intravenous solution depends on the nutritional, electrolyte, and fluid needs of the individual patient.

TABLE 9.6 Electrolytes in Blood Plasma and Selected Intravenous Solutions

		Normal Concentrations of Ions (mEq/L)			
	Blood Plasma	Normal Saline 0.9% NaCl	Lactated Ringer's Solution	Maintenance Solution	Replacement Solution (extracellular)
Purpose		Replaces fluid loss	Hydration	Maintains electrolytes and fluids	Replaces electrolytes
Cations					
Na^+	135–145	154	130	40	140
K^+	3.5–5.5		4	35	10
Ca^{2+}	4.5–5.5		3		5
Mg^{2+}	1.5–3.0				3
Total		154	137	75	158
Anions					
$Acetate^-$					47
Cl^-	95–105	154	109	40	103
HCO_3^-	22–28				
$Lactate^-$			28	20	
HPO_4^{2-}	1.8–2.3			15	
$Citrate^{3-}$					8
Total		154	137	75	158

QUESTIONS AND PROBLEMS

9.2 Electrolytes and Nonelectrolytes

LEARNING GOAL Identify solutes as electrolytes or nonelectrolytes.

9.7 KF is a strong electrolyte, and HF is a weak electrolyte. How is the solution of KF different from that of HF?

9.8 NaOH is a strong electrolyte, and CH_3OH is a nonelectrolyte. How is the solution of NaOH different from that of CH_3OH?

9.9 Write a balanced equation for the dissociation of each of the following strong electrolytes in water:
a. KCl
b. $CaCl_2$
c. K_3PO_4
d. $Fe(NO_3)_3$

9.10 Write a balanced equation for the dissociation of each of the following strong electrolytes in water:
a. LiBr
b. $NaNO_3$
c. $CuCl_2$
d. K_2CO_3

9.11 Indicate whether aqueous solutions of each of the following solutes contain only ions, only molecules, or mostly molecules and a few ions:
a. acetic acid, $HC_2H_3O_2$, a weak electrolyte
b. NaBr, a strong electrolyte
c. fructose, $C_6H_{12}O_6$, a nonelectrolyte

9.12 Indicate whether aqueous solutions of each of the following solutes contain only ions, only molecules, or mostly molecules and a few ions:
a. NH_4Cl, a strong electrolyte
b. ethanol, C_2H_5OH, a nonelectrolyte
c. HCN, hydrocyanic acid, a weak electrolyte

9.13 Classify the solute represented in each of the following equations as a strong, weak, or nonelectrolyte:

a. $K_2SO_4(s) \xrightarrow{H_2O} 2K^+(aq) + SO_4^{2-}(aq)$

b. $NH_3(g) + H_2O(l) \rightleftharpoons NH_4^+(aq) + OH^-(aq)$

c. $C_6H_{12}O_6(s) \xrightarrow{H_2O} C_6H_{12}O_6(aq)$

9.14 Classify the solute represented in each of the following equations as a strong, weak, or nonelectrolyte:

a. $CH_3OH(l) \xrightarrow{H_2O} CH_3OH(aq)$

b. $MgCl_2(s) \xrightarrow{H_2O} Mg^{2+}(aq) + 2Cl^-(aq)$

c. $HClO(aq) \rightleftharpoons H^+(aq) + ClO^-(aq)$

9.15 Calculate the number of equivalents in each of the following:
a. 1 mole of K^+
b. 2 moles of OH^-
c. 1 mole of Ca^{2+}
d. 3 moles of CO_3^{2-}

9.16 Calculate the number of equivalents in each of the following:
a. 1 mole of Mg^{2+}
b. 0.5 mole of H^+
c. 4 moles of Cl^-
d. 2 moles of Fe^{3+}

℞ Clinical Applications

9.17 An intravenous saline solution contains 154 mEq/L each of Na^+ and Cl^-. How many moles each of Na^+ and Cl^- are in 1.00 L of the saline solution?

9.18 An intravenous solution to replace potassium loss contains 40. mEq/L each of K^+ and Cl^-. How many moles each of K^+ and Cl^- are in 1.5 L of the solution?

9.19 An intravenous solution contains 40. mEq/L of Cl^- and 15 mEq/L of HPO_4^{2-}. If Na^+ is the only cation in the solution, what is the Na^+ concentration, in milliequivalents per liter?

9.20 A Ringer's solution contains the following concentrations (mEq/L) of cations: Na^+ 147, K^+ 4, and Ca^{2+} 4. If Cl^- is the only anion in the solution, what is the Cl^- concentration, in milliequivalents per liter?

9.21 When Amanda's blood was tested, the chloride level was 0.45 g/dL.
a. What is this value in milliequivalents per liter?
b. According to Table 9.6, is this value above, below, or within the normal range?

9.22 After dialysis, the level of magnesium in Amanda's blood was 0.0026 g/dL.
a. What is this value in milliequivalents per liter?
b. According to Table 9.6, is this value above, below, or within the normal range?

9.3 Solubility

The term *solubility* is used to describe the amount of a solute that can dissolve in a given amount of solvent. Many factors, such as the type of solute, the type of solvent, and the temperature, affect the solubility of a solute. **Solubility**, usually expressed in grams of solute in 100 g of solvent, is the maximum amount of solute that can be dissolved at a certain temperature. If a solute readily dissolves when added to the solvent, the solution does not contain the maximum amount of solute. We call this solution an **unsaturated solution**.

A solution that contains all the solute that can dissolve is a **saturated solution**. When a solution is saturated, the rate at which the solute dissolves becomes equal to the rate at which solid forms, a process known as *recrystallization*. Then there is no further change in the amount of dissolved solute in solution.

$$\text{Solute} + \text{solvent} \underset{\text{Solute recrystallizes}}{\overset{\text{Solute dissolves}}{\rightleftharpoons}} \text{saturated solution}$$

We can prepare a saturated solution by adding an amount of solute greater than that needed to reach solubility. Stirring the solution will dissolve the maximum amount of solute and leave the excess on the bottom of the container. Once we have a saturated solution, the addition of more solute will only increase the amount of undissolved solute.

LEARNING GOAL

Define solubility; distinguish between an unsaturated and a saturated solution. Identify an ionic compound as soluble or insoluble.

Additional solute can dissolve in an unsaturated solution, but not in a saturated solution.

▶ SAMPLE PROBLEM 9.3 Saturated Solutions

At 20 °C, the solubility of KCl is 34 g/100 g of H_2O. In the laboratory, a student mixes 75 g of KCl with 200. g of H_2O at a temperature of 20 °C.

a. How much of the KCl will dissolve?
b. Is the solution saturated or unsaturated?
c. What is the mass, in grams, of any solid KCl left undissolved on the bottom of the container?

SOLUTION

a. At 20 °C, KCl has a solubility of 34 g of KCl in 100 g of water. Using the solubility as a conversion factor, we can calculate the maximum amount of KCl that can dissolve in 200. g of water as follows:

$$200. \text{ g } H_2O \times \frac{34 \text{ g KCl}}{100 \text{ g } H_2O} = 68 \text{ g of KCl}$$

b. Because 75 g of KCl exceeds the maximum amount (68 g) that can dissolve in 200. g of water, the KCl solution is saturated.

c. If we add 75 g of KCl to 200. g of water and only 68 g of KCl can dissolve, there is 7 g (75 g − 68 g) of solid (undissolved) KCl on the bottom of the container.

STUDY CHECK 9.3

At 40 °C, the solubility of KNO_3 is 65 g/100 g of H_2O. How many grams of KNO_3 will dissolve in 120 g of H_2O at 40 °C?

ANSWER

78 g of KNO_3

Chemistry Link to **Health**

Gout and Kidney Stones: A Problem of Saturation in Body Fluids

The conditions of gout and kidney stones involve compounds in the body that exceed their solubility levels and form solid products. Gout affects adults, primarily men, over the age of 40. Attacks of gout may occur when the concentration of uric acid in blood plasma exceeds its solubility, which is 7 mg/100 mL of plasma at 37 °C. Insoluble deposits of needle-like crystals of uric acid can form in the cartilage, tendons, and soft tissues where they cause painful gout attacks. They may also form in the tissues of the kidneys, where they can cause renal damage. High levels of uric acid in the body can be caused by an increase in uric acid production, failure of the kidneys to remove uric acid, or a diet with an overabundance of foods containing purines, which are metabolized to uric acid in the body. Foods in the diet that contribute to high levels of uric acid include certain meats, sardines, mushrooms, asparagus, and beans. Drinking alcoholic beverages may also significantly increase uric acid levels and bring about gout attacks.

Treatment for gout involves diet changes and drugs. Medications, such as probenecid, which helps the kidneys eliminate uric acid, or allopurinol, which blocks the production of uric acid by the body may be useful.

Kidney stones are solid materials that form in the urinary tract. Most kidney stones are composed of calcium phosphate and calcium oxalate, although they can be solid uric acid. Insufficient water intake and high levels of calcium, oxalate, and phosphate in the urine can lead to the formation of kidney stones. When a kidney stone passes through the urinary tract, it causes considerable pain and discomfort, necessitating the use of painkillers and surgery. Sometimes ultrasound is used to break up kidney stones. Persons prone to kidney stones are advised to drink six to eight glasses of water every day to prevent saturation levels of minerals in the urine.

Gout occurs when uric acid exceeds its solubility.

Kidney stones form when calcium phosphate exceeds its solubility.

Effect of Temperature on Solubility

The solubility of most solids is greater as temperature increases, which means that solutions usually contain more dissolved solute at higher temperature. A few substances show little change in solubility at higher temperatures, and a few are less soluble (see Figure 9.5). For example, when you add sugar to iced tea, some undissolved sugar may form on the bottom of the glass. But if you add sugar to hot tea, many teaspoons of sugar are needed before solid sugar appears. Hot tea dissolves more sugar than does cold tea because the solubility of sugar is much greater at a higher temperature.

When a saturated solution is carefully cooled, it becomes a *supersaturated solution* because it contains more solute than the solubility allows. Such a solution is unstable, and if the solution is agitated or if a solute crystal is added, the excess solute will recrystallize to give a saturated solution again.

Conversely, the solubility of a gas in water decreases as the temperature increases. At higher temperatures, more gas molecules have the energy to escape from the solution. Perhaps you have observed the bubbles escaping from a cold carbonated soft drink as it warms. At high temperatures, bottles containing carbonated solutions may burst as more gas molecules leave the solution and increase the gas pressure inside the bottle. Biologists have found that increased temperatures in rivers and lakes cause the amount of dissolved oxygen to decrease until the warm water can no longer support a biological community. Electricity-generating plants are required to have their own ponds to use with their cooling towers to lessen the threat of thermal pollution in surrounding waterways.

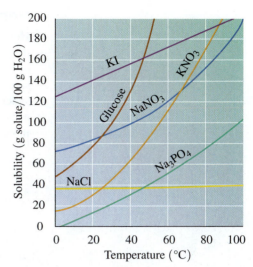

FIGURE 9.5 ▶ In water, most common solids are more soluble as the temperature increases.

Compare the solubility of $NaNO_3$ at 20 °C and 60 °C.

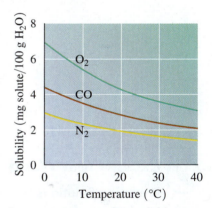

In water, gases are less soluble as the temperature increases.

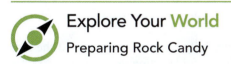

Explore Your World

Preparing Rock Candy

Need: one cup of water, three cups of granulated sugar, clean narrow glass or jar, wooden stick (skewer) or thick string that is the height of the glass, pencil, and food coloring (optional)

Process:

1. Place the water and two cups of sugar in a pan and begin heating and stirring. The sugar should all dissolve. Continue heating, but not boiling, adding small amounts of the remaining sugar and

Rock candy can be made from a saturated solution of sugar (sucrose).

stirring thoroughly each time, until some of the sugar no longer dissolves. There may be some sugar crystals on the bottom of the pan. Carefully pour the sugar solution into the glass or jar. Add two to three drops of food coloring, if desired.

2. Wet the wooden stick and roll it in granulated sugar to provide crystals for the sugar solution to attach to. Place the stick in the sugar solution. If using string, tape the string to a pencil so it will hang slightly above the bottom of the glass. Wet the lower half of the string, roll it in the granulated sugar, and place the pencil across the top of the glass with the string in the sugar solution. Place the glass and wooden stick or string in a place where it will not be disturbed. You should see sugar crystals grow over the next several days.

Questions

1. Why did more sugar dissolve as the solution was heated?
2. How did you know when you obtained a saturated solution?
3. Why did you see crystals forming on the stick or string over time?

Henry's Law

Henry's law states that the solubility of gas in a liquid is directly related to the pressure of that gas above the liquid. At higher pressures, there are more gas molecules available to enter and dissolve in the liquid. A can of soda is carbonated by using CO_2 gas at high pressure to increase the solubility of the CO_2 in the beverage. When you open the can at atmospheric pressure, the pressure on the CO_2 drops, which decreases the solubility of CO_2. As a result, bubbles of CO_2 rapidly escape from the solution. The burst of bubbles is even more noticeable when you open a warm can of soda.

CO_2 under high pressure

Pressure released

Lots of CO_2 dissolved in soda

CO_2 bubbles out of solution

Gas molecule

Fewer gas molecules dissolve

Gas at high pressure

Gas at low pressure

Cola

Cola

More gas molecules dissolve

When the pressure of a gas above a solution decreases, the solubility of that gas in the solution also decreases.

Soluble and Insoluble Ionic Compounds

In our discussion up to now, we have considered ionic compounds that dissolve in water. However, some ionic compounds do not dissociate into ions and remain as solids even in contact with water. The **solubility rules** give some guidelines about the solubility of ionic compounds in water.

Ionic compounds that are soluble in water typically contain at least one of the ions in Table 9.7. *Only an ionic compound containing a soluble cation or anion will dissolve in water.* Most ionic compounds containing Cl^- are soluble, but $AgCl$, $PbCl_2$, and Hg_2Cl_2 are insoluble. Similarly, most ionic compounds containing SO_4^{2-} are soluble, but a few are insoluble. Most other ionic compounds are insoluble (see Figure 9.6). In an insoluble ionic compound, the ionic bonds between its positive and negative ions are too strong for the polar water molecules to break. We can use the solubility rules to predict whether a solid ionic compound would be soluble or not. Table 9.8 illustrates the use of these rules.

TABLE 9.7 Solubility Rules for Ionic Compounds in Water

An ionic compound is soluble in water if it contains one of the following:
Positive Ions: Li^+, Na^+, K^+, Rb^+, Cs^+, NH_4^+
Negative Ions: NO_3^-, $C_2H_3O_2^-$
Cl^-, Br^-, I^- except when combined with Ag^+, Pb^{2+}, or Hg_2^{2+}
SO_4^{2-} except when combined with Ba^{2+}, Pb^{2+}, Ca^{2+}, Sr^{2+}, or Hg_2^{2+}
Ionic compounds that do not contain at least one of these ions are usually insoluble.

CdS

FeS

PbI_2

$Ni(OH)_2$

FIGURE 9.6 ▶ If an ionic compound contains a combination of a cation and an anion that are not soluble, that ionic compound is insoluble. For example, combinations of cadmium and sulfide, iron and sulfide, lead and iodide, and nickel and hydroxide do not contain any soluble ions. Thus, they form insoluble ionic compounds.

Q Why are each of these ionic compounds insoluble in water?

TABLE 9.8 Using Solubility Rules

Ionic Compound	Solubility in Water	Reasoning
K_2S	Soluble	Contains K^+
$Ca(NO_3)_2$	Soluble	Contains NO_3^-
$PbCl_2$	Insoluble	Is an insoluble chloride
NaOH	Soluble	Contains Na^+
$AlPO_4$	Insoluble	Contains no soluble ions

⚛ CORE CHEMISTRY SKILL

Using Solubility Rules

In medicine, insoluble $BaSO_4$ is used as an opaque substance to enhance X-rays of the gastrointestinal tract. $BaSO_4$ is so insoluble that it does not dissolve in gastric fluids (see Figure 9.7). Other ionic barium compounds cannot be used because they would dissolve in water, releasing Ba^{2+} which is poisonous.

▶ **SAMPLE PROBLEM 9.4** Soluble and Insoluble Ionic Compounds

Predict whether each of the following ionic compounds is soluble in water and explain why:

a. Na_3PO_4 **b.** $CaCO_3$

SOLUTION

a. The ionic compound Na_3PO_4 is soluble in water because any compound that contains Na^+ is soluble.
b. The ionic compound $CaCO_3$ is not soluble. The compound does not contain a soluble positive ion, which means that ionic compound containing Ca^{2+} and CO_3^{2-} is not soluble.

STUDY CHECK 9.4

In some electrolyte drinks, $MgCl_2$ is added to provide magnesium. Why would you expect $MgCl_2$ to be soluble in water?

ANSWER

$MgCl_2$ is soluble in water because ionic compounds that contain chloride are soluble unless they contain Ag^+, Pb^{2+}, or Hg_2^{2+}.

FIGURE 9.7 ▶ A barium sulfate-enhanced X-ray of the abdomen shows the lower gastrointestinal (GI) tract.

Q Is $BaSO_4$ a soluble or an insoluble substance?

Formation of a Solid

We can use solubility rules to predict whether a solid, called a *precipitate*, forms when two solutions containing soluble reactants are mixed as shown in Sample Problem 9.5.

▶ **SAMPLE PROBLEM 9.5** **Writing Equations for the Formation of an Insoluble Ionic Compound**

When solutions of NaCl and $AgNO_3$ are mixed, a white solid forms. Write the ionic and net ionic equations for the reaction.

SOLUTION

STEP 1 Write the ions of the reactants.

$$\textbf{Reactants}$$
$$\textbf{(initial combinations)}$$
$$Ag^+(aq) + NO_3^-(aq)$$

$$Na^+(aq) + Cl^-(aq)$$

STEP 2 Write the combinations of ions and determine if any are insoluble. When we look at the ions of each solution, we see that the combination of Ag^+ and Cl^- forms an insoluble ionic compound.

Mixture (new combinations)	Product	Soluble
$Ag^+(aq) + Cl^-(aq)$	AgCl	No
$Na^+(aq) + NO_3^-(aq)$	$NaNO_3$	Yes

STEP 3 Write the ionic equation including any solid. In the *ionic equation*, we show all the ions of the reactants. The products include the solid AgCl that forms along with the remaining ions Na^+ and NO_3^-.

$$Ag^+(aq) + NO_3^-(aq) + Na^+(aq) + Cl^-(aq) \longrightarrow AgCl(s) + Na^+(aq) + NO_3^-(aq)$$

STEP 4 Write the net ionic equation. To write a *net ionic equation*, we remove the Na^+ and NO_3^- ions, known as *spectator ions*, which are unchanged. This leaves only the ions and solid of the chemical reaction.

$$Ag^+(aq) + \underbrace{\cancel{NO_3^-(aq)} + \cancel{Na^+(aq)}}_{\text{Spectator ions}} + Cl^-(aq) \longrightarrow AgCl(s) + \underbrace{\cancel{Na^+(aq)} + \cancel{NO_3^-(aq)}}_{\text{Spectator ions}}$$

$$Ag^+(aq) + Cl^-(aq) \longrightarrow AgCl(s) \quad \text{Net ionic equation}$$

Cl⁻   NO₃⁻   Ag⁺   Na⁺

Insoluble ionic compound

Guide to Writing an Equation for the Formation of an Insoluble Ionic Compound

STEP 1
Write the ions of the reactants.

STEP 2
Write the combinations of ions and determine if any are insoluble.

STEP 3
Write the ionic equation including any solid.

STEP 4
Write the net ionic equation.

Type of Equation			
Chemical	$AgNO_3(aq)$	$+ NaCl(aq) \longrightarrow$	$AgCl(s) + NaNO_3(aq)$
Ionic	$Ag^+(aq) + NO_3^-(aq) +$	$Na^+(aq) + Cl^-(aq) \rightarrow$	$AgCl(s) + Na^+(aq) + NO_3^-(aq)$
Net Ionic	$Ag^+(aq)$	$+ Cl^-(aq) \longrightarrow$	$AgCl(s)$

STUDY CHECK 9.5

Predict whether a solid might form in each of the following mixtures of solutions. If so, write the net ionic equation for the reaction.

a. $NH_4Cl(aq) + Ca(NO_3)_2(aq)$ **b.** $Pb(NO_3)_2(aq) + KCl(aq)$

ANSWER

a. No solid forms because the products, $NH_4NO_3(aq)$ and $CaCl_2(aq)$, are soluble.

b. $Pb^{2+}(aq) + 2Cl^-(aq) \longrightarrow PbCl_2(s)$

QUESTIONS AND PROBLEMS

9.3 Solubility

LEARNING GOAL Define solubility; distinguish between an unsaturated and a saturated solution. Identify an ionic compound as soluble or insoluble.

Use the following table for problems 9.23 to 9.26:

Substance	Solubility (g/100 g H₂O)	
	20 °C	50 °C
KCl	34	43
$NaNO_3$	88	110
$C_{12}H_{22}O_{11}$ (sugar)	204	260

9.23 Determine whether each of the following solutions will be saturated or unsaturated at 20 °C:
a. adding 25 g of KCl to 100. g of H_2O
b. adding 11 g of $NaNO_3$ to 25 g of H_2O
c. adding 400. g of sugar to 125 g of H_2O

9.24 Determine whether each of the following solutions will be saturated or unsaturated at 50 °C:
a. adding 25 g of KCl to 50. g of H_2O
b. adding 150. g of $NaNO_3$ to 75 g of H_2O
c. adding 80. g of sugar to 25 g of H_2O

9.25 A solution containing 80. g of KCl in 200. g of H_2O at 50 °C is cooled to 20 °C.
a. How many grams of KCl remain in solution at 20 °C?
b. How many grams of solid KCl crystallized after cooling?

9.26 A solution containing 80. g of $NaNO_3$ in 75 g of H_2O at 50 °C is cooled to 20 °C.
a. How many grams of $NaNO_3$ remain in solution at 20 °C?
b. How many grams of solid $NaNO_3$ crystallized after cooling?

9.27 Explain the following observations:
a. More sugar dissolves in hot tea than in iced tea.
b. Champagne in a warm room goes flat.
c. A warm can of soda has more spray when opened than a cold one.

9.28 Explain the following observations:
a. An open can of soda loses its "fizz" faster at room temperature than in the refrigerator.
b. Chlorine gas in tap water escapes as the sample warms to room temperature.
c. Less sugar dissolves in iced coffee than in hot coffee.

9.29 Predict whether each of the following ionic compounds is soluble in water:
a. LiCl **b.** AgCl **c.** $BaCO_3$ **d.** K_2O **e.** $Fe(NO_3)_3$

9.30 Predict whether each of the following ionic compounds is soluble in water:
a. PbS **b.** KI **c.** Na_2S **d.** Ag_2O **e.** $CaSO_4$

9.31 Determine whether a solid forms when solutions containing the following ionic compounds are mixed. If so, write the ionic equation and the net ionic equation.
a. $KCl(aq)$ and $Na_2S(aq)$ **b.** $AgNO_3(aq)$ and $K_2S(aq)$
c. $CaCl_2(aq)$ and $Na_2SO_4(aq)$ **d.** $CuCl_2(aq)$ and $Li_3PO_4(aq)$

9.32 Determine whether a solid forms when solutions containing the following ionic compounds are mixed. If so, write the ionic equation and the net ionic equation.
a. $Na_3PO_4(aq)$ and $AgNO_3(aq)$
b. $K_2SO_4(aq)$ and $Na_2CO_3(aq)$
c. $Pb(NO_3)_2(aq)$ and $Na_2CO_3(aq)$
d. $BaCl_2(aq)$ and $KOH(aq)$

9.4 Solution Concentrations and Reactions

The amount of solute dissolved in a certain amount of solution is called the **concentration** of the solution. We will look at ways to express a concentration as a ratio of a certain amount of solute in a given amount of solution. The amount of a solute may be expressed in units of grams, milliliters, or moles. The amount of a solution may be expressed in units of grams, milliliters, or liters.

$$\text{Concentration of a solution} = \frac{\text{amount of solute}}{\text{amount of solution}}$$

LEARNING GOAL

Calculate the concentration of a solute in a solution; use concentration units to calculate the amount of solute or solution. Given the volume and concentration of a solution, calculate the amount of another reactant or product in a reaction.

Mass Percent (m/m) Concentration

Mass percent (m/m) describes the mass of the solute in grams for exactly 100 g of solution. In the calculation of mass percent (m/m), the units of mass of the solute and solution must be the same. If the mass of the solute is given as grams, then the mass of the solution must also be grams. The mass of the solution is the sum of the mass of the solute and the mass of the solvent.

$$\text{Mass percent (m/m)} = \frac{\text{mass of solute (g)}}{\text{mass of solute (g)} + \text{mass of solvent (g)}} \times 100\%$$

$$= \frac{\text{mass of solute (g)}}{\text{mass of solution (g)}} \times 100\%$$

Suppose we prepared a solution by mixing 8.00 g of KCl (solute) with 42.00 g of water (solvent). Together, the mass of the solute and mass of solvent give the mass of the solution (8.00 g + 42.00 g = 50.00 g). Mass percent is calculated by substituting the mass of the solute and the mass of the solution into the mass percent expression.

$$\frac{8.00 \text{ g KCl}}{50.00 \text{ g solution}} \times 100\% = 16.0\% \text{ (m/m) KCl solution}$$

$$\overbrace{8.00 \text{ g KCl} + 42.00 \text{ g H}_2\text{O}}$$

Solute   +   Solvent

Add 8.00 g of KCl

Add water until the
solution has a mass of 50.00 g

When water is added to 8.00 g of KCl to form 50.00 g of a KCl solution, the mass percent concentration is 16.0% (m/m).

Guide to Calculating Solution Concentration

STEP 1
State the given and needed quantities.

STEP 2
Write the concentration expression.

STEP 3
Substitute solute and solution quantities into the expression and calculate.

▶ **SAMPLE PROBLEM 9.6** Calculating Mass Percent (m/m) Concentration

What is the mass percent of NaOH in a solution prepared by dissolving 30.0 g of NaOH in 120.0 g of H_2O?

SOLUTION

STEP 1 State the given and needed quantities.

	Given	Need
ANALYZE THE PROBLEM	30.0 g of NaOH solute, 30.0 g NaOH + 120.0 g H_2O = 150.0 g of NaOH solution	mass percent (m/m)

STEP 2 Write the concentration expression.

$$\text{Mass percent (m/m)} = \frac{\text{grams of solute}}{\text{grams of solution}} \times 100\%$$

STEP 3 Substitute solute and solution quantities into the expression and calculate.

$$\text{Mass percent (m/m)} = \frac{30.0 \text{ g NaOH}}{150.0 \text{ g solution}} \times 100\%$$
$$= 20.0\% \text{ (m/m) NaOH solution}$$

STUDY CHECK 9.6

What is the mass percent (m/m) of NaCl in a solution made by dissolving 2.0 g of NaCl in 56.0 g of H_2O?

ANSWER

3.4% (m/m) NaCl solution

Volume Percent (v/v) Concentration

Because the volumes of liquids or gases are easily measured, the concentrations of their solutions are often expressed as **volume percent (v/v)**. The units of volume used in the ratio must be the same, for example, both in milliliters or both in liters.

$$1 \text{ mole of NaOH} = 40.00 \text{ g of NaOH}$$

$$\frac{1 \text{ mole NaOH}}{40.00 \text{ g NaOH}} \quad \text{and} \quad \frac{40.00 \text{ g NaOH}}{1 \text{ mole NaOH}}$$

$$\text{moles of NaOH} = 60.0 \text{ g } \cancel{\text{NaOH}} \times \frac{1 \text{ mole NaOH}}{40.00 \text{ g } \cancel{\text{NaOH}}}$$

$$= 1.50 \text{ moles of NaOH}$$

volume of solution $= 0.250$ L of NaOH solution

STEP 2 Write the concentration expression.

$$\text{Molarity (M)} = \frac{\text{moles of solute}}{\text{liters of solution}}$$

STEP 3 Substitute solute and solution quantities into the expression and calculate.

$$M = \frac{1.50 \text{ moles NaOH}}{0.250 \text{ L solution}} = \frac{6.00 \text{ moles NaOH}}{1 \text{ L solution}} = 6.00 \text{ M NaOH solution}$$

STUDY CHECK 9.9

What is the molarity of a solution that contains 75.0 g of KNO_3 dissolved in 0.350 L of solution?

ANSWER

2.12 M KNO_3 solution

Table 9.9 summarizes the types of units used in the various types of concentration expressions for solutions.

TABLE 9.9 Summary of Types of Concentration Expressions and Their Units

Concentration Units	Mass Percent (m/m)	Volume Percent (v/v)	Mass/Volume Percent (m/v)	Molarity (M)
Solute	g	mL	g	mole
Solution	g	mL	mL	L

Using Concentration as a Conversion Factor

In the preparation of solutions, we often need to calculate the amount of solute or solution. Then the concentration is useful as a conversion factor. Some examples of percent concentrations and molarity, their meanings, and conversion factors are given in Table 9.10. Some examples of using percent concentration or molarity as conversion factors are given in Sample Problems 9.10 and 9.11.

 CORE CHEMISTRY SKILL

Using Concentration as a Conversion Factor

TABLE 9.10 Conversion Factors from Concentrations

Percent Concentration	Meaning	Conversion Factors		
10% (m/m) KCl solution	10 g of KCl in 100 g of KCl solution	$\dfrac{10 \text{ g KCl}}{100 \text{ g solution}}$	and	$\dfrac{100 \text{ g solution}}{10 \text{ g KCl}}$
12% (v/v) ethanol solution	12 mL of ethanol in 100 mL of ethanol solution	$\dfrac{12 \text{ mL ethanol}}{100 \text{ mL solution}}$	and	$\dfrac{100 \text{ mL solution}}{12 \text{ mL ethanol}}$
5% (m/v) glucose solution	5 g of glucose in 100 mL of glucose solution	$\dfrac{5 \text{ g glucose}}{100 \text{ mL solution}}$	and	$\dfrac{100 \text{ mL solution}}{5 \text{ g glucose}}$
Molarity				
6.0 M HCl solution	6.0 moles of HCl in 1 liter of HCl solution	$\dfrac{6.0 \text{ moles HCl}}{1 \text{ L solution}}$	and	$\dfrac{1 \text{ L solution}}{6.0 \text{ moles HCl}}$

SAMPLE PROBLEM 9.10 **Using Mass/Volume Percent to Find Mass of Solute**

A topical antibiotic is 1.0% (m/v) clindamycin. How many grams of clindamycin are in 60. mL of the 1.0% (m/v) solution?

SOLUTION

Guide to Using Concentration to Calculate Mass or Volume

STEP 1
State the given and needed quantities.

STEP 2
Write a plan to calculate the mass or volume.

STEP 3
Write equalities and conversion factors.

STEP 4
Set up the problem to calculate the mass or volume.

STEP 1 State the given and needed quantities.

ANALYZE THE PROBLEM	Given	Need
	60. mL of 1.0% (m/v) clindamycin solution	grams of clindamycin

STEP 2 Write a plan to calculate the mass.

milliliters of solution — % (m/v) factor → grams of clindamycin

STEP 3 Write equalities and conversion factors. The percent (m/v) indicates the grams of a solute in every 100 mL of a solution. The 1.0% (m/v) can be written as two conversion factors.

$$100 \text{ mL of solution} = 1.0 \text{ g of clindamycin}$$

$$\frac{1.0 \text{ g clindamycin}}{100 \text{ mL solution}} \quad \text{and} \quad \frac{100 \text{ mL solution}}{1.0 \text{ g clindamycin}}$$

STEP 4 Set up the problem to calculate the mass. The volume of the solution is converted to mass of solute using the conversion factor that cancels mL.

$$60. \text{ mL solution} \times \frac{1.0 \text{ g clindamycin}}{100 \text{ mL solution}} = 0.60 \text{ g of clindamycin}$$

STUDY CHECK 9.10

In 2010, the FDA approved a 2.0% (m/v) morphine oral solution to treat severe or chronic pain. How many grams of morphine does a patient receive if 0.60 mL of 2.0% (m/v) morphine solution was ordered?

ANSWER

0.012 g of morphine

SAMPLE PROBLEM 9.11 **Using Molarity to Calculate Volume of Solution**

How many liters of a 2.00 M NaCl solution are needed to provide 67.3 g of NaCl?

SOLUTION

STEP 1 State the given and needed quantities.

ANALYZE THE PROBLEM	Given	Need
	67.3 g of NaCl, 2.00 M NaCl solution	liters of NaCl solution

STEP 2 Write a plan to calculate the volume.

grams of NaCl — Molar mass → moles of NaCl — Molarity → liters of NaCl solution

STEP 3 Write equalities and conversion factors.

$$1 \text{ mole of NaCl} = 58.44 \text{ g of NaCl}$$

$$\frac{1 \text{ mole NaCl}}{58.44 \text{ g NaCl}} \quad \text{and} \quad \frac{58.44 \text{ g NaCl}}{1 \text{ mole NaCl}}$$

$$1 \text{ L of NaCl solution} = 2.00 \text{ moles of NaCl}$$

$$\frac{1 \text{ L NaCl solution}}{2.00 \text{ moles NaCl}} \quad \text{and} \quad \frac{2.00 \text{ moles NaCl}}{1 \text{ L NaCl solution}}$$

STEP 4 Set up the problem to calculate the volume.

$$\text{liters of NaCl solution} = 67.3 \text{ g NaCl} \times \frac{1 \text{ mole NaCl}}{58.44 \text{ g NaCl}} \times \frac{1 \text{ L NaCl solution}}{2.00 \text{ moles NaCl}}$$

$$= 0.576 \text{ L of NaCl solution}$$

STUDY CHECK 9.11

How many milliliters of a 6.0 M HCl solution will provide 164 g of HCl?

ANSWER

750 mL of HCl solution

Chemical Reactions in Solution

When chemical reactions involve aqueous solutions, we use the balanced chemical equation, the molarity, and the volume to determine the moles or grams of the reactants or products. For example, we can determine the volume of a solution from the molarity and the grams of reactant as seen in Sample Problem 9.12.

▶**SAMPLE PROBLEM 9.12 Volume of a Solution in a Reaction**

Zinc reacts with HCl to produce hydrogen gas, H_2, and $ZnCl_2$.

$$Zn(s) + 2HCl(aq) \longrightarrow H_2(g) + ZnCl_2(aq)$$

How many liters of a 1.50 M HCl solution completely react with 5.32 g of zinc?

SOLUTION

STEP 1 State the given and needed quantities.

ANALYZE THE PROBLEM	Given	Need
	5.32 g of Zn, 1.50 M HCl solution	liters of HCl solution
	Equation	
	$Zn(s) + 2HCl(aq) \longrightarrow H_2(g) + ZnCl_2(aq)$	

STEP 2 Write a plan to calculate the needed quantity.

grams of Zn → Molar mass → moles of Zn → Mole–mole factor → moles of HCl → Molarity → liters of HCl solution

STEP 3 Write equalities and conversion factors including mole–mole and concentration factors.

$$1 \text{ mole of Zn} = 65.41 \text{ g of Zn}$$

$$\frac{1 \text{ mole Zn}}{65.41 \text{ g Zn}} \quad \text{and} \quad \frac{65.41 \text{ g Zn}}{1 \text{ mole Zn}}$$

$$1 \text{ mole of Zn} = 2 \text{ moles of HCl}$$

$$\frac{1 \text{ mole Zn}}{2 \text{ moles HCl}} \quad \text{and} \quad \frac{2 \text{ moles HCl}}{1 \text{ mole Zn}}$$

$$1 \text{ L of solution} = 1.50 \text{ moles of HCl}$$

$$\frac{1 \text{ L solution}}{1.50 \text{ moles HCl}} \quad \text{and} \quad \frac{1.50 \text{ moles HCl}}{1 \text{ L solution}}$$

⚛ CORE CHEMISTRY SKILL

Calculating the Quantity of a Reactant or Product for a Chemical Reaction in Solution

Guide to Calculations Involving Solutions in Chemical Reactions

STEP 1 State the given and needed quantities.

STEP 2 Write a plan to calculate the needed quantity or concentration.

STEP 3 Write equalities and conversion factors including mole–mole and concentration factors.

STEP 4 Set up the problem to calculate the needed quantity or concentration.

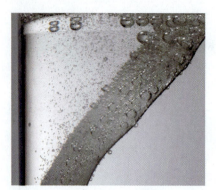

Zinc reacts when placed in a solution of HCl.

When a $BaCl_2$ solution is added to a Na_2SO_4 solution, $BaSO_4$, a white solid, forms.

STEP 4 Set up the problem to calculate the needed quantity.

$$5.32 \text{ g } \cancel{Zn} \times \frac{1 \text{ mole } \cancel{Zn}}{65.41 \text{ g } \cancel{Zn}} \times \frac{2 \text{ moles HCl}}{1 \text{ mole } \cancel{Zn}} \times \frac{1 \text{ L solution}}{1.50 \cancel{\text{ moles HCl}}} = 0.108 \text{ L of HCl solu}$$

STUDY CHECK 9.12

Using the reaction in Sample Problem 9.12, how many grams of zinc can react with 225 mL of a 0.200 M HCl solution?

ANSWER

1.47 g of Zn

▶ **SAMPLE PROBLEM 9.13** Volume of a Reactant in a Solution

How many milliliters of a 0.250 M $BaCl_2$ solution are needed to react with 0.0325 L of a 0.160 M Na_2SO_4 solution?

$$Na_2SO_4(aq) + BaCl_2(aq) \longrightarrow BaSO_4(s) + 2NaCl(aq)$$

SOLUTION

STEP 1 State the given and needed quantities.

	Given	Need
ANALYZE THE PROBLEM	0.0325 L of 0.160 M Na_2SO_4 solution 0.250 M $BaCl_2$ solution	milliliters of $BaCl_2$ solution
	Equation	
	$Na_2SO_4(aq) + BaCl_2(aq) \longrightarrow BaSO_4(s) + 2NaCl(aq)$	

STEP 2 Write a plan to calculate the needed quantity.

liters of Na_2SO_4 solution → **Molarity** → moles of Na_2SO_4 → **Mole–mole factor** → moles of $BaCl_2$

Molarity → liters of $BaCl_2$ solution → **Metric factor** → milliliters of $BaCl_2$ solution

STEP 3 Write equalities and conversion factors including mole–mole and concentration factors.

1 L of solution = 0.160 mole of Na_2SO_4	1 mole of Na_2SO_4 = 1 mole of $BaCl_2$
$\dfrac{1 \text{ L solution}}{0.160 \text{ mole } Na_2SO_4}$ and $\dfrac{0.160 \text{ mole } Na_2SO_4}{1 \text{ L solution}}$	$\dfrac{1 \text{ mole } Na_2SO_4}{1 \text{ mole } BaCl_2}$ and $\dfrac{1 \text{ mole } BaCl_2}{1 \text{ mole } Na_2SO_4}$

1 L of solution = 0.250 mole of $BaCl_2$	1 L = 1000 mL
$\dfrac{1 \text{ L solution}}{0.250 \text{ mole } BaCl_2}$ and $\dfrac{0.250 \text{ mole } BaCl_2}{1 \text{ L solution}}$	$\dfrac{1 \text{ L}}{1000 \text{ mL}}$ and $\dfrac{1000 \text{ mL}}{1 \text{ L}}$

STEP 4 Set up the problem to calculate the needed quantity.

$$0.0325 \text{ L } \cancel{\text{solution}} \times \frac{0.160 \cancel{\text{ mole } Na_2SO_4}}{1 \text{ L } \cancel{\text{solution}}} \times \frac{1 \cancel{\text{ mole } BaCl_2}}{1 \cancel{\text{ mole } Na_2SO_4}} \times \frac{1 \text{ L } \cancel{\text{solution}}}{0.250 \cancel{\text{ mole } BaCl_2}} \times \frac{1000 \text{ mL } BaCl_2 \text{ solution}}{1 \text{ L } \cancel{\text{solution}}}$$

$$= 20.8 \text{ mL of } BaCl_2 \text{ solution}$$

STUDY CHECK 9.13

For the reaction in Sample Problem 9.13, how many milliliters of a 0.330 M Na_2SO_4 solution are needed to react with 26.8 mL of a 0.216 M $BaCl_2$ solution?

ANSWER

17.5 mL of Na_2SO_4 solution

Figure 9.8 gives a summary of the pathways and conversion factors needed for substances including solutions involved in chemical reactions.

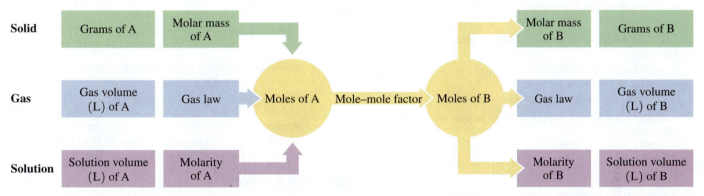

FIGURE 9.8 ▶ In calculations involving chemical reactions, substance A is converted to moles of A using molar mass (if solid), gas laws (if gas), or molarity (if solution). Then moles of A are converted to moles of substance B, which are converted to grams of solid, liters of gas, or liters of solution, as needed.

❓ What sequence of conversion factors would you use to calculate the number of grams of $CaCO_3$ needed to react with 1.50 L of a 2.00 M HCl solution in the reaction $CaCO_3(s) + 2HCl(aq) \longrightarrow CO_2(g) + H_2O(l) + CaCl_2(aq)$?

QUESTIONS AND PROBLEMS

9.4 Solution Concentrations and Reactions

LEARNING GOAL Calculate the concentration of a solute in a solution; use concentration units to calculate the amount of solute or solution. Given the volume and concentration of a solution, calculate the amount of another reactant or product in a reaction.

Interactive Video

Solutions

9.33 Calculate the mass percent (m/m) for the solute in each of the following:
   a. 25 g of KCl and 125 g of H_2O
   b. 12 g of sucrose in 225 g of tea solution
   c. 8.0 g of $CaCl_2$ in 80.0 g of $CaCl_2$ solution

9.34 Calculate the mass percent (m/m) for the solute in each of the following:
   a. 75 g of NaOH in 325 g of NaOH solution
   b. 2.0 g of KOH and 20.0 g of H_2O
   c. 48.5 g of Na_2CO_3 in 250.0 g of Na_2CO_3 solution

9.35 Calculate the mass/volume percent (m/v) for the solute in each of the following:
   a. 75 g of Na_2SO_4 in 250 mL of Na_2SO_4 solution
   b. 39 g of sucrose in 355 mL of a carbonated drink

9.36 Calculate the mass/volume percent (m/v) for the solute in each of the following:
   a. 2.50 g of LiCl in 40.0 mL of LiCl solution
   b. 7.5 g of casein in 120 mL of low-fat milk

9.37 Calculate the grams or milliliters of solute needed to prepare the following:
   a. 50. g of a 5.0% (m/m) KCl solution
   b. 1250 mL of a 4.0% (m/v) NH_4Cl solution
   c. 250. mL of a 10.0% (v/v) acetic acid solution

9.38 Calculate the grams or milliliters of solute needed to prepare the following:
   a. 150. g of a 40.0% (m/m) $LiNO_3$ solution
   b. 450 mL of a 2.0% (m/v) KOH solution
   c. 225 mL of a 15% (v/v) isopropyl alcohol solution

9.39 A mouthwash contains 22.5% (v/v) alcohol. If the bottle of mouthwash contains 355 mL, what is the volume, in milliliters, of alcohol?

9.40 A bottle of champagne is 11% (v/v) alcohol. If there are 750 mL of champagne in the bottle, what is the volume, in milliliters, of alcohol?

9.41 For each of the following solutions, calculate the:
   a. grams of 25% (m/m) $LiNO_3$ solution that contains 5.0 g of $LiNO_3$
   b. milliliters of 10.0% (m/v) KOH solution that contains 40.0 g of KOH
   c. milliliters of 10.0% (v/v) formic acid solution that contains 2.0 mL of formic acid

9.42 For each of the following solutions, calculate the:
  a. grams of 2.0% (m/m) NaCl solution that contains 7.50 g of NaCl
  b. milliliters of 25% (m/v) NaF solution that contains 4.0 g of NaF
  c. milliliters of 8.0% (v/v) ethanol solution that contains 20.0 mL of ethanol

9.43 Calculate the molarity of each of the following:
  a. 2.00 moles of glucose in 4.00 L of a glucose solution
  b. 4.00 g of KOH in 2.00 L of a KOH solution
  c. 5.85 g of NaCl in 400. mL of a NaCl solution

9.44 Calculate the molarity of each of the following:
  a. 0.500 mole of glucose in 0.200 L of a glucose solution
  b. 73.0 g of HCl in 2.00 L of a HCl solution
  c. 30.0 g of NaOH in 350. mL of a NaOH solution

9.45 Calculate the grams of solute needed to prepare each of the following:
  a. 2.00 L of a 1.50 M NaOH solution
  b. 4.00 L of a 0.200 M KCl solution
  c. 25.0 mL of a 6.00 M HCl solution

9.46 Calculate the grams of solute needed to prepare each of the following:
  a. 2.00 L of a 6.00 M NaOH solution
  b. 5.00 L of a 0.100 M $CaCl_2$ solution
  c. 175 mL of a 3.00 M $NaNO_3$ solution

9.47 For each of the following solutions, calculate the:
  a. liters of a 2.00 M KBr solution to obtain 3.00 moles of KBr
  b. liters of a 1.50 M NaCl solution to obtain 15.0 moles of NaCl
  c. milliliters of a 0.800 M $Ca(NO_3)_2$ solution to obtain 0.0500 mole of $Ca(NO_3)_2$

9.48 For each of the following solutions, calculate the:
  a. liters of a 4.00 M KCl solution to obtain 0.100 mole of KCl
  b. liters of a 6.00 M HCl solution to obtain 5.00 moles of HCl
  c. milliliters of a 2.50 M K_2SO_4 solution to obtain 1.20 moles of K_2SO_4

9.49 Answer the following for the reaction:

$$Pb(NO_3)_2(aq) + 2KCl(aq) \longrightarrow$$
$$PbCl_2(s) + 2KNO_3(aq)$$

  a. How many grams of $PbCl_2$ will be formed from 50.0 mL of a 1.50 M KCl solution?
  b. How many milliliters of a 2.00 M $Pb(NO_3)_2$ solution will react with 50.0 mL of a 1.50 M KCl solution?
  c. What is the molarity of 20.0 mL of a KCl solution that reacts completely with 30.0 mL of a 0.400 M $Pb(NO_3)_2$ solution?

9.50 Answer the following for the reaction:

$$NiCl_2(aq) + 2NaOH(aq) \longrightarrow$$
$$Ni(OH)_2(s) + 2NaCl(aq)$$

  a. How many milliliters of a 0.200 M NaOH solution are needed to react with 18.0 mL of a 0.500 M $NiCl_2$ solution?
  b. How many grams of $Ni(OH)_2$ are produced from the reaction of 35.0 mL of a 1.75 M NaOH solution and excess $NiCl_2$?

  c. What is the molarity of 30.0 mL of a $NiCl_2$ solution that reacts completely with 10.0 mL of a 0.250 M NaOH solution?

9.51 Answer the following for the reaction:

$$Mg(s) + 2HCl(aq) \longrightarrow H_2(g) + MgCl_2(aq)$$

  a. How many milliliters of a 6.00 M HCl solution are required to react with 15.0 g of magnesium?
  b. How many liters of hydrogen gas can form at STP when 0.500 L of a 2.00 M HCl solution reacts with excess magnesium?
  c. What is the molarity of a HCl solution if the reaction of 45.2 mL of the HCl solution with excess magnesium produces 5.20 L of H_2 gas at 735 mmHg and 25 °C?

9.52 Answer the following for the reaction:

$$CaCO_3(s) + 2HCl(aq) \longrightarrow$$
$$CO_2(g) + H_2O(l) + CaCl_2(aq)$$

  a. How many milliliters of a 0.200 M HCl solution can react with 8.25 g of $CaCO_3$?
  b. How many liters of CO_2 gas can form at STP when 15.5 mL of a 3.00 M HCl solution reacts with excess $CaCO_3$?
  c. What is the molarity of a HCl solution if the reaction of 200. mL of the HCl solution with excess $CaCO_3$ produces 12.0 L of CO_2 gas at 725 mmHg and 18 °C?

℞ Clinical Applications

9.53 A patient receives 100. mL of 20.% (m/v) mannitol solution every hour.
  a. How many grams of mannitol are given in 1 h?
  b. How many grams of mannitol does the patient receive in 12 h?

9.54 A patient receives 250 mL of a 4.0% (m/v) amino acid solution twice a day.
  a. How many grams of amino acids are in 250 mL of solution?
  b. How many grams of amino acids does the patient receive in 1 day?

9.55 A patient needs 100. g of glucose in the next 12 h. How many liters of a 5% (m/v) glucose solution must be given?

9.56 A patient received 2.0 g of NaCl in 8 h. How many milliliters of a 0.90% (m/v) NaCl (saline) solution were delivered?

9.57 A doctor orders 0.075 g of chlorpromazine, which is used to treat schizophrenia. If the stock solution is 2.5% (m/v), how many milliliters are administered to the patient?

9.58 A doctor orders 5 mg of compazine, which is used to treat nausea, vertigo, and migraine headaches. If the stock solution is 2.5% (m/v), how many milliliters are administered to the patient?

9.59 A $CaCl_2$ solution is given to increase blood levels of calcium. If a patient receives 5.0 mL of a 10.% (m/v) $CaCl_2$ solution, how many grams of $CaCl_2$ were given?

9.60 An intravenous solution of mannitol is used as a diuretic to increase the loss of sodium and chloride by a patient. If a patient receives 30.0 mL of a 25% (m/v) mannitol solution, how many grams of mannitol were given?

9.5 Dilution of Solutions

In chemistry and biology, we often prepare diluted solutions from more concentrated solutions. In a process called **dilution**, a solvent, usually water, is added to a solution, which increases the volume. As a result, the concentration of the solution decreases. In an everyday example, you are making a dilution when you add three cans of water to a can of concentrated orange juice.

1 can of orange juice concentrate   +   3 cans of water   =   4 cans of orange juice

Although the addition of solvent increases the volume, the amount of solute does not change; it is the same in the concentrated solution and the diluted solution (see Figure 9.9).

Grams or moles of solute = grams or moles of solute

Concentrated solution   Diluted solution

We can write this equality in terms of the concentration, C, and the volume, V. The concentration, C, may be percent concentration or molarity.

$$C_1 V_1 \;=\; C_2 V_2$$

Concentrated   Diluted
solution   solution

If we are given any three of the four variables (C_1, C_2, V_1, or V_2), we can rearrange the dilution expression to solve for the unknown quantity as seen in Sample Problem 9.14.

FIGURE 9.9 ▶ When water is added to a concentrated solution, there is no change in the number of particles. However, the solute particles spread out as the volume of the diluted solution increases.

◉ What is the concentration of the diluted solution after an equal volume of water is added to a sample of a 6 M HCl solution?

▶**SAMPLE PROBLEM 9.14** **Dilution of a Solution**

A doctor orders 1000. mL of a 35.0% (m/v) dextrose solution. If you have a 50.0% (m/v) dextrose solution, how many milliliters would you use to prepare 1000. mL of 35.0% (m/v) dextrose solution?

SOLUTION

STEP 1 Prepare a table of the concentrations and volumes of the solutions. For our problem analysis, we organize the solution data in a table, making sure that the units of concentration and volume are the same.

Guide to Calculating Dilution Quantities

STEP 1
Prepare a table of the concentrations and volumes of the solutions.

STEP 2
Rearrange the dilution expression to solve for the unknown quantity.

STEP 3
Substitute the known quantities into the dilution expression and calculate.

	Concentrated Solution	Diluted Solution	Know	Predict
ANALYZE THE PROBLEM	C_1 = 50.0% (m/v) dextrose	C_2 = 35.0% (m/v) dextrose	C_1 increases	
	V_1 = ? mL	V_2 = 1000. mL		V_1 decreases

STEP 2 Rearrange the dilution expression to solve for the unknown quantity.

$$C_1 V_1 = C_2 V_2$$

$$\frac{C_1 V_1}{C_1} = \frac{C_2 V_2}{C_1} \quad \text{Divide both sides by } C_1$$

$$V_1 = V_2 \times \frac{C_2}{C_1}$$

STEP 3 Substitute the known quantities into the dilution expression and calculate.

$$V_1 = 1000. \text{ mL} \times \frac{35.0\%}{50.0\%} = 700. \text{ mL of dextrose solution}$$

Concentration factor decreases volume

When the final volume (V_2) is multiplied by a ratio of the percent concentrations (concentration factor) that is less than 1, the initial volume (V_1) is less than the final volume (V_2) as predicted in Step 1.

STUDY CHECK 9.14

What initial volume of a 15% (m/v) mannose solution is needed to prepare 125 mL of a 3.0% (m/v) mannose solution?

ANSWER

25 mL of a 15% (m/v) mannose solution

▶ **SAMPLE PROBLEM 9.15 Molarity of a Diluted Solution**

What is the molarity of a solution when 75.0 mL of a 4.00 M KCl solution is diluted to a volume of 500. mL?

SOLUTION

STEP 1 Prepare a table of the concentrations and volumes of the solutions.

	Concentrated Solution	Diluted Solution	Know	Predict
ANALYZE THE PROBLEM	C_1 = 4.00 M KCl	C_2 = ? M KCl		C (molarity) decreases
	V_1 = 75.0 mL = 0.0750 L	V_2 = 500. mL = 0.500 L	V increases	

STEP 2 Rearrange the dilution expression to solve for the unknown quantity.

$$C_1 V_1 = C_2 V_2$$

$$\frac{C_1 V_1}{V_2} = \frac{C_2 V_2}{V_2} \quad \text{Divide both sides by } V_2$$

$$C_2 = C_1 \times \frac{V_1}{V_2}$$

STEP 3 Substitute the known quantities into the dilution expression and calculate.

$$C_2 = 4.00 \text{ M} \times \frac{75.0 \text{ mL}}{500. \text{ mL}} = 0.600 \text{ M (diluted KCl solution)}$$

Volume factor
decreases concentration

When the initial molarity (C_1) is multiplied by a ratio of the volumes (volume factor) that is less than 1, the molarity of the diluted solution decreases as predicted in Step 1.

STUDY CHECK 9.15

What is the molarity of a solution when 50.0 mL of a 4.00 M KOH solution is diluted to 200. mL?

ANSWER

1.00 M KOH solution

QUESTIONS AND PROBLEMS

9.5 Dilution of Solutions

LEARNING GOAL Describe the dilution of a solution; calculate the unknown concentration or volume when a solution is diluted.

9.61 To make tomato soup, you add one can of water to the condensed soup. Why is this a dilution?

9.62 A can of frozen lemonade calls for the addition of three cans of water to make a pitcher of the beverage. Why is this a dilution?

9.63 Calculate the final concentration of each of the following:
  a. 2.0 L of a 6.0 M HCl solution is added to water so that the final volume is 6.0 L.
  b. Water is added to 0.50 L of a 12 M NaOH solution to make 3.0 L of a diluted NaOH solution.
  c. A 10.0-mL sample of a 25% (m/v) KOH solution is diluted with water so that the final volume is 100.0 mL.
  d. A 50.0-mL sample of a 15% (m/v) H_2SO_4 solution is added to water to give a final volume of 250 mL.

9.64 Calculate the final concentration of each of the following:
  a. 1.0 L of a 4.0 M HNO_3 solution is added to water so that the final volume is 8.0 L.
  b. Water is added to 0.25 L of a 6.0 M NaF solution to make 2.0 L of a diluted NaF solution.
  c. A 50.0-mL sample of an 8.0% (m/v) KBr solution is diluted with water so that the final volume is 200.0 mL.
  d. A 5.0-mL sample of a 50.0% (m/v) acetic acid ($HC_2H_3O_2$) solution is added to water to give a final volume of 25 mL.

9.65 Determine the final volume, in milliliters, of each of the following:
  a. a 1.5 M HCl solution prepared from 20.0 mL of a 6.0 M HCl solution
  b. a 2.0% (m/v) LiCl solution prepared from 50.0 mL of a 10.0% (m/v) LiCl solution
  c. a 0.500 M H_3PO_4 solution prepared from 50.0 mL of a 6.00 M H_3PO_4 solution
  d. a 5.0% (m/v) glucose solution prepared from 75 mL of a 12% (m/v) glucose solution

9.66 Determine the final volume, in milliliters, of each of the following:
  a. a 1.00% (m/v) H_2SO_4 solution prepared from 10.0 mL of a 20.0% H_2SO_4 solution
  b. a 0.10 M HCl solution prepared from 25 mL of a 6.0 M HCl solution
  c. a 1.0 M NaOH solution prepared from 50.0 mL of a 12 M NaOH solution
  d. a 1.0% (m/v) $CaCl_2$ solution prepared from 18 mL of a 4.0% (m/v) $CaCl_2$ solution

9.67 Determine the initial volume, in milliliters, required to prepare each of the following:
  a. 255 mL of a 0.200 M HNO_3 solution using a 4.00 M HNO_3 solution
  b. 715 mL of a 0.100 M $MgCl_2$ solution using a 6.00 M $MgCl_2$ solution
  c. 0.100 L of a 0.150 M KCl solution using an 8.00 M KCl solution

9.68 Determine the initial volume, in milliliters, required to prepare each of the following:
  a. 20.0 mL of a 0.250 M KNO_3 solution using a 6.00 M KNO_3 solution
  b. 25.0 mL of a 2.50 M H_2SO_4 solution using a 12.0 M H_2SO_4 solution
  c. 0.500 L of a 1.50 M NH_4Cl solution using a 10.0 M NH_4Cl solution

℞ Clinical Applications

9.69 You need 500. mL of a 5.0% (m/v) glucose solution. If you have a 25% (m/v) glucose solution on hand, how many milliliters do you need?

9.70 A doctor orders 100. mL of 2.0% (m/v) ibuprofen. If you have 8.0% (m/v) ibuprofen on hand, how many milliliters do you need?

9.6 Properties of Solutions

The size and number of solute particles in different types of mixtures play an important role in determining the properties of that mixture.

Solutions

In the solutions discussed up to now, the solute was dissolved as small particles that are uniformly dispersed throughout the solvent to give a homogeneous solution. When you observe a solution, such as salt water, you cannot visually distinguish the solute from the solvent. The solution appears transparent, although it may have a color. The particles are so small that they go through filters and through *semipermeable membranes*. A semipermeable membrane allows solvent molecules such as water and very small solute particles to pass through, but does allow the passage of large solute molecules.

Colloids

The particles in a **colloid** are much larger than solute particles in a solution. Colloidal particles are large molecules, such as proteins, or groups of molecules or ions. Colloids, similar to solutions, are homogeneous mixtures that do not separate or settle out. Colloidal particles are small enough to pass through filters, but too large to pass through semipermeable membranes. Table 9.11 lists several examples of colloids.

TABLE 9.11 Examples of Colloids

Colloid	Substance Dispersed	Dispersing Medium
Fog, clouds, hair sprays	Liquid	Gas
Dust, smoke	Solid	Gas
Shaving cream, whipped cream, soapsuds	Gas	Liquid
Styrofoam, marshmallows	Gas	Solid
Mayonnaise, homogenized milk	Liquid	Liquid
Cheese, butter	Liquid	Solid
Blood plasma, paints (latex), gelatin	Solid	Liquid

Suspensions

Suspensions are heterogeneous, nonuniform mixtures that are very different from solutions or colloids. The particles of a suspension are so large that they can often be seen with the naked eye. They are trapped by filters and semipermeable membranes.

The weight of the suspended solute particles causes them to settle out soon after mixing. If you stir muddy water, it mixes but then quickly separates as the suspended particles settle to the bottom and leave clear liquid at the top. You can find suspensions among the medications in a hospital or in your medicine cabinet. These include Kaopectate, calamine lotion, antacid mixtures, and liquid penicillin. It is important to follow the instructions on the label that states "shake well before using" so that the particles form a suspension.

Water-treatment plants make use of the properties of suspensions to purify water. When chemicals such as aluminum sulfate or iron(III) sulfate are added to untreated water, they react with impurities to form large suspended particles called *floc*. In the water-treatment plant, a system of filters traps the suspended particles, but clean water passes through.

Table 9.12 compares the different types of mixtures and Figure 9.10 illustrates some properties of solutions, colloids, and suspensions.

TABLE 9.12 Comparison of Solutions, Colloids, and Suspensions

Type of Mixture	Type of Particle	Settling	Separation
Solution	Small particles such as atoms, ions, or small molecules	Particles do not settle	Particles cannot be separated by filters or semipermeable membranes
Colloid	Larger molecules or groups of molecules or ions	Particles do not settle	Particles can be separated by semipermeable membranes but not by filters
Suspension	Very large particles that may be visible	Particles settle rapidly	Particles can be separated by filters

Chemistry Link to **Health**
Colloids and Solutions in the Body

In the body, colloids are retained by semipermeable membranes. For example, the intestinal lining allows solution particles to pass into the blood and lymph circulatory systems. However, the colloids from foods are too large to pass through the membrane, and they remain in the intestinal tract. Digestion breaks down large colloidal particles, such as starch and protein, into smaller particles, such as glucose and amino acids that can pass through the intestinal membrane and enter the circulatory system. Certain foods, such as bran, a fiber, cannot be broken down by human digestive processes, and they move through the intestine intact.

Because large proteins, such as enzymes, are colloids, they remain inside cells. However, many of the substances that must be obtained by cells, such as oxygen, amino acids, electrolytes, glucose, and minerals, can pass through cellular membranes. Waste products, such as urea and carbon dioxide, pass out of the cell to be excreted.

- Solution
- Colloid
- Suspension

Filter

Semipermeable membrane

Settling
(a)　　(b)　　(c)

FIGURE 9.10 ▶ Properties of different types of mixtures: **(a)** suspensions settle out; **(b)** suspensions are separated by a filter; **(c)** solution particles go through a semipermeable membrane, but colloids and suspensions do not.

Ⓠ A filter can be used to separate suspension particles from a solution, but a semipermeable membrane is needed to separate colloids from a solution. Explain.

Boiling Point Elevation and Freezing Point Lowering

When we add a solute to water, it changes the vapor pressure, boiling point, and freezing point of pure water. Therefore, an aqueous solution will have a higher boiling point and a lower freezing point than that of pure water. These types of changes in physical properties, known as *colligative properties*, depend only on the concentration of solute particles in the solution.

We can illustrate how these changes in physical properties occur by comparing the number of evaporating solvent molecules in pure solvent with those in a solution with a nonvolatile solute in the solvent. In the solution, there are fewer solvent molecules at the surface because the solute that has been added takes up some of the space at the surface. As a result, fewer solvent molecules can evaporate compared to the pure solvent. Vapor pressure is lowered for the solution. If we add more solute molecules, the vapor pressure will be lowered even more.

Vapor pressure　　Lower vapor pressure

Pure solvent　　Solute and solvent

Ethylene glycol is added to a radiator to form an aqueous solution that has a lower freezing point than water.

The boiling point of a solvent is raised when a nonvolatile solute is added. The vapor pressure of a solvent must reach atmospheric pressure before it begins boiling. However, because the solute lowers the vapor pressure of the solvent, a temperature higher than the normal boiling point of the pure solvent is needed to cause the solution to boil.

The freezing point of a solvent is lowered when a nonvolatile solute is added. In this case, the solute particles prevent the organization of solvent molecules needed to form the solid state. Thus, a lower temperature is required before the molecules of the solvent can become organized enough to freeze.

Thus, when you spread salt on an icy sidewalk when temperatures drop below freezing, the particles from the salt combine with water to lower the freezing point, which causes the ice to melt. Another example is the addition of antifreeze, such as ethylene glycol HO—CH_2—CH_2—OH, to the water in a car radiator. Ethylene glycol forms many hydrogen bonds, which makes it very soluble in water. If an ethylene glycol and water mixture is about 50–50% by mass, it does not freeze until the temperature drops to about −30 °F, and does not boil unless the temperature reaches about 225 °F. The solution in the radiator prevents the water in the radiator from forming ice in cold weather or boiling over on a hot desert highway.

Insects and fish in climates with subfreezing temperatures control ice formation by producing biological antifreezes made of glycerol, proteins, and sugars, such as glucose, within their bodies. Some insects can survive temperatures below −60 °C. These forms of biological antifreezes may one day be applied to the long-term preservation of human organs.

The Alaska Upis beetle produces biological antifreeze to survive subfreezing temperatures.

Particles in Solution

A solute that is a nonelectrolyte dissolves as molecules, whereas a solute that is a strong electrolyte dissolves entirely as ions. The solute in antifreeze, ethylene glycol, $C_2H_6O_2$—a nonelectrolyte—dissolves as molecules.

Nonelectrolyte: 1 mole of $C_2H_6O_2(l)$ = 1 mole of $C_2H_6O_2(aq)$

However, when 1 mole of a strong electrolyte, such as NaCl or $CaCl_2$, dissolves in water, the NaCl solution will contain 2 moles of particles and the $CaCl_2$ solution will contain 3 moles of particles.

Strong electrolytes:

1 mole of NaCl(s) = $\underbrace{1 \text{ mole of } Na^+(aq) + 1 \text{ mole of } Cl^-(aq)}_{2 \text{ moles of particles } (aq)}$

1 mole of $CaCl_2$(s) = $\underbrace{1 \text{ mole of } Ca^{2+}(aq) + 2 \text{ moles of } Cl^-(aq)}_{3 \text{ moles of particles } (aq)}$

🕸 CORE CHEMISTRY SKILL

Calculating the Boiling Point/ Freezing Point of a Solution

Change in Boiling Point and Freezing Point

The change in boiling point or freezing point depends on the number of particles in the solution. One mole of an electrolyte such as glucose raises the boiling point of one kilogram of pure water (100.00 °C) by 0.51 °C, which gives a boiling point of 100.51 °C. If the solute is a strong electrolyte such as NaCl, one mole produces two moles of particles (ions). Then the boiling point of one kilogram of water is raised by 1.02 °C (2 × 0.51 °C), to give a boiling point of 101.02 °C.

The presence of solute particles also changes the freezing point. One mole of a non-electrolyte such as glucose lowers the freezing point (0.00 °C) of one kilogram of pure water by 1.86 °C, to give a freezing point of −1.86 °C. For NaCl, one mole dissociates to form two moles of particles (ions). Then the freezing point of one kilogram of water is lowered by 3.72 °C (2 × 1.86 °C), which gives a freezing point of −3.72 °C.

The effect of some solutes on freezing and boiling point is summarized in Table 9.13.

TABLE 9.13 Effect of Solute Concentration on Freezing and Boiling Points of 1 kg of Water

Substance in One Kilogram of Water	Type of Solute	Moles of Solute Particles in One Kilogram of Water	Freezing Point	Boiling Point
Pure water	None	0	0.00 °C	100.00 °C
1 mole of $C_2H_6O_2$	Nonelectrolyte	1	−1.86 °C	100.51 °C
1 mole of NaCl	Strong electrolyte	2	−3.72 °C	101.02 °C
1 mole of $CaCl_2$	Strong electrolyte	3	−5.58 °C	101.53 °C

A truck spreads calcium chloride on the road to melt ice and snow.

▶ **SAMPLE PROBLEM 9.16** Calculating the Freezing Point of a Solution

In the northern United States during freezing temperatures, $CaCl_2$ is spread on icy highways to melt the ice. Calculate the freezing point of a solution containing 0.50 mole of $CaCl_2$ in 1 kg of water.

SOLUTION

STEP 1 State the given and needed quantities.

ANALYZE THE PROBLEM	**Given**	**Need**
	0.50 mole of $CaCl_2$, 1 kg of water	freezing point of solution

STEP 2 Determine the number of moles of solute particles.

$$CaCl_2(s) \longrightarrow Ca^{2+}(aq) + 2Cl^-(aq) = 3 \text{ moles of solute particles}$$

1 mole of $CaCl_2$ = 3 moles of solute particles

$$\frac{1 \text{ mole } CaCl_2}{3 \text{ moles solute particles}} \quad \text{and} \quad \frac{3 \text{ moles solute particles}}{1 \text{ mole } CaCl_2}$$

STEP 3 Determine the temperature change using the moles of solute particles and the degrees Celsius change per mole of particles.

1 mole of solute particles = 1.86 °C

$$\frac{1.86 \text{ °C}}{1 \text{ mole solute particles}} \quad \text{and} \quad \frac{1 \text{ mole solute particles}}{1.86 \text{ °C}}$$

$$\text{Temperature change} = 0.50 \text{ mole } CaCl_2 \times \frac{3 \text{ moles solute particles}}{1 \text{ mole } CaCl_2} \times \frac{1.86 \text{ °C}}{1 \text{ mole solute particles}}$$

$$= 2.8 \text{ °C}$$

STEP 4 Subtract the temperature change from the freezing point. Finally, the freezing point lowering, ΔT_f, is subtracted from 0.0 °C to obtain the new freezing point of the $CaCl_2$ solution.

$$T_{\text{solution}} = T_{\text{water}} - \Delta T_f$$
$$= 0.0 \text{ °C} - 2.8 \text{ °C}$$
$$= -2.8 \text{ °C}$$

Calculating Freezing Point Lowering/Boiling Point Elevation

STEP 1
State the given and needed quantities.

STEP 2
Determine the number of moles of solute particles.

STEP 3
Determine the temperature change using the moles of solute particles and the degrees Celsius change per mole of particles.

STEP 4
Subtract the temperature change from the freezing point or add the temperature change to the boiling point.

Osmosis and Osmotic Pressure

The movement of water into and out of the cells of plants as well as the cells of our bodies is an important biological process that also depends on the solute concentration. In a process called **osmosis**, water molecules move through a semipermeable membrane from the solution with the lower concentration of solute into a solution with the higher solute concentration. In an osmosis apparatus, water is placed on one side of a semipermeable membrane and a sucrose (sugar) solution on the other side. The semipermeable membrane allows water molecules to flow back and forth but blocks the sucrose molecules because they cannot pass through the membrane. Because the sucrose solution has a higher solute concentration, more water molecules flow into the sucrose solution than out of the sucrose solution. The volume level of the sucrose solution rises as the volume level on the water side falls. The increase of water dilutes the sucrose solution to equalize (or attempt to equalize) the concentrations on both sides of the membrane.

Eventually the height of the sucrose solution creates sufficient pressure to equalize the flow of water between the two compartments. This pressure, called **osmotic pressure**, prevents the flow of additional water into the more concentrated solution. Then there is no further change in the volumes of the two solutions. The osmotic pressure depends on the concentration of solute particles in the solution. The greater the number of particles dissolved, the higher its osmotic pressure. In this example, the sucrose solution has a higher osmotic pressure than pure water, which has an osmotic pressure of zero.

Water flows into the solution with a higher solute concentration until the flow of water becomes equal in both directions.

In a process called *reverse osmosis*, a pressure greater than the osmotic pressure is applied to a solution so that it is forced through a purification membrane. The flow of water is reversed because water flows from an area of lower water concentration to an area of higher water concentration. The molecules and ions in solution stay behind, trapped by the membrane, while water passes through the membrane. This process of reverse osmosis is used in a few desalination plants to obtain pure water from sea (salt) water. However, the pressure that must be applied requires so much energy that reverse osmosis is not yet an economical method for obtaining pure water in most parts of the world.

Explore Your World

Everyday Osmosis

1. Place a few pieces of dried fruit such as raisins, prunes, or banana chips in water. Observe them after 1 hour or more. Look at them again the next day.
2. Place some grapes in a concentrated salt-water solution. Observe them after 1 hour or more. Look at them again the next day.
3. Place one potato slice in water and another slice in a concentrated salt-water solution. After 1 to 2 hours, observe the shapes and size of the slices. Look at them again the next day.

Questions

1. How did the shape of the dried fruit change after being in water? Explain.
2. How did the appearance of the grapes change after being in a concentrated salt solution? Explain.
3. How does the appearance of the potato slice that was placed in water compare to the appearance of the potato slice placed in salt water? Explain.
4. At the grocery store, why are sprinklers used to spray water on fresh produce such as lettuce, carrots, and cucumbers?

Osmolarity

Every molecule and every ion that dissolves in a solution contributes to its osmotic pressure. A solution with a higher concentration of dissolved particles has a higher osmotic pressure than a solution with fewer dissolved particles. Because the osmotic pressure depends on the number of particles in solution, which is equal to the number of osmoles. We use a concentration term *osmolarity* to indicate the number of osmoles dissolved in each liter of solution.

$$\text{Osmolarity (Osm)} = \frac{\text{number of osmoles}}{1 \text{ L of solution}}$$

When one mole of NaCl dissolves in one liter of solution, it produces one mole of Na^+ ions and one mole of Cl^- ions, or two osmoles. This would be a 1 M NaCl or a 2 Osm solution.

$$NaCl(s) \xrightarrow{H_2O} Na^+(aq) + Cl^-(aq)$$
1 mole   1 mole   1 mole   = 2 osmoles

When one mole of K_2SO_4 dissolves, two moles of K^+ ions and one mole of SO_4^{2-} ions or three osmoles are produced from each one mole of $K_2SO_4(s)$.

$$K_2SO_4(s) \xrightarrow{H_2O} 2K^+(aq) + SO_4^{2-}(aq)$$
1 mole   2 moles   1 mole   = 3 osmoles

Using the number of moles of ions as a conversion factor, we can convert the molarity of the solution to the osmolarity. For example, a 0.10 M K_2SO_4 solution would be a 0.30 Osm K_2SO_4 solution.

$$\frac{0.10 \text{ mole } K_2SO_4}{1 \text{ L solution}} \times \frac{3 \text{ osmoles}}{1 \text{ mole } K_2SO_4} = 0.30 \text{ Osm } K_2SO_4 \text{ solution}$$

The physiological solutions 0.9% (m/v) NaCl and 5% (m/v) glucose are isotonic solutions because they have the same concentration of particles and the same osmolarities as body fluids.

▶ **SAMPLE PROBLEM 9.17** Calculating the Osmolarity of a Solution

The osmolarity of normal blood serum is 0.30 Osm. Show that the osmolarity of 0.90% (m/v) NaCl solution is the same as that of normal serum.

SOLUTION

STEP **1** State the given and needed quantities.

	Given	Need
ANALYZE THE PROBLEM	0.90% (m/v) NaCl	osmolarity (Osm) of NaCl solution

STEP **2** Determine the number of osmoles in one mole of solute.

1 mole $NaCl(s) \longrightarrow$ 1 mole $Na^+(aq)$ + 1 mole $Cl^-(aq)$ = 2 moles of particles = 2 osmoles

STEP **3** Calculate the osmolarity (Osm).

$$\frac{0.90 \text{ g NaCl}}{100 \text{ mL solution}} \times \frac{1 \text{ mole NaCl}}{58.44 \text{ g NaCl}} \times \frac{2 \text{ osmoles}}{1 \text{ mole NaCl}} \times \frac{1000 \text{ mL}}{1 \text{ L}} = 0.30 \text{ Osm NaCl solution}$$

The osmolarity of 0.90% (m/v) NaCl solution is 0.30 Osm, which is the same as that of normal blood serum.

STUDY CHECK 9.17

Calculate the osmolarity of 5% (m/v) glucose solution. (The molar mass of the non-electrolyte glucose is 180 g/mole.)

ANSWER

0.3 Osm

Guide to Calculating Osmolarity

STEP **1**
State the given and needed quantities.

STEP **2**
Determine the number of osmoles in one mole of solute.

STEP **3**
Calculate the osmolarity (Osm).

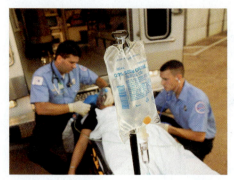

A 0.9% NaCl solution is isotonic with the solute concentration of the blood cells of the body.

Isotonic Solutions

Because the cell membranes in biological systems are semipermeable, osmosis is an ongoing process. The solutes in body solutions such as blood, tissue fluids, lymph, and plasma all exert osmotic pressure. Most intravenous (IV) solutions used in a hospital are **isotonic solutions**, which exert the same osmotic pressure as body fluids such as blood. The percent concentration typically used in IV solutions is mass/volume percent (m/v), which is a type of percent concentration we have already discussed. The most typical isotonic solutions are 0.9% (m/v) NaCl solution, or 0.9 g of NaCl/100 mL of solution, and 5% (m/v) glucose, or 5 g of glucose/100 mL of solution. Although they do not contain the same kinds of particles, a 0.9% (m/v) NaCl solution as well as a 5% (m/v) glucose solution both have the same osmolarity, 0.3 Osm. A red blood cell placed in an isotonic solution retains its volume because there is an equal flow of water into and out of the cell (see Figure 9.11a).

Hypotonic and Hypertonic Solutions

If a red blood cell is placed in a solution that is not isotonic, the differences in osmotic pressure inside and outside the cell can drastically alter the volume of the cell. When a red blood cell is placed in a **hypotonic solution**, which has a lower solute concentration (*hypo* means "lower than"), water flows into the cell by osmosis. The increase in fluid causes the cell to swell, and possibly burst—a process called **hemolysis** (see Figure 9.11b). A similar process occurs when you place dehydrated food, such as raisins or dried fruit, in water. The water enters the cells, and the food becomes plump and smooth.

If a red blood cell is placed in a **hypertonic solution**, which has a higher solute concentration (*hyper* means "greater than"), water flows out of the cell into the hypertonic solution by osmosis. Suppose a red blood cell is placed in a 10% (m/v) NaCl solution. Because the osmotic pressure in the red blood cell is the same as a 0.9% (m/v) NaCl solution, the 10% (m/v) NaCl solution has a much greater osmotic pressure. As water leaves the cell, it shrinks, a process called **crenation** (see Figure 9.11c). A similar process occurs when making pickles, which uses a hypertonic salt solution that causes the cucumbers to shrivel as they lose water.

FIGURE 9.11 ▶ **(a)** In an isotonic solution, a red blood cell retains its normal volume. **(b)** Hemolysis: In a hypotonic solution, water flows into a red blood cell, causing it to swell and burst. **(c)** Crenation: In a hypertonic solution, water leaves the red blood cell, causing it to shrink.

Q What happens to a red blood cell placed in a 4% NaCl solution?

Isotonic solution   Hypotonic solution   Hypertonic solution

(a) Normal   (b) Hemolysis   (c) Crenation

▶ **SAMPLE PROBLEM 9.18** Isotonic, Hypotonic, and Hypertonic Solutions

Describe each of the following solutions as isotonic, hypotonic, or hypertonic. Indicate whether a red blood cell placed in each solution will undergo hemolysis, crenation, or no change.

a. a 5% (m/v) glucose solution
b. a 0.2% (m/v) NaCl solution

SOLUTION

a. A 5% (m/v) glucose solution is isotonic. A red blood cell will not undergo any change.
b. A 0.2% (m/v) NaCl solution is hypotonic. A red blood cell will undergo hemolysis.

STUDY CHECK 9.18

What will happen to a red blood cell placed in a 10% (m/v) glucose solution?

ANSWER

The red blood cell will shrink (crenate).

Dialysis

Dialysis is a process that is similar to osmosis. In dialysis, a semipermeable membrane, called a dialyzing membrane, permits small solute molecules and ions as well as solvent water molecules to pass through, but it retains large particles, such as colloids. Dialysis is a way to separate solution particles from colloids.

Suppose we fill a cellophane bag with a solution containing NaCl, glucose, starch, and protein and place it in pure water. Cellophane is a dialyzing membrane, and the sodium ions, chloride ions, and glucose molecules will pass through it into the surrounding water. However, large colloidal particles, like starch and protein, remain inside. Water molecules will flow into the cellophane bag. Eventually the concentrations of sodium ions, chloride ions, and glucose molecules inside and outside the dialysis bag become equal. To remove more NaCl or glucose, the cellophane bag must be placed in a fresh sample of pure water.

Initial   Final

- Solution particles such as Na$^+$, Cl$^-$, glucose
- Colloidal particles such as protein, starch

Solution particles pass through a dialyzing membrane, but colloidal particles are retained.

Chemistry Link to **Health**

Dialysis by the Kidneys and the Artificial Kidney

The fluids of the body undergo dialysis by the membranes of the kidneys, which remove waste materials, excess salts, and water. In an adult, each kidney contains about 2 million nephrons. At the top of each nephron, there is a network of arterial capillaries called the *glomerulus*.

As blood flows into the glomerulus, small particles, such as amino acids, glucose, urea, water, and certain ions, will move through the capillary membranes into the nephron. As this solution moves through the nephron, substances still of value to the body (such as amino acids, glucose, certain ions, and 99% of the water) are reabsorbed. The major waste product, urea, is excreted in the urine.

Hemodialysis

If the kidneys fail to dialyze waste products, increased levels of urea can become life-threatening in a relatively short time. A person with kidney failure must use an artificial kidney, which cleanses the blood by **hemodialysis**.

A typical artificial kidney machine contains a large tank filled with water containing selected electrolytes. In the center of this dialyzing bath (dialysate), there is a dialyzing coil or membrane made of cellulose tubing. As the patient's blood flows through the dialyzing coil, the highly concentrated waste products dialyze out of the blood. No blood is lost because the membrane is not permeable to large particles such as red blood cells.

Dialysis patients do not produce much urine. As a result, they retain large amounts of water between dialysis treatments, which produces a strain on the heart. The intake of fluids for a dialysis patient may be restricted to as little as a few teaspoons of water a day. In the dialysis procedure, the pressure of the blood is increased as it circulates through the dialyzing coil so water can be squeezed out of the blood. For some dialysis patients, 2 to 10 L of water may be removed during one treatment. Dialysis patients have from two to three treatments a week, each treatment requiring about 5 to 7 h. Some of the newer treatments require less time. For many patients, dialysis is done at home with a home dialysis unit.

In the kidneys, each nephron contains a glomerulus where urea and waste products are removed to form urine.

During dialysis, waste products and excess water are removed from the blood.

QUESTIONS AND PROBLEMS

9.6 Properties of Solutions

LEARNING GOAL Identify a mixture as a solution, a colloid, or a suspension. Describe how the number of particles in a solution affects the freezing point, the boiling point, and the osmotic pressure of a solution.

9.71 Identify the following as characteristic of a solution, a colloid, or a suspension:
    a. a mixture that cannot be separated by a semipermeable membrane
    b. a mixture that settles out upon standing

9.72 Identify the following as characteristic of a solution, a colloid, or a suspension:
    a. Particles of this mixture remain inside a semipermeable membrane but pass through filters.
    b. The particles of solute in this solution are very large and visible.

9.73 In each pair, identify the solution that will have a lower freezing point. Explain.
    a. 1.0 mole of glycerol (nonelectrolyte) and 2.0 moles of ethylene glycol (nonelectrolyte) each in 1.0 kg of water
    b. 0.50 mole of KCl (strong electrolyte) and 0.50 mole of $MgCl_2$ (strong electrolyte) each in 1.0 kg of water

9.74 In each pair, identify the solution that will have a higher boiling point. Explain.
    a. 1.50 moles of LiOH (strong electrolyte) and 3.00 moles of KOH (strong electrolyte) each in 1.0 kg of water

    b. 0.40 mole of $Al(NO_3)_3$ (strong electrolyte) and 0.40 mole of CsCl (strong electrolyte) each in 1.0 kg of water

9.75 Calculate the freezing point of each of the following solutions:
    a. 1.36 moles of methanol, CH_3OH, a nonelectrolyte, added to 1.00 kg of water
    b. 640. g of the antifreeze propylene glycol, $C_3H_8O_2$, a nonelectrolyte, dissolved in 1.00 kg of water
    c. 111 g of KCl, a strong electrolyte, dissolved in 1.00 kg of water

9.76 Calculate the boiling point of each of the following solutions:
    a. 2.12 moles of glucose, $C_6H_{12}O_6$, a nonelectrolyte, added to 1.00 kg of water
    b. 110. g of sucrose, $C_{12}H_{22}O_{11}$, a nonelectrolyte, dissolved in 1.00 kg of water
    c. 146 g of $NaNO_3$, a strong electrolyte, dissolved in 1.00 kg of water

9.77 A 10% (m/v) starch solution is separated from a 1% (m/v) starch solution by a semipermeable membrane. (Starch is a colloid.)
    a. Which compartment has the higher osmotic pressure?
    b. In which direction will water flow initially?
    c. In which compartment will the volume level rise?

9.78 A 0.1% (m/v) albumin solution is separated from a 2% (m/v) albumin solution by a semipermeable membrane. (Albumin is a colloid.)

a. Which compartment has the higher osmotic pressure?
b. In which direction will water flow initially?
c. In which compartment will the volume level rise?

9.79 Indicate the compartment (**A** or **B**) that will increase in volume for each of the following pairs of solutions separated by a semi-permeable membrane:

A	B
a. 5% (m/v) sucrose	10% (m/v) sucrose
b. 8% (m/v) albumin	4% (m/v) albumin
c. 0.1% (m/v) starch	10% (m/v) starch

9.80 Indicate the compartment (**A** or **B**) that will increase in volume for each of the following pairs of solutions separated by a semi-permeable membrane:

A	B
a. 20% (m/v) starch	10% (m/v) starch
b. 10% (m/v) albumin	2% (m/v) albumin
c. 0.5% (m/v) sucrose	5% (m/v) sucrose

 Clinical Applications

9.81 What is the osmolarity of each of the following solutions?
a. hypertonic saline, NaCl, 3.0% (m/v) (strong electrolyte)
b. 50.% (m/v) dextrose ($C_6H_{12}O_6$), used to treat severe hypoglycemia

9.82 What is the osmolarity of each of the following solutions?
a. 3% (m/v) NaCl (strong electrolyte), used to treat hyponatremia
b. 2.5% (m/v) dextrose ($C_6H_{12}O_6$), used to hydrate cells

9.83 Are the following solutions isotonic, hypotonic, or hypertonic compared with a red blood cell?
a. distilled H_2O **b.** 1% (m/v) glucose
c. 0.9% (m/v) NaCl   **d.** 15% (m/v) glucose

9.84 Will a red blood cell undergo crenation, hemolysis, or no change in each of the following solutions?
a. 1% (m/v) glucose   **b.** 2% (m/v) NaCl
c. 5% (m/v) glucose   **d.** 0.1% (m/v) NaCl

9.85 Each of the following mixtures is placed in a dialyzing bag and immersed in distilled water. Which substances will be found outside the bag in the distilled water?
a. NaCl solution
b. starch solution (colloid) and alanine (an amino acid) solution
c. NaCl solution and starch solution (colloid)
d. urea solution

9.86 Each of the following mixtures is placed in a dialyzing bag and immersed in distilled water. Which substances will be found outside the bag in the distilled water?
a. KCl solution and glucose solution
b. albumin solution (colloid)
c. an albumin solution (colloid), KCl solution, and glucose solution
d. urea solution and NaCl solution

Clinical Update
Using Dialysis for Renal Failure

As a dialysis patient, Michelle has a 4-h dialysis treatment three times a week. When she arrives at the dialysis clinic, her weight, temperature, and blood pressure are taken and blood tests are done to determine the level of electrolytes and urea in her blood. In the dialysis center, tubes to the dialyzer are connected to the catheter she has had implanted. Blood is then pumped out of her body, through the dialyzer where it is filtered, and returned to her body. As Michelle's blood flows through the dialyzer, electrolytes from the dialysate move into her blood, and waste products in her blood move into the dialysate, which is continually renewed. To achieve normal serum electrolyte levels, dialysate fluid contains sodium, chloride, and magnesium levels that are equal to serum concentrations. These electrolytes are removed from the blood only if their concentrations are higher than normal. Typically, in dialysis patients, the potassium ion level is higher than normal. Therefore, initial dialysis may start with a low concentration of potassium ion in the dialysate. During dialysis excess fluid is removed by osmosis. A 4-h dialysis session requires at least 120 L of dialysis fluid. During dialysis, the electrolytes in the dialysate are adjusted until the electrolytes have the same levels as normal serum. Initially the dialysate solution prepared for Michelle's pre-dialysis blood tests shows that the electrolyte levels in her blood are HCO_3^- 24 mEq/L, K^+ 6.0 mEq/L, Na^+ 148 mEq/L, Ca^{2+} 3.0 mEq/L, Mg^{2+} 1.0 mEq/L, Cl^- 111.0 mEq/L.

A dialysis solution is prepared for Michelle that contains the following: HCO_3^- 35.0 mEq/L, K^+ 2.0 mEq/L, Na^+ 130 mEq/L, Ca^{2+} 5.0 mEq/L, Mg^{2+} 3.0 mEq/L, Cl^- 105.0 mEq/L, glucose 5.0%(m/v).

 Clinical Applications

9.87 **a.** Which electrolyte concentrations are higher than normal serum values in Michelle's pre-dialysis blood test (see Table 9.6)?
b. Which electrolyte concentrations are lower than normal serum values in Michelle's pre-dialysis blood test (see Table 9.6)?
c. Which electrolytes need to be increased by dialysis for Michelle's blood serum?
d. Which electrolytes are decreased by dialysis for Michelle's blood serum?

9.88 **a.** What is the total positive charge, in milliequivalents/L, of the electrolytes in the dialysate fluid?
b. What is the total negative charge, in milliequivalents/L, of the electrolytes in the dialysate fluid?
c. What is the net total charge, in milliequivalents/L, of the electrolytes in the dialysate fluid?
d. What is the osmolarity of the dialysate fluid?

SOLUTIONS

consist of a — **Solute** **Solvent**

give amounts as — **Concentration** of **Solute Particles (Osmoles)**

amount dissolved is — **Solubility**

as — **Electrolytes** **Nonelectrolytes**

m/m, v/v, m/v — **Percent**

mole/L — **Molarity**

change the — **Vapor Pressure, Freezing Point, Boiling Point, Osmotic Pressure**

the maximum amount that dissolves is — **Saturated**

dissociate 100% **Strong** slightly **Weak**

do not dissociate

add water for **Dilutions**

is used to calculate **Moles** **Volume**

CHAPTER REVIEW

9.1 Solutions
LEARNING GOAL Identify the solute and solvent in a solution; describe the formation of a solution.

- A solution forms when a solute dissolves in a solvent.
- In a solution, the particles of solute are evenly dispersed in the solvent.
- The solute and solvent may be solid, liquid, or gas.
- The polar O—H bond leads to hydrogen bonding between water molecules.
- An ionic solute dissolves in water, a polar solvent, because the polar water molecules attract and pull the ions into solution, where they become hydrated.
- The expression *like dissolves like* means that a polar or an ionic solute dissolves in a polar solvent while a nonpolar solute dissolves in a nonpolar solvent.

9.2 Electrolytes and Nonelectrolytes
LEARNING GOAL Identify solutes as electrolytes or nonelectrolytes.

Strong electrolyte

- Substances that produce ions in water are called electrolytes because their solutions will conduct an electrical current.
- Strong electrolytes are completely dissociated, whereas weak electrolytes are only partially ionized.
- Nonelectrolytes are substances that dissolve in water to produce only molecules and cannot conduct electrical currents.
- An equivalent (Eq) is the amount of an electrolyte that carries one mole of positive or negative charge.
- One mole of Na^+ is 1 Eq. One mole of Ca^{2+} has 2 Eq.

9.3 Solubility
LEARNING GOAL Define solubility; distinguish between an unsaturated and a saturated solution. Identify an ionic compound as soluble or insoluble.

Dissolved solute
Undissolved solute
Dissolving
Recrystallizing
Saturated solution

- The solubility of a solute is the maximum amount of a solute that can dissolve in 100 g of solvent.
- A solution that contains the maximum amount of dissolved solute is a saturated solution.
- A solution containing less than the maximum amount of dissolved solute is unsaturated.
- An increase in temperature increases the solubility of most solids in water, but decreases the solubility of gases in water.
- Ionic compounds that are soluble in water usually contain Li^+, Na^+, K^+, NH_4^+, NO_3^-, or acetate, $C_2H_3O_2^-$.

9.4 Solution Concentrations and Reactions
LEARNING GOAL Calculate the concentration of a solute in a solution; use concentration units to calculate the amount of solute or solution. Given the volume and concentration of a solution, calculate the amount of another reactant or product in a reaction.

Water added to make a solution   250 mL
5.0 g of KI   250 mL of KI solution

- Mass percent expresses the mass/mass (m/m) ratio of the mass of solute to the mass of solution multiplied by 100%.
- Percent concentration can also be expressed as volume/volume (v/v) and mass/volume (m/v) ratios.
- Molarity is the moles of solute per liter of solution.
- In calculations of grams or milliliters of solute or solution, the concentration is used as a conversion factor.
- Molarity (mole/L) is written as conversion factors to solve for moles of solute or volume of solution.

- When solutions are involved in chemical reactions, the moles of a substance in solution can be determined from the volume and molarity of the solution.
- When mass, volume, and molarities of substances in a reaction are given, the balanced equation is used to determine the quantities or concentrations of other substances in the reaction.

9.5 Dilution of Solutions

LEARNING GOAL Describe the dilution of a solution; calculate the unknown concentration or volume when a solution is diluted.

- In dilution, a solvent such as water is added to a solution, which increases its volume and decreases its concentration.

9.6 Properties of Solutions

LEARNING GOAL Identify a mixture as a solution, a colloid, or a suspension. Describe how the number of particles in a solution affects the freezing point, the boiling point, and the osmotic pressure of a solution.

Semipermeable membrane

- Colloids contain particles that pass through most filters but do not settle out or pass through permeable membranes.
- Suspensions have very large particles that settle out of solution.
- The particles in a solution lower the vapor pressure, raise the boiling point, lower the freezing point, and increase the osmotic pressure.
- In osmosis, solvent (water) passes through a semipermeable membrane from a solution with a lower osmotic pressure (lower solute concentration) to a solution with a higher osmotic pressure (higher solute concentration).
- Isotonic solutions have osmotic pressures equal to that of body fluids.
- In osmosis, solvent (water) passes through a selectively permeable membrane from a solution with a lower solute concentration to a solution with a higher concentration.
- Isotonic solutions have osmotic pressures equal to that of body fluids.
- A red blood cell maintains its volume in an isotonic solution but swells in a hypotonic solution, and shrinks in a hypertonic solution.
- In dialysis, water and small solute particles pass through a dialyzing membrane, while larger particles are retained.

KEY TERMS

colloid A mixture having particles that are moderately large. Colloids pass through filters but cannot pass through semipermeable membranes.

concentration A measure of the amount of solute that is dissolved in a specified amount of solution.

crenation The shriveling of a cell because water leaves the cell when the cell is placed in a hypertonic solution.

dialysis A process in which water and small solute particles pass through a semipermeable membrane.

dilution A process by which water (solvent) is added to a solution to increase the volume and decrease (dilute) the concentration of the solute.

electrolyte A substance that produces ions when dissolved in water; its solution conducts electricity.

equivalent (Eq) The amount of a positive or negative ion that supplies 1 mole of electrical charge.

hemodialysis A mechanical cleansing of the blood by an artificial kidney using the principle of dialysis.

hemolysis A swelling and bursting of red blood cells in a hypotonic solution because of an increase in fluid volume.

Henry's law The solubility of a gas in a liquid is directly related to the pressure of that gas above the liquid.

hydration The process of surrounding dissolved ions by water molecules.

hypertonic solution A solution that has a higher particle concentration and higher osmotic pressure than the cells of the body.

hypotonic solution A solution that has a lower particle concentration and lower osmotic pressure than the cells of the body.

isotonic solution A solution that has the same particle concentration and osmotic pressure as that of the cells of the body.

mass percent (m/m) The grams of solute in exactly 100 g of solution.

mass/volume percent (m/v) The grams of solute in exactly 100 mL of solution.

molarity (M) The number of moles of solute in exactly 1 L of solution.

nonelectrolyte A substance that dissolves in water as molecules; its solution does not conduct an electrical current.

osmosis The flow of a solvent, usually water, through a semipermeable membrane into a solution of higher solute concentration.

osmotic pressure The pressure that prevents the flow of water into the more concentrated solution.

saturated solution A solution containing the maximum amount of solute that can dissolve at a given temperature. Any additional solute will remain undissolved in the container.

solubility The maximum amount of solute that can dissolve in exactly 100 g of solvent, usually water, at a given temperature.

solubility rules A set of guidelines that states whether an ionic compound is soluble or insoluble in water.

solute The component in a solution that is present in the lesser amount.

solution A homogeneous mixture in which the solute is made up of small particles (ions or molecules) that can pass through filters and semipermeable membranes.

solvent The substance in which the solute dissolves; usually the component present in greater amount.

strong electrolyte A compound that ionizes completely when it dissolves in water. Its solution is a good conductor of electricity.

suspension A mixture in which the solute particles are large enough and heavy enough to settle out and be retained by both filters and semipermeable membranes.

unsaturated solution A solution that contains less solute than can be dissolved.

volume percent (v/v) A percent concentration that relates the volume of the solute in exactly 100 mL of solution.

weak electrolyte A substance that produces only a few ions along with many molecules when it dissolves in water. Its solution is a weak conductor of electricity.

⚛ CORE CHEMISTRY SKILLS

The chapter section containing each Core Chemistry Skill is shown in parentheses at the end of each heading.

Using Solubility Rules (9.3)

- Soluble ionic compounds contain Li^+, Na^+, K^+, NH_4^+, NO_3^-, or $C_2H_3O_2^-$ (acetate).
- Ionic compounds containing Cl^-, Br^-, or I^- are soluble, but if they are combined with Ag^+, Pb^{2+}, or Hg_2^{2+}, the ionic compounds are insoluble.
- Most ionic compounds containing SO_4^{2-} are soluble, but if SO_4^{2-} is combined with Ba^{2+}, Pb^{2+}, Ca^{2+}, Sr^{2+}, or Hg_2^{2+}, the ionic compounds are insoluble.
- Ionic compounds that do not contain at least one of these ions are usually insoluble.

Example: Is K_2SO_4 soluble or insoluble in water?
Answer: K_2SO_4 is soluble in water because it contains K^+.

Calculating Concentration (9.4)

The amount of solute dissolved in a certain amount of solution is called the concentration of the solution.

- Mass percent $(m/m) = \dfrac{\text{mass of solute}}{\text{mass of solution}} \times 100\%$

- Volume percent $(v/v) = \dfrac{\text{volume of solute}}{\text{volume of solution}} \times 100\%$

- Mass/volume percent $(m/v) = \dfrac{\text{grams of solute}}{\text{milliliters of solution}} \times 100\%$

- Molarity $(M) = \dfrac{\text{moles of solute}}{\text{liters of solution}}$

Example: What is the mass/volume percent (m/v) and the molarity (M) of 225 mL (0.225 L) of a LiCl solution that contains 17.1 g of LiCl?

Answer:

$$\text{Mass/volume percent } (m/v) = \frac{\text{grams of solute}}{\text{milliliters of solution}} \times 100\%$$

$$= \frac{17.1 \text{ g LiCl}}{225 \text{ mL solution}} \times 100\%$$

$$= 7.60\% \ (m/v) \text{ LiCl solution}$$

$$\text{moles of LiCl} = 17.1 \text{ g LiCl} \times \frac{1 \text{ mole LiCl}}{42.39 \text{ g LiCl}}$$

$$= 0.403 \text{ mole of LiCl}$$

$$\text{Molarity } (M) = \frac{\text{moles of solute}}{\text{liters of solution}} = \frac{0.403 \text{ mole LiCl}}{0.225 \text{ L solution}}$$

$$= 1.79 \text{ M LiCl solution}$$

Using Concentration as a Conversion Factor (9.4)

- When we need to calculate the amount of solute or solution, we use the mass/volume percent (m/v) or the molarity (M) as a conversion factor.
- For example, the concentration of a 4.50 M HCl solution means there are 4.50 moles of HCl in 1 L of HCl solution, which gives two conversion factors written as

$$\frac{4.50 \text{ moles HCl}}{1 \text{ L solution}} \quad \text{and} \quad \frac{1 \text{ L solution}}{4.50 \text{ moles HCl}}$$

Example: How many milliliters of a 4.50 M HCl solution will provide 1.13 moles of HCl?

Answer:

$$1.13 \text{ moles HCl} \times \frac{1 \text{ L solution}}{4.50 \text{ moles HCl}} \times \frac{1000 \text{ mL solution}}{1 \text{ L solution}}$$

$$= 251 \text{ mL of HCl solution}$$

Calculating the Quantity of a Reactant or Product for a Chemical Reaction in Solution (9.4)

- When chemical reactions involve aqueous solutions of reactants or products, we use the balanced chemical equation, the molarity, and the volume to determine the moles or grams of the reactants or products.

Example: How many grams of zinc metal will react with 0.315 L of a 1.20 M HCl solution?

$$Zn(s) + 2HCl(aq) \longrightarrow H_2(g) + ZnCl_2(aq)$$

Answer:

$$0.315 \text{ L solution} \times \frac{1.20 \text{ moles HCl}}{1 \text{ L solution}} \times \frac{1 \text{ mole Zn}}{2 \text{ moles HCl}} \times \frac{65.41 \text{ g Zn}}{1 \text{ mole Zn}}$$

$$= 12.4 \text{ g of Zn}$$

Calculating the Boiling Point/Freezing Point of a Solution (9.6)

- The particles in a solution raise the boiling point, lower the freezing point, and increase the osmotic pressure.
- The boiling point elevation is determined from the moles of particles in one kilogram of water.
- The freezing point lowering is determined from the moles of particles in one kilogram of water.

Example: What is the boiling point of a solution that contains 1.5 moles of the strong electrolyte KCl in 1.0 kg of water?

Answer: A solution of 1.5 moles of KCl in 1.0 kg of water contains 3.0 moles of particles (1.5 moles of K^+ and 1.5 moles of Cl^-) in 1.0 kg of water and has a boiling point change of

$$3.0 \text{ moles particles} \times \frac{0.51 \text{ °C}}{1 \text{ mole particles}} = 1.53 \text{ °C}$$

The boiling point would be 100.00 °C + 1.53 °C = 101.53 °C.

UNDERSTANDING THE CONCEPTS

The chapter sections to review are shown in parentheses at the end of each question.

9.89 Match the diagrams with the following: (9.1)
  a. a polar solute and a polar solvent
  b. a nonpolar solute and a polar solvent
  c. a nonpolar solute and a nonpolar solvent

     1   **2**

9.90 If all the solute is dissolved in diagram **1**, how would heating or cooling the solution cause each of the following changes? (9.3)
  a. **2** to **3**   **b.** **2** to **1**

   1   **2**   *Solid*   **3**

9.91 Select the diagram that represents the solution formed by a solute 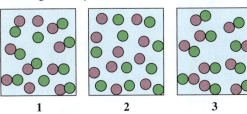 that is a (9.2)
  a. nonelectrolyte
  b. weak electrolyte
  c. strong electrolyte

   1   **2**   **3**

9.92 Select the container that represents the dilution of a 4% (m/v) KCl solution to give each of the following: (9.5)
  a. a 2% (m/v) KCl solution
  b. a 1% (m/v) KCl solution

4% (m/v) KCl   **1**   **2**   **3**

Use the following illustration of beakers and solutions for problems 9.93 and 9.94:

A   **B**

   1   **2**   **3**   **4**

9.93 Use the following types of ions: (9.3)

    Na^+ Cl^- Ag^+ NO_3^-

  a. Select the beaker (**1**, **2**, **3**, or **4**) that contains the products after the solutions in beakers **A** and **B** are mixed.
  b. If an insoluble ionic compound forms, write the ionic equation.
  c. If a reaction occurs, write the net ionic equation.

9.94 Use the following types of ions: (9.3)

    K^+ NO_3^- NH_4^+ Br^-

  a. Select the beaker (**1**, **2**, **3**, or **4**) that contains the products after the solutions in beakers **A** and **B** are mixed.

  b. If an insoluble ionic compound forms, write the ionic equation.
  c. If a reaction occurs, write the net ionic equation.

9.95 A pickle is made by soaking a cucumber in brine, a salt-water solution. What makes the smooth cucumber become wrinkled like a prune? (9.6)

9.96 Why do lettuce leaves in a salad wilt after a vinaigrette dressing containing salt is added? (9.6)

9.97 A semipermeable membrane separates two compartments, **A** and **B**. If the levels in **A** and **B** are equal initially, select the diagram that illustrates the final levels in **a** to **d**: (9.6)

	A	B
a.	2% (m/v) starch	8% (m/v) starch
b.	1% (m/v) starch	1% (m/v) starch
c.	5% (m/v) sucrose	1% (m/v) sucrose
d.	0.1% (m/v) sucrose	1% (m/v) sucrose

A   B   A   B   A   B

1   2   3

9.98 Select the diagram that represents the shape of a red blood cell when placed in each of the following **a** to **e**: (9.6)

1   2   3

Normal red blood cell

a. 0.9% (m/v) NaCl solution
b. 10% (m/v) glucose solution
c. 0.01% (m/v) NaCl solution
d. 5% (m/v) glucose solution
e. 1% (m/v) glucose solution

ADDITIONAL QUESTIONS AND PROBLEMS

9.99 Why does iodine dissolve in hexane, but not in water? (9.1)

9.100 How do temperature and pressure affect the solubility of solids and gases in water? (9.3)

9.101 Potassium nitrate has a solubility of 32 g of KNO_3 in 100 g of H_2O at 20 °C. Determine if each of the following forms an unsaturated or saturated solution at 20 °C: (9.3)
   a. adding 32 g of KNO_3 to 200. g of H_2O
   b. adding 19 g of KNO_3 to 50. g of H_2O
   c. adding 68 g of KNO_3 to 150. g of H_2O

9.102 Potassium chloride has a solubility of 43 g of KCl in 100 g of H_2O at 50 °C. Determine if each of the following forms an unsaturated or saturated solution at 50 °C: (9.3)
   a. adding 25 g of KCl to 100. g of H_2O
   b. adding 15 g of KCl to 25 g of H_2O
   c. adding 86 g of KCl to 150. g of H_2O

9.103 Indicate whether each of the following ionic compounds is soluble or insoluble in water: (9.3)
   a. KCl   **b.** $MgSO_4$ **c.** CuS
   d. $AgNO_3$ **e.** $Ca(OH)_2$

9.104 Indicate whether each of the following ionic compounds is soluble or insoluble in water: (9.3)
   a. $CuCO_3$ **b.** FeO   **c.** $Mg_3(PO_4)_2$
   d. $(NH_4)_2SO_4$ **e.** $NaHCO_3$

9.105 Write the net ionic equation to show the formation of a solid (insoluble ionic compound) when the following solutions are mixed. Write *none* if no solid forms. (9.3)
   a. $AgNO_3(aq)$ and $LiCl(aq)$
   b. $NaCl(aq)$ and $KNO_3(aq)$
   c. $Na_2SO_4(aq)$ and $BaCl_2(aq)$

9.106 Write the net ionic equation to show the formation of a solid (insoluble ionic compound) when the following solutions are mixed. Write *none* if no solid forms. (9.3)
   a. $Ca(NO_3)_2(aq)$ and $Na_2S(aq)$
   b. $Na_3PO_4(aq)$ and $Pb(NO_3)_2(aq)$
   c. $FeCl_3(aq)$ and $NH_4NO_3(aq)$

9.107 Calculate the mass percent (m/m) of a solution containing 15.5 g of Na_2SO_4 and 75.5 g of H_2O. (9.4)

9.108 Calculate the mass percent (m/m) of a solution containing 26 g of K_2CO_3 and 724 g of H_2O. (9.4)

9.109 How many milliliters of a 12% (v/v) propyl alcohol solution would you need to obtain 4.5 mL of propyl alcohol? (9.4)

9.110 An 80-proof brandy is a 40.% (v/v) ethanol solution. The "proof" is twice the percent concentration of alcohol in the beverage. How many milliliters of alcohol are present in 750 mL of brandy? (9.4)

9.111 How many liters of a 12% (m/v) KOH solution would you need to obtain 86.0 g of KOH? (9.4)

9.112 How many liters of a 5.0% (m/v) glucose solution would you need to obtain 75 g of glucose? (9.4)

9.113 What is the molarity of a solution containing 8.0 g of NaOH in 400. mL of NaOH solution? (9.4)

9.114 What is the molarity of a solution containing 15.6 g of KCl in 274 mL of KCl solution? (9.4)

9.115 How many grams of solute are in each of the following solutions? (9.4)
   a. 2.5 L of a 3.0 M $Al(NO_3)_3$ solution
   b. 75 mL of a 0.50 M $C_6H_{12}O_6$ solution
   c. 235 mL of a 1.80 M LiCl solution

9.116 How many grams of solute are in each of the following solutions? (9.4)
   a. 0.428 L of a 0.450 M K_2CO_3 solution
   b. 10.5 mL of a 2.50 M $AgNO_3$ solution
   c. 28.4 mL of a 6.00 M H_3PO_4 solution

9.117 Calculate the final concentration of the solution when water is added to prepare each of the following: (9.5)
   a. 25.0 mL of a 0.200 M NaBr solution is diluted to 50.0 mL
   b. 15.0 mL of a 12.0% (m/v) K_2SO_4 solution is diluted to 40.0 mL
   c. 75.0 mL of a 6.00 M NaOH solution is diluted to 255 mL

9.118 Calculate the final concentration of the solution when water is added to prepare each of the following: (9.5)

a. 25.0 mL of a 18.0 M HCl solution is diluted to 500. mL

b. 50.0 mL of a 15.0% (m/v) NH_4Cl solution is diluted to 125 mL

c. 4.50 mL of a 8.50 M KOH solution is diluted to 75.0 mL

9.119 What is the initial volume, in milliliters, needed to prepare each of the following diluted solutions? (9.5)

a. 250 mL of 3.0% (m/v) HCl from 10.0% (m/v) HCl

b. 500. mL of 0.90% (m/v) NaCl from 5.0% (m/v) NaCl

c. 350. mL of 2.00 M NaOH from 6.00 M NaOH

9.120 What is the initial volume, in milliliters, needed to prepare each of the following diluted solutions? (9.5)

a. 250 mL of 5.0% (m/v) glucose from 20.% (m/v) glucose

b. 45.0 mL of 1.0% (m/v) $CaCl_2$ from 5.0% (m/v) $CaCl_2$

c. 100. mL of 6.00 M H_2SO_4 from 18.0 M H_2SO_4

9.121 Calculate the freezing point of each of the following solutions: (9.6)

a. 0.580 mole of lactose, a nonelectrolyte, added to 1.00 kg of water

b. 45.0 g of KCl, a strong electrolyte, dissolved in 1.00 kg of water

c. 1.5 moles of K_3PO_4, a strong electrolyte, dissolved in 1.00 kg of water

9.122 Calculate the boiling point of each of the following solutions: (9.6)

a. 175 g of glucose, $C_6H_{12}O_6$, a nonelectrolyte, added to 1.00 kg of water

b. 1.8 moles of $CaCl_2$, a strong electrolyte, dissolved in 1.00 kg of water

c. 50.0 g of $LiNO_3$, a strong electrolyte, dissolved in 1.00 kg of water

℞ Clinical Applications

9.123 An antacid tablet, such as Amphojel, may be taken to reduce excess stomach acid, which is 0.20 M HCl. If one dose of Amphojel contains 450 mg of $Al(OH)_3$, what volume, in milliliters, of stomach acid will be neutralized? (9.4)

$$Al(OH)_3(s) + 3HCl(aq) \longrightarrow 3H_2O(l) + AlCl_3(aq)$$

9.124 Calcium carbonate, $CaCO_3$, reacts with stomach acid, (HCl, hydrochloric acid) according to the following equation: (9.4)

$$CaCO_3(s) + 2HCl(aq) \longrightarrow CO_2(g) + H_2O(l) + CaCl_2(aq)$$

Tums, an antacid, contains $CaCO_3$. If Tums is added to 20.0 mL of a 0.400 M HCl solution, how many grams of CO_2 gas are produced?

9.125 What is the osmolarity (Osm) of a half-normal 0.45% (m/v) NaCl solution? (9.6)

9.126 A Ringer's Injection solution contains Na^+ 147 mEq/L, K^+ 4 mEq/L, Ca^{2+} 4 mEq/L, and Cl^- 155 mEq/L. What is the osmolarity (Osm) of the solution? (9.6)

9.127 A patient on dialysis has a high level of urea, a high level of sodium, and a low level of potassium in the blood. Why is the dialyzing solution prepared with a high level of potassium but no sodium or urea? (9.6)

9.128 Why would a dialysis unit (artificial kidney) use isotonic concentrations of NaCl, KCl, $NaHCO_3$, and glucose in the dialysate? (9.6)

CHALLENGE QUESTIONS

The following groups of questions are related to the topics in this chapter. However, they do not all follow the chapter order, and they require you to combine concepts and skills from several sections. These questions will help you increase your critical thinking skills and prepare for your next exam.

9.129 In a laboratory experiment, a 10.0-mL sample of NaCl solution is poured into an evaporating dish with a mass of 24.10 g. The combined mass of the evaporating dish and NaCl solution is 36.15 g. After heating, the evaporating dish and dry NaCl have a combined mass of 25.50 g. (9.4)

a. What is the mass percent (m/m) of the NaCl solution?

b. What is the molarity (M) of the NaCl solution?

c. If water is added to 10.0 mL of the initial NaCl solution to give a final volume of 60.0 mL, what is the molarity of the diluted NaCl solution?

9.130 In a laboratory experiment, a 15.0-mL sample of KCl solution is poured into an evaporating dish with a mass of 24.10 g. The combined mass of the evaporating dish and KCl solution is 41.50 g. After heating, the evaporating dish and dry KCl have a combined mass of 28.28 g. (9.4)

a. What is the mass percent (m/m) of the KCl solution?

b. What is the molarity (M) of the KCl solution?

c. If water is added to 10.0 mL of the initial KCl solution to give a final volume of 60.0 mL, what is the molarity of the diluted KCl solution?

9.131 Potassium fluoride has a solubility of 92 g of KF in 100 g of H_2O at 18 °C. Determine if each of the following mixtures forms an unsaturated or saturated solution at 18 °C: (9.3)

a. adding 35 g of KF to 25 g of H_2O

b. adding 42 g of KF to 50. g of H_2O

c. adding 145 g of KF to 150. g of H_2O

9.132 Lithium chloride has a solubility of 55 g of LiCl in 100 g of H_2O at 25 °C. Determine if each of the following mixtures forms an unsaturated or saturated solution at 25 °C: (9.3)

a. adding 10 g of LiCl to 15 g of H_2O

b. adding 25 g of LiCl to 50. g of H_2O

c. adding 75 g of LiCl to 150. g of H_2O

9.133 A solution is prepared with 70.0 g of HNO_3 and 130.0 g of H_2O. The HNO_3 solution has a density of 1.21 g/mL. (9.4)

a. What is the mass percent (m/m) of the HNO_3 solution?

b. What is the total volume, in milliliters, of the solution?

c. What is the mass/volume percent (m/v) of the solution?

d. What is the molarity (M) of the solution?

9.134 A solution is prepared by dissolving 22.0 g of NaOH in 118.0 g of water. The NaOH solution has a density of 1.15 g/mL. (9.4)

a. What is the mass percent (m/m) of the NaOH solution?

b. What is the total volume, in milliliters, of the solution?

c. What is the mass/volume percent (m/v) of the solution?

d. What is the molarity (M) of the solution?

℞ **Clinical Applications**

9.135 A Pedialyte solution contains Na^+ 45 mEq/L, K^+ 20. mEq/L, Cl^- 35 mEq/L, $citrate^{3-}$ 30. mEq/L, and glucose ($C_6H_{12}O_6$) 25 g/L. (9.6)
   a. What is the total positive charge of the electrolytes?
   b. What is the total negative charge of the electrolytes?
   c. What is the osmolarity (Osm) of the solution?

9.136 A lactated Ringer's solution with 5% glucose contains Na^+ 130. mEq/L, K^+ 4 mEq/L, Ca^{2+} 3 mEq/L, Cl^- 109 mEq/L, $lactate^-$ 28 mEq/L, and glucose ($C_6H_{12}O_6$) 50. g/L. (9.6)
   a. What is the total positive charge of the electrolytes?
   b. What is the total negative charge of the electrolytes?
   c. What is the osmolarity (Osm) of the solution?

ANSWERS

Answers to Selected Questions and Problems

9.1 a. NaCl, solute; water, solvent
   b. water, solute; ethanol, solvent
   c. oxygen, solute; nitrogen, solvent

9.3 The polar water molecules pull the K^+ and I^- ions away from the solid and into solution, where they are hydrated.

9.5 a. water   **b.** CCl_4
   c. water   **d.** CCl_4

9.7 In a solution of KF, only the ions of K^+ and F^- are present in the solvent. In an HF solution, there are a few ions of H^+ and F^- present but mostly dissolved HF molecules.

9.9 a. $KCl(s) \xrightarrow{H_2O} K^+(aq) + Cl^-(aq)$

   b. $CaCl_2(s) \xrightarrow{H_2O} Ca^{2+}(aq) + 2Cl^-(aq)$

   c. $K_3PO_4(s) \xrightarrow{H_2O} 3K^+(aq) + PO_4^{3-}(aq)$

   d. $Fe(NO_3)_3(s) \xrightarrow{H_2O} Fe^{3+}(aq) + 3NO_3^-(aq)$

9.11 a. mostly molecules and a few ions
   b. ions only
   c. molecules only

9.13 a. strong electrolyte
   b. weak electrolyte
   c. nonelectrolyte

9.15 a. 1 Eq   **b.** 2 Eq
   c. 2 Eq   **d.** 6 Eq

9.17 0.154 mole of Na^+, 0.154 mole of Cl^-

9.19 55 mEq/L

9.21 a. 130 mEq/L   **b.** above the normal range

9.23 a. unsaturated   **b.** unsaturated
   c. saturated

9.25 a. 68 g of KCl   **b.** 12 g of KCl

9.27 a. The solubility of solid solutes typically increases as temperature increases.
   b. The solubility of a gas is less at a higher temperature.
   c. Gas solubility is less at a higher temperature and the CO_2 pressure in the can is increased.

9.29 a. soluble   **b.** insoluble   **c.** insoluble
   d. soluble   **e.** soluble

9.31 a. No solid forms.

   b. $2Ag^+(aq) + 2NO_3^-(aq) + 2K^+(aq) + S^{2-}(aq) \longrightarrow$
$Ag_2S(s) + 2K^+(aq) + 2NO_3^-(aq)$
$2Ag^+(aq) + S^{2-}(aq) \longrightarrow Ag_2S(s)$

   c. $Ca^{2+}(aq) + 2Cl^-(aq) + 2Na^+(aq) + SO_4^{2-}(aq) \longrightarrow$
$CaSO_4(s) + 2Na^+(aq) + 2Cl^-(aq)$
$Ca^{2+}(aq) + SO_4^{2-}(aq) \longrightarrow CaSO_4(s)$

   d. $3Cu^{2+}(aq) + 6Cl^-(aq) + 6Li^+(aq) + 2PO_4^{3-}(aq) \longrightarrow$
$Cu_3(PO_4)_2(s) + 6Li^+(aq) + 6Cl^-(aq)$
$3Cu^{2+}(aq) + 2PO_4^{3-}(aq) \longrightarrow Cu_3(PO_4)_2(s)$

9.33 a. 17% (m/m) KCl solution
   b. 5.3% (m/m) sucrose solution
   c. 10.% (m/m) $CaCl_2$ solution

9.35 a. 30.% (m/v) Na_2SO_4 solution
   b. 11% (m/v) sucrose solution

9.37 a. 2.5 g of KCl   **b.** 50. g of NH_4Cl
   c. 25.0 mL of acetic acid

9.39 79.9 mL of alcohol

9.41 a. 20. g of $LiNO_3$ solution
   b. 400. mL of KOH solution
   c. 20. mL of formic acid solution

9.43 a. 0.500 M glucose solution
   b. 0.0356 M KOH solution
   c. 0.250 M NaCl solution

9.45 a. 120. g of NaOH   **b.** 59.6 g of KCl
   c. 5.47 g of HCl

9.47 a. 1.50 L of KBr solution
   b. 10.0 L of NaCl solution
   c. 62.5 mL of $Ca(NO_3)_2$ solution

9.49 a. 10.4 g of $PbCl_2$
   b. 18.8 mL of $Pb(NO_3)_2$ solution
   c. 1.20 M KCl solution

9.51 a. 206 mL of HCl solution
   b. 11.2 L of H_2 gas
   c. 9.09 M HCl solution

9.53 a. 20. g of mannitol   **b.** 240 g of mannitol

9.55 2 L of glucose solution

9.57 3.0 mL of chlorpromazine solution

9.59 0.50 g of $CaCl_2$

9.61 Adding water (solvent) to the soup increases the volume and dilutes the tomato soup concentration.

9.63 a. 2.0 M HCl solution
   b. 2.0 M NaOH solution
   c. 2.5% (m/v) KOH solution
   d. 3.0% (m/v) H_2SO_4 solution

9.65 a. 80. mL of HCl solution
   b. 250 mL of LiCl solution
   c. 600. mL of H_3PO_4 solution
   d. 180 mL of glucose solution

9.67 a. 12.8 mL of the HNO_3 solution
   b. 11.9 mL of the $MgCl_2$ solution
   c. 1.88 mL of the KCl solution

9.69 1.0×10^2 mL

9.71 a. solution   **b.** suspension

9.73 a. 2.0 moles of ethylene glycol in 1.0 kg of water will have a lower freezing point because it has more particles in solution.

b. 0.50 mole of $MgCl_2$ in 1.0 kg of water has a lower freezing point because each $MgCl_2$ dissociates in water to give three particles, whereas each KCl dissociates to give only two particles.

9.75 a. $-2.53\,°C$ **b.** $-15.6\,°C$ **c.** $-5.54\,°C$

9.77 a. 10% (m/v) starch solution

b. from the 1% (m/v) starch solution into the 10% (m/v) starch solution

c. 10% (m/v) starch solution

9.79 a. B 10% (m/v) sucrose solution

b. A 8% (m/v) albumin solution

c. B 10% (m/v) starch solution

9.81 a. 1.0 Osm   **b.** 2.8 Osm

9.83 a. hypotonic   **b.** hypotonic
c. isotonic   **d.** hypertonic

9.85 a. NaCl   **b.** alanine
c. NaCl   **d.** urea

9.87 a. K^+, Na^+, Cl^- **b.** Ca^{2+}, Mg^{2+}
c. Ca^{2+}, Mg^{2+} **d.** K^+, Na^+, Cl^-

9.89 a. 1   **b.** 2   **c.** 1

9.91 a. 3   **b.** 1   **c.** 2

9.93 a. beaker 3

b. $Na^+(aq) + Cl^-(aq) + Ag^+(aq) + NO_3^-(aq) \longrightarrow$
$AgCl(s) + Na^+(aq) + NO_3^-(aq)$

c. $Ag^+(aq) + Cl^-(aq) \longrightarrow AgCl(s)$

9.95 The skin of the cucumber acts like a semipermeable membrane, and the more dilute solution inside flows into the brine solution.

9.97 a. 2   **b.** 1   **c.** 3   **d.** 2

9.99 Because iodine is a nonpolar molecule, it will dissolve in hexane, a nonpolar solvent. Iodine does not dissolve in water because water is a polar solvent.

9.101 a. unsaturated solution   **b.** saturated solution
c. saturated solution

9.103 a. soluble   **b.** soluble
c. insoluble   **d.** soluble
e. insoluble

9.105 a. $Ag^+(aq) + Cl^-(aq) \longrightarrow AgCl(s)$
b. none
c. $Ba^{2+}(aq) + SO_4^{2-}(aq) \longrightarrow BaSO_4(s)$

9.107 17.0% (m/m) Na_2SO_4 solution

9.109 38 mL of propyl alcohol solution

9.111 0.72 L of KOH solution

9.113 0.500 M NaOH solution

9.115 a. 1600 g of $Al(NO_3)_3$ **b.** 6.8 g of $C_6H_{12}O_6$
c. 17.9 g of LiCl

9.117 a. 0.100 M NaBr solution
b. 4.50% (m/v) K_2SO_4 solution
c. 1.76 M NaOH solution

9.119 a. 75 mL of 10.0% (m/v) HCl solution
b. 90. mL of 5.0% (m/v) NaCl solution
c. 117 mL of 6.00 M NaOH solution

9.121 a. $-1.08\,°C$ **b.** $-2.25\,°C$ **c.** $-11\,°C$

9.123 87 mL of HCl solution

9.125 0.15 Osm

9.127 A dialysis solution contains no sodium or urea so that these substances will flow out of the blood into the solution. High levels of potassium are maintained in the dialyzing solution so that the potassium will dialyze into the blood.

9.129 a. 11.6% (m/m) NaCl solution
b. 2.40 M NaCl solution
c. 0.400 M NaCl solution

9.131 a. saturated   **b.** unsaturated
c. saturated

9.133 a. 35.0% (m/m) HNO_3 solution
b. 165 mL
c. 42.4% (m/v) HNO_3 solution
d. 6.73 M HNO_3 solution

9.135 a. 65 mEq/L
b. 65 mEq/L
c. 0.25 Osm

10 Reaction Rates and Chemical Equilibrium

ANDREW WAS BORN 12 WEEKS EARLY WITH A

breathing problem called *infant respiratory distress syndrome* (IRDS). He was limp, purple, and not breathing. IRDS is caused by a lack of surfactant in underdeveloped lungs. Normally produced in the pulmonary alveoli, surfactants help the lungs inflate, and prevent the air sacs from collapsing. Without surfactants, a premature infant has difficulty breathing, which leads to decreased ventilation and hypoxia. Lack of oxygen can lead to the injury or death of cells and ultimately to irreversible brain damage. To prevent this, Andrew's metabolism needed to be slowed down.

At the hospital, Judy, a neonatal nurse, wrapped Andrew in a cooling blanket that lowered his body temperature to 33.5 °C. She attached electrodes to his head to monitor his brain activity. With a decrease in body temperature, Andrew's demand for oxygen was reduced. Artificial surfactants were administered to help him breathe more easily. When Andrew's oxygen levels in his bloodstream fell too low to maintain healthy tissues, Judy inserted a baby cannula in his nose that provided an air–oxygen mixture. Then more O_2 was picked up by Andrew's hemoglobin (Hb) at the lungs and released from the hemoglobin in the tissues.

$$Hb(aq) + O_2(g) \rightleftharpoons HbO_2(aq)$$

After Andrew successfully managed the three-day danger period, his body temperature was slowly restored to normal. Two weeks later, he was discharged from the hospital.

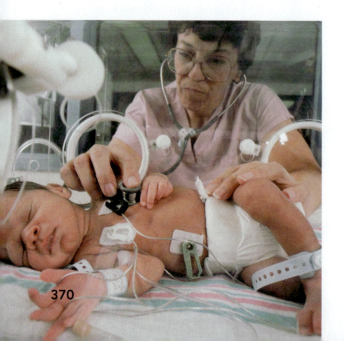

CAREER Neonatal Nurse

A neonatal nurse works with newborns that are premature, have birth defects, cardiac malformations, and surgical problems. Most neonatal nurses care for infants from the time of birth until they are discharged from the hospital.

A neonatal nurse monitors life support machines, medications, operates ventilators, and resuscitates a premature infant who stops breathing. Sufficient oxygen is provided for the tissues without injuring the organs. Many neonatal nurses take a national test to become part of a neonatal team or participate on an oxygenation team that provides heart–lung bypass for critically ill infants.

Earlier we looked at chemical reactions and determined the amounts of substances that react and the products that form. Now we are interested in how fast a reaction goes. If we know how fast a medication acts on the body, we can adjust the time over which the medication is taken. In construction, substances are added to cement to make it dry faster so that work can continue. Some reactions such as explosions or the formation of precipitates in a solution are very fast. When we roast a turkey or bake a cake, the reaction is slower. Some reactions such as the tarnishing of silver and the aging of the body are much slower (see Figure 10.1). We will see that some reactions need energy while other reactions produce energy. We burn gasoline in our automobile engines to produce energy to make our cars move. In this chapter, we will also look at the effect of changing the concentrations of reactants or products on the rate of reaction.

Up to now, we have considered a reaction as proceeding in a forward direction from reactants to products. However, in many reactions a reverse reaction also takes place as products collide to re-form reactants. When the forward and reverse reactions occur at the same rate, the amounts of reactants and products stay the same. When this balance in the rates of the forward and reverse reactions is reached, we say that the reaction has reached *equilibrium*. At equilibrium, both reactants and products are present. Some reaction mixtures contain mostly reactants and form only a few products, whereas others contain mostly products and a few reactants.

LOOKING AHEAD

10.1 Rates of Reactions 372
10.2 Chemical Equilibrium 377
10.3 Equilibrium Constants 380
10.4 Using Equilibrium Constants 383
10.5 Changing Equilibrium Conditions: Le Châtelier's Principle 387

♥ **Chemistry Link to Health** Oxygen–Hemoglobin Equilibrium and Hypoxia 389

♥ **Chemistry Link to Health** Homeostasis: Regulation of Body Temperature 392

℞ **Clinical Applications** 393

℞ **Clinical Update** An Iron-Rich Diet for Children's Anemia 393

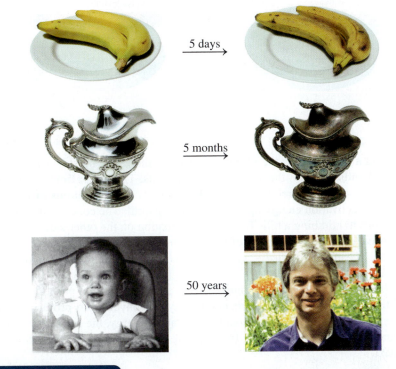

Reaction Rate Increases

5 days

5 months

50 years

FIGURE 10.1 ▶ Reaction rates vary greatly for everyday processes. A banana ripens in a few days, silver tarnishes in a few months, while the aging process of humans takes many years.

Ⓠ How would you compare the rates of the reaction that forms sugars in plants by photosynthesis with the reactions that digest sugars in the body?

CHAPTER READINESS*

🖩 KEY MATH SKILLS
- Solving Equations (1.4D)
- Writing Numbers in Scientific Notation (1.4F)

⚛ CORE CHEMISTRY SKILLS
- Using Significant Figures in Calculations (2.3)
- Balancing a Chemical Equation (7.1)
- Calculating Concentration (9.4)

*These Key Math Skills and Core Chemistry Skills from previous chapters are listed here for your review as you proceed to the new material in this chapter.

Describe how temperature, concentration, and catalysts affect the rate of a reaction.

10.1 Rates of Reactions

For a chemical reaction to take place, the molecules of the reactants must come in contact with each other. The **collision theory** indicates that a reaction takes place only when molecules collide with the proper orientation and sufficient energy. Many collisions can occur, but only a few actually lead to the formation of product. For example, consider the reaction of nitrogen and oxygen molecules (see Figure 10.2). To form nitrogen oxide (NO) product, the collisions between N_2 and O_2 molecules must place the atoms in the proper alignment. If the molecules are not aligned properly, no reaction takes place.

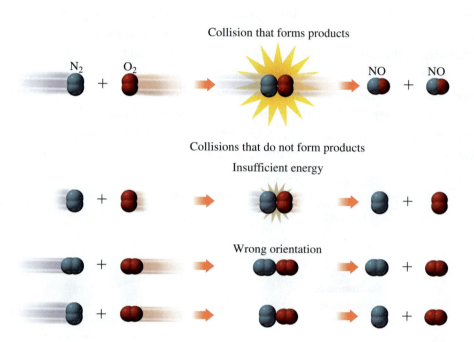

FIGURE 10.2 ▶ Reacting molecules must collide, have a minimum amount of energy, and have the proper orientation to form products.

Q What happens when reacting molecules collide with the minimum energy but don't have the proper orientation?

Activation Energy

Even when a collision has the proper orientation, there still must be sufficient energy to break the bonds between the atoms of the reactants. The **activation energy** is the minimum amount of energy required to break the bonds between atoms of the reactants. In Figure 10.3, activation energy appears as an energy hill. The concept of activation energy is analogous to climbing a hill. To reach a destination on the other side, we must have the energy needed to climb to the top of the hill. Once we are at the top, we can run down the other side. The energy needed to get us from our starting point to the top of the hill would be our activation energy.

In the same way, a collision must provide enough energy to push the reactants to the top of the energy hill. Then the reactants may be converted to products. If the energy provided by the collision is less than the activation energy, the molecules simply bounce apart and no reaction occurs. The features that lead to a successful reaction are summarized next.

Three Conditions Required for a Reaction to Occur

1. **Collision**   The reactants must collide.
2. **Orientation** The reactants must align properly to break and form bonds.
3. **Energy**   The collision must provide the energy of activation.

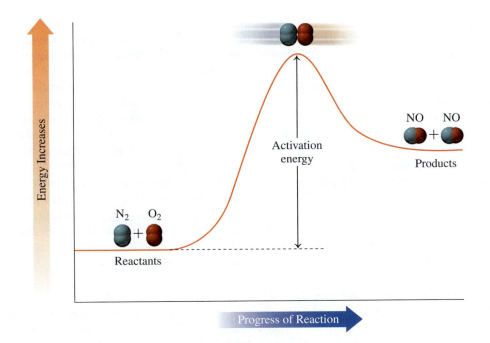

FIGURE 10.3 ▶ The activation energy is the minimum energy needed to convert the colliding molecules into product.

Q What happens in a collision of reacting molecules that have the proper orientation, but not the energy of activation?

Rate of Reaction

The **rate** (or speed) **of reaction** is determined by measuring the amount of a reactant used up, or the amount of a product formed, in a certain period of time.

$$\text{Rate of reaction} = \frac{\text{change in concentration of reactant or product}}{\text{change in time}}$$

We can describe the rate of reaction with the analogy of eating a pizza. When we start to eat, we have a whole pizza. As time goes by, there are fewer slices of pizza left. If we know how long it took to eat the pizza, we could determine the rate at which the pizza was consumed. Let's assume 4 slices are eaten every 8 minutes. That gives a rate of $\frac{1}{2}$ slice per minute. After 16 min, all 8 slices are gone.

Rate at Which Pizza Slices Are Eaten

Slices Eaten	0	4 slices	6 slices	8 slices
Time (min)	0	8 min	12 min	16 min

$$\text{Rate} = \frac{4 \text{ slices}}{8 \text{ min}} = \frac{1 \text{ slice}}{2 \text{ min}} = \frac{\frac{1}{2} \text{ slice}}{1 \text{ min}}$$

Reactions with low activation energies go faster than reactions with high activation energies. Some reactions go very fast, while others are very slow. For any reaction, the rate is affected by changes in temperature, changes in the concentration of the reactants, and the addition of catalysts.

Temperature

At higher temperatures, the increase in kinetic energy of the reactants makes them move faster and collide more often, and it provides more collisions with the required energy of activation. Reactions almost always go faster at higher temperatures. For every 10 °C increase in temperature, most reaction rates approximately double. If we want food to cook faster, we increase the temperature. When body temperature rises, there is an increase in the pulse rate, rate of breathing, and metabolic rate. If we are exposed to extreme heat, we may experience *heat stroke*, which is a condition that occurs when body temperature goes above 40.5 °C (105 °F). If the body loses its ability to regulate temperature, body temperature continues to rise, and may cause damage to the brain and internal organs. On the other hand, we slow down a reaction by decreasing the temperature. For example, we refrigerate perishable foods to make them last longer. In some cardiac surgeries, body temperature is decreased to 28 °C so the heart can be stopped and less oxygen is required by the brain. This is also the reason why some people have survived submersion in icy lakes for long periods of time. Cool water or an ice blanket may also be used to decrease the body temperature of a person with hyperthermia or heat stroke.

Concentrations of Reactants

For virtually all reactions, the rate of a reaction increases when the concentration of the reactants increases. When there are more reacting molecules, more collisions that form products can occur, and the reaction goes faster (see Figure 10.4). For example, a patient having difficulty breathing may be given a breathing mixture with a higher oxygen content than the atmosphere. The increase in the number of oxygen molecules in the lungs increases the rate at which oxygen combines with hemoglobin. The increased rate of oxygenation of the blood means that the patient can breathe more easily.

$$\text{Hb}(aq) \quad + \quad \text{O}_2(g) \quad \longrightarrow \quad \text{HbO}_2(aq)$$
Hemoglobin   Oxygen   Oxyhemoglobin

Catalysts

Another way to speed up a reaction is to lower the *energy of activation*. The energy of activation is the minimum energy needed to break apart the bonds of the reacting molecules. If a collision provides less than the activation energy, the bonds do not break and the reactant molecules bounce apart. A **catalyst** speeds up a reaction by providing an alternative pathway that has a lower energy of activation. When activation energy is lowered, more collisions provide sufficient energy for reactants to form product. During a reaction, a catalyst is not changed or consumed.

Reaction:

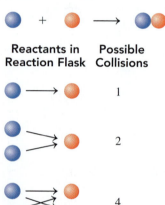

FIGURE 10.4 ▶ Increasing the concentration of a reactant increases the number of collisions that are possible.

Ⓠ Why does doubling the reactants increase the rate of reaction?

When a catalyst lowers the activation energy, the reaction occurs at a faster rate.

Catalysts have many uses in industry. In the manufacturing of margarine, hydrogen (H_2) is added to vegetable oils. Normally, the reaction is very slow because it has a high activation energy. However, when platinum (Pt) is used as a catalyst, the reaction occurs rapidly. In the body, biocatalysts called enzymes make most metabolic reactions proceed at rates necessary for proper cellular activity. Enzymes are added to laundry detergents to break down proteins (proteases), starches (amylases), or greases (lipases) that have stained clothes. Such enzymes function at the low temperatures that are used in home washing machines, and they are biodegradable as well.

The factors affecting reaction rates are summarized in Table 10.1.

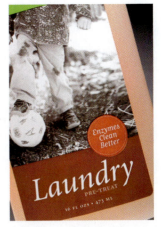

Enzymes in laundry detergent catalyze the removal of stains at low temperatures.

▶ SAMPLE PROBLEM 10.1 Factors That Affect the Rate of Reaction

Indicate whether the following changes will increase, decrease, or have no effect on the rate of reaction:

a. increasing the temperature
b. increasing the number of reacting molecules
c. adding a catalyst

SOLUTION

a. A higher temperature increases the kinetic energy of the particles, which increases the number of collisions and makes more collisions effective, causing an increase in the rate of reaction.
b. Increasing the number of reacting molecules increases the number of collisions and the rate of the reaction.
c. Adding a catalyst increases the rate of reaction by lowering the activation energy, which increases the number of collisions that form product.

STUDY CHECK 10.1

How does using an ice blanket on a patient affect the rate of metabolism in the body?

ANSWER

Lowering the temperature will decrease the rate of metabolism.

TABLE 10.1 Factors That Increase Reaction Rate

Factor	Reason
Increase temperature	More collisions, more collisions with energy of activation
Increase reactant concentration	More collisions
Add a catalyst	Lowers energy of activation

Chemistry Link to the **Environment**
Catalytic Converters

For over 30 years, manufacturers have been required to include catalytic converters in the exhaust systems of gasoline automobile engines. When gasoline burns, the products found in the exhaust of a car contain high levels of pollutants. These include carbon monoxide (CO) from incomplete combustion, hydrocarbons such as C_8H_{18} (octane) from unburned fuel, and nitrogen oxide (NO) from the reaction of N_2 and O_2 at the high temperatures reached within the engine. Carbon monoxide is toxic, and unburned hydrocarbons and nitrogen oxide are involved in the formation of smog and acid rain.

A catalytic converter consists of solid-particle catalysts, such as platinum (Pt) and palladium (Pd), on a ceramic honeycomb that provides a large surface area and facilitates contact with pollutants. As the pollutants pass through the converter, they react with the catalysts. Today, we all use unleaded gasoline because lead interferes with the ability of the Pt and Pd catalysts in the converter to react with the pollutants. The purpose of a catalytic converter is to lower the activation energy for reactions that convert each of these pollutants into substances such as CO_2, N_2, O_2, and H_2O, which are already present in the atmosphere.

Exhaust Gases
Hydrocarbons, C_8H_{18}
Carbon monoxide, CO
Nitrogen oxide, NO

Catalytic
converter

Catalyst

Tail Pipe Emissions
Water, H_2O
Carbon dioxide, CO_2
Nitrogen, N_2
Oxygen, O_2

$$2NO(g) \longrightarrow N_2(g) + O_2(g)$$

NO absorbed on catalyst

NO

Surface of metal (Pt, Pd) catalyst

NO dissociates

N_2 O_2

$$2CO(g) + O_2(g) \longrightarrow 2CO_2(g)$$

CO and O_2 absorbed on catalyst

CO

Surface of metal (Pt, Pd) catalyst

O_2 dissociates

CO_2

QUESTIONS AND PROBLEMS

10.1 Rates of Reactions

LEARNING GOAL Describe how temperature, concentration, and catalysts affect the rate of a reaction.

10.1 **a.** What is meant by the rate of a reaction?
   b. Why does bread grow mold more quickly at room temperature than in the refrigerator?

10.2 **a.** How does a catalyst affect the activation energy?
   b. Why is pure oxygen used in respiratory distress?

10.3 In the following reaction, what happens to the number of collisions when more $Br_2(g)$ molecules are added?

$$H_2(g) + Br_2(g) \longrightarrow 2HBr(g)$$

10.4 In the following reaction, what happens to the number of collisions when the temperature of the reaction is decreased?

$$2H_2(g) + CO(g) \longrightarrow CH_3OH(g)$$

10.5 How would each of the following change the rate of the reaction shown here?

$$2SO_2(g) + O_2(g) \longrightarrow 2SO_3(g)$$

a. adding some $SO_2(g)$
b. increasing the temperature
c. adding a catalyst
d. removing some $O_2(g)$

10.6 How would each of the following change the rate of the reaction shown here?

$$2NO(g) + 2H_2(g) \longrightarrow N_2(g) + 2H_2O(g)$$

a. adding some $NO(g)$
b. decreasing the temperature
c. removing some $H_2(g)$
d. adding a catalyst

10.2 Chemical Equilibrium

In earlier chapters, we considered the *forward reaction* in an equation and assumed that all of the reactants were converted to products. However, most of the time reactants are not completely converted to products because a *reverse reaction* takes place in which products collide to form the reactants. When a reaction proceeds in both a forward and reverse direction, it is said to be reversible. We have looked at other reversible processes. For example, the melting of solids to form liquids and the freezing of liquids to solids is a reversible physical change. Even in our daily life we have reversible events. We go from home to school and we return from school to home. We go up an escalator and we come back down. We put money in our bank account and we take money out.

An analogy for a forward and reverse reaction can be found in the phrase "We are going to the grocery store." Although we mention our trip in one direction, we know that we will also return home from the store. Because our trip has both a forward and reverse direction, we can say the trip is reversible. It is not very likely that we would stay at the store forever.

A trip to the grocery store can be used to illustrate another aspect of reversible reactions. Perhaps the grocery store is nearby and we usually walk. However, we can change our rate. Suppose that one day we drive to the store, which increases our rate and gets us to the store faster. Correspondingly, a car also increases the rate at which we return home.

Reversible Chemical Reactions

A **reversible reaction** proceeds in both the forward and reverse direction. That means there are two reaction rates: one is the rate of the forward reaction, and the other is the rate of the reverse reaction. When molecules begin to react, the rate of the forward reaction is faster than the rate of the reverse reaction. As reactants are consumed and products accumulate, the rate of the forward reaction decreases and the rate of the reverse reaction increases.

Equilibrium

Eventually, the rates of the forward and reverse reactions become equal; the reactants form products at the same rate that the products form reactants. A reaction reaches **chemical equilibrium** when no further change takes place in the concentrations of the reactants and products, even though the two reactions continue at equal but opposite rates.

At Equilibrium:

The rate of the forward reaction is equal to the rate of the reverse reaction.

No further changes occur in the concentrations of reactants and products, even though the two reactions continue at equal but opposite rates.

Let us look at the process as the reaction of H_2 and I_2 proceeds to equilibrium. Initially, only the reactants H_2 and I_2 are present. Soon, a few molecules of HI are produced by the forward reaction. With more time, additional HI molecules are produced. As the concentration of HI increases, more HI molecules collide and react in the reverse

LEARNING GOAL

Use the concept of reversible reactions to explain chemical equilibrium.

As a reaction progresses, the rate of the forward reaction decreases and that of the reverse reaction increases. At equilibrium, the rates of the forward and reverse reactions are equal.

Equilibrium is reached when there are no further changes in the concentrations of reactants and products.

	(a)	(b)	(c)	(d)	(e)
Concentration of Reactants	8 (4+4)	6 (3+3)	4 (2+2)	2 (1+1)	2 (1+1)
Concentration of Products	0	2	4	6	6

FIGURE 10.5 ▶ **(a)** Initially, the reaction flask contains only the reactants H_2 (white) and I_2 (purple). **(b)** The forward reaction between H_2 and I_2 begins to produce HI. **(c)** As the reaction proceeds, there are fewer molecules of H_2 and I_2 and more molecules of HI, which increases the rate of the reverse reaction. **(d)** At equilibrium, the concentrations of reactants H_2 and I_2 and product HI are constant. **(e)** The reaction continues with the rate of the forward reaction equal to the rate of the reverse reaction.

Q How do the rates of the forward and reverse reactions compare once a chemical reaction reaches equilibrium?

direction. As HI product builds up, the rate of the reverse reaction increases, while the rate of the forward reaction decreases. Eventually, the rates become equal, which means the reaction has reached equilibrium. Even though the concentrations remain constant at equilibrium, the forward and reverse reactions continue to occur. The forward and reverse reactions are usually shown together in a single equation by using a double arrow. A reversible reaction is two opposing reactions that occur at the same time (see Figure 10.5).

$$H_2(g) + I_2(g) \underset{\text{Reverse reaction}}{\overset{\text{Forward reaction}}{\rightleftharpoons}} 2HI(g)$$

SAMPLE PROBLEM 10.2 Reaction Rates and Equilibrium

Complete each of the following with *equal* or *not equal*, *faster* or *slower*, *change* or *do not change*:

a. Before equilibrium is reached, the concentrations of the reactants and products _____.
b. Initially, reactants placed in a container have a _____ rate of reaction than the rate of reaction of the products.
c. At equilibrium, the rate of the forward reaction is _____ to the rate of the reverse reaction.

SOLUTION

a. Before equilibrium is reached, the concentrations of the reactants and products *change*.
b. Initially, reactants placed in a container have a *faster* rate of reaction than the rate of reaction of the products.
c. At equilibrium, the rate of the forward reaction is *equal* to the rate of the reverse reaction.

STUDY CHECK 10.2

Complete the following statement with *change* or *do not change*:
At equilibrium, the concentrations of the reactants and products _____.

ANSWER

At equilibrium, the concentrations of the reactants and products *do not change*.

We can also set up a reaction starting with only reactants or with only products. Let's look at the initial reactions in each, the forward and reverse reactions, and the equilibrium mixture that forms (see Figure 10.6).

$$2SO_2(g) + O_2(g) \rightleftharpoons 2SO_3(g)$$

If we start with only the reactants SO_2 and O_2 in the container, the reaction to form SO_3 takes place until equilibrium is reached. However, if we start with only the product SO_3 in the container, the reaction to form SO_2 and O_2 takes place until equilibrium is reached. In both containers, the equilibrium mixture contains the same concentrations of SO_2, O_2, and SO_3.

(a)   (b)   (c)

$SO_2(g) + O_2(g)$ (initially) $2SO_2(g) + O_2(g) \rightleftharpoons 2SO_3(g)$ $SO_3(g)$ (initially)
(at equilibrium)

FIGURE 10.6 ▶ Sample **(a)** initially contains $SO_2(g)$ and $O_2(g)$. At equilibrium, sample **(b)** contains mostly $SO_3(g)$ and only small amounts of $SO_2(g)$ and $O_2(g)$, whereas sample **(c)** contains only $SO_3(g)$.

Q Why is the same equilibrium mixture obtained from $SO_2(g)$ and $O_2(g)$ as from $SO_3(g)$?

QUESTIONS AND PROBLEMS

10.2 Chemical Equilibrium

LEARNING GOAL Use the concept of reversible reactions to explain chemical equilibrium.

10.7 What is meant by the term *reversible reaction*?

10.8 When does a reversible reaction reach equilibrium?

10.9 Which of the following are at equilibrium?
   a. The rate of the forward reaction is twice as fast as the rate of the reverse reaction.
   b. The concentrations of the reactants and the products do not change.
   c. The rate of the reverse reaction does not change.

10.10 Which of the following are not at equilibrium?
   a. The rates of the forward and reverse reactions are equal.
   b. The rate of the forward reaction does not change.
   c. The concentrations of reactants and the products are not constant.

10.11 The following diagrams show the chemical reaction with time:

A $\rightleftharpoons$ B

If A is blue and B is orange, state whether or not the reaction has reached equilibrium in this time period and explain why.

| 1 h | 2 h | 3 h | 4 h |

10.12 The following diagrams show the chemical reaction with time:

C $\rightleftharpoons$ D

If C is blue and D is yellow, state whether or not the reaction has reached equilibrium in this time period and explain why.

| 1 h | 2 h | 3 h | 4 h |

LEARNING GOAL

Calculate the equilibrium constant for a reversible reaction given the concentrations of reactants and products at equilibrium.

At equilibrium, the number of people riding up the lift and the number of people skiing down the slope are constant.

⚛ CORE CHEMISTRY SKILL

Writing the Equilibrium Constant Expression

10.3 Equilibrium Constants

At equilibrium, the concentrations of the reactants and products are constant. We can use a ski lift as an analogy. Early in the morning, skiers at the bottom of the mountain begin to ride the ski lift up to the slopes. After the skiers reach the top of the mountain, they ski down. Eventually, the number of people riding up the ski lift becomes equal to the number of people skiing down the mountain. There is no further change in the number of skiers on the slopes; the system is at equilibrium.

Equilibrium Constant Expression

At equilibrium, the concentrations can be used to set up a relationship between the products and the reactants. Suppose we write a general equation for reactants A and B that form products C and D. The small italic letters are the coefficients in the balanced equation.

$$a\text{A} + b\text{B} \rightleftharpoons c\text{C} + d\text{D}$$

An **equilibrium constant expression** for a reversible chemical reaction multiplies the concentrations of the products together and divides by the concentrations of the reactants. Each concentration is raised to a power that is equal to its coefficient in the balanced chemical equation. The square bracket around each substance indicates that the concentration is expressed in moles per liter (M). For our general reaction, this is written as:

$$K_c = \frac{[\text{Products}]}{[\text{Reactants}]} = \frac{[\text{C}]^c [\text{D}]^d}{[\text{A}]^a [\text{B}]^b} \longleftarrow \text{Coefficients}$$

Equilibrium constant expression

We can now describe how to write the equilibrium constant expression for the reaction of H_2 and I_2 that forms HI. The balanced chemical equation is written with a double arrow between the reactants and the products.

$$H_2(g) + I_2(g) \rightleftharpoons 2HI(g)$$

We show the concentration of the products using brackets in the numerator and the concentrations of the reactants in brackets in the denominator and write any coefficient as an exponent of its concentration (a coefficient 1 is understood).

$$K_c = \frac{[\text{HI}]^2}{[\text{H}_2][\text{I}_2]} \longleftarrow \text{Coefficient of HI}$$

▶ **SAMPLE PROBLEM 10.3** **Writing Equilibrium Constant Expressions**

Write the equilibrium constant expression for the following reaction:

$$2SO_2(g) + O_2(g) \rightleftharpoons 2SO_3(g)$$

SOLUTION

STEP 1 Write the balanced chemical equation.

$$2SO_2(g) + O_2(g) \rightleftharpoons 2SO_3(g)$$

STEP 2 Write the concentrations of the products as the numerator and the reactants as the denominator.

$$\frac{[\text{Products}]}{[\text{Reactants}]} \longrightarrow \frac{[SO_3]}{[SO_2][O_2]}$$

STEP 3 Write any coefficient in the equation as an exponent.

$$K_c = \frac{[SO_3]^2}{[SO_2]^2[O_2]}$$

STUDY CHECK 10.3

Write the equilibrium constant expression for the following reaction:

$$2NO(g) + O_2(g) \rightleftharpoons 2NO_2(g)$$

ANSWER

$$K_c = \frac{[NO_2]^2}{[NO]^2[O_2]}$$

> **Guide to Writing the Equilibrium Constant Expression**
>
> **STEP 1**
> Write the balanced chemical equation.
>
> **STEP 2**
> Write the concentrations of the products as the numerator and the reactants as the denominator.
>
> **STEP 3**
> Write any coefficient in the equation as an exponent.

Calculating Equilibrium Constants

The **equilibrium constant, K_c,** is the numerical value obtained by substituting experimentally measured molar concentrations at equilibrium into the equilibrium constant expression. For example, the equilibrium constant expression for the reaction of H_2 and I_2 is written

$$H_2(g) + I_2(g) \rightleftharpoons 2HI(g) \qquad K_c = \frac{[HI]^2}{[H_2][I_2]}$$

In the first experiment, the molar concentrations for the reactants and products at equilibrium are found to be $[H_2] = 0.10$ M, $[I_2] = 0.20$ M, and $[HI] = 1.04$ M. When we substitute these values into the equilibrium constant expression, we obtain its numerical value.

In additional experiments 2 and 3, the mixtures have different equilibrium concentrations for the system at equilibrium at the same temperature. However, when these concentrations are used to calculate the equilibrium constant, we obtain the same value of K_c for each (see Table 10.2). *Thus, a reaction at a specific temperature can have only one value for the equilibrium constant.*

The units of K_c depend on the specific equation. In this example, the units of $[M]^2/[M]^2$ cancel out to give a value of 54. In other equations, the concentration units do not cancel. However, in this text, the numerical value will be given without any units as shown in Sample Problem 10.4.

⚛ **CORE CHEMISTRY SKILL**

Calculating an Equilibrium Constant

TABLE 10.2 Equilibrium Constant for $H_2(g) + I_2(g) \rightleftharpoons 2HI(g)$ at 427 °C

Experiment	Concentrations at Equilibrium			Equilibrium Constant
	$[H_2]$	$[I_2]$	$[HI]$	$K_c = \dfrac{[HI]^2}{[H_2][I_2]}$
1	0.10 M	0.20 M	1.04 M	$K_c = \dfrac{[1.04]^2}{[0.10][0.20]} = 54$
2	0.20 M	0.20 M	1.47 M	$K_c = \dfrac{[1.47]^2}{[0.20][0.20]} = 54$
3	0.30 M	0.17 M	1.66 M	$K_c = \dfrac{[1.66]^2}{[0.30][0.17]} = 54$

▶ **SAMPLE PROBLEM 10.4 Calculating an Equilibrium Constant**

The decomposition of dinitrogen tetroxide forms nitrogen dioxide.

$$N_2O_4(g) \rightleftharpoons 2NO_2(g)$$

What is the numerical value of K_c at 100 °C if a reaction mixture at equilibrium contains 0.45 M N_2O_4 and 0.31 M NO_2?

SOLUTION

STEP 1 State the given and needed quantities.

ANALYZE THE PROBLEM	Given	Need
	0.45 M N_2O_4, 0.31 M NO_2	K_c
	Equation	
	$N_2O_4(g) \rightleftharpoons 2NO_2(g)$	

STEP 2 Write the K_c expression for the equilibrium.

$$K_c = \frac{[NO_2]^2}{[N_2O_4]}$$

STEP 3 Substitute equilibrium (molar) concentrations and calculate K_c.

$$K_c = \frac{[0.31]^2}{[0.45]} = 0.21$$

STUDY CHECK 10.4

Calculate the numerical value of K_c if an equilibrium mixture contains 0.040 M NH_3, 0.60 M H_2, and 0.20 M N_2.

$$2NH_3(g) \rightleftharpoons 3H_2(g) + N_2(g)$$

ANSWER

$K_c = 27$

Guide to Calculating the K_c Value

STEP 1
State the given and needed quantities.

STEP 2
Write the K_c expression for the equilibrium.

STEP 3
Substitute equilibrium (molar) concentrations and calculate K_c.

QUESTIONS AND PROBLEMS

10.3 Equilibrium Constants

LEARNING GOAL Calculate the equilibrium constant for a reversible reaction given the concentrations of reactants and products at equilibrium.

10.13 Write the equilibrium constant expression for each of the following reactions:
a. $CH_4(g) + 2H_2S(g) \rightleftharpoons CS_2(g) + 4H_2(g)$
b. $2NO(g) \rightleftharpoons N_2(g) + O_2(g)$
c. $2SO_3(g) + CO_2(g) \rightleftharpoons CS_2(g) + 4O_2(g)$
d. $CH_4(g) + H_2O(g) \rightleftharpoons 3H_2(g) + CO(g)$

10.14 Write the equilibrium constant expression for each of the following reactions:
a. $2HBr(g) \rightleftharpoons H_2(g) + Br_2(g)$
b. $2BrNO(g) \rightleftharpoons Br_2(g) + 2NO(g)$
c. $CH_4(g) + Cl_2(g) \rightleftharpoons CH_3Cl(g) + HCl(g)$
d. $Br_2(g) + Cl_2(g) \rightleftharpoons 2BrCl(g)$

10.15 Write the equilibrium constant expression for the reaction in the diagram and calculate the numerical value of K_c. In the diagram, X atoms are orange and Y atoms are blue.

$$X_2(g) + Y_2(g) \rightleftharpoons 2XY(g)$$

Equilibrium
mixture

10.16 Write the equilibrium constant expression for the reaction in the diagram and calculate the numerical value of K_c. In the diagram, A atoms are red and B atoms are green.

$$2AB(g) \rightleftharpoons A_2(g) + B_2(g)$$

Equilibrium
mixture

10.17 What is the numerical value of K_c for the following reaction if the equilibrium mixture contains 0.030 M N_2O_4 and 0.21 M NO_2?

$$N_2O_4(g) \rightleftharpoons 2NO_2(g)$$

10.18 What is the numerical value of K_c for the following reaction if the equilibrium mixture contains 0.30 M CO_2, 0.033 M H_2, 0.20 M CO, and 0.30 M H_2O?

$$CO_2(g) + H_2(g) \rightleftharpoons CO(g) + H_2O(g)$$

10.19 What is the numerical value of K_c for the following reaction if the equilibrium mixture contains 0.51 M CO, 0.30 M H_2, 1.8 M CH_4, and 2.0 M H_2O?

$$CO(g) + 3H_2(g) \rightleftharpoons CH_4(g) + H_2O(g)$$

10.20 What is the numerical value of K_c for the following reaction if the equilibrium mixture contains 0.44 M N_2, 0.40 M H_2, and 2.2 M NH_3?

$$N_2(g) + 3H_2(g) \rightleftharpoons 2NH_3(g)$$

10.4 Using Equilibrium Constants

The values of K_c can be large or small. The size of the equilibrium constant depends on whether equilibrium is reached with more products than reactants, or more reactants than products. However, the size of an equilibrium constant does not affect how fast equilibrium is reached.

LEARNING GOAL

Use an equilibrium constant to predict the extent of reaction and to calculate equilibrium concentrations.

Equilibrium with a Large K_c

When a reaction has a large equilibrium constant, it means that the forward reaction produced a large amount of products when equilibrium was reached. Then the equilibrium mixture contains mostly products, which makes the concentrations of the products in the numerator higher than the concentrations of the reactants in the denominator. Thus at equilibrium, this reaction has a large K_c. Consider the reaction of SO_2 and O_2, which has a large K_c. At equilibrium, the reaction mixture contains mostly product and few reactants (see Figure 10.7).

$$2SO_2(g) + O_2(g) \rightleftharpoons 2SO_3(g)$$

$$K_c = \frac{[SO_3]^2}{[SO_2]^2[O_2]} \quad \frac{\text{Mostly product}}{\text{Few reactants}} = 3.4 \times 10^2$$

FIGURE 10.7 ▶ In the reaction of $SO_2(g)$ and $O_2(g)$, the equilibrium mixture contains mostly product $SO_3(g)$, which results in a large K_c.

🅠 Why does an equilibrium mixture containing mostly product have a large K_c?

$$2SO_2(g) + O_2(g) \rightleftharpoons 2SO_3(g)$$

Equilibrium with a Small K_c

When a reaction has a small equilibrium constant, the equilibrium mixture contains a high concentration of reactants and a low concentration of products. Then the equilibrium expression has a small number in the numerator and a large number in the denominator. Thus at equilibrium, this reaction has a small K_c. Consider the reaction for the formation of $NO(g)$ from $N_2(g)$ and $O_2(g)$, which has a small K_c (see Figure 10.8).

$$N_2(g) + O_2(g) \rightleftharpoons 2NO(g)$$

$$K_c = \frac{[NO]^2}{[N_2][O_2]} \quad \frac{\text{Few products}}{\text{Mostly reactants}} = 2 \times 10^{-9}$$

FIGURE 10.8 ▶ The equilibrium mixture contains a very small amount of the product NO and a large amount of the reactants N_2 and O_2, which results in a small K_c.

🅠 Does a reaction with a $K_c = 3.2 \times 10^{-5}$ contain mostly reactants or products at equilibrium?

$$N_2(g) + O_2(g) \rightleftharpoons 2NO(g)$$

A few reactions have equilibrium constants close to 1, which means they have about equal concentrations of reactants and products. Moderate amounts of reactants have been converted to products upon reaching equilibrium (see Figure 10.9).

FIGURE 10.9 ▶ At equilibrium, a reaction with a large K_c contains mostly products, whereas a reaction with a small K_c contains mostly reactants.

🅠 Does a reaction with a $K_c = 1.2$ contain mostly reactants, mostly products, or about equal amounts of both reactants and products at equilibrium?

Table 10.3 lists some equilibrium constants and the extent of their reaction.

TABLE 10.3 Examples of Reactions with Large and Small K_c Values

Reactants	Products	K_c	Equilibrium Mixture Contains
$2CO(g) + O_2(g) \rightleftharpoons$	$2CO_2(g)$	2×10^{11}	Mostly products
$2H_2(g) + S_2(g) \rightleftharpoons$	$2H_2S(g)$	1.1×10^7	Mostly products
$N_2(g) + 3H_2(g) \rightleftharpoons$	$2NH_3(g)$	1.6×10^2	Mostly products
$PCl_5(g) \rightleftharpoons$	$PCl_3(g) + Cl_2(g)$	1.2×10^{-2}	Mostly reactants
$N_2(g) + O_2(g) \rightleftharpoons$	$2NO(g)$	2×10^{-9}	Mostly reactants

Calculating Concentrations at Equilibrium

When we know the numerical value of the equilibrium constant and all the equilibrium concentrations except one, we can calculate the unknown concentration as shown in Sample Problem 10.5.

⚛ **CORE CHEMISTRY SKILL**

Calculating Equilibrium Concentrations

▶**SAMPLE PROBLEM 10.5** Calculating Concentration Using an Equilibrium Constant

For the reaction of carbon dioxide and hydrogen, the equilibrium concentrations are 0.25 M CO_2, 0.80 M H_2, and 0.50 M H_2O. What is the equilibrium concentration of $CO(g)$?

$$CO_2(g) + H_2(g) \rightleftharpoons CO(g) + H_2O(g) \qquad K_c = 0.11$$

SOLUTION

STEP 1 State the given and needed quantities.

	Given	Need
ANALYZE THE PROBLEM	0.25 M CO_2, 0.80 M H_2, 0.50 M H_2O	[CO]
	Equation	
	$CO_2(g) + H_2(g) \rightleftharpoons CO(g) + H_2O(g) \qquad K_c = 0.11$	

STEP 2 Write the K_c expression for the equilibrium and solve for the needed concentration.

$$K_c = \frac{[CO][H_2O]}{[CO_2][H_2]}$$

We rearrange K_c to solve for the unknown [CO] as follows:

Multiply both sides by $[CO_2][H_2]$.

$$K_c \times [CO_2][H_2] = \frac{[CO][H_2O]}{[\cancel{CO_2}][\cancel{H_2}]} \times [\cancel{CO_2}][\cancel{H_2}]$$

$$K_c[CO_2][H_2] = [CO][H_2O]$$

Divide both sides by $[H_2O]$.

$$K_c \frac{[CO_2][H_2]}{[H_2O]} = \frac{[CO][\cancel{H_2O}]}{[\cancel{H_2O}]}$$

$$[CO] = K_c \frac{[CO_2][H_2]}{[H_2O]}$$

Guide to Using the Equilibrium Constant

STEP 1
State the given and needed quantities.

STEP 2
Write the K_c expression for the equilibrium and solve for the needed concentration.

STEP 3
Substitute the equilibrium (molar) concentrations and calculate the needed concentration.

STEP **3** Substitute the equilibrium (molar) concentrations and calculate the needed concentration.

$$[CO] = K_c \frac{[CO_2][H_2]}{[H_2O]} = 0.11 \frac{[0.25][0.80]}{[0.50]} = 0.044 \text{ M}$$

STUDY CHECK 10.5

When the alkene ethene (C_2H_4) reacts with water vapor, the alcohol ethanol (C_2H_5OH) is produced. If an equilibrium mixture contains 0.020 M C_2H_4 and 0.015 M H_2O, what is the equilibrium concentration of C_2H_5OH? At 327 °C, the K_c is 9.0×10^3.

$$C_2H_4(g) + H_2O(g) \rightleftharpoons C_2H_5OH(g)$$

ANSWER

$[C_2H_5OH] = 2.7$ M

QUESTIONS AND PROBLEMS

10.4 Using Equilibrium Constants

LEARNING GOAL Use an equilibrium constant to predict the extent of reaction and to calculate equilibrium concentrations.

10.21 If the K_c for this reaction is 4, which of the following diagrams represents the molecules in an equilibrium mixture? In the diagrams, X atoms are orange and Y atoms are blue.

$$X_2(g) + Y_2(g) \rightleftharpoons 2XY(g)$$

A   B   C

10.22 If the K_c for this reaction is 2, which of the following diagrams represents the molecules in an equilibrium mixture? In the diagrams, A atoms are orange and B atoms are green.

$$2AB(g) \rightleftharpoons A_2(g) + B_2(g)$$

A   B   C

10.23 Indicate whether each of the following equilibrium mixtures contains mostly products or mostly reactants:
   a. $Cl_2(g) + NO(g) \rightleftharpoons 2NOCl(g)$ $K_c = 3.7 \times 10^8$

b. $2H_2(g) + S_2(g) \rightleftharpoons 2H_2S(g)$ $K_c = 1.1 \times 10^7$
   c. $3O_2(g) \rightleftharpoons 2O_3(g)$ $K_c = 1.7 \times 10^{-56}$

10.24 Indicate whether each of the following equilibrium mixtures contains mostly products or mostly reactants:
   a. $CO(g) + Cl_2(g) \rightleftharpoons COCl_2(g)$ $K_c = 5.0 \times 10^{-9}$
   b. $2HF(g) \rightleftharpoons H_2(g) + F_2(g)$ $K_c = 1.0 \times 10^{-95}$
   c. $2NO(g) + O_2(g) \rightleftharpoons 2NO_2(g)$ $K_c = 6.0 \times 10^{13}$

10.25 The equilibrium constant, K_c, for this reaction is 54.

$$H_2(g) + I_2(g) \rightleftharpoons 2HI(g)$$

If the equilibrium mixture contains 0.015 M I_2 and 0.030 M HI, what is the molar concentration of H_2?

10.26 The equilibrium constant, K_c, for the following reaction is 4.6×10^{-3}. If the equilibrium mixture contains 0.050 M NO_2, what is the molar concentration of N_2O_4?

$$N_2O_4(g) \rightleftharpoons 2NO_2(g)$$

10.27 The K_c for the following reaction at 100 °C is 2.0. If the equilibrium mixture contains 2.0 M NO and 1.0 M Br_2, what is the molar concentration of NOBr?

$$2NOBr(g) \rightleftharpoons 2NO(g) + Br_2(g)$$

10.28 The K_c for the following reaction at 225 °C is 1.7×10^2. If the equilibrium mixture contains 0.18 M H_2 and 0.020 M N_2, what is the molar concentration of NH_3?

$$3H_2(g) + N_2(g) \rightleftharpoons 2NH_3(g)$$

10.5 Changing Equilibrium Conditions: Le Châtelier's Principle

We have seen that when a reaction reaches equilibrium, the rates of the forward and reverse reactions are equal and the concentrations remain constant. Now we will look at what happens to a system at equilibrium when changes occur in reaction conditions, such as changes in concentration, volume, and temperature.

LEARNING GOAL

Use Le Châtelier's principle to describe the changes made in equilibrium concentrations when reaction conditions change.

Le Châtelier's Principle

When we alter any of the conditions of a system at equilibrium, the rates of the forward and reverse reactions will no longer be equal. We say that a *stress* is placed on the equilibrium. Then the system responds by changing the rate of the forward or reverse reaction in the direction that relieves that stress to reestablish equilibrium. We can use **Le Châtelier's principle**, which states that when a system at equilibrium is disturbed, the system will shift in the direction that will reduce that stress.

> ### Le Châtelier's Principle
> When a stress (change in conditions) is placed on a reaction at equilibrium, the equilibrium will shift in the direction that relieves the stress.

Suppose we have two water tanks connected by a pipe. When the water levels in the tanks are equal, water flows in the forward direction from Tank A to Tank B at the same rate as it flows in the reverse direction from Tank B to Tank A. Suppose we add more water to Tank A. With a higher level of water in Tank A, more water flows in the forward direction from Tank A to Tank B than in the reverse direction from Tank B to Tank A, which is shown with a longer arrow. Eventually, equilibrium is reached as the levels in both tanks become equal, but higher than before. Then the rate of water flows equally between Tank A and Tank B.

At equilibrium, the water levels are equal.

Water added to tank A increases the rate of the forward direction.

Equilibrium is reached again when the water levels are equal.

Tank A   Tank B   Tank A   Tank B   Tank A   Tank B

The stress of adding water to tank A increases the rate of the forward direction to reestablish equal water levels and equilibrium.

Effect of Concentration Changes on Equilibrium

We will now use the reaction of H_2 and I_2 to illustrate how a change in concentration disturbs the equilibrium and how the system responds to that stress.

$$H_2(g) + I_2(g) \rightleftharpoons 2HI(g)$$

Suppose that more of the reactant H_2 is added to the equilibrium mixture, which increases the concentration of H_2. Because a K_c cannot change for a reaction at a given temperature, adding more H_2 places a stress on the system (see Figure 10.10). Then the system relieves this stress by increasing the rate of the forward reaction. Thus, more products are formed until the system is again at equilibrium. According to Le Châtelier's principle, adding more reactant causes the system to *shift* in the direction of the products until equilibrium is reestablished.

⚛ CORE CHEMISTRY SKILL

Using Le Châtelier's Principle

Add H_2

$$H_2(g) + I_2(g) \rightleftharpoons 2HI(g)$$

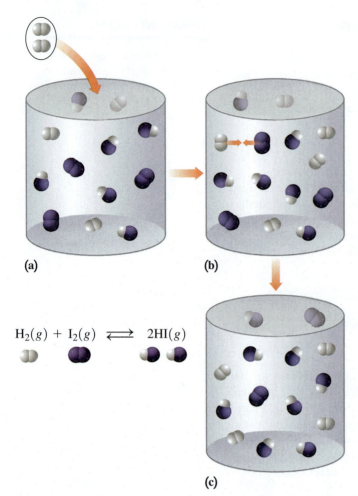

(a)

(b)

$$H_2(g) + I_2(g) \rightleftharpoons 2HI(g)$$

(c)

FIGURE 10.10 ▶ **(a)** The addition of H_2 places stress on the equilibrium system of $H_2(g) + I_2(g) \rightleftharpoons 2HI(g)$. **(b)** To relieve the stress, the forward reaction converts some reactants H_2 and I_2 to product HI. **(c)** A new equilibrium is established when the rates of the forward reaction and the reverse reaction become equal.

🔘 If more product HI is added, will the equilibrium shift in the direction of the products or reactants? Why?

TABLE 10.4 Effect of Concentration Changes on Equilibrium
$$H_2(g) + I_2(g) \rightleftharpoons 2HI(g)$$

Stress	Shift in the Direction of
Increase $[H_2]$	Products
Decrease $[H_2]$	Reactants
Increase $[I_2]$	Products
Decrease $[I_2]$	Reactants
Increase $[HI]$	Reactants
Decrease $[HI]$	Products

Suppose now that some H_2 is removed from the reaction mixture at equilibrium, which lowers the concentration of H_2 and slows the rate of the forward reaction. Using Le Châtelier's principle, we know that when some of the reactants are removed, the system will *shift* in the direction of the reactants until equilibrium is reestablished.

$$\overset{\text{Remove } H_2}{H_2(g) + I_2(g) \rightleftharpoons 2HI(g)}$$

The concentrations of the products of an equilibrium mixture can also increase or decrease. For example, if more HI is added, there is an increase in the rate of the reaction in the reverse direction, which converts some of the products to reactants. The concentration of the products decreases and the concentration of the reactants increases until equilibrium is reestablished. Using Le Châtelier's principle, we see that the addition of a product causes the system to *shift* in the direction of the reactants.

$$\overset{\text{Add HI}}{H_2(g) + I_2(g) \rightleftharpoons 2HI(g)}$$

In another example, some HI is removed from an equilibrium mixture, which decreases the concentration of the products. Then there is a *shift* in the direction of the products to reestablish equilibrium.

$$\overset{\text{Remove HI}}{H_2(g) + I_2(g) \rightleftharpoons 2HI(g)}$$

In summary, Le Châtelier's principle indicates that a stress caused by adding a substance at equilibrium is relieved when the equilibrium system shifts the reaction away from that substance. Adding more reactant causes an increase in the forward reaction to products. Adding more products causes an increase in the reverse reaction to reactants. When some of a substance is removed, the equilibrium system shifts in the direction of that substance. These features of Le Châtelier's principle are summarized in Table 10.4.

Effect of a Catalyst on Equilibrium

Sometimes a catalyst is added to a reaction to speed up a reaction by lowering the activation energy. As a result, the rates of both the forward and reverse reactions increase. The time required to reach equilibrium is shorter, but the same ratios of products and reactants are attained. Therefore, a catalyst speeds up the forward and reverse reactions, but it has no effect on the equilibrium mixture.

Effect of Volume Change on Equilibrium

If there is a change in the volume of a gas mixture at equilibrium, there will also be a change in the concentrations of those gases. Decreasing the volume will increase the concentration of gases, whereas increasing the volume will decrease their concentration. Then the system responds to reestablish equilibrium.

Let's look at the effect of decreasing the volume of the equilibrium mixture of the following reaction:

$$2CO(g) + O_2(g) \rightleftharpoons 2CO_2(g)$$

If we decrease the volume, all the concentrations increase. According to Le Châtelier's principle, the increase in concentration is relieved when the system shifts in the direction of the smaller number of moles.

$$\underset{\text{3 moles of gas}}{2CO(g) + O_2(g)} \quad \xrightarrow{\text{Decrease } V} \quad \underset{\text{2 moles of gas}}{2CO_2(g)}$$

On the other hand, when the volume of the equilibrium gas mixture increases, the concentrations of all the gases decrease. Then the system shifts in the direction of the greater number of moles to reestablish equilibrium (see Figure 10.11).

$$\underset{\text{3 moles of gas}}{2CO(g) + O_2(g)} \quad \xrightarrow{\text{Increase } V} \quad \underset{\text{2 moles of gas}}{2CO_2(g)}$$

When a reaction has the same number of moles of reactants as products, a volume change does not affect the equilibrium mixture because the concentrations of the reactants and products change in the same way.

$$\underset{\text{2 moles of gas}}{H_2(g) + I_2(g)} \rightleftharpoons \underset{\text{2 moles of gas}}{2HI(g)}$$

FIGURE 10.11 ▶ **(a)** A decrease in the volume of the container causes the system to shift in the direction of fewer moles of gas. **(b)** An increase in the volume of the container causes the system to shift in the direction of more moles of gas.

Q If you want to increase the products, should you increase or decrease the volume of the container?

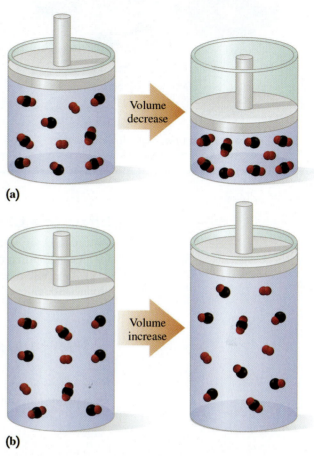

$$2CO(g) + O_2(g) \rightleftharpoons 2CO_2(g)$$

(a) Volume decrease

(b) Volume increase

Chemistry Link to **Health**
Oxygen–Hemoglobin Equilibrium and Hypoxia

The transport of oxygen involves an equilibrium between hemoglobin (Hb), oxygen, and oxyhemoglobin (HbO_2).

$$Hb(aq) + O_2(g) \rightleftharpoons HbO_2(aq)$$

When the O_2 level is high in the alveoli of the lung, the reaction shifts in the direction of the product HbO_2. In the tissues where O_2 concentration is low, the reverse reaction releases the oxygen from the hemoglobin. The equilibrium expression is written

$$K_c = \frac{[HbO_2]}{[Hb][O_2]}$$

At normal atmospheric pressure, oxygen diffuses into the blood because the partial pressure of oxygen in the alveoli is higher than that in the blood. At an altitude above 8000 ft, a decrease in the atmospheric pressure results in a significant reduction in the partial pressure of oxygen, which means that less oxygen is available for the blood and body tissues. The fall in atmospheric pressure at higher altitudes decreases the partial pressure of inhaled oxygen, and there is less driving pressure for gas exchange in the lungs. At an altitude of 18 000 ft, a person will obtain 29% less oxygen. When oxygen levels are lowered, a person may experience *hypoxia*, characterized by increased respiratory rate, headache, decreased mental acuteness, fatigue, decreased physical coordination, nausea, vomiting, and cyanosis. A similar problem occurs in persons with a history of lung disease that impairs gas diffusion in the alveoli or in persons with a reduced number of red blood cells, such as smokers.

According to Le Châtelier's principle, we see that a decrease in oxygen will shift the equilibrium in the direction of the reactants. Such a shift depletes the concentration of HbO_2 and causes the hypoxia.

$$Hb(aq) + O_2(g) \longleftarrow HbO_2(aq)$$

Immediate treatment of altitude sickness includes hydration, rest, and if necessary, descending to a lower altitude. The adaptation to lowered oxygen levels requires about 10 days. During this time the bone marrow increases red blood cell production, providing more red blood cells and more hemoglobin. A person living at a high altitude can have 50% more red blood cells than someone at sea level. This increase in hemoglobin causes a shift in the equilibrium back in the

Hypoxia may occur at high altitudes where the oxygen concentration is lower.

direction of HbO_2 product. Eventually, the higher concentration of HbO_2 will provide more oxygen to the tissues and the symptoms of hypoxia will lessen.

$$Hb(aq) + O_2(g) \longrightarrow HbO_2(aq)$$

For some who climb high mountains, it is important to stop and acclimatize for several days at increasing altitudes. At very high altitudes, it may be necessary to use an oxygen tank.

Effect of a Change in Temperature on Equilibrium

We can think of heat as a reactant or a product in a reaction. For example, in the equation for an endothermic reaction, heat is written on the reactant side. When the temperature of an endothermic reaction increases, the system responds by shifting in the direction of the products to remove heat.

$$\underset{\text{Increase } T}{N_2(g) + O_2(g) + \text{heat} \rightleftharpoons 2NO(g)}$$

If the temperature is decreased for an endothermic reaction, there is a decrease in heat. Then the system shifts in the direction of the reactants to add heat.

$$\underset{\text{Decrease } T}{N_2(g) + O_2(g) + \text{heat} \rightleftharpoons 2NO(g)}$$

In the equation for an exothermic reaction, heat is written on the product side. When the temperature of an exothermic reaction increases, the system responds by shifting in the direction of the reactants to remove heat.

$$\underset{\text{Increase } T}{2SO_2(g) + O_2(g) \rightleftharpoons 2SO_3(g) + \text{heat}}$$

If the temperature is decreased for an exothermic reaction, there is a decrease in heat. Then the system shifts in the direction of the products to add heat.

$$\underset{\text{Decrease } T}{2SO_2(g) + O_2(g) \rightleftharpoons 2SO_3(g) + \text{heat}}$$

Table 10.5 summarizes the ways we can use Le Châtelier's principle to determine the shift in equilibrium that relieves a stress caused by the change in a condition.

TABLE 10.5 Effects of Condition Changes on Equilibrium

Condition	Change (Stress)	Shift in the Direction of
Concentration	Add a reactant	Products (forward reaction)
	Remove a reactant	Reactants (reverse reaction)
	Add a product	Reactants (reverse reaction)
	Remove a product	Products (forward reaction)
Volume (container)	Decrease volume	Fewer moles of gas
	Increase volume	More moles of gas
Temperature	**Endothermic reaction**	
	Increase T	Products (forward reaction to remove heat)
	Decrease T	Reactants (reverse reaction to add heat)
	Exothermic reaction	
	Increase T	Reactants (reverse reaction to remove heat)
	Decrease T	Products (forward reaction to add heat)
Catalyst	Increases rates equally	No effect

▶ **SAMPLE PROBLEM 10.6 Using Le Châtelier's Principle**

Methanol, CH_3OH, is finding use as a fuel additive. Describe the effect of each of the following changes on the equilibrium mixture for the following reaction:

$$2CH_3OH(g) + 3O_2(g) \rightleftharpoons 2CO_2(g) + 4H_2O(g) + 1450 \text{ kJ}$$

a. adding more CO_2
b. adding more O_2
c. increasing the volume of the container
d. increasing the temperature
e. adding a catalyst

SOLUTION

a. When the concentration of the product CO_2 increases, the equilibrium shifts in the direction of the reactants.
b. When the concentration of the reactant O_2 increases, the equilibrium shifts in the direction of the products.
c. When the volume increases, the equilibrium shifts in the direction of the greater number of moles of gas, which is the products.
d. When the temperature is increased for an exothermic reaction, the equilibrium shifts in the direction of the reactants to remove heat.
e. When a catalyst is added, there is no change in the equilibrium mixture.

STUDY CHECK 10.6

Describe the effect of each of the following changes on the equilibrium mixture for the following reaction:

$$2HF(g) + Cl_2(g) + 357 \text{ kJ} \rightleftharpoons 2HCl(g) + F_2(g)$$

a. adding more Cl_2
b. decreasing the volume of the container
c. increasing the temperature

ANSWER

a. When the concentration of the reactant Cl_2 increases, the equilibrium shifts in the direction of the products.

b. There is no change in equilibrium mixture because the moles of reactant are equal to the moles of product.

c. When the temperature for an endothermic reaction increases, the equilibrium shifts to remove heat, which is in the direction of the products.

 # Chemistry Link to **Health**
Homeostasis: Regulation of Body Temperature

In a physiological system of equilibrium called *homeostasis*, changes in our environment are balanced by changes in our bodies. It is crucial to our survival that we balance heat gain with heat loss. If we do not lose enough heat, our body temperature rises. At high temperatures, the body can no longer regulate our metabolic reactions. If we lose too much heat, body temperature drops. At low temperatures, essential functions proceed too slowly.

The skin plays an important role in the maintenance of body temperature. When the outside temperature rises, receptors in the skin send signals to the brain. The temperature-regulating part of the brain stimulates the sweat glands to produce perspiration. As perspiration evaporates from the skin, heat is removed and the body temperature is decreased.

In cold temperatures, epinephrine is released, causing an increase in metabolic rate, which increases the production of heat. Receptors on the skin signal the brain to constrict the blood vessels. Less blood flows through the skin, and heat is conserved. The production of perspiration stops, thereby lessening the heat lost by evaporation.

Blood vessels dilate
• sweat production increases
• sweat evaporates
• skin cools

Blood vessels constrict and epinephrine is released
• metabolic activity increases
• muscular activity increases
• shivering occurs
• sweat production stops

QUESTIONS AND PROBLEMS

10.5 Changing Equilibrium Conditions: Le Châtelier's Principle

LEARNING GOAL Use Le Châtelier's principle to describe the changes made in equilibrium concentrations when reaction conditions change.

10.29 In the lower atmosphere, oxygen is converted to ozone (O_3) by the energy provided from lightning.

$$3O_2(g) + heat \rightleftharpoons 2O_3(g)$$

For each of the following changes at equilibrium, indicate whether the equilibrium shifts in the direction of products, reactants, or does not change:

a. adding more $O_2(g)$
b. adding more $O_3(g)$
c. increasing the temperature
d. increasing the volume of the container
e. adding a catalyst

10.30 Ammonia is produced by reacting nitrogen gas and hydrogen gas.

$$N_2(g) + 3H_2(g) \rightleftharpoons 2NH_3(g) + 92 \text{ kJ}$$

For each of the following changes at equilibrium, indicate whether the equilibrium shifts in the direction of products, reactants, or does not change:

a. removing some $N_2(g)$
b. decreasing the temperature
c. adding more $NH_3(g)$
d. adding more $H_2(g)$
e. increasing the volume of the container

10.31 Hydrogen chloride can be made by reacting hydrogen gas and chlorine gas.

$$H_2(g) + Cl_2(g) + heat \rightleftharpoons 2HCl(g)$$

For each of the following changes at equilibrium, indicate whether the equilibrium shifts in the direction of products, reactants, or does not change:

a. adding more $H_2(g)$
b. increasing the temperature
c. removing some $HCl(g)$
d. adding a catalyst
e. removing some $Cl_2(g)$

10.32 When heated, carbon monoxide reacts with water to produce carbon dioxide and hydrogen.

$$CO(g) + H_2O(g) \rightleftharpoons CO_2(g) + H_2(g) + \text{heat}$$

For each of the following changes at equilibrium, indicate whether the equilibrium shifts in the direction of products, reactants, or does not change:
a. decreasing the temperature
b. adding more $H_2(g)$
c. removing $CO_2(g)$ as its forms
d. adding more $H_2O(g)$
e. decreasing the volume of the container

℞ Clinical Applications

Use the following equation for the equilibrium of hemoglobin in the blood to answer problems 10.33 and 10.34:

$$Hb(aq) + O_2(g) \rightleftharpoons HbO_2(aq)$$

10.33 Athletes who train at high altitudes initially experience hypoxia, which causes their body to produce more hemoglobin. When an athlete first arrives at high altitude,
a. What is the stress on the hemoglobin equilibrium?
b. In what direction does the hemoglobin equilibrium shift?

10.34 A person who has been a smoker and has a low oxygen blood saturation uses an oxygen tank for supplemental oxygen. When oxygen is first supplied,
a. What is the stress on the hemoglobin equilibrium?
b. In what direction does the hemoglobin equilibrium shift?

Clinical Update
An Iron-Rich Diet for Children's Anemia

Today, Andrew is a thriving two-year old toddler. However, his mother is concerned that Andrew looks pale, seems to have some trouble breathing, has a lot of headaches, and generally seems tired. At the clinic, Andrew and his mother see Judy, his neonatal nurse when he was an infant. Judy notes his symptoms and takes a blood sample, which shows that Andrew has *iron-deficiency anemia*. Judy explains to his mother that Andrew's red-blood cell count is below normal, which means that he has a low concentration of hemoglobin in his blood.

Hemoglobin, present in our red blood cells, is an iron-containing protein that carries oxygen from our lungs to the muscles and tissues of our body. Each hemoglobin molecule contains four heme or iron-containing groups. Because each heme group can attach to one O_2 in the lungs, one hemoglobin can carry as many as four O_2 molecules. The transport of oxygen involves an equilibrium reaction between the reactants Hb and O_2 and the product HbO_2.

$$Hb(aq) + O_2(g) \rightleftharpoons HbO_2(aq)$$

The equilibrium expression can be written

$$K_c = \frac{[HbO_2]}{[Hb][O_2]}$$

In the alveoli of the lungs where the O_2 concentration is high, the forward reaction is faster, which shifts the equilibrium in the direction of the product HbO_2. As a result, O_2 binds to hemoglobin in the lungs.

$$Hb(aq) + O_2(g) \longrightarrow HbO_2(aq)$$

In the tissues and the muscles where the O_2 concentration is low, the reverse reaction is faster, which shifts the equilibrium in the direction of the reactant Hb and releases the oxygen from the hemoglobin.

$$Hb(aq) + O_2(g) \longleftarrow HbO_2(aq)$$

Judy recommends to Andrew's mother that his diet include more high iron-containing foods such as chicken, fish, spinach, iron-fortified cereal, eggs, peas, beans, peanut butter, and whole-grain bread. After three months of an iron-rich diet, Andrew's hemoglobin was within normal range.

In the lungs, Hb binds O_2.

O_2 is carried as HbO_2 by red cells from the lungs to the tissues and muscles.

In the tissues and muscles, HbO_2 releases O_2.

℞ Clinical Applications

10.35 For the hemoglobin equilibrium, indicate if each of the following changes shifts the equilibrium in the direction of the products, the reactants, or does not change:
a. increasing $[O_2]$
b. increasing $[HbO_2]$
c. decreasing $[Hb]$

10.36 For the hemoglobin equilibrium, indicate if each of the following changes shifts the equilibrium in the direction of the products, the reactants, or does not change:

a. decreasing $[O_2]$
b. increasing $[Hb]$
c. decreasing $[HbO_2]$

10.37 Andrew is diagnosed as being anemic. Why does Andrew not obtain sufficient oxygen in his tissues?

10.38 Andrew's diet is changed to include more iron-rich foods. How would an increase in iron affect his hemoglobin equilibrium?

CONCEPT MAP

REACTION RATES AND CHEMICAL EQUILIBRIUM

involves

Reaction Rates

are affected by

Concentrations of Reactants

Temperature

Catalyst

Reversible Reactions

when equal in rate give

Equilibrium Constant Expression

is written as

$$K_c = \frac{\text{Products}}{\text{Reactants}}$$

Small K_c Has Mostly Reactants

Large K_c Has Mostly Products

Le Châtelier's Principle

indicates that equilibrium adjusts for changes in

Concentration, Temperature, and Volume

CHAPTER REVIEW

10.1 Rates of Reactions
LEARNING GOAL
Describe how temperature, concentration, and catalysts affect the rate of a reaction.

- The rate of a reaction is the speed at which the reactants are converted to products.
- Increasing the concentrations of reactants, increasing the temperature, or adding a catalyst can increase the rate of a reaction.

10.2 Chemical Equilibrium
LEARNING GOAL Use the concept of reversible reactions to explain chemical equilibrium.

- Chemical equilibrium occurs in a reversible reaction when the rate of the forward reaction becomes equal to the rate of the reverse reaction.
- At equilibrium, no further change occurs in the concentrations of the reactants and products as the forward and reverse reactions continue.

10.3 Equilibrium Constants
LEARNING GOAL Calculate the equilibrium constant for a reversible reaction given the concentrations of reactants and products at equilibrium.

- An equilibrium constant, K_c, is the ratio of the concentrations of the products to the concentrations of the reactants, with each concentration raised to a power equal to its coefficient in the balanced chemical equation.

10.4 Using Equilibrium Constants
LEARNING GOAL Use an equilibrium constant to predict the extent of reaction and to calculate equilibrium concentrations.

- A large value of K_c indicates that an equilibrium mixture contains mostly products and few reactants, whereas a small value of K_c indicates that the equilibrium mixture contains mostly reactants.
- Equilibrium constants can be used to calculate the concentration of a component in the equilibrium mixture.

10.5 Changing Equilibrium Conditions: Le Châtelier's Principle
LEARNING GOAL Use Le Châtelier's principle to describe the changes made in equilibrium concentrations when reaction conditions change.

- When reactants are removed or products are added to an equilibrium mixture, the system shifts in the direction of the reactants.
- When reactants are added or products are removed from an equilibrium mixture, the system shifts in the direction of the products.

- A decrease in the volume of a reaction container causes a shift in the direction of the smaller number of moles of gas.
- An increase in the volume of a reaction container causes a shift in the direction of the greater number of moles of gas.

- Increasing the temperature of an endothermic reaction or decreasing the temperature of an exothermic reaction will cause the system to shift in the direction of products.
- Decreasing the temperature of an endothermic reaction or increasing the temperature of an exothermic reaction will cause the system to shift in the direction of reactants.

KEY TERMS

activation energy The energy that must be provided by a collision to break apart the bonds of the reacting molecules.
catalyst A substance that increases the rate of reaction by lowering the activation energy.
chemical equilibrium The point at which the rate of forward and reverse reactions are equal so that no further change in concentrations of reactants and products takes place.
collision theory A model for a chemical reaction stating that molecules must collide with sufficient energy and proper orientation to form products.
equilibrium constant, K_c The numerical value obtained by substituting the equilibrium concentrations of the components into the equilibrium constant expression.

equilibrium constant expression The ratio of the concentrations of products to the concentrations of reactants, with each component raised to an exponent equal to the coefficient of that compound in the balanced chemical equation.
Le Châtelier's principle When a stress is placed on a system at equilibrium, the equilibrium shifts to relieve that stress.
rate of reaction The speed at which reactants are used to form product(s).
reversible reaction A reaction in which a forward reaction occurs from reactants to products, and a reverse reaction occurs from products back to reactants.

⚛ CORE CHEMISTRY SKILLS

The chapter section containing each Core Chemistry Skill is shown in parentheses at the end of each heading.

Writing the Equilibrium Constant Expression (10.3)

- An equilibrium constant expression for a reversible reaction is written by multiplying the concentrations of the products in the numerator and dividing by the product of the concentrations of the reactants in the denominator.
- Each concentration is raised to a power equal to its coefficient in the balanced chemical equation:

$$K_c = \frac{[\text{Products}]}{[\text{Reactants}]} = \frac{[C]^c [D]^d}{[A]^a [B]^b} \text{Coefficients}$$

Example: Write the equilibrium constant expression for the following chemical reaction:

$$2NO_2(g) \rightleftharpoons N_2O_4(g)$$

Answer: $K_c = \dfrac{[N_2O_4]}{[NO_2]^2}$

Calculating an Equilibrium Constant (10.3)

- The equilibrium constant, K_c, is the numerical value obtained by substituting experimentally measured molar concentrations at equilibrium into the equilibrium constant expression.

Example: Calculate the numerical value of K_c for the following reaction when the equilibrium mixture contains 0.025 M NO_2 and 0.087 M N_2O_4:

$$2NO_2(g) \rightleftharpoons N_2O_4(g)$$

Answer: Write the equilibrium constant expression, substitute the molar concentrations, and calculate.

$$K_c = \frac{[N_2O_4]}{[NO_2]^2} = \frac{[0.087]}{[0.025]^2} = 140$$

Calculating Equilibrium Concentrations (10.4)

- To determine the concentration of a product or a reactant at equilibrium, we use the equilibrium constant expression to solve for the unknown concentration.

Example: Calculate the equilibrium concentration for CF_4 if $K_c = 2.0$, and the equilibrium mixture contains 0.10 M COF_2 and 0.050 M CO_2.

$$2COF_2(g) \rightleftharpoons CO_2(g) + CF_4(g)$$

Answer: Write the equilibrium constant expression.

$$K_c = \frac{[CO_2][CF_4]}{[COF_2]^2}$$

Rearrange the equation, substitute the molar concentrations, and calculate $[CF_4]$.

$$[CF_4] = \frac{K_c [COF_2]^2}{[CO_2]} = \frac{2.0 [0.10]^2}{[0.050]} = 0.40 \text{ M}$$

Using Le Châtelier's Principle (10.5)

- Le Châtelier's principle states that when a system at equilibrium is disturbed by changes in concentration, volume, or temperature, the system will shift in the direction that will reduce that stress.

Example: Nitrogen and oxygen form dinitrogen pentoxide in an exothermic, combination reaction.

$$2N_2(g) + 5O_2(g) \rightleftharpoons 2N_2O_5(g) + \text{heat}$$

For each of the following changes at equilibrium, indicate whether the equilibrium shifts in the direction of products, reactants, or does not change:

a. removing some $N_2(g)$
b. decreasing the temperature
c. increasing the volume of the container

Answer: **a.** Removing a reactant shifts the equilibrium in the direction of the reactants.

b. Decreasing the temperature shifts the equilibrium of an exothermic reaction in the direction of the products, which produces heat.

c. Increasing the volume of the container shifts the equilibrium in the direction of the greater number of moles of gas, which is in the direction of the reactants.

UNDERSTANDING THE CONCEPTS

The chapter sections to review are shown in parentheses at the end of each question.

10.39 Write the equilibrium constant expression for each of the following reactions: (10.3)
  a. $CH_4(g) + 2O_2(g) \rightleftharpoons CO_2(g) + 2H_2O(g)$
  b. $4NH_3(g) + 3O_2(g) \rightleftharpoons 2N_2(g) + 6H_2O(g)$
  c. $C(s) + 2H_2(g) \rightleftharpoons CH_4(g)$

10.40 Write the equilibrium constant expression for each of the following reactions: (10.3)
  a. $2C_2H_6(g) + 7O_2(g) \rightleftharpoons 4CO_2(g) + 6H_2O(g)$
  b. $2KHCO_3(s) \rightleftharpoons K_2CO_3(s) + CO_2(g) + H_2O(g)$
  c. $4NH_3(g) + 5O_2(g) \rightleftharpoons 4NO(g) + 6H_2O(g)$

10.41 Would the equilibrium constant, K_c, for the reaction in the diagrams have a large or small value? (10.4)

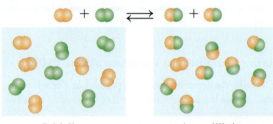

| Initially | At equilibrium |

10.42 Would the equilibrium constant, K_c, for the reaction in the diagrams have a large or small value? (10.4)

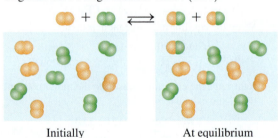

| Initially | At equilibrium |

10.43 Would T_2 be higher or lower than T_1 for the reaction shown in the diagrams? (10.5)

| $T_1 = 300\ ^\circ C$ | $T_2 = ?$ |

10.44 Would the reaction shown in the diagrams be exothermic or endothermic? (10.5)

| $T_1 = 100\ ^\circ C$ | $T_2 = 200\ ^\circ C$ |

ADDITIONAL QUESTIONS AND PROBLEMS

10.45 For each of the following changes at equilibrium, indicate whether the equilibrium shifts in the direction of products, reactants, or does not change: (10.5)

$$C_2H_4(g) + Cl_2(g) \rightleftharpoons C_2H_4Cl_2(g) + heat$$

  a. increasing the temperature of the reaction
  b. decreasing the volume of the reaction container
  c. adding a catalyst
  d. adding more $Cl_2(g)$

10.46 For each of the following changes at equilibrium, indicate whether the equilibrium shifts in the direction of products, reactants, or does not change: (10.5)

$$N_2(g) + O_2(g) + heat \rightleftharpoons 2NO(g)$$

  a. increasing the temperature of the reaction
  b. decreasing the volume of the reaction container
  c. adding a catalyst
  d. adding more $N_2(g)$

10.47 For each of the following reactions, indicate if the equilibrium mixture contains mostly products, mostly reactants, or both reactants and products: (10.4)
  a. $H_2(g) + Cl_2(g) \rightleftharpoons 2HCl(g)$ $K_c = 1.3 \times 10^{34}$
  b. $2NOBr(g) \rightleftharpoons 2NO(g) + Br_2(g)$ $K_c = 2.0$
  c. $2NOCl(g) \rightleftharpoons Cl_2(g) + 2NO(g)$ $K_c = 2.7 \times 10^{-9}$
  d. $C(s) + H_2O(g) \rightleftharpoons CO(g) + H_2(g)$ $K_c = 6.3 \times 10^{-1}$

10.48 For each of the following reactions, indicate if the equilibrium mixture contains mostly products, mostly reactants, or both reactants and products: (10.4)
  a. $2H_2O(g) \rightleftharpoons 2H_2(g) + O_2(g)$ $K_c = 4 \times 10^{-48}$
  b. $N_2(g) + 3H_2(g) \rightleftharpoons 2NH_3(g)$ $K_c = 0.30$
  c. $2SO_2(g) + O_2(g) \rightleftharpoons 2SO_3(g)$ $K_c = 1.2 \times 10^9$
  d. $H_2(g) + S(s) \rightleftharpoons 2H_2S(g)$ $K_c = 7.8 \times 10^5$

10.49 Consider the reaction: (10.3)

$$2NH_3(g) \rightleftharpoons N_2(g) + 3H_2(g)$$

  a. Write the equilibrium constant expression.
  b. What is the numerical value of K_c for the reaction if the concentrations at equilibrium are 0.20 M NH_3, 3.0 M N_2, and 0.50 M H_2?

10.50 Consider the reaction: (10.3)

$$2SO_2(g) + O_2(g) \rightleftharpoons 2SO_3(g)$$

  a. Write the equilibrium constant expression.
  b. What is the numerical value of K_c for the reaction if the concentrations at equilibrium are 0.10 M SO_2, 0.12 M O_2, and 0.60 M SO_3?

10.51 The K_c for the following reaction is 5.0 at 100 °C. If an equilibrium mixture contains 0.50 M NO_2, what is the molar concentration of N_2O_4? (10.3, 10.4)

$$2NO_2(g) \rightleftharpoons N_2O_4(g)$$

10.52 The K_c for the following reaction is 15 at 220 °C. If an equilibrium mixture contains 0.40 M CO and 0.20 M H_2, what is the molar concentration of CH_3OH? (10.3, 10.4)

$$CO(g) + 2H_2(g) \rightleftharpoons CH_3OH(g)$$

10.53 According to Le Châtelier's principle, does the equilibrium shift in the direction of products or reactants when O_2 is added to the equilibrium mixture of each of the following reactions? (10.5)
  a. $3O_2(g) \rightleftharpoons 2O_3(g)$
  b. $2CO_2(g) \rightleftharpoons 2CO(g) + O_2(g)$
  c. $2SO_2(g) + O_2(g) \rightleftharpoons 2SO_3(g)$
  d. $2SO_2(g) + 2H_2O(g) \rightleftharpoons H_2S(g) + 3O_2(g)$

10.54 According to Le Châtelier's principle, does the equilibrium shift in the direction of products or reactants when N_2 is added to the equilibrium mixture of each of the following reactions? (10.5)
  a. $2NH_3(g) \rightleftharpoons 3H_2(g) + N_2(g)$
  b. $N_2(g) + O_2(g) \rightleftharpoons 2NO(g)$
  c. $2NO_2(g) \rightleftharpoons N_2(g) + 2O_2(g)$
  d. $4NH_3(g) + 3O_2(g) \rightleftharpoons 2N_2(g) + 6H_2O(g)$

10.55 Would decreasing the volume of the container for each of the following reactions cause the equilibrium to shift in the direction of products, reactants, or not change? (10.5)
  a. $3O_2(g) \rightleftharpoons 2O_3(g)$
  b. $2CO_2(g) \rightleftharpoons 2CO(g) + O_2(g)$
  c. $P_4(g) + 5O_2(g) \rightleftharpoons P_4O_{10}(s)$
  d. $2SO_2(g) + 2H_2O(g) \rightleftharpoons 2H_2S(g) + 3O_2(g)$

10.56 Would increasing the volume of the container for each of the following reactions cause the equilibrium to shift in the direction of products, reactants, or not change? (10.5)
  a. $2NH_3(g) \rightleftharpoons 3H_2(g) + N_2(g)$
  b. $N_2(g) + O_2(g) \rightleftharpoons 2NO(g)$
  c. $N_2(g) + 2O_2(g) \rightleftharpoons 2NO_2(g)$
  d. $4NH_3(g) + 3O_2(g) \rightleftharpoons 2N_2(g) + 6H_2O(g)$

CHALLENGE QUESTIONS

The following groups of questions are related to the topics in this chapter. However, they do not all follow the chapter order, and they require you to combine concepts and skills from several sections. These questions will help you increase your critical thinking skills and prepare for your next exam.

10.57 For each of the following K_c values, indicate whether the equilibrium mixture contains mostly reactants, mostly products, or similar amounts of reactants and products: (10.4)
  a. $N_2(g) + O_2(g) \rightleftharpoons 2NO(g)$ $K_c = 1 \times 10^{-30}$
  b. $H_2(g) + Br_2(g) \rightleftharpoons 2HBr(g)$ $K_c = 2.0 \times 10^{19}$

10.58 For each of the following K_c values, indicate whether the equilibrium mixture contains mostly reactants, mostly products, or similar amounts of reactants and products: (10.4)
  a. $Cl_2(g) + 2NO(g) \rightleftharpoons 2NOCl(g)$ $K_c = 3.7 \times 10^8$
  b. $N_2(g) + 2H_2(g) \rightleftharpoons 2N_2H_4(g)$ $K_c = 7.4 \times 10^{-26}$

10.59 The K_c at 100 °C is 2.0 for the decomposition reaction of NOBr. (10.3, 10.4, 10.5)

$$2NOBr(g) \rightleftharpoons 2NO(g) + Br_2(g)$$

In an experiment, 1.0 mole of NOBr, 1.0 mole of NO, and 1.0 mole of Br_2 were placed in a 1.0 L container.
  a. Write the equilibrium constant expression for the reaction.
  b. Is the system at equilibrium?
  c. If not, will the rate of the forward or reverse reaction initially speed up?
  d. At equilibrium, which concentration(s) will be greater than 1.0 mole/L, and which will be less than 1.0 mole/L?

10.60 Consider the following reaction: (10.3, 10.4, 10.5)

$$PCl_5(g) \rightleftharpoons PCl_3(g) + Cl_2(g)$$

  a. Write the equilibrium constant expression for the reaction.
  b. Initially, 0.60 mole of PCl_5 is placed in a 1.0 L flask. At equilibrium, there is 0.16 mole of PCl_3 in the flask. What are the equilibrium concentrations of PCl_5 and Cl_2?
  c. What is the numerical value of the equilibrium constant, K_c, for the reaction?
  d. If 0.20 mole of Cl_2 is added to the equilibrium mixture, will the concentration of PCl_5 increase or decrease?

10.61 Indicate how each of the following will affect the equilibrium concentration of NH_3 in the following reaction: (10.3, 10.5)

$$2NH_3(g) + 46\ kJ \rightleftharpoons N_2(g) + 3H_2(g)$$

  a. adding more $H_2(g)$
  b. increasing the temperature of the reaction
  c. increasing the volume of the container
  d. decreasing the volume of the container
  e. adding a catalyst

10.62 Indicate how each of the following will affect the equilibrium concentration of NH_3 in the following reaction: (10.3, 10.5)

$$4NH_3(g) + 5O_2(g) \rightleftharpoons 4NO(g) + 6H_2O(g) + 906\ kJ$$

  a. adding more $O_2(g)$
  b. increasing the temperature of the reaction
  c. increasing the volume of the container
  d. adding more $NO(g)$
  e. removing some $H_2O(g)$

10.63 Indicate if you would increase or decrease the volume of the container to *increase* the yield of the products in each of the following: (10.5)
   a. $2SO_2(g) + O_2(g) \rightleftharpoons 2SO_3(g)$
   b. $2CH_4(g) \rightleftharpoons C_2H_2(g) + 3H_2(g)$
   c. $2H_2(g) + O_2(g) \rightleftharpoons 2H_2O(g)$

10.64 Indicate if you would increase or decrease the volume of the container to *increase* the yield of the products in each of the following: (10.5)
   a. $Cl_2(g) + 2NO(g) \rightleftharpoons 2NOCl(g)$
   b. $N_2(g) + 2H_2(g) \rightleftharpoons N_2H_4(g)$
   c. $N_2O_4(g) \rightleftharpoons 2NO_2(g)$

ANSWERS

Answers to Selected Questions and Problems

10.1 a. The rate of the reaction indicates how fast the products form or how fast the reactants are used up.
   b. At room temperature, the reactions involved in the growth of bread mold will proceed at a faster rate than at the lower temperature of the refrigerator.

10.3 The number of collisions will increase when the number of Br_2 molecules is increased.

10.5 a. increase   **b.** increase
   c. increase   **d.** decrease

10.7 A reversible reaction is one in which a forward reaction converts reactants to products, whereas a reverse reaction converts products to reactants.

10.9 a. not at equilibrium   **b.** at equilibrium
   c. at equilibrium

10.11 The reaction has reached equilibrium because the number of reactants and products does not change.

10.13 a. $K_c = \dfrac{[CS_2][H_2]^4}{[CH_4][H_2S]^2}$ **b.** $K_c = \dfrac{[N_2][O_2]}{[NO]^2}$

   c. $K_c = \dfrac{[CS_2][O_2]^4}{[SO_3]^2[CO_2]}$ **d.** $K_c = \dfrac{[H_2]^3[CO]}{[CH_4][H_2O]}$

10.15 $K_c = \dfrac{[XY]^2}{[X_2][Y_2]} = 36$

10.17 $K_c = 1.5$

10.19 $K_c = 260$

10.21 Diagram **B** represents the equilibrium mixture.

10.23 a. mostly products   **b.** mostly products
   c. mostly reactants

10.25 $[H_2] = 1.1 \times 10^{-3}$ M

10.27 $[NOBr] = 1.4$ M

10.29 a. Equilibrium shifts in the direction of the product.
   b. Equilibrium shifts in the direction of the reactants.
   c. Equilibrium shifts in the direction of the product.
   d. Equilibrium shifts in the direction of the reactants.
   e. No shift in equilibrium occurs.

10.31 a. Equilibrium shifts in the direction of the product.
   b. Equilibrium shifts in the direction of the product.
   c. Equilibrium shifts in the direction of the product.
   d. No shift in equilibrium occurs.
   e. Equilibrium shifts in the direction of the reactants.

10.33 a. The oxygen concentration is lowered.
   b. Equilibrium shifts in the direction of the reactants.

10.35 a. Equilibrium shifts in the direction of products.
   b. Equilibrium shifts in the direction of reactants.
   c. Equilibrium shifts in the direction of reactants.

10.37 Without enough iron, Andrew will not have sufficient hemoglobin. When Hb is decreased, the equilibrium shifts in the direction of the reactants, Hb and O_2.

10.39 a. $K_c = \dfrac{[CO_2][H_2O]^2}{[CH_4][O_2]^2}$ **b.** $K_c = \dfrac{[N_2]^2[H_2O]^6}{[NH_3]^4[O_2]^3}$

   c. $K_c = \dfrac{[CH_4]}{[H_2]^2}$

10.41 The equilibrium constant for the reaction would have a large value.

10.43 T_2 is lower than T_1.

10.45 a. Equilibrium shifts in the direction of the reactants.
   b. Equilibrium shifts in the direction of the products.
   c. There is no change in equilibrium.
   d. Equilibrium shifts in the direction of the products.

10.47 a. mostly products
   b. both reactants and products
   c. mostly reactants
   d. both reactants and products

10.49 a. $K_c = \dfrac{[N_2][H_2]^3}{[NH_3]^2}$ **b.** $K_c = 9.4$

10.51 $[N_2O_4] = 1.3$ M

10.53 a. Equilibrium shifts in the direction of the products.
   b. Equilibrium shifts in the direction of the reactants.
   c. Equilibrium shifts in the direction of the products.
   d. Equilibrium shifts in the direction of the reactants.

10.55 a. Equilibrium shifts in the direction of the products.
   b. Equilibrium shifts in the direction of the reactants.
   c. Equilibrium shifts in the direction of the products.
   d. Equilibrium shifts in the direction of the reactants.

10.57 a. A small K_c value indicates that the equilibrium mixture contains mostly reactants.
   b. A large K_c value indicates that the equilibrium mixture contains mostly products.

10.59 a. $K_c = \dfrac{[NO]^2[Br_2]}{[NOBr]^2}$
   b. When the concentrations are placed in the expression, the result is 1.0, which is not equal to K_c. The system is not at equilibrium.
   c. The rate of the forward reaction will increase.
   d. The $[Br_2]$ and $[NO]$ will increase and $[NOBr]$ will decrease.

10.61 a. increase   **b.** decrease
   c. decrease   **d.** increase
   e. no change

10.63 a. decrease   **b.** increase
   c. decrease

11

Acids and Bases

A 30-YEAR-OLD MAN HAS BEEN BROUGHT TO THE

emergency room after an automobile accident. The emergency room nurses are tending to the patient, Larry, who is unresponsive. A blood sample is taken then sent to Brianna, a clinical laboratory technician, who begins the process of analyzing the pH, the partial pressures of O_2 and CO_2, and the concentrations of glucose and electrolytes.

Within minutes, Brianna determines that Larry's blood pH is 7.30 and the partial pressure of CO_2 gas is above the desired level. Blood pH is typically in the range of 7.35 to 7.45, and a value less than 7.35 indicates a state of acidosis. Respiratory acidosis occurs because an increase in the partial pressure of CO_2 gas in the bloodstream prevents the biochemical buffers in blood from making a change in the pH.

Brianna recognizes these signs and immediately contacts the emergency room to inform them that Larry's airway may be blocked. In the emergency room, they provide Larry with an IV containing bicarbonate to increase the blood pH and begin the process of unblocking his airway. Shortly afterward, Larry's airway is cleared, and his blood pH and partial pressure of CO_2 gas return to normal.

CAREER Clinical Laboratory Technician

Clinical laboratory technicians, also known as medical laboratory technicians, perform a wide variety of tests on body fluids and cells that help in the diagnosis and treatment of patients. These tests range from determining blood concentrations of glucose and cholesterol to determining drug levels in the blood for transplant patients or a patient undergoing treatment. Clinical laboratory technicians also prepare specimens in the detection of cancerous tumors, and type blood samples for transfusions. Clinical laboratory technicians must also interpret and analyze the test results, which are then passed on to the physician.

11.1   Acids and Bases 400

11.2   Brønsted–Lowry Acids and Bases 403

11.3   Strengths of Acids and Bases 406

11.4   Dissociation Constants for Acids and Bases 411

11.5   Dissociation of Water 413

11.6   The pH Scale 416

❤   **Chemistry Link to Health** *Stomach Acid, HCl* 422

11.7   Reactions of Acids and Bases 423

❤   **Chemistry Link to Health** *Antacids* 424

11.8   Acid–Base Titration 425

11.9   Buffers 427

❤   **Chemistry Link to Health** *Buffers in the Blood Plasma* 430

℞   **Clinical Applications** 416, 422, 432, 437, 438, 441

℞   **Clinical Update** *Acid Reflux Disease* 432

Acids and bases are important substances in health, industry, and the environment. One of the most common characteristics of acids is their sour taste. Lemons and grapefruits taste sour because they contain acids such as citric and ascorbic acid (vitamin C). Vinegar tastes sour because it contains acetic acid. We produce lactic acid in our muscles when we exercise. Acid from bacteria turns milk sour in the production of yogurt and cottage cheese. We have hydrochloric acid in our stomachs that helps us digest food. Sometimes we take antacids, which are bases such as sodium bicarbonate or milk of magnesia, to neutralize the effects of too much stomach acid.

In the environment, the acidity, or pH, of rain, water, and soil can have significant effects. When rain becomes too acidic, it can dissolve marble statues and accelerate the corrosion of metals. In lakes and ponds, the acidity of water can affect the ability of plants and fish to survive. The acidity of soil around plants affects their

Citrus fruits are sour because of the presence of acids.

growth. If the soil pH is too acidic or too basic, the roots of the plant cannot take up some nutrients. Most plants thrive in soil with a nearly neutral pH, although certain plants, such as orchids, camellias, and blueberries, require a more acidic soil.

The pH of a solution describes its acidity. The lungs and the kidneys are the primary organs that regulate the pH of body fluids, including blood and urine. Major changes in the pH of the body fluids can severely affect biological activities within the cells. Buffers are present to prevent large fluctuations in pH.

CHAPTER READINESS*

🖩 **KEY MATH SKILLS**
- Solving Equations (1.4D)
- Writing Numbers in Scientific Notation (1.4F)

⚛ **CORE CHEMISTRY SKILLS**
- Writing Ionic Formulas (6.2)
- Balancing a Chemical Equation (7.1)

- Using Concentration as a Conversion Factor (9.4)
- Writing the Equilibrium Constant Expression (10.3)
- Calculating Equilibrium Concentrations (10.4)
- Using Le Châtelier's Principle (10.5)

*These Key Math Skills and Core Chemistry Skills from previous chapters are listed here for your review as you proceed to the new material in this chapter.

LEARNING GOAL

Describe and name acids and bases.

11.1 Acids and Bases

The term *acid* comes from the Latin word *acidus*, which means "sour." We are familiar with the sour tastes of vinegar and lemons and other common acids in foods.

In 1887, the Swedish chemist Svante Arrhenius was the first to describe **acids** as substances that produce hydrogen ions (H^+) when they dissolve in water. Because acids produce ions in water, they are also electrolytes. For example, hydrogen chloride dissociates in water to give hydrogen ions, H^+, and chloride ions, Cl^-. It is the hydrogen ions that give acids a sour taste, change the blue litmus indicator to red, and corrode some metals.

$$HCl(g) \xrightarrow{\;H_2O\;} H^+(aq) + Cl^-(aq)$$

Polar molecular compound   Dissociation   Hydrogen ion

Naming Acids

Acids dissolve in water to produce hydrogen ions, along with a negative ion that may be a simple nonmetal anion or a polyatomic ion. When an acid dissolves in water to produce a hydrogen ion and a simple nonmetal anion, the prefix *hydro* is used before the name of the nonmetal, and its *ide* ending is changed to *ic acid*. For example, hydrogen chloride (HCl) dissolves in water to form $HCl(aq)$, which is named hydrochloric acid. An exception is hydrogen cyanide (HCN), which as an acid is named hydrocyanic acid, $HCN(aq)$.

When an acid contains oxygen, it dissolves in water to produce a hydrogen ion and an oxygen-containing polyatomic anion. The most common form of an oxygen-containing acid has a name that ends with *ic acid*. The name of its polyatomic anion ends in *ate*. If the acid contains a polyatomic ion with an *ite* ending, its name ends in *ous acid*.

The halogens in Group 7A (17) can form more than two oxygen-containing acids. For chlorine, the common form is chloric acid, $HClO_3$, which contains the chlorate polyatomic ion (ClO_3^-). For the acid that contains one more oxygen atom than the common form, the prefix *per* is used; $HClO_4$ is named *perchloric acid*. When the polyatomic ion in the acid has one oxygen atom less than the common form, the suffix *ous* is used. Thus, $HClO_2$ is named *chlorous acid*; it contains the chlorite ion, ClO_2^-. The prefix *hypo* is used for the acid that has two oxygen atoms less than the common form; $HClO$ is named *hypochlorous acid*. The names of some common acids and their anions are listed in Table 11.1.

TABLE 11.1 Names of Common Acids and Their Anions

Acid	Name of Acid	Anion	Name of Anion
HCl	**Hydro**chlor**ic acid**	Cl^-	Chloride
HBr	**Hydro**brom**ic acid**	Br^-	Bromide
HI	**Hydro**iod**ic acid**	I^-	Iodide
HCN	**Hydro**cyan**ic acid**	CN^-	Cyanide
HNO_3	Nitr**ic acid**	NO_3^-	Nitrate
HNO_2	Nitr**ous acid**	NO_2^-	Nitrite
H_2SO_4	Sulfur**ic acid**	SO_4^{2-}	Sulfate
H_2SO_3	Sulfur**ous acid**	SO_3^{2-}	Sulfite
H_2CO_3	Carbon**ic acid**	CO_3^{2-}	Carbonate
$HC_2H_3O_2$	Acet**ic acid**	$C_2H_3O_2^-$	Acetate
H_3PO_4	Phosphor**ic acid**	PO_4^{3-}	Phosphate
H_3PO_3	Phosphor**ous acid**	PO_3^{3-}	Phosphite
$HClO_3$	Chlor**ic acid**	ClO_3^-	Chlorate
$HClO_2$	Chlor**ous acid**	ClO_2^-	Chlorite

Sulfuric acid dissolves in water to produce one or two H^+ and an anion.

Bases

You may be familiar with some household bases such as antacids, drain openers, and oven cleaners. According to the Arrhenius theory, **bases** are ionic compounds that dissociate into cations and hydroxide ions (OH^-) when they dissolve in water. They are another example of strong electrolytes. For example, sodium hydroxide is an Arrhenius base that dissociates completely in water to give sodium ions, Na^+, and hydroxide ions, OH^-.

NaOH(s)

$\quad\ominus$ OH⁻
$\quad\oplus$ Na⁺

Water

$$\text{NaOH}(s) \xrightarrow{\text{H}_2\text{O}} \text{Na}^+(aq) + \text{OH}^-(aq)$$

Ionic   Dissociation   Hydroxide
compound   ion

An Arrhenius base produces cations and OH⁻ anions in an aqueous solution.

Calcium hydroxide, $Ca(OH)_2$, is used in the food industry to produce beverages, and in dentistry as a filler for root canals.

Most Arrhenius bases are formed from Groups 1A (1) and 2A (2) metals, such as NaOH, KOH, LiOH, and $Ca(OH)_2$. The hydroxide ions (OH^-) give Arrhenius bases common characteristics, such as a bitter taste and a slippery feel. A base turns litmus indicator blue and phenolphthalein indicator pink. Table 11.2 compares some characteristics of acids and bases.

TABLE 11.2 Some Characteristics of Acids and Bases

Characteristic	Acids	Bases
Arrhenius	Produce H^+	Produce OH^-
Electrolytes	Yes	Yes
Taste	Sour	Bitter, chalky
Feel	May sting	Soapy, slippery
Litmus	Red	Blue
Phenolphthalein	Colorless	Pink
Neutralization	Neutralize bases	Neutralize acids

Naming Bases

Typical Arrhenius bases are named as *hydroxides*.

Base	Name
LiOH	Lithium **hydroxide**
NaOH	Sodium **hydroxide**
KOH	Potassium **hydroxide**
$Ca(OH)_2$	Calcium **hydroxide**
$Al(OH)_3$	Aluminum **hydroxide**

A soft drink contains H_3PO_4 and H_2CO_3.

> **SAMPLE PROBLEM 11.1** Names and Formulas of Acids and Bases
>
> **a.** Identify each of the following as an acid or a base and give its name:
>   **1.** H_3PO_4, ingredient in soft drinks
>   **2.** NaOH, ingredient in oven cleaner
> **b.** Write the formula for each of the following:
>   **1.** magnesium hydroxide, ingredient in antacids
>   **2.** hydrobromic acid, used industrially to prepare bromide compounds
>
> **SOLUTION**
>
> **a. 1.** acid, phosphoric acid   **2.** base, sodium hydroxide
> **b. 1.** $Mg(OH)_2$ **2.** HBr
>
> **STUDY CHECK 11.1**
>
> **a.** Identify as an acid or a base and give the name for H_2CO_3.
> **b.** Write the formula for iron(III) hydroxide.
>
> **ANSWER**
>
> **a.** acid, carbonic acid   **b.** $Fe(OH)_3$

QUESTIONS AND PROBLEMS

11.1 Acids and Bases

LEARNING GOAL Describe and name acids and bases.

11.1 Indicate whether each of the following statements is characteristic of an acid, a base, or both:
  a. has a sour taste
  b. neutralizes bases
  c. produces H^+ ions in water
  d. is named barium hydroxide
  e. is an electrolyte

11.2 Indicate whether each of the following statements is characteristic of an acid, a base, or both:
  a. neutralizes acids
  b. produces OH^- ions in water
  c. has a slippery feel
  d. conducts an electrical current in solution
  e. turns litmus red

11.3 Name each of the following acids or bases:
  a. HCl   **b.** $Ca(OH)_2$ **c.** $HClO_4$
  d. HNO_3 **e.** H_2SO_3 **f.** $HBrO_2$

11.4 Name each of the following acids or bases:
  a. $Al(OH)_3$ **b.** HBr   **c.** H_2SO_4
  d. KOH   **e.** HNO_2 **f.** $HClO_2$

11.5 Write formulas for each of the following acids and bases:
  a. rubidium hydroxide   **b.** hydrofluoric acid
  c. phosphoric acid   **d.** lithium hydroxide
  e. ammonium hydroxide   **f.** periodic acid

11.6 Write formulas for each of the following acids and bases:
  a. barium hydroxide   **b.** hydroiodic acid
  c. nitric acid   **d.** strontium hydroxide
  e. acetic acid   **f.** hypochlorous acid

11.2 Brønsted–Lowry Acids and Bases

LEARNING GOAL

Identify conjugate acid–base pairs for Brønsted–Lowry acids and bases.

In 1923, J. N. Brønsted in Denmark and T. M. Lowry in Great Britain expanded the definition of acids and bases to include bases that do not contain OH^- ions. A **Brønsted–Lowry acid** can donate a hydrogen ion, H^+, and a **Brønsted–Lowry base** can accept a hydrogen ion.

A Brønsted–Lowry acid is a substance that donates H^+.

A Brønsted–Lowry base is a substance that accepts H^+.

A free hydrogen ion, H^+, does not actually exist in water. Its attraction to polar water molecules is so strong that the H^+ bonds to a water molecule and forms a **hydronium ion, H_3O^+**.

$$H-\ddot{O}: + H^+ \longrightarrow \left[H-\ddot{O}-H \right]^+$$
$$\quad\; | \qquad\qquad\qquad\quad\; |$$
$$\quad\; H \qquad\qquad\qquad\quad H$$

Water   Hydrogen ion   Hydronium ion

We can write the formation of a hydrochloric acid solution as a transfer of H^+ from hydrogen chloride to water. By accepting an H^+ in the reaction, water is acting as a base according to the Brønsted–Lowry concept.

| HCl | + | H_2O | $\longrightarrow$ | H_3O^+ | + | Cl^- |

Hydrogen chloride   Water   Hydronium ion   Chloride ion

Acid   Base
(H^+ donor) (H^+ acceptor)   Acidic solution

In another reaction, ammonia, NH_3, acts as a base by accepting H^+ when it reacts with water. Because the nitrogen atom of NH_3 has a stronger attraction for H^+ than oxygen, water acts as an acid by donating H^+.

$$NH_3 \; + \; H_2O \; \rightleftharpoons \; NH_4^+ \; + \; OH^-$$

| Ammonia | Water | Ammonium ion | Hydroxide ion |

Base (H⁺ acceptor) Acid (H⁺ donor) Basic solution

▶ SAMPLE PROBLEM 11.2 Acids and Bases

In each of the following equations, identify the reactant that is a Brønsted–Lowry acid and the reactant that is a Brønsted–Lowry base:

a. $HBr(aq) + H_2O(l) \longrightarrow H_3O^+(aq) + Br^-(aq)$
b. $CN^-(aq) + H_2O(l) \rightleftharpoons HCN(aq) + OH^-(aq)$

SOLUTION

a. HBr, Brønsted–Lowry acid; H_2O, Brønsted–Lowry base
b. H_2O, Brønsted–Lowry acid; CN^-, Brønsted–Lowry base

STUDY CHECK 11.2

When HNO_3 reacts with water, water acts as a Brønsted–Lowry base. Write the equation for the reaction.

ANSWER

$$HNO_3(aq) + H_2O(l) \longrightarrow H_3O^+(aq) + NO_3^-(aq)$$

Conjugate acid–base pair

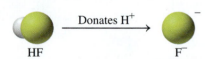

HF   F⁻

Conjugate acid–base pair

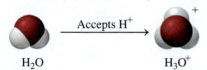

H_2O H_3O^+

HF, an acid, loses one H^+ to form its conjugate base F^-. Water acts as a base by gaining one H^+ to form its conjugate acid H_3O^+.

Conjugate Acid–Base Pairs

According to the Brønsted–Lowry theory, a **conjugate acid–base pair** consists of molecules or ions related by the loss of one H^+ by an acid, and the gain of one H^+ by a base. Every acid–base reaction contains two conjugate acid–base pairs because an H^+ is transferred in both the forward and reverse directions. When an acid such as HF loses one H^+, the conjugate base F^- is formed. When the base H_2O gains an H^+, its conjugate acid, H_3O^+, is formed.

Because the overall reaction of HF is reversible, the conjugate acid H_3O^+ can donate H^+ to the conjugate base F^- and re-form the acid HF and the base H_2O. Using the relationship of loss and gain of one H^+, we can now identify the conjugate acid–base pairs as HF/F^- along with H_3O^+/H_2O.

In another reaction, ammonia, NH_3, accepts H^+ from H_2O to form the conjugate acid NH_4^+ and conjugate base OH^-. Each of these conjugate acid–base pairs, NH_4^+/NH_3 and H_2O/OH^-, is related by the loss and gain of one H^+.

Ammonia, NH_3, acts as a base when it gains one H^+ to form its conjugate acid NH_4^+. Water acts as an acid by losing one H^+ to form its conjugate base OH^-.

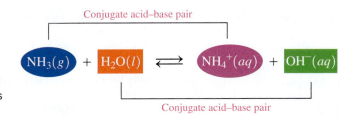

In these two examples, we see that water can act as an acid when it donates H^+ or as a base when it accepts H^+. Substances that can act as both acids and bases are **amphoteric** or *amphiprotic*. For water, the most common amphoteric substance, the acidic or basic behavior depends on the other reactant. Water donates H^+ when it reacts with a stronger base, and it accepts H^+ when it reacts with a stronger acid. Another example of an amphoteric substance is bicarbonate, HCO_3^-. With a base, HCO_3^- acts as an acid and donates one H^+ to give CO_3^{2-}. However, when HCO_3^- reacts with an acid, it acts as a base and accepts one H^+ to form H_2CO_3.

Amphoteric substances act as both acids and bases.

$$H_3O^+ \qquad\quad H_2O \qquad\quad OH^-$$
$$H_2CO_3 \xleftarrow{\text{Acts as a base}} HCO_3^- \xrightarrow{\text{Acts as an acid}} CO_3^{2-}$$

SAMPLE PROBLEM 11.3 Identifying Conjugate Acid–Base Pairs

Identify the conjugate acid–base pairs in the following reaction:
$$HBr(aq) + NH_3(aq) \rightleftharpoons Br^-(aq) + NH_4^+(aq)$$

SOLUTION

	Given		Need
ANALYZE THE PROBLEM	HBr	Br^-	conjugate acid–base pairs
	NH_3	NH_4^+	

STEP 1   Identify the reactant that loses H^+ as the acid.
In the reaction, HBr donates H^+ to form the product Br^-. Thus HBr is the acid and Br^- is its conjugate base.

STEP 2   Identify the reactant that gains H^+ as the base.
In the reaction, NH_3 gains H^+ to form the product NH_4^+. Thus, NH_3 is the base and NH_4^+ is its conjugate acid.

STEP 3   Write the conjugate acid–base pairs.
HBr/Br^- and NH_4^+/NH_3

STUDY CHECK 11.3

Identify the conjugate acid–base pairs in the following reaction:
$$HCN(aq) + SO_4^{2-}(aq) \rightleftharpoons CN^-(aq) + HSO_4^-(aq)$$

ANSWER

The conjugate acid–base pairs are HCN/CN^- and HSO_4^-/SO_4^{2-}.

Guide to Writing Conjugate Acid–Base Pairs

STEP 1
Identify the reactant that loses H^+ as the acid.

STEP 2
Identify the reactant that gains H^+ as the base.

STEP 3
Write the conjugate acid–base pairs.

QUESTIONS AND PROBLEMS

11.2 Brønsted–Lowry Acids and Bases

LEARNING GOAL Identify conjugate acid–base pairs for Brønsted–Lowry acids and bases.

11.7 Identify the reactant that is a Brønsted–Lowry acid and the reactant that is a Brønsted–Lowry base in each of the following:
   a. $HI(aq) + H_2O(l) \longrightarrow I^-(aq) + H_3O^+(aq)$
   b. $F^-(aq) + H_2O(l) \rightleftharpoons HF(aq) + OH^-(aq)$
   c. $H_2S(aq) + CH_3—CH_2—NH_2(aq) \rightleftharpoons$
   $\qquad\qquad HS^-(aq) + CH_3—CH_2—NH_3^+(aq)$

11.8 Identify the reactant that is a Brønsted–Lowry acid and the reactant that is a Brønsted–Lowry base in each of the following:
   a. $CO_3^{2-}(aq) + H_2O(l) \rightleftharpoons HCO_3^-(aq) + OH^-(aq)$
   b. $H_2SO_4(aq) + H_2O(l) \longrightarrow HSO_4^-(aq) + H_3O^+(aq)$
   c. $C_2H_3O_2^-(aq) + H_3O^+(aq) \rightleftharpoons HC_2H_3O_2(aq) + H_2O(l)$

11.9 Write the formula for the conjugate base for each of the following acids:
   a. HF **b.** H_2O **c.** $H_2PO_3^-$
   d. HSO_4^- **e.** $HClO_2$

11.10 Write the formula for the conjugate base for each of the following acids:
   a. HCO_3^- **b.** $CH_3—NH_3^+$ **c.** HPO_4^{2-}
   d. HNO_2 **e.** $HBrO$

11.11 Write the formula for the conjugate acid for each of the following bases:
   a. CO_3^{2-} **b.** H_2O **c.** $H_2PO_4^-$
   d. Br^- **e.** ClO_4^-

11.12 Write the formula for the conjugate acid for each of the following bases:
   a. SO_4^{2-} **b.** CN^- **c.** NH_3
   d. ClO_2^- **e.** HS^-

11.13 Identify the Brønsted–Lowry acid–base pairs in each of the following equations:
   a. $H_2CO_3(aq) + H_2O(l) \rightleftharpoons HCO_3^-(aq) + H_3O^+(aq)$
   b. $NH_4^+(aq) + H_2O(l) \rightleftharpoons NH_3(aq) + H_3O^+(aq)$
   c. $HCN(aq) + NO_2^-(aq) \rightleftharpoons CN^-(aq) + HNO_2(aq)$
   d. $CHO_2^-(aq) + HF(aq) \rightleftharpoons HCHO_2(aq) + F^-(aq)$

11.14 Identify the Brønsted–Lowry acid–base pairs in each of the following equations:
   a. $H_3PO_4(aq) + H_2O(l) \rightleftharpoons H_2PO_4^-(aq) + H_3O^+(aq)$
   b. $CO_3^{2-}(aq) + H_2O(l) \rightleftharpoons HCO_3^-(aq) + OH^-(aq)$
   c. $H_3PO_4(aq) + NH_3(aq) \rightleftharpoons H_2PO_4^-(aq) + NH_4^+(aq)$
   d. $HNO_2(aq) + CH_3—CH_2—NH_2(aq) \rightleftharpoons$
   $\qquad\qquad CH_3—CH_2—NH_3^+(aq) + NO_2^-(aq)$

11.15 When ammonium chloride dissolves in water, the ammonium ion NH_4^+ donates an H^+ to water. Write a balanced equation for the reaction of the ammonium ion with water.

11.16 When sodium carbonate dissolves in water, the carbonate ion CO_3^{2-} acts as a base. Write a balanced equation for the reaction of the carbonate ion with water.

LEARNING GOAL

Write equations for the dissociation of strong and weak acids; identify the direction of reaction.

11.3 Strengths of Acids and Bases

In the process called **dissociation**, an acid or a base separates into ions in water. The *strength* of an acid is determined by the moles of H_3O^+ that are produced for each mole of acid that dissociates. The *strength* of a base is determined by the moles of OH^- that are produced for each mole of base that dissolves. Strong acids and strong bases dissociate completely in water, whereas weak acids and weak bases dissociate only slightly, leaving most of the initial acid or base undissociated.

Strong and Weak Acids

Strong acids are examples of strong electrolytes because they donate H^+ so easily that their dissociation in water is essentially complete. For example, when HCl, a strong acid, dissociates in water, H^+ is transferred to H_2O; the resulting solution contains essentially only the ions H_3O^+ and Cl^-. We consider the reaction of HCl in H_2O as going 100% to products. Thus, one mole of a strong acid dissociates in water to yield one mole of H_3O^+ and one mole of its conjugate base. We write the equation for a strong acid such as HCl with a single arrow.

$$HCl(g) + H_2O(l) \longrightarrow H_3O^+(aq) + Cl^-(aq)$$

There are only six common strong acids, which are stronger acids than H_3O^+. All other acids are weak. Table 11.3 lists the relative strengths of acids and bases. **Weak acids** are weak electrolytes because they dissociate slightly in water, forming only a small amount of H_3O^+ ions. A weak acid has a strong conjugate base, which is why the reverse reaction is more prevalent. Even at high concentrations, weak acids produce low concentrations of H_3O^+ ions (see Figure 11.1).

Many of the products you use at home contain weak acids. Citric acid is a weak acid found in fruits and fruit juices such as lemons, oranges, and grapefruit. The vinegar used in salad dressings is typically a 5% (m/v) acetic acid, $HC_2H_3O_2$, solution. In water, a few $HC_2H_3O_2$ molecules donate H^+ to H_2O to form H_3O^+ ions and acetate ions $C_2H_3O_2^-$. The reverse reaction also takes place, which converts the H_3O^+ ions and acetate ions $C_2H_3O_2^-$ back to reactants. The formation of hydronium ions from vinegar is the reason we notice the sour taste of vinegar. We write the equation for a weak acid in an aqueous solution with a double arrow to indicate that the forward and reverse reactions are at equilibrium.

Weak acids are found in foods and household products.

$$\underset{\text{Acetic acid}}{HC_2H_3O_2(aq)} + H_2O(l) \rightleftharpoons \underset{\text{Acetate ion}}{C_2H_3O_2^-(aq)} + H_3O^+(aq)$$

TABLE 11.3 Relative Strengths of Acids and Bases

Acid		Conjugate Base	
Strong Acids			
Hydroiodic acid	HI	I^-	Iodide ion
Hydrobromic acid	HBr	Br^-	Bromide ion
Perchloric acid	$HClO_4$	ClO_4^-	Perchlorate ion
Hydrochloric acid	HCl	Cl^-	Chloride ion
Sulfuric acid	H_2SO_4	HSO_4^-	Hydrogen sulfate ion
Nitric acid	HNO_3	NO_3^-	Nitrate ion
Hydronium ion	H_3O^+	H_2O	Water
Weak Acids			
Hydrogen sulfate ion	HSO_4^-	SO_4^{2-}	Sulfate ion
Phosphoric acid	H_3PO_4	$H_2PO_4^-$	Dihydrogen phosphate ion
Nitrous acid	HNO_2	NO_2^-	Nitrite ion
Hydrofluoric acid	HF	F^-	Fluoride ion
Acetic acid	$HC_2H_3O_2$	$C_2H_3O_2^-$	Acetate ion
Carbonic acid	H_2CO_3	HCO_3^-	Bicarbonate ion
Hydrosulfuric acid	H_2S	HS^-	Hydrogen sulfide ion
Dihydrogen phosphate ion	$H_2PO_4^-$	HPO_4^{2-}	Hydrogen phosphate ion
Ammonium ion	NH_4^+	NH_3	Ammonia
Hydrocyanic acid	HCN	CN^-	Cyanide ion
Bicarbonate ion	HCO_3^-	CO_3^{2-}	Carbonate ion
Methylammonium ion	$CH_3-NH_3^+$	CH_3-NH_2	Methylamine
Hydrogen phosphate ion	HPO_4^{2-}	PO_4^{3-}	Phosphate ion
Water	H_2O	OH^-	Hydroxide ion

Acid Strength Increases (left vertical arrow)

Base Strength Increases (right vertical arrow)

FIGURE 11.1 ▶ A strong acid such as HCl is completely dissociated ($\approx 100\%$), whereas a weak acid such as $HC_2H_3O_2$ contains mostly molecules and a few ions.

🅀 What is the difference between a strong acid and a weak acid?

Diprotic Acids

Some weak acids, such as carbonic acid, are *diprotic acids* that have two H^+, which dissociate one at a time. For example, carbonated soft drinks are prepared by dissolving CO_2 in water to form carbonic acid, H_2CO_3. A weak acid such as H_2CO_3 reaches equilibrium between the mostly undissociated H_2CO_3 molecules and the ions H_3O^+ and HCO_3^-.

$$H_2CO_3(aq) + H_2O(l) \rightleftharpoons H_3O^+(aq) + HCO_3^-(aq)$$
Carbonic acid   Bicarbonate ion
(hydrogen carbonate)

Because HCO_3^- is also a weak acid, a second dissociation can take place to produce another hydronium ion and the carbonate ion, CO_3^{2-}.

$$HCO_3^-(aq) + H_2O(l) \rightleftharpoons H_3O^+(aq) + CO_3^{2-}(aq)$$
Bicarbonate ion   Carbonate ion
(hydrogen carbonate)

H_2CO_3 HCO_3^- CO_3^{2-}

Carbonic acid, a weak acid, loses one H^+ to form hydrogen carbonate ion, which loses a second H^+ to form carbonate ion.

Sulfuric acid, H_2SO_4, is also a diprotic acid. However, its first dissociation is complete (100%), which means H_2SO_4 is a strong acid. The product, hydrogen sulfate HSO_4^-, can dissociate again but only slightly, which means that the hydrogen sulfate ion is a weak acid.

$$H_2SO_4(aq) + H_2O(l) \longrightarrow H_3O^+(aq) + HSO_4^-(aq)$$
Sulfuric acid   Bisulfate ion
(hydrogen sulfate)

$$HSO_4^-(aq) + H_2O(l) \rightleftharpoons H_3O^+(aq) + SO_4^{2-}(aq)$$
Bisulfate ion   Sulfate ion
(hydrogen sulfate)

In summary, a strong acid such as HI in water dissociates completely to form an aqueous solution of the ions H_3O^+ and I^-. A weak acid such as HF dissociates only slightly in water to form an aqueous solution that consists mostly of HF molecules and a few H_3O^+ and F^- ions (see Figure 11.2).

Strong acid: $HI(aq) + H_2O(l) \longrightarrow H_3O^+(aq) + I^-(aq)$ Completely dissociated

Weak acid: $HF(aq) + H_2O(l) \rightleftharpoons H_3O^+(aq) + F^-(aq)$ Slightly dissociated

HF
F^-
H_3O^+

Hydrofluoric acid is the only halogen acid that is a weak acid.

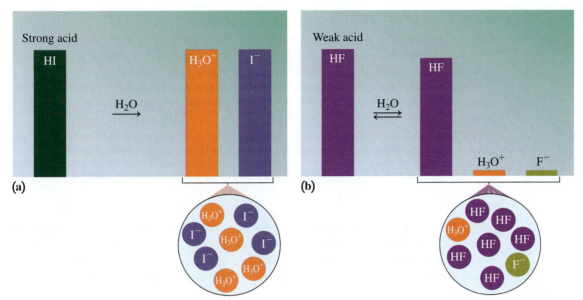

FIGURE 11.2 ▶ After dissociation in water, **(a)** the strong acid HI has high concentrations of H_3O^+ and I^-, and **(b)** the weak acid HF has a high concentration of HF and low concentrations of H_3O^+ and F^-.

 How do the heights of H_3O^+ and F^- compare to the height of the weak acid HF in the bar diagram for HF?

Strong and Weak Bases

As strong electrolytes, **strong bases** dissociate completely in water. Because these strong bases are ionic compounds, they dissociate in water to give an aqueous solution of metal ions and hydroxide ions. The Group 1A (1) hydroxides are very soluble in water, which can give high concentrations of OH^- ions. A few strong bases are less soluble in water, but what does dissolve dissociates completely as ions. For example, when KOH forms a KOH solution, it contains only the ions K^+ and OH^-.

$$KOH(s) \xrightarrow{H_2O} K^+(aq) + OH^-(aq)$$

Strong Bases

Lithium hydroxide LiOH
Sodium hydroxide NaOH
Potassium hydroxide KOH
Rubidium hydroxide RbOH
Cesium hydroxide CsOH
Calcium hydroxide $Ca(OH)_2$*
Strontium hydroxide $Sr(OH)_2$*
Barium hydroxide $Ba(OH)_2$*

*Low solubility, but they dissociate completely

Weak bases are weak electrolytes that are poor acceptors of hydrogen ions and produce very few ions in solution. A typical weak base, ammonia, NH_3, is found in window cleaners. In an aqueous solution, only a few ammonia molecules accept hydrogen ions to form NH_4^+ and OH^-.

$$NH_3(g) + H_2O(l) \rightleftharpoons NH_4^+(aq) + OH^-(aq)$$
Ammonia   Ammonium hydroxide

Bases in household products are used to remove grease and to open drains.

Bases in Household Products
Weak Bases
Window cleaner, ammonia, NH_3
Bleach, NaOCl
Laundry detergent, Na_2CO_3, Na_3PO_4
Toothpaste and baking soda, $NaHCO_3$
Baking powder, scouring powder, Na_2CO_3
Lime for lawns and agriculture, $CaCO_3$
Laxatives, antacids, $Mg(OH)_2$, $Al(OH)_3$

Strong Bases
Drain cleaner, oven cleaner, NaOH

Direction of Reaction

There is a relationship between the components in each conjugate acid–base pair. Strong acids have weak conjugate bases that do not readily accept H^+. As the strength of the acid decreases, the strength of its conjugate base increases.

In any acid–base reaction, there are two acids and two bases. However, one acid is stronger than the other acid, and one base is stronger than the other base. By comparing their relative strengths, we can determine the direction of the reaction. For example, the strong acid H_2SO_4 readily gives up H^+ to water. The hydronium ion H_3O^+ produced is a weaker acid than H_2SO_4, and the conjugate base HSO_4^- is a weaker base than water.

$$H_2SO_4(aq) + H_2O(l) \longrightarrow H_3O^+(aq) + HSO_4^-(aq) \quad \text{Mostly products}$$

Stronger acid	Stronger base	Weaker acid	Weaker base

Let's look at another reaction in which water donates one H^+ to carbonate, CO_3^{2-}, to form HCO_3^- and OH^-. From Table 11.3, we see that HCO_3^- is a stronger acid than H_2O. We also see that OH^- is a stronger base than CO_3^{2-}. To reach equilibrium, the stronger acid and stronger base react in the direction of the weaker acid and weaker base.

$$CO_3^{2-}(aq) + H_2O(l) \rightleftharpoons HCO_3^-(aq) + OH^-(aq) \quad \text{Mostly reactants}$$

Weaker base	Weaker acid	Stronger acid	Stronger base

▶ SAMPLE PROBLEM 11.4 Direction of Reaction

Does the equilibrium mixture of the following reaction contain mostly reactants or products?

$$HF(aq) + H_2O(l) \rightleftharpoons H_3O^+(aq) + F^-(aq)$$

SOLUTION

From Table 11.3, we see that HF is a weaker acid than H_3O^+ and that H_2O is a weaker base than F^-. Thus, the equilibrium mixture contains mostly reactants.

$$HF(aq) + H_2O(l) \rightleftharpoons H_3O^+(aq) + F^-(aq)$$

Weaker acid	Weaker base	Stronger acid	Stronger base

STUDY CHECK 11.4

Does the equilibrium mixture for reaction of nitric acid and water contain mostly reactants or products?

ANSWER

$$HNO_3(aq) + H_2O(l) \longrightarrow H_3O^+(aq) + NO_3^-(aq)$$

The equilibrium mixture contains mostly products because HNO_3 is a stronger acid than H_3O^+, and H_2O is a stronger base than NO_3^-.

QUESTIONS AND PROBLEMS

11.3 Strengths of Acids and Bases

LEARNING GOAL Write equations for the dissociation of strong and weak acids; identify the direction of reaction.

11.17 What is meant by the phrase "A strong acid has a weak conjugate base"?

11.18 What is meant by the phrase "A weak acid has a strong conjugate base"?

11.19 Identify the stronger acid in each of the following pairs:
   a. HBr or HNO_2
   b. H_3PO_4 or HSO_4^-
   c. HCN or H_2CO_3

11.20 Identify the stronger acid in each of the following pairs:
   a. NH_4^+ or H_3O^+
   b. H_2SO_4 or HCl
   c. H_2O or H_2CO_3

11.21 Identify the weaker acid in each of the following pairs:
   a. HCl or HSO_4^-
   b. HNO_2 or HF
   c. HCO_3^- or NH_4^+

11.22 Identify the weaker acid in each of the following pairs:
   a. HNO_3 or HCO_3^- **b.** HSO_4^- or H_2O **c.** H_2SO_4 or H_2CO_3

11.23 Predict whether each of the following reactions contains mostly reactants or products at equilibrium:
   a. $H_2CO_3(aq) + H_2O(l) \rightleftarrows HCO_3^-(aq) + H_3O^+(aq)$
   b. $NH_4^+(aq) + H_2O(l) \rightleftarrows NH_3(aq) + H_3O^+(aq)$
   c. $HNO_2(aq) + NH_3(aq) \rightleftarrows NO_2^-(aq) + NH_4^+(aq)$

11.24 Predict whether each of the following reactions contains mostly reactants or products at equilibrium:
   a. $H_3PO_4(aq) + H_2O(l) \rightleftarrows H_3O^+(aq) + H_2PO_4^-(aq)$
   b. $CO_3^{2-}(aq) + H_2O(l) \rightleftarrows OH^-(aq) + HCO_3^-(aq)$
   c. $HS^-(aq) + F^-(aq) \rightleftarrows HF(aq) + S^{2-}(aq)$

11.25 Write an equation for the acid–base reaction between ammonium ion and sulfate ion. Why does the equilibrium mixture contain mostly reactants?

11.26 Write an equation for the acid–base reaction between nitrous acid and hydroxide ion. Why does the equilibrium mixture contain mostly products?

11.4 Dissociation Constants for Acids and Bases

As we have seen, acids have different strengths depending on how much they dissociate in water. Because the dissociation of strong acids in water is essentially complete, the reaction is not considered to be an equilibrium situation. However, because weak acids in water dissociate only slightly, the ion products reach equilibrium with the undissociated weak acid molecules. For example, formic acid $HCHO_2$, the acid found in bee and ant stings, is a weak acid. Formic acid is a weak acid that dissociates in water to form hydronium ion, H_3O^+, and formate ion, CHO_2^-.

$$HCHO_2(aq) + H_2O(l) \rightleftarrows H_3O^+(aq) + CHO_2^-(aq)$$

HCHO$_2$

CHO$_2^-$

Formic acid, a weak acid, loses one H^+ to form formate ion.

Writing Dissociation Constants

An acid dissociation constant expression can be written for weak acids that gives the ratio of the concentrations of products to the weak acid reactants. As with other dissociation expressions, the molar concentration of the products is divided by the molar concentration of the reactants. Because water is a pure liquid with a constant concentration, it is omitted. The numerical value of the acid dissociation constant expression is the **acid dissociation constant, K_a**. For example, the acid dissociation constant expression for the equilibrium equation of formic acid shown above is written

$$K_a = \frac{[H_3O^+][CHO_2^-]}{[HCHO_2]}$$

The value of the K_a for formic acid at 25 °C is determined by experiment to be 1.8×10^{-4}. Thus, for the weak acid $HCHO_2$, the K_a is written

$$K_a = \frac{[H_3O^+][CHO_2^-]}{[HCHO_2]} = 1.8 \times 10^{-4} \quad \text{Acid dissociation constant}$$

The K_a for formic acid is small, which confirms that the equilibrium mixture of formic acid in water contains mostly reactants and only small amounts of the products. (Recall that the brackets in the K_a represent the molar concentrations of the reactants and products). Weak acids have small K_a values. However, strong acids, which are essentially 100% dissociated, have very large K_a values, but these values are not usually given. Table 11.4 gives K_a and K_b values for selected weak acids and bases.

TABLE 11.4 K_a and K_b Values for Selected Weak Acids and Bases

Acids		K_a
Phosphoric acid	H_3PO_4	7.5×10^{-3}
Nitrous acid	HNO_2	4.5×10^{-4}
Hydrofluoric acid	HF	3.5×10^{-4}
Formic acid	$HCHO_2$	1.8×10^{-4}
Acetic acid	$HC_2H_3O_2$	1.8×10^{-5}
Carbonic acid	H_2CO_3	4.3×10^{-7}
Hydrosulfuric acid	H_2S	9.1×10^{-8}
Dihydrogen phosphate	$H_2PO_4^-$	6.2×10^{-8}
Hydrocyanic acid	HCN	4.9×10^{-10}
Hydrogen carbonate	HCO_3^-	5.6×10^{-11}
Hydrogen phosphate	HPO_4^{2-}	2.2×10^{-13}
Bases		K_b
Methylamine	CH_3-NH_2	4.4×10^{-4}
Carbonate	CO_3^{2-}	2.2×10^{-4}
Ammonia	NH_3	1.8×10^{-5}

Let us now consider the dissociation of the weak base methylamine:

$$CH_3-NH_2(aq) + H_2O(l) \rightleftharpoons CH_3-NH_3^+(aq) + OH^-(aq)$$

As we did with the acid dissociation expression, the concentration of water is omitted from the base dissociation constant expression. The **base dissociation constant, K_b,** for methylamine is written

$$K_b = \frac{[CH_3-NH_3^+][OH^-]}{[CH_3-NH_2]} = 4.4 \times 10^{-4}$$

Table 11.5 summarizes the characteristics of acids and bases in terms of strength and equilibrium position.

TABLE 11.5 Characteristics of Acids and Bases

Characteristic	Strong Acids	Weak Acids
Equilibrium Position	Toward products	Toward reactants
K_a	Large	Small
$[H_3O^+]$ and $[A^-]$	100% of $[HA]$ dissociates	Small percent of $[HA]$ dissociates
Conjugate Base	Weak	Strong
Characteristic	Strong Bases	Weak Bases
Equilibrium Position	Toward products	Toward reactants
K_b	Large	Small
$[BH^+]$ and $[OH^-]$	100% of $[B]$ reacts	Small percent of $[B]$ reacts
Conjugate Acid	Weak	Strong

▶ SAMPLE PROBLEM 11.5 Writing an Acid Dissociation Constant Expression

Write the acid dissociation constant expression for the weak acid, nitrous acid.

SOLUTION

The equation for the dissociation of nitrous acid is written

$$HNO_2(aq) + H_2O(l) \rightleftharpoons H_3O^+(aq) + NO_2^-(aq)$$

The acid dissociation constant expression is written as the concentration of the products divided by the concentration of the undissociated weak acid.

$$K_a = \frac{[H_3O^+][NO_2^-]}{[HNO_2]}$$

STUDY CHECK 11.5

Write the acid dissociation constant expression for hydrogen phosphate.

ANSWER

$$K_a = \frac{[H_3O^+][PO_4^{3-}]}{[HPO_4^{2-}]}$$

QUESTIONS AND PROBLEMS

11.4 Dissociation Constants for Acids and Bases

LEARNING GOAL Write the expression for the dissociation constant of a weak acid or weak base.

11.27 Answer *true* or *false* for each of the following: A strong acid
  a. is completely dissociated in aqueous solution
  b. has a small value of K_a
  c. has a strong conjugate base
  d. has a weak conjugate base
  e. is slightly dissociated in aqueous solution

11.28 Answer *true* or *false* for each of the following: A weak acid
  a. is completely dissociated in aqueous solution
  b. has a small value of K_a
  c. has a strong conjugate base
  d. has a weak conjugate base
  e. is slightly dissociated in aqueous solution

11.29 Consider the following acids and their dissociation constants:

$$H_2SO_3(aq) + H_2O(l) \rightleftharpoons H_3O^+(aq) + HSO_3^-(aq)$$
$$K_a = 1.2 \times 10^{-2}$$

$$HS^-(aq) + H_2O(l) \rightleftharpoons H_3O^+(aq) + S^{2-}(aq)$$
$$K_a = 1.3 \times 10^{-19}$$

  a. Which is the stronger acid, H_2SO_3 or HS^-?
  b. What is the conjugate base of H_2SO_3?

  c. Which acid has the weaker conjugate base?
  d. Which acid has the stronger conjugate base?
  e. Which acid produces more ions?

11.30 Consider the following acids and their dissociation constants:

$$HPO_4^{2-}(aq) + H_2O(l) \rightleftharpoons H_3O^+(aq) + PO_4^{3-}(aq)$$
$$K_a = 2.2 \times 10^{-13}$$

$$HCHO_2(aq) + H_2O(l) \rightleftharpoons H_3O^+(aq) + CHO_2^-(aq)$$
$$K_a = 1.8 \times 10^{-4}$$

  a. Which is the weaker acid, HPO_4^{2-} or $HCHO_2$?
  b. What is the conjugate base of HPO_4^{2-}?
  c. Which acid has the weaker conjugate base?
  d. Which acid has the stronger conjugate base?
  e. Which acid produces more ions?

11.31 Phosphoric acid dissociates to form hydronium ion and dihydrogen phosphate. Phosphoric acid has a K_a of 7.5×10^{-3}. Write the equation for the reaction and the acid dissociation constant expression for phosphoric acid.

11.32 Aniline, $C_6H_5-NH_2$, a weak base with a K_b of 4.0×10^{-10}, reacts with water to form $C_6H_5-NH_3^+$ and hydroxide ion. Write the equation for the reaction and the base dissociation constant expression for aniline.

11.5 Dissociation of Water

LEARNING GOAL

Use the water dissociation constant expression to calculate the $[H_3O^+]$ and $[OH^-]$ in an aqueous solution.

In many acid–base reactions, water is *amphoteric*, which means that it can act either as an acid or as a base. In pure water, there is a forward reaction between two water molecules that transfers H^+ from one water molecule to the other. One molecule acts as an acid by losing H^+, and the water molecule that gains H^+ acts as a base. Every time H^+ is transferred between two water molecules, the products are one H_3O^+ and one OH^-, which react in the reverse direction to re-form two water molecules. Thus, equilibrium is reached between the conjugate acid–base pairs of water.

Writing the Water Dissociation Constant Expression, K_w

Using the equation for water at equilibrium, we can write its equilibrium constant expression that shows the concentrations of the products divided by the concentrations of the reactants. Recall that square brackets around the symbols indicate their concentrations in moles per liter (M).

$$H_2O(l) + H_2O(l) \rightleftharpoons H_3O^+(aq) + OH^-(aq)$$

$$K = \frac{[H_3O^+][OH^-]}{[H_2O][H_2O]}$$

By omitting the constant concentration of pure water, we can write the **water dissociation constant expression, K_w.**

$$K_w = [H_3O^+][OH^-]$$

Experiments have determined, that in pure water, the concentration of H_3O^+ and OH^- at 25 °C are each 1.0×10^{-7} M.

Pure water $[H_3O^+] = [OH^-] = 1.0 \times 10^{-7}$ M

When we place the $[H_3O^+]$ and $[OH^-]$ into the water dissociation constant expression, we obtain the numerical value of K_w, which is 1.0×10^{-14} at 25 °C. As before, the concentration units are omitted in the K_w value.

$$K_w = [H_3O^+][OH^-]$$
$$= [1.0 \times 10^{-7}][1.0 \times 10^{-7}] = 1.0 \times 10^{-14}$$

Neutral, Acidic, and Basic Solutions

The K_w value (1.0×10^{-14}) applies to any aqueous solution at 25 °C because all aqueous solutions contain both H_3O^+ and OH^- (see Figure 11.3). When the $[H_3O^+]$ and $[OH^-]$ in a solution are equal, the solution is **neutral**. However, most solutions are not neutral; they have different concentrations of $[H_3O^+]$ and $[OH^-]$. If acid is added to water, there is an increase in $[H_3O^+]$ and a decrease in $[OH^-]$, which makes an acidic solution. If base is added, $[OH^-]$ increases and $[H_3O^+]$ decreases, which gives a basic solution. However, for any aqueous solution, whether it is neutral, acidic, or basic, the product $[H_3O^+][OH^-]$ is equal to K_w (1.0×10^{-14}) at 25 °C (see Table 11.6).

FIGURE 11.3 ▶ In a neutral solution, $[H_3O^+]$ and $[OH^-]$ are equal. In acidic solutions, the $[H_3O^+]$ is greater than the $[OH^-]$. In basic solutions, the $[OH^-]$ is greater than the $[H_3O^+]$.

Q Is a solution that has a $[H_3O^+]$ of 1.0×10^{-3} M acidic, basic, or neutral?

TABLE 11.6 Examples of $[H_3O^+]$ and $[OH^-]$ in Neutral, Acidic, and Basic Solutions

Type of Solution	$[H_3O^+]$	$[OH^-]$	K_w
Neutral	1.0×10^{-7} M	1.0×10^{-7} M	1.0×10^{-14}
Acidic	1.0×10^{-2} M	1.0×10^{-12} M	1.0×10^{-14}
Acidic	2.5×10^{-5} M	4.0×10^{-10} M	1.0×10^{-14}
Basic	1.0×10^{-8} M	1.0×10^{-6} M	1.0×10^{-14}
Basic	5.0×10^{-11} M	2.0×10^{-4} M	1.0×10^{-14}

Using the K_w to Calculate $[H_3O^+]$ and $[OH^-]$ in a Solution

If we know the $[H_3O^+]$ of a solution, we can use the K_w to calculate the $[OH^-]$. If we know the $[OH^-]$ of a solution, we can calculate $[H_3O^+]$ from their relationship in the K_w, as shown in Sample Problem 11.6.

$$K_w = [H_3O^+][OH^-]$$

$$[OH^-] = \frac{K_w}{[H_3O^+]} \qquad [H_3O^+] = \frac{K_w}{[OH^-]}$$

> **CORE CHEMISTRY SKILL**
>
> Calculating $[H_3O^+]$ and $[OH^-]$ in Solutions

▶ **SAMPLE PROBLEM 11.6** Calculating the $[H_3O^+]$ of a Solution

A vinegar solution has a $[OH^-] = 5.0 \times 10^{-12}$ M at 25 °C. What is the $[H_3O^+]$ of the vinegar solution? Is the solution acidic, basic, or neutral?

SOLUTION

STEP 1 State the given and needed quantities.

ANALYZE THE PROBLEM	Given	Need
	$[OH^-] = 5.0 \times 10^{-12}$ M	$[H_3O^+]$

STEP 2 Write the K_w for water and solve for the unknown $[H_3O^+]$.

$$K_w = [H_3O^+][OH^-] = 1.0 \times 10^{-14}$$

Solve for $[H_3O^+]$ by dividing both sides by $[OH^-]$.

$$\frac{K_w}{[OH^-]} = \frac{[H_3O^+][\cancel{OH^-}]}{[\cancel{OH^-}]} = \frac{1.0 \times 10^{-14}}{[OH^-]}$$

$$[H_3O^+] = \frac{1.0 \times 10^{-14}}{[OH^-]}$$

STEP 3 Substitute the known $[OH^-]$ into the equation and calculate.

$$[H_3O^+] = \frac{1.0 \times 10^{-14}}{[5.0 \times 10^{-12}]} = 2.0 \times 10^{-3} \text{ M}$$

Because the $[H_3O^+]$ of 2.0×10^{-3} M is larger than the $[OH^-]$ of 5.0×10^{-12} M, the solution is acidic.

Guide to Calculating $[H_3O^+]$ and $[OH^-]$ in Aqueous Solutions

STEP 1
State the given and needed quantities.

STEP 2
Write the K_w for water and solve for the unknown $[H_3O^+]$ or $[OH^-]$.

STEP 3
Substitute the known $[H_3O^+]$ or $[OH^-]$ into the equation and calculate.

STUDY CHECK 11.6

What is the $[H_3O^+]$ of an ammonia cleaning solution with $[OH^-] = 4.0 \times 10^{-4}$ M? Is the solution acidic, basic, or neutral?

ANSWER

$[H_3O^+] = 2.5 \times 10^{-11}$ M, basic

QUESTIONS AND PROBLEMS

11.5 Dissociation of Water

LEARNING GOAL Use the water dissociation constant expression to calculate the $[H_3O^+]$ and $[OH^-]$ in an aqueous solution.

11.33 Why are the concentrations of H_3O^+ and OH^- equal in pure water?

11.34 What is the meaning and value of K_w at 25 °C?

11.35 In an acidic solution, how does the concentration of H_3O^+ compare to the concentration of OH^-?

11.36 If a base is added to pure water, why does the $[H_3O^+]$ decrease?

11.37 Indicate whether each of the following solutions is acidic, basic, or neutral:
a. $[H_3O^+] = 2.0 \times 10^{-5}$ M
b. $[H_3O^+] = 1.4 \times 10^{-9}$ M
c. $[OH^-] = 8.0 \times 10^{-3}$ M
d. $[OH^-] = 3.5 \times 10^{-10}$ M

11.38 Indicate whether each of the following solutions is acidic, basic, or neutral:
a. $[H_3O^+] = 6.0 \times 10^{-12}$ M
b. $[H_3O^+] = 1.4 \times 10^{-4}$ M
c. $[OH^-] = 5.0 \times 10^{-12}$ M
d. $[OH^-] = 4.5 \times 10^{-2}$ M

11.39 Calculate the $[H_3O^+]$ of each aqueous solution with the following $[OH^-]$:
a. coffee, 1.0×10^{-9} M
b. soap, 1.0×10^{-6} M

c. cleanser, 2.0×10^{-5} M
d. lemon juice, 4.0×10^{-13} M

11.40 Calculate the $[H_3O^+]$ of each aqueous solution with the following $[OH^-]$:
a. NaOH, 1.0×10^{-2} M
b. milk of magnesia, 1.0×10^{-5} M
c. aspirin, 1.8×10^{-11} M
d. seawater, 2.5×10^{-6} M

Rx Clinical Applications

11.41 Calculate the $[OH^-]$ of each aqueous solution with the following $[H_3O^+]$:
a. stomach acid, 4.0×10^{-2} M
b. urine, 5.0×10^{-6} M
c. orange juice, 2.0×10^{-4} M
d. bile, 7.9×10^{-9} M

11.42 Calculate the $[OH^-]$ of each aqueous solution with the following $[H_3O^+]$:
a. baking soda, 1.0×10^{-8} M
b. blood, 4.2×10^{-8} M
c. milk, 5.0×10^{-7} M
d. pancreatic juice, 4.0×10^{-9} M

LEARNING GOAL

Calculate pH from $[H_3O^+]$; given the pH, calculate the $[H_3O^+]$ and $[OH^-]$ of a solution.

11.6 The pH Scale

Personnel working in food processing, medicine, agriculture, spa and pool maintenance, soap manufacturing, and wine making measure the $[H_3O^+]$ and $[OH^-]$ of solutions. Although we have expressed H_3O^+ and OH^- as molar concentrations, it is more convenient to describe the acidity of solutions using the *pH scale*. On this scale, a number between 0 and 14 represents the H_3O^+ concentration for common solutions. A neutral solution has a pH of 7.0 at 25 °C. An acidic solution has a pH less than 7.0; a basic solution has a pH greater than 7.0 (see Figure 11.4).

Acidic solution	pH < 7.0	$[H_3O^+] > 1.0 \times 10^{-7}$ M
Neutral solution	pH = 7.0	$[H_3O^+] = 1.0 \times 10^{-7}$ M
Basic solution	pH > 7.0	$[H_3O^+] < 1.0 \times 10^{-7}$ M

When we relate acidity and pH, we are using an inverse relationship, which is when one component increases while the other component decreases. When an acid is added to pure water, the $[H_3O^+]$ (acidity) of the solution increases but its pH decreases. When a base is added to pure water, it becomes more basic, which means its acidity decreases and the pH increases.

In the laboratory, a pH meter is commonly used to determine the pH of a solution. There are also various indicators and pH papers that turn specific colors when placed in solutions of different pH values. The pH is found by comparing the color on the test paper or the color of the solution to a color chart (see Figure 11.5).

pH Value

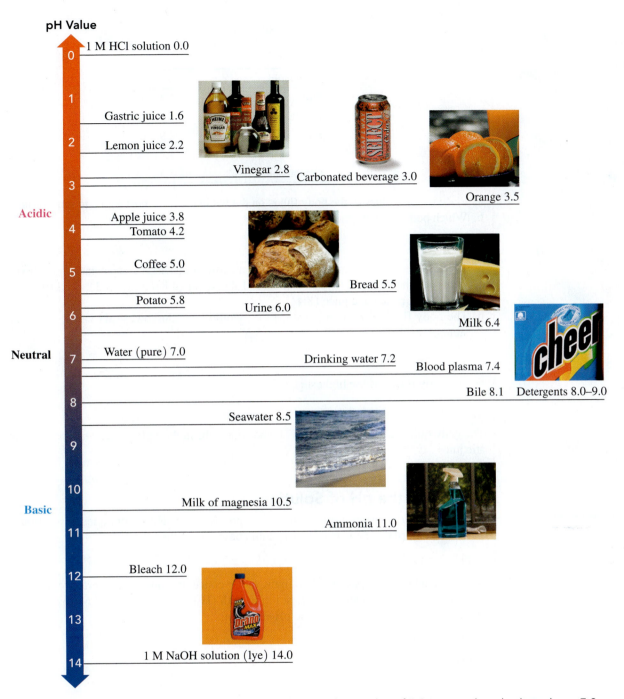

pH	
0	1 M HCl solution 0.0
1	
2	Gastric juice 1.6
	Lemon juice 2.2
3	Vinegar 2.8 · Carbonated beverage 3.0
	Orange 3.5
4	Apple juice 3.8
	Tomato 4.2
5	Coffee 5.0
	Bread 5.5
6	Potato 5.8 · Urine 6.0
	Milk 6.4
7	Water (pure) 7.0 · Drinking water 7.2 · Blood plasma 7.4
8	Bile 8.1 · Detergents 8.0–9.0
	Seawater 8.5
9	
10	Milk of magnesia 10.5
11	Ammonia 11.0
12	Bleach 12.0
13	
14	1 M NaOH solution (lye) 14.0

Acidic · **Neutral** · **Basic**

FIGURE 11.4 ▶ On the pH scale, values below 7.0 are acidic, a value of 7.0 is neutral, and values above 7.0 are basic.

Q Is apple juice an acidic, a basic, or a neutral solution?

(a)   **(b)**   **(c)**

FIGURE 11.5 ▶ The pH of a solution can be determined using **(a)** a pH meter, **(b)** pH paper, and **(c)** indicators that turn different colors corresponding to different pH values.

Q If a pH meter reads 4.00, is the solution acidic, basic, or neutral?

A dipstick is used to measure the pH of a urine sample.

▶ SAMPLE PROBLEM 11.7 pH of Solutions

Consider the pH of the following body fluids:

Body Fluid	pH
Stomach acid	1.4
Pancreatic juice	8.4
Sweat	4.8
Urine	5.3
Cerebrospinal fluid	7.3

a. Place the pH values of the body fluids on the list in order of most acidic to most basic.
b. Which body fluid has the highest $[H_3O^+]$?

SOLUTION

a. The most acidic body fluid is the one with the lowest pH, and the most basic is the body fluid with the highest pH: stomach acid (1.4), sweat (4.8), urine (5.3), cerebrospinal fluid (7.3), pancreatic juice (8.4).
b. The body fluid with the highest $[H_3O^+]$ would have the lowest pH value, which is stomach acid.

STUDY CHECK 11.7

Which body fluid has the highest $[OH^-]$?

ANSWER

The body fluid with the highest $[OH^-]$ would have the highest pH value, which is pancreatic juice.

KEY MATH SKILL

Calculating pH from $[H_3O^+]$

Calculating the pH of Solutions

The pH scale is a logarithmic scale that corresponds to the $[H_3O^+]$ of aqueous solutions. Mathematically, **pH** is the negative logarithm (base 10) of the $[H_3O^+]$.

$$pH = -\log[H_3O^+]$$

Essentially, the negative powers of 10 in the molar concentrations are converted to positive numbers. For example, a lemon juice solution with $[H_3O^+] = 1.0 \times 10^{-2}$ M has a pH of 2.00. This can be calculated using the pH equation:

$$pH = -\log[1.0 \times 10^{-2}]$$
$$pH = -(-2.00)$$
$$= 2.00$$

The number of *decimal places* in the pH value is the same as the number of significant figures in the $[H_3O^+]$. The number to the left of the decimal point in the pH value is the power of 10.

$$[H_3O^+] = \textbf{1.0} \times 10^{-2} \qquad pH = 2.\textbf{00}$$

Two SFs   Two SFs

If soil is too acidic, nutrients are not absorbed by crops. Then lime ($CaCO_3$), which acts as a base, may be added to increase the soil pH.

Because pH is a log scale, a change of one pH unit corresponds to a tenfold change in $[H_3O^+]$. It is important to note that the pH decreases as the $[H_3O^+]$ increases. For example, a solution with a pH of 2.00 has a $[H_3O^+]$ that is ten times greater than a solution with a pH of 3.00 and 100 times greater than a solution with a pH of 4.00. The pH of a solution is calculated from the $[H_3O^+]$ by using the *log* key and changing the sign as shown in Sample Problem 11.8.

> **SAMPLE PROBLEM 11.8** Calculating pH from $[H_3O^+]$

Aspirin, which is acetylsalicylic acid, was the first nonsteroidal anti-inflammatory drug (NSAID) used to alleviate pain and fever. If a solution of aspirin has a $[H_3O^+] = 1.7 \times 10^{-3}$ M, what is the pH of the solution?

Acidic H
that dissociates in
aqueous solution

Aspirin, acetylsalicylic acid, is a weak acid.

Guide to Calculating pH of an Aqueous Solution

STEP 1
State the given and needed quantities.

STEP 2
Enter the $[H_3O^+]$ into the pH equation and calculate.

STEP 3
Adjust the number of SFs on the *right* of the decimal point.

SOLUTION

STEP 1 State the given and needed quantities.

ANALYZE THE PROBLEM	Given	Need
	$[H_3O^+] = 1.7 \times 10^{-3}$ M	pH

STEP 2 Enter the $[H_3O^+]$ into the pH equation and calculate.

$$pH = -\log[H_3O^+] = -\log[1.7 \times 10^{-3}]$$

Calculator Procedure

$\boxed{+/-}$ $\boxed{\log}$ 1.7 $\boxed{\text{EE or EXP}}$ 3 $\boxed{+/-}$ $\boxed{=}$

Calculator Display

2.769551079

Be sure to check the instructions for your calculator.

STEP 3 Adjust the number of SFs on the *right* of the decimal point. In a pH value, the number to the *left* of the decimal point is an *exact* number derived from the power of 10. Thus, the two SFs in the coefficient determine that there are two SFs after the decimal point in the pH value.

STUDY CHECK 11.8

What is the pH of bleach with $[H_3O^+] = 4.2 \times 10^{-12}$ M?

ANSWER

pH = 11.38

When we need to calculate the pH from $[OH^-]$, we use the K_w to calculate $[H_3O^+]$, place it in the pH equation, and calculate the pH of the solution as shown in Sample Problem 11.9.

> **SAMPLE PROBLEM 11.9 Calculating pH from $[OH^-]$**
>
> What is the pH of an ammonia solution with $[OH^-] = 3.7 \times 10^{-3}$ M?
>
> **SOLUTION**
>
> **STEP 1** State the given and needed quantities.
>
> | ANALYZE THE PROBLEM | Given | Need |
> |---|---|---|
> | | $[OH^-] = 3.7 \times 10^{-3}$ M | $[H_3O^+]$, pH |
>
> **STEP 2** Enter the $[H_3O^+]$ into the pH equation and calculate. Because $[OH^-]$ is given for the ammonia solution, we have to calculate $[H_3O^+]$. Using the water dissociation constant expression, K_w, we divide both sides by $[OH^-]$ to obtain $[H_3O^+]$.
>
> $$K_w = [H_3O^+][OH^-] = 1.0 \times 10^{-14}$$
>
> $$\frac{K_w}{[OH^-]} = \frac{[H_3O^+][OH^-]}{[OH^-]}$$
>
> $$[H_3O^+] = \frac{1.0 \times 10^{-14}}{[3.7 \times 10^{-3}]} = 2.7 \times 10^{-12} \text{ M}$$
>
> Now, we enter the $[H_3O^+]$ into the pH equation.
>
> $$pH = -\log[H_3O^+] = -\log[2.7 \times 10^{-12}]$$
>
> **Calculator Procedure**   **Calculator Display**
>
> +/− log 2.7 EE or EXP 12 +/− =   11.56863624
>
> **STEP 3** Adjust the number of SFs on the *right* of the decimal point.
>
> 2.7 × 10⁻¹² M   pH = 11.**57**
> Two SFs   Two SFs to the *right* of the decimal point
>
> **STUDY CHECK 11.9**
>
> Calculate the pH of a sample of bile that has $[OH^-] = 1.3 \times 10^{-6}$ M.
>
> **ANSWER**
>
> pH = 8.11

A comparison of $[H_3O^+]$, $[OH^-]$, and their corresponding pH values is given in Table 11.7.

Calculating $[H_3O^+]$ from pH

If we are given the pH of the solution and asked to determine the $[H_3O^+]$, we need to reverse the calculation of pH.

$$[H_3O^+] = 10^{-pH}$$

For example, if the pH of a solution is 3.0, we can substitute it into this equation. The number of significant figures in $[H_3O^+]$ is equal to the number of decimal places in the pH value.

$$[H_3O^+] = 10^{-pH} = 10^{-3.0} = 1 \times 10^{-3} \text{ M}$$

KEY MATH SKILL

Calculating $[H_3O^+]$ from pH

TABLE 11.7 A Comparison of pH Values at 25 °C, $[H_3O^+]$, and $[OH^-]$

pH	$[H_3O^+]$	$[OH^-]$
0	10^0	10^{-14}
1	10^{-1}	10^{-13}
2	10^{-2}	10^{-12}
3	10^{-3}	10^{-11}
4	10^{-4}	10^{-10}
5	10^{-5}	10^{-9}
6	10^{-6}	10^{-8}
7	10^{-7}	10^{-7}
8	10^{-8}	10^{-6}
9	10^{-9}	10^{-5}
10	10^{-10}	10^{-4}
11	10^{-11}	10^{-3}
12	10^{-12}	10^{-2}
13	10^{-13}	10^{-1}
14	10^{-14}	10^0

Acidic

Neutral

Basic

Acids produce the sour taste of the fruits we eat.

For pH values that are not whole numbers, the calculation requires the use of the 10^x key, which is usually a *2nd function* key. On some calculators, this operation is done using the inverse log equation as shown in Sample Problem 11.10.

SAMPLE PROBLEM 11.10 Calculating $[H_3O^+]$ from pH

Calculate $[H_3O^+]$ for a urine sample, which has a pH of 7.5.

SOLUTION

STEP 1 State the given and needed quantities.

ANALYZE THE PROBLEM	Given	Need
	pH = 7.5	$[H_3O^+]$

STEP 2 Enter the pH value into the inverse log equation and calculate.

$$[H_3O^+] = 10^{-pH} = 10^{-7.5}$$

Calculator Procedure

[2nd] [log] [+/-] 7.5 [=]

Calculator Display

3.16227766 E −08

STEP 3 Adjust the SFs for the coefficient. Because the pH value 7.5 has one digit to the *right* of the decimal point, the coefficient for $[H_3O^+]$ is written with one SF.

$$[H_3O^+] = 3 \times 10^{-8}\,M$$
One SF

STUDY CHECK 11.10

What are the $[H_3O^+]$ and $[OH^-]$ of Diet Coke that has a pH of 3.17?

ANSWER

$[H_3O^+] = 6.8 \times 10^{-4}\,M$, $[OH^-] = 1.5 \times 10^{-11}\,M$

Guide to Calculating $[H_3O^+]$ from pH

STEP 1
State the given and needed quantities.

STEP 2
Enter the pH value into the inverse log equation and calculate.

STEP 3
Adjust the SFs for the coefficient.

The pH of Diet Coke is 3.17.

Chemistry Link to **Health**
Stomach Acid, HCl

Gastric acid, which contains HCl, is produced by parietal cells that line the stomach. When the stomach expands with the intake of food, the gastric glands begin to secrete a strongly acidic solution of HCl. In a single day, a person may secrete 2000 mL of gastric juice, which contains hydrochloric acid, mucins, and the enzymes pepsin and lipase.

The HCl in the gastric juice activates a digestive enzyme from the chief cells called *pepsinogen* to form *pepsin*, which breaks down proteins in food entering the stomach. The secretion of HCl continues until the stomach has a pH of about 2, which is the optimum for activating the digestive enzymes without ulcerating the stomach lining. In addition, the low pH destroys bacteria that reach the stomach. Normally, large quantities of viscous mucus are secreted within the stomach to protect its lining from acid and enzyme damage. Gastric acid may also form under conditions of stress when the nervous system activates the production of HCl. As the contents of the stomach move into the small intestine, cells produce bicarbonate that neutralizes the gastric acid until the pH is about 5.

Parietal cells in the lining of the stomach secrete gastric acid HCl.

QUESTIONS AND PROBLEMS

11.6 The pH Scale

LEARNING GOAL Calculate pH from $[H_3O^+]$; given the pH, calculate the $[H_3O^+]$ and $[OH^-]$ of a solution.

11.43 Why does a neutral solution have a pH of 7.0?

11.44 If you know the $[OH^-]$, how can you determine the pH of a solution?

11.45 State whether each of the following solutions is acidic, basic, or neutral:
- **a.** blood plasma, pH 7.38
- **b.** vinegar, pH 2.8
- **c.** coffee, pH 5.52
- **d.** tomatoes, pH 4.2
- **e.** chocolate cake, pH 7.6

11.46 State whether each of the following solutions is acidic, basic, or neutral:
- **a.** soda, pH 3.22
- **b.** shampoo, pH 5.7
- **c.** rain, pH 5.8
- **d.** honey, pH 3.9
- **e.** cheese, pH 5.2

11.47 A solution with a pH of 3 is 10 times more acidic than a solution with pH 4. Explain.

11.48 A solution with a pH of 10 is 100 times more basic than a solution with pH 8. Explain.

11.49 Calculate the pH of each solution given the following:
- **a.** $[H_3O^+] = 1 \times 10^{-4}$ M
- **b.** $[H_3O^+] = 3 \times 10^{-9}$ M
- **c.** $[OH^-] = 1 \times 10^{-5}$ M
- **d.** $[OH^-] = 2.5 \times 10^{-11}$ M
- **e.** $[H_3O^+] = 6.7 \times 10^{-8}$ M
- **f.** $[OH^-] = 8.2 \times 10^{-4}$ M

11.50 Calculate the pH of each solution given the following:
- **a.** $[H_3O^+] = 1 \times 10^{-8}$ M
- **b.** $[H_3O^+] = 5 \times 10^{-6}$ M
- **c.** $[OH^-] = 1 \times 10^{-2}$ M
- **d.** $[OH^-] = 8.0 \times 10^{-3}$ M
- **e.** $[H_3O^+] = 4.7 \times 10^{-2}$ M
- **f.** $[OH^-] = 3.9 \times 10^{-6}$ M

℞ Clinical Applications

11.51 Complete the following table for a selection of foods:

Food	$[H_3O^+]$	$[OH^-]$	pH	Acidic, Basic, or Neutral?
Rye bread		6.3×10^{-6} M		
Tomatoes			4.64	
Peas	6.2×10^{-7} M			

11.52 Complete the following table for a selection of foods:

Food	$[H_3O^+]$	$[OH^-]$	pH	Acidic, Basic, or Neutral?
Strawberries			3.90	
Soy milk				Neutral
Tuna fish (canned)	6.3×10^{-7} M			

11.53 A patient with severe metabolic acidosis has a blood plasma pH of 6.92. What is the $[H_3O^+]$ of the blood plasma?

11.54 A patient with respiratory alkalosis has a blood plasma pH of 7.58. What is the $[H_3O^+]$ of the blood plasma?

11.7 Reactions of Acids and Bases

Typical reactions of acids and bases include the reactions of acids with metals, carbonates or bicarbonates, and bases. For example, when you drop an antacid tablet in water, the bicarbonate ion and citric acid in the tablet react to produce carbon dioxide bubbles, water, and salt. A **salt** is an ionic compound that does not have H^+ as the cation or OH^- as the anion.

Acids and Metals

Acids react with certain metals to produce hydrogen gas (H_2) and a salt. Active metals include potassium, sodium, calcium, magnesium, aluminum, zinc, iron, and tin. In these single replacement reactions, the metal ion replaces the hydrogen in the acid.

$$Mg(s) + 2HCl(aq) \longrightarrow H_2(g) + MgCl_2(aq)$$
  Metal   Acid   Hydrogen   Salt

$$Zn(s) + 2HNO_3(aq) \longrightarrow H_2(g) + Zn(NO_3)_2(aq)$$
  Metal   Acid   Hydrogen   Salt

Acids React with Carbonates or Bicarbonates

When an acid is added to a carbonate or bicarbonate, the products are carbon dioxide gas, water, and a salt. The acid reacts with CO_3^{2-} or HCO_3^- to produce carbonic acid, H_2CO_3, which breaks down rapidly to CO_2 and H_2O.

$$2HCl(aq) + Na_2CO_3(aq) \longrightarrow CO_2(g) + H_2O(l) + 2NaCl(aq)$$
   Acid   Carbonate   Carbon   Water   Salt
                                            dioxide

$$HBr(aq) + NaHCO_3(aq) \longrightarrow CO_2(g) + H_2O(l) + NaBr(aq)$$
  Acid   Bicarbonate   Carbon   Water   Salt
                                         dioxide

Acids and Hydroxides: Neutralization

Neutralization is a reaction between a strong or weak acid with a strong base to produce a water and a salt. The H^+ of the acid and the OH^- of the base combine to form water. The salt is the combination of the cation from the base and the anion from the acid. We can write the following equation for the neutralization reaction between HCl and NaOH:

$$HCl(aq) + NaOH(aq) \longrightarrow H_2O(l) + NaCl(aq)$$
  Acid   Base   Water   Salt

If we write the strong acid HCl and the strong base NaOH as ions, we see that H^+ combines with OH^- to form water, leaving the ions Na^+ and Cl^- in solution.

$$H^+(aq) + Cl^-(aq) + Na^+(aq) + OH^-(aq) \longrightarrow H_2O(l) + Na^+(aq) + Cl^-(aq)$$

When we omit the ions that do not change during the reaction (*spectator ions*), we obtain the *net ionic equation*.

$$H^+(aq) + \cancel{Cl^-(aq)} + \cancel{Na^+(aq)} + OH^-(aq) \longrightarrow H_2O(l) + \cancel{Na^+(aq)} + \cancel{Cl^-(aq)}$$

The net ionic equation for the neutralization of H^+ and OH^- to form H_2O is

$$H^+(aq) + OH^-(aq) \longrightarrow H_2O(l)$$ Net ionic equation

Balancing Neutralization Equations

In a neutralization reaction, one H^+ always reacts with one OH^-. Therefore, a neutralization equation may need coefficients to balance the H^+ from the acid with the OH^- from the base as shown in Sample Problem 11.11.

LEARNING GOAL

Write balanced equations for reactions of acids with metals, carbonates or bicarbonates, and bases.

Magnesium reacts rapidly with acid and forms H_2 gas and a salt of magnesium.

⚛ **CORE CHEMISTRY SKILL**

Writing Equations for Reactions of Acids and Bases

When sodium bicarbonate (baking soda) reacts with an acid (vinegar), the products are carbon dioxide gas, water, and a salt.

Guide to Balancing an Equation for Neutralization

STEP 1
Write the reactants and products.

STEP 2
Balance the H⁺ in the acid with the OH⁻ in the base.

STEP 3
Balance the H_2O with the H⁺ and the OH⁻.

STEP 4
Write the salt from the remaining ions.

SAMPLE PROBLEM 11.11 Balancing Equations for Acids

Write the balanced equation for the neutralization of $HCl(aq)$ and $Ba(OH)_2(s)$.

SOLUTION

STEP 1 Write the reactants and products.

$$HCl(aq) + Ba(OH)_2(s) \longrightarrow H_2O(l) + salt$$

STEP 2 Balance the H⁺ in the acid with the OH⁻ in the base. Placing a coefficient of 2 in front of the HCl provides 2H⁺ for the 2OH⁻ from $Ba(OH)_2$.

$$2HCl(aq) + Ba(OH)_2(s) \longrightarrow H_2O(l) + salt$$

STEP 3 Balance the H_2O with the H⁺ and the OH⁻. Use a coefficient of 2 in front of H_2O to balance 2H⁺ and 2OH⁻.

$$2HCl(aq) + Ba(OH)_2(s) \longrightarrow 2H_2O(l) + salt$$

STEP 4 Write the salt from the remaining ions. Use the ions Ba^{2+} and $2Cl^-$ and write the formula for the salt as $BaCl_2$.

$$2HCl(aq) + Ba(OH)_2(s) \longrightarrow 2H_2O(l) + BaCl_2(aq)$$

STUDY CHECK 11.11

Write the balanced equation for the reaction between $H_2SO_4(aq)$ and $K_2CO_3(s)$.

ANSWER

$$H_2SO_4(aq) + K_2CO_3(s) \longrightarrow CO_2(g) + H_2O(l) + K_2SO_4(aq)$$

Chemistry Link to Health
Antacids

Antacids are substances used to neutralize excess stomach acid (HCl). Some antacids are mixtures of aluminum hydroxide and magnesium hydroxide. These hydroxides are not very soluble in water, so the levels of available OH⁻ are not damaging to the intestinal tract. However, aluminum hydroxide has the side effects of producing constipation and binding phosphate in the intestinal tract, which may cause weakness and loss of appetite. Magnesium hydroxide has a laxative effect. These side effects are less likely when a combination of the antacids is used.

$$Al(OH)_3(s) + 3HCl(aq) \longrightarrow 3H_2O(l) + AlCl_3(aq)$$

$$Mg(OH)_2(s) + 2HCl(aq) \longrightarrow 2H_2O(l) + MgCl_2(aq)$$

Antacids neutralize excess stomach acid.

Some antacids use calcium carbonate to neutralize excess stomach acid. About 10% of the calcium is absorbed into the bloodstream, where it elevates the level of serum calcium. Calcium carbonate is not recommended for patients who have peptic ulcers or a tendency to form kidney stones, which typically consist of an insoluble calcium salt.

$$CaCO_3(s) + 2HCl(aq) \longrightarrow CO_2(g) + H_2O(l) + CaCl_2(aq)$$

Still other antacids contain sodium bicarbonate. This type of antacid neutralizes excess gastric acid, increases blood pH, but also elevates sodium levels in the body fluids. It also is not recommended in the treatment of peptic ulcers.

$$NaHCO_3(s) + HCl(aq) \longrightarrow CO_2(g) + H_2O(l) + NaCl(aq)$$

The neutralizing substances in some antacid preparations are given in Table 11.8.

TABLE 11.8 Basic Compounds in Some Antacids

Antacid	Base(s)
Amphojel	$Al(OH)_3$
Milk of magnesia	$Mg(OH)_2$
Mylanta, Maalox, Di-Gel, Gelusil, Riopan	$Mg(OH)_2$, $Al(OH)_3$
Bisodol, Rolaids	$CaCO_3$, $Mg(OH)_2$
Titralac, Tums, Pepto-Bismol	$CaCO_3$
Alka-Seltzer	$NaHCO_3$, $KHCO_3$

QUESTIONS AND PROBLEMS

11.7 Reactions of Acids and Bases

LEARNING GOAL Write balanced equations for reactions of acids with metals, carbonates or bicarbonates, and bases.

11.55 Complete and balance the equation for each of the following reactions:
  a. $ZnCO_3(s) + HBr(aq) \longrightarrow$
  b. $Zn(s) + HCl(aq) \longrightarrow$
  c. $HCl(aq) + NaHCO_3(s) \longrightarrow$
  d. $H_2SO_4(aq) + Mg(OH)_2(s) \longrightarrow$

11.56 Complete and balance the equation for each of the following reactions:
  a. $KHCO_3(s) + HBr(aq) \longrightarrow$
  b. $Ca(s) + H_2SO_4(aq) \longrightarrow$
  c. $H_2SO_4(aq) + Ca(OH)_2(s) \longrightarrow$
  d. $Na_2CO_3(s) + H_2SO_4(aq) \longrightarrow$

11.57 Balance each of the following neutralization reactions:
  a. $HCl(aq) + Mg(OH)_2(s) \longrightarrow H_2O(l) + MgCl_2(aq)$
  b. $H_3PO_4(aq) + LiOH(aq) \longrightarrow H_2O(l) + Li_3PO_4(aq)$

11.58 Balance each of the following neutralization reactions:
  a. $HNO_3(aq) + Ba(OH)_2(s) \longrightarrow H_2O(l) + Ba(NO_3)_2(aq)$
  b. $H_2SO_4(aq) + Al(OH)_3(s) \longrightarrow H_2O(l) + Al_2(SO_4)_3(aq)$

11.59 Write a balanced equation for the neutralization of each of the following:
  a. $H_2SO_4(aq)$ and $NaOH(aq)$
  b. $HCl(aq)$ and $Fe(OH)_3(s)$
  c. $H_2CO_3(aq)$ and $Mg(OH)_2(s)$

11.60 Write a balanced equation for the neutralization of each of the following:
  a. $H_3PO_4(aq)$ and $NaOH(aq)$
  b. $HI(aq)$ and $LiOH(aq)$
  c. $HNO_3(aq)$ and $Ca(OH)_2(s)$

11.8 Acid–Base Titration

Suppose we need to find the molarity of a solution of HCl, which has an unknown concentration. We can do this by a laboratory procedure called **titration** in which we neutralize an acid sample with a known amount of base. In a titration, we place a measured volume of the acid in a flask and add a few drops of an **indicator**, such as phenolphthalein. An indicator is a compound that dramatically changes color when pH of the solution changes. In an acidic solution, phenolphthalein is colorless. Then we fill a buret with a NaOH solution of known molarity and carefully add NaOH solution to neutralize the acid in the flask (see Figure 11.6). We know that neutralization has taken place when the phenolphthalein in the solution changes from colorless to pink. This is called the neutralization **endpoint**. From the measured volume of the NaOH solution and its molarity, we calculate the number of moles of NaOH, the moles of acid, and use the measured volume of acid to calculate its concentration.

LEARNING GOAL

Calculate the molarity or volume of an acid or base solution from titration information.

FIGURE 11.6 ▶ The titration of an acid. A known volume of an acid is placed in a flask with an indicator and titrated with a measured volume of a base solution, such as NaOH, to the neutralization endpoint.

Q What data is needed to determine the molarity of the acid in the flask?

⚛ CORE CHEMISTRY SKILL

Calculating Molarity or Volume of an Acid or Base in a Titration

Guide to Calculations for an Acid–Base Titration

STEP 1
State the given and needed quantities and concentrations.

STEP 2
Write a plan to calculate the molarity or volume.

STEP 3
State equalities and conversion factors, including concentrations.

STEP 4
Set up the problem to calculate the needed quantity.

▶ **SAMPLE PROBLEM 11.12 Titration of an Acid**

If 16.3 mL of a 0.185 M $Sr(OH)_2$ solution is used to titrate the HCl in a 25.0-mL sample of gastric juice, what is the molarity of the HCl solution?

$$Sr(OH)_2(aq) + 2HCl(aq) \longrightarrow 2H_2O(l) + SrCl_2(aq)$$

SOLUTION

STEP 1 State the given and needed quantities and concentrations.

	Given	Need
ANALYZE THE PROBLEM	25.0 mL (0.0250 L) of HCl solution	molarity of the HCl solution
	16.3 mL of 0.185 M $Sr(OH)_2$ solution	
Neutralization Equation		
$Sr(OH)_2(aq) + 2HCl(aq) \longrightarrow 2H_2O(l) + SrCl_2(aq)$		

STEP 2 Write a plan to calculate the molarity.

mL of $Sr(OH)_2$ solution → **Metric factor** → L of $Sr(OH)_2$ solution → **Molarity** → moles of $Sr(OH)_2$ → **Mole–mole factor** → moles of HCl → **Divide by liters** → molarity of HCl solution

STEP 3 State equalities and conversion factors, including concentrations.

1 L of $Sr(OH)_2$ solution = 1000 mL of $Sr(OH)_2$ solution

$$\frac{1\ L\ Sr(OH)_2\ solution}{1000\ mL\ Sr(OH)_2\ solution} \quad and \quad \frac{1000\ mL\ Sr(OH)_2\ solution}{1\ L\ Sr(OH)_2\ solution}$$

1 L of $Sr(OH)_2$ solution = 0.185 mole of $Sr(OH)_2$

$$\frac{1\ L\ Sr(OH)_2\ solution}{0.185\ mole\ Sr(OH)_2} \quad and \quad \frac{0.185\ mole\ Sr(OH)_2}{1\ L\ Sr(OH)_2\ solution}$$

2 moles of HCl = 1 mole of $Sr(OH)_2$

$$\frac{2\ moles\ HCl}{1\ mole\ Sr(OH)_2} \quad and \quad \frac{1\ mole\ Sr(OH)_2}{2\ moles\ HCl}$$

STEP 4 Set up the problem to calculate the needed quantity.

$$16.3\ \cancel{mL\ Sr(OH)_2\ solution} \times \frac{1\ \cancel{L\ Sr(OH)_2\ solution}}{1000\ \cancel{mL\ Sr(OH)_2\ solution}} \times \frac{0.185\ \cancel{mole\ Sr(OH)_2}}{1\ \cancel{L\ Sr(OH)_2\ solution}} \times \frac{2\ moles\ HCl}{1\ \cancel{mole\ Sr(OH)_2}}$$

$$= 0.00603\ mole\ of\ HCl$$

$$molarity\ of\ HCl\ solution = \frac{0.00603\ mole\ HCl}{0.0250\ L\ HCl\ solution} = 0.241\ M\ HCl\ solution$$

Interactive Video

Acid-Base Titration

STUDY CHECK 11.12

What is the molarity of an HCl solution if 28.6 mL of a 0.175 M NaOH solution is needed to titrate a 25.0-mL sample of the HCl solution?

ANSWER

0.200 M HCl solution

QUESTIONS AND PROBLEMS

11.8 Acid–Base Titration

LEARNING GOAL Calculate the molarity or volume of an acid or base solution from titration information.

11.61 What is the molarity of a solution of HCl if 5.00 mL of the HCl solution is titrated with 28.6 mL of a 0.145 NaOH solution?

$$HCl(aq) + NaOH(aq) \longrightarrow H_2O(l) + NaCl(aq)$$

11.62 What is the molarity of the acetic acid solution if 29.7 mL of a 0.205 M KOH solution is required to titrate 25.0 mL of a solution of $HC_2H_3O_2$?

$$HC_2H_3O_2(aq) + KOH(aq) \longrightarrow H_2O(l) + KC_2H_3O_2(aq)$$

11.63 If 38.2 mL of a 0.163 M KOH solution is required to titrate 25.0 mL of a H_2SO_4 solution, what is the molarity of the H_2SO_4 solution?

$$H_2SO_4(aq) + 2KOH(aq) \longrightarrow 2H_2O(l) + K_2SO_4(aq)$$

11.64 If 32.8 mL of a 0.162 M NaOH solution is required to titrate 25.0 mL of a solution of H_2SO_4, what is the molarity of the H_2SO_4 solution?

$$H_2SO_4(aq) + 2NaOH(aq) \longrightarrow 2H_2O(l) + Na_2SO_4(aq)$$

11.65 A solution of 0.204 M NaOH is used to titrate 50.0 mL of a 0.0224 M H_3PO_4 solution. What volume, in milliliters, of the NaOH solution is required?

$$H_3PO_4(aq) + 3NaOH(aq) \longrightarrow 3H_2O(l) + Na_3PO_4(aq)$$

11.66 A solution of 0.312 M KOH is used to titrate 15.0 mL of a 0.186 M H_3PO_4 solution. What volume, in milliliters, of the KOH solution is required?

$$H_3PO_4(aq) + 3KOH(aq) \longrightarrow 3H_2O(l) + K_3PO_4(aq)$$

11.9 Buffers

The pH of water and most solutions changes drastically when a small amount of acid or base is added. However, when an acid or a base is added to a *buffer* solution, there is little change in pH. A **buffer solution** maintains the pH of a solution by neutralizing small amounts of added acid or base. In the human body, whole blood contains plasma, white blood cells and platelets, and red blood cells. Blood plasma contains buffers that maintain a consistent pH of about 7.4. If the pH of the blood plasma goes slightly above or below 7.4, changes in our oxygen levels and our metabolic processes can be drastic enough to cause death. Even though we obtain acids and bases from foods and cellular reactions, the buffers in the body absorb those compounds so effectively that the pH of our blood plasma remains essentially unchanged (see Figure 11.7).

H_2O

Buffer

LEARNING GOAL

Describe the role of buffers in maintaining the pH of a solution; calculate the pH of a buffer.

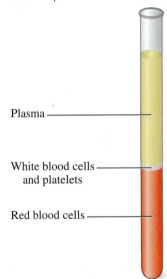

Plasma

White blood cells and platelets

Red blood cells

Whole blood consists of plasma, white blood cells and platelets, and red blood cells.

FIGURE 11.7 ▶ Adding an acid or a base to water changes the pH drastically, but a buffer resists pH change when small amounts of acid or base are added.

Q Why does the pH change several pH units when acid is added to water, but not when acid is added to a buffer?

In a buffer, an acid must be present to react with any OH^- that is added, and a base must be available to react with any added H_3O^+. However, that acid and base must not neutralize each other. Therefore, a combination of an acid–base conjugate pair is used in buffers. Most buffer solutions consist of nearly equal concentrations of a weak acid and a salt containing its conjugate base. Buffers may also contain a weak base and the salt of the weak base, which contains its conjugate acid.

FIGURE 11.8 ▶ The buffer described here consists of about equal concentrations of acetic acid ($HC_2H_3O_2$) and its conjugate base acetate ion ($C_2H_3O_2^-$). Adding H_3O^+ to the buffer neutralizes some $C_2H_3O_2^-$, whereas adding OH^- neutralizes some $HC_2H_3O_2$. The pH of the solution is maintained as long as the added amount of acid or base is small compared to the concentrations of the buffer components.

Q How does this acetic acid–acetate ion buffer maintain pH?

For example, a typical buffer can be made from the weak acid acetic acid ($HC_2H_3O_2$) and its salt, sodium acetate ($NaC_2H_3O_2$). As a weak acid, acetic acid dissociates slightly in water to form H_3O^+ and a very small amount of $C_2H_3O_2^-$. The addition of its salt, sodium acetate, provides a much larger concentration of acetate ion ($C_2H_3O_2^-$), which is necessary for its buffering capability.

$$HC_2H_3O_2(aq) + H_2O(l) \rightleftharpoons H_3O^+(aq) + C_2H_3O_2^-(aq)$$
Large amount   Large amount

We can now describe how this buffer solution maintains the $[H_3O^+]$. When a small amount of acid is added, the additional H_3O^+ combines with the acetate ion, $C_2H_3O_2^-$, causing the equilibrium to shift in the direction of the reactants, acetic acid and water. There will be a slight decrease in the $[C_2H_3O_2^-]$ and a slight increase in the $[HC_2H_3O_2]$, but both the $[H_3O^+]$ and pH are maintained (see Figure 11.8).

$$HC_2H_3O_2(aq) + H_2O(l) \longleftarrow H_3O^+(aq) + C_2H_3O_2^-(aq)$$
Equilibrium shifts in the
direction of the reactants

If a small amount of base is added to this same buffer solution, it is neutralized by the acetic acid, $HC_2H_3O_2$, which shifts the equilibrium in the direction of the products acetate ion and water. The $[HC_2H_3O_2]$ decreases slightly and the $[C_2H_3O_2^-]$ increases slightly, but again the $[H_3O^+]$ and thus the pH of the solution are maintained.

$$HC_2H_3O_2(aq) + OH^-(aq) \longrightarrow H_2O(l) + C_2H_3O_2^-(aq)$$
Equilibrium shifts in the
direction of the products

⚛ CORE CHEMISTRY SKILL

Calculating the pH of a Buffer

Calculating the pH of a Buffer

By rearranging the K_a expression to give $[H_3O^+]$, we can obtain the ratio of the acetic acid/acetate buffer.

$$K_a = \frac{[H_3O^+][C_2H_3O_2^-]}{[HC_2H_3O_2]}$$

Solving for $[H_3O^+]$ gives:

$$[H_3O^+] = K_a \times \frac{[HC_2H_3O_2]}{[C_2H_3O_2^-]} \quad \begin{array}{l} \longleftarrow \text{ Weak acid} \\ \longleftarrow \text{ Conjugate base} \end{array}$$

In this rearrangement of K_a, the weak acid is in the numerator and the conjugate base in the denominator. We can now calculate the $[H_3O^+]$ and pH for an acetic acid buffer as shown in Sample Problem 11.13.

▶**SAMPLE PROBLEM 11.13** Calculating the pH of a Buffer

The K_a for acetic acid, $HC_2H_3O_2$, is 1.8×10^{-5}. What is the pH of a buffer prepared with 1.0 M $HC_2H_3O_2$ and 1.0 M $C_2H_3O_2^-$?

$$HC_2H_3O_2(aq) + H_2O(l) \rightleftharpoons H_3O^+(aq) + C_2H_3O_2^-(aq)$$

SOLUTION

STEP 1 State the given and needed quantities.

	Given	**Need**
ANALYZE THE PROBLEM	1.0 M $HC_2H_3O_2$, 1.0 M $C_2H_3O_2^-$	pH
Equation		
$HC_2H_3O_2(aq) + H_2O(l) \rightleftharpoons H_3O^+(aq) + C_2H_3O_2^-(aq)$		

STEP 2 Write the K_a expression and rearrange for $[H_3O^+]$.

$$K_a = \frac{[H_3O^+][C_2H_3O_2^-]}{[HC_2H_3O_2]}$$

$$[H_3O^+] = K_a \times \frac{[HC_2H_3O_2]}{[C_2H_3O_2^-]}$$

STEP 3 Substitute $[HA]$ and $[A^-]$ into the K_a expression.

$$[H_3O^+] = 1.8 \times 10^{-5} \times \frac{[1.0]}{[1.0]}$$

$$[H_3O^+] = 1.8 \times 10^{-5} \, M$$

STEP 4 Use $[H_3O^+]$ to calculate pH. Placing the $[H_3O^+]$ into the pH equation gives the pH of the buffer.

$$pH = -\log[1.8 \times 10^{-5}] = 4.74$$

> **Guide to Calculating pH of a Buffer**
>
> **STEP 1**
> State the given and needed quantities.
>
> **STEP 2**
> Write the K_a expression and rearrange for $[H_3O^+]$.
>
> **STEP 3**
> Substitute $[HA]$ and $[A^-]$ into the K_a expression.
>
> **STEP 4**
> Use $[H_3O^+]$ to calculate pH.

STUDY CHECK 11.13

One of the conjugate acid–base pairs that buffers the blood plasma is $H_2PO_4^-/HPO_4^{2-}$, which has a K_a of 6.2×10^{-8}. What is the pH of a buffer that is prepared from 0.10 M $H_2PO_4^-$ and 0.50 M HPO_4^{2-}?

ANSWER

pH = 7.91

Because K_a is a constant at a given temperature, the $[H_3O^+]$ is determined by the $[HC_2H_3O_2]/[C_2H_3O_2^-]$ ratio. As long as the addition of small amounts of either acid or base changes the ratio of $[HC_2H_3O_2]/[C_2H_3O_2^-]$ only slightly, the changes in $[H_3O^+]$ will be small and the pH will be maintained. If a large amount of acid or base is added, the *buffering capacity* of the system may be exceeded. Buffers can be prepared from conjugate acid–base pairs such as $H_2PO_4^-/HPO_4^{2-}$, HPO_4^{2-}/PO_4^{3-}, HCO_3^-/CO_3^{2-}, or NH_4^+/NH_3. The pH of the buffer solution will depend on the conjugate acid–base pair chosen.

Using a common phosphate buffer for biological specimens, we can look at the effect of using different ratios of $[H_2PO_4^-]/[HPO_4^{2-}]$ on the $[H_3O^+]$ and pH. The K_a of $H_2PO_4^-$ is 6.2×10^{-8}. The equation and the $[H_3O^+]$ are written as follows:

$$H_2PO_4^-(aq) + H_2O(l) \rightleftharpoons H_3O^+(aq) + HPO_4^{2-}(aq)$$

$$[H_3O^+] = K_a \times \frac{[H_2PO_4^-]}{[HPO_4^{2-}]}$$

K_a	$\dfrac{[H_2PO_4^-]}{[HPO_4^{2-}]}$	Ratio	$[H_3O^+]$	pH
6.2×10^{-8}	$\dfrac{1.0\,M}{0.10\,M}$	$\dfrac{10}{1}$	6.2×10^{-7}	6.21
6.2×10^{-8}	$\dfrac{1.0\,M}{1.0\,M}$	$\dfrac{1}{1}$	6.2×10^{-8}	7.21
6.2×10^{-8}	$\dfrac{0.10\,M}{1.0\,M}$	$\dfrac{1}{10}$	6.2×10^{-9}	8.21

To prepare a phosphate buffer with a pH close to the pH of a biological sample, 7.4, we would choose concentrations that are about equal, such as 1.0 M $H_2PO_4^-$ and 1.0 M HPO_4^{2-}.

▶ **SAMPLE PROBLEM 11.14** **Preparation of Buffers**

What is the pH of a buffer made from 0.10 M formic acid ($HCHO_2$) and 0.10 M formate (CHO_2^-)? The K_a for formic acid is 1.8×10^{-4}.

SOLUTION

$$[H_3O^+] = K_a \times \frac{[HCHO_2]}{[CHO_2^-]}$$

$$[H_3O^+] = 1.8 \times 10^{-4} \times \frac{[0.10]}{[0.10]} = 1.8 \times 10^{-4}\,M$$

$$pH = -\log[1.8 \times 10^{-4}] = 3.74$$

STUDY CHECK 11.14

What is the pH of a buffer made from 0.10 M formic acid ($HCHO_2$) and 0.010 M formate (CHO_2^-)?

ANSWER

pH = 2.74

 # Chemistry Link to **Health**
Buffers in the Blood Plasma

The arterial blood plasma has a normal pH of 7.35 to 7.45. If changes in H_3O^+ lower the pH below 6.8 or raise it above 8.0, cells cannot function properly and death may result. In our cells, CO_2 is continually produced as an end product of cellular metabolism. Some CO_2 is carried to the lungs for elimination, and the rest dissolves in body fluids such as plasma and saliva, forming carbonic acid, H_2CO_3. As a weak acid, carbonic acid dissociates to give bicarbonate, HCO_3^-, and H_3O^+. More of the anion HCO_3^- is supplied by the kidneys to give an important buffer system in the body fluid—the H_2CO_3/HCO_3^- buffer.

$$CO_2(g) + H_2O(l) \rightleftharpoons H_2CO_3(aq) \rightleftharpoons$$
$$H_3O^+(aq) + HCO_3^-(aq)$$

Excess H_3O^+ entering the body fluids reacts with the HCO_3^-, and excess OH^- reacts with the carbonic acid.

$$H_2CO_3(aq) + H_2O(l) \longleftarrow H_3O^+(aq) + HCO_3^-(aq)$$
Equilibrium shifts in the direction of the reactants

$$H_2CO_3(aq) + OH^-(aq) \longrightarrow H_2O(l) + HCO_3^-(aq)$$
Equilibrium shifts in the direction of the products

For carbonic acid, we can write the equilibrium expression as

$$K_a = \frac{[H_3O^+][HCO_3^-]}{[H_2CO_3]}$$

To maintain the normal blood plasma pH (7.35 to 7.45), the ratio of $[H_2CO_3]/[HCO_3^-]$ needs to be about 1 to 10, which is obtained by the concentrations in the blood plasma of 0.0024 M H_2CO_3 and 0.024 M HCO_3^-.

$$[H_3O^+] = K_a \times \frac{[H_2CO_3]}{[HCO_3^-]}$$

$$[H_3O^+] = 4.3 \times 10^{-7} \times \frac{[0.0024]}{[0.024]}$$

$$= 4.3 \times 10^{-7} \times 0.10 = 4.3 \times 10^{-8} \text{ M}$$

$$pH = -\log[4.3 \times 10^{-8}] = 7.37$$

In the body, the concentration of carbonic acid is closely associated with the partial pressure of CO_2, P_{CO_2}. Table 11.9 lists the normal values for arterial blood. If the CO_2 level rises, increasing $[H_2CO_3]$, the equilibrium shifts to produce more H_3O^+, which lowers the pH. This condition is called *acidosis*. Difficulty with ventilation or gas diffusion can lead to respiratory acidosis, which can happen in emphysema or when an accident or depressive drugs affect the medulla of the brain.

A lowering of the CO_2 level leads to a high blood pH, a condition called *alkalosis*. Excitement, trauma, or a high temperature may cause a person to hyperventilate, which expels large amounts of CO_2. As the partial pressure of CO_2 in the blood falls below normal, the equilibrium shifts from H_2CO_3 to CO_2 and H_2O. This shift decreases the $[H_3O^+]$ and raises the pH. The kidneys also regulate H_3O^+ and HCO_3^-, but they do so more slowly than the adjustment made by the lungs during ventilation.

Table 11.10 lists some of the conditions that lead to changes in the blood pH and some possible treatments.

TABLE 11.9 Normal Values for Blood Buffer in Arterial Blood

P_{CO_2}	40 mmHg
H_2CO_3	2.4 mmoles/L of plasma
HCO_3^-	24 mmoles/L of plasma
pH	7.35 to 7.45

TABLE 11.10 Acidosis and Alkalosis: Symptoms, Causes, and Treatments

Respiratory Acidosis: $CO_2\uparrow$ pH$\downarrow$	
Symptoms:	Failure to ventilate, suppression of breathing, disorientation, weakness, coma
Causes:	Lung disease blocking gas diffusion (e.g., emphysema, pneumonia, bronchitis, asthma); depression of respiratory center by drugs, cardiopulmonary arrest, stroke, poliomyelitis, or nervous system disorders
Treatment:	Correction of disorder, infusion of bicarbonate
Metabolic Acidosis: $H^+\uparrow$ pH$\downarrow$	
Symptoms:	Increased ventilation, fatigue, confusion
Causes:	Renal disease, including hepatitis and cirrhosis; increased acid production in diabetes mellitus, hyperthyroidism, alcoholism, and starvation; loss of alkali in diarrhea; acid retention in renal failure
Treatment:	Sodium bicarbonate given orally, dialysis for renal failure, insulin treatment for diabetic ketosis
Respiratory Alkalosis: $CO_2\downarrow$ pH$\uparrow$	
Symptoms:	Increased rate and depth of breathing, numbness, light-headedness, tetany
Causes:	Hyperventilation because of anxiety, hysteria, fever, exercise; reaction to drugs such as salicylate, quinine, and antihistamines; conditions causing hypoxia (e.g., pneumonia, pulmonary edema, heart disease)
Treatment:	Elimination of anxiety-producing state, rebreathing into a paper bag
Metabolic Alkalosis: $H^+\downarrow$ pH$\uparrow$	
Symptoms:	Depressed breathing, apathy, confusion
Causes:	Vomiting, diseases of the adrenal glands, ingestion of excess alkali
Treatment:	Infusion of saline solution, treatment of underlying diseases

QUESTIONS AND PROBLEMS

11.9 Buffers

LEARNING GOAL Describe the role of buffers in maintaining the pH of a solution; calculate the pH of a buffer.

11.67 Which of the following represents a buffer system? Explain.
  a. NaOH and NaCl
  b. H_2CO_3 and $NaHCO_3$
  c. HF and KF
  d. KCl and NaCl

11.68 Which of the following represents a buffer system? Explain.
  a. $HClO_2$
  b. $NaNO_3$
  c. $HC_2H_3O_2$ and $NaC_2H_3O_2$
  d. HCl and NaOH

11.69 Consider the buffer system of hydrofluoric acid, HF, and its salt, NaF.

$$HF(aq) + H_2O(l) \rightleftharpoons H_3O^+(aq) + F^-(aq)$$

  a. The purpose of this buffer system is to:
    1. maintain $[HF]$ **2.** maintain $[F^-]$
    3. maintain pH
  b. The salt of the weak acid is needed to:
    1. provide the conjugate base
    2. neutralize added H_3O^+
    3. provide the conjugate acid
  c. If OH^- is added, it is neutralized by:
    1. the salt   **2.** H_2O **3.** H_3O^+
  d. When H_3O^+ is added, the equilibrium shifts in the direction of the:
    1. reactants   **2.** products   **3.** does not change

11.70 Consider the buffer system of nitrous acid, HNO_2, and its salt, $NaNO_2$.

$$HNO_2(aq) + H_2O(l) \rightleftharpoons H_3O^+(aq) + NO_2^-(aq)$$

a. The purpose of this buffer system is to:
  1. maintain $[HNO_2]$ 2. maintain $[NO_2^-]$
  3. maintain pH
b. The weak acid is needed to:
  1. provide the conjugate base   2. neutralize added OH^-
  3. provide the conjugate acid
c. If H_3O^+ is added, it is neutralized by:
  1. the salt   2. H_2O 3. OH^-
d. When OH^- is added, the equilibrium shifts in the direction of the:
  1. reactants   2. products   3. does not change

11.71 Nitrous acid has a K_a of 4.5×10^{-4}. What is the pH of a buffer solution containing 0.10 M HNO_2 and 0.10 M NO_2^-?

11.72 Acetic acid has a K_a of 1.8×10^{-5}. What is the pH of a buffer solution containing 0.15 M $HC_2H_3O_2$ and 0.15 M $C_2H_3O_2^-$?

11.73 Using Table 11.4 for K_a values, compare the pH of a HF buffer that contains 0.10 M HF and 0.10 M NaF with another HF buffer that contains 0.060 M HF and 0.120 M NaF.

11.74 Using Table 11.4 for K_a values, compare the pH of a H_2CO_3 buffer that contains 0.10 M H_2CO_3 and 0.10 M $NaHCO_3$ with another H_2CO_3 buffer that contains 0.15 M H_2CO_3 and 0.050 M $NaHCO_3$.

Rx Clinical Applications

11.75 Why would the pH of your blood plasma increase if you breathe fast?

11.76 Why would the pH of your blood plasma decrease if you hold your breath?

11.77 Someone with kidney failure excretes urine with large amounts of HCO_3^-. How would this loss of HCO_3^- affect the pH of the blood plasma?

11.78 Someone with severe diabetes obtains energy by the breakdown of fats, which produce large amounts of acidic substances. How would this affect the pH of the blood plasma?

 # Clinical Update
Acid Reflux Disease

Larry has not been feeling well lately. He tells his doctor that he has discomfort and a burning feeling in his chest, and a sour taste in his throat and mouth. At times, Larry says he feels bloated after a big meal, has a dry cough, is hoarse, and sometimes has a sore throat. He has tried antacids, but they do not bring any relief.

The doctor tells Larry that he thinks he has acid reflux. At the top of the stomach there is a valve, the lower esophageal sphincter, that normally closes after food passes through it. However, if the valve does not close completely, acid produced in the stomach to digest food can move up into the esophagus, a condition called *acid reflux*. The acid, which is hydrochloric acid, HCl, is produced in the stomach to kill bacteria, microorganisms, and to activate the enzymes we need to break down food.

If acid reflux occurs, the strong acid HCl comes in contact with the lining of the esophagus, where it causes irritation and produces a burning feeling in the chest. Sometimes the pain in the chest is called *heartburn*. If the HCl reflux goes high enough to reach the throat, a sour taste may be noticed in the mouth. If Larry's symptoms occur three or more times a week, he may have a chronic condition known as *acid reflux disease* or *gastroesophageal reflux disease* (GERD).

Larry's doctor orders an *esophageal pH test* in which the amount of acid entering the esophagus from the stomach is measured over 24 h. A probe that measures the pH is inserted into the lower esophagus above the esophageal sphincter. The pH measurements indicate a reflux episode each time the pH drops to 4 or less.

In the 24-h period, Larry has several reflux episodes and his doctor determines that he has chronic GERD. He and Larry discuss treatment for GERD, which includes eating smaller meals, not lying down for 3 h after eating, making dietary changes, and losing weight. Antacids may be used to neutralize the acid coming up from the stomach. Other medications known as *proton pump inhibitors* (PPIs), such as Prilosec and Nexium, may be used to suppress the production of HCl in the stomach (gastric parietal cells), which raises the pH in the stomach to between 4 and 5, and gives the esophagus time to heal. Nexium may be given in oral doses of 40 mg once a day for 4 weeks. In severe GERD cases, an artificial valve may be created at the top of the stomach to strength the lower esophageal sphincter.

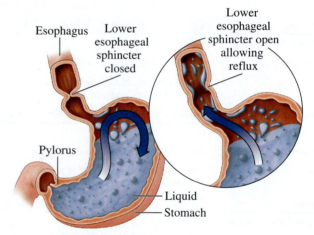

Rx Clinical Applications

11.79 At rest, the $[H_3O^+]$ of the stomach fluid is 2.0×10^{-4} M. What is the pH of the stomach fluid?

11.80 When food enters the stomach, HCl is released and the $[H_3O^+]$ of the stomach fluid rises to 4×10^{-2} M. What is the pH of the stomach fluid while eating?

11.81 In Larry's esophageal pH test, a pH value of 3.60 was recorded in the esophagus. What is the $[H_3O^+]$ in his esophagus?

11.82 After Larry had taken Nexium for 4 weeks, the pH in his stomach was raised to 4.52. What is the $[H_3O^+]$ in his stomach?

11.83 Write the balanced chemical equation for the neutralization reaction of stomach acid HCl with $CaCO_3$, an ingredient in some antacids.

11.84 Write the balanced chemical equation for the neutralization reaction of stomach acid HCl with $Al(OH)_3$, an ingredient in some antacids.

11.85 How many grams of $CaCO_3$ are required to neutralize 100. mL of stomach acid HCl, which is equivalent to 0.0400 M HCl?

11.86 How many grams of $Al(OH)_3$ are required to neutralize 150. mL of stomach acid HCl with a pH of 1.5?

CONCEPT MAP

ACIDS AND BASES

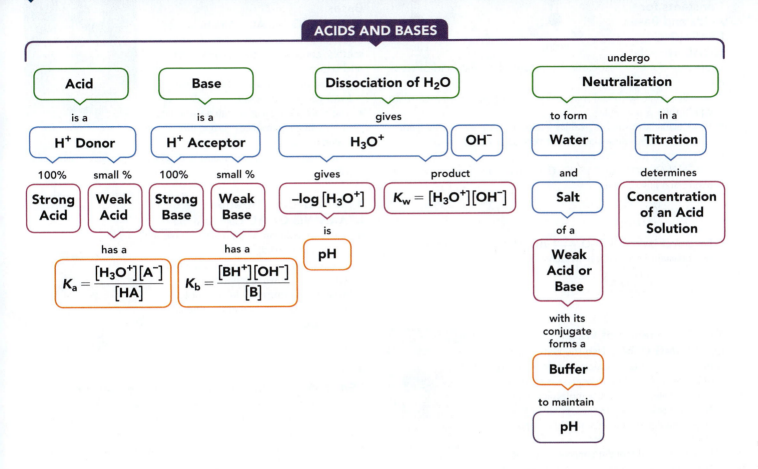

Acid → is a → **H⁺ Donor**
- 100% → **Strong Acid**
- small % → **Weak Acid** → has a → $K_a = \dfrac{[H_3O^+][A^-]}{[HA]}$

Base → is a → **H⁺ Acceptor**
- 100% → **Strong Base**
- small % → **Weak Base** → has a → $K_b = \dfrac{[BH^+][OH^-]}{[B]}$

Dissociation of H₂O → gives → **H_3O^+** and **OH^-**
- gives → $-\log[H_3O^+]$ → is → **pH**
- product → $K_w = [H_3O^+][OH^-]$

Neutralization (undergo)
- to form → **Water** and **Salt** → of a → **Weak Acid or Base** → with its conjugate forms a → **Buffer** → to maintain → **pH**
- in a → **Titration** → determines → **Concentration of an Acid Solution**

CHAPTER REVIEW

11.1 Acids and Bases
LEARNING GOAL Describe and name acids and bases.
- An Arrhenius acid produces H⁺ and an Arrhenius base produces OH⁻ in aqueous solutions.
- Acids taste sour, may sting, and neutralize bases.
- Bases taste bitter, feel slippery, and neutralize acids.
- Acids containing a simple anion use a *hydro* prefix, whereas acids with oxygen-containing polyatomic anions are named as *ic* or *ous* acids.

NaOH(s)

- ○ OH⁻
- ● Na⁺

— Water

$NaOH(s) \xrightarrow{H_2O} Na^+(aq) + OH^-(aq)$

Ionic compound   Dissociation   Hydroxide ion

11.2 Brønsted–Lowry Acids and Bases
LEARNING GOAL Identify conjugate acid–base pairs for Brønsted–Lowry acids and bases.

HCl + H₂O ⟶ H₃O⁺ + Cl⁻
Hydrogen chloride   Water   Hydronium ion   Chloride ion

Acid (H⁺ donor)   Base (H⁺ acceptor)   Acidic solution

- According to the Brønsted–Lowry theory, acids are H⁺ donors and bases are H⁺ acceptors.
- A conjugate acid–base pair is related by the loss or gain of one H⁺.
- For example, when the acid HF donates H⁺, the F⁻ is its conjugate base. The other acid–base pair would be H₃O⁺/H₂O.

$$HF(aq) + H_2O(l) \rightleftharpoons H_3O^+(aq) + F^-(aq)$$

11.3 Strengths of Acids and Bases
LEARNING GOAL Write equations for the dissociation of strong and weak acids; identify the direction of reaction.
- Strong acids dissociate completely in water, and the H⁺ is accepted by H₂O acting as a base.
- A weak acid dissociates slightly in water, producing only a small percentage of H₃O⁺.
- Strong bases are hydroxides of Groups 1A (1) and 2A (2) that dissociate completely in water.
- An important weak base is ammonia, NH₃.

HC₂H₃O₂
1 M

11.4 Dissociation Constants for Acids and Bases

HCHO₂   CHO₂⁻

LEARNING GOAL Write the expression for the dissociation constant of a weak acid or weak base.

- In water, weak acids and weak bases produce only a few ions when equilibrium is reached.
- Weak acids have small K_a values whereas strong acids, which are essentially 100% dissociated, have very large K_a values.
- The reaction for a weak acid can be written as $HA + H_2O \rightleftharpoons H_3O^+ + A^-$. The acid dissociation constant expression is written as

$$K_a = \frac{[H_3O^+][A^-]}{[HA]}.$$

- For a weak base, $B + H_2O \rightleftharpoons BH^+ + OH^-$, the base dissociation constant expression is written as

$$K_b = \frac{[BH^+][OH^-]}{[B]}.$$

11.5 Dissociation of Water

LEARNING GOAL Use the water dissociation constant expression to calculate the $[H_3O^+]$ and $[OH^-]$ in an aqueous solution.

$[H_3O^+] = [OH^-]$
Neutral solution

- In pure water, a few water molecules transfer H^+ to other water molecules, producing small, but equal, amounts of $[H_3O^+]$ and $[OH^-]$.
- In pure water, the molar concentrations of H_3O^+ and OH^- are each 1.0×10^{-7} mole/L.
- The *water dissociation constant expression*, K_w, $[H_3O^+][OH^-] = 1.0 \times 10^{-14}$ at 25 °C.
- In acidic solutions, the $[H_3O^+]$ is greater than the $[OH^-]$.
- In basic solutions, the $[OH^-]$ is greater than the $[H_3O^+]$.

11.6 The pH Scale

LEARNING GOAL Calculate pH from $[H_3O^+]$; given the pH, calculate the $[H_3O^+]$ and $[OH^-]$ of a solution.

- The pH scale is a range of numbers typically from 0 to 14, which represents the $[H_3O^+]$ of the solution.
- A neutral solution has a pH of 7.0. In acidic solutions, the pH is below 7.0; in basic solutions, the pH is above 7.0.
- Mathematically, pH is the negative logarithm of the hydronium ion concentration,

$$pH = -\log[H_3O^+].$$

11.7 Reactions of Acids and Bases

LEARNING GOAL Write balanced equations for reactions of acids with metals, carbonates or bicarbonates, and bases.

- An acid reacts with a metal to produce hydrogen gas and a salt.
- The reaction of an acid with a carbonate or bicarbonate produces carbon dioxide, water, and a salt.
- In neutralization, an acid reacts with a base to produce water and a salt.

11.8 Acid–Base Titration

LEARNING GOAL Calculate the molarity or volume of an acid or base solution from titration information.

- In a titration, an acid sample is neutralized with a known amount of a base.
- From the volume and molarity of the base, the concentration of the acid is calculated.

11.9 Buffers

LEARNING GOAL Describe the role of buffers in maintaining the pH of a solution; calculate the pH of a buffer.

- A buffer solution resists changes in pH when small amounts of an acid or a base are added.
- A buffer contains either a weak acid and its salt or a weak base and its salt.
- In a buffer, the weak acid reacts with added OH^-, and the anion of the salt reacts with added H_3O^+.
- Most buffer solutions consist of nearly equal concentrations of a weak acid and a salt containing its conjugate base.
- The pH of a buffer is calculated by solving the K_a expression for $[H_3O^+]$.

Buffer

KEY TERMS

acid A substance that dissolves in water and produces hydrogen ions (H^+), according to the Arrhenius theory. All acids are hydrogen ion donors, according to the Brønsted–Lowry theory.

acid dissociation constant, K_a The numerical value of the product of the ions from the dissociation of a weak acid divided by the concentration of the weak acid.

amphoteric Substances that can act as either an acid or a base in water.

base A substance that dissolves in water and produces hydroxide ions (OH^-) according to the Arrhenius theory. All bases are hydrogen ion acceptors, according to the Brønsted–Lowry theory.

base dissociation constant, K_b The numerical value of the product of the ions from the dissociation of a weak base divided by the concentration of the weak base.

Brønsted–Lowry acids and bases An acid is a hydrogen ion donor; a base is a hydrogen ion acceptor.

buffer solution A solution of a weak acid and its conjugate base or a weak base and its conjugate acid that maintains the pH by neutralizing added acid or base.

conjugate acid–base pair An acid and a base that differ by one H^+. When an acid donates a hydrogen ion, the product is its conjugate base, which is capable of accepting a hydrogen ion in the reverse reaction.

dissociation The separation of an acid or a base into ions in water.

endpoint The point at which an indicator changes color. For the indicator phenolphthalein, the color change occurs when the number of moles of OH^- is equal to the number of moles of H_3O^+ in the sample.

hydronium ion, H_3O^+ The ion formed by the attraction of a hydrogen ion, H^+, to a water molecule.

indicator A substance added to a titration sample that changes color when the pH of the solution changes.

neutral The term that describes a solution with equal concentrations of $[H_3O^+]$ and $[OH^-]$.

neutralization A reaction between an acid and a base to form water and a salt.

pH A measure of the $[H_3O^+]$ in a solution; $pH = -log[H_3O^+]$.

salt An ionic compound that contains a metal ion or NH_4^+ and a nonmetal or polyatomic ion other than OH^-.

strong acid An acid that completely dissociates in water.

strong base A base that completely dissociates in water.

titration The addition of base to an acid sample to determine the concentration of the acid.

water dissociation constant expression, K_w The product of $[H_3O^+]$ and $[OH^-]$ in solution; $K_w = [H_3O^+][OH^-]$.

weak acid An acid that is a poor donor of H^+ and dissociates only slightly in water.

weak base A base that is a poor acceptor of H^+ and produces only a small number of ions in water.

KEY MATH SKILLS

The chapter section containing each Key Math Skill is shown in parentheses at the end of each heading.

Calculating pH from $[H_3O^+]$ (11.6)

- The pH of a solution is calculated from the negative log of the $[H_3O^+]$.

$$pH = -log[H_3O^+]$$

Example: What is the pH of a solution that has $[H_3O^+] = 2.4 \times 10^{-11}$ M?

Answer: We substitute the given $[H_3O^+]$ into the pH equation and calculate the pH.

$$pH = -log[H_3O^+]$$

$\boxed{+/-}\,\boxed{log}\,2.4\,\boxed{EE\ or\ EXP}\,11\,\boxed{+/-}\,\boxed{=}$

$= 10.62$ (Two decimal places equal the 2 SFs in the $[H_3O^+]$ coefficient.)

Calculating $[H_3O^+]$ from pH (11.6)

- The calculation of $[H_3O^+]$ from the pH is done by reversing the pH calculation using the negative pH.

$$[H_3O^+] = 10^{-pH}$$

Example: What is the $[H_3O^+]$ of a solution with a pH of 4.80?

Answer: $[H_3O^+] = 10^{-pH}$
$= 10^{-4.80}$
$\boxed{2^{nd}}\,\boxed{log}\,\boxed{+/-}\,4.80\,\boxed{=}$
$= 1.6 \times 10^{-5}$ M

(2 SFs in the $[H_3O^+]$ equal the two decimal places in the pH.)

CORE CHEMISTRY SKILLS

The chapter section containing each Core Chemistry Skill is shown in parentheses at the end of each heading.

Identifying Conjugate Acid–Base Pairs (11.2)

- According to the Brønsted–Lowry theory, a conjugate acid–base pair consists of molecules or ions related by the loss of one H^+ by an acid, and the gain of one H^+ by a base.
- Every acid–base reaction contains two conjugate acid–base pairs because an H^+ is transferred in both the forward and reverse directions.
- When an acid such as HF loses one H^+, the conjugate base F^- is formed. When H_2O acts as a base, it gains one H^+, which forms its conjugate acid, H_3O^+.

Example: Identify the conjugate acid–base pairs in the following reaction:

$$H_2SO_4(aq) + H_2O(l) \rightleftharpoons HSO_4^-(aq) + H_3O^+(aq)$$

Answer: $H_2SO_4(aq) + H_2O(l) \rightleftharpoons HSO_4^-(aq) + H_3O^+(aq)$
Acid   Base   Conjugate base   Conjugate acid

Conjugate acid–base pairs: H_2SO_4/HSO_4^- and H_3O^+/H_2O

Calculating $[H_3O^+]$ and $[OH^-]$ in Solutions (11.5)

- For all aqueous solutions, the product of $[H_3O^+]$ and $[OH^-]$ is equal to the water dissociation constant expression, K_w.

$$K_w = [H_3O^+][OH^-]$$

- Because pure water contains equal numbers of OH^- ions and H_3O^+ ions each with molar concentrations of 1.0×10^{-7} M, the numerical value of K_w is 1.0×10^{-14} at 25 °C.

$$K_w = [H_3O^+][OH^-] = [1.0 \times 10^{-7}][1.0 \times 10^{-7}]$$
$$= 1.0 \times 10^{-14}$$

- If we know the $[H_3O^+]$ of a solution, we can use the K_w expression to calculate the $[OH^-]$. If we know the $[OH^-]$ of a solution, we can calculate the $[H_3O^+]$ using the K_w expression.

$$[OH^-] = \frac{K_w}{[H_3O^+]} \quad [H_3O^+] = \frac{K_w}{[OH^-]}$$

Example: What is the $[OH^-]$ in a solution that has $[H_3O^+] = 2.4 \times 10^{-11}$ M? Is the solution acidic or basic?

Answer: We solve the K_w expression for $[OH^-]$ and substitute in the known values of K_w and $[H_3O^+]$.

$$[OH^-] = \frac{K_w}{[H_3O^+]} = \frac{1.0 \times 10^{-14}}{[2.4 \times 10^{-11}]} = 4.2 \times 10^{-4} \text{ M}$$

Because the $[OH^-]$ is greater than the $[H_3O^+]$, this is a basic solution.

Writing Equations for Reactions of Acids and Bases (11.7)

- Acids react with certain metals to produce hydrogen gas (H_2) and a salt.

$$\underset{\text{Metal}}{Mg(s)} + \underset{\text{Acid}}{2HCl(aq)} \longrightarrow \underset{\text{Hydrogen}}{H_2(g)} + \underset{\text{Salt}}{MgCl_2(aq)}$$

- When an acid is added to a carbonate or bicarbonate, the products are carbon dioxide gas, water, and a salt.

$$\underset{\text{Acid}}{2HCl(aq)} + \underset{\text{Carbonate}}{Na_2CO_3(aq)} \longrightarrow \underset{\substack{\text{Carbon} \\ \text{dioxide}}}{CO_2(g)} + \underset{\text{Water}}{H_2O(l)} + \underset{\text{Salt}}{2NaCl(aq)}$$

- Neutralization is a reaction between a strong or weak acid with a strong base to produce water and a salt.

$$\underset{\text{Acid}}{HCl(aq)} + \underset{\text{Base}}{NaOH(aq)} \longrightarrow \underset{\text{Water}}{H_2O(l)} + \underset{\text{Salt}}{NaCl(aq)}$$

Example: Write the balanced chemical equation for the reaction of $ZnCO_3(s)$ and hydrobromic acid $HBr(aq)$.

Answer:

$$ZnCO_3(s) + 2HBr(aq) \longrightarrow CO_2(g) + H_2O(l) + ZnBr_2(aq)$$

Calculating Molarity or Volume of an Acid or Base in a Titration (11.8)

- In a titration, a measured volume of acid is neutralized by an NaOH solution of known molarity.

- From the measured volume of the NaOH solution required for titration and its molarity, the number of moles of NaOH, the moles of acid, and the concentration of the acid are calculated.

Example: A 15.0-mL sample of a H_2SO_4 solution is titrated with 24.0 mL of a 0.245 M NaOH solution. What is the molarity of the H_2SO_4 solution?

$$H_2SO_4(aq) + 2NaOH(aq) \longrightarrow 2H_2O(l) + Na_2SO_4(aq)$$

Answer:

$$24.0 \text{ mL NaOH solution} \times \frac{1 \text{ L NaOH solution}}{1000 \text{ mL NaOH solution}}$$
$$\times \frac{0.245 \text{ mole NaOH}}{1 \text{ L NaOH solution}} \times \frac{1 \text{ mole } H_2SO_4}{2 \text{ moles NaOH}} = 0.00294 \text{ mole of } H_2SO_4$$

$$\text{Molarity (M)} = \frac{0.00294 \text{ mole } H_2SO_4}{0.0150 \text{ L } H_2SO_4 \text{ solution}} = 0.196 \text{ M } H_2SO_4 \text{ solution}$$

Calculating the pH of a Buffer (11.9)

- A buffer solution maintains pH by neutralizing small amounts of added acid or base.
- Most buffer solutions consist of nearly equal concentrations of a weak acid and a salt containing its conjugate base such as acetic acid, $HC_2H_3O_2$, and its salt $NaC_2H_3O_2$.
- The $[H_3O^+]$ is calculated by solving the K_a expression for $[H_3O^+]$, then substituting the values of $[H_3O^+]$, $[HA]$, and K_a into the equation.

$$K_a = \frac{[H_3O^+][C_2H_3O_2^-]}{[HC_2H_3O_2]}$$

Solving for $[H_3O^+]$ gives:

$$[H_3O^+] = K_a \times \frac{[HC_2H_3O_2]}{[C_2H_3O_2^-]} \quad \begin{array}{l} \leftarrow \text{ Weak acid} \\ \leftarrow \text{ Conjugate base} \end{array}$$

- The pH of the buffer is calculated from the $[H_3O^+]$.

$$pH = -\log[H_3O^+]$$

Example: What is the pH of a buffer prepared with 0.40 M $HC_2H_3O_2$ and 0.20 M $C_2H_3O_2^-$, if the K_a of acetic acid is 1.8×10^{-5}?

Answer: $[H_3O^+] = K_a \times \dfrac{[HC_2H_3O_2]}{[C_2H_3O_2^-]} = 1.8 \times 10^{-5} \times \dfrac{[0.40]}{[0.20]}$

$$= 3.6 \times 10^{-5} \text{ M}$$

$$pH = -\log[3.6 \times 10^{-5}] = 4.44$$

UNDERSTANDING THE CONCEPTS

The chapter sections to review are shown in parentheses at the end of each question.

11.87 Determine if each of the following diagrams represents a strong acid or a weak acid. The acid has the formula HX. (11.3)

A   B

11.88 Adding a few drops of a strong acid to water will lower the pH appreciably. However, adding the same number of drops to a buffer does not appreciably alter the pH. Why? (11.9)

Water   Buffer

11.89 Identify each of the following as an acid or a base: (11.1)
    a. H_2SO_4 **b.** RbOH
    c. $Ca(OH)_2$ **d.** HI

11.90 Identify each of the following as an acid or a base: (11.1)
    a. $Sr(OH)_2$ **b.** H_2SO_3
    c. $HC_2H_3O_2$ **d.** CsOH

11.91 Complete the following table: (11.2)

Acid	Conjugate Base
H_2O	
	CN^-
HNO_2	
	$H_2PO_4^-$

11.92 Complete the following table: (11.2)

Base	Conjugate Acid
	HS^-
	H_3O^+
NH_3	
HCO_3^-	

℞ Clinical Applications

11.93 Sometimes, during stress or trauma, a person can start to hyperventilate. Then the person might breathe into a paper bag to avoid fainting. (11.9)
    a. What changes occur in the blood pH during hyperventilation?

b. How does breathing into a paper bag help return blood pH to normal?

Breathing into a paper bag can help a person who is hyperventilating.

11.94 In the blood plasma, pH is maintained by the carbonic acid–bicarbonate buffer system. (11.9)
    a. How is pH maintained when acid is added to the buffer system?
    b. How is pH maintained when base is added to the buffer system?

11.95 State whether each of the following solutions is acidic, basic, or neutral: (11.5)
    a. sweat, pH 5.2   **b.** tears, pH 7.5
    c. bile, pH 8.1   **d.** stomach acid, pH 2.5

11.96 State whether each of the following solutions is acidic, basic, or neutral: (11.5)
    a. saliva, pH 6.8   **b.** urine, pH 5.9
    c. pancreatic juice, pH 8.0   **d.** blood, pH 7.45

ADDITIONAL QUESTIONS AND PROBLEMS

11.97 Identify each of the following as an acid, base, or salt, and give its name: (11.1)
    a. $HBrO_2$ **b.** CsOH
    c. $Mg(NO_3)_2$ **d.** $HClO_4$

11.98 Identify each of the following as an acid, base, or salt, and give its name: (11.1)
    a. HNO_2 **b.** $MgBr_2$
    c. NH_3 **d.** Li_2SO_3

11.99 Complete the following table: (11.2)

Acid	Conjugate Base
HI	
	Cl^-
NH_4^+	
	HS^-

11.100 Complete the following table: (11.2)

Base	Conjugate Acid
F^-	
	$HC_2H_3O_2$
	HSO_3^-
ClO^-	

11.101 Using Table 11.3, identify the stronger acid in each of the following pairs: (11.3)
    a. HF or HCN   **b.** H_3O^+ or H_2S
    c. HNO_2 or $HC_2H_3O_2$ **d.** H_2O or HCO_3^-

11.102 Using Table 11.3, identify the stronger base in each of the following pairs: (11.3)
    a. H_2O or Cl^- **b.** OH^- or NH_3
    c. SO_4^{2-} or NO_2^- **d.** CO_3^{2-} or H_2O

11.103 Determine the pH for each of the following solutions: (11.6)
    a. $[H_3O^+] = 2.0 \times 10^{-8}$ M
    b. $[H_3O^+] = 5.0 \times 10^{-2}$ M
    c. $[OH^-] = 3.5 \times 10^{-4}$ M
    d. $[OH^-] = 0.0054$ M

11.104 Determine the pH for each of the following solutions: (11.6)
    a. $[OH^-] = 1.0 \times 10^{-7}$ M
    b. $[H_3O^+] = 4.2 \times 10^{-3}$ M
    c. $[H_3O^+] = 0.0001$ M
    d. $[OH^-] = 8.5 \times 10^{-9}$ M

11.105 Are the solutions in problem 11.103 acidic, basic, or neutral? (11.6)

11.106 Are the solutions in problem 11.104 acidic, basic, or neutral? (11.6)

11.107 Calculate the $[H_3O^+]$ and $[OH^-]$ for a solution with each of the following pH values: (11.6)
    a. 3.00   **b.** 6.2
    c. 8.85   **d.** 11.00

11.108 Calculate the $[H_3O^+]$ and $[OH^-]$ for a solution with each of the following pH values: (11.6)
    a. 10.00   **b.** 5.0
    c. 6.54   **d.** 1.82

11.109 Solution A has a pH of 4.5, and solution B has a pH of 6.7. (11.6)
   a. Which solution is more acidic?
   b. What is the $[H_3O^+]$ in each?
   c. What is the $[OH^-]$ in each?

11.110 Solution X has a pH of 9.5, and solution Y has a pH of 7.5. (11.6)
   a. Which solution is more acidic?
   b. What is the $[H_3O^+]$ in each?
   c. What is the $[OH^-]$ in each?

11.111 What is the $[OH^-]$ in a solution that contains 0.225 g of NaOH in 0.250 L of solution? (11.7)

11.112 What is the $[H_3O^+]$ in a solution that contains 1.54 g of HNO_3 in 0.500 L of solution? (11.7)

11.113 What is the pH of a solution prepared by dissolving 2.5 g of HCl in water to make 425 mL of solution? (11.6)

11.114 What is the pH of a solution prepared by dissolving 1.0 g of $Ca(OH)_2$ in water to make 875 mL of solution? (11.6)

CHALLENGE QUESTIONS

The following groups of questions are related to the topics in this chapter. However, they do not all follow the chapter order, and they require you to combine concepts and skills from several sections. These questions will help you increase your critical thinking skills and prepare for your next exam.

11.115 For each of the following: (11.2, 11.3)
   1. H_2S **2.** H_3PO_4
   a. Write the formula for the conjugate base.
   b. Write the K_a expression.
   c. Which is the weaker acid?

11.116 For each of the following: (11.2, 11.3)
   1. HCO_3^- **2.** $HC_2H_3O_2$
   a. Write the formula for the conjugate base.
   b. Write the K_a expression.
   c. Which is the stronger acid?

11.117 Using Table 11.3, identify the conjugate acid–base pairs in each of the following equations and whether the equilibrium mixture contains mostly products or mostly reactants: (11.2, 11.3)
   a. $NH_3(aq) + HNO_3(aq) \rightleftharpoons NH_4^+(aq) + NO_3^-(aq)$
   b. $H_2O(l) + HBr(aq) \rightleftharpoons H_3O^+(aq) + Br^-(aq)$

11.118 Using Table 11.3, identify the conjugate acid–base pairs in each of the following equations and whether the equilibrium mixture contains mostly products or mostly reactants: (11.2, 11.3)
   a. $HNO_2(aq) + HS^-(aq) \rightleftharpoons H_2S(g) + NO_2^-(aq)$
   b. $Cl^-(aq) + H_2O(l) \rightleftharpoons OH^-(aq) + HCl(aq)$

11.119 Complete and balance each of the following: (11.7)
   a. $ZnCO_3(s) + H_2SO_4(aq) \longrightarrow$
   b. $Al(s) + HNO_3(aq) \longrightarrow$

11.120 Complete and balance each of the following: (11.7)
   a. $H_3PO_4(aq) + Ca(OH)_2(s) \longrightarrow$
   b. $KHCO_3(s) + HNO_3(aq) \longrightarrow$

11.121 Determine each of the following for a 0.050 M KOH solution: (11.6, 11.7, 11.8)
   a. $[H_3O^+]$
   b. pH
   c. the balanced equation for the reaction with H_2SO_4
   d. milliliters of KOH solution required to neutralize 40.0 mL of a 0.035 M H_2SO_4 solution

11.122 Determine each of the following for a 0.10 M HBr solution: (11.6, 11.7, 11.8)
   a. $[H_3O^+]$
   b. pH
   c. the balanced equation for the reaction with LiOH
   d. milliliters of HBr solution required to neutralize 36.0 mL of a 0.25 M LiOH solution

11.123 One of the most acidic lakes in the United States is Little Echo Pond in the Adirondacks in New York. Recently, this lake had a pH of 4.2, well below the recommended pH of 6.5. (11.6, 11.8)
   a. What are the $[H_3O^+]$ and $[OH^-]$ of Little Echo Pond?
   b. What are the $[H_3O^+]$ and $[OH^-]$ of a lake that has a pH of 6.5?
   c. One way to raise the pH of an acidic lake (and restore aquatic life) is to add limestone ($CaCO_3$). How many grams of $CaCO_3$ are needed to neutralize 1.0 kL of the acidic water from the lake if the acid is sulfuric acid?

$$H_2SO_4(aq) + CaCO_3(s) \longrightarrow CO_2(g) + H_2O(l) + CaSO_4(aq)$$

A helicopter drops calcium carbonate on an acidic lake to increase its pH.

℞ Clinical Applications

11.124 The daily output of stomach acid (gastric juice) is 1000 mL to 2000 mL. Prior to a meal, stomach acid (HCl) typically has a pH of 1.42. (11.6, 11.7, 11.8)
   a. What is the $[H_3O^+]$ of the stomach acid?
   b. One chewable tablet of the antacid Maalox contains 600. mg of $CaCO_3$. Write the neutralization equation, and calculate the milliliters of stomach acid neutralized by two tablets of Maalox.
   c. The antacid milk of magnesia contains 400. mg of $Mg(OH)_2$ per teaspoon. Write the neutralization equation, and calculate the number of milliliters of stomach acid that are neutralized by 1 tablespoon of milk of magnesia (1 tablespoon = 3 teaspoons).

11.125 Calculate the volume, in milliliters, of a 0.150 M NaOH solution that will completely neutralize each of the following: (11.8)
   a. 25.0 mL of a 0.288 M HCl solution
   b. 10.0 mL of a 0.560 M H_2SO_4 solution

11.126 Calculate the volume, in milliliters, of a 0.215 M NaOH solution that will completely neutralize each of the following: (11.8)
  a. 3.80 mL of a 1.25 M HNO_3 solution
  b. 8.50 mL of a 0.825 M H_3PO_4 solution

11.127 A solution of 0.205 M NaOH is used to titrate 20.0 mL of a H_2SO_4 solution. If 45.6 mL of the NaOH solution is required to reach the endpoint, what is the molarity of the H_2SO_4 solution? (11.8)

$$H_2SO_4(aq) + 2NaOH(aq) \longrightarrow 2H_2O(l) + Na_2SO_4(aq)$$

11.128 A 10.0-mL sample of vinegar, which is an aqueous solution of acetic acid, $HC_2H_3O_2$, requires 16.5 mL of a 0.500 M NaOH solution to reach the endpoint in a titration. What is the molarity of the acetic acid solution? (11.8)

$$HC_2H_3O_2(aq) + NaOH(aq) \longrightarrow H_2O(l) + NaC_2H_3O_2(aq)$$

11.129 A buffer solution is made by dissolving H_3PO_4 and NaH_2PO_4 in water. (11.9)
  a. Write an equation that shows how this buffer neutralizes added acid.
  b. Write an equation that shows how this buffer neutralizes added base.
  c. Calculate the pH of this buffer if it contains 0.50 M H_3PO_4 and 0.20 M $H_2PO_4^-$. The K_a for H_3PO_4 is 7.5×10^{-3}.

11.130 A buffer solution is made by dissolving $HC_2H_3O_2$ and $NaC_2H_3O_2$ in water. (11.9)
  a. Write an equation that shows how this buffer neutralizes added acid.
  b. Write an equation that shows how this buffer neutralizes added base.
  c. Calculate the pH of this buffer if it contains 0.20 M $HC_2H_3O_2$ and 0.40 M $C_2H_3O_2^-$. The K_a for $HC_2H_3O_2$ is 1.8×10^{-5}.

ANSWERS

Answers to Selected Questions and Problems

11.1 a. acid   **b.** acid
  c. acid   **d.** base
  e. both

11.3 a. hydrochloric acid   **b.** calcium hydroxide
  c. perchloric acid   **d.** nitric acid
  e. sulfurous acid   **f.** bromous acid

11.5 a. RbOH   **b.** HF
  c. H_3PO_4 **d.** LiOH
  e. NH_4OH **f.** HIO_4

11.7 a. HI is the acid (hydrogen ion donor), and H_2O is the base (hydrogen ion acceptor).
  b. H_2O is the acid (hydrogen ion donor), and F^- is the base (hydrogen ion acceptor).
  c. H_2S is the acid (hydrogen ion donor), and $CH_3-CH_2-NH_2$ is the base (hydrogen ion acceptor).

11.9 a. F^- **b.** OH^-
  c. HPO_3^{2-} **d.** SO_4^{2-}
  e. ClO_2^-

11.11 a. HCO_3^- **b.** H_3O^+
  c. H_3PO_4 **d.** HBr
  e. $HClO_4$

11.13 a. The conjugate acid–base pairs are H_2CO_3/HCO_3^- and H_3O^+/H_2O.
  b. The conjugate acid–base pairs are NH_4^+/NH_3 and H_3O^+/H_2O.
  c. The conjugate acid–base pairs are HCN/CN^- and HNO_2/NO_2^-.
  d. The conjugate acid–base pairs are HF/F^- and $HCHO_2/CHO_2^-$.

11.15 $NH_4^+(aq) + H_2O(l) \rightleftarrows NH_3(aq) + H_3O^+(aq)$

11.17 A strong acid is a good hydrogen ion donor, whereas its conjugate base is a poor hydrogen ion acceptor.

11.19 a. HBr   **b.** HSO_4^- **c.** H_2CO_3

11.21 a. HSO_4^- **b.** HF   **c.** HCO_3^-

11.23 a. reactants   **b.** reactants   **c.** products

11.25 $NH_4^+(aq) + SO_4^{2-}(aq) \rightleftarrows NH_3(aq) + HSO_4^-(aq)$
  The equilibrium mixture contains mostly reactants because NH_4^+ is a weaker acid than HSO_4^-, and SO_4^{2-} is a weaker base than NH_3.

11.27 a. true   **b.** false   **c.** false
  d. true   **e.** false

11.29 a. H_2SO_3 **b.** HSO_3^-
  c. H_2SO_3 **d.** HS^-
  e. H_2SO_3

11.31 $H_3PO_4(aq) + H_2O(l) \rightleftarrows H_3O^+(aq) + H_2PO_4^-(aq)$

$$K_a = \frac{[H_3O^+][H_2PO_4^-]}{[H_3PO_4]}$$

11.33 In pure water, $[H_3O^+] = [OH^-]$ because one of each is produced every time a hydrogen ion is transferred from one water molecule to another.

11.35 In an acidic solution, the $[H_3O^+]$ is greater than the $[OH^-]$.

11.37 a. acidic   **b.** basic
  c. basic   **d.** acidic

11.39 a. 1.0×10^{-5} M   **b.** 1.0×10^{-8} M
  c. 5.0×10^{-10} M   **d.** 2.5×10^{-2} M

11.41 a. 2.5×10^{-13} M   **b.** 2.0×10^{-9} M
  c. 5.0×10^{-11} M   **d.** 1.3×10^{-6} M

11.43 In a neutral solution, the $[H_3O^+]$ is 1.0×10^{-7} M and the pH is 7.00, which is the negative value of the power of 10.

11.45 a. basic   **b.** acidic
  c. acidic   **d.** acidic
  e. basic

11.47 An increase or decrease of one pH unit changes the $[H_3O^+]$ by a factor of 10. Thus a pH of 3 is 10 times more acidic than a pH of 4.

11.49 a. 4.0   **b.** 8.5
  c. 9.0   **d.** 3.40
  e. 7.17   **f.** 10.92

11.51

Food	$[H_3O^+]$	$[OH^-]$	pH	Acidic, Basic, or Neutral?
Rye bread	1.6×10^{-9} M	6.3×10^{-6} M	8.80	Basic
Tomatoes	2.3×10^{-5} M	4.3×10^{-10} M	4.64	Acidic
Peas	6.2×10^{-7} M	1.6×10^{-8} M	6.21	Acidic

11.53 1.2×10^{-7} M

11.55 a. $ZnCO_3(s) + 2HBr(aq) \longrightarrow$
$$CO_2(g) + H_2O(l) + ZnBr_2(aq)$$
b. $Zn(s) + 2HCl(aq) \longrightarrow H_2(g) + ZnCl_2(aq)$
c. $HCl(aq) + NaHCO_3(s) \longrightarrow$
$$CO_2(g) + H_2O(l) + NaCl(aq)$$
d. $H_2SO_4(aq) + Mg(OH)_2(s) \longrightarrow 2H_2O(l) + MgSO_4(aq)$

11.57 a. $2HCl(aq) + Mg(OH)_2(s) \longrightarrow 2H_2O(l) + MgCl_2(aq)$
b. $H_3PO_4(aq) + 3LiOH(aq) \longrightarrow 3H_2O(l) + Li_3PO_4(aq)$

11.59 a. $H_2SO_4(aq) + 2NaOH(aq) \longrightarrow 2H_2O(l) + Na_2SO_4(aq)$
b. $3HCl(aq) + Fe(OH)_3(s) \longrightarrow 3H_2O(l) + FeCl_3(aq)$
c. $H_2CO_3(aq) + Mg(OH)_2(s) \longrightarrow 2H_2O(l) + MgCO_3(s)$

11.61 0.829 M HCl solution

11.63 0.124 M H_2SO_4 solution

11.65 16.5 mL

11.67 **b** and **c** are buffer systems. **b** contains the weak acid H_2CO_3 and its salt $NaHCO_3$. **c** contains HF, a weak acid, and its salt KF.

11.69 a. 3   **b.** 1 and 2
c. 3   **d.** 1

11.71 pH = 3.35

11.73 The pH of the 0.10 M HF/0.10 M NaF buffer is 3.46.
The pH of the 0.060 M HF/0.120 M NaF buffer is 3.76.

11.75 If you breathe fast, CO_2 is expelled and the equilibrium shifts to lower H_3O^+, which raises the pH.

11.77 If large amounts of HCO_3^- are lost, equilibrium shifts to higher H_3O^+, which lowers the pH.

11.79 pH = 3.70

11.81 2.5×10^{-4} M

11.83 $CaCO_3(s) + 2HCl(aq) \longrightarrow CO_2(g) + H_2O(l) + CaCl_2(aq)$

11.85 0.200 g of $CaCO_3$

11.87 a. This diagram represents a weak acid; only a few HX molecules separate into H_3O^+ and X^- ions.
b. This diagram represents a strong acid; all the HX molecules separate into H_3O^+ and X^- ions.

11.89 a. acid   **b.** base
c. base   **d.** acid

11.91

Acid	Conjugate Base
H_2O	OH^-
HCN	CN^-
HNO_2	NO_2^-
H_3PO_4	$H_2PO_4^-$

11.93 a. During hyperventilation, a person will lose CO_2 and the blood pH will rise.
b. Breathing into a paper bag will increase the CO_2 concentration and lower the blood pH.

11.95 a. acidic   **b.** basic
c. basic   **d.** acidic

11.97 a. acid, bromous acid
b. base, cesium hydroxide
c. salt, magnesium nitrate
d. acid, perchloric acid

11.99

Acid	Conjugate Base
HI	I^-
HCl	Cl^-
NH_4^+	NH_3
H_2S	HS^-

11.101 a. HF   **b.** H_3O^+
c. HNO_2 **d.** HCO_3^-

11.103 a. pH = 7.70
b. pH = 1.30
c. pH = 10.54
d. pH = 11.73

11.105 a. basic   **b.** acidic
c. basic   **d.** basic

11.107 a. $[H_3O^+] = 1.0 \times 10^{-3}$ M; $[OH^-] = 1.0 \times 10^{-11}$ M
b. $[H_3O^+] = 6 \times 10^{-7}$ M; $[OH^-] = 2 \times 10^{-8}$ M
c. $[H_3O^+] = 1.4 \times 10^{-9}$ M; $[OH^-] = 7.1 \times 10^{-6}$ M
d. $[H_3O^+] = 1.0 \times 10^{-11}$ M; $[OH^-] = 1.0 \times 10^{-3}$ M

11.109 a. Solution A
b. Solution A $[H_3O^+] = 3 \times 10^{-5}$ M;
Solution B $[H_3O^+] = 2 \times 10^{-7}$ M
c. Solution A $[OH^-] = 3 \times 10^{-10}$ M;
Solution B $[OH^-] = 5 \times 10^{-8}$ M

11.111 $[OH^-] = 0.0225$ M

11.113 pH = 0.80

11.115 a. 1. HS^-
      2. $H_2PO_4^-$
b. 1. $\dfrac{[H_3O^+][HS^-]}{[H_2S]}$
      2. $\dfrac{[H_3O^+][H_2PO_4^-]}{[H_3PO_4]}$
c. H_2S

11.117 a. HNO_3/NO_3^- and NH_4^+/NH_3; equilibrium mixture contains mostly products
b. HBr/Br^- and H_3O^+/H_2O; equilibrium mixture contains mostly products

11.119 a. $ZnCO_3(s) + H_2SO_4(aq) \longrightarrow$
$$CO_2(g) + H_2O(l) + ZnSO_4(aq)$$
b. $2Al(s) + 6HNO_3(aq) \longrightarrow 3H_2(g) + 2Al(NO_3)_3(aq)$

11.121 a. $[H_3O^+] = 2.0 \times 10^{-13}$ M
b. pH = 12.70
c. $2KOH(aq) + H_2SO_4(aq) \longrightarrow 2H_2O(l) + K_2SO_4(aq)$
d. 56 mL of the KOH solution

11.123 a. $[H_3O^+] = 6 \times 10^{-5}$ M; $[OH^-] = 2 \times 10^{-10}$ M
b. $[H_3O^+] = 3 \times 10^{-7}$ M; $[OH^-] = 3 \times 10^{-8}$ M
c. 3 g of $CaCO_3$

11.125 a. 48.0 mL of NaOH solution
b. 74.7 mL of NaOH solution

11.127 0.234 M H_2SO_4 solution

11.129 a. acid:
$$H_2PO_4^-(aq) + H_3O^+(aq) \longrightarrow H_3PO_4(aq) + H_2O(l)$$
b. base:
$$H_3PO_4(aq) + OH^-(aq) \longrightarrow H_2PO_4^-(aq) + H_2O(l)$$
c. pH = 1.72

CI.19 Consider the following reaction at equilibrium:

$$2H_2(g) + S_2(g) \rightleftharpoons 2H_2S(g) + \text{heat}$$

In a 10.0-L container, an equilibrium mixture contains 2.02 g of H_2, 10.3 g of S_2, and 68.2 g of H_2S. (7.5, 10.2, 10.3, 10.4, 10.5)

a. What is the numerical value of K_c for this equilibrium mixture?

b. If more H_2 is added to the equilibrium mixture, how will the equilibrium shift?

c. How will the equilibrium shift if the mixture is placed in a 5.00-L container with no change in temperature?

d. If a 5.00-L container has an equilibrium mixture of 0.300 mole of H_2 and 2.50 moles of H_2S, what is the $[S_2]$ if temperature remains constant?

CI.20 In wine-making, glucose ($C_6H_{12}O_6$) from grapes undergoes fermentation in the absence of oxygen to produce ethanol, C_2H_5OH, and carbon dioxide. A bottle of vintage port wine has a volume of 750 mL and contains 135 mL of ethanol which has a density of 0.789 g/mL. In 1.5 lb of grapes, there are 26 g of glucose. (2.7, 7.1, 7.5, 9.4)

When the glucose in grapes is fermented, ethanol is produced.

Port is a type of fortified wine that is produced in Portugal.

a. Calculate the volume percent (v/v) of ethanol in the port wine.

b. What is the molarity (M) of ethanol in the port wine?

c. Write the balanced chemical equation for the fermentation reaction of glucose in grapes.

d. How many grams of glucose from grapes are required to produce one bottle of port wine?

e. How many bottles of port wine can be produced from 1.0 ton of grapes (1 ton = 2000 lb)?

CI.21 A metal M with a mass of 0.420 g completely reacts with 34.8 mL of a 0.520 M HCl solution to form H_2 gas and aqueous MCl_3. (7.1, 7.5, 8.7, 11.7)

a. Write a balanced chemical equation for the reaction of the metal M(s) and HCl(aq).

b. What volume, in milliliters, of H_2 at 720. mmHg and 24 °C is produced?

c. How many moles of metal M reacted?

d. Using your results from part c, determine the molar mass and name of metal M.

e. Write the balanced chemical equation for the reaction.

When a metal reacts with a strong acid, bubbles of hydrogen gas form.

CI.22 A solution of HCl is prepared by diluting 15.0 mL of a 12.0 M HCl solution with enough water to make 750. mL of HCl solution. (9.4, 11.6, 11.7, 11.8)

a. What is the molarity of the HCl solution?

b. What is the $[H_3O^+]$ and pH of the HCl solution?

c. Write the balanced chemical equation for the reaction of HCl and $MgCO_3$.

d. How many milliliters of the diluted HCl solution is required to completely react with 350. mg of $MgCO_3$?

CI.23 A KOH solution is prepared by dissolving 8.57 g of KOH in enough water to make 850. mL of KOH solution. (9.4, 11.6, 11.7, 11.8)

a. What is the molarity of the KOH solution?

b. What is the $[H_3O^+]$ and pH of the KOH solution?

c. Write the balanced chemical equation for the neutralization of KOH by H_2SO_4.

d. How many milliliters of a 0.250 M H_2SO_4 solution is required to neutralize 10.0 mL of the KOH solution?

℞ Clinical Applications

CI.24 In a teaspoon (5.0 mL) of a liquid antacid, there are 400. mg of $Mg(OH)_2$ and 400. mg of $Al(OH)_3$. A 0.080 M HCl solution, which is similar to stomach acid, is used to neutralize 5.0 mL of the liquid antacid. (9.4, 11.6, 11.7, 11.8)

An antacid neutralizes stomach acid and raises the pH.

a. What is the pH of the HCl solution?

b. Write the balanced chemical equation for the neutralization of HCl and $Mg(OH)_2$.

c. Write the balanced chemical equation for the neutralization of HCl and $Al(OH)_3$.

d. How many milliliters of the HCl solution are needed to neutralize the $Mg(OH)_2$?

e. How many milliliters of the HCl solution are needed to neutralize the $Al(OH)_3$?

CI.25 A volume of 200.0 mL of a carbonic acid buffer for blood plasma is prepared that contains 0.403 g of $NaHCO_3$ and 0.0149 g of H_2CO_3. At body temperature (37 °C), the K_a of carbonic acid is 7.9×10^{-7}. (9.4, 11.6, 11.8, 11.9)

$$H_2CO_3(aq) + H_2O(l) \rightleftharpoons HCO_3^-(aq) + H_3O^+(aq)$$

a. What is the $[H_2CO_3]$?

b. What is the $[HCO_3^-]$?

c. What is the $[H_3O^+]$?

d. What is the pH of the buffer?

e. Write a balanced chemical equation that shows how this buffer neutralizes added acid.

f. Write a balanced chemical equation that shows how this buffer neutralizes added base.

CI.26 In the kidneys, the ammonia buffer system buffers high H_3O^+. Ammonia, which is produced in renal tubules from amino acids, combines with H^+ to be excreted as NH_4Cl. At body temperature (37 °C), the $K_a = 5.6 \times 10^{-10}$. A buffer solution with a volume of 125 mL contains 3.34 g of NH_4Cl and 0.0151 g of NH_3. (9.4, 11.6, 11.8, 11.9)

$$NH_4^+(aq) + H_2O(l) \rightleftharpoons NH_3(aq) + H_3O^+(aq)$$

a. What is the $[NH_4^+]$?
b. What is the $[NH_3]$?
c. What is the $[H_3O^+]$?
d. What is the pH of the buffer?
e. Write a balanced chemical equation that shows how this buffer neutralizes added acid.
f. Write a balanced chemical equation that shows how this buffer neutralizes added base.

ANSWERS

CI.19 a. $K_c = 248$
b. If H_2 is added, the equilibrium will shift in the direction of the products.
c. If the volume decreases, the equilibrium will shift in the direction of the products.
d. $[S_2] = 0.280$ M

CI.21 a. $2M(s) + 6HCl(aq) \longrightarrow 3H_2(g) + 2MCl_3(aq)$
b. 233 mL of H_2
c. 6.03×10^{-3} mole of M
d. 69.7 g/mole; gallium
e. $2Ga(s) + 6HCl(aq) \longrightarrow 3H_2(g) + 2GaCl_3(aq)$

CI.23 a. 0.180 M
b. $[H_3O^+] = 5.56 \times 10^{-14}$ M; pH = 13.255
c. $2KOH(aq) + H_2SO_4(aq) \longrightarrow 2H_2O(l) + K_2SO_4(aq)$
d. 3.60 mL

CI.25 a. 0.00120 M
b. 0.0240 M
c. 4.0×10^{-8} M
d. 7.40
e. $HCO_3^-(aq) + H_3O^+(aq) \longrightarrow H_2CO_3(aq) + H_2O(l)$
f. $H_2CO_3(aq) + OH^-(aq) \longrightarrow HCO_3^-(aq) + H_2O(l)$

12

Introduction to Organic Chemistry: Hydrocarbons

AT 4:35 A.M., A RESCUE CREW RESPONDED TO A

call about a house fire. At the scene, Jack, a firefighter/emergency medical technician (EMT) found Diane, a 62-year old woman, lying in the front yard of her house. In his assessment, Jack, reported that Diane had second- and third-degree burns over 40% of her body as well as a broken leg. He placed an oxygen re-breather mask on Diane to provide a high concentration of oxygen. Another firefighter/EMT, Nancy, began dressing the burns with sterile water and cling film, a first aid material made of polyvinyl chloride, which does not stick to the skin and is protective. Jack and his crew transported Diane to the burn center for further treatment.

At the scene of the fire, arson investigators used trained dogs to find traces of accelerants and fuel. Gasoline, which is often found at arson scenes, is a mixture of organic molecules called alkanes. Alkanes or hydrocarbons are chains of carbon and hydrogen atoms. The alkanes present in gasoline consist of a mixture of 5 to 8 carbon atoms in a chain. Alkanes are extremely combustible; they react with oxygen to form carbon dioxide, water, and large amounts of heat. Because alkanes undergo combustion reactions, they can be used to start arson fires.

CAREER Firefighter/Emergency Medical Technician

Firefighters/emergency medical technicians are first responders to fires, accidents, and other emergency situations. They are required to have an emergency medical technician certification in order to be able to treat seriously injured people. By combining the skills of a firefighter and an emergency medical technician, they increase the survival rates of the injured. The physical demands of firefighters are extremely high as they fight, extinguish, and prevent fires while wearing heavy protective clothing and gear. They also train for and participate in firefighting drills, and maintain fire equipment so that it is always working and ready.

Firefighters must also be knowledgeable about fire codes, arson, and the handling and disposal of hazardous materials. Since firefighters also provide emergency care for sick and injured people, they need to be aware of emergency medical and rescue procedures, as well as the proper methods for controlling the spread of infectious disease.

LOOKING AHEAD

12.1 Organic Compounds 444

12.2 Alkanes 447

12.3 Alkanes with Substituents 451

12.4 Properties of Alkanes 457

12.5 Alkenes and Alkynes 460

12.6 Cis–Trans Isomers 464

♥ **Chemistry Link to Health** *Cis–Trans Isomers for Night Vision* 467

12.7 Addition Reactions for Alkenes 468

♥ **Chemistry Link to Health** *Hydrogenation of Unsaturated Fats* 469

12.8 Aromatic Compounds 473

♥ **Chemistry Link to Health** *Some Common Aromatic Compounds in Nature and Medicine* 475

♥ **Chemistry Link to Health** *Polycyclic Aromatic Hydrocarbons (PAHs)* 477

℞ **Clinical Applications** 477

℞ **Clinical Update** *Diane's Treatment in the Burn Unit* 477

At the beginning of the nineteenth century, scientists classified chemical compounds as inorganic and organic. An inorganic compound was a substance that was composed of minerals, and an organic compound was a substance that came from an organism, thus the use of the word *organic*. Early scientists thought that some type of "vital force," which could be found only in living cells, was required to synthesize an organic compound. This idea was shown to be incorrect in 1828 when the German chemist Friedrich Wöhler synthesized urea, a product of protein metabolism, by heating an inorganic compound, ammonium cyanate.

$$NH_4CNO \xrightarrow{\text{Heat}} H_2N-\overset{\overset{\displaystyle O}{\|}}{C}-NH_2$$

Ammonium cyanate (inorganic)   Urea (organic)

The simplest organic compounds are the hydrocarbons that contain only the elements carbon and hydrogen. All the carbon-to-carbon bonds in a hydrocarbon known as an alkane are single $C-C$ bonds. Some common alkanes include methane (CH_4), propane (C_3H_8), and butane (C_4H_{10}).

Alkenes are hydrocarbons that contain one or more carbon-to-carbon double bonds ($C=C$). Because double bonds are very reactive, they easily add hydrogen atoms (hydrogenation) or water (hydration) to the carbon atoms in the double bond. One important compound containing a double bond is ethene (ethylene), which is used to ripen fruit when ready for market. A common compound with a triple bond is ethyne (acetylene), which burns at high temperatures and is used in welding metals.

Learning about the structures and reactions of organic molecules will provide you with a foundation for understanding the more complex molecules of biochemistry.

CHAPTER READINESS*

✪ CORE CHEMISTRY SKILLS

- Drawing Lewis Structures (6.6)
- Predicting Shape (6.8)
- Balancing a Chemical Equation (7.1)

*These Core Chemistry Skills from previous chapters are listed here for your review as you proceed to the new material in this chapter.

LEARNING GOAL

Identify properties characteristic of organic or inorganic compounds.

12.1 Organic Compounds

Organic chemistry is the study of carbon compounds. The element carbon has a special role because many carbon atoms can bond together to give a vast array of molecular compounds. **Organic compounds** always contain carbon and hydrogen, and sometimes other nonmetals such as oxygen, sulfur, nitrogen, phosphorus, or a halogen. We find organic compounds in many common products we use every day, such as gasoline, medicines, shampoos, plastics, and perfumes. The food we eat is composed of organic compounds such as carbohydrates, fats, and proteins that supply us with fuel for energy and the carbon atoms needed to build and repair the cells of our bodies.

We organize organic compounds by their *functional groups*, which are groups of atoms bonded in a specific way. Compounds that contain the same functional group have similar physical and chemical properties. The identification of functional groups allows us to classify organic compounds according to their structure, to name compounds within each family, and to predict their chemical reactions.

The formulas of organic compounds are written with carbon first, followed by hydrogen, and then any other elements. Organic compounds typically have low melting and boiling points, are not soluble in water, and are less dense than water. For example, vegetable oil, which is a mixture of organic compounds, does not dissolve in water but floats on top. Many organic compounds undergo combustion and burn vigorously in air. By contrast, many inorganic compounds have high melting and boiling points. Inorganic compounds that are ionic are usually soluble in water, and most do not burn in air. Table 12.1 contrasts some of the properties associated with organic and inorganic compounds, such as propane, C_3H_8, and sodium chloride, NaCl (see Figure 12.1).

Vegetable oil, a mixture of organic compounds, is not soluble in water.

TABLE 12.1 Some Properties of Organic and Inorganic Compounds

Property	Organic	Example: C_3H_8	Inorganic	Example: NaCl
Elements Present	C and H, sometimes O, S, N, P, or Cl (F, Br, I)	C and H	Most metals and nonmetals	Na and Cl
Particles	Molecules	C_3H_8	Mostly ions	Na^+ and Cl^-
Bonding	Mostly covalent	Covalent	Many are ionic, some covalent	Ionic
Polarity of Bonds	Nonpolar, unless a strongly electronegative atom is present	Nonpolar	Most are ionic or polar covalent, a few are nonpolar covalent	Ionic
Melting Point	Usually low	$-188\,°C$	Usually high	$801\,°C$
Boiling Point	Usually low	$-42\,°C$	Usually high	$1413\,°C$
Flammability	High	Burns in air	Low	Does not burn
Solubility in Water	Not soluble, unless a polar group is present	No	Most are soluble, unless nonpolar	Yes

$CH_3-CH_2-CH_3$

FIGURE 12.1 ▶ Propane, C_3H_8, is an organic compound, whereas sodium chloride, NaCl, is an inorganic compound.

ⓠ Why is propane used as a fuel?

Na^+

Cl^-

▸**SAMPLE PROBLEM 12.1** **Properties of Organic Compounds**

Indicate whether the following properties are more typical of organic or inorganic compounds:

a. is not soluble in water
b. has a high melting point
c. burns in air

SOLUTION

a. Many organic compounds are not soluble in water.
b. Inorganic compounds are more likely to have high melting points.
c. Organic compounds are more likely to be flammable.

STUDY CHECK 12.1

What elements are always found in organic compounds?

ANSWER

C and H

Representations of Carbon Compounds

Hydrocarbons are organic compounds that consist of only carbon and hydrogen. In organic molecules, every carbon atom has four bonds. In the simplest hydrocarbon, methane (CH_4), the carbon atom forms an octet by sharing its four valence electrons with four hydrogen atoms.

The most accurate representation of methane is the three-dimensional *space-filling model* (**a**) in which spheres show the relative size and shape of all the atoms. Another type of three-dimensional representation is the *ball-and-stick model* (**b**), where the atoms are shown as balls and the bonds between them are shown as sticks. In the ball-and-stick model of methane, CH_4, the covalent bonds from the carbon atom to each hydrogen atom are directed to the corners of a tetrahedron with bond angles of 109°. In the *wedge–dash model* (**c**), the three-dimensional shape is represented by symbols of the atoms with lines for bonds in the plane of the page, wedges for bonds that project out from the page, and dashes for bonds that are behind the page.

However, the three-dimensional models are awkward to draw and view for more complex molecules. Therefore, it is more practical to use their corresponding two-dimensional formulas. The **expanded structural formula (d)** shows all of the atoms and the bonds connected to each atom. A **condensed structural formula (e)** shows the carbon atoms each grouped with the attached number of hydrogen atoms.

(a)   (b)   (c)   (d)   (e)

Three-dimensional and two-dimensional representations of methane: (**a**) space-filling model, (**b**) ball-and-stick model, (**c**) wedge–dash model, (**d**) expanded structural formula, and (**e**) condensed structural formula.

The hydrocarbon ethane with two carbon atoms and six hydrogen atoms can be represented by a similar set of three- and two-dimensional models and formulas in which each carbon atom is bonded to another carbon and three hydrogen atoms. As in methane, each carbon atom in ethane retains a tetrahedral shape. A hydrocarbon is referred to as a *saturated hydrocarbon* when all the bonds in the molecule are single bonds.

Three-dimensional and two-dimensional representations of ethane: **(a)** space-filling model, **(b)** ball-and-stick model, **(c)** wedge–dash model, **(d)** expanded structural formula, and **(e)** condensed structural formula.

QUESTIONS AND PROBLEMS

12.1 Organic Compounds

LEARNING GOAL Identify properties characteristic of organic or inorganic compounds.

12.1 Identify each of the following as a formula of an organic or inorganic compound:
   a. KCl   **b.** C_4H_{10}
   c. C_2H_6O **d.** H_2SO_4
   e. $CaCl_2$ **f.** C_3H_7Cl

12.2 Identify each of the following as a formula of an organic or inorganic compound:
   a. $C_6H_{12}O_6$ **b.** K_3PO_4
   c. I_2 **d.** C_2H_6S
   e. $C_{10}H_{22}$ **f.** C_4H_9Br

12.3 Identify each of the following properties as more typical of an organic or inorganic compound:
   a. is soluble in water
   b. has a low boiling point
   c. contains carbon and hydrogen
   d. contains ionic bonds

12.4 Identify each of the following properties as more typical of an organic or inorganic compound:
   a. contains Li and F   **b.** is a gas at room temperature
   c. contains covalent bonds   **d.** produces ions in water

12.5 Match each of the following physical and chemical properties with ethane, C_2H_6, or sodium bromide, NaBr:
   a. boils at $-89\,°C$ **b.** burns vigorously in air
   c. is a solid at $250\,°C$ **d.** dissolves in water

12.6 Match each of the following physical and chemical properties with cyclohexane, C_6H_{12}, or calcium nitrate, $Ca(NO_3)_2$:
   a. melts at $500\,°C$
   b. is insoluble in water
   c. does not burn in air
   d. is a liquid at room temperature

12.7 How are the hydrogen atoms of methane, CH_4, arranged in space?

12.8 In a propane molecule with three carbon atoms, what is the shape around each carbon atom?

Propane

12.2 Alkanes

More than 90% of the compounds in the world are organic compounds. The large number of carbon compounds is possible because the covalent bond between carbon atoms (C—C) is very strong, allowing carbon atoms to form long, stable chains.

The **alkanes** are a type of hydrocarbon in which the carbon atoms are connected only by single bonds. One of the most common uses of alkanes is as fuels. Methane, used in gas heaters and gas cooktops, is an alkane with one carbon atom. The alkanes ethane, propane, and butane contain two, three, and four carbon atoms, respectively, connected in a row or a *continuous chain*. As we can see, the names for alkanes end in *ane*. Such names are part of the **IUPAC** (International Union of Pure and Applied Chemistry) **system** used by chemists to name organic compounds. Alkanes with five or more carbon atoms in a chain are named using Greek prefixes: *pent* (5), *hex* (6), *hept* (7), *oct* (8), *non* (9), and *dec* (10) (see Table 12.2).

LEARNING GOAL

Write the IUPAC names and draw the condensed or line-angle structural formulas for alkanes and cycloalkanes.

TABLE 12.2 IUPAC Names of the First 10 Alkanes

Number of Carbon Atoms	Molecular Formula	Condensed Structural Formula	Line-Angle Structural Formula
1	CH_4	CH_4	
2	C_2H_6	CH_3—CH_3	—
3	C_3H_8	CH_3—CH_2—CH_3	
4	C_4H_{10}	CH_3—CH_2—CH_2—CH_3	
5	C_5H_{12}	CH_3—CH_2—CH_2—CH_2—CH_3	
6	C_6H_{14}	CH_3—CH_2—CH_2—CH_2—CH_2—CH_3	
7	C_7H_{16}	CH_3—CH_2—CH_2—CH_2—CH_2—CH_2—CH_3	
8	C_8H_{18}	CH_3—CH_2—CH_2—CH_2—CH_2—CH_2—CH_2—CH_3	
9	C_9H_{20}	CH_3—CH_2—CH_2—CH_2—CH_2—CH_2—CH_2—CH_2—CH_3	
10	$C_{10}H_{22}$	CH_3—CH_2—CH_2—CH_2—CH_2—CH_2—CH_2—CH_2—CH_2—CH_3	

CORE CHEMISTRY SKILL

Naming and Drawing Alkanes

Condensed and Line-Angle Structural Formulas

In a condensed structural formula, each carbon atom and its attached hydrogen atoms are written as a group. A subscript indicates the number of hydrogen atoms bonded to each carbon atom.

$$H-\overset{\displaystyle H}{\underset{\displaystyle H}{C}}- \; = \; CH_3- \qquad\qquad -\overset{\displaystyle H}{\underset{\displaystyle H}{C}}- \; = \; -CH_2-$$

Expanded   Condensed   Expanded   Condensed

When an organic molecule consists of a chain of three or more carbon atoms, the carbon atoms do not lie in a straight line. Rather, they are arranged in a zigzag pattern.

A simplified structure called the **line-angle structural formula** shows a zigzag line in which carbon atoms are represented as the ends of each line and as corners. For example, in the line-angle structural formula of pentane, each line in the zigzag drawing represents a single bond. The carbon atoms on the ends are bonded to three hydrogen atoms. However, the carbon atoms in the middle of the carbon chain are each bonded to two carbons and two hydrogen atoms as shown in Sample Problem 12.2.

Guide to Drawing Structural Formulas for Alkanes

STEP 1
Draw the carbon chain.

STEP 2
Draw the expanded structural formula by adding the hydrogen atoms using single bonds to each of the carbon atoms.

STEP 3
Draw the condensed structural formula by combining the H atoms with each C atom.

STEP 4
Draw the line-angle structural formula as a zigzag line in which the ends and corners represent C atoms.

▶ **SAMPLE PROBLEM 12.2** Drawing Expanded, Condensed, and Line-Angle Structural Formulas for an Alkane

Draw the expanded, condensed, and line-angle structural formulas for pentane.

SOLUTION

STEP 1 Draw the carbon chain. A molecule of pentane has five carbon atoms in a continuous chain.

$$C-C-C-C-C$$

STEP 2 Draw the expanded structural formula by adding the hydrogen atoms using single bonds to each of the carbon atoms.

$$H-\overset{\displaystyle H}{\underset{\displaystyle H}{C}}-\overset{\displaystyle H}{\underset{\displaystyle H}{C}}-\overset{\displaystyle H}{\underset{\displaystyle H}{C}}-\overset{\displaystyle H}{\underset{\displaystyle H}{C}}-\overset{\displaystyle H}{\underset{\displaystyle H}{C}}-H$$

STEP 3 Draw the condensed structural formula by combining the H atoms with each C atom.

Expanded structural formula

Condensed structural formula

$CH_3-CH_2-CH_2-CH_2-CH_3$

STEP 4 Draw the line-angle structural formula as a zigzag line in which the ends and corners represent C atoms.

$CH_3-CH_2-CH_2-CH_2-CH_3$ Condensed structural formula

Line-angle structural formula

STUDY CHECK 12.2

Draw the condensed structural formula and give the name for the following line-angle structural formula:

ANSWER

$CH_3-CH_2-CH_2-CH_2-CH_2-CH_2-CH_3$ heptane

Conformations of Alkanes

Because an alkane has only single carbon–carbon bonds, the groups attached to each C are not in fixed positions. They can rotate freely about the bond connecting the carbon atoms. This motion is analogous to the independent rotation of the wheels of a toy car. Thus, different arrangements, known as *conformations*, occur during the rotation about a single bond.

Suppose we could look at butane, C_4H_{10}, as it rotates. Sometimes the —CH_3 groups line up in front of each other, and at other times they are opposite each other. As the —CH_3 groups turn around the single bond, the carbon chain in the condensed structural formulas may appear at different angles. For example, butane can be drawn using a variety of two-dimensional condensed structural formulas as shown in Table 12.3. All these condensed structural formulas represent the same compound with four carbon atoms.

TABLE 12.3 Some Structural Formulas for Butane, C_4H_{10}

Expanded Structural Formula

```
      H   H   H   H
      |   |   |   |
  H — C — C — C — C — H
      |   |   |   |
      H   H   H   H
```

Condensed Structural Formulas

$CH_3 — CH_2 — CH_2 — CH_3$

$\begin{array}{cc} CH_2 — CH_2 \\ | \quad\quad | \\ CH_3 \quad CH_3 \end{array}$

$\begin{array}{c} CH_3 \\ | \\ CH_2 — CH_2 \\ | \\ CH_3 \end{array}$

$\begin{array}{c} CH_3 \\ | \\ CH_2 \\ | \\ CH_2 \\ | \\ CH_3 \end{array}$

$\begin{array}{c} CH_3 — CH_2 \\ | \\ CH_2 — CH_3 \end{array}$

$\begin{array}{c} CH_3 \\ | \\ CH_2 — CH_2 — CH_3 \end{array}$

$CH_3 \quad CH_2$

$\quad CH_2 \quad CH_3$

Line-Angle Structural Formulas

Cycloalkanes

Hydrocarbons can also form cyclic or ring structures called **cycloalkanes**, which have two fewer hydrogen atoms than the corresponding alkanes. The simplest cycloalkane, cyclopropane (C_3H_6), has a ring of three carbon atoms bonded to six hydrogen atoms. Most often cycloalkanes are drawn using their line-angle structural formulas, which appear as simple geometric figures. As seen for alkanes, each corner of the line-angle structural formula for a cycloalkane represents a carbon atom.

The ball-and-stick models, condensed structural formulas, and line-angle structural formulas for several cycloalkanes are shown in Table 12.4. A cycloalkane is named by adding the prefix *cyclo* to the name of the alkane with the same number of carbon atoms.

TABLE 12.4 Formulas of Some Common Cycloalkanes

Name			
Cyclopropane	Cyclobutane	Cyclopentane	Cyclohexane

Ball-and-Stick Model

Condensed Structural Formula

| $\begin{array}{c} CH_2 \\ \diagup \diagdown \\ H_2C — CH_2 \end{array}$ | $\begin{array}{c} H_2C — CH_2 \\ \mid \quad\quad \mid \\ H_2C — CH_2 \end{array}$ | $\begin{array}{c} CH_2 \\ \diagup \quad \diagdown \\ H_2C \quad\quad CH_2 \\ \mid \quad\quad\quad \mid \\ H_2C — CH_2 \end{array}$ | $\begin{array}{c} CH_2 \\ \diagup \quad \diagdown \\ H_2C \quad\quad CH_2 \\ \mid \quad\quad\quad \mid \\ H_2C \quad\quad CH_2 \\ \diagdown \quad \diagup \\ CH_2 \end{array}$ |

Line-Angle Structural Formula

▶ **SAMPLE PROBLEM 12.3** Naming Alkanes and Cycloalkanes

Give the IUPAC name for each of the following:

a.
b.

SOLUTION

a. A chain with eight carbon atoms is octane.
b. The ring of six carbon atoms is named cyclohexane.

STUDY CHECK 12.3

What is the IUPAC name of the following compound?

ANSWER

cyclobutane

QUESTIONS AND PROBLEMS

12.2 Alkanes

LEARNING GOAL Write the IUPAC names and draw the condensed or line-angle structural formulas for alkanes and cycloalkanes.

12.9 Give the IUPAC name for each of the following alkanes and cycloalkanes:

a.
b. $CH_3 — CH_3$

c.
d.

12.10 Give the IUPAC name for each of the following alkanes and cycloalkanes:

a. CH_4
b.

c.
d.

12.11 Draw the condensed structural formula for alkanes or the line-angle structural formula for cycloalkanes for each of the following:
a. methane
b. ethane
c. pentane
d. cyclopropane

12.12 Draw the condensed structural formula for alkanes or the line-angle structural formula for cycloalkanes for each of the following:
a. propane
b. hexane
c. heptane
d. cyclopentane

12.3 Alkanes with Substituents

When an alkane has four or more carbon atoms, the atoms can be arranged so that a side group called a *branch* or **substituent** is attached to a carbon chain. For example, there are different ball-and-stick models for two compounds that have the molecular formula C_4H_{10}. One model is shown as a chain of four carbon atoms. In the other model, a carbon atom is attached as a branch or substituent to a carbon in a chain of three atoms (see Figure 12.2). An alkane with at least one branch is called a *branched alkane*. When the two compounds have the same molecular formula but different arrangements of atoms, they are called **structural isomers**.

LEARNING GOAL

Write the IUPAC names for alkanes with substituents and draw their condensed and line-angle structural formulas.

$$CH_3-CH_2-CH_2-CH_3$$

$$CH_3-\overset{\overset{\displaystyle CH_3}{|}}{CH}-CH_3$$

FIGURE 12.2 ▶ The structural isomers of C_4H_{10} have the same number and type of atoms but are bonded in a different order.

Q What makes these molecules structural isomers?

In another example, we can draw the condensed and line-angle structural formulas for three different structural isomers with the molecular formula C_5H_{12} as follows:

Structural Isomers of C_5H_{12}		
Condensed $\quad CH_3-CH_2-CH_2-CH_2-CH_3$	$CH_3-\overset{\overset{\displaystyle CH_3}{|}}{CH}-CH_2-CH_3$	$CH_3-\overset{\overset{\displaystyle CH_3}{|}}{\underset{\underset{\displaystyle CH_3}{|}}{C}}-CH_3$
Line-Angle		

SAMPLE PROBLEM 12.4 Structural Isomers

Identify each pair of formulas as structural isomers or the same molecule.

a. $\overset{\overset{\displaystyle CH_3}{|}}{CH_2}-\overset{\overset{\displaystyle CH_3}{|}}{CH_2}$ and $CH_2-CH_2-CH_3$
$\qquad\qquad\qquad\qquad\qquad\quad\; \overset{\overset{\displaystyle }{|}}{CH_3}$

b. and

SOLUTION

a. When we add up the number of C atoms and H atoms, they give the same molecular formula C_4H_{10}. The condensed structural formula on the left has a chain of four C atoms. Even though the $-CH_3$ ends are drawn up, they are part of the four-carbon chain. The condensed structural formula on the right also has a four-carbon chain even though one $-CH_3$ end is drawn down. Thus both condensed structural formulas represent the same molecule and are not structural isomers.

b. When we add up the number of C atoms and H atoms, they give the same molecular formula C_6H_{14}. The line-angle structural formula on the left has a five-carbon chain with a $-CH_3$ substituent on the second carbon of the chain. The line-angle structural formula on the right has a four-carbon chain with two $-CH_3$ substituents, one bonded to the second carbon and one bonded to the third carbon. Thus there is a different order of bonding of atoms, which represents structural isomers.

STUDY CHECK 12.4

Why does the following formula represent a different structural isomer of the molecules in Sample Problem 12.4, part **b**?

ANSWER

This formula represents a different structural isomer because the $-CH_3$ substituent is on the third carbon of the chain.

Substituents in Alkanes

In the IUPAC names for alkanes, a carbon branch is named as an **alkyl group**, which is an alkane that is missing one hydrogen atom. The alkyl group is named by replacing the *ane* ending of the corresponding alkane name with *yl*. Alkyl groups cannot exist on their own: They must be attached to a carbon chain. When a halogen atom is attached to a carbon chain, it is named as a *halo* group: *fluoro, chloro, bromo,* or *iodo*. Some of the common groups attached to carbon chains are illustrated in Table 12.5.

TABLE 12.5   Formulas and Names of Some Common Substituents

Formula	CH_3-		CH_3-CH_2-	
Name	methyl		ethyl	

Formula	$CH_3-CH_2-CH_2-$		$CH_3-CH-CH_3$	
Name	propyl		isopropyl	

Formula	$CH_3-CH_2-CH_2-CH_2-$	$CH_3-CH-CH_2-$	$CH_3-CH-CH_2-CH_3$	CH_3-C-CH_3
Name	butyl	isobutyl	*sec*-butyl	*tert*-butyl

Formula	$F-$	$Cl-$	$Br-$	$I-$
Name	fluoro	chloro	bromo	iodo

Naming Alkanes with Substituents

In the IUPAC system of naming, a carbon chain is numbered to give the location of the substituents. Let's take a look at how we use the IUPAC system to name the alkane shown in Sample Problem 12.5.

Interactive Video

Naming Alkanes

▶**SAMPLE PROBLEM 12.5** Writing IUPAC Names for Alkanes with Substituents

Give the IUPAC name for the following alkane:

$$CH_3-CH-CH_2-C-CH_2-CH_3$$

with CH_3 above the second carbon, Br above the fourth carbon, and CH_3 below the fourth carbon.

SOLUTION

ANALYZE THE PROBLEM	Given	Need
	six carbon chain, two methyl groups, one bromo group	IUPAC name

Guide to Naming Alkanes with Substituents

STEP 1
Write the alkane name for the longest chain of carbon atoms.

STEP 2
Number the carbon atoms starting from the end nearer a substituent.

STEP 3
Give the location and name for each substituent (alphabetical order) as a prefix to the name of the main chain.

STEP 1   Write the alkane name for the longest chain of carbon atoms.

$$CH_3-CH-CH_2-\overset{\displaystyle CH_3}{\underset{\displaystyle CH_3}{C}}-CH_2-CH_3 \qquad \text{hexane}$$

with a CH_3 branch above the second carbon and Br above the fourth carbon

STEP 2   Number the carbon atoms starting from the end nearer a substituent. Carbon 1 is the carbon atom nearer a methyl group, $-CH_3$, on the left.

$$CH_3-CH-CH_2-\overset{\displaystyle Br}{\underset{\displaystyle CH_3}{C}}-CH_2-CH_3 \qquad \text{hexane}$$

1   2   3   4   5   6

STEP 3   Give the location and name for each substituent (alphabetical order) as a prefix to the name of the main chain. The substituents, which are bromo and methyl groups, are listed in alphabetical order (bromo first, then methyl). A hyphen is placed between the number on the carbon chain and the substituent name. When there are two or more of the same substituent, a prefix (*di*, *tri*, *tetra*) is used in front of the name. However, these prefixes are not used to determine the alphabetical order of the substituents. Then commas are used to separate the numbers for the locations of the substituents.

$$CH_3-CH-CH_2-\overset{\displaystyle Br}{\underset{\displaystyle CH_3}{C}}-CH_2-CH_3 \qquad \text{4-bromo-2,4-dimethylhexane}$$

1   2   3   4   5   6

STUDY CHECK 12.5

Give the IUPAC name for the following compound:

ANSWER

4-isopropylheptane

Naming Cycloalkanes with Substituents

When one substituent is attached to a carbon atom in a cycloalkane, the name of the substituent is placed in front of the cycloalkane name. No number is needed for a single alkyl group or halogen atom because the carbon atoms in the cycloalkane are equivalent. However, if two or more substituents are attached, the ring is numbered by assigning carbon 1 to the substituent that comes first alphabetically. Then we count the carbon atoms in the ring in the direction (clockwise or counterclockwise) that gives the lower numbers to the substituents.

Methylcyclopentane   1,3-Dimethylcyclopentane

1-Chloro-3-methylcyclohexane

Haloalkanes

In a *haloalkane*, halogen atoms replace hydrogen atoms in an alkane. The halo substituents are numbered and arranged alphabetically, just as we did with the alkyl groups. Many times chemists use the common, traditional name for these compounds rather than the systematic IUPAC name. Simple haloalkanes are commonly named as alkyl halides; the carbon group is named as an alkyl group followed by the halide name.

Examples of Haloalkanes

Formula	CH_3-Cl	CH_3-CH_2-Br	$CH_3-CH-CH_3$ (F)	CH_3-C-CH_3 (Cl, CH_3)
IUPAC	Chloromethane	Bromoethane	2-Fluoropropane	2-Chloro-2-methylpropane
Common	Methyl chloride	Ethyl bromide	Isopropyl fluoride	*tert*-Butyl chloride

Drawing Condensed and Line-Angle Structural Formulas for Alkanes

The IUPAC name gives all the information needed to draw the condensed structural formula for an alkane. Suppose you are asked to draw the condensed structural formula for 2,3-dimethylbutane. The alkane name gives the number of carbon atoms in the longest chain. The names in the beginning indicate the substituents and where they are attached. We can break down the name in the following way:

2,3-Dimethylbutane

2,3-	Di	methyl	but	ane
Substituents on carbons 2 and 3	two identical groups	$-CH_3$ alkyl groups	four C atoms in the main chain	single (C—C) bonds

▶ **SAMPLE PROBLEM 12.6 Drawing Condensed Structures from IUPAC Names**

Draw the condensed and line-angle structural formulas for 2,3-dimethylbutane.

ANALYZE THE PROBLEM	Given	Need
	2,3-dimethylbutane	condensed and line-angle structural formulas

SOLUTION

STEP 1 **Draw the main chain of carbon atoms.** For butane, we draw a chain or a zigzag line of four carbon atoms.

C—C—C—C

STEP 2 **Number the chain and place the substituents on the carbons indicated by the numbers.** The first part of the name indicates two methyl groups —CH_3: one on carbon 2 and one on carbon 3.

Methyl Methyl
CH_3 CH_3
C—C—C—C
1   2   3   4

1 2 3 4

Guide to Drawing Structural Formulas for Alkanes with Substituents

STEP 1
Draw the main chain of carbon atoms.

STEP 2
Number the chain and place the substituents on the carbons indicated by the numbers.

STEP 3
For the condensed structural formula, add the correct number of hydrogen atoms to give four bonds to each C atom.

STEP **3** For the condensed structural formula, add the correct number of hydrogen atoms to give four bonds to each C atom.

$$CH_3-\overset{\overset{\displaystyle CH_3}{|}}{CH}-\overset{\overset{\displaystyle CH_3}{|}}{CH}-CH_3$$

2,3-Dimethylbutane

STUDY CHECK 12.6

Draw the condensed and line-angle structural formulas for 2-bromo-3-ethyl-4-methylpentane.

ANSWER

$$CH_3-\overset{\overset{\displaystyle Br}{|}}{CH}-\overset{\overset{\displaystyle CH_2}{|}}{\underset{\underset{\displaystyle CH_3}{|}}{CH}}-\overset{\overset{\displaystyle CH_3}{|}}{CH}-CH_3$$

QUESTIONS AND PROBLEMS

12.3 Alkanes with Substituents

LEARNING GOAL Write the IUPAC names for alkanes with substituents and draw their condensed and line-angle structural formulas.

12.13 Indicate whether each of the following pairs represent structural isomers or the same molecule:

a. $CH_3-\overset{\overset{\displaystyle CH_3}{|}}{CH}-CH_3$ and $\overset{\overset{\displaystyle CH_3}{|}}{\underset{\underset{\displaystyle CH_3}{|}}{CH}}-CH_3$

b. $CH_3-\overset{\overset{\displaystyle CH_3}{|}}{CH}-CH_2-CH_3$ and $\overset{\overset{\displaystyle CH_3}{|}}{CH_2}-\overset{\overset{\displaystyle CH_3}{|}}{CH_2}-CH_2$

c. (line-angle structure) and (line-angle structure)

12.14 Indicate whether each of the following pairs represent structural isomers or the same molecule:

a. $CH_3-\overset{\overset{\displaystyle CH_3}{|}}{\underset{\underset{\displaystyle CH_3}{|}}{C}}-CH_3$ and $\overset{\overset{\displaystyle CH_3}{|}}{\underset{\underset{\displaystyle CH_3}{|}}{CH}}-CH_2-CH_3$

b. $CH_3-\overset{\overset{\displaystyle CH_3}{|}}{CH}-\overset{\overset{\displaystyle CH_3}{|}}{CH}-\overset{\overset{\displaystyle CH_3}{|}}{CH_2}$ and $CH_3-\overset{\overset{\displaystyle CH_3}{|}}{CH}-CH_2-\overset{\overset{\displaystyle CH_3}{|}}{CH}-CH_3$

c. (line-angle structure) and (line-angle structure)

12.15 Give the IUPAC name for each of the following:

a. $CH_3-\overset{\overset{\displaystyle CH_3}{|}}{\underset{\underset{\displaystyle CH_3}{|}}{C}}-CH_3$ b. (line-angle structure)

c. $CH_3-\overset{\overset{\displaystyle CH_3}{|}}{CH}-CH_2-\overset{\overset{\displaystyle CH_3-\overset{\overset{\displaystyle CH_3}{|}}{\underset{\underset{\displaystyle CH_3}{|}}{C}}}{|}}{CH}-CH_2-\overset{\overset{\displaystyle CH_3}{|}}{CH}-CH_3$

d. (cyclobutane structure)   e. (cyclohexane with Br and Cl)

12.16 Give the IUPAC name for each of the following:

a. $CH_3-\overset{\overset{\displaystyle CH_3}{|}}{CH}-CH_2-CH_2-CH_3$

b. (line-angle structure)

c. $CH_3-CH_2-\overset{\overset{\displaystyle CH_2-CH_3}{|}}{\underset{\underset{\displaystyle CH_2-CH_3}{|}}{CH}}-CH_2-CH_3$

d. (cyclohexane structure)   e. (cyclopentane structure)

12.17 Draw the condensed structural formula for each of the following alkanes:
   a. 3,3-dimethylpentane
   b. 2,3,5-trimethylhexane
   c. 3-ethyl-5-isopropyloctane
   d. 1-bromo-2-chloroethane

12.18 Draw the condensed structural formula for each of the following alkanes:
   a. 3-ethylpentane
   b. 4-isopropyl-3-methylheptane
   c. 4-ethyl-2,2-dimethyloctane
   d. 2-bromopropane

12.19 Draw the line-angle structural formula for each of the following:
   a. 3-methylheptane
   b. 1-chloro-3-ethylcyclopentane
   c. bromocyclobutane
   d. 2,3-dichlorohexane

12.20 Draw the line-angle structural formula for each of the following:
   a. 1-bromo-2-methylpentane
   b. 1,2,3-trimethylcyclopropane
   c. ethylcyclohexane
   d. 4-chlorooctane

12.4 Properties of Alkanes

LEARNING GOAL

Identify the properties of alkanes and write a balanced chemical equation for combustion.

Many types of alkanes are the components of fuels that power our cars and oil that heats our homes. You may have used a mixture of hydrocarbons such as mineral oil as a laxative or petrolatum jelly to soften your skin. The differences in uses of many of the alkanes result from their physical properties, including solubility and density.

Some Uses of Alkanes

The first four alkanes—methane, ethane, propane, and butane—are gases at room temperature and are widely used as heating fuels.

Alkanes having five to eight carbon atoms (pentane, hexane, heptane, and octane) are liquids at room temperature. They are highly volatile, which makes them useful in fuels such as gasoline.

Liquid alkanes with 9 to 17 carbon atoms have higher boiling points and are found in kerosene, diesel, and jet fuels. Motor oil is a mixture of high-molecular-weight liquid hydrocarbons and is used to lubricate the internal components of engines. Mineral oil is a mixture of liquid hydrocarbons and is used as a laxative and a lubricant. Alkanes with 18 or more carbon atoms are waxy solids at room temperature. Known as paraffins, they are used in waxy coatings added to fruits and vegetables to retain moisture, inhibit mold, and enhance appearance. Petrolatum jelly, or Vaseline, is a semisolid mixture of hydrocarbons with more than 25 carbon atoms used in ointments and cosmetics and as a lubricant.

The solid alkanes that make up waxy coatings on fruits and vegetables help retain moisture, inhibit mold, and enhance appearance.

Melting and Boiling Points

Alkanes have the lowest melting and boiling points of all the organic compounds. This occurs because alkanes contain only the nonpolar bonds of C—C and C—H. Therefore, the attractions that occur between alkane molecules in the solid and liquid states are because of the relatively weak dispersion forces. As the number of carbon atoms increases, there is also an increase in the number of electrons, which increases the attraction because of the dispersion forces. Thus, alkanes with higher masses have higher melting and boiling points.

CH_4 CH_3—CH_3 CH_3—CH_2—CH_3 CH_3—CH_2—CH_2—CH_3 CH_3—CH_2—CH_2—CH_2—CH_3

Methane   Ethane   Propane   Butane   Pentane

bp = −164 °C   bp = −89 °C   bp = −42 °C   bp = 0.5 °C   bp = 36 °C

Number of Carbon Atoms Increases
Boiling Point Increases

The boiling points of branched alkanes are generally lower than the straight-chain isomers. The branched-chain alkanes tend to be more compact, which reduces the points of contact between the molecules. In an analogy, we can think of the carbon chains of straight-chain alkanes as pieces of licorice in a package. Because they have linear shapes, they can line up very close to each other, which gives many points of contact between the surface of the molecules. In our analogy, we can also think of branched alkanes as tennis balls in a can that, because of their spherical shapes, have only a small area of contact. One tennis ball represents an entire molecule. Because branched alkanes have fewer attractions, they have lower melting and boiling points.

There is more contact between the surfaces of hexane molecules (red and black licorice) than between the surfaces of 2,3-dimethylbutane molecules (tennis balls).

$CH_3-CH_2-CH_2-CH_2-CH_2-CH_3$

Hexane
bp = 69 °C

$$CH_3-CH_2-\overset{\overset{\displaystyle CH_3}{\displaystyle |}}{C}H-CH_2-CH_3$$

3-Methylpentane
bp = 63 °C

$$CH_3-\overset{\overset{\displaystyle CH_3}{\displaystyle |}}{C}H-\overset{\overset{\displaystyle CH_3}{\displaystyle |}}{C}H-CH_3$$

2,3-Dimethylbutane
bp = 58 °C

Number of Branches Increases
Boiling Point Decreases

Cycloalkanes have higher boiling points than the straight-chain alkanes with the same number of carbon atoms. Because rotation of carbon bonds is restricted, cycloalkanes maintain a rigid structure. Cycloalkanes with their rigid structures can be stacked closely together, which gives them many points of contact and therefore many attractions to each other.

We can compare the boiling points of straight-chain alkanes, branched-chain alkanes, and cycloalkanes with five carbon atoms as shown in Table 12.6.

Combustion of Alkanes

The carbon–carbon single bonds in alkanes are difficult to break, which makes them the least reactive family of organic compounds. However, alkanes burn readily in oxygen to produce carbon dioxide, water, and energy.

$$\text{Alkane}(g) + O_2(g) \xrightarrow{\Delta} CO_2(g) + H_2O(g) + \text{energy}$$

For example, methane is the natural gas we use to cook our food and heat our homes. The equation for the combustion of methane (CH_4) is written:

$$CH_4(g) + 2O_2(g) \xrightarrow{\Delta} CO_2(g) + 2H_2O(g) + \text{energy}$$
Methane

TABLE 12.6 Comparison of Boiling Points of Alkanes and Cycloalkanes with Five Carbons

Formula	Name	Boiling Point (°C)
Straight-Chain Alkane		
$CH_3-CH_2-CH_2-CH_2-CH_3$	Pentane	36
Branched-Chain Alkanes		
$\begin{array}{c} CH_3 \\ \vert \\ CH_3-CH-CH_2-CH_3 \end{array}$	2-Methylbutane	28
$\begin{array}{c} CH_3 \\ \vert \\ CH_3-C-CH_3 \\ \vert \\ CH_3 \end{array}$	Dimethylpropane	10
Cycloalkane		
(pentagon)	Cyclopentane	49

FIGURE 12.3 ▶ The propane fuel in the tank undergoes combustion, which provides energy.

Q What is the balanced equation for the combustion of propane?

In another example, propane is the gas used in portable heaters and gas barbecues (see Figure 12.3). The equation for the combustion of propane (C_3H_8) is written:

$$C_3H_8(g) + 5O_2(g) \xrightarrow{\Delta} 3CO_2(g) + 4H_2O(g) + \text{energy}$$
Propane

In the cells of our bodies, energy is produced by the combustion of glucose. Although a series of reactions is involved, we can write the overall combustion of glucose in our cells as follows:

$$C_6H_{12}O_6(aq) + 6O_2(g) \xrightarrow{\text{Enzymes}} 6CO_2(g) + 6H_2O(l) + \text{energy}$$
Glucose

Solubility and Density

Alkanes are nonpolar, which makes them insoluble in water. However, they are soluble in nonpolar solvents such as other alkanes. Alkanes have densities from 0.62 g/mL to about 0.79 g/mL, which is less than the density of water (1.0 g/mL).

If there is an oil spill in the ocean, the alkanes in the oil, which do not mix with water, form a thin layer on the surface that spreads over a large area. In April 2010, an explosion on an oil-drilling rig in the Gulf of Mexico caused the largest oil spill in U.S. history. At its maximum, an estimated 10 million liters of oil was leaked every day. Other major oil spills occurred in Queensland, Australia (2009), the coast of Wales (1996), the Shetland Islands (1993), and Alaska, from the *Exxon Valdez*, in 1989 (see Figure 12.4). If the crude oil reaches land, there can be considerable damage to beaches, shellfish, birds, and wildlife habitats. When animals such as birds are covered with oil, they must be cleaned quickly because ingestion of the hydrocarbons when they try to clean themselves is fatal.

Cleanup of oil spills includes mechanical, chemical, and microbiological methods. A boom may be placed around the leaking oil until it can be removed. Boats called skimmers then scoop up the oil and place it in tanks. In a chemical method, a substance that attracts oil is used to pick up oil, which is then scraped off into recovery tanks. Certain bacteria that ingest oil are also used to break oil down into less harmful products.

FIGURE 12.4 ▶ In oil spills, large quantities of oil spread out to form a thin layer on top of the ocean surface.

Q What physical properties cause oil to remain on the surface of water?

QUESTIONS AND PROBLEMS

12.4 Properties of Alkanes

LEARNING GOAL Identify the properties of alkanes and write a balanced chemical equation for combustion.

12.21 Heptane, used as a solvent for rubber cement, has a density of 0.68 g/mL and boils at 98 °C.
    a. Draw the condensed and line-angle structural formulas for heptane.
    b. Is heptane a solid, liquid, or gas at room temperature?
    c. Is heptane soluble in water?
    d. Will heptane float on water or sink?
    e. Write the balanced chemical equation for the complete combustion of heptane.

12.22 Nonane has a density of 0.79 g/mL and boils at 151 °C.
    a. Draw the condensed and line-angle structural formulas for nonane.
    b. Is nonane a solid, liquid, or gas at room temperature?
    c. Is nonane soluble in water?
    d. Will nonane float on water or sink?
    e. Write the balanced chemical equation for the complete combustion of nonane.

12.23 Write the balanced chemical equation for the complete combustion of each of the following compounds:
    a. ethane
    b. cyclopropane
    c. octane

12.24 Write the balanced chemical equation for the complete combustion of each of the following compounds:
    a. hexane   **b.** cyclopentane   **c.** butane

Butane in a portable burner undergoes combustion.

12.25 In each of the following pairs of hydrocarbons, which one would you expect to have the higher boiling point?
    a. pentane or heptane
    b. propane or cyclopropane
    c. hexane or 2-methylpentane

12.26 In each of the following pairs of hydrocarbons, which one would you expect to have the higher boiling point?
    a. propane or butane
    b. hexane or cyclohexane
    c. 2,2-dimethylpentane or heptane

LEARNING GOAL

Identify structural formulas as alkenes, cycloalkenes, and alkynes, and write their IUPAC names.

Bond angles = 120°
Ethene

H—C≡C—H
Bond angles = 180°
Ethyne

FIGURE 12.5 ► Ball-and-stick models of ethene and ethyne show the double or triple bonds and the bond angles.

Q Why are these compounds called unsaturated hydrocarbons?

12.5 Alkenes and Alkynes

Alkenes and *alkynes* are families of hydrocarbons that contain double and triple bonds, respectively. They are called *unsaturated hydrocarbons* because they do not contain the maximum number of hydrogen atoms, as do alkanes. They react with hydrogen gas to increase the number of hydrogen atoms to become alkanes, which are *saturated hydrocarbons*.

Identifying Alkenes and Alkynes

Alkenes contain one or more carbon–carbon double bonds that form when adjacent carbon atoms share two pairs of valence electrons. Recall that *a carbon atom always forms four covalent bonds*. In the simplest alkene, ethene, C_2H_4, two carbon atoms are connected by a double bond and each is also attached to two H atoms. This gives each carbon atom in the double bond a trigonal planar arrangement with bond angles of 120°. As a result, the ethene molecule is flat because the carbon and hydrogen atoms all lie in the same plane (see Figure 12.5).

Ethene, more commonly called ethylene, is an important plant hormone involved in promoting the ripening of fruit. Commercially grown fruit, such as avocados, bananas, and tomatoes, are often picked before they are ripe. Before the fruit is brought to market, it is exposed to ethylene to accelerate the ripening process. Ethylene also accelerates the breakdown of cellulose in plants, which causes flowers to wilt and leaves to fall from trees.

In an **alkyne**, a triple bond forms when two carbon atoms share three pairs of valence electrons. In the simplest alkyne, ethyne (C_2H_2), the two carbon atoms of the triple bond are each attached to one hydrogen atom, which gives a triple bond a linear geometry. Ethyne, commonly called acetylene, is used in welding where it reacts with oxygen to produce flames with temperatures above 3300 °C.

Fruit is ripened with ethene, a plant hormone.

A mixture of acetylene and oxygen undergoes combustion during the welding of metals.

Naming Alkenes and Alkynes

The IUPAC names for alkenes and alkynes are similar to those of alkanes. Using the alkane name with the same number of carbon atoms, the *ane* ending is replaced with *ene* for an alkene and *yne* for an alkyne (see Table 12.7). Cyclic alkenes are named as *cycloalkenes*.

TABLE 12.7 Comparison of Names for Alkanes, Alkenes, and Alkynes

Alkane	Alkene	Alkyne
CH_3-CH_3	$H_2C=CH_2$	$HC\equiv CH$
Ethane	Ethene (ethylene)	Ethyne (acetylene)
$CH_3-CH_2-CH_3$	$CH_3-CH=CH_2$	$CH_3-C\equiv CH$
Propane	Propene	Propyne

Examples of naming an alkene and an alkyne are seen in Sample Problem 12.7.

> **SAMPLE PROBLEM 12.7** Naming Alkenes and Alkynes

Write the IUPAC name for each of the following:

a. $$CH_3-\underset{\overset{|}{CH_3}}{CH}-CH=CH-CH_3$$

b. $CH_3-CH_2-C\equiv C-CH_2-CH_3$

SOLUTION

a.

	Given	Need
ANALYZE THE PROBLEM	five-carbon chain, double bond, methyl group	IUPAC name

STEP 1 Name the longest carbon chain that contains the double bond. There are five carbon atoms in the longest carbon chain containing the double bond. Replace the *ane* in the corresponding alkane name with *ene* to give pentene.

$$CH_3-\underset{\overset{|}{CH_3}}{CH}-CH=CH-CH_3 \qquad \text{pentene}$$

Explore Your World
Ripening Fruit

Obtain two unripe green bananas. Place one in a plastic bag and seal the bag. Leave the banana and the bag with a banana on the counter. Check the bananas twice a day to observe any difference in the ripening process.

Questions

1. What compound is used to ripen the bananas?
2. What are some possible reasons for any difference in the ripening rate?
3. If you wish to ripen an avocado, what procedure might you use?

Guide to Naming Alkenes and Alkynes

STEP 1
Name the longest carbon chain that contains the double or triple bond.

STEP 2
Number the carbon chain starting from the end nearer the double or triple bond.

STEP 3
Give the location and name for each substituent (alphabetical order) as a prefix to the alkene or alkyne name.

STEP 2 Number the carbon chain starting from the end nearer the double bond. Place the number of the first carbon in the double bond in front of the alkene name.

$$CH_3 - \underset{\underset{5}{|}}{\overset{\overset{CH_3}{|}}{CH}} - \underset{4}{CH} = \underset{3}{CH} - \underset{2}{CH} - \underset{1}{CH_3} \qquad \text{2-pentene}$$

Alkenes or alkynes with two or three carbons do not need numbers. For example, the double bond in ethene or propene must be between carbon 1 and carbon 2.

STEP 3 Give the location and name for each substituent (alphabetical order) as a prefix to the alkene name. The methyl group is located on carbon 4.

$$CH_3 - \underset{5}{\overset{\overset{CH_3}{|}}{CH}} - \underset{4}{CH} - \underset{3}{CH} = \underset{2}{CH} - \underset{1}{CH_3} \qquad \text{4-methyl-2-pentene}$$

b.

	Given	Need
ANALYZE THE PROBLEM	six carbon chain, triple bond	IUPAC name

STEP 1 Name the longest carbon chain that contains the triple bond. There are six carbon atoms in the longest chain containing the triple bond. Replace the *ane* in the corresponding alkane name with *yne* to give hexyne.

$$CH_3 - CH_2 - C \equiv C - CH_2 - CH_3 \qquad \text{hexyne}$$

STEP 2 Number the carbon chain starting from the end nearer the triple bond. Place the number of the first carbon in the triple bond in front of the alkyne name.

$$\underset{1}{CH_3} - \underset{2}{CH_2} - \underset{3}{C} \equiv \underset{4}{C} - \underset{5}{CH_2} - \underset{6}{CH_3} \qquad \text{3-hexyne}$$

STEP 3 Give the location and name for each substituent (alphabetical order) as a prefix to the alkyne name. There are no substituents in this formula.

STUDY CHECK 12.7

Name each of the following:

a. ⎯⎯≡⎯⎯/

b. (structure with Cl)

ANSWER

a. 2-pentyne

b. 2-chloro-1-hexene

Naming Cycloalkenes

Some alkenes called *cycloalkenes* have a double bond within a ring structure. If there is no substituent, the double bond does not need a number. If there is a substituent, the carbons in the double bond are numbered as 1 and 2, and the ring is numbered in the direction that will give the lower number to the substituent.

Cyclobutene   3-Methylcyclopentene

Chemistry Link to the **Environment**

Fragrant Alkenes

The odors you associate with lemons, oranges, roses, and lavender are because of volatile compounds that are synthesized by the plants. The pleasant flavors and fragrances of many fruits and flowers are often because of unsaturated compounds. They were some of the first kinds of compounds to be extracted from natural plant material. In ancient times, they were highly valued in their pure forms. Limonene and myrcene give the characteristic odors and flavors to lemons and bay leaves, respectively. Geraniol and citronellal give roses and lemongrass their distinct aromas. In the food and perfume industries, these compounds are extracted or synthesized and used as perfumes and flavorings.

The characteristic odor of a rose is because of geraniol, a 10-carbon alcohol with two double bonds.

$$CH_3-\underset{\underset{CH_3}{|}}{C}=CH-CH_2-CH_2-\underset{\underset{CH_3}{|}}{C}=CH-CH_2-OH$$
Geraniol, roses

$$CH_3-\underset{\underset{CH_3}{|}}{C}=CH-CH_2-CH_2-\underset{\overset{CH_2}{||}}{C}-CH=CH_2$$
Myrcene, bay leaves

$$CH_3-\underset{\underset{CH_3}{|}}{C}=CH-CH_2-CH_2-\underset{\underset{CH_3}{|}}{CH}-CH_2-\underset{\overset{O}{||}}{C}-H$$
Citronellal, lemongrass

Limonene, lemons and oranges

QUESTIONS AND PROBLEMS

12.5 Alkenes and Alkynes

LEARNING GOAL Identify structural formulas as alkenes, cycloalkenes, and alkynes, and write their IUPAC names.

12.27 Identify the following as alkanes, alkenes, cycloalkenes, or alkynes:

a. $H-\underset{\underset{H}{|}}{\overset{\overset{H}{|}}{C}}-\overset{\overset{H}{|}}{C}=\overset{\overset{H}{|}}{C}-H$ b. $CH_3-CH_2-C\equiv C-H$

c. ~~~~~   d.

12.28 Identify the following as alkanes, alkenes, cycloalkenes, or alkynes:

a.   b.

c. $CH_3-\underset{\underset{CH_3}{|}}{\overset{\overset{CH_3}{|}}{C}}=C-CH_3$ d. $\qquad-C\equiv CH$

12.29 Give the IUPAC name for each of the following:

a. $CH_3-\underset{\overset{CH_3}{|}}{C}=CH_2$ b.

c.   d.

12.30 Give the IUPAC name for each of the following:

a. $H_2C=CH-CH_2-CH_2-CH_2-CH_3$

b. $CH_3-C\equiv C-CH_2-CH_2-\underset{\underset{CH_3}{|}}{CH}-CH_3$

c.   d.

12.31 Draw the condensed structural formulas for **a** and **b** and line-angle structural formulas for **c** and **d**:
a. 1-pentene
b. 2-methyl-1-butene
c. 3-methylcyclohexene
d. 1-chloro-3-hexyne

12.32 Draw the condensed structural formulas for **a** and **b** and line-angle structural formulas for **c** and **d**:
a. 3-methyl-1-butyne
b. 3,4-dimethyl-1-pentene
c. 1,2-dichlorocyclopentene
d. 2-methyl-2-hexene

LEARNING GOAL

Draw the condensed and line-angle structural formulas and give the names for the cis–trans isomers of alkenes.

12.6 Cis–Trans Isomers

In any alkene, the double bond is rigid, which means there is no rotation around the double bond (see Explore Your World "Modeling Cis–Trans Isomers"). As a result, the atoms or groups are attached to the carbon atoms in the double bond on one side or the other, which gives two different structures called *geometric isomers* or *cis–trans isomers*.

For example, the formula for 1,2-dichloroethene can be drawn as two different molecules, which are cis–trans isomers. In the expanded structural formulas, the atoms bonded to the carbon atoms in the double bond have bond angles of 120°. When we draw 1,2-dichloroethene, we add the prefix *cis* or *trans* to denote whether the atoms bonded to the carbon atoms are on the same side or opposite sides of the molecule. In the **cis isomer**, the chlorine atoms are on the same side of the double bond. In the **trans isomer**, the chlorine atoms are on opposite sides of the double bond. *Trans* means "across," as in transcontinental; *cis* means "on this side."

$$Cl-CH=CH-Cl$$
1,2-Dichloroethene

Chlorine atoms are on the same side of the double bond.

cis-1,2-Dichloroethene

Chlorine atoms are on opposite sides of the double bond.

trans-1,2-Dichloroethene

Another example of a cis–trans isomer is 2-butene. If we look closely at 2-butene, we find that each carbon in the double bond is bonded to a $-CH_3$ group and a hydrogen atom. We can draw cis–trans isomers for 2-butene. In the *cis*-2-butene isomer, the $-CH_3$ groups are attached on the same side of the double bond. In the *trans*-2-butene isomer, the $-CH_3$ groups are attached to the double bond on opposite sides, as shown in their ball-and-stick models (see Figure 12.6).

FIGURE 12.6 ▶ Ball-and-stick models and line-angle structural formulas of the cis and trans isomers of 2-butene.

Q What feature in 2-butene accounts for the cis and trans isomers?

cis-2-Butene

trans-2-Butene

As with any pair of cis–trans isomers, *cis*-2-butene and *trans*-2-butene are different compounds with different physical properties and chemical properties. In general, trans isomers are more stable than their cis counterparts because the groups that are bigger than hydrogen atoms on the double bond are farther apart.

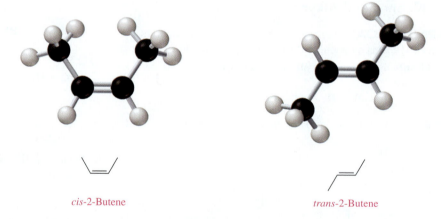

$$CH_3-CH=CH-CH_3$$
2-Butene

cis-2-Butene
(mp −139 °C; bp 3.7 °C)

trans-2-Butene
(mp −106 °C; bp 0.3 °C)

When the carbon atoms in the double bond are attached to two different atoms or groups of atoms, an alkene can have cis–trans isomers. For example, 3-hexene can be drawn with cis and trans isomers because there is one H atom and a $CH_3—CH_2—$ group attached to each carbon atom in the double bond. When you are asked to draw the formula for an alkene, it is important to consider the possibility of cis and trans isomers.

$$CH_3—CH_2 —CH = CH —CH_2—CH_3$$

3-Hexene

Same side   Opposite sides

cis-3-Hexene   trans-3-Hexene

Same side   Opposite sides

When an alkene has identical groups on the same carbon atom of the double bond, cis and trans isomers cannot be drawn. For example, 1,1-dichloropropene has just one condensed structural formula and does not form cis–trans isomers.

1,1-Dichloropropene

When identical groups are attached to carbon 1, there are no cis–trans isomers.

▶ SAMPLE PROBLEM 12.8 Identifying Cis–Trans Isomers

Identify each of the following as the cis or trans isomer and give its name:

a. Br   Cl

b.

SOLUTION

a. This is a cis isomer because the two halogen atoms attached to the carbon atoms of the double bond are on the same side. The name of the two-carbon alkene, starting with the bromo group on carbon 1, is *cis*-1-bromo-2-chloroethene.
b. This is a trans isomer because the two alkyl groups attached to the carbon atoms of the double bond are on opposite sides of the double bond. This isomer of the five-carbon alkene, 2-pentene, is named *trans*-2-pentene.

STUDY CHECK 12.8

Give the name for the following compound, including cis or trans:

ANSWER

trans-3-hexene

◆ Explore Your World

Modeling Cis–Trans Isomers

Because cis–trans isomerism is not easy to visualize, here are some things you can do to understand the difference in rotation around a single bond compared to a double bond and how it affects groups that are attached to the carbon atoms in the double bond.

Put the tips of your index fingers together. This is a model of a single bond. Consider the index fingers as a pair of carbon atoms, and think of your thumbs and other fingers as other parts of a carbon chain. While your index fingers are touching, twist your hands and change the position of your thumbs relative to each other. Notice how the relationship of your other fingers changes.

Now place the tips of your index fingers and middle fingers together in a model of a double bond. As you did before, twist your hands to move your thumbs away from each other. What happens? Can you change the location of your thumbs relative to each other without breaking the double bond? The difficulty of moving your hands with two fingers touching represents the lack of rotation about a double bond. You have made a model of a cis isomer when both thumbs point in the same direction. If you turn one hand over so one thumb points down and the other thumb points up, you have made a model of a trans isomer.

Cis-hands (cis-thumbs/fingers)

Trans-hands (trans-thumbs/fingers)

Using Gumdrops and Toothpicks to Model Cis–Trans Isomers

Obtain some toothpicks and yellow, green, and black gumdrops. The black gumdrops represent C atoms, the yellow gumdrops represent H atoms, and the green gumdrops represent Cl atoms. Place a toothpick between two black gumdrops. Use three more toothpicks to attach two yellow gumdrops and one green gumdrop to each black gumdrop carbon atom. Rotate one of the gumdrop carbon atoms to show the conformations of the attached H and Cl atoms.

Remove a toothpick and yellow gumdrop from each black gumdrop. Place a second toothpick between the carbon atoms, which makes a double bond. Try to twist the double bond of toothpicks. Can you do it? When you observe the location of the green gumdrops, does the model you made represent a cis or trans isomer? Why? If

your model is a cis isomer, how would you change it to a trans isomer? If your model is a trans isomer, how would you change it to a cis isomer?

Models from gumdrops represent cis and trans isomers.

Chemistry Link to the Environment

Pheromones in Insect Communication

Many insects emit minute quantities of chemicals called *pheromones* to send messages to individuals of the same species. Some pheromones warn of danger, others call for defense, mark a trail, or attract the opposite sex. In the past 40 yr, the structures of many pheromones have been chemically determined. One of the most studied is bom-

Pheromones allow insects to attract mates from a great distance.

bykol, the sex pheromone produced by the female silkworm moth. The bombykol molecule contains one cis double bond and one trans double bond. Even a few nanograms of bombykol will attract male silkworm moths from distances of over 1 km. The effectiveness of many of these pheromones depends on the cis or trans configuration of the double bonds in the molecules. A certain species will respond to one isomer but not the other.

Scientists are interested in synthesizing pheromones to use as non-toxic alternatives to pesticides. When placed in a trap, bombykol can be used to capture male silkworm moths. When a synthetic pheromone is released in a field, the males cannot locate the females, which disrupts the reproductive cycle. This technique has been successful with controlling the oriental fruit moth, the grapevine moth, and the pink bollworm.

Bombykol, sex attractant for the silkworm moth

Chemistry Link to **Health**

Cis–Trans Isomers for Night Vision

The retinas of the eyes consist of two types of cells: rods and cones. The rods on the edge of the retina allow us to see in dim light, and the cones, in the center, produce our vision in bright light. In the rods, there is a substance called *rhodopsin* that absorbs light. Rhodopsin is composed of *cis*-11-retinal, an unsaturated compound, attached to a protein. When rhodopsin absorbs light, the *cis*-11-retinal isomer is converted to its trans isomer, which changes its shape. The trans form no longer fits the protein, and it separates from the protein. The change from the cis to trans isomer and its separation from the protein generate an electrical signal that the brain converts into an image.

An enzyme (isomerase) converts the trans isomer back to the *cis*-11-retinal isomer and the rhodopsin re-forms. If there is a deficiency of rhodopsin in the rods of the retina, *night blindness* may occur. One common cause is a lack of vitamin A in the diet. In our diet, we obtain vitamin A from plant pigments containing β-carotene, which is found in foods such as carrots, squash, and spinach. In the small intestine, the β-carotene is converted to vitamin A, which can be converted to *cis*-11-retinal or stored in the liver for future use. Without a sufficient quantity of retinal, not enough rhodopsin is produced to enable us to see adequately in dim light.

Cis–Trans Isomers of Retinal

Cis double bond

Trans double bond

H

Light

Isomerase

cis-11-Retinal

trans-11-Retinal

QUESTIONS AND PROBLEMS

12.6 Cis–Trans Isomers

LEARNING GOAL Draw the condensed and line-angle structural formulas and give the names for the cis–trans isomers of alkenes.

12.33 Give the IUPAC name for each of the following, using cis or trans prefixes:

a.
$$CH_3 \quad CH_3$$
$$C=C$$
$$H \quad H$$

b.
$$CH_3-CH_2 \quad H$$
$$C=C$$
$$H \quad CH_2-CH_2-CH_2-CH_3$$

c.

12.34 Give the IUPAC name for each of the following, using cis or trans prefixes:

a.
$$CH_3 \quad CH_2-CH_3$$
$$C=C$$
$$H \quad H$$

b.
$$CH_3 \quad H$$
$$C=C$$
$$H \quad CH_2-CH_2-CH_2-CH_3$$

c.

12.35 Draw the condensed structural formula for each of the following:
 a. *trans*-1-bromo-2-chloroethene
 b. *cis*-2-hexene
 c. *trans*-3-heptene

12.36 Draw the condensed structural formula for each of the following:
 a. *cis*-1,2-difluoroethene
 b. *trans*-2-pentene
 c. *cis*-4-octene

12.37 Which of the following cannot have cis–trans isomers? Explain.
 a. $H_2C=CH-CH_3$
 b. $CH_3-CH_2-CH=CH-CH_3$
 c.

12.38 Which of the following cannot have cis–trans isomers? Explain.

a.
$$H \quad H$$
$$C=C$$
$$CH_3-CH_2 \quad CH_2-CH_3$$

b. $CH_3-CH_2-CH_2-CH=CH_2$

c.

12.7 Addition Reactions for Alkenes

The most characteristic reaction of alkenes is the **addition** of atoms or groups of atoms to the carbon atoms in a double bond. Addition occurs because double bonds are easily broken, providing electrons to form new single bonds.

The addition reactions have different names that depend on the type of reactant we add to the alkene, as Table 12.8 shows.

TABLE 12.8 Summary of Addition Reactions

Name of Addition Reaction	Reactants	Catalysts	Product
Hydrogenation	Alkene + H_2	Pt, Ni, or Pd	Alkane
Hydration	Alkene + H_2O	H^+ (strong acid)	Alcohol
Polymerization	Alkenes	High temperature, pressure	Polymer

Hydrogenation

In a reaction called **hydrogenation**, H atoms add to each of the carbon atoms in a double bond of an alkene. During hydrogenation, the double bonds are converted to single bonds in alkanes. A catalyst such as finely divided platinum (Pt), nickel (Ni), or palladium (Pd) is used to speed up the reaction.

Some examples of the hydrogenation of alkenes follow:

$$CH_3-CH=CH-CH_3 + H_2 \xrightarrow{Pt} CH_3-CH_2-CH_2-CH_3$$

2-Butene   Butane

Cyclohexene   Cyclohexane

SAMPLE PROBLEM 12.9 **Writing Equations for Hydrogenation**

Draw the structural formula for the product of each of the following hydrogenation reactions:

a. $CH_3-CH=CH_2 + H_2 \xrightarrow{Pt}$?   **b.** ⬠ $+ H_2 \xrightarrow{Pt}$?

SOLUTION

In an addition reaction, hydrogen adds to the double bond to give an alkane.

ANALYZE THE PROBLEM	**Given**	**Need**
	alkene + H_2	structural formula of product

a. $CH_3-CH_2-CH_3$ **b.** ⬠

STUDY CHECK 12.9

Draw the condensed structural formula for the product of the hydrogenation of 2-methyl-1-butene, using a platinum catalyst.

ANSWER

$$\overset{\displaystyle CH_3}{\underset{\displaystyle |}{CH_3-CH-CH_2-CH_3}}$$

Chemistry Link to Health

Hydrogenation of Unsaturated Fats

Vegetable oils such as corn oil or safflower oil are unsaturated fats composed of fatty acids that contain double bonds. The process of hydrogenation is used commercially to convert the double bonds in the unsaturated fats in vegetable oils to saturated fats such as margarine, which are more solid. Adjusting the amount of added hydrogen produces partially hydrogenated fats such as soft margarine, solid margarine in sticks, and shortenings, which are used in cooking. For example, oleic acid is a typical unsaturated fatty acid in olive oil and has a cis double bond at carbon 9. When oleic acid is hydrogenated, it is converted to stearic acid, a saturated fatty acid.

The unsaturated fats in vegetable oils are converted to saturated fats to make a more solid product.

Cis double bond

Oleic acid (found in olive oil and other unsaturated fats)

Single bond

Stearic acid (found in saturated fats)

Hydration

In **hydration**, an alkene reacts with water (H—OH). A hydrogen atom (H—) from water forms a bond with one carbon atom in the double bond, and the oxygen atom in —OH forms a bond with the other carbon. The reaction is catalyzed by a strong acid such as H_2SO_4, written as H^+. Hydration is used to prepare alcohols, which have the hydroxyl (—OH) functional group. When water (H—OH) adds to a symmetrical alkene, such as ethene, a single product is formed.

Interactive Video

Addition to an Asymmetric Bond

H—OH

Functional group of alcohols

Ethene

Ethanol (ethyl alcohol)

However, when H_2O adds to a double bond in an asymmetrical alkene, two products are possible. We can determine the prevalent product that forms using **Markovnikov's Rule**, named after the Russian chemist Vladimir Markovnikov. The rule states that when water adds to a double bond in which the carbon atoms are attached to different numbers of H atoms (an asymmetrical double bond), the H— from H—OH attaches to the carbon that has the *greater* number of H atoms and the —OH adds to the other carbon atom from the double bond. In the following example, the H— from H—OH attaches to the end carbon of the double bond, which has more hydrogen atoms, and the —OH adds to the middle carbon atom:

This C in the C═C has more H atoms.

HO—H

Propene

2-Propanol

▶**SAMPLE PROBLEM 12.10** Hydration

Draw the condensed structural formula for the product that forms in the following hydration reaction:

$$CH_3 - CH_2 - CH_2 - CH = CH_2 + H_2O \xrightarrow{H^+}$$

SOLUTION

ANALYZE THE PROBLEM	Given	Need
	hydration, asymmetrical alkene	condensed structural formula for the product

For an asymmetrical alkene, the H— from water (H—OH) adds to the carbon with the *greater* number of hydrogen atoms, and the —OH bonds to the carbon with fewer H atoms.

$$CH_3 - CH_2 - CH_2 - \overset{\overset{\text{OH}}{\downarrow}}{CH} = \overset{\overset{\text{H}}{\downarrow}}{CH_2} \xrightarrow{H^+} CH_3 - CH_2 - CH_2 - \overset{\overset{\text{OH}}{|}}{CH} - CH_3$$

STUDY CHECK 12.10

Draw the condensed structural formula for the product obtained by the hydration of 2-methyl-2-butene.

ANSWER

$$CH_3 - \overset{\overset{\text{OH}}{|}}{\underset{\underset{\text{CH}_3}{|}}{C}} - CH_2 - CH_3$$

FIGURE 12.7 ▶ Synthetic polymers are used to replace diseased veins and arteries.

Ⓠ Why are the substances in these plastic devices called polymers?

Addition of Alkenes: Polymerization

A **polymer** is a large molecule that consists of small repeating units called **monomers**. In the past hundred years, the plastics industry has made synthetic polymers that are in many of the materials we use every day, such as carpeting, plastic wrap, nonstick pans, plastic cups, and rain gear. In medicine, synthetic polymers are used to replace diseased or damaged body parts such as hip joints, pacemakers, teeth, heart valves, and blood vessels (see Figure 12.7). There are about 100 billion kg of plastics produced every year, which is about 15 kg for every person on Earth.

Many of the synthetic polymers are made by addition reactions of small alkene monomers. Many polymerization reactions require high temperature, a catalyst, and high pressure (over 1000 atm). In an addition reaction, a polymer grows longer as each monomer is added at the end of the chain. A polymer may contain as many as 1000 monomers. Polyethylene, a polymer made from ethylene monomers, is used in plastic bottles, film, and plastic dinnerware. More polyethylene is produced worldwide than any other polymer. Low-density polyethylene (LDPE) is flexible, breakable, less dense, and more branched than high-density polyethylene (HDPE). High-density polyethylene is stronger, more dense, and melts at a higher temperature than LDPE.

Ethene (ethylene) monomers   Polyethylene section

Table 12.9 lists several alkene monomers that are used to produce common synthetic polymers, and Figure 12.8 shows examples of each. The alkane-like nature of these plastic synthetic polymers makes them unreactive. Thus, they do not decompose easily (they are not biodegradable). As a result, they have become significant contributors to pollution, on land and in the oceans. Efforts are being made to make them more degradable.

TABLE 12.9 Some Alkenes and Their Polymers

Recycling Code	Monomer	Polymer Section	Common Uses
2 HDPE **4** LDPE	$H_2C{=}CH_2$ Ethene (ethylene)	Polyethylene (PE)	Plastic bottles, film, insulation materials, shopping bags
3 V	$H_2C{=}CH$—Cl Chloroethene (vinyl chloride)	Polyvinyl chloride (PVC)	Plastic pipes and tubing, garden hoses, garbage bags, shower curtains, credit cards, medical containers
5 PP	$H_2C{=}CH$—CH_3 Propene (propylene)	Polypropylene (PP)	Ski and hiking clothing, carpets, artificial joints, plastic bottles, food containers, medical face masks, tubing
	$F{-}C{=}C{-}F$ Tetrafluoroethene	Polytetrafluoroethylene (PTFE)	Nonstick coatings, Teflon
	$H_2C{=}C$—Cl 1,1-Dichloroethene	Polydichloroethylene (Saran)	Plastic film and wrap, Gore-Tex rainwear, medical implants
6 PS	$H_2C{=}CH$ Phenylethene (styrene)	—CH_2—CH—CH_2—CH—CH_2—CH— Polystyrene (PS)	Plastic coffee cups and cartons, insulation

You can identify the type of polymer used to manufacture a plastic item by looking for the recycling symbol (arrows in a triangle) found on the label or on the bottom of the plastic container. For example, the number 5 or the letters PP inside the triangle is the code for a polypropylene plastic. There are now many cities that maintain recycling programs that reduce the amount of plastic materials that are transported to landfills.

Today, products such as lumber, tables and benches, trash receptacles, and pipes used for irrigation systems are made from recycled plastics.

Tables, benches, and trash receptacles can be manufactured from recycled plastics.

Explore Your World

Polymers and Recycling Plastics

1. Make a list of the items you use or have in your room or home that are made of polymers.
2. Recycling information on the bottom or side of a plastic bottle includes a triangle with a code number that identifies the type of polymer used to make the plastic. Make a collection of several different kinds of plastic bottles. Try to find plastic items with each type of polymer.

Questions

1. What are the most common types of plastics among the plastic containers in your collection?
2. What are the monomers of some of the plastics you looked at?

Polyethylene

Polyvinyl chloride

Polypropylene

Polytetrafluoroethylene (Teflon)

Polydichloroethylene (Saran)

Polystyrene

FIGURE 12.8 ▶ Synthetic polymers provide a wide variety of items that we use every day.

Q What are some alkenes used to make the polymers in these plastic items?

▶ **SAMPLE PROBLEM 12.11** Polymers

A firefighter/EMT arrives at a home where a premature baby has been delivered. To prevent hypothermia during transport to the neonatal facility, she wraps the baby in cling wrap. Draw and name the monomer unit and draw a portion of the polymer formed from three monomer units for cling wrap, which is polydichloroethylene (ethene).

SOLUTION

$$H_2C\!=\!\underset{|}{\overset{Cl}{C}}\!-\!Cl$$

1,1-Dichloroethene

$$-\underset{\underset{H}{|}}{\overset{\overset{H}{|}}{C}}-\underset{\underset{Cl}{|}}{\overset{\overset{Cl}{|}}{C}}-\underset{\underset{H}{|}}{\overset{\overset{H}{|}}{C}}-\underset{\underset{Cl}{|}}{\overset{\overset{Cl}{|}}{C}}-\underset{\underset{H}{|}}{\overset{\overset{H}{|}}{C}}-\underset{\underset{Cl}{|}}{\overset{\overset{Cl}{|}}{C}}-$$

STUDY CHECK 12.11

Draw the condensed structural formula for the monomer used in the manufacturing of PVC.

ANSWER

$$H_2C\!=\!\underset{|}{\overset{Cl}{CH}}$$

QUESTIONS AND PROBLEMS

12.7 Addition Reactions for Alkenes

LEARNING GOAL Draw the condensed or line-angle structural formulas and give the names for the organic products of addition reactions of alkenes. Draw a condensed structural formula for a section of a polymer.

12.39 Draw the structural formula for the product in each of the following reactions using Markovnikov's rule when necessary:

a. $CH_3-CH_2-CH_2-CH=CH_2 + H_2 \xrightarrow{Pt}$
   $\quad\quad\quad\quad\quad\quad | $
   $\quad\quad\quad\quad\quad CH_3$

b. $H_2C=C-CH_2-CH_3 + H_2O \xrightarrow{H^+}$

c. $\diagup\!\!\diagdown\!\!\diagup + H_2 \xrightarrow{Pt}$

d. $\bigcirc\!\!\!\diagdown + H_2O \xrightarrow{H^+}$

12.40 Draw the structural formula for the product in each of the following reactions using Markovnikov's rule when necessary:

a. $CH_3-CH_2-CH=CH_2 + H_2O \xrightarrow{H^+}$

b. $\diagup\!\!\!\diagdown\!\!\!\diagup\!\!\!\diagdown + H_2 \xrightarrow{Pt}$

c. $\bigcirc + H_2 \xrightarrow{Pt}$

d. $\diagup\!\!\diagdown\!\!\diagup\!\!\diagdown + H_2O \xrightarrow{H^+}$

12.41 What is a polymer?

12.42 What is a monomer?

12.43 Write an equation that represents the formation of a portion of polypropylene from three of its monomers.

12.44 Write an equation that represents the formation of a portion of polystyrene from three of its monomers.

12.45 The plastic polyvinylidene difluoride, PVDF, is made from monomers of 1,1-difluoroethene. Draw the expanded structural formula for a portion of the polymer formed from three monomers of 1,1-difluoroethene.

12.46 The polymer polyacrylonitrile, PAN, used in the fabric material Orlon is made from monomers of acrylonitrile. Draw the expanded structural formula for a portion of the polymer formed from three monomers of acrylonitrile.

$$\begin{array}{c} CN \\ | \\ H_2C=CH \end{array}$$

Acrylonitrile

12.8 Aromatic Compounds

In 1825, Michael Faraday isolated a hydrocarbon called **benzene**, which consists of a ring of six carbon atoms with one hydrogen atom attached to each carbon. Because many compounds containing benzene had fragrant odors, the family of benzene compounds became known as **aromatic compounds**. Some common examples of aromatic compounds that we use for flavor are anisole from anise, estragole from tarragon, and thymol from thyme.

LEARNING GOAL

Describe the bonding in benzene; name aromatic compounds, and draw their line-angle structural formulas.

The space-filling model for benzene consists of a six-carbon ring with six hydrogen atoms.

Anise (anisole)   Tarragon (estragole)   Thyme (thymol)

The aroma and flavor of the herbs anise, tarragon, and thyme are because of aromatic compounds.

In benzene, each carbon atom uses three valence electrons to bond to the hydrogen atom and two adjacent carbons. That leaves one valence electron, which scientists first thought was shared in a double bond with an adjacent carbon. In 1865, August Kekulé proposed that the carbon atoms in benzene were arranged in a flat ring with alternating single and double bonds between the adjacent carbon atoms. There are two possible structural representations of benzene in which the double bonds can form between two different carbon atoms. If there were double bonds as in alkenes, then benzene should be much more reactive than it is.

However, unlike the alkenes and alkynes, aromatic hydrocarbons do not easily undergo addition reactions. If their reaction behavior is quite different, they must also differ in how the atoms are bonded in their structures. Today, we know that the six electrons are shared equally among the six carbon atoms. This unique feature of benzene makes it especially stable. Benzene is most often represented as a line-angle structural formula, which shows a hexagon with a circle in the center. Some of the ways to represent benzene are shown as follows:

Equivalent structures for benzene

Structural formulas for benzene

Naming Aromatic Compounds

Many compounds containing benzene have been important in chemistry for many years and still use their common names. Names such as toluene, aniline, and phenol are allowed by IUPAC rules.

Toluene
(methylbenzene)

Aniline
(aminobenzene)

Phenol
(hydroxybenzene)

When a benzene ring is a substituent, $-C_6H_5$, it is named as a phenyl group.

$$CH_3-CH-CH=CH_2$$

Phenyl group   3-Phenyl-1-butene

When benzene has only one substituent, the ring is not numbered. When there are two substituents, the benzene ring is numbered to give the lowest numbers to the substituents. When a common name can be used such as toluene, phenol, or aniline, the carbon atom attached to the methyl, hydroxyl, or amine group is numbered as carbon 1. In a common name, there are prefixes that are used to show the position of two substituents. The prefix **ortho** (*o*) indicates a 1,2-arrangement, **meta** (*m*) is a 1,3-arrangement, and **para** (*p*) is used for 1,4- arrangements.

Chlorobenzene

1,2-Dichlorobenzene
(*o*-dichlorobenzene)

1,3-Dichlorobenzene
(*m*-dichlorobenzene)

1,4-Dichlorobenzene
(*p*-dichlorobenzene)

The common name xylene is used for the isomers of dimethylbenzene.

CH$_3$ CH$_3$ CH$_3$

1,2-Dimethylbenzene   1,3-Dimethylbenzene   1,4-Dimethylbenzene
(*o*-xylene)   (*m*-xylene)   (*p*-xylene)

When there are three or more substituents attached to the benzene ring, they are numbered in the direction to give the lowest set of numbers and then named alphabetically.

► **SAMPLE PROBLEM 12.12** Naming Aromatic Compounds

Give the IUPAC name for the following:

CH$_3$

Cl

Br

SOLUTION

4-bromo-3-chlorotoluene

STUDY CHECK 12.12

Give the IUPAC and common name for the following compound:

CH$_2$—CH$_3$

CH$_2$—CH$_3$

ANSWER

1,3-diethylbenzene (*m*-diethylbenzene)

 Chemistry Link to **Health**

Some Common Aromatic Compounds in Nature and Medicine

Aromatic compounds are common in nature and in medicine. Toluene is used as a reactant to make drugs, dyes, and explosives such as TNT (trinitrotoluene). The benzene ring is found in some amino acids (the building blocks of proteins); in pain relievers such as aspirin, acetaminophen, and ibuprofen; and in flavorings such as vanillin.

Phenylalanine (amino acid)   Vanillin   Acetaminophen   Aspirin

Ibuprofen

Properties of Aromatic Compounds

The flat symmetrical structure of benzene allows the individual cyclic structures to be very close together, which contributes to the higher melting points and boiling points of benzene and its derivatives. For example, hexane melts at $-95\,°C$, whereas benzene melts at $6\,°C$. Among the disubstituted benzene compounds, the *para* isomers are more symmetric and have higher melting points than the *ortho* and *meta* isomers: o-xylene melts at $-26\,°C$ and m-xylene melts at $-48\,°C$, whereas p-xylene melts at $13\,°C$.

Aromatic compounds are less dense than water, although they are somewhat denser than other hydrocarbons. Halogenated benzene compounds are denser than water. Aromatic hydrocarbons are insoluble in water and are used as solvents for other organic compounds. Only those aromatic compounds containing strongly polar functional groups such as $-OH$ or $-COOH$ will be somewhat soluble in water. Benzene and other aromatic compounds are resistant to reactions that break up the aromatic system, although they are flammable, as are other hydrocarbon compounds.

QUESTIONS AND PROBLEMS

12.8 Aromatic Compounds

LEARNING GOAL Describe the bonding in benzene; name aromatic compounds, and draw their line-angle structural formulas.

12.47 Give the IUPAC name and any common name for each of the following:

12.48 Give the IUPAC name and any common name for each of the following:

12.49 Draw the structural formula for each of the following:
  a. aniline
  b. 1-bromo-3-chlorobenzene
  c. 1-ethyl-4-methylbenzene
  d. p-chlorotoluene

12.50 Draw the structural formula for each of the following:
  a. m-dibromobenzene
  b. o-chloroethylbenzene
  c. propylbenzene
  d. 1,2,4-trichlorobenzene

Chemistry Link to **Health**
Polycyclic Aromatic Hydrocarbons (PAHs)

Large aromatic compounds known as *polycyclic aromatic hydrocarbons* (PAHs) are formed by fusing together two or more benzene rings edge to edge. In a fused-ring compound, neighboring benzene rings share two carbon atoms. Naphthalene, with two benzene rings, is well known for its use in mothballs; anthracene, with three rings, is used in the manufacture of dyes.

Naphthalene   Anthracene   Phenanthrene

When a polycyclic compound contains phenanthrene, it may act as a carcinogen, a substance known to cause cancer.

Compounds containing five or more fused benzene rings such as benzo[a]pyrene are potent carcinogens. The molecules interact with the DNA in the cells, causing abnormal cell growth and cancer. Increased exposure to carcinogens increases the chance of DNA alterations in the cells. Benzo[a]pyrene, a product of combustion, has been identified in coal tar, tobacco smoke, barbecued meats, and automobile exhaust.

Benzo[a]pyrene

Aromatic compounds such as benzo[a]pyrene are strongly associated with lung cancers.

 # Clinical Update
Diane's Treatment in the Burn Unit

When Diane arrived at the hospital, she was transferred to the ICU burn unit. She had second-degree burns that caused damage to the underlying layers of skin and third-degree burns that caused damage to all the layers of the skin. Because body fluids are lost when deep burns occur, a lactated Ringer's solution was administered. The most common complications of burns are related to infection. To prevent infection, her skin was covered with a topical antibiotic. The next day Diane was placed in a tank to remove dressings, lotions, and damaged tissue. Dressings and ointments were changed every eight hours. Over a period of 3 months, grafts of Diane's unburned skin were used to cover burned areas. She remained in the burn unit for 3 months and then was discharged. However, Diane returned to the hospital for more skin grafts and plastic surgery.

The arson investigators determined that gasoline was the primary accelerant used to start the fire at Diane's house. Because there was a lot of paper and dry wood in the area, the fire spread quickly. Some of the hydrocarbons found in gasoline include hexane, heptane, octane, nonane, decane, and cyclohexane. Some other hydrocarbons in gasoline are isooctane, butane, 3-ethyltoluene, isopentane, toluene, and 1,3-dimethylbenzene.

Clinical Applications

12.51 The medications for Diane were contained in blister packs made of polychlorotrifluoroethylene (PCTFE). Draw the expanded structural formula for a portion of PCTFE polymer from three monomers of chlorotrifluoroethylene shown below:

Tablets are contained in blister packs made from polychlorotrifluoroethylene (PCTFE).

Chlorotrifluoroethylene

12.52 New polymers have been synthesized to replace PVC in IV bags and cling film. One of these is EVA, ethylene polyvinylacetate. Draw the expanded structural formula for a portion of EVA using an alternating sequence that has three of each monomer shown below:

Ethylene   Vinyl acetate

12.53 Write the balanced chemical equation for the complete combustion of each of the following hydrocarbons found in gasoline used to start a fire:
  a. nonane
  b. isopentane (2-methylbutane)
  c. 3-ethyltoluene

12.54 Write the balanced chemical equation for the complete combustion of each of the following hydrocarbons found in gasoline used to start a fire:
  a. isooctane (2,2,4-trimethylpentane)
  b. cyclohexane
  c. 1,3-dimethylbenzene

CONCEPT MAP

CHAPTER REVIEW

12.1 Organic Compounds
LEARNING GOAL Identify properties characteristic of organic or inorganic compounds.

- Organic compounds have covalent bonds, most form nonpolar molecules, have low melting points and low boiling points, are not very soluble in water, dissolve as molecules in solutions, and burn vigorously in air.
- Inorganic compounds are often ionic or contain polar covalent bonds and form polar molecules, have high melting and boiling points, are usually soluble in water, produce ions in water, and do not burn in air.
- In the simplest organic molecule, methane, CH_4, the C—H bonds that attach four hydrogen atoms to the carbon atom are directed to the corners of a tetrahedron with bond angles of 109°.
- In the expanded structural formula, a separate line is drawn for every bond.

12.2 Alkanes
LEARNING GOAL Write the IUPAC names and draw the condensed or line-angle structural formulas for alkanes and cycloalkanes.

- Alkanes are hydrocarbons that have only C—C single bonds.
- A condensed structural formula depicts groups composed of each carbon atom and its attached hydrogen atoms.
- A line-angle structural formula represents the carbon skeleton as ends and corners of a zigzag line or geometric figure.
- The IUPAC system is used to name organic compounds by indicating the number of carbon atoms.
- The name of a cycloalkane is written by placing the prefix *cyclo* before the alkane name with the same number of carbon atoms.

12.3 Alkanes with Substituents
LEARNING GOAL Write the IUPAC names for alkanes with substituents and draw their condensed and line-angle structural formulas.

- Structural isomers are compounds with the same molecular formulas that differ in the order in which their atoms are bonded.
- Substituents, which are attached to an alkane chain, include alkyl groups and halogen atoms (F, Cl, Br, or I).
- In the IUPAC system, alkyl substituents have names such as methyl, propyl, and isopropyl; halogen atoms are named as fluoro, chloro, bromo, or iodo.

12.4 Properties of Alkanes
LEARNING GOAL Identify the properties of alkanes and write a balanced chemical equation for combustion.

- Alkanes, which are nonpolar molecules, are not soluble in water, and usually less dense than water.
- Alkanes undergo combustion in which they react with oxygen to produce carbon dioxide, water, and energy.

12.5 Alkenes and Alkynes
LEARNING GOAL Identify structural formulas as alkenes, cycloalkenes, and alkynes, and write their IUPAC names.

- Alkenes are unsaturated hydrocarbons that contain carbon–carbon double bonds.
- Alkynes contain a carbon–carbon triple bond.
- The IUPAC names of alkenes end with *ene*, while alkyne names end with *yne*. The main chain is numbered from the end nearer the double or triple bond.

Bond angles = 120°
Ethene

12.6 Cis–Trans Isomers
LEARNING GOAL Draw the condensed and line-angle structural formulas and give the names for the cis–trans isomers of alkenes.

- Geometric or cis–trans isomers of alkenes occur when the carbon atoms in the double bond are connected to different atoms or groups.
- In the cis isomer, the similar groups are on the same side of the double bond, whereas in the trans isomer they are connected on opposite sides of the double bond.

cis-2-Butene

12.7 Addition Reactions for Alkenes
LEARNING GOAL Draw the condensed or line-angle structural formulas and give the names for the organic products of addition reactions of alkenes. Draw a condensed structural formula for a section of a polymer.

- The addition of small molecules to the double bond is a characteristic reaction of alkenes.
- Hydrogenation adds hydrogen atoms to the double bond of an alkene to yield an alkane.
- Hydration adds water to a double bond of an alkene to form an alcohol.
- When a different number of hydrogen atoms are attached to the carbons in a double bond, the H— from water adds to the carbon with the greater number of H atoms (Markovnikov's rule).
- Polymers are long-chain molecules that consist of many repeating units of smaller carbon molecules called monomers.
- Many materials that we use every day are made from synthetic polymers, including carpeting, plastic wrap, nonstick pans, and nylon.
- Many synthetic materials are made using addition reactions in which a catalyst links the carbon atoms from various kinds of alkene molecules (monomers).
- Many materials used in medicine are made from synthetic polymers, including tubing, IV containers, and face masks.

12.8 Aromatic Compounds

LEARNING GOAL Describe the bonding in benzene; name aromatic compounds, and draw their line-angle structural formulas.

Ibuprofen

- Most aromatic compounds contain benzene, C_6H_6, a cyclic structure containing six carbon atoms and six hydrogen atoms.
- The structure of benzene is represented as a hexagon with a circle in the center.
- The IUPAC system uses the names of benzene, toluene, aniline, and phenol.
- In the IUPAC name, two or more substituents are numbered and listed in alphabetical order. In the common name, with two substituents, the positions are shown by the prefixes *ortho* (1,2-), *meta* (1,3-), and *para* (1,4-).

SUMMARY OF NAMING

Family	Structure	IUPAC Name	Common Name
Alkane	$CH_3-CH_2-CH_3$	Propane	
		2-Methylbutane	Isopentane
Haloalkane	$CH_3-CH_2-CH_2-Cl$	1-Chloropropane	Propyl chloride
Cycloalkane		Cyclohexane	
Alkene	$CH_3-CH=CH_2$	Propene	Propylene
		cis-1,2-Dibromoethene	
		trans-1,2-Dibromoethene	
Cycloalkene		Cyclopropene	
Alkyne	$CH_3-C\equiv CH$	Propyne	
Aromatic		Methylbenzene; toluene	
		1,3-Dichlorobenzene	*m*-Dichlorobenzene

SUMMARY OF REACTIONS

The chapter sections to review are shown after the name of the reaction.

Combustion (12.4)

$$CH_3-CH_2-CH_3(g) + 5O_2(g) \xrightarrow{\Delta} 3CO_2(g) + 4H_2O(g) + \text{energy}$$

Propane

Hydrogenation (12.7)

$$H_2C=CH-CH_3 + H_2 \xrightarrow{Pt} CH_3-CH_2-CH_3$$

Propene   Propane

Hydration (12.7)

Markovnikov's Rule

$$H_2C=CH-CH_3 \ + \ H_2O \ \xrightarrow{\ H^+\ } \ CH_3-\overset{\overset{\displaystyle OH}{|}}{CH}-CH_3$$

Propene   2-Propanol

Polymerization (12.7)

$$H_2C=CH_2 \ + \ H_2C=CH_2 \ + \ H_2C=CH_2 \ \xrightarrow[\text{catalyst}]{\text{Heat, pressure,}} \ -CH_2-CH_2-CH_2-CH_2-CH_2-CH_2-$$

Ethene   Polyethylene

KEY TERMS

addition A reaction in which atoms or groups of atoms bond to a carbon–carbon double bond. Addition reactions include the addition of hydrogen (hydrogenation), and water (hydration).

alkane A hydrocarbon that contains only single bonds between carbon atoms.

alkene A hydrocarbon that contains one or more carbon–carbon double bonds ($C=C$).

alkyl group An alkane minus one hydrogen atom. Alkyl groups are named like the alkanes except a *yl* ending replaces *ane*.

alkyne A hydrocarbon that contains one or more carbon–carbon triple bonds ($C\equiv C$).

aromatic compound A compound that contains the ring structure of benzene.

benzene A ring of six carbon atoms, each of which is attached to a hydrogen atom, C_6H_6.

cis isomer An isomer of an alkene in which similar groups in the double bond are on the same side.

condensed structural formula A structural formula that shows the arrangement of the carbon atoms in a molecule but groups each carbon atom with its bonded hydrogen atoms

$$-CH_3, \ -CH_2-, \ \text{or} \ -\overset{|}{C}H-.$$

cycloalkane An alkane that is a ring or cyclic structure.

expanded structural formula A type of structural formula that shows the arrangement of the atoms by drawing each bond in the hydrocarbon.

hydration An addition reaction in which the components of water, $H-$ and $-OH$, bond to the carbon–carbon double bond to form an alcohol.

hydrocarbon An organic compound that contains only carbon and hydrogen.

hydrogenation The addition of hydrogen (H_2) to the double bond of alkenes to yield alkanes.

IUPAC system A system for naming organic compounds devised by the International Union of Pure and Applied Chemistry.

line-angle structural formula A simplified structure that shows a zig-zag line in which carbon atoms are represented as the ends of each line and as corners.

Markovnikov's rule When adding water to alkenes with different numbers of groups attached to the double bonds, the $H-$ adds to the carbon that has the greater number of hydrogen atoms.

meta A method of naming that indicates substituents at carbons 1 and 3 of a benzene ring.

monomer The small organic molecule that is repeated many times in a polymer.

organic compound A compound made of carbon that typically has covalent bonds, is nonpolar, has low melting and boiling points, is insoluble in water, and is flammable.

ortho A method of naming that indicates substituents at carbons 1 and 2 of a benzene ring.

para A method of naming that indicates substituents at carbons 1 and 4 of a benzene ring.

polymer A very large molecule that is composed of many small, repeating monomer units.

structural isomers Organic compounds in which identical molecular formulas have different arrangements of atoms.

substituent Groups of atoms such as an alkyl group or a halogen bonded to the main carbon chain or ring of carbon atoms.

trans isomer An isomer of an alkene in which similar groups in the double bond are on opposite sides.

⚛ CORE CHEMISTRY SKILLS

The chapter section containing each Core Chemistry Skill is shown in parentheses at the end of each heading.

Naming and Drawing Alkanes (12.2)

- The alkanes ethane, propane, and butane contain two, three, and four carbon atoms, respectively, connected in a row or a *continuous* chain.
- Alkanes with five or more carbon atoms in a chain are named using the prefixes *pent* (5), *hex* (6), *hept* (7), *oct* (8), *non* (9), and *dec* (10).

- In the condensed structural formula, the carbon and hydrogen atoms on the ends are written as $-CH_3$ and the carbon and hydrogen atoms in the middle are written as $-CH_2-$.

Example: **a.** What is the name of $CH_3-CH_2-CH_2-CH_3$?
          b. Draw the condensed structural formula for pentane.

Answer: **a.** An alkane with a four-carbon chain is named with the prefix *but* followed by *ane*, which is butane.
         b. Pentane is an alkane with a five-carbon chain. The carbon atoms on the ends are attached to three H atoms each, and the carbon atoms in the middle are attached to two H each. $CH_3-CH_2-CH_2-CH_2-CH_3$

Writing Equations for Hydrogenation, Hydration, and Polymerization (12.7)

- The addition of small molecules to the double bond is a characteristic reaction of alkenes.
- Hydrogenation adds hydrogen atoms to the double bond of an alkene to form an alkane.
- Hydration adds water to a double bond of an alkene to form an alcohol.
- When a different number of hydrogen atoms are attached to the carbons in a double bond, the H— from water adds to the carbon atom with the greater number of H atoms, and the —OH adds to the other carbon atom from the double bond.

Example: **a.** Draw the condensed structural formula for 2-methyl-2-butene.
b. Draw the condensed structural formula for the product of the hydrogenation of 2-methyl-2-butene.
c. Draw the condensed structural formula for the product of the hydration of 2-methyl-2-butene.

Answer: **a.** CH_3
$$CH_3-\overset{\overset{\displaystyle CH_3}{|}}{C}=CH-CH_3$$

b. When H_2 adds to a double bond, the product is an alkane with the same number of carbon atoms.
$$CH_3-\overset{\overset{\displaystyle CH_3}{|}}{CH}-CH_2-CH_3$$

c. When water adds to a double bond, the product is an alcohol, which has an —OH group. The H— from water adds to the carbon atom in the double bond that has the greater number of H atoms.
$$CH_3-\overset{\overset{\displaystyle CH_3}{|}}{\underset{\underset{\displaystyle OH}{|}}{C}}-CH_2-CH_3$$

UNDERSTANDING THE CONCEPTS

The chapter sections to review are shown in parentheses at the end of each question.

12.55 Match the following physical and chemical properties with potassium chloride, KCl, used in salt substitutes, or butane, C_4H_{10}, used in lighters: (12.1)

a. melts at $-138\,°C$
b. burns vigorously in air
c. melts at $770\,°C$
d. contains ionic bonds
e. is a gas at room temperature

12.56 Match the following physical and chemical properties with octane, C_8H_{18}, found in gasoline, or magnesium sulfate, $MgSO_4$, also called Epsom salts: (12.1)
a. contains only covalent bonds
b. melts at $1124\,°C$
c. is insoluble in water
d. is a liquid at room temperature
e. is a strong electrolyte

12.57 Identify the compounds in each of the following pairs as structural isomers or not structural isomers: (12.3)

a. and

b. and

12.58 Identify the compounds in each of the following pairs as structural isomers or not structural isomers: (12.3)

a.
$$CH_2-CH_2-CH_2$$
$$|\qquad\qquad |$$
$$CH_3\qquad CH_2-CH_3$$
and
$$CH_3\qquad\qquad CH_3$$
$$|\qquad\qquad\qquad |$$
$$CH_2-CH_2-CH_2-CH_2$$

b. and

12.59 Convert each of the following line-angle structural formulas to a condensed structural formula and give its IUPAC name: (12.3)

a. **b.**

12.60 Convert each of the following line-angle structural formulas to a condensed structural formula and give its IUPAC name: (12.3)

a. **b.**

12.61 Draw a portion of the polymer of Teflon, which is made from 1,1,2,2-tetrafluoroethene (use three monomers). (12.7)

Teflon is used as a nonstick coating on cooking pans.

12.62 A garden hose is made of polyvinyl chloride (PVC) from chloroethene (vinyl chloride). Draw a portion of the polymer (use three monomers) for PVC. (12.7)

A garden hose is made of polyvinyl chloride (PVC).

12.63 Give the number of carbon atoms and the types of carbon–carbon bonds for each of the following: (12.2, 12.3, 12.5)
a. propane   **b.** cyclopropane
c. propene   **d.** propyne

12.64 Give the number of carbon atoms and the types of carbon–carbon bonds for each of the following: (12.2, 12.3, 12.5)
a. butane   **b.** cyclobutane
c. cyclobutene   **d.** 2-butyne

ADDITIONAL QUESTIONS AND PROBLEMS

12.65 Give the IUPAC name for each of the following: (12.3)

a.
$$CH_3-CH_2-\overset{\overset{\displaystyle CH_3}{|}}{\underset{\underset{\displaystyle CH_3}{|}}{C}}-CH_3$$

b. CH_3-CH_2-Cl

c. $CH_3-CH_2-\overset{\overset{\displaystyle CH_3-CH_2}{|}}{CH}-CH_2-\overset{\overset{\displaystyle Br}{|}}{CH}-CH_3$

d.

12.66 Give the IUPAC name for each of the following: (12.3)

a.

b. $Cl-CH_2-\overset{\overset{\displaystyle Br}{|}}{CH}-CH_2-Br$

c. $CH_3-\overset{\overset{\displaystyle CH_3}{|}}{CH}-\underset{\underset{\underset{\underset{\displaystyle CH_3}{|}}{\displaystyle CH_2}}{|}}{\overset{|}{CH}}-CH_3$

d. $CH_3-CH_2-\overset{\overset{\displaystyle Cl}{|}}{\underset{\underset{\underset{\displaystyle CH_3}{|}}{\displaystyle CH_2}}{C}}-CH_2-CH_3$

12.67 Draw the condensed structural formula for alkanes or the line-angle structural formula for cycloalkanes for each of the following: (12.3, 12.5, 12.6)
a. 1,2-dibromocyclopentene
b. 2-hexyne
c. *cis*-2-heptene

12.68 Draw the condensed structural formula for alkanes or the line-angle structural formula for cycloalkanes for each of the following: (12.3, 12.5, 12.6)
a. *trans*-3-hexene
b. 2-bromo-3-chlorocyclohexene
c. 3-chloro-1-butyne

12.69 Give the IUPAC name for each of the following: (12.5, 12.6)

a.
$$\overset{\displaystyle CH_3}{\underset{\displaystyle H}{}}C=C\overset{\displaystyle H}{\underset{\displaystyle CH_2-CH_3}{}}$$

b.

c.

12.70 Give the IUPAC name for each of the following: (12.5, 12.6)

a. $H_2C=\overset{\overset{\displaystyle CH_3}{|}}{C}-CH_2-CH_2-CH_3$

b.

c.

12.71 Indicate if each of the following pairs represents structural isomers, cis–trans isomers, or identical compounds: (12.5, 12.6)

a.   and

b.
$$\overset{\displaystyle CH_3}{\underset{\displaystyle H}{}}C=C\overset{\displaystyle H}{\underset{\displaystyle CH_3}{}}\quad \text{and} \quad \overset{\displaystyle CH_3}{\underset{\displaystyle H}{}}C=C\overset{\displaystyle CH_3}{\underset{\displaystyle H}{}}$$

12.72 Indicate if each of the following pairs represents structural isomers, cis–trans isomers, or identical compounds: (12.5, 12.6)

a. $H_2C=\underset{\underset{\underset{\displaystyle CH_3}{|}}{\displaystyle CH_2-CH_2}}{\overset{\displaystyle CH}{}}$ and $CH_3-CH_2-CH_2-CH=CH_2$

b.   and

12.73 Write the IUPAC name, including cis or trans, for each of the following: (12.5, 12.6)

a.
$$\overset{\displaystyle CH_3-CH_2}{\underset{\displaystyle H}{}}C=C\overset{\displaystyle CH_2-CH_2-CH_3}{\underset{\displaystyle H}{}}$$

b.

c.

$$CH_3 \quad H$$
$$C=C$$
$$H \quad CH_2-CH_2-CH_2-CH_3$$

12.74 Write the IUPAC name, including cis or trans, for each of the following: (12.5, 12.6)

a.

$$CH_3$$
$$|$$
$$H \quad CH_2-CH-CH_3$$
$$C=C$$
$$CH_3-CH_2 \quad H$$

b.

c.

$$CH_3$$
$$|$$
$$CH_3-CH \quad H$$
$$C=C$$
$$H \quad CH_2-CH_2-CH_2-CH_3$$

12.75 Draw the condensed structural formulas for the cis and trans isomers for each of the following: (12.5, 12.6)
   a. 2-pentene   **b.** 3-hexene

12.76 Draw the condensed structural formulas for the cis and trans isomers for each of the following: (12.5, 12.6)
   a. 2-butene   **b.** 2-hexene

12.77 Write a balanced chemical equation for the complete combustion of each of the following: (12.4, 12.5)
   a. dimethylpropane
   b. cyclobutane
   c. 2-heptene

12.78 Write a balanced chemical equation for the complete combustion of each of the following: (12.4, 12.5)
   a. cycloheptane
   b. 2-methyl-1-pentene
   c. 3,3-dimethylhexane

12.79 Give the name for the product from the hydrogenation of each of the following: (12.7)
   a. 3-methyl-2-pentene
   b. 3-methylcyclohexene
   c. 2-butene

12.80 Give the name for the product from the hydrogenation of each of the following: (12.7)
   a. 1-hexene
   b. 2-methyl-2-butene
   c. 1-ethylcyclopentene

12.81 Draw the structural formula for the product of each of the following: (12.7)

a. $+ H_2 \xrightarrow{\text{Ni}}$

b. $+ H_2O \xrightarrow{H^+}$

c.
$$CH_3$$
$$|$$
$$CH_3-CH_2-C=CH_2 + H_2O \xrightarrow{H^+}$$

12.82 Draw the structural formula for the product of each of the following: (12.7)

a. $+ H_2O \xrightarrow{H^+}$

b. $CH_3-CH_2-CH_2-CH=CH_2 + H_2 \xrightarrow{\text{Ni}}$

c. $+ H_2O \xrightarrow{H^+}$

12.83 Copolymers contain more than one type of monomer. One copolymer used in medicine is made of alternating units of styrene and acrylonitrile. Draw the expanded structural formula for a section of the copolymer that would have three each of these alternating units. (12.7)

$$H_2C=CH \qquad H_2C=CH$$
Styrene   Acrylonitrile

12.84 Lucite, or Plexiglas, is a polymer of methyl methacrylate. Draw the expanded structural formula for a section of the polymer that is made from the addition of three of these monomers. (12.7)

$$CH_3 \quad O$$
$$| \qquad ||$$
$$H_2C=C-C-O-CH_3$$
Methyl methacrylate

12.85 Name each of the following aromatic compounds: (12.8)

a.   **b.**   **c.**

12.86 Name each of the following aromatic compounds: (12.8)

a.   **b.**   **c.**

12.87 Draw the structural formula for each of the following: (12.8)
   a. *p*-bromotoluene
   b. 2,6-dimethylaniline
   c. 1,4-dimethylbenzene

12.88 Draw the structural formula for each of the following: (12.8)
   a. ethylbenzene
   b. *m*-chloroaniline
   c. 1,2,4-trimethylbenzene

CHALLENGE QUESTIONS

12.89 If a female silkworm moth secretes 50 ng of bombykol, a sex attractant, how many molecules did she secrete? (See Chemistry Link to the Environment "Pheromones in Insect Communication.") (7.2, 12.6)

12.90 How many grams of hydrogen are needed to hydrogenate 30.0 g of 2-butene? (12.7)

12.91 Draw the condensed structural formula for and give the name of all the possible alkenes with molecular formula C_5H_{10} that have a five-carbon chain, including those with cis and trans isomers. (12.5, 12.6)

12.92 Draw the condensed structural formula for and give the name of all the possible alkenes with molecular formula C_6H_{12} that have a six-carbon chain, including those with cis and trans isomers. (12.5, 12.6)

12.93 Explosives used in mining contain TNT or 2,4,6-trinitrotoluene. (12.8)
   a. The functional group *nitro* is $-NO_2$. Draw the structural formula for 2,4,6-trinitrotoluene.
   b. TNT is actually a mixture of structural isomers of trinitrotoluene. Draw the structural formula for two other possible structural isomers.

Explosives containing TNT are used in mining.

12.94 Margarine is produced from the hydrogenation of vegetable oils, which contain unsaturated fatty acids. How many grams of hydrogen are required to completely saturate 75.0 g of oleic acid, $C_{18}H_{34}O_2$, which has one double bond? (12.7)

Margarines are produced by the hydrogenation of unsaturated fats.

ANSWERS

Answers to Selected Questions and Problems

12.1 a. inorganic   **b.** organic   **c.** organic
   d. inorganic   **e.** inorganic   **f.** organic

12.3 a. inorganic   **b.** organic
   c. organic   **d.** inorganic

12.5 a. ethane   **b.** ethane
   c. NaBr   **d.** NaBr

12.7 In methane, the covalent bonds from the carbon atom to each hydrogen atom are directed to the corners of a tetrahedron with bond angles of 109°.

12.9 a. pentane   **b.** ethane
   c. hexane   **d.** cycloheptane

12.11 a. CH_4
   b. CH_3-CH_3
   c. $CH_3-CH_2-CH_2-CH_2-CH_3$

   d. △

12.13 a. same molecule
   b. structural isomers of C_5H_{12}
   c. structural isomers of C_6H_{14}

12.15 a. dimethylpropane
   b. 2,3-dimethylpentane
   c. 4-*tert*-butyl-2,6-dimethylheptane
   d. methylcyclobutane
   e. 1-bromo-3-chlorocyclohexane

12.17 a.
$$CH_3-CH_2-\overset{\overset{\displaystyle CH_3}{|}}{\underset{\underset{\displaystyle CH_3}{|}}{C}}-CH_2-CH_3$$

   b.
$$CH_3-\overset{\overset{\displaystyle CH_3}{|}}{CH}-\overset{\overset{\displaystyle CH_3}{|}}{CH}-CH_2-\overset{\overset{\displaystyle CH_3}{|}}{CH}-CH_3$$

   c.
$$CH_3-CH_2-\overset{\overset{\displaystyle CH_2-CH_3}{|}}{CH}-CH_2-\overset{\overset{\displaystyle CH}{|}}{\underset{\underset{\displaystyle CH_3\,\,CH_3}{}}{CH}}-CH_2-CH_2-CH_3$$

   d. $Br-CH_2-CH_2-Cl$

12.19 a.

12.21 a. $CH_3-CH_2-CH_2-CH_2-CH_2-CH_2-CH_3$

  b. liquid
  c. no
  d. float
  e. $C_7H_{16}(g) + 11O_2(g) \xrightarrow{\Delta} 7CO_2(g) + 8H_2O(g) + energy$

12.23 a. $2C_2H_6(g) + 7O_2(g) \xrightarrow{\Delta} 4CO_2(g) + 6H_2O(g) + energy$

  b. $2C_3H_6(g) + 9O_2(g) \xrightarrow{\Delta} 6CO_2(g) + 6H_2O(g) + energy$

  c. $2C_8H_{18}(g) + 25O_2(g) \xrightarrow{\Delta}$
  $16CO_2(g) + 18H_2O(g) + energy$

12.25 a. heptane   **b.** cyclopropane   **c.** hexane

12.27 a. alkene   **b.** alkyne
  c. alkene   **d.** cycloalkene

12.29 a. 2-methylpropene   **b.** 4-bromo-2-pentyne
  c. 4-ethylcyclopentene   **d.** 4-ethyl-2-hexene

12.31 a. $H_2C=CH-CH_2-CH_2-CH_3$

  b. $H_2C=\overset{\overset{\displaystyle CH_3}{|}}{C}-CH_2-CH_3$

  c.

  d. Cl —

12.33 a. *cis*-2-butene
  b. *trans*-3-octene
  c. *cis*-3-heptene

12.35 a.

  b.

  c.

12.37 a and **c** cannot have cis–trans isomers because they each have two identical groups on at least one of the carbon atoms in the double bond.

12.39 a. $CH_3-CH_2-CH_2-CH_2-CH_3$

  b. $CH_3-\overset{\overset{\displaystyle CH_3}{|}}{\underset{\underset{\displaystyle OH}{|}}{C}}-CH_2-CH_3$

  c.

  d.

12.41 A polymer is a very large molecule composed of small units (monomers) that are repeated many times.

12.43

12.45

12.47 a. 2-chlorotoluene
  b. ethylbenzene
  c. 1,3,5-trichlorobenzene
  d. 1,3-dimethylbenzene (*m*-xylene)
  e. 3-bromo-5-chlorotoluene
  f. isopropylbenzene

12.49 a.   **b.**

  c.   **d.**

12.51

12.53

  a. $C_9H_{20}(l) + 14O_2(g) \xrightarrow{\Delta} 9CO_2(g) + 10H_2O(g) + energy$

  b. $C_5H_{12}(l) + 8O_2(g) \xrightarrow{\Delta} 5CO_2(g) + 6H_2O(g) + energy$

  c. $C_9H_{12}(l) + 12O_2(g) \xrightarrow{\Delta} 9CO_2(g) + 6H_2O(g) + energy$

12.55 a. butane
  b. butane
  c. potassium chloride
  d. potassium chloride
  e. butane

12.57 a. structural isomers
  b. not structural isomers

12.59 a. $CH_3-\overset{\overset{\displaystyle CH_3}{|}}{CH}-CH_2-\overset{\overset{\displaystyle CH_3}{|}}{CH}-CH_3$
  2,4-Dimethylpentane

  b. $CH_3-\overset{\overset{\displaystyle Cl}{|}}{CH}-\overset{\overset{\displaystyle CH_3}{|}}{CH}-\overset{\overset{\displaystyle Br}{|}}{CH}-CH_2-CH_3$
  4-Bromo-2-chloro-3-methylhexane

12.61

12.63 a. three carbon atoms; two carbon–carbon single bonds
  b. three carbon atoms; three carbon–carbon single bonds in a ring
  c. three carbon atoms; one carbon–carbon single bond; one carbon–carbon double bond
  d. three carbon atoms; one carbon–carbon single bond; one carbon–carbon triple bond

12.65 a. 2,2-dimethylbutane
   b. chloroethane
   c. 2-bromo-4-ethylhexane
   d. methylcyclopentane

12.67 a.

   b. $CH_3 - C \equiv C - CH_2 - CH_2 - CH_3$

   c.

12.69 a. *trans*-2-pentene
   b. 4-bromo-5-methyl-1-hexene
   c. 1-methylcyclopentene

12.71 a. structural isomers
   b. cis–trans isomers

12.73 a. *cis*-3-heptene
   b. *trans*-2-methyl-3-hexene
   c. *trans*-2-heptene

12.75

   a.

trans-2-Pentene

cis-2-Pentene

   b.

trans-3-Hexene

cis-3-Hexene

12.77 a. $C_5H_{12}(g) + 8O_2(g) \xrightarrow{\Delta} 5CO_2(g) + 6H_2O(g) +$ energy

   b. $C_4H_8(g) + 6O_2(g) \xrightarrow{\Delta} 4CO_2(g) + 4H_2O(g) +$ energy

   c. $2C_7H_{14}(l) + 21O_2(g) \xrightarrow{\Delta}$
      $14CO_2(g) + 14H_2O(g) +$ energy

12.79 a. 3-methylpentane   **b.** methylcyclohexane
   c. butane

12.81 a.

   b.

   c. $CH_3 - CH_2 - \overset{\overset{\displaystyle OH}{|}}{\underset{\underset{\displaystyle CH_3}{|}}{C}} - CH_3$

12.83

12.85 a. 3-methylaniline (*p*-methylaniline)
   b. 1-chloro-2-methylbenzene, 2-chlorotoluene
      (*o*-chlorotoluene)
   c. 1,2-difluorobenzene (*o*-difluorobenzene)

12.87 a.

   b.

   c.

12.89 1×10^{14} molecules of bombykol

12.91 a. $H_2C = CH - CH_2 - CH_2 - CH_3$ 1-Pentene

   b.

cis-2-Pentene

   c.

trans-2-Pentene

12.93 a.

   b.

Alcohols, Phenols, Thiols, and Ethers

AN EPIDURAL IS A REGIONAL ANESTHESIA THAT

will provide pain relief for Janet during her labor and delivery by blocking pain in the lower half of her body. Tom, a nurse anesthetist, prepares the medication for the epidural injection, which consists of a local anesthetic, chloroprocaine, and a small amount of fentanyl, a common opioid. Tom administers the anesthetic through a catheter into Janet's lower spine and in a few minutes, her pain subsides.

One of the earliest anesthetics used in medicine was diethyl ether, more commonly referred to as ether. Diethyl ether contains an ether functional group, which is an oxygen atom bonded by single bonds to two carbon groups. Today, ether is rarely used because it is extremely flammable, and produces undesirable side effects such as postanesthetic nausea and vomiting. Sevoflurane, which also has an ether functional group, is a more modern anesthetic that does not cause nausea and vomiting.

Ethoxyethane
(diethyl ether)

Sevoflurane

CAREER Nurse Anesthetist

More than 26 million people in the United States each year require anesthesia associated with a medical or dental procedure. Anesthesia is typically administered by a nurse anesthetist who provides care before, during, and after the procedure by giving medications to keep a patient asleep and pain-free while monitoring the patient's vital signs. A nurse anesthetist also obtains supplies, equipment, and an ample blood supply for a potential emergency, and interprets pre-surgical tests to determine how the anesthesia will affect the patient. A nurse anesthetist may also be required to insert artificial airways, administer oxygen, or work to prevent surgical shock during a procedure, working under the direction of the attending surgeon, dentist, or anesthesiologist.

In this chapter, we will look at organic compounds that contain functional groups with oxygen or sulfur atoms. Alcohols, which contain the hydroxyl group (—OH), are commonly found in nature and are used in industry and at home. For centuries, grains, vegetables, and fruits have been fermented to produce the ethanol present in alcoholic beverages. The hydroxyl group is important in biomolecules, such as sugars and starches, as well as in steroids, such as cholesterol and estradiol. Menthol is a cyclic alcohol with a minty odor and flavor that is used in cough drops, shaving creams, and ointments. The phenols contain the hydroxyl group attached to a benzene ring.

Ethers are compounds that contain an oxygen atom connected to two carbon atoms (—O—). Ethers are important solvents in chemistry and medical laboratories. Beginning in 1842, diethyl ether was used for about 100 years as a general anesthetic. Today, less flammable and more easily tolerated anesthetics are used. Thiols, which contain the —SH group, give the strong odors we associate with garlic and onions.

CHAPTER READINESS*

🔆 CORE CHEMISTRY SKILLS

- Naming and Drawing Alkanes (12.2)

*This Core Chemistry Skill from the previous chapter is listed here for your review as you proceed to the new material in this chapter.

13.1 Alcohols, Phenols, and Thiols

We can now classify and name alcohols, phenols, and thiols by their functional groups. In an **alcohol**, the functional group known as a hydroxyl group (—OH) replaces a hydrogen atom in a hydrocarbon. Oxygen (—O—) atoms are shown in red in the ball-and-stick models (see Figure 13.1). In a **phenol**, the hydroxyl group replaces a hydrogen atom attached to a benzene ring. A **thiol** contains a sulfur atom, shown in yellow-green in the ball-and-stick model, which makes a thiol similar to an alcohol except that —OH is replaced by a thiol group (—SH). Molecules of alcohols, phenols, and thiols have bent shapes around the oxygen or sulfur atom, similar to water.

LOOKING AHEAD

13.1 Alcohols, Phenols, and Thiols 489

🫀 **Chemistry Link to Health** *Some Important Alcohols and Phenols* 492

13.2 Ethers 495

🫀 **Chemistry Link to Health** *Ethers as Anesthetics* 496

13.3 Physical Properties of Alcohols, Phenols, and Ethers 497

🫀 **Chemistry Link to Health** *Hand Sanitizers and Ethanol* 500

13.4 Reactions of Alcohols and Thiols 501

🫀 **Chemistry Link to Health** *Methanol Poisoning* 503

🫀 **Chemistry Link to Health** *Oxidation of Alcohol in the Body* 505

℞ **Clinical Applications** 507, 512

℞ **Clinical Update** *Janet's New Diet Plan* 507

LEARNING GOAL

Give the IUPAC and common names for alcohols, phenols, and thiols; draw their condensed and line-angle structural formulas.

🔆 CORE CHEMISTRY SKILL

Identifying Alcohols, Phenols, and Thiols

CH_3—OH

—OH

Methanol

OH

OH

Phenol

CH_3—CH_2—SH

SH

Ethanethiol

FIGURE 13.1 ▶ An alcohol has a hydroxyl group (—OH) attached to carbon, and a phenol has a hydroxyl group (—OH) attached to a benzene ring. A thiol has a thiol group (—SH) attached to carbon.

Q How is an alcohol different from a thiol?

489

Naming Alcohols

In the IUPAC system, an alcohol is named by replacing the *e* of the corresponding alkane name with *ol*. The common name of a simple alcohol uses the name of the alkyl group followed by *alcohol*.

CH_3—H CH_3—OH CH_3—CH_2—H CH_3—CH_2—OH
Methane   Methanol   Ethane   Ethanol
                  (methyl alcohol)   (ethyl alcohol)

Alcohols with one or two carbon atoms do not require a number for the hydroxyl group. When an alcohol consists of a chain with 3 or more carbon atoms, the chain is numbered to give the position of the —OH group and any substituents on the chain. An alcohol with two —OH groups is named as a *diol*, and an alcohol with three —OH groups is named as a *triol*.

CH_3—CH_2—CH_2—OH CH_3—$\overset{\displaystyle OH}{\underset{}{CH}}$—$CH_3$ HO—CH_2—$\overset{\displaystyle OH}{\underset{}{CH}}$—$CH_2$—CH
3   2   1   1   2   3   1   2   3   4
        1-Propanol   2-Propanol   1,2-Butanediol
        (propyl alcohol)   (isopropyl alcohol)

We can also draw the line-angle structural formulas for alcohols as shown for 2-propanol, 2-butanol, and 1,2-butanediol.

2-Propanol   2-Butanol   1,2-Butanediol

A cyclic alcohol is named as a *cycloalkanol*. If there are substituents, the ring is numbered from carbon 1, which is the carbon attached to the —OH group. Compounds with no substituents on the ring do not require a number for the hydroxyl group.

Cyclohexanol   2-Methylcyclopentanol

Naming Phenols

The term *phenol* is the IUPAC name when a hydroxyl group (—OH) is bonded to a benzene ring. When there is a second substituent, the benzene ring is numbered starting from carbon 1, which is the carbon bonded to the —OH group. As we have seen for other aromatic compounds with 2 substituents, the terms *ortho*, *meta*, and *para* (abbreviated *o-*, *m-*, and *p-*) are used for the common names of simple phenols. The common name *cresol* is also used for methylphenols.

Phenol   3-Chlorophenol   4-Ethylphenol   3-Methylphenol
            (*m*-chlorophenol)   (*p*-ethylphenol)   (*m*-cresol)

SAMPLE PROBLEM 13.1 Naming Alcohols

Give the IUPAC name for the following:

$$CH_3-\overset{\overset{\displaystyle CH_3}{|}}{CH}-CH_2-\overset{\overset{\displaystyle OH}{|}}{CH}-CH_3$$

SOLUTION

	Given	Need
ANALYZE THE PROBLEM	alcohol, five carbon chain, methyl substituent	IUPAC name

STEP 1 Name the longest carbon chain attached to the —OH group by replacing the *e* in the corresponding alkane name with *ol*. To name the alcohol, the *e* in alkane name pentane is replaced by *ol*.

$$CH_3-\overset{\overset{\displaystyle CH_3}{|}}{CH}-CH_2-\overset{\overset{\displaystyle OH}{|}}{CH}-CH_3 \qquad \text{pentanol}$$

STEP 2 Number the chain starting at the end nearer to the —OH group. This carbon chain is numbered from right to left to give the position of the —OH group as carbon 2, which is shown as a prefix in the name 2-pentanol.

$$\underset{5}{CH_3}-\underset{4}{\overset{\overset{\displaystyle CH_3}{|}}{CH}}-\underset{3}{CH_2}-\underset{2}{\overset{\overset{\displaystyle OH}{|}}{CH}}-\underset{1}{CH_3} \qquad \text{2-pentanol}$$

STEP 3 Give the location and name of each substituent relative to the —OH group.

$$\underset{5}{CH_3}-\underset{4}{\overset{\overset{\displaystyle CH_3}{|}}{CH}}-\underset{3}{CH_2}-\underset{2}{\overset{\overset{\displaystyle OH}{|}}{CH}}-\underset{1}{CH_3} \qquad \text{4-methyl-2-pentanol}$$

STUDY CHECK 13.1

Give the IUPAC name for the following:

ANSWER

3-chloro-1-butanol

SAMPLE PROBLEM 13.2 Naming Phenols

Give the IUPAC and common names for the following:

OH
◯—Br

SOLUTION

	Given	Need
ANALYZE THE PROBLEM	phenol, bromo substituent	IUPAC and common names

---

Guide to Naming Alcohols and Phenols

STEP 1
Name the longest carbon chain attached to the —OH group by replacing the *e* in the corresponding alkane name with *ol*. Name an aromatic alcohol as a *phenol*.

STEP 2
Number the chain starting at the end nearer to the —OH group.

STEP 3
Give the location and name for each substituent relative to the —OH group.

Explore Your World
Alcohols in Household Products

Read the labels on household products such as sanitizers, mouthwashes, cold remedies, rubbing alcohol, and flavoring extracts. Look for names of alcohols, such as ethyl alcohol, isopropyl alcohol, thymol, and menthol.

Questions
1. What part of the name tells you that it is an alcohol?
2. What alcohol is usually meant by the term "alcohol"?
3. What is the percentage of alcohol in the products?
4. Draw the condensed structural formulas for the alcohols you find listed on the labels. You may need to use the Internet for some structures.

STEP 1 **Name an aromatic alcohol as a *phenol*.** The compound is a *phenol* because it contains an —OH group attached to a benzene ring.

phenol

STEP 2 **Number the chain starting at the end nearer to the —OH group.** For a phenol, the carbon atom attached to the —OH group is carbon 1.

phenol

STEP 3 **Give the location and name for each substituent relative to the —OH group.** For the common name, use the prefix *ortho* (*o*-).

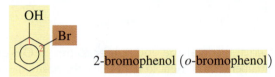

2-bromophenol (*o*-bromophenol)

STUDY CHECK 13.2

Give the IUPAC and common names for the following:

ANSWER

4-methylphenol (*p*-methylphenol; *p*-cresol)

 ## Chemistry Link to **Health**

Some Important Alcohols and Phenols

Methanol (*methyl alcohol*), the simplest alcohol, is found in many solvents and paint removers. If ingested, methanol is oxidized to formaldehyde, which can cause headaches, blindness, and death. Methanol is used to make plastics, medicines, and fuels. In car racing, it is used as a fuel because it is less flammable and has a higher octane rating than does gasoline.

Ethanol (*ethyl alcohol*) has been known since prehistoric times as an intoxicating product formed by the fermentation of grains, sugars, and starches.

$$C_6H_{12}O_6 \xrightarrow{\text{Fermentation}} 2CH_3—CH_2—OH + 2CO_2$$

Today, ethanol for commercial use is produced by reacting ethene and water at high temperatures and pressures. Ethanol is used as a solvent for perfumes, varnishes, and some medicines, such as tincture of iodine. Recent interest in alternative fuels has led to increased production of ethanol by the fermentation of sugars from grains such as corn, wheat, and rice. "Gasohol" is a mixture of ethanol and gasoline used as a fuel.

$$H_2C{=}CH_2 + H_2O \xrightarrow{\text{300 °C, 200 atm, H}^+} CH_3—CH_2—OH$$

1,2-Ethanediol (*ethylene glycol*) is used as an antifreeze in heating and cooling systems. It is also a solvent for paints, inks, and plastics, and it is used in the production of synthetic fibers such as Dacron. If ingested, it is extremely toxic. In the body, it is oxidized to oxalic acid, which forms insoluble salts in the kidneys that cause renal damage, convulsions, and death. Because its sweet taste is attractive to pets and children, ethylene glycol solutions must be carefully stored.

$$HO-CH_2-CH_2-OH \xrightarrow{[O]} HO-\underset{\underset{O}{\|}}{C}-\underset{\underset{O}{\|}}{C}-OH$$

1,2-Ethanediol
(ethylene glycol)

Oxalic acid

Antifreeze (ethylene glycol) raises the boiling point and decreases the freezing point of water in a radiator.

Phenols are found in several of the essential oils of plants, which produce the odor or flavor of the plant. Eugenol is found in cloves, vanillin in vanilla bean, isoeugenol in nutmeg, and thymol in thyme and mint. Thymol has a pleasant, minty taste and is used in mouthwashes and by dentists to disinfect a cavity before adding a filling compound.

1,2,3-Propanetriol (*glycerol* or *glycerin*), a trihydroxy alcohol, is a viscous liquid obtained from oils and fats during the production of soaps. The presence of several polar —OH groups makes it strongly attracted to water, a feature that makes glycerol useful as a skin softener in products such as skin lotions, cosmetics, shaving creams, and liquid soaps.

$$HO-CH_2-\underset{\underset{OH}{|}}{CH}-CH_2-OH$$

1,2,3-Propanetriol
(glycerol)

Bisphenol A (BPA) is used to make polycarbonate, a clear plastic that is used to manufacture beverage bottles, including baby bottles. Washing polycarbonate bottles with certain detergents or at high temperatures disrupts the polymer, causing small amounts of BPA to leach from the bottles. Because BPA is an estrogen mimic, there are concerns about the harmful effects from low levels of BPA. In 2008, Canada banned the use of polycarbonate baby bottles, which are now labeled "BPA free."

Bisphenol A (BPA)

Derivatives of phenol are found in the oils of nutmeg, thyme, cloves, and vanilla.

Vanillin

Eugenol

Thymol

Isoeugenol

Thiols

Thiols, also known as *mercaptans*, are a family of sulfur-containing organic compounds that have a *thiol* group (—SH). In the IUPAC system, thiols are named by adding *thiol* to the alkane name of the longest carbon chain and numbering the carbon chain from the end nearer the —SH group.

The spray of a skunk contains a mixture of thiols.

$$CH_3 - OH \qquad CH_3 - SH \qquad CH_3 - CH_2 - SH$$

$$\overset{SH}{\underset{|}{CH_3 - CH - CH_2 - CH_3}}$$

—OH   —SH   ⟍SH

$$\overset{SH}{\underset{|}{\diagup\diagdown}}$$

Methanol   Methanethiol   Ethanethiol   2-Butanethiol

An important property of thiols is a strong, sometimes disagreeable, odor. To help us detect natural gas (methane) leaks, a small amount of *tert*-butylthiol is added to the gas supply, which is normally odorless. There are thiols such as *trans*-2-butene-1-thiol in the spray emitted when a skunk senses danger.

$$\overset{CH_3}{\underset{H}{\diagdown}} C = C \overset{H}{\underset{CH_2 - SH}{\diagup}}$$

trans-2-Butene-1-thiol
(in skunk spray)

Methanethiol is the characteristic odor of oysters, cheddar cheese, and garlic. Garlic also contains 2-propene-1-thiol. The odor of onions is because of 1-propanethiol, which is also a lachrymator, a substance that makes eyes tear (see Figure 13.2).

$$CH_3 - SH$$
Methanethiol
(oysters and cheese)

$$CH_3 - CH_2 - CH_2 - SH$$
1-Propanethiol
(onions)

$$H_2C = CH - CH_2 - SH$$
2-Propene-1-thiol
(garlic)

FIGURE 13.2 ▶ Thiols are sulfur-containing compounds and often have strong odors.

Q How are the structures of thiols similar to alcohols?

QUESTIONS AND PROBLEMS

13.1 Alcohols, Phenols, and Thiols

LEARNING GOAL Give the IUPAC and common names for alcohols, phenols, and thiols; draw their condensed and line-angle structural formulas.

13.1 Give the IUPAC and common names for each of the following:

a. $CH_3 - CH_2 - OH$

b. $\overset{OH}{\underset{|}{CH_3 - CH_2 - CH - CH_3}}$

c. [line-angle structure with OH]

d. [cyclohexanol structure with OH and CH3]

e. [phenol ring structure with OH and F]

13.2 Give the IUPAC and common names for each of the following:

a.

b. $CH_3\!-\!CH_2\!-\!\overset{\overset{\displaystyle CH_3}{|}}{CH}\!-\!CH_2\!-\!OH$

c.

d.

e.

13.3 Draw the condensed or line-angle structural formula, if cyclic, for each of the following:
  a. 1-propanol
  b. 3-pentanol
  c. 2-methyl-2-butanol
  d. *p*-chlorophenol
  e. 2-bromo-5-chlorophenol

13.4 Draw the condensed or line-angle structural formula, if cyclic, for each of the following:
  a. 3-methyl-1-butanol
  b. 2,4-dichlorocyclohexanol
  c. 3-chloro-2-methyl-1-pentanol
  d. *o*-bromophenol
  e. 2,4-dimethylphenol

13.2 Ethers

An **ether** consists of an oxygen atom that is attached by single bonds to two carbon groups that are alkyl or aromatic groups.

LEARNING GOAL

Give the IUPAC and common names for ethers; draw their condensed or line-angle structural formulas.

$CH_3\!-\!O\!-\!CH_3$

Methoxymethane
(dimethyl ether)

$CH_3\!-\!CH_2\!-\!O\!-\!CH_3$

Methoxyethane
(ethyl methyl ether)

Methoxybenzene
(methyl phenyl ether)

Naming Ethers

In the common name of an ether, the names of the alkyl or aromatic groups attached to each side of the oxygen atom are written in alphabetical order, followed by the word *ether*.

Methyl   Propyl

Common name: Methyl propyl ether

In the IUPAC system, an ether is named with an *alkoxy* group made up of the smaller alkyl group and the oxygen atom, followed by the alkane name of the longer carbon chain.

Methoxy   Propane

IUPAC name: 1-Methoxypropane

Guide to Writing IUPAC Names for Ethers

STEP 1
Write the alkane name of the longer carbon chain.

STEP 2
Name the oxygen and smaller alkyl group as an alkoxy group.

STEP 3
Number the longer carbon chain from the end nearer the alkoxy group and give its location.

More examples of naming ethers with both IUPAC and common names follow:

$$CH_3-CH_2-O-CH_2-CH_3$$
Ethoxyethane
(diethyl ether)

$$CH_3-\overset{\overset{\displaystyle O-CH_3}{|}}{CH}-CH_2-CH_3$$
2-Methoxybutane

$$CH_3-CH_2-O-\bigcirc$$
Ethoxybenzene
(ethyl phenyl ether)

$$\bigcirc-O-\bigcirc$$
Phenoxybenzene
(diphenyl ether)

SAMPLE PROBLEM 13.3 Naming Ethers

Give the IUPAC name for the following:

$$CH_3-CH_2-O-CH_2-CH_2-CH_2-CH_3$$

SOLUTION

ANALYZE THE PROBLEM	Given	Need
	ether	IUPAC name

STEP 1 Write the alkane name of the longer carbon chain.

$$CH_3-CH_2-O-\underbrace{CH_2-CH_2-CH_2-CH_3}_{\text{Longer carbon chain}}$$ butane

STEP 2 Name the oxygen and smaller alkyl group as an alkoxy group.

$$\underset{\uparrow}{CH_3-CH_2-O}-CH_2-CH_2-CH_2-CH_3$$ ethoxybutane
Ethoxy group

STEP 3 Number the longer carbon chain from the end nearer the alkoxy group and give its location.

$$CH_3-CH_2-O-\underset{1}{CH_2}-\underset{2}{CH_2}-\underset{3}{CH_2}-\underset{4}{CH_3}$$ 1-ethoxybutane

STUDY CHECK 13.3

What is the IUPAC name of methyl phenyl ether?

ANSWER

methoxybenzene

Chemistry Link to Health
Ethers as Anesthetics

Anesthesia is the loss of sensation and consciousness. A general anesthetic is a substance that blocks signals to the awareness centers in the brain so the person has a loss of memory, a loss of feeling pain, and an artificial sleep. The term *ether* has been associated with anesthesia because diethyl ether was the most widely used anesthetic for more than a hundred years. Although it is easy to administer, ether is very volatile and highly flammable. A small spark in the operating room could cause an explosion. Since the 1950s, anesthetics such as Forane (isoflurane),

Forane
(isoflurane)

Forane (isoflurane) is an inhaled anesthetic.

Ethrane (enflurane), Suprane (desflurane), and Sevoflurane have been developed that are not as flammable. Most of these anesthetics retain the ether group, but the addition of halogen atoms reduces the volatility and flammability of the ethers.

Forane (isoflurane)
Ethrane (enflurane)
Suprane (desflurane)
Sevoflurane

QUESTIONS AND PROBLEMS

13.2 Ethers

LEARNING GOAL Give the IUPAC and common names for ethers; draw their condensed or line-angle structural formulas.

13.5 Give the IUPAC name and any common name for each of the following ethers:

a. $CH_3-O-CH_2-CH_3$ **b.**

c.
d. $CH_3-CH_2-CH_2-O-CH_3$

13.6 Give the IUPAC name and any common name for each of the following ethers:

a. $CH_3-CH_2-O-CH_2-CH_2-CH_3$

b.

c.
d. CH_3-O-CH_3

13.7 Draw the condensed or line-angle structural formula for each of the following:
a. ethyl propyl ether
b. cyclopropyl ethyl ether
c. methoxycyclopentane
d. 1-ethoxy-2-methylbutane
e. 2,3-dimethoxypentane

13.8 Draw the condensed or line-angle structural formula for each of the following:
a. diethyl ether
b. diphenyl ether
c. ethoxycyclohexane
d. 2-methoxy-2,3-dimethylbutane
e. 1,2-dimethoxybenzene

13.3 Physical Properties of Alcohols, Phenols, and Ethers

Alcohols are classified by the number of alkyl groups attached to the carbon atom bonded to the hydroxyl group (—OH). A **primary (1°) alcohol** has one alkyl group attached to the carbon atom bonded to the —OH group. The simplest alcohol, methanol (CH_3OH), which has a carbon attached to three H atoms but no alkyl group, is considered a primary alcohol; a **secondary (2°) alcohol** has two alkyl groups, and a **tertiary (3°) alcohol** has three alkyl groups.

LEARNING GOAL

Describe the classification of alcohols; describe the boiling points and solubility of alcohols, phenols, and ethers.

Primary (1°) alcohol

$$CH_3-\underset{\underset{H}{|}}{\overset{\overset{H}{|}}{C}}-OH$$

Secondary (2°) alcohol

$$CH_3-\underset{\underset{H}{|}}{\overset{\overset{CH_3}{|}}{C}}-OH$$

Tertiary (3°) alcohol

$$CH_3-\underset{\underset{CH_3}{|}}{\overset{\overset{CH_3}{|}}{C}}-OH$$

Carbon attached to —OH group

▶**SAMPLE PROBLEM 13.4** Classifying Alcohols

Classify each of the following alcohols as primary (1°), secondary (2°), or tertiary (3°):

a. $CH_3-CH_2-CH_2-OH$

b.

SOLUTION

a. The carbon atom bonded to the $-OH$ group is attached to one alkyl group, which makes this a primary (1°) alcohol.
b. The carbon atom bonded to the $-OH$ group is attached to three alkyl groups, which makes this a tertiary (3°) alcohol.

STUDY CHECK 13.4

Classify the following alcohol as primary (1°), secondary (2°), or tertiary (3°):

OH

ANSWER

secondary (2°)

Methanol
(methyl alcohol)

Hydrogen bonds form between alcohol molecules but not between ether molecules.

Boiling Points

Because there is a large electronegativity difference between the oxygen and hydrogen atoms in the $-OH$ group, the oxygen has a partially negative charge, and the hydrogen has a partially positive charge. As a result, hydrogen bonds form between the oxygen of one alcohol and hydrogen in the $-OH$ group of another alcohol. Hydrogen bonds cannot form between ether molecules because there are not any polar $-OH$ groups.

Alcohols have higher boiling points than do ethers of the same mass because alcohols require higher temperatures to provide sufficient energy to break the many hydrogen bonds. The boiling points of ethers are similar to those of alkanes because neither can form hydrogen bonds.

Methanol
(methyl alcohol)
in water

Solubility of Alcohols and Ethers in Water

The electronegativity of the oxygen atom in both alcohols and ethers influences their solubility in water. In alcohols, the atoms in the $-OH$ group can form hydrogen bonds with the H and O atoms of water. Alcohols with one to three carbon atoms are *miscible* in water, which means that any amount is completely soluble in water. However, the solubility provided by the polar $-OH$ group decreases as the number of carbon atoms increases. Alcohols with four carbon atoms are slightly soluble, and alcohols with five or more carbon atoms are not soluble.

Nonpolar carbon chain ⟶ CH_3-CH_2┤OH
Soluble in water

$CH_3-CH_2-CH_2-CH_2-CH_2-CH_2-CH_2-CH_2$┤$OH$
Insoluble in water

Dimethyl ether in water

Small alcohol and ether molecules are soluble in water because they form hydrogen bonds.

Although ethers can form hydrogen bonds with water, they do not form as many hydrogen bonds with water as do the alcohols. Ethers containing up to four carbon atoms are slightly soluble in water. Table 13.1 compares the boiling points and the solubility in water of some alcohols and ethers of similar mass.

TABLE 13.1 Boiling Points and Solubility of Some Alcohols and Ethers

Compound	Condensed Structural Formula	Number of Carbon Atoms	Boiling Point (°C)	Solubility in Water
Methanol	$CH_3—OH$	1	65	Soluble
Ethanol	$CH_3—CH_2—OH$	2	78	Soluble
1-Propanol	$CH_3—CH_2—CH_2—OH$	3	97	Soluble
1-Butanol	$CH_3—CH_2—CH_2—CH_2—OH$	4	118	Slightly soluble
1-Pentanol	$CH_3—CH_2—CH_2—CH_2—CH_2—OH$	5	138	Insoluble
Dimethyl ether	$CH_3—O—CH_3$	2	−23	Slightly soluble
Ethyl methyl ether	$CH_3—O—CH_2—CH_3$	3	8	Slightly soluble
Diethyl ether	$CH_3—CH_2—O—CH_2—CH_3$	4	35	Slightly soluble
Ethyl propyl ether	$CH_3—CH_2—O—CH_2—CH_2—CH_3$	5	64	Insoluble

Solubility and Boiling Point of Phenol

Phenol has a high boiling point (182 °C) because the —OH group allows phenol molecules to hydrogen bond with other phenol molecules. Phenol is slightly soluble in water because the —OH group can form hydrogen bonds with water molecules. In water, the —OH group of phenol ionizes slightly, which makes it a weak acid ($K_a = 1 \times 10^{-10}$). In fact, an early name for phenol was *carbolic acid*.

Phenol   Phenoxide ion

Phenol and Antiseptics

An *antiseptic* is a substance applied to the skin to kill microorganisms that cause infection. At one time, dilute solutions of phenol (carbolic acid) were used in hospitals as antiseptics. Joseph Lister (1827–1912) is considered a pioneer in antiseptic surgery and was the first to sterilize surgical instruments and dressings with phenol. Phenol was also used to disinfect wounds to prevent post-surgical infections such as gangrene. However, phenol is very corrosive and highly irritating to the skin; it can cause severe burns and ingestion can be fatal. Soon phenol solutions were replaced with other disinfectants. 4-Hexylresorcinol is a form of phenol used in topical antiseptics, throat lozenges, mouth washes, and throat sprays. Lysol, used to disinfect surfaces in a home or hospital, contains the antiseptics 2-phenylphenol and 2-benzyl-4-chlorophenol.

Joseph Lister was the first to use phenol to sterilize surgical instruments.

4-Hexylresorcinol   2-Phenylphenol   2-Benzyl-4-chlorophenol

Lysol, used as a disinfectant, contains phenol compounds.

Chemistry Link to Health

Hand Sanitizers and Ethanol

Hand sanitizers are used as an alternative to washing hands to kill most bacteria and viruses that spread colds and flu. As a gel or liquid solution, many hand sanitizers use ethanol as their active ingredient. Although safe for most adults, supervision is recommended when used by children because there is some concern about their risk to the health of children. After using an ethanol- or isopropyl alcohol-based hand sanitizer, children might ingest enough alcohol to make them sick.

In an alcohol-containing sanitizer, the amount of ethanol is typically 60% (v/v) but can be as high as 85% (v/v). This amount of

ethanol can make hand sanitizers a fire hazard in the home because ethanol is highly flammable. When ethanol undergoes combustion, it produces a transparent blue flame. When using an ethanol-containing sanitizer, it is important to rub hands until they are completely dry. It is also recommended that sanitizers containing ethanol be placed in storage areas that are away from heat sources in the home.

Some sanitizers are alcohol-free, but often the active ingredient is triclosan, which contains aromatic, ether, and phenol functional groups. The Food and Drug Administration is considering banning triclosan in personal-care products because when mixed with tap water for disposal, the triclosan that accumulates in the environment may promote the growth of antibiotic-resistant bacteria. Recent reports indicate that triclosan may disrupt the endocrine system and interfere with the function of estrogens, androgens, and thyroid hormones.

Hand sanitizers that contain ethanol are used to kill bacteria on the hands.

Triclosan is an antibacterial compound used in personal-care products.

QUESTIONS AND PROBLEMS

13.3 Physical Properties of Alcohols, Phenols, and Ethers

LEARNING GOAL Describe the classification of alcohols; describe the boiling points and solubility of alcohols, phenols, and ethers.

13.9 Classify each of the following alcohols as primary (1°), secondary (2°), or tertiary (3°):

a.

b. $CH_3-CH_2-CH_2-CH_2-OH$

c. $CH_3-\underset{\underset{CH_3}{|}}{\overset{\overset{OH}{|}}{C}}-CH_2-CH_3$ **d.**

13.10 Classify each of the following alcohols as primary (1°), secondary (2°), or tertiary (3°):

a.

b.

c.

d. $CH_3-CH_2-CH_2-\underset{\underset{CH_3}{|}}{\overset{\overset{CH_3}{|}}{C}}-OH$

13.11 Predict the compound with the higher boiling point in each of the following pairs:
   a. ethane or methanol   **b.** diethyl ether or 1-butanol
   c. 1-butanol or pentane

13.12 Predict the compound with the higher boiling point in each of the following pairs:
   a. 2-propanol and 2-butanol   **b.** dimethyl ether or ethanol
   c. dimethyl ether or diethyl ether

13.13 Are each of the following soluble, slightly soluble, or insoluble in water? Explain.
   a. CH_3-CH_2-OH
   b. CH_3-O-CH_3
   c. $CH_3-CH_2-CH_2-CH_2-CH_2-CH_2-OH$

13.14 Are each of the following soluble, slightly soluble, or insoluble in water? Explain.
   a. $CH_3-CH_2-CH_2-OH$
   b.
   c. $CH_3-CH_2-O-CH_2-CH_3$

13.15 Give an explanation for each of the following observations:
   a. Methanol is soluble in water, but ethane is not.
   b. 2-Propanol is soluble in water, but 1-butanol is only slightly soluble.
   c. 1-Propanol is soluble in water, but ethyl methyl ether is only slightly soluble.

13.16 Give an explanation for each of the following observations:
   a. Ethanol is soluble in water, but propane is not.
   b. Dimethyl ether is slightly soluble in water, but pentane is not.
   c. 1-Propanol is soluble in water, but 1-hexanol is not.

13.4 Reactions of Alcohols and Thiols

LEARNING GOAL

Write equations for the combustion, dehydration, and oxidation of alcohols and thiols.

Alcohols, similar to hydrocarbons, undergo combustion in the presence of oxygen. For example, in a restaurant, a flaming dessert may be prepared by pouring a liquor on fruit or ice cream and lighting it (see Figure 13.3). The combustion of the ethanol in the liquor proceeds as follows:

$$CH_3-CH_2-OH(g) + 3O_2(g) \xrightarrow{\Delta} 2CO_2(g) + 3H_2O(g) + energy$$

Dehydration of Alcohols to Form Alkenes

In a **dehydration** reaction, alcohols lose a water molecule when they are heated at a high temperature (180 °C) with an acid catalyst such as H_2SO_4. During the dehydration of an alcohol, H— and —OH are removed from *adjacent carbon atoms of the same alcohol* to produce a water molecule. A double bond forms between the same two carbon atoms to produce an alkene product.

FIGURE 13.3 ▶ A flaming dessert is prepared using an alcohol that undergoes combustion.

Q What is the equation for the complete combustion of the ethanol in the liquor?

The dehydration of a secondary alcohol can result in the formation of two products. **Saytzeff's rule** states that the major product is the one that forms by removing the hydrogen from the carbon atom that has the smaller number of hydrogen atoms. A hydrogen atom is easier to remove from the carbon atom adjacent to the carbon atom attached to the —OH group that has fewer hydrogen atoms.

⊗ **CORE CHEMISTRY SKILL**

Writing Equations for the Dehydration of Alcohols

Adjacent carbon with the smaller number of H atoms

CH₃—C—C—C—H →(H⁺, heat)

CH₃—C=C—C—H + H—OH
2-Butene (major product: 90%)

CH₃—C—C=C—H + H—OH
1-Butene (minor product: 10%)

2-Butanol

▶**SAMPLE PROBLEM 13.5** Dehydration of Alcohols

Draw the condensed structural formula for the major alkene produced by the dehydration of each of the following alcohols:

a. $CH_3-CH_2-CH_2-CH_2-OH \xrightarrow{H^+,\ heat}$

b. $CH_3-\underset{\underset{\displaystyle OH}{|}}{CH}-CH_2-CH_2-CH_3 \xrightarrow{H^+,\ heat}$

SOLUTION

a. The 1-butanol loses —OH from carbon 1 and H— from carbon 2 to form 1-butene. This is the only possible product.

$$CH_3 - CH_2 - CH = CH_2$$

b. For the dehydration of an asymmetrical alcohol, we use Saytzeff's rule to remove —OH from carbon 2 and H— from carbon 3, which has the smaller number of H atoms. The major product is 2-pentene.

$$CH_3 - CH = CH - CH_2 - CH_3$$

STUDY CHECK 13.5

What is the name of the alkene produced by the dehydration of cyclopentanol?

ANSWER

cyclopentene

CORE CHEMISTRY SKILL

Writing Equations for the Oxidation of Alcohols

The aldehyde functional group at the end of a chain has a C=O bonded to one carbon group and to H.

The ketone functional group in the middle of a chain has a C=O bonded to two carbon groups.

Oxidation of Alcohols

In organic chemistry, **oxidation** is a loss of hydrogen atoms or the addition of oxygen. When a compound is oxidized, there is an increase in the number of carbon–oxygen bonds. When a compound is reduced, there is a decrease in the number of carbon–oxygen bonds.

1 bond to O — CH_3-CH_2 (OH) Alcohol (1°) $\xrightarrow[\text{Reduction}]{\text{Oxidation}}$ 2 bonds to O — CH_3-C-H (O) Aldehyde $\xrightarrow[\text{Reduction}]{\text{Oxidation}}$ 3 bonds to O — CH_3-C-OH (O) Carboxylic acid

1 bond to O — CH_3-C-CH_3 (OH, H) Alcohol (2°) $\xrightarrow[\text{Reduction}]{\text{Oxidation}}$ 2 bonds to O — CH_3-C-CH_3 (O) Ketone — No further oxidation

An aldehyde or ketone is more oxidized than an alcohol; a carboxylic acid is more oxidized than an aldehyde.

Oxidation of Primary and Secondary Alcohols

The oxidation of a primary alcohol produces an aldehyde, which contains a double bond between oxygen and the carbon atom at the end of the chain. For example, the oxidation of methanol and ethanol occurs by removing two hydrogen atoms, one from the —OH group and another from the carbon that is bonded to the —OH group. The oxidized product contains the same number of carbon atoms as the reactant. The reaction is written with the symbol $[O]$ over the arrow to indicate that O is obtained from an oxidizing agent, such as $KMnO_4$ or $K_2Cr_2O_7$.

$$\underset{\substack{\text{Methanol} \\ \text{(methyl alcohol)}}}{\overset{\displaystyle \overset{\text{OH}}{\underset{\text{H}}{\mid}}}{\text{H}-\overset{\mid}{\underset{\mid}{\text{C}}}-\text{H}}} \xrightarrow{\text{[O]}} \underset{\substack{\text{Methanal} \\ \text{(formaldehyde)}}}{\overset{\displaystyle \overset{\text{O}}{\parallel}}{\text{H}-\text{C}-\text{H}}} + \text{H}_2\text{O}$$

$$\underset{\substack{\text{Ethanol} \\ \text{(ethyl alcohol)}}}{\overset{\displaystyle \overset{\text{OH}}{\underset{\text{H}}{\mid}}}{\text{CH}_3-\overset{\mid}{\underset{\mid}{\text{C}}}-\text{H}}} \xrightarrow{\text{[O]}} \underset{\substack{\text{Ethanal} \\ \text{(acetaldehyde)}}}{\overset{\displaystyle \overset{\text{O}}{\parallel}}{\text{CH}_3-\text{C}-\text{H}}} + \text{H}_2\text{O}$$

Aldehydes oxidize further by the addition of oxygen to form carboxylic acids, which have three carbon–oxygen bonds. This step occurs so readily that it is often difficult to isolate the aldehyde product during oxidation.

$$\underset{\substack{\text{Ethanal} \\ \text{(acetaldehyde)}}}{\overset{\displaystyle \overset{\text{O}}{\parallel}}{\text{CH}_3-\text{C}-\text{H}}} \xrightarrow{\text{[O]}} \underset{\substack{\text{Ethanoic acid} \\ \text{(acetic acid)}}}{\overset{\displaystyle \overset{\text{O}}{\parallel}}{\text{CH}_3-\text{C}-\text{OH}}}$$

$$\overset{\displaystyle \overset{\text{O}}{\parallel}}{\underset{}{-\text{C}}}\diagdown_{\text{OH}}$$

The carboxylic acid functional group at the end of a chain has a C=O bonded to one carbon group and to OH.

In the oxidation of secondary alcohols, the products are ketones. Two hydrogen atoms are removed, one from the —OH and the other from the carbon bonded to the —OH group. The result is a ketone that has the carbon–oxygen double bond attached to alkyl or aromatic groups on both sides. There is no further oxidation of a ketone because there are no hydrogen atoms attached to the carbon of the ketone group.

$$\underset{\substack{\text{2-Propanol} \\ \text{(isopropyl alcohol)}}}{\overset{\displaystyle \overset{\text{OH}}{\underset{\text{H}}{\mid}}}{\text{CH}_3-\overset{\mid}{\underset{\mid}{\text{C}}}-\text{CH}_3}} \xrightarrow{\text{[O]}} \underset{\substack{\text{Propanone} \\ \text{(dimethyl ketone; acetone)}}}{\overset{\displaystyle \overset{\text{O}}{\parallel}}{\text{CH}_3-\text{C}-\text{CH}_3}} + \text{H}_2\text{O}$$

Tertiary alcohols do not oxidize readily because there is no hydrogen atom on the carbon bonded to the —OH group. Because C—C bonds are usually too strong to oxidize, tertiary alcohols resist oxidation.

$$\underset{\substack{\text{Alcohol (3°)}}}{\overset{\displaystyle \overset{\text{OH}}{\underset{\text{CH}_3}{\mid}}}{\text{CH}_3-\overset{\mid}{\underset{\mid}{\text{C}}}-\text{CH}_3}} \xrightarrow{\text{[O]}} \text{No oxidation product readily forms}$$

No hydrogen on this carbon   No double bond forms

Chemistry Link to **Health**

Methanol Poisoning

Methanol, or "wood alcohol," is a highly toxic alcohol present in products such as windshield-washer fluid, Sterno, and paint strippers. Methanol is rapidly absorbed in the gastrointestinal tract. In the liver, it is metabolized to formaldehyde and then formic acid, a substance that causes nausea, severe abdominal pain, and blurred vision. Blindness can occur because the intermediate products destroy the retina of the eye. As little as 4 mL of methanol can produce blindness. The formic acid, which is not readily eliminated from the body, lowers blood pH so severely that just 30 mL of methanol can lead to coma and death.

The treatment for methanol poisoning involves giving sodium bicarbonate to neutralize the formic acid in the blood. In some cases, ethanol is given intravenously to the patient. The enzymes in the liver pick up ethanol molecules to oxidize instead of methanol molecules. This process gives time for the methanol to be eliminated via the lungs without the formation of its dangerous oxidation products.

> ► **SAMPLE PROBLEM 13.6** **Oxidation of Alcohols**
>
> Draw the condensed or line-angle structural formula for the aldehyde or ketone formed by the oxidation of each of the following:
>
> **a.** $CH_3-CH_2-\overset{\overset{\displaystyle OH}{|}}{CH}-CH_3$　　　　**b.** (line-angle structure with OH)
>
> **SOLUTION**
>
> **a.** This is a secondary (2°) alcohol, which oxidizes to a ketone.
>
> $CH_3-CH_2-\overset{\overset{\displaystyle O}{||}}{C}-CH_3$
>
> **b.** This is a primary (1°) alcohol, which oxidizes to an aldehyde.
>
> (line-angle structure with CHO, H labeled)
>
> **STUDY CHECK 13.6**
>
> Draw the condensed structural formula for the product formed by the oxidation of 2-pentanol.
>
> **ANSWER**
>
> $CH_3-\overset{\overset{\displaystyle O}{||}}{C}-CH_2-CH_2-CH_3$

Interactive Video

Oxidation of Alcohols

During vigorous exercise, lactic acid accumulates in the muscles and causes fatigue. When the activity level is decreased, oxygen enters the muscles. The secondary —OH group in lactic acid is oxidized to a ketone group in pyruvic acid, which eventually is oxidized to CO_2 and H_2O. The muscles in highly trained athletes are capable of taking up greater quantities of oxygen so that vigorous exercise can be maintained for longer periods of time.

Secondary alcohol　　　　　　　　　　　　　Ketone group

$CH_3-\overset{\overset{\displaystyle OH}{|}}{CH}-\overset{\overset{\displaystyle O}{||}}{C}-OH$　$\xrightarrow[\text{dehydrogenase}]{\text{Lactic acid}}$　$CH_3-\overset{\overset{\displaystyle O}{||}}{C}-\overset{\overset{\displaystyle O}{||}}{C}-OH$

Lactic acid　　　　　　　　　　　　　　　　Pyruvic acid

Oxidation of Thiols

Thiols also undergo oxidation by a loss of hydrogen atoms from the —SH groups. The oxidized product is called a **disulfide**.

$CH_3-S-H + H-S-CH_3 \xrightarrow{[O]} CH_3-S-S-CH_3 + H_2O$

Methanethiol　　　　　　　　　　　　　　Dimethyl disulfide

Much of the protein in the hair is cross-linked by disulfide bonds, which occur between the thiol groups of the amino acid cysteine:

Protein Chain$-CH_2-SH + HS-CH_2-$Protein Chain　$\xrightarrow{[O]}$

Cysteine side groups

Protein Chain$-CH_2-S-S-CH_2-$Protein Chain $+ H_2O$

Disulfide bond

Proteins in the hair take new shapes when disulfide bonds are reduced and oxidized.

When a person is given a "perm" ("permanent wave"), a reducing substance is used to break the disulfide bonds. While the hair is still wrapped around the curlers, an oxidizing substance is then applied that causes new disulfide bonds to form between different parts of the protein hair strands, which gives the hair a new shape.

Chemistry Link to **Health**
Oxidation of Alcohol in the Body

Ethanol is the most commonly abused drug in the United States. When ingested in small amounts, ethanol may produce a feeling of euphoria in the body despite the fact that it is a depressant. In the liver, enzymes such as alcohol dehydrogenase oxidize ethanol to acetaldehyde, a substance that impairs mental and physical coordination. If the blood alcohol concentration exceeds 0.4%, coma or death may occur. Table 13.2 gives some of the typical behaviors exhibited at various blood alcohol levels.

$$CH_3-CH_2-OH \xrightarrow{[O]} CH_3-\overset{\displaystyle O}{\overset{\displaystyle \|}{C}}-H \xrightarrow{[O]} 2CO_2 + H_2O$$

Ethanol   Ethanal
(ethyl alcohol) (acetaldehyde)

calculate the blood alcohol concentration (BAC). Several devices are used to measure the BAC. When a Breathalyzer is used, a suspected drunk driver exhales through a mouthpiece into a solution containing the orange Cr^{6+} ion. Any alcohol present in the exhaled air is oxidized, which reduces the orange Cr^{6+} to a green Cr^{3+}.

$$CH_3-CH_2-OH + Cr^{6+} \xrightarrow{[O]} CH_3-\overset{\displaystyle O}{\overset{\displaystyle \|}{C}}-OH + Cr^{3+}$$

Ethanol   Orange   Ethanoic acid   Green

The Alcosensor uses the oxidation of alcohol in a fuel cell to generate an electric current that is measured. The Intoxilyzer measures the amount of light absorbed by the alcohol molecules.

TABLE 13.2 Typical Behaviors Exhibited by a 150-lb Person Consuming Alcohol

Number of Beers (12 oz) or Glasses of Wine (5 oz) in 1 h	Blood Alcohol Level (% m/v)	Typical Behavior
1	0.025	Slightly dizzy, talkative
2	0.050	Euphoria, loud talking and laughing
4	0.10	Loss of inhibition, loss of coordination, drowsiness, legally intoxicated in most states
8	0.20	Intoxicated, quick to anger, exaggerated emotions
12	0.30	Unconscious
16–20	0.40–0.50	Coma and death

The acetaldehyde produced from ethanol in the liver is further oxidized to acetic acid, which is converted to carbon dioxide and water in the citric acid cycle. Thus, the enzymes in the liver can eventually break down ethanol, but the aldehyde and carboxylic acid intermediates can cause considerable damage while they are present within the cells of the liver.

A person weighing 150 lb requires about one hour to metabolize the alcohol in 12 ounces of beer. However, the rate of metabolism of ethanol varies between nondrinkers and drinkers. Typically, nondrinkers and social drinkers can metabolize 12 to 15 mg of ethanol/dL of blood in one hour, but an alcoholic can metabolize as much as 30 mg of ethanol/dL in one hour. Some effects of alcohol metabolism include an increase in liver lipids (fatty liver), gastritis, pancreatitis, ketoacidosis, alcoholic hepatitis, and psychological disturbances.

When alcohol is present in the blood, it evaporates through the lungs. Thus, the percentage of alcohol in the lungs can be used to

Sometimes alcoholics are treated with a drug called Antabuse (disulfiram), which prevents the oxidation of acetaldehyde to acetic acid. As a result, acetaldehyde accumulates in the blood, which causes nausea, profuse sweating, headache, dizziness, vomiting, and respiratory difficulties. Because of these unpleasant side effects, the person is less likely to use alcohol.

A Breathalyzer test is used to determine blood alcohol level.

QUESTIONS AND PROBLEMS

13.4 Reactions of Alcohols and Thiols

LEARNING GOAL Write equations for the combustion, dehydration, and oxidation of alcohols and thiols.

13.17 Write the balanced chemical equation for the complete combustion of each of the following:
    a. methanol   **b.** 2-butanol

13.18 Write the balanced chemical equation for the complete combustion of each of the following:
    a. cyclopentanol   **b.** 3-hexanol

13.19 Draw the condensed or line-angle structural formula for the alkene that is the major product from each of the following dehydration reactions:

13.20 Draw the condensed or line-angle structural formula for the alkene that is the major product from each of the following dehydration reactions:

    CH₃
    |
a. CH₃ — CH — CH₂ — OH $\xrightarrow{\text{H}^+,\ \text{heat}}$

    OH   CH₃
    | |
b. CH₃ — CH — CH — CH₂ — CH₃ $\xrightarrow{\text{H}^+,\ \text{heat}}$

c. (cyclohexanol with OH) $\xrightarrow{\text{H}^+,\ \text{heat}}$

d. (cyclopentane with OH and CH₃) $\xrightarrow{\text{H}^+,\ \text{heat}}$

13.21 What alcohol(s) could be used to produce each of the following compounds?
    a. CH₂＝CH₂   **b.** (propene line)   **c.** (cyclohexene)

13.22 What alcohol(s) could be used to produce each of the following compounds?
    a. (alkene line structure)

              CH₃
              |
    b. CH₃ — CH₂ — C＝CH — CH₃

    c. (cyclopentene)

13.23 Draw the condensed or line-angle structural formula for the aldehyde or ketone produced when each of the following alcohols is oxidized [O] (if no reaction, write *none*):
    a. CH₃ — CH₂ — CH₂ — CH₂ — CH₂ — OH

                OH
                |
    b. CH₃ — CH₂ — CH — CH₃

    c. (cyclohexane with OH)

    d. (branched chain with OH)

              CH₃
              |
    e. CH₃ — CH — CH₂ — CH₂ — OH

13.24 Draw the condensed or line-angle structural formula for the aldehyde or ketone produced when each of the following alcohols is oxidized [O] (if no reaction, write *none*):
    a. (cyclobutane with OH)
                OH
    b. (branched chain with OH)

                OH
                |
    c. CH₃ — CH₂ — C — CH₃   **d.** (cyclohexane OH/CH₃)
                |
                CH₃

    e. (cyclobutane with OH)

13.25 Draw the condensed or line-angle structural formula for the alcohol needed to give each of the following oxidation products:
           O
           ‖
    a. H — C — H   **b.** (cyclopentanone)   **c.** (ketone)

           O
           ‖
    d. (benzaldehyde C — H)   **e.** (methylcyclohexanone)

13.26 Draw the condensed or line-angle structural formula for the alcohol needed to give each of the following oxidation products:
           O
           ‖
    a. CH₃ — C — H   **b.** (ketone branched)   **c.** (cyclohexanone)

           O   CH₃   O
           ‖ | ‖
    d. CH₃ — CH₂ — C — H   **e.** CH₃ — CH — CH₂ — C — H

Clinical Update
Janet's New Diet Plan

At home, Janet decided to lose some weight after having her baby. For her new diet, she decided to eat more fruits and vegetables, including peppers and onions. Vegetables are low in calories, have no fat or cholesterol, contain fiber, vitamins, especially vitamin B_3 (niacin), and minerals. Peppers contain antioxidants, such as capsaicin, which gives hot peppers a burning taste. Onions contain fiber, folic acid, calcium, and antioxidants, which inhibit oxidation reactions in the body and act as protective agents. 2-Propene-1-thiol gives the taste and odor to garlic. Janet added ginger, which contains pungent compounds, such as gingerol and shogaol, which is a bioactive compound that has anti-nausea, anti-inflammatory, and anti-carcinogenic properties. Resveratrol, obtained from the skin of red grapes, may improve oxygenation of muscles.

Clinical Applications

13.27 a. Which of the functional groups alkene, alcohol, phenol, thiol, and ether are found in both gingerol and capsaicin?

b. Which of the functional groups alkene, alcohol, phenol, thiol, and ether are found in resveratrol from grapes?

c. What are the functional groups in 2-propene-1-thiol found in garlic?

13.28 a. Which of the functional groups alkene, alcohol, phenol, thiol, and ether are found in both gingerol and shogaol?

b. Which of the functional groups alkene, alcohol, phenol, thiol, and ether are found in capsaicin?

c. Write the balanced chemical equation for the reaction that would convert gingerol to shogaol.

Capsaicin

2-Propene-1-thiol

Gingerol

Shogaol

Resveratrol

ALCOHOLS, PHENOLS, THIOLS, AND ETHERS

with — Carbon–Sulfur Single Bonds

with — Carbon–Oxygen Single Bonds

are the — Thiols

are the — Alcohols · Phenols · Ethers

that undergo — Oxidation

that undergo — Dehydration · Oxidation

to form — Disulfides

to form — Alkenes

to change — 1° Alcohols · 2° Alcohols

to — Aldehydes · to — Ketones

which oxidize to — Carboxylic Acids

CHAPTER REVIEW

13.1 Alcohols, Phenols, and Thiols

LEARNING GOAL Give the IUPAC and common names for alcohols, phenols, and thiols; draw their condensed and line-angle structural formulas.

$$CH_3 - CH_2 - CH_2 - SH$$
1-Propanethiol
(onions)

- The functional group of an alcohol is the hydroxyl group (—OH) bonded to a carbon chain.
- In a phenol, the hydroxyl group is bonded to an aromatic ring.
- In thiols, the functional group is —SH, which is analogous to the —OH group of alcohols.
- In the IUPAC system, the names of alcohols have *ol* endings, and the location of the —OH group is given by numbering the carbon chain.
- A cyclic alcohol is named as a cycloalkanol.
- Simple alcohols are generally named by their common names, with the alkyl name preceding the term *alcohol*.
- An aromatic alcohol is named as a phenol.

13.2 Ethers

LEARNING GOAL Give the IUPAC and common names for ethers; draw their condensed or line-angle structural formulas.

- In an ether, an oxygen atom is connected by single bonds to two alkyl or aromatic groups.

- In the common names of ethers, the alkyl groups are listed alphabetically, followed by the word *ether*.
- In the IUPAC name of an ether, the smaller alkyl group with the oxygen is named as an alkoxy group and is attached to the longer alkane chain, which is numbered to give the location of the alkoxy group.

13.3 Physical Properties of Alcohols, Phenols, and Ethers

LEARNING GOAL Describe the classification of alcohols; describe the boiling points and solubility of alcohols, phenols, and ethers.

- Alcohols are classified according to the number of alkyl groups bonded to the carbon that holds the —OH group.
- In a primary (1°) alcohol, one group is attached to the hydroxyl carbon.
- In a secondary (2°) alcohol, two groups are attached to the hydroxyl carbon.
- In a tertiary (3°) alcohol, there are three groups bonded to the hydroxyl carbon.
- The —OH group allows alcohols to hydrogen bond, which causes alcohols to have higher boiling points than alkanes and ethers of similar mass.
- Short-chain alcohols and ethers can hydrogen bond with water, which makes them soluble.

13.4 Reactions of Alcohols and Thiols

LEARNING GOAL Write equations for the combustion, dehydration, and oxidation of alcohols and thiols.

- Alcohols undergo combustion with O_2 to form CO_2, H_2O, and energy.
- At high temperatures, alcohols dehydrate in the presence of an acid to yield alkenes.

- Primary alcohols are oxidized to aldehydes, which can oxidize further to carboxylic acids.
- Secondary alcohols are oxidized to ketones.
- Tertiary alcohols do not oxidize.
- Thiols undergo oxidation to form disulfides.

SUMMARY OF NAMING

Family	Structure	IUPAC Name	Common Name
Alcohol	CH_3—**OH**	Methanol	Methyl alcohol
Phenol	⬡—**OH**	Phenol	Phenol
Thiol	CH_3—**SH**	Methanethiol	
Ether	CH_3—**O**—CH_3	Methoxymethane	Dimethyl ether

SUMMARY OF REACTIONS

The chapter sections to review are shown after the name of the reaction.

Combustion of Alcohols (13.4)

$$CH_3\text{—}CH_2\text{—}OH + 3O_2 \xrightarrow{\Delta} 2CO_2 + 3H_2O + \text{energy}$$

Ethanol   Oxygen   Carbon   Water
                                 dioxide

Dehydration of Alcohols to Form Alkenes (13.4)

$$CH_3\text{—}CH_2\text{—}CH_2\text{—}OH \xrightarrow{H^+,\ heat} CH_3\text{—}CH\text{=}CH_2 + H_2O$$

1-Propanol   Propene

Oxidation of Primary Alcohols to Form Aldehydes (13.4)

$$\overset{\displaystyle OH}{\underset{\displaystyle}{CH_3\text{—}CH_2}} \xrightarrow{[O]} CH_3\text{—}\overset{\displaystyle O}{\underset{\displaystyle}{C}}\text{—}H + H_2O$$

Ethanol   Ethanal

Oxidation of Secondary Alcohols to Form Ketones (13.4)

$$\underset{\displaystyle}{CH_3}\overset{\displaystyle OH}{\underset{\displaystyle}{\text{—}CH\text{—}}}CH_3 \xrightarrow{[O]} CH_3\text{—}\overset{\displaystyle O}{\underset{\displaystyle}{C}}\text{—}CH_3 + H_2O$$

2-Propanol   Propanone

Oxidation of Aldehydes to Form Carboxylic Acids (13.4)

$$CH_3\text{—}\overset{\displaystyle O}{\underset{\displaystyle}{C}}\text{—}H \xrightarrow{[O]} CH_3\text{—}\overset{\displaystyle O}{\underset{\displaystyle}{C}}\text{—}OH$$

Ethanal   Ethanoic acid

KEY TERMS

alcohol An organic compound that contains the hydroxyl functional group (—OH) attached to a carbon chain.

dehydration A reaction that removes water from an alcohol in the presence of an acid to form alkenes at high temperatures.

disulfide A compound formed from thiols; disulfides contain the —S—S— functional group.

ether An organic compound in which an oxygen atom is bonded to two carbon groups that are alkyl or aromatic.

oxidation The loss of two hydrogen atoms from a reactant to give a more oxidized compound: primary alcohols oxidize to aldehydes, secondary alcohols oxidize to ketones. An oxidation can also be the addition of an oxygen atom, as in the oxidation of aldehydes to carboxylic acids.

phenol An organic compound that has a hydroxyl group (—OH) attached to a benzene ring.

primary (1°) alcohol An alcohol that has one alkyl group bonded to the alcohol's carbon atom.

Saytzeff's rule   In the dehydration of an alcohol, hydrogen is removed from the carbon that already has the smaller number of hydrogen atoms to form an alkene.

secondary (2°) alcohol   An alcohol that has two alkyl groups bonded to the carbon atom with the —OH group.

tertiary (3°) alcohol   An alcohol that has three alkyl groups bonded to the carbon atom with the —OH group.

thiol   An organic compound that contains a thiol group (—SH).

⚛ CORE CHEMISTRY SKILLS

The chapter section containing each Core Chemistry Skill is shown in parentheses at the end of each heading.

Identifying Alcohols, Phenols, and Thiols (13.1)

• Functional groups are specific groups of atoms in organic compounds, which undergo characteristic chemical reactions.
• Organic compounds with the same functional group have similar properties and reactions.

Example: Identify the functional group and classify the following molecule:

$$CH_3-CH_2-CH_2-CH_2-OH$$

Answer: The hydroxyl group (—OH) makes it an alcohol.

Naming Alcohols and Phenols (13.1)

• In the IUPAC system, an alcohol is named by replacing the *e* in the alkane name with *ol*.
• Simple alcohols are named with the alkyl name preceding the term *alcohol.*
• The carbon chain is numbered from the end nearer the —OH group and the location of the —OH is given in front of the name.
• A cyclic alcohol is named as a cycloalkanol.
• An aromatic alcohol is named as a phenol.

Example: Give the IUPAC name for the following:

$$CH_3-\overset{\overset{\displaystyle CH_3}{|}}{CH}-CH_2-OH$$

Answer: 2-methyl-1-propanol

Writing Equations for the Dehydration of Alcohols (13.4)

• At high temperatures, alcohols dehydrate in the presence of an acid to yield alkenes.
• Saytzeff's rule states that the major product from the dehydration of an asymmetrical alcohol is the one in which the —H atom is removed from the carbon atom that has the smaller number of H atoms.

Example: Draw the condensed structural formula for the organic product from the dehydration of 3-methyl-2-butanol.

Answer: $CH_3-\overset{\overset{\displaystyle CH_3}{|}}{C}=CH-CH_3$

Writing Equations for the Oxidation of Alcohols (13.4)

• Primary alcohols oxidize to aldehydes, which can oxidize further to carboxylic acids.
• Secondary alcohols oxidize to ketones.
• Tertiary alcohols do not oxidize.

Example: Draw the condensed structural formula for the product from the oxidation of 2-butanol.

Answer: $CH_3-\overset{\overset{\displaystyle O}{||}}{C}-CH_2-CH_3$

UNDERSTANDING THE CONCEPTS

The chapter sections to review are shown in parentheses at the end of each question.

13.29 Identify each of the following as an alcohol, a phenol, an ether, or a thiol: (13.1, 13.2)

a.   b.

c. $CH_3-\overset{\overset{\displaystyle SH}{|}}{CH}-CH_3$ d. $CH_3-\overset{\overset{\displaystyle OH}{|}}{\underset{\underset{\displaystyle CH_3}{|}}{C}}-CH_2-\overset{\overset{\displaystyle CH_3}{|}}{CH}-CH_3$

13.30 Identify each of the following as an alcohol, a phenol, an ether, or a thiol: (13.1, 13.2)

a.   b. $CH_3-CH_2-CH_2-SH$

c.   d.

13.31 Give the IUPAC and common names (if any) for each of the compounds in problem 13.29. (13.1, 13.2)

13.32 Give the IUPAC and common names (if any) for each of the compounds in problem 13.30. (13.1, 13.2)

13.33 Identify each of the following as an alcohol, a phenol, an ether, or a thiol: (13.1, 13.2)

a. $CH_3—CH_2—CH_2—O—CH_3$

b. $CH_3—CH_2—\overset{\overset{\displaystyle SH}{|}}{CH}—CH_3$

c. $CH_3—\overset{\overset{\displaystyle Br}{|}}{CH}—CH_2—\overset{\overset{\displaystyle OH}{|}}{CH}—CH_3$

d. (structure: meta-methylphenol)

13.34 Identify each of the following as an alcohol, a phenol, an ether, or a thiol: (13.1, 13.2)

a. $CH_3—CH_2—\overset{\overset{\displaystyle O—CH_3}{|}}{CH}—CH_2—CH_3$ **b.** (structure with SH)

c. (cyclohexane ring with OH, Cl, Cl)   **d.** (phenol ring with methyl)

13.35 Give the IUPAC and common names (if any) for each of the compounds in problem 13.33. (13.1, 13.2)

13.36 Give the IUPAC and common names (if any) for each of the compounds in problem 13.34. (13.1, 13.2)

ADDITIONAL QUESTIONS AND PROBLEMS

13.37 Draw the condensed or line-angle structural formula, if cyclic, for each of the following compounds: (13.1, 13.2)

a. 3-methylcyclopentanol   **b.** 4-chlorophenol
c. 2-methyl-3-pentanol   **d.** ethyl phenyl ether

13.38 Draw the condensed or line-angle structural formula, if cyclic, for each of the following compounds: (13.1, 13.2)

a. 3-methoxypentane   **b.** *m*-chlorophenol
c. 2,3-pentanediol   **d.** methyl propyl ether

13.39 Draw the condensed or line-angle structural formula, if cyclic, for each of the following compounds: (13.1, 13.2)

a. 3-pentanethiol   **b.** 2-methoxypentane
c. 2,4-dibromophenol   **d.** 2,3-dimethyl-2-butanol

13.40 Draw the condensed or line-angle structural formula, if cyclic, for each of the following compounds: (13.1, 13.2)

a. methanethiol   **b.** 3-methyl-2-butanol
c. 3,4-dichlorocyclohexanol **d.** 1-ethoxypropane

13.41 Give the IUPAC name for each of the following alcohols, phenols, and ethers: (13.1, 13.2)

a. (structure with OH)

b. $CH_3—\overset{\overset{\displaystyle OH}{|}}{\underset{\underset{\displaystyle CH_3}{|}}{C}}—CH_2—\overset{\overset{\displaystyle CH_3}{|}}{CH}—CH_3$

c. (phenol with Br)

d. $CH_3—\overset{\overset{\displaystyle O—CH_2—CH_3}{|}}{CH}—CH_2—CH_2—CH_3$

e. (cyclopentane with O)

13.42 Give the IUPAC name for each of the following alcohols, phenols, and ethers: (13.1, 13.2)

a. (cyclopentane with HO)

b. (structure with Br, Br, OH)

c. (structure with OH)

d. (cyclopropane with O)

e. $CH_3—\overset{\overset{\displaystyle O—CH_3}{|}}{CH}—CH_2—CH_3$

13.43 Draw the condensed structural formulas for all the alcohols with a molecular formula $C_4H_{10}O$. (13.1)

13.44 Draw the condensed structural formulas for all the ethers with a molecular formula $C_4H_{10}O$. (13.2)

13.45 Classify each of the following alcohols as primary (1°), secondary (2°), or tertiary (3°): (13.3)

a. (cyclohexane with OH)   **b.** (cyclohexane with CH₂OH)

c. $CH_3—\overset{\overset{\displaystyle CH_3}{|}}{CH}—CH_2—OH$

d. $CH_3—\overset{\overset{\displaystyle CH_3}{|}}{\underset{\underset{\displaystyle CH_3}{|}}{C}}—CH_2—\overset{\overset{\displaystyle OH}{|}}{CH}—CH_3$

e. $HO—CH_2—CH_2—CH_3$

f. (cyclopentane with OH)

13.46 Classify each of the following alcohols as primary (1°), secondary (2°), or tertiary (3°): (13.3)

a. (cyclopentane with HO)   **b.** (cyclohexane with OH)

c. $CH_3—\overset{\overset{\displaystyle CH_2—OH}{|}}{CH}—CH_2—CH_3$

d.
$$CH_3 - \overset{\overset{\displaystyle OH}{|}}{\underset{\underset{\displaystyle CH_3}{|}}{C}} - CH_2 - \overset{\overset{\displaystyle CH_3}{|}}{CH} - CH_3$$

e. $CH_3 - CH_2 - CH_2 - CH_2 - OH$

f.

13.47 Which compound in each of the following pairs would you expect to have the higher boiling point? Explain. (13.3)
  a. butane or 1-propanol
  b. 1-propanol or ethyl methyl ether
  c. ethanol or 1-butanol

13.48 Which compound in each of the following pairs would you expect to have the higher boiling point? Explain. (13.3)
  a. propane or ethyl alcohol
  b. 2-propanol or 2-pentanol
  c. methyl propyl ether or 1-butanol

13.49 Explain why each of the following compounds would be soluble or insoluble in water: (13.3)
  a. 2-propanol
  b. dipropyl ether
  c. 1-hexanol

13.50 Explain why each of the following compounds would be soluble or insoluble in water: (13.3)
  a. glycerol
  b. butane
  c. 1,3-hexanediol

13.51 Which compound in each pair would be more soluble in water? Explain. (13.3)
  a. butane or 1-propanol
  b. 1-propanol or ethyl methyl ether
  c. ethanol or 1-hexanol

13.52 Which compound in each pair would be more soluble in water? Explain. (13.3)
  a. ethane or ethanol
  b. 2-propanol or 2-pentanol
  c. methyl propyl ether or 1-butanol

13.53 Write the balanced chemical equation for the complete combustion of each of the following: (13.4)
  a. $CH_3 - CH_2 - CH_2 - CH_2 - OH + O_2 \xrightarrow{\Delta}$
  b. $+ O_2 \xrightarrow{\Delta}$
  c. $+ O_2 \xrightarrow{\Delta}$

13.54 Write the balanced chemical equation for the complete combustion of each of the following: (13.4)
  a. $CH_3 - CH_2 - CH_2 - CH_2 - OH + O_2 \xrightarrow{\Delta}$
  b. $+ O_2 \xrightarrow{\Delta}$
  c. $+ O_2 \xrightarrow{\Delta}$

13.55 Draw the condensed or line-angle structural formula, if cyclic, for each of the following naturally occurring compounds: (13.1, 13.2)
  a. 2,5-dichlorophenol, a defense pheromone of a grasshopper
  b. 3-methyl-1-butanethiol and *trans*-2-butene-1-thiol, a mixture that gives skunk scent its odor
  c. pentachlorophenol, a wood preservative

13.56 Dimethyl ether and ethyl alcohol both have the molecular formula C_2H_6O. One has a boiling point of $-24\ °C$, and the other, $79\ °C$. (13.1, 13.2, 13.3)
  a. Draw the condensed structural formula for each compound.
  b. Decide which boiling point goes with which compound and explain.

13.57 Draw the condensed or line-angle structural formula for the alkene (major product), aldehyde, ketone, or *none* produced in each of the following: (13.4)
  a. $CH_3 - CH_2 - CH_2 - OH \xrightarrow{H^+,\ heat}$
  b. $CH_3 - CH_2 - CH_2 - OH \xrightarrow{[O]}$
  c. $\xrightarrow{H^+,\ heat}$
  d. $\xrightarrow{H^+,\ heat}$
  e. $\xrightarrow{[O]}$

13.58 Draw the condensed or line-angle structural formula for the alkene (major product), aldehyde, ketone, or *none* produced in each of the following: (13.4)
  a. $\xrightarrow{H^+,\ heat}$
  b. $CH_3 - \overset{\overset{\displaystyle CH_3}{|}}{CH} - \overset{\overset{\displaystyle OH}{|}}{CH} - CH_3 \xrightarrow{H^+,\ heat}$
  c. $\xrightarrow{[O]}$
  d. $\xrightarrow{[O]}$
  e. $CH_3 - CH_2 - CH_2 - \overset{\overset{\displaystyle OH}{|}}{CH} - CH_3 \xrightarrow{H^+,\ heat}$

℞ Clinical Applications

13.59 Hexylresorcinol, an antiseptic ingredient used in mouth washes and throat lozenges, has the IUPAC name of 4-hexyl-1,3-benzenediol. Draw its condensed structural formula. (13.1)

13.60 Menthol, which has a minty flavor, is used in throat sprays and lozenges. Thymol is used as a topical antiseptic to destroy mold. (13.1)
  a. Give the IUPAC name for each.
  b. What is similar and what is different about their structures?

Menthol   Thymol

CHALLENGE QUESTIONS

The following groups of questions are related to the topics in this chapter. However, they do not all follow the chapter order, and they require you to combine concepts and skills from several sections. These questions will help you increase your critical thinking skills and prepare for your next exam.

13.61 A compound with the formula C_4H_8O is synthesized from 2-methyl-1-propanol and oxidizes easily to give a carboxylic acid. Draw the condensed structural formula for the compound. (13.4)

13.62 Methyl *tert*-butyl ether (MTBE), or 2-methoxy-2-methylpropane, has been used as a fuel additive for gasoline to boost the octane rating and to reduce CO emissions. (2.7, 7.5, 7.6, 7.7, 8.6, 13.4)
  a. If fuel mixtures are required to contain 2.7% oxygen by mass, how many grams of MTBE must be present in each 100. g of gasoline?
  b. How many liters of MTBE would be in 1.0 L of fuel if the density of both gasoline and MTBE is 0.740 g/mL?

Methyl *tert*-butyl ether (MTBE) is a gasoline additive.

  c. Write the balanced chemical equation for the complete combustion of MTBE.
  d. How many liters of air containing 21% (v/v) O_2 are required at STP to completely react (combust) 1.00 L of liquid MTBE?

13.63 Compound **A** is 1-propanol. When compound **A** is heated with strong acid, it dehydrates to form compound **B** (C_3H_6). When compound **A** is oxidized, compound **C** (C_3H_6O) forms. Draw the condensed structural formulas and give the IUPAC names for compounds **A**, **B**, and **C**. (13.4)

13.64 Compound **X** is 2-propanol. When compound **X** is heated with strong acid, it dehydrates to form compound **Y** (C_3H_6). When compound **X** is oxidized, compound **Z** (C_3H_6O) forms, which cannot be oxidized further. Draw the condensed structural formulas and give the IUPAC names for compounds **X**, **Y**, and **Z**. (13.4)

13.65 Sometimes several steps are needed to prepare a compound. Using a combination of the reactions we have studied, indicate how you might prepare the following from the starting substance given. For example, 2-propanol could be prepared from 1-propanol by first dehydrating the alcohol to give propene and then hydrating it again to give 2-propanol according to Markovnikov's rule, as follows: (13.4)

$$CH_3-CH_2-CH_2-OH \xrightarrow{H^+, heat} CH_3-CH=CH_2 + H_2O$$

1-Propanol   Propene

$$\xrightarrow{H^+} CH_3-\overset{\overset{\displaystyle OH}{|}}{CH}-CH_3$$

2-Propanol

  a. prepare 2-methylpropane from 2-methyl-2-propanol
  b. prepare $CH_3-\overset{\overset{\displaystyle O}{||}}{C}-CH_3$ from 1-propanol

13.66 As in problem 13.65, indicate how you might prepare the following from the starting substance given: (13.4)
  a. prepare 1-pentene from 1-pentanol
  b. prepare cyclohexane from cyclohexanol

ANSWERS

Answers to Selected Questions and Problems

13.1 a. ethanol (ethyl alcohol)
  b. 2-butanol (*sec*-butyl alcohol)
  c. 2-pentanol
  d. 4-methylcyclohexanol
  e. 3-fluorophenol (*m*-fluorophenol)

13.3 a. $CH_3-CH_2-CH_2-OH$
  b. $CH_3-CH_2-\overset{\overset{\displaystyle OH}{|}}{CH}-CH_2-CH_3$

  c. $CH_3-\overset{\overset{\displaystyle OH}{|}}{\underset{\underset{\displaystyle CH_3}{|}}{C}}-CH_2-CH_3$

  d.

  e.

13.5 a. methoxyethane (ethyl methyl ether)
  b. methoxycyclohexane (cyclohexyl methyl ether)
  c. ethoxycyclobutane (cyclobutyl ethyl ether)
  d. 1-methoxypropane (methyl propyl ether)

13.7 a. $CH_3-CH_2-O-CH_2-CH_2-CH_3$

  b.

  c.

  d. $CH_3-CH_2-O-CH_2-\overset{\overset{\displaystyle CH_3}{|}}{CH}-CH_2-CH_3$

  e. $CH_3-\overset{\overset{\displaystyle O-CH_3}{|}}{CH}-\overset{\overset{\displaystyle O-CH_3}{|}}{CH}-CH_2-CH_3$

13.9 a. 1°   **b.** 1°   **c.** 3°   **d.** 2°

13.11 a. methanol   **b.** 1-butanol   **c.** 1-butanol

13.13 a. Soluble; ethanol with a short carbon chain is soluble because the hydroxyl group forms hydrogen bonds with water.
  b. Slightly soluble; ethers with up to four carbon atoms are slightly soluble in water because they can form a few hydrogen bonds with water.
  c. Insoluble; an alcohol with a carbon chain of five or more carbon atoms is not soluble in water.

13.15 a. Methanol can form hydrogen bonds with water, but ethane cannot.
  b. 2-Propanol is more soluble because it has a shorter carbon chain.
  c. 1-Propanol is more soluble because it can form more hydrogen bonds.

13.17 a. $2CH_3-OH + 3O_2 \xrightarrow{\Delta} 2CO_2 + 4H_2O + energy$

  b. $CH_3-\overset{\overset{\displaystyle OH}{|}}{CH}-CH_2-CH_3 + 6O_2 \xrightarrow{\Delta}$
  $4CO_2 + 5H_2O + energy$

13.19 a. $CH_3-\overset{\overset{\displaystyle CH_3}{|}}{CH}-CH=CH_2$

  b.

  c.

  d. $CH_3-\overset{\overset{\displaystyle CH_3}{|}}{CH}-CH_2-CH=CH-CH_3$

13.21 a. CH_3-CH_2-OH

  b.

  c.

13.23 a. $CH_3-CH_2-CH_2-CH_2-\overset{\overset{\displaystyle O}{||}}{C}-H$

  b. $CH_3-CH_2-\overset{\overset{\displaystyle O}{||}}{C}-CH_3$

  c.

  d.

  e. $CH_3-\overset{\overset{\displaystyle CH_3}{|}}{CH}-CH_2-\overset{\overset{\displaystyle O}{||}}{C}-H$

13.25 a. CH_3-OH

  b.

  c.

  d.

  e.

13.27 a. Gingerol and capsaicin both have aromatic rings bonded to long hydrocarbon groups, with phenol and methoxy groups on the aromatic ring.
  b. Resveratrol contains phenol and alkene functional groups.
  c. 2-Propene-1-thiol contains alkene and thiol function groups.

13.29 a. alcohol   **b.** ether
  c. thiol   **d.** alcohol

13.31 a. 2-chloro-4-methylcyclohexanol
  b. methoxybenzene (methyl phenyl ether)
  c. 2-propanethiol
  d. 2,4-dimethyl-2-pentanol

13.33 a. ether   **b.** thiol
  c. alcohol   **d.** phenol

13.35 a. 1-methoxypropane (methyl propyl ether)
  b. 2-butanethiol
  c. 4-bromo-2-pentanol
  d. 3-methylphenol (*m*-methylphenol; *m*-cresol)

13.37 a.   **b.**

  c. $CH_3-\overset{\overset{\displaystyle CH_3}{|}}{CH}-\overset{\overset{\displaystyle OH}{|}}{CH}-CH_2-CH_3$

  d.

13.39 a.
$$CH_3-CH_2-\underset{\underset{SH}{|}}{CH}-CH_2-CH_3$$

b.
$$CH_3-\underset{\underset{O-CH_3}{|}}{CH}-CH_2-CH_2-CH_3$$

c.
(phenol with OH, Br at 2-position, Br at para-position)

d.
$$CH_3-\underset{\underset{OH}{|}}{\overset{\overset{CH_3}{|}}{C}}-\underset{\overset{CH_3}{|}}{CH}-CH_3$$

13.41 a. 2-methyl-2-propanol
b. 2,4-dimethyl-2-pentanol
c. 3-bromophenol
d. 2-ethoxypentane
e. methoxycyclopentane

13.43 $CH_3-CH_2-CH_2-CH_2-OH$

$$CH_3-\underset{\overset{CH_3}{|}}{CH}-CH_2-OH$$

$$CH_3-\underset{\overset{OH}{|}}{CH}-CH_2-CH_3$$

$$CH_3-\underset{\underset{CH_3}{|}}{\overset{\overset{OH}{|}}{C}}-CH_3$$

13.45 a. 2°　　　**b.** 1°　　　**c.** 1°
d. 2°　　　**e.** 1°　　　**f.** 3°

13.47 a. 1-propanol, hydrogen bonding
b. 1-propanol, hydrogen bonding
c. 1-butanol, greater molar mass

13.49 a. soluble, hydrogen bonding
b. insoluble, long carbon chain diminishes effect of hydrogen bonding of water to $-O-$
c. insoluble, long carbon chain diminishes effect of polar $-OH$ group on hydrogen bonding

13.51 a. 1-Propanol can form hydrogen bonds with its polar hydroxyl group.
b. An alcohol forms more hydrogen bonds than an ether.
c. Ethanol has a smaller number of carbon atoms.

13.65 a.
$$CH_3-\underset{\overset{OH}{|}}{\underset{\underset{CH_3}{|}}{C}}-CH_3 \xrightarrow{H^+,\ heat} CH_3-\underset{\overset{CH_3}{|}}{C}=CH_2 + H_2 \xrightarrow{Pt} CH_3-\underset{\overset{CH_3}{|}}{CH}-CH_3$$

b. $CH_3-CH_2-CH_2-OH \xrightarrow{H^+,\ heat} CH_3-CH=CH_2 + H_2O \xrightarrow{H^+,\ heat} CH_3-\underset{\overset{OH}{|}}{CH}-CH_3 \xrightarrow{[O]} CH_3-\overset{\overset{O}{||}}{C}-CH_3$

13.53 a. $CH_3-CH_2-CH_2-CH_2-OH + 6O_2 \xrightarrow{\Delta}$
$4CO_2 + 5H_2O + energy$

b. 2 $+ 15O_2 \xrightarrow{\Delta}$
$10CO_2 + 12H_2O + energy$

c. $+ 7O_2 \xrightarrow{\Delta} 5CO_2 + 5H_2O + energy$

13.55 a.
(phenol with OH, Cl at 2-position, Cl at 5-position)

b. $CH_3-\underset{\overset{CH_3}{|}}{CH}-CH_2-CH_2-SH$　　 (2-methyl-2-butene-like alkene with CH_2-SH)

c.
(phenol ring with OH and five Cl substituents)

13.57 a. $CH_3-CH=CH_2$

b. $CH_3-CH_2-\overset{\overset{O}{||}}{C}-H$

c. (trans-2-butene)

d. (cyclohexene)

e. (4-methylcyclohexanone)

13.59
(benzene ring with OH, OH, and $CH_2-CH_2-CH_2-CH_2-CH_2-CH_3$)

13.61 $CH_3-\underset{\overset{CH_3}{|}}{CH}-\overset{\overset{O}{||}}{C}-H$

13.63 $CH_3-CH_2-CH_2-OH$　　1-Propanol
A

$CH_3-CH=CH_2$　　Propene
B

$CH_3-CH_2-\overset{\overset{O}{||}}{C}-H$　　Propanal
C

14 Aldehydes, Ketones, and Chiral Molecules

RECENTLY, DIANA NOTICED THAT A BROWN MOLE
on her arm had changed appearance. For many years, it had been light brown in color, with a flat circular appearance. But over the last few weeks, Diana noticed that the mole had become raised, with irregular borders, and had darkened. She called her dermatologist for an appointment. Diana told Margaret, a dermatology nurse, that she had been going to tanning salons and had about 20 tanning sessions the previous year. She loved being outside but did not always apply sunscreen while in the sun or at the beach. Diana said she had no family history of malignant melanoma.

The risk factors for melanoma include frequent exposure to sun, severe sunburns at an early age, skin type, and family history. During Diana's skin exam, Margaret looked for other suspicious moles with nonuniform borders, changes in color, and changes in size. To treat the mole on Diana's arm, Margaret numbed the area, then removed a sample of skin tissue, which she sent to a lab for evaluation. Because the diagnosis indicated the presence of malignant melanoma cells, Margaret excised the entire mole including subcutaneous fat. Fortunately, the mole was not very large and no further treatment was needed. Margaret suggested that Diana return in six months for a follow-up skin check.

The number of cases of melanoma has been rising, unlike for many other types of cancer. Doctors think this change may be because of unprotected sun exposure, an increase in the use of tanning salons, and perhaps an increased awareness and detection of the disease.

CAREER Dermatology Nurse

A dermatology nurse performs many of the duties of dermatologists, including treating skin conditions, assisting in surgeries, performing biopsies and excisions, writing prescriptions, freezing skin lesions, and screening patients for skin cancer. To become a dermatology nurse, you first become a nurse or physician assistant and then specialize in dermatology. To be certified, the RN must have an additional two years of dermatology experience, with a minimum of 2000 h of work experience in dermatology, and pass an examination. Advanced training is available through colleges and universities, allied health schools, and medical schools.

LOOKING AHEAD

14.1 Aldehydes and Ketones 517

💙 **Chemistry Link to Health**
Some Important Aldehydes and Ketones 521

14.2 Physical Properties of Aldehydes and Ketones 523

14.3 Oxidation and Reduction of Aldehydes and Ketones 525

14.4 Hemiacetals and Acetals 527

14.5 Chiral Molecules 531

💙 **Chemistry Link to Health**
Enantiomers in Biological Systems 536

℞ **Clinical Applications** 522, 538, 539

℞ **Clinical Update** *Diana's Skin Protection Plan* 539

CHAPTER READINESS*

⚛ CORE CHEMISTRY SKILLS

- Naming and Drawing Alkanes (12.2)
- Naming Alcohols and Phenols (13.1)
- Writing Equations for the Oxidation of Alcohols (13.4)

*These Core Chemistry Skills from previous chapters are listed here for your review as you proceed to the new material in this chapter.

14.1 Aldehydes and Ketones

Aldehydes and ketones contain a **carbonyl group** that consists of a carbon–oxygen double bond with two groups of atoms attached to the carbon at angles of 120°. The oxygen atom with two lone pairs of electrons is much more electronegative than the carbon atom. Therefore, the carbonyl group has a strong dipole with a partial negative charge (δ^-) on the oxygen and a partial positive charge (δ^+) on the carbon. The polarity of the carbonyl group strongly influences the physical and chemical properties of aldehydes and ketones.

In an **aldehyde**, the carbon of the carbonyl group is bonded to at least one hydrogen atom. That carbon may also be bonded to another hydrogen atom, a carbon of an alkyl group, or an aromatic ring (see Figure 14.1). The aldehyde group may be written as separate atoms or as —CHO, with the double bond understood. In a **ketone**, the carbonyl group is bonded to two alkyl groups or aromatic rings. The keto group (C=O) can sometimes be written as CO. A line-angle structural formula may also be used to represent an aldehyde or ketone.

Formulas for C₃H₆O

Aldehyde

$$CH_3-CH_2-\overset{\overset{\displaystyle O}{\|}}{C}-H = CH_3-CH_2-CHO = $$

Ketone

$$CH_3-\overset{\overset{\displaystyle O}{\|}}{C}-CH_3 = CH_3-CO-CH_3 = $$

LEARNING GOAL

Identify compounds with carbonyl groups as aldehydes and ketones. Write the IUPAC and common names for aldehydes and ketones; draw their condensed or line-angle structural formulas.

FIGURE 14.1 ▶ The carbonyl group is found in aldehydes and ketones.

❓ If aldehydes and ketones both contain a carbonyl group, how can you differentiate between compounds from each family?

▶ **SAMPLE PROBLEM 14.1** Identifying Aldehydes and Ketones

Identify each of the following compounds as an aldehyde or ketone:

a.   **b.**   **c.**

SOLUTION

a. aldehyde   **b.** ketone   **c.** aldehyde

STUDY CHECK 14.1

Identify the following compound as an aldehyde or ketone:

ANSWER

ketone

Naming Aldehydes

In the IUPAC system, an aldehyde is named by replacing the *e* of the corresponding alkane name with *al*. No number is needed for the aldehyde group because it always appears at the end of the chain. The aldehydes with carbon chains of one to four carbons are often referred to by their common names, which end in *aldehyde* (see Figure 14.2). The roots (*form, acet, propion,* and *butyr*) of these common names are derived from Latin or Greek words.

	Methanal	Ethanal	Propanal	Butanal
IUPAC				
Common	(**form**aldehyde)	(**acet**aldehyde)	(**propion**aldehyde)	(**butyr**aldehyde)

FIGURE 14.2 ▶ In the structures of aldehydes, the carbonyl group is always the end carbon.

❓ Why is the carbon in the carbonyl group in aldehydes always at the end of the chain?

The IUPAC system names the aldehyde of benzene as benzaldehyde.

Benzaldehyde

▶ **SAMPLE PROBLEM 14.2 Naming Aldehydes**

Give the IUPAC name for each of the following aldehydes:

a. $CH_3-CH_2-\overset{\displaystyle CH_3}{\overset{\displaystyle |}{CH}}-CH_2-\overset{\displaystyle O}{\overset{\displaystyle ||}{C}}-H$ b.   Cl—◯—$\overset{\displaystyle O}{\overset{\displaystyle ||}{C}}$—H

SOLUTION

ANALYZE THE PROBLEM	Given	Need
	condensed structural formula of aldehyde	IUPAC name

Guide to Naming Aldehydes

STEP 1
Name the longest carbon chain by replacing the *e* in the alkane name with *al*.

STEP 2
Name and number any substituents by counting the carbonyl group as carbon 1.

a. **STEP 1** Name the longest carbon chain by replacing the *e* in the alkane name with *al*. The longest carbon chain containing the carbonyl group has five carbon atoms. It is named by replacing the *e* in the alkane name with *al* to give pentanal.

$CH_3-CH_2-\overset{\displaystyle CH_3}{\overset{\displaystyle |}{CH}}-CH_2-\overset{\displaystyle O}{\overset{\displaystyle ||}{C}}-H$ pentanal

STEP 2 Name and number any substituents by counting the carbonyl group as carbon 1. The substituent, which is the —CH$_3$ group on carbon 3, is methyl. The IUPAC name for this compound is 3-methylpentanal.

$\underset{5}{CH_3}-\underset{4}{CH_2}-\underset{3}{\overset{\displaystyle CH_3}{\overset{\displaystyle |}{CH}}}-\underset{2}{CH_2}-\underset{1}{\overset{\displaystyle O}{\overset{\displaystyle ||}{C}}}-H$ 3-methylpentanal

b. STEP 1 Name the longest carbon chain by replacing the *e* in the alkane name with *al*. The longest carbon chain consists of a benzene ring attached to a carbonyl group, which is named benzaldehyde.

benzaldehyde

STEP 2 Name and number any substituents by counting the carbonyl group as carbon 1. Counting from carbon 1 of the ring where the carbonyl group is attached, the chloro group is attached to carbon 4.

4-chlorobenzaldehyde

STUDY CHECK 14.2

What is the IUPAC name of the following compound?

ANSWER

5-methylhexanal

Naming Ketones

Aldehydes and ketones are some of the most important classes of organic compounds. Because they have played a major role in organic chemistry for more than a century, the common names for unbranched ketones are still in use. In the common names, the alkyl groups bonded to the carbonyl group are named as substituents and are listed alphabetically, followed by *ketone*. Acetone, which is another name for propanone, has been retained by the IUPAC system.

In the IUPAC system, the name of a ketone is obtained by replacing the *e* in the corresponding alkane name with *one*. Carbon chains with five carbon atoms or more are numbered from the end nearer the carbonyl group.

| Propanone | Butanone | 3-Pentanone |
| (dimethyl ketone; acetone) | (ethyl methyl ketone) | (diethyl ketone) |

For cyclic ketones, the prefix *cyclo* is used in front of the ketone name. Any substituent is located by numbering the ring starting with the carbonyl carbon as carbon 1. The ring is numbered in the direction to give substituents the lowest possible numbers.

Cyclopentanone   3-Methylcyclohexanone

Guide to Naming Ketones

STEP 1
Name the longest carbon chain by replacing the *e* in the alkane name with *one*.

STEP 2
Number the carbon chain starting from the end nearer the carbonyl group and indicate its location.

STEP 3
Name and number any substituents on the carbon chain.

SAMPLE PROBLEM 14.3 Naming Ketones

Give the IUPAC name for the following ketone:

$$CH_3 - CH - CH_2 - \overset{\displaystyle O}{\overset{\|}{C}} - CH_3$$
with CH_3 above the CH

SOLUTION

ANALYZE THE PROBLEM	Given	Need
	condensed structural formula of ketone	IUPAC name

STEP 1 Name the longest carbon chain by replacing the *e* in the alkane name with *one*. The longest chain has five carbon atoms, which is named pentanone.

$$CH_3 - CH - CH_2 - \overset{O}{\overset{\|}{C}} - CH_3 \qquad \text{pentanone}$$

STEP 2 Number the carbon chain starting from the end nearer the carbonyl group and indicate its location. Counting from the right, the carbonyl group is on carbon 2.

$$\underset{5}{CH_3} - \underset{4}{CH} - \underset{3}{CH_2} - \underset{2}{\overset{O}{\overset{\|}{C}}} - \underset{1}{CH_3} \qquad \text{2-pentanone}$$

STEP 3 Name and number any substituents on the carbon chain. Counting from the right, the methyl group is on carbon 4. The IUPAC name is 4-methyl-2-pentanone.

$$\underset{5}{CH_3} - \underset{4}{CH} - \underset{3}{CH_2} - \underset{2}{\overset{O}{\overset{\|}{C}}} - \underset{1}{CH_3} \qquad \text{4-methyl-2-pentanone}$$

STUDY CHECK 14.3

What is the IUPAC name of ethyl propyl ketone?

ANSWER

3-hexanone

Naming Compounds with Two Functional Groups

When a compound contains more than one functional group, we need to identify which group is used as the name of the compound and which group is named as a substituent. According to IUPAC rules for nomenclature, the more oxidized group will take priority. Table 14.1 lists the priorities for the functional groups we have studied, and the names of the functional groups as substituents. The functional group that is highest on the list is named as the compound, and any group lower on the list is named as a substituent. Examples are given for naming an alcohol, a ketone, and an aldehyde.

$$CH_3 - \overset{Cl}{\underset{|}{CH}} - CH_2 - OH$$
2-Chloro-1-propanol

$$CH_3 - \overset{OH}{\underset{|}{CH}} - CH_2 - \overset{O}{\overset{\|}{C}} - CH_3$$
4-Hydroxy-2-pentanone

$$CH_3 - \overset{O}{\overset{\|}{C}} - CH_2 - \overset{O}{\overset{\|}{C}} - H$$
3-Oxobutanal

TABLE 14.1 Priority of Functional Groups in IUPAC Names

	Functional Group	Name as a Substituent
Highest Priority	aldehyde	formyl
	ketone	oxo
	alcohol	hydroxy
	alkane	alkyl
Lowest Priority	halogen	halo

 Chemistry Link to **Health**

Some Important Aldehydes and Ketones

Formaldehyde, the simplest aldehyde, is a colorless gas with a pungent odor. An aqueous solution called *formalin*, which contains 40% formaldehyde, is used as a germicide and to preserve biological specimens. Industrially, it is a reactant in the synthesis of polymers used to make fabrics, insulation materials, carpeting, pressed wood products such as plywood, and plastics for kitchen counters. Exposure to formaldehyde fumes can irritate the eyes, nose, and upper respiratory tract and cause skin rashes, headaches, dizziness, and general fatigue.

Several naturally occurring aromatic aldehydes are used to flavor food and as fragrances in perfumes. Benzaldehyde is found in almonds, vanillin in vanilla beans, and cinnamaldehyde in cinnamon.

Benzaldehyde
(almond)

Vanillin
(vanilla)

Cinnamaldehyde
(cinnamon)

Methanal
(formaldehyde)

FIGURE 14.3 ▶ Acetone is used as a solvent in paint and nail polish removers.

Ⓠ What is the IUPAC name for acetone?

The simplest ketone, known as *acetone* or propanone (dimethyl ketone), is a colorless liquid with a mild odor that has wide use as a solvent in cleaning fluids, paint and nail polish removers, and rubber cement (see Figure 14.3). Acetone is extremely flammable, and care must be taken when using it. In the body, acetone may be produced in uncontrolled diabetes, fasting, and high-protein diets when large amounts of fats are metabolized for energy.

Muscone is a ketone used to make musk perfumes, and oil of spearmint contains carvone.

Muscone
(musk)

Carvone
(spearmint oil)

QUESTIONS AND PROBLEMS

14.1 Aldehydes and Ketones

LEARNING GOAL Identify compounds with carbonyl groups as aldehydes and ketones. Write the IUPAC and common names for aldehydes and ketones; draw their condensed or line-angle structural formulas.

14.1 Identify each of the following compounds as an aldehyde or a ketone:

a. $CH_3 - CH_2 - \overset{\overset{\displaystyle O}{\|}}{C} - CH_3$ b.

c.   d.

14.2 Identify each of the following compounds as an aldehyde or a ketone:

a.   b. $CH_3 - \overset{\overset{\displaystyle CH_3}{|}}{CH} - \overset{\overset{\displaystyle O}{\|}}{C} - H$

c.   d.

14.3 Indicate if each of the following pairs represents structural isomers or not:

a. $CH_3 - \overset{\overset{\displaystyle O}{\|}}{C} - CH_3$ and $CH_3 - CH_2 - \overset{\overset{\displaystyle O}{\|}}{C} - H$

b.   and

c. $CH_3 - \overset{\overset{\displaystyle O}{\|}}{C} - CH_2 - CH_3$ and

$CH_3 - \overset{\overset{\displaystyle O}{\|}}{C} - CH_2 - CH_2 - CH_3$

14.4 Indicate if each of the following pairs represents structural isomers or not:

a. $CH_3 - CH_2 - CH_2 - \overset{\overset{\displaystyle O}{\|}}{C} - H$ and

b.   and

c.   and

14.5 Give the IUPAC name for each of the following compounds:

a. $CH_3 - \overset{\overset{\displaystyle Br}{|}}{CH} - CH_2 - \overset{\overset{\displaystyle O}{\|}}{C} - H$ b.

c.   d.

14.6 Give the IUPAC name for each of the following compounds:

a.   b.

c.   d.

14.7 Give the common name for each of the following compounds:

a. $CH_3 - \overset{\overset{\displaystyle O}{\|}}{C} - H$ b.

c. $H - \overset{\overset{\displaystyle O}{\|}}{C} - H$

14.8 Give the common name for each of the following compounds:

a.

b. $CH_3 - CH_2 - \overset{\overset{\displaystyle O}{\|}}{C} - CH_2 - CH_3$

c. $CH_3 - CH_2 - \overset{\overset{\displaystyle O}{\|}}{C} - H$

14.9 Draw the condensed and line-angle structural formulas for each of the following compounds:
a. ethanal   b. 2-methyl-3-pentanone
c. butyl methyl ketone   d. 3-methylhexanal

14.10 Draw the condensed and line-angle structural formulas for each of the following compounds:
a. butyraldehyde   b. 3,4-dichloropentanal
c. 4-bromobutanone   d. acetone

℞ Clinical Applications

14.11 Anisaldehyde, from Korean mint or blue licorice, is a medicinal herb used in Chinese medicine. The IUPAC name of anisaldehyde is 4-methoxybenzaldehyde. Draw the line-angle structural formula for anisaldehyde.

14.12 The IUPAC name of ethyl vanillin, a synthetic compound used as a flavoring, is 3-ethoxy-4-hydroxybenzaldehyde. Draw the line-angle structural formula for ethyl vanillin.

14.2 Physical Properties of Aldehydes and Ketones

At room temperature, methanal (formaldehyde) and ethanal (acetaldehyde) are gases. Aldehydes and ketones containing 3 to 10 carbon atoms are liquids. The polar carbonyl group with a partially negative oxygen atom and a partially positive carbon atom has an influence on the boiling points and the solubility of aldehydes and ketones in water.

LEARNING GOAL

Describe the boiling points and solubilities of aldehydes and ketones.

Boiling Points of Aldehydes and Ketones

The polar carbonyl group in aldehydes and ketones provides dipole–dipole attractions, which alkanes do not have. Thus, aldehydes and ketones have higher boiling points than alkanes. However, aldehydes and ketones cannot form hydrogen bonds with each other as do alcohols. Thus, alcohols have higher boiling points than aldehydes and ketones of similar molar mass.

Dipole–dipole attractions in formaldehyde

Name	Butane	Propanal	Propanone	1-Propanol
Molar Mass	58	58	58	60
Family	Alkane	Aldehyde	Ketone	Alcohol
bp	0 °C	49 °C	56 °C	97 °C

Boiling Point Increases →

For aldehydes and ketones, the boiling points increase as the number of carbon atoms in the chain increases. As the molecules become larger, there are more electrons and more temporary dipoles (dispersion forces), which give higher boiling points.

Table 14.2 gives the boiling points and solubility of selected aldehydes and ketones.

TABLE 14.2 Boiling Points and Solubility of Selected Aldehydes and Ketones

Compound	Condensed Structural Formula	Number of Carbon Atoms	Boiling Point (°C)	Solubility in Water
Methanal (formaldehyde)	$H-CHO$	1	−21	Soluble
Ethanal (acetaldehyde)	CH_3-CHO	2	21	Soluble
Propanal (propionaldehyde)	CH_3-CH_2-CHO	3	49	Soluble
Propanone (acetone)	$CH_3-CO-CH_3$	3	56	Soluble
Butanal (butyraldehyde)	$CH_3-CH_2-CH_2-CHO$	4	75	Soluble
Butanone	$CH_3-CO-CH_2-CH_3$	4	80	Soluble
Pentanal	$CH_3-CH_2-CH_2-CH_2-CHO$	5	103	Slightly soluble
2-Pentanone	$CH_3-CO-CH_2-CH_2-CH_3$	5	102	Slightly soluble
Hexanal	$CH_3-CH_2-CH_2-CH_2-CH_2-CHO$	6	129	Not soluble
2-Hexanone	$CH_3-CO-CH_2-CH_2-CH_2-CH_3$	6	127	Not soluble

Solubility of Aldehydes and Ketones in Water

Aldehydes and ketones contain a polar carbonyl group (carbon–oxygen double bond), which has a partially negative oxygen atom and a partially positive carbon atom. Because the electronegative oxygen atom forms hydrogen bonds with water molecules, aldehydes

Hydrogen bonds

Acetaldehyde in water

Hydrogen bonds

Acetone in water

FIGURE 14.4 ▶ Acetaldehyde and acetone form hydrogen bonds with water.

🔵 Would you expect propanal to be soluble in water?

and ketones with one to four carbons are very soluble (see Figure 14.4). However, aldehydes and ketones with five or more carbon atoms are not soluble because longer hydrocarbon chains, which are nonpolar, diminish the solubility effect of the polar carbonyl group. Table 14.2 compares the solubility of some aldehydes and ketones.

▶ **SAMPLE PROBLEM 14.4** Boiling Point and Solubility

a. Arrange pentane, 2-butanol, and butanone, which have similar molar masses, in order of increasing boiling points. Explain.
b. Why is butanone soluble in water, but 2-hexanone is not?

SOLUTION

a. The only attractions between molecules of alkanes such as pentane are dispersion forces. With no dipole–dipole attractions or hydrogen bonds, pentane has the lowest boiling point of the three compounds. With a polar carbonyl group, butanone molecules form dipole–dipole attractions, but no hydrogen bonds. Butanone has a higher boiling point than pentane. Because molecules of 2-butanol can form hydrogen bonds with other butanol molecules, it has the highest boiling point of the three compounds. The actual boiling points are pentane (36 °C), butanone (80 °C), and 2-butanol (100 °C).
b. Butanone contains a carbonyl group with an electronegative oxygen atom that forms hydrogen bonds with water. 2-Hexanone also contains a carbonyl group, but its longer hydrocarbon chain reduces the impact on the solubility of the polar carbonyl group.

STUDY CHECK 14.4

If acetone molecules cannot hydrogen bond with each other, why is acetone soluble in water?

ANSWER

The oxygen atom in the carbonyl group of acetone forms hydrogen bonds with water molecules.

QUESTIONS AND PROBLEMS

14.2 Physical Properties of Aldehydes and Ketones

LEARNING GOAL Describe the boiling points and solubilities of aldehydes and ketones.

14.13 Which compound in each of the following pairs would have the higher boiling point? Explain.

a. $CH_3—CH_2—CH_3$ or $CH_3—\overset{\overset{\text{O}}{\|}}{C}—H$
b. propanal or pentanal
c. butanal or 1-butanol

14.14 Which compound in each of the following pairs would have the higher boiling point? Explain.

a. (structures shown) or
b. pentane or butanone
c. propanone or pentanone

14.15 Which compound in each of the following pairs would be more soluble in water? Explain.

a. $CH_3—\overset{\overset{\text{O}}{\|}}{C}—CH_2—CH_2—CH_3$ or

$CH_3—\overset{\overset{\text{O}}{\|}}{C}—\overset{\overset{\text{O}}{\|}}{C}—CH_2—CH_3$

b. propanal or pentanal
c. acetone or 2-pentanone

14.16 Which compound in each of the following pairs would be more soluble in water? Explain.

a. $CH_3—CH_2—CH_3$ or $CH_3—CH_2—CHO$
b. propanone or 3-hexanone
c. propane or propanone

14.17 Would you expect an aldehyde with a formula of $C_8H_{16}O$ to be soluble in water? Explain.

14.18 Would you expect an aldehyde with a formula of C_3H_6O to be soluble in water? Explain.

14.3 Oxidation and Reduction of Aldehydes and Ketones

LEARNING GOAL

Draw the condensed or line-angle structural formulas for the reactants and products in the oxidation or reduction of aldehydes and ketones.

Aldehydes oxidize readily to form carboxylic acids. In contrast, ketones do not undergo further oxidation.

$$CH_3-\overset{\overset{\displaystyle O}{\|}}{C}-H \xrightarrow{\text{Further oxidation}} CH_3-\overset{\overset{\displaystyle O}{\|}}{C}-OH$$

Ethanal → Ethanoic acid

$$CH_3-\overset{\overset{\displaystyle O}{\|}}{C}-CH_3 \xrightarrow{\text{Further oxidation}} \text{no reaction}$$

Propanone

Tollens' Test

The ease of oxidation of aldehydes allows certain mild oxidizing agents to oxidize the aldehyde functional group without oxidizing other functional groups. In the laboratory, **Tollens' test** may be used to distinguish between aldehydes and ketones. Tollens' reagent, which is a solution of Ag^+ ($AgNO_3$) and ammonia, oxidizes aldehydes, but not ketones. The silver ion is reduced and forms a layer called a "silver mirror" on the inside of the container.

$$CH_3-\overset{\overset{\displaystyle O}{\|}}{C}-H + 2Ag^+ \xrightarrow{[O]} 2Ag(s) + CH_3-\overset{\overset{\displaystyle O}{\|}}{C}-OH$$

Ethanal   Tollens'   Silver mirror   Ethanoic acid
(acetaldehyde) reagent   (acetic acid)

Commercially, a similar process is used to make mirrors by applying a solution of $AgNO_3$ and ammonia on glass with a spray gun (see Figure 14.5).

Another test, called **Benedict's test**, gives a positive test with compounds that have an aldehyde functional group and an adjacent hydroxyl group. When Benedict's solution containing Cu^{2+} ($CuSO_4$) is added to this type of aldehyde and heated, a brick-red solid of Cu_2O forms (see Figure 14.6). The test is negative with simple aldehydes and ketones.

$$CH_3-\overset{\overset{\displaystyle OH}{|}}{CH}-\overset{\overset{\displaystyle O}{\|}}{C}-H + 2Cu^{2+} \longrightarrow Cu_2O(s) + CH_3-\overset{\overset{\displaystyle OH}{|}}{CH}-\overset{\overset{\displaystyle O}{\|}}{C}-OH$$

2-Hydroxypropanal   Benedict's   Brick-red   2-Hydroxypropanoic acid
                    reagent   solid

Because many sugars such as glucose contain this type of aldehyde grouping, Benedict's reagent can be used to determine the presence of glucose in blood or urine.

D-Glucose + 2Cu²⁺ (Benedict's, blue) → D-Gluconic acid + Cu₂O(s) (brick red)

$$Ag^+ + 1\,e^- \longrightarrow Ag(s)$$

FIGURE 14.5 ▶ In Tollens' test, a "silver mirror" forms when the oxidation of an aldehyde reduces silver ions to metallic silver. The silvery surface of a mirror is formed in a similar way.

Q What is the product of the oxidation of an aldehyde?

Cu^{2+} $Cu_2O(s)$

FIGURE 14.6 ▶ The blue Cu^{2+} in Benedict's solution forms a brick-red solid of Cu_2O in a positive test for many sugars and aldehydes with adjacent hydroxyl groups.

Q Which test tube indicates that glucose is present?

SAMPLE PROBLEM 14.5 Tollens' Test

Draw the condensed structural formula for the product of oxidation, if any, when Tollens' reagent is added to each of the following compounds:

a. propanal   **b.** propanone   **c.** 2-methylbutanal

SOLUTION

Tollens' reagent will oxidize aldehydes but not ketones.

$$\textbf{a. } CH_3-CH_2-\overset{\overset{\textstyle O}{\|}}{C}-OH \qquad \textbf{b. } \text{no reaction} \qquad \textbf{c. } CH_3-CH_2-\overset{\overset{\textstyle CH_3}{|}}{CH}-\overset{\overset{\textstyle O}{\|}}{C}-OH$$

STUDY CHECK 14.5

Why does a silver mirror form when Tollens' reagent is added to a test tube containing benzaldehyde?

ANSWER

The oxidation of benzaldehyde reduces Ag^+ to metallic silver, which forms a silvery coating on the inside of the test tube.

Reduction of Aldehydes and Ketones

Aldehydes and ketones are reduced by hydrogen (H_2) or sodium borohydride $(NaBH_4)$. In the **reduction** of organic compounds, there is a decrease in the number of carbon–oxygen bonds. Aldehydes are reduced to primary alcohols, and ketones are reduced to secondary alcohols. A catalyst such as nickel, platinum, or palladium is needed for the addition of hydrogen.

Aldehydes Reduce to Primary Alcohols

$$CH_3-CH_2-\overset{\overset{\textstyle O}{\|}}{C}-H + \textbf{H}_2 \xrightarrow{Pt} CH_3-CH_2-\overset{\overset{\textstyle OH}{|}}{\underset{\underset{\textstyle \textbf{H}}{|}}{C}}-H$$

Propanal (propionaldehyde)   1-Propanol (1° alcohol) (propyl alcohol)

Ketones Reduce to Secondary Alcohols

$$CH_3-\overset{\overset{\textstyle O}{\|}}{C}-CH_3 + \textbf{H}_2 \xrightarrow{Ni} CH_3-\overset{\overset{\textstyle OH}{|}}{\underset{\underset{\textstyle \textbf{H}}{|}}{C}}-CH_3$$

Propanone (dimethyl ketone)   2-Propanol (2° alcohol) (isopropyl alcohol)

SAMPLE PROBLEM 14.6 Reduction of Carbonyl Groups

Write the equation for the reduction of cyclopentanone using hydrogen in the presence of a nickel catalyst.

SOLUTION

The reacting molecule is a cyclic ketone that has five carbon atoms. During the reduction, hydrogen atoms add to the carbon and oxygen in the carbonyl group, which reduces the ketone to the corresponding secondary alcohol.

Cyclopentanone   Cyclopentanol

STUDY CHECK 14.6

What is the name of the product obtained from the hydrogenation of 2-methylbutanal?

ANSWER

2-methyl-1-butanol

QUESTIONS AND PROBLEMS

14.3 Oxidation and Reduction of Aldehydes and Ketones

LEARNING GOAL Draw the condensed or line-angle structural formulas for the reactants and products in the oxidation or reduction of aldehydes and ketones.

14.19 Draw the condensed or line-angle structural formula, if cyclic, for the product of oxidation (if any) for each of the following compounds:
a. methanal
b. butanone
c. benzaldehyde
d. 3-methylcyclohexanone

14.20 Draw the condensed or line-angle structural formula, if cyclic, for the product of oxidation (if any) for each of the following compounds:
a. acetaldehyde
b. 3-methylbutanone
c. cyclohexanone
d. 3-methylbutanal

14.21 Which of the following compounds would react with Tollens' reagent, Benedict's reagent, both, or neither?

$$\text{a.} \quad \overset{\text{O}}{\overset{\|}{\diagup\diagup\!\!\!\diagdown\diagup\!\!\!\diagdown\text{C}}}\diagdown_{\text{H}} \qquad \text{b.} \quad CH_3-\overset{\overset{\text{O}}{\|}}{C}-CH_3$$

14.22 Which of the following compounds would react with Tollens' reagent, Benedict's reagent, both, or neither?

$$\text{c.} \quad CH_3-\overset{\overset{\text{OH}}{|}}{CH}-\overset{\overset{\text{O}}{\|}}{C}-H$$

$$\text{a.} \quad \overset{\text{O}}{\overset{\|}{\diagup\!\!\!\diagup\diagdown}} \qquad \text{b.} \quad CH_3-CH_2-\overset{\overset{\text{OH}}{|}}{CH}-\overset{\overset{\text{O}}{\|}}{C}-H$$

$$\text{c.} \quad CH_3-\overset{\overset{\text{O}}{\|}}{C}-H$$

14.23 Draw the condensed structural formula for the product formed when each of the following is reduced by hydrogen in the presence of a nickel catalyst:
a. butyraldehyde
b. acetone
c. 3-bromohexanal
d. 2-methyl-3-pentanone

14.24 Draw the condensed structural formula for the product formed when each of the following is reduced by hydrogen in the presence of a nickel catalyst:
a. ethyl propyl ketone
b. formaldehyde
c. 3-chloropentanal
d. 2-pentanone

14.4 Hemiacetals and Acetals

We have seen that the carbonyl group (C=O) is polar, which makes aldehydes and ketones very reactive. One of the most common reactions of aldehydes and ketones is the addition of one or two molecules of an alcohol to the carbonyl group.

LEARNING GOAL

Draw the condensed or line-angle structural formulas for the products of the addition of alcohols to aldehydes and ketones.

Hemiacetal and Acetal Formation

When one alcohol adds to an aldehyde or ketone in the presence of an acid catalyst, the product is a **hemiacetal**, which contains two functional groups on the same C atom: a hydroxyl group (—OH) and an alkoxy group (—OR). However, hemiacetals are generally unstable and react with a second molecule of the alcohol to form a stable *acetal* and water. The **acetal** has two alkoxy groups (—OR) attached to the same carbon atom. Commercially, compounds that are acetals are used to produce vitamins, dyes, pharmaceuticals, and perfumes.

$$\overset{\text{O}^{\delta-}}{\underset{\overset{\|}{\diagup}\delta+}{\overset{\|}{C}}} + HO-R \;\underset{}{\overset{H^+}{\rightleftharpoons}}\; \overset{\text{O}-H}{\underset{|}{-\overset{|}{\underset{|}{C}}-OR}} + HO-R \;\underset{}{\overset{H^+}{\rightleftharpoons}}\; \overset{\text{OR}}{\underset{|}{-\overset{|}{\underset{|}{C}}-OR}} + H-O-H$$

Aldehyde   Alcohol   Hemiacetal   Alcohol   Acetal
or ketone

In general, aldehydes are more reactive than ketones because the carbonyl carbon is more positive in aldehydes. Also, the presence of two alkyl groups in ketones makes it more difficult for an alcohol to form a bond with the carbon in the carbonyl group.

▶SAMPLE PROBLEM 14.7 Hemiacetals and Acetals

Identify each of the following as a hemiacetal or acetal:

a.
$$CH_3-CH_2-\overset{\displaystyle OH}{\underset{\displaystyle O-CH_3}{C}}-CH_3$$

b.
$$H-\overset{\displaystyle O-CH_3}{\underset{\displaystyle CH_3}{C}}-O-CH_3$$

c.
$$CH_3-\overset{\displaystyle OH}{\underset{\displaystyle O-CH_2-CH_3}{C}}-CH_3$$

SOLUTION

a. A hemiacetal has a carbon bonded to one alkoxy group and one hydroxyl group.
b. An acetal has a carbon bonded to two alkoxy groups.
c. A hemiacetal has a carbon bonded to one alkoxy group and one hydroxyl group.

STUDY CHECK 14.7

From the following descriptions, identify the compound as a hemiacetal or an acetal:

a. a molecule that contains a carbon atom attached to a hydroxyl group and an ethoxy group
b. a molecule that contains a carbon atom attached to two ethoxy groups

ANSWER

a. hemiacetal   b. acetal

Examples of the formation of a hemiacetal and acetal from an aldehyde and a ketone follow:

Hemiacetal and Acetal Formation from an Aldehyde

Ethanal + Methanol ⇌ Hemiacetal ⇌ Acetal + H_2O

Hemiacetal and Acetal Formation from an Ketone

Propanone + Ethanol ⇌ Hemiacetal ⇌ Acetal + H_2O

The reactions in the formation of hemiacetals and acetals are reversible. As predicted by Le Châtelier's principle, the system shifts in the direction of the products by removing water from the reaction mixture. The system shifts in the direction of the ketone or aldehyde by adding water.

SAMPLE PROBLEM 14.8 Hemiacetals and Acetals

Draw the condensed structural formulas for the hemiacetal and acetal formed when methanol adds to propanal.

SOLUTION

To form the hemiacetal, the hydrogen from methanol adds to the oxygen of the carbonyl group to form a new hydroxyl group. The remaining part of the methanol adds to the carbon atom in the carbonyl group. The acetal forms when a second molecule of methanol adds to the carbonyl carbon atom.

$$CH_3-CH_2-\overset{\overset{\displaystyle O}{\|}}{C}-H + HO-CH_3 \overset{H^+}{\rightleftharpoons} CH_3-CH_2-\overset{\overset{\displaystyle OH}{|}}{\underset{\underset{\displaystyle O-CH_3}{|}}{C}}-H + HO-CH_3 \overset{H^+}{\rightleftharpoons} CH_3-CH_2-\overset{\overset{\displaystyle O-CH_3}{|}}{\underset{\underset{\displaystyle O-CH_3}{|}}{C}}-H + H_2O$$

Propanal   Methanol   Hemiacetal   Methanol   Acetal

STUDY CHECK 14.8

Draw the condensed structural formula for the acetal formed when methanol adds to butanone.

ANSWER

$$CH_3-\overset{\overset{\displaystyle O-CH_3}{|}}{\underset{\underset{\displaystyle O-CH_3}{|}}{C}}-CH_2-CH_3$$

Cyclic Hemiacetals

One very important type of hemiacetal that can be isolated is a *cyclic hemiacetal* that forms when the carbonyl group and the —OH group are in the *same* molecule.

Open chain   Cyclic hemiacetal

The five- and six-atom cyclic hemiacetals and acetals are more stable than their open-chain isomers. The importance of understanding acetals is shown for glucose, a carbohydrate, which has both carbonyl and hydroxyl groups that can form acetal bonds. Glucose forms a cyclic hemiacetal when the hydroxyl group on carbon 5 bonds with the carbonyl group on carbon 1. The hemiacetal of glucose is so stable that almost all the glucose (99%) exists as the cyclic hemiacetal in aqueous solution.

Glucose   Formation of cyclic hemiacetal   Hemiacetal of glucose

An alcohol can add to the cyclic hemiacetal to form a cyclic acetal. This reaction is also very important in carbohydrate chemistry. It is the linkage that bonds glucose molecules to other glucose molecules in the formation of disaccharides and polysaccharides.

Maltose is a disaccharide consisting of two glucose molecules, and is produced from the hydrolysis of starch from grains. In maltose, an acetal bond (shown in red) links two glucose molecules. One glucose retains the cyclic hemiacetal bond (shown in green).

Maltose, a disaccharide, is produced from the hydrolysis of the starches in grains, such as barley.

α-Maltose

QUESTIONS AND PROBLEMS

14.4 Hemiacetals and Acetals

LEARNING GOAL Draw the condensed or line-angle structural formulas for the products of the addition of alcohols to aldehydes and ketones.

14.25 Indicate whether each of the following is a hemiacetal, acetal, or neither:

a. $CH_3-CH_2-O-CH_2-OH$

b.
$$CH_3-CH_2-CH_2-\overset{\displaystyle O-CH_3}{\underset{\displaystyle OH}{\overset{\displaystyle |}{\underset{\displaystyle |}{C}}}}-H$$

c.
$$CH_3-\overset{\displaystyle O-CH_2-CH_3}{\underset{\displaystyle O-CH_2-CH_3}{\overset{\displaystyle |}{\underset{\displaystyle |}{C}}}}-CH_2-CH_3$$

d.   **e.**

14.26 Indicate whether each of the following is a hemiacetal, acetal, or neither:

a. $CH_3-CH_2-O-CH_2-CH_3$

b. $HO-CH_2-CH_2-O-CH_2-CH_2-O-CH_3$

c.
$$CH_3-\overset{\displaystyle O-CH_2-CH_3}{\underset{\displaystyle OH}{\overset{\displaystyle |}{\underset{\displaystyle |}{C}}}}-CH_3$$

d.   **e.**

14.27 Draw the condensed structural formula for the hemiacetal formed by adding one methanol molecule to each of the following:

a. ethanal   **b.** propanone   **c.** butanal

14.28 Draw the condensed structural formula for the hemiacetal formed by adding one ethanol molecule to each of the following:

a. propanal   **b.** butanone   **c.** methanal

14.29 Draw the condensed structural formula for the acetal formed by adding a second methanol molecule to the compounds in problem 14.27.

14.30 Draw the condensed structural formula for the acetal formed by adding a second ethanol molecule to the compounds in problem 14.28.

14.5 Chiral Molecules

LEARNING GOAL

Identify chiral and achiral carbon atoms in an organic molecule.

Molecules are structural isomers when they have the same molecular formula, but different bonding arrangements.

Structural Isomers

C_2H_6O $CH_3 - CH_2 - OH$ $CH_3 - O - CH_3$
Ethanol Dimethyl ether

C_3H_6O
Propanal Propanone

Another group of isomers called *stereoisomers* has identical molecular formulas, too, but they are not structural isomers. In **stereoisomers**, the atoms are bonded in the same sequence but differ in the way they are arranged in space.

Chirality

Everything has a mirror image. If you hold your right hand up to a mirror, you see its mirror image, which matches your left hand (see Figure 14.7). If you turn your palms toward each other, one hand is the mirror image of the other. If you look at the palms of your hands, your thumbs are on opposite sides. If you then place your right hand over your left hand, you cannot match up all the parts of the hands: palms, backs, thumbs, and little fingers.

Interactive Video

Chirality

Left hand   Right hand

Mirror image of right hand

FIGURE 14.7 ▶ The left and right hands are chiral because they have mirror images that cannot be superimposed on each other.
◉ Why are your shoes chiral objects?

The thumbs and little fingers can be matched, but then the palms or backs of your hands are facing each other. Your hands are mirror images that cannot be superimposed on each other. When the mirror images cannot be completely matched, they are *nonsuperimposable*.

Objects such as hands that have nonsuperimposable mirror images are **chiral** (pronunciation *kai-ral*). Left and right shoes are chiral; left- and right-handed golf clubs are chiral. When we think of how difficult it is to put a left-hand glove on our right hand, put a right shoe on our left foot, or use left-handed scissors if we are right-handed, we begin to realize that certain properties of mirror images are very different.

When the mirror image of an object is identical and can be superimposed on the original, it is *achiral*. For example, the mirror image of a plain drinking glass is identical to the original glass, which means the mirror image can be superimposed on the glass (see Figure 14.8).

Chiral Carbon Atoms

A carbon compound is chiral if it has at least one carbon atom bonded to *four different atoms or groups*. This type of carbon atom is called a **chiral carbon** because there are two different ways that it can bond to four atoms or groups of atoms. The resulting structures

⚛ CORE CHEMISTRY SKILL

Identifying Chiral Molecules

FIGURE 14.8 ▶ Everyday objects such as gloves and shoes are chiral, but an unmarked bat and a plain glass are achiral.

ⓠ Why are some of the objects above chiral and others achiral?

are nonsuperimposable mirror images. Let's look at the mirror images of a carbon bonded to four different atoms (see Figure 14.9). If we line up the hydrogen and iodine atoms in the mirror images, the bromine and chlorine atoms appear on opposite sides. No matter how we turn the models, we cannot align all four atoms at the same time. When stereoisomers cannot be superimposed, they are called **enantiomers**.

FIGURE 14.9 ▶ **(a)** The enantiomers of a chiral molecule are mirror images. **(b)** The enantiomers of a chiral molecule cannot be superimposed on each other.

ⓠ Why is the carbon atom in this compound chiral?

If a molecule with two or more identical atoms bonded to the same atom is rotated, the atoms can be superimposed and the mirror images represent the same structure (see Figure 14.10).

FIGURE 14.10 ▶ The mirror images of an achiral compound can be superimposed on each other.

ⓠ Why can the mirror images of this compound be superimposed?

These are the same structures.

Explore Your World

Using Gumdrops and Toothpicks to Model Chiral Objects

Part 1: Achiral Objects

Obtain some toothpicks and orange, yellow, green, purple, and black gumdrops. Place four toothpicks into a black gumdrop making the ends of toothpicks the corners of a tetrahedron. Attach the gumdrops to the toothpicks: two orange, one green, and one yellow.

Using another black gumdrop, make a second model that is the mirror image of the original model. Now rotate one of the models and try to superimpose it on the other model. Are the models superimposable? If achiral objects have superimposable mirror images, are these models chiral or achiral?

Part 2: Chiral Objects

Using one of the original models, replace one orange gumdrop with a purple gumdrop. Now there are four different colors of gumdrops attached to the black gumdrop. Make its mirror image by replacing one orange gumdrop with a purple one on the second model. Now rotate one of the models, and try to superimpose it on the other model. Are the models superimposable? If chiral objects have nonsuperimposable mirror images, are these models chiral or achiral?

▶ **SAMPLE PROBLEM 14.9** Chiral Carbons

For each of the following, indicate whether the carbon in red is chiral or achiral:

a. Glycerol, which is used to sweeten and preserve foods and as a lubricant in soaps, creams, and hair care products.

$$HO-\overset{\overset{\displaystyle H}{|}}{\underset{\underset{\displaystyle H}{|}}{C}}-\overset{\overset{\displaystyle OH}{|}}{\underset{\underset{\displaystyle H}{|}}{C}}-\overset{\overset{\displaystyle H}{|}}{\underset{\underset{\displaystyle H}{|}}{C}}-OH$$

Glycerol

b. Monosodium glutamate (MSG), which is the salt of the amino acid glutamic acid used as a flavor enhancer in foods.

$$Na^+\ {}^-O-\overset{\overset{\displaystyle O}{\|}}{C}-\overset{\overset{\displaystyle H}{|}}{\underset{\underset{\displaystyle H}{|}}{C}}-\overset{\overset{\displaystyle H}{|}}{\underset{\underset{\displaystyle H}{|}}{C}}-\overset{\overset{\displaystyle NH_2}{|}}{\underset{\underset{\displaystyle H}{|}}{C}}-\overset{\overset{\displaystyle O}{\|}}{C}-OH$$

Monosodium glutamate (MSG)

c. Ibuprofen, which is a nonsteroidal anti-inflammatory drug used to relieve fever and pain.

$$CH_3-\overset{\overset{\displaystyle H}{|}}{\underset{\underset{\displaystyle CH_3}{|}}{C}}-\overset{\overset{\displaystyle H}{|}}{\underset{\underset{\displaystyle H}{|}}{C}}-\bigcirc-\overset{\overset{\displaystyle \overset{O}{\|}{-}C-OH}{}}{\underset{\underset{\displaystyle H}{|}}{C}}-CH_3$$

Ibuprofen

SOLUTION

a. Achiral. Two of the substituents on the carbon in red are the same:

Glycerol

b. Chiral. The carbon in red is bonded to four different groups:

Monosodium glutamate (MSG)

c. Chiral. The carbon in red is bonded to four different groups:

Ibuprofen

STUDY CHECK 14.9

Circle the chiral carbon of penicillamine, which is used in the treatment of rheumatoid arthritis.

ANSWER

CORE CHEMISTRY SKILL

Identifying D- and L- Fischer Projections

Drawing Fischer Projections

Emil Fischer devised a simplified system for drawing stereoisomers that shows the arrangements of the atoms around the chiral carbons. Fischer received the Nobel Prize in Chemistry in 1902 for his contributions to carbohydrate and protein chemistry. Now we use his model, called a **Fischer projection**, to represent a three-dimensional structure of enantiomers. Vertical lines represent bonds that project backward from a carbon atom and horizontal lines represent bonds that project forward. In this model, the most highly oxidized carbon is placed at the top and the intersections of vertical and horizontal lines represent a carbon atom that is usually chiral.

For glyceraldehyde, the only chiral carbon is the middle carbon. In the Fischer projection, the carbonyl group, which is the most highly oxidized group, is drawn at the top above the chiral carbon and the —CH₂OH group is drawn at the bottom. The —H and —OH groups can be drawn at each end of a horizontal line, but in two different ways. The stereoisomer that has the —OH group drawn to the left of the chiral atom is designated as the L stereoisomer. The stereoisomer with the —OH group drawn to the right of the chiral carbon represents the D stereoisomer (see Figure 14.11).

Fischer projections can also be drawn for compounds that have two or more chiral carbons. For example, in the mirror images of erythrose, both of the carbon atoms at the

Dash–Wedge Structures of Glyceraldehyde

Extend forward (wedge)

Mirror

Project back (dashed line)

Fischer Projections of Glyceraldehyde

Chiral carbon

L-Glyceraldehyde

D-Glyceraldehyde

FIGURE 14.11 ▶ In a Fischer projection, the chiral carbon atom is at the center, with horizontal lines for bonds that project forward and vertical lines for bonds that point away.

◉ Why does glyceraldehyde have only one chiral carbon atom?

intersections are chiral. To draw the mirror image for L-erythrose, we need to reverse the positions of *all* the —H and the —OH groups on the horizontal lines. For compounds with two or more chiral carbons, the designation as a D or L stereoisomer is determined by the position of the —OH group attached to the chiral carbon *farthest from the carbonyl group.*

L Stereoisomer

D Stereoisomer

L-Erythrose

D-Erythrose

▶ **SAMPLE PROBLEM 14.10 Fischer Projections**

Identify each of the following as the D or L stereoisomer:

a.   **b.**   **c.**

SOLUTION

a. When the —OH group is drawn to the left of the chiral carbon, it is the L stereoisomer.
b. When the —OH group is drawn to the right of the chiral carbon, it is the D stereoisomer.
c. When the —OH group is drawn to the right of the chiral carbon farthest from the top of the Fischer projection, it is the D stereoisomer.

STUDY CHECK 14.10

Draw the Fischer projections for the D and L stereoisomers of 2-hydroxypropanal and label the D and L isomers.

ANSWER

D-2-Hydroxypropanal   L-2-Hydroxypropanal

Chemistry Link to Health

Enantiomers in Biological Systems

Molecules in nature also have mirror images, and often one stereoisomer has a different biological effect than the other one. For some compounds, one enantiomer has a certain odor, and the other enantiomer has a completely different odor. For example, the oils that give the scent of spearmint and caraway seeds are *both* composed of carvone. However, carvone has one chiral carbon in the carbon ring indicated by an asterisk, which gives carvone two enantiomers. Olfactory receptors in the nose detect these enantiomers as two different odors. One enantiomer of carvone that is produced by the spearmint plant smells and tastes like spearmint, whereas its mirror image, produced by the caraway plant, has the odor and taste of caraway in rye bread. Thus, our senses of smell and taste are responsive to the chirality of molecules.

Spearmint

Caraway plant and seeds

Carvone extracted from spearmint

L-Carvone

D-Carvone

Carvone extracted from caraway plant and seeds

In the brain, one enantiomer of LSD affects the production of serotonin, which influences sensory perception and may lead to hallucinations. However, its enantiomer produces little effect in the brain. The behavior of nicotine and adrenaline (epinephrine) also depends upon only one of their enantiomers. For example, one enantiomer of nicotine is more toxic than the other. Only one enantiomer of epinephrine is responsible for the constriction of blood vessels.

Nicotine

Chiral carbon (shown with an asterisk *)

Adrenaline (epinephrine)

A substance used to treat Parkinson's disease is L-dopa, which is converted to dopamine in the brain, where it raises the serotonin level. However, the D-dopa enantiomer is not effective for the treatment of Parkinson's disease.

L-Dopa

D-Dopa

Many compounds in biological systems have only one enantiomer that is active. This happens because the enzymes and cell surface receptors on which metabolic reactions take place are themselves chiral. Thus, only one enantiomer interacts with its enzymes or receptors; the other is inactive. The chiral receptor fits the arrangement of the substituents in only one enantiomer; its mirror image does not fit properly (see Figure 14.12).

For many drugs, only one of the enantiomers is biologically active. However, for many years, drugs have been produced that were mixtures of their enantiomers. Today, drug researchers are using *chiral technology* to produce the active enantiomers of chiral drugs. Chiral catalysts are being designed that direct the formation of just one enantiomer rather than both. The active forms of several enantiomers are now being produced, such as L-dopa and naproxen. Naproxen is a nonsteroidal anti-inflammatory drug used to relieve pain, fever, and

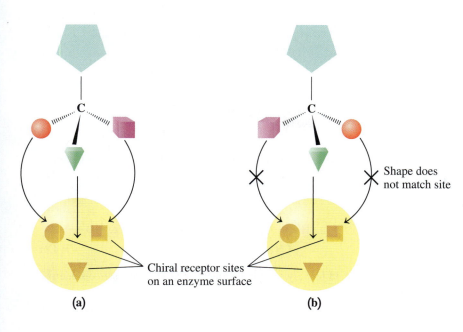

Ⓠ Why don't all the substituents of the mirror image of the active enantiomer fit into a chiral receptor site?

inflammation caused by osteoarthritis and tendinitis. The benefits of producing only the active enantiomer include using a lower dose, enhancing activity, reducing interactions with other drugs, and eliminating possible harmful side effects from the enantiomer.

The active enantiomer of the popular analgesic ibuprofen used in Advil, Motrin, and Nuprin has been produced. However, recent research shows that humans have an enzyme called *isomerase* that converts the inactive enantiomer of ibuprofen to its active form. Because of the lower cost of preparation, most manufacturers prepare ibuprofen as a mixture of inactive and active forms.

One enantiomer of ibuprofen is the active form, but its mirror image is inactive.

Active form of ibuprofen

Mirror image (inactive form)

QUESTIONS AND PROBLEMS

14.5 Chiral Molecules

LEARNING GOAL Identify chiral and achiral carbon atoms in an organic molecule.

14.31 Identify each of the following structures as chiral or achiral. If chiral, indicate the chiral carbon.

  a. $CH_3 - \overset{\overset{\displaystyle OH}{|}}{CH} - CH_3$ b.

  c. $CH_3 - \overset{\overset{\displaystyle Br}{|}}{CH} - \overset{\overset{\displaystyle O}{\|}}{C} - H$

  d. $CH_3 - CH_2 - \overset{\overset{\displaystyle OH}{|}}{\underset{\underset{\displaystyle CH_3}{|}}{C}} - CH_3$

14.32 Identify each of the following structures as chiral or achiral. If chiral, indicate the chiral carbon.

  a. $CH_3 - \overset{\overset{\displaystyle Cl}{|}}{\underset{\underset{\displaystyle CH_3}{|}}{C}} - CH_2 - \overset{\overset{\displaystyle Cl}{|}}{CH} - CH_3$

b. $CH_3-\overset{\overset{\displaystyle Br}{|}}{C}=CH-CH_3$

c. (structure with OH groups)

d. $Br-CH_2-\overset{\overset{\displaystyle Cl}{|}}{CH}-CH_3$

14.33 Draw the Fischer projection for each of the following dash–wedge structures:

a. (aldehyde; HO—C—Br, CH₃) **b.** (aldehyde; Cl—C—Br, OH) **c.** (aldehyde; HO—C—H, CH₂CH₃)

14.34 Draw the Fischer projection for each of the following dash–wedge structures:

a. (aldehyde; HO—C—Br, CH₂OH) **b.** (aldehyde; HO—C—H, CH₂OH) **c.** (aldehyde; H—C—OH, CH₂OH)

14.35 Indicate whether each pair of Fischer projections represents enantiomers or identical structures.

a. $\underset{CH_3}{\overset{CH_3}{Br-\!\!\!|\!\!\!-Cl}}$ and $\underset{CH_3}{\overset{CH_3}{Cl-\!\!\!|\!\!\!-Br}}$

b. (aldehyde) HO—H, CH₃ and (aldehyde) H—OH, CH₃

c. $\underset{H}{\overset{CH_3}{Cl-\!\!\!|\!\!\!-Br}}$ and $\underset{H}{\overset{CH_3}{Br-\!\!\!|\!\!\!-Cl}}$

d. (HO, C=O) H—OH, CH₃ and (HO, C=O) HO—H, CH₃

14.36 Indicate whether each pair of Fischer projections represents enantiomers or identical structures.

a. $\underset{CH_3}{\overset{CH_2OH}{Br-\!\!\!|\!\!\!-Cl}}$ and $\underset{CH_3}{\overset{CH_2OH}{Cl-\!\!\!|\!\!\!-Br}}$

b. (aldehyde) H—H, CH₃ and (aldehyde) H—H, CH₃

c. (CH₃, C=O) H—OH, CH₂CH₃ and (CH₃, C=O) HO—H, CH₂CH₃

d. (aldehyde) H—NH₂, CH₃ and (aldehyde) H₂N—H, CH₃

14.37 Identify each of the following as the D or L stereoisomer:

a. (CH₂OH, C=O) H—OH, CH₃ **b.** (aldehyde) H—OH, CH₃ **c.** (aldehyde) HO—H, CH₂OH

14.38 Identify each of the following as the D or L stereoisomer:

a. (aldehyde) HO—H, CH₂OH **b.** (aldehyde) HO—H, HO—H, CH₂OH **c.** (HO, C=O) H—OH, CH₂OH

Clinical Applications

14.39 Identify the chiral carbon in each of the following naturally occurring compounds:

a. citronellol; one enantiomer has the geranium odor

$$CH_3-\overset{\overset{\displaystyle CH_3}{|}}{C}=CH-CH_2-CH_2-\overset{\overset{\displaystyle CH_3}{|}}{CH}-CH_2-CH_2-OH$$

b. alanine, an amino acid

$$H_2N-\overset{\overset{\displaystyle CH_3}{|}}{CH}-\overset{\overset{\displaystyle O}{||}}{C}-OH$$

14.40 Identify the chiral carbon in each of the following naturally occurring compounds:

a. amphetamine (Benzedrine), stimulant, used in the treatment of hyperactivity

(benzene)—$CH_2-\overset{\overset{\displaystyle CH_3}{|}}{CH}-NH_2$

b. norepinephrine, increases blood pressure and nerve transmission

(dihydroxybenzene, HO, HO)—$\overset{\overset{\displaystyle OH}{|}}{CH}-CH_2-NH_2$

Clinical Update
Diana's Skin Protection Plan

After six months, Diana returns to the dermatology office for a follow-up skin check. There has been no change in the skin where the mole was excised and no other moles were found that were suspicious. Margaret reminded Diana to limit her exposure to the sun, especially between 10 A.M. and 3 P.M., and to wear protective clothing, including a hat, a long-sleeved shirt, and pants that cover her legs. On all exposed skin, Margaret tells Diana to use broad-spectrum sunscreen with an SPF of at least 15 every day. Sunscreen absorbs UV light radiation when the skin is exposed to sunlight and thus helps protect against sunburn. The SPF (sun protection factor) number, which ranges from 2 to 100, gives the amount of time for protected skin to sunburn compared to the time for unprotected skin to sunburn. The principal ingredients in sunscreens are usually aromatic molecules with carbonyl groups such as oxybenzone and avobenzone.

Clinical Applications

14.41 Oxybenzone is an effective sunscreen whose structural formula is shown.

  a. What functional groups are in oxybenzone?
  b. What is the molecular formula and molar mass of oxybenzone?
  c. If a bottle of sunscreen containing 178 mL has 6.0% (m/v) oxybenzone, how many grams of oxybenzone are present?

Sunscreen absorbs UV light, which protects against sunburn.

14.42 Avobenzone is a common ingredient in sunscreen. Its structural formula is shown.

  a. What functional groups are in avobenzone?
  b. What is the molecular formula and molar mass of avobenzone?
  c. If a bottle of sunscreen containing 236 mL has 3.0% (m/v) avobenzone, how many grams of avobenzone are present?

Oxybenzone

Avobenzone

CONCEPT MAP

ALDEHYDES, KETONES, AND CHIRAL MOLECULES

with — Carbon–Oxygen Double Bonds

can be — Chiral Compounds

are — Aldehydes — Ketones

with — Mirror Images

test positive with — Tollens' Test

react to form — 1° Alcohols — Hemiacetals

react to form — 2° Alcohols

drawn as — Fischer Projections

Benedict's Test — Carboxylic Acids — Acetals

CHAPTER REVIEW

14.1 Aldehydes and Ketones

LEARNING GOAL Identify compounds with carbonyl groups as aldehydes and ketones. Write the IUPAC and common names for aldehydes and ketones; draw their condensed or line-angle structural formulas.

Carbonyl group

- Aldehydes and ketones contain a carbonyl group ($C=O$), which is strongly polar.
- In aldehydes, the carbonyl group appears at the end of carbon chains attached to at least one hydrogen atom.
- In ketones, the carbonyl group occurs between two alkyl or aromatic groups.
- In the IUPAC system, the *e* in the corresponding alkane name is replaced with *al* for aldehydes and *one* for ketones. For ketones with more than four carbon atoms in the main chain, the carbonyl group is numbered to show its location.
- Many of the simple aldehydes and ketones use common names.
- Many aldehydes and ketones are found in biological systems, flavorings, and drugs.

14.2 Physical Properties of Aldehydes and Ketones

LEARNING GOAL Describe the boiling points and solubilites of aldehydes and ketones.

Hydrogen bonds

Acetone

- The polar carbonyl group in aldehydes and ketones gives higher boiling points than alkanes.
- The boiling points of aldehydes and ketones are lower than alcohols because aldehydes and ketones cannot hydrogen bond with each other.
- Aldehydes and ketones form hydrogen bonds with water molecules, which makes carbonyl compounds with one to four carbon atoms soluble in water.

14.3 Oxidation and Reduction of Aldehydes and Ketones

LEARNING GOAL Draw the condensed or line-angle structural formulas for the reactants and products in the oxidation or reduction of aldehydes and ketones.

- Primary alcohols can be oxidized to aldehydes, whereas secondary alcohols can oxidize to ketones.

- Aldehydes are easily oxidized to carboxylic acids, but ketones do not oxidize further.
- Aldehydes, but not ketones, react with Tollens' reagent to give "silver mirrors."
- In Benedict's test, aldehydes with adjacent hydroxyl groups reduce blue Cu^{2+} to give a brick-red Cu_2O solid.
- The reduction of aldehydes with hydrogen produces primary alcohols, whereas ketones are reduced to secondary alcohols.

14.4 Hemiacetals and Acetals

LEARNING GOAL Draw the condensed or line-angle structural formulas for the products of the addition of alcohols to aldehydes and ketones.

- Alcohols can add to the carbonyl group of aldehydes and ketones.
- The addition of one alcohol molecule forms a hemiacetal, whereas the addition of two alcohol molecules forms an acetal.
- Hemiacetals are not usually stable, except for cyclic hemiacetals, which are the most common form of simple sugars such as glucose.

14.5 Chiral Molecules

LEARNING GOAL Identify chiral and achiral carbon atoms in an organic molecule.

- Chiral molecules are molecules with mirror images that cannot be superimposed on each other. These types of stereoisomers are called enantiomers.
- A chiral molecule must have at least one chiral carbon, which is a carbon bonded to four different atoms or groups of atoms.
- The Fischer projection is a simplified way to draw the arrangements of atoms by placing the carbon atoms at the intersection of vertical and horizontal lines.
- The mirror images are labeled D or L to differentiate between enantiomers.

SUMMARY OF NAMING

Family	Structure	IUPAC Name	Common Name
Aldehyde	$H-\overset{\overset{\displaystyle O}{\|\|}}{C}-H$	Methanal	Formaldehyde
Ketone	$CH_3-\overset{\overset{\displaystyle O}{\|\|}}{C}-CH_3$	Propanone	Acetone; dimethyl ketone

SUMMARY OF REACTIONS

The chapter sections to review are shown after the name of the reaction.

Oxidation of Aldehydes to Form Carboxylic Acids (14.3)

$$CH_3-\overset{\overset{\textstyle O}{\|}}{C}-H \quad \xrightarrow{[O]} \quad CH_3-\overset{\overset{\textstyle O}{\|}}{C}-OH$$

Acetaldehyde   Acetic acid

Reduction of Aldehydes to Form Primary Alcohols (14.3)

$$CH_3-\overset{\overset{\textstyle O}{\|}}{C}-H \ + \ H_2 \quad \xrightarrow{Ni} \quad CH_3-\overset{\overset{\textstyle OH}{|}}{CH_2}$$

Acetaldehyde   Ethanol

Reduction of Ketones to Form Secondary Alcohols (14.3)

$$CH_3-\overset{\overset{\textstyle O}{\|}}{C}-CH_3 \ + \ H_2 \quad \xrightarrow{Ni} \quad CH_3-\overset{\overset{\textstyle OH}{|}}{CH}-CH_3$$

Acetone   2-Propanol

Addition of Alcohols to Form Hemiacetals and Acetals (14.4)

$$H-\overset{\overset{\textstyle O}{\|}}{C}-H \ + \ HO-CH_3 \ \underset{}{\overset{H^+}{\rightleftharpoons}} \ H-\overset{\overset{\textstyle O-CH_3}{|}}{\underset{\underset{\textstyle OH}{|}}{C}}-H \ + \ H_2O$$

Formaldehyde   Methanol   Hemiacetal

$$H-\overset{\overset{\textstyle O-CH_3}{|}}{\underset{\underset{\textstyle OH}{|}}{C}}-H \ + \ HO-CH_3 \ \underset{}{\overset{H^+}{\rightleftharpoons}} \ H-\overset{\overset{\textstyle O-CH_3}{|}}{\underset{\underset{\textstyle O-CH_3}{|}}{C}}-H \ + \ H_2O$$

Hemiacetal   Acetal

KEY TERMS

acetal The product of the addition of two alcohols to an aldehyde or ketone.

aldehyde An organic compound with a carbonyl functional group and at least one hydrogen attached to the carbon in the carbonyl group.

Benedict's test A test for aldehydes with adjacent hydroxyl groups in which Cu^{2+} ($CuSO_4$) ions in Benedict's reagent are reduced to a brick-red solid of Cu_2O.

carbonyl group A group that has a carbon–oxygen double bond with two groups of atoms attached to the carbon at angles of 120°.

chiral Objects or molecules that have nonsuperimposable mirror images.

chiral carbon A carbon atom that is bonded to four different atoms or groups.

enantiomers Stereoisomers that are mirror images that cannot be superimposed.

Fischer projection A system for drawing stereoisomers; an intersection of a vertical and horizontal line represents a carbon atom. A vertical line represents bonds that project backwards from a carbon atom and a horizontal line represents bonds that project forward. The most highly oxidized carbon is at the top.

hemiacetal The product of the addition of one alcohol to the double bond of the carbonyl group in aldehydes and ketones.

ketone An organic compound in which the carbonyl functional group is bonded to two alkyl or aromatic groups.

reduction A decrease in the number of carbon–oxygen bonds by the addition of hydrogen to a carbonyl bond. Aldehydes are reduced to primary alcohols; ketones to secondary alcohols.

stereoisomers Isomers that have atoms bonded in the same order, but with different arrangements in space.

Tollens' test A test for aldehydes in which the Ag^+ in Tollens' reagent is reduced to metallic silver, which forms a "silver mirror" on the walls of the container.

⚛ CORE CHEMISTRY SKILLS

The chapter section containing each Core Chemistry Skill is shown in parentheses at the end of each heading.

Naming Aldehydes and Ketones (14.1)

• In the IUPAC system, an aldehyde is named by replacing the *e* in the alkane name with *al* and a ketone by replacing the *e* with *one*.

• The position of a substituent on an aldehyde is indicated by numbering the carbon chain from the carbonyl group and given in front of the name.

• For a ketone, the carbon chain is numbered from the end nearer the carbonyl group.

Example: Give the IUPAC name for the following:

$$CH_3-\overset{\overset{\textstyle CH_3}{|}}{CH}-CH_2-\overset{\overset{\textstyle O}{\|}}{C}-CH_3$$

Answer: 4-methyl-2-pentanone

Identifying Chiral Molecules (14.5)

• Chiral molecules are molecules with mirror images that cannot be superimposed on each other. These types of stereoisomers are called enantiomers.

- A chiral molecule must have at least one chiral carbon, which is a carbon bonded to four different atoms or groups of atoms.

Example: Identify each of the following as chiral or achiral:

a. $CH_3—CH_2—\underset{\underset{Br}{|}}{CH}—CH_3$

b. $CH_3—CH_2—CH_2—Br$

c. $CH_3—\underset{\underset{Br}{|}}{CH}—CH_3$

Answer: Molecule **a** is chiral; molecules **b** and **c** are achiral.

Identifying D- and L-Fischer Projections (14.5)

- The Fischer projection is a simplified way to draw the arrangements of atoms by placing the carbon atoms at the intersection of vertical and horizontal lines.

- The names of the mirror images are labeled D or L to differentiate between enantiomers of carbohydrates.

Example: Identify each of the following as the D or L stereoisomer:

a.
```
      H     O
       \   //
        C
   HO ——|—— H
    H ——|—— OH
         CH2OH
```

b.
```
       CH2OH
        |
        C=O
   HO ——|—— H
   HO ——|—— H
         CH2OH
```

Answer: In **a**, the —OH group on the chiral carbon farthest from the carbonyl group is on the right; it is the D stereoisomer. In **b**, the —OH group on the chiral carbon farthest from the carbonyl group is on the left; it is the L stereoisomer.

UNDERSTANDING THE CONCEPTS

The chapter sections to review are shown in parentheses at the end of each question.

14.43 The compound cinnamaldehyde gives the flavor to cinnamon. Identify the functional groups in cinnamaldehyde. (14.1)

Cinnamaldehyde   Cinnamon sticks

14.44 The compound frambinone has the taste of raspberries and has been used in weight loss. Identify the functional groups in frambinone. (14.1)

$$HO—\hspace{-2pt}\bigcirc\hspace{-2pt}—CH_2—CH_2—\overset{\overset{O}{\|}}{C}—CH_3$$

Frambinone

14.45 Draw the condensed and line-angle structural formulas for each of the following: (14.1)
a. *trans*-2-hexenal, alarm pheromone of ants
b. 2,6-dimethyl-5-heptenal, communication pheromone of ants

14.46 Draw the condensed structural and line-angle structural formulas for each of the following: (14.1)
a. 4-methyl-3-heptanone, ant trail pheromone
b. 2-nonanone, moth sex attractant pheromone

14.47 Why does the C=O double bond have a dipole, whereas the C=C double bond does not? (14.1)

14.48 Why are aldehydes and ketones with one to four carbon atoms soluble in water? (14.2)

14.49 Which of the following will give a positive Tollens' test? (14.3)

a. $CH_3—CH_2—\overset{\overset{O}{\|}}{C}—H$

b. $CH_3—\underset{\underset{CH_3}{|}}{CH}—\overset{\overset{O}{\|}}{C}—H$

c. $CH_3—O—CH_2—CH_3$

14.50 Which of the following will give a positive Tollens' test? (14.3)

a. $CH_3—CH_2—CH_2—OH$

b. $CH_3—\underset{\underset{OH}{|}}{CH}—CH_3$

c.
```
     O
     ||
     C—H
    /\
```

ADDITIONAL QUESTIONS AND PROBLEMS

14.51 Give the IUPAC name for each of the following compounds: (14.1)

a.

b.
a structure with an aromatic ring bearing a C(=O)—H group and two Br substituents

c. Cl—CH$_2$—CH$_2$—C(=O)—H

d. a line-angle structure with a C=O and a Cl substituent

e. CH$_3$—CH$_2$—C(=O)—CH$_2$—CH(Cl)—CH$_3$

14.52 Give the IUPAC name for each of the following compounds: (14.1)

a. a line-angle ketone structure

b. an aromatic ring with C(=O)—H and Cl substituents

c. a cyclopentanone with Cl substituent

d. CH$_3$—CH(CH$_3$)—CH(CH$_3$)—CH$_2$—C(=O)—H

e.
an aromatic ring with C(=O)—CH$_3$

14.53 Draw the condensed structural formula or line-angle structural formula, if cyclic, for each of the following: (14.1)
a. 3-methylcyclopentanone   **b.** pentanal
c. ethyl methyl ketone   **d.** 4-methylhexanal
e. 4-oxopentanal

14.54 Draw the condensed structural formula or line-angle structural formula, if cyclic, for each of the following: (14.1)
a. 2-chlorobutanal   **b.** 2-methylcyclohexanone
c. 3,5-dimethylhexanal   **d.** 3-bromocyclopentanone
e. 4-hydroxy-2-pentanone

14.55 Which of the following aldehydes or ketones are soluble in water? (14.2)

a. CH$_3$—CH$_2$—C(=O)—H   **b.** CH$_3$—C(=O)—CH$_3$

c. CH$_3$—CH$_2$—C(=O)—CH$_2$—CH$_2$—CH$_3$

14.56 Which of the following aldehydes or ketones are soluble in water? (14.2)

a. CH$_3$—CH$_2$—C(=O)—CH$_3$ **b.** CH$_3$—C(=O)—H

c. CH$_3$—CH$_2$—CH(CH$_3$)—CH$_2$—C(=O)—H

14.57 In each of the following pairs of compounds, select the compound with the higher boiling point: (14.2)

a. CH$_3$—CH$_2$—CH$_2$—OH   or   CH$_3$—C(=O)—CH$_3$

b. CH$_3$—CH$_2$—CH$_2$—CH$_3$ or   CH$_3$—CH$_2$—C(=O)—H

c. CH$_3$—CH$_2$—OH   or   CH$_3$—C(=O)—H

14.58 In each of the following pairs of compounds, select the compound with the higher boiling point: (14.2)

a. CH$_3$—C(=O)—H   or   CH$_3$—CH$_2$—CH$_2$—CH$_2$—C(=O)—H

b. CH$_3$—CH$_2$—C(=O)—H   or   CH$_3$—CH(OH)—CH$_3$

c. CH$_3$—CH$_2$—CH$_2$—CH$_3$ or   CH$_3$—C(=O)—CH$_3$

14.59 Draw the condensed structural formula for the product, if any, when each of the following is oxidized: (14.3)

a. CH$_3$—CH$_2$—C(=O)—H   **b.** CH$_3$—CH$_2$—CH$_2$—C(=O)—H

c. a cyclohexanone line-angle structure

14.60 Draw the condensed structural formula for the product, if any, when each of the following is oxidized: (14.3)

a. CH$_3$—CH$_2$—C(=O)—CH$_3$

b.
an aromatic ring with a C(=O)H group

c. CH$_3$—CH(CH$_3$)—CH$_2$—C(=O)—H

14.61 Draw the condensed structural formula for the product when hydrogen and a nickel catalyst reduce each of the following: (14.3)

a. $CH_3-\overset{\overset{\displaystyle O}{\|}}{C}-CH_3$

b. $CH_2-\overset{\overset{\displaystyle O}{\|}}{C}-H$

c. $CH_3-\overset{\overset{\displaystyle CH_3}{|}}{CH}-CH_2-\overset{\overset{\displaystyle O}{\|}}{C}-CH_3$

14.62 Draw the condensed structural formula for the product when $NaBH_4$ reduces each of the following: (14.3)

a. $CH_3-\overset{\overset{\displaystyle O}{\|}}{C}-H$

b. (cyclopentanone with methyl group)

c. $H-\overset{\overset{\displaystyle O}{\|}}{C}-H$

14.63 Give the name of the alcohol, aldehyde, or ketone produced from each of the following reactions: (14.3)
a. oxidation of 1-propanol
b. oxidation of 2-pentanol
c. reduction of butanone
d. oxidation of cyclohexanol

14.64 Give the name of the alcohol, aldehyde, or ketone produced from each of the following reactions: (14.3)
a. reduction of butyraldehyde
b. oxidation of 3-methyl-2-pentanol
c. reduction of 4-methyl-2-hexanone
d. oxidation of 3-methylcyclopentanol

14.65 Identify the following as hemiacetals or acetals. Give the IUPAC names of the carbonyl compounds and alcohols used in their synthesis. (14.4)

a. $CH_3-CH_2-\overset{\overset{\displaystyle O-CH_3}{|}}{\underset{\underset{\displaystyle O-CH_3}{|}}{C}}-H$

b. $CH_3-CH_2-\overset{\overset{\displaystyle O-CH_2-CH_3}{|}}{\underset{\underset{\displaystyle OH}{|}}{C}}-CH_3$

c. CH_3-CH_2-O $O-CH_2-CH_3$ (cyclohexane ring)

14.66 Identify the following as hemiacetals or acetals. Give the IUPAC names of the carbonyl compounds and alcohols used in their synthesis. (14.4)

a. $CH_3-CH_2-\overset{\overset{\displaystyle O-CH_3}{|}}{\underset{\underset{\displaystyle OH}{|}}{C}}-H$

b. HO $O-CH-CH_3$ with CH_3 (cyclohexane ring)

c. $CH_3-\overset{\overset{\displaystyle O-CH_2-CH_2-CH_3}{|}}{\underset{\underset{\displaystyle O-CH_2-CH_2-CH_3}{|}}{C}}-H$

14.67 Circle the chiral carbons, if any, in each of the following compounds: (14.5)

a. $H-\overset{\overset{\displaystyle Cl}{|}}{\underset{\underset{\displaystyle Cl}{|}}{C}}-\overset{\overset{\displaystyle Cl}{|}}{\underset{\underset{\displaystyle H}{|}}{C}}-OH$

b. $CH_3-\overset{\overset{\displaystyle H}{|}}{C}=\overset{\overset{\displaystyle CH_3}{|}}{C}-CH_3$

c. $HO-CH_2-\overset{\overset{\displaystyle OH}{|}}{CH}-CH_2-OH$

d. $CH_3-\overset{\overset{\displaystyle NH_2}{|}}{CH}-\overset{\overset{\displaystyle O}{\|}}{C}-H$

e. $CH_3-CH_2-\overset{\overset{\displaystyle Br}{|}}{CH}-CH_2-CH_2-CH_3$

f. (cyclohexane with OH)

14.68 Circle the chiral carbons, if any, in each of the following compounds: (14.5)

a. $CH_3-\overset{\overset{\displaystyle O-CH_3}{|}}{CH}-CH_3$

b. $CH_3-\overset{\overset{\displaystyle OH}{|}}{CH}-\overset{\overset{\displaystyle O}{\|}}{C}-CH_3$

c. $CH_3-\overset{\overset{\displaystyle OH}{|}}{\underset{\underset{\displaystyle OH}{|}}{C}}-H$

d. $CH_3-\overset{\overset{\displaystyle CH_3}{|}}{CH}-\overset{\overset{\displaystyle O}{\|}}{C}-CH_3$

e. $CH_3-\overset{\overset{\displaystyle Br}{|}}{\underset{\underset{\displaystyle OH}{|}}{C}}-CH_2-CH_3$

f. (cyclohexane with Cl and Cl)

14.69 Identify each of the following pairs of Fischer projections as enantiomers or identical compounds: (14.5)

a. CH_2OH : $H-OH$; CH_2OH and CH_2OH : $HO-H$; CH_2OH

b. $\overset{H}{\underset{C}{\diagup}}{}^{O}$: $H-OH$; CH_2OH and $\overset{H}{\underset{C}{\diagup}}{}^{O}$: $HO-H$; CH_2OH

c. CH_2OH : $Cl-H$; CH_3 and CH_2OH : $H-Cl$; CH_3

d. OH : $H-OH$; CH_3 and OH : $HO-H$; CH_3

14.70 Identify each of the following pairs of Fischer projections as enantiomers or identical compounds: (14.5)

a.
$$CH_2OH \\ H—Cl \\ CH_2CH_3$$ and $$CH_2OH \\ Cl—H \\ CH_2CH_3$$

c.
$$CH_2OH \\ H—Cl \\ CH_3$$ and $$CH_2OH \\ H—Cl \\ CH_3$$

b.
$$CH_2OH \\ H—OH \\ CH_3$$ and $$CH_2OH \\ HO—H \\ CH_3$$

d.
$$\overset{H}{\underset{}{}}\overset{O}{\underset{\parallel}{C}} \\ H—OH \\ CH_3$$ and $$\overset{H}{\underset{}{}}\overset{O}{\underset{\parallel}{C}} \\ HO—H \\ CH_3$$

CHALLENGE QUESTIONS

The following groups of questions are related to the topics in this chapter. However, they do not all follow the chapter order, and they require you to combine concepts and skills from several sections. These questions will help you increase your critical thinking skills and prepare for your next exam.

Use the following condensed and line-angle structural formulas **A** to **F** to answer problems 14.71 and 14.72: (14.1, 14.5)

A $$CH_3—CH_2—\overset{O}{\underset{\parallel}{C}}—CH_2—CH_3$$

B $$CH_3—CH_2—CH_2—\overset{O}{\underset{\parallel}{C}}—CH_3$$

C $$CH_3—\overset{O}{\underset{\parallel}{C}}—CH_2—CH_2—CH_3$$

D $$CH_3—CH_2—CH_2—CH_2—\overset{O}{\underset{\parallel}{C}}—H$$

E   (line-angle cyclopentanone structure)

F   (line-angle cyclobutane with $\overset{O}{\underset{\parallel}{C}}—H$ substituent)

14.71 True or False?
a. **A** and **B** are structural isomers.
b. **D** and **F** are aldehydes.
c. **B** and **C** are the same compound.
d. **C** and **D** are structural isomers.

14.72 True or False?
a. **E** and **F** are structural isomers.
b. **A** is chiral.
c. **A** and **C** are the same compound.
d. **B** and **E** are ketones.

14.73 A compound with the formula C_4H_8O is made by oxidation of 2-butanol and cannot be oxidized further. Draw the condensed structural formula and give the IUPAC name for the compound. (14.1, 14.3)

14.74 A compound with the formula C_4H_8O is made by oxidation of 2-methyl-1-propanol and oxidizes easily to give a carboxylic acid. Draw the condensed structural formula and give the IUPAC name for the compound. (14.1, 14.3)

14.75 Draw the condensed structural formulas and give the IUPAC names for all the aldehydes and ketones that have the molecular formula C_4H_8O. (14.1)

14.76 Draw the condensed structural formulas and give the IUPAC names for all the aldehydes and ketones that have the molecular formula $C_5H_{10}O$. (14.1)

14.77 The common name of compound **A** is propyl alcohol. When compound **A** is heated with a strong acid, it dehydrates to form compound **B** (C_3H_6). When compound **A** is oxidized, compound **C** (C_3H_6O) forms. Draw the condensed structural formulas and give the IUPAC names for compounds **A**, **B**, and **C**. (14.1, 14.3)

14.78 The common name of compound **X** is isopropyl alcohol. When compound **X** is heated with a strong acid, it dehydrates to form compound **Y** (C_3H_6). When compound **X** is oxidized, compound **Z** (C_3H_6O) forms, which cannot be oxidized further. Draw the condensed structural formulas and give the IUPAC names for compounds **X**, **Y**, and **Z**. (14.1, 14.3)

ANSWERS

Answers to Selected Questions and Problems

14.1 a. ketone
c. ketone
b. aldehyde
d. aldehyde

14.3 a. structural isomers of C_3H_6O
b. structural isomers of $C_5H_{10}O$
c. not structural isomers

14.5 a. 3-bromobutanal
c. 2-methylcyclopentanone
b. 4-hydroxy-2-pentanone
d. 3-bromobenzaldehyde

14.7 a. acetaldehyde
c. formaldehyde
b. methyl propyl ketone

14.9 a. $$CH_3—\overset{O}{\underset{\parallel}{C}}—H$$

b. $$CH_3—\overset{CH_3}{\underset{\mid}{CH}}—\overset{O}{\underset{\parallel}{C}}—CH_2—CH_3$$

c. $$CH_3—\overset{O}{\underset{\parallel}{C}}—CH_2—CH_2—CH_2—CH_3$$

d. $CH_3-CH_2-CH_2-\underset{\underset{\textstyle CH_3}{|}}{CH}-CH_2-\overset{\overset{\textstyle O}{\|}}{C}-H$

(skeletal structure of 3-methyl aldehyde with O and H)

14.11

(structure: benzaldehyde with para methoxy group)

14.13 a. $CH_3-\overset{\overset{\textstyle O}{\|}}{C}-H$

Ethanal has a higher boiling point than propane because the polar carbonyl group in ethanal forms dipole–dipole attractions.

b. Pentanal has a longer carbon chain, more electrons, and more dispersion forces, which give it a higher boiling point.

c. 1-Butanol has a higher boiling point because it can hydrogen bond with other 1-butanol molecules.

14.15 a. $CH_3-\overset{\overset{\textstyle O}{\|}}{C}-\overset{\overset{\textstyle O}{\|}}{C}-CH_2-CH_3$ has two polar carbonyl groups and can form more hydrogen bonds with water.

b. Propanal has a shorter carbon chain than pentanal, in which the larger hydrocarbon chain reduces the impact on solubility of the polar carbonyl group.

c. Acetone has a shorter carbon chain than 2-pentanone, in which the larger hydrocarbon chain reduces the impact on solubility of the polar carbonyl group.

14.17 No. A hydrocarbon chain of eight carbon atoms reduces the impact on solubility of the polar carbonyl group.

14.19 a. $H-\overset{\overset{\textstyle O}{\|}}{C}-OH$ **b.** none

c. (benzoic acid structure: $\overset{\overset{\textstyle O}{\|}}{C}-OH$ on benzene ring)   **d.** none

14.21 a. Tollens' reagent   **b.** neither   **c.** both

14.23 a. $CH_3-CH_2-CH_2-CH_2-OH$

b. $CH_3-\underset{\underset{\textstyle OH}{|}}{CH}-CH_3$

c. $CH_3-CH_2-CH_2-\underset{\underset{\textstyle Br}{|}}{CH}-CH_2-CH_2-OH$

d. $CH_3-\underset{\underset{\textstyle CH_3}{|}}{CH}-\underset{\underset{\textstyle OH}{|}}{CH}-CH_2-CH_3$

14.25 a. hemiacetal   **b.** hemiacetal   **c.** acetal
d. hemiacetal
e. acetal

14.27 a. $CH_3-\overset{\overset{\textstyle O-CH_3}{|}}{\underset{\underset{\textstyle OH}{|}}{C}}-H$ **b.** $CH_3-\overset{\overset{\textstyle O-CH_3}{|}}{\underset{\underset{\textstyle OH}{|}}{C}}-CH_3$

c. $CH_3-CH_2-CH_2-\overset{\overset{\textstyle O-CH_3}{|}}{\underset{\underset{\textstyle OH}{|}}{C}}-H$

14.29 a. $CH_3-\overset{\overset{\textstyle O-CH_3}{|}}{\underset{\underset{\textstyle O-CH_3}{|}}{C}}-H$ **b.** $CH_3-\overset{\overset{\textstyle O-CH_3}{|}}{\underset{\underset{\textstyle O-CH_3}{|}}{C}}-CH_3$

c. $CH_3-CH_2-CH_2-\overset{\overset{\textstyle O-CH_3}{|}}{\underset{\underset{\textstyle O-CH_3}{|}}{C}}-H$

14.31 a. achiral
b. chiral

(structure with Br, labeled "Chiral carbon")

c. chiral

(structure: $CH_3-CH-\overset{\overset{\textstyle O}{\|}}{C}-H$ with Br, labeled "Chiral carbon")

d. achiral

14.33 a. (Fischer projection: CHO top, HO—left Br—right, CH_3 bottom)   **b.** (Fischer projection: CHO top, Cl—left Br—right, OH bottom)

c. (Fischer projection: CHO top, HO—left H—right, CH_2CH_3 bottom)

14.35 a. identical   **b.** enantiomers
c. enantiomers   **d.** enantiomers

14.37 a. D   **b.** D   **c.** L

14.39 a. $CH_3-\underset{\underset{\textstyle CH_3}{|}}{C}=CH-CH_2-CH_2-\underset{\underset{\textstyle CH_3}{|}}{CH}-CH_2-CH_2-OH$ (labeled "Chiral carbon")

b. $H_2N-\underset{\underset{\textstyle CH_3}{|}}{CH}-\overset{\overset{\textstyle O}{\|}}{C}-OH$ (labeled "Chiral carbon")

14.41 a. ether, phenol, ketone, aromatic
b. $C_{14}H_{12}O_3$, 228.2 g/mole
c. 10.7 g of oxybenzone

14.43 aromatic, alkene, aldehyde

14.45 a. $CH_3-CH_2-CH_2$

C=C with $CH_3-CH_2-CH_2$ and H on left carbon, $\overset{\displaystyle O}{\overset{\|}{C}}-H$ and H on right carbon

b. (structure: chain with C=C and aldehyde — drawn as skeletal: $CH_3-CH_2-CH_2$ chain with double bond then $\overset{O}{\overset{\|}{C}}-H$)

$CH_3-\overset{\displaystyle CH_3}{\overset{|}{C}}=CH-CH_2-CH_2-\overset{\displaystyle CH_3}{\overset{|}{CH}}-\overset{\displaystyle O}{\overset{\|}{C}}-H$

(skeletal structure with branched methyl, chain, and aldehyde $\overset{O}{\overset{\|}{C}}-H$)

14.47 The C=O double bond has a dipole because the oxygen atom is highly electronegative compared to the carbon atom. In the C=C double bond, both atoms have the same electronegativity, and there is no dipole.

14.49 a and b

14.51 a. 2-bromo-4-chlorocyclopentanone
  b. 2,4-dibromobenzaldehyde
  c. 3-chloropropanal
  d. 2-chloro-3-pentanone
  e. 5-chloro-3-hexanone

14.53 a. (cyclopentanone with methyl substituent, O double bond)

  b. $CH_3-CH_2-CH_2-CH_2-\overset{\displaystyle O}{\overset{\|}{C}}-H$

  c. $CH_3-CH_2-\overset{\displaystyle O}{\overset{\|}{C}}-CH_3$

  d. $CH_3-CH_2-\overset{\displaystyle CH_3}{\overset{|}{CH}}-CH_2-CH_2-\overset{\displaystyle O}{\overset{\|}{C}}-H$

  e. $CH_3-\overset{\displaystyle O}{\overset{\|}{C}}-CH_2-CH_2-\overset{\displaystyle O}{\overset{\|}{C}}-H$

14.55 a and b

14.57 a. $CH_3-CH_2-CH_2-OH$ **b.** $CH_3-CH_2-\overset{\displaystyle O}{\overset{\|}{C}}-H$
  c. CH_3-CH_2-OH

14.59 a. $CH_3-CH_2-\overset{\displaystyle O}{\overset{\|}{C}}-OH$

b. $CH_3-CH_2-CH_2-\overset{\displaystyle O}{\overset{\|}{C}}-OH$

c. no reaction

14.61 a. $CH_3-\overset{\displaystyle OH}{\overset{|}{CH}}-CH_3$

  b. (benzene ring)$-CH_2-CH_2-OH$

  c. $CH_3-\overset{\displaystyle CH_3}{\overset{|}{CH}}-CH_2-\overset{\displaystyle OH}{\overset{|}{CH}}-CH_3$

14.63 a. propanal   **b.** 2-pentanone
  c. 2-butanol   **d.** cyclohexanone

14.65 a. acetal; propanal and methanol
  b. hemiacetal; butanone and ethanol
  c. acetal; cyclohexanone and ethanol

14.67 a. $H-\overset{\displaystyle Cl}{\underset{\displaystyle Cl}{\overset{|}{\underset{|}{C}}}}-\overset{\displaystyle Cl}{\underset{\displaystyle H}{\overset{|}{\underset{|}{\textcircled{C}}}}}-OH$ **b.** none

  c. none   **d.** $CH_3-\overset{\displaystyle NH_2}{\overset{|}{\textcircled{C}H}}-\overset{\displaystyle O}{\overset{\|}{C}}-H$

  e. $CH_3-CH_2-\overset{\displaystyle Br}{\overset{|}{\textcircled{C}H}}-CH_2-CH_2-CH_3$
  f. none

14.69 a. identical   **b.** enantiomers
  c. enantiomers   **d.** identical

14.71 a. true   **b.** false   **c.** true   **d.** true

14.73 $CH_3-\overset{\displaystyle O}{\overset{\|}{C}}-CH_2-CH_3$ butanone

14.75 $CH_3-CH_2-CH_2-\overset{\displaystyle O}{\overset{\|}{C}}-H$ butanal

$CH_3-\overset{\displaystyle CH_3}{\overset{|}{CH}}-\overset{\displaystyle O}{\overset{\|}{C}}-H$ 2-methylpropanal

$CH_3-\overset{\displaystyle O}{\overset{\|}{C}}-CH_2-CH_3$ butanone

14.77 a. $CH_3-CH_2-CH_2-OH$ 1-propanol
  b. $CH_3-CH=CH_2$ propene

  c. $CH_3-CH_2-\overset{\displaystyle O}{\overset{\|}{C}}-H$ propanal

CI.27 A compound called butylated hydroxytoluene, or BHT, has been added to cereal and other foods since 1947 as an antioxidant. A common name for BHT is 2,6-di-*tert*-butyl-4-methylphenol. (2.6, 7.4, 7.5, 13.1)

a. Draw the line-angle structural formula for BHT.
b. BHT is produced from 4-methylphenol and 2-methylpropene. Draw the line-angle structural formulas for these reactants.
c. What are the molecular formula and molar mass of BHT?
d. The FDA (Food and Drug Administration) allows a maximum of 50. ppm of BHT added to cereal. How many milligrams of BHT could be added to a box of cereal that contains 15 oz of dry cereal?

CI.28 Used in sunless tanning lotions, the compound 1,3-dihydroxypropanone, or dihydroxyacetone (DHA), darkens the skin without exposure to sunlight. DHA reacts with amino acids in the outer surface of the skin. A typical drugstore lotion contains 4.0% (m/v) DHA. (2.6, 7.4, 7.5, 14.1)

A sunless tanning lotion contains DHA to darken the skin.

a. Draw the condensed structural formula for DHA.
b. What are the functional groups in DHA?
c. What are the molecular formula and molar mass of DHA?
d. A bottle of sunless tanning lotion contains 200 mL of lotion. How many milligrams of DHA are in a bottle?

CI.29 Acetone (propanone), a clear liquid solvent with an acrid odor, is used to remove nail polish, paints, and resins. It has a low boiling point and is highly flammable. (7.4, 7.5, 13.4, 14.1)

Acetone is a solvent used in polish remover.

a. Draw the condensed structural formula for propanone.
b. What are the molecular formula and molar mass of propanone?
c. Draw the condensed structural formula for the alcohol that can be oxidized to produce propanone.

CI.30 Acetone (propanone) has a density of 0.786 g/mL and a heat of combustion of 428 kcal/mole. Use your answers to problem CI.29 to solve the following: (7.1, 7.6, 7.9, 8.6, 14.1)
a. Write the equation for the complete combustion of propanone.
b. How much heat, in kilojoules, is released if 2.58 g of propanone reacts with oxygen?
c. How many grams of oxygen gas are needed to react with 15.0 mL of propanone?
d. How many liters of carbon dioxide gas are produced at STP in part **c**?

CI.31 One of the components of gasoline is octane, C_8H_{18}, which has a density of 0.803 g/mL. The combustion of 1 mole of octane provides 5510 kJ. A hybrid car has a fuel tank with a capacity of 11.9 gal and a gas mileage of 45 mi/gal. (2.6, 7.1, 7.5, 7.7, 7.9, 12.2)

Octane is one of the components of gasoline.

a. Write the balanced chemical equation for the combustion of octane.
b. Is the combustion of octane endothermic or exothermic?
c. How many moles of octane are in one tank of fuel, assuming it is all octane?
d. If the total mileage of this hybrid car for one year is 24 500 mi, how many kilograms of carbon dioxide would be produced from the combustion of the fuel, assuming it is all octane?

CI.32 Ionone is a compound that gives sweet violets their aroma. The small edible purple flowers of violets are used in salads and to make teas. An antioxidant called anthocyanin produces the blue and purple colors of violets. Liquid ionone has a density of 0.935 g/mL. (7.4, 7.7, 7.9, 8.6, 12.6, 13.1, 14.1)

Ionone

The aroma of violets is because of ionone.

a. What functional groups are present in ionone?
b. Is the double bond on the side chain cis or trans?
c. What are the molecular formula and molar mass of ionone?
d. How many moles are in 2.00 mL of ionone?
e. When ionone reacts with hydrogen in the presence of a platinum catalyst, hydrogen adds to the double bonds and converts the ketone group to an alcohol. What is the condensed structural formula and molecular formula for the product?
f. How many milliliters of hydrogen gas are needed at STP to completely react 5.0 mL of ionone?

CI.33 Butyraldehyde is a clear liquid solvent with an unpleasant odor. It has a low boiling point and is highly flammable. (14.1, 14.3)

The unpleasant odor of old gym socks is because of butyraldehyde.

a. Draw the condensed structural formula for butyraldehyde.
b. Draw the line-angle structural formula for butyraldehyde.
c. What is the IUPAC name of butyraldehyde?
d. Draw the condensed structural formula for the alcohol that is produced when butyraldehyde is reduced.

CI.34 Butyraldehyde has a density of 0.802 g/mL and a heat of combustion of 1520 kJ/mole. Use your answers to problem CI.33 to solve the following: (7.1, 7.7, 7.9, 8.6)
a. Write the balanced equation for the complete combustion of butyraldehyde.
b. How many grams of oxygen gas are needed to completely react 15.0 mL of butyraldehyde?
c. How many liters of carbon dioxide gas are produced at STP in part **b**?
d. Calculate the heat, in kilojoules, that is released from the combustion of butyraldehyde in part **b**.

ANSWERS

CI.27 a.

OH

b.

OH

4-Methylphenol

CH_3

$H_2C = C - CH_3$

2-Methylpropene

c. $C_{15}H_{24}O$, 220.4 g/mole   d. 21 mg

CI.29 a. $CH_3 - \overset{\overset{\displaystyle O}{\|}}{C} - CH_3$

b. C_3H_6O, 58.08 g/mole

c. $CH_3 - \overset{\overset{\displaystyle OH}{|}}{CH} - CH_3$

CI.31 a. $2C_8H_{18}(l) + 25O_2(g) \xrightarrow{\Delta}$
$16CO_2(g) + 18H_2O(g) + 11\ 020\ kJ$

b. exothermic
c. 317 moles of octane
d. 5.10×10^3 kg of CO_2

CI.33 a. $CH_3 - CH_2 - CH_2 - \overset{\overset{\displaystyle O}{\|}}{C} - H$

b.

c. butanal
d. $CH_3 - CH_2 - CH_2 - CH_2 - OH$

15

Carbohydrates

DURING HER ANNUAL PHYSICAL EXAMINATION,
Kate, a 64-year old woman, reported that she was bothered by blurry vision, frequent
need to urinate, and in the past year she had gained 22 lb. She had tried to lose weight
and increase her exercise for the past 6 months without success. Her diet was high in
carbohydrates. For dinner, Kate typically ate two cups of pasta and three to four slices
of bread with butter or olive oil. She also ate eight to ten pieces of fresh fruit per day at
meals and as snacks. A physical examination showed that her fasting blood glucose level
was 178 mg/dL, indicating type 2 diabetes. She was referred to the diabetes specialty
clinic, where she met Paula, a diabetic nurse. Paula explained to Kate that complex
carbohydrates are long chains of glucose molecules that we obtain from ingesting
breads and grains. They are broken down in the body into glucose, which is a simple
carbohydrate or a monosaccharide.

CAREER Diabetes Nurse

Diabetes nurses teach patients about diabetes, so they can self-
manage and control their condition. This includes education on
proper diets and nutrition for both diabetic and pre-diabetic patients.
Diabetes nurses help patients learn to monitor their medication,
blood sugar levels, and to look for symptoms like diabetic nerve
damage and vision loss. Diabetes nurses may also work with
patients who have been hospitalized because of complications
from their disease. This requires a thorough knowledge of the
endocrine system, as this system is often involved with obesity and
other diseases, resulting in some overlap between diabetes and
endocrinology nursing.

C arbohydrates are the most abundant of all the organic compounds
in nature. In plants, energy from the
Sun converts carbon dioxide and water into
the carbohydrate glucose. Polysaccharides
are made when many glucose molecules link
to form long-chain polymers of starch that
store energy or link in a different way to form
cellulose to build the structure of the plant.
About 65% of the foods in our diet consist of
carbohydrates. Each day, we utilize carbohydrates in foods such as bread, pasta, potatoes,
and rice. Other carbohydrates called disaccharides include sucrose (table sugar)
and lactose in milk. During digestion and cellular metabolism, carbohydrates are
converted into glucose, which is oxidized further in our cells to provide our bodies
with energy and to provide the cells with carbon atoms for building molecules of
proteins, lipids, and nucleic acids. In addition to providing the structural frame-
work of plants, cellulose has other important uses too. The wood in our furniture,
the pages in this book, and the cotton in our clothing are all made of cellulose.

Carbohydrates contained in foods
such as pasta and bread provide
energy for the body.

LOOKING AHEAD

15.1   Carbohydrates 551
15.2   Fischer Projections of
       Monosaccharides 554
♡   **Chemistry Link to
       Health** *Hyperglycemia and
       Hypoglycemia* 557
15.3   Haworth Structures of
       Monosaccharides 558
15.4   Chemical Properties of
       Monosaccharides 561
♡   **Chemistry Link to Health**
       Testing for Glucose 563
15.5   Disaccharides 564
♡   **Chemistry Link to Health**
       *How Sweet Is My
       Sweetener?* 566
♡   **Chemistry Link to Health**
       *Blood Types and
       Carbohydrates* 567
15.6   Polysaccharides 570
℞   **Clinical Applications** 554,
       558, 570, 572, 573
℞   **Clinical Update** *Kate's
       Program for Type 2
       Diabetes* 573

CHAPTER READINESS*

⚛ CORE CHEMISTRY SKILLS
- Naming Alcohols and Phenols (13.1)
- Writing Equations for the Oxidation
  of Alcohols (13.4)

- Naming Aldehydes and Ketones (14.1)

*These Core Chemistry Skills from previous chapters are listed here for your review as you proceed to
the new material in this chapter.

15.1 Carbohydrates

Carbohydrates such as table sugar, lactose, and cellulose are all made of carbon, hydrogen,
and oxygen. Simple sugars, which have formulas of $C_n(H_2O)_n$, were once thought to be
hydrates of carbon, thus the name *carbohydrate*. In a series of reactions called *photosynthesis*, energy from the Sun is used to combine the carbon atoms from carbon dioxide (CO_2)
and the hydrogen and oxygen atoms of water (H_2O) into the carbohydrate glucose.

$$6CO_2 + 6H_2O + \text{energy} \underset{\text{Respiration}}{\overset{\text{Photosynthesis}}{\rightleftharpoons}} \underset{\text{Glucose}}{C_6H_{12}O_6} + 6O_2$$

In the body, glucose is oxidized in a series of metabolic reactions known as *respiration*,
which releases chemical energy to do work in the cells. Carbon dioxide and water are produced
and returned to the atmosphere. The combination of photosynthesis and respiration is called
the *carbon cycle*, in which energy from the Sun is stored in plants by photosynthesis and made
available to us when the carbohydrates in our diets are metabolized (see Figure 15.1).

LEARNING GOAL

Classify a monosaccharide as an
aldose or a ketose, and indicate the
number of carbon atoms.

Photosynthesis

$CO_2 + H_2O$

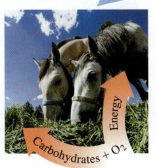

Respiration

FIGURE 15.1 ▶ During photosynthesis, energy from the Sun combines CO_2 and H_2O to
form glucose ($C_6H_{12}O_6$) and O_2. During respiration in the body, carbohydrates are
oxidized to CO_2 and H_2O, while energy is produced.

◉ What are the reactants and products of respiration?

Types of Carbohydrates

The simplest carbohydrates are the **monosaccharides**. A monosaccharide cannot be split or hydrolyzed into smaller carbohydrates. One of the most common carbohydrates, glucose, $C_6H_{12}O_6$, is a monosaccharide. A **disaccharide** consists of two monosaccharide units joined together, which can be split into two monosaccharide units. For example, ordinary table sugar, sucrose, $C_{12}H_{22}O_{11}$, is a disaccharide that can be split by water (hydrolysis) in the presence of an acid or an enzyme to give one molecule of glucose and one molecule of another monosaccharide, fructose.

$$C_{12}H_{22}O_{11} + H_2O \xrightarrow{\text{H}^+ \text{ or enzyme}} C_6H_{12}O_6 + C_6H_{12}O_6$$

Sucrose   Glucose   Fructose

A **polysaccharide** is a carbohydrate that contains many monosaccharide units, which is called a *polymer*. In the presence of an acid or an enzyme, a polysaccharide can be completely hydrolyzed to yield many monosaccharide molecules.

Example	Type of Carbohydrate	Products of Hydrolysis

 Honey contains the monosaccharides fructose and glucose.

Monosaccharide + H_2O $\xrightarrow{\text{H}^+ \text{ or enzyme}}$ no hydrolysis

 Milk contains lactose, which is a disaccharide.

Disaccharide + H_2O $\xrightarrow{\text{H}^+ \text{ or enzyme}}$ two monosaccharide molecules

 Cotton consists of the polysaccharide cellulose.

Polysaccharide + many H_2O $\xrightarrow{\text{H}^+ \text{ or enzyme}}$ many monosaccharide molecules

Monosaccharides

A monosaccharide contains several hydroxyl groups attached to a chain of three to seven carbon atoms that also contains an aldehyde or a ketone group. Thus, a monosaccharide is known as a polyhydroxy aldehyde or polyhydroxy ketone. In an **aldose**, the first carbon in the chain is an aldehyde, whereas a **ketose** has a ketone as the second carbon atom.

Erythrulose, used in sunless tanning lotions, reacts with amino acids or proteins in the skin to produce a bronze color.

Monosaccharides are also classified by the number of carbon atoms. A monosaccharide with three carbon atoms is a *triose*, one with four carbon atoms is a *tetrose*; a *pentose* has five carbons, and a *hexose* contains six carbons. We can use both classification systems to indicate the aldehyde or ketone group and the number of carbon atoms. An aldopentose is a five-carbon monosaccharide that is an aldehyde; a ketohexose is a six-carbon monosaccharide that is a ketone.

Glyceraldehyde (aldotriose)   Threose (aldotetrose)   Ribose (aldopentose)   Fructose (ketohexose)

► SAMPLE PROBLEM 15.1 Monosaccharides

Classify each of the following monosaccharides as an aldopentose, ketopentose, aldohexose, or ketohexose:

a. Ribulose

b. Glucose

SOLUTION

a. Ribulose has five carbon atoms (pentose) and is a ketone, which makes it a ketopentose.
b. Glucose has six carbon atoms (hexose) and is an aldehyde, which makes it an aldohexose.

STUDY CHECK 15.1

Classify the following monosaccharide, erythrose, as an aldotetrose, ketotetrose, aldopentose, or ketopentose:

ANSWER
aldotetrose

QUESTIONS AND PROBLEMS

15.1 Carbohydrates

LEARNING GOAL Classify a monosaccharide as an aldose or a ketose, and indicate the number of carbon atoms.

15.1 What reactants are needed for photosynthesis and respiration?

15.2 What is the relationship between photosynthesis and respiration?

15.3 What is a monosaccharide? A disaccharide?

15.4 What is a polysaccharide?

15.5 What functional groups are found in all monosaccharides?

15.6 What is the difference between an aldose and a ketose?

15.7 What are the functional groups and number of carbons in a ketopentose?

15.8 What are the functional groups and number of carbons in an aldohexose?

℞ Clinical Applications

15.9 Classify each of the following monosaccharides as an aldopentose, ketopentose, aldohexose, or ketohexose:

a. Psicose is a carbohydrate present in low amounts in foods.

$$
\begin{array}{c}
CH_2OH \\
| \\
C{=}O \\
| \\
H{-}C{-}OH \\
| \\
H{-}C{-}OH \\
| \\
H{-}C{-}OH \\
| \\
CH_2OH
\end{array}
$$

Psicose

b. Lyxose is a component of bacterial glycolipids.

$$
\begin{array}{c}
H{}{\diagdown}{}O \\
C \\
| \\
HO{-}C{-}H \\
| \\
HO{-}C{-}H \\
| \\
H{-}C{-}OH \\
| \\
CH_2OH
\end{array}
$$

Lyxose

15.10 Classify each of the following monosaccharides as an aldopentose, ketopentose, aldohexose, or ketohexose:

a. A solution of xylose is given to a patient to test its absorption by the intestines.

$$
\begin{array}{c}
H{}{\diagdown}{}O \\
C \\
| \\
H{-}C{-}OH \\
| \\
HO{-}C{-}H \\
| \\
H{-}C{-}OH \\
| \\
CH_2OH
\end{array}
$$

Xylose

b. Tagatose is a carbohydrate found in fruit that is similar in sweetness to sugar.

$$
\begin{array}{c}
CH_2OH \\
| \\
C{=}O \\
| \\
HO{-}C{-}H \\
| \\
HO{-}C{-}H \\
| \\
H{-}C{-}OH \\
| \\
CH_2OH
\end{array}
$$

Tagatose

15.2 Fischer Projections of Monosaccharides

LEARNING GOAL

Identify and draw the D and L configurations of the Fischer projections for common monosaccharides.

L-Glyceraldehyde   D-Glyceraldehyde

A Fischer projection for the simplest aldose, glyceraldehyde, is drawn with vertical and horizontal lines that represent the carbon chain. The aldehyde group (the most oxidized carbon) is placed at the top of the vertical line and the —H and —OH groups are on the horizontal intersecting line. In L-glyceraldehyde, the letter L is assigned to the enantiomer with the —OH group on the left of the chiral carbon. In D-glyceraldehyde, the —OH group is on the right. The carbon atom in the —CH₂OH group at the bottom of the Fischer projection is not chiral, because it does not have four different groups bonded to it.

The most common monosaccharides contain five or six carbon atoms with several chiral carbons. A chiral carbon atom is attached to four different atoms or groups. Each Fischer projection of a monosaccharide can be drawn as a mirror image, which gives a pair of enantiomers. By convention, the —OH group farthest from the aldehyde or ketone group is used to determine the D or L configuration of a monosaccharide. The following are the Fischer projections for the D and L enantiomers of ribose, a five-carbon monosaccharide, and the D and L enantiomers of glucose, a six-carbon monosaccharide. The vertical carbon chain is numbered starting from the top carbon.

In each pair of mirror images, it is important to see that all of the —OH groups on chiral carbon atoms are reversed so that they appear on the opposite sides of the molecule. For example, in L-ribose, all of the —OH groups drawn on the left side of the vertical line are drawn on the right side in the mirror image of D-ribose.

SAMPLE PROBLEM 15.2 Fischer Projections for Monosaccharides

Ribulose, which is used in various brands of artificial sweeteners, has the following Fischer projection:

```
        CH₂OH
         |
         C=O
         |
    H ——— OH
         |
    H ——— OH
         |
        CH₂OH
```

Identify the compound as D- or L-ribulose.

Guide to Identifying D- or L-Monosaccharides

STEP 1
Number the carbon chain starting at the top of the Fischer projection.

STEP 2
Locate the chiral carbon farthest from the top of the Fischer projection.

STEP 3
Identify the position of the —OH group as D- or L-.

SOLUTION

	Given	**Need**
ANALYZE THE PROBLEM	Fischer projection of ribulose	identify as D- or L-ribulose

STEP 1 Number the carbon chain starting at the top of the Fischer projection.

```
        CH₂OH
        1|
         C=O
        2|
    H ——— OH
        3|
    H ——— OH
        4|
        CH₂OH
        5
```

STEP 2 Locate the chiral carbon farthest from the top of the Fischer projection. The chiral carbon farthest from the top is carbon 4.

$$
\begin{array}{c}
\underset{1}{\text{CH}_2\text{OH}} \\
| \\
\underset{2}{\text{C}}=\text{O} \\
| \\
\text{H}\!-\!\!\underset{3}{}\!\!-\!\text{OH} \\
| \\
\boxed{\text{H}\!-\!\!\underset{4}{}\!\!-\!\text{OH}} \\
| \\
\underset{5}{\text{CH}_2\text{OH}}
\end{array}
$$

STEP 3 Identify the position of the —OH group as D- or L-. In this Fischer projection, the —OH group is drawn on the right of carbon 4, which makes it D-ribulose.

STUDY CHECK 15.2

Draw and name the Fischer projection for the mirror image of the ribulose in Sample Problem 15.2.

ANSWER

$$
\begin{array}{c}
\text{CH}_2\text{OH} \\
| \\
\text{C}=\text{O} \\
| \\
\text{HO}\!-\!\!\!\!-\!\text{H} \\
| \\
\text{HO}\!-\!\!\!\!-\!\text{H} \\
| \\
\text{CH}_2\text{OH}
\end{array}
$$

L-Ribulose

Some Important Monosaccharides

D-Glucose, D-galactose, and D-fructose are the most important monosaccharides. They are all hexoses with the molecular formula $C_6H_{12}O_6$ and are isomers of each other. Although we can draw Fischer projections for their D and L enantiomers, the D enantiomers are more commonly found in nature and used in the cells of the body. The Fischer projections for the D enantiomers are drawn as follows:

D-Glucose   D-Galactose   D-Fructose

D-Glucose

The most common hexose, **D-glucose**, $C_6H_{12}O_6$, also known as dextrose and blood sugar, is found in fruits, vegetables, corn syrup, and honey (see Figure 15.2). D-glucose is a building block of the disaccharides sucrose, lactose, and maltose, and polysaccharides such as amylose, cellulose, and glycogen.

In the body, glucose normally occurs at a concentration of 70 to 90 mg/dL (1 dL = 100 mL) of blood. Excess glucose is converted to glycogen and stored in the liver and muscle. When the amount of glucose exceeds the amount is needed for energy in the body or stored as glycogen, the excess glucose is converted to fat, which can be stored in unlimited amounts.

FIGURE 15.2 ▶ The sweet taste of honey is because of the monosaccharides D-glucose and D-fructose.

Q What are some differences in the Fischer projections of D-glucose and D-fructose?

D-Glucose   D-Fructose

D-Galactose

D-Galactose, $C_6H_{12}O_6$, is an aldohexose that is obtained from the disaccharide lactose, which is found in milk and milk products. D-Galactose is important in the cellular membranes of the brain and nervous system. The only difference in the Fischer projections of D-glucose and D-galactose is the arrangement of the —OH group on carbon 4.

In a condition called *galactosemia*, an enzyme needed to convert D-galactose to D-glucose is missing. The accumulation of D-galactose in the blood and tissues can lead to cataracts, mental retardation, failure to thrive, and liver disease. The treatment for galactosemia is the removal of all foods containing D-galactose, mainly milk and milk products as well as breast milk, from the diet. However, soy milk does not contain lactose or D-galactose, and may be given to infants with galactosemia. If this is done for an infant immediately after birth, the damaging effects of D-galactose accumulation can be avoided.

D-Fructose

In contrast to D-glucose and D-galactose, **D-fructose**, $C_6H_{12}O_6$, is a ketohexose. The structure of D-fructose differs from glucose at carbons 1 and 2 by the location of the carbonyl group. D-Fructose is the sweetest of the carbohydrates, almost twice as sweet as sucrose (table sugar). This characteristic makes D-fructose popular with dieters because less fructose, and therefore fewer calories, is needed to provide a pleasant taste. D-Fructose, also called levulose and fruit sugar, is found in fruit juices and honey (see Figure 15.2).

D-Fructose is also obtained as one of the hydrolysis products of sucrose, the disaccharide known as table sugar. High-fructose corn syrup (HFCS) is a sweetener that is produced by using an enzyme to break down sucrose to D-glucose and D-fructose. An HFCS mixture containing about 50% D-fructose and 50% D-glucose is used in soft drinks and many foods, such as baked goods.

A food label shows that high fructose corn syrup is the sweetener in this product.

Chemistry Link to **Health**

Hyperglycemia and Hypoglycemia

Kate's doctor ordered an oral glucose tolerance test (OGTT) to evaluate her body's ability to return to normal glucose concentrations (70 to 90 mg/dL) in response to the ingestion of a specified amount of glucose. After Kate fasted for 12 h, she drinks a solution containing 75 g of glucose. A blood sample is taken immediately, followed by more blood samples each half-hour for 2 h, and then every hour for a total of 5 h. After her test, Kate was told that her blood glucose was 178 mg/dL, which indicates hyperglycemia. The term *glyc* or *gluco* refers to "sugar." The prefix *hyper* means above or over; *hypo* means below or under. Thus, the blood sugar level in *hyperglycemia* is above normal and in *hypoglycemia* it is below normal.

An example of a disease that can cause hyperglycemia is *type 2 diabetes*, which occurs when the pancreas is unable to produce sufficient quantities of insulin. As a result, glucose levels in the body fluids can rise as high as 350 mg/dL. Kate's symptoms of type 2 diabetes include thirst, excessive urination, and increased appetite. In older adults, type 2 diabetes is sometimes a consequence of excessive weight gain.

When a person is hypoglycemic, the blood glucose level rises and then decreases rapidly to levels as low as 40 mg/dL. In some cases, hypoglycemia is caused by overproduction of insulin by the pancreas. Low blood glucose can cause dizziness, general weakness, and muscle tremors. A diet may be prescribed that consists of several small meals high in protein and low in carbohydrate. Some hypoglycemic patients are finding success with diets that include more complex carbohydrates rather than simple sugars.

A glucose solution is given to determine blood glucose levels.

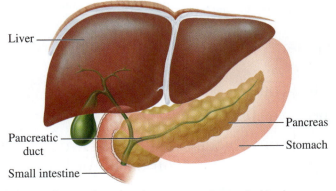

The insulin produced in the pancreas is needed in the digestive system for the metabolism of glucose.

QUESTIONS AND PROBLEMS

15.2 Fischer Projections of Monosaccharides

LEARNING GOAL Identify and draw the D and L configurations of the Fischer projections for common monosaccharides.

15.11 Identify each of the following as the D or L enantiomer:

a.

Threose

b.

Xylulose

c.

Mannose

d.

Allose

15.12 Identify each of the following as the D or L enantiomer:

a.

Arabinose

b.

Sorbose

c.

Lyxose

d.

Ribose

15.13 Draw the Fischer projection for the other enantiomer of **a** to **d** in problem 15.11.

15.14 Draw the Fischer projection for the other enantiomer of **a** to **d** in problem 15.12.

15.15 Draw the Fischer projections for D-glucose and L-glucose.

15.16 Draw the Fischer projections for D-fructose and L-fructose.

℞ Clinical Applications

15.17 An infant with galactosemia can utilize D-glucose in milk but not D-galactose. How does the Fischer projection of D-galactose differ from that of D-glucose?

15.18 D-Fructose is the sweetest monosaccharide. How does the Fischer projection of D-fructose differ from that of D-glucose?

15.19 Identify the monosaccharide that fits each of the following descriptions:
   a. is also called blood sugar
   b. is not metabolized in a condition known as galactosemia

15.20 Identify a monosaccharide that fits each of the following descriptions:
   a. found in high blood levels in diabetes
   b. is also called fruit sugar

LEARNING GOAL

Draw and identify the Haworth structures for monosaccharides.

⚛ CORE CHEMISTRY SKILL

Drawing Haworth Structures

15.3 Haworth Structures of Monosaccharides

Up until now, we have drawn the Fischer projections for monosaccharides as open chains. However, the most stable form of pentoses and hexoses are five- or six-atom rings. These rings, known as **Haworth structures**, are the cyclic hemiacetals produced from the reaction of a carbonyl group and a hydroxyl group in the *same* molecule. We will now show how to draw the Haworth structure for D-glucose from its Fischer projection.

Drawing Haworth Structures

To convert a Fischer projection to a Haworth structure, turn the Fischer projection clockwise by 90°. The —H and —OH groups on the right of the vertical carbon chain are now below the horizontal carbon chain. Those on the left of the open chain are now above the horizontal carbon chain.

Fold the horizontal carbon chain into a hexagon, rotate the groups on carbon 5, and bond the O on carbon 5 to carbon 1. With carbons 2 and 3 as the base of a hexagon, move the remaining carbons upward. Rotate the groups on carbon 5 so that the —OH group

D-Glucose (open chain)

is close to carbon 1. To complete the Haworth structure, draw a bond between the oxygen of the —OH group on carbon 5 to carbon 1 to form a hemiacetal.

Rotation of groups on carbon 5 ⇌ Carbon-5 oxygen bonds to carbon 1 ⇌ Cyclic hemiacetal structure

Because the new —OH group can be drawn above or below the plane of the Haworth structure, there are two forms of D-glucose. These different forms, called *anomers*, differ only by the position of the —OH group at carbon 1. In the α (alpha) anomer, the —OH group is drawn below the plane of the ring. In the β (beta) anomer, the —OH group is drawn above the plane of the ring. By convention, the carbon atoms in the ring are drawn as corners.

Hydroxyl group on new chiral carbon

← Anomeric carbon
α Anomer
α-D-Glucose

Mutarotation of α- and β-D-Glucose

In an aqueous solution, the Haworth structure of α-D-glucose opens to give the open chain of D-glucose, which has an aldehyde group. At any given time, there is only a trace amount of the open chain because it closes quickly to form a stable cyclic structure. However, when the open chain closes again it can form β-D-glucose. In this process called *mutarotation*, each anomer converts to the open chain and back again. As the ring opens and closes, the —OH group on carbon 1 can form either the α or β anomer. An aqueous glucose solution contains a mixture of 36% α-D-glucose and 64% β-D-glucose.

β Anomer
OH
← Anomeric carbon
β-D-Glucose

α-D-Glucose (36%) ⇌ D-Glucose open chain (trace) — Open chain with aldehyde group ⇌ β-D-Glucose (64%) — β Anomer

Haworth Structures of Galactose

Galactose is an aldohexose that differs from glucose only in the arrangement of the —OH group on carbon 4. Thus, its Haworth structure is similar to glucose, except that the —OH group on carbon 4 is drawn above the ring. Galactose also exists as α and β anomers.

D-Galactose

Open chain of D-galactose

α-D-Galactose

β-D-Galactose

Haworth Structures of Fructose

In contrast to glucose and galactose, fructose is a ketohexose. The Haworth structure for fructose is a five-atom ring with carbon 2 at the right corner of the ring. The cyclic structure forms when the —OH group on carbon 5 reacts with carbon 2 in the carbonyl group. The new —OH group on carbon 2 gives the α and β anomers of fructose.

D-Fructose

Open chain of D-fructose

α-D-Fructose

β-D-Fructose

▶ **SAMPLE PROBLEM 15.3** **Drawing Haworth Structures for Sugars**

D-Mannose, a carbohydrate found in immunoglobulins, has the following Fischer projection. Draw the Haworth structure for β-D-mannose.

D-Mannose

Guide to Drawing Haworth Structures

STEP 1
Turn the Fischer projection clockwise by 90°.

STEP 2
Fold the horizontal carbon chain into a hexagon, rotate the groups on carbon 5, and bond the O on carbon 5 to carbon 1.

STEP 3
Draw the new —OH group on carbon 1 below the ring to give the α anomer or above the ring to give the β anomer.

SOLUTION

STEP 1 Turn the Fischer projection clockwise by 90°.

STEP 2 Fold the horizontal carbon chain into a hexagon, rotate the groups on carbon 5, and bond the O on carbon 5 to carbon 1.

STEP 3 Draw the new —OH group on carbon 1 above the ring to give the β anomer.

STUDY CHECK 15.3

Draw the Haworth structure for α-D-mannose.

ANSWER

QUESTIONS AND PROBLEMS

15.3 Haworth Structures of Monosaccharides

LEARNING GOAL Draw and identify the Haworth structures for monosaccharides.

15.21 What are the kind and number of atoms in the ring portion of the Haworth structure of glucose?

15.22 What are the kind and number of atoms in the ring portion of the Haworth structure of fructose?

15.23 Draw the Haworth structures for α- and β-D-glucose.

15.24 Draw the Haworth structures for α- and β-D-fructose.

15.25 Identify each of the following as the α or β anomer:

a.

b.

15.26 Identify each of the following as the α or β anomer:

a.

b.

15.4 Chemical Properties of Monosaccharides

Monosaccharides contain functional groups that can undergo chemical reactions. In an aldose, the aldehyde group can be oxidized to a carboxylic acid. The carbonyl group in both an aldose and a ketose can be reduced to give a hydroxyl group. The hydroxyl groups can react with other compounds to form a variety of derivatives that are important in biological structures.

LEARNING GOAL

Identify the products of oxidation or reduction of monosaccharides; determine whether a carbohydrate is a reducing sugar.

Oxidation of Monosaccharides

Although monosaccharides exist mostly in cyclic forms, we have seen that a small amount of the open-chain form is always present, which provides an aldehyde group. An aldehyde group with an adjacent hydroxyl can be oxidized to a carboxylic acid by an oxidizing agent such as Benedict's reagent. The sugar acids are named by replacing the *ose* ending of the monosaccharide with *onic acid*. Then the Cu^{2+} is reduced to Cu^+, which forms a brick-red precipitate of Cu_2O. A carbohydrate that reduces another substance is called a **reducing sugar**.

Open chain of D-glucose, a reducing sugar

D-Gluconic acid

Fructose, a ketohexose, is also a reducing sugar. Usually a ketone cannot be oxidized. However, in a basic Benedict's solution, a rearrangement occurs between the ketone group on carbon 2 and the hydroxyl group on carbon 1. As a result, fructose is converted to glucose, which produces an aldehyde group with an adjacent hydroxyl that can be oxidized.

D-Fructose (ketose)

D-Glucose (aldose)

Reduction of Monosaccharides

The reduction of the carbonyl group in monosaccharides produces sugar alcohols, which are also called *alditols*. D-Glucose is reduced to D-glucitol, better known as D-sorbitol. The sugar alcohols are named by replacing the *ose* ending of the monosaccharide with *itol*. Sugar alcohols such as D-sorbitol, D-xylitol from D-xylose, and D-mannitol from D-mannose are used as sweeteners in many sugar-free products such as diet drinks and sugarless gum as well as products for people with diabetes. However, there are some side effects of these sugar substitutes. Some people experience some discomfort such as gas and diarrhea from the ingestion of sugar alcohols. The development of cataracts in diabetics is attributed to the accumulation of D-sorbitol in the lens of the eye.

D-glucitol or D-sorbitol is used as a low-calorie sweetener in diet drinks and sugarless gum.

D-Glucose

D-Glucitol or D-Sorbitol

▶ **SAMPLE PROBLEM 15.4 Reducing Sugars**

Why is D-glucose called a reducing sugar?

SOLUTION

The aldehyde group with an adjacent hydroxyl of D-glucose is easily oxidized by Benedict's reagent. A carbohydrate that reduces Cu^{2+} to Cu^+ is called a reducing sugar.

STUDY CHECK 15.4

A solution containing a tablet of Benedict's reagent turns brick red with a urine sample. According to Table 15.1, what might this result indicate?

ANSWER

The brick-red color of the Benedict's reagent shows a high level of reducing sugar (probably glucose) in the urine, which may indicate type 2 diabetes.

Benedict's solution gives a brick red precipitate with reducing sugars.

Chemistry Link to **Health**

Testing for Glucose

Normally, blood glucose flows through the kidneys and is reabsorbed into the bloodstream. However, if the blood plasma level exceeds about 160 mg of glucose/dL the kidneys cannot reabsorb all of the glucose, and it spills over into the urine, a condition known as *glucosuria*. A symptom of diabetes is a high level of glucose in the urine.

Benedict's test can be used to determine the presence of glucose in urine. The amount of copper(I) oxide (Cu_2O) formed is proportional to the amount of reducing sugar present in the urine. Low to moderate levels of reducing sugar turn the solution green; solutions with high glucose levels turn Benedict's reagent yellow or brick red.

In another clinical test, the presence of glucose in the urine can be detected using a paper strip containing *o*-methylaniline and two enzymes glucose oxidase and peroxidase. When the paper strip comes in contact with any glucose in the urine, glucose and oxygen are converted by glucose oxidase to gluconic acid and hydrogen peroxide.

Then peroxidase converts the hydrogen peroxide into a compound that reacts with *o*-methylaniline in the test strip to form a color ranging from green to a dark brown. The intensity of the color depends on the amount of glucose present in the urine. Table 15.1 lists some colors associated with the concentration of glucose in the urine.

$$H_2O_2 + \text{dye } (o\text{-methylaniline}) \xrightarrow{\text{Peroxidase}} \text{colored products}$$

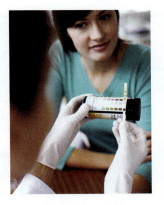

o-Methylaniline

The color of the dye *o*-methylaniline on a test strip determines the glucose level in urine.

D-Glucose $+ O_2 \xrightarrow{\text{Glucose oxidase}}$ D-Gluconic acid $+ H_2O_2$ (Hydrogen peroxide) (Oxidized)

TABLE 15.1 Glucose Oxidase Test Results

	Glucose Present in Urine	
	% (m/v)	mg/dL
Blue	0	0
Blue-green	0.10	100
Green	0.25	250
Green-brown	0.50	500
Brown	1.00	1000
Dark-brown	2.00	2000

QUESTIONS AND PROBLEMS

15.4 Chemical Properties of Monosaccharides

LEARNING GOAL Identify the products of oxidation or reduction of monosaccharides; determine whether a carbohydrate is a reducing sugar.

15.27 Draw the Fischer projection for D-xylitol produced when D-xylose is reduced.

D-Xylose

15.28 Draw the Fischer projection for D-mannitol produced when D-mannose is reduced.

D-Mannose

15.29 Draw the Fischer projection for the oxidation and the reduction products of D-arabinose. What are the names of the sugar acid and the sugar alcohol produced?

D-Arabinose

15.30 Draw the Fischer projection for the oxidation and the reduction products of D-ribose. What are the names of the sugar acid and sugar alcohol produced?

D-Ribose

LEARNING GOAL

Describe the monosaccharide units and linkages in disaccharides.

15.5 Disaccharides

A disaccharide is composed of two monosaccharides linked together. The most common disaccharides are maltose, lactose, and sucrose. When two monosaccharides combine in a dehydration reaction, the product is a disaccharide. The reaction occurs between the hydroxyl group on carbon 1 and one of the hydroxyl groups on a second monosaccharide.

$$\text{Glucose + glucose} \xrightarrow{\text{Maltose synthase}} \text{maltose} + H_2O$$
$$\text{Glucose + galactose} \xrightarrow{\text{Lactose synthase}} \text{lactose} + H_2O$$
$$\text{Glucose + fructose} \xrightarrow{\text{Sucrose synthase}} \text{sucrose} + H_2O$$

Maltose, or malt sugar, is obtained from starch and is found in germinating grains. When maltose in barley and other grains is hydrolyzed by yeast enzymes, glucose is obtained, which can undergo fermentation to give ethanol. Maltose is used in cereals, candies, and the brewing of beverages.

In the Haworth structure of a disaccharide, a **glycosidic bond** is a hemiacetal bond that connects two monosaccharides. In maltose, a glycosidic bond forms between the —OH groups of carbons 1 and 4 of two α-D-glucose molecules with a loss of a water molecule. The glycosidic bond in maltose is designated as an $\alpha(1 \rightarrow 4)$ linkage to show that an alpha —OH group on carbon 1 is joined to carbon 4 of the second glucose molecule. Because the second glucose molecule still has a free —OH group on carbon 1, it can form an open chain, which allows maltose to form both α and β anomers. The open chain provides an aldehyde group that can be oxidized, making maltose a reducing sugar.

CH_2OH ... (structures)

α-D-Glucose   + α-D-Glucose

$\downarrow$

$\alpha(1\rightarrow4)$-Glycosidic bond

$+ \; H_2O$

α Anomer

α-Maltose, a disaccharide

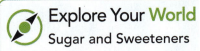
Lactose, milk sugar, is a disaccharide found in milk and milk products (see Figure 15.3). The bond in lactose is a $\beta(1\rightarrow4)$-glycosidic bond because the —OH group on carbon 1 of β-D-galactose forms a glycosidic bond with the —OH group on carbon 4 of a D-glucose molecule. Because D-glucose still has a free —OH group on carbon 1, it can form an open chain, which allows lactose to form both α and β anomers. The open chain provides an aldehyde group that can be oxidized, making lactose a reducing sugar.

Lactose makes up 6 to 8% of human milk and about 4 to 5% of cow's milk, and it is used in products that attempt to duplicate mother's milk. When a person does not produce sufficient quantities of the enzyme lactase, which is needed to hydrolyze lactose, it remains undigested when it enters the colon. Then bacteria in the colon digest the lactose in a fermentation process that creates large amounts of gas including carbon dioxide and

FIGURE 15.3 ▶ Lactose, a disaccharide found in milk and milk products, contains galactose and glucose.

Q What type of glycosidic bond links galactose and glucose in lactose?

CH_2OH ... β-D-Galactose   + α-D-Glucose

$\downarrow$

CH_2OH ... $\beta(1\rightarrow4)$-Glycosidic bond $+ \; H_2O$ α Anomer

α-Lactose, a disaccharide

FIGURE 15.4 ▶ Sucrose, a disaccharide obtained from sugar beets and sugar cane, contains glucose and fructose.

Q Why is sucrose a nonreducing sugar?

methane, which cause bloating and abdominal cramps. In some commercial milk products, lactase has already been added to break down lactose.

Sucrose consists of an α-D-glucose and a β-D-fructose molecule joined by an $\alpha, \beta(1 \rightarrow 2)$-glycosidic bond (see Figure 15.4). Unlike maltose and lactose, the glycosidic bond in sucrose is between carbon 1 of glucose and carbon 2 of fructose. Thus, sucrose cannot form an open chain and cannot be oxidized. Sucrose cannot react with Benedict's reagent and is not a reducing sugar.

The sugar we use to sweeten our cereal, coffee, or tea is sucrose. Most of the sucrose for table sugar comes from sugar cane (20% by mass) or sugar beets (15% by mass). Both the raw and refined forms of sugar are sucrose. Some estimates indicate that each person in the United States consumes an average of 68 kg (150 lb) of sucrose every year, either by itself or in a variety of food products.

Chemistry Link to **Health**

How Sweet Is My Sweetener?

Although many of the monosaccharides and disaccharides taste sweet, they differ considerably in their degree of sweetness. Dietetic foods contain sweeteners that are noncarbohydrate or carbohydrates that are sweeter than sucrose. Some examples of sweeteners compared with sucrose are shown in Table 15.2.

Sucralose, which is known as Splenda, is made from sucrose by replacing some of the hydroxyl groups with chlorine atoms.

Aspartame, which is marketed as NutraSweet or Equal, is used in a large number of sugar-free products. It is a noncarbohydrate sweetener made of aspartic acid and a methyl ester of phenylalanine. It does have some caloric value, but it is so sweet that a very small quantity is needed. However, phenylalanine, one of the breakdown products, poses a danger to anyone who cannot metabolize it properly, a condition called *phenylketonuria* (PKU).

Sucralose (Splenda)

Aspartame (NutraSweet)

Another artificial sweetener, Neotame, is a modification of the aspartame structure. The addition of a large alkyl group to the amine group prevents enzymes from breaking the amide bond between aspartic acid and phenylalanine. Thus, phenylalanine is not produced when Neotame is used as a sweetener. Very small amounts of Neotame are needed because it is about 10 000 times sweeter than sucrose.

Large alkyl group
to modify Aspartame   Neotame

TABLE 15.2 Relative Sweetness of Sugars and Artificial Sweeteners

	Sweetness Relative to Sucrose (= 100)
Monosaccharides	
Galactose	30
Glucose	75
Fructose	175
Disaccharides	
Lactose	16
Maltose	33
Sucrose	100
Sugar Alcohols	
Sorbitol	60
Maltitol	80
Xylitol	100
Artificial Sweeteners (Noncarbohydrate)	
Aspartame	18 000
Saccharin	45 000
Sucralose	60 000
Neotame	1 000 000

Saccharin, which is marketed as Sweet'N Low, has been used as a noncarbohydrate artificial sweetener for more than 60 yr. The use of saccharin has been banned in Canada because studies indicate that it may cause bladder tumors. However, it has still been approved by the FDA for use in the United States.

Saccharin (Sweet'N Low)

Artificial sweeteners may be used as sugar substitutes.

 # Chemistry Link to **Health**
Blood Types and Carbohydrates

Every individual's blood can be typed as one of four blood groups: A, B, AB, and O. Although there is some variation among ethnic groups in the United States, the incidence of blood types in the general population is about 43% O, 40% A, 12% B, and 5% AB.

The blood types A, B, and O are determined by terminal saccharides attached to the surface of red blood cells. Blood type O has three terminal monosaccharides: *N*-acetylglucosamine, galactose, and fucose. Blood type A contains the same three monosaccharides, but in addition, a molecule of *N*-acetylgalactosamine is attached to galactose in the saccharide chain. Blood type B also contains the same three monosaccharides, but in addition, a second molecule of galactose is attached to the saccharide chain. Blood type AB consists of the same monosaccharides found in blood types A and B. The structures of these monosaccharides are as follows:

N-Acetylglucosamine (*N*-AcGlu)   *N*-Acetylgalactosamine (*N*-AcGal)

← *N*-Acetyl →

L-Fucose (Fuc)   D-Galactose (Gal)

Because there is a different monosaccharide in type A blood than in type B blood, persons with type A blood produce antibodies against type B, and vice versa. For example, if a person with type A blood receives a transfusion of type B blood, the donor red blood cells are treated as if they are foreign invaders. An immune reaction occurs when the body sees the foreign saccharides on the red blood cells and makes antibodies against these donor red blood cells. The red blood cells will then clump together, or agglutinate, resulting in kidney failure, circulatory collapse, and death. The same thing will happen if a person with type B blood receives type A blood.

Because type O blood has only the three common terminal monosaccharides, a person with type O produces antibodies against blood types A, B, and AB. However, persons with blood types A, B, and AB can receive type O blood. Thus, persons with type O blood are *universal donors*. Because type AB blood contains all the terminal monosaccharides, a person with type AB blood produces no antibodies to type A, B, or O blood. Persons with type AB blood are *universal recipients*. Table 15.3 summarizes the compatibility of blood groups for transfusion.

Terminal Saccharides for Each Blood Type

Red blood cell surface

N-Acetylglucosamine   *N*-Acetylgalactosamine

Fucose   Galactose

Blood from a donor is screened to make sure that there is an exact match with the blood type of the recipient.

TABLE 15.3 Compatibility of Blood Groups

Blood Type	Produces Antibodies Against	Can Receive
A	B, AB	A, O
B	A, AB	B, O
AB universal recipient	None	A, B, AB, O
O universal donor	A, B, AB	O

▶ SAMPLE PROBLEM 15.5
Glycosidic Bonds in Disaccharides

Melibiose is a disaccharide that is 30 times sweeter than sucrose.

a. What are the monosaccharide units in melibiose?
b. What type of glycosidic bond links the monosaccharides?
c. Identify the structure as α- or β-melibiose.

SOLUTION

a. First monosaccharide
(left)

When the —OH group on carbon 4 is above the plane, it is D-galactose. When the —OH group on carbon 1 is below the plane, it is α-D-galactose.

Second monosaccharide
(right)

When the —OH group on carbon 4 is below the plane, it is α-D-glucose.

b. Type of glycosidic bond

The —OH group at carbon 1 of α-D-galactose bonds with the —OH group on carbon 6 of glucose, which makes it an α(1 → 6)-glycosidic bond.

c. Name of disaccharide

The —OH group on carbon 1 of glucose is below the plane, which α-melibiose.

STUDY CHECK 15.5

Cellobiose is a disaccharide composed of two D-glucose molecules connected by a β(1 → 4)-glycosidic linkage. Draw the Haworth structure for β-cellobiose.

ANSWER

QUESTIONS AND PROBLEMS

15.5 Disaccharides

LEARNING GOAL Describe the monosaccharide units and linkages in disaccharides.

15.31 For each of the following, give the monosaccharide units produced by hydrolysis, the type of glycosidic bond, and the name of the disaccharide including α or β:

a.

b.

15.32 For each of the following, give the monosaccharide units produced by hydrolysis, the type of glycosidic bond, and the name of the disaccharide including α or β:

a.

b.

15.33 Indicate whether each disaccharide in problem 15.31 is a reducing sugar or not.

15.34 Indicate whether each disaccharide in problem 15.32 is a reducing sugar or not.

℞ Clinical Applications

15.35 Identify the disaccharide that fits each of the following descriptions:
   a. ordinary table sugar
   b. found in milk and milk products

   c. also called malt sugar
   d. hydrolysis gives galactose and glucose

15.36 Identify the disaccharide that fits each of the following descriptions:
   a. not a reducing sugar
   b. composed of two glucose units
   c. also called milk sugar
   d. hydrolysis gives glucose and fructose

LEARNING GOAL

Describe the structural features of amylose, amylopectin, glycogen, and cellulose.

15.6 Polysaccharides

A polysaccharide is a polymer of many monosaccharides joined together. Four important polysaccharides—*amylose, amylopectin, cellulose,* and *glycogen*—are all polymers of D-glucose that differ only in the type of glycosidic bonds and the amount of branching in the molecule.

Starch

Starch, a storage form of glucose in plants, is found as insoluble granules in rice, wheat, potatoes, beans, and cereals. Starch is composed of two kinds of polysaccharides, amylose and amylopectin. **Amylose**, which makes up about 20% of starch, consists of 250 to 4000 α-D-glucose molecules connected by $\alpha(1 \rightarrow 4)$-glycosidic bonds in a continuous chain. Sometimes called a straight-chain polymer, polymers of amylose are actually coiled in helical fashion (see Figure 15.5a).

Amylopectin, which makes up as much as 80% of starch, is a branched-chain polysaccharide. Like amylose, the glucose molecules are connected by $\alpha(1 \rightarrow 4)$-glycosidic bonds. However, at about every 25 glucose units, there is a branch of glucose molecules attached by an $\alpha(1 \rightarrow 6)$-glycosidic bond between carbon 1 of the branch and carbon 6 in the main chain (see Figure 15.5b).

Starches hydrolyze easily in water and acid to give smaller saccharides, called *dextrins*, which then hydrolyze to maltose and finally glucose. In our bodies, these complex carbohydrates are digested by the enzymes amylase (in saliva) and maltase (in the intestine). The glucose obtained provides about 50% of our nutritional calories.

$$\text{Amylose, amylopectin} \xrightarrow{\text{H}^+ \text{ or amylase}} \text{dextrins} \xrightarrow{\text{H}^+ \text{ or amylase}} \text{maltose} \xrightarrow{\text{H}^+ \text{ or maltase}} \text{many D-glucose units}$$

Glycogen

Glycogen, or animal starch, is a polymer of glucose that is stored in the liver and muscle of animals. It is hydrolyzed in our cells at a rate that maintains the blood level of glucose and provides energy between meals. The structure of glycogen is very similar to that of amylopectin found in plants, except that glycogen is more highly branched. In glycogen, the glucose units are joined by $\alpha(1 \rightarrow 4)$-glycosidic bonds, and branches occurring about every 10 to 15 glucose units are attached by $\alpha(1 \rightarrow 6)$-glycosidic bonds.

Cellulose

Cellulose is the major structural material of wood and plants. Cotton is almost pure cellulose. In cellulose, glucose molecules form a long unbranched chain similar to that of amylose. However, the glucose units in cellulose are linked by $\beta(1 \rightarrow 4)$-glycosidic bonds. The cellulose chains do not form coils like amylose but are aligned in parallel rows that

(a) Unbranched chain of amylose

$\alpha(1\rightarrow4)$-Glycosidic bond

Amylose

Glucose monomers

Amylopectin, glycogen

$\alpha(1\rightarrow6)$-Glycosidic bond to branch

$\alpha(1\rightarrow4)$-Glycosidic bond

(b) Branched chain of amylopectin

FIGURE 15.5 ▶ The structure of amylose **(a)** is a straight-chain polysaccharide of glucose units, and the structure of amylopectin **(b)** is a branched chain of glucose.

Ⓠ What are the two types of glycosidic bonds that link glucose molecules in amylopectin?

are held in place by hydrogen bonds between hydroxyl groups in adjacent chains, making cellulose insoluble in water. This gives a rigid structure to the cell walls in wood and fiber that is more resistant to hydrolysis than are the starches (see Figure 15.6).

Humans have an enzyme called α-amylase in saliva and pancreatic juices that hydrolyze the $\alpha(1\rightarrow4)$-glycosidic bonds of starches, but not the $\beta(1\rightarrow4)$-glycosidic bonds of cellulose. Thus, humans cannot digest cellulose. Animals such as horses, cows, and goats can obtain glucose from cellulose because their digestive systems contain bacteria that provide enzymes such as cellulase to hydrolyze $\beta(1\rightarrow4)$-glycosidic bonds.

Cellulose

$\beta(1 \rightarrow 4)$-Glycosidic bond

FIGURE 15.6 ▶ The polysaccharide cellulose is composed of glucose units connected by $\beta(1 \rightarrow 4)$-glycosidic bonds.

Q Why are humans unable to digest cellulose?

Explore Your World
Polysaccharides

Read the nutrition label on a box of crackers, cereal, bread, chips, or pasta. The major ingredient in crackers is flour, which contains starch. Chew on a single cracker for 4 or 5 min. Note how the taste changes as you chew the cracker. An enzyme (amylase) in your saliva breaks apart the bonds in starch.

Questions

1. How are carbohydrates listed on the label?
2. What other carbohydrates are listed?
3. How did the taste of the cracker change during the time that you chewed it?
4. What happens to the starches in the cracker as the amylase enzyme in your saliva reacts with the amylose and amylopectin?

▶ **SAMPLE PROBLEM 15.6   Structures of Polysaccharides**

Identify the polysaccharide described by each of the following:

a. a polysaccharide that is stored in the liver and muscle tissues
b. an unbranched polysaccharide containing $\beta(1 \rightarrow 4)$-glycosidic bonds
c. a starch containing $\alpha(1 \rightarrow 4)$- and $\alpha(1 \rightarrow 6)$-glycosidic bonds

SOLUTION

a. glycogen   **b.** cellulose   **c.** amylopectin, glycogen

STUDY CHECK 15.6

Cellulose and amylose are both unbranched glucose polymers. How do they differ?

ANSWER

Cellulose contains glucose units connected by $\beta(1 \rightarrow 4)$-glycosidic bonds, whereas the glucose units in amylose are connected by $\alpha(1 \rightarrow 4)$-glycosidic bonds.

QUESTIONS AND PROBLEMS

15.6 Polysaccharides

LEARNING GOAL Describe the structural features of amylose, amylopectin, glycogen, and cellulose.

15.37 Describe the similarities and differences in the following:
 a. amylose and amylopectin
 b. amylopectin and glycogen

15.38 Describe the similarities and differences in the following:
 a. amylose and cellulose
 b. cellulose and glycogen

℞ Clinical Applications

15.39 Give the name of one or more polysaccharides that matches each of the following descriptions:
 a. not digestible by humans
 b. the storage form of carbohydrates in plants
 c. contains only $\alpha(1 \rightarrow 4)$-glycosidic bonds
 d. the most highly branched polysaccharide

15.40 Give the name of one or more polysaccharides that matches each of the following descriptions:
   a. the storage form of carbohydrates in animals
   b. contains only $\beta(1 \rightarrow 4)$-glycosidic bonds
   c. contains both $\alpha(1 \rightarrow 4)$- and $\alpha(1 \rightarrow 6)$-glycosidic bonds
   d. produces maltose during digestion

Clinical Update
Kate's Program for Type 2 Diabetes

At Kate's next appointment, Paula showed Kate how to use a glucose meter. She instructed Kate to measure her blood glucose level twice a day before and after breakfast and dinner. Paula explains to Kate that her pre-meal blood glucose level should be 110 mg/dL or less, and if it increases by more than 50 mg/dL, she needs to lower the amount of carbohydrates she consumes.

Kate and Paula proceed to plan several meals. Because a meal should contain about 45 to 60 g of carbohydrates, they combined fruits and vegetables that have high and low levels of carbohydrates in the same meal to stay within the recommended range. Kate and Paula also discuss the fact that complex carbohydrates in the body take longer to break down into glucose, and therefore, raise the blood sugar level more gradually.

Kate increased her exercise to walking 30 minutes twice a day. She began to change her diet by eating 6 small meals a day consisting of more fruits and vegetables without starch such as green beans and broccoli, $\frac{1}{4}$ cup of whole grains, and $\frac{1}{4}$ cup of chicken or fish. Kate also decreased the amounts of breads and pasta because she knew carbohydrates would raise her blood sugar.

After three months, Kate reported that she had lost 10 lb and that her blood glucose had dropped to 146 mg/dL. Her blurry vision had improved and need to urinate had decreased.

Clinical Applications

15.41 Kate's blood volume is 3.9 L. Before treatment, if her blood glucose was 178 mg/dL, how many grams of glucose were in her blood?

15.42 Kate's blood volume is 3.9 L. After three months of diet and exercise, if her blood glucose is 146 mg/dL, how many grams of glucose are in her blood?

15.43 For breakfast, Kate had 1 cup of orange juice (23 g carbohydrate), 2 slices of wheat toast (24 g carbohydrate), 2 tablespoons of grape jam (26 g carbohydrate), and coffee with sugar substitute (0 g carbohydrate).
   a. Has Kate remained within the limit of 45 to 60 g for carbohydrate?
   b. Using the energy value of 4 kcal/g for carbohydrate, calculate the total kilocalories from carbohydrates in Kate's breakfast, rounded to the tens place.

15.44 The next day, Kate had 1 cup of cereal (15 g carbohydrate) with skim milk (7 g carbohydrate), 1 banana (17 g carbohydrate), and 1/2 cup of orange juice (12 g carbohydrate) for breakfast.
   a. Has Kate remained within the limit of 45 to 60 g for carbohydrate?
   b. Using the energy value of 4 kcal/g for carbohydrate, calculate the total kilocalories from carbohydrates in Kate's breakfast, rounded to the tens place.

CONCEPT MAP

CHAPTER REVIEW

15.1 Carbohydrates

LEARNING GOAL Classify a monosaccharide as an aldose or a ketose, and indicate the number of carbon atoms.

Aldehyde

Erythrose, an aldose

- Carbohydrates are classified as monosaccharides (simple sugars), disaccharides (two monosaccharide units), or polysaccharides (many monosaccharide units).
- Monosaccharides are polyhydroxy aldehydes (aldoses) or ketones (ketoses).
- Monosaccharides are also classified by their number of carbon atoms: triose, tetrose, pentose, or hexose.

15.2 Fischer Projections of Monosaccharides

LEARNING GOAL Identify and draw the D and L configurations of the Fischer projections for common monosaccharides.

L-Glucose   D-Glucose

- In a D enantiomer, the —OH group is on the right of the chiral carbon farthest from the carbonyl group; the —OH group is on the left in the L enantiomer.
- Important monosaccharides are the aldohexoses, glucose and galactose, and the ketohexose, fructose.

15.3 Haworth Structures of Monosaccharides

LEARNING GOAL Draw and identify the Haworth structures for monosaccharides.

α-D-Glucose

- The predominant form of a monosaccharide is a ring of five or six atoms.
- The cyclic structure forms when an —OH group (usually the one on carbon 5 in hexoses) reacts with the carbonyl group of the same molecule.
- The formation of a new hydroxyl group on carbon 1 gives α and β anomers of the cyclic monosaccharide.

15.4 Chemical Properties of Monosaccharides

LEARNING GOAL Identify the products of oxidation or reduction of monosaccharides; determine whether a carbohydrate is a reducing sugar.

D-Gluconic acid

- The aldehyde group in an aldose can be oxidized to a carboxylic acid, while the carbonyl group in an aldose or a ketose can be reduced to give a hydroxyl group.
- Monosaccharides that are reducing sugars have an aldehyde group in the open chain that can be oxidized.

15.5 Disaccharides

LEARNING GOAL Describe the monosaccharide units and linkages in disaccharides.

- Disaccharides are two monosaccharide units joined together by a glycosidic bond.
- In the common disaccharides maltose, lactose, and sucrose, there is at least one glucose unit.
- Maltose and lactose form α and β anomers, which makes them reducing sugars.
- Sucrose does not have α and β anomers and is not a reducing sugar.

15.6 Polysaccharides

LEARNING GOAL Describe the structural features of amylose, amylopectin, glycogen, and cellulose.

- Polysaccharides are polymers of monosaccharide units.
- Amylose is an unbranched chain of glucose with α(1 → 4)-glycosidic bonds, and amylopectin is a branched polymer of glucose with α(1 → 4)- and α(1 → 6)-glycosidic bonds.
- Glycogen is similar to amylopectin with more branching.
- Cellulose is also a polymer of glucose, but in cellulose, the glycosidic bonds are β(1 → 4)-bonds.

SUMMARY OF CARBOHYDRATES

Carbohydrate	Food Sources	Monosaccharide Components
Monosaccharides		
Glucose	Fruit juices, honey, corn syrup	
Galactose	Lactose hydrolysis	
Fructose	Fruit juices, honey, sucrose hydrolysis	
Disaccharides		**Monosaccharide Components**
Maltose	Germinating grains, starch hydrolysis	Glucose + glucose
Lactose	Milk, yogurt, ice cream	Glucose + galactose
Sucrose	Sugar cane, sugar beets	Glucose + fructose
Polysaccharides		
Amylose	Rice, wheat, grains, cereals	Unbranched polymer of glucose joined by α(1 → 4)-glycosidic bonds
Amylopectin	Rice, wheat, grains, cereals	Branched polymer of glucose joined by α(1 → 4)- and α(1 → 6)-glycosidic bonds
Glycogen	Liver, muscles	Highly branched polymer of glucose joined by α(1 → 4)- and α(1 → 6)-glycosidic bonds
Cellulose	Plant fiber, bran, beans, celery	Unbranched polymer of glucose joined by β(1 → 4)-glycosidic bonds

SUMMARY OF REACTIONS

The chapter sections to review are shown after the name of the reaction.

Oxidation and Reduction of Monosaccharides (15.4)

D-Glucitol   D-Glucose   D-Gluconic acid

Formation of Disaccharides (15.5)

Monosaccharide   Monosaccharide   Disaccharide

Hydrolysis of Polysaccharides (15.6)

Amylose, amylopectin $\xrightarrow{\text{H}^+ \text{ or enzymes}}$ many D-glucose units

KEY TERMS

aldose A monosaccharide that contains an aldehyde group.

amylopectin A branched-chain polymer of starch composed of glucose units joined by $\alpha(1 \rightarrow 4)$- and $\alpha(1 \rightarrow 6)$-glycosidic bonds.

amylose An unbranched polymer of starch composed of glucose units joined by $\alpha(1 \rightarrow 4)$-glycosidic bonds.

carbohydrate A simple or complex sugar composed of carbon, hydrogen, and oxygen.

cellulose An unbranched polysaccharide composed of glucose units linked by $\beta(1 \rightarrow 4)$-glycosidic bonds that cannot be hydrolyzed by the human digestive system.

disaccharide A carbohydrate composed of two monosaccharides joined by a glycosidic bond.

fructose A monosaccharide that is also called levulose and fruit sugar and is found in honey and fruit juices; it is combined with glucose in sucrose.

galactose A monosaccharide that occurs combined with glucose in lactose.

glucose An aldohexose found in fruits, vegetables, corn syrup, and honey that is also known as blood sugar and dextrose. The most prevalent monosaccharide in the diet. Most polysaccharides are polymers of glucose.

glycogen A polysaccharide formed in the liver and muscles for the storage of glucose as an energy reserve. It is composed of

glucose in a highly branched polymer joined by $\alpha(1 \rightarrow 4)$- and $\alpha(1 \rightarrow 6)$-glycosidic bonds.

glycosidic bond The bond that forms when the hydroxyl group of one monosaccharide reacts with the hydroxyl group of another monosaccharide. It is the type of bond that links monosaccharide units in di- or polysaccharides.

Haworth structure The ring structure of a monosaccharide.

ketose A monosaccharide that contains a ketone group.

lactose A disaccharide consisting of glucose and galactose found in milk and milk products.

maltose A disaccharide consisting of two glucose units; it is obtained from the hydrolysis of starch and is found in germinating grains.

monosaccharide A polyhydroxy compound that contains an aldehyde or ketone group.

polysaccharide A polymer of many monosaccharide units, usually glucose. Polysaccharides differ in the types of glycosidic bonds and the amount of branching in the polymer.

reducing sugar A carbohydrate with an aldehyde group capable of reducing the Cu^{2+} in Benedict's reagent.

sucrose A disaccharide composed of glucose and fructose; a nonreducing sugar, commonly called table sugar or "sugar."

⚛ CORE CHEMISTRY SKILLS

Identifying ᴅ- and ʟ-Fischer Projections (15.2)

- The Fischer projection is a simplified way to draw the arrangements of atoms by placing the carbon atoms at the intersection of vertical and horizontal lines.
- The names of the mirror images are labeled ᴅ or ʟ to differentiate between enantiomers of carbohydrates.

Example: Identify each of the following as the ᴅ or ʟ enantiomer:

a.
```
     H    O
      \ //
       C
  H —— OH
  HO —— H
  H —— OH
     CH₂OH
```

b.
```
     CH₂OH
       |
       C = O
  H —— OH
  HO —— H
  HO —— H
     CH₂OH
```

Answer: In **a**, the —OH group on the chiral carbon farthest from the carbonyl group is on the right; it is the ᴅ enantiomer.

In **b**, the —OH group on the chiral carbon farthest from the carbonyl group is on the left; it is the ʟ enantiomer.

Drawing Haworth Structures (15.3)

- The Haworth structure shows the ring structure of a monosaccharide.
- Groups on the right side of the Fischer projection of the monosaccharide are below the plane of the ring, those on the left are above the plane.

- The new hemiacetal —OH group that forms is the α anomer if it is below the plane of the ring, or the β anomer if it is above the plane.

Example: Draw the Haworth structure for β-ᴅ-idose.

```
     O     H
      \\  /
        C
  HO —— H
  H —— OH
  HO —— H
  H —— OH
     CH₂OH
```

Answer: In the β-anomer, the new —OH group is above the plane of the ring.

```
         CH₂OH
           O
    HO         OH
        H
        H    OH
     H           H

        OH   H
```

UNDERSTANDING THE CONCEPTS

The chapter sections to review are shown in parentheses at the end of each question.

15.45 Isomaltose, obtained from the breakdown of starch, has the following Haworth structure: (15.3, 15.4, 15.5)

```
        CH₂OH
          O
   H          H
    H
    OH   H
HO
          O
   H    OH  CH₂
              O
         H          H
          H
          OH   H
       HO          OH

         H    OH
```
Isomaltose

a. Is isomaltose a mono-, di-, or polysaccharide?
b. What are the monosaccharides in isomaltose?
c. What is the glycosidic link in isomaltose?
d. Is this the α or β anomer of isomaltose?
e. Is isomaltose a reducing sugar?

15.46 Sophorose, a carbohydrate found in certain types of beans, has the following Haworth structure: (15.3, 15.4, 15.5)

Sophorose

a. Is sophorose a mono-, di-, or polysaccharide?
b. What are the monosaccharides in sophorose?
c. What is the glycosidic link in sophorose?
d. Is this the α or β anomer of sophorose?
e. Is sophorose a reducing sugar?

15.47 Melezitose, a carbohydrate secreted by insects, has the following Haworth structure: (15.3, 15.4, 15.5)

Melezitose

a. Is melezitose a mono-, di-, or trisaccharide?
b. What ketohexose and aldohexose are present in melezitose?
c. Is melezitose a reducing sugar?

15.48 What are the disaccharides and polysaccharides present in each of the following? (15.5, 15.6)

(a)   (b)

(c)   (d)

ADDITIONAL QUESTIONS AND PROBLEMS

15.49 What are the differences in the Fischer projections of D-fructose and D-galactose? (15.2)

15.50 What are the differences in the Fischer projections of D-glucose and D-fructose? (15.2)

15.51 What are the differences in the Fischer projections of D-galactose and L-galactose? (15.2)

15.52 What are the differences in the Haworth structures of α-D-glucose and β-D-glucose? (15.3)

15.53 The sugar D-gulose is a sweet-tasting syrup. (15.2, 15.3)

D-Gulose

a. Draw the Fischer projection for L-gulose.
b. Draw the Haworth structures for α- and β-D-gulose.

15.54 Use the Fischer projection for D-gulose in problem 15.53 to answer each of the following: (15.2, 15.4)
a. Draw the Fischer projection and name the product formed by the reduction of D-gulose.
b. Draw the Fischer projection and name the product formed by the oxidation of D-gulose.

15.55 D-Sorbitol, a sweetener found in seaweed and berries, contains only hydroxyl functional groups. When D-sorbitol is oxidized, it forms D-glucose. Draw the Fischer projection for D-sorbitol. (15.2, 15.4)

15.56 Raffinose is a trisaccharide found in Australian manna and in cottonseed meal. It is composed of three different monosaccharides. Identify the monosaccharides in raffinose. (15.3)

Raffinose

15.57 If α-galactose is dissolved in water, β-galactose is eventually present. Explain how this occurs. (15.4)

15.58 Why are lactose and maltose reducing sugars, but sucrose is not? (15.5)

CHALLENGE QUESTIONS

The following groups of questions are related to the topics in this chapter. However, they do not all follow the chapter order, and they require you to combine concepts and skills from several sections. These questions will help you increase your critical thinking skills and prepare for your next exam.

15.59 α-Cellobiose is a disaccharide obtained from the hydrolysis of cellulose. It is quite similar to maltose except it has a β(1 → 4)-glycosidic bond. Draw the Haworth structure for α-cellobiose. (15.3, 15.5)

15.60 The disaccharide trehalose found in mushrooms is composed of two α-D-glucose molecules joined by an α(1 → 1)-glycosidic bond. Draw the Haworth structure for trehalose. (15.3, 15.5)

15.61 Gentiobiose is found in saffron. (15.3, 15.4, 15.5)
  a. Gentiobiose contains two glucose molecules linked by a β(1 → 6)-glycosidic bond. Draw the Haworth structure for β-gentiobiose.
  b. Is gentiobiose a reducing sugar? Explain.

15.62 Identify the Fischer projection **A** to **D** that matches each of the following: (15.1, 15.2)
  a. the L enantiomer of mannose   **b.** a ketopentose
  c. an aldopentose   **d.** a ketohexose

Fischer projection A:
H—C=O
H——OH
HO——H
H——OH
CH₂OH
A

Fischer projection B:
H—C=O
H——OH
H——OH
HO——H
HO——H
CH₂OH
B

Fischer projection C:
CH₂OH
C=O
HO——H
H——OH
CH₂OH
C

Fischer projection D:
CH₂OH
C=O
H——OH
HO——H
HO——H
CH₂OH
D

ANSWERS

Answers to Selected Questions and Problems

15.1 Photosynthesis requires CO_2, H_2O, and the energy from the Sun. Respiration requires O_2 from the air and glucose from our foods.

15.3 Monosaccharides can be a chain of three to eight carbon atoms, one in a carbonyl group as an aldehyde or ketone, and the rest attached to hydroxyl groups. A monosaccharide cannot be split or hydrolyzed into smaller carbohydrates. A disaccharide consists of two monosaccharide units joined together that can be split.

15.5 Hydroxyl groups are found in all monosaccharides along with a carbonyl on the first or second carbon that gives an aldehyde or ketone functional group.

15.7 A ketopentose contains hydroxyl and ketone functional groups and has five carbon atoms.

15.9 a. ketohexose   **b.** aldopentose

15.11 a. D   **b.** D   **c.** L   **d.** D

15.13 a.
H—C=O
H——OH
HO——H
CH₂OH

b.
CH₂OH
C=O
H——OH
HO——H
CH₂OH

c.
H—C=O
HO——H
HO——H
H——OH
H——OH
CH₂OH

d.
H—C=O
HO——H
HO——H
HO——H
HO——H
CH₂OH

15.15
H—C=O
H——OH
HO——H
H——OH
H——OH
CH₂OH
D-Glucose

H—C=O
HO——H
H——OH
HO——H
HO——H
CH₂OH
L-Glucose

15.17 In D-galactose, the —OH group on carbon 4 extends to the left. In D-glucose, this —OH group goes to the right.

15.19 a. glucose   **b.** galactose

15.21 In the cyclic structure of glucose, there are five carbon atoms and an oxygen atom.

15.23

α-D-Glucose   β-D-Glucose

15.25 a. α anomer   **b.** α anomer

15.27

CH₂OH
H——OH
HO——H
H——OH
CH₂OH
D-Xylitol

15.29 Oxidation product: Reduction product:

Fischer projection (Oxidation product):

HO—C=O (top)
HO—H
H—OH
H—OH
CH₂OH

D-Arabinonic acid

Fischer projection (Reduction product):

CH₂OH
HO—H
H—OH
H—OH
CH₂OH

D-Arabitol

15.31 a. galactose and glucose; $\beta(1 \rightarrow 4)$-glycosidic bond; β-lactose
    b. glucose and glucose; $\alpha(1 \rightarrow 4)$-glycosidic bond; α-maltose

15.33 a. is a reducing sugar   **b.** is a reducing sugar

15.35 a. sucrose   **b.** lactose
    c. maltose   **d.** lactose

15.37 a. Amylose is an unbranched polymer of glucose units joined by $\alpha(1 \rightarrow 4)$-glycosidic bonds; amylopectin is a branched polymer of glucose joined by $\alpha(1 \rightarrow 4)$- and $\alpha(1 \rightarrow 6)$-glycosidic bonds.
    b. Amylopectin, which is produced in plants, is a branched polymer of glucose, joined by $\alpha(1 \rightarrow 4)$- and $\alpha(1 \rightarrow 6)$-glycosidic bonds. The branches in amylopectin occur about every 25 glucose units. Glycogen, which is produced in animals, is a highly branched polymer of glucose, joined by $\alpha(1 \rightarrow 4)$- and $\alpha(1 \rightarrow 6)$-glycosidic bonds. The branches in glycogen occur about every 10 to 15 glucose units.

15.39 a. cellulose   **b.** amylose, amylopectin
    c. amylose   **d.** glycogen

15.41 6.9 of glucose

15.43 a. Kate's breakfast had 73 g of carbohydrate. She still needs to cut down the amount of carbohydrate.
    b. 290 kcal

15.45 a. disaccharide   **b.** α-D-glucose
    c. $\alpha(1 \rightarrow 6)$-glycosidic bond   **d.** α
    e. is a reducing sugar

15.47 a. trisaccharide
    b. two glucose and one fructose
    c. Melezitose has no free —OH groups on the glucose or fructose molecules; like sucrose it is not a reducing sugar.

15.49 D-Fructose is a ketohexose, whereas D-galactose is an aldohexose. In the Fischer projection of D-galactose, the —OH group on carbon 4 is drawn on the left; in fructose, the —OH group is drawn on the right.

15.51 L-Galactose is the mirror image of D-galactose. In the Fischer projection of D-galactose, the —OH groups on carbon 2 and carbon 5 are drawn on the right side, but they are drawn on the left for carbon 3 and carbon 4. In L-galactose, the —OH groups are reversed; carbons 2 and 5 have —OH groups drawn on the left, and carbons 3 and 4 have —OH groups drawn on the right.

15.53 a.

Fischer projection:

H—C=O (top)
HO—H
HO—H
H—OH
HO—H
CH₂OH

L-Gulose

    b.

α-D-Gulose β-D-Gulose

15.55

CH₂OH
H—OH
HO—H
H—OH
H—OH
CH₂OH

15.57 When α-galactose forms an open-chain structure, it can close to form either α- or β-galactose.

15.59

(Haworth structure of a disaccharide with CH₂OH, OH, H, HO groups joined by an O glycosidic linkage)

15.61 a.

(Haworth structure of gentiobiose, two pyranose rings joined through a CH₂ group and O)

    b. Yes. Gentiobiose is a reducing sugar. The ring on the right can open up to form an aldehyde that can be oxidized.

16

Carboxylic Acids and Esters

MAUREEN, A SURGICAL TECHNICIAN, BEGINS

preparing for Robert's heart surgery. After Maureen places all of the surgical instruments into an autoclave for sterilization, she prepares the room by ensuring that all of the equipment is working properly. She also determines that the room is sterile, as this will minimize the chance of an infection. Right before surgery begins, Maureen shaves Robert's chest and disinfects the incision sites.

After the surgery, Maureen applies Indermil, which is a type of liquid bandage, to Robert's incision sites. Liquid bandages are tissue adhesives that seal surgical or wound incisions on a patient. Stitches and staples are not required and scarring is minimal. The polymer in a liquid bandage is typically dissolved in an alcohol-based solvent. The alcohol also acts as an antiseptic.

Indermil is a cyanoester or cyanoacrylate, as it contains a cyano group ($C\equiv N$) and an ester functional group. Esters have a carbonyl group ($C=O$), which has a single bond to a carbon group on one side of the carbonyl and an oxygen atom on the other side. The oxygen atom is then bonded to a carbon group by a single bond. Cyanoacrylates are a group of adhesives that include "Super Glue" and Indermil, which is butyl cyanoacrylate. The *ate* in butyl cyanoacrylate indicates that an ester is present in the molecule, and the *butyl* indicates the four-carbon group that is bonded to the oxygen atom.

In water and body fluids, these adhesives rapidly form strong chains that join the edges of surfaces and hold them in place.

Indermil

CAREER Surgical Technician

Surgical technicians prepare the operating room by creating a sterile environment. This includes setting up surgical instruments and equipment, and ensuring that all of the equipment is working properly. A sterile environment is critical to the patient's recovery, as it helps lower the chance of an infection. They also prepare patients for surgery by washing, shaving, and disinfecting incision sites. During the surgery, a surgical technician provides the sterile instruments and supplies to the surgeons and surgical assistants.

arboxylic acids are weak acids. They have a sour or tart taste, produce hydronium ions in water, and neutralize bases. You encounter carboxylic acids when you use a salad dressing containing vinegar, which is a solution of acetic acid and water, or experience the sour taste of citric acid in a grapefruit or lemon. When a carboxylic acid combines with an alcohol, an ester and water are produced. Fats and oils are esters of glycerol and fatty acids, which are long-chain carboxylic acids. Esters produce the pleasant aromas and flavors of many fruits, such as bananas, strawberries, and oranges.

LOOKING AHEAD

16.1 Carboxylic Acids 581

♡ **Chemistry Link to Health** *Alpha Hydroxy Acids* 583

16.2 Properties of Carboxylic Acids 585

♡ **Chemistry Link to Health** *Carboxylic Acids in Metabolism* 589

16.3 Esters 590

♡ **Chemistry Link to Health** *Salicylic Acid from a Willow Tree* 591

16.4 Naming Esters 593

16.5 Properties of Esters 596

℞ **Clinical Applications** 599, 602

℞ **Clinical Update** *Liquid Bandages* 599

CHAPTER READINESS*

⚛ CORE CHEMISTRY SKILLS

- Writing Equations for Reactions of Acids and Bases (11.7)
- Naming and Drawing Alkanes (12.2)

*These Core Chemistry Skills from previous chapters are listed here for your review as you proceed to the new material in this chapter.

16.1 Carboxylic Acids

In a **carboxylic acid**, the carbon atom of a carbonyl group is attached to a hydroxyl group, which forms a **carboxyl group.** The carboxyl functional group may be attached to an alkyl group or an aromatic group. Some ways to represent the carboxyl group in carboxylic acids are the following:

LEARNING GOAL

Write the IUPAC and common names for carboxylic acids and draw their condensed and line-angle structural formulas.

Carbonyl group

Hydroxyl group

Carboxyl group

$$CH_3-\overset{\overset{\displaystyle O}{\|}}{C}-OH$$

Ethanoic acid
(acetic acid)

$$\overset{\overset{\displaystyle O}{\|}}{\diagup}\diagup\diagdown OH$$

Propanoic acid
(propionic acid)

$$CH_3-CH_2-CH_2-\overset{\overset{\displaystyle O}{\|}}{C}-OH$$

Butanoic acid
(butyric acid)

IUPAC Names of Carboxylic Acids

The IUPAC names of carboxylic acids replace the *e* of the corresponding alkane with *oic acid*. If there are substituents, the carbon chain is numbered beginning with the carboxyl carbon.

⚛ CORE CHEMISTRY SKILL

Naming Carboxylic Acids

$$H-\overset{\overset{\displaystyle O}{\|}}{C}-OH$$

Methanoic acid

$$CH_3-\overset{\overset{\displaystyle CH_3}{|}}{CH}-\overset{\overset{\displaystyle O}{\|}}{C}-OH$$

2-Methylpropanoic acid

$$CH_3-\overset{\overset{\displaystyle OH}{|}}{CH}-CH_2-\overset{\overset{\displaystyle O}{\|}}{C}-OH$$

3-Hydroxybutanoic acid

The simplest aromatic carboxylic acid is named benzoic acid. With the carboxyl carbon bonded to carbon 1, the ring is numbered in the direction that gives substituents the smallest possible numbers. As before, the prefixes *ortho*, *meta*, and *para* may be used to show the position of one other substituent.

Benzoic acid

4-Aminobenzoic acid
(*p*-aminobenzoic acid; PABA)

3,4-Dichlorobenzoic acid

Many carboxylic acids are still named by their common names, which use prefixes: *form*, *acet*, *propion*, *butyr*. When using the common names, the Greek letters alpha (α), beta (β), and gamma (γ) are assigned to the carbons adjacent to the carboxyl carbon.

$$
\begin{array}{cccc}
& CH_3 & & O \\
& | & & \| \\
CH_3- & CH- & CH_2- & C-OH
\end{array}
$$

IUPAC	4	3	2	1
Common		γ	β	α

Formic acid is injected under the skin during bee or red ant stings and other insect bites. Acetic acid is the oxidation product of the ethanol in wines and apple cider. The resulting solution of acetic acid and water is known as vinegar. Propionic acid is obtained from the fats of dairy products. Butyric acid gives the foul odor to rancid butter (see Table 16.1).

A red ant sting contains formic acid that irritates the skin.

TABLE 16.1 IUPAC and Common Names of Selected Carboxylic Acids

Condensed Structural Formula	IUPAC Name	Common Name	Ball-and-Stick Model
$H-\overset{\displaystyle O}{\overset{\|}{C}}-OH$	Methanoic acid	Formic acid	
$CH_3-\overset{\displaystyle O}{\overset{\|}{C}}-OH$	Ethanoic acid	Acetic acid	
$CH_3-CH_2-\overset{\displaystyle O}{\overset{\|}{C}}-OH$	Propanoic acid	Propionic acid	
$CH_3-CH_2-CH_2-\overset{\displaystyle O}{\overset{\|}{C}}-OH$	Butanoic acid	Butyric acid	

▶ **SAMPLE PROBLEM 16.1   Naming Carboxylic Acids**

Give the IUPAC and common name for the following carboxylic acid:

SOLUTION

	Given	Need
ANALYZE THE PROBLEM	carboxylic acid	IUPAC and common name

STEP 1   Identify the longest carbon chain and replace the *e* in the corresponding alkane name with *oic acid*. The IUPAC name of a carboxylic acid with four carbons is butanoic acid; the common name is butyric acid.

butanoic acid

(butyric acid)

STEP 2 Name and number any substituents by counting the carboxyl group as carbon 1. With a methyl group on the second carbon, the IUPAC name is 2-methylbutanoic acid. For the common name, the Greek letter α specifies the carbon atom next to the carboxyl carbon, α-methylbutyric acid.

2-methylbutanoic acid

(α-methylbutyric acid)

4 3 2 1
γ β α

STUDY CHECK 16.1

Give the IUPAC and common name for the following:

ANSWER

3-chlorobenzoic acid (*m*-chlorobenzoic acid)

Guide to Naming Carboxylic Acids

STEP 1
Identify the longest carbon chain and replace the *e* in the corresponding alkane name with *oic acid.*

STEP 2
Name and number any substituents by counting the carboxyl group as carbon 1.

Preparation of Carboxylic Acids

Carboxylic acids can be prepared from primary alcohols or aldehydes. For example, when ethyl alcohol in wine is exposed to oxygen in the air, vinegar is produced. The oxidation process converts the ethyl alcohol (1° alcohol) to acetaldehyde, and then to acetic acid, the carboxylic acid in vinegar.

$$CH_3-CH_2 \xrightarrow{[O]} CH_3-C-H \xrightarrow{[O]} CH_3-C-OH$$

Ethanol
(ethyl alcohol)

Ethanal
(acetaldehyde)

Ethanoic acid
(acetic acid)

The sour taste of vinegar is because of ethanoic acid (acetic acid).

♡ Chemistry Link to **Health**
Alpha Hydroxy Acids

Alpha hydroxy acids (AHAs), found in fruits, milk, and sugar cane, are naturally occurring carboxylic acids with a hydroxyl group (—OH) on the carbon atom that is adjacent to the carboxyl group. Cleopatra, Queen of Egypt, reportedly bathed in sour milk to smooth her skin. Dermatologists have been using products with high concentrations (20 to 70%) of AHAs to remove acne scars and in skin peels to reduce irregular pigmentation and age spots. Lower concentrations (8 to 10%) of AHAs are added to skin care products for the purpose of smoothing fine lines, improving skin texture, and cleansing pores. Several different AHAs may be found in skin care products singly or in combination. Glycolic acid and lactic acid are most frequently used.

Recent studies indicate that products with AHAs increase sensitivity of the skin to sun and UV radiation. It is recommended that a sunscreen with a sun protection factor (SPF) of at least 15 be used when treating the skin with products that include AHAs. Products containing AHAs at concentrations under 10% and pH values greater than 3.5 are generally considered safe. However, the Food and Drug Administration (FDA) has received reports of AHAs causing skin irritation including blisters, rashes, and discoloration of the skin. The FDA does not require product safety reports from cosmetic manufacturers, although they are responsible for marketing safe products. The FDA advises that you test any product containing AHAs on a small area of skin before you use it on a large area.

Alpha hydroxy carboxylic acids are used in many skin care products.

Alpha Hydroxy Acid (Source)	Condensed Structural Formula
Glycolic acid (sugar cane)	$HO-CH_2-\overset{\overset{\textstyle O}{\|\|}}{C}-OH$
Lactic acid (sour milk)	$CH_3-\overset{\overset{\textstyle OH}{\|}}{CH}-\overset{\overset{\textstyle O}{\|\|}}{C}-OH$
Tartaric acid (grapes)	$HO-\overset{\overset{\textstyle O}{\|\|}}{C}-\overset{\overset{\textstyle OH}{\|}}{CH}-\overset{\overset{\textstyle OH}{\|}}{CH}-\overset{\overset{\textstyle O}{\|\|}}{C}-OH$
Malic acid (apples)	$HO-\overset{\overset{\textstyle O}{\|\|}}{C}-CH_2-\overset{\overset{\textstyle OH}{\|}}{CH}-\overset{\overset{\textstyle O}{\|\|}}{C}-OH$
Citric acid (citrus fruits)	$HO-\overset{\overset{\textstyle CH_2-COOH}{\|}}{\underset{\underset{\textstyle CH_2-COOH}{\|}}{C}}-COOH$

QUESTIONS AND PROBLEMS

16.1 Carboxylic Acids

LEARNING GOAL Write the IUPAC and common names for carboxylic acids and draw their condensed and line-angle structural formulas.

16.1 What carboxylic acid is responsible for the pain of an ant sting?

16.2 What carboxylic acid is found in vinegar?

16.3 Draw the condensed structural formula and give the IUPAC name for each of the following:
  a. a carboxylic acid that has the formula $C_6H_{12}O_2$, with no substituents
  b. a carboxylic acid that has the formula $C_6H_{12}O_2$, with one ethyl substituent

16.4 Draw the condensed structural formula and give the IUPAC name for each of the following:
  a. a carboxylic acid that has the formula $C_5H_{10}O_2$, with no substituents
  b. a carboxylic acid that has the formula $C_5H_{10}O_2$, with two methyl substituents

16.5 Give the IUPAC and common name, if any, for each of the following carboxylic acids:

  a. $CH_3-\overset{\overset{\textstyle O}{\|\|}}{C}-OH$

  b. (line-angle structure) $\longrightarrow OH$ with O double bond

  c. (line-angle structure with branch) $\longrightarrow OH$ with O

  d. (line-angle structure) $\overset{\overset{\textstyle O}{\|\|}}{C}-OH$ with two Br substituents on ring

16.6 Give the IUPAC and common name, if any, for each of the following carboxylic acids:

  a. $H-\overset{\overset{\textstyle O}{\|\|}}{C}-OH$

  b. (line-angle structure) $\overset{\overset{\textstyle O}{\|\|}}{} OH$ with Br substituent

  c. (benzene ring with) $\overset{\overset{\textstyle O}{\|\|}}{C}-OH$ and Cl substituent

  d. $CH_3-CH_2-\overset{\overset{\textstyle CH_3}{\|}}{CH}-\overset{\overset{\textstyle O}{\|\|}}{C}-OH$

16.7 Draw the condensed structural formula for each of the following carboxylic acids:
  a. 2-chloroethanoic acid
  b. 3-hydroxypropanoic acid
  c. α-methylbutyric acid
  d. 3,5-dibromoheptanoic acid

16.8 Draw the condensed structural formula for each of the following carboxylic acids:
  a. pentanoic acid
  b. 3-ethylbenzoic acid
  c. α-hydroxyacetic acid
  d. 2,4-dibromobutanoic acid

16.9 Draw the condensed or line-angle structural formula for the carboxylic acid formed by the oxidation of each of the following:

a. CH_3-OH

b. $CH_3-\overset{\overset{\displaystyle O}{\|}}{C}-H$

c. [branched chain structure with OH]

d. [cyclopentane with CH₂OH]

16.10 Draw the condensed or line-angle structural formula for the carboxylic acid formed by the oxidation of each of the following:

a. [line-angle structure with OH]

b. [line-angle structure with CHO]

c. $CH_3-\overset{\overset{\displaystyle CH_3}{|}}{CH}-CH_2-\overset{\overset{\displaystyle O}{\|}}{C}-H$

d. [benzene ring with CH_2-CH_2-OH]

16.2 Properties of Carboxylic Acids

Carboxylic acids are among the most polar organic compounds because their functional group consists of two polar groups: a hydroxyl group ($-OH$) and a carbonyl group ($C=O$). The $-OH$ group is similar to the functional group in alcohols, and the $C=O$ is similar to the functional group of aldehydes and ketones.

LEARNING GOAL

Describe the boiling points, solubility, dissociation, and neutralization of carboxylic acids.

[Two structural diagrams showing polar groups with δ⁺ and δ⁻ charges, labeled "Two polar groups"]

Boiling Points

The polar carboxyl groups allow carboxylic acids to form several hydrogen bonds with other carboxylic acid molecules. This effect of hydrogen bonds gives carboxylic acids higher boiling points than alcohols, ketones, and aldehydes of similar molar mass.

	$CH_3-CH_2-\overset{\overset{\displaystyle O}{\|}}{C}-H$	$CH_3-CH_2-CH_2-OH$	$CH_3-\overset{\overset{\displaystyle O}{\|}}{C}-OH$
Name	Propanal	1-Propanol	Ethanoic acid
Molar Mass	58	60	60
Family	Aldehyde	Alcohol	Carboxylic acid
bp	49 °C	97 °C	118 °C

Boiling Point Increases →

A dimer of two ethanoic acid molecules

An important reason for the higher boiling points of carboxylic acids is that two carboxylic acids form hydrogen bonds between their carboxyl groups, resulting in a *dimer*. As a dimer, the mass of the carboxylic acid is effectively doubled, which means that a higher temperature is required to reach the boiling point. Table 16.2 lists the boiling points for some selected carboxylic acids.

▶**SAMPLE PROBLEM 16.2** Boiling Points of Carboxylic Acids

Match each of the compounds 2-butanol, pentane, propanoic acid with a boiling point of 141 °C, 100 °C, or 36 °C. (They have about the same molar mass.)

SOLUTION

The boiling point increases when the molecules of a compound can form hydrogen bonds or have dipole–dipole attractions. Pentane has the lowest boiling point, 36 °C,

Acetic acid crystals form at a freezing point of 16.5 °C.

FIGURE 16.1 ▶ Acetic acid forms hydrogen bonds with water molecules.

🔍 Why do the atoms in the carboxyl group form hydrogen bonds with water molecules?

because alkanes cannot form hydrogen bonds or dipole–dipole attractions. 2-Butanol has a higher boiling point, 100 °C, than pentane because an alcohol can form hydrogen bonds. Propanoic acid has the highest boiling point, 141 °C, because carboxylic acids can form stable dimers through hydrogen bonding to increase their effective molar mass and therefore their boiling points.

STUDY CHECK 16.2

Why would methanoic acid (molar mass 46, bp 101 °C) have a higher boiling point than ethanol (molar mass 46, bp 78 °C)?

ANSWER

Two methanoic acid molecules form a dimer, which gives an effective molar mass that is double that of a single acid molecule. Thus, a higher boiling point is required than for ethanol.

Solubility in Water

Carboxylic acids with one to five carbons are soluble in water because the carboxyl group forms hydrogen bonds with several water molecules (see Figure 16.1). However, as the length of the hydrocarbon chain increases, the nonpolar portion reduces the solubility of the carboxylic acid in water. Carboxylic acids having more than five carbons are not very soluble in water. Table 16.2 lists the solubility for some selected carboxylic acids.

TABLE 16.2 Boiling Points, Solubilities, and Acid Dissociation Constants for Selected Carboxylic Acids

IUPAC Name	Condensed Structural Formula	Boiling Point (°C)	Solubility in Water	Acid Dissociation Constant (at 25 °C)
Methanoic acid	$\overset{\overset{\textstyle O}{\|\|}}{H-C-OH}$	101	Soluble	1.8×10^{-4}
Ethanoic acid	$\overset{\overset{\textstyle O}{\|\|}}{CH_3-C-OH}$	118	Soluble	1.8×10^{-5}
Propanoic acid	$\overset{\overset{\textstyle O}{\|\|}}{CH_3-CH_2-C-OH}$	141	Soluble	1.3×10^{-5}
Butanoic acid	$\overset{\overset{\textstyle O}{\|\|}}{CH_3-CH_2-CH_2-C-OH}$	164	Soluble	1.5×10^{-5}
Pentanoic acid	$\overset{\overset{\textstyle O}{\|\|}}{CH_3-CH_2-CH_2-CH_2-C-OH}$	187	Soluble	1.5×10^{-5}
Hexanoic acid	$\overset{\overset{\textstyle O}{\|\|}}{CH_3-CH_2-CH_2-CH_2-CH_2-C-OH}$	205	Slightly soluble	1.4×10^{-5}
Benzoic acid	$\overset{\overset{\textstyle O}{\|\|}}{C-OH}$ (on benzene ring)	250	Slightly soluble	6.4×10^{-5}

Acidity of Carboxylic Acids

An important property of carboxylic acids is their dissociation in water. When a carboxylic acid dissociates in water, H^+ is transferred to a water molecule to form a negatively charged **carboxylate ion** and a positively charged hydronium ion (H_3O^+). Carboxylic acids are more acidic than most other organic compounds including phenols. However, they are weak acids. The acid dissociation constants of some carboxylic acids are given in Table 16.2.

Carboxylic Acid   **Carboxylate Ion**

$$CH_3-\overset{O}{\overset{\|}{C}}-OH + H_2O \rightleftharpoons CH_3-\overset{O}{\overset{\|}{C}}-O^- + H_3O^+$$

Ethanoic acid   Ethanoate ion   Hydronium
(acetic acid)   (acetate ion)   ion

► SAMPLE PROBLEM 16.3 Dissociation of Carboxylic Acids in Water

Write the balanced chemical equation for the dissociation of propanoic acid in water.

SOLUTION

ANALYZE THE PROBLEM	Given	Need
	propanoic acid	chemical equation for dissociation in water

A chemical equation for the dissociation of a carboxylic acid includes the reactants, a carboxylic acid and water, and the products, carboxylate and hydronium ions.

$$CH_3-CH_2-\overset{O}{\overset{\|}{C}}-OH + H_2O \rightleftharpoons CH_3-CH_2-\overset{O}{\overset{\|}{C}}-O^- + H_3O^+$$

Propanoic acid   Propanoate ion
(propionic acid)   (propionate ion)

STUDY CHECK 16.3

Write the balanced chemical equation for the dissociation of formic acid in water.

ANSWER

$$H-\overset{O}{\overset{\|}{C}}-OH + H_2O \rightleftharpoons H-\overset{O}{\overset{\|}{C}}-O^- + H_3O^+$$

Neutralization of Carboxylic Acids

Because carboxylic acids are weak acids, they are completely neutralized by strong bases such as NaOH and KOH. The products are a **carboxylate salt** and water. The carboxylate ion is named by replacing the *ic acid* ending of the acid name with *ate*.

$$H-\overset{O}{\overset{\|}{C}}-OH + NaOH \longrightarrow H-\overset{O}{\overset{\|}{C}}-O^- Na^+ + H_2O$$

Methanoic acid   Sodium methanoate
(formic acid)   (sodium formate)

Benzoic acid + KOH ⟶ Potassium benzoate + H_2O

FIGURE 16.2 ▶ Carboxylate salts are often used as preservatives and flavor enhancers in soups and seasonings.

🅠 What is the carboxylate salt produced by the neutralization of butanoic acid and lithium hydroxide?

Sodium propionate, a preservative, is added to bread, cheeses, and bakery items to inhibit the spoilage of the food by microorganisms. Sodium benzoate, an inhibitor of mold and bacteria, is added to juices, margarine, relishes, salads, and jams. Monosodium glutamate (MSG) is added to meats, fish, vegetables, and bakery items to enhance flavor, although it causes headache in some people (see Figure 16.2).

$$CH_3—CH_2—\overset{\displaystyle O}{\overset{\|}{C}}—O^-\ Na^+$$

Sodium propanoate
(sodium propionate)

Sodium benzoate

$$HO—\overset{\displaystyle O}{\overset{\|}{C}}—CH_2—CH_2—\overset{\displaystyle NH_2}{\overset{|}{C}H}—\overset{\displaystyle O}{\overset{\|}{C}}—O^-\ Na^+$$

Monosodium glutamate

Carboxylate salts are ionic compounds with strong attractions between positively charged metal ions such as Li^+, Na^+, and K^+ and the negatively charged carboxylate ion. Like most salts, the carboxylate salts are solids at room temperature, have high melting points, and are usually soluble in water.

▶ **SAMPLE PROBLEM 16.4 Neutralization of Carboxylic Acid**

Write the balanced chemical equation for the neutralization of propanoic acid (propionic acid) with sodium hydroxide.

SOLUTION

ANALYZE THE PROBLEM	Given	Need
	propanoic acid	neutralization equation

A chemical equation for the neutralization of carboxylic acid includes the reactants, a carboxylic acid and a base, and the products, a carboxylate salt and water.

$$CH_3—CH_2—\overset{\displaystyle O}{\overset{\|}{C}}—OH + NaOH \longrightarrow CH_3—CH_2—\overset{\displaystyle O}{\overset{\|}{C}}—O^-\ Na^+ + H_2O$$

Propanoic acid   Sodium   Sodium propanoate
(propionic acid)   hydroxide   (sodium propionate)

STUDY CHECK 16.4

What carboxylic acid will give potassium butanoate (potassium butyrate) when it is neutralized by KOH?

ANSWER

butanoic acid (butyric acid)

Chemistry Link to **Health**

Carboxylic Acids in Metabolism

Several carboxylic acids are part of the metabolic processes within our cells. For example, during glycolysis, a molecule of glucose is broken down into two molecules of pyruvic acid, or actually, its carboxylate ion, pyruvate. During strenuous exercise when oxygen levels are low (anaerobic), pyruvic acid is reduced to give lactic acid or the lactate ion.

$$CH_3-\overset{O}{\overset{||}{C}}-\overset{O}{\overset{||}{C}}-OH + 2H \xrightarrow{\text{Reduction}} CH_3-\overset{OH}{\overset{|}{CH}}-\overset{O}{\overset{||}{C}}-OH$$

Pyruvic acid   Lactic acid

During exercise, pyruvic acid is converted to lactic acid in the muscles.

In the *citric acid cycle*, also called the Krebs cycle, di- and tricarboxylic acids are oxidized and decarboxylated (loss of CO_2) to produce energy for the cells of the body. These carboxylic acids are normally referred to by their common names. At the start of the citric acid cycle, citric acid with six carbons is converted to five-carbon α-ketoglutaric acid. Citric acid is also the acid that gives the sour taste to citrus fruits such as lemons and grapefruits.

$$HO-\overset{\overset{\displaystyle COOH}{|}\,\overset{\displaystyle CH_2}{|}}{\underset{\overset{\displaystyle CH_2}{|}\,\underset{\displaystyle COOH}{|}}{C}}-COOH \xrightarrow{[O]} \begin{matrix} COOH \\ | \\ CH_2 \\ | \\ CH_2 \\ | \\ C=O \\ | \\ COOH \end{matrix} + CO_2$$

Citric acid α-Ketoglutaric acid

The citric acid cycle continues as α-ketoglutaric acid loses CO_2 to give a four-carbon succinic acid. Then a series of reactions converts succinic acid to oxaloacetic acid. We see that some of the functional groups we have studied, along with reactions such as hydration and oxidation, are part of the metabolic processes that take place in our cells.

$$\begin{matrix} COOH \\ | \\ CH_2 \\ | \\ CH_2 \\ | \\ COOH \end{matrix} \xrightarrow{[O]} \begin{matrix} COOH \\ | \\ C-H \\ || \\ H-C \\ | \\ COOH \end{matrix} \xrightarrow{H_2O} \begin{matrix} COOH \\ | \\ HO-C-H \\ | \\ CH_2 \\ | \\ COOH \end{matrix} \xrightarrow{[O]} \begin{matrix} COOH \\ | \\ C=O \\ | \\ CH_2 \\ | \\ COOH \end{matrix}$$

Succinic acid   Fumaric acid   Malic acid   Oxaloacetic acid

At the pH of the aqueous environment in the cells, the carboxylic acids are dissociated, which means it is actually the carboxylate ions that take part in the reactions of the citric acid cycle. For example, in water, succinic acid is in equilibrium with its carboxylate ion, succinate.

$$\begin{matrix} COOH \\ | \\ CH_2 \\ | \\ CH_2 \\ | \\ COOH \end{matrix} + 2H_2O \rightleftharpoons \begin{matrix} COO^- \\ | \\ CH_2 \\ | \\ CH_2 \\ | \\ COO^- \end{matrix} + 2H_3O^+$$

Succinic acid   Succinate ion

Citric acid gives the sour taste to citrus fruits.

QUESTIONS AND PROBLEMS

16.2 Properties of Carboxylic Acids

LEARNING GOAL Describe the boiling points, solubility, dissociation, and neutralization of carboxylic acids.

16.11 Identify the compound in each of the following pairs that has the higher boiling point. Explain.
   a. ethanoic acid (acetic acid) or butanoic acid
   b. 1-propanol or propanoic acid
   c. butanone or butanoic acid

16.12 Identify the compound in each of the following pairs that has the higher boiling point. Explain.
   a. propanone (acetone) or propanoic acid
   b. propanoic acid or hexanoic acid
   c. ethanol or ethanoic acid (acetic acid)

16.13 Identify the compound in each of the following groups that is most soluble in water. Explain.
  a. propanoic acid, hexanoic acid, benzoic acid
  b. pentane, 1-hexanol, propanoic acid

16.14 Identify the compound in each of the following groups that is most soluble in water. Explain.
  a. butanone, butanoic acid, butane
  b. acetic acid, pentanoic acid, octanoic acid

16.15 Write the balanced chemical equation for the dissociation of each of the following carboxylic acids in water:
  a. butanoic acid

$$CH_3 \overset{\displaystyle CH_3}{\underset{\displaystyle |}{\,}} \quad$$

  b. $CH_3 \!-\! \overset{\overset{\displaystyle CH_3}{\displaystyle |}}{C}\!H \!-\! \overset{\overset{\displaystyle O}{\displaystyle \|}}{C} \!-\! OH$

16.16 Write the balanced chemical equation for the dissociation of each of the following carboxylic acids in water:

  a. $CH_3 \!-\! CH_2 \!-\! CH_2 \!-\! CH_2 \!-\! \overset{\overset{\displaystyle O}{\displaystyle \|}}{C} \!-\! OH$

  b. α-hydroxyacetic acid

16.17 Write the balanced chemical equation for the reaction of each of the following carboxylic acids with NaOH:
  a. pentanoic acid
  b. 2-chloropropanoic acid
  c. benzoic acid

16.18 Write the balanced chemical equation for the reaction of each of the following carboxylic acids with KOH:
  a. hexanoic acid
  b. 2-methylbutanoic acid
  c. p-chlorobenzoic acid

16.19 Give the IUPAC and common names, if any, of the carboxylate salts produced in problem 16.17.

16.20 Give the IUPAC and common names, if any, of the carboxylate salts produced in problem 16.18.

LEARNING GOAL

Write a balanced chemical equation for the formation of an ester.

16.3 Esters

A carboxylic acid reacts with an alcohol to form an **ester** and water. In an ester, the —H of the carboxylic acid is replaced by an alkyl group. Fats and oils in our diets contain esters of glycerol and fatty acids, which are long-chain carboxylic acids. The aromas and flavors of many fruits including bananas, oranges, and strawberries are due to esters.

Carboxylic Acid	Ester
$CH_3 \!-\! \overset{\overset{\displaystyle O}{\displaystyle \|}}{C} \!-\! O \!-\! H$	$CH_3 \!-\! \overset{\overset{\displaystyle O}{\displaystyle \|}}{C} \!-\! O \!-\! CH_3$
Ethanoic acid (acetic acid)	Methyl ethanoate (methyl acetate)

Esterification

In a reaction called **esterification**, an ester is produced when a carboxylic acid and an alcohol react in the presence of an acid catalyst (usually H_2SO_4) and heat. In esterification, the —OH group from the carboxylic acid and the —H from the alcohol combine to form water. An excess of the alcohol reactant is used to shift the equilibrium in the direction of the formation of the ester product.

$$CH_3 \!-\! \overset{\overset{\displaystyle O}{\displaystyle \|}}{C} \!-\! OH + H \!-\! O \!-\! CH_3 \;\underset{}{\overset{H^+, \text{ heat}}{\rightleftharpoons}}\; CH_3 \!-\! \overset{\overset{\displaystyle O}{\displaystyle \|}}{C} \!-\! O \!-\! CH_3 + H \!-\! OH$$

Ethanoic acid (acetic acid)   Methanol (methyl alcohol)   Methyl ethanoate (methyl acetate)

For example, the ester propyl ethanoate, which has the flavor and odor of pears, can be prepared using ethanoic acid and 1-propanol. The equation for this esterification is written as

$$CH_3 \!-\! \overset{\overset{\displaystyle O}{\displaystyle \|}}{C} \!-\! OH + H \!-\! O \!-\! CH_2 \!-\! CH_2 \!-\! CH_3 \;\underset{}{\overset{H^+, \text{ heat}}{\rightleftharpoons}}\; CH_3 \!-\! \overset{\overset{\displaystyle O}{\displaystyle \|}}{C} \!-\! O \!-\! CH_2 \!-\! CH_2 \!-\! CH_3 + H_2O$$

Ethanoic acid (acetic acid)   1-Propanol (propyl alcohol)   Propyl ethanoate (propyl acetate)

> **SAMPLE PROBLEM 16.5** Writing Esterification Equations

An ester that has the smell of pineapple can be synthesized from butanoic acid and methanol. Write the balanced chemical equation for the formation of this ester.

SOLUTION

	Given	Need
ANALYZE THE PROBLEM	butanoic acid, methanol	esterification equation

In an esterification equation, a carboxylic acid and an alcohol react to form an ester and water. The ester product of the esterification of butanoic acid and methanol is methyl butanoate.

$$CH_3-CH_2-CH_2-\overset{\overset{\displaystyle O}{\|}}{C}-\textbf{OH} + \textbf{H}-O-CH_3 \underset{}{\overset{H^+,\text{ heat}}{\rightleftharpoons}} CH_3-CH_2-CH_2-\overset{\overset{\displaystyle O}{\|}}{C}-O-CH_3 + \textbf{H}_2\textbf{O}$$

Butanoic acid   Methanol   Methyl butanoate

STUDY CHECK 16.5

The ester that smells like plums can be synthesized from methanoic acid and 1-butanol. Write the balanced chemical equation for the formation of this ester.

ANSWER

$$H-\overset{\overset{\displaystyle O}{\|}}{C}-OH + H-O-CH_2-CH_2-CH_2-CH_3 \overset{H^+,\text{ heat}}{\rightleftharpoons}$$

$$H-\overset{\overset{\displaystyle O}{\|}}{C}-O-CH_2-CH_2-CH_2-CH_3 + H_2O$$

 ## Chemistry Link to **Health**
Salicylic Acid from a Willow Tree

For many centuries, relief from pain and fever was obtained by chewing on the leaves or a piece of bark from the willow tree. By the 1800s, chemists discovered that salicin was the agent in the bark responsible for the relief of pain. However, the body converts salicin to salicylic acid, which has a carboxyl group and a hydroxyl group that irritates the stomach lining. In 1899, the Bayer chemical company in Germany produced an ester of salicylic acid and acetic acid, called acetylsalicylic acid (aspirin), which is less irritating. In some aspirin preparations, a buffer is added to neutralize the carboxylic acid group. Today, aspirin is used as an analgesic (pain reliever), antipyretic (fever reducer), and anti-inflammatory agent. Many people take a daily low-dose aspirin, which has been found to lower the risk of heart attack and stroke.

The discovery of salicin in the leaves and bark of the willow tree led to the development of aspirin.

Oil of wintergreen, or methyl salicylate, has a pungent, minty odor and flavor. Because it can pass through the skin, methyl salicylate is used in skin ointments, where it acts as a counterirritant, producing heat to soothe sore muscles.

Ointments containing methyl salicylate are used to soothe sore muscles.

Chemistry Link to the **Environment**

Plastics

Terephthalic acid (an aromatic acid with two carboxyl groups) is produced in large quantities for the manufacture of polyesters such as Dacron. When terephthalic acid reacts with ethylene glycol, ester bonds form on both ends of the molecules, allowing many molecules to combine into a long polyester polymer.

Dacron, a synthetic material first produced by DuPont in the 1960s, is a polyester used to make permanent press fabrics, carpets, and clothes. Permanent press is a chemical process in which fabrics are permanently shaped and treated for wrinkle resistance. In medicine, artificial blood vessels and valves are made of Dacron, which is biologically inert and does not clot the blood.

Dacron is a polyester used in permanent press clothing.

A section of the polyester Dacron

The polyester can also be made into a film called Mylar and a plastic known as PETE (polyethyleneterephthalate). PETE is used for plastic soft drink and water bottles as well as for peanut butter jars, containers of salad dressings, shampoos, and dishwashing liquids. Today, PETE (recycling symbol "1") is the most widely recycled of all the plastics. Every year, more than 1.5×10^9 lb (6.8×10^8 kg) of PETE is being recycled. After PETE is separated from other plastics, it is used to make useful items, including polyester fabric for T-shirts and coats, carpets, fill for sleeping bags, doormats, and containers for tennis balls.

Polyester, in the form of the plastic PETE, is used to make soft drink bottles.

QUESTIONS AND PROBLEMS

16.3 Esters

LEARNING GOAL Write a balanced chemical equation for the formation of an ester.

16.21 Identify each of the following as an aldehyde, a ketone, a carboxylic acid, or an ester:

a. $CH_3 - \overset{\overset{O}{\|}}{C} - H$

b. $CH_3 - \overset{\overset{O}{\|}}{C} - O - CH_3$

c.

d. $CH_3 - CH_2 - \overset{\overset{O}{\|}}{C} - OH$

16.22 Identify each of the following as an aldehyde, a ketone, a carboxylic acid, or an ester:

a. $CH_3 - \overset{\overset{O}{\|}}{C} - OH$

b. $CH_3 - \overset{\overset{O}{\|}}{C} - O - CH_2 - CH_3$

c. (line-angle structure with H)

d. $CH_3 - \overset{\overset{CH_3}{|}}{CH} - \overset{\overset{O}{\|}}{C} - O - CH_2 - CH_3$

16.23 Draw the condensed structural formula for the ester formed when each of the following reacts with ethyl alcohol:
a. acetic acid   b. butyric acid
c. benzoic acid

16.24 Draw the condensed structural formula for the ester formed when each of the following reacts with methyl alcohol:
a. formic acid   b. propionic acid
c. 2-methylpentanoic acid

16.25 Draw the condensed or line-angle structural formula for the ester formed in each of the following reactions:

a. (line-angle) $\overset{O}{\|}$ ... $OH + HO$ (line-angle) $\xrightarrow{H^+, heat}$

b.

$CH_3 - CH_2 - CH_2 - CH_2 - \overset{\overset{O}{\|}}{C} - OH + HO - \overset{\overset{CH_3}{|}}{CH} - CH_3 \xrightarrow{H^+, heat}$

16.26 Draw the condensed or line-angle structural formula for the ester formed in each of the following reactions:

a. (line-angle) $\overset{O}{\|}$ ... $OH + HO$ (line-angle) $\xrightarrow{H^+, heat}$

b. (benzene ring)$- \overset{\overset{O}{\|}}{C} - OH + HO - CH_2 - CH_2 - CH_2 - CH_3 \xrightarrow{H^+, heat}$

16.27 Give the IUPAC and common names, if any, of the carboxylic acid and alcohol needed to produce each of the following esters:

a. $H - \overset{\overset{O}{\|}}{C} - O - CH_3$

b. $CH_3 - CH_2 - \overset{\overset{O}{\|}}{C} - O - CH_2 - CH_3$

c. (line-angle structure) $\overset{O}{\|}$—O—

d. $CH_3 - \overset{\overset{CH_3}{|}}{CH} - CH_2 - \overset{\overset{O}{\|}}{C} - O - CH_2 - CH_3$

16.28 Give the IUPAC and common names, if any, of the carboxylic acid and alcohol needed to produce each of the following esters:

a. $CH_3 - CH_2 - \overset{\overset{O}{\|}}{C} - O - CH_2 - CH_3$

b. (line-angle structure) $\overset{O}{\|}$—O—

c. $CH_3 - CH_2 - \overset{\overset{}{}}{CH} - \overset{\overset{O}{\|}}{C} - O - CH_3$ with CH_3 below the CH

d. (line-angle structure) $\overset{O}{\|}$—O—

16.4 Naming Esters

The name of an ester consists of two words that are derived from the names of the alcohol and the acid in that ester. The first word indicates the *alkyl* part from the alcohol. The second word is the *carboxylate* from the carboxylic acid. The IUPAC names of esters use the IUPAC names of the acids, while the common names of esters use the common names of the acids. Let's take a look at the following ester, which has a fruity odor. We start by separating the ester bond to identify the alkyl part from the alcohol and the carboxylate part from the acid. Then we name the ester as an alkyl carboxylate.

LEARNING GOAL

Write the IUPAC and common names for esters; draw condensed and line-angle structural formulas.

Methyl ethanoate
(methyl acetate)

The following examples of some typical esters show the IUPAC as well as the common names of esters:

$$CH_3-\overset{\overset{\displaystyle O}{\|}}{C}-O-CH_2-CH_2$$

Ethyl ethanoate
(ethyl acetate)

$$CH_3-CH_2-\overset{\overset{\displaystyle O}{\|}}{C}-O-CH_3$$

Methyl propanoate
(methyl propionate)

$$\overset{\overset{\displaystyle O}{\|}}{C}-O-CH_2-CH_3$$

Ethyl benzoate

Many of the fragrances of perfumes and flowers, and the flavors of fruits, are due to esters. Small esters are volatile so we can smell them and soluble in water so we can taste them. Several esters and their flavors and odor are listed in Table 16.3.

TABLE 16.3 Some Esters in Fruits and Flavorings

Condensed Structural Formula and Name	Flavor/Odor
$CH_3-\overset{\overset{O}{\|}}{C}-O-CH_2-CH_2-CH_3$ Propyl ethanoate (propyl acetate)	Pears
$CH_3-\overset{\overset{O}{\|}}{C}-O-CH_2-CH_2-CH_2-CH_2-CH_3$ Pentyl ethanoate (pentyl acetate)	Bananas
$CH_3-\overset{\overset{O}{\|}}{C}-O-CH_2-CH_2-CH_2-CH_2-CH_2-CH_2-CH_2-CH_3$ Octyl ethanoate (octyl acetate)	Oranges
$CH_3-CH_2-CH_2-\overset{\overset{O}{\|}}{C}-O-CH_2-CH_3$ Ethyl butanoate (ethyl butyrate)	Pineapples
$CH_3-CH_2-CH_2-\overset{\overset{O}{\|}}{C}-O-CH_2-CH_2-CH_2-CH_2-CH_3$ Pentyl butanoate (pentyl butyrate)	Apricots

Esters such as ethyl butanoate provide the odor and flavor of many fruits such as pineapples.

▶ SAMPLE PROBLEM 16.6 Naming Esters

What are the IUPAC and common names of the following ester?

$$CH_3-CH_2-\overset{\displaystyle O}{\overset{\displaystyle \|}{C}}-O-CH_2-CH_2-CH_3$$

SOLUTION

ANALYZE THE PROBLEM	Given	Need
	ester	IUPAC and common names

STEP 1 Write the name for the carbon chain from the alcohol as an *alkyl* group. The alcohol part of the ester is from propanol (propyl alcohol). The alkyl group is propyl.

$$CH_3-CH_2-\overset{\displaystyle O}{\overset{\displaystyle \|}{C}}-O-CH_2-CH_2-CH_3 \qquad \text{propyl}$$

STEP 2 Change the *ic acid* of the acid name to *ate*. The carboxylic acid part of the ester is from propanoic (propionic) acid, which becomes propanoate (propionate). The ester is named propyl propanoate (propyl propionate). Replacing the *ic acid* in the common name propionic acid with *ate* gives propionate. The common name for the ester is propyl propionate.

$$CH_3-CH_2-\overset{\displaystyle O}{\overset{\displaystyle \|}{C}}-O-CH_2-CH_2-CH_3 \qquad \text{propyl propanoate}$$
$$\text{(propyl propionate)}$$

STUDY CHECK 16.6

Draw the line-angle structural formula for ethyl heptanoate that gives odor and flavor to grapes.

ANSWER

Guide to Naming Esters

STEP 1
Write the name for the carbon chain from the alcohol as an *alkyl* group.

STEP 2
Change the *ic acid* of the acid name to *ate*.

The odor of grapes is due to ethyl heptanoate.

QUESTIONS AND PROBLEMS

16.4 Naming Esters

LEARNING GOAL Write the IUPAC and common names for esters; draw condensed and line-angle structural formulas.

16.29 Give the IUPAC name and common names, if any, for each of the following esters:

a. $H-\overset{\displaystyle O}{\overset{\displaystyle \|}{C}}-O-CH_3$

b. $CH_3-CH_2-\overset{\displaystyle O}{\overset{\displaystyle \|}{C}}-O-CH_2-CH_3$

c. (line-angle structure)

d. $CH_3-CH_2-CH_2-CH_2-\overset{\displaystyle O}{\overset{\displaystyle \|}{C}}-O-CH_2-\overset{\displaystyle CH_3}{\overset{\displaystyle |}{C}H}-CH_3$

16.30 Give the IUPAC name and common names, if any, for each of the following esters:

a. $CH_3-CH_2-CH_2-\overset{\displaystyle O}{\overset{\displaystyle \|}{C}}-O-CH_2-CH_3$

b. $CH_3-CH_2-CH_2-CH_2-CH_2-\overset{\displaystyle O}{\overset{\displaystyle \|}{C}}-O-CH_3$

c. [structure: isobutyl group with C=O and O-CH₃]

d. $CH_3-CH_2-\overset{\displaystyle O}{\overset{\displaystyle \|}{C}}-O-CH_2-CH_2-CH_2-CH_3$

16.31 Draw the condensed structural formula for each of the following:
a. methyl acetate   b. butyl formate
c. ethyl pentanoate   d. 2-bromopropyl propanoate

16.32 Draw the condensed structural formula for each of the following:
a. hexyl acetate   b. propyl formate
c. ethyl 2-hydroxybutanoate   d. methyl benzoate

16.33 What is the ester responsible for the flavor and odor of each of the following fruits?
a. banana   b. orange
c. apricot

16.34 What flavor would you notice if you smelled or tasted each of the following?
a. ethyl butanoate   b. propyl acetate
c. octyl acetate

LEARNING GOAL

Describe the boiling points and solubility of esters; draw the condensed structural formulas for the hydrolysis products.

16.5 Properties of Esters

Esters have boiling points higher than those of alkanes and ethers, but lower than those of alcohols and carboxylic acids of similar mass. Because ester molecules do not have hydroxyl groups, they cannot hydrogen bond to each other.

$$CH_3-CH_2-CH_2-CH_3 \qquad H-\overset{\displaystyle O}{\overset{\displaystyle \|}{C}}-O-CH_3 \qquad CH_3-CH_2-CH_2-OH \qquad CH_3-\overset{\displaystyle O}{\overset{\displaystyle \|}{C}}-OH$$

Name	Butane	Methyl methanoate	1-Propanol	Ethanoic acid
Molar Mass	58	60	60	60
Family	Alkane	Ester	Alcohol	Carboxylic acid
bp	0 °C	32 °C	97 °C	118 °C

Boiling Point Increases →

Solubility in Water

Esters with two to five carbon atoms are soluble in water. The partially negative oxygen of the carbonyl group forms hydrogen bonds with the partially positive hydrogen atoms of water molecules. The solubility of esters decreases as the number of carbon atoms increases.

Acid Hydrolysis of Esters

When esters are heated with water in the presence of a strong acid, usually H_2SO_4 or HCl, *hydrolysis* occurs. In **hydrolysis**, water reacts with the ester to form a carboxylic acid and an alcohol. Therefore, hydrolysis is the reverse of the esterification reaction. During acid hydrolysis, a water molecule provides the —OH group to convert the carbonyl group of the ester to a carboxyl group. A large quantity of water is used to shift the equilibrium in the direction of the carboxylic acid and alcohol products. When hydrolysis of biological esters occurs in the cells, an enzyme replaces the acid as the catalyst.

—— Hydrogen bonds

Esters with 2 to 5 carbon atoms are soluble because they form hydrogen bonds with water.

$$CH_3-\overset{\displaystyle O}{\overset{\displaystyle \|}{C}}-O-CH_3 + H-OH \overset{H^+, \text{ heat}}{\rightleftharpoons} CH_3-\overset{\displaystyle O}{\overset{\displaystyle \|}{C}}-OH + HO-CH_3$$

Methyl ethanoate   Water   Ethanoic acid   Methanol
(methyl acetate)   (acetic acid)   (methyl alcohol)

▶ SAMPLE PROBLEM 16.7 Acid Hydrolysis of Esters

Aspirin that has been stored for a long time may undergo hydrolysis in the presence of water and heat. What are the hydrolysis products of aspirin?

Aspirin
(acetylsalicylic acid)

Aspirin stored in a warm, humid place may undergo hydrolysis.

SOLUTION

ANALYZE THE PROBLEM	Given	Need
	aspirin	hydrolysis products

To write the hydrolysis products, separate the compound at the ester bond. Complete the formula of the carboxylic acid by adding —OH (from water) to the carbonyl group and —H to complete the alcohol. The acetic acid in the products gives the odor of vinegar to a sample of aspirin that has hydrolyzed.

Aspirin + H—OH ⇌ (H⁺, heat) Salicylic acid + HO—C—CH₃ Acetic acid

Separate here

STUDY CHECK 16.7

What are the names of the products from the acid hydrolysis of ethyl propanoate (ethyl propionate)?

ANSWER

propanoic acid and ethanol (propionic acid and ethyl alcohol)

Base Hydrolysis of Esters (Saponification)

When an ester undergoes hydrolysis with a strong base such as NaOH or KOH, the products are the carboxylate salt and the corresponding alcohol. This base hydrolysis is also called **saponification**, which refers to the reaction of a long-chain fatty acid with NaOH to make soap. Thus, a carboxylic acid, which is produced in acid hydrolysis, is converted to its carboxylate salt when neutralized by a strong base.

Ester + strong base ⟶ carboxylate salt + alcohol

$$CH_3-C(=O)-O-CH_3 + NaOH \xrightarrow{Heat} CH_3-C(=O)-O^- Na^+ + HO-CH_3$$

Methyl ethanoate (methyl acetate) + Sodium hydroxide ⟶ Sodium ethanoate (sodium acetate) + Methanol (methyl alcohol)

⊗ CORE CHEMISTRY SKILL

Hydrolyzing Esters

Ethyl acetate is the solvent in fingernail polish.

▶SAMPLE PROBLEM 16.8 Base Hydrolysis of Esters

Ethyl acetate is a solvent used in fingernail polish, plastics, and lacquers. Write the balanced chemical equation for the hydrolysis of ethyl acetate with NaOH.

SOLUTION

ANALYZE THE PROBLEM	Given	Need
	ester, base	carboxylate salt, alcohol

Ethyl ethanoate (ethyl acetate)   Sodium ethanoate (sodium acetate)   Ethanol (ethyl alcohol)

Interactive Video

Hydrolysis of Esters

STUDY CHECK 16.8

Draw the condensed structural formulas for the products from the hydrolysis of methyl benzoate with KOH.

ANSWER

$$ \text{C}_6\text{H}_5-\overset{\overset{\displaystyle O}{\|}}{\text{C}}-\text{O}^-\text{ K}^+ \;+\; \text{HO}-\text{CH}_3 $$

QUESTIONS AND PROBLEMS

16.5 Properties of Esters

LEARNING GOAL Describe the boiling points and solubility of esters; draw the condensed structural formulas for the hydrolysis products.

16.35 For each of the following pairs of compounds, select the compound that has the higher boiling point:

a. $CH_3-\overset{\overset{\displaystyle O}{\|}}{C}-O-CH_3$ or $CH_3-CH_2-\overset{\overset{\displaystyle O}{\|}}{C}-OH$

b. $CH_3-\overset{\overset{\displaystyle O}{\|}}{C}-O-CH_3$ or $CH_3-CH_2-CH_2-CH_2-OH$

c. (line-angle structure)   or   (line-angle ester structure)

16.36 For each of the following pairs of compounds, select the compound that has the higher boiling point:

a. $H-\overset{\overset{\displaystyle O}{\|}}{C}-O-CH_3$ or $CH_3-CH_2-CH_2-OH$

b. H (line-angle ester)   or   (line-angle acid with OH)

c. $CH_3-O-CH_2-CH_3$ or $H-\overset{\overset{\displaystyle O}{\|}}{C}-O-CH_3$

16.37 Draw the condensed or line-angle structural formulas for the products from the acid- or base-catalyzed hydrolysis of each of the following compounds:

a. $CH_3-CH_2-\overset{\overset{\displaystyle O}{\|}}{C}-O-CH_3 + NaOH \xrightarrow{\text{Heat}}$

b. (acetate ester line-angle) $+ H_2O \underset{\xrightarrow{H^+,\text{ heat}}}{\rightleftharpoons}$

c. $CH_3-CH_2-CH_2-\overset{\overset{\displaystyle O}{\|}}{C}-O-CH_2-CH_3 + H_2O \underset{\xrightarrow{H^+,\text{ heat}}}{\rightleftharpoons}$

d. (benzoate) $\overset{\overset{\displaystyle O}{\|}}{C}-O-CH_2-CH_3 + NaOH \xrightarrow{\text{Heat}}$

e. (benzoate ester line-angle) $+ H_2O \underset{\xrightarrow{H^+,\text{ heat}}}{\rightleftharpoons}$

16.38 Draw the condensed or line-angle structural formulas for the products from the acid- or base-catalyzed hydrolysis of each of the following compounds:

a. $CH_3-CH_2-\overset{\overset{\displaystyle O}{\|}}{C}-O-CH_2-CH_2-CH_2-CH_3 + H_2O \underset{\xrightarrow{H^+,\text{ heat}}}{\rightleftharpoons}$

b. H (formate ester line-angle) $+ NaOH \xrightarrow{\text{Heat}}$

c. $CH_3-CH_2-\overset{\overset{\displaystyle O}{\|}}{C}-O-CH_3 + H_2O \underset{}{\overset{H^+,\ heat}{\rightleftharpoons}}$

d. $CH_3-CH_2-\overset{\overset{\displaystyle O}{\|}}{C}-O-\bigcirc + H_2O \underset{}{\overset{H^+,\ heat}{\rightleftharpoons}}$

e. [structure] $+ NaOH \overset{Heat}{\rightarrow}$

℞ Clinical Update
Liquid Bandages

The liquid bandage used to close Robert's surgical incisions is also available in pharmacies for home use in closing wounds. The liquid hardens quickly when it comes in contact with blood and tissue, stops bleeding, and holds the edges of the wound together as skin heals. In a few days, the plastic bandage sloughs off and there is no need to remove stitches or staples. Anyone applying liquid bandage needs to be aware that contact of the liquid with gloves or other surfaces will cause them to adhere. Persons with an allergy to plastic should not use liquid bandage products.

The polymer in the liquid bandage consists of repeating units of Indermil. Indermil can be produced by the esterification reaction of 2-cyano-2-propenoic acid and 1-butanol.

$H_2C=\overset{\overset{\displaystyle CN}{|}}{C}-\overset{\overset{\displaystyle O}{\|}}{C}-OH$
2-Cyano-2-propenoic acid

℞ Clinical Applications

16.39 a. Draw the condensed structural formulas for the reactants and products from the reaction between 2-cyano-2-propenoic acid and 1-butanol.
   b. What is the IUPAC name of the ester formed?

16.40 a. Draw the condensed structural formulas for the products from the acid hydrolysis of the ester in problem 16.39.
   b. Draw the condensed structural formulas for the products from the base hydrolysis with NaOH of the ester in problem 16.39.

A spray containing a liquid bandage applied to a wound closes the wound quickly and stops bleeding.

CONCEPT MAP

CARBOXYLIC ACIDS AND ESTERS

Carboxylic Acids

have a → **Carboxyl Group** → forms hydrogen bonds and are → **Soluble in Water Up to 5 C Atoms**

are → **Polar** → and dissociate as → **Weak Acids**

are neutralized by → **Strong Bases** → to form → **Carboxylate Salts**

and → **Alcohols** → combine to form / hydrolyze to form → **Esters** → saponify to form → **Carboxylate Salts** and **Alcohols**

CHAPTER REVIEW

16.1 Carboxylic Acids
LEARNING GOAL Write the IUPAC and common names for carboxylic acids and draw their condensed and line-angle structural formulas.

- A carboxylic acid contains the carboxyl functional group, which is a hydroxyl group connected to a carbonyl group.
- The IUPAC name of a carboxylic acid is obtained by replacing the *e* in the alkane name with *oic acid*.
- The common names of carboxylic acids with one to four carbon atoms are formic acid, acetic acid, propionic acid, and butyric acid.

16.2 Properties of Carboxylic Acids
LEARNING GOAL Describe the boiling points, solubility, dissociation, and neutralization of carboxylic acids.

Hydrogen bonds

- The carboxyl group contains polar bonds of O—H and C=O, which makes a carboxylic acid with one to five carbon atoms soluble in water.
- As weak acids, carboxylic acids dissociate slightly by donating H^+ to water to form carboxylate and hydronium ions.
- Carboxylic acids are neutralized by base, producing a carboxylate salt and water.

16.3 Esters
LEARNING GOAL Write a balanced chemical equation for the formation of an ester.
- In an ester, an alkyl or aromatic group replaces the H of the hydroxyl group of a carboxylic acid.

- In the presence of a strong acid, a carboxylic acid reacts with an alcohol to produce an ester and a molecule of water from the —OH removed from the carboxylic acid, and the —H removed from the alcohol molecule.

16.4 Naming Esters
LEARNING GOAL Write the IUPAC and common names for esters; draw condensed and line-angle structural formulas.
- The names of esters consist of two words: the alkyl part from the alcohol and the name of the carboxylate obtained by replacing *ic acid* with *ate*.

Methyl ethanoate
(methyl acetate)

16.5 Properties of Esters
LEARNING GOAL
Describe the boiling points and solubility of esters; draw the condensed structural formulas for the hydrolysis products.

Aspirin
(acetylsalicylic acid)

- Esters have boiling points that are lower than alcohols and carboxylic acids, but higher than alkanes.
- Esters with two to five carbon atoms are soluble in water.
- Esters undergo acid hydrolysis by adding water to yield the carboxylic acid and alcohol.
- Base hydrolysis, or saponification, of an ester produces the carboxylate salt and an alcohol.

SUMMARY OF NAMING

Family	Structure	IUPAC Name	Common Name
Carboxylic acid	CH_3—C(=O)—OH	Ethanoic acid	Acetic acid
Carboxylate salt	CH_3—C(=O)—O^- Na^+	Sodium ethanoate	Sodium acetate
Ester	CH_3—C(=O)—O—CH_3	Methyl ethanoate	Methyl acetate

SUMMARY OF REACTIONS

The chapter sections to review are shown after the name of the reaction.

Dissociation of a Carboxylic Acid in Water (16.2)

$$CH_3-\overset{\displaystyle O}{\overset{\|}{C}}-OH + H_2O \rightleftharpoons CH_3-\overset{\displaystyle O}{\overset{\|}{C}}-O^- + H_3O^+$$

Ethanoic acid   Ethanoate ion   Hydronium
(acetic acid)   (acetate ion)   ion

Neutralization of a Carboxylic Acid (16.2)

$$CH_3-CH_2-\overset{\displaystyle O}{\overset{\|}{C}}-OH + NaOH \longrightarrow CH_3-CH_2-\overset{\displaystyle O}{\overset{\|}{C}}-O^- Na^+ + H_2O$$

Propanoic acid   Sodium   Sodium propanoate
(propionic acid)   hydroxide   (sodium propionate)

Esterification: Carboxylic Acid and an Alcohol (16.3)

$$CH_3-\overset{\displaystyle O}{\overset{\|}{C}}-OH + HO-CH_3 \underset{}{\overset{H^+, heat}{\rightleftharpoons}} CH_3-\overset{\displaystyle O}{\overset{\|}{C}}-O-CH_3 + H_2O$$

Ethanoic acid   Methanol   Methyl ethanoate
(acetic acid)   (methyl alcohol)   (methyl acetate)

Acid Hydrolysis of an Ester (16.5)

$$CH_3-\overset{\displaystyle O}{\overset{\|}{C}}-O-CH_3 + H-OH \underset{}{\overset{H^+, heat}{\rightleftharpoons}} CH_3-\overset{\displaystyle O}{\overset{\|}{C}}-OH + HO-CH_3$$

Methyl ethanoate   Ethanoic acid   Methanol
(methyl acetate)   (acetic acid)   (methyl alcohol)

Base Hydrolysis of an Ester (Saponification) (16.5)

$$CH_3-CH_2-\overset{\displaystyle O}{\overset{\|}{C}}-O-CH_3 + NaOH \overset{Heat}{\longrightarrow} CH_3-CH_2-\overset{\displaystyle O}{\overset{\|}{C}}-O^- Na^+ + HO-CH_3$$

Methyl propanoate   Sodium   Sodium propanoate   Methanol
(methyl propionate)   hydroxide   (sodium propionate)   (methyl alcohol)

KEY TERMS

acid hydrolysis The splitting of an ester molecule in the presence of a strong acid to produce a carboxylic acid and an alcohol.

base hydrolysis (saponification) The splitting of an ester molecule by a strong base to produce a carboxylate salt and an alcohol.

carboxyl group A functional group found in carboxylic acids composed of carbonyl and hydroxyl groups.

$$-\overset{\displaystyle O}{\overset{\|}{C}}-OH$$

Carboxyl group

carboxylate ion The anion produced when a carboxylic acid dissociates in water.

carboxylate salt The product of neutralization of a carboxylic acid, which is a carboxylate ion and a metal ion from the base.

carboxylic acid An organic compound containing the carboxyl group.

ester An organic compound in which an alkyl or aromatic group replaces the hydrogen atom in a carboxylic acid.

esterification The formation of an ester from a carboxylic acid and an alcohol with the elimination of a molecule of water in the presence of an acid catalyst.

⚛ CORE CHEMISTRY SKILLS

The chapter section containing each Core Chemistry Skill is shown in parentheses at the end of each heading.

Naming Carboxylic Acids (16.1)

- The IUPAC name of a carboxylic acid is obtained by replacing the *e* in the corresponding alkane name with *oic acid*.
- The common names of carboxylic acids with one to four carbon atoms are formic acid, acetic acid, propionic acid, and butyric acid.

Example: Give the IUPAC name for the following:

$$CH_3-CH-CH_2-\overset{\overset{\displaystyle Cl}{|}}{\underset{\underset{\displaystyle CH_3}{|}}{C}}-CH_2-\overset{\overset{\displaystyle O}{\|}}{C}-OH$$

Answer: 3-chloro-3,5-dimethylhexanoic acid

Hydrolyzing Esters (16.5)

- Esters undergo acid hydrolysis by adding water to produce a carboxylic acid and an alcohol.
- Esters undergo base hydrolysis, or saponification, to produce a carboxylate salt and an alcohol.

Example: Draw the condensed structural formulas for the products from the **(a)** acid and **(b)** base hydrolysis (NaOH) of ethyl butanoate.

Answer:

a. $CH_3-CH_2-CH_2-\overset{\overset{\displaystyle O}{\|}}{C}-OH \ + \ HO-CH_2-CH_3$

b. $CH_3-CH_2-CH_2-\overset{\overset{\displaystyle O}{\|}}{C}-O^- \ Na^+ \ + \ HO-CH_2-CH_3$

UNDERSTANDING THE CONCEPTS

The chapter sections to review are shown in parentheses at the end of each question.

16.41 Draw the condensed structural formulas and give the IUPAC names of two structural isomers of the carboxylic acids that have the molecular formula $C_4H_8O_2$. (16.1)

16.42 Draw the condensed structural formulas and give the IUPAC names of four structural isomers of the carboxylic acids that have the molecular formula $C_5H_{10}O_2$. (16.1)

16.43 Draw the condensed structural formulas and give the IUPAC names of two structural isomers of the esters that have the molecular formula $C_3H_6O_2$. (16.3, 16.4)

16.44 Draw the condensed structural formulas and give the IUPAC names of four structural isomers of the esters that have the molecular formula $C_4H_8O_2$. (16.3, 16.4)

℞ Clinical Applications

16.45 A strawberry nutritional drink used for a liquid diet is flavored with methyl butanoate. (16.1, 16.3, 16.4, 16.5)
  a. Draw the condensed structural formula for methyl butanoate.

b. Give the IUPAC name of the carboxylic acid and the alcohol used to prepare methyl butanoate.
c. Write a balanced chemical equation for the acid hydrolysis of methyl butanoate.
d. Write a balanced chemical equation for the base hydrolysis of methyl butanoate with NaOH.

16.46 The drug cocaine hydrochloride hydrolyzes in air to give methyl benzoate. Its odor, which smells like pineapple guava, is used to train drug-sniffing dogs. (16.1, 16.3, 16.4, 16.5)

a. Draw the condensed structural formula for methyl benzoate.
b. Give the name of the carboxylic acid and alcohol used to prepare methyl benzoate.
c. Write a balanced chemical equation for the acid hydrolysis of methyl benzoate.
d. Write a balanced chemical equation for the base hydrolysis of methyl benzoate with NaOH.

ADDITIONAL QUESTIONS AND PROBLEMS

16.47 Give the IUPAC and common names, if any, for each of the following compounds: (16.1, 16.4)

a. $CH_3-\overset{\overset{\displaystyle CH_3}{|}}{CH}-CH_2-\overset{\overset{\displaystyle O}{\|}}{C}-OH$

b.
$$\underset{\text{benzene ring}}{\bigcirc}-\overset{\overset{\displaystyle O}{\|}}{C}-O-CH_2-CH_3$$

c. $CH_3-CH_2-\overset{\overset{\displaystyle O}{\|}}{C}-O-CH_2-CH_3$

d.
$$\underset{\underset{\displaystyle Cl}{|}}{\bigcirc}-\overset{\overset{\displaystyle O}{\|}}{C}-OH$$

e.

f. $CH_3-\overset{\overset{\displaystyle O}{\|}}{C}-O-\overset{\overset{\displaystyle CH_3}{|}}{CH}-CH_3$

16.48 Give the IUPAC and common names, if any, for each of the following compounds: (16.1, 16.4)

a. $CH_3-\overset{\overset{\displaystyle CH_3}{|}}{CH}-CH_2-CH_2-\overset{\overset{\displaystyle O}{\|}}{C}-OH$

b.

c.

d. $CH_3-CH_2-CH_2-\overset{\overset{\displaystyle O}{\|}}{C}-O-CH_3$

e. $CH_3-\overset{\overset{\displaystyle CH_3}{|}}{CH}-CH_2-\overset{\overset{\displaystyle O}{\|}}{C}-O-CH_2-CH_3$

f. $CH_3-\overset{\overset{\displaystyle CH_3}{|}}{CH}-CH_2-\overset{\overset{\displaystyle OH}{|}}{CH}-\overset{\overset{\displaystyle O}{\|}}{C}-OH$

16.49 Draw the line-angle structural formulas for two methyl esters that have the molecular formula $C_5H_{10}O_2$. (16.3)

16.50 Draw the line-angle structural formulas for the carboxylic acid and the ester that have the molecular formula $C_2H_4O_2$. (16.1, 16.3)

16.51 Draw the condensed structural formula for each of the following: (16.1, 16.4)
 a. methyl hexanoate
 b. *p*-chlorobenzoic acid
 c. β-chloropropionic acid
 d. ethyl butanoate
 e. 3-methylpentanoic acid
 f. ethyl benzoate

16.52 Draw the condensed structural formula for each of the following: (16.1, 16.4)
 a. α-bromobutyric acid
 b. ethyl butyrate
 c. 2-methyloctanoic acid
 d. 3,5-dimethylhexanoic acid
 e. propyl acetate
 f. 3,4-dibromobenzoic acid

16.53 For each of the following pairs, identify the compound that would have the higher boiling point. Explain. (16.2, 16.5)

 a. $CH_3-CH_2-CH_2-OH$ or $CH_3-\overset{\overset{\displaystyle O}{\|}}{C}-OH$

 b. $CH_3-CH_2-CH_2-CH_3$ or $CH_3-\overset{\overset{\displaystyle O}{\|}}{C}-OH$

16.54 For each of the following pairs, identify the compound that would have the higher boiling point. Explain. (16.2, 16.5)

 a. $CH_3-\overset{\overset{\displaystyle OH}{|}}{CH}-CH_3$ or $H-\overset{\overset{\displaystyle O}{\|}}{C}-O-CH_3$

 b. $H-\overset{\overset{\displaystyle O}{\|}}{C}-O-CH_3$ or $CH_3-CH_2-CH_2-CH_3$

16.55 Acetic acid, methyl formate, and 1-propanol all have the same molar mass. The possible boiling points are 32 °C, 97 °C, and 118 °C. Match the compounds with the boiling points and explain your choice. (16.2, 16.5)

16.56 Propionic acid, 1-butanol, and butyraldehyde all have the same molar mass. The possible boiling points are 76 °C, 118 °C, and 141 °C. Match the compounds with the boiling points and explain your choice. (16.2, 16.5)

16.57 Which of the following compounds are soluble in water? (16.2, 16.5)

 a. $CH_3-CH_2-\overset{\overset{\displaystyle O}{\|}}{C}-O^-\ Na^+$

 b.

 c. $CH_3-CH_2-CH_2-OH$

 d. $CH_3-CH_2-\overset{\overset{\displaystyle O}{\|}}{C}-OH$

16.58 Which of the following compounds are soluble in water? (16.2, 16.5)

 a. $CH_3-CH_2-CH_2-\overset{\overset{\displaystyle O}{\|}}{C}-OH$

 b. $CH_3-\overset{\overset{\displaystyle O}{\|}}{C}-O-CH_3$

 c. $CH_3-CH_2-CH_2-CH_3$

 d.

16.59 Draw the condensed structural formulas for the products from each of the following reactions: (16.2, 16.3)

 a. $CH_3-CH_2-\overset{\overset{\displaystyle O}{\|}}{C}-OH + H_2O \ \rightleftharpoons$

 b. $CH_3-CH_2-\overset{\overset{\displaystyle O}{\|}}{C}-OH + KOH \ \longrightarrow$

 c.
$\overset{H^+,\ heat}{\rightleftharpoons}$

 d.
$+ HO-CH_2-CH_3 \ \overset{H^+,\ heat}{\rightleftharpoons}$

16.60 Draw the condensed structural formulas for the products from each of the following reactions: (16.2, 16.3)

 a. $CH_3-\overset{\overset{\displaystyle O}{\|}}{C}-OH + NaOH \ \longrightarrow$

 b. $CH_3-\overset{\overset{\displaystyle O}{\|}}{C}-OH + H_2O \ \rightleftharpoons$

 c.
$OH + KOH \ \longrightarrow$

d. $CH_3\!-\!\underset{\underset{CH_3}{|}}{CH}\!-\!\overset{\overset{O}{\|}}{C}\!-\!OH + HO\!-\!CH_3 \underset{\longleftarrow}{\overset{H^+,\ heat}{\rightleftharpoons}}$

16.61 Give the IUPAC names of the carboxylic acid and alcohol needed to produce each of the following esters: (16.3)

a. $CH_3\!-\!\underset{\underset{CH_3}{|}}{CH}\!-\!CH_2\!-\!\overset{\overset{O}{\|}}{C}\!-\!O\!-\!CH_3$

b. benzene ring with $\overset{\overset{O}{\|}}{C}\!-\!O\!-\!CH_2\!-\!CH_3$ and Cl substituent

c. $CH_3CH_2CH_2CH_2\overset{\overset{O}{\|}}{C}\!-\!O\!-\!CH_2CH_3$

16.62 Give the IUPAC names of the carboxylic acid and alcohol needed to produce each of the following esters: (16.3)

a. $CH_3\!-\!CH_2\!-\!CH_2\!-\!\overset{\overset{O}{\|}}{C}\!-\!O\!-\!CH_2\!-\!CH_3$

b. $CH_3CH_2\overset{\overset{O}{\|}}{C}\!-\!O\!-$ benzene ring with Cl substituent

c. $CH_3\!-\!\underset{\underset{CH_3}{|}}{CH}\!-\!\underset{\underset{CH_3}{|}}{CH}\!-\!\overset{\overset{O}{\|}}{C}\!-\!O\!-\!CH_3$

16.63 Draw the condensed structural formulas for the products from each of the following reactions: (16.5)

a. $CH_3\!-\!CH_2\!-\!\overset{\overset{O}{\|}}{C}\!-\!O\!-\!\underset{\underset{CH_3}{|}}{CH}\!-\!CH_3 + H_2O \underset{\longleftarrow}{\overset{H^+,\ heat}{\rightleftharpoons}}$

b. $CH_3\!-\!\underset{\underset{CH_3}{|}}{CH}\!-\!\overset{\overset{O}{\|}}{C}\!-\!O\!-\!CH_2\!-\!CH_2\!-\!CH_3 + NaOH \xrightarrow{Heat}$

16.64 Draw the condensed structural formulas for the products from each of the following reactions: (16.5)

a. $CH_3\!-\!CH_2\!-\!\overset{\overset{O}{\|}}{C}\!-\!O\!-\!\underset{\underset{CH_3}{|}}{CH}\!-\!CH_3 + NaOH \xrightarrow{Heat}$

b. $CH_3\!-\!\underset{\underset{CH_3}{|}}{CH}\!-\!\overset{\overset{O}{\|}}{C}\!-\!O\!-\!CH_2\!-\!CH_2\!-\!CH_3 + H_2O \underset{\longleftarrow}{\overset{H^+,\ heat}{\rightleftharpoons}}$

CHALLENGE QUESTIONS

The following groups of questions are related to the topics in this chapter. However, they do not all follow the chapter order, and they require you to combine concepts and skills from several sections. These questions will help you increase your critical thinking skills and prepare for your next exam.

16.65 Using the reactions we have studied, indicate how you might prepare the following from the starting substance given: (12.7, 16.1, 16.3)
 a. acetic acid from ethene
 b. butyric acid from 1-butanol

16.66 Using the reactions we have studied, indicate how you might prepare the following from the starting substance given: (16.1, 16.3)
 a. pentanoic acid from 1-pentanol
 b. ethyl acetate from two molecules of ethanol

16.67 Methyl benzoate is not soluble in water; however, when it is heated with KOH, the ester forms soluble products. When HCl is added to neutralize the basic solution, a white solid forms. Draw the condensed structural formulas for the reactants and products when methyl benzoate and KOH react. Explain what happens. (16.4, 16.5)

16.68 Hexanoic acid is not soluble in water. However, when hexanoic acid is added to a solution of NaOH, a soluble product forms. Draw the condensed structural formulas for the reactants and products when hexanoic acid and NaOH react. Explain what happens. (16.4, 16.5)

16.69 Propyl acetate is an ester that gives the odor and flavor of pears. (9.4, 16.3, 16.4, 16.5)
 a. Draw the condensed structural formula for propyl acetate.
 b. Write a balanced chemical equation for the formation of propyl acetate.
 c. Write a balanced chemical equation for the hydrolysis of propyl acetate with HCl.
 d. Write a balanced chemical equation for the hydrolysis of propyl acetate with NaOH.
 e. How many milliliters of a 0.208 M NaOH solution is needed to completely hydrolyze (saponify) 1.58 g of propyl acetate?

16.70 Ethyl octanoate is a flavor component of mangos. (9.4, 16.3, 16.4, 16.5)
 a. Draw the condensed structural formula for ethyl octanoate.
 b. Write a balanced chemical equation for the formation of ethyl octanoate.
 c. Write a balanced chemical equation for the hydrolysis of ethyl octanoate with HCl.
 d. Write a balanced chemical equation for the hydrolysis of ethyl octanoate with NaOH.
 e. How many milliliters of a 0.315 M NaOH solution is needed to completely hydrolyze (saponify) 2.84 g of ethyl octanoate?

ANSWERS

Answers to Selected Questions and Problems

16.1 methanoic acid (formic acid)

16.3 a.

$$CH_3-CH_2-CH_2-CH_2-CH_2-\overset{\displaystyle O}{\overset{\|}{C}}-OH, \text{ hexanoic acid}$$

b. $CH_3-CH_2-\overset{\displaystyle CH_3-CH_2}{\overset{|}{CH}}-\overset{\displaystyle O}{\overset{\|}{C}}-OH,$ 2-ethylbutanoic acid

16.5 a. ethanoic acid (acetic acid)
b. butanoic acid (butyric acid)
c. 3-methylhexanoic acid
d. 3,4-dibromobenzoic acid

16.7 a. $Cl-CH_2-\overset{\displaystyle O}{\overset{\|}{C}}-OH$

b. $HO-CH_2-CH_2-\overset{\displaystyle O}{\overset{\|}{C}}-OH$

c. $CH_3-CH_2-\underset{\displaystyle CH_3}{\overset{\displaystyle O}{\overset{\|}{C}}}-OH$ where CH is bonded to CH₃

$$CH_3-CH_2-\underset{\overset{|}{CH_3}}{CH}-\overset{\displaystyle O}{\overset{\|}{C}}-OH$$

d. $CH_3-CH_2-\underset{\overset{|}{Br}}{CH}-CH_2-\underset{\overset{|}{Br}}{CH}-CH_2-\overset{\displaystyle O}{\overset{\|}{C}}-OH$

16.9 a. $H-\overset{\displaystyle O}{\overset{\|}{C}}-OH$ **b.** $CH_3-\overset{\displaystyle O}{\overset{\|}{C}}-OH$

c. (isovaleric structure with OH)   **d.** (cyclopentane carboxylic acid with OH)

16.11 a. Butanoic acid has a greater molar mass and would have a higher boiling point.
b. Propanoic acid can form dimers, effectively doubling the molar mass, which gives propanoic acid a higher boiling point.
c. Butanoic acid can form dimers, effectively doubling the molar mass, which gives butanoic acid a higher boiling point.

16.13 a. Propanoic acid has the smallest alkyl group, which makes it most soluble.
b. Propanoic acid forms more hydrogen bonds with water, which makes it most soluble.

16.15 a. $CH_3-CH_2-CH_2-\overset{\displaystyle O}{\overset{\|}{C}}-OH + H_2O \rightleftharpoons$

$$CH_3-CH_2-CH_2-\overset{\displaystyle O}{\overset{\|}{C}}-O^- + H_3O^+$$

b. $CH_3-\underset{\overset{|}{CH_3}}{CH}-\overset{\displaystyle O}{\overset{\|}{C}}-OH + H_2O \rightleftharpoons$

$$CH_3-\underset{\overset{|}{CH_3}}{CH}-\overset{\displaystyle O}{\overset{\|}{C}}-O^- + H_3O^+$$

16.17 a.

$$CH_3-CH_2-CH_2-CH_2-\overset{\displaystyle O}{\overset{\|}{C}}-OH + NaOH \longrightarrow$$

$$CH_3-CH_2-CH_2-CH_2-\overset{\displaystyle O}{\overset{\|}{C}}-O^- Na^+ + H_2O$$

b. $CH_3-\underset{\overset{|}{Cl}}{CH}-\overset{\displaystyle O}{\overset{\|}{C}}-OH + NaOH \longrightarrow$

$$CH_3-\underset{\overset{|}{Cl}}{CH}-\overset{\displaystyle O}{\overset{\|}{C}}-O^- Na^+ + H_2O$$

c. (benzoic acid) $\overset{\displaystyle O}{\overset{\|}{C}}-OH$ + NaOH $\longrightarrow$ (benzoate) $\overset{\displaystyle O}{\overset{\|}{C}}-O^- Na^+$ + H_2O

16.19 a. sodium pentanoate
b. sodium 2-chloropropanoate (sodium α-chloropropionate)
c. sodium benzoate

16.21 a. aldehyde   **b.** ester
c. ketone   **d.** carboxylic acid

16.23 a. $CH_3-\overset{\displaystyle O}{\overset{\|}{C}}-O-CH_2-CH_3$

b. $CH_3-CH_2-CH_2-\overset{\displaystyle O}{\overset{\|}{C}}-O-CH_2-CH_3$

c. (benzene ring)$-\overset{\displaystyle O}{\overset{\|}{C}}-O-CH_2-CH_3$

16.25 a. (ester skeletal structure)

b. $CH_3-CH_2-CH_2-CH_2-\overset{\displaystyle O}{\overset{\|}{C}}-O-\underset{\overset{|}{CH_3}}{CH}-CH_3$

16.27 a. methanoic acid (formic acid) and methanol (methyl alcohol)
b. propanoic acid (propionic acid) and ethanol (ethyl alcohol)
c. butanoic acid (butyric acid) and methanol (methyl alcohol)
d. 3-methylbutanoic acid (β-methylbutyric acid) and ethanol (ethyl alcohol)

16.29 a. methyl methanoate (methyl formate)
  b. ethyl propanoate (ethyl propionate)
  c. methyl butanoate (methyl butyrate)
  d. 2-methylpropyl pentanoate

16.31 a. $CH_3 - \overset{\displaystyle O}{\overset{\|}{C}} - O - CH_3$

  b. $H - \overset{\displaystyle O}{\overset{\|}{C}} - O - CH_2 - CH_2 - CH_2 - CH_3$

  c. $CH_3 - CH_2 - CH_2 - CH_2 - \overset{\displaystyle O}{\overset{\|}{C}} - O - CH_2 - CH_3$

  d. $CH_3 - CH_2 - \overset{\displaystyle O}{\overset{\|}{C}} - O - CH_2 - \overset{\displaystyle Br}{\overset{\|}{CH}} - CH_3$

16.33 a. pentyl ethanoate (pentyl acetate)
  b. octyl ethanoate (octyl acetate)
  c. pentyl butanoate (pentyl butyrate)

16.35 a. $CH_3 - CH_2 - \overset{\displaystyle O}{\overset{\|}{C}} - OH$
  b. $CH_3 - CH_2 - CH_2 - CH_2 - OH$

  c.

16.37 a. $CH_3 - CH_2 - \overset{\displaystyle O}{\overset{\|}{C}} - O^- \ Na^+ \ + \ HO - CH_3$

  b.

  c. $CH_3 - CH_2 - CH_2 - \overset{\displaystyle O}{\overset{\|}{C}} - OH \ + \ HO - CH_2 - CH_3$

  d. $- \overset{\displaystyle O}{\overset{\|}{C}} - O^- \ Na^+ \ + \ HO - CH_2 - CH_3$

  e.

16.39 a. $H_2C = \overset{\displaystyle CN}{\overset{|}{C}} - \overset{\displaystyle O}{\overset{\|}{C}} - OH \ + \ HO - CH_2 - CH_2 - CH_2 - CH_3 \ \underset{}{\overset{H^+,\ heat}{\rightleftharpoons}}$

$H_2C = \overset{\displaystyle CN}{\overset{|}{C}} - \overset{\displaystyle O}{\overset{\|}{C}} - O - CH_2 - CH_2 - CH_2 - CH_3 \ + \ H_2O$

  b. butyl 2-cyano-2-propenoate

16.41 $CH_3 - CH_2 - CH_2 - \overset{\displaystyle O}{\overset{\|}{C}} - OH$ butanoic acid $CH_3 - \overset{\displaystyle CH_3}{\overset{|}{CH}} - \overset{\displaystyle O}{\overset{\|}{C}} - OH$ 2-methylpropanoic acid

16.43 $CH_3 - \overset{\displaystyle O}{\overset{\|}{C}} - O - CH_3$ methyl ethanoate $H - \overset{\displaystyle O}{\overset{\|}{C}} - O - CH_2 - CH_3$ ethyl methanoate

16.45 a. $CH_3 - CH_2 - CH_2 - \overset{\displaystyle O}{\overset{\|}{C}} - O - CH_3$
  b. butanoic acid and methanol

  c. $CH_3 - CH_2 - CH_2 - \overset{\displaystyle O}{\overset{\|}{C}} - O - CH_3 \ + \ H_2O \ \overset{H^+,\ heat}{\rightleftharpoons}$

$CH_3 - CH_2 - CH_2 - \overset{\displaystyle O}{\overset{\|}{C}} - OH \ + \ HO - CH_3$

  d. $CH_3 - CH_2 - CH_2 - \overset{\displaystyle O}{\overset{\|}{C}} - O - CH_3 \ + \ NaOH \ \overset{Heat}{\longrightarrow}$

$CH_3 - CH_2 - CH_2 - \overset{\displaystyle O}{\overset{\|}{C}} - O^- \ Na^+ \ + \ HO - CH_3$

16.47 a. 3-methylbutanoic acid (β-methylbutyric acid)
  b. ethyl benzoate
  c. ethyl propanoate (ethyl propionate)
  d. 2-chlorobenzoic acid (*o*-chlorobenzoic acid)
  e. 4-hydroxypentanoic acid
  f. 2-propyl ethanoate (isopropyl acetate)

16.49

16.51 a. $CH_3 - CH_2 - CH_2 - CH_2 - CH_2 - \overset{\displaystyle O}{\overset{\|}{C}} - O - CH_3$

  b.

  c. $Cl - CH_2 - CH_2 - \overset{\displaystyle O}{\overset{\|}{C}} - OH$

  d. $CH_3 - CH_2 - CH_2 - \overset{\displaystyle O}{\overset{\|}{C}} - O - CH_2 - CH_3$

  e. $CH_3 - CH_2 - \overset{\displaystyle CH_3}{\overset{|}{CH}} - CH_2 - \overset{\displaystyle O}{\overset{\|}{C}} - OH$

  f.

16.53 a. Ethanoic acid has a higher boiling point than 1-propanol because two molecules of ethanoic acid hydrogen bond to form a dimer, which effectively doubles the molar mass and requires a higher temperature to reach the boiling point.
  b. Ethanoic acid forms hydrogen bonds, but butane does not.

16.55 Of the three compounds, methyl formate would have the lowest boiling point since it only has dipole–dipole attractions. Both acetic acid and 1-propanol can form hydrogen bonds, but because acetic acid can form dimers and double the effective molar mass, it has the highest boiling point. Methyl formate, 32 °C; 1-propanol, 97 °C; acetic acid, 118 °C.

16.57 a, c, and **d** are soluble in water.

16.59 a. $CH_3-CH_2-\overset{\overset{\displaystyle O}{\|}}{C}-O^- + H_3O^+$

b. $CH_3-CH_2-\overset{\overset{\displaystyle O}{\|}}{C}-O^-\ K^+ + H_2O$

c. $+ H_2O$

d. $+ H_2O$

16.61 a. 3-methylbutanoic acid and methanol
b. 3-chlorobenzoic acid and ethanol
c. hexanoic acid and ethanol

16.63 a. $CH_3-CH_2-\overset{\overset{\displaystyle O}{\|}}{C}-OH + HO-\overset{\overset{\displaystyle CH_3}{|}}{CH}-CH_3$

b. $CH_3-\overset{\overset{\displaystyle CH_3}{|}}{CH}-\overset{\overset{\displaystyle O}{\|}}{C}-O^-\ Na^+ + HO-CH_2-CH_2-CH_3$

16.65 a. $H_2C{=}CH_2 + H_2O \xrightarrow{\ H^+\ }$

$CH_3-CH_2-OH \xrightarrow{[O]} CH_3-\overset{\overset{\displaystyle O}{\|}}{C}-OH$

b. $CH_3-CH_2-CH_2-CH_2-OH \xrightarrow{[O]}$

$CH_3-CH_2-CH_2-\overset{\overset{\displaystyle O}{\|}}{C}-OH$

16.67 $-\overset{\overset{\displaystyle O}{\|}}{C}-O-CH_3 + KOH \xrightarrow{\ Heat\ }$

$-\overset{\overset{\displaystyle O}{\|}}{C}-O^-\ K^+ + HO-CH_3$

In KOH solution, the ester undergoes saponification to form the carboxylate salt, potassium benzoate, and methanol, which are soluble in water. When HCl is added, the salt is converted to benzoic acid, which is insoluble.

16.69 a. $CH_3-\overset{\overset{\displaystyle O}{\|}}{C}-O-CH_2-CH_2-CH_3$

b. $CH_3-\overset{\overset{\displaystyle O}{\|}}{C}-OH + HO-CH_2-CH_2-CH_3 \underset{\longleftarrow}{\overset{H^+,\ heat}{\rightleftharpoons}}$

$CH_3-\overset{\overset{\displaystyle O}{\|}}{C}-O-CH_2-CH_2-CH_3 + H_2O$

c. $CH_3-\overset{\overset{\displaystyle O}{\|}}{C}-O-CH_2-CH_2-CH_3 + H_2O \overset{H^+,\ heat}{\rightleftharpoons}$

$CH_3-\overset{\overset{\displaystyle O}{\|}}{C}-OH + HO-CH_2-CH_2-CH_3$

d. $CH_3-\overset{\overset{\displaystyle O}{\|}}{C}-O-CH_2-CH_2-CH_3 + NaOH \xrightarrow{\ Heat\ }$

$CH_3-\overset{\overset{\displaystyle O}{\|}}{C}-O^-\ Na^+ + HO-CH_2-CH_2-CH_3$

e. 74.4 mL of a 0.208 M NaOH solution

17

Lipids

REBECCA LEARNED OF HER FAMILY'S HYPER-
cholesterolemia after her mother died of a heart attack at 44. Her mother had a total cholesterol level of 600 mg/dL, which is three times the normal level. Rebecca learned that the lumps under her mother's skin and around the cornea of her eyes, called *xanthomas*, were caused by cholesterol that was stored throughout her body. In familial hypercholesterolemia (FH), genetic mutations prevent the removal of cholesterol from the bloodstream. As a result, low-density lipoprotein (LDL) accumulates in the blood and a person with FH can develop cardiovascular disease early in life. In adults with FH, cholesterol levels may be greater than 300 mg/dL, and LDL levels may be greater than 220 mg/dL. At the lipid clinic, Rebecca's blood tests showed that she had a total cholesterol level of 420 mg/dL and an LDL-cholesterol level of 275 mg/dL. Rebecca was diagnosed with FH. She learned that from birth, cholesterol has been accumulating throughout her arteries. FH is a genetic condition: If one parent has it, there is a 50 percent chance that a child will inherit the disorder. FH is caused by a mutation that blocks the removal of LDL-cholesterol from the blood resulting in the formation of cholesterol deposits on the arterial walls.

At age 39, Rebecca discovered a painful lump that was identified as calcified cholesterol. After her diagnosis, Rebecca met with Susan, a clinical lipid specialist at the lipid clinic where she informed Rebecca about managing risk factors that can lead to heart attack and stroke. Susan told Rebecca about medications she would prescribe, and then followed the results.

CAREER Clinical Lipid Specialist

Clinical lipid specialists work with patients who have lipid disorders such as high cholesterol, high triglycerides, coronary heart disease, obesity, and FH. At a lipid clinic, a clinical lipid specialist reviews a patient's lipid profile, which includes total cholesterol, high-density lipoprotein (HDL), and low-density lipoprotein (LDL). If a lipid disorder is identified, the lipid specialist assesses the patient's current diet and exercise program. The lipid specialist diagnoses and determines treatment including dietary changes such as reducing salt intake, increasing the amount of fiber in the diet, and lowering the amount of fat. He or she also discusses drug therapy using lipid-lowering medications that remove LDL-cholesterol to help patients achieve and maintain good health.

Allied health professionals such as nurses, nurse practitioners, pharmacists, and dietitians are certified by a clinical lipid specialist program for specialized care of patients with lipid disorders.

When we talk of fats and oils, waxes, steroids, and cholesterol, we are discussing lipids. Lipids are naturally occurring compounds that vary considerably in structure but share the common feature of being soluble in nonpolar solvents, but not in water. Fats, which are one family of lipids, have many functions in the body, such as storing energy and protecting and insulating internal organs. Because lipids are not soluble in water, they are important in cellular membranes that function to separate the internal contents of cells from the external environment. Other types of lipids are found in nerve fibers and in hormones, which act as chemical messengers.

Many people are concerned about the amounts of saturated fats and cholesterol in our diets. Researchers suggest that saturated fats and cholesterol are associated with diseases such as diabetes; cancers of the breast, pancreas, and colon; and *atherosclerosis*, a condition in which deposits of lipid materials called *plaque* accumulate in the coronary blood vessels. In atherosclerosis, plaque restricts the flow of blood to the tissue, causing necrosis (death). An accumulation of plaque in the heart could result in a *myocardial infarction* (heart attack).

The American Institute for Cancer Research (AICR) has recommended that we increase the fiber and starch content of our diets by adding more vegetables, fruits, and whole grains as well as foods with low levels of fat and cholesterol such as fish, poultry, lean meats, and low-fat dairy products. The AICR has also suggested that we limit our intake of foods high in fat and cholesterol such as eggs, nuts, fatty or organ meats, cheeses, butter, and coconut and palm oil.

LOOKING AHEAD

17.1 Lipids 609
17.2 Fatty Acids 610
♥ **Chemistry Link to Health**
Omega-3 Fatty Acids in Fish Oils 615
17.3 Waxes and Triacylglycerols 617
17.4 Chemical Properties of Triacylglycerols 621
♥ **Chemistry Link to Health**
Converting Unsaturated Fats to Saturated Fats: Hydrogenation and Interesterification 622
17.5 Phospholipids 627
♥ **Chemistry Link to Health**
Infant Respiratory Distress Syndrome (IRDS) 630
17.6 Steroids: Cholesterol, Bile Salts, and Steroid Hormones 632
♥ **Chemistry Link to Health**
Anabolic Steroids 636
17.7 Cell Membranes 638
Rx **Clinical Applications** 610, 616, 620, 631, 637, 640, 644
Rx **Clinical Update** *Rebecca's Program to Lower Cholesterol in Familial Hypercholesterolemia (FH)* 640

CHAPTER READINESS*

⚛ CORE CHEMISTRY SKILLS

- Writing Equations for Hydrogenation, Hydration, and Polymerization (12.7)
- Naming Alcohols and Phenols (13.1)
- Naming Carboxylic Acids (16.1)
- Hydrolyzing Esters (16.5)

*These Core Chemistry Skills from previous chapters are listed here for your review as you proceed to the new material in this chapter.

17.1 Lipids

Lipids are a family of biomolecules that have the common property of being soluble in organic solvents but not in water. The word *lipid* comes from the Greek word *lipos*, meaning "fat" or "lard." Typically, the lipid content of a cell can be extracted using a nonpolar solvent such as ether or chloroform. Lipids are an important feature in cell membranes and steroid hormones.

Types of Lipids

Within the lipid family, there are specific structures that distinguish the different types of lipids. Lipids such as waxes, triacylglycerols, glycerophospholipids, and sphingolipids are esters that can be hydrolyzed to give fatty acids along with other molecules. Triacylglycerols and glycerophospholipids contain the alcohol *glycerol*, whereas sphingolipids contain the amino alcohol *sphingosine*. Steroids, which have a completely different structure, do not contain fatty acids and cannot be hydrolyzed. Steroids are characterized by the *steroid*

LEARNING GOAL

Describe the classes of lipids.

nucleus of four fused carbon rings. Figure 17.1 illustrates the types and general structure of lipids we will discuss in this chapter.

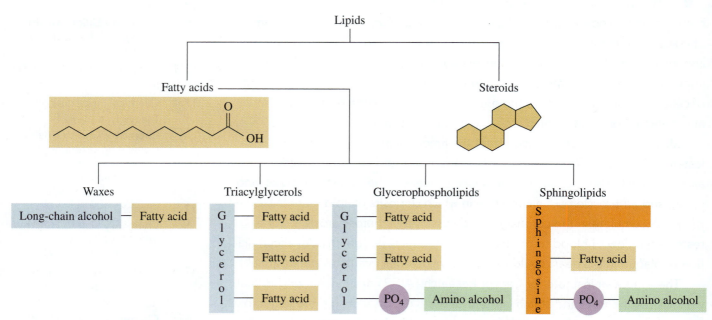

FIGURE 17.1 ▶ Lipids are naturally occurring compounds in cells and tissues, which are soluble in organic solvents but not in water.

Q What chemical property do waxes, triacylglycerols, and steroids have in common?

QUESTIONS AND PROBLEMS

17.1 Lipids

LEARNING GOAL Describe the classes of lipids.

17.1 Lipids are not soluble in water. Are lipids polar or nonpolar molecules?

17.2 Which of the following solvents might be used to dissolve an oil stain?
   a. water
   b. CCl_4
   c. diethyl ether
   d. benzene
   e. NaCl solution

R **Clinical Applications**

17.3 What are some functions of lipids in the body?

17.4 What are some of the different kinds of lipids?

LEARNING GOAL

Draw the condensed or line-angle structural formula for a fatty acid and identify it as saturated or unsaturated.

 CORE CHEMISTRY SKILL

Identifying Fatty Acids

17.2 Fatty Acids

A **fatty acid** contains a long, unbranched carbon chain with a carboxylic acid group at one end. Although the carboxylic acid part is hydrophilic, the long hydrophobic carbon chain makes fatty acids insoluble in water.

Most naturally occurring fatty acids have an even number of carbon atoms, usually between 12 and 20. An example of a fatty acid is lauric acid, a 12-carbon acid found in coconut oil. In a line-angle structural formula of a fatty acid, the ends and bends of the line are the carbon atoms. The structural formula of lauric acid can be drawn in several forms.

Drawing Structural Formulas for Lauric Acid

Ball-and-stick model

$$CH_3-(CH_2)_{10}-\overset{\overset{\displaystyle O}{\|}}{C}-OH \qquad CH_3-(CH_2)_{10}-COOH$$

$$CH_3-CH_2-CH_2-CH_2-CH_2-CH_2-CH_2-CH_2-CH_2-CH_2-CH_2-C\overset{\displaystyle O}{\diagdown}_{OH}$$

Condensed structural formulas

Line-angle structural formula

A **saturated fatty acid (SFA)** contains only carbon–carbon single bonds, which make the properties of a long-chain fatty acid similar to those of an alkane. An **unsaturated fatty acid** contains one or more carbon–carbon double bonds. In a **monounsaturated fatty acid (MUFA)**, the long carbon chain has one double bond, which makes its properties similar to those of an alkene. A **polyunsaturated fatty acid (PUFA)** has at least two carbon–carbon double bonds. Table 17.1 lists some of the typical fatty acids in lipids. In the lipids of plants and animals, about half of the fatty acids are saturated and half are unsaturated.

Cis and Trans Isomers of Unsaturated Fatty Acids

Unsaturated fatty acids can be drawn as *cis* and *trans* isomers. For example, oleic acid, an 18-carbon monounsaturated fatty acid found in olives, has one double bond starting at carbon 9. We can show its cis and trans structures using its line-angle structural formulas. The cis structure is the more prevalent isomer found in naturally occurring unsaturated fatty acids. In the cis isomer, the carbon chain has a "kink" at the double bond site. The trans isomer of oleic acid, *elaidic acid*, is a straight chain without a kink at the double bond site.

Almost all naturally occurring unsaturated fatty acids have one or more cis double bonds.

The human body is capable of synthesizing some fatty acids from carbohydrates or other fatty acids. However, humans cannot synthesize sufficient amounts of polyunsaturated fatty acids such as linoleic acid, linolenic acid, and arachidonic acid. Because they must be obtained from the diet, they are known as *essential fatty acids* (EFAs). In infants, a deficiency of EFAs can cause skin dermatitis. However, the role of fatty acids in adult nutrition is not well understood. Adults do not usually have a deficiency of EFAs.

Explore Your **World**
Solubility of Fats and Oils

Place some water in a small bowl. Add a drop of vegetable oil. Then add a few more drops of the oil. Record your observations. Now add a few drops of liquid soap and mix. Record your observations.

Place a small amount of fat such as margarine, butter, shortening, or vegetable oil on a dish or plate. Run water over it. Record your observations. Mix some soap with the fat substance and run water over it again. Record your observations.

Questions
1. Do the drops of oil in the water separate or do they come together? Explain.
2. How does the soap affect the oil layer?
3. Why don't the fats on the dish or plate wash off with water?
4. In general, what is the solubility of lipids in water?
5. Why does soap help to wash the fats off the plate?

TABLE 17.1 Structures and Melting Points of Common Fatty Acids

Name	Carbon Atoms: Double Bonds	Present in	Melting Point (°C)	Structures
Saturated Fatty Acids				
Lauric acid	12:0	Coconut	44	CH_3—$(CH_2)_{10}$—COOH
Myristic acid	14:0	Nutmeg	55	CH_3—$(CH_2)_{12}$—COOH
Palmitic acid	16:0	Palm	63	CH_3—$(CH_2)_{14}$—COOH
Stearic acid	18:0	Animal fat	69	CH_3—$(CH_2)_{16}$—COOH
Monounsaturated Fatty Acids				
Palmitoleic acid	16:1	Butter	0	CH_3—$(CH_2)_5$—CH=CH—$(CH_2)_7$—COOH
Oleic acid	18:1	Olives, pecan, grapeseed	14	CH_3—$(CH_2)_7$—CH=CH—$(CH_2)_7$—COOH
Polyunsaturated Fatty Acids				
Linoleic acid	18:2	Soybean, safflower, sunflower	−5	CH_3—$(CH_2)_4$—CH=CH—CH_2—CH=CH—$(CH_2)_7$—COOH
Linolenic acid	18:3	Corn	−11	CH_3—CH_2—CH=CH—CH_2—CH=CH—CH_2—CH=CH—$(CH_2)_7$—COOH
Arachidonic acid	20:4	Meat, eggs, fish	−50	CH_3—$(CH_2)_3$—$(CH_2$—CH=CH$)_4$—$(CH_2)_3$—COOH

Physical Properties of Fatty Acids

The saturated fatty acids fit closely together in a regular pattern, which allows many dispersion forces between the carbon chains. These normally weak intermolecular forces of attraction can be significant when molecules of fatty acids are close together. As a result, a significant amount of energy and high temperatures are required to separate the fatty acids before melting occurs. As the length of the carbon chain increases, more interactions occur between the fatty acids, requiring higher temperatures to melt. Saturated fatty acids are usually solids at room temperature (see Figure 17.2).

In unsaturated fatty acids, the cis double bonds cause the carbon chain to bend or kink, giving the molecules an irregular shape. As a result, unsaturated fatty acids cannot stack as closely as saturated fatty acids, and thus have fewer interactions between carbon

Stearic acid, mp 69 °C

Oleic acid, mp 14 °C

(a)

(b)

FIGURE 17.2 ▶ **(a)** In saturated fatty acids, the molecules fit closely together to give high melting points. **(b)** In unsaturated fatty acids, molecules cannot fit closely together, resulting in lower melting points.

◎ Why does the cis double bond affect the melting points of unsaturated fatty acids?

chains. We might think of saturated fatty acids as chips with regular shapes that stack closely together in a can. Similarly, irregularly shaped chips would be like unsaturated fatty acids that do not fit closely together. Consequently, less energy is required to separate the molecules, making the melting points of unsaturated fats lower than those of saturated fats. Most unsaturated fats are liquid oils at room temperature.

▶ **SAMPLE PROBLEM 17.1 Structures and Properties of Fatty Acids**

Consider the line-angle structural formula for vaccenic acid, a fatty acid found in dairy products and human milk.

a. Why is this substance an acid?
b. How many carbon atoms are in vaccenic acid?
c. Is the fatty acid saturated, monounsaturated, or polyunsaturated?
d. Give the shorthand notation for the number of carbon atoms and double bonds in vaccenic acid.
e. Is it most likely to be solid or liquid at room temperature?
f. Would it be soluble in water?

SOLUTION

a. Vaccenic acid contains a carboxylic acid group. b. It contains 18 carbon atoms.
c. It is a monounsaturated fatty acid (MUFA). d. 18:1
e. It is liquid at room temperature.
f. No. Its long hydrocarbon chain makes it insoluble in water.

STUDY CHECK 17.1

Palmitoleic acid is a fatty acid with the following condensed structural formula:

$$CH_3-(CH_2)_5-CH=CH-(CH_2)_7-\overset{\overset{\displaystyle O}{\|}}{C}-OH$$

a. How many carbon atoms are in palmitoleic acid?
b. Is the fatty acid saturated, monounsaturated, or polyunsaturated?
c. Give the shorthand notation for the number of carbon atoms and double bonds in palmitoleic acid.
d. Is it most likely to be solid or liquid at room temperature?

ANSWER

a. 16   b. monounsaturated   c. 16:1   d. liquid

Prostaglandins

Prostaglandins are hormone-like substances produced in small amounts in most cells of the body. The prostaglandins, also known as *eicosanoids*, are formed from arachidonic acid, the polyunsaturated fatty acid with 20 carbon atoms (*eicos* is the Greek word for 20). Swedish chemists first discovered prostaglandins and named them "prostaglandin E" (soluble in ether) and "prostaglandin F" (soluble in phosphate buffer or *fosfat* in Swedish). The various kinds of prostaglandins differ by the substituents attached to the five-carbon ring. Prostaglandin E (PGE) has a ketone group on carbon 9, whereas prostaglandin F (PGF) has a hydroxyl group. The number of double bonds is shown as a subscript 1 or 2.

Although prostaglandins are broken down quickly, they have potent physiological effects. Some prostaglandins increase blood pressure, and others lower blood pressure. Other prostaglandins stimulate contraction and relaxation in the smooth muscle of the uterus. When tissues are injured, arachidonic acid is converted to prostaglandins that produce inflammation and pain in the area.

Arachidonic acid

Analgesics

PGF₂

When tissues are injured, prostaglandins are produced, which cause pain and inflammation.

Pain, fever, inflammation

The treatment of pain, fever, and inflammation is based on inhibiting the enzymes that convert arachidonic acid to prostaglandins. Several nonsteroidal anti-inflammatory drugs (NSAIDs), such as aspirin, block the production of prostaglandins and in doing so decrease pain and inflammation and reduce fever (antipyretics). Ibuprofen has similar anti-inflammatory and analgesic effects. Other NSAIDs include naproxen (Aleve and Naprosyn), ketoprofen (Actron), and nabumetone (Relafen). Although NSAIDs are helpful, their long-term use can result in liver, kidney, and gastrointestinal damage.

Aspirin

Ibuprofen (Advil, Motrin)

Naproxen (Aleve, Naprosyn)

Chemistry Link to **Health**
Omega-3 Fatty Acids in Fish Oils

Because unsaturated fats are now recognized as being more beneficial to health than saturated fats, American diets have changed to include more unsaturated fats and less saturated fatty acids. This change is a response to research that indicates that atherosclerosis and heart disease are associated with high levels of fats in the diet. However, the Inuit people of Alaska have a diet with high levels of unsaturated fats as well as high levels of blood cholesterol, but a very low occurrence of atherosclerosis and heart attacks. The fats in the Inuit diet are primarily unsaturated fats from fish, rather than from land animals.

Both fish and vegetable oils have high levels of unsaturated fats. The fatty acids in vegetable oils are *omega-6 fatty acids* (ω-6 fatty acids), in which the first double bond occurs at carbon 6 counting from the methyl end of the carbon chain. Omega is the last letter in the Greek alphabet and is used to denote the end. Two common omega-6 acids are linoleic acid (LA) and arachidonic acid (AA). However, the fatty acids in fish oils are mostly the omega-3 type, in which the first double

Cold water fish are a good source of omega-3 fatty acids.

bond occurs at the third carbon counting from the methyl group. Three common *omega-3 fatty acids* (or ω-3 fatty acids) in fish are linolenic acid (ALA), eicosapentaenoic acid (EPA), and docosahexaenoic acid (DHA).

In atherosclerosis and heart disease, cholesterol forms plaques that adhere to the walls of the blood vessels. Blood pressure rises as blood has to squeeze through a smaller opening in the blood vessel. As more plaque forms, there is also a possibility of blood clots blocking the blood vessels and causing a heart attack. Omega-3 fatty acids lower the tendency of blood platelets to stick together, thereby reducing the possibility of blood clots. However, high levels of omega-3 fatty acids can increase bleeding if the ability of the platelets to form blood clots is reduced too much. It does seem that a diet that includes fish such as salmon, tuna, and herring can provide higher amounts of the omega-3 fatty acids, which help lessen the possibility of developing heart disease.

Omega-6 Fatty Acids

Linoleic acid (LA)

Arachidonic acid (AA)

Omega-3 Fatty Acids

Linolenic acid (ALA)

Eicosapentaenoic acid (EPA)

Docosahexaenoic acid (DHA)

QUESTIONS AND PROBLEMS

17.2 Fatty Acids

LEARNING GOAL Draw the condensed or line-angle structural formula for a fatty acid and identify it as saturated or unsaturated.

17.5 Describe some similarities and differences in the structures of a saturated fatty acid and an unsaturated fatty acid.

17.6 Stearic acid and linoleic acid each have 18 carbon atoms. Why does stearic acid melt at 69 °C but linoleic acid melts at −5 °C?

17.7 Draw the line-angle structural formula for each of the following fatty acids:
  a. palmitic acid   **b.** oleic acid

17.8 Draw the line-angle structural formula for each of the following fatty acids:
  a. stearic acid   **b.** linoleic acid

17.9 For each of the following fatty acids, give the shorthand notation for the number of carbon atoms and double bonds, and classify as saturated, monounsaturated, or polyunsaturated:
  a. lauric acid   **b.** linolenic acid
  c. palmitoleic acid   **d.** stearic acid

17.10 For each of the following fatty acids, give the shorthand notation for the number of carbon atoms and double bonds, and classify as saturated, monounsaturated, or polyunsaturated:
  a. linoleic acid   **b.** palmitic acid
  c. myristic acid   **d.** oleic acid

17.11 How does the structure of a fatty acid with a cis double bond differ from the structure of a fatty acid with a trans double bond?

17.12 How does the double bond influence the dispersion forces that can form between the hydrocarbon chains of fatty acids?

℞ Clinical Applications

17.13 What is the difference in the location of the first double bond in an omega-3 and an omega-6 fatty acid (see Chemistry Link to Health "Omega-3 Fatty Acids in Fish Oils")?

17.14 What are some sources of omega-3 and omega-6 fatty acids (see Chemistry Link to Health "Omega-3 Fatty Acids in Fish Oils")?

17.15 Compare the structures and functional groups of arachidonic acid and prostaglandin PGE_1.

17.16 Compare the structures and functional groups of PGF_1 and PGF_2.

17.17 What are some effects of prostaglandins in the body?

17.18 How does an anti-inflammatory drug reduce inflammation?

17.3 Waxes and Triacylglycerols

Waxes are found in many plants and animals. Natural waxes are found on the surface of fruits, and on the leaves and stems of plants where they help prevent loss of water and damage from pests. Waxes on the skin, fur, and feathers of animals provide a waterproof coating. A **wax** is an ester of a saturated fatty acid and a long-chain alcohol, each containing from 14 to 30 carbon atoms.

The formulas of some common waxes are given in Table 17.2. Beeswax obtained from honeycombs and carnauba wax from palm trees are used to give a protective coating to furniture, cars, and floors. Jojoba wax is used in making candles and cosmetics such as lipstick. Lanolin, a mixture of waxes obtained from wool, is used in hand and facial lotions to aid retention of water, softening the skin.

LEARNING GOAL

Draw the condensed or line-angle structural formula for a wax or triacylglycerol produced by the reaction of a fatty acid and an alcohol or glycerol.

TABLE 17.2 Some Typical Waxes

Type	Condensed Structural Formula	Source	Uses
Beeswax	$CH_3-(CH_2)_{14}-\overset{\displaystyle O}{\overset{\|}{C}}-O-(CH_2)_{29}-CH_3$	Honeycomb	Candles, shoe polish, wax paper
Carnauba wax	$CH_3-(CH_2)_{24}-\overset{\displaystyle O}{\overset{\|}{C}}-O-(CH_2)_{29}-CH_3$	Brazilian palm tree	Waxes for furniture, cars, floors, shoes
Jojoba wax	$CH_3-(CH_2)_{18}-\overset{\displaystyle O}{\overset{\|}{C}}-O-(CH_2)_{19}-CH_3$	Jojoba bush	Candles, soaps, cosmetics

Waxes are esters of long-chain alcohols and fatty acids.

Triacylglycerols

In the body, fatty acids are stored as **triacylglycerols**, also called *triglycerides*, which are triesters of glycerol (a trihydroxy alcohol) and fatty acids. The general formula of a triacylglycerol follows:

Triacylglycerol

Jojoba wax is obtained from the seed of the jojoba bush.

In a triacylglycerol, three hydroxyl groups of glycerol form ester bonds with the carboxyl groups of three fatty acids. For example, glycerol and three molecules of stearic acid form a triacylglycerol. In the name, glycerol is named *glyceryl* and the fatty acids are named as carboxylates. For example, stearic acid is named as stearate, which gives the name glyceryl tristearate. The common name of this compound is tristearin.

Tristearin consists of glycerol with three ester bonds to stearic acid molecules.

Glycerol   3 Stearic acid molecules   Glyceryl tristearate (tristearin)

⚙ **CORE CHEMISTRY SKILL**

Drawing Structures for Triacylglycerols

Prior to hibernation, a polar bear eats food with a high caloric content.

Triacylglycerols are used to thicken creams and lotions.

Guide to Drawing Triacylglycerols

STEP 1
Draw the condensed structural formulas for glycerol and the fatty acids.

STEP 2
Form ester bonds between the hydroxyl groups on glycerol and the carboxyl groups on each fatty acid.

Most naturally occurring triacylglycerols contain glycerol bonded to two or three different fatty acids, typically palmitic acid, oleic acid, linoleic acid, and stearic acid. For example, a mixed triacylglycerol might be made from stearic acid, oleic acid, and palmitic acid. One possible structure for this mixed triacylglycerol follows:

$$CH_2-O-\overset{\overset{\displaystyle O}{\|}}{C}-(CH_2)_{16}-CH_3 \quad \text{Stearic acid}$$
$$CH-O-\overset{\overset{\displaystyle O}{\|}}{C}-(CH_2)_7-CH=CH-(CH_2)_7-CH_3 \quad \text{Oleic acid}$$
$$CH_2-O-\overset{\overset{\displaystyle O}{\|}}{C}-(CH_2)_{14}-CH_3 \quad \text{Palmitic acid}$$

A mixed triacylglycerol

Triacylglycerols are the major form of energy storage for animals. Animals that hibernate eat large quantities of plants, seeds, and nuts that are high in calories. Prior to hibernation, these animals, such as polar bears, gain as much as 14 kg per week. As the external temperature drops, the animal goes into hibernation. The body temperature drops to nearly freezing, and cellular activity, respiration, and heart rate are drastically reduced. Animals that live in extremely cold climates hibernate for 4 to 7 months. During this time, stored fat is the only source of energy.

▶ **SAMPLE PROBLEM 17.2** Drawing the Structure for a Triacylglycerol

Draw the condensed structural formula for glyceryl tripalmitoleate (tripalmitolein), which is used in cosmetic creams and lotions.

SOLUTION

ANALYZE THE PROBLEM	Given	Need
	glyceryl tripalmitoleate (tripalmitolein)	condensed structural formula

Glyceryl tripalmitoleate (tripalmitolein) is the triacylglycerol that contains ester bonds between glycerol and three palmitoleic acid molecules.

STEP 1 Draw the condensed structural formulas for glycerol and the fatty acids.

$$CH_2-OH + HO-\overset{\overset{\displaystyle O}{\|}}{C}-(CH_2)_7-CH=CH-(CH_2)_5-CH_3 \quad \text{Palmitoleic acid}$$
$$CH-OH + HO-\overset{\overset{\displaystyle O}{\|}}{C}-(CH_2)_7-CH=CH-(CH_2)_5-CH_3 \quad \text{Palmitoleic acid}$$
$$CH_2-OH + HO-\overset{\overset{\displaystyle O}{\|}}{C}-(CH_2)_7-CH=CH-(CH_2)_5-CH_3 \quad \text{Palmitoleic acid}$$

Glycerol

STEP 2 Form ester bonds between the hydroxyl groups on glycerol and the carboxyl groups on each fatty acid.

$$CH_2-O-\overset{\overset{\displaystyle O}{\|}}{C}-(CH_2)_7-CH=CH-(CH_2)_5-CH_3$$
$$CH-O-\overset{\overset{\displaystyle O}{\|}}{C}-(CH_2)_7-CH=CH-(CH_2)_5-CH_3$$
$$CH_2-O-\overset{\overset{\displaystyle O}{\|}}{C}-(CH_2)_7-CH=CH-(CH_2)_5-CH_3$$

Glyceryl tripalmitoleate (tripalmitolein)

STUDY CHECK 17.2

Draw the condensed structural formula for the triacylglycerol containing three molecules of myristic acid (14:0).

ANSWER

$$CH_2-O-\overset{\overset{\displaystyle O}{\|}}{C}-(CH_2)_{12}-CH_3$$
$$CH-O-\overset{\overset{\displaystyle O}{\|}}{C}-(CH_2)_{12}-CH_3$$
$$CH_2-O-\overset{\overset{\displaystyle O}{\|}}{C}-(CH_2)_{12}-CH_3$$

Melting Points of Fats and Oils

A **fat** is a triacylglycerol that is solid at room temperature, and it usually comes from animal sources such as meat, whole milk, butter, and cheese.

An **oil** is a triacylglycerol that is usually a liquid at room temperature and is obtained from a plant source. Olive oil and peanut oil are monounsaturated because they contain large amounts of oleic acid. Oils from corn, cottonseed, safflower seed, and sunflower seed are polyunsaturated because they contain large amounts of fatty acids with two or more double bonds (see Figure 17.3).

Glyceryl trioleate (triolein)

FIGURE 17.3 ▶ Vegetable oils such as olive oil, corn oil, and safflower oil contain unsaturated fats.

Q Why is olive oil a liquid at room temperature?

Palm oil and coconut oil are solids at room temperature because they consist mostly of saturated fatty acids. Coconut oil is 92% saturated fats, about half of which is lauric acid, which contains 12 carbon atoms rather than 18 carbon atoms found in the stearic acid of animal sources. Thus coconut oil has a melting point that is higher than typical vegetable oils, but not as high as fats from animal sources that contain stearic acid. The amounts of saturated, monounsaturated, and polyunsaturated fatty acids in some typical fats and oils are listed in Figure 17.4.

Saturated fatty acids have higher melting points than unsaturated fatty acids because they pack together more tightly. Animal fats usually contain more saturated fatty acids than do vegetable oils. Therefore, the melting points of animal fats are higher than those of vegetable oils.

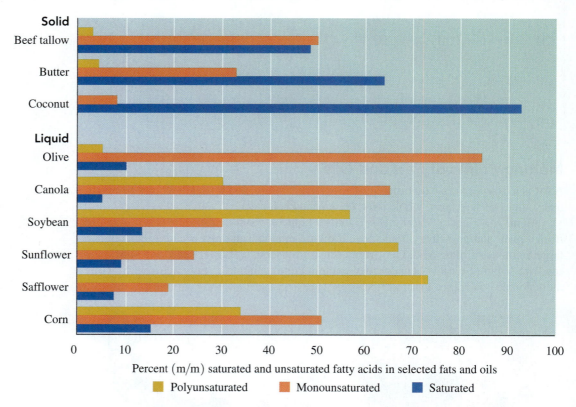

FIGURE 17.4 ▶ Vegetable oils are liquids at room temperature because they have a higher percentage of unsaturated fatty acids than do animal fats.

Ⓠ Why is butter a solid at room temperature, whereas canola oil is a liquid?

QUESTIONS AND PROBLEMS

17.3 Waxes and Triacylglycerols

LEARNING GOAL Draw the condensed or line-angle structural formula for a wax or triacylglycerol produced by the reaction of a fatty acid and an alcohol or glycerol.

17.19 Draw the condensed structural formula for the ester in beeswax that is formed from myricyl alcohol, $CH_3-(CH_2)_{29}-OH$, and palmitic acid.

17.20 Draw the condensed structural formula for the ester in jojoba wax that is formed from arachidic acid, a 20-carbon saturated fatty acid, and 1-docosanol, $CH_3-(CH_2)_{21}-OH$.

17.21 Draw the condensed structural formula for a triacylglycerol that contains stearic acid and glycerol.

17.22 Draw the condensed structural formula for a mixed triacylglycerol that contains two palmitic acid molecules and one oleic acid molecule on the center carbon of glycerol.

℞ Clinical Applications

17.23 Caprylic acid is an 8-carbon saturated fatty acid that occurs in coconut oil (10%) and palm kernel oil (4%). Draw the condensed structural formula for glyceryl tricaprylate (tricaprylin).

17.24 Linoleic acid is a 18-carbon unsaturated fatty acid with two double bonds that occurs in many vegetable oils including safflower oil (75%) and poppyseed oil (75%). Draw the condensed structural formula for glyceryl trilinoleate (trilinolein).

17.25 Safflower oil is polyunsaturated, whereas olive oil is monounsaturated. Why would safflower oil have a lower melting point than olive oil?

17.26 Olive oil is monounsaturated, whereas butter fat is saturated. Why does olive oil have a lower melting point than butter fat?

17.27 How does the percentage of monounsaturated and polyunsaturated fatty acids in sunflower oil compare to that of safflower oil?

17.28 How does the percentage of monounsaturated and polyunsaturated fatty acids in olive oil compare to that of canola oil?

17.4 Chemical Properties of Triacylglycerols

The chemical reactions of triacylglycerols involve the hydrogenation of the double bonds in the fatty acids, and the hydrolysis and saponification of the ester bonds between glycerol and the fatty acids.

LEARNING GOAL

Draw the condensed or line-angle structural formula for the products of a triacylglycerol that undergoes hydrogenation, hydrolysis, or saponification.

Hydrogenation

In the **hydrogenation** reaction, hydrogen gas is bubbled through the heated oil typically in the presence of a nickel catalyst. As a result, H atoms add to one or more carbon–carbon double bonds to form carbon–carbon single bonds.

$$-CH=CH- + H_2 \xrightarrow{Ni} \begin{array}{c} H \quad H \\ | \quad | \\ -C-C- \\ | \quad | \\ H \quad H \end{array}$$

For example, when hydrogen adds to all of the double bonds of glyceryl trioleate (triolein) using a nickel catalyst, the product is the saturated fat glyceryl tristearate (tristearin).

Double bonds ↓

$$CH_2-O-\overset{O}{\overset{||}{C}}-(CH_2)_7-CH=CH-(CH_2)_7-CH_3$$
$$CH-O-\overset{O}{\overset{||}{C}}-(CH_2)_7-CH=CH-(CH_2)_7-CH_3 + 3H_2 \xrightarrow{Ni}$$
$$CH_2-O-\overset{O}{\overset{||}{C}}-(CH_2)_7-CH=CH-(CH_2)_7-CH_3$$

Glyceryl trioleate
(triolein)

Single bonds ↓

$$CH_2-O-\overset{O}{\overset{||}{C}}-(CH_2)_7-CH_2-CH_2-(CH_2)_7-CH_3$$
$$CH-O-\overset{O}{\overset{||}{C}}-(CH_2)_7-CH_2-CH_2-(CH_2)_7-CH_3$$
$$CH_2-O-\overset{O}{\overset{||}{C}}-(CH_2)_7-CH_2-CH_2-(CH_2)_7-CH_3$$

Glyceryl tristearate
(tristearin)

In commercial hydrogenation, the addition of hydrogen is stopped before all the double bonds in a liquid vegetable oil become completely saturated. Complete hydrogenation gives a very brittle product, whereas the partial hydrogenation of a liquid vegetable oil changes it to a soft, semisolid fat. As it becomes more saturated, the melting point increases, and the substance becomes more solid at room temperature. By controlling the amount of hydrogen, manufacturers can produce various types of products such as soft margarines, solid stick margarines, and solid shortenings (see Figure 17.5). Although these products now contain more saturated fatty acids than the original oils, they contain no cholesterol, unlike similar products from animal sources, such as butter and lard.

⚛ **CORE CHEMISTRY SKILL**

Drawing the Products for the Hydrogenation, Hydrolysis, and Saponification of a Triacylglycerol

Vegetable oils   Tub (soft)   Stick margarine
(liquids)   margarine   (solid)

FIGURE 17.5 ▶ Many soft margarines, stick margarines, and solid shortenings are produced by the partial hydrogenation of vegetable oils.

◉ How does hydrogenation change the structure of the fatty acids in the vegetable oils?

Chemistry Link to **Health**

Converting Unsaturated Fats to Saturated Fats: Hydrogenation and Interesterification

During the early 1900s, margarine became a popular replacement for the highly saturated fats such as butter and lard. Margarine is produced by partially hydrogenating the unsaturated fats in vegetable oils such as safflower oil, corn oil, canola oil, cottonseed oil, and sunflower oil.

Hydrogenation and Trans Fats

In vegetable oils, the unsaturated fats usually contain cis double bonds. As hydrogenation occurs, double bonds are converted to single bonds. However, a small amount of the cis double bonds are converted to trans double bonds because they are more stable, which causes a change in the overall structure of the fatty acids. If the label on a product states that the oils have been "partially hydrogenated," that product will also contain trans fatty acids. In the United States, it is estimated that 2 to 4% of our total calories comes from trans fatty acids.

The concern about trans fatty acids is that their altered structure may make them behave like saturated fatty acids in the body. In the 1980s, research indicated that trans fatty acids have an effect on blood cholesterol similar to that of saturated fats, although study results vary. Several studies reported that trans fatty acids raise the levels of LDL-cholesterol, and lower the levels of HDL-cholesterol. (LDL and HDL are described in section 17.6.)

Foods containing naturally occurring trans fat include milk, beef, and eggs. Foods that contain trans fatty acids from the hydrogenation process include deep-fried foods, bread, baked goods, cookies, crackers, chips, stick and soft margarines, and vegetable shortening. The American Heart Association recommends that margarine should have no more

than 2 g of saturated fat per tablespoon and a liquid vegetable oil should be the first ingredient. They also recommend the use of soft margarine, which is only slightly hydrogenated and therefore has fewer trans fatty acids. Currently, the amount of trans fats is included on the Nutrition Facts label on food products. In the United States, a food label for a product that has less than 0.5 g of trans fat in one serving can read "0 g of trans fat."

The best advice may be to reduce total fat in the diet by using fats and oils sparingly, cooking with little or no fat, substituting olive oil or canola oil for other oils, and limiting the use of coconut oil and palm oil, which are high in saturated fatty acids.

Nutrition Facts
Serving Size 5 oz. (144g)
Servings Per Container 4

Amount Per Serving

Calories 310   **Calories** from Fat 100

	% Daily Value*
Total Fat 15g	21%
Saturated Fat 2.6g	17%
Trans Fat 1g	
Cholesterol 118mg	39%
Sodium 560mg	28%
Total Carbohydrate 12g	4%
Dietary Fiber 1g	4%
Sugars 1g	
Protein 24g	

Nutrition Facts label includes the grams of trans fat in one serving.

H   H

cis-Fatty acid

H_2/Ni

H H

Ni catalyst

H_2 Isomerization

Undesired side product (*trans*-fatty acid)

Addition of H_2

Desired saturated product

Interesterification

Interesterification is a newer process used to change unsaturated vegetable oils into products that have the properties of solid and semisolid saturated fats. During the process of interesterification, lipase enzymes are used to hydrolyze ester bonds in triacylglycerols of vegetable oils so that glycerol and fatty acids are formed. Then the saturated fatty acids recombine with glycerol. For example, an unsaturated

oleic acid in a vegetable oil could be replaced by a saturated stearic acid, which results in a more saturated fat with a higher melting point. The saturated products in the mixture are separated by differences in melting points. As a result of bypassing the hydrogenation process of converting double bonds to single bonds, there are no trans fatty acids present in the solid or semisolid fats products. Such products may have a label that reads "no trans fats."

Simplified Example of Interesterification

Mixed triacylglycerols are unsaturated and have lower melting points.

A new mixture of triacylglycerols includes saturated triacylglycerols with higher melting points, as well as unsaturated triacylglycerols.

Hydrolysis

Triacylglycerols are hydrolyzed (split by water) in the presence of strong acids such as HCl or H_2SO_4, or digestive enzymes called *lipases*. The products of hydrolysis of the ester bonds are glycerol and three fatty acids. The polar glycerol is soluble in water, but the fatty acids with their long hydrocarbon chains are not.

Saponification

Saponification occurs when a fat is heated with a strong base such as NaOH to form glycerol and the sodium salts of the fatty acids, which is soap. When NaOH is used, a solid soap is produced that can be molded into a desired shape; KOH produces a softer, liquid soap. An oil that is polyunsaturated produces a softer soap. Names like "coconut" or "avocado shampoo" tell you the sources of the oil used in the reaction.

Fat or oil + strong base $\xrightarrow{\text{Heat}}$ glycerol + salts of fatty acids (soap)

$$
\begin{array}{l}
\text{CH}_2\text{—O—}\overset{\displaystyle O}{\overset{\displaystyle \|}{\text{C}}}\text{—(CH}_2)_{14}\text{—CH}_3 \\[4pt]
\text{CH—O—}\overset{\displaystyle O}{\overset{\displaystyle \|}{\text{C}}}\text{—(CH}_2)_{14}\text{—CH}_3 + \textbf{3NaOH} \\[4pt]
\text{CH}_2\text{—O—}\overset{\displaystyle O}{\overset{\displaystyle \|}{\text{C}}}\text{—(CH}_2)_{14}\text{—CH}_3
\end{array}
\xrightarrow{\text{Heat}}
\begin{array}{l}
\text{CH}_2\text{—OH} \quad \text{Na}^+\ {}^-\text{O—}\overset{\displaystyle O}{\overset{\displaystyle \|}{\text{C}}}\text{—(CH}_2)_{14}\text{—CH}_3 \\[4pt]
\text{CH—OH} + \text{Na}^+\ {}^-\text{O—}\overset{\displaystyle O}{\overset{\displaystyle \|}{\text{C}}}\text{—(CH}_2)_{14}\text{—CH}_3 \\[4pt]
\text{CH}_2\text{—OH} \quad \text{Na}^+\ {}^-\text{O—}\overset{\displaystyle O}{\overset{\displaystyle \|}{\text{C}}}\text{—(CH}_2)_{14}\text{—CH}_3
\end{array}
$$

Glyceryl tripalmitate   Glycerol   3 Sodium palmitate
(tripalmitin)   (soap)

The reactions for fatty acids and triacylglycerols that are similar to the reactions of hydrogenation of alkenes, esterification, hydrolysis, and saponification are summarized in Table 17.3.

TABLE 17.3 Summary of Organic and Lipid Reactions

Reaction	Organic Reactants and Products	Lipid Reactants and Products
Esterification	Carboxylic acid + alcohol $\xrightarrow{\text{H}^+,\ \text{heat}}$ ester + water	3 Fatty acids + glycerol $\xrightarrow{\text{Enzyme}}$ triacylglycerol (fat) + 3 water
Hydrogenation	Alkene (double bond) + hydrogen $\xrightarrow{\text{Pt}}$ alkane (single bonds)	Unsaturated fat (double bonds) + hydrogen $\xrightarrow{\text{Ni}}$ saturated fat (single bonds)
Hydrolysis	Ester + water $\xrightarrow{\text{H}^+,\ \text{heat}}$ carboxylic acid + alcohol	Triacylglycerol (fat) + 3 water $\xrightarrow{\text{Enzyme}}$ 3 fatty acids + glycerol
Saponification	Ester + sodium hydroxide $\xrightarrow{\text{Heat}}$ sodium salt of carboxylic acid + alcohol	Triacylglycerol (fat) + 3 sodium hydroxide $\xrightarrow{\text{Heat}}$ 3 sodium salts of fatty acid (soaps) + glycerol

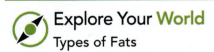

Explore Your World
Types of Fats

Read the labels on food products that contain fats, such as butter, margarine, vegetable oils, peanut butter, and potato chips. Look for terms such as saturated, monounsaturated, polyunsaturated, and partially or fully hydrogenated.

Questions

1. What type(s) of fats or oils are in the product?
2. How many grams of saturated, monounsaturated, and polyunsaturated fats are there in one serving of the product?
3. What percentage of the total fat is saturated fat? Unsaturated fat?

4. The label on a container of peanut butter states that the cottonseed and canola oils used to make the peanut butter have been fully hydrogenated. What are the typical products that would form when hydrogen is added?
5. For each packaged food, determine the following:
   a. How many grams of fat are in one serving of the food?
   b. Using the caloric value for fat (9 kcal/g), how many Calories (kilocalories) come from the fat in one serving?
   c. What is the percentage of fat in one serving?

Chemistry Link to the **Environment**

Biodiesel as an Alternative Fuel

Biodiesel is a name of a nonpetroleum fuel that can be used in place of diesel fuel. Biodiesel is produced from renewable biological resources such as vegetable oils (primarily soybean), waste vegetable oils from restaurants, and some animal fats. Biodiesel is nontoxic and biodegradable.

Biodiesel is prepared from triacylglycerols and alcohols (usually ethanol) to form ethyl esters and glycerol. The glycerol that separates from the fat is used in soaps and other products. The reaction of triacylglycerols is catalyzed by a base such as NaOH or KOH at low temperatures.

Triacylglycerol + 3 ethanol ⟶

3 ethyl esters (biodiesel) + glycerol

Compared to diesel fuel from petroleum, biodiesel burns in an engine to produce much lower levels of carbon dioxide emissions, particulates, unburned hydrocarbons, and aromatic hydrocarbons that cause lung cancer. Because biodiesel has extremely low sulfur content, it does not contribute to the formation of the sulfur oxides that produce acid rain. The energy output from the combustion of biodiesel is almost the same as energy produced by the combustion of petroleum diesel.

In many cases, diesel engines need only slight modification to use biodiesel. Manufacturers of diesel cars, trucks, boats, and tractors have different suggestions for the percentage of biodiesel to use, ranging from 2% (B2) blended with standard diesel fuel to using 100% pure biodiesel (B100). For example, B20 is 20% biodiesel by volume, blended with 80% petroleum diesel by volume. In 2013, 4.9×10^9 L of biodiesel were produced in the United States. Fuel stations in Europe and the United States are now stocking biodiesel fuel.

Biodiesel 20 contains 20% ethyl esters and 80% standard diesel fuel.

$$CH_2-O-\overset{\overset{\displaystyle O}{\|}}{C}-(CH_2)_{12}-CH_3$$
$$CH-O-\overset{\overset{\displaystyle O}{\|}}{C}-(CH_2)_7-CH=CH-(CH_2)_7-CH_3 + 3CH_3-CH_2-OH \xrightarrow{\text{NaOH catalyst}}$$
$$CH_2-O-\overset{\overset{\displaystyle O}{\|}}{C}-(CH_2)_{16}-CH_3$$

Triacylglycerol from vegetable oil   Ethanol

$$CH_2-OH \qquad CH_3-CH_2-O-\overset{\overset{\displaystyle O}{\|}}{C}-(CH_2)_{12}-CH_3$$
$$CH-OH + CH_3-CH_2-O-\overset{\overset{\displaystyle O}{\|}}{C}-(CH_2)_7-CH=CH-(CH_2)_7-CH_3$$
$$CH_2-OH \qquad CH_3-CH_2-O-\overset{\overset{\displaystyle O}{\|}}{C}-(CH_2)_{16}-CH_3$$

Glycerol   Ethyl esters used for biodiesel

▶ **SAMPLE PROBLEM 17.3** **Reactions of Lipids During Digestion**

Write the equation for the reaction catalyzed by the enzyme lipase that hydrolyzes glyceryl trilaurate (trilaurin) during the digestion process.

SOLUTION

ANALYZE THE PROBLEM	Given	Need
	glyceryl trilaurate	chemical equation for hydrolysis

glyceryl trilaurate is an ester of glycerol and three lauric acid molecules (12:0). When the ester undergoes hydrolysis by lipase, the products are glycerol and three lauric acid molecules.

$$
\begin{array}{l}
CH_2-O-\overset{\overset{\displaystyle O}{\|}}{C}-(CH_2)_{10}-CH_3 \\
\quad\quad\quad\overset{\displaystyle O}{\|} \\
CH-O-\overset{\overset{\displaystyle O}{\|}}{C}-(CH_2)_{10}-CH_3 \quad + \quad 3H_2O \xrightarrow{\text{Lipase}} \\
\quad\quad\quad\overset{\displaystyle O}{\|} \\
CH_2-O-\overset{\overset{\displaystyle O}{\|}}{C}-(CH_2)_{10}-CH_3
\end{array}
$$

Glyceryl trilaurate
(trilaurin)

$$
\begin{array}{ll}
CH_2-OH & HO-\overset{\overset{\displaystyle O}{\|}}{C}-(CH_2)_{10}-CH_3 \\
& \quad\quad\overset{\displaystyle O}{\|} \\
CH-OH \; + & HO-\overset{\overset{\displaystyle O}{\|}}{C}-(CH_2)_{10}-CH_3 \\
& \quad\quad\overset{\displaystyle O}{\|} \\
CH_2-OH & HO-\overset{\overset{\displaystyle O}{\|}}{C}-(CH_2)_{10}-CH_3
\end{array}
$$

Glycerol   3 Lauric acid
                  molecules

STUDY CHECK 17.3

What is the name of the product formed when a triacylglycerol containing oleic acid (18:1) and linoleic acid (18:2) is completely hydrogenated?

ANSWER

glyceryl tristearate (tristearin)

QUESTIONS AND PROBLEMS

17.4 Chemical Properties of Triacylglycerols

LEARNING GOAL Draw the condensed or line-angle structural formula for the products of a triacylglycerol that undergoes hydrogenation, hydrolysis, or saponification.

17.29 Identify each of the following processes as hydrogenation, hydrolysis, or saponification and give the products:
   a. the reaction of palm oil with KOH
   b. the reaction of glyceryl trilinoleate from safflower oil with water and HCl

17.30 Identify each of the following processes as hydrogenation, hydrolysis, or saponification and give the products:
   a. the reaction of corn oil and hydrogen (H_2) with a nickel catalyst
   b. the reaction of glyceryl tristearate with water in the presence of lipase enzyme

17.31 Write the balanced chemical equation for the hydrogenation of glyceryl tripalmitoleate, a fat containing glycerol and three palmitoleic acid molecules.

17.32 Write the balanced chemical equation for the hydrogenation of glyceryl trilinolenate, a fat containing glycerol and three linolenic acid molecules.

17.33 Write the balanced chemical equation for the acid hydrolysis of glyceryl trimyristate (trimyristin).

17.34 Write the balanced chemical equation for the acid hydrolysis of glyceryl trioleate (triolein).

17.35 Write the balanced chemical equation for the NaOH saponification of glyceryl trimyristate (trimyristin).

17.36 Write the balanced chemical equation for the NaOH saponification of glyceryl trioleate (triolein).

17.37 Draw the condensed structural formula for the product of the hydrogenation of the following triacylglycerol:

$$
\begin{array}{l}
CH_2-O-\overset{\overset{\displaystyle O}{\|}}{C}-(CH_2)_{16}-CH_3 \\
\quad\quad\quad\overset{\displaystyle O}{\|} \\
CH-O-\overset{\overset{\displaystyle O}{\|}}{C}-(CH_2)_7-CH=CH-(CH_2)_7-CH_3 \\
\quad\quad\quad\overset{\displaystyle O}{\|} \\
CH_2-O-\overset{\overset{\displaystyle O}{\|}}{C}-(CH_2)_{16}-CH_3
\end{array}
$$

17.38 Draw the condensed structural formulas for all the products that would be obtained when the triacylglycerol in problem 17.37 undergoes complete hydrolysis.

17.5 Phospholipids

LEARNING GOAL

Draw the structure of a phospholipid containing glycerol or sphingosine.

The **phospholipids** are a family of lipids similar in structure to triacylglycerols; they include glycerophospholipids and sphingomyelins. In a **glycerophospholipid**, two fatty acids form ester bonds with the first and second hydroxyl groups of glycerol. The third hydroxyl group forms an ester with phosphoric acid, which forms another phosphoester bond with an amino alcohol. In a *sphingomyelin*, sphingosine replaces glycerol. We can compare the general structures of a triacylglycerol, a glycerophospholipid, and a sphingolipid as follows:

Triacylglycerol   Glycerophospholipid   Sphingomyelin

Amino Alcohols

Three amino alcohols found in glycerophospholipids are choline, serine, and ethanolamine. In the body, at a physiological pH of 7.4, these amino alcohols are ionized.

$$HO-CH_2-CH_2-\overset{+}{\underset{CH_3}{\overset{CH_3}{\underset{|}{\overset{|}{N}}}}}-CH_3 \qquad HO-CH_2-\overset{\overset{+}{NH_3}}{\underset{|}{CH}}-\overset{O}{\overset{||}{C}}-O^- \qquad HO-CH_2-CH_2-\overset{+}{NH_3}$$

Choline   Serine   Ethanolamine

Lecithins and *cephalins* are two types of glycerophospholipids that are particularly abundant in brain and nerve tissues as well as in egg yolks, wheat germ, and yeast. Lecithins contain choline, and cephalins usually contain ethanolamine and sometimes serine. In the following structural formulas, the fatty acid that is used in each example is palmitic acid:

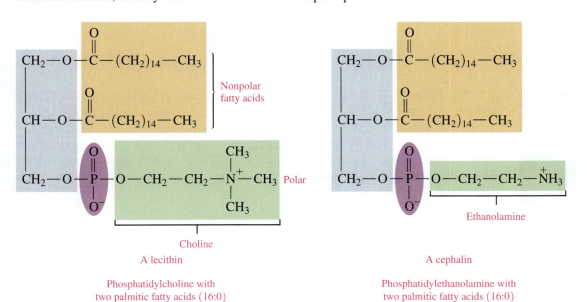

A lecithin

Phosphatidylcholine with two palmitic fatty acids (16:0)

A cephalin

Phosphatidylethanolamine with two palmitic fatty acids (16:0)

Glycerophospholipids contain both polar and nonpolar regions, which allow them to interact with both polar and nonpolar substances. The ionized amino alcohol and phosphate portion, called "the head," is polar and strongly attracted to water (see Figure 17.6). The hydrocarbon chains of the two fatty acids are the nonpolar "tails" of the glycerophospholipid, which are only soluble in other nonpolar substances, mostly lipids.

Choline   Glycerol   Two palmitic
     Phosphate   fatty acids (16:0)

(a) Components of a typical glycerophospholipid

Choline   Phosphoric acid   Glycerol   Fatty acids

(b) Glycerophospholipid

Polar head   Nonpolar tails

Polar head

Nonpolar tails

(c) Simplified way to draw a glycerophospholipid

FIGURE 17.6 ▶ **(a)** The components of a typical glycerophospholipid: an amino alcohol, phosphoric acid, glycerol, and two fatty acids. **(b)** In a glycerophospholipid, a polar "head" contains the ionized amino alcohol and phosphate, while the hydrocarbon chains of two fatty acids make up the nonpolar "tails." **(c)** A simplified drawing indicates the polar region and the nonpolar region.

Q Why are glycerophospholipids polar?

Poisonous snake venom contains phospholipases that hydrolyze phospholipids in red blood cells.

Snake venom is produced by the modified saliva glands of poisonous snakes. When a snake bites, venom is ejected through the fang of the snake. The venom of the eastern diamondback rattlesnake and the Indian cobra contains *phospholipases*, which are enzymes that catalyze the hydrolysis of the fatty acid on the center carbon of glycerophospholipids in the red blood cells. The resulting product, called *lysophospholipid*, causes breakdown of the red blood cell membranes. This makes them permeable to water, which causes hemolysis of the red blood cells.

▶ SAMPLE PROBLEM 17.4 Drawing Glycerophospholipid Structures

Draw the condensed structural formula for the cephalin that contains two stearic acids, phosphate, and serine as the ionized amino alcohol.

SOLUTION

	Given	Need
ANALYZE THE PROBLEM	cephalin, two stearic acids (18:0), phosphate, serine (ionized)	condensed structural formula

$$CH_2—O—\overset{\overset{\textstyle O}{\|}}{C}—(CH_2)_{16}—CH_3$$

Glycerol $CH—O—\overset{\overset{\textstyle O}{\|}}{C}—(CH_2)_{16}—CH_3$ } Stearic acids

$$CH_2—O—\overset{\overset{\textstyle O}{\|}}{\underset{\underset{\textstyle O^-}{\|}}{P}}—O—CH_2—\overset{\overset{\textstyle \overset{+}{N}H_3}{|}}{CH}—\overset{\overset{\textstyle O}{\|}}{C}—O^-$$

Phosphate · Serine

STUDY CHECK 17.4

Draw the condensed structural formula for the lecithin that contains two myristic acids phosphate, and choline as the ionized amino alcohol.

ANSWER

$$CH_2—O—\overset{\overset{\textstyle O}{\|}}{C}—(CH_2)_{12}—CH_3$$

$$CH—O—\overset{\overset{\textstyle O}{\|}}{C}—(CH_2)_{12}—CH_3$$

$$CH_2—O—\overset{\overset{\textstyle O}{\|}}{\underset{\underset{\textstyle O^-}{\|}}{P}}—O—CH_2—CH_2—\overset{\overset{\textstyle CH_3}{|}}{\underset{\underset{\textstyle CH_3}{|}}{\overset{+}{N}}}—CH_3$$

$$HO—CH—CH=CH—(CH_2)_{12}—CH_3$$
$$\overset{|}{CH—NH_2}$$
$$\overset{|}{CH_2—OH}$$
Sphingosine

Sphingosine, found in sphingomyelins, is a long-chain amino alcohol, which replaces glycerol. In a **sphingomyelin**, the amine group of sphingosine forms an amide bond to a fatty acid and the hydroxyl group forms an ester bond with phosphate, which forms another phosphoester bond to choline or ethanolamine. The sphingomyelins are abundant in the white matter of the myelin sheath, a coating surrounding the nerve cells that increases the speed of nerve impulses and insulates and protects the nerve cells.

Myelin sheath · Nerve fiber (axon)

Normal myelin sheath

Damaged myelin sheath

A sphingomyelin containing myristic acid and choline

In multiple sclerosis, sphingomyelin is lost from the myelin sheath, which protects the neurons in the brain and spinal cord. As the disease progresses, the myelin sheath deteriorates. Scars form on the neurons and impair the transmission of nerve signals. The symptoms of multiple sclerosis include various levels of muscle weakness with loss of coordination and vision, depending on the amount of damage. The cause of multiple sclerosis is not yet known, although some researchers suggest that a virus is involved. Several studies also suggest that adequate levels of vitamin D may lessen the severity or lower the risk of developing multiple sclerosis.

When the myelin sheath loses sphingomyelin, it deteriorates and the transmission of nerve signals is impaired.

▶ **SAMPLE PROBLEM 17.5** Sphingomyelin

The sphingomyelin found in eggs contains sphingosine, palmitic acid, the 16-carbon saturated fatty acid, and the ionized amino alcohol choline. Draw the condensed structural formula for this sphingomyelin.

SOLUTION

	Given	Need
ANALYZE THE PROBLEM	sphingosine, palmitic acid (16:0), choline (ionized)	condensed structural formula of the sphingomyelin

STUDY CHECK 17.5

Stearic acid is found in sphingomyelin in the brain. Draw the condensed structural formula for this sphingomyelin using ethanolamine as the ionized amino alcohol.

ANSWER

Chemistry Link to **Health**
Infant Respiratory Distress Syndrome (IRDS)

When an infant is born, an important key to its survival is proper lung function. In the lungs, there are many tiny air sacs called *alveoli*, where the exchange of O_2 and CO_2 takes place. Upon birth of a mature infant, surfactant is released into the lung tissues where it lowers the surface tension in the alveoli, which helps the air sacs inflate. The production of a *pulmonary surfactant*, which is a mixture of phospholipids including lecithin and sphingomyelin produced by specific lung cells, occurs in a fetus after 24 to 28 weeks of pregnancy. If an infant is born prematurely before 28 weeks of gestation, the low level of surfactant and immature lung development lead to a high risk of *Infant Respiratory Distress Syndrome* (IRDS). Without sufficient surfactant, the air sacs collapse and have to reopen with each breath. As a result, alveoli cells are damaged, less oxygen is taken in, and more carbon dioxide is retained, which can lead to hypoxia and acidosis.

One way to determine the maturity of the lungs of a fetus is to measure the *lecithin–sphingomyelin (L/S) ratio*. A ratio of 2.5 indicates mature fetal lung function, an L/S ratio of 2.4 to 1.6 indicates a low risk, and a ratio of less than 1.5 indicates a high risk of IRDS. Before the initiation of an early delivery, the L/S ratio of the amniotic fluid is measured. If the L/S ratio is low, steroids may be given to the mother to assist the lung development and production of surfactant in the fetus. Once a premature infant is born, treatment includes the use of steroids to help maturation of the lungs, the application of surfactants, and the administration of supplemental oxygen with ventilation to help minimize damage to the lungs.

A premature infant with respiratory distress is treated with a surfactant and oxygen.

Without sufficient surfactant in the lungs of a premature infant, the alveoli collapse, which decreases pulmonary function.

QUESTIONS AND PROBLEMS

17.5 Phospholipids

LEARNING GOAL Draw the structure of a phospholipid containing glycerol or sphingosine.

17.39 Describe the similarities and differences between triacylglycerols and glycerophospholipids.

17.40 Describe the similarities and differences between lecithins and cephalins.

17.41 Draw the condensed structural formula for the cephalin that contains two palmitic acids, phosphate, and ethanolamine as the ionized amino alcohol.

17.42 Draw the condensed structural formula for the lecithin that contains two palmitic acids, phosphate, and choline as the ionized amino alcohol.

℞ Clinical Applications

17.43 Identify the following glycerophospholipid, which is found in nerves and spinal cord in the body, as a lecithin or cephalin, and list its components:

$$CH_2-O-\overset{\overset{\displaystyle O}{\|}}{C}-(CH_2)_7-CH=CH-(CH_2)_7-CH_3$$
$$CH-O-\overset{\overset{\displaystyle O}{\|}}{C}-(CH_2)_{16}-CH_3$$
$$CH_2-O-\overset{\overset{\displaystyle O}{\|}}{\underset{\underset{\displaystyle O^-}{|}}{P}}-O-CH_2-CH_2-\overset{+}{N}H_3$$

17.44 Identify the following glycerophospholipid, which helps conduct nerve impulses in the body, as a lecithin or cephalin, and list its components:

$$CH_2-O-\overset{\overset{\displaystyle O}{\|}}{C}-(CH_2)_{14}-CH_3$$
$$CH-O-\overset{\overset{\displaystyle O}{\|}}{C}-(CH_2)_{16}-CH_3$$
$$CH_2-O-\overset{\overset{\displaystyle O}{\|}}{\underset{\underset{\displaystyle O^-}{|}}{P}}-O-CH_2-CH_2-\overset{\underset{\displaystyle CH_3}{|}}{\overset{\overset{\displaystyle CH_3}{|}}{\overset{+}{N}}}-CH_3$$

17.45 Identify the following features of this phospholipid, which is abundant in the myelin sheath that surrounds nerve cells:

$$HO-CH-CH=CH\text{⁓⁓⁓⁓⁓}$$
$$CH-\overset{\overset{\displaystyle H}{|}}{N}-\overset{\overset{\displaystyle O}{\|}}{C}\text{⁓⁓⁓⁓⁓}$$
$$CH_2-O-\overset{\overset{\displaystyle O}{\|}}{\underset{\underset{\displaystyle O^-}{|}}{P}}-O\text{⁓}\overset{+}{N}H_3$$

a. Is the phospholipid formed from glycerol or sphingosine?
b. What is the fatty acid?
c. What type of bond connects the fatty acid?
d. What is the ionized amino alcohol?

17.46 Identify the following features of this phospholipid, which is needed for the brain and nerve tissues:

a. Is the phospholipid formed from glycerol or sphingosine?
b. What is the fatty acid?
c. What type of bond connects the fatty acid?
d. What is the ionized amino alcohol?

17.6 Steroids: Cholesterol, Bile Salts, and Steroid Hormones

Steroids are compounds containing the *steroid nucleus*, which consists of three cyclohexane rings and one cyclopentane ring fused together. The four rings in the steroid nucleus are designated A, B, C, and D. The carbon atoms are numbered beginning with the carbons in ring A, and in steroids like cholesterol, ending with two methyl groups.

Steroid nucleus   Steroid numbering system

Cholesterol

Cholesterol

Cholesterol, which is one of the most important and abundant steroids in the body, is a *sterol* because it contains an oxygen atom as a hydroxyl group (—OH) on carbon 3. Like many steroids, cholesterol has a double bond between carbon 5 and carbon 6, methyl groups at carbon 10 and carbon 13, and a carbon chain at carbon 17. In other steroids, the oxygen atom forms a carbonyl group (C=O) at carbon 3.

Cholesterol is a component of cellular membranes, myelin sheath, and brain and nerve tissue. It is also found in the liver and bile salts; large quantities of it are found in the skin, and some of it becomes vitamin D when the skin is exposed to direct sunlight. In the adrenal gland, cholesterol is used to synthesize steroid hormones. The liver synthesizes sufficient cholesterol for the body from fats, carbohydrates, and proteins. Additional cholesterol is obtained from meat, milk, and eggs in the diet. There is no cholesterol in vegetable and plant products.

Cholesterol in the Body

If a diet is high in cholesterol, the liver produces less cholesterol. A typical daily American diet includes 400 to 500 mg of cholesterol, one of the highest in the world. The American Heart Association has recommended that we consume no more than 300 mg of cholesterol a day. Researchers suggest that saturated fats and cholesterol are associated with diseases such as diabetes; cancers of the breast, pancreas, and colon; and atherosclerosis. In atherosclerosis, deposits of a protein–lipid complex (plaque) accumulate in the coronary blood vessels, restricting the flow of blood to the tissue and causing necrosis (death) of the

tissue (see Figure 17.7). In the heart, plaque accumulation could result in a *myocardial infarction* (heart attack). Other factors that may also increase the risk of heart disease are family history, lack of exercise, smoking, obesity, diabetes, gender, and age. The cholesterol contents of some typical foods are listed in Table 17.4.

TABLE 17.4 Cholesterol Content of Some Foods

Food	Serving Size	Cholesterol (mg)
Liver (beef)	3 oz	370
Large egg	1	200
Lobster	3 oz	175
Fried chicken	$3\frac{1}{2}$ oz	130
Hamburger	3 oz	85
Chicken (no skin)	3 oz	75
Fish (salmon)	3 oz	40
Whole milk	1 cup	35
Butter	1 tablespoon	30
Skim milk	1 cup	5
Margarine	1 tablespoon	0

(a)

(b)

FIGURE 17.7 ▶ Excess cholesterol forms plaque that can block an artery, resulting in a heart attack. **(a)** A cross section of a normal, open artery shows no buildup of plaque. **(b)** A cross section of an artery that is almost completely clogged by atherosclerotic plaque.

 What property of cholesterol would cause it to form deposits along the coronary arteries?

Clinically, cholesterol levels are considered elevated if the total plasma cholesterol level exceeds 200 mg/dL. Saturated fats in the diet may stimulate the production of cholesterol by the liver. A diet that is low in foods containing cholesterol and saturated fats appears to be helpful in reducing the serum cholesterol level. The AICR has recommended that our diet contain more fiber and starch by adding more vegetables, fruits, whole grains, and moderate amounts of foods with low levels of fat and cholesterol such as fish, poultry, lean meats, and low-fat dairy products. AICR also suggests that we limit our intake of foods high in cholesterol such as eggs, nuts, French fries, fatty or organ meats, cheeses, butter, and coconut and palm oil.

▶**SAMPLE PROBLEM 17.6** Cholesterol

Refer to the structure of cholesterol for each of the following questions:

a. What part of cholesterol is the steroid nucleus?
b. What features have been added to the steroid nucleus in cholesterol?
c. What classifies cholesterol as a sterol?

SOLUTION

a. The four fused rings form the steroid nucleus.
b. The cholesterol molecule contains a hydroxyl group (—OH) on the first ring, one double bond in the second ring, methyl groups (—CH₃) at carbons 10 and 13, and a branched carbon chain.
c. The hydroxyl group determines the sterol classification.

STUDY CHECK 17.6

Why is cholesterol in the lipid family?

ANSWER

Cholesterol is not soluble in water; it is classified with the lipid family.

Bile Salts

The *bile salts* in the body are synthesized from cholesterol in the liver and stored in the gallbladder. When bile is secreted into the small intestine, the bile salts mix with the water-insoluble fats and oils in our diets. The bile salts with their nonpolar and polar regions act much like soaps, breaking down large globules of fat into smaller droplets. The smaller droplets containing fat have a larger surface area to react with lipases, which are the enzymes that digest fat. The bile salts also help with the absorption of cholesterol into the intestinal mucosa.

When large amounts of cholesterol accumulate in the gallbladder, cholesterol can become solid, which forms gallstones (see Figure 17.8). Gallstones are composed of almost 100% cholesterol, with some calcium salts, fatty acids, and glycerophospholipids. Normally, small stones pass through the bile duct into the duodenum, the first part of the small intestine immediately beyond the stomach. If a large stone passes into the bile duct, it can get stuck, and the pain can be severe. If the gallstone obstructs the duct, bile cannot be excreted. Then bile pigments known as bilirubin will not be able to pass through the bile duct into the duodenum. They will back up into the liver and be excreted via the blood, causing jaundice (*hyperbilirubinemia*), which gives a yellow color to the skin and the whites of the eyes.

FIGURE 17.8 ▶ Gallstones form in the gallbladder when cholesterol levels are high.

Q What type of steroid is stored in the gallbladder?

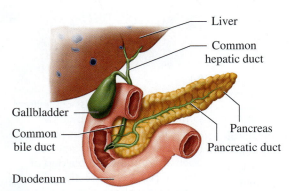

Gallstones formed in the gallbladder usually pass through the bile duct into the duodenum. If too large, they may obstruct the bile duct causing pain and blocking bile.

Sodium glycocholate (a bile salt)

Lipoproteins: Transporting Lipids

In the body, lipids must be moved through the bloodstream to tissues where they are stored, used for energy, or used to make hormones. However, most lipids are nonpolar and insoluble in the aqueous environment of blood. They are made more soluble by combining them with phospholipids and proteins to form water-soluble complexes called **lipoproteins**. In general, lipoproteins are spherical particles with an outer surface of polar proteins and phospholipids that surround hundreds of nonpolar molecules of triacylglycerols and cholesteryl esters (see Figure 17.9). Cholesteryl esters are the prevalent form of cholesterol in the blood. They are formed by the esterification of the hydroxyl group in cholesterol with a fatty acid.

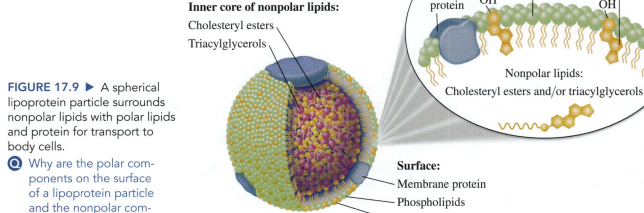

FIGURE 17.9 ▶ A spherical lipoprotein particle surrounds nonpolar lipids with polar lipids and protein for transport to body cells.

Q Why are the polar components on the surface of a lipoprotein particle and the nonpolar components at the center?

Ester bond

Cholesteryl ester

There are a variety of lipoproteins, which differ in density, lipid composition, and function. They include chylomicrons, very-low-density lipoproteins (VLDLs), low-density lipoproteins (LDLs), and high-density lipoproteins (HDLs). The density of the lipoproteins increases as the percentage of protein in each type also increases (see Table 17.5).

TABLE 17.5 Composition and Properties of Plasma Lipoproteins

	Chylomicrons	VLDL	LDL	HDL
Density (g/mL)	0.940	0.950–1.006	1.006–1.063	1.063–1.210
	Composition (% by mass)			
Type of Lipid				
Triacylglycerols	86	55	6	4
Phospholipids	7	18	22	24
Cholesterol	2	7	8	2
Cholesteryl esters	3	12	42	15
Protein	2	8	22	55

Two important lipoproteins are the LDL and HDL, which transport cholesterol. The LDL carries cholesterol to the tissues where it can be used for the synthesis of cell membranes and steroid hormones. When the LDL exceeds the amount of cholesterol needed by the tissues, the LDL deposits cholesterol in the arteries (plaque), which can restrict blood flow and increase the risk of developing heart disease and/or myocardial infarctions (heart attacks). This is why LDL is called "bad" cholesterol. The HDL picks up cholesterol from the tissues and carries it to the liver, where it can be converted to bile salts, which are eliminated from the body. This is why HDL is called "good" cholesterol. Other lipoproteins include chylomicrons that carry triacylglycerols from the intestines to the liver, muscle, and adipose tissues, and VLDL that carries the triacylglycerols synthesized in the liver to the adipose tissues for storage (see Figure 17.10).

Because high cholesterol levels are associated with the onset of atherosclerosis and heart disease, a doctor may order a *lipid panel* as part of a health examination. A lipid panel is a blood test that measures serum lipid levels including cholesterol, triglycerides, HDL, and LDL. The results of a lipid panel are used to evaluate a patient's risk of heart disease and to help a doctor determine the type of treatment needed.

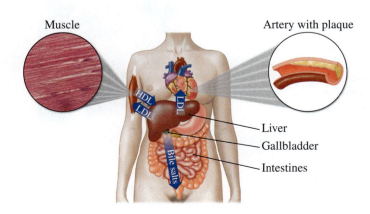

Muscle

Artery with plaque

Liver

Gallbladder

Intestines

FIGURE 17.10 ▶ High- and low-density lipoproteins transport cholesterol between the tissues and the liver.

What type of lipoprotein transports cholesterol to the liver?

Lipid Panel	Recommended Level	Greater Risk of Heart Disease
Total Cholesterol	Less than 200 mg/dL	Greater than 240 mg/dL
Triglycerides (triacylglycerols)	Less than 150 mg/dL	Greater than 200 mg/dL
HDL ("good" cholesterol)	Greater than 60 mg/dL	Less than 40 mg/dL
LDL ("bad" cholesterol)	Less than 100 mg/dL	Greater than 160 mg/dL
Cholesterol/HDL Ratio	Less than 4	Greater than 7

Steroid Hormones

The word *hormone* comes from the Greek "to arouse" or "to excite." Hormones are chemical messengers that serve as a communication system from one part of the body to another. The *steroid* hormones, which include the sex hormones and the adrenocortical hormones, are closely related in structure to cholesterol and depend on cholesterol for their synthesis.

Two of the male sex hormones, *testosterone* and *androsterone*, promote the growth of muscle and facial hair, and the maturation of the male sex organs and of sperm.

The *estrogens*, a group of female sex hormones, direct the development of female sexual characteristics: the uterus increases in size, fat is deposited in the breasts, and the pelvis broadens. *Progesterone* prepares the uterus for the implantation of a fertilized egg. If an egg is not fertilized, the levels of progesterone and estrogen drop sharply, and menstruation follows. Synthetic forms of the female sex hormones are used in birth control pills. As with other kinds of steroids, side effects include weight gain and a greater risk of forming blood clots. The structures of some steroid hormones are shown below:

Testosterone (androgen) (produced in testes) — Estradiol (estrogen) (produced in ovaries) — Progesterone (produced in ovaries) — Norethindrone (synthetic progestin)

Chemistry Link to Health
Anabolic Steroids

Some of the physiological effects of testosterone are to increase muscle mass and decrease body fat. Derivatives of testosterone called *anabolic steroids* that enhance these effects have been synthesized. Although they have some medical uses, anabolic steroids have been used in high dosages by some athletes in an effort to increase muscle mass. Such use is banned by most sports organizations.

Use of anabolic steroids in attempting to improve athletic strength can cause numerous side effects: in males—a reduction in testicle size, low sperm count and infertility, male pattern baldness, and breast development; in females—facial hair, deepening of the voice, male pattern baldness, breast atrophy, and menstrual dysfunction. Possible long-term consequences of anabolic steroid use in both men and women include liver disease and tumors, depression, and heart complications, with an increased risk of prostate cancer for men.

High doses of anabolic steroids, which are banned by sports organizations, are used to increase muscle mass.

Methandienone

Oxandrolone

Nandrolone

Stanozolol

Adrenal Corticosteroids

The adrenal glands, located on the top of each kidney, produce a large number of compounds known as the *corticosteroids*. *Cortisone* increases the blood glucose level and stimulates the synthesis of glycogen in the liver. *Aldosterone* is responsible for the regulation of electrolytes and water balance by the kidneys. *Cortisol* is released under stress to increase blood sugar and regulate carbohydrate, fat, and protein metabolism. Synthetic corticosteroid drugs such as *prednisone* are derived from cortisone and used medically for reducing inflammation and treating asthma and rheumatoid arthritis, although health problems can result from long-term use.

The adrenal glands on the kidneys produce corticosteroids.

Cortisone
(produced in adrenal gland)

Aldosterone (mineralocorticoid)
(produced in adrenal gland)

Cortisol
(produced in adrenal cortex)

Prednisone
(synthetic corticoid)

QUESTIONS AND PROBLEMS

17.6 Steroids: Cholesterol, Bile Salts, and Steroid Hormones

LEARNING GOAL Draw the structures of steroids.

17.47 Draw the structure for the steroid nucleus.

17.48 Draw the structure for cholesterol.

℞ Clinical Applications

17.49 What is the function of bile salts in digestion?

17.50 Why are lipoproteins needed to transport lipids in the bloodstream?

17.51 How do chylomicrons differ from VLDL?

17.52 How does LDL differ from HDL?

17.53 Why is LDL called "bad" cholesterol?

17.54 Why is HDL called "good" cholesterol?

17.55 What are the similarities and differences between the steroid hormones estradiol and testosterone?

17.56 What are the similarities and differences between the adrenal hormone cortisone and the synthetic corticoid prednisone?

17.57 Which of the following are steroid hormones?
  a. cholesterol   b. cortisol
  c. estradiol   d. testosterone

17.58 Which of the following are adrenal corticosteroids?
  a. prednisone   b. aldosterone
  c. cortisol   d. testosterone

17.7 Cell Membranes

The membrane of a cell separates the contents of a cell from the external fluids. It is *semi-permeable* so that nutrients can enter the cell and waste products can leave. The main components of a cell membrane are the glycerophospholipids and sphingolipids. Earlier in this chapter, we saw that the phospholipids consist of a nonpolar region, or hydrocarbon "tail," with two long-chain fatty acids and a polar region, or ionic "head" of phosphate and an ionized amino alcohol.

In a cell (plasma) membrane, two layers of phospholipids are arranged with their hydrophilic heads at the outer and inner surfaces of the membrane, and their hydrophobic tails in the center. This double layer arrangement of phospholipids is called a **lipid bilayer** (see Figure 17.11). The outer layer of phospholipids is in contact with the external fluids, and the inner layer is in contact with the internal contents of the cell.

Most of the phospholipids in the lipid bilayer contain unsaturated fatty acids. Because of the kinks in the carbon chains at the cis double bonds, the phospholipids do not fit closely together. As a result, the lipid bilayer is not a rigid, fixed structure, but one that is dynamic and fluid-like. This liquid-like bilayer also contains proteins, carbohydrates, and cholesterol molecules. For this reason, the model of biological membranes is referred to as the **fluid mosaic model** of membranes.

In the fluid mosaic model, proteins known as *peripheral proteins* emerge on just one of the surfaces, outer or inner. The *integral proteins* extend through the entire lipid bilayer and appear on both surfaces of the membrane. Some proteins and lipids on the outer surface of the cell membrane are attached to carbohydrates. These carbohydrate chains project into the surrounding fluid environment where they are responsible for cell recognition and communication with chemical messengers such as hormones and neurotransmitters. In animals, cholesterol molecules embedded among the phospholipids make up 20 to 25% of the lipid bilayer. Because cholesterol molecules are large and rigid, they reduce the flexibility of the lipid bilayer and add strength to the cell membrane.

FIGURE 17.11 ▶ In the fluid mosaic model of a cell membrane, proteins and cholesterol are embedded in a lipid bilayer of phospholipids. The bilayer forms a membrane-type barrier with polar heads at the membrane surfaces and the nonpolar tails in the center away from the water.

Q What types of fatty acids are found in the phospholipids of the lipid bilayer?

Interactive Video

Membrane Structure

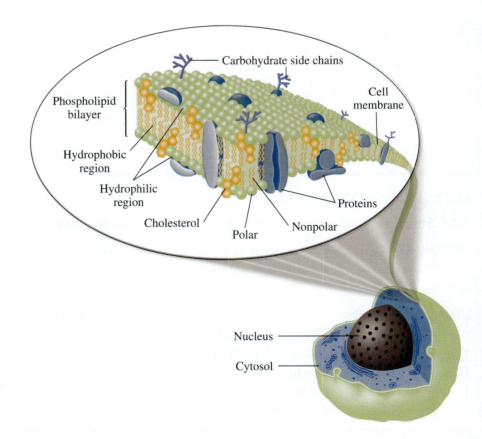

▶ **SAMPLE PROBLEM 17.7** Lipid Bilayer in Cell Membranes

Describe the role of phospholipids in the lipid bilayer.

SOLUTION

Phospholipids consist of polar and nonpolar parts. In a cell membrane, an alignment of the nonpolar sections toward the center with the polar sections on the outside produces a barrier that prevents the contents of a cell from mixing with the fluids on the outside of the cell.

STUDY CHECK 17.7

What is the function of cholesterol in the cell membrane?

ANSWER

Cholesterol adds strength and rigidity to the cell membrane.

Transport through Cell Membranes

Although a nonpolar membrane separates aqueous solutions, it is necessary that certain substances can enter and leave the cell. The main function of a cell membrane is to allow the movement (transport) of ions and molecules on one side of the membrane to the other side. This transport of materials into and out of a cell is accomplished in several ways.

Diffusion (Passive) Transport

In the simplest transport mechanism called *diffusion* or *passive transport*, molecules can diffuse from a higher concentration to a lower concentration. For example, small molecules such as O_2, CO_2, urea, and water diffuse via passive transport through cell membranes. If their concentrations are greater outside the cell than inside, they diffuse into the cell. If their concentrations are higher within the cell, they diffuse out of the cell.

Facilitated Transport

In *facilitated transport*, proteins that extend from one side of the bilayer membrane to the other provide a channel through which certain substances can diffuse more rapidly than by passive diffusion to meet cellular needs. These protein channels allow transport of chloride ion (Cl^-), bicarbonate ion (HCO_3^-), and glucose molecules in and out of the cell.

Active Transport

Certain ions such as K^+, Na^+, and Ca^{2+} move across a cell membrane *against* their concentration gradients. For example, the K^+ concentration is greater inside a cell, and the Na^+ concentration is greater outside. However, in the conduction of nerve impulses and contraction of muscles, K^+ moves into the cell, and Na^+ moves out by a process known as *active transport*.

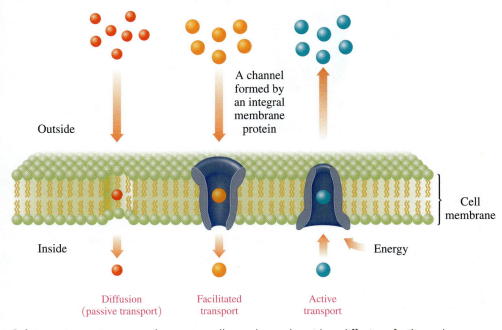

Substances are transported across a cell membrane by either diffusion, facilitated transport, or active transport.

QUESTIONS AND PROBLEMS

17.7 Cell Membranes

LEARNING GOAL Describe the composition and function of the lipid bilayer in cell membranes.

 Clinical Applications

17.59 What is the function of the lipid bilayer in a cell membrane?

17.60 Describe the structure of a lipid bilayer.

17.61 How do molecules of cholesterol affect the structure of cell membranes?

17.62 How do the unsaturated fatty acids in the phospholipids affect the structure of cell membranes?

17.63 Where are proteins located in cell membranes?

17.64 What is the difference between peripheral and integral proteins?

17.65 Identify the type of transport described by each of the following:
   a. A molecule moves through a protein channel.
   b. O_2 moves into the cell from a higher concentration outside the cell.

17.66 Identify the type of transport described by each of the following:
   a. An ion moves from low to high concentration in the cell.
   b. Carbon dioxide moves through a cell membrane.

Clinical Update

Rebecca's Program to Lower Cholesterol in Familial Hypercholesterolemia (FH)

At the lipid clinic, Susan told Rebecca how to maintain a diet with less beef and chicken, more fish with omega-3 oils, low-fat dairy products, no egg yolks, and no coconut or palm oils. Rebecca maintained her new diet containing lower quantities of fats and increased quantities of fiber for the next year. She also increased her exercise using a treadmill and cycling and lost 35 lb. When Rebecca returned to the lipid clinic to check her progress with Susan, a new set of blood tests indicated that her total cholesterol had dropped from 420 to 390 mg/dL and her LDL had dropped from 275 to 255 mg/dL.

Because Rebecca's changes in diet and exercise did not sufficiently lower her cholesterol level, Susan prescribed a medication to help lower blood cholesterol levels. The most common medications used

for treating high LDL-cholesterol are the statins lovastatin (Mevacor), pravastatin (Pravachol), simvastatin (Zocor), atorvastatin (Lipitor), and rosuvastatin (Crestor). For some FH patients, statin therapy may be combined with fibrates such as gemfibrozil or fenofibrate that reduce the synthesis of enzymes that break down fats in the blood.

Rebecca tried different statins, one at a time. One statin caused muscle aches and Susan prescribed pravastatin (Pravachol), 80 mg once a day, which was effective. Later, Susan added fenofibrate (TriCor), one 145-mg tablet, each day to the Pravachol. Rebecca understands that her medications and diet and exercise plan is a lifelong process and its impact is to help her live to a much older age than her mother. Because Rebecca was diagnosed with FH, both her children were tested for FH. Her older son was diagnosed with FH, and is also being treated with a statin. Her younger son does not have FH.

Pravastatin (Pravachol)

Fenofibrate (TriCor)

 Clinical Applications

17.67 Identify the functional groups in Pravachol.

17.68 Identify the functional groups in TriCor.

17.69 Six months after Rebecca was using the Pravachol, her blood test showed that a 5.0-mL blood sample contained a total cholesterol of 18 mg.
   a. How many grams of Pravachol did Rebecca consume in 1 week?
   b. What was her total cholesterol in mg/dL?

17.70 Five months later, Rebecca added the fibrate TriCor to the statin, her blood test showed that a 5.0-mL blood sample contained a total cholesterol of 14 mg.
   a. How many grams of TriCor did Rebecca consume in 1 week?
   b. What was her total cholesterol in mg/dL?

CONCEPT MAP

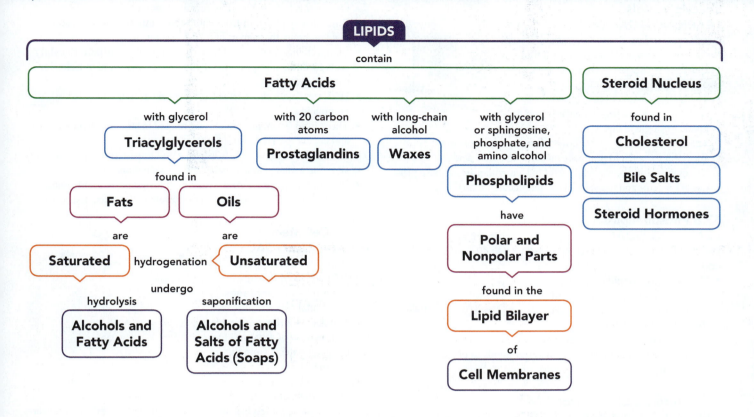

LIPIDS

contain

Fatty Acids ———— **Steroid Nucleus**

with glycerol → **Triacylglycerols**

with 20 carbon atoms → **Prostaglandins**

with long-chain alcohol → **Waxes**

with glycerol or sphingosine, phosphate, and amino alcohol → **Phospholipids**

found in → **Cholesterol**, **Bile Salts**, **Steroid Hormones**

found in → **Fats**, **Oils**

are → **Saturated** — hydrogenation — **Unsaturated**

undergo

hydrolysis → **Alcohols and Fatty Acids**

saponification → **Alcohols and Salts of Fatty Acids (Soaps)**

have → **Polar and Nonpolar Parts**

found in the → **Lipid Bilayer**

of → **Cell Membranes**

CHAPTER REVIEW

17.1 Lipids
LEARNING GOAL Describe the classes of lipids.
- Lipids are nonpolar compounds that are not soluble in water.
- Classes of lipids include waxes, triacylglycerols, glycerophospholipids, sphingolipids, and steroids.

17.2 Fatty Acids
LEARNING GOAL Draw the condensed or line-angle structural formula for a fatty acid and identify it as saturated or unsaturated.
- Fatty acids are unbranched carboxylic acids that typically contain an even number (12 to 20) of carbon atoms.

- Fatty acids may be saturated, monounsaturated with one double bond, or polyunsaturated with two or more double bonds.
- The double bonds in unsaturated fatty acids are almost always cis.

17.3 Waxes and Triacylglycerols
LEARNING GOAL Draw the condensed or line-angle structural formula for a wax or triacylglycerol produced by the reaction of a fatty acid and an alcohol or glycerol.

Triacylglycerol

- A wax is an ester of a long-chain fatty acid and a long-chain alcohol.
- The triacylglycerols are esters of glycerol with three long-chain fatty acids.
- Fats contain more saturated fatty acids and have higher melting points than most vegetable oils.

17.4 Chemical Properties of Triacylglycerols

LEARNING GOAL Draw the condensed or line-angle structural formula for the products of a triacylglycerol that undergoes hydrogenation, hydrolysis, or saponification.

Shortening (solid)

Tub (soft) margarine   Stick margarine (soft and solid)

- The hydrogenation of unsaturated fatty acids of a triacylglycerol converts double bonds to single bonds.
- The hydrolysis of the ester bonds in triacylglycerols in the presence of a strong acid produces glycerol and fatty acids.
- In saponification, a triacylglycerol heated with a strong base produces glycerol and the salts of the fatty acids (soap).

17.5 Phospholipids

LEARNING GOAL Draw the structure of a phospholipid containing glycerol or sphingosine.

Phospholipid

Glycerol — Fatty acid

Glycerol — Fatty acid

Glycerol — PO₄ — Amino alcohol

- Glycerophospholipids are esters of glycerol with two fatty acids and a phosphate group attached to an ionized amino alcohol.
- In a sphingomyelin, the amino alcohol sphingosine forms an amide bond with a fatty acid, and phosphoester bonds to phosphate and an ionized amino alcohol.

17.6 Steroids: Cholesterol, Bile Salts, and Steroid Hormones

LEARNING GOAL Draw the structures of steroids.

Steroid nucleus

- Steroids are lipids containing the steroid nucleus, which is a fused structure of four rings.
- Steroids include cholesterol, bile salts, and steroid hormones.

- Lipids, which are nonpolar, are transported through the aqueous environment of the blood by forming lipoproteins.
- Bile salts, synthesized from cholesterol, mix with water-insoluble fats and break them apart during digestion.
- Lipoproteins, such as chylomicrons and LDL, transport triacylglycerols from the intestines and the liver to fat cells and muscles for storage and energy.
- HDL transports cholesterol from the tissues to the liver for elimination.
- The steroid hormones are closely related in structure to cholesterol and depend on cholesterol for their synthesis.
- The sex hormones, such as estrogen and testosterone, are responsible for sexual characteristics and reproduction.
- The adrenal corticosteroids, such as aldosterone and cortisone, regulate water balance and glucose levels in the cells, respectively.

17.7 Cell Membranes

LEARNING GOAL Describe the composition and function of the lipid bilayer in cell membranes.

Phospholipid bilayer

- All animal cells are surrounded by a semipermeable membrane that separates the cellular contents from the external fluids.
- The membrane is composed of two rows of phospholipids in a lipid bilayer.
- Proteins and cholesterol are embedded in the lipid bilayer, and carbohydrates are attached to its surface.
- Nutrients and waste products move through the cell membrane using passive transport (diffusion), facilitated transport, or active transport.

SUMMARY OF REACTIONS

The chapter sections to review are shown after the name of the reaction.

Esterification (17.3)

Glycerol + 3 fatty acid molecules $\xrightarrow{\text{Enzyme}}$ triacylglycerol + 3H₂O

Hydrogenation of Triacylglycerols (17.4)

Triacylglycerol (unsaturated) + H₂ $\xrightarrow{\text{Ni}}$ triacylglycerol (saturated)

Hydrolysis of Triacylglycerols (17.4)

Triacylglycerol + 3H₂O $\xrightarrow{\text{H}^{+}\text{ or lipase}}$ glycerol + 3 fatty acid molecules

Saponification of Triacylglycerols (17.4)

Triacylglycerol + 3NaOH $\xrightarrow{\text{Heat}}$ glycerol + 3 sodium salts of fatty acids (soaps)

KEY TERMS

cholesterol The most prevalent of the steroid compounds; needed for cellular membranes and the synthesis of vitamin D, hormones, and bile salts.

fat A triacylglycerol that is solid at room temperature and usually comes from animal sources.

fatty acid A long-chain carboxylic acid found in many lipids.

fluid mosaic model The concept that cell membranes are lipid bilayer structures that contain an assortment of polar lipids and proteins in a dynamic, fluid arrangement.

glycerophospholipid A polar lipid of glycerol attached to two fatty acids and a phosphate group connected to an ionized amino alcohol such as choline, serine, or ethanolamine.

hydrogenation The addition of hydrogen to unsaturated fats.

lipid bilayer A model of a cell membrane in which phospholipids are arranged in two rows.

lipids A family of compounds that is nonpolar in nature and not soluble in water; includes prostaglandins, waxes, triacylglycerols, phospholipids, and steroids.

lipoprotein A polar complex composed of a combination of nonpolar lipids with glycerophospholipids and proteins to form a polar complex that can be transported through body fluids.

monounsaturated fatty acid (MUFA) A fatty acid with one double bond.

oil A triacylglycerol that is usually a liquid at room temperature and is obtained from a plant source.

phospholipid A polar lipid of glycerol or sphingosine attached to fatty acids and a phosphate group connected to an amino alcohol.

polyunsaturated fatty acid (PUFA) A fatty acid that contains two or more double bonds.

prostaglandins A number of compounds derived from arachidonic acid that regulate several physiological processes.

saturated fatty acid (SFA) A fatty acid that has no double bonds, which has a higher melting point than unsaturated lipids, and is usually solid at room temperature.

sphingomyelin A compound in which the amine group of sphingosine forms an amide bond to a fatty acid and the hydroxyl group forms an ester bond with phosphate, which forms another phosphoester bond to an ionized amino alcohol.

steroids Types of lipid containing a multicyclic ring system.

triacylglycerols A family of lipids composed of three fatty acids bonded through ester bonds to glycerol, a trihydroxy alcohol.

unsaturated fatty acid A fatty acid that contains one or more carbon–carbon double bonds, which has a lower melting point than saturated fatty acids, and is usually liquid at room temperature.

wax The ester of a long-chain alcohol and a long-chain saturated fatty acid.

⚛ CORE CHEMISTRY SKILLS

Chapter section containing each Core Chemistry Skill is shown in parentheses at the end of each heading.

Identifying Fatty Acids (17.2)

Fatty acids are unbranched carboxylic acids that typically contain an even number (12 to 20) of carbon atoms.

- Fatty acids may be saturated, monounsaturated with one double bond, or polyunsaturated with two or more double bonds.
- The double bonds in unsaturated fatty acids are almost always cis.

Example: State the number of carbon atoms, saturated or unsaturated, and name of the following:

Answer: 16 carbon atoms, saturated, palmitic acid

Drawing Structures for Triacylglycerols (17.3)

- Triacylglycerols are esters of glycerol with three long-chain fatty acids.

Example: Draw and name the triacylglycerol formed from the esterification of glycerol and palmitic acid.

Answer:

Glyceryl tripalmitate (tripalmitin)

Drawing the Products for the Hydrogenation, Hydrolysis, and Saponification of a Triacylglycerol (17.4)

- The hydrogenation of unsaturated fatty acids of a triacylglycerol in the presence of a Pt or Ni catalyst converts double bonds to single bonds.
- The hydrolysis of the ester bonds in triacylglycerols in the presence of a strong acid produces glycerol and fatty acids.
- In saponification, a triacylglycerol heated with a strong base produces glycerol and the salts of the fatty acids (soap).

Example: Identify each of the following as hydrogenation, hydrolysis, or saponification and state the products:

    a. the reaction of palm oil with NaOH

    b. the reaction of glyceryl trilinoleate from corn oil with water in the presence of an acid catalyst

    c. the reaction of corn oil and H_2 using a nickel catalyst

Answer:
    a. The reaction of palm oil with NaOH is saponification, and the products are glycerol and the potassium salts of the fatty acids, which is soap.

    b. In hydrolysis, glyceryl trilinoleate reacts with water in the presence of an acid catalyst, which splits the ester bonds to produce glycerol and three molecules of linoleic acid.

    c. In hydrogenation, H_2 adds to double bonds in corn oil, which produces a more saturated, and thus more solid, fat.

Identifying the Steroid Nucleus (17.6)

- The steroid nucleus consists of three cyclohexane rings and one cyclopentane ring fused together.

Example: Why are cholesterol, sodium glycocholate (a bile salt), and cortisone (a corticosteroid) all considered steroids?

Answer: They all contain the steroid nucleus of three six-carbon rings and one five-carbon ring fused together.

UNDERSTANDING THE CONCEPTS

The chapter sections to review are shown in parentheses at the end of each question.

17.71 Palmitic acid is obtained from palm oil as glyceryl tripalmitate (tripalmitin). Draw the condensed structural formula for glyceryl tripalmitate. (17.2, 17.3)

Palm fruit from palm trees are a source of palm oil.

17.72 Jojoba wax in candles consists of a 20-carbon saturated fatty acid and a 20-carbon saturated alcohol. Draw the condensed structural formula for jojoba wax. (17.2, 17.3)

Candles contain jojoba wax.

℞ Clinical Applications

17.73 Identify each of the following as a saturated, monounsaturated, polyunsaturated, omega-3, or omega-6 fatty acid: (17.2)

a. $CH_3-(CH_2)_7-CH=CH-(CH_2)_7-\overset{\overset{\displaystyle O}{\|}}{C}-OH$

b. linoleic acid

c. $CH_3-CH_2-(CH=CH-CH_2)_5-CH_2-CH_2-\overset{\overset{\displaystyle O}{\|}}{C}-OH$

17.74 Identify each of the following as a saturated, monounsaturated, polyunsaturated, omega-3, or omega-6 fatty acid: (17.2)

a. $CH_3-(CH_2)_4-CH=CH-CH_2-CH=CH-(CH_2)_7-\overset{\overset{\displaystyle O}{\|}}{C}-OH$

b. linolenic acid

c. $CH_3-(CH_2)_{14}-\overset{\overset{\displaystyle O}{\|}}{C}-OH$

Salmon is a good source of omega-3 unsaturated fatty acids.

ADDITIONAL QUESTIONS AND PROBLEMS

17.75 Among the ingredients in lipstick are beeswax, carnauba wax, hydrogenated vegetable oils, and glyceryl tricaprate (tricaprin). (17.1, 17.2, 17.3)
   a. What types of lipids have been used?
   b. Draw the condensed structural formula for glyceryl tricaprate (tricaprin). Capric acid is a saturated 10-carbon fatty acid.

17.76 Because peanut oil floats on the top of peanut butter, the peanut oil in many brands of peanut butter is hydrogenated and the solid is mixed into the peanut butter to give a solid product that does not separate. If a triacylglycerol in peanut oil that contains one oleic acid and two linoleic acids is completely hydrogenated, draw the condensed structural formula for the product. (17.3, 17.4)

17.77 Trans fats are produced during the hydrogenation of their unsaturated fatty acids. (17.2)
   a. What is the typical configuration of the double bond in a monounsaturated fatty acid?
   b. How does a trans fatty acid differ from a cis fatty acid?
   c. Draw the condensed structural formula for elaidic acid.

17.78 One mole of glyceryl trioleate (triolein) is completely hydrogenated. (7.6, 7.7, 8.6, 17.3, 17.4)
   a. Draw the condensed structural formula for the product.
   b. How many moles of hydrogen are required?
   c. How many grams of hydrogen are required?
   d. How many liters of hydrogen gas are needed if the reaction is run at STP?

℞ Clinical Applications

17.79 The total kilocalories and grams of fat for some typical meals at fast-food restaurants are listed here. Calculate the number of kilocalories and the percentage of total kilocalories from fat (1 gram of fat = 9 kcal). Round answers to the tens place. Would you expect the fats to be mostly saturated or unsaturated? Why? (17.2, 17.3)
   a. a chicken dinner, 830 kcal, 46 g of fat
   b. a quarter-pound cheeseburger, 520 kcal, 29 g of fat
   c. pepperoni pizza (three slices), 560 kcal, 18 g of fat

17.80 The total kilocalories and grams of fat for some typical meals at fast-food restaurants are listed here. Calculate the number of kilocalories and the percentage of total kilocalories from fat (1 gram of fat = 9 kcal). Round answers to the tens place. Would you expect the fats to be mostly saturated or unsaturated? Why? (17.2, 17.3)
  a. a beef burrito, 470 kcal, 21 g of fat
  b. deep-fried fish (three pieces), 480 kcal, 28 g of fat
  c. a jumbo hot dog, 180 kcal, 18 g of fat

17.81 Identify each of the following as a fatty acid, soap, triacylglycerol, wax, glycerophospholipid, sphingolipid, or steroid: (17.1, 17.2, 17.3, 17.5, 17.6)
  a. beeswax   **b.** cholesterol
  c. lecithin   **d.** glyceryl tripalmitate (tripalmitin)
  e. sodium stearate   **f.** safflower oil

17.82 Identify each of the following as a fatty acid, soap, triacylglycerol, wax, glycerophospholipid, sphingolipid, or steroid: (17.1, 17.2, 17.3, 17.5, 17.6)
  a. sphingomyelin   **b.** whale blubber
  c. adipose tissue   **d.** progesterone
  e. cortisone   **f.** stearic acid

17.83 Identify the components (**1** to **6**) contained in each of the following lipids (**a** to **d**): (17.1, 17.2, 17.3, 17.5, 17.6)
  1. glycerol   **2.** fatty acid
  3. phosphate   **4.** amino alcohol
  5. steroid nucleus   **6.** sphingosine

  a. estrogen   **b.** cephalin
  c. wax   **d.** triacylglycerol

17.84 Identify the components (**1** to **6**) contained in each of the following lipids (**a** to **d**): (17.1, 17.2, 17.3, 17.5, 17.6)
  1. glycerol   **2.** fatty acid
  3. phosphate   **4.** amino alcohol
  5. steroid nucleus   **6.** sphingosine

  a. glycerophospholipid **b.** sphingomyelin
  c. aldosterone   **d.** linoleic acid

17.85 Which of the following are found in cell membranes? (17.7)
  a. cholesterol   **b.** triacylglycerols
  c. carbohydrates

17.86 Which of the following are found in cell membranes? (17.7)
  a. proteins   **b.** waxes
  c. phospholipids

CHALLENGE QUESTIONS

The following groups of questions are related to the topics in this chapter. However, they do not all follow the chapter order, and they require you to combine concepts and skills from several sections. These questions will help you increase your critical thinking skills and prepare for your next exam.

17.87 Draw the condensed structural formula for a glycerophospholipid that contains two stearic acids and a phosphate bonded to ethanolamine. (17.2, 17.5)

17.88 Sunflower seed oil can be used to make margarine. A triacylglycerol in sunflower seed oil contains two linoleic acids and one oleic acid. (17.2, 17.3, 17.5)
  a. Draw the condensed structural formulas for two isomers of the triacylglycerol in sunflower seed oil.
  b. Using one of the isomers, write the reaction that would be used when sunflower seed oil is used to make solid margarine.

Sunflower oil is obtained from the seeds of the sunflower.

17.89 Match the lipoprotein (**1** to **4**) with its description (**a** to **d**). (17.6)
  1. chylomicrons   **2.** VLDL
  3. LDL   **4.** HDL

  a. "good" cholesterol
  b. transports most of the cholesterol to the cells
  c. carries triacylglycerols from the intestine to the fat cells
  d. transports cholesterol to the liver

17.90 Match the lipoprotein (**1** to **4**) with its description (**a** to **d**). (17.6)
  1. chylomicrons   **2.** VLDL
  3. LDL   **4.** HDL

  a. has the greatest abundance of protein
  b. "bad" cholesterol
  c. carries triacylglycerols synthesized in the liver to the muscles
  d. has the lowest density

17.91 A sink drain can become clogged with solid fat such as glyceryl tristearate (tristearin). (7.1, 7.6, 7.7, 9.4, 17.3, 17.4)
  A sink drain can become clogged with saturated fats.
  a. How would adding lye (NaOH) to the sink drain remove the blockage?
  b. Write a balanced chemical equation for the reaction that occurs.
  c. How many milliliters of a 0.500 M NaOH solution are needed to completely saponify 10.0 g of glyceryl tristearate (tristearin)?

17.92 One of the triacylglycerols in olive oil is glyceryl tripalmitole-ate (tripalmitolein). (7.1, 7.6, 7.7, 8.6, 9.4, 17.3, 17.4)

    a. Draw the condensed structural formula for glyceryl tripal-mitoleate (tripalmitolein).

    b. How many liters of H_2 gas at STP are needed to completely saturate 100 g of glyceryl tripalmitoleate (tripalmitolein)?

    c. How many milliliters of a 0.250 M NaOH solution are needed to completely saponify 100 g of glyceryl tripalmi-toleate (tripalmitolein)?

Olive oil contains glyceryl tripalmitoleate (tripalmitolein).

ANSWERS

Answers to Selected Questions and Problems

17.1 Because lipids are not soluble in water, a polar solvent, they are nonpolar molecules.

17.3 Lipids provide energy, protection, and insulation for the organs in the body. Lipids are also an important part of cell membranes.

17.5 All fatty acids contain a long chain of carbon atoms with a carboxylic acid group. Saturated fatty acids contain only carbon–carbon single bonds; unsaturated fatty acids contain one or more double bonds.

17.7   **a.** palmitic acid

O
‖
CH₃—(CH₂)₁₄—C—OH (structure drawn)

    b. oleic acid

(structure drawn)

17.9   **a.** (12:0), saturated   **b.** (18:3), polyunsaturated
      c. (16:1), monounsaturated   **d.** (18:0), saturated

17.11 In a cis fatty acid, the hydrogen atoms are on the same side of the double bond, which produces a kink in the carbon chain. In a trans fatty acid, the hydrogen atoms are on opposite sides of the double bond, which gives a carbon chain without any kink.

17.13 In an omega-3 fatty acid, there is a double bond beginning at carbon 3, counting from the methyl group, whereas in an omega-6 fatty acid, there is a double bond beginning at carbon 6, counting from the methyl group.

17.15 Arachidonic acid and PGE₁ are both carboxylic acids with 20 carbon atoms. The differences are that arachidonic acid has four cis double bonds and no other functional groups, whereas PGE₁ has one trans double bond, one ketone functional group, and two hydroxyl functional groups. In addition, a part of the PGE₁ chain forms a cyclopentane ring.

17.17 Prostaglandins raise or lower blood pressure, stimulate con-traction and relaxation of smooth muscle, and may cause inflammation and pain.

17.19 CH_3—$(CH_2)_{14}$—$\overset{\displaystyle O}{\overset{\displaystyle \|}{C}}$—O—$(CH_2)_{29}$—$CH_3$

17.21

$$CH_2-O-\overset{O}{\overset{\|}{C}}-(CH_2)_{16}-CH_3$$
$$CH-O-\overset{O}{\overset{\|}{C}}-(CH_2)_{16}-CH_3$$
$$CH_2-O-\overset{O}{\overset{\|}{C}}-(CH_2)_{16}-CH_3$$

17.23

$$CH_2-O-\overset{O}{\overset{\|}{C}}-(CH_2)_{6}-CH_3$$
$$CH-O-\overset{O}{\overset{\|}{C}}-(CH_2)_{6}-CH_3$$
$$CH_2-O-\overset{O}{\overset{\|}{C}}-(CH_2)_{6}-CH_3$$

17.25 Safflower oil has a lower melting point since it contains fatty acids with two or three double bonds; olive oil contains a large amount of oleic acid, which has only one double bond (mono-unsaturated).

17.27 Sunflower oil has about 24% monounsaturated fats, whereas safflower oil has about 18%. Sunflower oil has about 66% polyunsaturated fats, whereas safflower oil has about 73%.

17.29   **a.** The reaction of palm oil with KOH is saponification; the products are glycerol and the potassium salts of the fatty acids, which are soaps.

    b. The reaction of glyceryl trilinoleate from safflower oil with water and HCl is hydrolysis, which splits the ester bonds to produce glycerol and three molecules of linoleic acid.

17.31

$$CH_2-O-\overset{O}{\overset{\|}{C}}-(CH_2)_7-CH=CH-(CH_2)_5-CH_3$$
$$CH-O-\overset{O}{\overset{\|}{C}}-(CH_2)_7-CH=CH-(CH_2)_5-CH_3 \ + \ 3H_2$$
$$CH_2-O-\overset{O}{\overset{\|}{C}}-(CH_2)_7-CH=CH-(CH_2)_5-CH_3$$

$$\xrightarrow{\text{Ni}}$$

$$CH_2-O-\overset{O}{\overset{\|}{C}}-(CH_2)_{14}-CH_3$$
$$CH-O-\overset{O}{\overset{\|}{C}}-(CH_2)_{14}-CH_3$$
$$CH_2-O-\overset{O}{\overset{\|}{C}}-(CH_2)_{14}-CH_3$$

17.33

$$CH_2-O-\overset{\displaystyle O}{\overset{\|}{C}}-(CH_2)_{12}-CH_3$$
$$CH-O-\overset{\displaystyle O}{\overset{\|}{C}}-(CH_2)_{12}-CH_3 \ + \ 3H_2O \ \xrightarrow{H^+, \ heat}$$
$$CH_2-O-\overset{\displaystyle O}{\overset{\|}{C}}-(CH_2)_{12}-CH_3$$

$$CH_2-OH$$
$$CH-OH \ + \ 3HO-\overset{\displaystyle O}{\overset{\|}{C}}-(CH_2)_{12}-CH_3$$
$$CH_2-OH$$

17.35

$$CH_2-O-\overset{\displaystyle O}{\overset{\|}{C}}-(CH_2)_{12}-CH_3$$
$$CH-O-\overset{\displaystyle O}{\overset{\|}{C}}-(CH_2)_{12}-CH_3 \ + \ 3NaOH \ \xrightarrow{Heat}$$
$$CH_2-O-\overset{\displaystyle O}{\overset{\|}{C}}-(CH_2)_{12}-CH_3$$

$$CH_2-OH$$
$$CH-OH \ + \ 3Na^+ \ {}^-O-\overset{\displaystyle O}{\overset{\|}{C}}-(CH_2)_{12}-CH_3$$
$$CH_2-OH$$

17.37

$$CH_2-O-\overset{\displaystyle O}{\overset{\|}{C}}-(CH_2)_{16}-CH_3$$
$$CH-O-\overset{\displaystyle O}{\overset{\|}{C}}-(CH_2)_{16}-CH_3$$
$$CH_2-O-\overset{\displaystyle O}{\overset{\|}{C}}-(CH_2)_{16}-CH_3$$

17.39 A triacylglycerol consists of glycerol and three fatty acids. A glycerophospholipid also contains glycerol, but has only two fatty acids. The hydroxyl group on the third carbon of glycerol is attached by a phosphoester bond to an ionized amino alcohol.

17.41

$$CH_2-O-\overset{\displaystyle O}{\overset{\|}{C}}-(CH_2)_{14}-CH_3$$
$$CH-O-\overset{\displaystyle O}{\overset{\|}{C}}-(CH_2)_{14}-CH_3$$
$$CH_2-O-\overset{\displaystyle O}{\overset{\|}{\underset{\underset{\textstyle O^-}{\displaystyle |}}{P}}}-O-CH_2-CH_2-\overset{+}{N}H_3$$

17.43 This glycerophospholipid is a cephalin. It contains glycerol, oleic acid, stearic acid, a phosphate, and ethanolamine.

17.45 a. sphingosine **b.** palmitic acid
c. an amide bond **d.** ethanolamine

17.47

17.49 Bile salts act to emulsify fat globules, allowing the fat to be more easily digested.

17.51 Chylomicrons have a lower density than VLDLs. They pick up triacylglycerols from the intestine, whereas VLDLs transport triacylglycerols synthesized in the liver.

17.53 "Bad" cholesterol is the cholesterol carried by LDL that can form deposits in the arteries called plaque, which narrows the arteries.

17.55 Both estradiol and testosterone contain the steroid nucleus and a hydroxyl group. Testosterone has a ketone group, a double bond, and two methyl groups. Estradiol has an aromatic ring, a hydroxyl group in place of the ketone, and a methyl group.

17.57 b, c, and **d**

17.59 The lipid bilayer in a cell membrane surrounds the cell and separates the contents of the cell from the external fluids.

17.61 Because the molecules of cholesterol are large and rigid, they reduce the flexibility of the lipid bilayer and add strength to the cell membrane.

17.63 The peripheral proteins in the membrane emerge on the inner or outer surface only, whereas the integral proteins extend through the membrane to both surfaces.

17.65 Substances move through cell membranes by diffusion (passive transport), facilitated transport, and active transport.
a. facilitated transport
b. diffusion (passive transport)

17.67 alkene, alcohol, ester, carboxylic acid

17.69 a. 0.56 g of Pravachol **b.** 360 mg/dL

17.71

$$CH_2-O-\overset{\displaystyle O}{\overset{\|}{C}}-(CH_2)_{14}-CH_3$$
$$CH-O-\overset{\displaystyle O}{\overset{\|}{C}}-(CH_2)_{14}-CH_3$$
$$CH_2-O-\overset{\displaystyle O}{\overset{\|}{C}}-(CH_2)_{14}-CH_3$$

17.73 a. monounsaturated
b. polyunsaturated, omega-6
c. polyunsaturated, omega-3

17.75 a. Beeswax and carnauba are waxes. Vegetable oil and glyceryl tricaprate (tricaprin) are triacylglycerols.

b.
$$CH_2-O-\overset{\displaystyle O}{\overset{\|}{C}}-(CH_2)_8-CH_3$$
$$CH-O-\overset{\displaystyle O}{\overset{\|}{C}}-(CH_2)_8-CH_3$$
$$CH_2-O-\overset{\displaystyle O}{\overset{\|}{C}}-(CH_2)_8-CH_3$$
Glyceryl tricaprate (tricaprin)

17.77 a. A typical unsaturated fatty acid has a cis double bond.
b. A cis unsaturated fatty acid contains hydrogen atoms on the same side of each double bond. A trans unsaturated fatty acid has hydrogen atoms on opposite sides of the double bond that forms during hydrogenation.

c.
$$CH_3-(CH_2)_6-CH_2 \quad \overset{H}{\underset{}{\diagdown}} C=C \overset{CH_2-(CH_2)_6-\overset{\displaystyle O}{\overset{\|}{C}}-OH}{\underset{H}{\diagup}}$$

17.79 a. 410 kcal from fat; 49% fat
  b. 260 kcal from fat; 50.% fat
  c. 160 kcal from fat; 29% fat

17.81 a. Beeswax is a wax.
  b. Cholesterol is a steroid.
  c. Lecithin is a glycerophospholipid.
  d. Glyceryl tripalmitate is a triacylglycerol.
  e. Sodium stearate is a soap.
  f. Safflower oil is a triacylglycerol.

17.83 a. 5   **b.** 1, 2, 3, 4
  c. 2   **d.** 1, 2

17.85 a and c

17.87

$$CH_2-O-\overset{\overset{\displaystyle O}{\|}}{C}-(CH_2)_{16}-CH_3$$
$$CH-O-\overset{\overset{\displaystyle O}{\|}}{C}-(CH_2)_{16}-CH_3$$
$$CH_2-O-\overset{\overset{\displaystyle O}{\|}}{P}-O-CH_2-CH_2-\overset{+}{N}H_3$$
$$|$$
$$O^-$$

17.89 a. (**4**) HDL   **b.** (**3**) LDL
  c. (**1**) chylomicrons   **d.** (**4**) HDL

17.91 a. Adding NaOH would saponify lipids such as glyceryl tristearate (tristearin), forming glycerol and salts of the fatty acids that are soluble in water and would wash down the drain.

b.
$$CH_2-O-\overset{\overset{\displaystyle O}{\|}}{C}-(CH_2)_{16}-CH_3$$
$$CH-O-\overset{\overset{\displaystyle O}{\|}}{C}-(CH_2)_{16}-CH_3 + 3NaOH \xrightarrow{\text{Heat}}$$
$$CH_2-O-\overset{\overset{\displaystyle O}{\|}}{C}-(CH_2)_{16}-CH_3$$

$$CH_2-OH$$
$$CH-OH + 3Na^+\ {}^-O-\overset{\overset{\displaystyle O}{\|}}{C}-(CH_2)_{16}-CH_3$$
$$CH_2-OH$$
Glycerol   Salts of stearic acid

c. 67.3 mL of a 0.500 M NaOH solution

18

Amines and Amides

LANCE, AN ENVIRONMENTAL HEALTH PRACTITIONER,
is collecting soil and water samples at a ranch to test for the presence and concentration of any pesticides and pharmaceuticals. Ranchers use pesticides to increase food production and pharmaceuticals to treat and prevent animal-related diseases. Due to the common use of these chemicals, they may pass into the soil and water supply, potentially contaminating the environment and causing health problems.

Recently, the sheep on the ranch were treated with a pharmaceutical dewormer, fenbendazole, to destroy any gastrointestinal worms. Fenbendazole contains several functional groups: aromatic rings, an ester, an amine, and imidazole, a heterocyclic amine. Heterocyclic amines are carbon-based rings where one or more of the carbon atoms have been replaced by a nitrogen atom. Imidazole is a five-atom ring that contains two nitrogen atoms.

Lance detects small amounts of fenbendazole in the soil. He advises the rancher to decrease the dosage he administers to his sheep in order to reduce the amounts currently being detected in the soil. Lance then indicates he will be back in a month to re-test the soil and water.

Fenbendazole   Imidazole

CAREER Environmental Health Practitioner

Environmental health practitioners (EHPs) monitor environmental pollution to protect the health of the public. By using specialized equipment, EHPs measure pollution levels in soil, air, and water, as well as noise and radiation levels. EHPs can specialize in a specific area, such as air quality or hazardous and solid waste. For instance, air quality experts monitor indoor air for allergens, mold, and toxins; they measure outdoor air pollutants created by businesses, vehicles, and agriculture. Since EHPs obtain samples with potentially hazardous materials, they must be knowledgeable about safety protocols and wear personal protective equipment. EHPs also recommend methods to diminish various pollutants, and may assist in cleanup and remediation efforts.

649

LOOKING AHEAD

18.1 Amines 650

18.2 Properties of Amines 656

18.3 Heterocyclic Amines 661

💗 **Chemistry Link to Health**
Synthesizing Drugs 663

18.4 Neurotransmitters 664

18.5 Amides 671

💗 **Chemistry Link to Health** *Amides in Health and Medicine* 674

18.6 Hydrolysis of Amides 676

℞ **Clinical Applications** 661, 664, 670, 678, 681, 683

℞ **Clinical Update** *Testing Soil and Water Samples for Chemicals* 678

A mines and amides are organic compounds that contain nitrogen. Many nitrogen-containing compounds are important to life as components of amino acids, proteins, and nucleic acids (DNA and RNA). Many amines that exhibit strong physiological activity are used in medicine as decongestants, anesthetics, and sedatives. Examples include dopamine, histamine, epinephrine, and amphetamine.

Alkaloids such as caffeine, nicotine, cocaine, and digitalis, which demonstrate powerful physiological activity, are naturally occurring amines obtained from plants. In amides, the functional group consists of a carbonyl group attached to an amine. In biochemistry, the amide bond that links amino acids in a protein is called a peptide bond. Some medically important amides include acetaminophen (Tylenol) used to reduce fever; phenobarbital, a sedative and anticonvulsant medication; and penicillin, an antibiotic.

CHAPTER READINESS*

⚛ CORE CHEMISTRY SKILLS

- Writing Equations for Reactions of Acids and Bases (10.6)

- Naming and Drawing Alkanes (11.2)

*These Core Chemistry Skills from previous chapters are listed here for your review as you proceed to the new material in this chapter.

LEARNING GOAL

Name amines using IUPAC and common names; draw the condensed or line-angle structural formulas given the names. Classify amines as primary (1°), secondary (2°), or tertiary (3°).

18.1 Amines

Amines are derivatives of ammonia (NH_3) in which the nitrogen atom, which has one lone pair of electrons, has three bonds to hydrogen atoms. In an amine, the nitrogen atom is bonded to one, two, or three alkyl or aromatic groups.

Naming Amines

In the IUPAC names for amines, the *e* in the corresponding alkane name is replaced with *amine*.

CH_4 CH_3-NH_2 CH_3-CH_3 $CH_3-CH_2-NH_2$

Methane   Methanamine   Ethane   Ethanamine

When the amine has a chain of three or more carbon atoms, it is numbered to show the position of the $-NH_2$ group and any other substituents.

$$CH_3-\underset{3}{CH_2}-\underset{2}{CH_2}-\underset{1}{NH_2} \qquad \underset{1}{CH_3}-\underset{2}{CH}(NH_2)-\underset{3}{CH_3}$$

1-Propanamine   2-Propanamine

$$\underset{1}{CH_3}-\underset{2}{CH}(NH_2)-\underset{3}{CH_2}-\underset{4}{CH_3} \qquad \underset{4}{CH_3}-\underset{3}{CH}(CH_3)-\underset{2}{CH_2}-\underset{1}{CH_2}-NH_2$$

2-Butanamine   3-Methyl-1-butanamine

If there is an alkyl group attached to the nitrogen atom, the prefix *N*- and the alkyl name are placed in front of the amine name. If there are two alkyl groups bonded to the N atom, the prefix *N*- is used for each and they are listed alphabetically.

Longest carbon chain — Alkyl groups attached to N atom — Longest carbon chain — Alkyl groups listed alphabetically

N-Methylethanamine   *N*,*N*-Dimethyl-1-propanamine   *N*-Ethyl-*N*-methyl-1-butanamine

▶ **SAMPLE PROBLEM 18.1 IUPAC Names for Amines**

Give the IUPAC name for the following amine:

$$CH_3 - CH_2 - CH_2 - CH_2 - \overset{\overset{\displaystyle H}{|}}{N} - CH_3$$

SOLUTION

STEP 1 Name the longest carbon chain bonded to the N atom by replacing the *e* of its alkane name with *amine*. The longest carbon chain bonded to the N atom has four carbon atoms, which is named by replacing the *e* in the alkane name with *amine* to give butanamine.

$$CH_3 - CH_2 - CH_2 - CH_2 - \overset{\overset{\displaystyle H}{|}}{N} - CH_3 \qquad \text{butanamine}$$

STEP 2 Number the carbon chain to show the position of the amine group and other substituents. The N atom in the amine group is attached to carbon 1 of butanamine.

$$\underset{4}{CH_3} - \underset{3}{CH_2} - \underset{2}{CH_2} - \underset{1}{CH_2} - \overset{\overset{\displaystyle H}{|}}{N} - CH_3 \qquad \text{1-butanamine}$$

STEP 3 Any alkyl group attached to the nitrogen atom is indicated by the prefix *N*- and the alkyl name, which is placed in front of the amine name. Alkyl groups attached to the N atom are listed alphabetically.

$$\underset{4}{CH_3} - \underset{3}{CH_2} - \underset{2}{CH_2} - \underset{1}{CH_2} - \overset{\overset{\displaystyle H}{|}}{N} - CH_3 \qquad \textit{N}\text{-methyl-1-butanamine}$$

Guide to the IUPAC Naming of Amines

STEP 1
Name the longest carbon chain bonded to the N atom by replacing the *e* of its alkane name with *amine*.

STEP 2
Number the carbon chain to show the position of the amine group and other substituents.

STEP 3
Any alkyl group attached to the nitrogen atom is indicated by the prefix *N*- and the alkyl name, which is placed in front of the amine name.

STUDY CHECK 18.1

Draw the condensed structural formula for *N*-ethyl-1-propanamine.

ANSWER

$$CH_3 - CH_2 - CH_2 - \overset{\overset{\displaystyle H}{|}}{N} - CH_2 - CH_3$$

Common Names of Amines

The common names of amines are often used when the alkyl groups are not branched. The alkyl groups bonded to the nitrogen atom are listed in alphabetical order. The prefixes *di* and *tri* are used to indicate two and three identical groups.

Methylamine   Dimethylamine   Ethylmethylpropylamine

▶ SAMPLE PROBLEM 18.2 Common Names of Amines

Give a common name for each of the following amines:

a. $CH_3-CH_2-NH_2$

b.
$$CH_3-\overset{\overset{\displaystyle CH_3}{|}}{N}-CH_3$$

SOLUTION

a. This amine has one ethyl group attached to the nitrogen atom; its name is ethylamine.
b. The common name for an amine with three methyl groups attached to the nitrogen atom is trimethylamine.

STUDY CHECK 18.2

Draw the condensed structural formula for butyldimethylamine.

ANSWER

$$CH_3-CH_2-CH_2-CH_2-\overset{\overset{\displaystyle CH_3}{|}}{N}-CH_3$$

Naming Compounds with Two Functional Groups

When a compound contains more than one functional group, we need to identify which group is used for the name of the compound and which group is named as a substituent. According to IUPAC rules for nomenclature, an oxygen-containing group will take priority over an $-NH_2$ group. Therefore, the $-NH_2$ group is named as the substituent, *amino*. Table 18.1 lists the priorities for the major functional groups, and the names of the functional groups as substituents. The functional group that is highest on the list is named as the compound, and any group lower on the list is named as a substituent. Examples are given for naming an alcohol, ketone, and carboxylic acid that also contain an amine group.

$$CH_3-\overset{\overset{\displaystyle NH_2}{|}}{CH}-CH_2-OH$$
2-Amino-1-propanol

$$CH_3-\overset{\overset{\displaystyle NH_2}{|}}{CH}-CH_2-\overset{\overset{\displaystyle O}{||}}{C}-CH_3$$
4-Amino-2-pentanone

$$CH_3-\overset{\overset{\displaystyle NH_2}{|}}{CH}-CH_2-\overset{\overset{\displaystyle O}{||}}{C}-OH$$
3-Aminobutanoic acid

TABLE 18.1 Priority of Functional Groups in IUPAC Names

	Functional Group	Name of Compound	Name as a Substituent
Highest Priority	carboxylic acid	oic acid	
	ester	oate	
	amide	amide	amido
	aldehyde	al	formyl
	ketone	one	oxo
	alcohol	ol	hydroxy
	amine	amine	amino
	alkane	ane	alkyl
Lowest Priority	halide		halo

▶ SAMPLE PROBLEM 18.3 IUPAC Names for Compounds with Two Functional Groups

Give the IUPAC name for the following compound, which is used in the production of methadone:

$$CH_3-\overset{\overset{\displaystyle OH}{|}}{CH}-CH_2-NH_2$$

SOLUTION

STEP **1** Identify the functional group with the highest priority and use the longest carbon chain to give the compound name. Because the hydroxyl group has a higher priority than the amine group, the compound is named as an alcohol.

$$CH_3-\underset{\underset{OH}{|}}{CH}-CH_2-NH_2 \qquad \text{propanol}$$

STEP **2** Number the carbon chain, and give the position and name of the main group and the substituent group on the carbon chain.

$$\underset{3}{CH_3}-\underset{2}{\underset{\underset{OH}{|}}{CH}}-\underset{1}{CH_2}-NH_2 \qquad \text{1-amino-2-propanol}$$

> **Guide to Naming Compounds with Two Functional Groups**
>
> **STEP 1**
> Identify the functional group with the highest priority and use the longest carbon chain to give the compound name.
>
> **STEP 2**
> Number the carbon chain, and give the position and name of the main group and the substituent group on the carbon chain.

STUDY CHECK 18.3

Draw the condensed structural formula for 3-aminopentanal.

ANSWER

$$CH_3-CH_2-\underset{\underset{NH_2}{|}}{CH}-CH_2-\overset{\overset{O}{\|}}{C}-H$$

Aromatic Amines

The aromatic amines use the name *aniline*, which is approved by IUPAC. Aniline is the simplest aromatic amine; it is used to make many industrial chemicals.

Aniline 4-Bromoaniline (*p*-bromoaniline) *N*-Methylaniline *N,N*-Dimethylaniline

Aniline, which was discovered in 1826 when it was first isolated from indigo plants, is used to make many dyes, which give color to wool, cotton, and silk fibers, as well as blue jeans. It is also used to make the polymer polyurethane and in the synthesis of the pain reliever acetaminophen.

Indigo

Indigo used in blue dyes can be obtained from tropical plants such as *Indigofera tinctoria*.

Classification of Amines

Amines are classified by counting the number of carbon atoms directly bonded to the nitrogen atom. In a primary (1°) amine, the nitrogen atom is bonded to one alkyl group. In a secondary (2°) amine, the nitrogen atom is bonded to two alkyl groups. In a tertiary (3°) amine, the nitrogen atom is bonded to three alkyl groups. In each of the following models of ammonia and amines, the atoms are arranged around the nitrogen atom (blue) in a trigonal pyramidal shape:

Ammonia	Primary (1°) amine	Secondary (2°) amine	Tertiary (3°) amine
H—N̈—H │ H	CH₃—N̈—H │ H	CH₃—N̈—CH₃ │ H	CH₃—N̈—CH₃ │ CH₃

Ammonia | Methanamine (methylamine) | N-Methylmethanamine (dimethylamine) | N,N-Dimethylmethanamine (trimethylamine)

Line-Angle Structural Formulas for Amines

We can draw line-angle structural formulas for amines just as we have for other organic compounds. In the line-angle structural formula for an amine, we show the hydrogen atoms bonded to the N atom. For example, we can draw the following line-angle structural formulas and classify each:

1-Propanamine (propylamine)
Primary (1°) amine

N-Ethyl-1-propanamine (ethylpropylamine)
Secondary (2°) amine

N-Ethyl-N-methyl-1-propanamine (ethylmethylpropylamine)
Tertiary (3°) amine

▶ **SAMPLE PROBLEM 18.4** Classifying Amines

Classify each of the following amines as primary (1°), secondary (2°), or tertiary (3°):

a. (cyclohexyl)—NH₂

b. CH₃—N(CH₃)—CH₂—CH₃

c. (phenyl)—N(H)—CH₃

d. (line-angle amine)

SOLUTION

a. This is a primary (1°) amine because there is one alkyl group (cyclohexyl) attached to the nitrogen atom.

b. This is a tertiary (3°) amine. There are three alkyl groups (two methyls and one ethyl) attached to the nitrogen atom.

c. This is a secondary (2°) amine with two carbon groups, methyl and phenyl, bonded to the nitrogen atom.

d. The nitrogen atom in this line-angle structural formula is bonded to two alkyl groups, which makes it a secondary (2°) amine.

STUDY CHECK 18.4

Classify the following amine as primary (1°), secondary (2°), or tertiary (3°):

$$CH_3-CH_2-\underset{\underset{CH_3}{|}}{N}-CH_2-CH_2-CH_3$$

ANSWER

tertiary (3°)

QUESTIONS AND PROBLEMS

18.1 Amines

LEARNING GOAL Name amines using IUPAC and common names; draw the condensed or line-angle structural formulas given the names. Classify amines as primary (1°), secondary (2°), or tertiary (3°).

18.1 What is a primary amine?

18.2 What is a tertiary amine?

18.3 Classify each of the following amines as primary (1°), secondary (2°), or tertiary (3°):

a. $CH_3-CH_2-CH_2-NH_2$ **b.** $CH_3-\underset{\underset{CH_3}{|}}{N}-CH_2-CH_3$

c. (line-angle structure) NH_2

d. (benzene ring with) $\underset{\underset{CH_3}{|}}{N}-CH_3$

e. $CH_3-\underset{\underset{CH_3}{|}}{CH}-\underset{\underset{CH_3}{|}}{N}-CH_2-CH_3$

18.4 Classify each of the following amines as primary (1°), secondary (2°), or tertiary (3°):

a. $CH_3-CH_2-\underset{\underset{NH_2}{|}}{CH}-CH_3$

b. $CH_3-CH_2-\underset{\underset{CH_2-CH_2-CH_3}{|}}{N}-CH_2-CH_3$

c. (line-angle structure with) $\underset{\underset{H}{|}}{N}$

d. (benzene ring with) $\underset{\underset{CH_3}{|}}{CH}-NH_2$

e. $CH_3-\underset{\underset{CH_3}{|}}{\overset{\overset{H}{|}}{N}}-\underset{\underset{CH_3}{|}}{C}-CH_3$

18.5 Write the IUPAC and common names for each of the following:

a. $CH_3-CH_2-NH_2$

b. $CH_3-\underset{\underset{H}{\overset{\overset{H}{|}}{}}}{N}-CH_2-CH_2-CH_3$

c. (line-angle structure with) N

d. $CH_3-\underset{\underset{NH_2}{|}}{CH}-CH_3$

18.6 Write the IUPAC and common names for each of the following:

a. $CH_3-CH_2-CH_2-NH_2$

b. $CH_3-\underset{\underset{H}{\overset{\overset{H}{|}}{}}}{N}-CH_2-CH_3$

c. (line-angle structure with) NH_2

d. $CH_3-CH_2-\underset{\underset{CH_2-CH_3}{|}}{N}-CH_2-CH_3$

18.7 Write the IUPAC name for each of the following molecules that have two functional groups:

a. $CH_3-\underset{\underset{NH_2}{|}}{CH}-CH_2-CH_2-\overset{\overset{O}{\|}}{C}-OH$

b. (benzene ring with) $\underset{}{NH_2}$ and Cl

c. $H_2N-CH_2-CH_2-\overset{\overset{O}{\|}}{C}-H$

d. $CH_3-\underset{\underset{NH_2}{|}}{CH}-CH_2-\underset{\underset{OH}{|}}{CH}-CH_2-CH_3$

18.8 Write the IUPAC name for each of the following molecules that have two functional groups:

a.
$$CH_3 - \overset{\overset{\displaystyle O}{\|}}{C} - \overset{\overset{\displaystyle NH_2}{|}}{CH} - CH_3$$

b.
$$CH_3 - \overset{\overset{\displaystyle NH_2}{|}}{CH} - CH_2 - CH_2 - CH_2 - OH$$

c. (structure showing benzene ring with N(H)(CH₃) group and Br substituent)

d.
$$CH_3 - \overset{\overset{\displaystyle NH_2}{|}}{CH} - \overset{\overset{\displaystyle O}{\|}}{C} - H$$

18.9 Draw the condensed structural formula for each of the following amines:
a. 2-chloroethanamine
b. *N*-methylaniline
c. butylpropylamine
d. 2-aminobutanal

18.10 Draw the condensed structural formula for each of the following amines:
a. dimethylamine
b. *p*-chloroaniline
c. *N,N*-diethylaniline
d. 1-amino-3-pentanone

18.2 Properties of Amines

LEARNING GOAL

Describe the boiling points and solubility of amines; write equations for the dissociation and neutralization of amines.

Amines contain polar N—H bonds, which allow primary and secondary amines to form hydrogen bonds with each other, while all amines can form hydrogen bonds with water. However, nitrogen is not as electronegative as oxygen, which means that the hydrogen bonds in amines are weaker than the hydrogen bonds in alcohols.

Most hydrogen bonds

Hydrogen bonds

Primary (1°) amine

Hydrogen bond

Secondary (2°) amine

No hydrogen bonds

Tertiary (3°) amine

Boiling Points of Amines

Amines have boiling points that are higher than alkanes but lower than alcohols. Primary (1°) amines, with two N—H bonds, can form more hydrogen bonds, and thus have higher boiling points than secondary (2°) amines of the same mass. It is not possible for tertiary (3°) amines to hydrogen bond with each other since they have no N—H bonds. Tertiary amines have lower boiling points than primary or secondary amines of the same mass.

$$CH_3 - CH_2 - CH_2 - NH_2$$
Propylamine (1°)
bp 48 °C

$$CH_3 - CH_2 - \overset{\overset{\displaystyle H}{|}}{N} - CH_3$$
Ethylmethylamine (2°)
bp 37 °C

$$CH_3 - \overset{\overset{\displaystyle CH_3}{|}}{N} - CH_3$$
Trimethylamine (3°)
bp 3 °C

Boiling Point Decreases →

Solubility of Amines in Water

Amines with one to six carbon atoms, including tertiary amines, are soluble because they form several hydrogen bonds with water (see Figure 18.1). Generally, the primary amines are most soluble, and tertiary amines are least soluble. As the number of carbon atoms in an amine increases in the nonpolar alkyl portions, the effect of hydrogen bonding is diminished.

Most hydrogen bonds

Hydrogen bonds

Primary (1°) amine

Fewest hydrogen bonds

Hydrogen bonds

Secondary (2°) amine

Hydrogen bond

Tertiary (3°) amine

FIGURE 18.1 ▶ Primary, secondary, and tertiary amines form hydrogen bonds with water molecules, but primary amines form the most and tertiary amines form the fewest.

Ⓠ Why do tertiary (3°) amines form fewer hydrogen bonds with water than primary amines?

SAMPLE PROBLEM 18.5 Boiling Points and Solubility of Amines

The compounds trimethylamine and ethylmethylamine have the same molar mass. Why is the boiling point of trimethylamine (3 °C) lower than that of ethylmethylamine (37 °C)?

SOLUTION

With polar N—H bonds, ethylmethylamine molecules form hydrogen bonds with each other. Thus, a higher temperature is required to break the hydrogen bonds and form a gas. However, trimethylamine, which is a tertiary amine, does not have N—H bonds and cannot hydrogen bond with other trimethylamine molecules. It does not need as high a temperature to form a gas.

STUDY CHECK 18.5

Why is
$$CH_3-CH_2-\overset{\overset{\displaystyle H}{\displaystyle |}}{N}-CH_2-CH_3$$ more soluble in water than

$$CH_3-CH_2-CH_2-CH_2-\overset{\overset{\displaystyle H}{\displaystyle |}}{N}-CH_2-CH_2-CH_3?$$

ANSWER

Hydrogen bonding makes amines with six or fewer carbon atoms soluble in water. When there are seven or more carbon atoms in the alkyl portions of an amine, the longer non-polar hydrocarbon chains diminish the solubility effect of the polar amine group.

Amines React as Bases in Water

Ammonia (NH_3) acts as a Brønsted–Lowry base by accepting H^+ from water to produce an ammonium ion (NH_4^+) and a hydroxide ion (OH^-).

$$H-\overset{\overset{\displaystyle H}{\displaystyle |}}{\underset{\displaystyle |}{\overset{\displaystyle ..}{N}}}-H + \text{HOH} \rightleftharpoons H-\overset{\overset{\displaystyle H}{\displaystyle |}}{\underset{\displaystyle |}{\overset{\displaystyle +}{N}}}-H + OH^-$$

Ammonia   Ammonium   Hydroxide
                     ion   ion

All of the amines we have discussed in this chapter are also Brønsted–Lowry bases because the lone pair of electrons on the nitrogen atom accepts H^+ from water. In the reaction of an amine with water, the products are a positively charged alkylammonium ion and a negatively charged hydroxide ion. The organic product is named by adding *ammonium ion* to the name of its alkyl group.

Reaction of a Primary Amine with Water

$$CH_3 - \overset{H}{\underset{H}{\overset{..}{N}}} - H + H_2O \rightleftharpoons CH_3 - \overset{H}{\underset{H}{\overset{+}{N}}} - H + OH^-$$

Methylamine   Methylammonium   Hydroxide
ion   ion

Reaction of a Secondary Amine with Water

$$CH_3 - \overset{..}{\underset{H}{N}} - CH_3 + H_2O \rightleftharpoons CH_3 - \overset{H}{\underset{H}{\overset{+}{N}}} - CH_3 + OH^-$$

Dimethylamine   Dimethylammonium   Hydroxide
ion   ion

Reaction of a Tertiary Amine with Water

$$CH_3 - \overset{..}{\underset{CH_3}{N}} - CH_3 + H_2O \rightleftharpoons CH_3 - \overset{H}{\underset{CH_3}{\overset{+}{N}}} - CH_3 + OH^-$$

Trimethylamine   Trimethylammonium   Hydroxide
ion   ion

The amines in fish react with the acid in lemon to neutralize the "fishy" odor.

Neutralization of an Amine

When you squeeze lemon juice on fish, the "fishy" odor is removed by converting the amines to their ammonium salts. In a *neutralization reaction*, an amine acts as a base and reacts with an acid to form an **ammonium salt**. The lone pair of electrons on the nitrogen atom accepts H^+ from an acid to give an ammonium salt; no water is formed. An ammonium salt is named by using its alkylammonium ion name followed by the name of the negative ion.

| Amine | Acid | Ammonium Salt |

$$CH_3 - \overset{..}{\underset{H}{N}} - H + H - Cl \longrightarrow CH_3 - \overset{H}{\underset{H}{\overset{+}{N}}} - H \ Cl^-$$

Methylamine   Methylammonium chloride

$$CH_3 - \overset{..}{\underset{H}{N}} - CH_3 + H - Cl \longrightarrow CH_3 - \overset{H}{\underset{H}{\overset{+}{N}}} - CH_3 \ Cl^-$$

Dimethylamine   Dimethylammonium chloride

In a **quaternary ammonium salt**, a nitrogen atom is bonded to four carbon groups, which classifies it as a quaternary (4°) amine. As in other ammonium salts, the nitrogen atom has a positive charge. Choline, a component of glycerophospholipids, is a quaternary ammonium ion. The quaternary salts differ from other ammonium salts because the nitrogen atom is not bonded to an H atom.

$$CH_3 - \overset{\overset{\displaystyle CH_3}{|}}{\underset{\underset{\displaystyle CH_3}{|}}{\overset{+}{N}}} - CH_3 \ Cl^-$$

Tetramethylammonium chloride

$$HO - CH_2 - CH_2 - \overset{\overset{\displaystyle CH_3}{|}}{\underset{\underset{\displaystyle CH_3}{|}}{\overset{+}{N}}} - CH_3$$

Choline

Properties of Ammonium Salts

Ammonium salts are ionic compounds with strong attractions between the positively charged ammonium ion and an anion, usually chloride. Like most salts, ammonium salts are solid at room temperature, odorless, and soluble in water and body fluids. For this reason, amines that are large molecules that are intended to be used as drugs are converted to their ammonium salts, which are soluble in water and body fluids. The ammonium salt of ephedrine is used as a bronchodilator and in decongestant products such as Sudafed. The ammonium salt of diphenhydramine is used in products such as Benadryl for relief of itching and pain from skin irritations and rashes (see Figure 18.2). In pharmaceuticals, the naming of the ammonium salt follows an older method of giving the amine name followed by the name of the acid.

FIGURE 18.2 ▶ Decongestants and products that relieve itchy skin often contain ammonium salts.

Q Why are ammonium salts used in drugs rather than the biologically active amines?

Ephedrine hydrochloride
Ephedrine HCl
Sudafed

Diphenhydramine hydrochloride
Diphenylhydramine HCl
Benadryl

When an ammonium salt reacts with a strong base such as NaOH, it is converted back to the amine, which is also called the free amine or free base.

$$CH_3 - \overset{+}{N}H_3 \ Cl^- + NaOH \longrightarrow CH_3 - NH_2 + NaCl + H_2O$$

The narcotic cocaine is typically extracted from coca leaves using an acidic solution to give a white, solid ammonium salt, which is cocaine hydrochloride. It is the salt of cocaine (cocaine hydrochloride) that is smuggled and used illegally on the street. "Crack cocaine" is the free amine or free base of the amine obtained by treating the cocaine hydrochloride with NaOH and ether, a process known as "free-basing." The solid product is known as "crack cocaine" because it makes a cracking noise when heated. The free amine is rapidly absorbed when smoked and gives stronger highs than the cocaine hydrochloride, which makes crack cocaine more addictive.

Coca leaves are a source of cocaine.

Cocaine hydrochloride

Cocaine ("free base"; crack cocaine)

Crack cocaine is obtained by treating cocaine hydrochloride with NaOH and ether.

> **SAMPLE PROBLEM 18.6** Reactions of Amines
>
> Write a balanced chemical equation that shows ethylamine:
>
> **a.** acting as a weak base in water
> **b.** neutralized by HCl
>
> **SOLUTION**
>
> **a.** $CH_3—CH_2—NH_2 + H_2O \rightleftharpoons CH_3—CH_2—\overset{+}{N}H_3 + OH^-$
> **b.** $CH_3—CH_2—NH_2 + HCl \longrightarrow CH_3—CH_2—\overset{+}{N}H_3\ Cl^-$
>
> **STUDY CHECK 18.6**
>
> Draw the condensed structural formula for the ammonium salt formed by the reaction of trimethylamine and HCl.
>
> **ANSWER**
>
> $$CH_3—\overset{\overset{\displaystyle CH_3}{|}}{\underset{\underset{\displaystyle CH_3}{|}}{\overset{+}{N}}}—H\ Cl^-$$

QUESTIONS AND PROBLEMS

18.2 Properties of Amines

LEARNING GOAL Describe the boiling points and solubility of amines; write equations for the dissociation and neutralization of amines.

18.11 Identify the compound in each pair that has the higher boiling point. Explain.
  a. $CH_3—CH_2—NH_2$ or $CH_3—CH_2—OH$
  b. $CH_3—NH_2$ or $CH_3—CH_2—CH_2—NH_2$
  c. $CH_3—\overset{\overset{\displaystyle CH_3}{|}}{N}—CH_3$ or $CH_3—CH_2—CH_2—NH_2$

18.12 Identify the compound in each pair that has the higher boiling point. Explain.
  a. $CH_3—CH_2—CH_2—CH_3$ or $CH_3—CH_2—CH_2—NH_2$
  b. $CH_3—NH_2$ or $CH_3—CH_2—NH_2$
  c. $CH_3—CH_2—CH_2—OH$ or $CH_3—\overset{\overset{\displaystyle NH_2}{|}}{CH}—CH_3$

18.13 Propylamine (59 g/mole) has a boiling point of 48 °C, and ethylmethylamine (59 g/mole) has a boiling point of 37 °C. Butane (58 g/mole) has a much lower boiling point of −1 °C. Explain.

18.14 Assign the boiling point of 3 °C, 48 °C, or 97 °C to the appropriate compound: 1-propanol, propylamine, and trimethylamine.

18.15 Indicate if each of the following is soluble in water. Explain.
  a. $CH_3—CH_2—NH_2$
  b. $CH_3—\overset{\overset{\displaystyle H}{|}}{N}—CH_3$
  c. $CH_3—CH_2—CH_2—\overset{\overset{\displaystyle CH_2—CH_2—CH_3}{|}}{N}—CH_2—CH_2—CH_3$
  d. $CH_3—\overset{\overset{\displaystyle NH_2}{|}}{CH}—CH_2—CH_3$

18.16 Indicate if each of the following is soluble in water. Explain.
  a. $CH_3—CH_2—CH_2—NH_2$
  b. $CH_3—CH_2—CH_2—\overset{\overset{\displaystyle H}{|}}{N}—CH_2—CH_3$
  c. $CH_3—\overset{\overset{\displaystyle NH_2}{|}}{CH}—CH_3$
  d. (diphenylamine structure with N—H)

18.17 Write a balanced chemical equation for the dissociation of each of the following amines in water:
  a. methylamine   **b.** dimethylamine
  c. aniline

18.18 Write a balanced chemical equation for the dissociation of each of the following amines in water:
  a. diethylamine   **b.** propylamine
  c. N-methylaniline

18.19 Draw the condensed structural formula for the ammonium salt obtained when each of the amines in problem 18.17 reacts with HCl.

18.20 Draw the condensed structural formula for the ammonium salt obtained when each of the amines in problem 18.18 reacts with HCl.

℞ Clinical Applications

18.21 Novocain, a local anesthetic, is the ammonium salt of procaine.

The aroma of pepper is due to piperidine, a heterocyclic amine.

$$H_2N—\overset{O}{\overset{\|}{\text{◯—C}}}—O—CH_2—CH_2—N\begin{smallmatrix}CH_2—CH_3\\ \\CH_2—CH_3\end{smallmatrix}$$

Procaine

a. Draw the condensed structural formula for the ammonium salt (procaine hydrochloride) formed when procaine reacts with HCl. (*Hint:* The tertiary amine reacts with HCl.)
b. Why is procaine hydrochloride used rather than procaine?

18.22 Lidocaine (Xylocaine) is used as a local anesthetic and cardiac depressant.

Lidocaine (Xylocaine)

a. Draw the condensed structural formula for the ammonium salt formed when lidocaine reacts with HCl.
b. Why is the ammonium salt of lidocaine used rather than the amine?

18.3 Heterocyclic Amines

A **heterocyclic amine** is a cyclic organic compound that consists of a ring of five or six atoms, of which one or two are nitrogen atoms. Of the five-atom rings, the simplest one is pyrrolidine, which is a ring of four carbon atoms and one nitrogen atom, all with single bonds. Pyrrole is a five-atom ring with one nitrogen atom and two double bonds. Imidazole is a five-atom ring that contains two nitrogen atoms. Piperidine is a six-atom heterocyclic ring with a nitrogen atom. Some of the pungent aroma and taste of black pepper that we use to season our food is due to piperidine. Purine and pyrimidine rings are found in DNA and RNA. In purine, the structures of 6-atom pyrimidine and 5-atom imidazole are combined. Heterocyclic amines with two or three double bonds have aromatic properties similar to benzene.

5-Atom Heterocyclic Amines

Pyrrolidine   Pyrrole   Imidazole

6-Atom Heterocyclic Amines

Piperidine   Pyridine   Pyrimidine   Purine

▶**SAMPLE PROBLEM 18.7** Heterocyclic Amines

Identify the heterocyclic amines that are part of the structure of nicotine.

Nicotine

SOLUTION

Nicotine contains two heterocyclic rings. The 6-atom ring with one N atom and three double bonds is pyridine, and the 5-atom ring with one N atom and no double bonds is pyrrolidine. The N atom in the pyrrolidine ring is bonded to a methyl group ($-CH_3$).

STUDY CHECK 18.7

Sedamine is used as a sleep aid. Identify the heterocyclic amine that is part of the structure of sedamine.

Sedamine

ANSWER

piperidine

Alkaloids: Amines in Plants

Alkaloids are physiologically active nitrogen-containing compounds produced by plants. The term *alkaloid* refers to the "alkali-like" or basic characteristics we have seen for amines. Certain alkaloids are used in anesthetics, in antidepressants, and as stimulants, and many are habit forming.

As a stimulant, nicotine increases the level of adrenaline in the blood, which increases the heart rate and blood pressure. Nicotine is addictive because it activates pleasure centers in the brain. Nicotine has a simple alkaloid structure that includes a pyrrolidine ring. Coniine, which is obtained from poison hemlock, is an extremely toxic alkaloid that contains a piperidine ring.

Coniine, which causes respiratory paralysis, is a poisonous alkaloid from hemlock.

Nicotine   Coniine

Caffeine is a purine that is a central nervous system stimulant. Present in coffee, tea, soft drinks, energy drinks, chocolate, and cocoa, caffeine increases alertness, but it may cause nervousness and insomnia. Caffeine is also used in certain pain relievers to counteract the drowsiness caused by an antihistamine (see Figure 18.3).

Caffeine

FIGURE 18.3 ▶ Caffeine is a stimulant found in coffee, tea, energy drinks, and chocolate.

🅠 Why is caffeine an alkaloid?

Several alkaloids are used in medicine. Quinine, obtained from the bark of the cinchona tree, has been used to treat malaria since the 1600s. Atropine from nightshade (belladonna) is used in low concentrations to accelerate slow heart rates and to dilate the eyes during eye examinations.

Quinine

Atropine

For many centuries, morphine and codeine, alkaloids found in the opium poppy plant, have been used as effective painkillers (see Figure 18.4). Codeine, which is structurally similar to morphine, is used in some prescription painkillers and cough syrups. Heroin, obtained by a chemical modification of morphine, is strongly addictive and is not used medically. The structure of the prescription drug OxyContin (oxycodone) used to relieve severe pain is similar to heroin. Today, there are an increasing number of deaths from Oxy-Contin abuse because its physiological effects are also similar to those of heroin.

Morphine

Codeine

Heroin

OxyContin

FIGURE 18.4 ▶ The green, unripe poppy seed capsule contains a milky sap (opium) that is the source of the alkaloids morphine and codeine.

ⓠ Where is the piperidine ring in the structures of morphine and codeine?

♡ Chemistry Link to **Health**

Synthesizing Drugs

One area of research in pharmacology is the synthesis of compounds that retain the anesthetic characteristic of naturally occurring alkaloids, such as cocaine and morphine, without the addictive side effects. For example, cocaine is an effective anesthetic, but after taking it on a regular basis, the user can become addicted. Research chemists modified the structure of cocaine but kept the phenyl group and nitrogen atom. The synthetic products procaine and lidocaine retain the anesthetic qualities of the natural alkaloid without the addictive side effects.

The structure of morphine was also modified to make a synthetic alkaloid, meperidine, or Demerol, which acts as an effective painkiller.

Cocaine

Procaine (Novocain)

Lidocaine (Xylocaine)

Meperidine (Demerol)

QUESTIONS AND PROBLEMS

18.3 Heterocyclic Amines

LEARNING GOAL Identify heterocyclic amines; distinguish between the types of heterocyclic amines.

18.23 Name the heterocyclic amines in each of the following:

a. b. c.

18.24 Name the heterocyclic amines in each of the following:

a. b. c.

Rx Clinical Applications

18.25 Ritalin (methylphenidate) is a stimulant that may be prescribed for attention deficit hyperactivity disorder (ADHD). What is the heterocyclic amine in Ritalin?

Ritalin

18.26 Niacin, which is also known as vitamin B_3 and nicotinic acid, is found in many foods such as fish, beef, milk, and eggs. What is the heterocyclic amine in niacin?

Niacin

18.27 Low levels of serotonin in the brain appear to be associated with depressed states. What is the heterocyclic amine in serotonin?

Serotonin

18.28 Histamine causes inflammation and itchy skin in an allergic reaction. What is the heterocyclic amine in histamine?

$CH_2 - CH_2 - NH_2$

Histamine

LEARNING GOAL

Describe the role of amines as neurotransmitters.

18.4 Neurotransmitters

A **neurotransmitter** is a chemical compound that transmits an impulse from a nerve cell (neuron) to a target cell such as another nerve cell, a muscle cell, or a gland cell. A typical neuron consists of a cell body and numerous filaments called *dendrites* at one end, and an axon that ends at the *axon terminal* at the opposite end. The axon terminals and the dendrites of other nerve cells form junctions called *synapses*. When an electrical signal reaches the axon terminal of a nerve cell, neurotransmitters are released into the synapse, which are taken up by the dendrites in nearby nerve cells. Thus, an alternating series of electrical impulses and chemical transmitters move information through a network of nerve cells in a very short period of time.

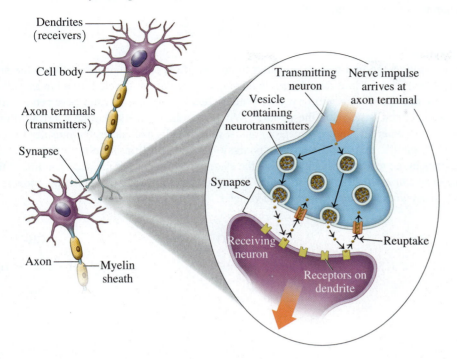

A nerve cell (neuron) consists of a cell body and filaments called axons and dendrites that form junctions (synapses) with nearby nerve cells to transmit nerve impulses.

Neurotransmitters at the Synapse

Within a nerve cell, a neurotransmitter is synthesized and stored in vesicles at the end of the axon terminal. There are many vesicles in a single filament, and each vesicle may contain several thousand molecules of a neurotransmitter. When a nerve impulse arrives at the nerve cell, it stimulates the vesicles to release the neurotransmitter into the synapse. The neurotransmitter molecules diffuse across the synapse to their receptor sites on the dendrites of another nerve cell. Neurotransmitters can be *excitatory*, which means they stimulate the receptors to send more nerve impulses, or *inhibitory*, which means they decrease the activity of the receptors. The binding of an excitatory neurotransmitter opens ion channels in nearby nerve cells. A flow of positive ions creates new electrical impulses that stimulate additional nerve cells to release the neurotransmitter from their vesicles into the synapse.

Termination of Neurotransmitter Action

Between nerve impulses, the neurotransmitters bound to the receptors are quickly removed to allow new signals to come from the adjacent nerve cells. The removal of neurotransmitters from the receptors can be done in different ways.

1. The neurotransmitter diffuses away from the synapse.
2. Enzymes in the receptors break down the neurotransmitter.
3. Reuptake returns the neurotransmitter to the vesicles where it is stored.

Amine Neurotransmitters

Neurotransmitters contain nitrogen atoms as amines and alkylammonium ions. Most are synthesized in a few steps from compounds such as amino acids obtained from our diets. The amino groups are usually ionized to form ammonium cations, and carboxyl groups are ionized to form carboxylate anions. Important amine neurotransmitters include acetylcholine, dopamine, norepinephrine (noradrenaline), epinephrine (adrenaline), serotonin, histamine, glutamate, and GABA.

Acetylcholine

Acetylcholine, the first neurotransmitter to be identified, communicates between the nervous system and the muscle, where it is involved in regulating muscle activation as well as learning and short-term memory. It is synthesized by forming an ester between choline and acetate, and is stored in the vesicles. When stimulated, acetylcholine is released into the synapse where it binds to receptors on the muscle cells and causes the muscles to contract. To enable continual nerve transmission, acetylcholine is quickly degraded by enzymes in the receptors that hydrolyze the ester bond. The loss of the acetylcholine at the receptors causes muscle cells to relax. The resulting choline and acetate are converted back to acetylcholine and stored in the vesicles.

In older adults, a decrease in acetylcholine produces gaps in short-term memory. In Alzheimer's disease, the levels of acetylcholine may decrease by 90%, which causes severe loss of reasoning and motor function. Medications that are cholinesterase inhibitors such as Aricept are used to slow the breakdown of acetylcholine in order to maintain the acetylcholine levels in the brain.

Donepezil hydrochloride (Aricept)

Cholinesterase inhibitors, such as Aricept, slow the enzymatic breakdown of acetylcholine.

Nerve poisons such as Sarin, Soman, and Parathion bind to the acetylcholinesterase enzyme and inhibit its action. As a result, acetylcholine remains in the synapse and nerve transmissions stop. Because acetylcholine cannot be released, the muscles in the body cannot relax, and convulsions and respiratory failure soon occur.

Amphetamine
(Benzedrine, Adderall)

Methamphetamine
(Methedrine)

Catecholamines

The word catecholamine refers to the catechol part (3,4-dihydroxyphenyl group) of these aromatic amines. The most important catecholamine neurotransmitters are dopamine, norepinephrine, and epinephrine, which are closely related in structure and all are synthesized from the amino acid tyrosine. In the diet, tyrosine is found in meats, nuts, eggs, and cheese.

Amphetamine and methamphetamine are synthetic central nervous system stimulants that increase the levels of excitatory catecholamine neurotransmitters particularly

Neurotransmitters dopamine, norepinephrine, and epinephrine are synthesized from the amino acid tyrosine after it is converted to L-dopa.

dopamine and norepinephrine. Amphetamine is used in the treatment of ADHD to improve cognition and decrease hyperactivity.

Dopamine

Dopamine, which is produced in the nerve cells of the midbrain, works as a natural stimulant, to give us energy and feelings of enjoyment. It plays a role in controlling muscle movement, regulation of the sleep–wake cycle, and helps to improve cognition, attention, memory, and learning. High levels of dopamine may be involved in addictive behavior and schizophrenia. Cocaine and amphetamine block the reuptake of dopamine into the vesicles of the nerve cell. As a result, dopamine remains in the synapse longer. The addiction to cocaine may be a result of the extended exposure to high levels of dopamine in the synapses.

L-Dopa is used to increase dopamine levels in the brain.

> **SAMPLE PROBLEM 18.8**
>
> Place the following in order of occurrence for nerve impulses:
>
> **a.** Neurotransmitters diffuse across synapse to receptors on dendrites.
> **b.** Neurotransmitters move away from receptors.
> **c.** An electrical signal reaches the axon terminal of a nerve cell.
> **d.** Reuptake moves neurotransmitters into the vesicles for storage.
> **e.** Vesicles release neurotransmitters into the synapse of nearby nerve cells.
> **f.** Neurotransmitters stimulate receptors to send new nerve impulse.
>
> **SOLUTION**
>
> **c, e, a, f, b, d**
>
> **STUDY CHECK 18.8**
>
> How does an excitatory neurotransmitter send a nerve impulse at the receptor?
>
> **ANSWER**
>
> When the neurotransmitter attaches to the receptor, ion channels open and positive ions flow to nearby nerve cells creating new electrical impulses.

In persons with Parkinson's disease, the midbrain nerve cells lose their ability to produce dopamine. As dopamine levels drop, there is a decrease in motor coordination, resulting in a slowing of movement and shuffling, rigidity of muscle, loss of cognition, and dementia. Although dopamine cannot cross the blood–brain barrier, persons with Parkinson's disease are given L-dopa, the precursor of dopamine, which does cross the blood–brain barrier.

Norepinephrine and Epinephrine

Norepinephrine (noradrenaline) and epinephrine (adrenaline) are hormonal neurotransmitters that play a role in sleep, attention and focus, and alertness. Epinephrine is synthesized from norepinephrine by the addition of a methyl group to the amine group. Norepinephrine (noradrenaline) and epinephrine (adrenaline) are normally produced in the adrenal glands, and are produced in large quantities when the stress of physical threat causes the fight-or-flight response. Then they cause an increase in blood pressure and heart rate, constrict blood vessels, dilate airways, and stimulate the breakdown of glycogen, which provides glucose and energy for the body. Because of its physiological effects, epinephrine is administered during cardiac arrest, and used as a bronchodilator during allergy or asthma attacks. As a neurotransmitter, low levels of norepinephrine as well as dopamine contribute to *attention deficit disorder* (ADD). Medications such as Ritalin or Dexedrine may be prescribed to increase levels of norepinephrine and dopamine.

Serotonin

Serotonin (5-hydroxytryptamine) helps us to relax, sleep deeply and peacefully, think rationally, and gives us a feeling of well-being and calmness. Serotonin is synthesized from the amino acid tryptophan, which can cross the blood–brain barrier. A diet which contains foods such as eggs, fish, cheese, turkey, chicken, and beef, which have high levels of tryptophan, will increase serotonin levels. Foods with a low level of tryptophan, such as whole wheat, will lower serotonin levels. Psychedelic drugs such as LSD and mescaline stimulate the action of serotonin at its receptors.

Tryptophan (amino acid) → Serotonin + CO_2

Low levels of serotonin in the brain may be associated with depression, anxiety disorders, obsessive–compulsive disorder, and eating disorders. Many antidepressant drugs, such as fluoxetine (Prozac) and paroxetine (Paxil), are selective serotonin reuptake inhibitors (SSRIs). When the reuptake of serotonin is slowed, it remains longer at the receptors, where it continues its action; the net effect is as if additional quantities of serotonin were taken.

Prozac is one of the selective serotonin reuptake inhibitors (SSRIs) used to slow the reuptake of serotonin.

Fluoxetine hydrochloride (Prozac)

Paroxetine hydrochloride (Paxil)

Histamine

Histamine is synthesized in the nerve cells in the hypothalamus from the amino acid histidine, when a carboxylate group is converted to CO_2. Histamine is produced by the immune system in response to pathogens and invaders, or injury. When histamine combines with histamine receptors, it causes allergic reactions, which may include inflammation, watery eyes, itchy skin, and hay fever. Histamine can also cause smooth muscle constriction, such as the closing of the trachea in persons allergic to shellfish. Histamine is also stored and released in the cells of the stomach, where it stimulates acid production. Antihistamines, such as Benadryl, Zantac, and Tagamet, are used to block the histamine receptors and stop the allergic reactions.

Histidine

Histidine decarboxylase

Histamine + CO_2

Glutamate

Glutamate is the most abundant neurotransmitter in the nervous system, where it is used to stimulate over 90% of the synapses. When glutamate binds to its receptor cells, it stimulates the synthesis of nitrogen oxide (NO), also a neurotransmitter in the brain. As NO reaches the transmitting nerve cells, more glutamate is released. Glutamate and NO are thought to be involved in learning and memory. Glutamate is used in many fast excitatory synapses in the brain and spinal cord. The reuptake of glutamate out of the synapse and back into the nerve cell occurs rapidly, which keeps glutamate levels low. If the reuptake of glutamate does not take place fast enough, a condition called *excitotoxicity* occurs in which excess glutamate at the receptors can destroy brain cells. In Lou Gehrig's disease (ALS), the production of an excessive amount of glutamate causes the degeneration of nerve cells in the spinal cord. As a result, a person with Lou Gehrig's disease suffers increasing weakness and muscular atrophy. When the reuptake of glutamate is too rapid, the levels of glutamate fall too low in the synapse, which may result in mental illness such as schizophrenia.

Glutamate

Gamma(γ)-Aminobutyric Acid or GABA

Gamma(γ)-aminobutyric acid or GABA, which is produced from glutamate, is the most common inhibitory neurotransmitter in the brain. GABA produces a calming effect and reduces anxiety by inhibiting the ability of nerve cells to send electrical signals to nearby nerve cells. It is involved in the regulation of muscle tone, sleep, and anxiety. GABA can be obtained as a nutritional supplement. Medications such as benzodiazepines,

GABA is the major inhibitory neurotransmitter.

and barbiturates such as phenobarbital, are used to increase GABA levels at the GABA receptors. Alcohol, sedatives, and tranquilizers increase the inhibitory effects of GABA. Caffeine decreases the GABA levels in the synapses, leading to conditions of anxiety and sleep problems.

$$H_3\overset{+}{N}-\underset{\underset{\underset{O^-}{\overset{\|}{C}}}{|}}{CH}-CH_2-CH_2-\overset{O}{\overset{\|}{C}}-O^- \longrightarrow H_3\overset{+}{N}-CH_2-CH_2-CH_2-\overset{O}{\overset{\|}{C}}-O^- + CO_2$$

Glutamate   Gamma(γ)-aminobutyric acid (GABA)

Table 18.2 summarizes the properties and functions of selected neurotransmitters we have discussed.

TABLE 18.2 Selected Neurotransmitters

Amine Transmitters	Synthesized from	Site of Synthesis	Function	Effect Enhanced by
Acetylcholine	Acetyl CoA and choline	Central nervous system	Excitatory: regulates muscle activation, learning, and short-term memory	Nicotine
Dopamine	Tyrosine	Central nervous system	Excitatory and inhibitory: regulates muscle movement, cognition, sleep, mood, and learning; deficiency leads to Parkinson's disease and schizophrenia	L-dopa, amphetamines, cocaine
Norepinephrine	Tyrosine	Central nervous system	Excitatory and inhibitory: sleep, focus, and alertness	Ritalin, Dexedrine
Epinephrine	Tyrosine	Adrenal glands	Excitatory: plays a role in sleep and being alert, and is involved in the fight-or-flight response	Ritalin, Dexedrine
Serotonin	Tryptophan	Central nervous system	Inhibitory: regulates anxiety, eating, mood, sleep, learning, and memory	LSD; Prozac and Paxil block its action to relieve anxiety
Histamine	Histidine	Central nervous system: hypothalamus	Inhibitory: involved in allergic reactions, inflammation, and hay fever	Antihistamines
Amino Acid Transmitters				
Glutamate		Central nervous system: spinal cord	Excitatory: involved in learning and memory; main excitatory neurotransmitter in brain	Alcohol
GABA	Glutamate	Central nervous system: brain, hypothalamus	Inhibitory: regulates muscle tone, sleep, and anxiety	Alcohol, sedatives, tranquilizers; synthesis blocked by antianxiety drugs (benzodiazepines); caffeine decreases GABA levels in synapse

QUESTIONS AND PROBLEMS

18.4 Neurotransmitters

LEARNING GOAL Describe the role of amines as neurotransmitters.

18.29 What is a neurotransmitter?

18.30 Where are the neurotransmitters stored in a neuron?

18.31 When is a neurotransmitter released into the synapse?

18.32 What happens to a neurotransmitter once it is in the synapse?

18.33 Why is it important to remove a neurotransmitter from its receptor?

18.34 What are three ways in which a neurotransmitter can be separated from a receptor?

℞ Clinical Applications

18.35 What is the role of acetylcholine?

18.36 What are some physiological effects of low levels of acetylcholine?

18.37 What is the function of dopamine in the body?

18.38 What are some physiological effects of low levels of dopamine?

18.39 What is the function of serotonin in the body?

18.40 What are the physiological effects of low serotonin?

18.41 What is the function of histamine in the body?

18.42 How do antihistamines stop the action of histamine?

18.43 Why is it important that the levels of glutamate in the synapse remain low?

18.44 What happens if there is an excess of glutamate in the synapse?

18.45 What is the function of GABA in the body?

18.46 What is the effect of caffeine on GABA levels?

18.5 Amides

The **amides** are derivatives of carboxylic acids in which an amino group replaces the hydroxyl group.

LEARNING GOAL

Draw the amide product from amidation, and give the IUPAC and common names.

Carboxylic Acid   **Amide**

Ethanoic acid
(acetic acid)

Ethanamide
(acetamide)

Preparation of Amides

An amide is produced in a reaction called **amidation**, or *condensation*, in which a carboxylic acid reacts with ammonia or a primary (1°) or secondary (2°) amine. A molecule of water is eliminated, and the fragments of the carboxylic acid and amine molecules join to form the amide, much like the formation of an ester. Because a tertiary (3°) amine does not contain a hydrogen atom, it cannot undergo amidation.

⚛ CORE CHEMISTRY SKILL

Forming Amides

Amide bond

$$CH_3-CH_2-\overset{\overset{\displaystyle O}{\|}}{C}-OH + H-\overset{\overset{\displaystyle H}{|}}{N}-H \xrightarrow{\text{Heat}} CH_3-CH_2-\overset{\overset{\displaystyle O}{\|}}{C}-\overset{\overset{\displaystyle H}{|}}{N}-H + H_2O$$

Propanoic acid   Ammonia   Propanamide
(propionic acid)   (propionamide)

$$CH_3-CH_2-\overset{\overset{\displaystyle O}{\|}}{C}-OH + H-\overset{\overset{\displaystyle H}{|}}{N}-CH_3 \xrightarrow{\text{Heat}} CH_3-CH_2-\overset{\overset{\displaystyle O}{\|}}{C}-\overset{\overset{\displaystyle H}{|}}{N}-CH_3 + H_2O$$

Propanoic acid   Methylamine   *N*-Methylpropanamide
(propionic acid)   (*N*-methylpropionamide)

▶SAMPLE PROBLEM 18.9 Amidation

Draw the condensed structural formula for the amide product in each of the following reactions:

a. (benzene ring)$-\overset{\overset{\displaystyle O}{\|}}{C}-OH + NH_3 \xrightarrow{\text{Heat}}$

b. $CH_3-\overset{\overset{\displaystyle O}{\|}}{C}-OH + H_2N-CH_2-CH_3 \xrightarrow{\text{Heat}}$

SOLUTION

The condensed structural formula for the amide product can be drawn by attaching the carbonyl group from the acid to the nitrogen atom of the amine. The —OH group is removed from the acid and —H from the amine to form water.

a. (benzene ring)—C(=O)—NH₂

b. $CH_3—C(=O)—N(H)—CH_2—CH_3$

STUDY CHECK 18.9

Draw the condensed structural formulas for the carboxylic acid and amine needed to prepare the following amide. (*Hint*: Separate the N and C=O of the amide group, and add —H and —OH to give the original amine and carboxylic acid.)

$H—C(=O)—N(CH_3)—CH_3$

ANSWER

$H—C(=O)—OH$ and $H—N(CH_3)—CH_3$

Naming Amides

In the IUPAC and common names for amides, the *oic acid* or *ic acid* from the corresponding carboxylic acid name is replaced with *amide*. We can diagram the name of an amide in the following way:

From butanoic acid (butyric acid) → $CH_3—CH_2—CH_2—C(=O)—NH_2$ ← From ammonia

IUPAC Butanamide
Common Butyramide

$H—C(=O)—NH_2$ Methanamide (formamide)

$CH_3—C(=O)—NH_2$ Ethanamide (acetamide)

(benzene)—C(=O)—NH₂ Benzamide

When alkyl groups are attached to the nitrogen atom, the prefix *N-* or *N, N-* precedes the name of the amide, depending on whether there are one or two groups. We can diagram the name of a substituted amide in the following way:

From butanoic acid (butyric acid) → $CH_3—CH_2—CH_2—C(=O)—N(CH_3)—CH_3$ ← From dimethylamine

IUPAC N,N-Dimethylbutanamide
Common N,N-Dimethylbutyramide

O H
‖ |
$CH_3-C-N-CH_3$

N-Methylethanamide
(*N*-methylacetamide)

O CH₃
‖ |
$CH_3-CH_2-C-N-CH_3$

N,N-Dimethylpropanamide
(*N,N*-dimethylpropionamide)

O
‖
C—N—CH₃
|
H

N-Methylbenzamide

CH₃
|
$CH_3-CH-CH_2-CH_2-C-NH_2$
                     ‖
                     O

4-Methylpentanamide

▶ **SAMPLE PROBLEM 18.10** Naming Amides

Give the IUPAC name for the following amide:

O H
‖ |
$CH_3-CH_2-CH_2-C-N-CH_2-CH_3$

SOLUTION

	Given	Need
ANALYZE THE PROBLEM	amide	IUPAC name

STEP 1 Replace *oic acid* (IUPAC) or *ic acid* (common) in the carboxyl name with *amide*.

O H
‖ |
$CH_3-CH_2-CH_2-C-N-CH_2-CH_3$ butanamide

STEP 2 Name each substituent on the N atom using the prefix *N-* and the alkyl name.

O H
‖ |
$CH_3-CH_2-CH_2-C-N-CH_2-CH_3$ *N*-ethyl butanamide

STUDY CHECK 18.10

Draw the condensed structural formula for *N,N*-dimethylbenzamide.

ANSWER

O CH₃
‖ |
C—N—CH₃

Guide to Naming Amides

STEP 1
Replace *oic acid* (IUPAC) or *ic acid* (common) in the carboxyl name with *amide*.

STEP 2
Name each substituent on the N atom using the prefix *N-* and the alkyl name.

Physical Properties of Amides

The amides do not have the properties of bases that we saw for the amines. Only methanamide is a liquid at room temperature, while the other amides are solids. For primary (1°) amides, the —NH₂ group can form more hydrogen bonds, which gives primary amides the highest melting points. The melting points of the secondary (2°) amides are lower because they form fewer hydrogen bonds. Because tertiary (3°) amides cannot form hydrogen bonds, they have the lowest melting points (see Table 18.3).

TABLE 18.3 Melting Points of Selected Amides with the Same Molar Mass (73.0 g/mole)

Primary (1°)	Secondary (2°)	Tertiary (3°)
Propanamide 80. °C	*N*-Methylethanamide 28 °C	*N*,*N*-Dimethylmethanamide −61 °C

Melting Point Decreases →

Hydrogen bonds

Hydrogen bonding between molecules of a primary amide.

    The amides with one to five carbon atoms are soluble in water because they can hydrogen bond with water molecules.

Hydrogen bonds

Primary (1°) amide

Hydrogen bonds

Secondary (2°) amide

Hydrogen bond

Tertiary (3°) amide

In water, primary amides form more hydrogen bonds than secondary and tertiary amides.

♡ Chemistry Link to **Health**

Amides in Health and Medicine

The simplest natural amide is urea, an end product of protein metabolism in the body. The kidneys remove urea from the blood and excrete it in urine. If the kidneys malfunction, urea is not removed and builds to a toxic level, a condition called *uremia*. Urea is also used as a component of fertilizer to increase nitrogen in the soil.

$$H_2N - \overset{\displaystyle O}{\overset{\displaystyle \|}{C}} - NH_2$$

Urea

Synthetic amides are used as substitutes for sugar. Saccharin is a very powerful sweetener and is used as a sugar substitute. The sweetener aspartame is made from two amino acids, aspartic acid and phenylalanine, joined by an amide bond.

Saccharin

(Luminal), pentobarbital (Nembutal), and secobarbital (Seconal). Other amides, such as meprobamate and diazepam, act as sedatives and tranquilizers.

Amides are found in synthetic sweeteners, such as aspartame, and pain relievers, such as acetaminophen.

Phenobarbital
(Luminal)

Pentobarbital
(Nembutal)

Aspartic acid   Phenylalanine   Methyl ester
Aspartame

Secobarbital
(Seconal)

The compounds phenacetin and acetaminophen, which is used in Tylenol, reduce fever and pain, but they have little anti-inflammatory effect.

Phenacetin

Meprobamate
(Miltown)

Acetaminophen

Many barbiturates are cyclic amides of barbituric acid that act as sedatives in small dosages or sleep inducers in larger dosages. They are often habit forming. Barbiturate drugs include phenobarbital

Diazepam
(Valium)

QUESTIONS AND PROBLEMS

18.5 Amides

LEARNING GOAL Draw the amide product from amidation, and give the IUPAC and common names.

18.47 Draw the condensed structural formula for the amide formed in each of the following reactions:

a. $CH_3-C(=O)-OH + NH_3 \xrightarrow{Heat}$

b. $CH_3-C(=O)-OH + H_2N-CH_2-CH_3 \xrightarrow{Heat}$

c. $\langle\text{C}_6H_5\rangle-C(=O)-OH + H_2N-CH_2-CH_2-CH_3 \xrightarrow{Heat}$

18.48 Draw the condensed structural formula for the amide formed in each of the following reactions:

a. $CH_3-CH_2-CH_2-CH_2-C(=O)-OH + NH_3 \xrightarrow{Heat}$

b. $CH_3-CH(CH_3)-C(=O)-OH + H_2N-CH_2-CH_3 \xrightarrow{Heat}$

c. $CH_3-CH_2-C(=O)-OH + H_2N-\langle\text{C}_6H_5\rangle \xrightarrow{Heat}$

18.49 Give the IUPAC and common names (if any) for each of the following amides:

a. $\underset{\displaystyle CH_3}{} - \overset{\displaystyle O}{\overset{\displaystyle \|}{C}} - \overset{\displaystyle H}{\overset{\displaystyle |}{N}} - CH_3$

b. [structure: propyl chain with C=O and NH₂]

c. $H - \overset{\displaystyle O}{\overset{\displaystyle \|}{C}} - NH_2$

d. [benzene ring] $- \overset{\displaystyle O}{\overset{\displaystyle \|}{C}} - \overset{\displaystyle H}{\overset{\displaystyle |}{N}} - CH_3$

18.50 Give the IUPAC and common names (if any) for each of the following amides:

a. $CH_3 - CH_2 - \overset{\displaystyle O}{\overset{\displaystyle \|}{C}} - \overset{\displaystyle H}{\overset{\displaystyle |}{N}} - CH_2 - CH_3$

b. [structure: pentyl chain with C=O and NH₂]

c. $CH_3 - \overset{\displaystyle O}{\overset{\displaystyle \|}{C}} - \overset{\displaystyle CH_3}{\overset{\displaystyle |}{N}} - CH_2 - CH_2 - CH_3$

d. [benzene ring] $- \overset{\displaystyle O}{\overset{\displaystyle \|}{C}} - \overset{\displaystyle CH_2 - CH_3}{\overset{\displaystyle |}{N}} - CH_2 - CH_3$

18.51 Draw the condensed structural formula for each of the following amides:
a. propionamide
b. pentanamide
c. *N*-ethylbenzamide
d. *N*-ethylbutyramide

18.52 Draw the condensed structural formula for each of the following amides:
a. *N*-ethyl-*N*-methylbenzamide
b. 3-methylbutanamide
c. hexanamide
d. *N*-propylpentanamide

18.53 For each of the following pairs, identify the compound that has the higher melting point. Explain.
a. ethanamide or *N*-methylethanamide
b. butane or propionamide
c. *N,N*-dimethylpropanamide or *N*-methylpropanamide

18.54 For each of the following pairs, identify the compound that has the higher melting point. Explain.
a. propane or ethanamide
b. *N*-methylethanamide or propanamide
c. *N*-ethylethanamide or *N,N*-dimethylethanamide

18.6 Hydrolysis of Amides

In a reverse reaction of amidation, **hydrolysis** occurs when water and an acid or a base split an amide. In acid hydrolysis of an amide, the products are the carboxylic acid and the ammonium salt. In base hydrolysis, the products are the carboxylate salt and the amine or ammonia.

Acid Hydrolysis of Amides

Amide · Carboxylic Acid · Ammonium Salt

Ethanamide (acetamide) → Ethanoic acid (acetic acid) + Ammonium chloride

Base Hydrolysis of Amides

Amide · Carboxylate Salt · Amine

N-Methylpropanamide (*N*-methylpropionamide) → Sodium propanoate, a salt (sodium propionate) + Methanamine (methylamine)

▶**SAMPLE PROBLEM 18.11** **Hydrolysis of Amides**

Draw the condensed structural formulas and give the IUPAC names for the products of the hydrolysis of *N*-methylpentanamide with NaOH.

SOLUTION

	Given	Need
ANALYZE THE PROBLEM	hydrolysis of *N*-methylpentanamide with NaOH	products, condensed structural formulas, IUPAC names

In hydrolysis, the amide bond is broken between the carboxyl carbon atom and the nitrogen atom. When NaOH is used, the products are the carboxylate salt and an amine.

$$\boxed{\text{NaOH}}$$

$$\underset{\textit{N-Methylpentanamide}}{CH_3-CH_2-CH_2-CH_2-\overset{\overset{\displaystyle O}{\|}}{C}\!\vdots\!\overset{\overset{\displaystyle H}{|}}{N}-CH_3} \xrightarrow{\text{Heat}}$$

$$\underset{\text{Sodium pentanoate}}{CH_3-CH_2-CH_2-CH_2-\overset{\overset{\displaystyle O}{\|}}{C}-\boxed{O^-\,Na^+}} + \underset{\text{Methanamine}}{\boxed{H}\!-\!\overset{\overset{\displaystyle H}{|}}{N}-CH_3}$$

STUDY CHECK 18.11

Draw the condensed structural formulas for the products obtained from the hydrolysis of *N*-methylbutyramide with HBr.

ANSWER

$$CH_3-CH_2-CH_2-\overset{\overset{\displaystyle O}{\|}}{C}-OH \quad \text{and} \quad CH_3-\overset{+}{N}H_3\ Br^-$$

QUESTIONS AND PROBLEMS

18.6 Hydrolysis of Amides

LEARNING GOAL Write balanced chemical equations for the hydrolysis of amides.

18.55 Draw the condensed structural formulas for the products from the hydrolysis of each of the following with HCl:

a. $CH_3-\overset{\overset{\displaystyle O}{\|}}{C}-NH_2$

b. $CH_3-CH_2-\overset{\overset{\displaystyle O}{\|}}{C}-NH_2$

c. $CH_3-CH_2-CH_2-\overset{\overset{\displaystyle O}{\|}}{C}-\overset{\overset{\displaystyle H}{|}}{N}-CH_3$

d. $\underset{}{\overset{\overset{\displaystyle O}{\|}}{\underset{}{\text{⬡}}\,C-NH_2}}$

18.56 Draw the condensed structural formulas for the products from the hydrolysis of each of the following with NaOH:

a. $CH_3-CH_2-\overset{\overset{\displaystyle CH_3}{|}}{C}H-\overset{\overset{\displaystyle O}{\|}}{C}-NH_2$

b. $CH_3-CH_2-CH_2-\overset{\overset{\displaystyle O}{\|}}{C}-\overset{\overset{\displaystyle CH_2-CH_3}{|}}{N}-CH_2-CH_3$

c. $\text{⬡}-\overset{\overset{\displaystyle O}{\|}}{C}-\overset{\overset{\displaystyle CH_3}{|}}{N}-CH_2-CH_2-CH_2-CH_3$

d. $CH_3-\overset{\overset{\displaystyle Cl}{|}}{C}H-\overset{\overset{\displaystyle O}{\|}}{C}-\overset{\overset{\displaystyle CH_3}{|}}{N}-CH_2-CH_3$

Clinical Update
Testing Soil and Water Samples for Chemicals

Lance, an environmental health practitioner, returned to the sheep ranch to obtain more soil and water samples. When he arrived at the ranch, he noticed that the owners were spraying the sheep because they had infestation of flies and maggots. Lance was told that the insecticide they were spraying on the sheep was called dicyclanil, a potent insect growth regulator. Lance was also informed that the sheep were being treated with enrofloxacin to counteract a respiratory infection.

Because high levels of these chemicals could be hazardous if they exceed acceptable environmental standards, Lance collected samples of soil and water to test for contaminants or breakdown products to evaluate in the laboratory. He will send the test results to the rancher,

A soil bag is filled with soil from areas where sheep were sprayed with dicyclanil.

who will use those results to adjust the levels of the drugs, order protective equipment, and do a cleanup, if necessary.

Clinical Applications

18.57 Name the functional groups in dicyclanil. Identify the heterocyclic amine in dicyclanil.

18.58 Name the functional groups in enrofloxacin.

18.59 The recommended application for dicyclanil for an adult sheep is 65 mg/kg of body mass. If dicyclanil is supplied in a spray with a concentration of 50. mg/mL, how many milliliters of the spray are required to treat a 70.-kg adult sheep?

18.60 The recommended dose for enrofloxacin for sheep is 30. mg/kg of body mass for 5 days. Enrofloxacin is supplied in 50.-mL vials with a concentration of 100. mg/mL. How many vials are needed to treat a 64-kg sheep for 5 days?

Dicyclanil

Enrofloxacin

CONCEPT MAP

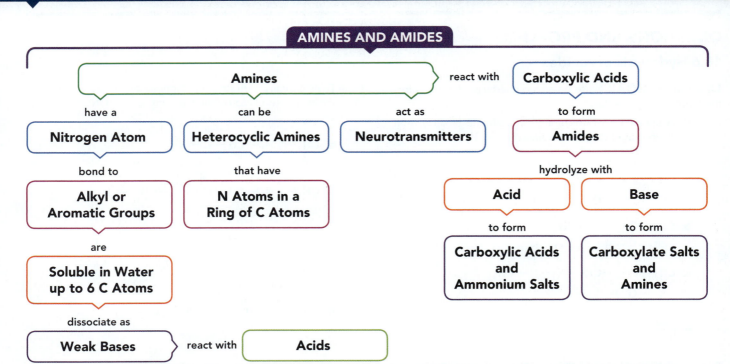

AMINES AND AMIDES

Amines — react with → **Carboxylic Acids**

have a → **Nitrogen Atom**

can be → **Heterocyclic Amines**

act as → **Neurotransmitters**

to form → **Amides**

bond to → **Alkyl or Aromatic Groups**

that have → **N Atoms in a Ring of C Atoms**

hydrolyze with → **Acid** / **Base**

are → **Soluble in Water up to 6 C Atoms**

Acid — to form → **Carboxylic Acids and Ammonium Salts**

Base — to form → **Carboxylate Salts and Amines**

dissociate as → **Weak Bases** — react with → **Acids**

CHAPTER REVIEW

18.1 Amines
LEARNING GOAL Name amines using IUPAC and common names; draw the condensed or line-angle structural formulas given the names. Classify amines as primary (1°), secondary (2°), or tertiary (3°).

Dimethylamine

- In the IUPAC system, name the longest carbon chain bonded to the N atom by replacing the *e* of its alkane name with *amine*. Groups attached to the nitrogen atom use the *N-* prefix.
- When other functional groups are present, the —NH$_2$ is named as an amino group.
- In the common names of simple amines, the alkyl groups are listed alphabetically followed by *amine*.
- A nitrogen atom attached to one, two, or three alkyl or aromatic groups forms a primary (1°), secondary (2°), or tertiary (3°) amine.

18.2 Properties of Amines
LEARNING GOAL Describe the boiling points and solubility of amines; write equations for the dissociation and neutralization of amines.

Hydrogen bonds

- Primary and secondary amines form hydrogen bonds, which make their boiling points higher than those of alkanes of similar mass, but lower than those of alcohols.
- Amines with up to six carbon atoms are soluble in water.
- In water, amines act as weak bases because the nitrogen atom accepts H$^+$ a proton from water to produce ammonium and hydroxide ions.
- When amines react with acids, they form ammonium salts. As ionic compounds, ammonium salts are solids, soluble in water, and odorless.
- Quaternary (4°) ammonium salts contain four carbon groups bonded to the nitrogen atom.

18.3 Heterocyclic Amines
LEARNING GOAL Identify heterocyclic amines; distinguish between the types of heterocyclic amines.

- Heterocyclic amines are cyclic organic compounds that contain one or more nitrogen atoms in the ring.

- Heterocyclic amines typically consist of five or six atoms and one or more nitrogen atoms.
- Many heterocyclic compounds are known for their physiological activity.
- Alkaloids such as caffeine and nicotine are physiologically active amines derived from plants.

18.4 Neurotransmitters
LEARNING GOAL Describe the role of amines as neurotransmitters.

- Neurotransmitters are chemicals that transfer a signal between nerve cells.

18.5 Amides
LEARNING GOAL Draw the amide product from amidation, and give their IUPAC and common names.

Ethanamide (acetamide)

- Amides are derivatives of carboxylic acids in which the hydroxyl group is replaced by —NH$_2$ or a primary or secondary amine group.
- Amides are formed when carboxylic acids react with ammonia or primary or secondary amines in the presence of heat.
- Amides are named by replacing the *oic acid* or *ic acid* from the carboxylic acid name with *amide*. Any carbon group attached to the nitrogen atom is named using the *N-* prefix.

18.6 Hydrolysis of Amides
LEARNING GOAL Write balanced chemical equations for the hydrolysis of amides.

$$CH_3-\overset{\overset{O}{\|}}{C}-NH_2 + H_2O + HCl \longrightarrow CH_3-\overset{\overset{O}{\|}}{C}-OH + NH_4^+Cl^-$$

Ethanamide (acetamide)   Ethanoic acid (acetic acid)   Ammonium chloride

- Hydrolysis of an amide by an acid produces a carboxylic acid and an ammonium salt.
- Hydrolysis of an amide by a base produces the carboxylate salt and an amine.

SUMMARY OF NAMING

Family	Structure	IUPAC Name	Common Name
Amine	$CH_3-CH_2-NH_2$	Ethanamine	Ethylamine
	$CH_3-CH_2-NH-CH_3$	*N*-Methylethanamine	Ethylmethylamine
Ammonium salt	$CH_3-CH_2-\overset{+}{N}H_3\ Cl^-$	Ethylammonium chloride	Ethylammonium chloride
Amide	$CH_3-\overset{\overset{O}{\|}}{C}-NH_2$	Ethanamide	Acetamide

SUMMARY OF REACTIONS

The chapter sections to review are shown after the name of the reaction.

Dissociation of an Amine in Water (18.2)

$$CH_3-\underset{\underset{\text{H}}{|}}{\overset{\overset{\text{H}}{|}}{N}} + H_2O \rightleftharpoons CH_3-\underset{\underset{\text{H}}{|}}{\overset{\overset{\text{H}}{|}}{\overset{+}{N}}}-H + OH^-$$

Methylamine   Methylammonium   Hydroxide
                       ion   ion

Neutralization of an Amine (18.2)

$$CH_3-\underset{\underset{\text{H}}{|}}{\overset{\overset{\text{H}}{|}}{N}} + HCl \longrightarrow CH_3-\underset{\underset{\text{H}}{|}}{\overset{\overset{\text{H}}{|}}{\overset{+}{N}}}-H\ Cl^-$$

Methylamine   Methylammonium chloride

Amidation: Carboxylic Acid and an Amine (18.5)

$$CH_3-CH_2-\overset{\overset{\text{O}}{\|}}{C}-OH + H-\overset{\overset{\text{H}}{|}}{N}-H \xrightarrow{\text{Heat}} CH_3-CH_2-\overset{\overset{\text{O}}{\|}}{C}-\overset{\overset{\text{H}}{|}}{N}-H + H_2O$$

Propanoic acid   Ammonia   Propanamide
(propionic acid)   (propionamide)

$$CH_3-CH_2-\overset{\overset{\text{O}}{\|}}{C}-OH + H-\overset{\overset{\text{H}}{|}}{N}-CH_3 \xrightarrow{\text{Heat}} CH_3-CH_2-\overset{\overset{\text{O}}{\|}}{C}-\overset{\overset{\text{H}}{|}}{N}-CH_3 + H_2O$$

Propanoic acid   Methanamine   *N*-Methylpropanamide
(propionic acid)   (methylamine)   (*N*-methylpropionamide)

Acid Hydrolysis of an Amide (18.6)

$$CH_3-\overset{\overset{\text{O}}{\|}}{C}-NH_2 + H_2O + HCl \xrightarrow{\text{Heat}} CH_3-\overset{\overset{\text{O}}{\|}}{C}-OH + NH_4^+\ Cl^-$$

Ethanamide   Ethanoic acid   Ammonium
(acetamide)   (acetic acid)   chloride

Base Hydrolysis of an Amide (18.6)

$$CH_3-CH_2-\overset{\overset{\text{O}}{\|}}{C}-\overset{\overset{\text{H}}{|}}{N}-CH_3 + NaOH \xrightarrow{\text{Heat}} CH_3-CH_2-\overset{\overset{\text{O}}{\|}}{C}-O^-\ Na^+ + H_2N-CH_3$$

N-Methylpropanamide   Sodium propanoate   Methanamine
(*N*-methylpropionamide)   (sodium propionate)   (methylamine)

KEY TERMS

alkaloid An amine having physiological activity that is produced in plants.

amidation The formation of an amide from a carboxylic acid and ammonia or an amine.

amide An organic compound containing the carbonyl group attached to an amino group or a substituted nitrogen atom.

amine An organic compound containing a nitrogen atom attached to one, two, or three alkyl or aromatic groups.

ammonium salt An ionic compound produced from an amine and an acid.

heterocyclic amine A cyclic organic compound that contains one or more nitrogen atoms in the ring.

hydrolysis The splitting of a molecule by the addition of water. Amides yield the corresponding carboxylic acid and amine, or their salts.

neurotransmitter A chemical compound that transmits an impulse from a nerve cell (neuron) to a target cell such as another nerve cell, a muscle cell, or a gland cell.

quaternary ammonium salt An ammonium salt in which the nitrogen atom is bonded to four carbon groups.

⊛ CORE CHEMISTRY SKILLS

The chapter section containing each Core Chemistry Skill is shown in parentheses at the end of each heading.

Forming Amides (18.5)

- Amides are formed when carboxylic acids react with ammonia or primary or secondary amines in the presence of heat.

Example: Draw the condensed structural formula for the amide product of the reaction of 3-methylbutanoic acid and ethylamine.

Answer:

$$CH_3 — CH — CH_2 — \overset{\overset{\textstyle O}{\|}}{C} — \overset{\overset{\textstyle H}{|}}{N} — CH_2 — CH_3$$
(with CH_3 branch on the second carbon)

Hydrolyzing Amides (18.6)

- An amide undergoes acid hydrolysis to produce a carboxylic acid and an ammonium salt.

- An amide undergoes base hydrolysis to produce the carboxylate salt and an amine.

Example: Draw the condensed structural formulas for the products from the **(a)** acid **(HCl)** and **(b)** base **(NaOH)** hydrolysis of *N*-ethylbutanamide.

Answer:

a. $CH_3 — CH_2 — CH_2 — \overset{\overset{\textstyle O}{\|}}{C} — OH + CH_3 — CH_2 — \overset{+}{N}H_3\ Cl^-$

b. $CH_3 — CH_2 — CH_2 — \overset{\overset{\textstyle O}{\|}}{C} — O^-\ Na^+ + CH_3 — CH_2 — NH_2$

UNDERSTANDING THE CONCEPTS

The chapter sections to review are shown in parentheses at the end of each question.

℞ Clinical Applications

18.61 The sweetener aspartame is made from two amino acids: aspartic acid and phenylalanine. Identify the functional groups in aspartame. (16.1, 16.3, 18.2, 18.5)

Aspartame

18.62 Some aspirin substitutes contain phenacetin to reduce fever. Identify the functional groups in phenacetin. (13.2, 18.5)

Phenacetin

18.63 Neo-Synephrine is the active ingredient in some nose sprays used to reduce the swelling of nasal membranes. Identify the functional groups in Neo-Synephrine. (13.1, 18.1)

Neo-Synephrine

18.64 Melatonin is a naturally occurring compound in plants and animals, where it regulates the biological time clock. Melatonin is sometimes used to counteract jet lag. Identify the functional groups in melatonin. (13.2, 18.1, 18.5)

Melatonin

18.65 What is an excitatory neurotransmitter? (18.4)

18.66 What is an inhibitory neurotransmitter? (18.4)

18.67 Identify the structural components that are the same in dopamine, norepinephrine, and epinephrine. (18.4)

18.68 Identify the structural components that are different in dopamine, norepinephrine, and epinephrine. (18.4)

ADDITIONAL QUESTIONS AND PROBLEMS

18.69 Give the IUPAC and common names (if any) and classify each of the following compounds as a primary (1°), secondary (2°), tertiary (3°) amine, or as a quaternary (4°) ammonium salt: (18.1, 18.2)

a. $CH_3-CH_2-\overset{\displaystyle CH_2-CH_3}{\overset{\displaystyle |+}{\underset{\displaystyle CH_2-CH_3}{N}}}-CH_2-CH_3 \ Br^-$

b. $CH_3-CH_2-CH_2-CH_2-CH_2-NH_2$

c. $CH_3-CH_2-CH_2-\overset{\displaystyle H}{\underset{\displaystyle |}{N}}-CH_2-CH_3$

18.70 Give the IUPAC and common names (if any) and classify each of the following compounds as a primary (1°), secondary (2°), tertiary (3°) amine, or as a quaternary (4°) ammonium salt: (18.1, 18.2)

a. $\overset{\displaystyle CH_3}{\underset{\displaystyle |}{N}}-CH_2-CH_3$ (on benzene ring)

b. $CH_3-\overset{\displaystyle CH_3}{\underset{\displaystyle |}{CH}}-CH_2-\overset{\displaystyle CH_3}{\underset{\displaystyle |}{N}}-CH_2-CH_3$

c. $CH_3-\overset{\displaystyle CH_2-CH_3}{\overset{\displaystyle |+}{\underset{\displaystyle CH_3}{N}}}-CH_2-CH_3 \ Cl^-$

18.71 Draw the condensed structural formula for each of the following compounds: (18.1, 18.2)
a. 3-pentanamine
b. cyclohexylamine
c. dimethylammonium chloride
d. triethylamine

18.72 Draw the condensed structural formula for each of the following compounds: (18.1, 18.2)
a. 3-amino-2-hexanol
b. tetramethylammonium bromide
c. N,N-dimethylaniline
d. butylethylmethylamine

18.73 In each of the following pairs, indicate the compound that has the higher boiling point. Explain. (18.1, 18.2)
a. 1-butanol or butanamine
b. ethylamine or dimethylamine

18.74 In each of the following pairs, indicate the compound that has the higher boiling point. Explain. (18.1, 18.2)
a. butylamine or diethylamine
b. butane or propylamine

18.75 In each of the following pairs, indicate the compound that is more soluble in water. Explain. (18.1, 18.2)
a. ethylamine or dibutylamine
b. trimethylamine or N-ethylcyclohexylamine

18.76 In each of the following pairs, indicate the compound that is more soluble in water. Explain. (18.1, 18.2, 18.5)
a. butylamine or pentane   b. butyramide or hexane

18.77 Give the IUPAC name for each of the following amides: (18.5)

a. $CH_3-\overset{\displaystyle O}{\overset{\displaystyle ||}{C}}-\overset{\displaystyle H}{\underset{\displaystyle |}{N}}-CH_2-CH_3$

b. $CH_3-CH_2-\overset{\displaystyle O}{\overset{\displaystyle ||}{C}}-NH_2$

c. $CH_3-\overset{\displaystyle CH_3}{\underset{\displaystyle |}{CH}}-CH_2-\overset{\displaystyle O}{\overset{\displaystyle ||}{C}}-NH_2$

18.78 Give the IUPAC name for each of the following amides: (18.5)

a. $CH_3-CH_2-CH_2-CH_2-\overset{\overset{\displaystyle O}{\|}}{C}-NH_2$

b. $CH_3-\overset{\overset{\displaystyle O}{\|}}{C}-\overset{\overset{\displaystyle CH_3}{|}}{N}-CH_2-CH_2-CH_2-CH_3$

c. $CH_3-\overset{\overset{\displaystyle O}{\|}}{C}-\overset{\overset{\displaystyle CH_3}{|}}{N}-CH_3$

18.79 Draw the condensed structural formulas for the products of the following reactions: (18.2)

a. $CH_3-CH_2-\overset{\overset{\displaystyle CH_3}{|}}{\underset{+}{N}}H_2\ Cl^-\ +\ NaOH \longrightarrow$

b. $CH_3-CH_2-NH-CH_3\ +\ H_2O \rightleftharpoons$

18.80 Draw the condensed structural formulas for the products of the following reactions: (18.2)

a. $CH_3-CH_2-NH-CH_3\ +\ HCl \longrightarrow$

b. $CH_3-CH_2-CH_2-\overset{+}{N}H_3\ Cl^-\ +\ NaOH \longrightarrow$

Clinical Applications

18.81 Voltaren (diclofenac) is indicated for acute and chronic treatment of the symptoms of rheumatoid arthritis. Name the functional groups in the voltaren molecule. (18.1)

Voltaren

18.82 Toradol (ketorolac) is used in dentistry to relieve pain. Name the functional groups in toradol. (18.3, 18.5)

Toradol

18.83 Give the name of the alkaloid described in each of the following: (18.3)

a. from the bark of the cinchona tree and used in malaria treatment

b. found in tobacco

c. found in coffee and tea

d. a painkiller found in the opium poppy plant

18.84 Identify the heterocyclic amine(s) in each of the following: (18.3)

a. caffeine   b. Demerol (meperidine)

c. coniine   d. quinine

18.85 What is the structural difference between tryptophan and serotonin? (18.4)

18.86 What is the structural difference between histidine and histamine? (18.4)

18.87 What does the abbreviation SSRI signify? (18.4)

18.88 Give an example of an SSRI and its role in treating depression. (18.4)

CHALLENGE QUESTIONS

The following groups of questions are related to the topics in this chapter. However, they do not all follow the chapter order, and they require you to combine concepts and skills from several sections. These questions will help you increase your critical thinking skills and prepare for your next exam.

18.89 There are four amine isomers with the molecular formula C_3H_9N. Draw their condensed structural formulas. Give the common name and classify each as a primary (1°), secondary (2°), or tertiary (3°) amine. (18.1)

18.90 There are four amide isomers with the molecular formula C_3H_7NO. Draw their condensed structural formulas. (18.5)

Clinical Applications

18.91 Use the Internet to look up the structural formula for the following medicinal drugs. List the functional groups in each compound. (18.1, 18.3, 18.5)

a. Keflex, an antibiotic (cefalexin)

b. Inderal, a β-channel blocker used to treat heart irregularities (propranolol)

c. Ibuprofen, an anti-inflammatory agent

d. Aldomet (methyldopa)

e. OxyContin (oxycodone), a narcotic pain reliever

f. Triamterene, a diuretic

18.92 Kevlar is a lightweight polymer used in tires and bulletproof vests. Part of the strength of Kevlar is due to hydrogen bonds between polymer chains. The polymer chain is: (16.1, 18.1, 18.5)

Poly-paraphenylene terephthalamide (Kevlar)

a. Draw the condensed structural formulas for the carboxylic acid and amine that polymerize to make Kevlar.

b. What feature of Kevlar will give the hydrogen bonds between the polymer chains?

18.93 Why is L-dopa, not dopamine, given to persons with low dopamine levels? (18.4)

18.94 How does cocaine increase the dopamine levels in the synapse? (18.4)

ANSWERS

Answers to Selected Questions and Problems

18.1 In a primary amine, there is one alkyl group (and two hydrogens) attached to a nitrogen atom.

18.3 a. primary (1°)   **b.** secondary (2°)
c. primary (1°)   **d.** tertiary (3°)
e. tertiary (3°)

18.5 a. ethanamine (ethylamine)
b. N-methyl-1-propanamine (methylpropylamine)
c. N-ethyl-N-methylethanamine (diethylmethylamine)
d. 2-propanamine (isopropylamine)

18.7 a. 4-aminopentanoic acid
b. 2-chloroaniline
c. 3-aminopropanal
d. 5-amino-3-hexanol

18.9 a. $Cl-CH_2-CH_2-NH_2$

b.

$$\begin{array}{c} H \\ | \\ N-CH_3 \end{array}$$

(benzene ring)

c. $CH_3-CH_2-CH_2-CH_2-\overset{\overset{\displaystyle H}{|}}{N}-CH_2-CH_2-CH_3$

d. $CH_3-CH_2-\overset{\overset{\displaystyle NH_2}{|}}{C}H-\overset{\overset{\displaystyle O}{||}}{C}-H$

18.11 a. CH_3-CH_2-OH has a higher boiling point because the $-OH$ group forms stronger hydrogen bonds than the $-NH_2$ group.
b. $CH_3-CH_2-CH_2-NH_2$ has the higher boiling point because it has a greater molar mass.
c. $CH_3-CH_2-CH_2-NH_2$ has the higher boiling point because it is a primary amine that forms hydrogen bonds. A tertiary amine cannot form hydrogen bonds with other tertiary amines.

18.13 As a primary amine, propylamine can form two hydrogen bonds, which gives it the highest boiling point. Ethylmethylamine, a secondary amine, can form one hydrogen bond, and butane cannot form hydrogen bonds. Thus, butane has the lowest boiling point of the three compounds.

18.15 a. Yes, amines with fewer than seven carbon atoms are soluble in water.
b. Yes, amines with fewer than seven carbon atoms are soluble in water.
c. No, an amine with nine carbon atoms is not soluble in water.
d. Yes, amines with fewer than seven carbon atoms are soluble in water.

18.17 a. $CH_3-NH_2 + H_2O \rightleftharpoons CH_3-\overset{+}{N}H_3 + OH^-$

b. $CH_3-\overset{\overset{\displaystyle H}{|}}{N}-CH_3 + H_2O \rightleftharpoons CH_3-\overset{\overset{\displaystyle H}{|}}{\underset{\underset{\displaystyle H}{|}}{\overset{+}{N}}}-CH_3 + OH^-$

18.19

c. (aniline) $NH_2 + H_2O \rightleftharpoons$ (anilinium) $\overset{+}{N}H_3 + OH^-$

18.19 a. $CH_3-\overset{+}{N}H_3\ Cl^-$

b. $CH_3-\overset{+}{N}H_2-CH_3\ Cl^-$

c. (benzene ring) $\overset{+}{N}H_3\ Cl^-$

18.21 a. H_2N- (benzene ring) $-\overset{\overset{\displaystyle O}{||}}{C}-O-CH_2-CH_2-\overset{\overset{\displaystyle CH_2-CH_3}{|}}{\underset{\underset{\displaystyle CH_2-CH_3}{|}}{\overset{+}{N}}}-H\ Cl^-$

b. The ammonium salt (Novocain) is more soluble in aqueous body fluids than procaine.

18.23 a. piperidine   **b.** pyrimidine   **c.** pyrrole

18.25 piperidine

18.27 pyrrole

18.29 A neurotransmitter is a chemical compound that transmits an impulse from a nerve cell to a target cell.

18.31 When a nerve impulse reaches the axon terminal, it stimulates the release of neurotransmitters into the synapse.

18.33 A neurotransmitter must be removed from its receptor so that new signals can come from the nerve cells.

18.35 Acetylcholine is a neurotransmitter that communicates between the nervous system and muscle cells.

18.37 Dopamine is a neurotransmitter that controls muscle movement, regulates the sleep–wake cycle, and helps to improve cognition, attention, memory, and learning.

18.39 Serotonin is a neurotransmitter that helps to decrease anxiety, improve mood, learning, and memory; it also reduces appetite, and induces sleep.

18.41 Histamine is a neurotransmitter that causes allergic reactions, which may include inflammation, watery eyes, itchy skin, and hay fever.

18.43 Excess glutamate in the synapse can lead to destruction of brain cells.

18.45 GABA is a neurotransmitter that regulates muscle tone, sleep, and anxiety.

18.47 a. $CH_3-\overset{\overset{\displaystyle O}{||}}{C}-NH_2$

b. $CH_3-\overset{\overset{\displaystyle O}{||}}{C}-\overset{\overset{\displaystyle H}{|}}{N}-CH_2-CH_3$

c. (benzene ring) $-\overset{\overset{\displaystyle O}{||}}{C}-\overset{\overset{\displaystyle H}{|}}{N}-CH_2-CH_2-CH_3$

18.49 a. N-methylethanamide (N-methylacetamide)
b. butanamide (butyramide)
c. methanamide (formamide)
d. N-methylbenzamide

18.51 a. $CH_3-CH_2-\overset{\overset{\displaystyle O}{\|}}{C}-NH_2$

b. $CH_3-CH_2-CH_2-CH_2-\overset{\overset{\displaystyle O}{\|}}{C}-NH_2$

c. ⬡$-\overset{\overset{\displaystyle O}{\|}}{C}-\overset{\overset{\displaystyle H}{|}}{N}-CH_2-CH_3$

d. $CH_3-CH_2-CH_2-\overset{\overset{\displaystyle O}{\|}}{C}-\overset{\overset{\displaystyle H}{|}}{N}-CH_2-CH_3$

18.53 a. Ethanamide has the higher melting point because it forms more hydrogen bonds as a primary amide than *N*-methylethanamide, which is a secondary amide.

b. Propionamide has the higher melting point because it forms hydrogen bonds, but butane does not.

c. *N*-methylpropanamide, a secondary amide, has a higher melting point because it can form hydrogen bonds, whereas *N*,*N*-dimethylpropanamide, a tertiary amide, cannot form hydrogen bonds.

18.55 a. $CH_3-\overset{\overset{\displaystyle O}{\|}}{C}-OH + NH_4^+ \ Cl^-$

b. $CH_3-CH_2-\overset{\overset{\displaystyle O}{\|}}{C}-OH + NH_4^+ \ Cl^-$

c. $CH_3-CH_2-CH_2-\overset{\overset{\displaystyle O}{\|}}{C}-OH + CH_3-\overset{+}{N}H_3 \ Cl^-$

d. ⬡$-\overset{\overset{\displaystyle O}{\|}}{C}-OH + NH_4^+ \ Cl^-$

18.57 amine, pyrimidine

18.59 91 mL

18.61 amine, carboxylic acid, amide, aromatic, ester

18.63 amine, aromatic, alcohol, phenol

18.65 Excitatory neurotransmitters open ion channels and stimulate the receptors to send more signals.

18.67 Dopamine, norepinephrine, and epinephrine all have catechol (3,4-dihydroxyphenyl) and amine components.

18.69 a. tetraethylammonium bromide; quaternary (4°) ammonium salt

b. 1-pentanamine (pentylamine); primary (1°)

c. *N*-ethyl-1-propanamine; (ethylpropylamine); secondary (2°)

18.71 a. $CH_3-CH_2-\overset{\overset{\displaystyle NH_2}{|}}{CH}-CH_2-CH_3$

b. ⬡ with NH_2

c. $CH_3-\overset{\overset{\displaystyle CH_3}{|+}}{N}H_2 \ Cl^-$

d. $CH_3-CH_2-\overset{\overset{\displaystyle CH_2-CH_3}{|}}{N}-CH_2-CH_3$

18.73 a. An alcohol with an —OH group such as 1-butanol forms stronger hydrogen bonds than an amine, and has a higher boiling point than an amine.

b. Ethylamine, a primary amine, forms more hydrogen bonds and has a higher boiling point than dimethylamine, which forms fewer hydrogen bonds as a secondary amine.

18.75 a. Ethylamine is a small amine that is soluble because it forms hydrogen bonds with water. Dibutylamine has two large nonpolar alkyl groups that decrease its solubility in water.

b. Trimethylamine is a small tertiary amine that is soluble because it hydrogen bonds with water. *N*-ethylcyclohexylamine has a large nonpolar cycloalkyl group that decreases its solubility in water.

18.77 a. *N*-ethylethanamide   **b.** propanamide
c. 3-methylbutanamide

18.79 a. $CH_3-CH_2-\overset{\overset{\displaystyle H}{|}}{N}-CH_3 + NaCl + H_2O$

b. $CH_3-CH_2-\overset{+}{N}H_2-CH_3 + OH^-$

18.81 carboxylate salt, aromatic, amine

18.83 a. quinine   **b.** nicotine
c. caffeine   **d.** morphine, codeine

18.85 Tryptophan contains a carboxylic acid group that is not present in serotonin. Serotonin has a hydroxyl group (—OH) on the aromatic ring that is not present in tryptophan.

18.87 SSRI stands for selective serotonin reuptake inhibitor.

18.89 $CH_3-CH_2-CH_2-NH_2$
Propylamine (1°)

$CH_3-CH_2-\overset{\overset{\displaystyle H}{|}}{N}-CH_3$
Ethylmethylamine (2°)

$CH_3-\overset{\overset{\displaystyle CH_3}{|}}{N}-CH_3$
Trimethylamine (3°)

$CH_3-\overset{\overset{\displaystyle CH_3}{|}}{CH}-NH_2$
Isopropylamine (1°)

18.91 a. aromatic, amine, amide, carboxylic acid, cycloalkene
b. aromatic, ether, alcohol, amine
c. aromatic, carboxylic acid
d. phenol, amine, carboxylic acid
e. aromatic, ether, alcohol, amine, ketone
f. aromatic, amine

18.93 Dopamine is needed in the brain, where it is important in controlling muscle movement. Since dopamine cannot cross the blood–brain barrier, persons with low levels of dopamine are given L-dopa, which can cross the blood–brain barrier, where it is converted to dopamine.

CI.35 The plastic known as PETE (**p**oly**e**thylene**te**rephthalate) is used to make plastic soft drink bottles and containers for salad dressing, shampoos, and dishwashing liquids. PETE is a polymer of terephthalic acid and ethylene glycol. Today, PETE is the most widely recycled of all the plastics. In one year, 1.5×10^9 lb of PETE are recycled. After it is separated from other plastics, PETE can be used in polyester fabric, door mats, and tennis ball containers. The density of PETE is 1.38 g/mL. (2.5, 2.7, 16.3)

Terephthalic acid   Ethylene glycol

Plastic bottles made of PETE are ready to be recycled.

a. Draw the condensed structural formula for the ester formed from one molecule of terephthalic acid and one molecule of ethylene glycol.
b. Draw the condensed structural formula for the product formed when a second molecule of ethylene glycol reacts with the ester you drew in part **a**.
c. How many kilograms of PETE are recycled in one year?
d. What volume, in liters, of PETE is recycled in one year?
e. Suppose a landfill holds 2.7×10^7 L of recycled PETE. If all the PETE that is recycled in a year were placed instead in landfills, how many would it fill?

CI.36 Epibatidine is one of the alkaloids that the Ecuadorian poison dart frog (*Epipedobates tricolor*) secretes through its skin. Natives of the rainforest prepare poison darts by rubbing the tips on the skin of the poison dart frogs. The effect of a very small amount of the poison can paralyze or kill an animal. As a pain reliever, epibatidine is 200 times more effective than morphine. Although a therapeutic dose has been calculated as 2.5 mg/kg, epibatidine has adverse effects. It is expected that more research to chemically modify the epibatidine molecule will produce an important pain reliever. (7.4, 7.5, 18.3)

a. What two heterocyclic amines are in the structure of epibatidine?
b. What is the molecular formula of epibatidine?
c. What is the molar mass of epibatidine?
d. How many grams of epibatidine would be given to a 60.-kg person if the dose is 2.5 mg/kg?
e. How many molecules of epibatidine would be given to a 60.-kg person for the dose in part **d**?

CI.37 The insect repellent DEET is an amide that can be made from the amidation of 3-methylbenzoic acid with diethylamine. A 6.0-fl oz can of DEET repellent contains 25% DEET (m/v)(1 qt = 32 fl oz). (7.4, 7.5, 9.4, 18.5)

a. Draw the condensed structural formula for DEET.
b. Give the molecular formula for DEET.
c. What is the molar mass of DEET?
d. How many grams of DEET are in one spray can?
e. How many molecules of DEET are in one spray can?

DEET is used in insect repellent.

CI.38 Glyceryl trimyristate (trimyristin) is found in the seeds of the nutmeg (*Myristica fragrans*). Trimyristin is used as a lubricant and fragrance in soaps and shaving creams. Isopropyl myristate is used to increase absorption of skin creams. Draw the condensed structural formula for each of the following: (16.1, 16.2, 16.3, 16.4, 16.5)

Nutmeg contains high levels of glyceryl trimyristate.

a. myristic acid (14:0)
b. glyceryl trimyristate (trimyristin)
c. isopropyl myristate
d. products from the hydrolysis of glyceryl trimyristate with an acid catalyst
e. products from the saponification of glyceryl trimyristate with KOH
f. reactant and product for oxidation of myristyl alcohol to myristic acid

Epibatidine

Natives in the South American rainforests obtain poison for blow darts from the alkaloids secreted by poison dart frogs.

CI.39 Panose is a trisaccharide that is being considered as a possible sweetener by the food industry. (15.4, 15.5, 15.6)

Panose

A   B   C

Hyaluronic acid

a. What are the monosaccharide units **A**, **B**, and **C** in panose?
b. What type of glycosidic bond connects monosaccharides **A** and **B**?
c. What type of glycosidic bond connects monosaccharides **B** and **C**?
d. Is the structure drawn as α- or β-panose?
e. Why would panose be a reducing sugar?

CI.40 Hyaluronic acid (HA), a polymer of about 25 000 disaccharide units, is a natural component of eye and joint fluid as well as skin and cartilage. Due to the ability of HA to absorb water, it is used in skin care products and injections to smooth wrinkles and for treatment of arthritis. The repeating disaccharide units in HA consist of D-gluconic acid and N-acetyl-D-glucosamine. N-Acetyl-D-glucosamine is an amide derived from acetic acid and D-glucosamine, in which an amine group ($-NH_2$) replaces the hydroxyl on carbon 2 of D-glucose. Another natural polymer called chitin is found in the shells of crabs and lobsters. Chitin is made of repeating units of N-acetyl-D-glucosamine connected by $\beta(1 \rightarrow 4)$-glycosidic bonds. (15.4, 15.5, 15.6, 18.5)

The shells of crabs and lobsters contain chitin.

a. Draw the Haworth structures for the product of the oxidation reaction of the hydroxyl group on carbon 6 in β-D-glucose to form β-D-gluconic acid.
b. Draw the Haworth structure for β-D-glucosamine.
c. Draw the Haworth structure for the amide of β-D-glucosamine and acetic acid.
d. What are the two types of glycosidic bonds that link the monosaccharides in hyaluronic acid?
e. Draw the structure for a section of chitin with two N-acetyl-D-glucosamine units linked by $\beta(1 \rightarrow 4)$-glycosidic bonds.

ANSWERS

CI.35 a. HO$-$C(=O)$-$C$_6$H$_4-$C(=O)$-$O$-$CH$_2-$CH$_2-$OH

b.

HO$-$CH$_2-$CH$_2-$O$-$C(=O)$-$C$_6$H$_4-$C(=O)$-$O$-$CH$_2-$CH$_2-$OH

c. 6.8×10^8 kg of PETE
d. 4.9×10^8 L of PETE
e. 18 landfills

CI.37 a.

b. $C_{12}H_{17}NO$
c. 191.3 g/mole
d. 44 g of DEET
e. 1.4×10^{23} molecules

CI.39 a. **A**, **B**, and **C** are all glucose.
b. An $\alpha(1 \rightarrow 6)$-glycosidic bond links **A** and **B**.
c. An $\alpha(1 \rightarrow 4)$-glycosidic bond links **B** and **C**.
d. β-panose
e. Panose is a reducing sugar because it has a free hydroxyl group on carbon 1 of structure **C**, which allows glucose **C** to form an aldehyde.

19

Amino Acids and Proteins

EDITH IS HAVING TROUBLE COMPLETING SIMPLE

daily tasks and even remembering who her husband is at times. Edith's doctor suspects that Edith may be in the early stages of Alzheimer's disease. Edith is referred to a neurologist who administers tests to assess her cognitive impairment. Victoria, a radiology technician, explains to Edith that she is scheduled for a positron emission tomography (PET) scan of her brain.

Patients with Alzheimer's have impaired brain function caused by the accumulation of beta-amyloid proteins that form clumps or plaques that block transmission in nerve cells. Proteins like beta-amyloid consist of chains of amino acids. There are 20 different amino acids commonly found in proteins. As the name implies, amino acids contain an amino (amine) functional group and a carboxylic acid group. Each amino acid has a unique side chain, or R group, which distinguishes it from the other amino acids that make up proteins.

CAREER Radiology Technician

Radiology technicians work with radiologists to produce images of the body that allow for the diagnosis and treatment of certain medical conditions. Technicians operate imaging equipment such as X-ray, computed tomography (CT), and positron emission tomography (PET). During the PET procedure, the technician works with the patient by explaining each step of the imaging procedure, answering questions, and monitoring the patient's physical condition. A patient is instructed to remove jewelry, clothing, and any other items that could interfere with the equipment. The technician positions the patient and covers parts of the body not being filmed. The technician may inject contrast agents to improve image quality. Radiology technicians maintain good radiation safety practice and serve as an important liaison between patient and physician. Once the imaging process is complete, the radiology technician reviews the images with radiologists, and makes additional images when necessary. A radiology technician may also maintain patient records.

Preparation for a career as a radiology technician involves a certificate program that takes one to two years, a two-year associate's degree, or a four-year bachelor's degree.

The word "protein" is derived from the Greek word *proteios*, meaning "first." Proteins are made up from 20 different amino acids arranged in a specific order. The ordering determines the characteristics of the protein and its biological action. Proteins provide structure in membranes, build cartilage and connective tissue, transport oxygen in blood and muscle, direct biological reactions as enzymes, defend the body against infection, and control metabolic processes as hormones. They can even be a source of energy.

All of these different protein functions depend on the structures and chemical behavior of amino acids, the building blocks of proteins. We will see how peptide bonds link amino acids and how the sequence of the amino acids in these protein polymers directs the formation of their unique three-dimensional structures.

LOOKING AHEAD

19.1 Proteins and Amino Acids 689

♥ **Chemistry Link to Health**
Essential Amino Acids 693

19.2 Amino Acids as Acids and Bases 694

19.3 Formation of Peptides 697

♥ **Chemistry Link to Health**
Polypeptides in the Body 699

19.4 Protein Structure: Primary and Secondary Levels 701

♥ **Chemistry Link to Health**
Protein Sequencing 702

♥ **Chemistry Link to Health**
Protein Secondary Structures and Alzheimer's Disease 705

19.5 Protein Structure: Tertiary and Quaternary Levels 706

♥ **Chemistry Link to Health**
Sickle Cell Anemia 710

19.6 Protein Hydrolysis and Denaturation 711

℞ **Clinical Applications** 694, 700, 706, 714, 718

℞ **Clinical Update** *Alzheimer's Diagnosis* 714

CHAPTER READINESS*

▦ KEY MATH SKILL

- Calculating pH from $[H_3O^+]$ (11.6)

⚛ CORE CHEMISTRY SKILLS

- Writing Equations for Reactions of Acids and Bases (11.7)
- Naming Carboxylic Acids (16.1)
- Forming Amides (18.5)

*This Key Math Skill and Core Chemistry Skills from previous chapters are listed here for your review as you proceed to the new material in this chapter.

19.1 Proteins and Amino Acids

Protein molecules, compared with many of the compounds we have studied, can be gigantic. Insulin has a molar mass of 5800, and hemoglobin has a molar mass of about 67 000. Some virus proteins are even larger, having molar masses of more than 40 million. Even though proteins can be huge, they all contain the same 20 amino acids. Every protein is a polymer built from these 20 different amino acid building blocks, repeated numerous times, with the specific sequence of the amino acids determining the characteristics of the protein and its biological action.

The many kinds of proteins perform different functions in the body. Some proteins form structural components such as cartilage, muscles, hair, and nails. Wool, silk, feathers, and horns in animals are made of proteins (see Figure 19.1). Proteins that function as enzymes regulate biological reactions such as digestion and cellular metabolism. Other proteins, such as hemoglobin and myoglobin, transport oxygen in the blood and muscle. Table 19.1 gives examples of proteins that are classified by their functions.

Amino Acids

Proteins are composed of building blocks called *amino acids*. The general structure of an **amino acid** consists of a central carbon atom called the α carbon, which is attached to an ammonium group ($-NH_3^+$) and a carboxylate group ($-COO^-$). The α carbon is also bonded to a hydrogen atom ($-H$) and a side chain called an R group. All of the 20 amino acids present in human proteins have this general structure except for proline in which the amine group is part of a ring structure. The differences in all of the 20 amino acids are due to the unique characteristics of the R groups.

LEARNING GOAL

Classify proteins by their functions. Give the name and abbreviations for an amino acid, and draw its zwitterion.

FIGURE 19.1 ▶ The horns of animals are made of proteins.

🔍 What class of protein would be in horns?

TABLE 19.1 Classification of Some Proteins and Their Functions

Class of Protein	Function	Examples
Structural	Provide structural components	*Collagen* is in tendons and cartilage. *Keratin* is in hair, skin, wool, and nails.
Contractile	Make muscles move	*Myosin* and *actin* contract muscle fibers.
Transport	Carry essential substances throughout the body	*Hemoglobin* transports oxygen. *Lipoproteins* transport lipids.
Storage	Store nutrients	*Casein* stores protein in milk. *Ferritin* stores iron in the spleen and liver.
Hormone	Regulate body metabolism and the nervous system	*Insulin* regulates blood glucose level. *Growth hormone* regulates body growth.
Enzyme	Catalyze biochemical reactions in the cells	*Sucrase* catalyzes the hydrolysis of sucrose. *Trypsin* catalyzes the hydrolysis of proteins.
Protection	Recognize and destroy foreign substances	*Immunoglobulins* stimulate immune responses.

⚛ **CORE CHEMISTRY SKILL**

Drawing the Zwitterion for an Amino Acid

At physiological pH, the ionized ammonium and carboxylate groups give an amino acid a balance of positive and negative charge, which gives an overall zero charge. This neutral amino acid, which is called a **zwitterion**, occurs at a specific pH value known as its **isoelectric point (pI)**. Because amino acids as zwitterions are charged, they have properties similar to salts: they have high melting points and are soluble in water, but not nonpolar solvents. In the zwitterion of alanine, the ammonium group (blue) has a positive charge, the carboxylate group (pink) has a negative charge, and the R group (yellow) is a methyl substituent, $-CH_3$.

The zwitterion of alanine is neutral at its pI 6.0.

The ball-and-stick model of alanine shows the positively and negatively charged groups at its pI.

Classification of Amino Acids

We classify amino acids using their specific R groups, which determine their properties in aqueous solution. The **nonpolar amino acids** have hydrogen, alkyl, or aromatic R groups, which make them *hydrophobic* ("water fearing"). The **polar amino acids** have R groups that interact with water, which makes them *hydrophilic* ("water loving"). The *polar neutral* amino acids contain hydroxyl ($-OH$), thiol ($-SH$), or amide ($-CONH_2$) R groups. The R group of a polar **acidic amino acid** contains a carboxylate group ($-COO^-$). The R group of a polar **basic amino acid** contains an ammonium group ($-NH_3^+$). The structures of the 20 α-amino acids, their groups, names, three-letter and one-letter abbreviations, and pI values are listed in Table 19.2.

Using Table 19.2, we can summarize the different types of amino acid R groups, their polarity, and interaction with water as follows:

Type of Amino Acid	Number	Type of R Groups	Interaction with Water
Nonpolar	9	Nonpolar	Hydrophobic
Polar, neutral	6	Contain O and S atoms, but no charge	Hydrophilic
Polar, acidic	2	Contain carboxylate groups, negative charge	Hydrophilic
Polar, basic	3	Contain ammonium groups, positive charge	Hydrophilic

TABLE 19.2 Structures, Names, Abbreviations, and Isoelectric Points (pI) of 20 Common Amino Acids at Physiological pH (7.4)

Nonpolar Amino Acids (hydrophobic)

Glycine (Gly, G)
6.0

Alanine (Ala, A)
6.0

*Valine (Val, V)
6.0

*Leucine (Leu, L)
6.0

*Isoleucine (Ile, I)
6.0

*Phenylalanine (Phe, F)
5.5

*Methionine (Met, M)
5.7

Proline (Pro, P)
6.3

*Tryptophan (Trp, W)
5.9

Polar Amino Acids (hydrophilic)

Amino Acids with Neutral R Groups

Serine (Ser, S)
5.7

*Threonine (Thr, T)
5.6

Tyrosine (Tyr, Y)
5.7

Cysteine (Cys, C)
5.1

Asparagine (Asn, N)
5.4

Glutamine (Gln, Q)
5.7

Amino Acids with Charged R Groups

Acidic (negative charge)   Basic (positive charge)

Aspartate (Asp, D)
2.8

Glutamate (Glu, E)
3.2

*Histidine (His, H)
7.6

*Lysine (Lys, K)
9.7

Arginine (Arg, R)
10.8

*Essential amino acids

▶ **SAMPLE PROBLEM 19.1** **Structural Formulas of Amino Acids**

Draw the zwitterion for each of the following amino acids:

a. serine

b. aspartate

SOLUTION

ANALYZE THE PROBLEM	Given	Need
	serine, aspartate	draw the zwitterion for each

a.
$$
\begin{array}{c}
OH \\
| \\
CH_2 \quad O \\
| \quad \parallel \\
H_3\overset{+}{N}-C-C-O^- \\
| \\
H
\end{array}
$$

b.
$$
\begin{array}{c}
O \quad O^- \\
\diagdown C \diagup \\
| \\
CH_2 \quad O \\
| \quad \parallel \\
H_3\overset{+}{N}-C-C-O^- \\
| \\
H
\end{array}
$$

STUDY CHECK 19.1

Draw the zwitterion for leucine.

ANSWER

$$
\begin{array}{c}
CH_3 \quad CH_3 \\
\diagdown \quad \diagup \\
CH \\
| \\
CH_2 \quad O \\
| \quad \parallel \\
H_3\overset{+}{N}-C-C-O^- \\
| \\
H
\end{array}
$$

Amino Acid Abbreviations

Amino acids have both three-letter and one-letter abbreviations as seen in Table 19.2. The three-letter abbreviations, which were used initially, represent letters from the amino acid names as closely as possible. As scientists began to list the order of amino acids in longer chains of amino acids, the abbreviations were reduced to one letter to allow the faster transfer of data. Of the 20 amino acids, 11 have one-letter abbreviations that are the same as the first letter in their names. However, nine amino acids use different letters. Arginine R and tyrosine Y use the second letters in their names. Phenylalanine is F, which sounds like the first letters of its name. The other amino acids use single letters that are part of their names or have sounds similar to parts of their name. Lysine is K, which is near L in the alphabet.

▶ **SAMPLE PROBLEM 19.2** **Classification of Amino Acids**

Using Table 19.2, indicate each of the following for the amino acid shown:

$$
\begin{array}{c}
\bigcirc \\
| \\
CH_2 \quad O \\
| \quad \parallel \\
H_3\overset{+}{N}-C-C-O^- \\
| \\
H
\end{array}
$$

a. name, three-letter, and one-letter abbreviations
b. polar or nonpolar

c. has a neutral, acidic, or basic R group
d. interaction with water as hydrophobic or hydrophilic

SOLUTION

a. phenylalanine, Phe, F   **b.** nonpolar
c. neutral   **d.** hydrophobic

STUDY CHECK 19.2

Using Table 19.2, indicate each of the following for the amino acid shown:

$$H_3\overset{+}{N}-\overset{\overset{\displaystyle OH}{\underset{\displaystyle CH_2}{|}}}{\underset{\displaystyle H}{\overset{|}{C}}}-\overset{\displaystyle O}{\overset{\displaystyle \|}{C}}-O^-$$

a. name, three-letter, and one-letter abbreviations
b. polar or nonpolar
c. has a neutral, acidic, or basic R group
d. interaction with water as hydrophobic or hydrophilic

ANSWER

a. serine, Ser, S   **b.** polar
c. neutral   **d.** hydrophilic

Amino Acid Stereoisomers

All of the α-amino acids except for glycine are chiral because the α carbon is attached to four different groups. Thus, amino acids can exist as D and L stereoisomers called *enantiomers*. We draw Fischer projections for α-amino acids by placing the carboxylate group at the top and the R group at the bottom. In the L enantiomer of an amino acid, the $-NH_3^+$ group is on the left, and in the D enantiomer, the $-NH_3^+$ group is on the right. In biological systems, the only amino acids incorporated into proteins are the L enantiomers. There are D amino acids found in nature, but not in proteins.

L-Alanine   D-Alanine

In the Fischer projections of amino acids such as alanine, the $-NH_3^+$ group appears on the left or right of the chiral carbon to give L or D enantiomers.

 Chemistry Link to **Health**

Essential Amino Acids

Of the 20 amino acids typically used to build proteins in the body, only 11 can be synthesized in the body. The other nine amino acids, designated in Table 19.2 with asterisks and listed in Table 19.3, are called the **essential amino acids** because they must be obtained from the diet. In addition to the essential amino acids required by adults, infants and growing children also require arginine, cysteine, and tyrosine.

Complete proteins, which contain all of the essential amino acids, are found in most animal products, such as eggs, milk, meat, fish, and poultry. However, gelatin and plant proteins such as grains, beans, and nuts are *incomplete proteins* because they are deficient in one or more of the essential amino acids. Diets that rely on plant foods for protein must combine protein sources to obtain all the essential amino acids. Some examples of *complementary protein* sources include rice and beans, or a peanut butter sandwich on whole grain bread. Rice and wheat contain the amino acid methionine that is deficient in beans and peanuts, whereas beans and peanuts are rich in lysine that is lacking in grain (see Table 19.4).

Complete proteins such as eggs, milk, meat, and fish contain all of the essential amino acids. Incomplete proteins from plants such as grains, beans, and nuts are deficient in one or more essential amino acids.

TABLE 19.3 Essential Amino Acids for Adults

Histidine (His, H)	Phenylalanine (Phe, F)
Isoleucine (Ile, I)	Threonine (Thr, T)
Leucine (Leu, L)	Tryptophan (Trp, W)
Lysine (Lys, K)	Valine (Val, V)
Methionine (Met, M)	

TABLE 19.4 Amino Acid Deficiencies in Selected Vegetables and Grains

Food Source	Amino Acid Deficiency
Wheat, rice, oats	Lysine
Corn	Lysine, tryptophan
Beans	Methionine, tryptophan
Peas, peanuts	Methionine
Almonds, walnuts	Lysine, tryptophan
Soy	Methionine

QUESTIONS AND PROBLEMS

19.1 Proteins and Amino Acids

LEARNING GOAL Classify proteins by their functions. Give the name and abbreviations for an amino acid, and draw its zwitterion.

19.1 Classify each of the following proteins according to its function:
   a. hemoglobin, oxygen carrier in the blood
   b. collagen, a major component of tendons and cartilage
   c. keratin, a protein found in hair
   d. amylases that catalyze the hydrolysis of starch

19.2 Classify each of the following proteins according to its function:
   a. insulin, which is needed for glucose utilization
   b. antibodies, disable foreign proteins
   c. casein, milk protein
   d. lipases that catalyze the hydrolysis of lipids

19.3 Draw the zwitterion and give the three- and one-letter abbreviation for each of the following amino acids:
   a. isoleucine   b. glutamine
   c. glutamate   d. proline

19.4 Draw the zwitterion and give the three- and one-letter abbreviation for each of the following amino acids:
   a. lysine   b. arginine
   c. methionine   d. tyrosine

19.5 Classify each of the amino acids in problem 19.3 as polar or nonpolar. If polar, indicate if the R group is neutral, acidic, or basic. Indicate if each is hydrophobic or hydrophilic.

19.6 Classify each of the amino acids in problem 19.4 as polar or nonpolar. If polar, indicate if the R group is neutral, acidic, or basic. Indicate if each is hydrophobic or hydrophilic.

℞ **Clinical Applications**

19.7 Give the name of the essential amino acid that has the following abbreviation:
   a. His   b. V   c. K   d. Ile

19.8 Give the name of the essential amino acid that has the following abbreviation:
   a. Trp   b. Met   c. F   d. W

19.9 Draw the Fischer projection for each of the following essential amino acids:
   a. L-serine   b. L-leucine

19.10 Draw the Fischer projection for each of the following essential amino acids:
   a. L-threonine   b. L-isoleucine

19.11 Explain why each of the following pairs are complementary proteins:
   a. corn and peas   b. rice and soy

19.12 Explain why each of the following pairs are complementary proteins:
   a. beans and oats   b. almonds and peanuts

19.2 Amino Acids as Acids and Bases

LEARNING GOAL

Using the zwitterion for an amino acid at its isoelectric point, draw its ionized structures at pH values above or below its isoelectric point.

The charged groups on an amino acid act as weak acids and bases, which means the groups can lose or gain H^+. Thus, the overall charge on an amino acid depends on the pH of the solution. At the isoelectric point (pI), an amino acid exists as a zwitterion with an overall charge of zero. However, an amino acid becomes a positive ion if it is placed in a more acidic solution (has a lower pH) than its pI. If that same amino acid is placed in a solution that is more basic (has a higher pH) than its pI, it becomes a negative ion.

The pI values for nonpolar and polar neutral amino acids range from pH 5.1 to 6. For example, alanine is a zwitterion at its pI of 6.0 with a carboxylate group ($-COO^-$) and an ammonium group ($-NH_3^+$), which give it an overall charge of zero. When alanine is placed in a solution that is more acidic, with a lower pH than its pI (pH < 6.0), the carboxylate group ($-COO^-$) of alanine gains H^+, which forms the carboxylic acid

(—COOH). Because the —NH$_3^+$ group retains a charge of 1+, alanine has an overall positive charge (1+) at a pH lower than its pI of 6.0.

Zwitterion of alanine
pH = 6.0
(charge = 0)

Alanine
pH < 6.0
(charge = 1+)

When alanine is placed in a solution that is more basic, with a higher pH than its pI (pH > 6.0), the —NH$_3^+$ group of alanine loses H$^+$ and forms an amino group (—NH$_2$), which has no charge. Because the carboxylate group (—COO$^-$) has a charge of 1−, alanine has an overall negative charge (1−) at a pH higher than 6.0.

Zwitterion of alanine
pH = 6.0
(charge = 0)

Alanine
pH > 6.0
(charge = 1−)

The overall charge due to carboxylic acid or carboxylate groups and ammonium or amino groups for amino acids in solutions with pH below pI, at the pI, or above pI are summarized in Table 19.5.

TABLE 19.5 Ionized Forms of Nonpolar and Polar Neutral Amino Acids

Solution	pH < pI (acidic)	pH = pI	pH > pI (basic)
Change in H$^+$	[H$^+$] increases	No change	[H$^+$] decreases
Carboxylic Acid/Carboxylate	—COOH	—COO$^-$	—COO$^-$
Ammonium/Amino	—NH$_3^+$	—NH$_3^+$	—NH$_2$
Overall Charge	1+	0	1−

Ionized Forms of Polar Acidic and Polar Basic Amino Acids

The pI values of the polar acidic amino acids are around pH 3. For example, the aspartate zwitterion has a pI of 2.8. However, as pH values change, the ammonium group (—NH$_3^+$), the carboxylate group (—COO$^-$), and the carboxylic acid (—COOH) R group can lose or gain H$^+$, which changes the overall charge. For example, at pH 7, which is above the pI for aspartate, the R group loses H$^+$ to form carboxylate and gives aspartate an overall charge of 1−. When the pH value increases further, the ammonium group loses H$^+$, which gives aspartate an overall change of 2−. At pH values below 2.8, the carboxylate group on the α carbon gains H$^+$, which gives aspartate an overall 1+ charge.

Aspartate
pH < 2.8
(charge = 1+)

Zwitterion of aspartate
pH = 2.8
(charge = 0)

Aspartate
pH = 7
(charge = 1−)

Aspartate
pH > 10
(charge = 2−)

The pI values of the polar basic amino acids (lysine, arginine, and histidine) are from pH 8 to 11. At pH values of 8 to 11, the amines in the R groups are not ionized, which gives an overall charge of zero. At lower pH values, the amines ($-NH_2$) in the R groups gain H^+ to form ammonium groups ($-NH_3^+$). With one carboxylate group ($-COO^-$) and two ammonium groups ($-NH_3^+$), the basic amino acids have an overall 1+ charge at pH values below their pIs. When the pH is lowered further, the α-carboxylate group ($-COO^-$) gains H^+. With a carboxylic acid group ($-COOH$) and two ammonium groups ($-NH_3^+$), the basic amino acids at very low pH values have an overall charge of 2+. If the pH increases above the pI, H^+ is lost to give ions with a 1− charge.

▶ SAMPLE PROBLEM 19.3 Amino Acids in Acidic or Basic Solution

The pI of glycine is 6.0. Draw the structural formula and state the overall charge for glycine at **a.** pH 6.0 and at **b.** pH 8.0.

SOLUTION

ANALYZE THE PROBLEM	Given	Need
	glycine, pI 6.0 **a.** pH 6.0, **b.** pH 8.0	structural formula, overall charge

a. At a pH of 6.0, glycine has an ammonium group and a carboxylate group, which give it an overall change of zero (0).

$$H_3\overset{+}{N}-\overset{\overset{\displaystyle H}{|}}{\underset{\underset{\displaystyle H}{|}}{C}}-\overset{\overset{\displaystyle O}{||}}{C}-O^-\qquad \text{Charge 0 at pH 6.0}$$

b. At a pH of 8.0 (basic solution), the $-NH_3^+$ group loses H^+ to become $-NH_2$, which has no charge. Because the carboxylate group ($-COO^-$) remains ionized, the overall charge of glycine at pH 8.0 is negative (1−).

$$H_2N-\overset{\overset{\displaystyle H}{|}}{\underset{\underset{\displaystyle H}{|}}{C}}-\overset{\overset{\displaystyle O}{||}}{C}-O^-\qquad \text{Charge 1− at pH 8.0}$$

STUDY CHECK 19.3

Draw the structural formula for glycine at pH 3.0 and give the overall charge.

ANSWER

$$H_3\overset{+}{N}-\overset{\overset{\displaystyle H}{|}}{\underset{\underset{\displaystyle H}{|}}{C}}-\overset{\overset{\displaystyle O}{||}}{C}-OH\qquad \text{Charge 1+ at pH 3.0}$$

Ball-and-stick model of glycine at its pI of 6.0.

QUESTIONS AND PROBLEMS

19.2 Amino Acids as Acids and Bases

LEARNING GOAL Using the zwitterion for an amino acid at its isoelectric point, draw its ionized structures at pH values above or below its isoelectric point.

19.13 Draw the zwitterion for each of the following amino acids:
 a. Val   **b.** C
 c. threonine   **d.** A

19.14 Draw the zwitterion for each of the following amino acids:
 a. phenylalanine   **b.** leucine
 c. S   **d.** Asn

19.15 Draw the ionized form for each of the amino acids in problem 19.13 at a pH below 1.0.

19.16 Draw the ionized form for each of the amino acids in problem 19.14 at a pH above 12.0.

19.17 Would each of the following ionized forms of valine exist at a pH above, below, or at its pI?

a.

$$CH_3 \quad CH_3$$
$$\diagdown \quad \diagup$$
$$CH \quad O$$
$$| \qquad \parallel$$
$$H_2N—C—C—O^-$$
$$|$$
$$H$$

b.

$$CH_3 \quad CH_3$$
$$\diagdown \quad \diagup$$
$$CH \quad O$$
$$| \qquad \parallel$$
$$H_3\overset{+}{N}—C—C—OH$$
$$|$$
$$H$$

c.

$$CH_3 \quad CH_3$$
$$\diagdown \quad \diagup$$
$$CH \quad O$$
$$| \qquad \parallel$$
$$H_3\overset{+}{N}—C—C—O^-$$
$$|$$
$$H$$

19.18 Would each of the following ionized forms of serine exist at a pH above, below, or at its pI?

a.

$$OH$$
$$|$$
$$CH_2 \quad O$$
$$| \qquad \parallel$$
$$H_3\overset{+}{N}—C—C—O^-$$
$$|$$
$$H$$

b.

$$OH$$
$$|$$
$$CH_2 \quad O$$
$$| \qquad \parallel$$
$$H_3\overset{+}{N}—C—C—OH$$
$$|$$
$$H$$

c.

$$OH$$
$$|$$
$$CH_2 \quad O$$
$$| \qquad \parallel$$
$$H_2N—C—C—O^-$$
$$|$$
$$H$$

19.3 Formation of Peptides

LEARNING GOAL

Draw the structure for a peptide, give its three-letter and one-letter abbreviations, and name.

When a carboxylic acid and an amine react through a condensation reaction, they form an amide bond. Because amino acids have the same functional groups, they also react to form an amide bond, called a **peptide bond**. The linking of two or more amino acids by peptide bonds forms a **peptide**. Two amino acids form a *dipeptide*, three amino acids form a *tripeptide*, and four amino acids form a *tetrapeptide*. A chain of five amino acids is a *pentapeptide*, and longer chains of amino acids are called *polypeptides*.

In the condensation reaction for the formation of the dipeptide glycylalanine (Gly–Ala, GA) (see Figure 19.2), the O atom is removed from the carboxylate group

Glycine   Alanine   Glycylalanine (Gly–Ala, GA)   Water

Amide group

Peptide bond

FIGURE 19.2 ▶ A peptide bond between glycine and alanine as zwitterions forms the dipeptide glycylalanine.

ⓠ What functional groups in glycine and alanine form the peptide bond?

($—COO^-$) of glycine, which combines with two H atoms removed from the ammonium group ($—NH_3^+$) of alanine to produce H_2O. When the peptide bonds have formed, the remaining parts of the amino acids are called *amino acid residues*.

In this dipeptide, the amino acid glycine written on the left with a free $—NH_3^+$ group is called the **N-terminal amino acid** or **N-terminus**. The amino acid alanine written on the right with a free $—COO^-$ group is called the **C-terminal amino acid** or **C-terminus**. By convention, chains of peptides are written starting with the N-terminal amino acid (the N-terminus) on the left, and ending with the C-terminal amino acid (or C-terminus) on the right.

N-terminus   Peptide bond   C-terminus

$$H \quad H \quad O \qquad\qquad H \quad CH_3 \ O \qquad\qquad\qquad H \quad H \quad O \qquad CH_3 \ O$$
$$| \quad | \quad \parallel \qquad\qquad | \qquad | \quad \parallel \qquad\qquad\qquad | \quad | \quad \parallel \qquad\quad | \quad \parallel$$
$$H—N^+—C—C—O^- \ + \ H—N^+—C—C—O^- \ \longrightarrow \ H—N^+—C—\boxed{C—N}—C—C—O^- \ + \ H_2O$$
$$| \quad | \qquad\qquad\qquad | \quad | \qquad\qquad\qquad\qquad | \quad | \qquad\quad | \quad |$$
$$H \quad H \qquad\qquad\qquad H \quad H \qquad\qquad\qquad\qquad H \quad H \qquad H \quad H$$

Glycine   Alanine   Glycylalanine (Gly–Ala, GA)

Peptide bond

The backbone of a peptide consists of the repeating sequence —N—C—C—.

From alanine
alanyl

From glycine
glycyl

From serine
serine

Alanylglycylserine
(Ala–Gly–Ser, AGS)

In the diagram of the dipeptide glycylalanine, the glycine residue is the N-terminus and the alanine residue is the C-terminus. The **backbone** of the dipeptide is the repeating sequence of the blue **N** from the ammonium group, the black **C** from the α carbon attached to an R group, and the magenta **C** from the carboxylate group.

Naming Peptides

The name of a peptide begins with the names of the N-terminal amino acid residue and all the following amino acid residues up to the C-terminal amino acid in which the *ine* or *ate* endings are replaced with *yl*. The C-terminal amino acid residue retains its complete amino acid name. For example, a tripeptide consisting of alanine, glycine, and serine residues is named as alan**yl**glyc**yl**serine. For convenience, the order of amino acids in the peptide is written from left to right as a sequence of three-letter or one-letter abbreviations.

▶ **SAMPLE PROBLEM 19.4** Drawing a Peptide

Draw the structure and give the name for the tripeptide Gly–Ser–Met.

SOLUTION

ANALYZE THE PROBLEM	Given	Need
	Gly–Ser–Met	tripeptide structure, name

STEP 1 Draw the structures for each amino acid in the peptide, starting with the N-terminus.

Gly, G
N-terminus

Ser, S

Met, M
C-terminus

STEP 2 Remove the O atom from the carboxylate group of the N-terminus and two H atoms from the ammonium group in the adjacent amino acid. Repeat this process until the C-terminus is reached.

Gly, G
N-terminus

Ser, S

Met, M
C-terminus

Guide to Drawing a Peptide

STEP 1
Draw the structures for each amino acid in the peptide, starting with the N-terminus.

STEP 2
Remove the O atom from the carboxylate group of the N-terminus and two H atoms from the ammonium group in the adjacent amino acid.

STEP 3
Use peptide bonds to connect the amino acid residues.

STEP 3 Use peptide bonds to connect the amino acid residues.

The tripeptide is named by replacing the last syllable of each amino acid name with *yl*, starting with the N-terminus. The C-terminus retains its complete amino acid name.

N-terminus glycine is named glycyl

serine is named seryl

C-terminus methionine keeps its full name

The tripeptide is named glycylserylmethionine.

STUDY CHECK 19.4

Draw the structure and give the name for Phe–Thr, a section in glucagon, which is a peptide hormone that increases blood glucose levels.

ANSWER

Phenylalanylthreonine

 ## Chemistry Link to **Health**

Polypeptides in the Body

Enkephalins and endorphins are natural painkillers produced in the body. They are polypeptides that bind to receptors in the brain to give relief from pain. This effect appears to be responsible for the runner's high, for temporary loss of pain when severe injury occurs, and for the analgesic effects of acupuncture.

The *enkephalins*, which are found in the thalamus and the spinal cord, are pentapeptides, the smallest molecules with opiate activity. The short amino acid sequence of met-enkephalin is incorporated into the longer amino acid sequence of the endorphins.

Four groups of *endorphins* have been identified: α-endorphin contains 16 amino acids, β-endorphin contains 31 amino acids, γ-endorphin has 17 amino acids, and δ-endorphin has 27 amino acids.

Endorphins may produce their sedating effects by preventing the release of substance P, a polypeptide with 11 amino acids, which has been found to transmit pain impulses to the brain.

Two hormones produced by the pituitary gland are the nonapeptides (peptides with nine amino acids) oxytocin and vasopressin. Oxytocin stimulates uterine contractions in labor, and vasopressin is an antidiuretic hormone that regulates blood pressure by adjusting the amount of water reabsorbed by the kidneys. The structures of these nonapeptides are very similar. Only the amino acids in positions 3 and 8 are different. However, the difference of two amino acids greatly affects how the two hormones function in the body.

met-Enkephalin

α-Endorphin

| Tyr–Gly–Gly–Phe–Met┼Thr–Ser–Glu–Lys–Ser–Gln–Thr–Pro–Leu–Val–Thr |

└─ met-Enkephalin ─┘

Leu

Glu–Gly–Lys–Lys–Tyr–Ala–Asn–Lys–Ile–Ile–Ala–Asn–Lys–Phe

β-Endorphin

Oxytocin
Vasopressin

Oxytocin, a nonapeptide used to initiate labor, was the first hormone to be synthesized in the laboratory.

QUESTIONS AND PROBLEMS

19.3 Formation of Peptides

LEARNING GOAL Draw the structure for a peptide, give its three-letter and one-letter abbreviations, and name.

19.19 Draw the structure for each of the following peptides, and give the three-letter and one-letter abbreviations for their names:
  a. alanylcysteine   **b.** serylphenylalanine
  c. glycylalanylvaline   **d.** valylisoleucyltryptophan

19.20 Draw the structure for each of the following peptides, and give the three-letter and one-letter abbreviations for their names:
  a. prolylaspartate
  b. threonylleucine
  c. methionylglutaminyllysine
  d. histidylglycylglutamylisoleucine

℞ Clinical Applications

19.21 Refer to the structure of met-enkephalin (Chemistry Link to Health: Polypeptides in the Body) to answer each of the following:
  a. What is the C-terminus of met-enkephalin?
  b. What is the N-terminus of met-enkephalin?

  c. Write the amino acid order for met-enkephalin using single-letter abbreviations.

19.22 Refer to the structure of β-endorphin (Chemistry Link to Health: Polypeptides in the Body) to answer each of the following:
  a. What is the C-terminus of β-endorphin?
  b. What is the N-terminus of β-endorphin?
  c. Write the amino acid order for β-endorphin using single-letter abbreviations.

19.23 Peptides isolated from rapeseed that may lower blood pressure have the following sequence of amino acids. Draw the structure for each peptide and write the one-letter abbreviations.
  a. Arg–Ile–Tyr
  b. Val–Trp–Ile–Ser

19.24 Peptides from sweet potato with antioxidant properties have the following sequence of amino acids. Draw the structure for each peptide and write the one-letter abbreviations.
  a. Asp–Cys–Gly–Tyr
  b. Asn–Tyr–Asp–Glu–Tyr

19.4 Protein Structure: Primary and Secondary Levels

LEARNING GOAL

Describe the primary and secondary structures of a protein.

A **protein** is a polypeptide of 50 or more amino acids that has biological activity. Each protein in our cells has a unique sequence of amino acids that determines its three-dimensional structure and biological function.

Primary Structure

The **primary structure** of a protein is the particular sequence of amino acids held together by peptide bonds. For example, a hormone that stimulates the thyroid to release thyroxine is a tripeptide with the amino acid sequence Glu–His–Pro, EHP.

Although five other sequences of the same three amino acids are possible, such as His–Pro–Glu or Pro–His–Glu, they do not produce hormonal activity. Thus, the biological function of both peptides and proteins depends on the specific sequence of the amino acids.

The first protein to have its primary structure determined was insulin, which was accomplished by Frederick Sanger in 1953. Since that time, scientists have determined the amino acid sequences of many proteins. Insulin is a hormone that regulates the glucose level in the blood. In the primary structure of human insulin, there are two polypeptide chains. In chain A, there are 21 amino acids, and in chain B there are 30 amino acids. The polypeptide chains are held together by *disulfide bonds* formed by the thiol groups of the cysteine amino acids in each of the chains (see Figure 19.3). Today, human insulin with this exact structure is produced in large quantities through genetic engineering for the treatment of diabetes.

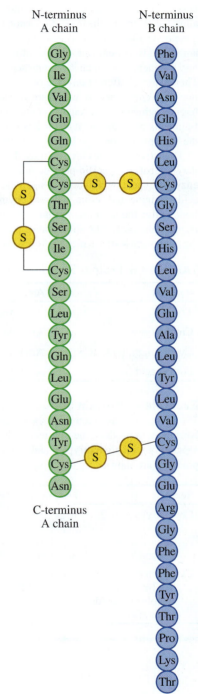

FIGURE 19.3 ▶ The sequence of amino acids in human insulin is the primary structure.

🔵 What kinds of bonds occur in the primary structure of a protein?

▶ **SAMPLE PROBLEM 19.5** Primary Structure

What are the three-letter and one-letter abbreviations of the tetrapeptide that contains two valines, one proline, and one histidine if the N-terminus is histidine and the C-terminus is proline?

SOLUTION

The tetrapeptide starts with the N-terminus, histidine, followed by two valine residues, and ends with the C-terminus, proline.

Three-letter abbreviations: His–Val–Val–Pro

One-letter abbreviations: HVVP

STUDY CHECK 19.5

What are the three-letter and one-letter abbreviations of a tripeptide containing two glycines and one tyrosine, if the N-terminus is tyrosine?

ANSWER

Tyr–Gly–Gly (YGG)

Chemistry Link to **Health**

Protein Sequencing

A protein is a very large molecule, which has hundreds of amino acids. The unique sequence of amino acids in a primary structure allows us to predict the three-dimensional structure of a protein. Using a method called *protein sequencing*, scientists determine the order of amino acids. An enzyme or reagent is used to hydrolyze the protein into fragments for which the amino acid order (sequence) is obtained. Then using a different enzyme or reagent, the protein is hydrolyzed into different fragments, which are also sequenced. Finally, all the different fragments are arranged to find where they overlap. Only protein fragments of 20 amino acids or less can be accurately sequenced, so the large protein must be hydrolyzed into smaller pieces.

Digestive enzymes are often used to produce fragments because they hydrolyze specific peptide bonds. For example, the digestive enzyme trypsin only hydrolyzes peptide bonds after the basic amino acids arginine and lysine, whereas chymotrypsin hydrolyzes peptide bonds after the aromatic amino acids phenylalanine, tyrosine, and tryptophan. Table 19.6 shows some protein sequencing reagents and the amino acids after which hydrolysis occurs.

TABLE 19.6 Protein Sequencing Reagents

Reagent	Amino Acids Where Hydrolysis Occurs
Trypsin	After Arg and Lys (R or K)
Chymotrypsin	After Phe, Tyr, and Trp (F, Y, or W)
Cyanogen bromide (CNBr)	After Met (M)
Formic acid	After Asp (D)

Example of Protein Sequencing

The hormone α-melanotropin is a 13-amino acid peptide that stimulates cells to produce the pigment melanin. If the peptide is treated separately with chymotrypsin and cyanogen bromide, the fragments produced are shown.

Reagent	Fragments Produced
Chymotrypsin hydrolyzes peptide bonds after Phe, Tyr, and Trp.	Arg–Trp Ser–Tyr Gly–Lys–Pro–Val Ser–Met–Glu–His–Phe
Cyanogen bromide (CNBr) hydrolyzes peptide bonds after Met.	Ser–Tyr–Ser–Met Glu–His–Phe–Arg–Trp–Gly–Lys–Pro–Val

Now we can match the overlapping sections of amino acids from different fragments to determine their sequence in α-melanotropin. The pair Ser–Met is found in the fragments Ser–Tyr–Ser–Met and Ser–Met–Glu–His–Phe, which we can align in our series of fragments.

Ser–Tyr
Ser–Tyr–Ser–Met
    Ser–Met–Glu–His–Phe

From this group of fragments, we can write a sequence of seven amino acid residues as

Ser–Tyr–Ser–Met–Glu–His–Phe

The sequence Glu–His–Phe is also found in the longer fragment Glu–His–Phe–Arg–Trp–Gly–Lys–Pro–Val. By overlapping the two matching sections of amino acid residues, we obtain the complete sequence of amino acid residues.

Ser–Tyr–Ser–Met–Glu–His–Phe
       Glu–His–Phe–Arg–Trp–Gly–Lys–Pro–Val

Thus, the primary structure of the 13 amino acid residues in α-melanotropin is written as

Ser–Tyr–Ser–Met–Glu–His–Phe–Arg–Trp–Gly–Lys–Pro–Val

Now we can use this primary structure of α-melanotropin to see where chymotrypsin and CNBr reagent hydrolyzed peptide bonds to give the fragments we used to determine its sequence.

Secondary Structure

The **secondary structure** of a protein describes the structure that forms when amino acids form hydrogen bonds between the atoms in the backbone within a single polypeptide chain or between polypeptide chains. The most common types of secondary structures are the *alpha helix* and the *beta-pleated sheet*.

Alpha Helix

In an **alpha helix (α helix)**, hydrogen bonds form between the hydrogen atoms attached to the backbone nitrogen atoms (N—H), and the oxygen atoms in the backbone carbonyl (C=O) four amino acids away in the α helix (see Figure 19.4). The formation of many hydrogen bonds along the polypeptide chain gives the characteristic right-handed spiral shape of an alpha helix. All the residues of the different amino acids in the polypeptide extend to the outside of the helix.

C-terminus

Peptide backbone of primary structure

- ● Carbon
- ● Oxygen
- ● Nitrogen
- ● R group
- ○ Hydrogen

Hydrogen bonds of secondary structure

N-terminus

FIGURE 19.4 ▶ The α helix acquires a coiled shape of a right-handed spiral because of the hydrogen bonds between the hydrogen of the N—H group in one turn of the polypeptide and the oxygen in the C=O group in the next turn.

Q What are the partial charges of the H in N—H and the O in C=O that allows for hydrogen bonding?

Beta-Pleated Sheet

Another type of secondary structure found in proteins is the **beta-pleated sheet (β-pleated sheet)**. In a β-pleated sheet, short zigzagging lengths of polypeptide chain called β-strands are held together side by side by hydrogen bonds that form between oxygen atoms of the backbone carbonyl groups (C=O) in one section of the polypeptide chain, and the hydrogen atoms on the backbone nitrogen groups (N—H) in a nearby section of the polypeptide chain. A β-pleated sheet can form between adjacent polypeptide chains or within the same polypeptide chain when the rigid structure of the amino acid proline causes a bend in the polypeptide chain.

The tendency to form various kinds of secondary structures depends on the amino acids in a particular segment of the polypeptide chain. Typically, β-pleated sheets contain mostly amino acids with small residues such as glycine, valine, alanine, and serine, which extend above and below the β-pleated sheet. The α-helical regions in a protein have higher amounts of amino acids with large residues such as histidine, leucine, and methionine. The hydrogen bonds holding the β-pleated sheets tightly in place account for the strength and durability of fibrous proteins such as silk (see Figure 19.5).

In some proteins, the polypeptide chain consists mostly of α helices, whereas other proteins consist mostly of β-pleated sheets. However, in most proteins, there are sections of both α helices and β-pleated sheets. The sections of the polypeptide chain with no definite secondary structure are called *random coils*.

The secondary structure in silk is a β-pleated sheet.

Alpha helix

Beta-pleated sheet

Protein with alpha helices
and beta-pleated sheets

A ribbon model of a protein shows
the regions of alpha helices and
beta-pleated sheets.

C-terminus

Hydrogen bonds
between peptide
backbones

● Carbon
● Oxygen
● Nitrogen
● R group
● Hydrogen

N-terminus

FIGURE 19.5 ▶ Hydrogen bonds between β-strands form a β-pleated sheet.

Q How do the hydrogen bonds differ between a β-pleated sheet and an α helix?

The regions of the α helices and β-pleated sheets are shown in a ribbon model in which the coiled portions represent the α helical backbone, and the long arrows that look like a piece of fettuccine represent the β-strands in a β-pleated sheet. Regions that are not α helices or β-pleated sheets are random regions indicated by thick lines.

Collagen

Collagen, the most abundant protein in the body, makes up as much as one-third of all protein in vertebrates. It is found in connective tissue, blood vessels, skin, tendons, ligaments, the cornea of the eye, and cartilage. The strong structure of collagen is a result of three helices woven together like a braid to form a **triple helix** (see Figure 19.6).

Collagen has a high content of glycine (33%), proline (22%), and alanine (12%), and smaller amounts of hydroxyproline and hydroxylysine, which are modified forms of proline and lysine. The —OH groups on these modified amino acids provide additional hydrogen bonds between the peptide chains to give strength to the collagen triple helix. When several triple helices wrap together as a braid, they form the fibrils that make up connective tissues and tendons. When a diet is deficient in vitamin C, collagen fibrils are weakened because the enzymes needed to form hydroxyproline and hydroxylysine require vitamin C. Collagen becomes less elastic as a person ages because additional bonds form between the fibrils. Bones, cartilage, and tendons become more brittle, and wrinkles are seen as the skin loses elasticity.

OH
|
CH
|
H_2C CH_2 O
|+ | ‖
H_2N — CH — C — O^-

Hydroxyproline

$\overset{+}{N}H_3$
|
CH_2
|
H — C — OH
|
CH_2
|
CH_2 O
| ‖
$H_3\overset{+}{N}$ — CH — C — O^-

Hydroxylysine

Hydroxyproline and hydroxylysine
provide additional hydrogen bonds
in the triple helices of collagen.

SAMPLE PROBLEM 19.6 Identifying Protein Structures

Identify the secondary structure (α helix, β-pleated sheet, or triple helix) described in each of the following statements:

a. a structure that has hydrogen bonds between adjacent polypeptide chains
b. three helical polypeptides woven together
c. a peptide chain with a coiled or corkscrew shape that is held in place by hydrogen bonds

SOLUTION

a. β-pleated sheet
b. triple helix
c. α helix

STUDY CHECK 19.6

Which attractive force holds secondary structures together in proteins?

ANSWER

hydrogen bonding

Triple helix   3 peptide chains

FIGURE 19.6 ▶ Collagen fibers are triple helices of polypeptide chains held together by hydrogen bonds.

◉ What are some of the amino acids in collagen that form hydrogen bonds between the polypeptide chains?

 # Chemistry Link to **Health**

Protein Secondary Structures and Alzheimer's Disease

Alzheimer's disease is a form of dementia in which a person has increasing memory loss and inability to handle daily tasks. Alzheimer's usually occurs after age 60 and is irreversible. Although researchers are still investigating its causes, Alzheimer's patients have distinctly different brain tissue from people who do not have the disease. In the brain of a normal person, small beta-amyloid proteins, made up of 42 amino acids, exist in the alpha helical form. In the brain of a person with Alzheimer's, the beta-amyloid proteins change shape from the normal alpha helices that are soluble to insoluble, sticky beta-pleated sheets, forming clusters of protein fragments called *plaques*. The diagnosis of Alzheimer's disease is based on the presence of plaques and neurofibrillary tangles in the neurons that affect the transmission of nerve signals.

There is no cure for Alzheimer's disease, but there are medications that can slow its progression or lessen symptoms for a limited time. Medications like donepezil (Aricept) and rivastigmine (Exelon) help keep the levels of nerve transmitters high in the brain, which improves learning and memory in patients.

In patients with Alzheimer's disease, beta-amyloid proteins change from **(a)** a normal alpha-helical shape to **(b)** beta-pleated sheets that stick together and form plaques in the brain.

(a)   (b)

Normal   Alzheimer's

Neuron

Beta-amyloid plaque

Neurofibrillary tangles

In an Alzheimer's brain, beta-amyloid plaques and neurofibrillary tangles damage the neurons and interfere with nerve signals.

QUESTIONS AND PROBLEMS

19.4 Protein Structure: Primary and Secondary Levels

LEARNING GOAL Describe the primary and secondary structures of a protein.

19.25 What type of bonding occurs in the primary structure of a protein?

19.26 How can two proteins with exactly the same number and type of amino acids have different primary structures?

19.27 Two peptides each contain one valine residue and two methionine residues. What are their possible primary structures?

19.28 What are the two different types of secondary protein structure?

19.29 What happens to the primary structure of a protein when a protein forms a secondary structure?

19.30 In an α helix, how does bonding occur between the amino acids in the polypeptide chain?

19.31 What is the difference in bonding between an α helix and a β-pleated sheet?

19.32 How is the structure of a β-pleated sheet different from that of a triple helix?

℞ Clinical Applications

19.33 Write the three-letter sequence for the amino acid residues in the octapeptide angiotensin II, a hormone involved in regulating blood pressure in humans, if treatment with chymotrypsin and trypsin gives the following fragments (see Chemistry Link to Health: Protein Sequencing):

Reagent	Fragments Produced
Chymotrypsin	Ile–His–Pro–Phe
	Asp–Arg–Val–Tyr
Trypsin	Asp–Arg
	Val–Tyr–Ile–His–Pro–Phe

19.34 Write the three-letter sequence for the amino acid residues in somatostatin, a peptide that inhibits the release of growth hormone, if treatment with chymotrypsin and trypsin gives the following fragments (see Chemistry Link to Health: Protein Sequencing):

Reagent	Fragments Produced
Chymotrypsin	Phe
	Trp
	Lys–Thr–Phe
	Thr–Ser–Cys
	Ala–Gly–Cys–Lys–Asn–Phe
Trypsin	Ala–Gly–Cys–Lys
	Asn–Phe–Phe–Trp–Lys
	Thr–Phe–Thr–Ser–Cys

19.5 Protein Structure: Tertiary and Quaternary Levels

LEARNING GOAL

Describe the tertiary and quaternary structures of a protein.

⚛ CORE CHEMISTRY SKILL

Identifying the Primary, Secondary, Tertiary, and Quaternary Structures of Proteins

The **tertiary structure** of a protein involves attractions and repulsions between the amino acid residues in the polypeptide chain. As interactions occur between the residues in different parts of the peptide chain, segments of the chain twist and bend to give the protein its specific three-dimensional shape.

Interactions Between Residues in Tertiary Structures

The tertiary structure of a protein is stabilized by interactions between the amino acid residues in one region of the polypeptide chain and the residues in other regions of the protein (see Figure 19.7). The stabilizing interactions of tertiary structures are detailed as follows:

1. **Hydrophilic interactions** occur between the external aqueous environment and the residues of polar amino acid residues. Sections of the polypeptide chain with polar residues are pulled to the outer surface of a protein where the residues interact with the polar water molecules.

2. **Hydrophobic interactions** occur between amino acid residues that have nonpolar residues. Within a protein, the amino acid residues with nonpolar residues are pushed toward each other and repelled by the hydrophilic interactions in water. This *hydrophobic effect* forms a nonpolar center at the interior of the protein.

3. **Salt bridges** are ionic attractions between the charges of the acidic and basic residues of amino acid residues. For example, the positively charged residue of lysine forms a salt bridge (ionic bond) with the negatively charged residue of aspartate.

4. **Hydrogen bonds** form between the H of a polar residue and the O or N of a second polar amino acid residue. For example, a hydrogen bond occurs between the —OH groups of two serines or between the —OH of serine and the =O in asparagine.

5. **Disulfide bonds** (—S—S—) are covalent bonds that form when the —SH groups of two cysteine residues are oxidized (H removed). In some proteins, there may be several disulfide bonds between the cysteine residues in the polypeptide chain; in others, there may be none.

FIGURE 19.7 ▶ Interactions between amino acid residues fold a polypeptide into a specific three-dimensional shape called its tertiary structure.

Q Why would one section of the polypeptide chain be pushed to the center whereas another section would be pulled to the surface?

C-terminus

N-terminus

FIGURE 19.8 ▶ The ribbon model represents the tertiary structure of the polypeptide chain of myoglobin, a globular protein.

Q Would hydrophilic amino acids be found on the outside or inside of the myoglobin structure?

α Helix

α-Keratin

FIGURE 19.9 ▶ The fibrous proteins of *α*-keratin wrap together to form fibrils of hair and wool.

Q Why does hair have a large amount of cysteine amino acids?

> **SAMPLE PROBLEM 19.7 Interaction Between Residues in Tertiary Structures**
>
> What type of interaction would you expect between the residues of each of the following amino acids in a tertiary structure of a protein?
>
> **a.** cysteine and cysteine   **b.** glutamate and lysine
> **c.** tyrosine and water
>
> **SOLUTION**
>
> | ANALYZE THE PROBLEM | Given | Need |
> |---|---|---|
> | | pairs of amino acids | type of interaction between residues |
>
> **a.** Two cysteines, each containing —SH, will form a disulfide bond.
> **b.** The interaction of the —COO⁻ in the residue of glutamate and the —NH₃⁺ in the residue of lysine will form an ionic bond called a salt bridge.
> **c.** The residue in tyrosine has an —OH group that is attracted to water by hydrophilic interactions.
>
> **STUDY CHECK 19.7**
>
> Would you expect to find valine and leucine on the outside or the inside of the tertiary structure? Why?
>
> **ANSWER**
>
> Both valine and leucine have nonpolar residues and would be found on the nonpolar inside of the tertiary structure.

Globular and Fibrous Proteins

A group of proteins known as **globular proteins** have compact, spherical shapes because sections of the polypeptide chain fold over on top of each other due to the various interactions between amino acid residues. It is the globular proteins that carry out the work of the cells: functions such as synthesis, transport, and metabolism.

Myoglobin is a globular protein that stores oxygen in skeletal muscle. High concentrations of myoglobin are found in the muscles of sea mammals, such as seals and whales allowing them to stay under the water for a long time. Myoglobin contains 153 amino acids in a single polypeptide chain with about three-fourths of the chain in the *α* helix secondary structure. The polypeptide chain, including its helical regions, forms a compact tertiary structure by folding upon itself (see Figure 19.8). Within the tertiary structure, oxygen (O_2) binds to an iron ion located in an organic compound called a *heme* within the protein.

The **fibrous proteins** are proteins that consist of long, thin, fiber-like shapes. They are typically involved in the structure of cells and tissues. Two types of fibrous protein are the *α*- and *β*-keratins. The *α*-keratins are the proteins that make up hair, wool, skin, and nails. In hair, three *α* helices coil together like a braid to form a fibril. Within the fibril, the *α* helices are held together by disulfide (—S—S—) linkages between the residues of the many cysteine amino acid residues in hair. Several fibrils bind together to form a strand of hair (see Figure 19.9). The *β*-keratins are the type of proteins found in the feathers of birds and scales of reptiles. In *β*-keratins, the proteins consist of large amounts of a *β*-pleated sheet structure.

Quaternary Structure: Hemoglobin

Although many proteins are biologically active as tertiary structures, most proteins require two or more tertiary structures to be biologically active. When a biologically active protein consists of two or more polypeptide chains or subunits, the structural level is called **quaternary structure**. Hemoglobin, a globular protein that transports oxygen in blood, consists of four polypeptide chains: two *α*-chains with 141 amino acids, and two *β*-chains with

146 amino acids. Although the α-chains and β-chains have different sequences of amino acids, they both form similar tertiary structures with similar shapes (see Figure 19.10).

In the quaternary structure, the subunits are held together by the same interactions that stabilize their tertiary structures, such as hydrogen bonds and salt bridges between R groups of amino acid residues, disulfide bonds, and hydrophobic interactions. Each subunit of hemoglobin is a globular protein with an embedded heme group, which contains one iron ion that can bind an oxygen molecule. In the adult hemoglobin molecule, all four subunits $(\alpha_2\beta_2)$ *must* be combined for hemoglobin to properly function as an oxygen carrier. Therefore, the complete quaternary structure of hemoglobin can bind and transport up to four molecules of oxygen.

Hemoglobin and myoglobin have similar biological functions. Hemoglobin carries oxygen in the blood, whereas myoglobin carries oxygen in muscle. Myoglobin, a single polypeptide chain with a molar mass of 17 000, has about one-fourth the molar mass of hemoglobin (67 000). The tertiary structure of the single polypeptide myoglobin is almost identical to the tertiary structure of each of the subunits of hemoglobin. Myoglobin carries one molecule of oxygen, whereas hemoglobin carries four oxygen molecules. The similarity in tertiary structures allows each protein to bind and release oxygen in a similar manner. Table 19.7 and Figure 19.11 summarize the structural levels of proteins.

FIGURE 19.10 ▶ In the ribbon model of hemoglobin, the quaternary structure is made up of four polypeptide subunits—two (orange) are α-chains and two (red) are β-chains. The heme groups (green) in the four subunits bind oxygen.

Q What is the difference between a tertiary structure and a quaternary structure?

TABLE 19.7 Summary of Structural Levels in Proteins

Structural Level	Characteristics
Primary	Peptide bonds join amino acids in a specific sequence in a polypeptide.
Secondary	The α helix or β-pleated sheet, forms by hydrogen bonding between the backbone atoms in the peptide bonds along the chain.
Tertiary	A polypeptide folds into a compact, three-dimensional shape stabilized by interactions (hydrogen bonds, salt bridges, hydrophobic, hydrophilic, disulfide) between amino acid residues to form a biologically active protein.
Quaternary	Two or more protein subunits combine and are stabilized by interactions (hydrogen bonds, salt bridges, hydrophobic) between amino acid residues to form a biologically active protein.

(a) Primary structure

(b) Secondary structure

C-terminus

(c) Tertiary structure

N-terminus

(d) Quaternary structure

FIGURE 19.11 ▶ Proteins consist of **(a)** primary, **(b)** secondary, **(c)** tertiary, and often times **(d)** quaternary structural levels.

Q What is the difference between a primary structure and a tertiary structure?

Interactive Video

Different Levels of Protein Structure

▶**SAMPLE PROBLEM 19.8 Identifying Protein Structure**

Indicate whether the following interactions are responsible for primary, secondary, tertiary, or quaternary protein structures:

a. disulfide bonds that form between portions of a protein chain
b. peptide bonds that form a chain of amino acids
c. hydrogen bonds between the H of a peptide bond and the O of a peptide bond four amino acids away

SOLUTION

ANALYZE THE PROBLEM	Given	Need
	interactions of amino acid residues	identify structural level of protein

a. Disulfide bonds are a type of interaction between amino acid residues found in the tertiary and quaternary levels of protein structure.

b. The peptide bonds in the sequence of amino acids form the primary level of protein structure.

c. The hydrogen bonds between the peptide bonds along the polypeptide chain form the secondary structures of α helix or β-pleated sheet.

STUDY CHECK 19.8

What structural level is represented by the hydrophobic side chains of the amino acid residues at the center of a globular protein?

ANSWER

tertiary structure

Chemistry Link to Health

Sickle Cell Anemia

Sickle cell anemia is a disease caused by an abnormality in the shape of one of the subunits of the hemoglobin protein. In the β-chain, the sixth amino acid, glutamate, which is polar acidic, is replaced by valine, a nonpolar amino acid.

Because valine has a nonpolar residue, it is attracted to the nonpolar regions within the beta hemoglobin chains. The affected red blood cells (RBCs) change from a rounded shape to a crescent shape, which interferes with their ability to transport adequate quantities of oxygen. Hydrophobic interactions also cause sickle cell hemoglobin molecules to stick together. They form insoluble fibers of sickle cell hemoglobin that clog capillaries, where they cause inflammation, pain, and organ damage. Critically low oxygen levels may occur in the affected tissues.

In sickle cell anemia, both genes for the altered hemoglobin must be inherited. However, both sickled cells and normal cells are found in persons who carry one gene for sickle cell hemoglobin, a condition known as *sickle cell trait* that provides some resistance to malaria.

Polar acidic amino acid

Normal β-chain: Val–His–Leu–Thr–Pro–Glu–Glu–Lys–

Sickled β-chain: Val–His–Leu–Thr–Pro–Val–Glu–Lys–

Nonpolar amino acid

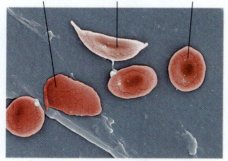

RBC beginning to sickle   Sickled RBC   Normal RBC

Diagnosing Sickle Cell Anemia—Electrophoresis

Proteins can be isolated from each other and used to diagnose diseases such as sickle cell anemia by a technique called *electrophoresis*. In electrophoresis, used to identify and diagnose sickle cell anemia, samples containing normal hemoglobin and sickle cell hemoglobin proteins are placed on a gel and an electric current is applied. The proteins move along the gel based on their charge, size, and shape.

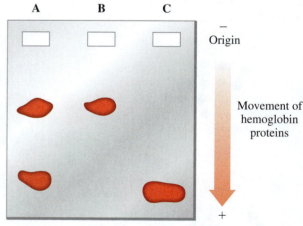

In electrophoresis, hemoglobin samples from patients with sickle cell trait (**A**), sickle cell anemia (**B**), and normal hemoglobin (**C**) are placed on a gel and an electric field is applied. The differences in the movement of the abnormal and normal hemoglobin proteins identify the condition of sickle cell trait or anemia.

QUESTIONS AND PROBLEMS

19.5 Protein Structure: Tertiary and Quaternary Levels

LEARNING GOAL Describe the tertiary and quaternary structures of a protein.

19.35 What type of interaction would you expect between the following groups in a tertiary structure?
a. cysteine and cysteine
b. glutamate and lysine
c. serine and aspartate
d. leucine and leucine

19.36 What type of interaction would you expect between the following groups in a tertiary structure?
a. phenylalanine and isoleucine
b. aspartate and histidine
c. asparagine and tyrosine
d. alanine and proline

19.37 A portion of a polypeptide chain contains the following sequence of amino acids:

–Leu–Val–Cys–Asp–

a. Which amino acid can form a disulfide bond?
b. Which amino acids are likely to be found on the inside of the protein structure? Why?
c. Which amino acids would be found on the outside of the protein? Why?
d. How does the primary structure of a protein affect its tertiary structure?

19.38 About one-half of the 153 amino acids in myoglobin have nonpolar residues.
a. Where would you expect those amino acids to be located in the tertiary structure?
b. Where would you expect the polar residues to be in the tertiary structure?
c. Why is myoglobin more soluble in water than silk or wool?

19.39 Indicate whether each of the following statements describes the primary, secondary, tertiary, or quaternary protein structure:
a. Residues interact to form disulfide bonds or ionic bonds.
b. Peptide bonds join the amino acids in a polypeptide chain.
c. Several polypeptides in a β-pleated sheet are held together by hydrogen bonds between adjacent chains.
d. Hydrogen bonding between amino acid residues in the same polypeptide gives a coiled shape to the protein.

19.40 Indicate whether each of the following statements describes the primary, secondary, tertiary, or quaternary protein structure:
a. Hydrophobic amino acid residues seeking a nonpolar environment move toward the inside of the folded protein.
b. Hydrophilic amino acid residues move to the polar aqueous environment outside the protein.
c. An active protein contains four tertiary subunits.
d. In sickle cell anemia, valine replaces glutamate in the β-chain.

19.6 Protein Hydrolysis and Denaturation

LEARNING GOAL

Describe the hydrolysis and denaturation of proteins.

Recall that peptide bonds are formed through condensation reactions. Similarly, they can be broken through hydrolysis reactions yielding individual amino acids. This process occurs in the stomach when enzymes such as pepsin or trypsin catalyze the hydrolysis of proteins to give amino acids. This hydrolysis breaks up the primary structure by breaking the covalent peptide bonds that link the amino acids. In the digestion of proteins, the amino acids are absorbed through the intestinal walls and carried to the cells, where they can be used to synthesize new proteins.

Alanylglycylserine (Ala–Gly–Ser, AGS)

Alanine (Ala, A)   Glycine (Gly, G)   Serine (Ser, S)

Denaturation of Proteins

Denaturation of a protein occurs when there is a change that disrupts the interactions between residues that stabilize the secondary, tertiary, or quaternary structure. However, the covalent amide bonds of the primary structure are not affected.

The loss of secondary and tertiary structures occurs when conditions change, such as increasing the temperature or making the pH very acidic or basic. If the pH changes, the basic and acidic residues lose their ionic charges and cannot form salt bridges, which causes a change in the shape of the protein. Denaturation can also occur by adding certain organic compounds or heavy metal ions, or through mechanical agitation. When the interactions between the residues are disrupted, a globular protein unfolds like a wet spaghetti noodle. With the loss of its overall shape (tertiary structure), the protein is no longer biologically active (see Figure 19.12).

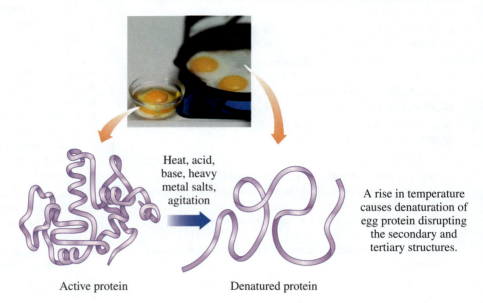

FIGURE 19.12 ▶ Denaturation of a protein occurs when the interactions of residues that stabilize secondary, tertiary, or quaternary structures are disrupted, which destroys the shape and renders the protein biologically inactive.

Q What are some ways in which proteins are denatured?

Heat, acid, base, heavy metal salts, agitation

A rise in temperature causes denaturation of egg protein disrupting the secondary and tertiary structures.

Active protein   Denatured protein

Heat

Whenever you cook food, you are using heat to denature protein. Hydrogen bonds and hydrophobic interactions between nonpolar residues are disrupted. Few proteins can remain biologically active above 50 °C. The nutritional value of the proteins in food is not changed, but they are more digestible. High temperatures are also used to disinfect surgical instruments and gowns by denaturing the proteins of any bacteria present.

Acids and Bases

Like a cooked egg, the denatured proteins in milk form more of a semisolid when denatured. In the preparation of yogurt and cheese, bacteria that produce lactic acid are added to denature the proteins by changing the pH. A change in pH breaks down hydrogen bonds and disrupts the ionic bonds (salt bridges). Tannic acid, a weak acid used in burn ointments, is applied to the site of the burn to coagulate proteins, which forms a protective cover and prevents further loss of fluid from the burn.

Organic Compounds

Ethanol and isopropyl alcohol act as disinfectants by exchanging the bacterial protein's hydrogen bonds to water with their own and disrupting the side chain intramolecular hydrogen bonding. An alcohol swab is used to clean wounds or to prepare the skin for an injection because the alcohol passes through the cell walls and coagulates the proteins inside the bacteria.

Heavy Metal Ions

In hospitals, a dilute (1%) solution of $AgNO_3$ is placed in the eyes of newborn babies to destroy the bacteria that cause gonorrhea. Heavy metal ions such as Ag^+, Pb^{2+}, and Hg^{2+} denature protein by forming bonds with ionic residues or reacting with disulfide ($-S-S-$) bonds. If heavy metals are ingested, they act as poisons by severely denaturing body proteins and disrupting metabolic reactions. An antidote is a high-protein food, such as milk, eggs, or cheese, that combines with the heavy metal ions until the stomach can be pumped.

Agitation

The whipping of cream and the beating of egg whites are examples of using mechanical agitation to denature protein. The whipping action stretches the polypeptide chains until the stabilizing interactions are disrupted. Table 19.8 summarizes protein denaturation.

TABLE 19.8 Protein Denaturation

Denaturing Agent	Bonds Disrupted	Examples
Heat Above 50 °C	Hydrogen bonds; hydrophobic interactions between nonpolar residues	Cooking food and autoclaving surgical items
Acids and Bases	Hydrogen bonds between polar residues; salt bridges	Lactic acid from bacteria, which denatures milk protein in the preparation of yogurt and cheese
Organic Compounds	Hydrophobic interactions	Ethanol and isopropyl alcohol, which disinfect wounds and prepare the skin for injections
Heavy Metal Ions Ag^+, Pb^{2+}, and Hg^{2+}	Disulfide bonds in proteins by forming ionic bonds	Mercury and lead poisoning
Agitation	Hydrogen bonds and hydrophobic interactions by stretching polypeptide chains and disrupting stabilizing interactions	Whipped cream, meringue made from egg whites

▶ **SAMPLE PROBLEM 19.9 Denaturation of Proteins**

Describe the denaturation process in each of the following:

a. An appetizer known as ceviche is prepared without heat by placing slices of raw fish in a solution of lemon or lime juice. After 3 or 4 h, the fish appears to be "cooked."
b. When baking scalloped potatoes, the added milk curdles (forms solids).

SOLUTION

a. The acids in lemon or lime juice break down the hydrogen bonds between polar residues and disrupt salt bridges, which denature the proteins of the fish.
b. The heat during baking breaks apart hydrogen bonds and hydrophobic interactions between nonpolar residues in the milk proteins. When the milk denatures, the proteins become insoluble and form solids called curds.

STUDY CHECK 19.9

Why is a dilute solution of $AgNO_3$ used to disinfect the eyes of newborn infants?

ANSWER

The heavy metal Ag^+ denatures the proteins in bacteria that cause gonorrhea.

Explore Your World

Denaturation of Milk Protein

Pour some milk in five glasses. Add the following to the milk samples in glasses 1 to 4. The fifth glass of milk is a reference sample.

1. Vinegar, drop by drop. Stir.
2. One-half teaspoon of meat tenderizer. Stir.
3. One teaspoon of fresh pineapple juice. (Canned juice has been heated and cannot be used.)
4. One teaspoon of fresh pineapple juice after the juice is heated to boiling.

Questions

1. How did the appearance of the milk change in each of the samples?
2. What enzyme is listed on the package label of the tenderizer?
3. How does the effect of the heated pineapple juice compare with that of the fresh juice? Explain.
4. Why is cooked pineapple used when making gelatin (a protein) desserts?

QUESTIONS AND PROBLEMS

19.6 Protein Hydrolysis and Denaturation

LEARNING GOAL Describe the hydrolysis and denaturation of proteins.

19.41 What products would result from the complete hydrolysis of Gly–Ala–Ser?

19.42 Would the hydrolysis products of the tripeptide Ala–Ser–Gly be the same or different from the products in problem 19.41? Explain.

19.43 What dipeptides could be produced from the partial hydrolysis of His–Met–Gly–Val?

19.44 What tripeptides could be produced from the partial hydrolysis of Ser–Leu–Gly–Gly–Ala?

19.45 What structural level of a protein is affected by hydrolysis?

19.46 What structural level of a protein is affected by denaturation?

Clinical Applications

19.47 Indicate the changes in the secondary and tertiary structural levels of proteins for each of the following:
   a. An egg placed in water at 100 °C is soft-boiled after 3 min.
   b. Prior to giving an injection, the skin is wiped with an alcohol swab.
   c. Surgical instruments are placed in a 120 °C autoclave.
   d. During surgery, a wound is closed by cauterization (heat).

19.48 Indicate the changes in the secondary and tertiary structural levels of proteins for each of the following:
   a. Tannic acid is placed on a burn.
   b. Milk is heated to 60 °C to make yogurt.
   c. To avoid spoilage, seeds are treated with a solution of $HgCl_2$.
   d. Hamburger is cooked at high temperatures to destroy *E. coli* bacteria that may cause intestinal illness.

Clinical Update
Alzheimer's Diagnosis

In preparation for the PET scan, Victoria gives Edith an injection of a radioactive fluorine compound called Vizamyl (flutemetamol F-18). The activity of the F-18 was 4.0 mCi. The PET scan for Edith started 90 min following the IV injection.

Vizamyl

Fluorine-18, which has a half-life of 110 min, decays by positron emission to stable oxygen-18. Vizamyl specifically binds to the beta-amyloid proteins, which are detected by the PET scans.

Beta-amyloid refers to proteins containing 40 amino acid residues, which are found as amyloid plaque in the brains of Alzheimer's patients.

Edith and her husband return to the clinic to learn the results of her PET scan. A PET scan of the brain indicates the level of plaque formation in the brain of adults with cognitive declines. Victoria shows Edith and her husband the PET scan images and points out dark regions in the brain where the Vizamyl has identified beta-amyloid plaque formation. Edith is diagnosed with early Alzheimer's.

Edith is prescribed an acetylcholinesterase inhibitor that can slow the progression of the disease by keeping levels of the neurotransmitter acetylcholine high, but will not cure it. Edith's husband is relieved to have a diagnosis so that he can better assist Edith in the future.

Normal   Mild cognitive impairment   Alzheimer's disease

 Clinical Applications

19.49 When Edith leaves the clinic 5.5 h after her injection of Vizamyl F-18, what is the activity of the radioisotope in her body?

19.50 Write the balanced nuclear equation for the positron emission by F-18 to form O-18.

19.51 What is the difference between the secondary structures of the beta-amyloid protein in a normal adult brain and the brain of an adult with Alzheimer's disease?

19.52 What causes the formation of beta-amyloid plaques in Alzheimer's disease?

19.53 Determine the amino acid sequence of a peptide section of beta-amyloid containing 10 amino acid residues when it is treated with chymotrypsin and trypsin to give the following fragments:

Reagent	Fragments Produced from Hydrolysis
Chymotrypsin	Glu–Phe Glu–Val Arg–His–Asp–Ser–Gly–Tyr
Trypsin	Glu–Phe–Arg His–Asp–Ser–Gly–Tyr–Glu–Val

19.54 Determine the amino acid sequence of a peptide section of beta-amyloid containing 10 amino acid residues when it is treated with chymotrypsin and trypsin to give the following fragments:

Reagent	Fragments Produced from Hydrolysis
Chymotrypsin	Phe Ala–Glu–Asp His–His–Gln–Lys–Leu–Val–Phe
Trypsin	His–His–Gln–Lys Leu–Val–Phe–Phe–Ala–Glu–Asp

AMINO ACIDS AND PROTEINS

Proteins

contain

Amino Acids

that have

Ammonium, Carboxylate, and R Groups

that form

Zwitterions

at their

Isoelectric Points (pI)

contain peptide bonds between

Amino Acids

in a specific order as the

Primary Structure

and hydrogen bonds as the

Secondary Structure

with interactions that give

Tertiary and Quaternary Structures

undergo

Hydrolysis

to give

Amino Acids

or

Denaturation

when

Proteins Change 2°, 3°, 4° Shape

from

Heat, Acids and Bases, Organic Compounds, Heavy Metal Ions, or Agitation

CHAPTER REVIEW

19.1 Proteins and Amino Acids

LEARNING GOAL Classify proteins by their functions. Give the name and abbreviations for an amino acid, and draw its zwitterion.

- Some proteins are enzymes or hormones, whereas others are important in structure, transport, protection, storage, and muscle contraction.
- A group of 20 amino acids provides the molecular building blocks of proteins.
- Attached to the central α carbon of each amino acid are a hydrogen atom, an ammonium group, a carboxylate group, and a unique R group.
- The R group gives an amino acid the property of being nonpolar, polar, acidic, or basic.

19.2 Amino Acids as Acids and Bases

LEARNING GOAL Using the zwitterion for an amino acid at its isoelectric point, draw its ionized structures at pH values above or below its isoelectric point.

- Amino acids exist as positive ions at pH values below their pI values, and as negative ions at pH values above their pI values.
- At the isoelectric point, ionized amino acids have an overall charge of zero.

19.3 Formation of Peptides

LEARNING GOAL Draw the structure for a peptide, give its three-letter and one-letter abbreviations, and name.

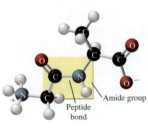

Peptide bond / Amide group

- Peptides form when an amide bond links the carboxylate group of one amino acid and the ammonium group of a second amino acid.
- Long chains of amino acids that are biologically active are called proteins.
- The primary structure of a protein is its sequence of amino acids joined by peptide bonds.
- Peptides are named from the N-terminus by replacing the last syllable of each amino acid name with *yl* followed by the amino acid name of the C-terminus.

19.4 Protein Structure: Primary and Secondary Levels

LEARNING GOAL Describe the primary and secondary structures of a protein.

- Amino acid sequences can be determined by examining overlapping peptide fragments.
- In the secondary structure, hydrogen bonds between atoms in the peptide bonds produce a characteristic shape such as an α helix or β-pleated sheet.
- The most abundant form of protein in the body is collagen, which is composed of fibrils of triple helices that are hydrogen bonded.

Peptide backbone of primary structure

Hydrogen bonds of secondary structure

19.5 Protein Structure: Tertiary and Quaternary Levels

LEARNING GOAL Describe the tertiary and quaternary structures of a protein.

- In globular proteins, the polypeptide chain, including α helical and β-pleated sheet regions, folds upon itself to form a tertiary structure.

C-terminus

N-terminus

- A tertiary structure is stabilized by interactions that push amino acids with hydrophobic residues to the center and pull amino acids with hydrophilic residues to the surface, and by interactions between amino acids with residues that form hydrogen bonds, disulfide bonds, and salt bridges.
- In a quaternary structure, two or more tertiary subunits are joined together for biological activity, held by the same interactions found in tertiary structures.

19.6 Protein Hydrolysis and Denaturation

LEARNING GOAL Describe the hydrolysis and denaturation of proteins.

- Hydrolysis of a protein occurs when peptide bonds in the primary structure are broken by enzyme action to produce amino acids.
- Denaturation of a protein destroys the secondary, tertiary, or quaternary structures of a protein with a loss of biological activity.
- Denaturation is caused by high temperatures, acids or bases, organic compounds, metal ions, or agitation.

Active protein → Heat, acid, base, heavy metal salts, agitation → Denatured protein

KEY TERMS

acidic amino acid An amino acid that has an R group with a carboxylate group ($-COO^-$).

α(alpha) helix A secondary level of protein structure, in which hydrogen bonds connect the $N-H$ of one peptide bond with the $C=O$ of a peptide bond farther along in the chain to form a coiled or corkscrew structure.

amino acid The building block of proteins, consisting of a hydrogen atom, an ammonium group, a carboxylate group, and a unique R group attached to the α carbon.

backbone The repeating sequence of $N-C-C$ atoms from the amino acid residues in a protein.

basic amino acid An amino acid that contains an amine R group.

β(beta)-pleated sheet A secondary level of protein structure that consists of hydrogen bonds between peptide links in parallel polypeptide chains.

C-terminus (C-terminal amino acid) The end amino acid in a peptide chain with a free carboxylate group ($-COO^-$).

collagen The most abundant form of protein in the body, which is composed of fibrils of triple helices that are hydrogen bonded together between $-OH$ groups of hydroxyproline and hydroxylysine.

denaturation The loss of secondary, tertiary, and quaternary protein structure caused by heat, acids, bases, organic compounds, heavy metals, and/or agitation.

disulfide bond Covalent $-S-S-$ bond that forms between the $-SH$ groups of two cysteines in a protein, which stabilizes tertiary and quaternary structures.

essential amino acid Amino acid that must be supplied by the diet because it is not synthesized by the body.

fibrous protein A protein that is insoluble in water; consisting of polypeptide chains with α helices or β-pleated sheets, and comprising the fibers of hair, wool, skin, nails, and silk.

globular protein Protein that acquires a compact shape from attractions between the residues of the amino acids in the protein.

hydrogen bond The interaction between water and the polar residues such as $-OH$, $-NH_3^+$, and $-COO^-$ on the outside surface of a polypeptide chain.

hydrophilic interaction The attraction between polar residues on the protein surface and water.

hydrophobic interaction The attraction between nonpolar residues on the inside of a globular protein.

isoelectric point (pI) The pH at which an amino acid exists as a zwitterion with a net charge of zero.

N-terminus (N-terminal amino acid) The first amino acid in a peptide with a free $-NH_3^+$ group.

nonpolar amino acid Amino acid with a nonpolar R group containing only C and H atoms.

peptide The combination of two or more amino acids joined by peptide bonds; dipeptide, tripeptide, and so on.

peptide bond The amide bond in peptides that joins the carboxylate group of one amino acid with the ammonium group in the next amino acid.

polar amino acid (neutral) Amino acid with a polar R group.

primary structure The specific sequence of the amino acid residues in a protein.

protein A polypeptide of 50 or more amino acid residues that has biological activity.

quaternary structure A protein structure in which two or more protein subunits form an active protein.

salt bridge The attraction between the ionized residues of basic and acidic amino acids in the tertiary structure of a protein.

secondary structure The formation of an α helix or β-pleated sheet by hydrogen bonds.

tertiary structure The folding of the secondary structure of a protein into a compact structure that is stabilized by the interactions of residues such as ionic and disulfide bonds.

triple helix The protein structure found in collagen consisting of three helical polypeptide chains woven together like a braid.

zwitterion The ionized form of an amino acid at its pI that has an ammonium group ($-NH_3^+$) and a carboxylate group ($-COO^-$).

⚛ CORE CHEMISTRY SKILLS

The chapter section containing each Core Chemistry Skill is shown in parentheses at the end of each heading.

Drawing the Zwitterion for an Amino Acid (19.1)

- The central α carbon of each amino acid is bonded to an ammonium group ($-NH_3^+$), a carboxylate group ($-COO^-$), a hydrogen atom, and a unique R group.
- The R group gives an amino acid the property of being nonpolar, polar, acidic, or basic.
- At the isoelectric point (pI), an amino acid has an overall charge of zero.
- Amino acids exist as positive ions at pH values below their pI values, and as negative ions at pH values above their pI values.

Example: Draw the zwitterion for cysteine.

Answer:

$$\begin{array}{c} SH \\ | \\ CH_2 \quad O \\ | \qquad || \\ H_3\overset{+}{N}-C-C-O^- \\ | \\ H \end{array}$$

Identifying the Primary, Secondary, Tertiary, and Quaternary Structures of Proteins (19.4, 19.5)

- The primary structure of a protein is the sequence of amino acids joined by peptide bonds.

- In the secondary structures of proteins, hydrogen bonds between atoms in the peptide bonds produce an alpha helix or a beta-pleated sheet.
- The tertiary structure of a protein is stabilized by residues that form hydrogen bonds, disulfide bonds, and salt bridges, and hydrophobic residues that move to the center and hydrophilic residues that move to the surface.
- In a quaternary structure, two or more tertiary subunits are combined for biological activity, held by the same interactions found in tertiary structures.

Example: Identify the following as characteristic of the primary, secondary, tertiary, or quaternary structure of a protein:
- **a.** The residues of two amino acids interact to form a salt bridge.
- **b.** Eight amino acids form peptide bonds.
- **c.** A polypeptide forms an alpha helix.
- **d.** Two amino acids with hydrophobic residues move toward the inside of the folded protein.
- **e.** A protein with biological activity contains four tertiary polypeptide subunits.

Answer:
- **a.** tertiary, quaternary
- **b.** primary
- **c.** secondary
- **d.** tertiary
- **e.** quaternary

UNDERSTANDING THE CONCEPTS

The chapter sections to review are shown in parentheses at the end of each question.

19.55 Seeds and vegetables are often deficient in one or more essential amino acids. The following table shows which essential amino acids are present in each food. (19.1)

Source	Lysine	Tryptophan	Methionine
Oatmeal	No	Yes	Yes
Rice	No	Yes	Yes
Garbanzo beans	Yes	No	Yes
Lima beans	Yes	No	No
Cornmeal	No	No	Yes

Use the table to decide if each food combination provides the essential amino acids lysine, tryptophan, and methionine.
- **a.** rice and garbanzo beans
- **b.** lima beans and cornmeal
- **c.** a salad of garbanzo beans and lima beans

19.56 Use the table in problem 19.55 to decide if each food combination provides the essential amino acids lysine, tryptophan, and methionine. (19.1)
- **a.** rice and lima beans
- **b.** rice and oatmeal
- **c.** oatmeal and lima beans

Oatmeal is deficient in the essential amino acid lysine.

Use the following condensed structural formulas of cysteine (**1** to **4**) to answer problems 19.57 and 19.58:

$$\begin{array}{c} SH \\ | \\ CH_2 \quad O \\ | \qquad || \\ H_2N-CH-C-O^- \\ \textbf{(1)} \end{array} \qquad \begin{array}{c} SH \\ | \\ CH_2 \quad O \\ | \qquad || \\ H_3\overset{+}{N}-CH-C-OH \\ \textbf{(2)} \end{array}$$

$$\begin{array}{c} SH \\ | \\ CH_2 \quad O \\ | \qquad || \\ H_3\overset{+}{N}-CH-C-O^- \\ \textbf{(3)} \end{array} \qquad \begin{array}{c} SH \\ | \\ CH_2 \quad O \\ | \qquad || \\ H_2N-CH-C-OH \\ \textbf{(4)} \end{array}$$

19.57 If cysteine, an amino acid prevalent in hair, has a pI of 5.1, which condensed structural formula would it have in solutions with each the following pH values? (19.2)
  a. pH = 10.5   **b.** pH = 5.1
  c. pH = 1.8

The proteins in hair contain many cysteine residues that form disulfide bonds.

19.58 If cysteine, an amino acid prevalent in hair, has a pI of 5.1, which condensed structural formula would it have in solutions with each of the following pH values? (19.2)
  a. pH = 2.0   **b.** pH = 3.5
  c. pH = 9.1

19.59 Each of three peptides contains one valine residue and two serine residues. Use their three-letter and one-letter abbreviations to write the three possible peptides. (19.3, 19.4)

19.60 Each of three peptides contains one glycine residue, one alanine residue, and two isoleucine residues. In this peptide, the N-terminus is glycine. Use their three-letter and one-letter abbreviations to write the three possible peptides. (19.3, 19.4)

19.61 Identify the amino acids and the type of interaction that occurs between the following amino acid residues in a tertiary protein structure: (19.5)

  a. $-CH_2-\overset{\overset{\displaystyle O}{\|}}{C}-NH_2$ and $HO-CH_2-$
  b. $-CH_2-SH$ and $HS-CH_2-$
  c. $-CH_2-\overset{\overset{\displaystyle CH_3}{|}}{CH}-CH_3$ and CH_3-

19.62 What type of interaction would you expect between the residues of the following amino acids in a tertiary structure? (19.2, 19.5)
  a. threonine and glutamine
  b. valine and alanine
  c. arginine and glutamate

ADDITIONAL QUESTIONS AND PROBLEMS

19.63 Draw the condensed structural formula for each of the following amino acids at pH 4.0: (19.1, 19.2)
  a. serine   **b.** alanine   **c.** lysine

19.64 Draw the condensed structural formula for each of the following amino acids at pH 11.0 : (19.1, 19.2)
  a. cysteine   **b.** aspartate   **c.** valine

19.65 **a.** Draw the structure for –Ser–Lys–Asp–. (19.3, 19.4, 19.5)
  b. Would you expect to find this segment at the center or at the surface of a globular protein? Why?

19.66 **a.** Draw the structure for –Val–Ala–Leu–. (19.3, 19.4, 19.5)
  b. Would you expect to find this segment at the center or at the surface of a globular protein? Why?

19.67 **a.** Where in the body is collagen found? (19.4)
  b. What type of structure is used to form collagen?

19.68 **a.** What are some functions of collagen? (19.4)
  b. What amino acids give strength to collagen?

19.69 Would you expect a polypeptide with a high content of His, Met, and Leu to have more α-helical sections or β-pleated sheet sections? (19.4)

19.70 Why would a polypeptide with a high content of Val, Pro, and Ser be likely to have more α-helical sections than β-pleated sheet sections? (19.4)

19.71 If serine was replaced by valine in a protein, how would the tertiary structure be affected? (19.5)

19.72 If glycine was replaced by alanine in a protein, how would the tertiary structure be affected? (19.5)

19.73 The amino acids lysine, proline, and glutamate are found in a protein. Which of these amino acids would: (19.5)
  a. be found in hydrophobic regions?
  b. be found in hydrophilic regions?
  c. form salt bridges?

19.74 The amino acids histidine, phenylalanine, and serine are found in a protein. Which of these amino acids would: (19.5)
  a. be found in hydrophobic regions?
  b. be found in hydrophilic regions?
  c. form hydrogen bonds?

19.75 In the preparation of meringue for a pie, a few drops of lemon juice are added and the egg whites are whipped. What causes the meringue to form? (19.6)

19.76 How does denaturation of a protein differ from its hydrolysis? (19.6)

℞ Clinical Applications

19.77 Aspartame, which is used in artificial sweeteners, contains the following dipeptide: (19.3)

Aspartame is an artificial sweetener.

  a. What are the amino acid residues in the dipeptide?
  b. How would you name the dipeptide in aspartame?
  c. Give the three-letter and one-letter abbreviations for the dipeptide in aspartame.

19.78 The tripeptide shown has a strong attraction for Cu^{2+} and is present in human blood and saliva.

a. What are the amino acid residues?
b. How would you name this tripeptide?
c. Give the three-letter and one-letter abbreviations for the tripeptide.

CHALLENGE QUESTIONS

The following groups of questions are related to the topics in this chapter. However, they do not all follow the chapter order, and they require you to combine concepts and skills from several sections. These questions will help you increase your critical thinking skills and prepare for your next exam.

19.79 Indicate the overall charge of each amino acid at the following pH values as 0, 1+, or 1−. (19.1, 19.2)
a. serine at pH 5.7
b. threonine at pH 2.0
c. isoleucine at pH 3.0
d. leucine at pH 9.0

19.80 Indicate the overall charge of each amino acid at the following pH values as 0, 1+, or 1−. (19.1, 19.2)
a. tyrosine at pH 3.0
b. glycine at pH 10.0
c. phenylalanine at pH 8.5
d. methionine at pH 5.7

19.81 What are some differences between each of the following? (19.1, 19.2, 19.3, 19.4, 19.5)
a. secondary and tertiary protein structures
b. essential and nonessential amino acids
c. polar and nonpolar amino acids
d. dipeptides and tripeptides

19.82 What are some differences between each of the following? (19.1, 19.2, 19.3, 19.4, 19.5)
a. an ionic bond (salt bridge) and a disulfide bond
b. fibrous and globular proteins
c. α helix and β-pleated sheet
d. tertiary and quaternary structures of proteins

ANSWERS

Answers to Selected Questions and Problems

19.1 a. transport
b. structural
c. structural
d. enzyme

19.3 a.

19.5 a. nonpolar; hydrophobic
b. polar, neutral; hydrophilic
c. polar, acidic; hydrophilic
d. nonpolar; hydrophobic

19.7 a. histidine
b. valine
c. lysine
d. isoleucine

19.9 a.

19.11 a. Lysine and tryptophan are lacking in corn but supplied by peas; methionine is lacking in peas but supplied by corn.
b. Lysine is lacking in rice but supplied by soy; methionine is lacking in soy but supplied by rice.

19.13 a.

c.
$$\text{CH}_3$$
$$\text{HO}-\text{CH}\quad\text{O}$$
$$\text{H}_3\overset{+}{\text{N}}-\underset{\underset{\text{H}}{|}}{\text{C}}-\overset{\parallel}{\text{C}}-\text{O}^-$$

d.
$$\text{CH}_3\quad\text{O}$$
$$\text{H}_3\overset{+}{\text{N}}-\underset{\underset{\text{H}}{|}}{\text{C}}-\overset{\parallel}{\text{C}}-\text{O}^-$$

19.15 a.
$$\text{CH}_3\;\;\text{CH}_3$$
$$\text{CH}\quad\text{O}$$
$$\text{H}_3\overset{+}{\text{N}}-\underset{\underset{\text{H}}{|}}{\text{C}}-\overset{\parallel}{\text{C}}-\text{OH}$$

b.
$$\text{SH}$$
$$\text{CH}_2\quad\text{O}$$
$$\text{H}_3\overset{+}{\text{N}}-\underset{\underset{\text{H}}{|}}{\text{C}}-\overset{\parallel}{\text{C}}-\text{OH}$$

c.
$$\text{CH}_3$$
$$\text{HO}-\text{CH}\quad\text{O}$$
$$\text{H}_3\overset{+}{\text{N}}-\underset{\underset{\text{H}}{|}}{\text{C}}-\overset{\parallel}{\text{C}}-\text{OH}$$

d.
$$\text{CH}_3\quad\text{O}$$
$$\text{H}_3\overset{+}{\text{N}}-\underset{\underset{\text{H}}{|}}{\text{C}}-\overset{\parallel}{\text{C}}-\text{OH}$$

19.17 a. above its pI   **b.** below its pI   **c.** at its pI

19.19 a.
$$\text{CH}_3\quad\text{O}\qquad\qquad\overset{\displaystyle\text{SH}}{\overset{|}{\text{CH}_2}}\quad\text{O}$$
$$\text{H}_3\overset{+}{\text{N}}-\underset{\underset{\text{H}}{|}}{\text{C}}-\overset{\parallel}{\text{C}}-\text{NH}-\underset{\underset{\text{H}}{|}}{\text{C}}-\overset{\parallel}{\text{C}}-\text{O}^-$$
Ala–Cys, AC

b.
Ser–Phe, SF

c.
$$\text{Gly–Ala–Val, GAV}$$

d.
$$\text{Val–Ile–Trp, VIW}$$

19.21 a. Methionine, Met, is the C-terminus of met-enkephalin.
  b. Tyrosine, Tyr, is the N-terminus of met-enkephalin.
  c. YGGFM

19.23 a.
RIY

b.
VWIS

19.25 Amide bonds, which are covalent, form to connect the amino acids that make up the protein.

19.27 Val–Met–Met, VMM; Met–Val–Met, MVM; Met–Met–Val, MMV

19.29 The primary structure remains unchanged and intact as hydrogen bonds form between carbonyl oxygen atoms and amino hydrogen atoms in the secondary structure.

19.31 In the α helix, hydrogen bonds form between the carbonyl oxygen atom and the amino hydrogen atom in the next turn of the helix. In the β-pleated sheet, hydrogen bonds occur between parallel peptides or sections of a long polypeptide chain.

19.33 Asp–Arg–Val–Tyr–Ile–His–Pro–Phe

19.35 a. disulfide bond   **b.** salt bridge
  c. hydrogen bond   **d.** hydrophobic interaction

19.37 a. cysteine
  b. Leucine and valine will be found on the inside of the protein because they are hydrophobic.
  c. The cysteine and aspartate would be on the outside of the protein because they are polar.
  d. The order of the amino acids (the primary structure) provides the residues whose interactions determine the tertiary structure of the protein.

19.39 a. tertiary and quaternary   **b.** primary
  c. secondary   **d.** secondary

19.41 The products would be the amino acids glycine, alanine, and serine.

19.43 His–Met, Met–Gly, Gly–Val

19.45 Hydrolysis splits the peptide bonds in the primary structure.

19.47 a. Placing an egg in boiling water coagulates the proteins of the egg because the heat disrupts hydrogen bonds and hydrophobic interactions.

   b. The alcohol on the swab coagulates the proteins of any bacteria present by forming hydrogen bonds and disrupting hydrophobic interactions.

   c. The heat from an autoclave will coagulate the proteins of any bacteria on the surgical instruments by disrupting hydrogen bonds and hydrophobic interactions.

   d. Heat will coagulate the surrounding proteins to close the wound by disrupting hydrogen bonds and hydrophobic interactions.

19.49 0.50 mCi

19.51 The secondary structure of beta-amyloid protein in the brain of a normal person is alpha-helical whereas the secondary structure in the brain of a person with Alzheimer's changes to beta-pleated sheet.

19.53 Glu–Phe–Arg–His–Asp–Ser–Gly–Tyr–Glu–Val

19.55 a. yes   **b.** no   **c.** no

19.57 a. (1)   **b.** (3)   **c.** (2)

19.59 Val–Ser–Ser (VSS), Ser–Ser–Val (SSV), Ser–Val–Ser (SVS)

19.61 a. asparagine and serine, hydrogen bond
   b. cysteine and cysteine, disulfide bond
   c. leucine and alanine, hydrophobic interaction

19.63 a.

$$H_3\overset{+}{N}-\underset{\underset{H}{|}}{\overset{\overset{CH_2}{|}}{C}}-\overset{O}{\overset{||}{C}}-OH \quad\quad (with\ OH\ on\ CH_2)$$

   b.

$$H_3\overset{+}{N}-\underset{\underset{H}{|}}{\overset{\overset{CH_3}{|}}{C}}-\overset{O}{\overset{||}{C}}-OH$$

   c.

$$H_3\overset{+}{N}-\underset{\underset{H}{|}}{\overset{\overset{CH_2-CH_2-CH_2-CH_2-\overset{+}{N}H_3}{|}}{C}}-\overset{O}{\overset{||}{C}}-OH$$

19.65 a.

$$H_3\overset{+}{N}-\underset{H}{C}-\overset{O}{\overset{||}{C}}-NH-\underset{H}{C}-\overset{O}{\overset{||}{C}}-NH-\underset{H}{C}-\overset{O}{\overset{||}{C}}-O^-$$

   b. This segment contains polar residues, which would be found on the surface of a globular protein where they hydrogen bond with water.

19.67 a. Collagen is found in connective tissue, blood vessels, skin, tendons, ligaments, the cornea of the eye, and cartilage.
   b. A triple helix is the structure found in collagen.

19.69 α helical

19.71 Serine is a polar amino acid, whereas valine is a nonpolar amino acid. Serine would move to the outside surface of the protein where it can form hydrogen bonds with water. However, valine, which is nonpolar, would be pushed to the center of the tertiary structure where it is stabilized by forming hydrophobic interactions.

19.73 a. proline   **b.** lysine, glutamate
   c. lysine, glutamate

19.75 The acid from the lemon juice and the mechanical whipping (agitation) denature the proteins of the egg white, which turn into solids as meringue.

19.77 a. aspartate and phenylalanine
   b. aspartylphenylalanine
   c. Asp–Phe, DF

19.79 a. 0   **c.** 1+
   b. 1+   **d.** 1−

19.81 a. In the secondary structure of proteins, hydrogen bonds form an alpha helix or a pleated sheet; the tertiary structure is determined by hydrogen bonds as well as by disulfide bonds and salt bridges.

   b. Nonessential amino acids can be synthesized by the body; essential amino acids must be supplied by the diet.

   c. Polar amino acids have hydrophilic R groups, whereas nonpolar amino acids have hydrophobic R groups.

   d. A dipeptide contains two amino acids, but a tripeptide contains three amino acids.

20

Enzymes and Vitamins

NOAH, A 6-YEAR-OLD BOY, IS HAVING SEVERE

diarrhea, abdominal pain, and intestinal growling two hours after he eats. Noah is also underweight for his age. His mother makes an appointment for Noah to see Emma, his physician assistant. Emma suspects that Noah may be lactose intolerant, which occurs due to an enzyme deficiency of lactase. A hydrogen breath test (HBT) is scheduled for Noah in a few days. Until then, Emma suggests that Noah's mother limit the amount of milk and milk products in Noah's diet.

The disaccharide in milk is lactose, which is broken down by *lactase* in the intestinal tract to glucose and galactose that are a source of energy. The enzyme lactase is a biological catalyst that is also a protein. When there is a lack of the enzyme, lactose is not broken down and remains in the intestinal tract. In the intestines, the lactose undergoes fermentation by bacteria to products that include gases such as H_2, CH_4, and CO_2, causing nausea, abdominal cramps, and diarrhea. The severity of the symptoms depends on how much lactose is present in the food and how much lactase a person produces.

CAREER Physician Assistant

A physician assistant, commonly referred to as a PA, helps a doctor by examining and treating patients, as well as prescribing medications. Many physician assistants take on the role of the primary caregiver. Their duties would also include obtaining patient medical records and histories, diagnosing illnesses, educating and counseling patients, and referring the patient, when needed, to a specialist. Due to this diversity, physician assistants must be knowledgeable about a variety of medical conditions. Physician assistants may also help the doctor during major surgery.

Physician assistants can work in clinics, hospitals, health maintenance organizations, private practices, or take on a more administrative role that involves hiring new PAs and acting as the go-between for the hospital and patient or their family.

Every second, thousands of chemical reactions occur in the cells of our body. For example, many reactions occur to digest the food we eat, convert the products to chemical energy, and synthesize proteins and other macromolecules in our cells. In the laboratory, we can carry out chemical reactions that hydrolyze polysaccharides, fats, or proteins, but we must use a strong acid or base, high temperatures, and long reaction times. In the cells of our body, these reactions must take place at much faster rates that meet our physiological and metabolic needs. To make this happen, enzymes catalyze the chemical reactions in our cells, with a different enzyme for each reaction. Digestive enzymes in the mouth, stomach, and small intestine catalyze the hydrolysis of carbohydrate, fats, and proteins. Enzymes in the mitochondria extract energy from biomolecules to give us energy.

Every enzyme responds to what comes into the cells and to what the cells need. Enzymes keep reactions going when our cells need certain products, and turn off reactions when those products are not needed.

Many enzymes require cofactors to function properly. Cofactors are inorganic metal ions (minerals) or organic compounds such as vitamins. We obtain minerals such as zinc (Zn^{2+}) and iron (Fe^{3+}) and vitamins from our diets. A lack of minerals and vitamins can lead to certain nutritional diseases. For example, rickets is a deficiency of vitamin D, and scurvy occurs when a diet is low in vitamin C.

LOOKING AHEAD

20.1 Enzymes and Enzyme Action 723

20.2 Classification of Enzymes 726

♡ Chemistry Link to Health *Isoenzymes As Diagnostic Tools* 728

20.3 Factors Affecting Enzyme Activity 729

20.4 Regulation of Enzyme Activity 732

20.5 Enzyme Inhibition 735

20.6 Enzyme Cofactors and Vitamins 739

℞ Clinical Applications 729, 732, 735, 739, 744, 745, 748, 749, 750

℞ Clinical Update *Noah's Diet for Lactose Intolerance* 744

CHAPTER READINESS*

⚛ CORE CHEMISTRY SKILLS

• Interpreting Graphs (1.4E)

• Identifying the Primary, Secondary, Tertiary, and Quaternary Structures of Proteins (19.4, 19.5)

*These Core Chemistry Skills from previous chapters are listed here for your review as you proceed to the new material in this chapter.

20.1 Enzymes and Enzyme Action

Biological catalysts known as **enzymes** are needed for most chemical reactions that take place in the body. A *catalyst* increases the rate of a reaction by changing the way a reaction takes place but is itself not changed at the end of the reaction. An uncatalyzed reaction in a cell may take place eventually, but not at a rate fast enough for survival. For example, the acid in our stomachs would hydrolyze proteins in our diets without a catalyst, but without digestive enzymes, we would be unable to form amino acids fast enough to meet the body's requirements. The chemical reactions in our cells occur at incredibly fast rates under the mild conditions of pH 7.4 and a body temperature of 37 °C.

Enzymes act as catalysts by lowering the activation energy for a chemical reaction (see Figure 20.1). Less energy is required to convert reactant molecules to products, which increases the rate of a biochemical reaction compared to the rate of the uncatalyzed reaction. The rates of enzyme-catalyzed reactions are much faster than the rates of the uncatalyzed reactions. Some enzymes can increase the rate of a biological reaction by a factor of a billion, a trillion, or even a hundred million trillion compared to the rate of the uncatalyzed reaction. For example, an enzyme in the blood called carbonic anhydrase catalyzes the rapid interconversion of carbon dioxide and water to bicarbonate and H^+. In one second, one molecule of carbonic anhydrase can catalyze the reaction of about one million molecules of carbon dioxide. Carbonic anhydrase also catalyzes the reverse reaction, converting bicarbonate and H^+ to carbon dioxide and water.

$$CO_2 + H_2O \underset{}{\overset{\text{Carbonic anhydrase}}{\rightleftharpoons}} HCO_3^- + H^+$$

LEARNING GOAL

Describe enzymes and their role in enzyme-catalyzed reactions.

FIGURE 20.1 ▶ The enzyme carbonic anhydrase lowers the activation energy for the reversible reaction that converts CO_2 and H_2O to bicarbonate and H^+.

Q Why are enzymes needed in biological reactions?

723

Active site

Substrate

■	Lactose
■	Trp
■	Tyr
■	Gln
■	Glu
■	His
■	Asn

Amino acids in active site

FIGURE 20.2 ▶ Enzymes like lactase have an active site where the substrate fits for catalysis to occur. The quaternary structure of lactase consists of four subunits. The substrate, lactose (gray), is held in place in the active site by hydrogen bonds with amino acid side chains.

Q Why does an enzyme catalyze a reaction for only certain substrates?

Enzymes and Active Sites

Nearly all enzymes are globular proteins. Each has a unique three-dimensional shape that recognizes and binds a small group of reacting molecules, which are called **substrates**. The tertiary structure of an enzyme plays an important role in how that enzyme catalyzes reactions.

In a catalyzed reaction, an enzyme must bind to a substrate in a way that favors catalysis. A typical enzyme is much larger than its substrate. However, within the enzyme's tertiary structure is a region called the **active site**, in which the substrate or substrates are held while the reaction takes place. The active site is often a small pocket within the larger tertiary structure that closely fits the substrate. Within the active site of an enzyme, residues of specific amino acids interact with functional groups of the substrate to form hydrogen bonds, salt bridges, and hydrophobic interactions.

Figure 20.2 shows the folded structure of the enzyme lactase. Lactase hydrolyzes the disaccharide lactose to the monosaccharides glucose and galactose. The protein backbone of lactase is represented by a ribbon. As lactase folds into its tertiary structure, the pocket that forms in one part of its surface is its active site. This is where the hydrolysis of lactose occurs. At least six residues are involved in the binding of the lactose substrate to the lactase enzyme.

Like a hand in a glove, lactose, the substrate for lactase, fits snugly into its active site. Other disaccharides will not fit into the active site. Enzymes demonstrate various types of *substrate specificity*. Three categories of substrate specificity are outlined in Table 20.1.

TABLE 20.1 Types of Substrate Specificity

Type	Reaction Type	Example
Absolute	catalyzes one type of reaction for one substrate	Urease catalyzes only the hydrolysis of urea.
Group	catalyzes one type of reaction for similar substrates	Hexokinase adds a phosphate group to hexoses.
Linkage	catalyzes one type of reaction for a specific type of bond	Chymotrypsin catalyzes the hydrolysis of peptide bonds.

> ▶ **SAMPLE PROBLEM 20.1** The Enzyme Active Site
>
> What is the function of the active site in an enzyme?
>
> **SOLUTION**
>
> The R groups of amino acid residues within the active site of an enzyme bind the substrate by forming hydrogen bonds, salt bridges, and hydrophobic interactions and catalyze the reaction.
>
> **STUDY CHECK 20.1**
>
> Which is a larger molecule, glucose or hexokinase?
>
> **ANSWER**
>
> Hexokinase. Typically, enzymes are large protein molecules containing many amino acid residues, and substrates are small molecules such as the monosaccharide glucose.

This ribbon representation shows the change in the shape of the enzyme hexokinase as the glucose molecule binds to its active site where it undergoes phosphorylation.

Enzyme-Catalyzed Reaction

The combination of an enzyme and a substrate within the active site forms an **enzyme–substrate (ES) complex** that catalyzes the reaction with lower activation energy. Within the active site, R groups on the amino acid residues catalyze the reaction to form the **enzyme–product (EP) complex**. Then the products are released from the enzyme so it can bind to another substrate molecule. We can write the catalyzed reaction of an enzyme (E) with a substrate (S) to form product (P) as follows:

E + S	$\rightleftharpoons$	ES complex	$\longrightarrow$	EP complex	$\longrightarrow$	E + P
Enzyme and Substrate		Enzyme–Substrate Complex		Enzyme–Product Complex		Enzyme and Product

In the hydrolysis of the disaccharide lactose by the enzyme lactase, a molecule of lactose binds to the active site of lactase. In this ES complex, the glycosidic bond of lactose is in a position that is favorable for *hydrolysis*, which is the splitting by water of a large molecule into smaller parts. Groups on the amino acid residues in the active site then catalyze the hydrolysis of lactose, which produces the monosaccharides glucose and galactose. Because the structures of the products are no longer attracted to the active site, they are released, which allows the enzyme lactase to react with another lactose molecule (see Figure 20.3).

E + S	$\rightleftharpoons$	ES complex	$\longrightarrow$	EP complex	$\longrightarrow$	E + P
Lactase + Lactose		Lactase–Lactose Complex		Lactase–Glucose–Galactose Complex		Lactase + Glucose + Galactose

Models of Enzyme Action

An early theory of enzyme action, called the *lock-and-key model*, described the active site as having a rigid, nonflexible shape. According to the lock-and-key model, the shape of the active site was analogous to a lock, and its substrate was the key that specifically fit that lock. However, this model was a static one that did not include the flexibility of the tertiary shape of an enzyme and the way we now know that the active site can adjust to the shape of a substrate.

In the dynamic model of enzyme action, called the **induced-fit model**, the flexibility of the active site allows it to adapt to the shape of the substrate. At the same time, the shape of the substrate may be modified to better fit the geometry of the active site. As a result, the fit of both the active site and the substrate provides the best alignment for the catalysis of the substrate. In the induced-fit model, substrate and enzyme work together to acquire a geometrical arrangement that lowers the activation energy (see Figure 20.3).

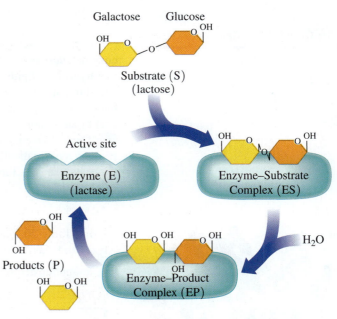

FIGURE 20.3 ▶ A flexible active site in lactase and the flexible substrate lactose adjust to provide the best fit for the hydrolysis reaction. Once the disaccharide is hydrolyzed, the monosaccharide products are released from the enzyme, which is ready to bind another lactose.

◉ Why does the enzyme-catalyzed hydrolysis of lactose go faster than the hydrolysis of lactose in a test tube?

> ▶ **SAMPLE PROBLEM 20.2** The Induced-Fit Model
>
> How does the induced-fit model explain the binding of the substrate at the active site?
>
> **SOLUTION**
>
> In the induced-fit model, the shapes of the substrate and the active site adjust so that the substrate is in the optimum position needed for the enzyme to carry out reaction catalysis.
>
> **STUDY CHECK 20.2**
>
> How does the lock-and-key model explain the binding of the substrate at an active site?
>
> **ANSWER**
>
> In the lock-and-key model, the substrate fits perfectly into the active site of the enzyme similar to a key fitting into a lock. We know today that most enzymes do not have a rigid active site and that the active site flexes to accommodate the chemical reaction being catalyzed.

QUESTIONS AND PROBLEMS

20.1 Enzymes and Enzyme Action

LEARNING GOAL Describe enzymes and their role in enzyme-catalyzed reactions.

20.1 Why do chemical reactions in the body require enzymes?

20.2 How do enzymes make chemical reactions in the body proceed at faster rates?

20.3 Match the terms, (1) enzyme–substrate complex, (2) enzyme, and (3) substrate, with each of the following:
a. has a tertiary structure that recognizes the substrate
b. the combination of an enzyme with the substrate
c. has a structure that fits the active site of an enzyme

20.4 Match the terms, (1) active site, (2) induced-fit model, and (3) lock-and-key model with each of the following:
a. an active site that has a rigid shape
b. the portion of an enzyme where catalytic activity occurs
c. an active site that adapts to the shape of a substrate

20.5 **a.** Write an equation that represents an enzyme-catalyzed reaction.
b. How is the active site different from the whole enzyme structure?

20.6 **a.** How does an enzyme speed up the reaction of a substrate?
b. After the products have formed, what happens to the enzyme?

LEARNING GOAL

Classify enzymes and give their names.

⚛ **CORE CHEMISTRY SKILL**

Classifying Enzymes

The ribbon structure for alanine transaminase, an aminotransferase, contains 495 amino acid residues.

20.2 Classification of Enzymes

The names of enzymes describe the compound or the reaction that is catalyzed. The actual names of enzymes are derived by replacing the end of the name of the reaction or reacting compound with the suffix *ase*. For example, an *oxidase* is an enzyme that catalyzes an oxidation reaction, and a *dehydrogenase* removes hydrogen atoms. These enzymes are classified as *oxidoreductases* because they catalyze the loss or gain of hydrogen or oxygen.

Often the name of the enzyme can be used to predict its class and function. The enzyme *sucrase* is a catalyst in the hydrolysis of sucrose, and *lipase* catalyzes reactions that hydrolyze lipids. Some enzymes use names that end in the suffix *in*, such as *papain* found in papaya; *rennin* found in milk; and *pepsin* and *trypsin*, enzymes that catalyze the hydrolysis of proteins. These enzymes are classified as *hydrolases* because they use water to split large molecules into smaller ones.

The Enzyme Commission of the International Union of Biochemistry and Molecular Biology systematically classifies enzymes according to the six general types of reactions they catalyze (see Table 20.2).

SAMPLE PROBLEM 20.3 Classifying Enzymes

Using Table 20.2, identify the chemical reaction each of the following enzymes catalyzes and classify the enzyme:

a. aminotransferase

b. lactate dehydrogenase

SOLUTION

ANALYZE THE PROBLEM	Given	Need
	name of the enzyme	type of reaction catalyzed, class of enzyme

a. An aminotransferase catalyzes the transfer of an amino group between two substrates, which is classified as a transferase.
b. Lactate dehydrogenase catalyzes the removal of two H atoms from lactate, which is classified as an oxidoreductase.

STUDY CHECK 20.3

What is the name and classification of the enzyme that catalyzes the hydrolysis of lipids?

ANSWER

An enzyme that hydrolyzes a lipid is a lipase, which is classified as a hydrolase.

TABLE 20.2 Classification of Enzymes

Class	Examples of Reaction Catalyzed
1. Oxidoreductases	

Catalyze oxidation–reduction reactions

Oxidases catalyze the oxidation of a substrate.

Dehydrogenases catalyze the removal or addition of two H atoms and utilize a coenzyme.

$$CH_3-CH_2-OH + NAD^+ \xrightarrow{\text{Alcohol dehydrogenase}} CH_3-\overset{\displaystyle O}{\overset{\|}{C}}-H + NADH + H^+$$

Ethanol — Coenzyme — Ethanal — Coenzyme

2. Transferases

Catalyze the transfer of a functional group between two compounds

Transaminases catalyze the transfer of an amino group from one substrate to another ATP is utilized.

Kinases catalyze the transfer of phosphate groups from one substrate to another.

$$CH_3-\overset{\overset{\displaystyle +}{\overset{NH_3}{|}}}{CH}-COO^- + {}^-OOC-\overset{\displaystyle O}{\overset{\|}{C}}-CH_2-CH_2-COO^- \underset{\text{Alanine transaminase}}{\rightleftharpoons} CH_3-\overset{\displaystyle O}{\overset{\|}{C}}-COO^- + {}^-OOC-\overset{\overset{\displaystyle +}{\overset{NH_3}{|}}}{CH}-CH_2-CH_2-COO^-$$

Alanine — α-Ketoglutarate — Pyruvate — Glutamate

3. Hydrolases

Catalyze hydrolysis (add H_2O) reactions that split a compound into two products

Proteases catalyze the hydrolysis of peptide bonds in proteins.

Lipases catalyze the hydrolysis of ester bonds in lipids.

Nucleases catalyze the hydrolysis of the phosphate ester bonds in nucleic acids.

$$-NH-\overset{\overset{\displaystyle R}{|}}{CH}-\overset{\displaystyle O}{\overset{\|}{C}}-NH-\overset{\overset{\displaystyle R}{|}}{CH}-COO^- + H_2O \xrightarrow{\text{Protease}} -NH-\overset{\overset{\displaystyle R}{|}}{CH}-\overset{\displaystyle O}{\overset{\|}{C}}-O^- + H_3\overset{+}{N}-\overset{\overset{\displaystyle R}{|}}{CH}-COO^-$$

Polypeptide — Shorter polypeptide — Amino acid

4. Lyases

Catalyze the addition or removal of a group without hydrolysis

Decarboxylases catalyze the removal of CO_2 from a substrate.

Deaminases catalyze the removal of NH_3 from a substrate.

Dehydratases catalyze the removal of H_2O from a substrate.

Hydratases catalyze the addition of H_2O to a substrate.

$$CH_3-\overset{\displaystyle O}{\overset{\|}{C}}-COO^- + H^+ \xrightarrow{\text{Pyruvate decarboxylase}} CH_3-\overset{\displaystyle O}{\overset{\|}{C}}-H + CO_2$$

Pyruvate — Ethanal — Carbon dioxide

5. Isomerases

Catalyze the rearrangement (isomerization) of atoms within a substrate

Isomerases catalyze rearrangement reactions.

Epimerases catalyze rearrangements between carbohydrates.

$$\underset{\text{Maleate}}{\overset{\displaystyle {}^-OOC \quad COO^-}{\underset{\displaystyle H \qquad H}{C=C}}} \underset{\text{isomerase}}{\overset{\text{Maleate}}{\rightleftharpoons}} \underset{\text{Fumarate}}{\overset{\displaystyle {}^-OOC \quad H}{\underset{\displaystyle H \qquad COO^-}{C=C}}}$$

6. Ligases

Catalyze the joining of two substrates using ATP energy (see Section 22.2)

Synthetases catalyze the formation of a bond between two substrates utilizing the energy of ATP.

Carboxylases catalyze the formation of a bond between CO_2 and a substrate utilizing the energy of ATP.

$${}^-OOC-\overset{\displaystyle O}{\overset{\|}{C}}-CH_3 + CO_2 + ATP \xrightarrow{\text{Pyruvate carboxylase}} {}^-OOC-\overset{\displaystyle O}{\overset{\|}{C}}-CH_2-COO^- + ADP + P_i + H^+$$

Pyruvate — Oxaloacetate

Chemistry Link to **Health**

Isoenzymes As Diagnostic Tools

Isoenzymes are different forms of an enzyme that catalyze the same reaction in different cells or tissues of the body. They consist of quaternary structures with slight variations in the amino acids in the polypeptide subunits. For example, there are five isoenzymes of *lactate dehydrogenase* (LDH) that catalyze the conversion between lactate and pyruvate.

$$\underset{\text{Lactate}}{CH_3-\underset{\underset{OH}{|}}{CH}-COO^-} + NAD^+ \underset{\xleftarrow{\hspace{1cm}}}{\overset{\text{Lactate}}{\underset{\text{dehydrogenase}}{\xrightarrow{\hspace{1cm}}}}} \underset{\text{Pyruvate}}{CH_3-\underset{\overset{O}{||}}{C}-COO^-} + NADH + H^+$$

A myocardial infarction may be indicated by an increase in the levels of creatine kinase (CK) and lactate dehydrogenase (LDH).

Each LDH isoenzyme contains a mix of polypeptide subunits, M and H. In the liver and muscle, lactate is converted to pyruvate by the LDH_5 isoenzyme with four M subunits designated M_4. In the heart, the same reaction is catalyzed by the LDH_1 isoenzyme (H_4) containing four H subunits. Different combinations of the M and H subunits are found in the LDH isoenzymes of the brain, red blood cells, kidneys, and white blood cells.

The different forms of an enzyme allow a medical diagnosis of damage or disease to a particular organ or tissue. In healthy tissues, isoenzymes function within the cells. However, when a disease damages a particular organ, cells die, which releases their contents including the isoenzymes into the blood. Measurements of the elevated levels of specific isoenzymes in the blood serum help to identify the disease and its location in the body. For example, an elevation in serum LDH_5, M_4, indicates liver damage or disease. When a *myocardial infarction* or heart attack damages heart muscle, an increase in the level of LDH_1 (H_4) isoenzyme is detected in the blood serum (see Table 20.3).

Isoenzymes of Lactate Dehydrogenase	Highest Levels Found in the Following:
H M	
H_4 (LDH_1)	Heart, kidneys
H_3M (LDH_2)	Red blood cells, heart, kidney, brain
H_2M_2 (LDH_3)	Brain, lung, white blood cells
HM_3 (LDH_4)	Lung, skeletal muscle
M_4 (LDH_5)	Skeletal muscle, liver

The different isoenzymes of lactate dehydrogenase (LDH) indicate damage to different organs in the body.

Another isoenzyme used diagnostically is creatine kinase (CK), which consists of two types of polypeptide subunits. Subunit B is prevalent in the brain, and subunit M predominates in muscle. Normally CK_3 (subunits MM) is present at low levels in the blood serum. However, in a patient who has suffered a myocardial infarction, the level of CK_2 (subunits MB) is elevated within 4 to 6 h and reaches a peak in about 24 h. Table 20.4 lists some enzymes used to diagnose tissue damage and diseases of certain organs.

TABLE 20.3 Isoenzymes of Lactate Dehydrogenase and Creatine Kinase

Isoenzyme	Abundant in	Subunits
Lactate Dehydrogenase (LDH)		
LDH_1	Heart, kidneys	H_4
LDH_2	Red blood cells, heart, kidney, brain	H_3M
LDH_3	Brain, lung, white blood cells	H_2M_2
LDH_4	Lung, skeletal muscle	HM_3
LDH_5	Skeletal muscle, liver	M_4
Creatine Kinase (CK)		
CK_1	Brain, lung	BB
CK_2	Heart muscle	MB
CK_3	Skeletal muscle, red blood cells	MM

TABLE 20.4 Serum Enzymes Used in Diagnosis of Tissue Damage

Condition	Diagnostic Enzymes Elevated
Heart attack or liver disease (cirrhosis, hepatitis)	Lactate dehydrogenase (LDH) Aspartate transaminase (AST)
Heart attack	Creatine kinase (CK)
Hepatitis	Alanine transaminase (ALT)
Liver (carcinoma) or bone disease (rickets)	Alkaline phosphatase (ALP)
Pancreatic disease	Pancreatic amylase (PA) Cholinesterase (CE) Lipase (LPS)
Prostate carcinoma	Acid phosphatase (ACP) Prostate-specific antigen (PSA)

QUESTIONS AND PROBLEMS

20.2 Classification of Enzymes

LEARNING GOAL Classify enzymes and give their names.

20.7 What type of reaction is catalyzed by each of the following classes of enzymes?
  a. oxidoreductases   **b.** transferases
  c. hydrolases

20.8 What type of reaction is catalyzed by each of the following classes of enzymes?
  a. lyases   **b.** isomerases
  c. ligases

20.9 What is the name of the class of enzymes that catalyzes each of the following reactions?
  a. hydrolyzing sucrose
  b. adding oxygen
  c. converting glucose-6-phosphate to fructose-6-phosphate
  d. moving an amino group from one molecule to another

20.10 What is the name of the class of enzymes that catalyzes each of the following reactions?
  a. adding water to a double bond
  b. removing hydrogen atoms from a substrate
  c. splitting peptide bonds in proteins
  d. converting a tertiary alcohol to a secondary alcohol

20.11 Classify the enzyme that catalyzes each of the following reactions:

a. $CH_3-\overset{\overset{O}{\|}}{C}-COO^- + H^+ \longrightarrow CH_3-\overset{\overset{O}{\|}}{C}-H + CO_2$

b. $CH_3-\overset{\overset{+}{NH_3}}{\underset{|}{C}H}-COO^- + {}^-OOC-\overset{\overset{O}{\|}}{C}-CH_2-CH_3 \rightleftharpoons$
$CH_3-\overset{\overset{O}{\|}}{C}-COO^- + {}^-OOC-\overset{\overset{+}{NH_3}}{\underset{|}{C}H}-CH_2-CH_3$

20.12 Classify the enzyme that catalyzes each of the following reactions:

a. $CH_3-\overset{\overset{O}{\|}}{C}-COO^- + CO_2 + ATP \longrightarrow$
${}^-OOC-CH_2-\overset{\overset{O}{\|}}{C}-COO^- + ADP + P_i + H^+$

b. $CH_3-CH_2-OH + NAD^+ \longrightarrow$
$CH_3-\overset{\overset{O}{\|}}{C}-H + NADH + H^+$

20.13 Predict the name of the enzyme that catalyzes each of the following reactions:
  a. oxidizes succinate
  b. combines glutamate and ammonia to form glutamine
  c. removes 2H from an alcohol

20.14 Predict the name of the enzyme that catalyzes each of the following reactions:
  a. hydrolyzes sucrose
  b. transfers an amino group from aspartate
  c. removes a carboxylate group from pyruvate

℞ Clinical Applications

20.15 Name the enzyme that is indicated by each of the following abbreviations:
  a. PSA   **b.** CK   **c.** CE

20.16 Name the enzyme that is indicated by each of the following abbreviations:
  a. ALP   **b.** AST   **c.** PA

20.17 What are isoenzymes?

20.18 How is the LDH isoenzyme in the heart different from the LDH isoenzyme in the liver?

20.19 A patient arrives in the emergency room complaining of chest pains. What enzymes might be present in the patient's blood serum?

20.20 A patient who is an alcoholic has elevated levels of LDH and AST. What condition might be indicated?

20.3 Factors Affecting Enzyme Activity

The **activity** of an enzyme describes how fast an enzyme catalyzes the reaction that converts a substrate to product. This activity is strongly affected by reaction conditions, which include the temperature, pH, concentration of the enzyme, and concentration of the substrate.

LEARNING GOAL

Describe the effect of changes of temperature, pH, concentration of enzyme, and concentration of substrate on enzyme activity.

⚛ CORE CHEMISTRY SKILL

Identifying Factors Affecting Enzyme Activity

Temperature

Enzymes are very sensitive to temperature. At low temperatures, most enzymes show little activity because there is not a sufficient amount of energy for the catalyzed reaction to take place. At higher temperatures, enzyme activity increases as reacting molecules move faster causing more collisions with enzymes. Enzymes are most active at **optimum temperature**, which is 37 °C, or body temperature, for most enzymes (see Figure 20.4). At temperatures above 50 °C, the tertiary structures, and thus the shapes of most proteins are

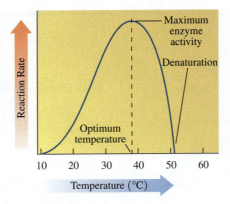

FIGURE 20.4 ▶ An enzyme attains maximum activity at its optimum temperature, usually 37 °C. Lower temperatures slow the rate of reaction, and temperatures above 50 °C denature most enzymes, with a loss of catalytic activity.

Q Why is 37 °C the optimum temperature for many enzymes?

Thermophiles survive in the high temperatures (50 °C to 120 °C) of a hot spring.

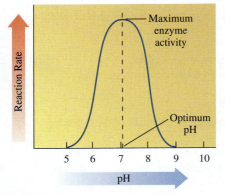

FIGURE 20.5 ▶ Enzymes are most active at their optimum pH. At a higher or lower pH, denaturation of the enzyme causes a loss of catalytic activity.

Q Why does the digestive enzyme pepsin have an optimum pH of 2.0?

destroyed causing a loss of enzyme activity. For this reason, equipment in hospitals and laboratories is sterilized in autoclaves where the high temperatures denature the enzymes in harmful bacteria.

Certain organisms, known as thermophiles, live in environments where temperatures range from 50 °C to 120 °C. In order to survive in these extreme conditions, thermophiles have enzymes with tertiary structures that are not destroyed by such high temperatures. Some research shows that their enzymes are very similar to ordinary enzymes except that they contain more hydrogen bonds and salt bridges that stabilize their tertiary structures at high temperatures and resist unfolding and the loss of enzymatic activity.

pH

Enzymes are most active at their **optimum pH**, the pH that maintains the proper tertiary structure of the protein (see Figure 20.5). If a pH value is above or below the optimum pH, the interactions between the R groups of amino acid residues are disrupted, which destroys the tertiary structure and the active site. As a result, the enzyme no longer binds substrate, and no catalysis occurs. Small changes in pH are reversible, which allows an enzyme to regain its tertiary or quaternary structure and biological activity. However, large variations from optimum pH permanently destroy the structure of the enzyme.

Enzymes in most cells have optimum pH values at physiological pH around 7.4. However, enzymes in the stomach have a low optimum pH because they hydrolyze proteins at the acidic pH in the stomach. For example, pepsin, a digestive enzyme in the stomach, has an optimum pH of 1.5 to 2.0. Between meals, the pH in the stomach is 4 to 5, and pepsin shows little or no digestive activity. When food enters the stomach, the secretion of HCl lowers the pH to about 2, which activates the digestive enzyme pepsin. Table 20.5 lists the optimum pH values for selected enzymes.

TABLE 20.5 Optimum pH for Selected Enzymes

Enzyme	Location	Substrate	Optimum pH
Pepsin	stomach	peptide bonds	1.5–2.0
Lactase	GI tract	lactose	6.0
Sucrase	small intestine	sucrose	6.2
Amylase	pancreas	amylose	6.7–7.0
Urease	liver	urea	7.0
Trypsin	small intestine	peptide bonds	7.7–8.0
Lipase	pancreas	lipid (ester bonds)	8.0
Arginase	liver	arginine	9.7

Enzyme and Substrate Concentration

In any catalyzed reaction, the substrate must first bind with the enzyme to form the enzyme–substrate complex. For a particular substrate concentration, an increase in enzyme concentration increases the rate of the catalyzed reaction. At higher enzyme concentrations, more molecules are available to bind substrate and catalyze the reaction. As long as the substrate concentration is greater than the enzyme concentration, there is a direct relationship between the enzyme concentration and enzyme activity (see Figure 20.6a). In most enzyme-catalyzed reactions, the concentration of the substrate is much greater than the concentration of the enzyme.

When the enzyme concentration is kept constant, the addition of more substrate will increase the rate of the reaction. If the substrate concentration is high, the substrate can bind with all of the available enzyme molecules. Then the rate of the reaction reaches its maximum, and the addition of more substrate does not increase the rate further (see Figure 20.6b).

Explore Your World
Enzyme Activity

The enzymes on the surface of a freshly cut apple, avocado, or banana react with oxygen in the air to turn the surface brown. An antioxidant, such as vitamin C in lemon juice, prevents the browning reaction. Cut an apple, an avocado, or a banana into several slices. Place one slice in a plastic zipper bag, squeeze out all the air, and close the zipper lock. Dip another slice in lemon juice. Sprinkle another slice with a crushed vitamin C tablet. Leave another slice alone as a control. Observe the surface of each of your samples. Record your observations immediately, then every hour for 6 h or longer.

Questions

1. Which slice(s) shows the most oxidation (a brown color)?
2. Which slice(s) shows little or no oxidation?
3. How was the browning reaction on each slice affected by treatment with an antioxidant?

FIGURE 20.6 ▶ **(a)** Increasing the enzyme concentration increases the rate of reaction. **(b)** Increasing the substrate concentration increases the rate of reaction until all the enzyme molecules are combined with substrate.

Q What happens to the rate of reaction when all the available enzymes are attached to substrate molecules?

▶ **SAMPLE PROBLEM 20.4** Factors Affecting Enzymatic Activity

Describe the effect each of the following changes would have on the rate of the reaction that is catalyzed by urease:

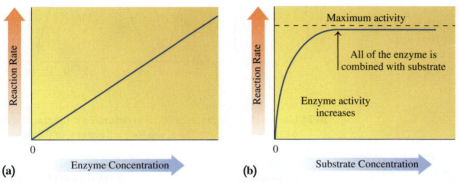

a. increasing the urea concentration   **b.** lowering the temperature to 10 °C

SOLUTION

a. An increase in urea concentration will increase the rate of reaction until all the enzyme molecules bind to urea. Then no further increase in rate occurs.
b. Because 10 °C is lower than the optimum temperature of 37 °C, there is a decrease in the rate of the reaction.

STUDY CHECK 20.4

If urease has an optimum pH of 7.0, what is the effect of lowering the pH of a urease sample to 3.0?

ANSWER

At a pH lower than the optimum pH, the hydrogen bonds and salt bridges of urease will be disrupted, resulting in the denaturation of the enzyme, loss of tertiary and quaternary structure, and a decrease in its biological activity.

QUESTIONS AND PROBLEMS

20.3 Factors Affecting Enzyme Activity

LEARNING GOAL Describe the effect of changes of temperature, pH, concentration of enzyme, and concentration of substrate on enzyme activity.

℞ Clinical Applications

20.21 Trypsin, a protease that hydrolyzes polypeptides, functions in the small intestine at an optimum pH of 7.7 to 8.0. How is the rate of a trypsin-catalyzed reaction affected by each of the following conditions?
 a. lowering the concentration of polypeptides
 b. changing the pH to 3.0
 c. running the reaction at 75 °C
 d. adding more trypsin

20.22 Pepsin, a protease that hydrolyzes polypeptides, functions in the stomach at an optimum pH of 1.5 to 2.0. How is the rate of a pepsin-catalyzed reaction affected by each of the following conditions?

Trypsin, a protease containing 247 amino acid residues, hydrolyzes peptides after lysine or arginine residues.

 a. increasing the concentration of polypeptides
 b. changing the pH to 5.0
 c. running the reaction at 0 °C
 d. using less pepsin

20.23 Use the graph to estimate the optimum pH for pepsin, lactase, sucrase, and trypsin.

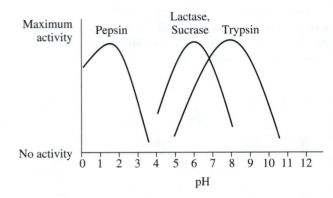

20.24 Use the graph in problem 20.23 to determine if the reaction rate will be the optimum rate or not for each enzyme at the following pH values:
 a. trypsin, pH 5.0   **b.** lactase, pH 5.0
 c. pepsin, pH 4.0   **d.** trypsin, pH 8.0
 e. sucrase, pH 2.0

LEARNING GOAL

Describe the role of allosteric enzymes, feedback control, and covalent modification in regulating enzyme activity.

20.4 Regulation of Enzyme Activity

In enzyme-catalyzed reactions, substances are produced in the amounts and at the times they are needed in a cell. Therefore the rates of enzyme-catalyzed reactions are controlled by regulatory enzymes that increase the reaction rate when more of a particular substance is needed, and decrease the reaction rate when that substance is not needed. Enzyme activity can be regulated by allosteric enzymes, feedback control, and covalent modifications.

Positive Allosteric Regulation

Allosteric site   Active site   Substrate

Products   Products

Negative Allosteric Regulation

Enzyme   Substrate

FIGURE 20.7 ▶ A positive regulator changes the shape of the active site allowing the substrate to bind more effectively and increasing the reaction rate. A negative regulator changes the shape of the active site preventing the binding of the substrate and decreasing the reaction rate.

Allosteric Enzymes

Many enzymes are **allosteric enzymes**, which bind with a regulator molecule that is different from the substrate. The regulator binds to the enzyme at an *allosteric site*, which is a different location than the active site. As a result, the shape of the enzyme changes, which causes a change in the shape of the active site. There are both positive and negative regulators. A *positive regulator* changes the shape of the active site to allow the substrate to bind more effectively, which increases the rate of the catalyzed reaction. A *negative regulator* changes the shape of the active site to prevent the proper binding of the substrate, which decreases the rate of the catalyzed reaction (see Figure 20.7).

Feedback Control

In **feedback control**, the end product of a series of reactions acts as a negative regulator (see Figure 20.8). When the end product is present in sufficient amounts for the needs of the cell, end product molecules act as negative regulators and bind to the allosteric site within the first enzyme (E_1) in the reaction series. Then the substrate cannot bind to the active site and production of all of the intermediate compounds in the subsequent reaction sequence stops.

The end product binds with the allosteric enzyme, which makes it inactive.

FIGURE 20.8 ▶ In feedback control, the end product binds to a regulatory site on the allosteric (first) enzyme in the reaction sequence, which prevents the formation of all intermediate compounds needed in the synthesis of the end product.

◉ Do the intermediate enzymes in a reaction sequence have regulatory sites?

When the level of end product is low, the regulator dissociates from the allosteric enzyme (E_1), which unblocks the active site allowing the enzyme to bind with the initial substrate once again. Feedback control allows the enzyme-catalyzed reactions to operate only when the end product is needed by the cell. Thus, feedback control prevents the accumulation of intermediate products as well as end product, thereby conserving energy and materials in the cell.

An example of feedback control is the reaction sequence in which the amino acid threonine is converted to the amino acid isoleucine. When the level of isoleucine is high in the cell, some of the isoleucine binds to the allosteric enzyme threonine deaminase (E_1). The binding of isoleucine changes the shape of the threonine deaminase, which prevents threonine from binding to its active site. As a result, the entire reaction sequence does not function. As isoleucine is utilized in the cell and its concentration decreases, isoleucine molecules are released from the allosteric site on threonine deaminase. The shape of the deaminase returns to its active form, which allows the enzyme-catalyzed reaction sequence to convert threonine to isoleucine.

Covalent Modification

Covalent modification is another way in which enzymes are modified when covalent bonds to a group on the polypeptide chain are formed or broken. As a regulatory mechanism, covalent modification is reversible.

Zymogens (Proenzymes)

Many enzymes are active as soon as they are synthesized and fold into their tertiary or quaternary structures. However, **zymogens**, or *proenzymes*, are produced as inactive forms and stored for later use. Zymogens include digestive enzymes, protein hormones, such as insulin, and blood clotting enzymes (see Table 20.6). For example, proteases, which are digestive enzymes that hydrolyze protein, are produced as larger, inactive forms. Once a zymogen is formed, it is transported to the part of the body where the active form is needed. Then the zymogen is converted to its active form by a covalent modification, typically the removal of a polypeptide section, which uncovers its active site. The pancreatic zymogens are stored in *zymogen granules*, which have membranes that are resistant to enzymatic digestion while in the pancreas. If zymogen activation should occur in the pancreas, the proteins within the tissues of the pancreas would undergo digestion, which would cause inflammation and could result in a painful condition called *pancreatitis*.

The ribbon representation of chymotrypsin shows six cysteines (green) that form three disulfide bonds (yellow).

TABLE 20.6 Examples of Zymogens and Their Active Forms

Zymogen (Inactive Enzyme)	Produced in	Activated in	Enzyme (Active)
Chymotrypsinogen	pancreas	small intestine	chymotrypsin
Pepsinogen	gastric chief cells	stomach	pepsin
Trypsinogen	pancreas	small intestine	trypsin
Fibrinogen	blood	damaged tissues	fibrin
Prothrombin	blood	damaged tissues	thrombin
Proinsulin	pancreas	pancreas	insulin

The proteases trypsin and chymotrypsin are produced as zymogens and stored in the pancreas. After food is ingested, hormones trigger the release of the zymogens from the pancreas for transport to the small intestine. There the zymogens are converted into active digestive enzymes by proteases that remove peptide sections from the protein chains. A hexapeptide from the zymogen trypsinogen is removed by a peptidase to form the active digestive enzyme trypsin. As more trypsin forms, it in turn removes peptide sections to activate trypsinogen.

Trypsin also activates the zymogen chymotrypsinogen, which consists of 245 amino acids, by removing two dipeptides to give the active enzyme chymotrypsin, which has three polypeptide sections held together by disulfide bonds. As an active protease, chymotrypsin splits the peptide bonds after the hydrophobic amino acid residues tryptophan, tyrosine, and phenylalanine.

Once formed, trypsin catalyzes the removal of dipeptides from inactive chymotrypsinogen and trypsinogen to give the active proteases chymotrypsin and trypsin.

The protein hormone insulin is initially synthesized in the pancreas as a zymogen called proinsulin. When the polypeptide chain of 33 amino acids is removed by peptidases, insulin becomes biologically active.

The removal of a polypeptide chain from proinsulin produces the active form of insulin.

Phosphorylation

Another common covalent modification is the addition or removal of a phosphate group, which can induce a structural change in an enzyme and change its catalytic activity. Almost one-third of all enzymes are regulated through addition or removal of a phosphate group. An inactive enzyme can be activated by the addition of a phosphate from ATP in a reaction catalyzed by a kinase (see Figure 20.9a). For enzymes that are inactive when phosphorylated, a phosphatase catalyzes the hydrolysis of phosphate and that enzyme becomes active (see Figure 20.9b).

FIGURE 20.9 ▶ Phosphorylation is a type of covalent modification in which an enzyme is deactivated or activated. **(a)** A kinase can activate an inactive enzyme by phosphorylation. **(b)** A phosphatase can activate an inactive enzyme by removal of phosphate.

Q What is the difference between a kinase and a phosphatase if they both transfer phosphates?

▶ **SAMPLE PROBLEM 20.5** Enzyme Regulation

How is the rate of a reaction sequence regulated in feedback control?

SOLUTION

When the end product of a reaction sequence is produced at sufficient levels for the cell, some product molecules bind to the allosteric enzyme (E_1) in the sequence, which shuts down all the reactions that follow and stops the synthesis of intermediate products.

STUDY CHECK 20.5

Why is pepsin, a digestive enzyme, produced as a zymogen?

ANSWER

Pepsin hydrolyzes proteins in the foods we ingest. It is synthesized as a zymogen, pepsinogen, to prevent its digestion of the proteins that make up the organs in the body.

QUESTIONS AND PROBLEMS

20.4 Regulation of Enzyme Activity

LEARNING GOAL Describe the role of allosteric enzymes, feedback control, and covalent modification in regulating enzyme activity.

20.25 How does an allosteric enzyme function as a regulatory enzyme?

20.26 What is the difference between a negative regulator and a positive regulator?

20.27 In feedback control, how does the end product of a reaction sequence regulate enzyme activity?

20.28 Why are the second or third enzymes in a reaction sequence not used as regulatory enzymes?

℞ Clinical Applications

20.29 Indicate if the following statements describe enzyme regulation by (1) an allosteric enzyme, (2) a zymogen, or (3) covalent modification:
  a. The enzyme activity increases due to phosphorylation.
  b. Fibrinogen in the blood forms fibrin in damaged tissues.
  c. A positive regulator stimulates enzyme action.

20.30 Indicate if the following statements describe enzyme regulation by (1) an allosteric enzyme, (2) a zymogen, or (3) covalent modification:
  a. An end product attaches to the regulatory site of the first enzyme in the reaction sequence.
  b. Proinsulin forms in the pancreas.
  c. Phosphorylase kinase deactivates pyruvate dehydrogenase.

20.31 Why is the active form of thrombin, which helps blood clot, produced from prothrombin only when injury and bleeding occur?

20.32 The zymogen trypsinogen produced in the pancreas is activated in the small intestine, where it catalyzes the digestion of proteins. Explain how the activation of the zymogen in the pancreas can lead to an inflammation of the pancreas called pancreatitis.

20.5 Enzyme Inhibition

LEARNING GOAL

Describe competitive and noncompetitive inhibition, and reversible and irreversible inhibition.

Inhibitors are substances that cause enzymes to lose catalytic activity. Although inhibitors act differently, they all prevent the active site from binding with a substrate. An enzyme with a *reversible inhibitor* can regain enzymatic activity, but an *irreversible inhibitor* causes the permanent loss of enzymatic activity.

Reversible Inhibition

In **reversible inhibition**, the inhibitor causes a loss of enzymatic activity that can be reversed. A reversible inhibitor can act in different ways but does not form covalent bonds with the enzyme. Reversible inhibition can be competitive or noncompetitive. In *competitive inhibition*, an inhibitor competes for the active site, whereas in *noncompetitive inhibition*, the inhibitor acts on another site that is not the active site.

Competitive Inhibitors

A **competitive inhibitor** has a chemical structure and polarity that is similar to that of the substrate. Thus, a competitive inhibitor competes with the substrate for the active site on the enzyme. When the inhibitor occupies the active site, the substrate cannot bind to the enzyme and no reaction can occur (see Figure 20.10). As long as the concentration of the inhibitor is substantial, there is a loss of enzyme activity. However, adding more substrate displaces the competitive inhibitor. As more enzyme molecules bind to substrate (ES), enzyme activity is regained.

FIGURE 20.10 ▶ With a structure similar to the substrate of an enzyme, a competitive inhibitor (I) also fits the active site and competes with the substrate when both are present.

Q Why does increasing the substrate concentration reverse the inhibition by a competitive inhibitor?

Malonate, which has a structure and polarity similar to that of succinate, competes for the active site on the enzyme succinate dehydrogenase. As long as malonate, a competitive inhibitor, occupies the active site, no reaction occurs. When more of the substrate succinate is added, malonate is displaced from the active site, and the inhibition is reversed.

Some bacterial infections are treated with competitive inhibitors called *antimetabolites*. Sulfanilamide, one of the first sulfa drugs, competes with *p*-aminobenzoic acid (PABA), which is an essential substance (metabolite) in the growth cycle of bacteria.

Noncompetitive Inhibitors

The structure of a **noncompetitive inhibitor** does not resemble the substrate and does not compete for the active site. Instead, a noncompetitive inhibitor binds to a site on the enzyme that is not the active site. When bonded, the noncompetitive inhibitor distorts the shape of the enzyme. Inhibition occurs because the substrate cannot fit in the altered active site or it does not fit properly. Without the proper alignment of substrate, no catalysis can take place (see Figure 20.11). A noncompetitive inhibitor prevents catalysis in a similar manner as a negative regulator of an allosteric enzyme. Because a noncompetitive inhibitor is not competing for the active site, the addition of more substrate does not reverse the effect of a noncompetitive inhibitor. Examples of noncompetitive inhibitors are the heavy metal ions Pb^{2+}, Ag^+, and Hg^{2+} that bond with amino acid side groups such as —COO^- or —OH. However, the effect of a metallic noncompetitive inhibitor can be reversed by using chemical reagents known as *chelators*, which bind these heavy metals, and remove them from the body. Then the enzyme regains biological activity.

Active Site

Enzyme–Substrate Enzyme–Product
Complex (ES)   Complex (EP)

Products (P)

Active Site

The change in shape of the
active site caused by a
noncompetitive inhibitor prevents
the binding of substrate

Enzyme–Inhibitor
Complex (EI)

FIGURE 20.11 ▶ A noncompetitive inhibitor (I) binds to an enzyme at a site other than the active site, which distorts the enzyme and active site and prevents the proper binding and catalysis of the substrate at the active site.

Q Why does an increase in the substrate concentration not reverse inhibition by a noncompetitive inhibitor?

Irreversible Inhibition

In irreversible inhibition, a molecule causes an enzyme to lose all enzymatic activity. Most **irreversible inhibitors** are toxic substances that destroy enzymes. Usually an irreversible inhibitor forms a covalent bond with an amino acid side group within the active site, which prevents the substrate from binding to the active site, thereby preventing catalytic activity.

E—CH₂—OH + F—P=O ⟶ E—CH₂—O—P=O + HF

Enzyme–Serine

Diisopropyl fluorophosphate
(DFP)

Enzyme–Serine covalently
bonded to DFP

Insecticides and nerve gases act as irreversible inhibitors of acetylcholinesterase, an enzyme needed for nerve conduction. The compound diisopropyl fluorophosphate (DFP) forms a covalent bond with the —CH₂OH group of a serine residue in the active site. When acetylcholinesterase is inhibited, the transmission of nerve impulses is blocked, and paralysis occurs.

Antibiotics produced by bacteria, mold, or yeast are irreversible inhibitors used to stop bacterial growth. For example, penicillin inhibits an enzyme needed for the formation of cell walls in bacteria, but not human cell membranes. With an incomplete cell wall, bacteria cannot survive and the infection is stopped. However, some bacteria are resistant to penicillin because they produce penicillinase, an enzyme that breaks down penicillin. The penicillinase hydrolyzes the four-atom ring converting penicillin to penicillinoic acid, which is inactive. Over the years, derivatives of penicillin to which bacteria have not yet become resistant have been produced. Examples of some irreversible enzyme inhibitors are listed in Table 20.7.

Penicillinase

Penicillin

Penicillinoic acid

TABLE 20.7 Examples of Irreversible Enzyme Inhibitors

Name	Structure	Source	Inhibitory Action
Cyanide	CN^-	bitter almonds	bonds to iron in the heme group of cytochrome c oxidase, an enzyme in electron transport
Allopurinol		drug	inhibits xanthine oxidase from forming uric acid
Parathion		insecticide	inhibits cholinesterase from breaking down acetylcholine, resulting in continual nerve transmission
Penicillin		*Penicillium* fungus	inhibits enzymes that build cell walls in bacteria

R Groups for Penicillin Derivatives

Penicillin G   Penicillin V   Ampicillin   Amoxicillin

A summary of competitive, noncompetitive, and irreversible inhibitor characteristics is shown in Table 20.8.

TABLE 20.8 Summary of Competitive, Noncompetitive, and Irreversible Inhibitors

Characteristics	Competitive	Noncompetitive	Irreversible
Shape of Inhibitor	similar shape to the substrate	does not have a similar shape to the substrate	does not have a similar shape to the substrate
Binding to Enzyme	competes for and binds at the active site	binds away from the active site to change the shape of the enzyme and its activity	forms a covalent bond with the enzyme
Reversibility	adding more substrate reverses the inhibition	not reversed by adding more substrate, but by a chemical change that removes the inhibitor	permanent, not reversible

Guide to Determining Type of Enzyme Inhibition

STEP 1
Compare the structure of the inhibitor to that of the substrate.

STEP 2
Describe the characteristics of the inhibitor.

STEP 3
Assign the type of inhibition based on the characteristics.

▶ **SAMPLE PROBLEM 20.6 Enzyme Inhibition**

State the type of inhibition in the following:

a. The inhibitor has a structure similar to that of the substrate.
b. The inhibitor binds to the surface of the enzyme, changing its shape in such a way that it cannot bind to substrate.

SOLUTION

a. **STEP 1** Compare the structure of the inhibitor to that of the substrate. This inhibitor has a structure similar to that of the substrate.

 STEP 2 Describe the characteristics of the inhibitor. This inhibitor would compete with the substrate for the active site.

 STEP 3 Assign the type of inhibition based on the characteristics. This type of inhibition is competitive inhibition, which is reversed by increasing the concentration of the substrate.

b. **STEP 1** Compare the structure of the inhibitor to that of the substrate. This inhibitor does not have a structure similar to the substrate.

STEP **2** Describe the characteristics of the inhibitor. This inhibitor binds to the surface of the enzyme where it changes the shape of the enzyme and the active site.

STEP **3** Assign the type of inhibition based on the characteristics. This type of inhibition is noncompetitive inhibition.

STUDY CHECK 20.6

What type of inhibition occurs when aspirin, also called acetylsalicylic acid, forms a covalent bond with serine in the active site of the enzyme cyclooxygenase?

ANSWER

irreversible inhibition

QUESTIONS AND PROBLEMS

20.5 Enzyme Inhibition

LEARNING GOAL Describe competitive and noncompetitive inhibition, and reversible and irreversible inhibition.

20.33 Indicate whether each of the following describes a competitive or a noncompetitive enzyme inhibitor:
   a. The inhibitor has a structure similar to the substrate.
   b. The effect of the inhibitor cannot be reversed by adding more substrate.
   c. The inhibitor competes with the substrate for the active site.
   d. The structure of the inhibitor is not similar to the substrate.
   e. The addition of more substrate reverses the inhibition.

20.34 Oxaloacetate is an inhibitor of succinate dehydrogenase.
   a. Would you expect oxaloacetate to be a competitive or a noncompetitive inhibitor? Why?
   b. Would oxaloacetate bind to the active site or elsewhere on the enzyme?
   c. How would you reverse the effect of the inhibitor?

Succinate   Oxaloacetate

℞ Clinical Applications

20.35 Methanol and ethanol are oxidized by alcohol dehydrogenase. In methanol poisoning, ethanol is given intravenously to prevent the formation of formaldehyde that has toxic effects.
   a. Draw the condensed structural formulas for methanol and ethanol.
   b. Would ethanol compete with methanol for the active site or bind to a different site on the enzyme?
   c. Would ethanol be a competitive or noncompetitive inhibitor of methanol oxidation?

20.36 In humans, the antibiotic amoxicillin (a type of penicillin) is used to treat certain bacterial infections.
   a. Does the antibiotic inhibit human enzymes?
   b. Why does the antibiotic kill bacteria but not humans?
   c. Is amoxicillin a reversible or irreversible inhibitor?

Amoxicillin is a derivative of the antibiotic penicillin.

20.6 Enzyme Cofactors and Vitamins

For many enzymes, their polypeptide chains are biologically active. However, there are also enzymes in which the polypeptide chain is inactive and cannot catalyze a reaction. An inactive enzyme becomes active when it combines with a **cofactor**, which is a nonprotein component such as a vitamin or a metal ion. If the cofactor is an organic molecule, it is known as a **coenzyme**. A cofactor binds to an enzyme in a way that prepares the active site to take part in the catalysis of its substrate.

Metal Ions as Cofactors

The metal ions from the minerals that we obtain from foods in our diet have various functions in enzyme catalysis. Metal ion cofactors such as Fe^{2+} and Cu^{2+} are often required by enzymes involved in the loss or gain of electrons (oxidoreductases). Other metal ions such as Zn^{2+} stabilize the amino acid residues in the active site of hydrolases. Some of the metal ion cofactors that are required by enzymes are listed in Table 20.9.

The enzyme carboxypeptidase is produced in the pancreas and moves into the small intestine where it catalyzes the hydrolysis of the C-terminal amino acid with an aromatic residue in a protein (see Figure 20.12).

LEARNING GOAL

Describe the types of cofactors found in enzymes.

TABLE 20.9 Enzymes and the Metal Ions Required as Cofactors

Metal Ion	Enzymes Requiring Metal Ion Cofactors
Cu^{2+}/Cu^+	Cytochrome oxidase
Fe^{2+}/Fe^{3+}	Catalase Cytochrome oxidase
Zn^{2+}	Alcohol dehydrogenase Carbonic anhydrase Carboxypeptidase A
Mg^{2+}	Glucose-6-phosphatase Hexokinase
Mn^{2+}	Arginase
Ni^{2+}	Urease

FIGURE 20.12 ▶
Carboxypeptidase requires a Zn^{2+} cofactor for the hydrolysis of the peptide bond of a C-terminal aromatic amino acid.

◉ Why is Zn^{2+} a cofactor for carboxypeptidase?

The active site includes a pocket that fits the bulky hydrophobic amino acid residue on a protein substrate. In the center of the active site, a Zn^{2+} cofactor is bonded to the nitrogen atom in each of two histidine residues, and an oxygen atom in the residue of glutamic acid. The Zn^{2+} promotes the hydrolysis of the peptide bond by stabilizing the partial negative charge of the oxygen in the carbonyl group of the peptide bond undergoing hydrolysis.

The ribbon representation of carboxypeptidase shows a Zn^{2+} cofactor (orange sphere) in the center of the active site, held in place by amino acid residues in the active site.

Vitamin C (ascorbic acid)

FIGURE 20.13 ▶ Oranges, lemons, peppers, and tomatoes contain the water-soluble vitamin, vitamin C (ascorbic acid), which is an antioxidant.

◉ What happens to the excess vitamin C that may be consumed in one day?

▶**SAMPLE PROBLEM 20.7 Cofactors**

Indicate whether each of the following enzymes is active with or without a cofactor:

a. an enzyme that needs Mg^{2+} for catalytic activity
b. a polypeptide chain that is biologically active
c. an enzyme that binds to vitamin B_6 to become active

SOLUTION

a. The enzyme would be active with the metal ion Mg^{2+} cofactor.
b. An active enzyme that is only a polypeptide chain does not require a cofactor.
c. An enzyme that requires vitamin B_6 is active with a cofactor.

STUDY CHECK 20.7

Which cofactor for the enzymes in Sample Problem 20.7 would be called a coenzyme?

ANSWER

vitamin B_6

Vitamins and Coenzymes

Vitamins are organic molecules that are essential for normal health and growth. They are required in trace amounts and need to be obtained from the diet because vitamins are not synthesized in the body. Before vitamins were discovered, it was known that lime juice prevented the disease scurvy in sailors, and that cod liver oil could prevent rickets. In 1912, scientists found that in addition to carbohydrates, fats, and proteins, certain other factors called vitamins must be obtained from the diet. Vitamin B_1 (thiamine) was the first B vitamin to be identified, thus the abbreviation B_1.

Vitamins are classified into two groups by solubility: water-soluble and fat-soluble. **Water-soluble vitamins** have polar groups such as —OH and —COOH, which make them soluble in the aqueous environment of the cells. The **fat-soluble vitamins** are nonpolar compounds, which are soluble in the fat (lipid) components of the body such as fat deposits and cell membranes.

Water-Soluble Vitamins

Because water-soluble vitamins cannot be stored in the body, any excess amounts are excreted in the urine each day. Therefore, the water-soluble vitamins must be in the foods of our daily diets (see Figure 20.13). Because many water-soluble vitamins are easily destroyed by heat, oxygen, and ultraviolet light, care must be taken in food preparation, processing, and storage. Because refining grains such as wheat causes a loss of vitamins, during the 1940s, the Committee on Food and Nutrition of the National Research Council began to recommend dietary enrichment of cereal grains. Vitamin B_1 (thiamine), vitamin B_2 (riboflavin), and iron were in the first group of added nutrients recommended. The Recommended Daily Allowance (RDA) for many vitamins and minerals appears on food product labels. Individuals eating balanced meals including fresh produce and whole grains can readily achieve the U.S. RDAs.

Many of the water-soluble vitamins are precursors of cofactors required by many enzymes to carry out certain aspects of catalytic action (see Table 20.10). The coenzymes do not remain bonded to a particular enzyme, but are used repeatedly by different enzyme molecules to facilitate an enzyme-catalyzed reaction (see Figure 20.14). Thus, only small amounts of coenzymes are required in the cells. Table 20.11 gives the structures of the water-soluble vitamins.

CORE CHEMISTRY SKILL

Describing the Role of Cofactors

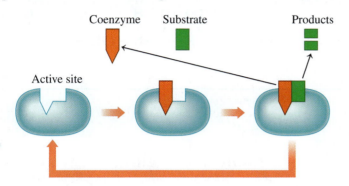

FIGURE 20.14 ► A coenzyme is required so that an enzyme can become active.

Q What is the function of water-soluble vitamins in enzymes?

TABLE 20.10 Water-Soluble Vitamins, Coenzymes, Functions, Sources and RDA, and Deficiency Symptoms

Vitamin	Coenzyme	Transfer Function	Sources and RDA (Adults)	Deficiency Symptoms
B_1 (Thiamine)	Thiamine pyrophosphate (TPP)	aldehyde groups	liver, yeast, whole grain bread, cereals, milk (1.2 mg)	beriberi: fatigue, poor appetite, weight loss
B_2 (Riboflavin)	Flavin adenine dinucleotide (FAD); flavin mononucleotide (FMN)	electrons	beef, liver, chicken, eggs, green leafy vegetables, dairy foods, peanuts, whole grains (1.2 to 1.8 mg)	dermatitis; dry skin; red, sore tongue; cataracts
B_3 (Niacin)	Nicotinamide adenine dinucleotide (NAD^+); nicotinamide adenine dinucleotide phosphate ($NADP^+$)	electrons	brewer's yeast, chicken, beef, fish, liver, brown rice, whole grains (14 to 18 mg)	pellagra: dermatitis, muscle fatigue, loss of appetite, diarrhea, mouth sores
B_5 (Pantothenic acid)	Coenzyme A	acetyl groups	salmon, beef, liver, eggs, brewer's yeast, whole grains, fresh vegetables (5 mg)	fatigue, retarded growth, muscle cramps, anemia
B_6 (Pyridoxine)	Pyridoxal phosphate (PLP)	amino groups	meat, liver, fish, nuts, whole grains, spinach (1.3 to 2.0 mg)	dermatitis, fatigue, anemia, retarded growth
B_9 (Folic acid)	Tetrahydrofolate (THF)	methyl groups	green leafy vegetables, beans, meat, seafood, yeast, asparagus, whole grains enriched with folic acid (400 mcg)	abnormal red blood cells, anemia, intestinal tract disturbances, loss of hair, growth impairment, depression
B_{12} (Cobalamin)	Methylcobalamin	methyl groups, hydrogen	liver, beef, kidney, chicken, fish, milk products (2.0 to 2.6 mcg)	pernicious anemia, malformed red blood cells, nerve damage
C (Ascorbic acid)	Ascorbic acid	electrons	blueberries, citrus fruits, strawberries, cantaloupe, tomatoes, peppers, broccoli, cabbage, spinach (75 to 90 mg)	scurvy: bleeding gums, weakened connective tissues, slow-healing wounds, anemia
H (Biotin)	Biocytin	carbon dioxide	liver, yeast, nuts, eggs (30 mcg)	dermatitis, loss of hair, fatigue, anemia, depression

TABLE 20.11 Structures of Water-Soluble Vitamins

B₁ (Thiamine)

B₂ (Riboflavin)

B₃ (Niacin)

B₅ (Pantothenic acid)

B₆ (Pyridoxine)

B₁₂ (Cobalamin)

C (Ascorbic acid)

H (Biotin)

B₉ (Folic acid)

Fat-Soluble Vitamins

The fat-soluble vitamins—A, D, E, and K—are not involved as coenzymes in catalytic reactions, but they are important in processes such as vision, formation of bone, protection from oxidation, and proper blood clotting (see Table 20.12). Because the fat-soluble vitamins are stored in the body, and not eliminated, it is possible to take too much, which could be toxic primarily in the liver and fatty tissues. Table 20.13 gives the structures of the fat-soluble vitamins.

TABLE 20.12 Function, Sources and RDA, and Deficiency Symptoms of Fat-Soluble Vitamins

Vitamin	Function	Sources and RDA (Adults)	Deficiency Symptoms
A (Retinol)	formation of visual pigments, synthesis of RNA	yellow and green fruits and vegetables (800 mcg)	night blindness, immune system repression, slowed growth, rickets
D (Cholecalciferol)	regulation of absorption of P and Ca during bone growth	sunlight, cod liver oil, enriched milk, eggs (5 to 10 mcg)	rickets, weak bone structure, osteomalacia
E (Tocopherol)	antioxidant; prevents oxidation of vitamin A and unsaturated fatty acids	meats, whole grains, vegetables (15 mg)	hemolysis, anemia
K (Menaquinone)	synthesis of zymogen prothrombin for blood clotting	liver, spinach, cauliflower (9 to 120 mcg)	prolonged bleeding time, bruising

TABLE 20.13 Structures of Fat-Soluble Vitamins

Vitamin A (Retinol)	
Vitamin D (Cholecalciferol)	
Vitamin E (Tocopherol)	
Vitamin K (Menaquinone)	

The orange pigment (carotene) in carrots is used to synthesize vitamin A (retinol), an antioxidant, in the body.

Antioxidants

The production of energy by cells occurs through chemical oxidation. During this process, reactive oxygen compounds called *free radicals*, such as $NO^{\bullet}$, $OH^{\bullet}$, and $O_2^{\bullet-}$ are formed. These molecules are called free radicals because they have an unpaired electron. Because electrons are more stable when they are paired, free radicals react readily. An overabundance of free radicals can cause cellular and DNA damage such as aging, inflammation, cataracts, and cancer.

The body uses *antioxidants* to defend against free radicals. These antioxidants include vitamins C, E, and beta-carotene, a precursor to vitamin A. Many face creams and serums contain vitamin E to protect against free radicals. The tannins and flavonoids found in tea leaves and wine have been shown to have antioxidant properties.

The body also produces antioxidant enzymes such as superoxide dismutase that reacts with free radicals damaging membranes, proteins, and neurons. A genetic mutation in this enzyme is responsible for the disease *Amyotrophic Lateral Sclerosis* (ALS) commonly called Lou Gehrig's disease. Another antioxidant enzyme is glutathione peroxidase, which uses the micronutrient selenium as a cofactor.

Sunflower seeds, almonds, and spinach contain vitamin E, which is an antioxidant.

Vitamins and other small molecules in foods act as antioxidants, which can prevent oxidative damage to cells.

> **SAMPLE PROBLEM 20.8 Vitamins**
>
> Why is it more important to get regular, daily amounts of vitamins B_1 and B_2, but not vitamins A or D?
>
> **SOLUTION**
>
> Water-soluble vitamins like vitamin B_1 (thiamine) and vitamin B_2 (riboflavin) are not stored in the body, whereas fat-soluble vitamins such as vitamin A (retinol) and vitamin D (cholecalciferol) are stored in the liver and body fat. Any excess of thiamine or riboflavin is eliminated in the urine and must be replenished each day from the diet.
>
> **STUDY CHECK 20.8**
>
> Why are fresh fruits rather than cooked fruits recommended as a source of vitamin C?
>
> **ANSWER**
>
> Water-soluble vitamins such as vitamin C are easily destroyed by heat.

QUESTIONS AND PROBLEMS

20.6 Enzyme Cofactors and Vitamins

LEARNING GOAL Describe the types of cofactors found in enzymes.

20.37 Is the enzyme described in each of the following statements active with or without a cofactor?
   a. requires vitamin B_1 (thiamine)
   b. needs Zn^{2+} for catalytic activity
   c. its active form consists of two polypeptide chains

20.38 Is the enzyme described in each of the following statements active with or without a cofactor?
   a. requires vitamin B_2 (riboflavin)
   b. its active form is composed of 155 amino acid residues
   c. uses Cu^{2+} during catalysis

20.39 Identify the vitamin that is a component of each of the following coenzymes:
   a. coenzyme A
   b. tetrahydrofolate (THF)
   c. NAD^+

20.40 Identify the vitamin that is a component of each of the following coenzymes:
   a. thiamine pyrophosphate
   b. FAD
   c. pyridoxal phosphate

Rx Clinical Applications

20.41 What vitamin may be deficient in the following conditions?
   a. rickets
   b. scurvy
   c. pellagra

20.42 What vitamin may be deficient in the following conditions?
   a. poor night vision
   b. pernicious anemia
   c. beriberi

20.43 The RDA for vitamin B_6 (pyridoxine) is 1.3 to 2.0 mg. Why will it not improve your nutrition to take 100 mg of pyridoxine daily?

20.44 The RDA for vitamin C (ascorbic acid) is 75 to 90 mg. If you take 1000 mg of vitamin C daily, what happens to the vitamin C you do not need?

Rx Clinical Update
Noah's Diet for Lactose Intolerance

When Noah and his mother return to the clinic, Emma administers the hydrogen breath test (HBT) after Noah has fasted for 8 h. First, the technician has Noah breathe into a balloon to determine a base level of hydrogen (H_2). Then Noah drinks a solution containing lactose and more breath samples are collected and measured for hydrogen over the next 3 h. Hydrogen is present in the breath when the bacteria in the colon are fermenting lactose and producing hydrogen (H_2).

Lactose intolerance is confirmed if the hydrogen levels rise 20 ppm above baseline levels over a 3-h period after ingesting the lactose solution. The results of the test shown as the black line on the graph show that Noah's levels were 130 ppm, so Emma and the attending physician concluded that Noah has a problem digesting lactose, which means he has *lactose intolerance*.

Treatment of Lactose Intolerance

Emma tells Noah's mother that he will need to avoid products that contain lactose, including milk and milk products such as cheese, butter, and ice cream. A person who is lactose intolerant should also know that some foods that are not dairy products contain lactose. For example, many baked goods, cereals, breakfast drinks, salad dressings, and even lunchmeat can contain lactose. Food labels must be read carefully to see if the ingredients include "milk" or "lactose."

Another way to combat lactose intolerance is to use the enzyme lactase with meals. Lactase is available in many forms, such as tablets that are taken with meals, or drops that are added to milk. When lactase is added to milk that is left in the refrigerator for 24 h, the lactose level is reduced by 70 to 90%. Lactase pills or chewable tablets are taken when a person begins to eat a meal that contains dairy foods.

Lactaid contains lactase that aids the digestion of lactose.

℞ Clinical Applications

20.45 Using the graph for the average hydrogen breath test, estimate
  a. the baseline ppm at 60 min
  b. the hydrogen ppm for Noah at 60 min

20.46 Using the graph for the average hydrogen breath test, estimate
  a. the baseline ppm at 90 min
  b. the hydrogen ppm for Noah at 90 min

20.47 Noah's mother makes him some hot chocolate, to which she adds a tablet of lactase. A few hours after Noah drinks the hot chocolate, he has symptoms of lactose intolerance. Explain why the lactase was ineffective.

20.48 Noah's mother adds a tablet of lactase to a glass of milk and places it in the refrigerator for 24 h. The next day Noah drinks the milk and has no symptoms of lactose intolerance. Explain why the lactase was effective.

CONCEPT MAP

ENZYMES AND VITAMINS

- are → **Proteins**
  - with → **Tertiary or Quaternary Structures**
    - that have an → **Active Site**
      - that fits the → **Substrate**
        - to form an → **ES Complex** → to form → **EP Complex** → to form → **E + Product (P)**

- have → **Activity**
  - affected by → **pH**, **Temperature**, **Concentrations**, **Inhibitors**
  - controlled by → **Allosteric Enzymes**, **Feedback Control**, **Zymogens**, **Covalent Modification**

- may need → **Cofactors**
  - such as → **Metal Ions**, **Vitamins**
    - which are → **Water-Soluble**, **Fat-Soluble**

CHAPTER REVIEW

20.1 Enzymes and Enzyme Action

LEARNING GOAL Describe enzymes and their role in enzyme-catalyzed reactions.

- Enzymes are globular proteins that act as biological catalysts by lowering activation energy and accelerating the rate of cellular reactions.
- Within the tertiary structure of an enzyme, a small pocket called the active site binds the substrate.
- In the lock-and-key model, an early theory of enzyme action, a substrate precisely fits the shape of the active site.
- In the induced-fit model, both the active site and the substrate undergo changes in their shapes to give the best fit for efficient catalysis.
- In the enzyme–substrate complex, catalysis takes place when amino acid residues in the active site of an enzyme react with a substrate.
- When the products of catalysis are released, the enzyme can bind to another substrate molecule.

20.2 Classification of Enzymes

LEARNING GOAL Classify enzymes and give their names.

- The names of most enzymes ending in *ase* describe the compound or reaction catalyzed by the enzyme.
- Enzymes are classified by the type of reaction they catalyze, such as oxidoreductase, transferase, or isomerase.

20.3 Factors Affecting Enzyme Activity

LEARNING GOAL Describe the effect of changes of temperature, pH, concentration of enzyme, and concentration of substrate on enzyme activity.

- The optimum temperature at which most enzymes are effective is usually 37 °C, and the optimum pH is usually 7.4.
- The rate of an enzyme-catalyzed reaction decreases as temperature and pH go above or below the optimum temperature and pH values.
- An increase in the enzyme concentration increases the rate of reaction.
- An increase in substrate concentration increases the reaction rate of an enzyme-catalyzed reaction, but a maximum rate is reached when all of the enzyme molecules are combined with substrate.

20.4 Regulation of Enzyme Activity

LEARNING GOAL Describe the role of allosteric enzymes, feedback control, and covalent modification in regulating enzyme activity.

- Allosteric enzymes change their activity when they bind to regulator molecules.
- In feedback control, the end product of an enzyme-catalyzed reaction acts as a negative regulator and binds with the first enzyme of the reaction sequence.
- Covalent modification regulates enzymes by adding or removing a covalently bonded group.
- Insulin and most digestive enzymes are produced as inactive forms called zymogens.
- Production of zymogens and phosphorylation are types of covalent modification.

20.5 Enzyme Inhibition

LEARNING GOAL Describe competitive and noncompetitive inhibition, and reversible and irreversible inhibition.

Enzyme–Substrate Complex

- An inhibitor reduces the activity of an enzyme or makes it inactive.
- An inhibitor can be reversible or irreversible.
- A competitive inhibitor has a structure similar to the substrate and competes for the active site.
- When the active site is occupied, the enzyme cannot catalyze the reaction of the substrate.
- A noncompetitive inhibitor attaches to the enzyme away from the active site, changing the shape of both the enzyme and its active site.
- An irreversible inhibitor forms a covalent bond within the active site that permanently prevents catalytic activity.

20.6 Enzyme Cofactors and Vitamins

LEARNING GOAL Describe the types of cofactors found in enzymes.

Coenzyme   Products

- Some enzymes are biologically active as proteins only, whereas other enzymes require a nonprotein component called a cofactor.
- A cofactor may be a metal ion, such as Cu^{2+} or Fe^{2+}, or an organic molecule or a vitamin called a coenzyme.
- A vitamin is a small organic molecule needed for health and normal growth that is obtained in small amounts from the diet.
- The water-soluble vitamins are B and C, and they function as coenzymes. Vitamin B is essential for the workings of certain enzymes in the body, and vitamin C is an antioxidant.
- The fat-soluble vitamins are A, D, E, and K. Vitamin A is important for vision, vitamin D for proper bone growth, vitamin E is an antioxidant, and vitamin K is required for proper blood clotting.
- Antioxidants neutralize the highly reactive oxygen free radicals generated during oxidative processes.

KEY TERMS

active site A pocket in a part of the tertiary enzyme structure that binds to a substrate and catalyzes a reaction.

activity The rate at which an enzyme catalyzes the reaction that converts a substrate to a product.

allosteric enzyme An enzyme that regulates the rate of a reaction when a regulator molecule attaches to a site other than the active site.

antibiotic A substance usually produced by bacteria, mold, or yeast that inhibits the growth of bacteria.

coenzyme An organic molecule, usually a vitamin, required as a cofactor in enzyme action.

cofactor A metal ion or an organic molecule that is necessary for a biologically functional enzyme.

competitive inhibitor A molecule that has a structure similar to a substrate and that inhibits enzyme action by competing for the active site.

covalent modification Regulation of an enzyme that involves forming or breaking covalent bonds to a group on the polypeptide chain.

enzyme A globular protein, sometimes with a cofactor, that catalyzes a biological reaction.

enzyme–product (EP) complex An intermediate consisting of an enzyme that binds to a product in an enzyme-catalyzed reaction.

enzyme–substrate (ES) complex An intermediate consisting of an enzyme that binds to a substrate in an enzyme-catalyzed reaction.

fat-soluble vitamin A vitamin that is not soluble in water and can be stored in the liver and body fat.

feedback control A type of inhibition in which an end product inhibits the first enzyme in a sequence of enzyme-catalyzed reactions.

induced-fit model A model of enzyme action in which the shape of a substrate and the active site of the enzyme adjust to give an optimal fit.

inhibitor A substance that makes an enzyme inactive by interfering with its ability to react with a substrate.

irreversible inhibitor A compound or metal ion that causes the loss of enzymatic activity by forming a covalent bond near or at the active site.

noncompetitive inhibitor An inhibitor that does not resemble the substrate and attaches to the enzyme away from the active site to prevent the binding of the substrate.

optimum pH The pH at which an enzyme is most active.

optimum temperature The temperature at which an enzyme is most active.

reversible inhibition The loss of enzymatic activity by an inhibitor whose effect can be reversed.

substrate The molecule that reacts in the active site in an enzyme-catalyzed reaction.

vitamin An organic molecule that is essential for normal health and growth, and obtained in small amounts from the diet.

water-soluble vitamin A vitamin that is soluble in water; cannot be stored in the body; is easily destroyed by heat, ultraviolet light, and oxygen; and functions as a coenzyme.

zymogen An inactive form of an enzyme that is activated by the removal of a peptide portion from one end of the protein.

⚛ CORE CHEMISTRY SKILLS

Describing Enzyme Action (20.1)

- Enzymes are biological catalysts that lower the activation energy and accelerate the rate of cellular reactions.
- Within the tertiary structure of an enzyme, a small pocket called the active site binds the substrate.
- In the induced-fit model of enzyme action, the active site and the substrate change their shapes for efficient catalysis.
- When the products of catalysis are released, the enzyme can bind to another substrate molecule.

Example: Match the terms (1) enzyme, (2) substrate, (3) active site, and (4) induced-fit model with each of the following:
  a. an active site that adapts to the shape of a substrate
  b. has a structure that fits the active site of an enzyme
  c. the portion of an enzyme where catalytic activity occurs
  d. has a tertiary structure that recognizes the substrate

Answer: **a.** (4) induced-fit model   **b.** (2) substrate
  c. (3) active site   **d.** (1) enzyme

Classifying Enzymes (20.2)

An enzyme can be classified from its name or the equation for the catalyzed reaction. Enzymes have six general classes: oxidoreductase, transferase, hydrolase, lyase, isomerase, and ligase.

Example: Match the enzyme names (1) DNA ligase, (2) HIV protease, (3) protein kinase, and (4) glucose oxidase with one of the following classifications:
  a. oxidoreductase   **b.** transferase
  c. hydrolase   **d.** ligase

Answer: **a.** (4) glucose oxidase   **b.** (3) protein kinase
  c. (2) HIV protease   **d.** (1) DNA ligase

Identifying Factors Affecting Enzyme Activity (20.3)

- The activity of many enzymes is regulated by allosteric enzymes, feedback control, and covalent modification including production of zymogens and phosphorylation.
- The rate of an enzyme-catalyzed reaction is affected by changes in temperature, pH, enzyme, and substrate concentration.
- Molecules called inhibitors decrease enzyme activity by binding in the active site (competitive inhibition) or at another site on the enzyme (noncompetitive inhibition).

Example: Lactase, the enzyme that hydrolyzes lactose, operates at an optimal pH of 6.0 and an optimal temperature of 37 °C. Would the following changes increase, decrease, or have no effect on the activity of lactase?
  a. lowering the pH to 2
  b. raising the temperature above 65 °C
  c. greatly increasing the amount of lactose available
  d. introducing a competitive inhibitor of lactase

Answer: **a.** decrease   **b.** decrease   **c.** increase   **d.** decrease

Describing the Role of Cofactors (20.6)

- Metal ions can be cofactors that stabilize the active site of enzymes and are vital for catalysis.
- Many vitamins are coenzymes necessary for catalysis by some enzymes.

Example: Match the coenzymes (1) NAD^+, (2) FAD, (3) coenzyme A, and (4) THF with one of the following vitamins:
    a. riboflavin (B_2)   **b.** niacin (B_3)
    c. folic acid (B_9)   **d.** pantothenic acid (B_5)

Answer: **a.** (2) FAD   **b.** (1) NAD^+
              c. (4) THF   **d.** (3) coenzyme A

UNDERSTANDING THE CONCEPTS

The chapter sections to review are shown in parentheses at the end of each question.

20.49 Fresh pineapple contains the enzyme bromelain that degrades proteins. (20.3)
    a. The directions on a gelatin (protein) package say not to add fresh pineapple. However, canned pineapple that has been heated to high temperatures can be added. Why?
    b. Fresh pineapple can be used as a marinade to tenderize tough meat. Why?

Fresh pineapple contains the enzyme bromelain.

20.50 Vitamin C, also called ascorbic acid, can act as a coenzyme and an antioxidant. (20.6)
    a. Is vitamin C a water-soluble or a fat-soluble vitamin? How do you know?
    b. How do antioxidants protect cells from damage?

Rose hips are rich in vitamin C.

℞ Clinical Applications

20.51 Ethylene glycol ($HO-CH_2-CH_2-OH$) is a major component of antifreeze. If ingested, it is first converted to $HOOC-CHO$ (oxoethanoic acid) and then to $HOOC-COOH$ (oxalic acid), which is toxic. (20.1, 20.4)

    a. What class of enzyme catalyzes both of the reactions of ethylene glycol?
    b. The treatment for the ingestion of ethylene glycol is an intravenous solution of ethanol. How might this help prevent toxic levels of oxalic acid in the body?

Ethylene glycol is added to a radiator to prevent freezing and boiling.

20.52 Adults who are lactose intolerant cannot break down the disaccharide in milk products. To help digest dairy food, a product known as Lactaid can be ingested prior to eating dairy products. (20.1, 20.3)
    a. What is the name of the enzyme present in Lactaid, and what is the major class of this enzyme?
    b. What might happen to the enzyme if the digestion product were stored in a warm area?
    c. A label on a bottle of Lactaid recommends it is stored at room temperature (68 °F to 77 °F) and kept away from heat and moisture. Why should Lactaid be stored at cool temperatures and dry conditions?

The disaccharide lactose is present in milk products.

ADDITIONAL QUESTIONS AND PROBLEMS

20.53 Why do the cells in the body have so many enzymes? (20.1)

20.54 Are all the possible enzymes present at the same time in a cell? (20.1)

20.55 How are enzymes different from the catalysts used in chemistry laboratories? (20.1)

20.56 Why do enzymes function only under mild conditions? (20.1)

20.57 How does an enzyme change the activation energy for a reaction in a cell? (20.1)

20.58 Why do most enzyme-catalyzed reactions proceed quickly? (20.1)

20.59 How does the lock-and-key model explain that sucrose hydrolyzes sucrose but not lactose? (20.1)

20.60 How does the induced-fit model of enzyme action allow an enzyme to catalyze a reaction of a group of substrates? (20.1)

20.61 Indicate whether each of the following would be a substrate (S) or an enzyme (E): (20.2)
a. lactose   **b.** lactase   **c.** lipase
d. trypsin   **e.** pyruvate   **f.** transaminase

20.62 Indicate whether each of the following would be a substrate (S) or an enzyme (E): (20.2)
a. glucose   **b.** hydrolase   **c.** maleate isomerase
d. alanine   **e.** amylose   **f.** amylase

20.63 Give the substrate for each of the following enzymes: (20.2)
a. urease   **b.** succinate dehydrogenase
c. aspartate transaminase   **d.** phenylalanine hydroxylase

20.64 Give the substrate for each of the following enzymes: (20.2)
a. maltase   **b.** fructose oxidase
c. phenolase   **d.** sucrase

20.65 Predict the major class for each of the following enzymes: (20.2)
a. acyltransferase   **b.** oxidase
c. lipase   **d.** decarboxylase

20.66 Predict the major class for each of the following enzymes: (20.2)
a. cis–trans isomerase   **b.** reductase
c. carboxylase   **d.** peptidase

20.67 What is meant by the optimum temperature for an enzyme? (20.3)

20.68 What is meant by the optimum pH for an enzyme? (20.3)

20.69 Indicate how each of the following will affect an enzyme-catalyzed reaction if the enzyme has an optimum temperature of 37 °C and an optimum pH of 7.0: (20.3)
a. heating the reaction mixture to 100 °C
b. placing the reaction mixture in ice
c. adjusting the pH of the reaction mixture to pH 2.0

20.70 Indicate how each of the following will affect an enzyme-catalyzed reaction if the enzyme has an optimum temperature of 37 °C and an optimum pH of 8.0: (20.3)
a. decreasing the temperature of the reaction mixture from 37 °C to 15 °C
b. adjusting the pH of the reaction mixture to pH 5.0
c. adjusting the pH of the reaction mixture to pH 10.0

20.71 Indicate whether the enzyme is saturated or not saturated with substrate in each of the following conditions: (20.3)
a. adding more substrate does not increase the rate of reaction
b. doubling the substrate concentration doubles the rate of reaction

20.72 Indicate whether each of the following enzymes would be functional: (20.3)
a. pepsin, a digestive enzyme, at pH 2.0
b. an enzyme at 37 °C, if the enzyme is from a type of thermophilic bacteria that has an optimum temperature of 100 °C

20.73 What is an allosteric enzyme? (20.4)

20.74 Why can some regulator molecules speed up a reaction, whereas others slow it down? (20.4)

20.75 In feedback control, what type of regulator slows down the catalytic activity of the reaction series? (20.4)

20.76 Why is covalent modification used to regulate the activity of an enzyme? (20.4)

20.77 How does reversible inhibition differ from irreversible inhibition? (20.5)

20.78 How does competitive reversible inhibition differ from noncompetitive reversible inhibition? (20.5)

20.79 Match the type of inhibitor (**1** to **3**) with the following statements (**a** to **d**): (20.5)
1. competitive inhibitor
2. noncompetitive inhibitor
3. irreversible inhibitor

a. forms a covalent bond with an amino acid residue in the active site
b. has a structure similar to the substrate
c. the addition of more substrate reverses the inhibition
d. bonds to the surface of the enzyme, causing a change in the shape of the enzyme and active site

20.80 Match the type of inhibitor (**1** to **3**) with the following statements (**a** to **d**): (20.5)
1. competitive inhibitor
2. noncompetitive inhibitor
3. irreversible inhibitor

a. has a structure that is not similar to the substrate
b. the addition of more substrate does not reverse the inhibition, but the removal of the inhibitor by chemical reaction can return activity to the enzyme
c. the inhibition is permanent, and it cannot be reversed
d. competes with the substrate for the active site

20.81 Which of the following statements describe an enzyme that requires a cofactor? (20.6)
a. contains Mg^{2+} in the active site
b. has catalytic activity as a tertiary protein structure
c. requires folic acid for catalytic activity

20.82 Which of the following statements describes an enzyme that requires a cofactor? (20.6)
a. contains riboflavin (vitamin B_2)
b. has four subunits of polypeptide chains
c. requires Fe^{3+} in the active site for catalytic activity

℞ Clinical Applications

20.83 Match the following coenzymes (**1** to **3**) with their vitamins (**a** to **c**): (20.6)
1. NAD^+ **2.** thiamine pyrophosphate (TPP)
3. coenzyme A

a. pantothenic acid (B_5)   **b.** niacin (B_3)
c. thiamine (B_1)

20.84 Match the following coenzymes (**1** to **3**) with their vitamins (**a** to **c**): (20.6)
 1. pyridoxal phosphate   **2.** tetrahydrofolate (THF)
 3. FAD

 a. folic acid   **b.** riboflavin (B$_2$)   **c.** pyridoxine

20.85 Why are only small amounts of vitamins needed in the cells when there are several enzymes that require coenzymes? (20.6)

20.86 Why is there a daily requirement for vitamins? (20.6)

20.87 Match each of the following symptoms or conditions (**1** to **3**) with a vitamin deficiency (**a** to **c**): (20.6)
 1. night blindness   **2.** weak bone structure   **3.** pellagra

 a. niacin   **b.** vitamin A   **c.** vitamin D

20.88 Match each of the following symptoms or conditions (**1** to **3**) with a vitamin deficiency (**a** to **c**): (20.6)
 1. bleeding   **2.** anemia   **3.** scurvy

 a. cobalamin   **b.** vitamin C   **c.** vitamin K

20.89 If a blood test indicates a high level of LDH and CK, what could be the cause? (20.2)

20.90 If a blood test indicates a high level of ALT, what could be the cause? (20.2)

20.91 Many drugs are competitive inhibitors of enzymes. When scientists design inhibitors to serve as drugs, why do you suppose they choose to design competitive inhibitors instead of noncompetitive inhibitors? (20.5)

20.92 When lead acts as a poison, it can do so by either replacing another ion (such as zinc) in the active site of an enzyme or it can react with cysteine side chains to form covalent bonds. Which of these is irreversible and why? (20.5)

20.93 **a.** What type of an inhibitor is the antibiotic ampicillin? (20.5)
 b. Why is ampicillin used to treat bacterial infections?

20.94 A gardener using Parathion develops a headache, dizziness, nausea, blurred vision, excessive salivation, and muscle twitching. (20.5)
 a. What might be happening to the gardener?
 b. Why must humans be careful when using insecticides?

20.95 The zymogen pepsinogen is produced in the gastric chief cells of the stomach. (20.4)
 a. How and where does pepsinogen become the active form, pepsin?
 b. Why are proteases such as pepsin produced in inactive forms?

20.96 Thrombin is an enzyme that helps produce blood clotting when an injury and bleeding occur. (20.4)
 a. What would be the name of the zymogen of thrombin?
 b. Why would the active form of thrombin be produced only when an injury to tissue occurs?

CHALLENGE QUESTIONS

The following groups of questions are related to the topics in this chapter. However, they do not all follow the chapter order, and they require you to combine concepts and skills from several sections. These questions will help you increase your critical thinking skills and prepare for your next exam.

20.97 Lactase is an enzyme that hydrolyzes lactose to glucose and galactose. (20.1, 20.2)
 a. What are the reactants and products of the reaction?
 b. Draw an energy diagram for the reaction with and without lactase.
 c. How does lactase make the reaction go faster?

20.98 Maltase is an enzyme that hydrolyzes maltose into two glucose molecules. (20.1, 20.2)
 a. What are the reactants and products of the reaction?
 b. Draw an energy diagram for the reaction with and without maltase.
 c. How does maltase make the reaction go faster?

20.99 What class of enzyme would catalyze each of the following reactions? (20.2)

 a. $CH_3-\overset{\displaystyle O}{\overset{\|}{C}}-H \longrightarrow CH_3-\overset{\displaystyle O}{\overset{\|}{C}}-OH$

 b. $H_3\overset{+}{N}-CH_2-\overset{\displaystyle O}{\overset{\|}{C}}-\overset{\displaystyle H}{\overset{|}{N}}-\overset{\displaystyle CH_3}{\overset{|}{CH}}-\overset{\displaystyle O}{\overset{\|}{C}}-O^- + H_2O \longrightarrow$
 $H_3\overset{+}{N}-CH_2-\overset{\displaystyle O}{\overset{\|}{C}}-O^- + H_3\overset{+}{N}-\overset{\displaystyle CH_3}{\overset{|}{CH}}-\overset{\displaystyle O}{\overset{\|}{C}}-O^-$

 c. $CH_3-CH=CH-CH_3 + H_2O \longrightarrow$
 $CH_3-CH_2-\overset{\displaystyle OH}{\overset{|}{CH}}-CH_3$

20.100 What class of enzyme would catalyze each of the following reactions? (20.2)

 a. $CH_3-\overset{\displaystyle O}{\overset{\|}{C}}-\overset{\displaystyle O}{\overset{\|}{C}}-OH \longrightarrow CH_3-\overset{\displaystyle O}{\overset{\|}{C}}-OH + CO_2$

 b. $CH_3-\overset{\displaystyle O}{\overset{\|}{C}}-\overset{\displaystyle O}{\overset{\|}{C}}-OH + CO_2 + ATP \longrightarrow$
 $HO-\overset{\displaystyle O}{\overset{\|}{C}}-CH_2-\overset{\displaystyle O}{\overset{\|}{C}}-\overset{\displaystyle O}{\overset{\|}{C}}-OH + ADP + P_i$

 c. glucose-6-phosphate $\longrightarrow$ fructose-6-phosphate

℞ Clinical Applications

20.101 Cadmium is a poisonous metal used in industries that produce batteries and plastics. Cadmium ions (Cd^{2+}) are inhibitors of the enzyme hexokinase. Increasing the concentration of glucose or ATP, the substrates of hexokinase, or Mg^{2+}, the cofactor of hexokinase, does not change the rate of the cadmium-inhibited reaction. Is cadmium a competitive or noncompetitive inhibitor? Explain. (20.5, 20.6)

20.102 Beano contains an enzyme that breaks down polysaccharides into smaller, more digestible sugars, which diminishes the intestinal gas formation that can occur after eating foods such as vegetables and beans. (20.1, 20.2, 20.5)

    a. The label says "contains alpha-galactosidase." What class of enzyme is this?

    b. What is the substrate for the enzyme?

    c. The directions indicate you should not cook with or heat Beano. Why?

Beano contains an enzyme that breaks down carbohydrates.

ANSWERS TO SELECTED QUESTIONS AND PROBLEMS

20.1 Chemical reactions can occur without enzymes, but the rates are too slow. Catalyzed reactions, which are many times faster, provide the amounts of products needed by the cell at a particular time.

20.3 **a.** (2) enzyme
    b. (1) enzyme–substrate complex
    c. (3) substrate

20.5 **a.** $E + S \rightleftharpoons ES \longrightarrow EP \longrightarrow E + P$
    b. The active site is a region or pocket within the tertiary structure of an enzyme that accepts the substrate, aligns the substrate for reaction, and catalyzes the reaction.

20.7 **a.** oxidation–reduction
    b. transfer of a group from one substance to another
    c. hydrolysis (splitting) of molecules with the addition of water

20.9 **a.** hydrolase   **b.** oxidoreductase
    c. isomerase   **d.** transferase

20.11 **a.** lyase   **b.** transferase

20.13 **a.** succinate oxidase
    b. glutamine synthetase
    c. alcohol dehydrogenase

20.15 **a.** prostate-specific antigen   **b.** creatine kinase
    c. cholinesterase

20.17 Isoenzymes are slightly different forms of an enzyme that catalyze the same reaction in different organs and tissues of the body.

20.19 A doctor might run tests for the enzymes CK and LDH to determine if the patient had a heart attack.

20.21 **a.** The reaction will be slower.
    b. The reaction will slow or stop because the enzyme will be denatured at low pH.
    c. The reaction will slow or stop because the high temperature will denature the enzyme.
    d. The reaction will go faster as long as there are polypeptides to react.

20.23 pepsin, pH 2; lactase, pH 6; sucrase, pH 6; trypsin, pH 8

20.25 When a regulator molecule binds to an allosteric site, the shape of the enzyme is altered, which makes the active site more reactive or less reactive, and thereby increases or decreases the rate of the reaction.

20.27 In feedback control, the product binds to the first enzyme in a series and changes the shape of the active site. If the active site can no longer bind the substrate effectively, the reaction will stop.

20.29 **a.** (3) covalent modification   **b.** (2) a zymogen
    c. (1) an allosteric enzyme

20.31 In order to conserve material and energy and to prevent clotting in the bloodstream, thrombin is produced from prothrombin only at a wound site.

20.33 **a.** competitive   **b.** noncompetitive
    c. competitive   **d.** noncompetitive
    e. competitive

20.35 **a.** methanol, CH_3-OH; ethanol, CH_3-CH_2-OH
    b. Ethanol competes with methanol for the active site in the enzyme.
    c. Ethanol is a competitive inhibitor.

20.37 **a.** active with a cofactor
    b. active with a cofactor
    c. does not require a cofactor

20.39 **a.** pantothenic acid (vitamin B_5)
    b. folic acid
    c. niacin (vitamin B_5)

20.41 **a.** vitamin D (cholecalciferol)
    b. vitamin C (ascorbic acid)
    c. vitamin B_3 (niacin)

20.43 Vitamin B_6 is a water-soluble vitamin, which means that each day any excess of vitamin B_6 is eliminated from the body.

20.45 **a.** 20 ppm H_2 **b.** 40 ppm H_2

20.47 Heating the milk in the hot chocolate will denature the protein enzyme, lactase. Since the enzyme is no longer active, Noah will suffer from the symptoms of lactose intolerance.

20.49 **a.** The enzyme bromelain found in fresh pineapple breaks down protein, which means that the gelatin dessert would not turn solid upon cooking. The high temperatures used to prepare canned pineapple denature the enzyme so it no longer catalyzes the hydrolysis of protein.
    b. The enzyme in fresh pineapple juice can be used to tenderize tough meat because the enzyme breaks down proteins.

20.51 **a.** oxidoreductase
    b. Ethanol competes with ethylene glycol for the active site of the alcohol dehydrogenase enzyme, saturating the active site, which allows ethylene glycol to be removed from the body without producing oxalic acid.

20.53 The many different reactions that take place in cells require different enzymes because enzymes react with only a certain type of substrate.

20.55 Enzymes are catalysts that are proteins and function only at mild temperature and pH. Catalysts used in chemistry laboratories are usually inorganic materials that function at high temperatures and in strongly acidic or basic conditions.

20.57 An enzyme lowers the activation energy for a reaction.

20.59 Sucrose fits the shape of the active site in sucrose, but lactose does not.

20.61 a. S   b. E   c. E
       d. E   e. S   f. E

20.63 a. urea   b. succinate
       c. aspartate   d. phenylalanine

20.65 a. transferase   b. oxidoreductase
       c. hydrolase   d. lyase

20.67 The optimum temperature for an enzyme is the temperature at which the enzyme is fully active and most effective.

20.69 a. The rate of catalysis will slow and stop as a high temperature denatures the enzyme.
       b. The rate of the catalyzed reaction will slow as temperature is lowered.
       c. The enzyme will not be functional at pH 2.0.

20.71 a. saturated   b. unsaturated

20.73 An allosteric enzyme contains sites for regulators that alter the structure of the active site of an enzyme, which speeds up or slows down the rate of the catalyzed reaction.

20.75 In feedback control, a negative regulator slows down the catalytic activity.

20.77 In reversible inhibition, the inhibitor can dissociate from the enzyme, whereas in irreversible inhibition, the inhibitor forms a strong covalent bond with the enzyme and does not dissociate. Irreversible inhibitors act as poisons to enzymes.

20.79 a. (3) irreversible inhibitor
       b. (1) competitive inhibitor
       c. (1) competitive inhibitor
       d. (2) noncompetitive inhibitor

20.81 a. requires a cofactor
       b. does not require a cofactor
       c. requires a cofactor (coenzyme)

20.83 a. (3) coenzyme A   b. (1) NAD^+
       c. (2) thiamine pyrophosphate (TPP)

20.85 A vitamin combines with an enzyme only when the enzyme and coenzyme are needed to catalyze a reaction. When the enzyme is not needed, the vitamin dissociates for use by other enzymes in the cell.

20.87 a. niacin, (3) pellagra
       b. vitamin A, (1) night blindness
       c. vitamin D, (2) weak bone structure

20.89 A heart attack may be the cause.

20.91 When designing an inhibitor, the substrate of an enzyme usually is known even if the structure of the enzyme is not. It is easier to design a molecule that resembles the substrate (competitive) than to find an inhibitor that binds to a second site on an enzyme (noncompetitive).

20.93 a. Antibiotics such as ampicillin are irreversible inhibitors.
       b. Antibiotics inhibit enzymes needed to form cell walls in bacteria, not humans.

20.95 a. When pepsinogen enters the stomach, the low pH cleaves a peptide from its protein chain to form pepsin.
       b. An active protease would digest the proteins of the stomach rather than the proteins in foods.

20.97 a. The reactants are lactose and water and the products are glucose and galactose.
       b.

       c. By lowering the energy of activation, the enzyme furnishes a lower energy pathway by which the reaction can take place.

20.99 a. oxidoreductase   b. hydrolase
       c. lyase

20.101 Cadmium would be a noncompetitive inhibitor because increasing the substrate and cofactor has no effect on the rate. This implies that the cadmium is binding to another site on the enzyme.

21

Nucleic Acids and Protein Synthesis

ELLEN HAS FOUND A PEA-SIZED LUMP IN HER

breast. A needle biopsy confirms that Ellen has breast cancer. She undergoes a lumpectomy, during which the surgeon removes the tumor along with a small margin of surrounding normal tissue. The surgeon also makes an incision under her arm and removes the sentinel lymph nodes. Because cancer cells are found in the sentinel node, more lymph nodes are removed. He sends the excised tumor and lymph nodes to Lisa, a histology technician.

Lisa prepares the tissue sample to be viewed by a pathologist. Tissue preparation requires Lisa to cut the tissue into very thin sections, normally 0.001 mm, which are mounted onto microscope slides. She treats the tissue on the slides with a dye to stain the cells, which enables the pathologist to distinguish abnormal cells more easily.

When a person's DNA (deoxyribonucleic acid) is damaged, it may result in mutations that promote the abnormal cell growth found in cancer. Cancer as well as genetic diseases can be a result of mutations caused by environmental and hereditary factors.

CAREER Histology Technician

A histology technician studies the microscopic make-up of tissues, cells, and bodily fluids with the purpose of detecting and identifying the presence of a specific disease. They determine blood types and the concentrations of drugs and other substances in the blood. Histologists also help establish a rationale for why a patient may not be responding to his or her treatment. Sample preparation is a critical component of a histologist's job, as they prepare tissue samples from humans, animals, and plants. The tissue samples are cut, using specialized equipment, into extremely thin sections which are then mounted, and stained using various chemical dyes. The dyes provide contrast for the cells to be viewed and help highlight any abnormalities that may exist. Utilization of various dyes requires the histologist to be familiar with solution preparation and the handling of potentially hazardous chemicals.

LOOKING AHEAD

21.1 Components of Nucleic Acids 754

21.2 Primary Structure of Nucleic Acids 759

21.3 DNA Double Helix 761

21.4 DNA Replication 763

21.5 RNA and Transcription 766

21.6 The Genetic Code and Protein Synthesis 771

Chemistry Link to Health *Many Antibiotics Inhibit Protein Synthesis* 774

21.7 Genetic Mutations 776

21.8 Recombinant DNA 780

21.9 Viruses 782

Chemistry Link to Health *Cancer* 785

Clinical Applications 758, 775, 779, 786, 787, 791

Clinical Update *Ellen's Medical Treatment Following Breast Cancer Surgery* 786

Nucleic acids are large molecules found in the nuclei of cells that store information and direct activities for cellular growth and reproduction. Deoxyribonucleic acid (DNA), the genetic material in the nucleus of a cell, contains all the information needed for the development of a complete living organism. The way you grow, your hair, your eyes, your physical appearance, and all the activities of all the cells in your body are determined by a set of directions contained within the DNA of your cells.

All of the genetic information in the cell is called the *genome*. Every time a cell divides, the information in the genome is copied and passed on to the new cells. This replication process must duplicate the genetic instructions exactly. Some sections of DNA called *genes* contain the information to make a particular protein.

When a cell requires protein, another type of nucleic acid, ribonucleic acid (RNA), interprets the genetic information in DNA and carries that information to the ribosomes, where the synthesis of protein takes place. However, mistakes may occur that lead to mutations that affect the synthesis of a certain protein.

CHAPTER READINESS*

⚛ CORE CHEMISTRY SKILLS

- Forming Amides (18.5)
- Drawing the Zwitterion for an Amino Acid (19.1)
- Identifying the Primary, Secondary, Tertiary, and Quaternary Structures of Proteins (19.4, 19.5)
- Identifying Factors Affecting Enzyme Activity (20.3)

*These Core Chemistry Skills from previous chapters are listed here for your review as you proceed to the new material in this chapter.

LEARNING GOAL

Describe the bases and ribose sugars that make up the nucleic acids DNA and RNA.

FIGURE 21.1 ▶ The general structure of a nucleotide includes a nitrogen-containing base, a sugar, and a phosphate group.

❓ In a nucleotide, what types of groups are bonded to a five-carbon sugar?

21.1 Components of Nucleic Acids

There are two closely related types of nucleic acids: *deoxyribonucleic acid* (**DNA**) and *ribonucleic acid* (**RNA**). Both are unbranched polymers of repeating monomer units known as *nucleotides*. Each nucleotide has three components: a base that contains nitrogen, a five-carbon sugar, and a phosphate group (see Figure 21.1). A DNA molecule may contain several million nucleotides; smaller RNA molecules may contain up to several thousand.

Bases

The nitrogen-containing **bases** in nucleic acids are derivatives of the heterocyclic amines *pyrimidine* or *purine*. A pyrimidine has a single ring with two nitrogen atoms, and a purine has two rings each with two nitrogen atoms. They are basic because the nitrogen atoms are H^+ acceptors.

Pyrimidine   Purine

In DNA, the purine bases with double rings are adenine (A) and guanine (G), and the pyrimidine bases with single rings are cytosine (C) and thymine (T). RNA contains the same bases, except thymine (5-methyluracil) is replaced by uracil (U) (see Figure 21.2).

Pyrimidines

Cytosine (C)
(DNA and RNA)

Uracil (U)
(RNA only)

Thymine (T)
(DNA only)

Purines

Adenine (A)
(DNA and RNA)

Guanine (G)
(DNA and RNA)

FIGURE 21.2 ▶ DNA contains the bases A, G, C, and T; RNA contains A, G, C, and U.

◉ Which bases are found in DNA?

Pentose Sugars

In RNA, the five-carbon sugar is *ribose*, which gives the letter R in the abbreviation RNA. The atoms in the pentose sugars are numbered with primes ($1'$, $2'$, $3'$, $4'$, and $5'$) to differentiate them from the atoms in the bases. In DNA, the five-carbon sugar is *deoxyribose*, which is similar to ribose except that there is no hydroxyl group (—OH) on $C2'$. The *deoxy* prefix means "without oxygen" and provides the letter D in DNA.

Nucleosides and Nucleotides

A **nucleoside** is composed of one of the nitrogen-containing bases and one of the sugars, either ribose or deoxyribose. A nitrogen atom of the base is connected by a β-N-glycosidic bond to the $C1'$ of the sugar. For example, the combination of adenine, a purine, and ribose forms the nucleoside adenosine.

Pentose Sugars in RNA and DNA

Ribose in RNA

Deoxyribose in DNA

The five-carbon pentose sugar found in RNA is ribose and in DNA, deoxyribose.

A base forms a β-N-glycosidic bond with ribose or deoxyribose to form a nucleoside.

When a phosphate group adds to a nucleoside, a *nucleotide* is produced. Thus, a **nucleotide** is composed of a base, a sugar, and a phosphate group, which forms a phosphoester bond with the $C5'$ OH group of the sugar. Other hydroxyl groups on ribose can also form phosphate esters, but only $5'$ monophosphate nucleotides are found in RNA and DNA. All the nucleotides in RNA and DNA are shown in Figure 21.3.

Phosphate + Nucleoside ⟶ Nucleotide + H_2O

The addition of a phosphate group to a nucleoside (adenosine) forms a nucleotide (adenosine monophosphate, AMP).

Adenosine monophosphate (AMP)
Deoxyadenosine monophosphate (dAMP)

Guanosine monophosphate (GMP)
Deoxyguanosine monophosphate (dGMP)

Cytidine monophosphate (CMP)
Deoxycytidine monophosphate (dCMP)

Uridine monophosphate (UMP)

Deoxythymidine monophosphate (dTMP)

FIGURE 21.3 ▶ The nucleotides of RNA (shown in black) are similar to those of DNA (shown in magenta), except in DNA the sugar is deoxyribose and deoxythymidine replaces uridine.

Ⓠ What are two differences in the nucleotides of RNA and DNA?

Table 21.1 summarizes the components in DNA and RNA.

TABLE 21.1 Components in DNA and RNA

Component	DNA	RNA
Bases	A, G, C, and T	A, G, C, and U
Sugar	Deoxyribose	Ribose
Nucleoside	Base + deoxyribose	Base + ribose
Nucleotide	Base + deoxyribose + phosphate	Base + ribose + phosphate
Nucleic Acid	Polymer of deoxyribose nucleotides	Polymer of ribose nucleotides

Naming Nucleosides and Nucleotides

The name of a nucleoside that contains a purine ends with *osine*, whereas a nucleoside that contains a pyrimidine ends with *idine*. The names of nucleosides of DNA add *deoxy* to the beginning of their names. The corresponding nucleotides in RNA and DNA are named by adding *monophosphate* to the end of the nucleoside name. Although the letters A, G, C, U, and T represent the bases, they are often used in the abbreviations of the respective nucleosides and nucleotides. The names of the bases, nucleosides, and nucleotides in DNA and RNA and their abbreviations are listed in Table 21.2.

TABLE 21.2 Nucleosides and Nucleotides in DNA and RNA

Base	Nucleosides	Nucleotides
DNA		
Adenine (A)	Deoxyadenosine (A)	Deoxyadenosine monophosphate (dAMP)
Guanine (G)	Deoxyguanosine (G)	Deoxyguanosine monophosphate (dGMP)
Cytosine (C)	Deoxycytidine (C)	Deoxycytidine monophosphate (dCMP)
Thymine (T)	Deoxythymidine (T)	Deoxythymidine monophosphate (dTMP)
RNA		
Adenine (A)	Adenosine (A)	Adenosine monophosphate (AMP)
Guanine (G)	Guanosine (G)	Guanosine monophosphate (GMP)
Cytosine (C)	Cytidine (C)	Cytidine monophosphate (CMP)
Uracil (U)	Uridine (U)	Uridine monophosphate (UMP)

Formation of Di- and Triphosphonucleotides

When one or two more phosphate groups add to a monophosphate nucleotide, a di- or triphosphate nucleotide is produced. For example, adding one phosphate group to AMP gives ADP (*adenosine diphosphate*). Adding another phosphate group to ADP gives ATP (*adenosine triphosphate*) (see Figure 21.4). Of the triphosphates, ATP is of particular interest because it is the major source of energy for most energy-requiring activities in the cell. In other examples, phosphate is added to GMP to yield GDP and GTP, which is part of the citric acid cycle.

FIGURE 21.4 ▶ The addition of one or two more phosphate groups to AMP forms adenosine diphosphate (ADP) and adenosine triphosphate (ATP).

◉ How does the structure of deoxyguanosine triphosphate (dGTP) differ from ATP?

SAMPLE PROBLEM 21.1 Nucleotides

For each of the following nucleotides, identify the components and whether the nucleotide is found in DNA only, RNA only, or both DNA and RNA:

a. deoxyguanosine monophosphate (dGMP)
b. adenosine monophosphate (AMP)

SOLUTION

a. This nucleotide of deoxyribose, guanine, and a phosphate group is only found in DNA.
b. This nucleotide of ribose, adenine, and a phosphate group is only found in RNA.

STUDY CHECK 21.1

What is the name and abbreviation of the DNA nucleotide of cytosine?

ANSWER

deoxycytidine monophosphate (dCMP)

QUESTIONS AND PROBLEMS

21.1 Components of Nucleic Acids

LEARNING GOAL Describe the bases and ribose sugars that make up the nucleic acids DNA and RNA.

21.1 Identify each of the following bases as a purine or a pyrimidine:
   a. thymine
   b.

21.2 Identify each of the following bases as a purine or a pyrimidine:
   a. guanine
   b.

21.3 Identify each of the bases in problem 21.1 as a component of DNA only, RNA only, or both DNA and RNA.

21.4 Identify each of the bases in problem 21.2 as a component of DNA only, RNA only, or both DNA and RNA.

21.5 What are the names and abbreviations of the four nucleotides in DNA?

21.6 What are the names and abbreviations of the four nucleotides in RNA?

21.7 Identify each of the following as a nucleoside or a nucleotide:
   a. adenosine
   b. deoxycytidine
   c. uridine
   d. cytidine monophosphate

21.8 Identify each of the following as a nucleoside or a nucleotide:
   a. deoxythymidine
   b. guanosine
   c. deoxyadenosine monophosphate
   d. uridine monophosphate

21.9 State whether each of the following components is present in (1) DNA only, (2) RNA only, or (3) both DNA and RNA:
   a. phosphate
   b. ribose
   c. deoxycytidine monophosphate
   d. adenine

21.10 State whether each of the following components is present in (1) DNA only, (2) RNA only, or (3) both DNA and RNA:
   a. deoxyribose
   b. guanosine monophosphate
   c. uracil
   d. UMP

℞ Clinical Applications

21.11 In the genetic disease *adenosine deaminase deficiency*, there is an accumulation of adenosine. Draw the condensed structural formula for deoxyadenosine monophosphate.

21.12 In the genetic disease *uridine monophosphate synthase deficiency*, symptoms include anemia, cardiac malformations, and infections. Draw the condensed structural formula for uridine monophosphate.

21.13 In Lesch–Nyhan syndrome, a deficiency of *guanine transferase* causes an overproduction of uric acid. Draw the condensed structural formula for guanosine monophosphate.

21.14 A deficiency of *adenine transferase* causes a lack of adenine for purine synthesis and a high level of adenine in the urine. Draw the condensed structural formula for adenosine monophosphate.

21.2 Primary Structure of Nucleic Acids

LEARNING GOAL

Describe the primary structures of RNA and DNA.

The **nucleic acids** are polymers of many nucleotides in which the 3′ hydroxyl group of the sugar in one nucleotide bonds to the phosphate group on the 5′ carbon atom in the sugar of the next nucleotide. This connection between a phosphate and sugars in adjacent nucleotides is referred to as a **phosphodiester linkage**. As more nucleotides are added, a backbone forms that consists of alternating sugar and phosphate groups. The bases, which are attached to each sugar, extend out from the sugar–phosphate backbone.

A phosphodiester linkage forms between the 3′ hydroxyl group in the sugar of one nucleotide and the phosphate group on the 5′ carbon atom in the sugar of the next nucleotide.

Each nucleic acid has its own unique sequence of bases, which is known as its **primary structure**. It is this sequence of bases that carries the genetic information. In any nucleic acid, the sugar at one end has an unreacted or free 5′ phosphate terminal end, and the sugar at the other end has a free 3′ hydroxyl group.

A nucleic acid sequence is read from the sugar with the free 5′ phosphate to the sugar with the free 3′ hydroxyl group. The order of nucleotides in a nucleic acid is often written using the letters of the bases. For example, the nucleotide sequence starting with adenine (free 5′ phosphate end) in the section of RNA shown in Figure 21.5 is A C G U.

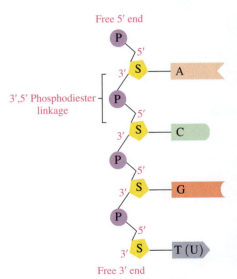

In the primary structure of nucleic acids, each sugar in a sugar–phosphate backbone is attached to a base.

FIGURE 21.5 ▶ In the primary structure of RNA, A, C, G, and U are connected by 3′,5′ phosphodiester linkages.

◉ Where are the free 5′ phosphate and 3′ hydroxyl groups?

▶SAMPLE PROBLEM 21.2 **Bonding of Nucleotides**

Draw the condensed structural formula for an RNA dinucleotide formed by joining the 3′ OH group of adenosine monophosphate and the 5′ phosphate group of cytidine monophosphate.

SOLUTION

The dinucleotide is drawn by connecting the 3′ hydroxyl group on the adenosine 5′ monophosphate with the 5′ phosphate group on the cytidine monophosphate.

STUDY CHECK 21.2

What type of linkage connects the two nucleotides in Sample Problem 21.2?

ANSWER

A 3′,5′ phosphodiester linkage connects the 3′ OH group in the ribose of AMP and the 5′ carbon in the ribose of CMP.

QUESTIONS AND PROBLEMS

21.2 Primary Structure of Nucleic Acids

LEARNING GOAL Describe the primary structures of RNA and DNA.

21.15 What nucleic acid subunits are connected in a 3′,5′ phosphodiester linkage in a polynucleotide?

21.16 What is the difference in the 3′ end and the 5′ end of a polynucleotide chain?

21.17 What components join together to form the backbone of a nucleic acid?

21.18 What component in the backbone of a nucleic acid is bonded to a nitrogen base?

21.19 What component in a nucleic acid determines the 5′ free end?

21.20 What component in a nucleic acid determines the 3′ free end?

21.21 Draw the condensed structural formula for the dinucleotide 5′ G C 3′ that would be in RNA.

21.22 Draw the condensed structural formula for the dinucleotide 5′ A T 3′ that would be in DNA.

21.3 DNA Double Helix

LEARNING GOAL

Describe the double helix of DNA.

During the 1940s, biologists determined that the bases in DNA from a variety of organisms had a specific relationship: the amount of adenine (A) was equal to the amount of thymine (T), and the amount of guanine (G) was equal to the amount of cytosine (C) (see Table 21.3). Eventually, scientists determined that adenine is paired (1:1) with thymine, and guanine is paired (1:1) with cytosine. This relationship, known as *Chargaff's rules*, can be summarized as follows:

Number of purine molecules = Number of pyrimidine molecules

Adenine (A) = Thymine (T)

Guanine (G) = Cytosine (C)

TABLE 21.3 Percentages of Bases in the DNAs of Selected Organisms

Organism	%A	%T	%G	%C
Human	30	30	20	20
Chicken	28	28	22	22
Salmon	28	28	22	22
Corn (maize)	27	27	23	23
Neurospora	23	23	27	27

In 1953, James Watson and Francis Crick proposed that DNA was a **double helix** that consisted of two polynucleotide strands winding about each other like a spiral staircase. The sugar–phosphate backbones are analogous to the outside railings of the stairs, with the bases arranged like steps along the inside. One strand goes from the 5′ to 3′ direction, and the other strand goes in the 3′ to 5′ direction.

CORE CHEMISTRY SKILL

Writing the Complementary DNA Strand

Complementary Base Pairs

Each of the bases along one polynucleotide strand forms hydrogen bonds to only one specific base on the opposite DNA strand. Adenine forms hydrogen bonds to thymine only, and guanine bonds to cytosine only (see Figure 21.6). The pairs AT and GC are called **complementary base pairs**. Because of structural limitations, there are only two kinds of stable base pairs. The bases that bind utilizing two hydrogen bonds are adenine and thymine, and the bases that bind utilizing three hydrogen bonds are cytosine and guanine. *No other stable base pairs occur.* For example, adenine does not form hydrogen bonds with cytosine or guanine; cytosine does not form hydrogen bonds with adenine or thymine. This explains why DNA has equal amounts of A and T bases and equal amounts of G and C.

Adenine–Thymine Base Pair
(two hydrogen bonds)

Adenine   Thymine

Guanine–Cytosine Base Pair
(three hydrogen bonds)

Guanine   Cytosine

Sugar–phosphate
backbone

FIGURE 21.6 ▶ In the model shown, the sugar–phosphate backbone is represented by a ribbon with hydrogen bonds between complementary base pairs.

Q Why are GC base pairs more stable than AT base pairs?

▷ SAMPLE PROBLEM 21.3 Complementary Base Pairs

Write the complementary base sequence for the following segment of a strand of DNA:

5′ A C G A T C T 3′

SOLUTION

ANALYZE THE PROBLEM	Given	Need
	5′ A C G A T C T 3′	complementary base sequence

The complementary base pairs are A–T and C–G. The complementary strand is written in the opposite direction, from the 3′ end to the 5′ end.

Original segment of DNA: 5′ A C G A T C T 3′

Complementary segment: 3′ T G C T A G A 5′

STUDY CHECK 21.3

STUDY CHECK 21.3

What sequence of bases is complementary to a DNA segment with a base sequence of
5′ G G T T A A C C 3′?

ANSWER

3′ C C A A T T G G 5′

QUESTIONS AND PROBLEMS

21.3 DNA Double Helix

LEARNING GOAL Describe the double helix of DNA.

21.23 List three structural characteristics of DNA.

21.24 What is meant by double helix?

21.25 How are the two strands of nucleic acid in DNA held together?

21.26 What is meant by complementary base pairing?

21.27 Write the base sequence in a complementary DNA segment if
each original segment has the following base sequence:
  a. 5′ A A A A A A 3′
  b. 5′ G G G G G G 3′

  c. 5′ A G T C C A G G T 3′
  d. 5′ C T G T A T A C G T T A 3′

21.28 Write the base sequence in a complementary DNA segment if
each original segment has the following base sequence:
  a. 5′ T T T T T T 3′
  b. 5′ C C C C C C C C C 3′
  c. 5′ A T G G C A 3′
  d. 5′ A T A T G C G C T A A A 3′

21.4 DNA Replication

The function of DNA in the cells of animals and plants as well as in bacteria is to preserve
genetic information. As cells divide, copied strands of DNA are produced that transfer
genetic information to the new cells.

LEARNING GOAL

Describe the process of DNA
replication.

DNA Replication

In DNA **replication**, the strands in the original or *parent* DNA molecule separate to allow
the synthesis of complementary DNA strands. The process begins with the unwinding of a
portion of the double helix by breaking the hydrogen bonds between the complementary
bases. The resulting single strands act as templates for the synthesis of new complementary strands of DNA (see Figure 21.7).

Within the nucleus, nucleoside triphosphates of the four types of bases (dATP, dTTP,
dGTP, and dCTP) are available so that each exposed base on the template strand can form
hydrogen bonds with its complementary base. For example, T in the template strand
hydrogen bonds with A, and G on the template strand hydrogen bonds with C. As the
hydrogen bonds form base pairs, phosphodiester linkages are formed between the
nucleotides.

Eventually, the entire double helix of the parent DNA is copied. In each new DNA,
one strand of the double helix is from the parent DNA, and one is a newly synthesized
DNA strand. This process produces two new daughter DNA strands, which are exact
copies of the parent DNA. In DNA replication, complementary base pairing ensures the
correct placement of bases in the daughter DNA strands.

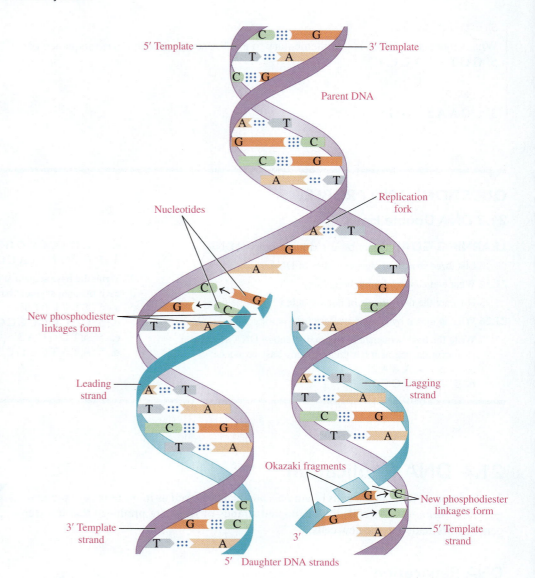

FIGURE 21.7 ▶ In DNA replication, the separate strands of the parent DNA are the templates for the synthesis of complementary strands, producing two exact copies of DNA.

Q How many strands of the parent DNA are contained in each of the daughter DNA?

Direction of Replication

Now that we have seen the overall process, we can take a look at some of the details of DNA replication, which requires the interaction of many enzymes and proteins as well as the parent DNA strands (see Figure 21.8). The unwinding of DNA by *helicase* occurs simultaneously in several sections along the parent DNA molecule. The separated strands are held open by a small protein called *single-strand binding protein* so that *DNA polymerase* can bind to the exposed bases. As a result, DNA polymerase can catalyze the replication process at each of these open DNA sections called **replication forks**. However, DNA polymerase only moves in the 5′ to 3′ direction, which means it catalyzes the formation of phosphodiester linkages between the hydroxyl group at the end of the growing nucleic acid and the phosphate group of a nucleoside triphosphate. The new DNA strand that grows in the 5′ to 3′ direction, the *leading strand*, is synthesized continuously.

However, the other new DNA strand, which is the *lagging strand*, is synthesized discontinuously in short, separate segments. To initiate synthesis on the lagging strand, the enzyme *primase* produces short complementary RNA fragments, called *primers*. These RNA primers serve as starting points for DNA polymerase to begin extending the complementary DNA fragments at the 3′ end until the polymerase reaches the next primer. As a result, DNA replication on the lagging strand consists of DNA segments called **Okazaki fragments**. Eventually DNA polymerase replaces the RNA primers in each segment with the corresponding DNA. Finally *DNA ligase* connects the Okazaki fragments by phosphodiester linkages, forming a daughter lagging strand, which matches the leading DNA strand. The enzymes and proteins required for replication are summarized in Table 21.4.

Direction of Replication

TABLE 21.4 Enzymes and Proteins in DNA Replication

Enzymes and Proteins		
1. Helicase	Helicase breaks the hydrogen bonds of the parent DNA strands at the *replication forks*, which gives two separate DNA strands.	
2. Single-strand Binding Protein	Single-strand binding proteins attach to the separated parent strands to keep them apart and the bases exposed.	
	Leading Strand 5′ to 3′	**Lagging Strand 3′ to 5′**
3. Primase		Primase synthesizes short RNA segments called primers that are starting points for DNA polymerase.
4. DNA Polymerase	DNA polymerase catalyzes the formation of phosphodiester linkages on the new DNA strands between the 3′ ends of the growing chains and available complementary nucleotides (dATP, dTTP, dGTP, and dCTP).	
	DNA polymerase adds nucleotides continuously in the 5′ to 3′ direction to a growing DNA chain.	At each primer, DNA polymerase forms short, separate segments (Okazaki fragments) until it reaches the next primer and stops.
5. DNA Ligase		DNA ligase joins the Okazaki fragments.

FIGURE 21.8 ▶ DNA replication occurs continuously in the 5′ to 3′ direction on the leading strand and discontinuously on the lagging strand in the 5′ to 3′ direction. Smaller Okazaki fragments are joined by DNA ligase.

🔎 Why are the Okazaki fragments formed only for the lagging strand?

▶**SAMPLE PROBLEM 21.4** **Direction of DNA Replication**

In an original DNA strand, a segment has the base sequence 5′ A G T C C G 3′.

a. What is the sequence of nucleotides in the daughter DNA strand that is complementary to this segment?

b. Why would the complementary sequence in the daughter DNA strand be synthesized as Okazaki fragments that require a DNA ligase?

SOLUTION

a. Only one possible nucleotide can pair with each base in the original segment. Thymine will pair only with adenine, whereas cytosine pairs only with guanine to give the complementary base sequence: 3′ T C A G G C 5′.

b. Because DNA polymerase only adds nucleotides in the 5′ to 3′ direction, DNA on the lagging strand is synthesized as short Okazaki fragments, which are joined by DNA ligase.

STUDY CHECK 21.4

How many daughter strands are formed during the replication of DNA?

ANSWER

Two daughter strands are formed, one from each strand of the DNA double helix.

QUESTIONS AND PROBLEMS

21.4 DNA Replication

LEARNING GOAL Describe the process of DNA replication.

21.29 What is the function of the enzyme helicase in DNA replication?

21.30 What is the function of the enzyme DNA polymerase in DNA replication?

21.31 What process ensures that the replication of DNA produces identical copies?

21.32 Why are Okazaki fragments formed in the synthesis of the lagging strand?

21.33 Match each component with one of the following descriptions:
   (1) lagging strand
   (2) helicase
   (3) primase
   (4) replication fork

   a. unwinds the DNA helix
   b. synthesizes primers at the replication fork
   c. point in DNA where nucleotides add to daughter DNA strand
   d. daughter DNA synthesized from short sections called Okazaki fragments

21.34 Match each component with one of the following descriptions:
   (1) leading strand
   (2) DNA ligase
   (3) single-strand binding protein
   (4) DNA polymerase

   a. catalyzes the formation of phosphodiester linkages between nucleotides
   b. daughter DNA synthesized continuously in 5′ to 3′ direction
   c. attaches to unwound strands to keep them open
   d. combines Okazaki fragments to form daughter DNA strand

21.35 Answer each of the following for a segment of a template strand 3′ G C T C C A T G 5′:
   a. Write the sequence of the new DNA segment.
   b. Will the production of this new DNA segment require the synthesis of Okazaki fragments?

21.36 Answer each of the following for a segment of a template strand 5′ A A G T C G T G 3′:
   a. Write the sequence of the new DNA segment.
   b. Will the production of this new DNA segment require the synthesis of Okazaki fragments?

LEARNING GOAL

Identify the different types of RNA; describe the synthesis of mRNA.

Small subunit   +   Large subunit

Ribosome

FIGURE 21.9 ▶ A typical ribosome consists of a small subunit and a large subunit. The subunit shapes shown contain both protein and rRNA.

🔍 Why would there be many thousands of ribosomes in a cell?

21.5 RNA and Transcription

Ribonucleic acid, RNA, which makes up most of the nucleic acid found in the cell, is involved with transmitting the genetic information needed to operate the cell. Similar to DNA, RNA molecules are unbranched polymers of nucleotides. However, RNA differs from DNA in several important ways:

1. The sugar in RNA is ribose rather than the deoxyribose found in DNA.
2. In RNA, the base uracil replaces thymine.
3. RNA molecules are single stranded, not double stranded.
4. RNA molecules are much smaller than DNA molecules.

Types of RNA

There are three major types of RNA in the cells: *messenger RNA*, *ribosomal RNA*, and *transfer RNA*. Ribosomal RNA (**rRNA**), the most abundant type of RNA, is combined with proteins to form ribosomes. Ribosomes, which are the sites for protein synthesis, consist of two subunits: a large subunit and a small subunit (see Figure 21.9). Cells that synthesize large numbers of proteins have thousands of ribosomes.

Messenger RNA (**mRNA**) carries genetic information from the DNA, located in the nucleus of the cell, to the ribosomes, located in the *cytosol*, the liquid outside the nucleus. A *gene* is a segment of DNA that produces a separate mRNA used to synthesize a protein needed in the cell.

Transfer RNA (**tRNA**), the smallest of the RNA molecules, interprets the genetic information in mRNA and brings specific amino acids to the ribosome for protein synthesis. Only tRNA can translate the genetic information in the mRNA into the amino acid sequence that makes a protein. There can be more than one tRNA for each of the 20 amino acids. The structures of all of the transfer RNAs are similar, consisting of 70 to 90 nucleotides. Hydrogen bonds between some complementary bases in the strand produce loops that give some double-stranded regions. The types of RNA molecules in humans are summarized in Table 21.5.

TABLE 21.5 Types of RNA Molecules in Humans

Type	Abbreviation	Percentage of Total RNA	Function in the Cell
Ribosomal RNA	rRNA	80	major component of the ribosomes; site of protein synthesis
Messenger RNA	mRNA	5	carries information for protein synthesis from the DNA to the ribosomes
Transfer RNA	tRNA	15	brings specific amino acids to the site of protein synthesis

Although the structure of tRNA in three dimensions is complex, we can draw tRNA as a two-dimensional cloverleaf (see Figure 21.10a). In the three-dimensional model, the RNA chain has more twists that shows the L-shape of tRNA (see Figure 21.10b). All tRNA molecules have a 3′ end with the nucleotide sequence ACC, which is known as the *acceptor stem*. An enzyme attaches an amino acid to the 3′ end of the acceptor stem by forming an ester bond with the free —OH group of the acceptor stem. Each tRNA contains an **anticodon**, which is a series of three bases that complements three bases on mRNA.

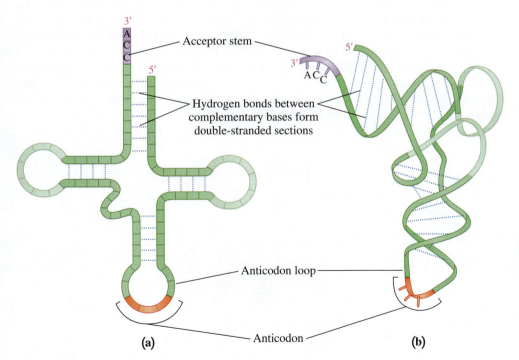

Acceptor stem

Hydrogen bonds between complementary bases form double-stranded sections

Anticodon loop

Anticodon

(a)   (b)

FIGURE 21.10 ▶ A typical tRNA molecule has an acceptor stem at the 3′ end that attaches to an amino acid and an anticodon loop that complements a codon on mRNA.

Q Why will different tRNAs have different bases in the anticodon loop?

RNA and Protein Synthesis

We now look at the overall processes involved in transferring genetic information encoded in the DNA to the production of proteins. In the nucleus, genetic information for the synthesis of a protein is copied from a gene in DNA to make mRNA, a process called **transcription**. The mRNA molecules move out of the nucleus into the cytosol, where they bind with the ribosomes. Then in a process called **translation**, tRNA molecules convert the information in the mRNA into amino acids, which are placed in the proper sequence to synthesize a protein (see Figure 21.11).

FIGURE 21.11 ▶ The genetic information in DNA is replicated in cell division and used to produce messenger RNA that codes for amino acids used in protein synthesis at the ribosomes.

Q What is the difference between transcription and translation?

Transcription: Synthesis of mRNA

Transcription begins when the section of a DNA molecule that contains the gene to be copied unwinds. Within this unwound portion of DNA called a *transcription bubble*, the 5′ to 3′ open strand is the *DNA informational strand*, whereas the 3′ to 5′ is the *DNA template strand*. *RNA polymerase* uses the DNA template strand to form the new mRNA using bases that are complementary to the DNA template: C and G form pairs, T (in DNA) pairs with A (in mRNA), and A (in DNA) pairs with U (in mRNA). When the RNA polymerase reaches the termination site (a sequence of nucleotides that is a stop signal), transcription ends, and the new mRNA is released. The unwound portion of the DNA returns to its double helix structure (see Figure 21.12).

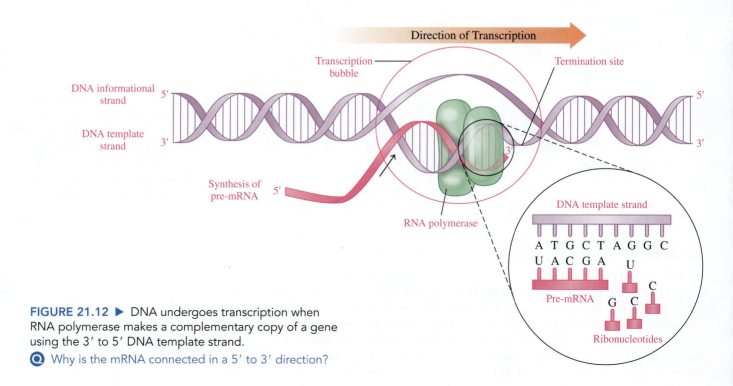

FIGURE 21.12 ▶ DNA undergoes transcription when RNA polymerase makes a complementary copy of a gene using the 3′ to 5′ DNA template strand.

Q Why is the mRNA connected in a 5′ to 3′ direction?

SAMPLE PROBLEM 21.5 RNA Synthesis

The sequence of bases in a part of the DNA template strand is 3′ C G A T C A 5′. What corresponding mRNA is produced?

SOLUTION

To form the mRNA, the bases in the DNA template are paired with their complementary bases: G with C, C with G, T with A, and A with U.

DNA template strand: 3′ C G A T C A 5′

Transcription: ↓ ↓ ↓ ↓ ↓ ↓

Complementary base sequence in mRNA: 5′ G C U A G U 3′

STUDY CHECK 21.5

What is the DNA template strand segment that codes for the mRNA segment with the nucleotide sequence 5′ G G G U U U A A A 3′?

ANSWER

3′ C C C A A A T T T 5′

CORE CHEMISTRY SKILL

Writing the mRNA Segment for a DNA Template

Processing of mRNA

The DNA in plants and animals (eukaryotes) contains sections known as *exons* and *introns*. **Exons**, which code for proteins, are mixed in with sections called **introns** that do not code for proteins. A newly formed mRNA called a *pre-mRNA* or *heterogeneous nuclear RNA* (hnRNA) is a copy of the entire DNA template, including the noncoding introns. However, the pre-mRNA exists for only a short time before it is processed. The introns are cut out and the remaining exons spliced together by *spliceosome*. The function of introns is not well understood. They may regulate transcription to allow different proteins to be synthesized from the same gene or have a role in genetic expression. This processing of pre-mRNA produces a mature mRNA that leaves the nucleus to deliver the genetic information to the ribosomes for the synthesis of protein (see Figure 21.13). The removal of introns in eukaryotes offers the cell another chance to check the mRNA before it exits the nucleus, preserving the DNA sequence.

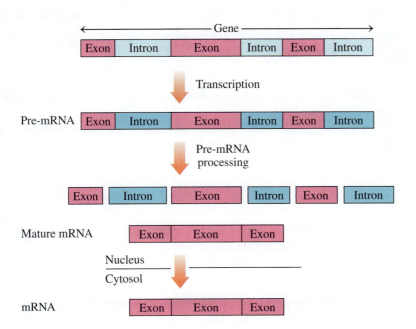

FIGURE 21.13 ▶ A pre-mRNA, containing copies of the exons and introns from the gene, is processed to remove the introns to form a mature mRNA that codes for a protein.

Q What is the difference between exons and introns?

Regulation of Transcription: Transcription Factors

The synthesis of mRNA occurs when cells require a particular protein; it does not occur randomly. The regulation of mRNA synthesis is controlled at the transcription level.

In eukaryotes (plants and animals), the transcription of a gene requires the RNA polymerase to bind to DNA. However, RNA polymerase cannot do this alone. A group of

RNA polymerase

Promoter region

DNA

Activator

Transcription factors

Gene

Transcription

mRNA

Protein

Transcription factors at the promoter region bind RNA polymerase to DNA, which activates the transcription of a gene.

protein complexes called a **transcription factor** must first recognize and bind to a *promoter region* (small nucleotide sequences) in front of the start site for the gene. Proteins called *activators* bind with the transcription factor complex; the function of the activators is to increase the rate of RNA transcription. Thus transcription factors and activators work together to regulate the binding and activity of RNA polymerase at the specific gene for the transcription of a particular mRNA for that protein. Sometimes, another regulatory protein called a *repressor* blocks the activator and slows down the rate of transcription. Although all cells have the same set of genes, different transcription factors activate different genes that produce proteins for different tissues and organs. Transcription factors have a role in cancer if they activate genes that cause cell division. Mutations in transcription factors may lead to diabetes, inflammation, cancer, and autoimmune diseases.

> ► **SAMPLE PROBLEM 21.6 Transcription**
>
> Describe why transcription will or will not take place in each of the following conditions:
>
> **a.** There are no transcription factors bound at the promoter region.
> **b.** An activator binds to a transcription factor.
>
> **SOLUTION**
>
> **a.** Transcription will not take place as long as there are no transcription factors to bind and activate the RNA polymerase.
> **b.** Transcription will take place when the activated transcription factor binds to the promoter region on the DNA, which makes the RNA polymerase begin transcription.
>
> **STUDY CHECK 21.6**
>
> Where in a cell does pre-mRNA processing take place?
>
> **ANSWER**
>
> The processing of pre-mRNA to mature mRNA takes place in the nucleus before the mRNA can move into the cytosol and the ribosomes.

QUESTIONS AND PROBLEMS

21.5 RNA and Transcription

LEARNING GOAL Identify the different types of RNA; describe the synthesis of mRNA.

21.37 What are the three different types of RNA?

21.38 What are the functions of each type of RNA?

21.39 What is the composition of a ribosome?

21.40 What is the smallest RNA?

21.41 What is meant by the term "transcription"?

21.42 What bases in mRNA are used to complement the bases A, T, G, and C in DNA?

21.43 Write the corresponding section of mRNA produced from the following section of DNA template strand:

3′ C C G A A G G T T C A C 5′

21.44 Write the corresponding section of mRNA produced from the following section of DNA template strand:

3′ T A C G G C A A G C T A 5′

21.45 What are introns and exons?

21.46 What kind of processing do pre-mRNA molecules undergo before they leave the nucleus?

21.47 A pre-mRNA segment has the following base sequence. If underlined sections **A**, **C**, and **D** are introns, and **B**, **E**, and **F** are exons, what is the base sequence of the mature mRNA produced after pre-mRNA processing?

5′ <u>ACC</u>	GGC	<u>ACA</u>	<u>UUC</u>	GGA	<u>UCG</u> 3′
A	B	C	D	E	F

21.48 A pre-mRNA segment has the following base sequence. If underlined sections **B**, **D**, and **F** are introns, and **A**, **C**, and **E** are exons, what is the base sequence of the mature mRNA produced after pre-mRNA processing?

5′ GAC	<u>UAU</u>	GGC	<u>AAC</u>	GGC	<u>GUC</u> 3′
A	B	C	D	E	F

21.49 What is a transcription factor?

21.50 How do transcription factors control protein synthesis at the transcription level?

21.51 What is an activator?

21.52 What is a repressor?

21.6 The Genetic Code and Protein Synthesis

LEARNING GOAL

Use the genetic code to write the amino acid sequence for a segment of mRNA.

The overall function of the different types of RNA in the cell is to facilitate the task of synthesizing proteins. After the genetic information encoded in DNA is transcribed and processed into mature mRNA molecules, they move out of the nucleus to the ribosomes in the cytosol. At the ribosomes, the genetic information in the mRNA is translated into a sequence of amino acids in protein.

Genetic Code

The **genetic code** consists of a series of three nucleotides (triplets) in mRNA called **codons** that specify the amino acids and their sequence in a protein. Early work on protein synthesis showed that repeating triplets of uracil (UUU) produced a polypeptide that contained only phenylalanine. Therefore, a sequence of 5′ UUU UUU UUU 3′ codes for three phenylalanines.

Interactive Video

Protein Synthesis

Codons in mRNA: 5′ UUU   UUU   UUU 3′

↓   ↓   ↓

Amino acid sequence: Phe — Phe — Phe

Codons have been determined for all 20 amino acids. A total of 64 codons are possible from the triplet combinations of A, G, C, and U. Three of these, UGA, UAA, and UAG, are stop signals that code for the termination of protein synthesis. All the other three-base codons shown in Table 21.6 specify amino acids. Thus one amino acid can have several codons. For example, glycine has four codons: GGU, GGC, GGA, and GGG. The triplet AUG has two roles in protein synthesis. At the beginning of an mRNA, the codon AUG signals the start of protein synthesis. In the middle of a series of codons, the AUG codon specifies the amino acid methionine.

⚛ CORE CHEMISTRY SKILL

Writing the Amino Acid for an mRNA Codon

Translation

Once an mRNA is synthesized and processed, it migrates out of the nucleus into the cytosol to the ribosomes. In the *translation* process, tRNA molecules, amino acids, and enzymes convert the mRNA codons into amino acids to build a protein.

Activation of tRNA

Each tRNA molecule contains a loop called the *anticodon*, which is a triplet of bases that complements a codon in mRNA. An amino acid is attached to the acceptor stem of each tRNA by an enzyme called *aminoacyl–tRNA synthetase*. Each amino acid has a different synthetase (see Figure 21.14). Activation of tRNA occurs when aminoacyl–tRNA synthetase forms an ester bond between the carboxylate group of its amino acid and the hydroxyl group on the acceptor stem. Each synthetase then checks the tRNA–amino acid combination and hydrolyzes any incorrect combinations.

TABLE 21.6 Codons in mRNA: The Genetic Code for Amino Acids

First Letter	Second Letter				Third Letter
	U	C	A	G	
U	UUU ⎱Phe (F) UUC ⎰ UUA ⎱Leu (L) UUG ⎰	UCU ⎫ UCC ⎬Ser (S) UCA ⎪ UCG ⎭	UAU ⎱Tyr (Y) UAC ⎰ UAA STOP[b] UAG STOP[b]	UGU ⎱Cys (C) UGC ⎰ UGA STOP[b] UGG Trp (W)	U C A G
C	CUU ⎫ CUC ⎬Leu (L) CUA ⎪ CUG ⎭	CCU ⎫ CCC ⎬Pro (P) CCA ⎪ CCG ⎭	CAU ⎱His (H) CAC ⎰ CAA ⎱Gln (Q) CAG ⎰	CGU ⎫ CGC ⎬Arg (R) CGA ⎪ CGG ⎭	U C A G
A	AUU ⎫ AUC ⎬Ile (I) AUA ⎭ AUG START[a]/ Met (M)	ACU ⎫ ACC ⎬Thr (T) ACA ⎪ ACG ⎭	AAU ⎱Asn (N) AAC ⎰ AAA ⎱Lys (K) AAG ⎰	AGU ⎱Ser (S) AGC ⎰ AGA ⎱Arg (R) AGG ⎰	U C A G
G	GUU ⎫ GUC ⎬Val (V) GUA ⎪ GUG ⎭	GCU ⎫ GCC ⎬Ala (A) GCA ⎪ GCG ⎭	GAU ⎱Asp (D) GAC ⎰ GAA ⎱Glu (E) GAG ⎰	GGU ⎫ GGC ⎬Gly (G) GGA ⎪ GGG ⎭	U C A G

START[a] codon signals the initiation of a peptide chain.
STOP[b] codons signal the end of a peptide chain.

FIGURE 21.14 ▶ An activated tRNA with anticodon AGU bonds to serine at the acceptor stem.

Q What is the codon for serine for this tRNA?

Initiation and Chain Elongation

Protein synthesis begins when mRNA binds to a ribosome. The first codon in an mRNA is a *start codon*, AUG, which forms hydrogen bonds with methionine–tRNA. Another tRNA hydrogen bonds to the next codon, placing a second amino acid adjacent to methionine. A peptide bond forms between the C terminus of methionine and the N terminus of the second amino acid (see Figure 21.15). The initial tRNA detaches from the ribosome,

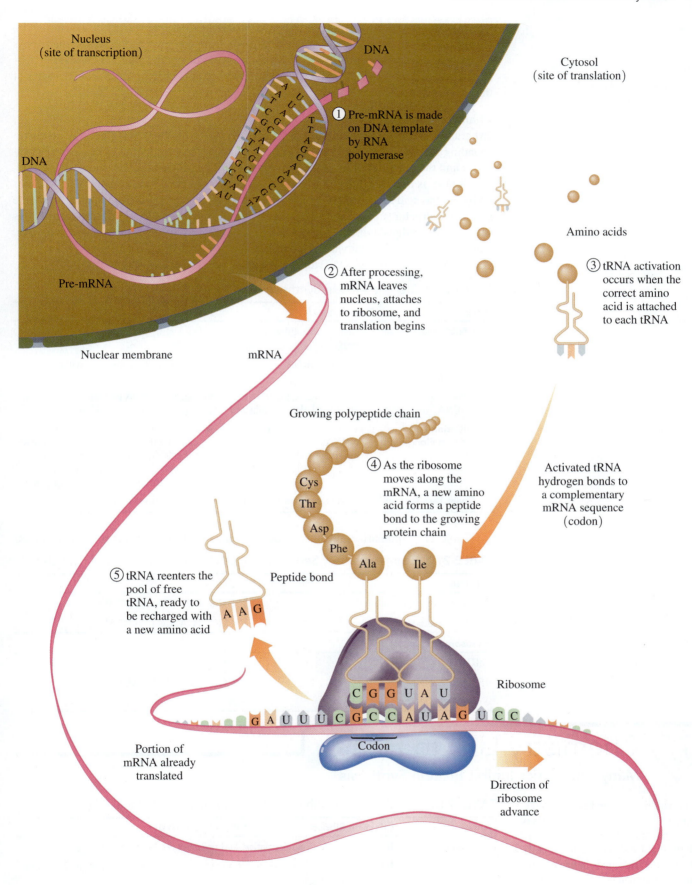

FIGURE 21.15 ▶ In the translation process, the mRNA synthesized by transcription attaches to a ribosome, and tRNAs pick up their amino acids, bind to the appropriate codon, and place them in a growing peptide chain.

◉ How is the correct amino acid placed in the peptide chain?

which shifts to the next available codon, a process called *translocation*. During *chain elongation*, the ribosome moves along the mRNA from codon to codon so that the tRNAs can attach new amino acids to the growing polypeptide chain. Sometimes several ribosomes, called a polysome, translate the same strand of mRNA to produce several copies of the polypeptide at the same time.

Chain Termination

Eventually, a ribosome encounters a codon—UAA, UGA, or UAG—that has no corresponding tRNAs. These are *stop codons*, which signal the termination of polypeptide synthesis and the release of the polypeptide chain from the ribosome. The initial amino acid, methionine, is usually removed from the beginning of the polypeptide chain. The R groups on the amino acid residues in the new polypeptide chain form hydrogen bonds to give the secondary structures of α helices, β-pleated sheets, or triple helices and form interactions such as salt bridges and disulfide bonds to produce tertiary and quaternary structures, which make it a biologically active protein.

Table 21.7 summarizes the steps in protein synthesis.

TABLE 21.7 Steps in Protein Synthesis

Step	Site: Materials	Process
1. DNA Transcription	Nucleus: nucleotides, RNA polymerase	A DNA template is used to produce mRNA.
2. Translation of mRNA	Ribosome: mRNA	mRNA binds to ribosomes where translation begins.
3. Activation of tRNA	Cytosol: amino acids, tRNAs, aminoacyl–tRNA synthetase	Molecules of tRNA pick up specific amino acids according to their anticodons.
4. Initiation and Chain Elongation	Ribosome: Met–tRNA, mRNA, aminoacyl–tRNAs	A start codon binds the first tRNA carrying the amino acid methionine to the mRNA. Successive tRNAs bind to and detach from the ribosome as they add an amino acid to the polypeptide.
5. Chain Termination	Ribosome: stop codon on mRNA	The protein is released from the ribosome.

Table 21.8 summarizes the nucleotide and amino acid sequences in protein synthesis.

TABLE 21.8 Complementary Sequences in DNA, mRNA, tRNA, and Peptides

Nucleus	
DNA informational strand	5′ GCG AGT GGA TAC 3′
DNA template strand	3′ CGC TCA CCT ATG 5′
Ribosome (cytosol)	
mRNA	5′ GCG AGU GGA UAC 3′
tRNA anticodons	3′ CGC UCA CCU AUG 5′
Polypeptide amino acids	Ala —Ser—Gly—Tyr

Chemistry Link to **Health**
Many Antibiotics Inhibit Protein Synthesis

Several antibiotics stop bacterial infections by interfering with the synthesis of proteins needed by the bacteria. Some antibiotics act only on bacterial cells, binding to the ribosomes in bacteria but not those in human cells. A description of some of these antibiotics is given in Table 21.9.

TABLE 21.9 Antibiotics That Inhibit Protein Synthesis in Bacterial Cells

Antibiotic	Effect on Ribosomes to Inhibit Protein Synthesis
Chloramphenicol	Inhibits peptide bond formation and prevents the binding of tRNA
Erythromycin	Inhibits peptide chain growth by preventing the translocation of the ribosome along the mRNA
Puromycin	Causes release of an incomplete protein by ending the growth of the polypeptide early
Streptomycin	Prevents the proper attachment of the initial tRNA
Tetracycline	Prevents the binding of tRNA

▸**SAMPLE PROBLEM 21.7** Protein Synthesis

Use three-letter and one-letter abbreviations to write the amino acid sequence for the peptide from the mRNA sequence of 5′ UCA AAA GCC CUU 3′.

SOLUTION

Each of the codons specifies a particular amino acid. Using Table 21.6, we write a peptide with the following amino acid sequence:

mRNA codons: 5′ UCA AAA GCC CUU 3′

Amino acid sequence: Ser — Lys — Ala — Leu , SKAL

STUDY CHECK 21.7

Use three-letter and one-letter abbreviations to write the amino acid sequence for the peptide from the mRNA sequence of 5′ GGG AGC AGU GAG GUU 3′.

ANSWER

Gly–Ser–Ser–Glu–Val, GSSEV

QUESTIONS AND PROBLEMS

21.6 The Genetic Code and Protein Synthesis

LEARNING GOAL Use the genetic code to write the amino acid sequence for a segment of mRNA.

21.53 What is a codon?

21.54 What is the genetic code?

21.55 What amino acid is coded for by each of the following mRNA codons?
a. CUU **b.** UCA **c.** GGU **d.** AGG

21.56 What amino acid is coded for by each of the following mRNA codons?
a. AAA **b.** UUC **c.** CGG **d.** GCA

21.57 When does the codon AUG signal the start of a protein? When does it code for the amino acid methionine?

21.58 The codons UGA, UAA, and UAG do not code for amino acids. What is their role as codons in mRNA?

21.59 What is the difference between a *codon* and an *anticodon*?

21.60 Why are there at least 20 different tRNAs?

21.61 What are the three steps of translation?

21.62 Where does protein synthesis take place?

21.63 Use three-letter and one-letter abbreviations to write the amino acid sequence for the peptide from each of the following mRNA sequences:
a. 5′ ACC ACA ACU 3′
b. 5′ UUU CCG UUC CCA 3′
c. 5′ UAC GGG AGA UGU 3′

21.64 Use three-letter and one-letter abbreviations to write the amino acid sequence for the peptide from each of the following mRNA sequences:
a. 5′ AAA CCC UUG GCC 3′
b. 5′ CCU CGC AGC CCA UGA 3′
c. 5′ AUG CAC AAG GAA GUA CUG 3′

21.65 How is a peptide chain extended?

21.66 What is meant by "translocation"?

21.67 The following sequence is a portion of the DNA template strand:

3′ GCT TTT CAA AAA 5′

a. Write the corresponding mRNA segment.
b. What are the anticodons of the tRNAs?
c. Write the three-letter and one-letter abbreviations for this segment in the peptide chain.

21.68 The following sequence is a portion of the DNA template strand:

3′ TGT GGG GTT ATT 5′

a. Write the corresponding mRNA segment.
b. What are the anticodons of the tRNAs?
c. Write the three-letter and one-letter abbreviations for this segment in the peptide chain.

℞ Clinical Applications

21.69 The following is a segment of the DNA template that codes for human insulin:

3′ TTT GTG AAC CAA CAC CTG 5′

a. Write the corresponding mRNA segment.
b. Write the three-letter and one-letter abbreviations for this corresponding peptide segment.

21.70 The following is a segment of the DNA template that codes for human insulin:

3′ TGC GGC TCA CAC CTG GTG 5′

a. Write the corresponding mRNA segment.
b. Write the three-letter and one-letter abbreviations for the corresponding peptide segment.

LEARNING GOAL

Identify the type of change in DNA for a point mutation, a deletion mutation, and an insertion mutation.

21.7 Genetic Mutations

A **mutation** is a change in the nucleotide sequence of DNA. Such a change may alter the sequence of amino acids, affecting the structure and function of a protein in a cell. Mutations may result from X-rays, overexposure to sun (ultraviolet (UV) light), chemicals called *mutagens*, and possibly some viruses. If a mutation occurs in a somatic cell (a cell other than a reproductive cell), the altered DNA is limited to that cell and its daughter cells. If the mutation affects DNA that controls the growth of the cell, cancer could result. If a mutation occurs in a germ cell (egg or sperm), then all DNA produced will contain the same genetic change. When a mutation severely alters proteins or enzymes, the new cells may not survive or the person may exhibit a disease or condition that is a result of a genetic defect.

Types of Mutations

Consider a triplet of bases CCG in the template strand of DNA, which produces the codon GGC in mRNA. At the ribosome, tRNA would place the amino acid glycine in the peptide chain (see Figure 21.16a). Now, suppose that T replaces the first C in the DNA triplet, which gives TCG as the triplet. Then the codon produced in the mRNA is AGC, which brings the tRNA with the amino acid serine to add to the peptide chain. The replacement of one base in the template strand of DNA with another is called a **point mutation**. When there is a change of a nucleotide in the codon, a different amino acid may be inserted into the polypeptide. However, if a point mutation does not change the amino acid, it is a *silent mutation*. A point mutation is the most common way in which mutations occur (see Figure 21.16b).

In a **deletion mutation**, a base is deleted from the normal order of bases in the template strand of DNA. Suppose that an A is deleted from the triplet AAA giving a new triplet of AAC (see Figure 21.16c). The next triplet becomes CGA rather than CCG, and so on. All the triplets shift by one base, which changes all the codons that follow and leads to a different sequence of amino acids from that point.

In an **insertion mutation**, a base is inserted into the normal order of bases in the template strand of DNA. Suppose a T is inserted into the triplet AAA, which gives a new triplet of AAT. The next triplet becomes ACC rather than CCG, and so on. All the triplets shift by one base, which changes all the codons that follow and leads to a different sequence of amino acids from that point.

Explore Your World

A Model for DNA Replication and Mutation

1. Cut out 16 rectangular pieces of paper. Using 8 rectangular pieces for DNA strand 1, label two each of the following nucleotide symbols: A═, T═, G≡, and C≡.
2. Using the other 8 rectangular pieces for DNA strand 2, label two of each of the following nucleotide symbols: ═A, ═T, ≡G, and ≡C.
3. Place the pieces for strand 1 in random order.
4. Using the DNA segment strand 1 you made in part 3, select the correct bases to build the complementary segment of DNA strand 2.
5. Using the rectangular pieces for nucleotides, put together a DNA segment using a template strand of A T T G C C. What is the mRNA that would form from this segment of DNA? What is the dipeptide that would form from this mRNA?
6. In the DNA segment of part 5, change the G to an A. What is the mRNA that would form from this segment of DNA? What is the dipeptide that forms? How could this change in codons lead to a mutation?

SAMPLE PROBLEM 21.8 Mutations

An mRNA has the sequence of codons 5′ CCC AGA GCC 3′. If a point mutation in the DNA changes the mRNA codon of AGA to GGA, how is the amino acid sequence affected in the resulting protein?

SOLUTION

The mRNA sequence 5′ CCC AGA GCC 3′ codes for the following amino acids: proline, arginine, and alanine. When the point mutation occurs, the new sequence of the mRNA codons is 5′ CCC GGA GCC 3′, which codes for proline, glycine, and alanine. The basic amino acid arginine is replaced by the nonpolar amino acid glycine.

	Normal			After Point Mutation		
mRNA codons:	5′ CCC	AGA	GCC 3′	5′ CCC	GGA	GCC 3′
Amino acid sequence:	Pro	Arg	Ala	Pro	Gly	Ala

STUDY CHECK 21.8

How might the protein made from this mRNA be affected by this mutation?

ANSWER

Because the point mutation replaces a polar basic amino acid with a nonpolar neutral amino acid, the tertiary structure may be altered sufficiently to cause the resulting protein to be less effective or nonfunctional.

(a) Normal DNA and protein synthesis

(b) Point mutation

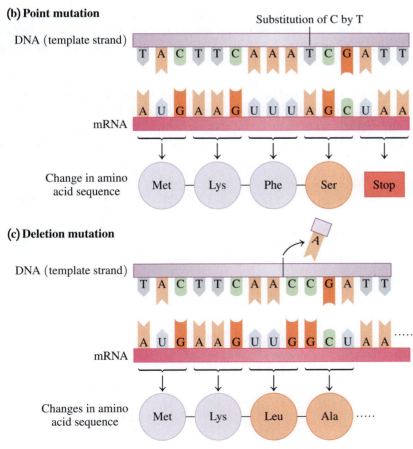

(c) Deletion mutation

FIGURE 21.16 ▶ An alteration in the DNA template strand produces a change in the sequence of amino acids in the protein, which may result in a mutation. **(a)** A normal DNA leads to the correct amino acid order in a protein. **(b)** In a point mutation, the change of a base in DNA leads to a change in the mRNA codon and possibly a change in one amino acid. **(c)** The deletion of a base causes a deletion mutation, which changes the mRNA codons that follow the mutation and produces a different amino acid sequence.

Q When would a point muta-tion cause protein synthesis to stop?

Effect of Mutations

Some mutations do not cause a significant change in the primary structure of a protein and the protein is able to maintain biological activity. However, if the mutation causes a change to an amino acid critical to protein structure or function, the protein loses biological activity. If the protein is an enzyme, it may no longer bind to its substrate or react with the substrate at the active site. When an altered enzyme cannot catalyze a reaction, certain substances may accumulate until they act as poisons in the cell, or substances vital to survival may not be synthesized. If a defective enzyme occurs in a major metabolic pathway or is involved in the building of a cell membrane, the mutation can be lethal. When a protein deficiency is hereditary, the condition is called a **genetic disease**.

Genetic Diseases

A genetic disease is the result of a defective enzyme caused by a mutation in its genetic code. For example, *phenylketonuria* (PKU) results when DNA cannot direct the synthesis of the enzyme phenylalanine hydroxylase, required for the conversion of phenylalanine to tyrosine. In an attempt to break down the phenylalanine, other enzymes in the cells convert it to phenylpyruvate. If phenylalanine and phenylpyruvate accumulate in the blood of an infant, it can lead to severe brain damage and mental retardation. If PKU is detected in a newborn baby, a diet is prescribed that eliminates all foods that contain phenylalanine. Preventing the buildup of phenylpyruvate ensures normal growth and development.

The amino acid tyrosine is needed in the formation of melanin, the pigment that gives the color to our skin and hair. If the enzyme that converts tyrosine to melanin is defective, no melanin is produced and a genetic disease known as *albinism* results. Persons and animals with no melanin have no skin, eye, or hair pigment (see Figure 21.17). Table 21.10 lists some other common genetic diseases and the type of metabolism or area affected.

FIGURE 21.17 ▶ A peacock with albinism does not produce the melanin needed to make bright colors for its feathers.

ⓠ Why are traits such as albinism related to the gene?

TABLE 21.10 Some Genetic Diseases

Genetic Disease	Result
Galactosemia	In galactosemia, the transferase enzyme required for the metabolism of galactose-1-phosphate is absent, resulting in the accumulation of galactose-1-phosphate, which leads to cataracts and mental retardation. Galactosemia occurs in about 1 in every 50 000 births.
Cystic fibrosis (CF)	Cystic fibrosis is caused by a mutation in the gene for the protein that regulates the production of stomach fluids and mucus. CF is one of the most common inherited diseases in children, in which thick mucus secretions make breathing difficult and block pancreatic function.
Down syndrome	Down syndrome is the leading cause of mental retardation, occurring in about 1 of every 800 live births; the mother's age strongly influences its occurrence. Mental and physical problems, including heart and eye defects, are the result of the formation of three chromosomes (trisomy), usually number 21, instead of a pair.
Familial hypercholesterolemia (FH)	Familial hypercholesterolemia occurs when there is a mutation of a gene on chromosome 19, which produces high cholesterol levels that lead to early coronary heart disease in people 30 to 40 years old.
Muscular dystrophy (MD) (Duchenne)	Muscular dystrophy, Duchenne form, is caused by a mutation in the X chromosome. This muscle-destroying disease appears at about age 5, with death by age 20, and occurs in about 1 of 10 000 males.
Huntington's disease (HD)	Huntington's disease affects the nervous system, leading to total physical impairment. It is the result of a mutation in a gene on chromosome 4, which can now be mapped to test people in families with a history of HD. There are about 30 000 people with Huntington's disease in the United States.
Sickle cell anemia	Sickle cell anemia is caused by a defective form of hemoglobin resulting from a mutation in a gene on chromosome 11. It decreases the oxygen-carrying ability of red blood cells, which take on a sickled shape, causing anemia and plugged capillaries from red blood cell aggregation. In the United States, about 72 000 people are affected by sickle cell anemia.
Hemophilia	Hemophilia is the result of one or more defective blood clotting factors that lead to poor coagulation, excessive bleeding, and internal hemorrhages. There are about 20 000 hemophilia patients in the United States.
Tay–Sachs disease	Tay–Sachs disease is the result of a defective hexosaminidase A, which causes an accumulation of gangliosides and leads to mental retardation, loss of motor control, and early death.

QUESTIONS AND PROBLEMS

21.7 Genetic Mutations

LEARNING GOAL Identify the type of change in DNA for a point mutation, a deletion mutation, and an insertion mutation.

21.71 What is a point mutation?

21.72 How does a point mutation for an enzyme affect the order of amino acids in that protein?

21.73 What is the effect of a deletion mutation on the amino acid sequence of a polypeptide?

21.74 How can a mutation decrease the activity of a protein?

21.75 How is protein synthesis affected if the normal base sequence TTT in the DNA template strand is changed to TTC?

21.76 How is protein synthesis affected if the normal base sequence CCC in the DNA template strand is changed to ACC?

21.77 Consider the following segment of mRNA produced by the normal order of DNA nucleotides:

5′ ACA UCA CGG GUA 3′

a. What is the amino acid order produced from this mRNA?
b. What is the amino acid order if a point mutation changes UCA to ACA?
c. What is the amino acid order if a point mutation changes CGG to GGG?
d. What happens to protein synthesis if a point mutation changes UCA to UAA?

e. What is the amino acid order if an insertion mutation adds a G to the beginning of the mRNA segment?
f. What is the amino acid order if a deletion mutation removes the A at the beginning of the mRNA segment?

21.78 Consider the following segment of mRNA produced by the normal order of DNA nucleotides:

5′ CUU AAA CGA GUU 3′

a. What is the amino acid order produced from this mRNA?
b. What is the amino acid order if a point mutation changes CUU to CCU?
c. What is the amino acid order if a point mutation changes CGA to AGA?
d. What happens to protein synthesis if a point mutation changes AAA to UAA?
e. What is the amino acid order if an insertion mutation adds a G to the beginning of the mRNA segment?
f. What is the amino acid order if a deletion mutation removes the C at the beginning of the mRNA segment?

℞ Clinical Applications

21.79 a. A point mutation changes a codon in the mRNA for an enzyme from GCC to GCA. Why is there no change in the amino acid order in the protein?

b. In sickle cell anemia, a point mutation in the mRNA for hemoglobin results in the replacement of glutamate with valine in the resulting hemoglobin molecule. Why does the replacement of one amino acid cause such a drastic change in biological function?

21.80 a. A point mutation in the mRNA for an enzyme results in the replacement of leucine with alanine in the resulting enzyme molecule. Why does this change in amino acids have little effect on the biological activity of the enzyme?

b. A point mutation in mRNA replaces cytosine in the codon UCA with adenine. How would this substitution affect the amino acid order in the protein?

LEARNING GOAL

Describe the preparation and uses of recombinant DNA.

21.8 Recombinant DNA

Techniques in the field of genetic engineering permit scientists to cut and recombine DNA fragments to form **recombinant DNA**. The technology of recombinant DNA is used to produce important medicines like human insulin for diabetics, the antiviral substance interferon, blood clotting factor VIII, and human growth hormone.

Preparing Recombinant DNA

Much of the work with recombinant DNA is done with *Escherichia coli* (*E. coli*) bacteria. Some of the DNA in bacterial cells exists as small, circular double-stranded DNA structures called *plasmids*, which are easy to isolate and capable of replication. Initially, *E. coli* cells are soaked in a detergent solution to disrupt the plasma membrane releasing the plasmids. A *restriction enzyme* is used to cut the double strands of DNA between specific bases in the DNA sequence (see Figure 21.18). For example, the restriction enzyme EcoR1 (pronounced "Echo-R-One") recognizes the base sequences GAATTC on both strands, and cuts both DNA strands between the G and A.

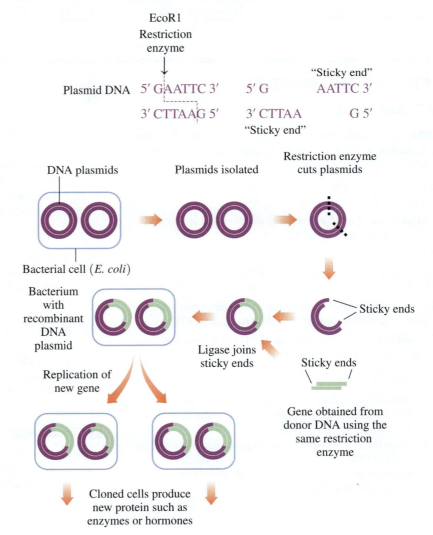

FIGURE 21.18 ▶ Recombinant DNA is formed by placing a gene from another organism in a plasmid DNA of the bacterium, which causes the bacterium to produce a nonbacterial protein such as insulin or growth hormone.

Q How can recombinant DNA help a person with a genetic disease?

The same restriction enzymes are used to cut a piece of DNA called donor DNA from a gene of a different organism, such as the gene that produces insulin or growth hormone. When the donor DNA is mixed with the cut plasmids, the nucleotides in their "sticky ends" join by forming complementary base pairs to make *recombinant DNA*. The resulting altered plasmids containing the recombinant DNA are placed in a fresh culture of *E. coli* bacteria. The *E. coli* that take up the plasmids are then selected. As the recombined cells divide and replicate, they produce the protein from the inserted gene in the plasmids.

Plasmid DNA	Donor DNA	Recombinant DNA
5' G	AATTC 3' $\longrightarrow$	5' GAATTC 3'
3' CTTAA	G 5' $\longrightarrow$	3' CTTAAG 5'

In a single day, one *E. coli* bacterium is capable of producing a million copies of itself including the recombinant DNA, a process known as *gene cloning*. If the inserted DNA codes for the human insulin protein, the altered plasmids begin to synthesize human insulin. Bacterial cells with the recombinant DNA can produce large quantities of the insulin protein, which is then collected and purified. Table 21.11 lists some of the products developed through recombinant DNA technology that are now used therapeutically.

TABLE 21.11 Therapeutic Products of Recombinant DNA

Product	Therapeutic Use
Human insulin	Treat diabetes
Erythropoietin (EPO)	Treat anemia; stimulate production of erythrocytes
Human growth hormone (HGH)	Stimulate growth
Interferon	Treat cancer and viral disease
Tumor necrosis factor (TNF)	Destroy tumor cells
Monoclonal antibodies	Transport drugs needed to treat cancer and transplant rejection
Epidermal growth factor (EGF)	Stimulate healing of wounds and burns
Human blood clotting factor VIII	Treat hemophilia; allows blood to clot normally
Interleukins	Stimulate immune system; treat cancer
Prourokinase	Destroy blood clots; treat myocardial infarctions
Influenza vaccine	Prevent influenza
Hepatitis B virus (HBV) vaccine	Prevent viral hepatitis

Polymerase Chain Reaction

Before gene cloning can occur, a purified gene has to be isolated. In 1987, a process called the **polymerase chain reaction (PCR)** made it possible to produce multiple copies of a gene (amplify) in a short time. In the PCR technique, a sequence of a DNA molecule is selected to copy, and the DNA is heated to separate the strands. RNA primers hydrogen bond to a small group of complementary nucleotides on each strand end of the sequence to be copied. The DNA strands with their primers are mixed with a heat-stable DNA polymerase and the four deoxyribonucleotides, and undergo repeated cycles of heating and cooling to produce complementary strands for the DNA section. Then the process is repeated with the new batch of DNA. After several cycles of the PCR process, millions of copies of the initial DNA section are produced (see Figure 21.19).

Genetic Testing

PCR allows screening for defective genes whose sequence is known. For example, there are several defects in two known breast cancer genes, called BRCA1 and BRCA2, that correlate to a higher risk of breast cancer. Patients are screened for the defects in these genes by using a DNA sample from their blood or saliva. PCR amplifies the defective genes while incorporating a fluorescent label which is visible if the test is positive.

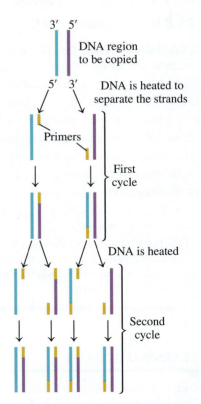

FIGURE 21.19 ▶ Each cycle of the polymerase chain reaction doubles the number of copies of the DNA section.

🔍 Why are the DNA strands heated at the start of each cycle?

FIGURE 21.20 ▶ Bands on film represent DNA fingerprints that can be used to identify a person involved in a crime.

🅠 What causes DNA fragments to appear on X-ray film?

DNA Fingerprinting

DNA fingerprinting or *DNA profiling* uses PCR to identify individuals based on a set of 13 hereditary traits. The chance that two individuals of the same ethnic background have the same 13 genetic traits is 1 in 575 trillion unless they are identical twins. Only a very small sample size is needed from blood, skin, saliva, or semen. Fluorescent or radioactive isotopes are incorporated into the amplified DNA during the PCR process. The DNA is cut into smaller pieces by restriction enzymes, which are placed on a gel and separated using electrophoresis. The banding pattern on the gel is called a DNA fingerprint.

One application of DNA fingerprinting is in forensic science, where DNA samples are used to connect a suspect with a crime (see Figure 21.20). Recently, DNA fingerprinting has been used to gain the release of individuals who were wrongly convicted. Other applications of DNA fingerprinting are determining the biological parents of a child, establishing the identity of a deceased person, and matching recipients with organ donors.

The Human Genome

The Human Genome Project, completed in 2003, showed that our DNA is composed of 3 billion bases and 21 000 genes coding for protein, but represents only 3% of the total DNA. Since then researchers have identified stretches of DNA that code for other RNA molecules. Much of our DNA regulates genes and serves as recognition sites for proteins like transcription factors and polymerase enzymes. To date, almost 80% of our genome has been assigned a function allowing scientists to better understand human diseases caused by errors in DNA replication, transcription, or regulation.

QUESTIONS AND PROBLEMS

21.8 Recombinant DNA

LEARNING GOAL Describe the preparation and uses of recombinant DNA.

21.81 Why are *E. coli* bacteria used in recombinant DNA procedures?

21.82 What is a plasmid?

21.83 How are plasmids obtained from *E. coli*?

21.84 Why are restriction enzymes mixed with the plasmids?

21.85 How is a gene for a particular protein inserted into a plasmid?

21.86 Why is DNA polymerase useful in criminal investigations?

21.87 What is a DNA fingerprint?

21.88 What beneficial proteins are produced from recombinant DNA technology?

21.89 The Acl1 restriction enzyme will cleave DNA between A and C (A/C) in the 5′ to 3′ direction. Draw the resulting DNA sections with the "sticky ends" when the following DNA segment is cleaved by Acl1:

5′ A A C G T T 3′
3′ T T G C A A 5′

21.90 The Pci1 restriction enzyme will cleave DNA between A and C (A/C) in the 5′ to 3′ direction. Draw the resulting DNA sections with the "sticky ends" when the following DNA segment is cleaved by Pci1:

5′ A C A T G T 3′
3′ T G T A C A 5′

21.91 Write the DNA sequence for each of the following "sticky ends":
a. 5′ G G C T 3′   b. 5′ A A T G C G 3′
c. 5′ T T C C G A 3′

21.92 Write the DNA sequence for each of the following "sticky ends":
a. 5′ T C C T C T 3′   b. 5′ G G C A C T T 3′
c. 5′ T A G C A T 3′

21.9 Viruses

LEARNING GOAL

Describe the methods by which a virus infects a cell.

Viruses are small particles of 3 to 200 genes that cannot replicate without a host cell. A typical virus contains a nucleic acid, DNA or RNA, but not both, inside a protein coat. A virus does not have the necessary material such as nucleotides and enzymes to make proteins and grow. The only way a virus can replicate (make additional copies of itself) is to invade a host cell and take over the machinery and materials necessary for protein synthesis and growth. Some infections caused by viruses invading human cells are listed in Table 21.12. There are also viruses that attack bacteria, plants, and animals.

TABLE 21.12 Some Diseases Caused by Viral Infection

Disease	Virus
Common cold	Coronavirus (over 100 types), rhinovirus (over 110 types)
Influenza	Orthomyxovirus
Warts	Papovavirus
Herpes	Herpesvirus
HPV	Human papilloma virus
Leukemia, cancers, AIDS	Retrovirus
Hepatitis	Hepatitis A virus (HAV), hepatitis B virus (HBV), hepatitis C virus (HCV)
Mumps	Paramyxovirus
Epstein–Barr	Epstein–Barr virus (EBV)
Chicken pox (shingles)	*Varicella zoster* virus (VZV)

A viral infection begins when an enzyme in the protein coat of the virus makes a hole in the outside of the host cell, allowing the viral nucleic acid to enter and mix with the materials in the host cell (see Figure 21.21). If the virus contains DNA, the host cell begins to replicate the viral DNA in the same way it would replicate normal DNA. Viral DNA produces viral RNA, and a protease processes proteins to produce a protein coat to form a viral particle that leaves the cell. The cell synthesizes so many virus particles that it eventually releases new viruses to infect more cells.

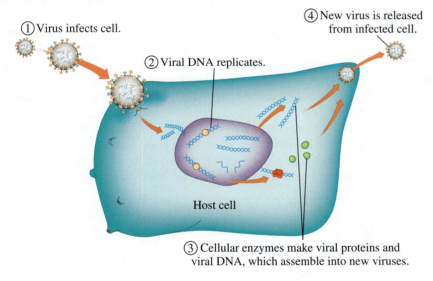

① Virus infects cell.

② Viral DNA replicates.

④ New virus is released from infected cell.

Host cell

③ Cellular enzymes make viral proteins and viral DNA, which assemble into new viruses.

FIGURE 21.21 ▶ After a virus attaches to the host cell, it injects its viral DNA and uses the host cell's machinery and materials to make viral mRNA, new viral DNA, and viral proteins. The newly assembled viruses are released to infect other cells.

Q Why does a virus need a host cell for replication?

Vaccines are inactive forms of viruses that boost the immune response by causing the body to produce antibodies to the virus. Several childhood diseases, such as polio, mumps, chicken pox, and measles, can be prevented through the use of vaccines.

Reverse Transcription

A virus that contains RNA as its genetic material is a **retrovirus**. Once inside the host cell, it must first make viral DNA using a process known as *reverse transcription*. A retrovirus contains a polymerase enzyme called *reverse transcriptase* that uses the viral RNA template to synthesize complementary strands of DNA. Once produced, the single DNA strands form double-stranded DNA using the nucleotides present in the host cell. This newly formed viral DNA, called a *provirus*, integrates with the DNA of the host cell (see Figure 21.22).

AIDS

During the early 1980s, a disease called *acquired immune deficiency syndrome*, commonly known as AIDS, began to claim an alarming number of lives. We now know that the HIV virus (human immunodeficiency virus) causes the disease (see Figure 21.23). HIV is a retrovirus that infects and destroys T4 lymphocyte cells, which are involved in the immune response. After the HIV binds to receptors on the surface of a T4 cell, the virus injects viral RNA into the

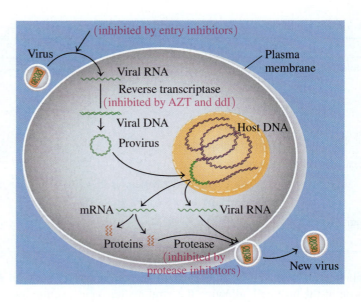

FIGURE 21.22 ▶ After a retrovirus injects its viral RNA into a cell, it forms a DNA strand by reverse transcription. The single-stranded DNA forms a double-stranded DNA called a provirus, which is incorporated into the host cell DNA. When the cell replicates, the provirus produces the viral RNA needed to produce more virus particles.

Q What is reverse transcription?

FIGURE 21.23 ▶ The HIV virus causes AIDS, which destroys the immune system in the body.

Q Is HIV a DNA virus or an RNA retrovirus?

host cell. As a retrovirus, the genes of the viral RNA direct the formation of viral DNA, which is then incorporated into the host's genome so it can replicate as part of the host cell's DNA. The gradual depletion of T4 cells reduces the ability of the immune system to destroy harmful organisms. The AIDS syndrome is characterized by opportunistic infections such as *Pneumocystis carinii*, which causes pneumonia, and *Kaposi's sarcoma*, a skin cancer.

Treatment for AIDS is based on attacking the HIV at different points in its life cycle, including cell entry, reverse transcription, and protein synthesis. Nucleoside analogs mimic the structures of the nucleosides used for DNA synthesis, and are able to successfully inhibit the reverse transcriptase enzyme. For example, the drug AZT (3′-azido-2′-deoxythymidine) is similar to thymidine, and ddI (2′,3′-dideoxyinosine) is similar to guanosine. Two other drugs are 2′,3′-dideoxycytidine (ddC) and 2′,3′-didehydro-2′,3′-dideoxythymidine (d4T). Such compounds are found in the "cocktails" that are providing extended remission of HIV infections. When a nucleoside analog is incorporated into viral DNA, the lack of a hydroxyl group on the 3′ carbon in the sugar prevents the formation of the sugar–phosphate bonds and stops the replication of the virus.

Today, people with HIV and AIDS are treated with a combination of drugs that include entry inhibitors, reverse transcriptase inhibitors, and protease inhibitors. Entry inhibitors attach to the surface of either the lymphocyte or HIV virus, which blocks entry into the cell. Entry inhibitors include enfuvirtide (Fuzeon) and maraviroc (Selzentry). Protease inhibitors prevent the proper cutting and formation of proteins used by the virus to make more copies of its own proteins. Protease inhibitors include saquinavir (Invirase), ritonavir (Norvir), fosamprenavir (Lexiva), and several others. When patients become resistant to certain drugs, different combinations are used to prolong life expectancy.

▶ **SAMPLE PROBLEM 21.9** Viruses

Why are viruses unable to replicate on their own?

SOLUTION

Viruses contain only packets of DNA or RNA, but not the necessary replication machinery that includes enzymes and nucleosides.

STUDY CHECK 21.9

What are the essential parts of a virus?

ANSWER

nucleic acid (DNA or RNA) and a protein coat

Lexiva metabolizes slowly to provide amprenavir, an HIV-protease inhibitor.

Chemistry Link to **Health**

Cancer

Normally, cells in the body undergo an orderly and controlled cell division. When cells begin to grow and multiply without control, they invade neighboring cells and appear as a tumor. If these tumors are limited, they are benign. When they invade other tissues and interfere with normal functions of the body, the tumors are cancerous. Cancer can be caused by chemical and environmental substances, by ultraviolet or medical radiation, or by *oncogenic viruses*, which are associated with human cancers.

Some reports estimate that 70 to 80% of all human cancers are initiated by chemical and environmental substances. A *carcinogen* is any substance that increases the chance of inducing a tumor. Known

carcinogens include aniline dyes, cigarette smoke, and asbestos. More than 90% of all persons with lung cancer are smokers. A carcinogen causes cancer by reacting with molecules in a cell, probably DNA, and altering the growth of that cell. Some known carcinogens are listed in Table 21.13.

TABLE 21.13 Some Chemical and Environmental Carcinogens

Carcinogen	Tumor Site
Aflatoxin	Liver
Aniline dyes	Bladder
Arsenic	Skin, lungs
Asbestos	Lungs, respiratory tract
Cadmium	Prostate, kidneys
Chromium	Lungs
Nickel	Lungs, sinuses
Nitrites	Stomach
Vinyl chloride	Liver

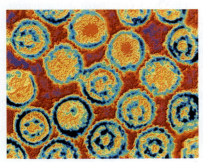

Epstein–Barr virus (EBV), herpesvirus 4, causes cancer in humans.

Skin cancer has become one of the most prevalent forms of cancer. It appears that DNA damage in the areas of the skin exposed to ultra-violet radiation may eventually cause mutations. The cells lose their ability to control protein synthesis. This type of uncontrolled cell division becomes skin cancer. The incidence of *malignant melanoma*, one of the most serious skin cancers, has been rapidly increasing. Some possible factors for this increase may be the popularity of sun tanning as well as the reduction of the ozone layer, which absorbs much of the harmful radiation from sunlight.

Oncogenic viruses cause cancer when cells are infected. Several viruses associated with human cancers are listed in Table 21.14. Some cancers such as retinoblastoma and breast cancer appear to occur more frequently within families. There is some indication that a missing or defective gene may be responsible.

TABLE 21.14 Human Cancers Caused by Oncogenic Viruses

Virus	Disease
RNA Viruses	
Human T-cell lymphotropic virus-type 1 (HTLV-1)	Leukemia
DNA Viruses	
Epstein–Barr virus (EBV)	Burkitt's lymphoma (cancer of white blood B cells) Nasopharyngeal carcinoma Hodgkin's disease
Hepatitis B virus (HBV)	Liver cancer
Herpes simplex virus (HSV, type 2)	Cervical and uterine cancer
Papilloma virus (HPV)	Cervical and colon cancer, genital warts

QUESTIONS AND PROBLEMS

21.9 Viruses

LEARNING GOAL Describe the methods by which a virus infects a cell.

21.93 What type of genetic information is found in a virus?

21.94 Why do viruses need to invade a host cell?

℞ Clinical Applications

21.95 A specific virus contains RNA as its genetic material.
   a. Why would reverse transcription be used in the life cycle of this type of virus?
   b. What is the name of this type of virus?

21.96 What is the purpose of a vaccine?

21.97 How do nucleoside analogs disrupt the life cycle of the HIV virus?

21.98 How do protease inhibitors disrupt the life cycle of the HIV virus?

Clinical Update
Ellen's Medical Treatment Following Breast Cancer Surgery

Ellen's oncologist told Ellen that the cells in her breast tumor and surrounding tissue tested positive for estrogen receptor (ER), which verified that she had breast cancer. Many breast tumors are estrogen positive because they require estrogen for their growth. Estrogen is a hormone that travels through the bloodstream and activates estrogen receptors in the cells of the breast and ovaries. The bonding of estrogen (activator) and the estrogen receptor (transcription factor) to DNA increase the production of mammary cells and potential mutations that can lead to cancer. High levels of the estrogen receptor appear in more than 60% of all breast cancer cases.

Because Ellen is 45 years old and has a family history of breast and ovarian cancer, she was also tested for altered genes BRCA1 and BRCA2. Normally, these genes suppress tumor growth by repairing DNA defects. However, if the mutated genes are inherited, a person's cells lose the ability to suppress tumor growth, and the risk for breast and ovarian as well as other cancers becomes much greater. Both parents can carry a BRCA mutation and pass it on to their sons and daughters. Ellen was relieved that her test results for mutated BRCA1 and BRCA2 were negative.

The estrogen receptor is a dimer with a binding region for estrogen or tamoxifen.

After Ellen completed a radiation series, she discussed the choice of drugs available for the treatment of breast cancer. Drugs such as tamoxifen and raloxifene block the binding of estrogen to the estrogen receptor, which prevents the growth of cancers that are estrogen positive. Other drugs such as anastrozole (Arimidex) and letrozole (Femara) are aromatase inhibitors (AIs) that prevent the growth of new tumors by blocking the synthesis of aromatase (estrogen synthetase), an enzyme that produces estrogen. Aromatase inhibitors are used primarily for post-menopausal women whose ovaries no longer produce estrogen. Ellen and her oncologist agreed upon the use of tamoxifen, which she will take for the next five years to prevent breast cancer from recurring after her surgery.

℞ Clinical Applications

21.99 What are estrogen receptors?

21.100 How do estrogen and the estrogen receptor influence cancer growth of mammary cells?

21.101 How does tamoxifen reduce the potential of breast cancer?

21.102 How does letrozole reduce the potential of breast cancer?

21.103 The following is a segment of the template strand of human BRCA1 gene:

   3′ TGG AAT TAT CTG CTC TTC GCG 5′

   a. Write the corresponding mRNA segment.
   b. Write the three-letter and one-letter abbreviations for the corresponding peptide segment.
   c. If there is a point mutation in the fourth nucleotide triplet and A replaces **G**, what is the change, if any, in the amino acid sequence?

21.104 The following is a segment of the template strand of human BRCA1 gene:

   3′ ACA TAT TTT GCA AAT TTT GCA 5′

   a. Write the corresponding mRNA segment.
   b. Write the three-letter and one-letter abbreviations for the corresponding peptide segment.
   c. If there is a point mutation in the second nucleotide triplet and C replaces **A**, what is the change, if any, in the amino acid sequence?

Tamoxifen slows down transcription by blocking the binding of estrogen to estrogen receptors.

CONCEPT MAP

NUCLEIC ACIDS AND PROTEIN SYNTHESIS

Nucleic Acids are **DNA** and **RNA**

DNA *contains* **Deoxynucleotides A, T, G, C** *arranged as a* **Double Helix** *with* **Complementary Base Pairs A–T, G–C** *with an order called* **Genetic Code**

RNA *contains* **Nucleotides A, U, G, C** *with three types* **mRNA** *and* **tRNA** *and* **rRNA**

triplets of bases are **Codons** *place the proper* / *produce a* **Protein**

Protein Synthesis *uses* **Codons** *specific for* **Amino Acids** *produce a* **Protein** *using* **Transcription** **Translation**

Mutations *change in a base causes* *such as* **Point Mutation, Deletion Mutation, Insertion Mutation** *can lead to* **Genetic Disease**

Viruses *contain* **DNA** **RNA** *use* **Reverse Transcription** *reproduce using* **Cellular Materials**

CHAPTER REVIEW

21.1 Components of Nucleic Acids
LEARNING GOAL Describe the bases and ribose sugars that make up the nucleic acids DNA and RNA.

- Nucleic acids, such as deoxyribonucleic acid (DNA) and ribonucleic acid (RNA), are polymers of nucleotides.
- A nucleoside is a combination of a pentose sugar and a base.
- A nucleotide is composed of three parts: a pentose sugar, a base, and a phosphate group.
- In DNA, the sugar is deoxyribose and the base can be adenine, thymine, guanine, or cytosine.
- In RNA, the sugar is ribose, and uracil replaces thymine.

21.2 Primary Structure of Nucleic Acids
LEARNING GOAL Describe the primary structures of RNA and DNA.

- Each nucleic acid has its own unique sequence of bases known as its primary structure.

- In a nucleic acid polymer, the 3′ OH group of each ribose in RNA or deoxyribose in DNA forms a phosphodiester linkage to the phosphate group of the 5′ carbon atom of the sugar in the next nucleotide to give a backbone of alternating sugar and phosphate groups.
- There is a free 5′ phosphate at one end of the polymer and a free 3′ OH group at the other end.

21.3 DNA Double Helix
LEARNING GOAL Describe the double helix of DNA.

- A DNA molecule consists of two strands of nucleotides that are wound around each other like a spiral staircase.
- The two strands are held together by hydrogen bonds between complementary base pairs, A with T, and G with C.

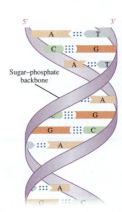

Sugar–phosphate backbone

21.4 DNA Replication
LEARNING GOAL Describe the process of DNA replication.

- During DNA replication, DNA polymerase makes new DNA strands along each of the original DNA strands that serve as templates.
- Complementary base pairing ensures the correct pairing of bases to give identical copies of the original DNA.

21.5 RNA and Transcription
LEARNING GOAL Identify the different types of RNA; describe the synthesis of mRNA.

RNA polymerase

- The three types of RNA differ by function in the cell: ribosomal RNA makes up most of the structure of the ribosomes, messenger RNA carries genetic information from the DNA to the ribosomes, and transfer RNA places the correct amino acids in a growing peptide chain.
- Transcription is the process by which RNA polymerase produces mRNA from one strand of DNA.
- Transcription factors at the promoter region bind RNA polymerase to DNA, which activates the transcription of a gene.
- The bases in the mRNA are complementary to the DNA, except A in DNA is paired with U in RNA.
- The production of mRNA occurs when certain proteins are needed in the cell.

21.6 The Genetic Code and Protein Synthesis
LEARNING GOAL Use the genetic code to write the amino acid sequence for a segment of mRNA.

- The genetic code consists of a series of codons, which are sequences of three bases that specify the order for the amino acids in a protein.
- There are 64 codons for the 20 amino acids, which means there are multiple codons for most amino acids.
- The codon AUG signals the start of transcription, and codons UAG, UGA, and UAA signal it to stop.
- Proteins are synthesized at the ribosomes in a translation process that includes three steps: initiation, chain elongation, and termination.

- During translation, tRNAs bring the appropriate amino acids to the ribosome, and peptide bonds form to join the amino acids in a peptide chain.
- When the polypeptide is released, it takes on its secondary and tertiary structures and becomes a functional protein in the cell.

21.7 Genetic Mutations
LEARNING GOAL Identify the type of change in DNA for a point mutation, a deletion mutation, and an insertion mutation.

- A genetic mutation is a change of one or more bases in the DNA sequence that alters the structure and ability of the resulting protein to function properly.
- In a point mutation, one codon is altered, and in an insertion mutation or a deletion mutation, a base is added or removed, which changes all the codons after the base change.

21.8 Recombinant DNA
LEARNING GOAL Describe the preparation and uses of recombinant DNA.

- A recombinant DNA is prepared by inserting a DNA segment—a gene—into plasmid DNA present in *E. coli* bacteria.
- As the altered bacterial cells replicate, the protein expressed by the foreign DNA segment is produced.
- In criminal investigation, large quantities of DNA are obtained from smaller amounts by the polymerase chain reaction.

21.9 Viruses
LEARNING GOAL Describe the methods by which a virus infects a cell.

Host cell

- Viruses containing DNA or RNA must invade host cells to use the machinery within the cell for the synthesis of more viruses.
- For a retrovirus containing RNA, a viral DNA is synthesized by reverse transcription using the nucleotides and enzymes in the host cell.
- In the treatment of AIDS, entry inhibitors block the virus from entering the cell, nucleoside analogs inhibit the reverse transcriptase of the HIV virus, and protease inhibitors disrupt the catalytic activity of protease needed to produce proteins for the synthesis of more viruses.

KEY TERMS

anticodon The triplet of bases in the center loop of tRNA that is complementary to a codon on mRNA.

base A nitrogen-containing compound found in DNA and RNA: adenine (A), thymine (T), cytosine (C), guanine (G), and uracil (U).

codon A sequence of three bases in mRNA that specifies a certain amino acid to be placed in a protein. A few codons signal the start or stop of protein synthesis.

complementary base pairs In DNA, adenine is always paired with thymine (A and T or T and A), and guanine is always paired with cytosine (G and C or C and G). In forming RNA, adenine is always paired with uracil (A and U or U and A).

deletion mutation A mutation that deletes a base from a DNA sequence.

DNA Deoxyribonucleic acid; the genetic material of all cells containing nucleotides with deoxyribose, phosphate, and the four bases: adenine, thymine, guanine, and cytosine.

double helix The helical shape of the double chain of DNA that is like a spiral staircase with a sugar–phosphate backbone on the outside and base pairs like stair steps on the inside.

exons The sections in a DNA template that code for proteins.

genetic code The sequence of codons in mRNA that specifies the amino acid order for the synthesis of protein.

genetic disease A physical malformation or metabolic dysfunction caused by a mutation in the base sequence of DNA.

insertion mutation A mutation that inserts a base in a DNA sequence.

introns The sections in DNA that do not code for proteins.

mRNA Messenger RNA; produced in the nucleus from DNA to carry the genetic information to the ribosomes for the construction of a protein.

mutation A change in the DNA base sequence that alters the formation of a protein in the cell.

nucleic acid A large molecule composed of nucleotides; found as a double helix in DNA and as the single strands of RNA.

nucleoside The combination of a pentose sugar and a base.

nucleotide Building block of a nucleic acid consisting of a base, a pentose sugar (ribose or deoxyribose), and a phosphate group.

Okazaki fragment A short segment formed by DNA polymerase in the daughter DNA strand that runs in the 3′ to 5′ direction.

phosphodiester linkage The phosphate link that joins the 3′ hydroxyl group in one nucleotide to the phosphate group on the 5′ carbon atom in the next nucleotide.

point mutation A mutation that replaces one base in a DNA with a different base.

polymerase chain reaction (PCR) A procedure in which a strand of DNA is copied many times by mixing it with primers, DNA polymerase and a mixture of deoxyribonucleotides and subjecting it to repeated cycles of heating and cooling.

primary structure The sequence of nucleotides in nucleic acids.

recombinant DNA DNA combined from different organisms to form new, synthetic DNA.

replication The process of duplicating DNA by pairing the bases on each parent strand with their complementary bases.

replication forks The open sections in unwound DNA strands where DNA polymerase begins the replication process.

retrovirus A virus that contains RNA as its genetic material and that synthesizes a complementary DNA strand inside a cell.

RNA Ribonucleic acid; a type of nucleic acid that is a single strand of nucleotides containing ribose, phosphate, and the four bases: adenine, cytosine, guanine, and uracil.

rRNA Ribosomal RNA; the most prevalent type of RNA and a major component of the ribosomes.

transcription The transfer of genetic information from DNA by the formation of mRNA.

transcription factor A protein that binds to DNA and controls transcription. It often binds with an activator.

translation The interpretation of the codons in mRNA as amino acids in a peptide.

tRNA Transfer RNA; an RNA that places a specific amino acid into a peptide chain at the ribosome so that a protein can be made. There is one or more tRNA for each of the 20 different amino acids.

virus A small particle containing DNA or RNA in a protein coat that requires a host cell for replication.

CORE CHEMISTRY SKILLS

The chapter section containing each Core Chemistry Skill is shown in parentheses at the end of each heading.

Writing the Complementary DNA Strand (21.3)

- During DNA replication, new DNA strands are made along each of the original DNA strands.
- The new strand of DNA is made by forming hydrogen bonds with the bases in the template strand: A with T and T with A; C with G and G with C.

Example: Write the complementary base sequence for the following DNA segment:

5′ A T T C G G T A C 3′

Answer: 3′ T A A G C C A T G 5′

Writing the mRNA Segment for a DNA Template (21.5)

- Transcription is the process that produces mRNA from one strand of DNA.

- The bases in the mRNA are complementary to the DNA, expect that A in DNA is paired with U in RNA.

Example: What is the mRNA produced for the DNA segment
5′ C G C A T G T C A 3′?

Answer: 3′ G C G U A C A G U 5′

Writing the Amino Acid for an mRNA Codon (21.6)

- The genetic code consists of a sequence of three bases (codons) that specifies the order for the amino acids in a protein.
- The codon AUG signals the start of transcription and codons UAG, UGA, and UAA signal it to stop.

Example: Use three-letter and one-letter abbreviations to write the amino acid sequence you would expect in a peptide for the mRNA sequence 5′ CCG UAU GGG 3′.

Answer: Pro–Tyr–Gly, PYG

UNDERSTANDING THE CONCEPTS

The chapter sections to review are given in parentheses at the end of each question.

21.105 Answer the following questions for the given section of DNA: (21.4, 21.5, 21.6)

a. Complete the bases in the parent and new strands.

Parent strand: | A | | G | T | | | C | T |

New strand: | | C | | | G | C | G | | |

b. Using the new strand as a template, write the mRNA sequence.

c. Write the three-letter symbols for the amino acids that would go into the peptide from the mRNA you wrote in part **b**.

21.106 Suppose a mutation occurs in the DNA section in problem 21.105, and the first base in the parent chain, adenine, is replaced by guanine. (21.4, 21.5, 21.6, 21.7)

    a. What type of mutation has occurred?

    b. Using the new strand that results from this mutation, write the order of bases in the altered mRNA.

    c. Write the three-letter symbols for the amino acids that would go into the peptide from the mRNA you wrote in part **b**.

    d. What effect, if any, might this mutation have on the structure and/or function of the resulting protein?

ADDITIONAL QUESTIONS AND PROBLEMS

21.107 Identify each of the following bases as a pyrimidine or a purine: (21.1)

    a. cytosine   **b.** adenine

    c. uracil   **d.** thymine

    e. guanine

21.108 Indicate if each of the bases in problem 21.107 is found in DNA only, RNA only, or both DNA and RNA. (21.1)

21.109 Identify the base and sugar in each of the following nucleosides: (21.1)

    a. deoxythymidine   **b.** adenosine

    c. cytidine   **d.** deoxyguanosine

21.110 Identify the base and sugar in each of the following nucleotides: (21.1)

    a. CMP   **b.** dAMP

    c. dTMP   **d.** UMP

21.111 How do the bases thymine and uracil differ? (21.1)

21.112 How do the bases cytosine and uracil differ? (21.1)

21.113 Draw the condensed structural formula for CMP. (21.1)

21.114 Draw the condensed structural formula for dGMP. (21.1)

21.115 What is similar about the primary structure of RNA and DNA? (21.2)

21.116 What is different about the primary structure of RNA and DNA? (21.2)

21.117 If the DNA double helix in salmon contains 28% adenine, what is the percentage of thymine, guanine, and cytosine? (21.3)

21.118 If the DNA double helix in humans contains 20% cytosine, what is the percentage of guanine, adenine, and thymine? (21.3)

21.119 In DNA, how many hydrogen bonds form between adenine and thymine? (21.3)

21.120 In DNA, how many hydrogen bonds are formed between guanine and cytosine? (21.3)

21.121 Write the complementary base sequence for each of the following DNA segments: (21.4)

    a. 5′ G A C T T A G G C 3′

    b. 3′ T G C A A A C T A G C T 5′

    c. 5′ A T C G A T C G A T C G 3′

21.122 Write the complementary base sequence for each of the following DNA segments: (21.4)

    a. 5′ T T A C G G A C C G C 3′

    b. 5′ A T A G C C C T T A C T G G 3′

    c. 3′ G G C C T A C C T T A A C G A C G 5′

21.123 In DNA replication, what is the difference between the synthesis of the leading strand and the synthesis of the lagging strand? (21.4)

21.124 How are the Okazaki fragments joined to the growing DNA strand? (21.4)

21.125 After the replication of a DNA, where are the original DNA strands located in the daughter DNA molecules? (21.4)

21.126 How can replication occur at several places along a DNA double helix? (21.4)

21.127 Match the following statements with rRNA, mRNA, or tRNA: (21.5)

    a. is the smallest type of RNA

    b. makes up the highest percentage of RNA in the cell

    c. carries genetic information from the nucleus to the ribosomes

21.128 Match the following statements with rRNA, mRNA, or tRNA: (21.5)

    a. combines with proteins to form ribosomes

    b. brings amino acids to the ribosomes for protein synthesis

    c. acts as a template for protein synthesis

21.129 What are the possible codons for each of the following amino acids? (21.6)

    a. threonine   **b.** serine

    c. cysteine

21.130 What are the possible codons for each of the following amino acids? (21.6)

    a. valine   **b.** arginine

    c. histidine

21.131 What is the amino acid for each of the following codons? (21.6)

    a. AAG   **b.** AUU   **c.** CGA

21.132 What is the amino acid for each of the following codons? (21.6)

    a. CAA   **b.** GGC   **c.** AAC

21.133 What is the anticodon on tRNA for each of the following codons in an mRNA? (21.6)

    a. AGC   **b.** UAU   **c.** CCA

21.134 What is the anticodon on tRNA for each of the following codons in an mRNA? (21.6)

    a. GUG   **b.** CCC   **c.** GAA

℞ Clinical Applications

21.135 Endorphins are polypeptides that reduce pain. What is the amino acid order for the endorphin leucine enkephalin (leu-enkephalin), which has the following mRNA? (21.5, 21.6)

    5′ AUG UAC GGU GGA UUU CUA UAA 3′

21.136 Endorphins are polypeptides that reduce pain. What is the amino acid order for the endorphin methionine enkephalin (met-enkephalin), which has the following mRNA? (21.5, 21.6)

    5′ AUG UAC GGU GGA UUU AUG UAA 3′

CHALLENGE QUESTIONS

The following groups of questions are related to the topics in this chapter. However, they do not all follow the chapter order, and they require you to combine concepts and skills from several sections. These questions will help you increase your critical thinking skills and prepare for your next exam.

21.137 Oxytocin is a peptide that contains nine amino acids. How many nucleotides would be found in the mRNA for this peptide? (21.6)

21.138 A polypeptide contains 36 amino acids. How many nucleotides would be found in the mRNA for this polypeptide? (21.6)

21.139 What is the difference between a DNA virus and a retrovirus? (21.9)

21.140 Why are there no base pairs in DNA between adenine and guanine or thymine and cytosine? (21.3)

21.141 Match each of the following processes (**1** to **5**) with one of the items (**a** to **e**): (21.4, 21.5, 21.6)

(1) replication of DNA   (2) transcription
(3) translation   (4) recombinant DNA
(5) reverse transcription

a. Okazaki fragments
b. mRNA is synthesized from nuclear DNA
c. viruses
d. restriction enzymes
e. tRNA molecules bond to anticodons

21.142 Match each of the following processes (**1** to **5**) with one of the items (**a** to **e**): (21.4, 21.5, 21.6)

(1) replication of DNA   (2) transcription
(3) translation   (4) recombinant DNA
(5) reverse transcription

a. amino acids are linked together
b. RNA template is used to synthesize DNA
c. helicase unwinds DNA
d. genetic information is transferred from DNA
e. sticky ends join new DNA segment

ANSWERS

Answers to Selected Questions and Problems

21.1 **a.** pyrimidine   **b.** pyrimidine

21.3 **a.** DNA   **b.** both DNA and RNA

21.5 deoxyadenosine monophosphate (dAMP), deoxythymidine monophosphate (dTMP), deoxycytidine monophosphate (dCMP), and deoxyguanosine monophosphate (dGMP)

21.7 **a.** nucleoside   **b.** nucleoside
       c. nucleoside   **d.** nucleotide

21.9 **a.** (3) both DNA and RNA
       b. (2) RNA only
       c. (1) DNA only
       d. (3) both DNA and RNA

21.11

21.13

21.15 The nucleotides in nucleic acid polymers are held together by phosphodiester linkages between the 3′ OH group of a sugar (ribose or deoxyribose) and a phosphate group on the 5′ carbon of another sugar.

21.17 –sugar–phosphate–sugar–phosphate–

21.19 the free 5′ phosphate on the 5′ carbon of ribose or deoxyribose of a nucleic acid

21.21

Guanosine (G)

Cytidine (C

21.23 Structural features of DNA include that it is shaped like a double helix, it contains a sugar–phosphate backbone, the nitrogen-containing bases are hydrogen bonded between strands, and the strands run in opposite directions. A forms two hydrogen bonds to T, and G forms three hydrogen bonds to C.

21.25 The two DNA strands are held together by hydrogen bonds between the complementary bases in each strand.

21.27 **a.** 3′ T T T T T T 5′   **b.** 3′ C C C C C C 5′
       c. 3′ T C A G G T C C A 5′
       d. 3′ G A C A T A T G C A A T 5′

21.29 The enzyme helicase unwinds the DNA helix so that the parent DNA strands can be replicated into daughter DNA strands.

21.31 Once the DNA strands separate, the DNA polymerase pairs each of the bases with its complementary base and produces two exact copies of the original DNA.

21.33 **a.** (2) helicase **b.** (3) primase
c. (4) replication fork **d.** (1) lagging strand

21.35 **a.** 5′ CGAGGTAC 3′ **b.** No

21.37 ribosomal RNA, messenger RNA, and transfer RNA

21.39 A ribosome consists of a small subunit and a large subunit that contain rRNA combined with proteins.

21.41 In transcription, the sequence of nucleotides on a DNA template (one strand) is used to produce the base sequence of a messenger RNA.

21.43 5′ GGC UUC CAA GUG 3′

21.45 In eukaryotic cells, genes contain sections called exons that code for proteins and sections called introns that do not code for proteins.

21.47 5′ GGC GGA UCG 3′

21.49 A transcription factor is a molecule that binds to DNA and regulates transcription.

21.51 An activator binds to transcription factors and increases the rate of RNA transcription.

21.53 A codon is a three-base sequence in mRNA that codes for a specific amino acid in a protein.

21.55 **a.** leucine (Leu) **b.** serine (Ser)
c. glycine (Gly) **d.** arginine (Arg)

21.57 When AUG is the first codon, it signals the start of protein synthesis. Thereafter, AUG codes for methionine.

21.59 A codon is a base triplet in the mRNA. An anticodon is the complementary triplet on a tRNA for a specific amino acid.

21.61 initiation, chain elongation, and termination

21.63 **a.** Thr–Thr–Thr, TTT
b. Phe–Pro–Phe–Pro, FPFP
c. Tyr–Gly–Arg–Cys, YGRC

21.65 The new amino acid is joined by a peptide bond to the growing peptide chain. The ribosome moves to the next codon, which attaches to a tRNA carrying the next amino acid.

21.67 **a.** 5′ CGA AAA GUU UUU 3′
b. GCU, UUU, CAA, AAA
c. Arg–Lys–Val–Phe, RKVF

21.69 **a.** 5′AAA CAC UUG GUU GUG GAC 3′
b. Lys–His–Leu–Val–Val–Asp, KHLVVD

21.71 In a point mutation, a base in DNA is replaced by a different base.

21.73 In a deletion mutation caused by the deletion of a base, all the codons from the mutation onward are changed, which changes the order of amino acids in the rest of the polypeptide chain.

21.75 The normal triplet TTT forms a codon AAA, which codes for lysine. The mutation TTC forms a codon AAG, which also codes for lysine. There is no effect on the amino acid sequence.

21.77 **a.** Thr–Ser–Arg–Val
b. Thr–Thr–Arg–Val
c. Thr–Ser–Gly–Val
d. Thr — STOP. Protein synthesis would terminate early. If this occurs early in the formation of the polypeptide, the resulting protein will probably be nonfunctional.
e. The new protein will contain the sequence Asp–Ile–Thr–Gly.
f. The new protein will contain the sequence His–His–Gly.

21.79 **a.** GCC and GCA both code for alanine.
b. A vital ionic interaction in the tertiary structure of hemoglobin cannot be formed when the polar glutamic acid is replaced by valine, which is nonpolar. The resulting hemoglobin is malformed and less capable of carrying oxygen.

21.81 *E. coli* bacterial cells contain several small circular plasmids of DNA that can be isolated easily. After the recombinant DNA is formed, *E. coli* multiply rapidly, producing many copies of the recombinant DNA in a relatively short time.

21.83 *E. coli* can be soaked in a detergent solution that disrupts the plasma membrane and releases the cell contents, including the plasmids, which are collected.

21.85 When a gene has been obtained using a restriction enzyme, it is mixed with plasmids that have been cut by the same enzyme. When mixed together, the sticky ends of the DNA fragments bond with the sticky ends of the plasmid DNA to form a recombinant DNA.

21.87 In DNA fingerprinting, restriction enzymes cut a sample DNA into fragments, which are sorted by size using gel electrophoresis. A radioactive probe that adheres to specific DNA sequences exposes an X-ray film and creates a pattern of dark and light bands called a DNA fingerprint.

21.89 The bold sections represent the "sticky ends" of the cleaved bases.

5′ AA **CGTT** 3′

3′ TT**GC** AA 5′

21.91 **a.** 3′ CCGA 5′ **b.** 3′ TTACGC 5′
c. 3′ AAGGCT 5′

21.93 DNA or RNA, but not both

21.95 **a.** A viral RNA is used to synthesize a viral DNA to produce the proteins for the protein coat, which allows the virus to replicate and leave the cell.
b. retrovirus

21.97 Nucleoside analogs such as AZT and ddI are similar to the nucleosides required to make viral DNA in reverse transcription. However, they interfere with the ability of the DNA to form and thereby disrupt the life cycle of the HIV virus.

21.99 Estrogen receptors are transcription factors that bind to DNA and increase the production of mammary cells, which can lead to mutations and cancer.

21.101 Tamoxifen blocks the binding of estrogen to the estrogen receptor, which prevents binding and activation of the gene.

21.103 **a.** 5′ ACC UUA AUA GAC GAG AAG CGC 3′
b. Thr–Leu–Ile–Asp–Glu–Lys–Arg, TLIDEKR
c. There is no change, Asp is still the fourth amino acid residue.

21.105 a.

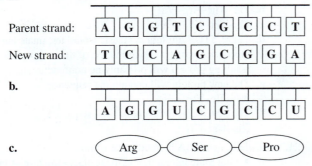

Parent strand: A G G T C G C C T

New strand: T C C A G C G G A

b.

A G G U C G C C U

c. Arg   Ser   Pro

21.107 a. pyrimidine   **b.** purine
   c. pyrimidine   **d.** purine
   e. pyrimidine

21.109 a. thymine and deoxyribose
   b. adenine and ribose
   c. cytosine and ribose
   d. guanine and deoxyribose

21.111 They are both pyrimidines, but thymine has a methyl group.

21.113

(structure of a nucleotide showing phosphate group, CH_2, ribose sugar with OH OH, and cytosine base with NH_2)

$$^-O-\overset{\overset{\displaystyle O}{\|}}{\underset{\underset{\displaystyle O^-}{}}{P}}-O-CH_2$$

21.115 They are both polymers of nucleotides connected through phosphodiester linkages between alternating sugar and phosphate groups, with bases extending out from each sugar.

21.117 28% T, 22% G, and 22% C

21.119 two

21.121 a. 3′ C T G A A T C C G 5′
   b. 5′ A C G T T T G A T C G A 3′
   c. 3′ T A G C T A G C T A G C 5′

21.123 DNA polymerase synthesizes the leading strand continuously in the 5′ to 3′ direction. The lagging strand is synthesized in small segments called Okazaki fragments because it must grow in the 3′ to 5′ direction and DNA polymerase can only work in the 5′ to 3′ direction.

21.125 One strand of the parent DNA is found in each of the two copies of the daughter DNA molecule.

21.127 a. tRNA   **b.** rRNA   **c.** mRNA

21.129 a. ACU, ACC, ACA, and ACG
   b. UCU, UCC, UCA, UCG, AGU, and AGC
   c. UGU and UGC

21.131 a. lysine   **b.** isoleucine   **c.** arginine

21.133 a. UCG   **b.** AUA   **c.** GGU

21.135 START–Tyr–Gly–Gly–Phe–Leu–STOP

21.137 Three nucleotides are needed to code for each amino acid, plus the start and stop codons consisting of three nucleotides each, which makes a minimum total of 33 nucleotides.

21.139 A DNA virus attaches to a cell and injects viral DNA that uses the host cell to produce copies of the DNA to make viral RNA. A retrovirus injects viral RNA from which complementary DNA is produced by reverse transcription.

21.141 a. (1) replication of DNA
   b. (2) transcription
   c. (5) reverse transcription
   d. (4) recombinant DNA
   e. (3) translation

CI.41 Aromasin is a drug that is used to inhibit the activity of the enzyme aromatase (estrogen synthetase). In the ovaries and mammary glands, aromatase converts testosterone to estrogen. Aromasin is used to treat breast cancer because it binds irreversibly to the active site of the enzyme, preventing the synthesis of estrogen and slowing the growth of estrogen-related cancers. Aromasin has the molecular formula $C_{20}H_{24}O_2$. (7.5, 12.5, 13.1, 14.1, 17.6, 20.1, 20.4)

Aromasin

a. What are the functional groups in aromasin?
b. What are the functional groups in testosterone?
c. What are the functional groups in estrogen?
d. Why is the enzyme that converts testosterone to estrogen called aromatase?
e. Why would aromasin compete with testosterone, the precursor of estrogen?
f. What is the molar mass of aromasin?
g. If one tablet contains 25 mg of aromasin and there are 30 tablets in a package, how many moles of aromasin are in the package?

Testosterone → Aromatase → Estrogen

CI.42 Thalassemia is an inherited genetic mutation that limits the production of the beta chain needed for the formation of hemoglobin. If low levels of the beta chain are produced, there is a shortage of red blood cells (anemia). As a result, the body does not have sufficient amounts of oxygen. In one form of thalassemia, a single nucleotide is deleted in the DNA that codes for the beta chain. This mutation involves the deletion of thymine (T) from section 91 in the following informational strand of normal DNA: (21.4, 21.5, 21.6, 21.7, 21.8)

89	90	91	92	93	94	
AGT	GAG	CTG	CAC	TGT	GAC	A ...

The ribbon structure of hemoglobin shows the four polypeptide subunits; two (orange) are α-chains and two (red) are β-chains. The heme groups (green) in the four subunits bind oxygen.

a. Write the complementary (template) strand for this normal DNA segment.
b. Write the mRNA sequence from normal DNA using the template strand in part **a**.
c. What amino acids are placed in the beta chain by this portion of mRNA?
d. What is the order of nucleotides in the mutation?
e. Write the template strand for the mutated DNA segment.
f. Write the mRNA sequence from the mutated DNA segment using the template strand in part **e**.
g. What amino acids are placed in the beta chain by the mutated DNA segment?
h. What type of mutation occurs in this form of thalassemia?
i. How might the properties of this segment of the beta chain be different from the properties of the normal protein?
j. How might the level of structure in hemoglobin be affected if beta chains are not produced?

Hypothalamus   Pituitary gland

The hypothalamus secretes GnRF.

Use the following information for CI.43 and CI.44:
In response to signals from the nervous system, the hypothalamus secretes a polypeptide hormone known as gonadotropin-releasing factor (GnRF), which stimulates the pituitary gland to release other hormones into the bloodstream. Two of these hormones are luteinizing hormone (LH) and follicle-stimulating hormone (FSH).

The mRNA for the GnRF contains the codon sequence:
5′ GAA CAC UGG UCC UAU GGC CUU AGG CCA GGA 3′
(19.1, 19.3, 19.4, 20.5, 21.6, 21.7)

CI.43 a. Write the three-letter abbreviations for the sequence of amino acid residues in the decapeptide GnRF.
b. Write the one-letter abbreviations for the decapeptide GnRF.
c. If the fourth triplet UCC is changed to UUC, what type of mutation has occurred in the mRNA?
d. What is the change in the amino acid sequence in the mutated GnRF?
e. How could the tertiary structure and biological behavior of the mutated GnRF change?
f. When the level of LH or FSH is high in the bloodstream, the hypothalamus stops secreting GnRF. What type of regulation of proteins does this represent?

CI.44 Use the amino acid sequence you determined in CI.43 for the GnRF to answer the following: (19.1, 19.2, 19.3, 19.4)
  a. What amino acid is the N-terminus?
  b. What amino acid is the C-terminus?
  c. Which amino acids in GnRF are nonpolar?
  d. Which amino acids in GnRF are polar neutral?
  e. Draw the condensed structural formulas for the acidic amino acids at physiological pH.
  f. Draw the condensed structural formulas for the basic amino acids at physiological pH.

CI.45 A segment of the DNA template from BRCA1 mutated gene has the nucleotide sequence: 3′ A C A T A T T T T G C A A A T T T T G C A T G C 5′ (21.5, 21.6, 21.7)
  a. Write the corresponding section of mRNA produced from the segment of the BRCA1 mutated gene.
  b. What are the tRNA anticodons?
  c. Write the three-letter abbreviations for the amino acid residues in the peptide for this segment.

CI.46 A segment of the DNA template from BRCA2 mutated gene has the nucleotide sequence: 3′ T T C A A A G A G C A A G G G C T G A C T C T G 5′ (21.5, 21.6, 21.7)
  a. Write the corresponding section of mRNA produced from the segment of the BRCA2 mutated gene.
  b. What are the tRNA anticodons?
  c. Write the three-letter abbreviations for the amino acid residues in the peptide for this segment.

ANSWERS

CI.41 a. ketone, alkene, cycloalkene
  b. alkene, cycloalkene, alcohol, ketone
  c. phenol, alcohol
  d. The enzyme aromatase converts a six-carbon cycloalkene into an aromatic ring.
  e. Aromasin has a steroid structure similar to that of testosterone, which binds with aromatase at the active site.
  f. 296.4 g/mole
  g. 2.5×10^{-3} mole

CI.43 a. Glu–His–Trp–Ser–Tyr–Gly–Leu–Arg–Pro–Gly
  b. EHWSYGLRRPG
  c. a point mutation
  d. serine is replaced with phenylalanine

  e. Serine has a polar —OH group, whereas phenylalanine is nonpolar. The polar serine would have been on the outside of the normal peptide, whereas the phenylalanine will move to the inside of the mutated GnRF. This could change the tertiary structure of the decapeptide, and possibly cause a loss in biological activity.
  f. feedback control

CI.45 a. 5′ UGU AUA AAA CGU UUA AAA CGU ACG 3′
  b. ACA UAU UUU GCA AAU UUU GCA UGC
  c. Cys–Ile–Lys–Arg–Leu–Lys–Arg–Thr

22

Metabolic Pathways for Carbohydrates

PHILIP, WHO IS 8 MONTHS OLD, WAS BROUGHT TO the hepatology unit with symptoms that included convulsions, lethargy, difficulty breathing, and diarrhea. Blood tests indicated that Philip had very low blood glucose, low blood pH, high lactate levels, and high liver glycogen. During examination, Barbara, a clinical lipid specialist, noted that Philip was small for his age, had a doll-like face from fat deposits, and a very large liver causing an extended abdomen. Because of his characteristic doll-like face and large amount of glycogen in his liver, Philip was diagnosed with a glycogen storage disease type I (GSD I), also known as *von Gierke's disease*, in which a genetic disorder produces a defective enzyme *glucose-6-phosphatase*. Without this enzyme, glucose-6-phosphate cannot be degraded to glucose but is stored as glycogen in large amounts in the liver.

CAREER Hepatology Nurse

Hepatology nursing is a specialty of nursing that emphasizes liver health, prevention of illness, and the care of clients with liver-related health problems that can have viral, genetic, and metabolic causes.

The hepatology nurse provides care for patients with liver-related conditions in clinics, outreach centers, or hospitals. Nursing care involves diagnosing illnesses, ordering and analyzing laboratory tests, developing appropriate treatment plans, providing patient education, and giving instruction in preventative care. In addition, a hepatology nurse may be responsible for documenting patient medical records, clinical research, and drug testing.

LOOKING AHEAD

22.1   Metabolism and Energy 798

♥   **Chemistry Link to Health**
ATP Energy and Ca²⁺ Needed to Contract Muscles 803

22.2   Important Coenzymes in Metabolic Pathways 804

22.3   Digestion of Carbohydrates 808

22.4   Glycolysis: Oxidation of Glucose 810

22.5   Pathways for Pyruvate 816

22.6   Glycogen Synthesis and Degradation 819

♥   **Chemistry Link to Health**
Glycogen Storage Diseases (GSDs) 822

22.7   Gluconeogenesis: Glucose Synthesis 824

℞   **Clinical Applications** 804, 816, 819, 824, 829, 833

℞   **Clinical Update** *Philip's Diet for von Gierke's Disease* 829

When we eat food, the polysaccharides, lipids, and proteins are digested to smaller molecules that can be absorbed into the cells of our body. As the glucose, fatty acids, and amino acids are broken down further, the energy is transferred to molecules in our cells such as adenosine triphosphate (ATP). Our cells use the energy stored in ATP when they do work such as contracting muscles, synthesizing large molecules, sending nerve impulses, and moving substances across cell membranes.

All the chemical reactions that take place in cells to break down or build molecules are known as *metabolism*. A *metabolic pathway* is a series of linked reactions each catalyzed by a specific enzyme. In this and the following chapters, we will look at these pathways and the way they produce energy and cellular compounds.

CHAPTER READINESS*

⚛ CORE CHEMISTRY SKILLS

- Identifying D- and L-Fischer Projections (15.2)
- Describing Enzyme Action (20.1)
- Classifying Enzymes (20.2)
- Identifying Factors Affecting Enzyme Activity (20.3)
- Describing the Role of Cofactors (20.6)

*These Core Chemistry Skills from previous chapters are listed here for your review as you proceed to the new material in this chapter.

LEARNING GOAL

Describe the three stages of catabolism, the structure of ATP, and the role of ATP.

22.1 Metabolism and Energy

The term **metabolism** refers to all the chemical reactions that provide energy and the substances required for continued cell growth. There are two types of metabolic reactions: *catabolic* and *anabolic*. In **catabolic reactions**, complex molecules are broken down to small ones with an accompanying release of energy. In **anabolic reactions**, energy in the cell is used to join small molecules to build large ones. We can think of catabolism as consisting of three stages (see Figure 22.1).

Stage 1 Catabolism begins with the processes of **digestion** in which enzymes in the digestive tract hydrolyze large molecules into smaller ones. The polysaccharides break down to monosaccharides, fats break down to glycerol and fatty acids, and the proteins yield amino acids. These digestion products diffuse into the bloodstream for transport to cells.

Stage 2 Within the cells, catabolic reactions continue as the digestion products are broken down further to yield two- and three-carbon compounds such as pyruvate and acetyl CoA.

Stage 3 The major production of energy takes place in the mitochondria, as the two-carbon acetyl group is oxidized in the citric acid cycle, which produces reduced coenzymes NADH, NADPH, and $FADH_2$. As long as the cells have oxygen, the hydrogen ions and electrons from the reduced coenzymes are transferred to electron transport to synthesize ATP.

Stages of Catabolism

FIGURE 22.1 ▶ In the three stages of catabolism, large molecules from foods are digested and degraded to give smaller molecules that can be oxidized to produce energy.

Q Where is most of the ATP energy produced in the cells?

Identify each of the following as catabolic or anabolic:

a. digestion of lipids
b. synthesis of lactase
c. hydrolysis of sucrose
d. synthesis of adenine monophosphate from adenine, ribose, and phosphate

SOLUTION

a. The breakdown of large molecules involves catabolic reactions.
b. The synthesis of large molecules involves anabolic reactions.
c. The breakdown of sucrose to smaller molecules is a catabolic reaction.
d. The combination of small molecules to give a large molecule is an anabolic reaction.

STUDY CHECK 22.1

Identify the oxidation of glucose to CO_2 and H_2O as catabolic or anabolic.

ANSWER

catabolic

Cell Structure for Metabolism

To understand the relationships among metabolic reactions, we need to look at where these metabolic reactions take place in the cells of plants and animals. The cells in plants and animals are *eukaryotic* cells, which have a nucleus that contains DNA (see Figure 22.2). Single-celled organisms such as bacteria are *prokaryotic* cells, which have no nucleus.

In animals, a *cell membrane* separates the materials inside the cell from the aqueous environment surrounding the cell. The *nucleus* contains the genes that control DNA replication and protein synthesis. The **cytosol**, the fluid part of the cell, is an aqueous solution of electrolytes and enzymes that catalyze many of the chemical reactions in the cell.

Within the cytosol are small structures called *organelles* that carry out specific functions in the cell. The *ribosomes* are the sites of protein synthesis. *Lysosomes* contain enzymes that break down recyclable cellular structures that are no longer needed by the cell. The **mitochondria** are the energy-producing factories of the cells. A mitochondrion has an outer membrane and an inner membrane, with an intermembrane space between them. The fluid section surrounded by the inner membrane is called the *matrix*. Enzymes located in the matrix and along the inner membrane catalyze the oxidation of carbohydrates, fats, and amino acids. All of these oxidation pathways eventually produce CO_2, H_2O, and energy, which are used to form energy-rich compounds. Table 22.1 summarizes some of the functions of the cellular components in animal cells.

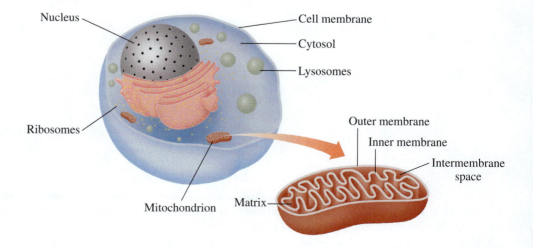

FIGURE 22.2 ▶ The diagram illustrates the major components of a typical eukaryotic cell of animals and plants.

🔵 What is the function of the mitochondrion in a cell?

TABLE 22.1 Functions of Components in Animal Cells

Component	Description and Function
Cell membrane	Separates the contents of a cell from the external environment and contains structures that communicate with other cells
Cytosol	Is the fluid part of the cytoplasm that contains enzymes for many of the cell's chemical reactions
Lysosome	Contains hydrolytic enzymes that digest and recycle old cell structures
Mitochondrion	Contains the structures for the synthesis of ATP from energy-producing reactions
Nucleus	Contains genetic information for the replication of DNA and the synthesis of protein
Ribosome	Is the site of protein synthesis using mRNA templates

In our cells, the energy released from the oxidation of the food we eat is stored in the form of a "high-energy" compound called *adenosine triphosphate* (ATP). The **ATP** molecule is composed of the base adenine, a ribose sugar, and three phosphate groups (see Figure 22.3).

FIGURE 22.3 ▶ Adenosine triphosphate (ATP) hydrolyzes to form ADP and AMP, along with a release of energy.

◉ How many phosphate groups are in adenosine monophosphate (AMP)?

Hydrolysis of ATP Yields Energy

Adenosine triphosphate undergoes hydrolysis, which breaks one of its phosphodiester linkages, to yield adenosine diphosphate (**ADP**), an inorganic phosphate group HPO_4^{2-}, abbreviated P_i, and energy needed for cellular metabolism. The hydrolysis of ATP molecules can provide 7.3 kcal/mole (31 kJ/mole).

$$ATP \longrightarrow ADP + P_i + 7.3 \text{ kcal/mole (31 kJ/mole)}$$

We can draw the hydrolysis of ATP as an exothermic reaction on an energy curve.

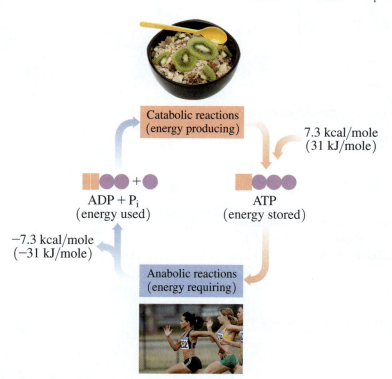

The ADP can also hydrolyze to form adenosine monophosphate (AMP) and an inorganic phosphate (P_i). The abbreviated equation is written as follows:

$$ADP \longrightarrow AMP + P_i + 7.3 \text{ kcal/mole (31 kJ/mole)}$$

Every time we contract muscles, move substances across cellular membranes, send nerve signals, or synthesize an enzyme, we use energy from ATP hydrolysis. In a cell that is doing work (anabolic processes), 1 to 2 million ATP molecules may be hydrolyzed in one second. The amount of ATP hydrolyzed in one day can be as much as our body mass, even though only about 1 g of ATP is present in all our cells at any given time.

When we take in food, the resulting catabolic reactions provide energy to regenerate ATP in our cells. Then 7.3 kcal/mole (31 kJ/mole) is used to synthesize ATP from ADP and P_i (see Figure 22.4).

$$ADP + P_i + 7.3 \text{ kcal/mole (31 kJ/mole)} \longrightarrow ATP$$

ATP Drives Reactions

Many of the reactions essential to a cell do not proceed spontaneously, but they can be made to proceed by combining them with a reaction that releases energy for their use. Often the energy released by the hydrolysis of ATP is used to run a reaction that requires energy. For example, the glucose obtained from the digestion of carbohydrates must add a phosphate group to start its breakdown in the cell. However, the energy needed to add a phosphate group to glucose is 3.3 kcal/mole (14 kJ/mole),

FIGURE 22.4 ▶ ATP, the energy-storage molecule, links energy-producing reactions with energy-requiring reactions in the cells.

🔵 What type of reaction provides energy for ATP synthesis?

which means that the reaction does not occur spontaneously. When this energy-requiring reaction is paired with the energy-releasing hydrolysis of ATP, which releases 7.3 kcal/mole of energy, the reaction can take place.

ATP	$\longrightarrow$ ADP + P_i + 7.3 kcal/mole (31 kJ/mole)	Provides energy
Glucose + P_i + 3.3 kcal/mole (14 kJ/mole) $\longrightarrow$	glucose-6-phosphate	Requires energy
Overall: ATP + glucose	$\longrightarrow$ ADP + glucose-6-phosphate + 4.0 kcal/mole (17 kJ/mole)	

▶ **SAMPLE PROBLEM 22.2 ATP and Energy**

The reaction of glutamate (Glu) with ammonia (NH_3) produces the amino acid glutamine (Gln). The reaction requires 3.4 kcal/mole.

a. Is the formation of glutamine a catabolic or an anabolic reaction?
b. Write the equation for the formation of glutamine (Gln) including the energy.
c. Write the equation for the hydrolysis of ATP including the energy.
d. Write the overall equation for the combined reactions including the net energy change.

SOLUTION

a. anabolic
b. Glu + NH_3 + 3.4 kcal/mole $\longrightarrow$ Gln
c. ATP $\longrightarrow$ ADP + P_i + 7.3 kcal/mole
d. Glu + NH_3 + ATP $\longrightarrow$ Gln + ADP + P_i + 3.9 kcal/mole

STUDY CHECK 22.2

Why are anabolic reactions that require energy coupled with the hydrolysis of a high-energy compound such as ATP?

ANSWER

The hydrolysis of a high-energy compound such as ATP provides energy to drive reactions that require energy.

Chemistry Link to **Health**
ATP Energy and Ca^{2+} Needed to Contract Muscles

Our muscles consist of thousands of parallel fibers. Within these muscle fibers are filaments composed of two kinds of proteins, myosin and actin. Arranged in alternating rows, the thick filaments of the protein myosin overlap the thin filaments containing the protein actin. During muscle contraction, the thin filaments (actin) slide inward over the thick filaments (myosin), which shortens the muscle fibers.

The calcium ion, Ca^{2+}, and ATP play an important role in muscle contraction. An increase in the Ca^{2+} concentration in the muscle fibers causes the filaments to slide, whereas a decrease stops the process. In a relaxed muscle, the Ca^{2+} concentration is low. When a nerve impulse reaches the muscle, the calcium channels in the membrane surrounding the muscle fibers open to allow Ca^{2+} to flow into the fluid surrounding the filaments. The muscle contracts as myosin binds to actin and pulls the filaments inward. The energy for the contraction is provided by the hydrolysis of ATP to ADP + P_i.

Muscles contract when myosin binds to actin.

Muscle contraction continues as long as both ATP and Ca^{2+} levels are high around the filaments. When the nerve impulse ends, the calcium channels close. The Ca^{2+} concentration decreases as energy from ATP pumps the remaining Ca^{2+} out of the filaments, back across the membrane, causing the muscle to relax. In *rigor mortis*, Ca^{2+} concentration remains high within the muscle fibers, causing a continued state of rigidity. After approximately 72 h, the Ca^{2+} concentration decreases due to cellular deterioration, and the muscles relax.

Muscle contraction uses the energy from the breakdown of ATP.

QUESTIONS AND PROBLEMS

22.1 Metabolism and Energy

LEARNING GOAL Describe the three stages of catabolism, the structure of ATP, and the role of ATP.

22.1 What stage of catabolism involves the digestion of polysaccharides?

22.2 What stage of catabolism involves the conversion of small molecules to CO_2, H_2O, and energy for the synthesis of ATP?

22.3 What is meant by a catabolic reaction in metabolism?

22.4 What is meant by an anabolic reaction in metabolism?

22.5 Identify each of the following as a catabolic or an anabolic reaction:
a. synthesis of lipids from glycerol and fatty acids
b. glucose adds P_i to form glucose-6-phosphate
c. hydrolysis of ATP to ADP and P_i
d. digestion of proteins in the stomach

22.6 Identify each of the following as a catabolic or an anabolic reaction:
a. digestion of fats to fatty acids and glycerol
b. hydrolysis of proteins into amino acids
c. synthesis of nucleic acids from nucleotides
d. glucose and galactose form the disaccharide lactose

22.7 Why is ATP considered an energy-rich compound?

22.8 What is meant when we say that the hydrolysis of ATP is used to "drive" a reaction?

22.9 Phosphoenolpyruvate (PEP) is a high-energy compound that releases 14.8 kcal/mole of energy when it hydrolyzes to pyruvate and P_i. This reaction can be coupled with the synthesis of ATP from ADP and P_i.
a. Write an equation for the energy-releasing reaction of PEP.
b. Write an equation for the energy-requiring reaction that forms ATP.
c. Write the overall equation for the combined reaction including the net energy change.

22.10 The phosphorylation of glycerol to glycerol-3-phosphate requires 2.2 kcal/mole and is driven by the hydrolysis of ATP.
a. Write an equation for the energy-releasing reaction of ATP.
b. Write an equation for the energy-requiring reaction that forms glycerol-3-phosphate.
c. Write the overall equation for the combined reaction including the net energy change.

℞ Clinical Applications

22.11 A 185-lb person bicycling vigorously on a stationary bicycle uses 2100 kJ. If the molar mass of ATP is 507 g/mole, how many grams of ATP are hydrolyzed to provide this amount of energy?

22.12 A 185-lb person bicycling moderately on a stationary bicycle uses 1300 kJ. If the molar mass of ATP is 507 g/mole, how many grams of ATP are hydrolyzed to provide this amount of energy?

LEARNING GOAL

Describe the components and functions of the coenzymes NAD^+, $NADP^+$, FAD, and coenzyme A.

22.2 Important Coenzymes in Metabolic Pathways

Several metabolic reactions that extract energy from our food involve oxidation and reduction reactions. Therefore, we will review several important coenzymes in their oxidized and reduced forms. In chemistry, oxidation is often association with the loss of H atoms, whereas reduction is associated with the gain of H atoms. Often, we represent two H atoms as two hydrogen ions ($2H^+$) and two electrons ($2\,e^-$). In both types of reactions, coenzymes are required to carry the hydrogen ions and electrons from or to the reacting substrate. A coenzyme that gains hydrogen ions and electrons is reduced, whereas a coenzyme that loses hydrogen ions and electrons to a substrate is oxidized.

In general, oxidation reactions produce energy, and reduction reactions require energy. Table 22.2 summarizes the characteristics of oxidation and reduction.

CORE CHEMISTRY SKILL

Identifying Important Coenzymes in Metabolism

TABLE 22.2 Characteristics of Oxidation and Reduction in Metabolic Pathways

Oxidation	Reduction
Loss of electrons (e^-)	Gain of electrons (e^-)
Loss of hydrogen (H or H^+ and e^-)	Gain of hydrogen (H or H^+ and e^-)
Gain of oxygen	Loss of oxygen
Produces energy	Requires energy input

NAD$^+$

NAD$^+$ (nicotinamide adenine dinucleotide) is an important coenzyme in which the vitamin *niacin* provides the *nicotinamide* group, which is bonded to ribose and the nucleotide adenosine diphosphate (ADP) (see Figure 22.5). The oxidized form of NAD$^+$ undergoes reduction when a carbon atom in the nicotinamide ring reacts with 2H (two hydrogen ions and two electrons), leaving one H^+.

The NAD$^+$ coenzyme is required in dehydrogenation reactions that produce carbon–oxygen (C=O) double bonds, such as the oxidation of alcohols to aldehydes and ketones. An example of an oxidation–reduction reaction is the oxidation of ethanol in the liver to ethanal and the reduction of NAD$^+$ to NADH + H^+.

FIGURE 22.5 ▶ The coenzyme NAD$^+$ (nicotinamide adenine dinucleotide), which consists of adenosine diphosphate, nicotinamide from the vitamin niacin, and ribose, is reduced to NADH + H^+ by adding a hydrogen ion and two electrons to NAD$^+$. The coenzyme NADP$^+$ is similar to NAD$^+$ except that a 2′ OH group is replaced by a phosphate. The reduced form of NADP$^+$ is NADPH.

Why is the conversion of NAD$^+$ to NADH and H^+ called a reduction?

NADP$^+$ (nicotinamide adenine dinucleotide phosphate) is a coenzyme used in anabolic reactions, such as lipid and nucleic acid synthesis, which require a source of hydrogen ions and electrons. The coenzyme NADP$^+$ is similar to NAD$^+$ except that a 2' OH group is replaced by a phosphate group. The reduced form of NADP$^+$ is NADPH.

FAD

FAD (flavin adenine dinucleotide) is a coenzyme that contains the nucleotide adenosine diphosphate and riboflavin. Riboflavin, also known as vitamin B$_2$, consists of ribitol (a sugar alcohol) and flavin. The oxidized form of FAD undergoes reduction when the two nitrogen atoms in the flavin part of the FAD coenzyme react with two hydrogen atoms ($2H^+ + 2\,e^-$), reducing FAD to FADH$_2$ (see Figure 22.6).

FIGURE 22.6 ▶ The coenzyme FAD (flavin adenine dinucleotide) made from riboflavin (vitamin B$_2$) and adenosine diphosphate is reduced to FADH$_2$ by adding two hydrogen atoms.

Q What is the type of reaction in which FAD accepts hydrogen?

FAD is used as a coenzyme when a dehydrogenation reaction converts a carbon–carbon single bond to a carbon–carbon (C=C) double bond. An example of a reaction in the citric acid cycle that reduces FAD is the conversion of the carbon–carbon single bond in succinate to a double bond in fumarate and FADH$_2$.

Coenzyme A

Coenzyme A (CoA) is made up of several components: pantothenic acid (vitamin B_5), phosphorylated ADP, and aminoethanethiol (see Figure 22.7).

Aminoethanethiol · Pantothenic acid · Phosphorylated ADP · **Coenzyme A**

FIGURE 22.7 ▶ Coenzyme A is derived from a phosphorylated ADP and pantothenic acid bonded by an amide bond to aminoethanethiol, which contains the —SH reactive part of the molecule.

Q What part of coenzyme A reacts with a two-carbon acetyl group?

An important function of coenzyme A is to prepare small acyl groups (represented by the letter A in the name), such as acetyl, for reactions with enzymes. The reactive feature of coenzyme A is the thiol group (—SH), which bonds to a two-carbon acetyl group to produce the energy-rich thioester **acetyl CoA**.

Acetyl group · Coenzyme A · Acetyl CoA (thioester)

In biochemistry, several abbreviations are used for coenzyme A and acetyl coenzyme A. For discussions in this text, we will use CoA for coenzyme A and acetyl CoA when the acetyl group is bonded to the sulfur atom (—S—) in coenzyme A. In equations, we will show the —SH group in coenzyme A as HS—CoA.

Types of Metabolic Reactions

Many reactions within the cells are similar to the types of reactions in organic chemistry such as hydration, dehydration (condensation), hydrolysis, hydrogenation, oxidation, and reduction. In the laboratory, organic reactions typically require strong acids (low pH), high temperatures, and/or metallic catalysts. However, metabolic reactions take place at body temperature and physiological pH, only requiring enzymes and often a coenzyme. Table 22.3 gives some enzymes and coenzymes, as well as their metabolic reactions.

TABLE 22.3 Enzymes and Coenzymes in Metabolic Reactions

Reaction	Enzyme	Coenzyme
Oxidation	Dehydrogenase	NAD^+, $NADP^+$, FAD
Reduction	Dehydrogenase	$NADH + H^+$, $NADPH + H^+$, $FADH_2$
Hydration	Hydrase	
Dehydration	Dehydrase	
Rearrangement	Isomerase, epimerase	
Transfer of phosphate group	Phosphatase, kinase	ATP, GDP, ADP
Transfer of acetyl group	Acetyl CoA transferase	CoA
Decarboxylation	Decarboxylase	
Hydrolysis	Protease, lipase, synthetase	ADP, GDP

> ### SAMPLE PROBLEM 22.3 Coenzymes
>
> Describe the reactive part of each of the following coenzymes and the way each participates in metabolic pathways:
>
> **a.** FAD **b.** NAD^+
>
> #### SOLUTION
>
> **a.** The oxidized form of FAD undergoes reduction when two nitrogen atoms in the flavin part react with $2H^+$ and $2\ e^-$ to give $FADH_2$. The coenzyme FAD is utilized in oxidation reactions that produce carbon–carbon ($C=C$) double bonds.
> **b.** The oxidized form of NAD^+ undergoes reduction when a carbon atom in the nicotinamide part reacts with $2H^+$ and $2\ e^-$, to give NADH and H^+. The coenzyme NAD^+ is utilized in oxidation reactions that produce carbon–oxygen ($C=O$) double bonds.
>
> #### STUDY CHECK 22.3
>
> Describe the reactive part of coenzyme A and how it participates in metabolic reactions.
>
> #### ANSWER
>
> In coenzyme A, the thiol group ($-SH$) of aminoethanethiol combines with an acetyl group to form acetyl coenzyme A. The HS$-$CoA participates in the transfer of acyl groups, usually acetyl groups.

QUESTIONS AND PROBLEMS

22.2 Important Coenzymes in Metabolic Pathways

LEARNING GOAL Describe the components and functions of the coenzymes NAD^+, $NADP^+$, FAD, and coenzyme A.

22.13 Identify one or more coenzymes that contain each of the following components:
  a. pantothenic acid **b.** niacin
  c. ribitol

22.14 Identify one or more coenzymes that contain each of the following components:
  a. riboflavin **b.** adenine
  c. aminoethanethiol

22.15 Give the abbreviation for each of the following:
  a. the reduced form of NAD^+
  b. the oxidized form of $FADH_2$

22.16 Give the abbreviation for each of the following:
  a. the reduced form of FAD
  b. the oxidized form of NADPH

22.17 What coenzyme picks up hydrogen when a carbon–carbon double bond is formed?

22.18 What coenzyme picks up hydrogen when a carbon–oxygen double bond is formed?

22.3 Digestion of Carbohydrates

LEARNING GOAL

Give the sites and products of the digestion of carbohydrates.

In stage 1 of catabolism, foods undergo digestion, a process that converts large molecules to smaller ones that can be absorbed by the body.

Digestion of Carbohydrates

We begin the digestion of carbohydrates as soon as we chew food. Enzymes produced in the salivary glands hydrolyze some of the α-glycosidic bonds in amylose and amylopectin, producing maltose, glucose, and smaller polysaccharides called dextrins, which contain three to eight glucose units. After swallowing, the partially digested starches enter the acidic environment of our stomach, where the low pH stops further carbohydrate digestion (see Figure 22.8).

In the small intestine, which has a pH of about 8, enzymes produced in the pancreas hydrolyze the remaining dextrins to maltose and glucose. Then enzymes produced in the mucosal cells that line the small intestine hydrolyze maltose, lactose, and sucrose. The resulting monosaccharides are absorbed through the intestinal wall into the bloodstream, which carries them to the liver, where the hexoses fructose and galactose are converted to glucose. Glucose is the primary energy source for muscle contractions, red blood cells, and the brain.

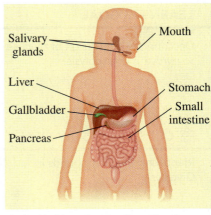

Carbohydrates begin digestion in the mouth, proteins in the stomach and small intestine, and lipids in the small intestine.

FIGURE 22.8 ▶ In stage 1 of catabolism, the digestion of carbohydrates begins in the mouth and is completed in the small intestine.

Q Why is there little or no digestion of carbohydrates in the stomach?

▶**SAMPLE PROBLEM 22.4** Digestion of Carbohydrates

Indicate the carbohydrate that undergoes digestion in each of the following sites:

a. mouth **b.** stomach **c.** small intestine

SOLUTION

a. starches amylose and amylopectin ($\alpha(1\rightarrow4)$-glycosidic bonds only)
b. essentially no digestion of carbohydrates **c.** dextrins, maltose, sucrose, and lactose

STUDY CHECK 22.4

Describe the digestion of amylose, a polymer of glucose molecules joined by $\alpha(1\rightarrow4)$-glycosidic bonds.

ANSWER

The digestion of amylose begins in the mouth when salivary amylase hydrolyzes some of the $\alpha(1\rightarrow4)$-glycosidic bonds. In the small intestine, pancreatic amylase hydrolyzes more glycosidic bonds, and finally maltose is hydrolyzed by maltase to yield glucose.

QUESTIONS AND PROBLEMS

22.3 Digestion of Carbohydrates

LEARNING GOAL Give the sites and products of the digestion of carbohydrates.

22.19 What is the general type of reaction that occurs during the digestion of carbohydrates?

22.20 Why is α-amylase produced in the salivary glands and in the pancreas?

22.21 Complete the following equations by filling in the missing words:
a. _____ + H_2O ⟶ galactose + glucose
b. Sucrose + H_2O ⟶ _____ + _____
c. Maltose + H_2O ⟶ glucose + _____

22.22 Give the site and the enzyme for each of the reactions in problem 22.21.

22.4 Glycolysis: Oxidation of Glucose

The major source of energy for the body is the glucose produced when we digest the carbohydrates in our food or from glycogen, a polysaccharide stored in the liver and skeletal muscle. Glucose in the bloodstream enters our cells where it undergoes degradation in a pathway called *glycolysis*. Early organisms used glycolysis to produce energy from simple nutrients long before there was any oxygen in Earth's atmosphere. Glycolysis is an **anaerobic** process; no oxygen is required.

In **glycolysis**, a six-carbon glucose molecule is broken down to yield two molecules of three-carbon pyruvate. All the reactions in glycolysis take place in the cytosol of the cell where the enzymes for glycolysis are located. In the first five reactions (1 to 5), called the *energy-investing phase*, energy is obtained from the hydrolysis of two ATP, which is needed to form sugar phosphates (see Figure 22.9). In reactions 4 and 5, a six-carbon sugar phosphate is split to yield two molecules of three-carbon sugar phosphate. In the last five reactions (6 to 10), called the *energy-generating phase*, energy is obtained from the hydrolysis of the energy-rich phosphate compounds and used to synthesize four ATP.

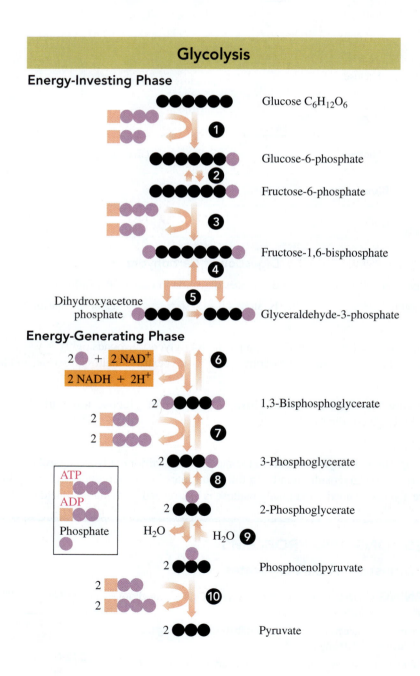

FIGURE 22.9 ▶ In glycolysis, the six-carbon glucose molecule is degraded to yield two three-carbon pyruvate molecules. A net of two ATP is produced along with two NADH.

ⓠ Where in the glycolysis pathway is glucose cleaved to yield two three-carbon compounds?

Energy-Investing Reactions: 1 to 5

As we describe the reactions in glycolysis, recall the names of enzymes that catalyze reactions as outlined in Table 22.3.

Reaction 1 Phosphorylation

In the initial reaction, a phosphate group is transferred from ATP to glucose producing glucose-6-phosphate and ADP. The enzyme that catalyzes this reaction is called a *hexokinase*, *hexo* because glucose is a hexose sugar and *kinase* because it uses the energy of ATP to transfer the phosphate group.

$$\text{P} = -\overset{\displaystyle O}{\underset{\displaystyle O^-}{\overset{\|}{\underset{|}{P}}}} - O^- = -PO_3^{2-}$$

Reaction 2 Isomerization

Glucose-6-phosphate, the aldose from reaction 1, is converted by *phosphoglucose isomerase* to fructose-6-phosphate, which is a ketose.

Reaction 3 Phosphorylation

The hydrolysis of another ATP provides a second phosphate group, which is transferred to fructose-6-phosphate producing fructose-1,6-bisphosphate. The word *bisphosphate* is used to show that the two phosphate groups are on different carbons in fructose and not connected to each other. This reaction is catalyzed by a second kinase enzyme called *phosphofructokinase*.

Reaction 4 Cleavage

Fructose-1,6-bisphosphate is split by *aldolase* into two three-carbon phosphate isomers: dihydroxyacetone phosphate and glyceraldehyde-3-phosphate.

Reaction 5 Isomerization

Because dihydroxyacetone phosphate is a ketone, it cannot react further. However, it undergoes isomerization by *triose phosphate isomerase* producing a second molecule of glyceraldehyde-3-phosphate, which can be oxidized. Now all six carbon atoms from glucose are contained in two identical triose phosphates.

Glyceraldehyde-3-phosphate

1,3-Bisphosphoglycerate

3-Phosphoglycerate

2-Phosphoglycerate

Phosphoenolpyruvate

Pyruvate

Energy-Generating Reactions: 6 to 10

In our discussion of glycolysis from this point, the two molecules of glyceraldehyde-3-phosphate produced in step 5 are undergoing the same reactions. For simplicity, we show the structures and reactions for only one three-carbon molecule for reactions 6 to 10.

Reaction 6 Oxidation and Phosphorylation

The aldehyde group of each glyceraldehyde-3-phosphate is oxidized by *glyceraldehyde-3-phosphate dehydrogenase* to a carboxyl group. The coenzyme NAD^+ is reduced to NADH and H^+. Then a phosphate group (P_i) is transferred to each of the new carboxyl groups to form two molecules of 1,3-bisphosphoglycerate, which is a high-energy compound.

Reaction 7 Phosphate Transfer

A phosphate group from each 1,3-bisphosphoglycerate is transferred to two ADP molecules by *phosphoglycerate kinase* yielding two molecules of the high-energy compound ATP. At this point in glycolysis, two ATP are produced, which balance the two ATP consumed in reactions 1 and 3.

Reaction 8 Isomerization

Two 3-phosphoglycerate molecules undergo isomerization by *phosphoglycerate mutase*, which moves the phosphate group from carbon 3 to carbon 2, yielding two molecules of 2-phosphoglycerate. The enzyme here is a specific type of isomerase called a *mutase* because the functional group merely shifts from one carbon to another.

Reaction 9 Dehydration

Each of the phosphoglycerate molecules undergoes dehydration (loss of water) by the enzyme *enolase* producing two phosphoenolpyruvate molecules, a high-energy compound.

Reaction 10 Phosphate Transfer

In a second direct substrate phosphorylation, phosphate groups from two phosphoenol-pyruvate molecules are transferred by *pyruvate kinase* to yield two ADP, two pyruvate, and two ATP. Here, a fourth kinase enzyme is involved because a phosphate is transferred with ATP production.

Summary of Glycolysis

In the glycolysis pathway, a six-carbon glucose molecule is converted to two three-carbon pyruvates. Initially, two ATP are required to form fructose-1,6-bisphosphate. In later reactions (7 and 10), phosphate transfers produce a total of four ATP. Overall, glycolysis yields two ATP and two NADH when a glucose molecule is converted to two pyruvates.

$$C_6H_{12}O_6 + \boxed{2\ NAD^+} + \boxed{2\ ADP} + 2P_i \longrightarrow 2CH_3 - \overset{\overset{\displaystyle O}{\|}}{C} - COO^- + \boxed{2\ NADH} + \boxed{2\ ATP} + 4H^+ + 2H_2O$$

Glucose   Pyruvate

Stage 1 Polysaccharides

Stage 2 Monosaccharides

2 ATP → 2 ADP

Glycolysis

Glucose

NAD⁺ → NADH

4 ADP → 4 ATP

2 Pyruvate

Glucose obtained from the digestion of polysaccharides is degraded in glycolysis to pyruvate.

▶ **SAMPLE PROBLEM 22.5** Reactions in Glycolysis

Identify each of the following reactions as an isomerization, phosphorylation, or dehydration:

a. A phosphate group is transferred to ADP to form ATP.
b. 3-Phosphoglycerate is converted to 2-phosphoglycerate.
c. A water molecule is removed from 2-phosphoglycerate.

SOLUTION

a. phosphorylation
b. isomerization
c. dehydration

STUDY CHECK 22.5

Indicate the reaction and enzyme that catalyzes each of the reactions in Sample Problem 22.5.

ANSWER

a. Phosphorylation in reaction 7 is catalyzed by phosphoglycerate kinase and in reaction 10 by pyruvate kinase.
b. Isomerization in reaction 8 is catalyzed by phosphoglycerate mutase.
c. Dehydration in reaction 9 is catalyzed by enolase.

Fructose and Galactose Enter Glycolysis

Other monosaccharides in our diet such as fructose and galactose also enter glycolysis, but first they must be converted to intermediates that can enter into the glycolytic pathway.

Fructose

In the muscles and kidneys, fructose is phosphorylated to fructose-6-phosphate, which enters glycolysis in reaction 3, where its movement through glycolysis is regulated by the enzyme phosphofructokinase. In the liver, fructose is converted to glyceraldehyde-3-phosphate, which enters glycolysis at reaction 6. Because this is after the main regulation at step 3, any fructose that enters the liver must continue through glycolysis.

Galactose

In a series of four enzymatic steps, galactose reacts with ATP to yield glucose-1-phosphate, which is converted to glucose-6-phosphate. Glucose-6-phosphate enters glycolysis at reaction 2.

Galactose and fructose form intermediates that enter the glycolysis pathway to be metabolized.

Regulation of Glycolysis

Metabolic pathways such as glycolysis do not run at the same rates all the time. The amount of glucose that is broken down is controlled by the requirements in the cells for pyruvate, ATP, and other intermediates of glycolysis. Within the 10-step pathway of glycolysis, the three enzymatic reactions 1, 3, and 10 are irreversible. These irreversible reactions respond to the levels of ATP and other products.

Reaction 1 Hexokinase

The amount of glucose entering the glycolysis pathway decreases when high levels of glucose-6-phosphate are present in the cell. This phosphorylation product inhibits hexokinase, which prevents glucose from reacting with ATP. This inhibition of the first enzyme in a pathway is an example of feedback control, which is a type of enzyme regulation.

Reaction 3 Phosphofructokinase

The reaction catalyzed by phosphofructokinase is a major control point for glycolysis. Because this is an irreversible reaction, once fructose-1,6-bisphosphate is formed, it must continue through the remaining reactions to pyruvate. As an allosteric enzyme, phosphofructokinase is inhibited by high levels of ATP and activated by high levels of ADP and AMP. High levels of ADP and AMP indicate that the cell has used up much of its ATP. As a regulator, phosphofructokinase increases the rate of pyruvate production for ATP synthesis when the cell needs to replenish ATP, and slows or stops the reaction when ATP is plentiful.

Reaction 10 Pyruvate Kinase

In the last reaction of glycolysis, high levels of ATP as well as acetyl CoA inhibit pyruvate kinase, which is another allosteric enzyme.

Reactions 1, 3, and 10 of glycolysis are examples of how metabolic pathways shut off enzymes to stop the production of molecules that are not needed. Pyruvate, which can be used to synthesize ATP, responds to ATP levels in the cell. When ATP levels are high, enzymes in glycolysis slow or stop the synthesis of pyruvate. With phosphofructokinase and pyruvate kinase inhibited by ATP, glucose-6-phosphate accumulates and inhibits reaction 1, and glucose does not enter the glycolysis pathway. The glycolysis pathway is shut down until ATP is once again needed in the cell. When ATP levels are low or AMP/ADP levels are high, these enzymes are activated and pyruvate production starts again.

▶**SAMPLE PROBLEM 22.6** Regulation of Glycolysis

How is glycolysis regulated by each of the following enzymes?

a. hexokinase   **b.** phosphofructokinase   **c.** pyruvate kinase

SOLUTION

a. High levels of glucose-6-phosphate inhibit hexokinase, which stops the addition of a phosphate group to glucose in reaction 1.
b. Phosphofructokinase, which catalyzes the formation of fructose-1,6-bisphosphate, is inhibited by high levels of ATP, and activated by high levels of ADP and AMP.
c. High levels of ATP or acetyl CoA inhibit pyruvate kinase, which stops the formation of pyruvate in reaction 10.

STUDY CHECK 22.6

Name the molecule that inhibits hexokinase by feedback regulation in step 1 of glycolysis.

ANSWER

glucose-6-phosphate

The Pentose Phosphate Pathway

The **pentose phosphate pathway** is an alternative pathway for the oxidation of glucose, which produces the coenzyme NADPH and five-carbon pentoses. The NADPH, which is the reduced form of $NADP^+$, is an important coenzyme required in the anabolic pathways such as the biosynthesis of nucleic acids, cholesterol, and fatty acids in the liver and fat (adipose) cells. The pentose phosphate pathway begins with glucose-6-phosphate from reaction 1 in glycolysis, which is converted to ribulose-5-phosphate and requires two $NADP^+$. Ribulose-5-phosphate is isomerized by *phosphopentose isomerase* to ribose-5-phosphate, an important component of nucleotides such as ATP, GTP, UTP, NAD^+, FAD, as well as RNA.

Glucose-6-phosphate + $2NADP^+$ + H_2O ⟶ ribose-5-phosphate + 2NADPH + $2H^+$ + CO_2

Several steps follow as ribose-5-phosphate is converted to sugar phosphates with three-, four-, five-, six-, and seven-carbon atoms, and eventually to fructose-6-phosphate (6C) and glyceraldehyde-3-phosphate (3C), both intermediates that can be metabolized in the glycolysis pathway. In this series of reactions, three ribose-5-phosphate molecules are converted to two hexose molecules and one triose molecule.

3 Ribose-5-phosphate ⟶ 2 fructose-6-phosphate + glyceraldehyde-3-phosphate

We can write the overall reaction of the pentose phosphate pathway as

3 Glucose-6-phosphate + $6NADP^+$ + $3H_2O$ ⟶

2 fructose-6-phosphate + glyceraldehyde-3-phosphate + 6NADPH + $6H^+$ + $3CO_2$

The importance of the pentose phosphate pathway is to supply NADPH and pentose sugars for biosynthesis, and utilize the remaining three- and six-carbon intermediates in glycolysis.

Pentose phosphate pathway

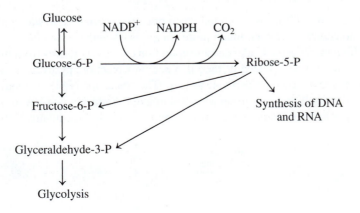

The pentose phosphate pathway converts glucose-6-P to ribose-5-P, which is needed for the synthesis of DNA and RNA. Ribose-5-P can also return to glycolysis as needed.

QUESTIONS AND PROBLEMS

22.4 Glycolysis: Oxidation of Glucose

LEARNING GOAL Describe the conversion of glucose to pyruvate in glycolysis.

22.23 What is the starting compound of glycolysis?

22.24 What is the three-carbon product of glycolysis?

22.25 How is ATP used in the initial steps of glycolysis?

22.26 How many ATP are used in the initial steps of glycolysis?

22.27 What three-carbon intermediates are obtained when fructose-1,6-bisphosphate splits?

22.28 Why does one of the three-carbon intermediates undergo isomerization?

22.29 How does substrate phosphorylation account for the production of ATP in glycolysis?

22.30 Why are there two ATP molecules formed for one molecule of glucose?

22.31 Indicate the enzyme(s) that catalyze(s) each of the following reactions in glycolysis:
  a. phosphorylation
  b. direct transfer of a phosphate group

22.32 Indicate the enzyme(s) that catalyze(s) each of the following reactions in glycolysis:
  a. isomerization
  b. formation of a three-carbon ketone and a three-carbon aldehyde

22.33 How many ATP or NADH are produced (or required) in each of the following steps in glycolysis?
  a. glucose to glucose-6-phosphate
  b. glyceraldehyde-3-phosphate to 1,3-bisphosphoglycerate
  c. glucose to pyruvate

22.34 How many ATP or NADH are produced (or required) in each of the following steps in glycolysis?
  a. 1,3-bisphosphoglycerate to 3-phosphoglycerate
  b. fructose-6-phosphate to fructose-1,6-bisphosphate
  c. phosphoenolpyruvate to pyruvate

22.35 Which step(s) in glycolysis involve(s) the following?
  a. The first ATP molecule is hydrolyzed.
  b. Direct substrate phosphorylation occurs.
  c. Six-carbon sugar splits into two three-carbon molecules.

22.36 Which step(s) in glycolysis involve(s) the following?
  a. Isomerization takes place.
  b. NAD^+ is reduced.
  c. A second ATP molecule is synthesized.

22.37 How do galactose and fructose, obtained from the digestion of carbohydrates, enter glycolysis?

22.38 What are three enzymes that regulate glycolysis?

22.39 Indicate whether each of the following would activate or inhibit phosphofructokinase:
  a. low levels of ATP   **b.** high levels of ATP

22.40 Indicate whether each of the following would activate or inhibit pyruvate kinase:
  a. low levels of ATP   **b.** high levels of ATP

22.41 What is the initial substrate for the pentose phosphate pathway?

22.42 What are the end products of the pentose phosphate pathway?

22.43 What is the purpose of producing NADPH in the pentose phosphate pathway?

22.44 What is the purpose of producing ribose-5-phosphate in the pentose phosphate pathway?

℞ Clinical Applications

22.45 Table sugar, which is the disaccharide sucrose, contains the monosaccharides glucose and fructose. After digestion of sucrose, how do each of the monosaccharides enter glycolysis?

22.46 Milk sugar, which is the disaccharide lactose, contains the monosaccharides glucose and galactose. After digestion of lactose, how do each of the monosaccharides enter glycolysis?

LEARNING GOAL

Give the conditions for the conversion of pyruvate to lactate, ethanol, and acetyl coenzyme A.

22.5 Pathways for Pyruvate

The pyruvate produced from glucose can now enter pathways that continue to extract energy. The available pathway depends on whether there is sufficient oxygen in the cell. Under **aerobic** conditions, oxygen is available to convert pyruvate to acetyl coenzyme A (acetyl CoA) and CO_2. When oxygen levels are low, pyruvate is reduced to lactate. In yeast cells, pyruvate is reduced to ethanol and CO_2.

Aerobic Conditions

In glycolysis, two ATP were generated when one glucose molecule was converted to two pyruvate molecules. However, much more energy is obtained from glucose when oxygen levels are high in the cells. Under aerobic conditions, pyruvate moves from the cytosol into the mitochondria to be oxidized further. In a complex reaction, pyruvate is oxidized, and a carbon atom is removed from pyruvate as CO_2. The coenzyme NAD^+ is reduced during the oxidation. The resulting two-carbon acetyl compound is attached to CoA, producing acetyl CoA, an important intermediate in many metabolic pathways (see Figure 22.10).

$$CH_3-\overset{\overset{\displaystyle O}{\|}}{C}-\overset{\overset{\displaystyle O}{\|}}{C}-O^- + HS-CoA + NAD^+ \xrightarrow[\text{dehydrogenase}]{\text{Pyruvate}} CH_3-\overset{\overset{\displaystyle O}{\|}}{C}-S-CoA + CO_2 + NADH$$

Pyruvate   Acetyl CoA

FIGURE 22.10 ▶ Pyruvate is converted to acetyl CoA under aerobic conditions and to lactate or ethanol (in certain microorganisms) under anaerobic conditions.

🔘 During vigorous exercise, why does lactate accumulate in the muscles?

Anaerobic Conditions

When we engage in strenuous exercise, the oxygen stored in our muscle cells is quickly depleted. Under anaerobic conditions, pyruvate remains in the cytosol where it is reduced to lactate. The product NAD^+ is used to oxidize glyceraldehyde-3-phosphate in the glycolysis pathway, which produces a small but needed amount of ATP.

$$CH_3-\underset{\underset{\text{Pyruvate (oxidized)}}{}}{\overset{\overset{O}{\|}}{C}}-\overset{\overset{O}{\|}}{C}-O^- + \boxed{NADH + H^+} \underset{\xrightarrow{\text{dehydrogenase}}}{\overset{\text{Lactate}}{\rightleftharpoons}} CH_3-\underset{\underset{\text{Lactate (reduced)}}{\underset{H}{|}}}{\overset{\overset{OH}{|}}{C}}-\overset{\overset{O}{\|}}{C}-O^- + \boxed{NAD^+}$$

The accumulation of lactate causes the muscles to tire and become sore. After exercise, a person continues to breathe rapidly to repay the *oxygen debt* incurred during exercise. Most of the lactate is transported to the liver, where it is converted back into pyruvate. Under anaerobic conditions, the only ATP production in glycolysis occurs during the steps that phosphorylate ADP directly, giving a net gain of only two ATP.

After vigorous exercise, rapid breathing helps to repay the oxygen debt.

$$C_6H_{12}O_6 + \boxed{2\ ADP} + 2P_i \longrightarrow 2CH_3-\underset{\underset{\text{Lactate}}{}}{\overset{\overset{OH}{|}}{CH}}-COO^- + \boxed{2\ ATP}$$
Glucose

Bacteria also convert pyruvate to lactate under anaerobic conditions. In the preparation of kimchee and sauerkraut, cabbage is covered with salt brine. The glucose obtained from the starches in the cabbage is converted to lactate. The acid environment acts as a

Olives are cured in a vinegar and salt brine.

preservative that prevents the growth of other bacteria. The pickling of olives and cucumbers gives similar products. When cultures of bacteria that produce lactate are added to milk, the acid denatures the milk proteins to give sour cream and yogurt.

Fermentation

Some microorganisms, particularly yeast, convert sugars to ethanol under anaerobic conditions by a process called **fermentation**. After pyruvate is formed in glycolysis, a carbon atom is removed in the form of CO_2 (**decarboxylation**). The NAD^+ for continued glycolysis is regenerated when the ethanal is reduced to ethanol.

$$CH_3-\overset{\overset{O}{\|}}{C}-\overset{\overset{O}{\|}}{C}-O^- + H^+ \xrightarrow[\text{decarboxylase}]{\text{Pyruvate}} CH_3-\overset{\overset{O}{\|}}{C}-H + CO_2$$

Pyruvate   Ethanal (acetaldehyde)

$$CH_3-\overset{\overset{O}{\|}}{C}-H + NADH + H^+ \xrightarrow[\text{dehydrogenase}]{\text{Alcohol}} CH_3-\overset{\overset{H}{|}}{\underset{H}{C}}-OH + NAD^+$$

Ethanal (acetaldehyde)   Ethanol

Beer is produced by the fermentation of pyruvate from barley malt, which gives carbon dioxide and ethanol.

The process of fermentation by yeast is one of the oldest known chemical reactions. Enzymes in the yeast convert the sugars in a variety of carbohydrate sources to glucose and then to ethanol. The evolution of CO_2 gas produces bubbles in beer, sparkling wines, and champagne. The type of carbohydrate used determines the taste associated with a particular alcoholic beverage. Beer is made from the fermentation of barley malt, wine and champagne from the sugars in grapes, vodka from potatoes or grain, sake from rice, and whiskeys from corn or rye. Fermentation produces solutions of about 15% alcohol by volume. At this concentration, the alcohol kills the yeast and fermentation stops.

▶ **SAMPLE PROBLEM 22.7 Pathways for Pyruvate**

Identify the pathway(s) that has each of the following characteristics:

a. In this pathway, NAD^+ is reduced to $NADH + H^+$.
b. The product of this pathway contains three carbon atoms.
c. NADH is the oxidizing agent in this anaerobic pathway to give a two-carbon molecule.
d. CO_2 is a product of this aerobic pathway.

SOLUTION

a. NAD^+ is used to oxidize pyruvate to acetyl CoA with the loss of one carbon atom as CO_2.
b. Pyruvate is reduced to a three-carbon molecule of lactate by lactate dehydrogenase and NADH.
c. Under anaerobic conditions, pyruvate is reduced to ethanol, a two-carbon molecule, and CO_2 by NADH.
d. Under aerobic conditions, pyruvate is oxidized to acetyl CoA and CO_2 by NAD^+.

STUDY CHECK 22.7

After strenuous exercise, lactate is oxidized back to pyruvate by lactate dehydrogenase using NAD^+. Write an equation to show this reaction.

ANSWER

$$CH_3-\overset{\overset{\displaystyle OH}{|}}{CH}-\overset{\overset{\displaystyle O}{\|}}{C}-O^- + \boxed{NAD^+} \xrightarrow{\text{Lactate dehydrogenase}} CH_3-\overset{\overset{\displaystyle O}{\|}}{C}-\overset{\overset{\displaystyle O}{\|}}{C}-O^- + \boxed{NADH + H^+}$$

QUESTIONS AND PROBLEMS

22.5 Pathways for Pyruvate

LEARNING GOAL Give the conditions for the conversion of pyruvate to lactate, ethanol, and acetyl coenzyme A.

22.47 What condition is needed in the cell to convert pyruvate to acetyl CoA?

22.48 What coenzymes are needed for the oxidation of pyruvate to acetyl CoA?

22.49 Write the overall equation for the conversion of pyruvate to acetyl CoA.

22.50 What are the possible products of pyruvate under anaerobic conditions?

22.51 Indicate which of the pathways for pyruvate (1) acetyl CoA, (2) lactate, and/or (3) ethanol occur under each of the following conditions:
   a. The reaction is catalyzed by alcohol dehydrogenase.
   b. NAD^+ is reduced.
   c. A three-carbon compound is produced.
   d. CO_2 is produced.

22.52 Indicate which of the pathways for pyruvate (1) acetyl CoA, (2) lactate, and/or (3) ethanol occur under each of the following conditions:
   a. NAD^+ is produced.
   b. $HS-CoA$ is required.
   c. NADH is required.
   d. The reaction is catalyzed by pyruvate decarboxylase.

22.53 In fermentation, a carbon atom is removed from pyruvate. What is the compound formed with that carbon atom?

22.54 In fermentation, what enzymes and coenzymes are used to produce ethanol?

Clinical Applications

22.55 After a marathon, a runner has muscle pain and cramping. What might have occurred in the muscle cells to cause this?

22.56 Some students decided to make some wine by placing yeast and grape juice in a container with a tight lid. A few weeks later, the container exploded. What reaction could account for the explosion?

22.57 A defective *pyruvate dehydrogenase* causes a buildup of lactate in the body and lactic acidosis, which lead to neurological problems. In addition, the production of cellular energy is diminished. Write the chemical equation for the conversion of pyruvate to lactate.

22.58 Defective *pyruvate decarboxylase*, an enzyme in the pyruvate dehydrogenase complex, is a rare disorder that occurs in infancy and leads to an elevated level of pyruvate and lactate in the blood and urine. The inability to convert pyruvate to acetyl CoA and CO_2 leads to lack of energy, general weakness, and developmental delay. Write the chemical equation for the conversion of pyruvate to acetyl CoA.

22.6 Glycogen Synthesis and Degradation

LEARNING GOAL

Describe the synthesis and breakdown of glycogen.

You have just eaten a large meal that supplies you with all the glucose you need to produce pyruvate and ATP by glycolysis. Any excess glucose is used to replenish your energy reserves by synthesizing glycogen, which is stored in your muscles and liver. Glycogen is a polymer of glucose with $\alpha(1 \rightarrow 4)$-glycosidic bonds and multiple branches attached by $\alpha(1 \rightarrow 6)$-glycosidic bonds. When glycogen stores are full, any remaining glucose is converted to triacylglycerols and stored as body fat. When your diet does not supply sufficient glucose and your blood glucose is low, the glycogen in your muscles is converted to glucose for energy, and the glucose from glycogen in your liver is released into the bloodstream to raise your blood glucose levels. During conditions of fasting, glycogen breakdown supplies nearly all the glucose for the body.

Glycogen Synthesis: Glycogenesis

Glycogenesis is the metabolic process of converting glucose molecules into glycogen. When glucose-6-phosphate, which is produced in reaction 1 of glycolysis, is not needed in the cell, it can be stored as glycogen.

Glucose-6-phosphate

Phosphoglucomutase ❶

Glucose-1-phosphate

Pyrophosphorylase ❷

UDP-glucose

▲ *Activated* by insulin
▼ *Inhibited* by glucagon (liver)
and epinephrine (muscle)

Glycogen synthase ❸

Glucose adds to glycogen chain

FIGURE 22.11 ▶ In glycogenesis, glucose is used to synthesize glycogen.

🅠 What is the function of UTP in glycogen synthesis?

🕸 CORE CHEMISTRY SKILL

Identifying the Compounds and Enzymes in Glycogenesis and Glycogenolysis

Reaction 1 Isomerization

Glycogen synthesis begins when the enzyme *phosphoglucomutase* converts glucose-6-phosphate to the isomer glucose-1-phosphate. A mutase is a type of isomerase that shifts the phosphate functional group between carbon atoms (see Figure 22.11).

Reaction 2 Activation

Before glucose-1-phosphate can be added to the glycogen chain, it must be activated. Energy is released when *pyrophosphorylase* catalyzes the reaction of the high-energy compound UTP (uridine triphosphate), which transfers UMP to glucose-1-phosphate to give UDP-glucose (uridine diphosphate-glucose) and pyrophosphate, PP_i.

Reaction 3 Glycogen Synthesis (Glucose Transfer to Glycogen)

Glycogen synthase catalyzes the breaking of the phosphate bond to glucose in UDP-glucose, releasing glucose, which forms an $\alpha(1 \rightarrow 4)$-glycosidic bond with the end of a glycogen chain.

Glycogenolysis

Glycogen is a highly branched polysaccharide of glucose monomers with both $\alpha(1 \rightarrow 4)$- and $\alpha(1 \rightarrow 6)$-glycosidic bonds. Glucose is the primary energy source for muscle contractions, red blood cells, and the brain. When blood glucose is depleted, the glycogen stored in the muscle and liver is converted to glucose molecules in a process called **glycogenolysis**.

Glycogen phosphorylase **①** and **②**

▲ *Activated* by glucagon (liver)
and epinephrine (muscle)
▼ *Inhibited* by insulin

Glycogen

Glucose-1-phosphate

+

Glycogen with one glucose removed

Phosphoglucomutase **③**

Glucose-6-phosphate

→ Glycolysis

Glucose-6-phosphatase **④** Liver and
kidney only

Glucose

+ P → Bloodstream

Reaction 1 Phosphorolysis (Hydrolysis and Phosphorylation)

Glucose molecules are removed one by one from the ends of the glycogen chain and phosphorylated by *glycogen phosphorylase* to yield glucose-1-phosphate.

Reaction 2 Hydrolysis $\alpha(1 \rightarrow 6)$

Glycogen phosphorylase continues to cleave $\alpha(1 \rightarrow 4)$-links until one glucose remains bonded to the main chain by an $\alpha(1 \rightarrow 6)$-glycosidic bond. A debranching enzyme $\alpha(1 \rightarrow 6)$-*glycosidase* breaks $\alpha(1 \rightarrow 6)$-glycosidic bonds so that branches of glucose molecules can be hydrolyzed by reaction 1.

Reaction 3 Isomerization

The glucose-1-phosphate molecules are converted to glucose-6-phosphate molecules, which enter the glycolysis pathway at reaction 2.

Reaction 4 Dephosphorylation

Free glucose is needed for energy by the brain and muscle. Although glucose can diffuse across cell membranes, charged glucose phosphate cannot. Only cells in the liver and kidneys have a *glucose-6-phosphatase* that hydrolyzes the glucose-6-phosphate to yield free glucose.

> **SAMPLE PROBLEM 22.8** **Glycogen Metabolism**
>
> Identify each of the following as part of the reaction pathways of glycogenolysis or glycogenesis:
>
> **a.** Glucose-1-phosphate is converted to glucose-6-phosphate.
> **b.** Glucose-1-phosphate forms UDP-glucose.
> **c.** The pathway that is activated by insulin.
>
> **SOLUTION**
>
> **a.** glycogenolysis   **b.** glycogenesis   **c.** glycogenesis
>
> **STUDY CHECK 22.8**
>
> Why do cells in the liver and kidneys provide glucose to raise blood glucose levels, but cells in skeletal muscle do not?
>
> **ANSWER**
>
> Only the cells in the liver and kidneys provide glucose-6-phosphatase, which is needed to catalyze the hydrolysis of glucose-6-phosphate to yield free glucose.

Regulation of Glycogen Metabolism

The brain, skeletal muscles, and red blood cells require large amounts of glucose every day to function properly. To protect the brain, hormones with opposing actions control blood glucose levels. When glucose is low, *glucagon*, a hormone produced in the pancreas, is secreted into the bloodstream. Glucagon signals cells in the liver to increase the rate of glycogenolysis, which raises blood glucose levels. At the same time, glucagon inhibits the synthesis of glycogen.

Glycogen in skeletal muscle is broken down quickly when the body requires a "burst of energy," often referred to as "fight or flight." *Epinephrine* released from the adrenal glands converts glycogen phosphorylase from an inactive to an active form. The secretion of only a few molecules of epinephrine results in the breakdown of a huge number of glycogen molecules.

Soon after we eat and digest a meal, our blood glucose level rises, which stimulates the pancreas to secrete the hormone *insulin* into our bloodstream. Insulin signals cells to use glucose by increasing glycogen synthesis and oxidation reactions such as glycolysis. At the same time, insulin inhibits the synthesis of glucose, which we will discuss in the next section.

 # Chemistry Link to **Health**

Glycogen Storage Diseases (GSDs)

Glycogen storage diseases (GSDs) occur when a defective enzyme is involved in a pathway for glycogen storage or degradation. Different types of GSDs are listed in Table 22.4. For example, in Hers' disease (GSD VI), liver phosphorylase is deficient and glycogen cannot be completely degraded to glucose. As a result, glycogen accumulates in the liver and a person with Hers' disease has hypoglycemia. Severe GSDs are detected in infancy, and life expectancy is usually short. Less severe types are detected in adulthood.

There are no cures for GSDs, although diet therapy may be used to treat symptoms. For some GSD III patients, liver transplantation has been successful.

A micrograph shows an excess of stored glycogen (blue) in a liver biopsy of a patient with Cori's disease.

TABLE 22.4 Types of Glycogen Storage Diseases (GSDs)

Type	Organ	Defective Enzyme	Disease	Specifics
0	Liver, muscle	Glycogen synthase	Glycogen synthase deficiency	Liver type severe, lack of muscle glycogen, exercise intolerant
I	Liver, kidneys	Glucose-6-phosphatase	*von Gierke's*, cannot convert glucose-6-phosphate to glucose	Glycogen accumulation, liver enlargement, hypoglycemic, short life expectancy
II	Lysosomes of all organs	$\alpha(1\rightarrow 4)$-phosphatase	*Pompe's*	Glycogen accumulation heart, heart failure, significant muscle weakness, short life expectancy
III	Liver, muscle	Glycogen debranching enzyme	*Cori's*, cannot completely degrade glycogen to glucose	Lack of glycogen degradation, cannot hydrolyze $\alpha(1\rightarrow 6)$-glycosidic bonds, hypoglycemic, muscle weakness
IV	Liver	Glycogen branching enzyme	*Andersen's*, cannot form $\alpha(1\rightarrow 6)$-glycogen branches	Abnormal, unbranched glycogen accumulation, short life expectancy due to heart or liver failure
V	Muscle	Glycogen phosphorylase	*McArdle's*, cannot degrade glycogen in muscle to glucose	Exercise intolerant, muscle cramps due to exercise
VI	Liver	Glycogen phosphorylase	*Hers'*, cannot degrade glycogen in liver to glucose	Mild impact

A summary of the processes of glycogenesis and glycogenolysis indicates that glucose-6-phosphate and glucose-1-phosphate are intermediates of both processes, but UDP-glucose is only involved in glycogenesis.

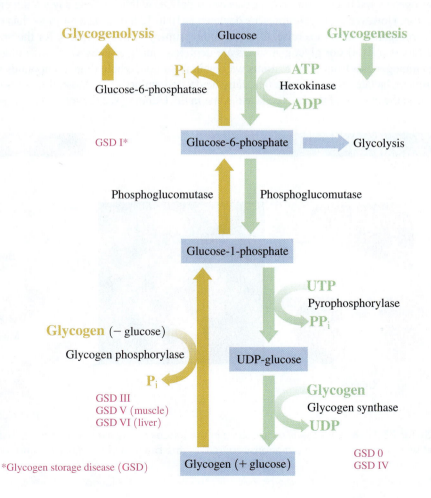

Glucose-6-phosphate and glucose-1-phosphate are intermediates of both glycogenesis and glycogenolysis.

QUESTIONS AND PROBLEMS

22.6 Glycogen Synthesis and Degradation

LEARNING GOAL Describe the synthesis and breakdown of glycogen.

22.59 What is meant by the term *glycogenesis*?

22.60 What is meant by the term *glycogenolysis*?

22.61 How do muscle cells use glycogen to provide energy?

22.62 How does the liver raise blood glucose levels?

22.63 What is the function of glycogen phosphorylase?

22.64 Why is the enzyme phosphoglucomutase used in both glycogenolysis and glycogenesis?

22.65 Indicate whether each of the following hormones activates or inhibits glycogenesis:
   a. insulin   **b.** glucagon   **c.** epinephrine

22.66 Indicate whether each of the following hormones activates or inhibits glycogenolysis:
   a. insulin   **b.** glucagon   **c.** epinephrine

℞ Clinical Applications

22.67 Diabetics often substitute fructose for glucose. Why is it acceptable for diabetics to include fructose in their diet?

22.68 Glycogen storage diseases are the result of a defective enzyme involved in pathways for glycogen storage or degradation. What is the effect of a defective debranching enzyme in *Cori's disease* (GSD III)?

22.69 Glycogen storage diseases are the result of a defective enzyme involved in pathways for glycogen storage or degradation. What is the effect of a defective liver *glycogen phosphorylase* in *Hers' disease* (GSD VI)?

22.70 Glycogen storage diseases are the result of a defective enzyme involved in pathways for glycogen storage or degradation. What is the effect of a defective *glycogen synthase enzyme* (GSD 0)?

LEARNING GOAL

Describe how glucose is synthesized from noncarbohydrate molecules.

22.7 Gluconeogenesis: Glucose Synthesis

Glycogen stored in our liver and muscles can supply us with about one day's requirement of glucose. However, glycogen stores are depleted in 10 to 12 h if we fast for more than one day or participate in heavy exercise. Glucose is the primary source of energy for the brain and red blood cells. If our glycogen stores are depleted, our liver cells synthesize glucose by **gluconeogenesis** from carbon atoms we obtain from noncarbohydrate compounds such as pyruvate, lactate, glycerol from fats, fatty acids, and amino acids. Most glucose is synthesized in the cytosol of the liver cells and some in the kidneys (see Figure 22.12).

FIGURE 22.12 ▶ Glucose is synthesized in the tissues of the liver and kidneys. Tissues that use glucose as their main energy source are the brain, skeletal muscles, and red blood cells.

Q Why does the body need a pathway for the synthesis of glucose from noncarbohydrate sources?

To begin the metabolic process of gluconeogenesis, the carbon atoms from noncarbohydrate food sources are converted to pyruvate. Many of the compounds and reactions in gluconeogenesis are the same in glycolysis and catalyzed by the same enzymes. There are 10 reactions in glycolysis and 11 reactions in gluconeogenesis. Three reactions (1, 3, and 10) in glycolysis, which are irreversible reactions, are catalyzed by different enzymes in gluconeogenesis.

Converting Pyruvate to Phosphoenolpyruvate

To start the synthesis of glucose from pyruvate, two catalyzed reactions are needed to replace reaction 10 in glycolysis. In the first step, *pyruvate carboxylase* uses the energy of ATP hydrolysis to catalyze the addition of CO_2 to pyruvate to produce a four-carbon compound oxaloacetate. In the second step, *phosphoenolpyruvate carboxykinase* uses the energy of hydrolysis of the high-energy compound GTP to convert oxaloacetate to phosphoenolpyruvate. Molecules of phosphoenolpyruvate now use the same enzymes of the next several reverse reactions in glycolysis to form fructose-1,6-bisphosphate.

Converting Fructose-1,6-Bisphosphate to Fructose-6-Phosphate

The second irreversible reaction in glycolysis (reaction 3) is bypassed when *fructose-1,6-bisphosphatase* cleaves a phosphate group from fructose-1,6-bisphosphate by hydrolysis with water. The product fructose-6-phosphate undergoes the reversible reaction 2 of glycolysis to yield glucose-6-phosphate.

Converting Glucose-6-Phosphate to Glucose (Reaction 1)

In the final irreversible reaction, the phosphate group of glucose-6-phosphate is hydrolyzed by a different enzyme *glucose-6-phosphatase* to form glucose.

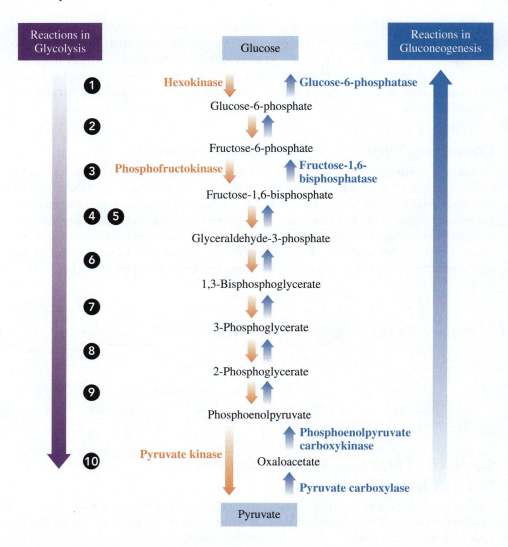

FIGURE 22.13 ▶ In gluconeogenesis, four different enzymes (in blue) are used to replace the enzymes that catalyze the three irreversible reactions of glycolysis (1, 3, and 10). All the other reactions are catalyzed in both directions by the same enzymes used for glycolysis.

🅠 Why are 11 enzymes required for gluconeogenesis and only 10 for glycolysis?

A summary of the reactions and different enzymes in gluconeogenesis and glycolysis is shown in Figure 22.13. The overall equation for gluconeogenesis is written as follows:

$$2\text{ Pyruvate } + \text{ 4 ATP} + \text{2 GTP} + \text{2 NADH} + 2\text{H}^+ + 6\text{H}_2\text{O} \longrightarrow$$
$$\text{glucose} + \text{4 ADP} + \text{2 GDP} + 6\text{P}_i + \text{2 NAD}^+$$

Energy Cost of Gluconeogenesis

The pathway of gluconeogenesis consists of seven reversible reactions of glycolysis and four new reactions that replace the three irreversible reactions. If all the reactions were simply the reverse of glycolysis, gluconeogenesis would not be energetically favorable. However, by using energy obtained from four ATP, two GTP, and two NADH, gluconeogenesis can take place.

Lactate and the Cori Cycle

When a person exercises vigorously, anaerobic conditions in the muscle reduce pyruvate to lactate. At the same time, NADH is converted to NAD$^+$, so that a small amount of ATP is formed when oxygen is lacking. Lactate is an important source of carbon atoms for gluconeogenesis. In the **Cori cycle**, lactate is transported to the liver where it is oxidized to pyruvate, which is used to synthesize glucose. Glucose enters the bloodstream and returns to the muscle to rebuild glycogen stores. The Cori cycle is very active when a person has just completed a period of vigorous exercise (see Figure 22.14).

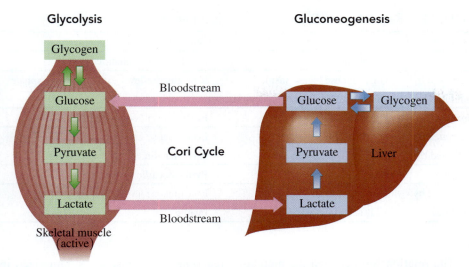

FIGURE 22.14 ▶ In the Cori cycle, lactate from glycolysis in the muscles enters the bloodstream and travels to the liver where it is converted to glucose. The glucose travels through the bloodstream to muscles to produce energy.

Q Why is lactate formed in the muscle converted to glucose in the liver?

SAMPLE PROBLEM 22.9 Gluconeogenesis

The conversion of fructose-1,6-bisphosphate to fructose-6-phosphate is an irreversible reaction using a glycolytic enzyme. How does gluconeogenesis make this reaction happen?

SOLUTION

This reaction is catalyzed by fructose-1,6-bisphosphatase, which cleaves a phosphate group using a hydrolysis reaction, a reaction that is energetically favorable.

STUDY CHECK 22.9

Why is hexokinase in glycolysis replaced by glucose-6-phosphatase in gluconeogenesis?

ANSWER

The reaction catalyzed by hexokinase in glycolysis is irreversible.

Regulation of Gluconeogenesis

Gluconeogenesis is a pathway that protects the brain and nervous system from experiencing a loss of glucose, which causes impairment of function. It is also a pathway that is utilized when vigorous activity depletes blood glucose and glycogen stores. Thus, the level of carbohydrate available from the diet controls gluconeogenesis. When a diet is high in carbohydrate, the gluconeogenesis pathway is not utilized. However, when a diet is low in carbohydrate, the pathway is very active.

As long as conditions in a cell favor glycolysis, there is no synthesis of glucose. But when the cell requires the synthesis of glucose, glycolysis is turned off. The same three reactions that control glycolysis also control gluconeogenesis, but with different enzymes. Let's look at how high levels of certain compounds activate or inhibit the two processes (see Table 22.5).

TABLE 22.5 Regulation of Glycolysis and Gluconeogenesis

	Glycolysis	**Gluconeogenesis**
Enzyme	Hexokinase	Glucose-6-phosphatase
Activated by	High glucose levels, insulin	Low glucose levels, glucose-6-phosphate
Inhibited by	Glucose-6-phosphate, epinephrine	
Enzyme	Phosphofructokinase	Fructose-1,6-bisphosphatase
Activated by	AMP, insulin	Low glucose levels, glucagon
Inhibited by	ATP, glucagon	AMP, insulin
Enzyme	Pyruvate kinase	Pyruvate carboxylase
Activated by	Fructose-1,6-bisphosphate	Low glucose levels, glucagon
Inhibited by	ATP, acetyl CoA	Insulin

The relationship between the metabolic reactions of glucose are summarized in Figure 22.15.

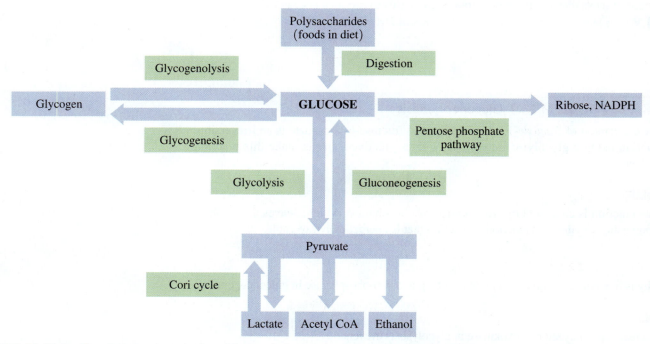

FIGURE 22.15 ▶ Glycolysis involves the breakdown of glucose, and gluconeogenesis involves the synthesis of glucose from noncarbohydrates. The pentose phosphate pathway converts glucose to ribose and provides NADPH. Glycogenolysis degrades glycogen to glucose whereas glycogenesis produces glycogen from glucose.

Q Why does glycogenesis occur after the digestion of a meal high in carbohydrates?

QUESTIONS AND PROBLEMS

22.7 Gluconeogenesis: Glucose Synthesis

LEARNING GOAL Describe how glucose is synthesized from noncarbohydrate molecules.

22.71 What is the function of gluconeogenesis in the body?

22.72 What enzymes in glycolysis are not used in gluconeogenesis?

22.73 What enzymes in glycolysis are used in gluconeogenesis?

22.74 How is the lactate produced in skeletal muscle used for glucose synthesis?

22.75 Indicate whether each of the following activates or inhibits gluconeogenesis:
a. low glucose levels
b. glucagon
c. insulin
d. AMP

22.76 Indicate whether each of the following activates or inhibits glycolysis:
a. low glucose levels
b. insulin
c. epinephrine
d. ATP

Clinical Applications

22.77 Low carbohydrate diets ask dieters to lower or eliminate their intake of carbohydrates. Since we need glucose to fuel the brain, gluconeogenesis will produce glucose under these conditions. What carbohydrate store is lowered (and the source of weight loss) in people who do not eat carbohydrates?

22.78 When would gluconeogenesis be most active, after a meal, or when you wake up in the morning? Explain your reasoning.

Clinical Update
Philip's Diet for von Gierke's Disease

Much of the metabolism of carbohydrates depends on the storage and degradation of glycogen stored in the liver. If glucose-6-phosphatase is defective, the liver cannot provide the body with glucose. In *von Gierke's disease*, the huge amounts of glycogen that accumulate lead to an enlarged liver. Because Philip cannot produce sufficient glucose, he is hypoglycemic and weak.

The hepatology nurse, Barbara, began dietary management by giving Philip frequent feedings of glucose or starch by nasogastric tube to raise blood glucose levels. A stomach tube (gastrostomy tube) was also used. Philip showed a rapid improvement in physical behavior. During the day, Philip was fed cornstarch, which is easily digested to provide small, but continuous, amounts of glucose in the blood. Foods containing fructose or galactose were avoided because they are converted to glucose-6-phosphate, which Philip cannot metabolize. As Philip grows older, he can be physically active, but should not participate in contact sports to avoid damage to his liver. As a young child, Philip continues to thrive.

Clinical Applications

22.79 What are some symptoms of *von Gierke's disease*?

22.80 Write the chemical equation for the reaction catalyzed by glucose-6-phosphatase.

22.81 What is the impact of a defective glucose-6-phosphatase in *von Gierke's disease* (GSD I) on blood glucose and stored glycogen?

22.82 Explain why Philip's condition requires that he is fed cornstarch every few hours.

CONCEPT MAP

METABOLIC PATHWAYS FOR CARBOHYDRATES

Digestion of Carbohydrates

yields

Glucose

reacts by → **Pentose Phosphate Pathway** → to yield → **Nucleotides and NADPH**

is oxidized by → **Glycolysis** → to yield → **Pyruvate**, **NADH**, **ATP**

Pyruvate is reduced to → **Lactate** → to give → **Gluconeogenesis**

Pyruvate undergoes oxidation to → **Acetyl CoA** → undergoes

CO$_2$

NADH

hydrolyzes glycogen to

undergoes → **Glycogenesis** → to store as → **Glycogen** → undergoes → **Glycogenolysis**

CHAPTER REVIEW

22.1 Metabolism and Energy

LEARNING GOAL Describe the three stages of catabolism, the structure of ATP, and the role of ATP.

- Metabolism includes all the catabolic and anabolic reactions that occur in the cells.
- Catabolic reactions degrade large molecules into smaller ones with an accompanying release of energy.
- Anabolic reactions require energy to synthesize larger molecules from smaller ones.
- The three stages of catabolism are digestion of food, degradation of monomers such as glucose to pyruvate, and the extraction of energy from the two- and three-carbon compounds from stage 2.
- Many of the metabolic enzymes are present in the cytosol of the cell where metabolic reactions take place.
- Energy obtained from catabolic reactions is stored primarily in adenosine triphosphate (ATP), a high-energy compound.
- ATP is hydrolyzed when energy is required by anabolic reactions in the cells.

22.2 Important Coenzymes in Metabolic Pathways

LEARNING GOAL Describe the components and functions of the coenzymes NAD$^+$, NADP, FAD, and coenzyme A.

- NAD$^+$, NADP$^+$, and FAD are the oxidized forms of coenzymes that participate in oxidation–reduction reactions.
- When NAD$^+$, NADP$^+$, and FAD pick up hydrogen ions and electrons, they are reduced to NADH + H$^+$, NADPH + H$^+$, and FADH$_2$.
- Coenzyme A contains a thiol group (—SH) that usually bonds with a two-carbon acetyl group (acetyl CoA).

22.3 Digestion of Carbohydrates

LEARNING GOAL Give the sites and products of the digestion of carbohydrates.

- The digestion of carbohydrates is a series of reactions that breaks down polysaccharides into hexose monomers such as glucose, galactose, and fructose.
- The hexose monomers are absorbed through the intestinal wall into the bloodstream to be carried to cells where they provide energy and carbon atoms for the synthesis of new molecules.

22.4 Glycolysis: Oxidation of Glucose

LEARNING GOAL Describe the conversion of glucose to pyruvate in glycolysis.

Glucose-6-phosphate

- Glycolysis, which occurs in the cytosol, consists of 10 reactions that degrade glucose (six carbons) to two pyruvate molecules (three carbons each).
- The overall series of reactions yields two molecules of the reduced coenzyme NADH and two ATP.
- The pentose phosphate pathway utilizes glucose-6-phosphate to supply NADPH for the biosynthesis of pentose sugars, fatty acids, cholesterol, and amino acids.

22.5 Pathways for Pyruvate

LEARNING GOAL Give the conditions for the conversion of pyruvate to lactate, ethanol, and acetyl coenzyme A.

- Under aerobic conditions, pyruvate is oxidized in the mitochondria to acetyl CoA.
- In the absence of oxygen, pyruvate is reduced to lactate and NAD$^+$ is regenerated for the continuation of glycolysis, whereas microorganisms such as yeast reduce pyruvate to ethanol, a process known as fermentation.

22.6 Glycogen Synthesis and Degradation

LEARNING GOAL Describe the synthesis and breakdown of glycogen.

- When blood glucose levels are high, glycogenesis converts glucose to glycogen, which is stored in the liver.
- Glycogenolysis breaks down glycogen to glucose when glucose and ATP levels are low.

22.7 Gluconeogenesis: Glucose Synthesis

LEARNING GOAL Describe how glucose is synthesized from noncarbohydrate molecules.

- When blood glucose levels are low and glycogen stores in the liver are depleted, gluconeogenesis occurs, which synthesizes glucose from noncarbohydrate compounds such as pyruvate.
- Gluconeogenesis utilizes many of the same enzymes as glycolysis.

SUMMARY OF KEY REACTIONS

The chapter sections to review are shown after the name of the reaction.

Hydrolysis of ATP (22.1)

$$ATP \longrightarrow ADP + P_i + 7.3 \text{ kcal/mole } (31 \text{ kJ/mole})$$

Hydrolysis of ADP (22.1)

$$ADP \longrightarrow AMP + P_i + 7.3 \text{ kcal/mole } (31 \text{ kJ/mole})$$

Formation of ATP (22.1)

$$ADP + P_i + 7.3 \text{ kcal/mole } (31 \text{ kJ/mole}) \longrightarrow ATP$$

Reduction of NAD$^+$, NADP$^+$, and FAD (22.2)

$$NAD^+ + 2H^+ + 2\,e^- \longrightarrow NADH + H^+$$
$$NADP^+ + 2H^+ + 2\,e^- \longrightarrow NADPH + H^+$$
$$FAD + 2H^+ + 2\,e^- \longrightarrow FADH_2$$

Glycolysis (22.4)

$$C_6H_{12}O_6 + 2ADP + 2P_i + 2NAD^+ \longrightarrow$$

Glucose

$$2CH_3 - \overset{\displaystyle O}{\overset{\|}{C}} - COO^- + 2ATP + 2NADH + 4H^+$$

Pyruvate

Pentose Phosphate Pathway (22.4)

$$\text{Glucose-6-P} + 2NADP^+ + H_2O \longrightarrow$$
$$\text{ribose-5-P} + 2NADPH + 2H^+ + CO_2$$

Oxidation of Pyruvate to Acetyl CoA (22.5)

$$CH_3 - \overset{\displaystyle O}{\overset{\|}{C}} - COO^- + NAD^+ + HS - CoA \xrightarrow{\text{Pyruvate dehydrogenase}}$$

Pyruvate

$$CH_3 - \overset{\displaystyle O}{\overset{\|}{C}} - S - CoA + NADH + CO_2$$

Acetyl CoA

Reduction of Pyruvate to Lactate (22.5)

$$CH_3 - \overset{\displaystyle O}{\overset{\|}{C}} - COO^- + NADH + H^+ \longrightarrow$$

Pyruvate

$$CH_3 - \overset{\displaystyle OH}{\overset{|}{C}}H - COO^- + NAD^+$$

Lactate

Oxidation of Glucose to Lactate (22.5)

$$\text{Glucose} + 2ADP + 2P_i \longrightarrow 2\text{lactate} + 2ATP$$

Reduction of Pyruvate to Ethanol (22.5)

$$CH_3 - \overset{\displaystyle O}{\overset{\|}{C}} - COO^- + NADH + 2H^+ \longrightarrow$$

Pyruvate

$$CH_3 - CH_2 - OH + NAD^+ + CO_2$$

Ethanol

Glycogenesis (22.6)

$$\text{UDP-glucose} + \text{glycogen} \longrightarrow \text{glycogen–glucose} + UDP$$

Glycogenolysis (22.6)

$$\text{Glycogen–glucose} \longrightarrow \text{glycogen} + \text{glucose}$$

Gluconeogenesis (22.7)

$$2 \text{ Pyruvate} + 4ATP + 2GTP + 2NADH + 2H^+ + 6H_2O \longrightarrow$$
$$\text{glucose} + 4ADP + 2GDP + 6P_i + 2NAD^+$$

KEY TERMS

acetyl CoA The compound that forms when a two-carbon acetyl unit bonds to coenzyme A.

ADP Adenosine diphosphate, formed by the hydrolysis of ATP; consists of adenine, a ribose sugar, and two phosphate groups.

aerobic An oxygen-containing environment in the cells.

anabolic reaction A metabolic reaction that requires energy to build large molecules from small molecules.

anaerobic A condition in cells when there is no oxygen.

ATP Adenosine triphosphate, a high-energy compound that stores energy in the cells; consists of adenine, a ribose sugar, and three phosphate groups.

catabolic reaction A metabolic reaction that produces energy for the cell by the degradation and oxidation of glucose and other molecules.

coenzyme A (CoA) A coenzyme that transports acyl and acetyl groups.

Cori cycle A cyclic process in which lactate produced in muscle is transferred to the liver to be converted to glucose, which can be used again by muscle.

cytosol The fluid of the cell, which is an aqueous solution of electrolytes and enzymes.

decarboxylation The loss of a carbon atom in the form of CO_2.

digestion The processes in the gastrointestinal tract that break down large food molecules to smaller ones that pass through the intestinal membrane into the bloodstream.

FAD A coenzyme (flavin adenine dinucleotide) for dehydrogenase enzymes that forms carbon–carbon double bonds.

fermentation The anaerobic conversion of glucose by enzymes in yeast to yield alcohol and CO_2.

gluconeogenesis The synthesis of glucose from noncarbohydrate compounds.

glycogenesis The synthesis of glycogen from glucose molecules.

glycogenolysis The breakdown of glycogen into glucose molecules.

glycolysis The 10 oxidation reactions of glucose that yield two pyruvate molecules.

metabolism All the chemical reactions in living cells that carry out molecular and energy transformations.

mitochondrion The organelle of cells where energy-producing reactions take place.

NAD$^+$ The hydrogen acceptor used in oxidation reactions that form carbon–oxygen double bonds.

pentose phosphate pathway A metabolic pathway that oxidizes glucose to produce NADPH for anabolic reactions and five-carbon sugars required for the synthesis of nucleotides, DNA, and RNA.

⚛ CORE CHEMISTRY SKILLS

The chapter section containing each Core Chemistry Skill is shown in parentheses at the end of each heading.

Identifying Important Coenzymes in Metabolism (22.2)

- ATP is a nucleotide that transfers energy through metabolic reactions.
- NAD$^+$, NADP$^+$, and FAD are the oxidized forms of the coenzymes that move electrons and H$^+$ through metabolic reactions.
- CoA is a coenzyme that moves two-carbon acetyl groups through metabolic reactions.

Example: Provide the formulas of the reduced forms of the coenzymes that move electrons and H$^+$ through metabolism.

Answer: NADH, NADPH, and FADH$_2$

Identifying the Compounds in Glycolysis (22.4)

- Glycolysis, which occurs in the cytosol, consists of 10 reactions that degrade glucose (6C) to two pyruvate (3C).
- The overall series of reactions in glycolysis yields two NADH and two ATP.

Example: Identify the reaction(s) and compounds in glycolysis that have each of the following:
   a. requires ATP
   b. converts a six-carbon compound to two three-carbon compounds
   c. converts ADP to ATP

Answer: a. The phosphorylation of glucose in reaction 1 and fructose-6-phosphate in reaction 3 each require one ATP.
   b. In reaction 4, the six-carbon fructose-1,6-bisphosphate is cleaved into two three-carbon compounds.
   c. Phosphate transfer in reactions 7 and 10 converts ADP to ATP.

Identifying the Compounds and Enzymes in Glycogenesis and Glycogenolysis (22.6)

- Glucose undergoes glycogenesis when blood glucose levels are high and is stored as glycogen in the liver.
- Glycogenolysis breaks down glycogen to glucose when levels of glucose or ATP are low.

Example: Indicate which of the processes glycogenesis and/or glycogenolysis involve each of the following compounds:
   a. glucose-1-phosphate
   b. UDP-glucose
   c. glycogen phosphorylase
   d. UTP

Answer: a. glycogenesis, glycogenolysis
   b. glycogenesis
   c. glycogenolysis
   d. glycogenesis

UNDERSTANDING THE CONCEPTS

The chapter sections to review are given in parentheses at the end of each question.

22.83 On a hike, you expend 350 kcal/h. How many moles of ATP will you use if you hike for 2.5 h? (22.1)

Vigorous hiking can expend 350 kcal per hour.

22.84 Identify each of the following as a six-carbon or a three-carbon compound and arrange them in the order in which they occur in glycolysis: (22.4)
   a. 3-phosphoglycerate
   b. pyruvate
   c. glucose-6-phosphate
   d. glucose
   e. fructose-1,6-bisphosphate

22.85 Indicate whether each of the following enzymes is utilized in (1) glycogenesis but not glycogenolysis, (2) glycogenolysis but not glycogenesis, or (3) both glycogenesis and glycogenolysis: (22.6)
   a. pyrophosphorylase   b. phosphoglucomutase
   c. glycogen phosphorylase

22.86 Indicate whether each of the following enzymes is utilized in (1) glycogenesis but not glycogenolysis, (2) glycogenolysis but not glycogenesis, or (3) both glycogenesis and glycogenolysis: (22.6)
   a. glycogen synthase
   b. glucose-6-phosphatase
   c. debranching enzyme

22.87 Indicate whether each of the following enzymes is utilized in (1) glycolysis but not gluconeogenesis, (2) gluconeogenesis but not glycolysis, or (3) both glycolysis and gluconeogenesis: (22.4, 22.7)
   a. glucose-6-phosphatase   b. aldolase
   c. phosphofructokinase   d. phosphoglycerate mutase

22.88 Indicate whether each of the following enzymes is utilized in (1) glycolysis but not gluconeogenesis, (2) gluconeogenesis but not glycolysis, or (3) both glycolysis and gluconeogenesis: (22.4, 22.7)
   a. hexokinase   b. pyruvate kinase
   c. enolase   d. pyruvate carboxylase

ADDITIONAL QUESTIONS AND PROBLEMS

22.89 What is meant by the term metabolism? (22.1)

22.90 How do catabolic reactions differ from anabolic reactions? (22.1)

22.91 What stage of catabolism involves the digestion of large food polymers? (22.1)

22.92 What stage of catabolism degrades monomers such as glucose into smaller molecules? (22.1)

22.93 What type of cell has a nucleus? (22.1)

22.94 What is the function of each of the following cell components? (22.1)
a. cell membrane   **b.** mitochondria   **c.** cytosol

22.95 What is the full name of ATP? (22.1)

22.96 What is the full name of ADP? (22.1)

22.97 Write the abbreviated equation for the hydrolysis of ATP to ADP. (22.1)

22.98 Write the abbreviated equation for the hydrolysis of ADP to AMP. (22.1)

22.99 What are the high- and low-energy forms of the coenzyme FAD? (22.2)

22.100 What type of reaction uses FAD as the coenzyme? (22.2)

22.101 What are the high- and low-energy forms of the coenzyme NAD^+? (22.2)

22.102 What type of reaction uses NAD^+ as the coenzyme? (22.2)

22.103 Write the abbreviation for the reduced form of each of the following: (22.2)
a. FAD   **b.** NAD^+ **c.** $NADP^+$

22.104 What is the name of the vitamin in the structure of each of the following? (22.2)
a. FAD   **b.** NAD^+ **c.** coenzyme A

22.105 How and where does lactose undergo digestion in the body? What are the products? (22.3)

22.106 How and where does sucrose undergo digestion in the body? What are the products? (22.3)

22.107 What are the reactant and product of glycolysis? (22.4)

22.108 What is the coenzyme used in glycolysis? (22.4)

22.109 **a.** In glycolysis, which reactions involve phosphorylation? (22.4)
b. Which reactions involve a direct substrate phosphorylation to generate ATP?

22.110 How do ADP and ATP regulate the glycolysis pathway? (22.4)

22.111 What reaction and enzyme in glycolysis convert a hexose bisphosphate into two three-carbon intermediates? (22.4)

22.112 How does the investment and generation of ATP give a net gain of ATP for glycolysis? (22.4)

22.113 What compound is converted to fructose-6-phosphate by phosphoglucose isomerase? (22.4)

22.114 What product forms when glyceraldehyde-3-phosphate adds a phosphate group? (22.4)

22.115 When is pyruvate converted to lactate in the body? (22.5)

22.116 When pyruvate is used to form acetyl CoA or ethanol in fermentation, the product has only two carbon atoms. What happened to the third carbon? (22.5)

22.117 How does phosphofructokinase regulate the rate of glycolysis? (22.5)

22.118 How does pyruvate kinase regulate the rate of glycolysis? (22.5)

22.119 When does the rate of glycogenolysis increase in the cells? (22.6)

22.120 If glucose-1-phosphate is the product from glycogen breakdown, how does it enter glycolysis? (22.6)

℞ Clinical Applications

22.121 What is the end product of glycogenolysis in the liver? (22.6)

22.122 What is the end product of glycogenolysis in skeletal muscle? (22.6)

22.123 Indicate whether each of the following conditions would increase or decrease the rate of glycogenolysis in the liver: (22.6)
a. low blood glucose level
b. secretion of insulin
c. secretion of glucagon
d. high levels of ATP

22.124 Indicate whether each of the following conditions would increase or decrease the rate of glycogenesis in the liver: (22.6)
a. low blood glucose level
b. secretion of insulin
c. secretion of glucagon
d. high levels of ATP

22.125 Indicate whether each of the following conditions would increase or decrease the rate of gluconeogenesis: (22.7)
a. high blood glucose level
b. secretion of insulin
c. secretion of glucagon
d. high levels of ATP

22.126 Indicate whether each of the following conditions would increase or decrease the rate of glycolysis: (22.4)
a. high blood glucose level
b. secretion of insulin
c. secretion of glucagon
d. high levels of ATP

CHALLENGE QUESTIONS

The following groups of questions are related to the topics in this chapter. However, they do not all follow the chapter order, and they require you to combine concepts and skills from several sections. These questions will help you increase your critical thinking skills and prepare for your next exam.

22.127 Why is glucose provided by glycogenolysis in the liver but not in skeletal muscle? (22.6)

22.128 When does the rate of glycogenesis increase in the cells? (22.6)

22.129 How do the hormones insulin and glucagon affect the rates of glycogenesis, glycogenolysis, and glycolysis? (22.4, 22.6)

22.130 What is the function of gluconeogenesis? (22.7)

22.131 Where does the Cori cycle operate? (22.7)

22.132 Identify each of the following as part of glycolysis, glycogenolysis, glycogenesis, or gluconeogenesis: (22.4, 22.6, 22.7)
   a. Glycogen is broken down to glucose in the liver.
   b. Glucose is synthesized from noncarbohydrate sources.

   c. Glucose is degraded to pyruvate.
   d. Glycogen is synthesized from glucose.

22.133 The average daily diet of an adult woman is 2.0×10^3 kcal. The molar mass of ATP is 507 g/mole. (22.1)
   a. If all the energy in her diet is converted to ATP, how many kg of ATP are synthesized in one day?
   b. If the average amount of ATP in the body is 250 g, what is the lifetime, in minutes, of ATP?

22.134 A teaspoon containing 4.2 g of sucrose is added to a cup of tea. (22.1)
   a. How much energy, in kilocalories, are in the sucrose if 1 g of sucrose provides 4 kcal?
   b. How many grams of ATP (507 g/mole) are produced if all the energy in the sucrose is converted to ATP?

ANSWERS

Answers to Selected Questions and Problems

22.1 The digestion of polysaccharides takes place in stage 1.

22.3 In metabolism, a catabolic reaction breaks apart large molecules, releasing energy.

22.5 **a.** anabolic   **b.** anabolic
   c. catabolic   **d.** catabolic

22.7 When a phosphate group is cleaved from ATP, sufficient energy is released for energy-requiring processes in the cell.

22.9 **a.** PEP $\longrightarrow$ pyruvate + P_i + 14.8 kcal/mole
   b. ADP + P_i + 7.3 kcal/mole $\longrightarrow$ ATP
   c. PEP + ADP $\longrightarrow$ ATP + pyruvate + 7.5 kcal/mole

22.11 3.4×10^4 g

22.13 **a.** coenzyme A   **b.** NAD$^+$, NADP$^+$
   c. FAD

22.15 **a.** NADH   **b.** FAD

22.17 FAD

22.19 Hydrolysis is the main reaction involved in the digestion of carbohydrates.

22.21 **a.** lactose   **b.** glucose and fructose
   c. glucose

22.23 glucose

22.25 ATP is required in phosphorylation reactions.

22.27 glyceraldehyde-3-phosphate and dihydroxyacetone phosphate

22.29 ATP is produced in glycolysis by transferring a phosphate group from 1,3-bisphosphoglycerate and from phosphoenolpyruvate directly to ADP.

22.31 **a.** hexokinase; phosphofructokinase
   b. phosphoglycerate kinase; pyruvate kinase

22.33 **a.** 1 ATP required   **b.** 1 NADH produced
   c. 2 ATP and 2 NADH produced

22.35 **a.** In reaction 1, a hexokinase uses ATP to phosphorylate glucose.

   b. In reactions 7 and 10, phosphate groups are transferred from 1,3-bisphosphoglycerate and phosphoenolpyruvate directly to ADP to produce ATP.
   c. In reaction 4, the six-carbon molecule fructose-1,6-bisphosphate is split into two three-carbon molecules, glyceraldehyde-3-phosphate and dihydroxyacetone phosphate.

22.37 In a series of enzymatic reactions, galactose is phosphorylated to yield glucose-1-phosphate, which is converted to glucose-6-phosphate, which enters glycolysis in reaction 2. In the muscles, fructose is phosphorylated to fructose-6-phosphate, which enters glycolysis in reaction 3, where its movement through glycolysis is regulated by the enzyme phosphofructokinase. In the liver, fructose is phosphorylated to fructose-1-phosphate, which is converted to glyceraldehyde-3-phosphate, which enters glycolysis at reaction 6.

22.39 **a.** activate   **b.** inhibit

22.41 Glucose-6-phosphate is the initial substrate for the pentose phosphate pathway.

22.43 The pentose phosphate pathway produces NADPH required for anabolic reactions.

22.45 Sucrose contains the monosaccharides glucose and fructose. Once hydrolyzed during digestion, glucose directly enters glycolysis at step 1 and fructose enters glycolysis either at step 3 in the muscle and kidney or step 6 in the liver.

22.47 Aerobic (oxygen) conditions are needed.

22.49 The oxidation of pyruvate converts NAD$^+$ to NADH and produces acetyl CoA and CO_2.

$$CH_3-\overset{\overset{\displaystyle O}{\|}}{C}-COO^- + NAD^+ + HS-CoA \xrightarrow{\text{Pyruvate dehydrogenase}}$$

$$CH_3-\overset{\overset{\displaystyle O}{\|}}{C}-S-CoA + NADH + CO_2$$

22.51 **a.** (3) ethanol   **b.** (1) acetyl CoA
     c. (2) lactate   **d.** (1) acetyl CoA,
                                (3) ethanol

22.53 carbon dioxide, CO_2

22.55 During strenuous exercise, under anaerobic conditions, pyruvate is converted to lactate. The accumulation of lactate causes the muscles to tire and become sore.

22.57
$$CH_3-\overset{\overset{\textstyle O}{\|}}{C}-\overset{\overset{\textstyle O}{\|}}{C}-O^- + NADH + H^+ \longrightarrow$$
$$CH_3-\overset{\overset{\textstyle OH}{|}}{C}H-\overset{\overset{\textstyle O}{\|}}{C}-O^- + NAD^+$$

22.59 Glycogenesis is the synthesis of glycogen from glucose molecules.

22.61 Muscle cells break down glycogen to glucose-6-phosphate, which enters glycolysis.

22.63 Glycogen phosphorylase cleaves the glycosidic bonds at the ends of glycogen chains to remove glucose as glucose-1-phosphate.

22.65 **a.** activates   **b.** inhibits   **c.** inhibits

22.67 The movement of glucose out of the bloodstream and into the cells is regulated by insulin whereas fructose is not. Fructose can move into the cells and be degraded in glycolysis.

22.69 When the glycogen phosphorylase enzyme in the liver is defective, glycogen in the liver cannot be broken down to glucose.

22.71 When there are no glycogen stores remaining in the liver, gluconeogenesis synthesizes glucose from noncarbohydrate compounds such as pyruvate and lactate.

22.73 phosphoglucose isomerase, aldolase, triose phosphate isomerase, glyceraldehyde-3-phosphate dehydrogenase, phosphoglycerate kinase, phosphoglycerate mutase, and enolase

22.75 **a.** activates   **b.** activates
     c. inhibits   **d.** inhibits

22.77 People on low carbohydrate diets do not store normal amounts of glycogen and therefore lose this weight and the water weight used to hydrolyze the glycogen.

22.79 Some of the symptoms of von Gierke's disease are: liver enlargement due to glycogen accumulation, and hypoglycemia, which can lead to a shortened life expectancy.

22.81 Glycogen cannot be degraded completely to glucose causing low blood glucose. Glycogen accumulates as stored glycogen in the liver. Lower insulin levels inhibits glycolysis and activates gluconeogenesis.

22.83 120 moles of ATP

22.85 **a.** (1) glycogenesis but not glycogenolysis
     b. (3) both glycogenesis and glycogenolysis
     c. (2) glycogenolysis but not glycogenesis

22.87 **a.** (2) gluconeogenesis but not glycolysis
     b. (3) both glycolysis and gluconeogenesis
     c. (1) glycolysis but not gluconeogenesis
     d. (3) both glycolysis and gluconeogenesis

22.89 Metabolism includes all the reactions in cells that provide energy and material for cell growth.

22.91 stage 1

22.93 eukaryotic cell

22.95 adenosine triphosphate

22.97 $ATP \longrightarrow ADP + P_i + 7.3$ kcal/mole (31 kJ/mole)

22.99 High energy is the reduced form, $FADH_2$; low energy is the oxidized form, FAD.

22.101 High energy is the reduced form, NADH; low energy is the oxidized form, NAD^+.

22.103 **a.** $FADH_2$ **b.** $NADH + H^+$
     c. $NADPH + H^+$

22.105 Lactose undergoes digestion in the small intestine to yield glucose and galactose.

22.107 Glucose is the reactant and pyruvate is the product of glycolysis.

22.109 **a.** Reactions 1 and 3 involve phosphorylation of hexoses with ATP.
     b. Reactions 7 and 10 involve direct substrate phosphorylation that generates ATP.

22.111 Reaction 4, which converts fructose-1,6-bisphosphate into two three-carbon intermediates, is catalyzed by aldolase.

22.113 glucose-6-phosphate

22.115 Pyruvate is converted to lactate when oxygen is not present in the cell (anaerobic conditions) to regenerate NAD^+ for glycolysis.

22.117 Phosphofructokinase is an allosteric enzyme that is activated by high levels of AMP and ADP because the cell needs to produce more ATP. When ATP levels are high due to a decrease in energy needs, ATP inhibits phosphofructokinase, which reduces its catalysis of fructose-6-phosphate.

22.119 The rate of glycogenolysis increases when blood glucose levels are low and glucagon has been secreted, which accelerates the breakdown of glycogen.

22.121 glucose

22.123 **a.** increase   **b.** decrease
     c. increase   **d.** decrease

22.125 **a.** decrease   **b.** decrease
     c. increase   **d.** decrease

22.127 The cells in the liver, but not skeletal muscle, contain a phosphatase enzyme needed to convert glucose-6-phosphate to free glucose that can diffuse through cell membranes into the bloodstream. Glucose-6-phosphate, which is the end product of glycogenolysis in muscle cells, cannot diffuse easily across cell membranes.

22.129 Insulin increases the rate of glycogenesis and glycolysis and decreases the rate of glycogenolysis. Glucagon decreases the rate of glycogenesis and glycolysis and increases the rate of glycogenolysis.

22.131 The Cori cycle is a cyclic process that involves the transfer of lactate from muscle to the liver where glucose is synthesized, which can be used again by the muscle.

22.133 **a.** 140 kg   **b.** 2.6 min

Metabolism and Energy Production

NATALIE WAS RECENTLY DIAGNOSED WITH MILD
pulmonary emphysema due to secondhand cigarette smoke. She has been referred to Angela, an exercise physiologist, who begins to assess Natalie's condition by connecting her to an electrocardiogram (ECG or EKG), a pulse oximeter, and a blood pressure cuff. The ECG records the electrical activity of Natalie's heart, which is used to measure the rate and rhythm of her heartbeat, and possible presence of heart damage. The pulse oximeter measures her pulse and the saturation level of oxygen in her arterial blood (the percentage of hemoglobin that is saturated with O_2). The blood pressure cuff determines the pressure exerted by the heart in pumping her blood.

To determine possible heart disease, Natalie has an exercise stress test on a treadmill to measure how her heart rate and blood pressure respond to exertion by walking faster as the slope of the treadmill is increased. Electrical leads are attached to measure the heart rate and blood pressure first at rest and then on the treadmill. Additional equipment using a face mask collects expired air and measures Natalie's maximal volume of oxygen uptake, or $V_{O_2\ max}$.

A pulse oximeter measures the pulse and the O_2 saturation in the blood.

CAREER Exercise Physiologist

Exercise physiologists work with athletes as well as patients who have been diagnosed with diabetes, heart disease, pulmonary disease, or other chronic disabilities or diseases. Patients who have been diagnosed with one of these diseases are often prescribed exercise as a form of treatment, and they are referred to an exercise physiologist. The exercise physiologist evaluates the patient's overall health and then creates a customized exercise program for that individual. The program for an athlete might focus on reducing the number of injuries, whereas a program for a cardiac patient would focus on strengthening the heart muscles. The exercise physiologist also monitors the patient for improvement and determines if the exercise is helping to reduce or reverse the progression of the disease.

O xygen is necessary for catabolism and the production of ATP. In the mitochondria, the reactions associated with electron transport are coupled
with oxidative phosphorylation to produce ATP. The pyruvate obtained
from the degradation of glucose during glycolysis is converted to acetyl CoA when
oxygen is plentiful in the cell and to lactate when oxygen levels are low. Although
glycolysis produces a small amount of ATP, most of the ATP in the cells is produced in
stage 3 of catabolism during the conversion of pyruvate. In a process known as *respiration*, oxygen is required to complete the oxidation of glucose to CO_2 and H_2O.

In the *citric acid cycle*, a series of catabolic reactions in the mitochondria oxidizes the two carbon atoms in the acetyl component of acetyl CoA to two molecules
of carbon dioxide. The reduced coenzymes NADH and $FADH_2$ produced in the
citric acid cycle enter *electron transport*, or the *respiratory chain*, where they provide
hydrogen ions and electrons that combine with oxygen (O_2) to form H_2O. The
energy transferred during electron transport is used to synthesize ATP from ADP.

LOOKING AHEAD

23.1   The Citric Acid Cycle 837
23.2   Electron Transport and
       ATP 844
♡♡   **Chemistry Link to
       Health** *Toxins: Inhibitors of
       Electron Transport* 847
♡♡   **Chemistry Link to
       Health** *Uncouplers of ATP
       Synthesis* 849
23.3   ATP Energy from
       Glucose 851
♡♡   **Chemistry Link to
       Health** *Efficiency of ATP
       Production* 854
℞   **Clinical Applications** 844,
       850, 855, 859
℞   **Clinical Update** *Improving
       Natalie's Overall Fitness* 855

CHAPTER READINESS*

⊛ CORE CHEMISTRY SKILLS
- Writing Equations for Hydrogenation, Hydration, and Polymerization (12.7)
- Classifying Enzymes (20.2)
- Identifying Important Coenzymes in Metabolism (22.2)
- Identifying the Compounds in Glycolysis (22.4)

*These Core Chemistry Skills from previous chapters are listed here for your review as you proceed to
the new material in this chapter.

23.1 The Citric Acid Cycle

The citric acid cycle is a series of reactions that connects the intermediate acetyl CoA
from the catabolic pathways in stage 2 with electron transport and the synthesis of ATP in
stage 3. As a central pathway in metabolism, the **citric acid cycle** uses the two-carbon
acetyl group of acetyl CoA to produce CO_2, and reduced coenzymes NADH and $FADH_2$
(see Figure 23.1).

The citric acid cycle is named for the six-carbon citrate ion from citric acid $(C_6H_8O_7)$,
a tricarboxylic acid, which forms in the first reaction. The citric acid cycle is also known
as the *tricarboxylic acid (TCA) cycle* or the *Krebs cycle*, named for H. A. Krebs, who recognized it in 1937 as the major pathway for the production of energy.

Overview of the Citric Acid Cycle

Six carbons move through the eight reactions of the citric acid cycle, with each turn producing oxaloacetate (four carbons) and $2CO_2$ (see Figure 23.2). Each turn of the cycle
contains four oxidation reactions producing the reduced coenzymes NADH and $FADH_2$
from the energy released during the reactions. One GTP (converted to ATP in the cell) is
also produced during the citric acid cycle from the energy transferred during coenzyme A
hydrolysis.

Eight reactions take place in the citric acid cycle that oxidize acetyl CoA from pyruvate or fatty acids and produce CO_2 and the high-energy compounds $FADH_2$, NADH, and
GTP (see Figure 23.3). Reactions involved in the citric acid cycle include condensation
(dehydration), hydration, oxidation, reduction, and hydrolysis.

LEARNING GOAL

Describe the oxidation of acetyl
CoA in the citric acid cycle.

⊛ CORE CHEMISTRY SKILL

Describing the Reactions in the
Citric Acid Cycle

Stages of Catabolism

Stage 1
Digestion and
hydrolysis

Stage 2
Degradation and
some oxidation to
smaller molecules

Stage 3
Oxidation to CO_2,
H_2O, and energy
for ATP synthesis

FIGURE 23.1 ▶ The citric acid cycle connects the catabolic pathways that begin with the digestion and degradation of foods in stages 1 and 2 with the oxidation of substrates in stage 3 that generates most of the energy for ATP synthesis.

ⓠ Why is the citric acid cycle called a central metabolic pathway?

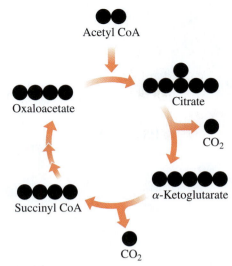

FIGURE 23.2 ▶ In the citric acid cycle, two carbon atoms are removed as CO_2 from six-carbon citrate to give four-carbon succinyl CoA, which is converted to four-carbon oxaloacetate.

Q How many carbon atoms are removed in one turn of the citric acid cycle?

Citric acid (citrate) provides the sour taste of citrus fruits such as lemons, limes, oranges, and grapefruits.

Reaction 1   Formation of Citrate

In the first reaction, *citrate synthase* catalyzes the condensation of an acetyl group (2C) from acetyl CoA with oxaloacetate (4C) to yield citrate (6C) and coenzyme A. The energy to form citrate is provided by the hydrolysis of the high-energy thioester bond in acetyl CoA.

$$CH_3-\overset{\overset{O}{\|}}{C}-S-CoA \; + \; \underset{\underset{COO^-}{|}}{\overset{\overset{COO^-}{|}}{\underset{CH_2}{C=O}}} \; + \; H_2O \; \xrightarrow{\text{Citrate synthase}} \; HO-\underset{\underset{COO^-}{|}}{\overset{\overset{\overset{COO^-}{|}}{CH_2}}{C}}-COO^- \; + \; HS-CoA \; + \; H^+$$

Acetyl CoA   Oxaloacetate   Citrate

Reaction 2   Isomerization

The citrate formed in reaction 1 is a tertiary alcohol, which cannot be oxidized. In reaction 2, citrate is rearranged to its isomer isocitrate, a secondary alcohol that can be oxidized. Initially, *aconitase* catalyzes the dehydration of citrate (tertiary alcohol) to yield *cis*-aconitate, which is followed by a hydration that forms isocitrate (secondary alcohol).

$$HO-\overset{\overset{\overset{COO^-}{|}}{\overset{CH_2}{|}}}{\underset{\underset{COO^-}{|}}{\underset{H-C-H}{C}}}-COO^- \; \xrightarrow[H_2O]{\text{Aconitase}} \; \overset{\overset{\overset{COO^-}{|}}{\overset{CH_2}{|}}}{\underset{\underset{COO^-}{|}}{\underset{C-H}{C}}}-COO^- \; \xrightarrow[H_2O]{\text{Aconitase}} \; H-\overset{\overset{\overset{COO^-}{|}}{\overset{CH_2}{|}}}{\underset{\underset{COO^-}{|}}{\underset{HO-C-H}{C}}}-COO^-$$

Citrate   *cis*-Aconitate   Isocitrate
(3° alcohol)   (2° alcohol)

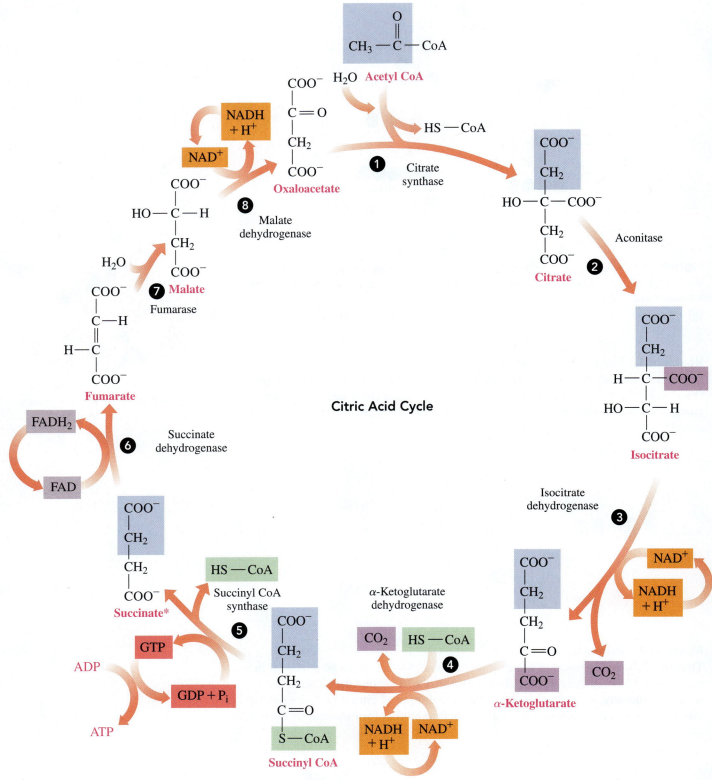

*Succinate is a symmetrical compound.

FIGURE 23.3 ▶ In the citric acid cycle, oxidation reactions produce two CO_2 and reduced coenzymes NADH and $FADH_2$, GTP, and regenerate oxaloacetate.

Q What type of enzyme in the citric acid cycle produces reduced coenzymes?

Reaction 3   Oxidation and Decarboxylation

In reaction 3, both an oxidation and a decarboxylation take place for the first time in the citric acid cycle. The secondary alcohol group in isocitrate (6C) is oxidized to a ketone by *isocitrate dehydrogenase*. A *decarboxylation* removes one carbon from isocitrate by converting a carboxylate group (COO^-) to a CO_2 molecule. The ketone product is named α-ketoglutarate (5C) because the ketone is next to (alpha to) the carboxyl group. During this oxidation, a dehydrogenase removes hydrogen ions and electrons, which are used to reduce NAD^+ to NADH and H^+.

Isocitrate → α-Ketoglutarate

Reaction 4   Decarboxylation and Oxidation

In a reaction catalyzed by *α-ketoglutarate dehydrogenase*, α-ketoglutarate (5C) undergoes decarboxylation. The four-carbon product combines with coenzyme A to yield succinyl CoA. The oxidation of the thiol group ($-SH$) in HS$-$CoA provides hydrogen that is transferred to NAD^+ to form a second molecule of NADH and H^+.

α-Ketoglutarate → Succinyl CoA

Reaction 5   Hydrolysis

In reaction 5, *succinyl CoA synthetase* catalyzes the hydrolysis of the thioester bond in succinyl CoA to yield succinate and HS$-$CoA. The energy from hydrolysis is transferred to the condensation of phosphate and GDP (guanosine diphosphate) forming GTP, a high-energy compound similar to ATP.

Succinyl CoA → Succinate

Eventually in the cell, the hydrolysis of GTP to GDP provides energy for the condensation of phosphate with ADP forming ATP. This reaction is the only time in the citric acid cycle that ATP is produced by a direct transfer of a phosphate group. The reaction between GTP and ADP regenerates GDP that is used again in the citric acid cycle.

$$GTP + ADP \longrightarrow GDP + ATP$$

Reaction 6   Oxidation

In reaction 6, *succinate dehydrogenase* catalyzes the oxidation of succinate to yield fumarate, a compound with a carbon–carbon (C=C) double bond. In this oxidation, the 2H lost from succinate are used to reduce the coenzyme FAD to $FADH_2$. This is the only reaction in the citric acid cycle in which FAD is reduced to $FADH_2$.

Reaction 7   Hydration

In reaction 7, a hydration catalyzed by *fumarase* adds water to the double bond of fumarate to yield malate, which is a secondary alcohol.

Reaction 8   Oxidation

In reaction 8, the last step of the citric acid cycle, *malate dehydrogenase* catalyzes the oxidation of the hydroxyl group (—OH) in malate to a carbonyl group (C=O) yielding oxaloacetate. For the third time in the citric acid cycle, an oxidation by a dehydrogenase provides hydrogen ions and electrons for the reduction of NAD^+ to NADH and H^+.

Malic acid (malate) produces the sour taste of green apples and rhubarb.

Products from One Turn of the Citric Acid Cycle

2 CO_2
3 NADH and $3H^+$
1 $FADH_2$
1 GTP (1 ATP)
1 HS—CoA

Summary of Products from the Citric Acid Cycle

We have seen that the citric acid cycle begins when a two-carbon acetyl group from acetyl CoA combines with four-carbon oxaloacetate to form six-carbon citrate. Through oxidation, reduction, and decarboxylation, two carbon atoms are removed to yield two CO_2 and a four-carbon compound that undergoes reactions to regenerate oxaloacetate.

In the four oxidation reactions for one turn of the citric acid cycle, three NAD^+ are reduced to three NADH and one FAD is reduced to one $FADH_2$. One GDP is converted to one GTP, which is used to convert one ADP and P_i to ATP. We can write an overall chemical equation for one complete turn of the citric acid cycle as follows:

$$\text{Acetyl CoA} + 3NAD^+ + FAD + GDP \text{ (or ADP)} + P_i + 2H_2O \longrightarrow$$
$$2CO_2 + 3NADH + 3H^+ + FADH_2 + GTP \text{ (or ATP)} + HS-CoA$$

Up to this point, we have seen that when a molecule of glucose undergoes oxidation, it yields two acetyl CoA that would go through two turns of the citric acid cycle producing several reduced coenzymes and 2 ATP in the process.

Regulation of the Citric Acid Cycle

The primary function of the citric acid cycle is to produce high-energy compounds like NADH and $FADH_2$ for ATP synthesis. When the cell needs energy, low levels of ATP or high levels of ADP stimulate the conversion of pyruvate to acetyl CoA, which increases the rate of the citric acid cycle. When ATP or NADH levels are high, citrate synthase is inhibited, and the production of acetyl CoA from pyruvate decreases.

In the citric acid cycle, the enzymes that catalyze reactions 3 and 4 respond to allosteric activation and feedback inhibition. In reaction 3, isocitrate dehydrogenase is activated by high levels of ADP and inhibited by high levels of ATP and NADH. In reaction 4, α-ketoglutarate dehydrogenase is activated by high levels of ADP and inhibited by high levels of NADH and succinyl CoA (see Figure 23.4).

FIGURE 23.4 ▶ High levels of ADP activate enzymes for the production of acetyl CoA and the citric acid cycle, whereas high levels of ATP, NADH, and succinyl CoA inhibit enzymes in the citric acid cycle.

◉ How do high levels of ATP affect the rate of the citric acid cycle?

▶**SAMPLE PROBLEM 23.1** The Citric Acid Cycle

When one acetyl CoA moves through one turn of the citric acid cycle, how many of each of the following is produced?

a. NADH   **b.** CO_2

SOLUTION

a. One turn of the citric acid cycle produces three molecules of NADH.
b. Two molecules of CO_2 are produced by the decarboxylation of isocitrate and α-ketoglutarate.

STUDY CHECK 23.1

When one acetyl CoA moves through one turn of the citric acid cycle, how many $FADH_2$ would be produced?

ANSWER

one $FADH_2$

QUESTIONS AND PROBLEMS

23.1 The Citric Acid Cycle

LEARNING GOAL Describe the oxidation of acetyl CoA in the citric acid cycle.

23.1 What other names are used for the citric acid cycle?

23.2 What compounds are needed to start the citric acid cycle?

23.3 What are the products from one turn of the citric acid cycle?

23.4 What compound is regenerated in each turn of the citric acid cycle?

23.5 Identify the reaction(s) of the citric acid cycle that involve(s)
a. oxidation and decarboxylation
b. dehydration
c. reduction of NAD^+

23.6 Identify the reaction(s) of the citric acid cycle that involve(s)
a. reduction of FAD
b. direct phosphate transfer
c. hydration

23.7 Refer to the diagram of the citric acid cycle to answer each of the following:
  a. What are the six-carbon compounds?
  b. How is the number of carbon atoms decreased?
  c. What is the five-carbon compound?
  d. In which reactions are secondary alcohols oxidized?

23.8 Refer to the diagram of the citric acid cycle to answer each of the following:
  a. What is the yield of CO_2 molecules?
  b. What are the four-carbon compounds?
  c. What is the yield of GTP molecules?
  d. What are the decarboxylation reactions?

23.9 Indicate the name of the enzyme that catalyzes each of the following reactions in the citric acid cycle:
  a. joins acetyl CoA to oxaloacetate
  b. forms a carbon–carbon double bond
  c. adds water to fumarate

23.10 Indicate the name of the enzyme that catalyzes each of the following reactions in the citric acid cycle:
  a. isomerizes citrate
  b. oxidizes and decarboxylates α-ketoglutarate
  c. hydrolyzes succinyl CoA

23.11 Indicate the coenzyme that accepts hydrogen in each of the following:
  a. isocitrate $\longrightarrow$ α-ketoglutarate
  b. succinate $\longrightarrow$ fumarate

23.12 Indicate the coenzyme that accepts hydrogen in each of the following:
  a. malate $\longrightarrow$ oxaloacetate
  b. α-ketoglutarate $\longrightarrow$ succinyl CoA

23.13 What enzymes in the citric acid cycle are allosteric enzymes?

23.14 Why does the rate of the oxidation of pyruvate affect the rate of the citric acid cycle?

23.15 How do high levels of ADP affect the rate of the citric acid cycle?

23.16 How do high levels of NADH affect the rate of the citric acid cycle?

℞ Clinical Applications

23.17 An enzyme deficiency in the citric acid cycle causes a buildup of malate. Symptoms of the enzyme deficiency include polycythemia, severe neurological problems, and seizures. Which enzyme in the citric acid cycle is deficient?

23.18 An enzyme deficiency in the citric acid cycle produces a large amount of α-ketoglutarate in the blood and urine. Symptoms of the enzyme deficiency include neurological degeneration, rigid muscles, and encephalopathy. Which enzyme in the citric acid cycle is deficient?

LEARNING GOAL

Describe the transfer of hydrogen ions and electrons in electron transport and the process of oxidative phosphorylation in ATP synthesis.

23.2 Electron Transport and ATP

At this point in stage 3 of catabolism, for each glucose molecule that completes glycolysis, the oxidation of two pyruvate, and the citric acid cycle, four ATP, ten NADH, and two $FADH_2$ are produced.

From One Glucose	ATP	Reduced Coenzymes	
Glycolysis	2	2 NADH	
Oxidation of 2 Pyruvate		2 NADH	
Citric Acid Cycle with 2 Acetyl CoA	2	6 NADH	2 $FADH_2$
Total for One Glucose	4	10 NADH	2 $FADH_2$

The reduced coenzymes NADH and $FADH_2$ produced from glycolysis, the oxidation of pyruvate, and the citric acid cycle are oxidized to provide the energy for the synthesis of significant amounts of ATP. In **electron transport**, or the *respiratory chain*, hydrogen ions and electrons from NADH and $FADH_2$ are passed from one electron acceptor or electron carrier to the next until they combine with oxygen to form H_2O. The energy released during electron transport is used to synthesize ATP from ADP and P_i, a process called *oxidative phosphorylation*. As long as oxygen is available for the mitochondria in the cell, electron transport and oxidative phosphorylation function to synthesize most of the ATP produced in the cell.

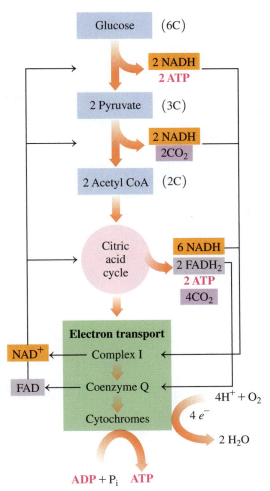

The enzymes and electron carriers for electron transport are located along the inner membrane of the mitochondria.

A mitochondrion contains an inner and outer membrane. Along the highly folded inner membrane are the enzymes and electron carriers required for electron transport. Embedded within these membranes are five distinct protein complexes, which are numbered I, II, III, IV, and V. Four of the protein complexes (I, III, IV, and V) extend through the inner mitochondrial membrane, with one end of each complex in the matrix and the other end in the intermembrane space. Two mobile electron carriers, coenzyme Q and cytochrome *c*, carry electrons between these protein complexes bound to the inner membrane (see Figure 23.5).

Complex I

Electron transport begins when hydrogen ions and electrons are transferred from NADH to complex I. The loss of hydrogen from NADH regenerates NAD^+, which becomes available to oxidize more substrates in oxidative

The reduced coenzymes NADH and $FADH_2$ that provide hydrogen ions and electrons in electron transport are regenerated as NAD^+ and FAD.

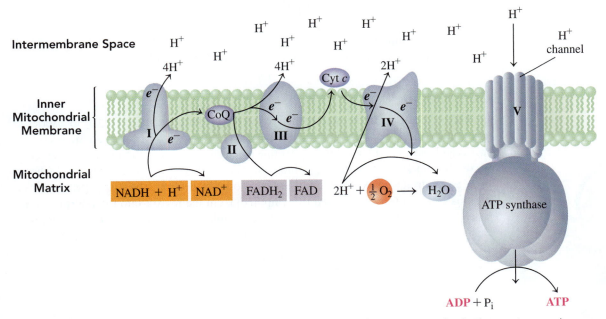

FIGURE 23.5 ▶ In electron transport, the oxidation of NADH and $FADH_2$ provides hydrogen ions and electrons that eventually react with oxygen to form water.

Q What pathway is the major source of NADH for electron transport?

Quinone

$$CH_3-O \overset{O}{\underset{O}{\bigcirc}} (CH_2-CH=\overset{CH_3}{\underset{|}{C}}-CH_2)_{10}H$$

$$CH_3-O$$

$$2H^+ + 2\,e^-$$

Oxidized coenzyme Q (CoQ)

$$CH_3-O \overset{OH}{\underset{OH}{\bigcirc}} (CH_2-CH=\overset{CH_3}{\underset{|}{C}}-CH_2)_{10}H$$

$$CH_3-O$$

Reduced coenzyme Q (CoQH$_2$)

FIGURE 23.6 ▶ The electron carrier CoQ is reduced to CoQH$_2$ when it accepts 2H$^+$ and 2 e$^-$ from NADH + H$^+$ or FADH$_2$.

Q How does reduced coenzyme CoQH$_2$ compare to the oxidized form?

pathways such as the citric acid cycle. The hydrogen ions and electrons are transferred to the first mobile electron carrier **coenzyme Q (CoQ)**, which is not strongly associated with a particular complex. Thus, CoQH$_2$ can carry electrons from complexes I and II to complex III (see Figure 23.6).

During the electron transfer to CoQ, H$^+$ ions are pumped through complex I into the intermembrane space, producing a reservoir of H$^+$ called a **hydrogen ion gradient**. Each time two electrons pass from NADH to CoQ, a total of 4H$^+$ are pumped across the mitochondrial membrane. This movement of hydrogen ions produces a charge separation on opposite sides of the membrane. The overall reaction sequence in complex I is written as follows:

$$\boxed{NADH + H^+} + CoQ \longrightarrow \boxed{NAD^+} + CoQH_2$$

Complex II

Complex II consists of the enzyme succinate dehydrogenase from the citric acid cycle. In complex II, CoQ obtains hydrogen and electrons directly from FADH$_2$ that was generated by the conversion of succinate to fumarate in the citric acid cycle. This produces CoQH$_2$ and regenerates the oxidized coenzyme FAD, which becomes available again to oxidize more substrates in oxidative pathways. The overall reaction sequence in complex II is written as follows:

$$\boxed{FADH_2} + CoQ \longrightarrow \boxed{FAD} + CoQH_2$$

Because complex II is at a lower energy than complex I, the electrons from FADH$_2$ enter electron transport at a lower energy level than those from NADH.

Complex III

In complex III, two electrons are transferred from the mobile carrier CoQH$_2$ to a series of iron-containing proteins called **cytochromes (cyt)**. Eventually, electrons are transferred to two cytochrome c, which is another mobile electron carrier that can move between complexes III and IV. Cytochrome c, which contains Fe^{3+}/Fe^{2+}, is reduced to Fe^{2+} when it gains an electron, and oxidized to Fe^{3+} when it loses an electron. The energy generated during this electron transfer is used to pump 4H$^+$ from the matrix into the intermembrane space, increasing the high-energy hydrogen ion gradient. As a mobile carrier, cytochrome c carries electrons to complex IV. The overall reaction in complex III is written as follows:

$$CoQH_2 + 2cyt\,c\,(Fe^{3+}) \longrightarrow CoQ + 2H^+ + 2cyt\,c\,(Fe^{2+})$$

(Oxidized)   (Reduced)

Cytochrome c carries one electron when Fe^{3+} is reduced to Fe^{2+} (orange sphere). The heme group (gray) holds the iron in place.

Complex IV

At complex IV, four electrons from four cytochrome c are passed to other electron carriers until the electrons combine with hydrogen ions and oxygen (O$_2$) to form two molecules of water. The overall reaction in complex IV is written as follows:

$$4\,e^- + 4H^+ + O_2 \longrightarrow 2H_2O$$

This equation may also be written as:

$$2\,e^- + 2H^+ + \tfrac{1}{2}O_2 \longrightarrow H_2O$$

At complex IV, energy is used to pump H^+ from the mitochondrial matrix into the intermembrane space, increasing the hydrogen ion gradient further. Overall, the reduced coenzymes NADH and $FADH_2$ from the citric acid cycle enter electron transport to provide hydrogen ions and electrons that react with oxygen, producing water and regenerating the oxidized coenzymes NAD^+ and FAD.

▶ SAMPLE PROBLEM 23.2 Oxidation and Reduction

Identify each of the following steps in electron transport as oxidation or reduction:

a. $CoQH_2 \longrightarrow CoQ + 2H^+ + 2\,e^-$
b. $\text{cyt } c\ (Fe^{3+}) + e^- \longrightarrow \text{cyt } c\ (Fe^{2+})$

SOLUTION

a. The loss of electrons is oxidation.
b. The gain of an electron is reduction.

STUDY CHECK 23.2

What is the final substance that accepts electrons in electron transport?

ANSWER

oxygen (O_2)

Chemistry Link to **Health**

Toxins: Inhibitors of Electron Transport

Several substances can inhibit the electron carriers in the different complexes of electron transport. Rotenone, a product from a plant root used as an insecticide, and the painkillers Amytal and Demerol block electron transport between complexes I and CoQ. Another inhibitor is the antibiotic antimycin A, which blocks the flow of electrons between complex III and cytochrome c. Another group of compounds, including cyanide (CN^-) and carbon monoxide, block the flow of electrons between cytochrome c and complex IV. Oligomycin, a common antibiotic, inhibits electron carriers by blocking complex V, ATP synthase. Oligomycin, a common antibiotic, inhibits electron carriers by blocking complex V, ATP synthase. The toxic nature of these compounds makes it clear that organisms rely heavily on the process of electron transport.

Rotenone

Amytal

Demerol

Antimycin A

When an inhibitor blocks a step in electron transport, the carriers preceding that step are unable to transfer electrons, and remain in their reduced forms. All the carriers after the blocked step remain oxidized without a source of electrons. Thus, any of these inhibitors can shut down electron transport. Consequently, respiration stops, and the cells die.

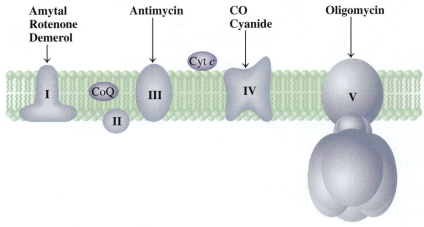

When an inhibitor blocks a step in electron transport, ATP synthesis stops.

Oxidative Phosphorylation

We have seen that energy is generated when electrons from the oxidation of substrates flow through electron transport. Now we will look at how that energy is coupled with the production of ATP in the process called **oxidative phosphorylation**.

In 1978, Peter Mitchell received the Nobel Prize in chemistry for his theory called the *chemiosmotic model*, which links the energy from electron transport to a hydrogen ion gradient that drives the synthesis of ATP. In the model, the complexes I, III, and IV act as hydrogen ion pumps by pushing H^+ ions out of the matrix and into the intermembrane space, producing a hydrogen ion gradient.

To equalize the pH and the electrical charge between the intermembrane space and the matrix, H^+ must return to the matrix. However, H^+ cannot move through the inner membrane. Instead, H^+ must return to the matrix by passing through a fifth protein complex in the inner membrane called **ATP synthase**, also called *complex V*. The flow of H^+ from the intermembrane space through the ATP synthase generates energy that is used to synthesize ATP from ADP and P_i. This process of oxidative phosphorylation couples the energy from electron transport to the synthesis of ATP.

$$ADP + P_i + \text{energy} \xrightarrow{\text{ATP synthase}} ATP$$

Electron Transport and ATP Synthesis

When NADH enters electron transport at complex I, the energy transferred from its oxidation can be used to synthesize 2.5 ATP. When $FADH_2$ enters electron transport at complex II, which is at a lower energy level, its oxidation provides energy for the synthesis of 1.5 ATP. Old values of 3 ATP from NADH and 2 ATP from $FADH_2$ are still found in some chemistry texts and are often used in biology. However, the ATP values are now considered to be somewhat less than earlier calculations. Current research indicates that the oxidation of one NADH yields 2.5 ATP and one $FADH_2$ yields 1.5 ATP.

Reduced Coenzyme		Oxidized Coenzyme		ATP Output
NADH + H^+	$\longrightarrow$	NAD^+	+	2.5 ATP
$FADH_2$	$\longrightarrow$	FAD	+	1.5 ATP

▶ **SAMPLE PROBLEM 23.3** **ATP Synthesis**

Why does the oxidation of NADH provide energy for the formation of 2.5 ATP molecules, whereas $FADH_2$ produces 1.5 ATP molecules?

SOLUTION

The oxidation of NADH at complex I provides electrons and hydrogen ions (H^+), which are pumped from the matrix into the intermembrane space eventually producing enough energy for the synthesis of 2.5 ATP molecules. However, $FADH_2$ is oxidized at complex II, which provides energy for the synthesis of only 1.5 ATP molecules.

STUDY CHECK 23.3

How do hydrogen ions return to the matrix?

ANSWER

Hydrogen ions return to the matrix by passing through ATP synthase, complex V.

Chemistry Link to **Health**
Uncouplers of ATP Synthase

Some types of compounds called *uncouplers* separate the electron transport system from ATP synthase. They do this by providing an alternate route for hydrogen ions to return to the matrix. The electrons are transported to O_2 in electron transport, but ATP is not formed by ATP synthase.

Some uncouplers transport H^+ through the inner mitochondrial membrane, which is normally impermeable to H^+. Compounds such as dicumarol and 2,4-dinitrophenol (DNP) are hydrophobic and bind with H^+ to carry them across the inner membrane. An antibiotic, oligomycin, blocks the channel, which does not allow any H^+ ions to return to the matrix. By removing H^+ ions or blocking the channel, there is no H^+ flow to generate energy for ATP synthesis.

When there is no mechanism for ATP synthesis, the energy of electron transport is released as heat. Certain animals that are adapted to cold climates have developed their own uncoupling system, which allows them to use electron transport energy for heat production. These animals have large amounts of a tissue called *brown fat*, which contains a high concentration of mitochondria. This tissue is brown because of the color of iron in the cytochromes of the mitochondria. The hydrogen ion pumps still operate in brown fat, but a protein called thermogenin, embedded in the inner mitochondrial membrane of brown adipose tissues, allows the H^+ to bypass ATP synthase. Heat rather than ATP is produced.

Dicumarol

2,4-Dinitrophenol (DNP)

Oligomycin

In newborn babies, brown fat is used to generate heat because babies have a small mass but large surface area, and they need to produce more heat than do adults. The brown fat deposits are located near major blood vessels, which carry the warmed blood to the body. Most adults have little or no brown fat, although someone who works outdoors in a cold climate will develop some brown fat deposits.

Plants also use uncouplers. In early spring, heat is used to warm early shoots of plants under the snow, which helps them melt the snow around the plants. Some plants, such as skunk cabbage, use uncoupling agents to volatize fragrant compounds that attract insects to pollinate the plants.

Brown fat helps babies to keep warm.

Regulation of Electron Transport and Oxidative Phosphorylation

Electron transport is regulated by the availability of ADP, P_i, oxygen (O_2), and NADH. Low levels of any of these compounds will decrease the activity of electron transport and the formation of ATP. When a cell is active and ATP is consumed rapidly, the elevated levels of ADP will activate the synthesis of ATP. Therefore, the activity of electron transport is strongly dependent on the availability of ADP for ATP synthesis.

QUESTIONS AND PROBLEMS

23.2 Electron Transport and ATP

LEARNING GOAL Describe the transfer of hydrogen ions and electrons in electron transport and the process of oxidative phosphorylation in ATP synthesis.

23.19 Is cyt c (Fe^{3+}) the abbreviation for the oxidized or reduced form of cytochrome c?

23.20 Is $FADH_2$ the abbreviation for the oxidized or reduced form of flavin adenine dinucleotide?

23.21 Identify each of the following as oxidation or reduction:
a. $NADH \longrightarrow NAD^+ + H^+ + 2\,e^-$
b. $CoQ + 2H^+ + 2\,e^- \longrightarrow CoQH_2$

23.22 Identify each of the following as oxidation or reduction:
a. cyt c (Fe^{2+}) $\longrightarrow$ cyt c (Fe^{3+}) $+ e^-$
b. $FAD + 2H^+ + 2\,e^- \longrightarrow FADH_2$

23.23 What reduced coenzyme provides hydrogen and electrons for electron transport at complex I?

23.24 What reduced coenzyme provides hydrogen and electrons for electron transport at complex II?

23.25 Arrange the following in the order in which they appear in electron transport: cytochrome c (Fe^{3+}), $FADH_2$, CoQ.

23.26 Arrange the following in the order in which they appear in electron transport: O_2, NAD^+, FAD.

23.27 How are electrons carried from complex I to complex III?

23.28 How are electrons carried from complex III to complex IV?

23.29 How is NADH oxidized in electron transport?

23.30 How is $FADH_2$ oxidized in electron transport?

23.31 Complete each of the following reactions in electron transport:
a. $NADH + H^+ + \underline{\quad} \longrightarrow \underline{\quad} + CoQH_2$
b. $CoQH_2 + 2cyt\ c\ (Fe^{3+}) \longrightarrow CoQ + \underline{\quad} + \underline{\quad}$

23.32 Complete each of the following reactions in electron transport:
a. $CoQ + \underline{\quad} \longrightarrow \underline{\quad} + FAD$
b. $4cyt\ c\ (Fe^{3+}) + 4H^+ + O_2 \longrightarrow 4cyt\ c\ (Fe^{2+}) + \underline{\quad}$

23.33 What is meant by the term oxidative phosphorylation?

23.34 How is the hydrogen ion gradient established?

23.35 According to the chemiosmotic model, how does the hydrogen ion gradient provide energy to synthesize ATP?

23.36 How does the phosphorylation of ADP occur?

23.37 How are glycolysis and the citric acid cycle linked to the production of ATP by electron transport?

23.38 Why does $FADH_2$ provide energy to synthesize 1.5 ATP via electron transport, whereas NADH provides energy to synthesize 2.5 ATP?

℞ Clinical Applications

23.39 Potassium cyanide is a potent poison that kills by inhibiting electron transport when CN^- binds to the Fe^{3+} in the cytochrome heme groups. Why would this stop electron transport?

23.40 Coenzyme Q is sold as a dietary supplement called CoQ10 with recommended doses of 22 mg to 400 mg. It is said to boost energy and recovery from exercise. Based on its role in electron transport, explain how this might be possible.

23.41 Increasing thermogenesis has been thought to be a way to lose weight. In fact, 2,4-dinitrophenol is available as a supplement most often used by bodybuilders to burn fat. This dangerous drug is also marketed as a pesticide and kills insects in a similar manner. What might be a side effect of using this compound?

23.42 Oligomycin is an antibiotic that inhibits ATP synthase. If ATP synthase is not operable, what happens to the energy from electron transport?

23.3 ATP Energy from Glucose

The total ATP for the complete oxidation of glucose under aerobic conditions is calculated by combining the ATP produced from glycolysis, the oxidation of pyruvate, the citric acid cycle, and electron transport.

LEARNING GOAL

Account for the ATP produced by the complete oxidation of glucose.

ATP from Glycolysis

In glycolysis, the oxidation of glucose stores energy in two NADH molecules, as well as two ATP molecules from direct phosphate transfer. From glycolysis, glucose produces a total of seven ATP: five ATP from two NADH (malate–aspartate shuttle), and two ATP from direct phosphate transfer.

$$\text{Glucose} \longrightarrow 2 \text{ pyruvate } + \boxed{\text{2 ATP}} + \boxed{\text{2 NADH}} \boxed{\text{(5 ATP)}}$$

Malate–Aspartate Shuttle

Because glycolysis occurs in the cytosol, the NADH it produces cannot pass through the mitochondrial inner membrane. However, the hydrogen ions and electrons from NADH in the cytosol of heart and liver cells can be transferred to compounds in the *malate–aspartate shuttle* called *transporters*, which can move in and out of the mitochondria. In the cytosol, *malate dehydrogenase* catalyzes the reaction of oxaloacetate and NADH to yield malate and NAD^+. Then a transporter binds the malate and carries it across the mitochondrial membrane into the matrix, where *malate dehydrogenase* in the matrix oxidizes malate back to oxaloacetate. The oxidation provides hydrogen ions and electrons that are used to reduce NAD^+ to NADH, which can now enter electron transport to synthesize ATP (see Figure 23.7). Because the oxaloacetate produced in the matrix cannot cross the mitochondrial membrane, it is converted back to aspartate, which moves out of matrix back into the cytosol, where transamination converts it to oxaloacetate. The resulting NAD^+ can participate again in glycolysis in the cytosol.

Cytosol

FIGURE 23.7 ▶ The malate–aspartate shuttle transfers the energy stored in NADH formed during glycolysis to transporters that move from the cytosol into the mitochondrial matrix where NADH is regenerated for use in electron transport.

◉ Why does the NADH produced by glycolysis utilize the malate–aspartate shuttle?

ATP from the Oxidation of Two Pyruvate

Under aerobic conditions, pyruvate enters the mitochondria, where it is oxidized to give acetyl CoA, CO_2, and NADH. Because glucose yields two pyruvate, two NADH enter electron transport; thus the oxidation of two pyruvate leads to the production of five ATP.

$$2 \text{ Pyruvate} \longrightarrow 2 \text{ acetyl CoA} + 2CO_2 + \boxed{2 \text{ NADH} \quad (5 \text{ ATP})}$$

ATP from the Citric Acid Cycle

The two acetyl CoA produced from two pyruvate now enter the citric acid cycle. Each acetyl CoA makes one turn of the citric acid cycle and produces two CO_2, three NADH, one $FADH_2$, and one ATP (from GTP) by direct phosphate transfer. Thus, the two acetyl CoA initially from one glucose produce a total of six NADH, two $FADH_2$, and two ATP. In electron transport, six NADH produce 15 ATP, and two $FADH_2$ produce 3 ATP. In two turns of the citric acid cycle, a total of 20 ATP are produced.

$$6 \text{ NADH} \times 2.5 \text{ ATP/NADH} = 15 \text{ ATP}$$
$$2 \text{ FADH}_2 \times 1.5 \text{ ATP/FADH}_2 = 3 \text{ ATP}$$
$$2 \text{ GTP} \times 1 \text{ ATP/GTP} = 2 \text{ ATP}$$
$$\overline{\text{Total (two turns)} = 20 \text{ ATP}}$$

The overall equation for the reaction of two acetyl CoA is

$$2 \text{ Acetyl CoA} \longrightarrow 4CO_2 + 20 \text{ ATP} \text{ (two turns of the citric acid cycle)}$$

ATP from the Complete Oxidation of Glucose

⊗ **CORE CHEMISTRY SKILL**

Calculating the ATP Produced from Glucose

The total ATP production for the complete oxidation of glucose is calculated by combining the ATP produced from glycolysis plus the oxidation of pyruvate plus the citric acid cycle (see Figure 23.8). The ATP produced for these reactions is given in Table 23.1.

TABLE 23.1 ATP Produced by the Complete Oxidation of Glucose

Pathway	Reaction	Coenzymes	ATP Yield
Glycolysis	Oxidation of glyceraldehyde-3-phosphate	2 NADH	5 ATP
	Direct phosphorylation (2 triose phosphate)		2 ATP
	Summary: $C_6H_{12}O_6 \longrightarrow$ 2 pyruvate + 2H_2O Glucose		**7 ATP**
Oxidation and Decarboxylation	2 Pyruvate $\longrightarrow$ 2 acetyl CoA	2 NADH	**5 ATP**
Citric Acid Cycle (two turns)	Oxidation of 2 isocitrate	2 NADH	5 ATP
	Oxidation of 2 α-ketoglutarate	2 NADH	5 ATP
	2 Direct phosphate transfers (2 GTP)		2 ATP
	Oxidation of 2 succinate	2 FADH_2	3 ATP
	Oxidation of 2 malate	2 NADH	5 ATP
	Summary: 2 Acetyl CoA $\longrightarrow$ 4CO_2 + 2H_2O		**20 ATP**
Total Yield	$C_6H_{12}O_6 + 6O_2 \longrightarrow 6CO_2 + 6H_2O$ Glucose		**32 ATP**

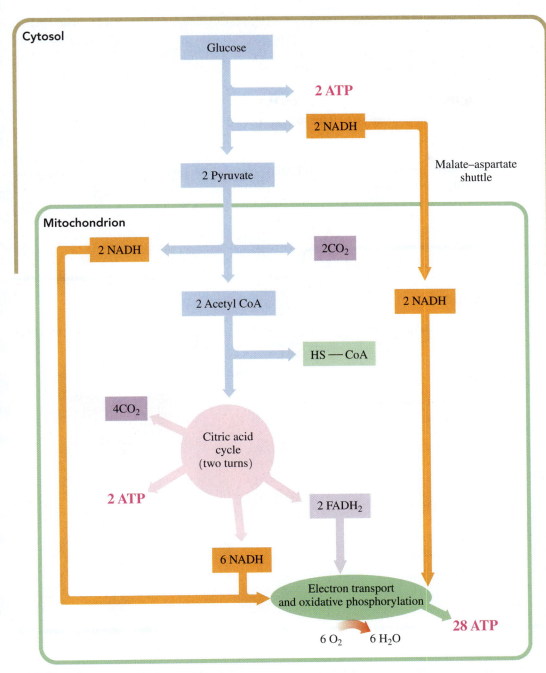

FIGURE 23.8 ▶ The complete oxidation of glucose from glycolysis, citric acid cycle, and electron transport yields a maximum of 32 ATP.

🔘 Which metabolic pathway produces most of the ATP from the oxidation of glucose?

▶ **SAMPLE PROBLEM 23.4 ATP Production**

As Natalie is walking on the treadmill during her fitness test, how many ATP are produced during each of the following oxidations?

a. two pyruvate to two acetyl CoA
b. one glucose to two acetyl CoA

SOLUTION

	Given	Need
ANALYZE THE PROBLEM	**a.** two pyruvate to two acetyl CoA	number of ATP
	b. one glucose to two acetyl CoA	number of ATP

a. The oxidation of two pyruvate to two acetyl CoA produces two NADH, which yields five ATP. We calculate this as:

$$2 \text{ NADH} \times 2.5 \text{ ATP/NADH} = 5 \text{ ATP}$$

b. Seven ATP are produced, two by direct phosphorylation and five from the two NADH, when glucose is oxidized to two pyruvate. Five ATP (from two NADH) are synthesized from the oxidation of two pyruvate to two acetyl CoA. Thus, a total of 12 ATP are produced when glucose is oxidized to yield two acetyl CoA.

STUDY CHECK 23.4

What are the sources of ATP for two turns of the citric acid cycle?

ANSWER

Six NADH provide 15 ATP, two $FADH_2$ provide three ATP, and two direct phosphate transfers provide two ATP.

 Chemistry Link to **Health**
Efficiency of ATP Production

In a laboratory, a calorimeter is used to measure the heat energy from the combustion of glucose. In a calorimeter, 1 mole of glucose produces 690 kcal.

$$C_6H_{12}O_6 + 6O_2 \longrightarrow 6CO_2 + 6H_2O + 690 \text{ kcal}$$

We can compare the amount of energy produced from 1 mole of glucose in a calorimeter with the ATP energy produced in the mitochondria from glucose. We use the energy of the hydrolysis of ATP (7.3 kcal/mole of ATP). Because 1 mole of glucose generates energy for up to 32 moles of ATP, the total energy from the oxidation of 1 mole of glucose in the cells would be 230 kcal/mole.

$$\frac{32 \text{ moles ATP}}{1 \text{ mole glucose}} \times \frac{7.3 \text{ kcal}}{1 \text{ mole ATP}} = 230 \text{ kcal}/1 \text{ mole of glucose}$$

Compared to the energy produced by burning glucose in a calorimeter, our cells are about 33% efficient in converting the total available chemical energy in glucose to ATP.

$$\frac{230 \text{ kcal (cells)}}{690 \text{ kcal (calorimeter)}} \times 100\% = 33\%$$

The rest of the energy from glucose produced during the oxidation of glucose in our cells is lost as heat.

Calorimeter	Cells
Energy produced by 1 mole of glucose (690 kcal)	Stored as ATP (230 kcal)
	Lost as heat (460 kcal)

QUESTIONS AND PROBLEMS

23.3 ATP Energy from Glucose

LEARNING GOAL Account for the ATP produced by the complete oxidation of glucose.

23.43 How many turns of the citric acid cycle are required to oxidize one molecule of glucose?

23.44 Under aerobic conditions, what is the maximum number of ATP that can be produced from one glucose molecule?

23.45 What is the energy yield in ATP associated with each of the following?
a. $NADH \longrightarrow NAD^+$
b. glucose $\longrightarrow$ 2 pyruvate
c. 2 pyruvate $\longrightarrow$ 2 acetyl CoA $+ 2CO_2$

23.46 What is the energy yield in ATP associated with each of the following?
a. $FADH_2 \longrightarrow FAD$
b. glucose $+ 6O_2 \longrightarrow 6CO_2 + 6H_2O$
c. acetyl CoA $\longrightarrow 2CO_2$

Clinical Update
Improving Natalie's Overall Fitness

Natalie's exercise stress test results indicate that she has a $V_{O_2 max}$ of 30 mL/kg min, which Angela, her exercise physiologist, classifies in the fair to poor range for her age. Natalie's blood oxygen measured 89%. The normal values for pulse oximeter readings are 95 to 100%, which means that Natalie's O_2 saturation is considered

Low-intensity exercises are used at the beginning of Natalie's exercise program.

low. Thus, Natalie does not have an adequate amount of O_2 in her blood, and may be hypoxic. This may be the reason she has noticed a shortness of breath and a dry cough. Her doctor diagnosed her with *interstitial lung disease*, which is scarring of the tissue of the lungs.

Angela teaches Natalie to inhale and exhale slower and deeper to fill the lungs with more air and thus more oxygen. Angela also develops a workout program with the goal of increasing Natalie's overall fitness level. They begin with low-intensity exercises that utilize smaller muscles instead of larger muscles, which require more O_2 and can deplete a significant amount of the O_2 in her blood. During the exercises, Angela continues to monitor Natalie's heart rate, blood O_2

level, and blood pressure to ensure that Natalie is exercising at a level that will enable her to become stronger without breaking down muscle due to a lack of oxygen.

As Natalie's $V_{O_2 max}$ improves, Angela modifies her workouts to include larger muscle groups. Eventually Natalie will take a second exercise stress test to check her progress.

℞ Clinical Applications

23.47 How would low oxygen levels affect the production of ATP?

23.48 If Natalie has low levels of NADH, how would her production of ATP be affected?

23.49 Natalie's low O_2 gives her only a 24% efficiency of ATP production from glucose. How many moles of ATP would she obtain from 25 g of glucose if glucose has a molar mass of 180.2 g/mole? (see Chemistry Link to Health "Efficiency of ATP Production")

23.50 Natalie's exercise program improves her O_2 blood level to give her a 30.% efficiency of ATP production from glucose. How many moles of ATP would she obtain from 25 g of glucose if glucose has a molar mass of 180.2 g/mole? (see Chemistry Link to Health "Efficiency of ATP Production")

CONCEPT MAP

METABOLISM AND ENERGY PRODUCTION

Acetyl CoA

enters the

Citric Acid Cycle

to yield

GTP   **NADH**   **FADH$_2$**   **CO$_2$**

that enter

Electron Transport

is converted to

provide energy for

ATP Synthase

provide

H$^+$ and Electrons

which produces

ATP

to

O$_2$

to produce

H$_2$O

CHAPTER REVIEW

23.1 The Citric Acid Cycle
LEARNING GOAL

Describe the oxidation of acetyl CoA in the citric acid cycle.

- In a sequence of reactions called the citric acid cycle, an acetyl group is combined with oxaloacetate to yield citrate.
- Citrate undergoes oxidation and decarboxylation to yield two CO_2, GTP, three NADH, and $FADH_2$ with the regeneration of oxaloacetate.
- The direct phosphate transfer of ADP by GTP yields ATP.

23.2 Electron Transport and ATP
LEARNING GOAL

Describe the transfer of hydrogen ions and electrons in electron transport and the process of oxidative phosphorylation in ATP synthesis.

- The reduced coenzymes NADH and $FADH_2$ from various metabolic pathways are oxidized to NAD^+ and FAD when their electrons are transferred through the electron transport system.

- The protein complexes in electron transport act as hydrogen ion pumps producing an H^+ gradient across the inner mitochondrial membrane.
- As the hydrogen ions return to the matrix by way of ATP synthase, energy is generated.
- This energy is used to drive the synthesis of ATP in a process known as oxidative phosphorylation.
- The ADP and ATP levels in the cells control the activity of electron transport.

23.3 ATP Energy from Glucose
LEARNING GOAL

Account for the ATP produced by the complete oxidation of glucose.

Calorimeter	Cells
Energy produced by 1 mole of glucose (690 kcal)	Stored as ATP (230 kcal)
	Lost as heat (460 kcal)

- The oxidation of NADH yields 2.5 ATP, and $FADH_2$ yields 1.5 ATP.
- The energy from the NADH produced in the cytosol is transferred into the matrix via a shuttle. The malate–aspartate shuttle is used in the heart and liver.
- Under aerobic conditions, the complete oxidation of glucose yields a maximum of 32 ATP from the oxidation of the reduced coenzymes NADH and $FADH_2$ by electron transport, oxidative phosphorylation, and from direct phosphate transfer.

SUMMARY OF KEY REACTIONS

The chapter sections to review are shown after the name of the reaction.

Citric Acid Cycle (23.1)

$$\text{Acetyl CoA} + 3NAD^+ + FAD + GDP + P_i + 2H_2O \longrightarrow$$
$$2CO_2 + 3NADH + 3H^+ + FADH_2 + GTP + HS{-}CoA$$

Electron Transport and Oxidative Phosphorylation (23.2)

$$NADH + H^+ \longrightarrow NAD^+ + 2.5\ ATP$$
$$FADH_2 \longrightarrow FAD + 1.5\ ATP$$

Phosphorylation of ADP (23.2)

$$ADP + P_i \longrightarrow ATP$$

Complete Oxidation of Glucose (23.3)

$$\underset{\text{Glucose}}{C_6H_{12}O_6} + 6O_2 + 32\ ADP + 32P_i \longrightarrow 6CO_2 + 6H_2O + 32\ ATP$$

KEY TERMS

ATP synthase An enzyme complex (V) that links the energy released by hydrogen ions returning to the matrix with the synthesis of ATP from ADP and P_i.

citric acid cycle A series of oxidation reactions in the mitochondria that converts acetyl CoA to CO_2 and yields NADH and $FADH_2$. It is also called the tricarboxylic acid cycle or the Krebs cycle.

coenzyme Q (CoQ) A mobile carrier that transfers electrons from NADH and $FADH_2$ to complex III.

cytochrome (cyt) An iron-containing protein that transfers electrons from $CoQH_2$ to oxygen.

electron transport A series of reactions in the mitochondria that transfers electrons from NADH and $FADH_2$ to electron carriers, and finally to O_2, which produces H_2O. Energy changes during these transfers provide energy for ATP synthesis.

hydrogen ion gradient A separation of charge across a membrane caused by the pumping of hydrogen ions from the matrix into the intermembrane space.

oxidative phosphorylation The synthesis of ATP using the energy of the hydrogen ions and electrons from the NADH and $FADH_2$ that enter electron transport to produce a hydrogen ion gradient.

⚛ CORE CHEMISTRY SKILLS

The chapter section containing each Core Chemistry Skill is shown in parentheses at the end of each heading.

Describing the Reactions in the Citric Acid Cycle (23.1)

- In the initial reaction of the citric acid cycle, an acetyl group combines with oxaloacetate to yield citrate.
- Citrate undergoes several reactions including oxidation, decarboxylation, and hydration to yield two CO_2, GTP, three NADH, one $FADH_2$, and to form another oxaloacetate.

Example: Identify the compound(s) in the citric acid cycle that undergo each of the following changes:
  a. loses a CO_2 molecule
  b. adds water

Answer: a. Isocitrate (6C) undergoes oxidation and decarboxylation to form α-ketoglutarate (5C), and α-ketoglutarate (5C) undergoes oxidation and decarboxylation to form succinyl CoA (4C).
  b. Fumarate, which has a double bond, adds an H_2O molecule to form malate.

Calculating the ATP Produced from Glucose (23.3)

- The reduced coenzymes NADH and $FADH_2$ from various metabolic pathways are oxidized to NAD^+ and FAD when their H^+ ions and electrons are transferred to the electron transport system.
- The energy released is used to synthesize ATP from ADP and P_i.

- The final acceptor, O_2, combines with H^+ ions and electrons to yield H_2O.
- The protein complexes I, III, and IV in electron transport move hydrogen ions into the intermembrane space, which produces the H^+ gradient.
- As the H^+ ions return to the matrix by way of ATP synthase, ATP energy is generated in a process known as oxidative phosphorylation.
- The oxidation of NADH yields 2.5 ATP, and the oxidation of $FADH_2$ yields 1.5 ATP.
- Under aerobic conditions, the complete oxidation of glucose yields a maximum of 32 ATP.

Example: Calculate the ATP produced from each of the following:
  a. one glucose to two pyruvate
  b. one NADH to one NAD^+
  c. complete oxidation of one glucose to $6CO_2$ and $6H_2O$

Answer: a. Glucose is converted to two pyruvate during glycolysis, which produces 2 ATP and 2 NADH for a total of 7 ATP.
  b. One NADH is converted to one NAD^+ in the electron transport system, which produces 2.5 ATP.
  c. Glucose is completely oxidized to $6CO_2$ and $6H_2O$ in glycolysis, citric acid cycle, and electron transport, which produces a maximum of 32 ATP.

UNDERSTANDING THE CONCEPTS

The chapter sections to review are given in parentheses at the end of each question.

23.51 Identify each of the following as a substance that is part of the citric acid cycle, electron transport, or both: (23.1, 23.2)
  a. succinate
  b. $CoQH_2$
  c. FAD
  d. cyt *c* (Fe^{2+})
  e. citrate

23.52 Identify each of the following as a substance that is part of the citric acid cycle, electron transport, or both: (23.1, 23.2)
  a. succinyl CoA
  b. acetyl CoA
  c. malate
  d. NAD^+
  e. α-ketoglutarate

23.53 Complete the names of the missing compounds in the citric acid cycle: (23.1)
  a. citrate ⟶ _____
  b. succinyl CoA ⟶ _____
  c. malate ⟶ _____

23.54 Complete the names of the missing compounds in the citric acid cycle: (23.1)
  a. oxaloacetate ⟶ _____
  b. fumarate ⟶ _____
  c. isocitrate ⟶ _____

23.55 Identify the reactant and product for each of the following enzymes in the citric acid cycle: (23.1)
  a. aconitase
  b. succinate dehydrogenase
  c. fumarase

23.56 Identify the reactant and product for each of the following enzymes in the citric acid cycle: (23.1)
  a. isocitrate dehydrogenase
  b. succinyl CoA synthetase
  c. malate dehydrogenase

23.57 For each of the given enzymes (**a** to **c**), indicate which of the following are needed: NAD^+, H_2O, FAD, GDP. (23.1)
  a. aconitase
  b. succinate dehydrogenase
  c. isocitrate dehydrogenase

23.58 For each of the given enzymes (**a** to **c**), indicate which of the following are needed: NAD^+, H_2O, FAD, GDP. (23.1)
  a. fumarase
  b. succinyl CoA synthetase
  c. malate dehydrogenase

23.59 Identify the type(s) of reaction(s)—(1) oxidation, (2) decarboxylation, (3) hydrolysis, (4) hydration—catalyzed by each of the following enzymes (**a** to **c**): (23.1)
  a. aconitase
  b. succinate dehydrogenase
  c. isocitrate dehydrogenase

23.60 Identify the type(s) of reaction(s)—(1) oxidation, (2) decarboxylation, (3) hydrolysis, (4) hydration—catalyzed by each of the following enzymes (**a** to **c**): (23.1)
  a. fumarase
  b. α-ketoglutarate dehydrogenase
  c. malate dehydrogenase

23.61 How many H^+ are pumped across the inner mitochondrial membrane when one NADH undergoes oxidation via electron transport? (23.2)

23.62 How many H^+ are pumped across the inner mitochondrial membrane when one $FADH_2$ undergoes oxidation via electron transport? (23.2)

23.63 What is the maximum number of ATP produced by energy generated when electrons flow from NADH to oxygen (O_2)? (23.3)

23.64 What is the maximum number of ATP produced by energy generated when electrons flow from $FADH_2$ to oxygen (O_2)? (23.3)

ADDITIONAL QUESTIONS AND PROBLEMS

23.65 What is the main function of the citric acid cycle in energy production? (23.1)

23.66 Most metabolic pathways are not considered cycles. Why the citric acid cycle is considered a metabolic cycle? (23.1)

23.67 If there are no reactions in the citric acid cycle that use oxygen, O_2, why does the cycle operate only in aerobic conditions? (23.1)

23.68 What products of the citric acid cycle are needed for electron transport? (23.1)

23.69 Identify the compounds in the citric acid cycle that have the following: (23.1)
  a. six carbon atoms   **b.** five carbon atoms
  c. a keto group

23.70 Identify the compounds in the citric acid cycle that have the following: (23.1)
  a. four carbon atoms   **b.** a hydroxyl group
  c. a carbon–carbon double bond

23.71 In which reaction of the citric acid cycle does each of the following occur? (23.1)
  a. A five-carbon keto acid is decarboxylated.
  b. A carbon–carbon double bond is hydrated.
  c. NAD^+ is reduced.
  d. A secondary hydroxyl group is oxidized.

23.72 In which reaction of the citric acid cycle does each of the following occur? (23.1)
  a. FAD is reduced.
  b. A six-carbon keto acid is decarboxylated.
  c. A carbon–carbon double bond is formed.
  d. GDP undergoes direct phosphate transfer.

23.73 Indicate the coenzyme(s) for each of the following reactions: (23.1)
  a. isocitrate $\longrightarrow$ α-ketoglutarate
  b. α-ketoglutarate $\longrightarrow$ succinyl CoA

23.74 Indicate the coenzyme(s) for each of the following reactions: (23.1)
  a. succinate $\longrightarrow$ fumarate
  b. malate $\longrightarrow$ oxaloacetate

23.75 How does each of the following regulate the citric acid cycle? (23.1)
  a. high levels of NADH
  b. high levels of ATP

23.76 How does each of the following regulate the citric acid cycle? (23.1)
  a. high levels of ADP
  b. low levels of NADH

23.77 At which complexes in the electron transport system are hydrogen ions pumped into the intermembrane space? (23.2)

23.78 What is the effect of hydrogen ion accumulation in the intermembrane space? (23.2)

23.79 Which complex in electron transport is inhibited by each of the following? (23.2)
  a. Amytal and rotenone   **b.** antimycin A
  c. cyanide and carbon monoxide

23.80 a. When an inhibitor blocks electron transport, how are the coenzymes that precede the blocked site affected? (23.2)
  b. When an inhibitor blocks electron transport, how are the coenzymes that follow the blocked site affected?

23.81 In the chemiosmotic model, how is energy provided to synthesize ATP? (23.2)

23.82 Where does the synthesis of ATP take place in electron transport? (23.2)

23.83 Why do hydrogen ions tend to leave the intermembrane space and return to the matrix within a mitochondrion? (23.2)

23.84 Why do the enzyme complexes that pump hydrogen ions extend across the mitochondrial membrane from the matrix to the intermembrane space? (23.2)

23.85 Where is ATP synthase for oxidative phosphorylation located in the cell? (23.2)

23.86 How does the NADH generated in the cytosol during glycolysis get moved into the matrix? (23.3)

23.87 How many ATP are produced when glucose is oxidized to pyruvate compared to when glucose is oxidized to CO_2 and H_2O? (23.3)

23.88 Considering the efficiency of ATP synthesis, how many kilocalories of energy would be conserved from the complete oxidation of 4.0 moles of glucose? (23.3)

23.89 How is the energy from the hydrogen ion gradient utilized by ATP synthase? (23.2)

23.90 In electron transport, would the solution in the space between the outer and inner mitochondrial membrane be more or less acidic than the solution in the matrix? (23.2)

23.91 Why would a bear that is hibernating have more brown fat than one that is active? (23.2)

23.92 Why would an animal that lives in a warm climate have less brown fat than a similar animal that lives in a cold climate? (23.2)

CHALLENGE QUESTIONS

The following groups of questions are related to the topics in this chapter. However, they do not all follow the chapter order, and they require you to combine concepts and skills from several sections. These questions will help you increase your critical thinking skills and prepare for your next exam.

23.93 Using the value 7.3 kcal/mole for ATP, how many kilocalories can be produced from the ATP provided by the reaction of 1 mole of glucose in each of the following? (23.1, 23.3)
  a. glycolysis
  b. oxidation of pyruvate to acetyl CoA
  c. citric acid cycle
  d. complete oxidation to CO_2 and H_2O

23.94 In a calorimeter, the combustion of 1 mole of glucose produces 690 kcal. What percentage of ATP energy is produced from 1 mole of glucose by each of the reactions in problem 23.93 **a** to **d**? (23.1, 23.3)

23.95 What does it mean to say that the cell is 33% efficient in storing the energy from the complete combustion of glucose? (23.3)

23.96 If acetyl CoA has a molar mass of 809 g/mole, how many moles of ATP are produced when 1.0 μg of acetyl CoA completes the citric acid cycle? (23.3)

Clinical Applications

23.97 A person's basal metabolic rate (BMR) gives the number of kilocalories utilized in one day to maintain weight. To lose weight, caloric intake needs to be lower or activity level can be increased. The resting BMR can be calculated in kilocalories by the following formula: (23.3)

Women: BMR kcal = 655 + (4.35 × weight lb) + (4.70 × height in.) − (4.70 × age in years)
  a. If a woman weighs 115 lb, is 5 ft 4 in. tall, and is 21 years old, what is her basal metabolic rate, rounded to the nearest 10 kilocalories?
  b. If the molar mass of ATP is 507 g/mole, how many kilograms of ATP is used in one day?

23.98 A person's basal metabolic rate (BMR) gives the number of kilocalories utilized in one day to maintain weight. To lose weight, caloric intake needs to be lower or activity level can be increased. The resting BMR can be calculated in kilocalories by the following formula: (23.3)

Men: BMR kcal = 66 + (6.23 × weight lb) + (12.7 × height in.) − (6.80 × age in years)
  a. If a man weighs 184 lb, is 6 ft 1 in. tall, and is 32 years old, what is his basal metabolic rate, rounded to the nearest 10 kilocalories?
  b. If the molar mass of ATP is 507 g/mole, how many kilograms of ATP is used in one day?

ANSWERS TO SELECTED QUESTIONS AND PROBLEMS

23.1 Krebs cycle and tricarboxylic acid cycle

23.3 $2CO_2$, 3 NADH + 3H$^+$, FADH$_2$, GTP (ATP), and HS—CoA

23.5 a. Two reactions, reactions 3 and 4, involve oxidation and decarboxylation.
  b. Reaction 6 involves dehydration.
  c. Reactions 3, 4, and 8 involve reduction of NAD$^+$.

23.7 a. citrate and isocitrate
  b. A carbon atom is lost as CO_2 in decarboxylation.
  c. α-ketoglutarate
  d. reactions 3 and 8

23.9 a. citrate synthase
  b. succinate dehydrogenase and aconitase
  c. fumarase

23.11 a. NAD$^+$ **b.** FAD

23.13 Isocitrate dehydrogenase and α-ketoglutarate dehydrogenase are allosteric enzymes.

23.15 High levels of ADP increase the rate of the citric acid cycle.

23.17 malate dehydrogenase

23.19 oxidized

23.21 a. oxidation   **b.** reduction

23.23 NADH

23.25 FADH$_2$, CoQ, cytochrome c (Fe^{3+})

23.27 The mobile carrier CoQ transfers electrons from complex I to complex III.

23.29 NADH transfers electrons to complex I to give NAD$^+$.

23.31 a. $NADH + H^+ + CoQ \longrightarrow NAD^+ + CoQH_2$
b. $CoQH_2 + 2cyt\ c\ (Fe^{3+}) \longrightarrow$
$$CoQ + 2cyt\ c\ (Fe^{2+}) + 2H^+$$

23.33 In oxidative phosphorylation, the energy from the oxidation reactions in electron transport is used to synthesize ATP from ADP and P_i.

23.35 As hydrogen ions return to the lower energy environment in the matrix, they pass through ATP synthase where they release energy to drive the synthesis of ATP.

23.37 Glycolysis and the citric acid cycle produce the reduced coenzymes NADH and $FADH_2$, which enter electron transport and release hydrogen ions and electrons that are used to generate energy for the synthesis of ATP.

23.39 If CN^- binds to the heme of a cytochrome, electrons cannot reduce Fe^{3+} to Fe^{2+} and will not be transported, stopping electron transport.

23.41 Because dinitrophenol induces thermogenesis and inhibits ATP synthase, it raises body temperature to unsafe levels and can cause constant sweating.

23.43 Two. In glycolysis, one glucose molecule forms two pyruvate, which oxidize to give 2 acetyl CoA.

23.45 a. 2.5 ATP   **b.** 7 ATP   **c.** 5 ATP

23.47 Electron transport requires oxygen. A low level of oxygen will decrease the activity of electron transport and the formation of ATP.

23.49 3.2 moles of ATP

23.51 a. citric acid cycle   **b.** electron transport
c. both   **d.** electron transport
e. citric acid cycle

23.53 a. isocitrate   **b.** succinate
c. oxaloacetate

23.55 a. citrate, isocitrate   **b.** succinate, fumarate
c. fumarate, malate

23.57 a. Aconitase uses H_2O.
b. Succinate dehydrogenase uses FAD.
c. Isocitrate dehydrogenase uses NAD^+.

23.59 a. (4) hydration reaction
b. (1) oxidation reaction
c. (1) oxidation and (2) decarboxylation reaction

23.61 $10\ H^+$

23.63 2.5 ATP

23.65 The oxidation reactions of the citric acid cycle produce a source of reduced coenzymes for electron transport and ATP synthesis.

23.67 The oxidized coenzymes NAD^+ and FAD needed for the citric acid cycle are regenerated by electron transport, which requires oxygen.

23.69 a. citrate, isocitrate   **b.** α-ketoglutarate
c. α-ketoglutarate, succinyl CoA, oxaloacetate

23.71 a. In reaction 4, α-ketoglutarate, a five-carbon keto acid, is decarboxylated.
b. In reactions 2 and 7, double bonds in aconitate and fumarate are hydrated.
c. NAD^+ is reduced in reactions 3, 4, and 8.
d. In reactions 3 and 8, a secondary hydroxyl group in isocitrate and malate is oxidized.

23.73 a. NAD^+ **b.** NAD^+ and CoA

23.75 a. High levels of NADH inhibit isocitrate dehydrogenase and α-ketoglutarate dehydrogenase to slow the rate of the citric acid cycle.
b. High levels of ATP inhibit isocitrate dehydrogenase to slow the rate of the citric acid cycle.

23.77 complexes I, III, and IV

23.79 a. electron flow from complex I to CoQ
b. electron flow from complex III to cyt c
c. electron flow from cytochrome c to complex IV

23.81 Energy is released as hydrogen ions flow through ATP synthase back to the matrix and utilized for the synthesis of ATP.

23.83 Hydrogen ions flow through ATP synthase into the matrix where the H^+ concentration is lower.

23.85 ATP synthase is a protein complex, which spans the inner mitochondrial membrane.

23.87 The oxidation of glucose to pyruvate produces 7 ATP, whereas the oxidation of glucose to CO_2 and H_2O produces a maximum of 32 ATP.

23.89 As hydrogen ions from the hydrogen ion gradient move through the ATP synthase to return to the matrix, energy is released and used to synthesize ATP by ATP synthase.

23.91 A hibernating bear has more brown fat because it can be used during the winter for heat rather than ATP energy.

23.93 a. 51 kcal   **b.** 37 kcal
c. 150 kcal   **d.** 230 kcal

23.95 If the combustion of glucose produces 690 kcal, but only 230 kcal (from 32 ATP) in cells, the efficiency of glucose use in the cells is 230 kcal/690 kcal or 33%.

23.97 a. 1360 kcal   **b.** 94.5 kg

24

Metabolic Pathways for Lipids and Amino Acids

LUKE IS 48 YEARS OLD AND WORKS AS A PARAMEDIC.

Recently, blood work from his annual physical examination indicated a plasma cholesterol level of 256 mg/dL. Clinically, cholesterol levels are considered elevated if the total plasma cholesterol level exceeds 200 mg/dL. Luke's doctor ordered a liver profile that showed elevated liver enzymes: *Alanine transaminase* (ALT) 282 Units/L (normal ALT 5 to 35 Units/L) and *aspartate transaminase* (AST) 226 Units/L (normal AST 5 to 50 Units/L). Luke's doctor ordered a medication to lower Luke's plasma cholesterol.

During Luke's career as a paramedic, he was exposed several times to blood and was accidently stuck by a needle containing infected blood. Luke takes 8 to 10 ibuprofen tablets per month for pain and uses herbs, garlic, ginkgo, and antioxidants. Although herbs, antioxidants, and ibuprofen can cause liver inflammation, they would not usually cause the elevation of liver enzymes reported in Luke's blood tests. A hepatitis profile showed that Luke was positive for antibodies to both hepatitis B and C. His doctor diagnosed Luke with *chronic hepatitis C virus* (HCV) infection. Hepatitis C is an infection caused by a virus that attacks the liver and leads to inflammation. Most people infected with the hepatitis C virus have no symptoms. Hepatitis C is usually passed by contact with contaminated blood or by needles shared during illegal drug use. In *autoimmune hepatitis*, the immune system of a person's body destroys cells in the liver. As part of his treatment, Luke attended a class on living with hepatitis C given by Belinda, a public health nurse.

CAREER Public Health Nurse (PHN)

Hepatitis C virus is a common cause of liver disease and a major health problem worldwide. Patients diagnosed with HCV require lifelong monitoring and are usually cared for by specialist teams including a public health nurse. A public health nurse works in public health departments, correctional facilities, occupational health facilities, schools, and organizations that aim to improve health at the community level. They often focus on high-risk populations such as the elderly, the homeless, teen mothers, and those at risk for a communicable disease such as hepatitis.

LOOKING AHEAD

24.1   Digestion of
        Triacylglycerols 862
24.2   Oxidation of Fatty
        Acids 865
24.3   ATP and Fatty Acid
        Oxidation 870
        **Chemistry Link to
        Health** *Stored Fat and
        Obesity* 871
24.4   Ketogenesis and Ketone
        Bodies 873
        **Chemistry Link to
        Health** *Diabetes and
        Ketone Bodies* 875
24.5   Fatty Acid Synthesis 876
24.6   Degradation of Proteins
        and Amino Acids 880
24.7   Urea Cycle 884
24.8   Fates of the Carbon Atoms
        from Amino Acids 886
24.9   Synthesis of Amino
        Acids 888
        **Chemistry Link to
        Health** *Phenylketonuria
        (PKU)* 890
        Clinical Applications 865,
        873, 875, 880, 886, 892, 896
        Clinical Update *Treatment
        of Luke's Hepatitis C* 892

C arbohydrate metabolism involves glucose as the primary fuel for the synthesis of ATP. However, lipids and proteins also play an important role in metabolism and energy production. In this chapter, we look at how the digestion of lipids produces fatty acids and glycerol and how the digestion of proteins yields amino acids. When our caloric intake exceeds the metabolic needs of our bodies, excess carbohydrates and fatty acids are converted to triacylglycerols and added to our fat cells of adipose tissue. Almost all of our stored energy is in the form of triacylglycerols in our fat cells, which can store unlimited quantities of fat. This fact has become quite apparent in the large number of people in the United States that are considered obese. We will see that the fatty acids in triacylglycerols produce more ATP when used for energy than a glucose molecule; however, they are not the preferred energy source of our bodies. This is why it is more difficult to lose weight (burn fat) than to store it.

The digestion and degradation of dietary proteins as well as body proteins provide amino acids, which are needed to synthesize nitrogen-containing compounds in our cells, such as new proteins and nucleic acids. Although amino acids are not considered a primary source of fuel, energy can be extracted from amino acids if glycogen and fat reserves have been depleted. When a person is fasting or starving, the breakdown of the body's own proteins eventually destroys essential body tissues, particularly muscles.

CHAPTER READINESS*

⚛ CORE CHEMISTRY SKILLS

- Identifying Fatty Acids (17.2)
- Drawing the Zwitterion for an Amino Acid (19.1)
- Identifying Important Coenzymes in Metabolism (22.3)
- Identifying the Compounds in Glycolysis (22.4)

- Identifying the Compounds and Enzymes in Glycogenesis and Glycogenolysis (22.6)
- Describing the Reactions in the Citric Acid Cycle (23.1)
- Calculating the ATP Produced from Glucose (23.3)

*These Core Chemistry Skills from previous chapters are listed here for your review as you proceed to the new material in this chapter.

LEARNING GOAL

Describe the sites and products obtained from the digestion of triacylglycerols.

24.1 Digestion of Triacylglycerols

Our adipose tissue is made of fat cells called *adipocytes*, which store triacylglycerols (see Figure 24.1). Let's compare the amount of energy stored in the fat cells to the energy from glucose, glycogen, and protein. A typical 70-kg (150-lb) person has about 140 000 kcal of energy stored as fat, 24 000 kcal as protein, 720 kcal as glycogen reserves, and 80 kcal as blood glucose. Therefore, the energy available from stored fats is about 85% of the total energy available in the body. Thus, body fat is our major source of stored energy.

Digestion of Dietary Fats

Just as oil and water do not mix, dietary fats do not readily mix with the aqueous environment of the small intestine where digestion begins. Natural emulsifiers, called bile salts containing hydrophobic and hydrophilic regions, are secreted from the gallbladder into the small intestine. These molecules are able to interact with both the hydrophobic fat

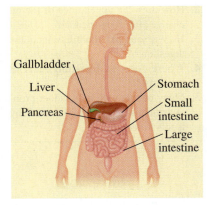

FIGURE 24.1 ▶ The fat cells (adipocytes) that make up adipose tissue are capable of storing unlimited quantities of triacylglycerols.

Q What are some sources of fats in our diet?

$$CH_2-O-\overset{\overset{\textstyle O}{\|}}{C}-(CH_2)_{16}-CH_3$$
$$CH-O-\overset{\overset{\textstyle O}{\|}}{C}-(CH_2)_{16}-CH_3$$
$$CH_2-O-\overset{\overset{\textstyle O}{\|}}{C}-(CH_2)_{16}-CH_3$$

A triacylglycerol

globules and the aqueous solution in the small intestine. In a process called *emulsification*, the bile salts break the fat globules into smaller droplets called *micelles* (pronounced *my-cells*). Emulsification also occurs in the creation of some sauces like a creamy salad dressing where oil and water are mixed with egg which provides a phospholipid emulsifier.

Next, *pancreatic lipases* released from the pancreas hydrolyze triacylglycerols to yield monoacylglycerols and fatty acids, which are absorbed into the intestinal lining, where they recombine to form triacylglycerols. The resulting nonpolar compounds are coated with phospholipids and proteins to form lipoproteins called *chylomicrons*, which makes them polar and soluble in the aqueous environment of the lymph and bloodstream (see Figure 24.2).

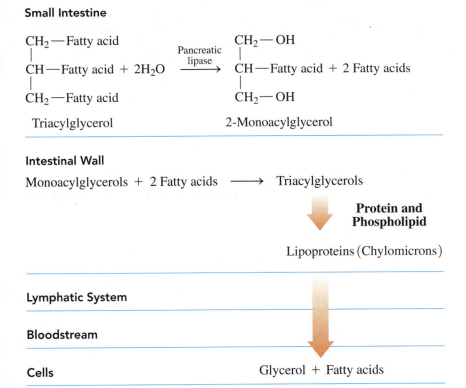

Small Intestine

$$\begin{array}{l}CH_2-\text{Fatty acid}\\CH-\text{Fatty acid} + 2H_2O\\CH_2-\text{Fatty acid}\end{array} \xrightarrow[\text{lipase}]{\text{Pancreatic}} \begin{array}{l}CH_2-OH\\CH-\text{Fatty acid} + \text{2 Fatty acids}\\CH_2-OH\end{array}$$

Triacylglycerol   2-Monoacylglycerol

Intestinal Wall

Monoacylglycerols + 2 Fatty acids $\longrightarrow$ Triacylglycerols

Protein and Phospholipid

Lipoproteins (Chylomicrons)

Lymphatic System

Bloodstream

Cells   Glycerol + Fatty acids

FIGURE 24.2 ▶ The digestion of fats begins in the small intestine when bile salts emulsify fats that undergo hydrolysis to monoacylglycerols and fatty acids.

Q What kinds of enzymes are secreted from the pancreas into the small intestine to hydrolyze triacylglycerols?

In the cells, lipases hydrolyze the triacylglycerols to yield glycerol and free fatty acids, which can be used for energy production. Fatty acids, which are the preferred fuel of the heart, are oxidized to acetyl CoA molecules for ATP synthesis. However, the brain and red blood cells cannot utilize fatty acids. Fatty acids cannot diffuse across the blood–brain barrier, and red blood cells have no mitochondria, which are where fatty acids are oxidized. Therefore, glucose and glycogen are the primary sources of energy for the brain and red blood cells.

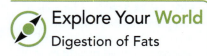

Explore Your World
Digestion of Fats

Place some water and several drops of vegetable oil in a container with a top. Cap the container and shake. Observe. Add a few drops of liquid soap or detergent to the oil and water, cap the container again, and shake. Observe.

Questions

1. Why does the oil separate from the water?
2. How does the appearance of the oil change after soap is added?
3. How is soap like the bile salts in the digestion of fats?
4. Where does fat digestion occur in the body?
5. Many people with gallbladder problems take supplemental lipase. Why is this necessary?

Utilization of Fat Stores

When blood glucose is depleted and glycogen stores are low, the process of fat utilization is stimulated when the hormones glucagon or epinephrine are secreted into the bloodstream where they bind to receptors on the membrane of adipose tissue. A hormone-sensitive lipase within the fat cells catalyzes the hydrolysis of triacylglycerols to glycerol and free fatty acids, which then diffuse into the bloodstream and bind with plasma proteins (albumin) to be transported to the tissues, muscles, and fat cells. Most of the glycerol goes into the liver, where it is metabolized.

Metabolism of Glycerol

Enzymes in the liver convert glycerol to dihydroxyacetone phosphate in two steps. In the first step, glycerol is phosphorylated using ATP to yield glycerol-3-phosphate. In the second step, the secondary hydroxyl group is oxidized to yield dihydroxyacetone phosphate, which is an intermediate in several metabolic pathways including glycolysis and gluconeogenesis.

$$CH_2-OH$$
$$CH-OH \quad + \quad \boxed{ATP} \quad \xrightarrow{\text{Glycerol kinase}} \quad CH_2-OH$$
$$CH_2-OH$$

Glycerol $+$ ATP → Glycerol-3-phosphate $+$ ADP

Glycerol-3-phosphate $+$ NAD⁺ → Dihydroxyacetone phosphate $+$ NADH + H⁺ (via Glycerol-3-phosphate dehydrogenase)

→ Glycolysis   Gluconeogenesis

The overall reaction for the metabolism of glycerol is written as follows:

Glycerol $+$ ATP $+$ NAD$^+$ ⟶ dihydroxyacetone phosphate $+$ ADP $+$ NADH $+$ H$^+$

▶ **SAMPLE PROBLEM 24.1** **Fats and Digestion**

Answer each of the following for the digestion of triacylglycerols:

a. Where does it take place?
b. What enzyme is involved?
c. What are the products of digestion?

SOLUTION

a. the small intestine
b. pancreatic lipase
c. monoacylglycerols and fatty acids

STUDY CHECK 24.1

How are the nonpolar triacylglycerols emulsified so that they can be digested?

ANSWER

The triacylglycerols entering the small intestine are emulsified by bile salts into smaller droplets of fat that can react with the lipases.

QUESTIONS AND PROBLEMS

24.1 Digestion of Triacylglycerols

LEARNING GOAL Describe the sites and products obtained from the digestion of triacylglycerols.

24.1 What is the role of bile salts in lipid digestion?

24.2 How are insoluble triacylglycerols transported to the tissues and fat cells?

24.3 When are fats released from fat stores?

24.4 What happens to the glycerol produced from the hydrolysis of triacylglycerols in adipose tissues?

24.5 How is glycerol converted to an intermediate of glycolysis?

24.6 How can glycerol be used to synthesize glucose?

Ⓡ Clinical Applications

A person with Duchenne muscular dystrophy cannot convert glycerol to glycerol-3-phosphate.

24.7 What enzyme would be defective?

24.8 Why would a person with this enzyme deficiency have high blood glycerol levels?

24.2 Oxidation of Fatty Acids

A large amount of energy is obtained when fatty acids undergo oxidation in the mitochondria to yield acetyl CoA. In fat catabolism, fatty acids undergo **beta oxidation** (**β oxidation**), which removes two-carbon segments containing the alpha and beta carbon from the carboxyl end of the fatty acid.

LEARNING GOAL

Describe the metabolic pathway of β oxidation.

$$\underset{\substack{\beta \text{ oxidation}\\ \text{occurs here}}}{\downarrow}$$

$$CH_3-(CH_2)_{14}-\underset{\beta}{CH_2}-\underset{\alpha}{CH_2}-\overset{\displaystyle O}{\overset{\displaystyle \|}{C}}-OH$$

Stearic acid

Each cycle in β oxidation produces an acetyl CoA and a fatty acid that is shorter by two carbons. The cycle repeats until the original fatty acid is completely degraded to two-carbon units that form acetyl CoA that can enter the citric acid cycle in the same way as the acetyl CoA derived from glucose.

Fatty Acid Activation

The fatty acids, which are produced in the cytosol, must be transported through the inner mitochondrial membrane before they can undergo β oxidation in the matrix. In an *activation* process using ATP and catalyzed by *acyl CoA synthetase*, a fatty acid is combined with CoA to yield a high-energy fatty acyl CoA. The energy released by the hydrolysis of two high-energy bonds of ATP is used to drive the reaction, which gives AMP and two inorganic phosphates ($2P_i$). In our discussion of fatty acid activation, we will use the terms *acyl CoA* and *acetyl CoA*. The term *acyl* refers to a long-chain fatty acid that is bonded to coenzyme A, whereas *acetyl* refers to a two-carbon acetyl group that is bonded to coenzyme A.

$$CH_3-(CH_2)_n-CH_2-CH_2-\overset{\displaystyle O}{\overset{\displaystyle \|}{C}}-OH + ATP + HS-CoA \xrightarrow{\substack{\text{Acyl CoA}\\ \text{synthetase}}}$$

Fatty acid

$$CH_3-(CH_2)_n-CH_2-CH_2-\overset{\displaystyle O}{\overset{\displaystyle \|}{C}}-S-CoA + AMP + 2P_i + H_2O$$

Fatty acyl CoA

Transport of Fatty Acyl CoA into the Mitochondria

The acyl CoA molecules formed in the cytosol cannot pass through the inner mitochondrial membrane into the matrix where β oxidation of fatty acids takes place. A transport system called the *carnitine shuttle* is used to carry fatty acids into the mitochondria. In the cytosol, *carnitine acyltransferase* catalyzes the transfer of a fatty acyl group to the hydroxyl group of carnitine to produce fatty acyl carnitine, which passes through the inner mitochondrial membrane into the matrix.

In the mitochondrial matrix, another *carnitine acyltransferase* catalyzes the reverse reaction that transfers the fatty acyl group to CoA to reform fatty acyl CoA. The carnitine is released and returns to the cytosol. Thus, the carnitine shuttle moves fatty acyl CoA from the cytosol into the matrix where the fatty acid can undergo β oxidation (see Figure 24.3).

FIGURE 24.3 ▶ In the carnitine shuttle system, fatty acids are activated and transported from the cytosol through the inner mitochondrial membrane into the matrix.

Q Why is carnitine needed to transport a fatty acid into the matrix?

Reactions of the β Oxidation Cycle

In the mitochondrial matrix, fatty acyl CoA molecules undergo β oxidation, which is a cycle of four reactions that convert the $-CH_2-$ of the β-carbon (carbon 3) in a long-chain fatty acyl group into a keto group. Once the β-keto group is formed, a two-carbon acetyl CoA is split from the original fatty acyl chain, which gives a shortened fatty acyl chain.

Reaction 1   Oxidation

In the first step of β oxidation, *acyl CoA dehydrogenase* catalyzes the transfer of hydrogen atoms from the α- and β-carbons of the activated fatty acid to form a trans carbon–carbon double bond and the reduced coenzyme $FADH_2$. Recall that oxidation can be the addition of oxygen *or* removal of hydrogen.

$$CH_3-(CH_2)_n-\underset{\beta}{CH_2}-\underset{\alpha}{CH_2}-\overset{\displaystyle O}{\overset{\|}{C}}-S-CoA \ + \ \boxed{FAD} \ \xrightarrow{\underset{\text{dehydrogenase}}{\text{Acyl CoA}}} \ CH_3-(CH_2)_n-\underset{\underset{H}{|}}{\overset{\overset{H}{|}}{\underset{\beta}{C}}}=\underset{\alpha}{C}-\overset{\displaystyle O}{\overset{\|}{C}}-S-CoA \ + \ \boxed{FADH_2}$$

Fatty acyl CoA   *trans*-Enoyl CoA

Reaction 2   Hydration

In the second step, a hydration reaction catalyzed by *enoyl CoA hydratase* adds the components of water to the trans double bond, which forms a hydroxyl group (—OH) on the β-carbon.

$$CH_3-(CH_2)_n-\underset{\underset{H}{|}}{\overset{\overset{H}{|}}{\underset{\beta}{C}}}=\underset{\alpha}{C}-\overset{\displaystyle O}{\overset{\|}{C}}-S-CoA \ + \ H_2O \ \xrightarrow{\underset{\text{hydratase}}{\text{Enoyl CoA}}} \ CH_3-(CH_2)_n-\underset{\underset{H}{|}}{\overset{\overset{OH}{|}}{\underset{\beta}{C}}}-\underset{\underset{H}{|}}{\overset{\overset{H}{|}}{\underset{\alpha}{C}}}-\overset{\displaystyle O}{\overset{\|}{C}}-S-CoA$$

trans-Enoyl CoA   3-Hydroxyacyl CoA

Reaction 3   Oxidation

In the third step, the secondary hydroxyl group on the β-carbon, which is carbon 3, is oxidized by *3-hydroxyacyl CoA dehydrogenase* to yield a ketone. The hydrogen atoms removed in the oxidation are transferred to NAD$^+$ to yield a β-keto or 3-keto group and the reduced coenzyme NADH.

$$CH_3-(CH_2)_n-\underset{\underset{H}{|}}{\overset{\overset{OH}{|}}{\underset{\beta}{C}}}-\underset{\underset{H}{|}}{\overset{\overset{H}{|}}{\underset{\alpha}{C}}}-\overset{\displaystyle O}{\overset{\|}{C}}-S-CoA \ + \ \boxed{NAD^+} \ \xrightarrow{\underset{\text{dehydrogenase}}{\text{3-Hydroxyacyl CoA}}} \ CH_3-(CH_2)_n-\underset{\beta}{\overset{\overset{\displaystyle O}{\|}}{C}}-\underset{\underset{H}{|}}{\overset{\overset{H}{|}}{\underset{\alpha}{C}}}-\overset{\displaystyle O}{\overset{\|}{C}}-S-CoA$$

3-Hydroxyacyl CoA β-Ketoacyl CoA $+$ $\boxed{NADH + H^+}$

Reaction 4   Cleavage (Thiolysis)

In the fourth step of β oxidation, the C_α—C_β bond is cleaved by *β-ketoacyl CoA thiolase* to yield a two-carbon acetyl CoA and a new fatty acyl CoA that is shortened by two carbon atoms. This new, shorter fatty acyl CoA repeats the four steps of the β oxidation cycle until the original fatty acid is completely degraded to two-carbon units of acetyl CoA.

$$CH_3-(CH_2)_n-\underset{\beta}{\overset{\overset{\displaystyle O}{\|}}{C}}-\underset{\underset{H}{|}}{\overset{\overset{H}{|}}{\underset{\alpha}{C}}}-\overset{\displaystyle O}{\overset{\|}{C}}-S-CoA \ + \ HS-CoA \ \xrightarrow{\underset{\text{thiolase}}{\beta\text{-Ketoacyl CoA}}}$$

β-Ketoacyl CoA

$$CH_3-(CH_2)_{n-2}-\overset{\displaystyle O}{\overset{\|}{C}}-S-CoA \ + \ CH_3-\overset{\displaystyle O}{\overset{\|}{C}}-S-CoA$$

Fatty acyl CoA   Acetyl CoA
(2 C atoms shorter)

Fatty Acid Length Determines Cycle Repeats

The number of carbon atoms in a fatty acid determines the number of times the cycle repeats and the number of acetyl CoA units it produces. For example, the complete β oxidation of capric acid (C_{10}) produces five acetyl CoA groups, which is equal to one-half the number of carbon atoms in the chain. Because the final turn of the cycle produces two acetyl CoA units, the total number of times the cycle repeats is one less than the total number of acetyl groups it produces. Therefore, the C_{10} fatty acid goes through the cycle four times (see Figure 24.4).

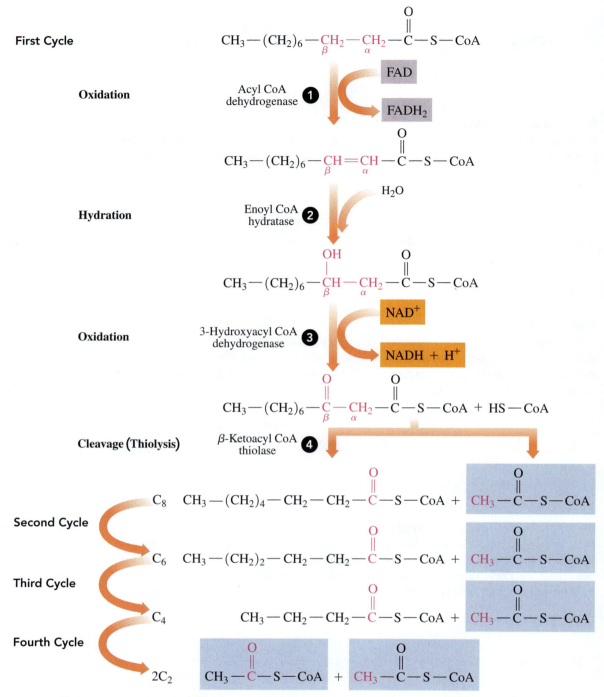

FIGURE 24.4 ▶ Capric acid (C_{10}) undergoes four oxidation cycles that repeat reactions 1 to 4 and yield five acetyl CoA molecules, four NADH, and four $FADH_2$.

❓ How many NADH and $FADH_2$ molecules are produced in one turn of the fatty acid cycle of β oxidation?

For capric acid, the overall equation for the four cycles of β oxidation is

Caproyl (C_{10}) CoA + 4HS—CoA + 4NAD$^+$ + 4FAD $\longrightarrow$

5acetyl CoA + 4NADH + 4H$^+$ + 4FADH$_2$

Most fatty acids have an even numbers of carbon atoms. However, some odd-numbered chains of fatty acids are produced by other organisms and by bacteria. Essentially an odd-numbered fatty acid goes through the same four steps of β oxidation until the final cycle, in which the remaining fatty acyl CoA is cleaved, to yield a propionyl CoA (C_3 group) and an acetyl CoA.

Fatty Acid	Number of Carbon Atoms	Number of Acetyl CoA	Number of β Oxidation Cycles
Myristic acid	14	7	6
Palmitic acid	16	8	7
Stearic acid	18	9	8

Oxidation of Unsaturated Fatty Acids

We have shown the β oxidation sequence of reactions for saturated fatty acids with an even number of carbon atoms. However, the fats in our diets, particularly the oils, contain unsaturated fatty acids, which have one or more cis double bonds. The hydration reaction adds water to trans double bonds, not cis. When the double bond in an unsaturated fatty acid is ready for hydration, an isomerase forms a trans double bond between the α- and β-carbon atoms, which is the arrangement needed for the hydration reaction.

Because the isomerization provides the trans double bond for the hydration in reaction 2, it bypasses the first reaction. Therefore, the energy released by the β oxidation of an unsaturated fatty acid is slightly less because no $FADH_2$ is produced in that cycle. For unsaturated fatty acids, we will decrease the total $FADH_2$ yield by one for each double bond.

▶ **SAMPLE PROBLEM 24.2** β **Oxidation**

Match each of the following (**a** to **d**) with one of the reactions (**1** to **4**) in the β oxidation cycle:
(1) first oxidation   (2) hydration   (3) second oxidation   (4) cleavage (thiolysis)

a. Water is added to a trans double bond.
b. An acetyl CoA is removed.
c. FAD is reduced to $FADH_2$.
d. A 3-hydroxyacyl CoA is converted to 3-ketoacyl CoA.

SOLUTION

a. (2) hydration   **b.** (4) cleavage (thiolysis)   **c.** (1) first oxidation
d. (3) second oxidation

STUDY CHECK 24.2

Determine the number of β oxidation cycles and number of acetyl CoA molecules produced for cerotic acid (C_{26}), a fatty acid found in beeswax and carnauba wax.

ANSWER

Cerotic acid (C_{26}) requires 12 β oxidation cycles, and produces 13 acetyl CoA molecules.

QUESTIONS AND PROBLEMS

24.2 Oxidation of Fatty Acids

LEARNING GOAL Describe the metabolic pathway of β oxidation.

24.9 Where in the cell is a fatty acid activated?

24.10 What is the function of carnitine in the β oxidation of fatty acids?

24.11 What coenzymes are required for β oxidation?

24.12 When does an isomerization occur during the β oxidation of a fatty acid?

24.13 In each of the following acyl CoA molecules, identify the β-carbon:

a.

$$CH_3 - CH_2 - CH_2 - CH_2 - CH_2 - CH_2 - CH_2 - \overset{\overset{\displaystyle O}{\|}}{C} - S - CoA$$

b.

24.14 In each of the following acyl CoA molecules, identify the β-carbon:

a. $CH_3 - (CH_2)_{14} - CH_2 - CH_2 - \overset{\overset{\displaystyle O}{\|}}{C} - S - CoA$

b.

24.15 Draw the condensed or line-angle structural formula for the product(s) when each of the following undergoes the indicated reaction:

a.

Enoyl CoA hydratase

b.

$$CH_3 - (CH_2)_6 - CH_2 - CH_2 - \overset{\overset{\displaystyle O}{\|}}{C} - S - CoA \xrightarrow{\text{Acyl CoA dehydrogenase}}$$

24.16 Draw the condensed or line-angle structural formula for the product(s) when each of the following undergoes the indicated reaction:

a.

β-Ketoacyl CoA thiolase

b.

$$CH_3 - (CH_2)_8 - \overset{\overset{\displaystyle OH}{|}}{\underset{\underset{\displaystyle H}{|}}{C}} - \overset{\overset{\displaystyle H}{|}}{\underset{\underset{\displaystyle H}{|}}{C}} - \overset{\overset{\displaystyle O}{\|}}{C} - S - CoA \xrightarrow{\text{3-Hydroxyacyl CoA dehydrogenase}}$$

24.17 Caprylic acid (octanoic acid) is a saturated C_8 fatty acid found in coconut and palm oil as well as cow, goat, and human milk.
  a. Draw the condensed structural formula for the activated form of caprylic acid.
  b. Indicate the α- and β-carbon atoms in caprylic acid.
  c. State the number of β oxidation cycles for the complete oxidation of caprylic acid.
  d. State the number of acetyl CoA units obtained from the complete oxidation of caprylic acid.

24.18 Lignoceric acid is a saturated C_{24} fatty acid found in small amounts in peanut oil.
  a. Draw the line-angle structural formula for the activated form of lignoceric acid.
  b. Indicate the α- and β-carbon atoms in lignoceric acid.
  c. State the number of β oxidation cycles for the complete oxidation of lignoceric acid.
  d. State the number of acetyl CoA units obtained from the complete oxidation of lignoceric acid.

24.3 ATP and Fatty Acid Oxidation

The total energy yield from the oxidation of a particular fatty acid depends on the number of β oxidation cycles needed for the long-chain fatty acid. After the initial input of two ATP, each β oxidation cycle produces one NADH, one FADH$_2$, and one acetyl CoA. Each NADH generates sufficient energy to synthesize 2.5 ATP, whereas each FADH$_2$ provides energy for the synthesis of 1.5 ATP. Thus, each β oxidation cycle produces a total of four ATP. However, the greatest amount of energy produced from a fatty acid is generated by the production of the acetyl CoA molecules that enter the citric acid cycle. For every acetyl CoA that enters the citric acid cycle, a total of 10 ATP are synthesized.

We have seen that capric acid, C_{10}, goes through four turns of the β oxidation cycle, which produces five acetyl CoA units, four NADH, and four FADH$_2$. The initial activation of capric acid requires the energy of two ATP. The total ATP produced is calculated as follows:

ATP Production from β Oxidation for Capric Acid (C$_{10}$)		
Citric acid cycle: 5 acetyl CoA $\times \dfrac{10 \text{ ATP}}{\text{acetyl CoA}}$		= 50 ATP
β oxidation: 4 NADH $\times \dfrac{2.5 \text{ ATP}}{\text{NADH}}$		= 10 ATP
4 FADH$_2$ $\times \dfrac{1.5 \text{ ATP}}{\text{FADH}_2}$		= 6 ATP
Activation of capric acid:		= −2 ATP
Total		= 64 ATP

♥ Chemistry Link to **Health**
Stored Fat and Obesity

The storage of fat is an important survival feature in the lives of many animals. In hibernating animals, large amounts of stored fat provide the energy for the entire hibernation period, which could be several months. In camels, large amounts of food are stored in the camel's hump, which is actually a huge fat deposit. When food resources are low, the camel can survive months without food or water by utilizing the fat reserves in the hump. Migratory birds preparing to fly long distances also store large amounts of fat. Whales are kept warm by a layer of body fat called "blubber," which can be as thick as 2 ft. Blubber also provides energy when whales must survive long periods of starvation. Penguins also have blubber, which protects them from the cold and provides energy when they are incubating their eggs.

Humans also have the capability to store large amounts of fat, although they do not hibernate or usually have to survive for long periods without food. When humans survived on sparse diets that were mostly vegetarian, about 20% of the dietary calories were from fat. Today, a typical diet includes more dairy products and foods with high fat levels, and as much as 60% of the calories are from fat. The U.S. Public Health Service now estimates that in the United States more than one-third of adults are obese. Obesity is defined as a body weight that is more than 20% over an ideal weight. Obesity is a major factor in health problems such as diabetes, heart disease, high blood pressure, stroke, and gallstones, as well as some cancers and forms of arthritis.

To maintain a constant weight, the energy intake (calories in food) must balance the energy expended (calories used by the body). Body weight and food intake are regulated by two "hunger hormones" called ghrelin and leptin. Ghrelin, an appetite-stimulating hormone of 28 amino acid residues, is secreted by an empty stomach and travels to the brain where it makes you feel hungry. After you eat a meal, the stomach is stretched, and ghrelin secretion stops. In people who are obese or have a high calorie intake, the ghrelin levels are low, whereas in people who are fasting, the ghrelin levels are high.

Leptin, a protein, is secreted mainly in the fat cells, also called *adipose*, and travels to the brain where it makes you feel full. The more adipose tissue present, the more leptin you produce. Obese patients have high levels of leptin, but they may be leptin-resistant, which means that they do not experience a sense of fullness that leptin signals to the brain in normal adults. Leptin acts on the liver and skeletal muscles, where it stimulates fatty acid oxidation in the mitochondria, which decreases fat stores.

One way we might control our appetites is by avoiding high-fat foods. When we eat foods high in fat, we tend to eat more. Eating a diet rich in whole grains or high in protein suppresses ghrelin more than a diet high in fat. Sleep deprivation also causes ghrelin levels to rise which can lead to overeating.

Marine mammals have thick layers of blubber that serve as insulation as well as energy storage.

A camel stores large amounts of fat in its hump.

Leptin, shown here as a ribbon model, is an appetite-repressing hormone that consists of 146 amino acid residues formed in the fat cells.

►SAMPLE PROBLEM 24.3 ATP Production from β Oxidation

How many ATP will be produced from the β oxidation of palmitic acid, a C_{16} saturated fatty acid?

SOLUTION

ANALYZE THE PROBLEM	Given	Need
	β oxidation of palmitic acid (C_{16})	total ATP produced

Palmitic acid (C_{16}) requires seven β oxidation cycles, which produce seven NADH and seven $FADH_2$. The total number of acetyl CoA is eight. The activation of palmitic acid decreases the total produced by two ATP.

ATP Production from β Oxidation for Palmitic Acid (C_{16})

Citric acid cycle: 8 ~~acetyl CoA~~ $\times \dfrac{10 \text{ ATP}}{\text{acetyl CoA}}$		= 80 ATP
β oxidation: 7 ~~NADH~~ $\times \dfrac{2.5 \text{ ATP}}{\text{NADH}}$		= 17.5 ATP
7 ~~FADH$_2$~~ $\times \dfrac{1.5 \text{ ATP}}{\text{FADH}_2}$		= 10.5 ATP
Activation of palmitic acid:		= −2 ATP
Total		= 106 ATP

STUDY CHECK 24.3

Compare the total ATP from the reduced coenzymes and from acetyl CoA in the β oxidation of palmitic acid.

ANSWER

Eight acetyl CoA units yield 80 ATP whereas seven NADH and seven $FADH_2$ yield 28 ATP.

Explore Your World

Fat Storage and Blubber

Obtain four plastic freezer bags, masking tape, and some solid vegetable shortening (fat) used for cooking. Fill a bucket or container with enough water to cover both of your hands. Add ice until the water feels very cold.

Place 3 or 4 tablespoons of the shortening in one of the plastic bags. Place another plastic bag inside the first bag containing the fat. Tape the top edges of the two bags together, leaving the inside bag open. Using the remaining two plastic bags, place one inside the other, and tape the top edges together leaving the inside bag open. Now place one hand inside the bag with the vegetable shortening and distribute the fat around until a layer of about 2/3 in. (2 cm) of the fat in the inner bag covers your hand. Place your other hand inside the other double bag and submerge both your hands in the ice water. Measure the time it takes for one hand to feel uncomfortably cold. Remove your hands before they get too cold.

Questions

1. How effective is the double bag with "blubber" in protecting your hand from the cold?
2. How would increasing the amount of vegetable shortening affect your results?
3. How does "blubber" help an animal survive starvation?
4. Why would animals in warm climates, such as camels and migratory birds, need to store fat?

QUESTIONS AND PROBLEMS

24.3 ATP and Fatty Acid Oxidation

LEARNING GOAL Calculate the total ATP produced by the complete oxidation of a fatty acid.

24.19 Why is the energy of fatty acid activation from ATP to AMP considered the same as the hydrolysis of 2 ATP $\longrightarrow$ 2 ADP?

24.20 What is the number of ATP molecules obtained from each acetyl CoA in the citric acid cycle?

℞ Clinical Applications

24.21 Behenic acid is a saturated fatty acid found in peanut and canola oils. Answer each of the following (**a** to **c**) for behenic acid:

a. How many cycles of β oxidation are needed?
b. How many acetyl CoA units are produced?
c. How many ATP can be generated from the β oxidation of behenic acid?

24.22 Stearic acid is a saturated fatty acid found in animal products. Answer each of the following (**a** to **c**) for stearic acid:

a. How many cycles of β oxidation are needed?
b. How many acetyl CoA units are produced?
c. How many ATP can be generated from the β oxidation of stearic acid?

24.23 Oleic acid is a monounsaturated fatty acid common in animal and vegetable oils. Answer each of the following (**a** to **c**) for oleic acid:

a. How many cycles of β oxidation are needed?
b. How many acetyl CoA units are produced?
c. How many ATP can be generated from the β oxidation of oleic acid?

24.24 Palmitoleic acid is a monounsaturated fatty acid common in animal and vegetable oils. Answer each of the following (**a** to **c**) for palmitoleic acid:

a. How many cycles of β oxidation are needed?
b. How many acetyl CoA units are produced?
c. How many ATP can be generated from the β oxidation of palmitoleic acid?

24.4 Ketogenesis and Ketone Bodies

LEARNING GOAL

Describe the pathway of ketogenesis.

When carbohydrates are not available to meet energy needs, the body breaks down fatty acids, which undergo β oxidation to acetyl CoA. Normally, acetyl CoA would enter the citric acid cycle for further oxidation and energy production. However, when large quantities of fatty acids are degraded, too much acetyl CoA is produced and the citric acid cycle cannot oxidize it all. As a result, high levels of acetyl CoA accumulate in the liver. Then, acetyl CoA molecules combine in a pathway known as **ketogenesis** to form compounds called **ketone bodies** (see Figure 24.5). Ketone bodies are produced in the liver and transported to the cells in the heart, brain, and skeletal muscle.

⚛ CORE CHEMISTRY SKILL

Describing How Ketone Bodies are Formed

Reaction 1 Condensation
In ketogenesis, two molecules of acetyl CoA combine to form acetoacetyl CoA and HS—CoA. This condensation is in the reverse direction of the last step of β oxidation.

Reaction 2 Hydrolysis
The hydrolysis of acetoacetyl CoA forms acetoacetate, a ketone body, and HS—CoA. Acetoacetate can enter the citric acid cycle by reforming acetyl CoA for energy production or break down into other ketone bodies.

Reaction 3 Hydrogenation (Reduction)
Acetoacetate is reduced by 2H from NADH + H⁺ to β-hydroxybutyrate, which is considered a ketone body even though it does not contain a keto group.

Reaction 4 Decarboxylation
Acetoacetate can also undergo decarboxylation to yield acetone, a ketone body, and CO_2.

FIGURE 24.5 ▶ In ketogenesis, molecules combine to produce ketone bodies: acetoacetate, β-hydroxybutyrate, and acetone.

🅠 What condition in the body leads to the formation of ketone bodies?

$$CH_3-\overset{\displaystyle O}{\overset{\|}{C}}-S-CoA \;+\; CH_3-\overset{\displaystyle O}{\overset{\|}{C}}-S-CoA$$

Acetyl CoA   Acetyl CoA

❶ HS—CoA

$$CH_3-\overset{\displaystyle O}{\overset{\|}{C}}-CH_2-\overset{\displaystyle O}{\overset{\|}{C}}-S-CoA$$

Acetoacetyl CoA

❷ HS—CoA

$$CH_3-\overset{\displaystyle O}{\overset{\|}{C}}-CH_2-\overset{\displaystyle O}{\overset{\|}{C}}-O^-$$

Acetoacetate

NADH + H⁺

❸

NAD⁺

❹ CO₂

$$CH_3-\overset{\displaystyle OH}{\overset{\|}{C}H}-CH_2-\overset{\displaystyle O}{\overset{\|}{C}}-O^- \qquad CH_3-\overset{\displaystyle O}{\overset{\|}{C}}-CH_3$$

β-Hydroxybutyrate   Acetone

A ketone test strip indicates the level of ketone bodies in a urine sample.

Ketosis

The accumulation of ketone bodies may lead to a condition called **ketosis**, which occurs in severe diabetes, diets high in fat and low in carbohydrates, alcoholism, and starvation. Because two of the ketone bodies are carboxylic acids, they can lower the blood pH below 7.4. This condition is called **acidosis** and often accompanies ketosis. A drop in blood pH can interfere with the ability of the blood to carry oxygen and cause breathing difficulties.

▶ **SAMPLE PROBLEM 24.4** **Ketogenesis**

The process called ketogenesis takes place in the liver.

a. What are some conditions that promote ketogenesis?
b. What are the names of the three compounds called ketone bodies?
c. What ketone bodies are responsible for the acidosis that occurs in ketogenesis?

SOLUTION

a. When excess acetyl CoA cannot be processed by the citric acid cycle, acetyl CoA molecules enter the ketogenesis pathway and form ketone bodies.
b. The ketone bodies are acetoacetate, β-hydroxybutyrate, and acetone.
c. The ketone bodies acetoacetate and β-hydroxybutyrate, which are carboxylic acids, can decrease the pH of the blood (metabolic acidosis).

STUDY CHECK 24.4

Which ketone bodies contain each of the following functional groups?

a. ketone   **b.** alcohol

ANSWER

a. Acetone contains a ketone group.
b. β-Hydroxybutyrate contains an alcohol group.

Chemistry Link to **Health**
Diabetes and Ketone Bodies

Blood glucose is elevated within 30 min following a meal containing carbohydrates. The elevated level of glucose stimulates the secretion of the hormone *insulin* from the pancreas, which increases the flow of glucose into muscle and adipose tissue for the synthesis of glycogen. As blood glucose levels drop, the secretion of insulin decreases. When blood glucose is low, another hormone, *glucagon*, is secreted by the pancreas, which stimulates the breakdown of glycogen in the liver to yield glucose.

In *diabetes mellitus*, glucose cannot be utilized or stored as glycogen, because insulin is not secreted or does not function properly. In type 1, *insulin-dependent diabetes*, which often begins in childhood, the pancreas produces inadequate levels of insulin. This type of diabetes can result from damage to the pancreas by viral infections or from genetic mutations. In type 2, *insulin-resistant diabetes*, which usually occurs in adults, insulin is produced, but insulin receptors are not responsive. Thus, a person with type 2 diabetes will not respond to insulin therapy. *Gestational diabetes* can occur during pregnancy, but blood glucose levels usually return to normal after the baby is born.

Pregnant women with diabetes tend to gain weight and have large babies.

In all types of diabetes, insufficient amounts of glucose are available in the muscle, liver, and adipose tissue. As a result, liver cells synthesize glucose from noncarbohydrate sources via gluconeogenesis and use fatty acids for energy by breaking down fat, which elevates levels of acetyl CoA. Excess acetyl CoA undergoes ketogenesis, and ketone bodies accumulate in the blood. A person with uncontrolled diabetes can go into ketosis. Common symptoms of ketosis include an odor of acetone on the breath and lack of motor coordination due to low levels of glucose reaching the brain.

In uncontrolled diabetes, the concentration of blood glucose exceeds the ability of the kidney to reabsorb glucose, and glucose appears in the urine. High levels of glucose increase the osmotic pressure in the blood, which leads to an increase in urine output. Symptoms of diabetes include excessive thirst and frequent urination. Treatment for diabetes includes diet changes to limit carbohydrate intake and may require medication such as a daily injection of insulin or pills taken by mouth.

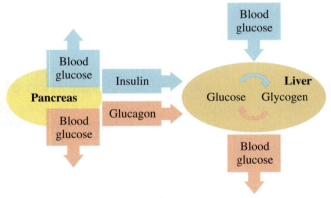

Type 1 diabetes can be treated with injections of insulin.

QUESTIONS AND PROBLEMS
24.4 Ketogenesis and Ketone Bodies

LEARNING GOAL Describe the pathway of ketogenesis.

24.25 What is ketogenesis?

24.26 If a person were fasting, why would they have high levels of acetyl CoA?

24.27 What type of reaction converts acetoacetate to 3-hydroxybutyrate?

24.28 How is acetone formed from acetoacetate?

℞ Clinical Applications

24.29 Diabetics often display signs of ketosis if insulin levels are not maintained. What is ketosis?

24.30 Why do diabetics produce high levels of ketone bodies?

Describe the biosynthesis of fatty acids from acetyl CoA.

24.5 Fatty Acid Synthesis

When the body has met all its energy needs and the glycogen stores are full, acetyl CoA from the breakdown of carbohydrates and fatty acids is used to synthesize new fatty acids in the cytosol. In the pathway called **lipogenesis**, two-carbon acetyl units are linked together to give a 16-carbon fatty acid, palmitic acid. Although the reactions appear much like the reverse of the reactions we discussed in fatty acid oxidation, the synthesis of fatty acids proceeds in a separate pathway with different enzymes. Fatty acid oxidation occurs in the mitochondria and uses FAD and NAD^+, whereas fatty acid synthesis occurs in the cytosol and uses the reduced coenzyme NADPH. The structure of NADPH is similar to NADH, except it has a phosphate group.

Synthesis of Acyl Carrier Protein (ACP)

In β oxidation, acetyl and acyl groups are activated using coenzyme A (HS—CoA). In fatty acid synthesis, an acyl carrier protein (HS—ACP) activates the acyl compounds. HS—ACP contains the thiol and pantothenic acid (vitamin B_5) groups found in acetyl CoA but now these groups are attached to a protein.

Aminoethanethiol   Pantothenic acid

Acyl carrier protein (ACP)
(HS—ACP)

Preparation of Activated Carriers

Before fatty acid synthesis can begin, the activated carriers must be synthesized. The synthesis of a three-carbon malonyl ACP requires the synthesis of malonyl CoA, when acetyl CoA combines with bicarbonate. The hydrolysis of ATP provides the energy for the reaction.

For fatty acid synthesis, the activated forms acetyl ACP and malonyl ACP are produced when the acyl group is combined with HS—ACP.

Synthesis of Fatty Acids (Palmitate)

The synthesis of a fatty acid in the cytosol requires a cycle of four reactions that adds two-carbon acetyl units to a growing carbon chain until it contains a total of 16 carbon atoms (palmitate).

Reaction 1   Condensation

In the first reaction, *3-ketoacyl ACP synthase* catalyzes the condensation of acetyl ACP and malonyl ACP to yield four-carbon acetoacetyl ACP and CO_2.

Reaction 2   Reduction

In the second reaction, *3-ketoacyl ACP reductase* reduces the 3-keto group using 2H from NADPH + H^+ to yield 3-hydroxyacyl ACP, an alcohol, and the oxidized coenzyme $NADP^+$. In the cytosol, NADPH is used to provide hydrogen for reduction reactions.

Reaction 3   Dehydration

In the third reaction, *3-hydroxyacyl ACP dehydrase* catalyzes the dehydration of the hydroxyl group to form a trans double bond in *trans*-2-enoyl ACP.

Reaction 4   Reduction

In the fourth reaction, *enoyl ACP reductase* uses hydrogen from NADPH + H^+ to reduce the double bond to a single bond, which forms butyryl ACP, a saturated four-carbon compound, which is two carbon atoms longer that the original acetyl ACP.

Cycle of Fatty Acid Synthesis Repeats

The cycle of fatty acid synthesis repeats with the four-carbon butyryl ACP condensing with another malonyl ACP to produce a six-carbon hexanoyl ACP. After seven cycles of fatty acid synthesis, the product, C_{16} palmitoyl ACP, is hydrolyzed to yield palmitate and HS—ACP (see Figure 24.6). The overall equation for the synthesis of palmitate from acetyl CoA is written as

$$8 \text{ Acetyl CoA} + 14\text{NADPH} + 7\text{ATP} \longrightarrow$$
$$\text{palmitate} + 14\text{NADP}^+ + 8\text{HS}\text{—CoA} + 7\text{ADP} + 7\text{P}_i + 6\text{H}_2\text{O}$$

Longer and Shorter Fatty Acids

Palmitate is the first fatty acid produced by fatty acid synthesis. However, shorter and longer fatty acids are also produced in cells. Shorter fatty acids are released earlier in the fatty acid synthesis process before there are 16 carbon atoms in the chain. Longer fatty acids are produced with special enzymes that add two-carbon acetyl units to the carboxyl end of the fatty acid chain.

Regulation of Fatty Acid Synthesis

Fatty acid synthesis takes place primarily in the adipose tissue, where triacylglycerols are formed and stored. The hormone *insulin* stimulates the formation of fatty acids. When blood glucose is high, insulin moves glucose into the cells. In the cell, insulin stimulates glycolysis and the oxidation of pyruvate, thereby producing acetyl CoA for fatty acid synthesis. By adding two carbons to the growing fatty acid chain by using three-carbon malonyl units, the transport of acyl groups into the matrix of the mitochondria is blocked, preventing their oxidation.

FIGURE 24.6 ▶ In fatty acid synthesis (lipogenesis), two-carbon units from acetyl CoA are added together to form palmitate.

Q Identify each of the reactions 1 to 4 as reduction, dehydration, or condensation.

Comparison of β Oxidation and Fatty Acid Synthesis

We have seen that many of the steps in the synthesis of palmitate are similar to those that occur in the β oxidation of palmitate. Synthesis combines two-carbon acetyl units to make long carbon chains, whereas β oxidation removes two-carbon acetyl units from long carbon chains. Synthesis of fatty acids involves reduction and dehydration, whereas β oxidation of fatty acids involves oxidation and hydration. We can distinguish between the two pathways by comparing some of their features in Table 24.1.

TABLE 24.1 A Comparison of β Oxidation and Fatty Acid Synthesis

	β Oxidation	Fatty Acid Synthesis (Lipogenesis)
Site	mitochondrial matrix	cytosol
Activated by	glucagon low blood glucose	insulin high blood glucose
Activator	coenzyme A (HS—CoA)	acyl carrier protein (HS—ACP)
Initial Substrate	fatty acid	acetyl CoA
Initial Coenzymes	FAD, NAD$^+$	NADPH + H$^+$
Types of Reactions	oxidation hydration cleavage	reduction dehydration condensation
Function	cleaves two-carbon acetyl group	adds two-carbon acetyl group
Final Product	acetyl CoA	palmitate (C_{16}) or other fatty acids
Final Coenzymes	FADH$_2$, NADH + H$^+$	NADP$^+$

▶**SAMPLE PROBLEM 24.5 Fatty Acid Synthesis**

Malonyl ACP is required for the elongation of fatty acid chains.

a. Complete the following equations for the formation of malonyl ACP from the starting material:

Acetyl CoA + HCO$_3^-$ + ATP $\longrightarrow$

Malonyl CoA + HS—ACP $\longrightarrow$

b. What enzymes catalyze these reactions?

SOLUTION

a. Acetyl CoA combines with bicarbonate to form malonyl CoA, which reacts with ACP to form malonyl ACP.

Acetyl CoA + HCO$_3^-$ + ATP $\longrightarrow$ malonyl CoA + ADP + P$_i$ + H$^+$

Malonyl CoA + HS—ACP $\longrightarrow$ malonyl ACP + HS—CoA

b. The enzyme for the first reaction is acetyl CoA carboxylase. The enzyme for the second reaction is malonyl CoA transacylase.

STUDY CHECK 24.5

If malonyl ACP is a three-carbon acyl group, why are only two carbon atoms added each time malonyl ACP is combined with a fatty acid chain?

ANSWER

In each cycle of fatty acid synthesis, a two-carbon acetyl group from the three-carbon group in malonyl ACP adds to the growing fatty acid chain and one carbon forms CO_2.

QUESTIONS AND PROBLEMS

24.5 Fatty Acid Synthesis

LEARNING GOAL Describe the biosynthesis of fatty acids from acetyl CoA.

24.31 Where does fatty acid synthesis occur in the cell?

24.32 What compound is involved in the activation of acyl compounds in fatty acid synthesis?

24.33 What are the starting materials for fatty acid synthesis?

24.34 What is the function of malonyl ACP in fatty acid synthesis?

24.35 Identify the reaction (**a** to **c**) catalyzed by each of the following enzymes (**1** to **3**):

1. acetyl CoA carboxylase
2. acetyl CoA transacylase
3. malonyl CoA transacylase

a. converts malonyl CoA to malonyl ACP
b. combines acetyl CoA with bicarbonate to give malonyl CoA
c. converts acetyl CoA to acetyl ACP

24.36 Identify the reaction (**a** to **d**) catalyzed by each of the following enzymes (**1** to **4**):
1. 3-ketoacyl ACP synthase
2. 3-ketoacyl ACP reductase
3. 3-hydroxyacyl ACP dehydrase
4. enoyl ACP reductase

a. catalyzes the dehydration of an alcohol
b. converts a carbon–carbon double bond to a carbon–carbon single bond
c. combines a two-carbon acetyl group with a three-carbon acyl group accompanied by the loss of CO_2
d. reduces a keto group to a hydroxyl group

24.37 Determine the number of each of the following components involved in the synthesis of one molecule of capric acid, a C_{10} fatty acid:
a. HCO_3^- b. ATP
c. acetyl CoA   d. malonyl ACP
e. NADPH   f. CO_2 removed

24.38 Determine the number of each of the following components involved in the synthesis of one molecule of myristic acid, a C_{14} fatty acid:
a. HCO_3^- b. ATP
c. acetyl CoA   d. malonyl ACP
e. NADPH   f. CO_2 removed

℞ Clinical Applications

24.39 Triclosan, which is used in antiseptic hand washes and lotions to inhibit the growth of bacteria, is an inhibitor of enoyl ACP reductase.

a. What reaction in fatty acid synthesis is catalyzed by enoyl ACP reductase?
b. If fatty acid synthesis is required for the formation of bacterial membranes, why is triclosan used to control the growth of bacteria?

24.40 Researchers have synthesized a compound from biotin called CABI that inhibits the catalytic activity of acetyl CoA carboxylase in the cytosol. Mice without acetyl CoA carboxylase activity were found to lose weight even though they ate more food.

CABI

Biotin

a. What reaction in fatty acid synthesis is catalyzed by acetyl CoA carboxylase?
b. How might CABI be useful in reducing obesity?

Describe the hydrolysis of dietary protein and the reactions of transamination and oxidative deamination in the degradation of amino acids.

24.6 Degradation of Proteins and Amino Acids

The major role of protein in the diet is to provide amino acids for the synthesis of new proteins for the body and nitrogen atoms for the synthesis of compounds such as nucleotides. We have seen that carbohydrates and lipids are major sources of energy, but when they are not available, amino acids are degraded to substrates that enter energy-producing pathways.

In stage 1, the digestion of proteins begins in the stomach, where hydrochloric acid (HCl) at pH 2 denatures proteins and activates enzymes such as *pepsin* that begin to hydrolyze peptide bonds. Polypeptides move out of the stomach into the small intestine, where *trypsin* and *chymotrypsin* complete the hydrolysis of the peptides to amino acids. The amino acids are absorbed through the intestinal walls into the bloodstream for transport to the cells (see Figure 24.7).

▶ **SAMPLE PROBLEM 24.6** Digestion of Proteins

What are the sites and end products for the digestion of proteins?

SOLUTION

The digestion of proteins begins in the stomach and is completed in the small intestine to yield amino acids.

STUDY CHECK 24.6

What is the function of HCl in the stomach?

ANSWER

HCl denatures proteins and activates enzymes such as pepsin.

Protein Turnover

Our bodies are constantly replacing old proteins with new ones. The process of breaking down proteins and synthesizing new proteins is called **protein turnover**. Many types of proteins, including enzymes, hormones, and hemoglobin, are synthesized in the cells and then degraded. For example, the hormone *insulin* has a half-life of 10 min, whereas the half-life of *lactate dehydrogenase* is about 2 days and hemoglobin is 120 days. Damaged and ineffective proteins are also degraded and replaced. Although most amino acids are used to build proteins, other compounds also require nitrogen for their synthesis, as seen in Table 24.2 (see Figure 24.8).

TABLE 24.2 Nitrogen-Containing Compounds

Type of Compound	Example
Nonessential amino acids	Alanine, aspartate, cysteine, glycine
Proteins	Muscle protein, enzymes
Neurotransmitters	Acetylcholine, dopamine, serotonin
Amino alcohols	Choline, ethanolamine
Heme	Hemoglobin, cytochrome *c*
Hormones	Thyroxine, epinephrine, insulin
Nucleotides (nucleic acids)	Purines, pyrimidines

Usually, we maintain a nitrogen balance in the cells so that the amount of protein we break down is equal to the amount that is reused. A diet that is high in protein, however, has a positive nitrogen balance because it supplies more nitrogen than we need. Because the body cannot store nitrogen, the excess is excreted as urea. Such high protein diets put extra demands on the liver and kidneys. A diet that does not provide sufficient protein has a negative nitrogen balance, which is a condition that occurs during starvation and fasting.

Energy from Amino Acids

Normally, only a small amount (about 10%) of our energy needs is supplied by amino acids. However, more energy is extracted from amino acids in conditions such as fasting or starvation, when carbohydrate and fat stores are exhausted. If amino acids remain the only source of energy for a long period of time, the breakdown of body proteins eventually leads to a destruction of essential body tissues. In *anorexia*, the loss of protein decreases muscle mass and may severely weaken the heart muscle and impair heart function.

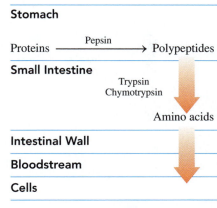

FIGURE 24.7 ▶ Proteins are hydrolyzed to polypeptides in the stomach and to amino acids in the small intestine.

🔘 What enzyme, secreted into the small intestine, hydrolyzes peptides?

FIGURE 24.8 ▶ Proteins are used in the synthesis of nitrogen-containing compounds or degraded to urea and carbon skeletons that enter other metabolic pathways.

🔘 What are some compounds that require nitrogen for their synthesis?

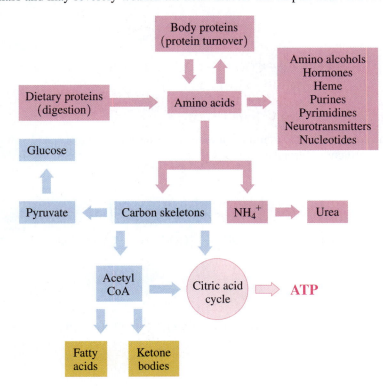

> **SAMPLE PROBLEM 24.7** **Nitrogen Balance**

With a positive nitrogen balance, why are excess amino acids excreted?

SOLUTION

Because the body cannot store nitrogen, amino acids that are not needed for the synthesis of proteins are excreted.

STUDY CHECK 24.7

Under what condition does the body have a negative nitrogen balance?

ANSWER

In conditions such as fasting or starvation, a diet insufficient in protein leads to a negative nitrogen balance.

Degradation of Amino Acids

When dietary protein exceeds the nitrogen needed for protein synthesis, the excess amino acids are degraded. The α-amino group is removed to yield an α-keto acid, which can be converted to an intermediate for other metabolic pathways. The carbon atoms from amino acids are used in the citric acid cycle as well as for the synthesis of fatty acids, ketone bodies, and glucose.

Transamination

The degradation of amino acids occurs primarily in the liver. In a **transamination** reaction, an α-amino group is transferred from an amino acid to an α-keto acid, usually α-ketoglutarate. A new amino acid and a new α-keto acid are produced.

We can write an equation to show the transfer of the amino group from alanine to α-ketoglutarate to yield glutamate, the new amino acid, and the α-keto acid pyruvate. The enzymes for the transfer of amino groups are known as *transaminases* or *aminotransferases*. Pyruvate can now enter the citric acid cycle for the production of energy.

$$CH_3-\overset{\overset{+}{NH_3}}{\underset{}{CH}}-COO^- \ + \ ^-OOC-\overset{\overset{O}{\|}}{C}-CH_2-CH_2-COO^- \ \underset{\longleftarrow}{\overset{\text{Alanine transaminase}}{\longrightarrow}}$$

Alanine α-Ketoglutarate

$$CH_3-\overset{\overset{O}{\|}}{C}-COO^- \ + \ ^-OOC-\overset{\overset{+}{NH_3}}{\underset{}{CH}}-CH_2-CH_2-COO^-$$

Pyruvate   Glutamate

> **SAMPLE PROBLEM 24.8** **Transamination**

Write the equation for the transamination of glutamate and oxaloacetate by drawing the condensed structural formulas.

SOLUTION

$$^-OOC-\overset{\overset{+}{NH_3}}{\underset{}{CH}}-CH_2-CH_2-COO^- \ + \ ^-OOC-\overset{\overset{O}{\|}}{C}-CH_2-COO^- \ \underset{\longleftarrow}{\overset{\text{Aspartate transaminase}}{\longrightarrow}}$$

Glutamate   Oxaloacetate

$$^-OOC-\overset{\overset{O}{\|}}{C}-CH_2-CH_2-COO^- \ + \ ^-OOC-\overset{\overset{+}{NH_3}}{\underset{}{CH}}-CH_2-COO^-$$

α-Ketoglutarate   Aspartate

Aspartate transaminase (AST) catalyzes the reversible transfer of an amino group between glutamate and aspartate.

What are some other possible names for the enzyme that catalyzes the reaction in Sample Problem 24.8?

ANSWER

glutamate aminotransferase, glutamate transaminase, aspartate aminotransferase

Oxidative Deamination

In a process called **oxidative deamination**, the amino group $(-NH_3^+)$ in glutamate is removed as an ammonium ion, NH_4^+. The deamination reaction produces α-ketoglutarate, which can enter transamination with an amino acid. The reaction is catalyzed by *glutamate dehydrogenase*, which uses NAD^+ as a coenzyme.

$$\underset{\text{Glutamate}}{{}^-OOC-\overset{\overset{+}{\underset{|}{NH_3}}}{CH}-CH_2-CH_2-COO^-} + H_2O + \boxed{NAD^+} \underset{\text{dehydrogenase}}{\overset{\text{Glutamate}}{\rightleftarrows}}$$

$$\underset{\alpha\text{-Ketoglutarate}}{{}^-OOC-\overset{\overset{O}{\underset{||}{}}}{C}-CH_2-CH_2-COO^-} + NH_4^+ + \boxed{NADH + H^+}$$

Through transamination, the amino group from any amino acid can be used to form glutamate, which undergoes oxidative deamination, converting the amino group to an ammonium ion.

▶ **SAMPLE PROBLEM 24.9** Transamination and Oxidative Deamination

Indicate whether each of the following represents a transamination or an oxidative deamination:

a. Glutamate is converted to α-ketoglutarate and NH_4^+.
b. Alanine and α-ketoglutarate react to form pyruvate and glutamate.

SOLUTION

a. Oxidative deamination occurs when the $-NH_3^+$ group in glutamate is removed as an ammonium ion, NH_4^+.
b. Transamination occurs when an amino group is transferred from an amino acid to an α-keto acid such as α-ketoglutarate.

Is the reaction catalyzed by glutamate dehydrogenase, which requires NAD^+, an example of transamination or oxidative deamination?

ANSWER

oxidative deamination

QUESTIONS AND PROBLEMS

24.6 Degradation of Proteins and Amino Acids

LEARNING GOAL Describe the hydrolysis of dietary protein and the reactions of transamination and oxidative deamination in the degradation of amino acids.

24.41 Where do dietary proteins undergo digestion in the body?

24.42 What is meant by protein turnover?

24.43 What are some nitrogen-containing compounds that need amino acids for their synthesis?

24.44 What is the fate of the amino acids obtained from a high protein diet?

24.45 What are the reactants and products in transamination reactions?

24.46 What types of enzymes catalyze transamination reactions?

24.47 Draw the condensed structural formula for the α-keto acid produced from each of the following in transamination:

$$\overset{\overset{+}{N}H_3}{\underset{|}{}}$$

a. $H-\overset{|}{C}H-COO^-$ Glycine

$$\overset{\overset{+}{N}H_3}{\underset{|}{}}$$

b. $HS-CH_2-\overset{|}{C}H-COO^-$ Cysteine

$$\overset{CH_3}{\underset{|}{}} \quad \overset{\overset{+}{N}H_3}{\underset{|}{}}$$

c. $CH_3-\overset{|}{C}H-\overset{|}{C}H-COO^-$ Valine

24.48 Draw the condensed structural formula for the α-keto acid produced from each of the following in transamination:

$$\overset{\overset{+}{N}H_3}{\underset{|}{}}$$

a. $^-OOC-CH_2-\overset{|}{C}H-COO^-$ Aspartate

$$\overset{CH_3}{\underset{|}{}} \quad \overset{\overset{+}{N}H_3}{\underset{|}{}}$$

b. $CH_3-CH_2-\overset{|}{C}H-\overset{|}{C}H-COO^-$ Isoleucine

$$\overset{\overset{+}{N}H_3}{\underset{|}{}}$$

c. $HO-CH_2-\overset{|}{C}H-COO^-$ Serine

24.49 Write the equation, using condensed structural formulas, for the oxidative deamination of glutamate.

24.50 How do all 20 amino acids produce ammonium ions in oxidative deamination?

24.7 Urea Cycle

LEARNING GOAL

Describe the formation of urea from an ammonium ion.

The ammonium ion, which is the end product of amino acid degradation, is toxic if it is allowed to accumulate. Thus, in the liver, the **urea cycle** converts ammonium ions to urea, which is transported to the kidneys to form urine.

$$2NH_4^+ + CO_2 \longrightarrow H_2N-\overset{\overset{O}{\|}}{C}-NH_2 + 2H^+ + H_2O$$
$$\text{Urea}$$

In one day, a typical adult may excrete about 25 to 30 g of urea in the urine. This amount increases when a diet is high in protein. If urea is not properly excreted, it builds up quickly to a toxic level. To detect renal disease, the *blood urea nitrogen* (BUN) level is measured. If the BUN is high, protein intake must be reduced, and hemodialysis may be needed to remove toxic nitrogen waste from the blood.

Urea Cycle

The urea cycle in the liver cells consists of reactions that take place in both the mitochondria and cytosol (see Figure 24.9). In preparation for the urea cycle, ammonium ions react with carbon dioxide and water, using the energy from two ATP to yield carbamoyl phosphate.

$$NH_4^+ + CO_2 + \boxed{2\ ATP} + H_2O \xrightarrow[\text{synthetase}]{\text{Carbamoyl phosphate}} H_2N-\overset{\overset{O}{\|}}{C}-O-\overset{\overset{O}{\|}}{\underset{\underset{O^-}{|}}{P}}-O^- + \boxed{2\ ADP} + P_i + 3H^+$$
$$\text{Carbamoyl phosphate}$$

Reaction 1   Transfer of the Carbamoyl Group

In the mitochondrial matrix, reaction 1 utilizes *ornithine transcarbamylase* to catalyze the transfer of the carbamoyl group from carbamoyl phosphate to ornithine (an amino acid not found in proteins) to yield citrulline, which is transported across the mitochondrial membrane by the citrulline transporter protein into the cytosol. The hydrolysis of the high-energy phosphate bond in carbamoyl phosphate provides the energy to drive the reaction.

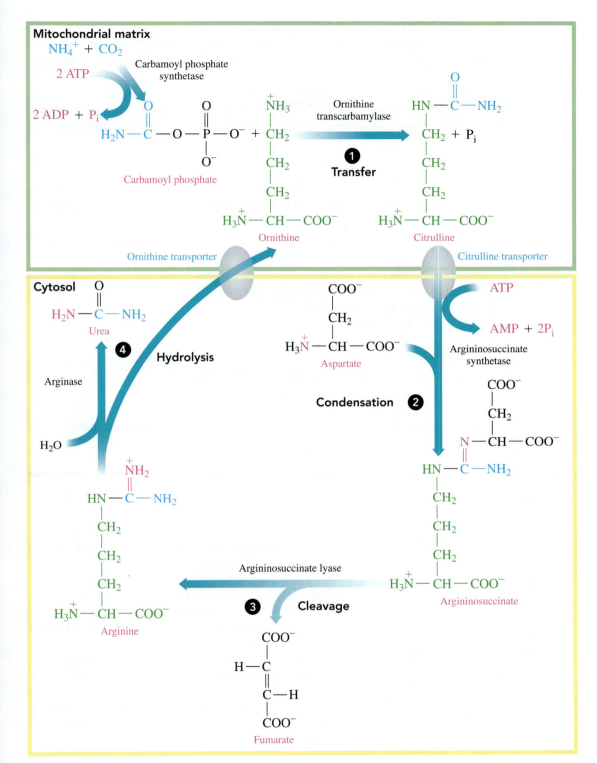

FIGURE 24.9 ▶ In the urea cycle, urea is formed from a carbon and nitrogen (blue) from carbamoyl phosphate (initially an ammonium ion from oxidative deamination) and a nitrogen atom from aspartate (magenta).

🔘 Where in the cell is urea formed?

Reaction 2 Condensation of Citrulline with Aspartate

In the cytosol, reaction 2, a condensation of citrulline with aspartate catalyzed by *argininosuccinate synthetase*, produces argininosuccinate. The energy for the reaction is supplied by the hydrolysis of two phosphate bonds in ATP to yield AMP and two inorganic phosphates. The nitrogen atom in aspartate becomes one of the nitrogen atoms in the urea molecule that is produced in the final reaction.

Reaction 3   Cleavage of Argininosuccinate

Reaction 3 in the cytosol catalyzed by *argininosuccinate lyase* splits (cleaves) argininosuccinate to yield arginine, an amino acid, and fumarate, a citric acid cycle intermediate.

Reaction 4   Hydrolysis of Arginine to Form Urea

Reaction 4 catalyzed by *arginase* is the hydrolysis of arginine to yield urea and ornithine. The ornithine returns to the mitochondrial matrix through the ornithine transporter protein to repeat the urea cycle.

▶ **SAMPLE PROBLEM 24.10** Urea Cycle

Indicate the reaction in the urea cycle where each of the following compounds is a reactant:

a. aspartate   **b.** ornithine   **c.** arginine

SOLUTION

a. Aspartate and citrulline undergo condensation in reaction 2.
b. A carbamoyl group is transferred to ornithine in reaction 1.
c. Arginine is cleaved in reaction 4.

STUDY CHECK 24.10

Name the products of each reaction in Sample Problem 24.10.

ANSWER

a. argininosuccinate   **b.** citrulline   **c.** urea and ornithine

---

QUESTIONS AND PROBLEMS

24.7 Urea Cycle

LEARNING GOAL Describe the formation of urea from an ammonium ion.

24.51 Draw the condensed structural formula for urea.

24.52 Draw the condensed structural formula for carbamoyl phosphate.

24.53 What is the source of carbon in urea?

24.54 How much ATP energy is required to drive one turn of the urea cycle?

℞ **Clinical Applications**

24.55 Why does the body convert NH_4^+ to urea?

24.56 Why would a person on a high-protein diet be instructed to drink large quantities of water?

Use the following information for problems 24.57 and 24.58:

Research indicates that *sudden infant death syndrome* may be the result of a deficiency of any one of the enzymes in the urea cycle. The *urea cycle disorders* (UCD) are a result of a genetic mutation that leads to a deficient enzyme. When the urea cycle is disrupted *hyperammonemia* (high ammonia levels) can cause irreversible changes in the brain.

24.57 In addition to ammonia, what intermediate of the urea cycle would be elevated if an infant has a deficiency of *argininosuccinate synthetase*?

24.58 In addition to ammonia, what intermediate of the urea cycle would be elevated if an infant has a deficiency of *argininosuccinate lyase*?

LEARNING GOAL

Describe where carbon atoms from amino acids enter the citric acid cycle or other pathways.

24.8 Fates of the Carbon Atoms from Amino Acids

The carbon skeletons from the transamination of amino acids are used as intermediates in the citric acid cycle or other metabolic pathways. We can classify the amino acids according to the number of carbon atoms in those intermediates (see Figure 24.10). The amino acids that provide three-carbon compounds are converted to pyruvate. The amino acids with four carbon atoms are converted to oxaloacetate, and the five-carbon amino acids provide α-ketoglutarate. Some amino acids are listed twice because they can enter different pathways to form citric acid cycle intermediates.

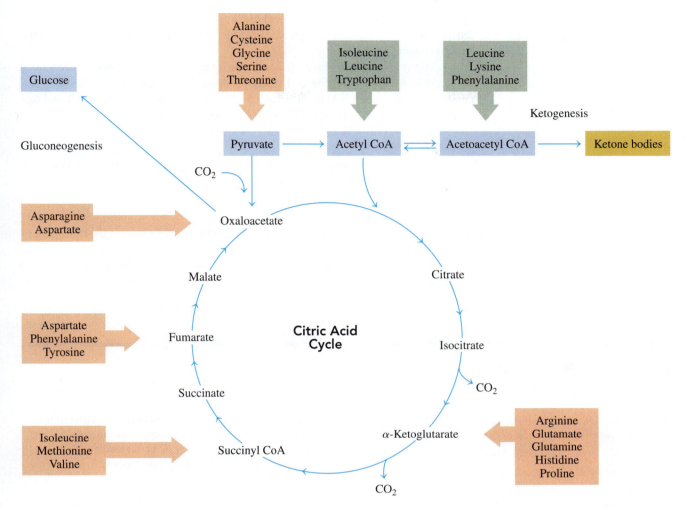

FIGURE 24.10 ► Carbon atoms from degraded amino acids are converted to the intermediates of the citric acid cycle or other pathways. Glucogenic amino acids (pink boxes) produce carbon skeletons that can form glucose, and ketogenic amino acids (green boxes) can produce ketone bodies.

🔵 Why is aspartate glucogenic, but leucine ketogenic?

A **glucogenic amino acid** generates pyruvate, α-ketoglutarate, succinyl CoA, fumarate, or oxaloacetate, which can be used to synthesize glucose by gluconeogenesis. A **ketogenic amino acid** produces acetoacetyl CoA or acetyl CoA, which can enter the ketogenesis pathway to form ketone bodies or the lipogenesis pathway to form fatty acids. Some amino acids can be both glucogenic and ketogenic.

► **SAMPLE PROBLEM 24.11 Degradation of Amino Acids**

Identify the citric acid cycle component and the number of ATP produced by each of the following amino acids:

a. proline   **b.** tyrosine   **c.** tryptophan

SOLUTION

	Given	Need
ANALYZE THE PROBLEM	proline, tyrosine, tryptophan	ATP produced via the citric acid cycle

a. Proline is converted to the citric acid cycle intermediate α-ketoglutarate. The reactions in the remaining part of the citric acid cycle from α-ketoglutarate to oxaloacetate produce two NADH, one GTP, and one $FADH_2$. The two NADH provide five ATP, one GTP provides one ATP, and one $FADH_2$ provides 1.5 ATP, for a total of 7.5 ATP from proline.

b. Tyrosine is converted to the citric acid cycle intermediate fumarate. The remaining reactions of the citric acid cycle from fumarate to oxaloacetate produce one NADH, which provides 2.5 ATP.

c. Tryptophan is converted to the citric acid cycle intermediate acetyl CoA. The reactions in the citric acid cycle starting with acetyl CoA produce three NADH, one GTP, and one $FADH_2$. The three NADH provide 7.5 ATP, one GTP provides one ATP, and one $FADH_2$ provides 1.5 ATP, for a total of 10 ATP from tryptophan.

STUDY CHECK 24.11

Why does the citric acid cycle component from leucine supply more ATP than the intermediate from phenylalanine?

ANSWER

Leucine forms the citric acid cycle intermediate acetyl CoA that enters at the beginning of the citric acid cycle to provide 10 ATP. Phenylalanine forms the citric acid cycle intermediate fumarate that enters later in the citric acid cycle to produce one NADH, which is used to provide 2.5 ATP.

QUESTIONS AND PROBLEMS

24.8 Fates of the Carbon Atoms from Amino Acids

LEARNING GOAL Describe where carbon atoms from amino acids enter the citric acid cycle or other pathways.

24.59 What is the function of a glucogenic amino acid?

24.60 What is the function of a ketogenic amino acid?

24.61 What component of the citric acid cycle can be produced from the carbon atoms of each of the following amino acids?
  a. alanine
  b. asparagine
  c. valine
  d. glutamine

24.62 What component of the citric acid cycle can be produced from the carbon atoms of each of the following amino acids?
  a. leucine
  b. threonine
  c. cysteine
  d. arginine

24.9 Synthesis of Amino Acids

LEARNING GOAL

Illustrate how some nonessential amino acids are synthesized from intermediates in the citric acid cycle and other metabolic pathways.

TABLE 24.3 Essential and Nonessential Amino Acids in Adults

Essential	Nonessential
Histidine	Alanine
Isoleucine	Arginine
Leucine	Asparagine
Lysine	Aspartate
Methionine	Cysteine
Phenylalanine	Glutamate
Threonine	Glutamine
Tryptophan	Glycine
Valine	Proline
	Serine
	Tyrosine

Plants and bacteria such as *E. coli* produce all of their amino acids using NH_4^+ and NO_3^-. However, humans can synthesize only 9 of the 20 amino acids found in their proteins. The nonessential amino acids are synthesized in the body, whereas the essential amino acids must be obtained from the diet (see Table 24.3). The amino acids arginine, cysteine, and tyrosine are essential in diets for infants and children due to their rapid growth requirements, but they are not essential amino acids for adults.

Some Pathways for Amino Acid Synthesis

A variety of pathways are involved in the synthesis of nonessential amino acids. When the body synthesizes nonessential amino acids, the α-keto acid carbon skeletons are obtained from the citric acid cycle or glycolysis and converted to amino acids by transamination (see Figure 24.11).

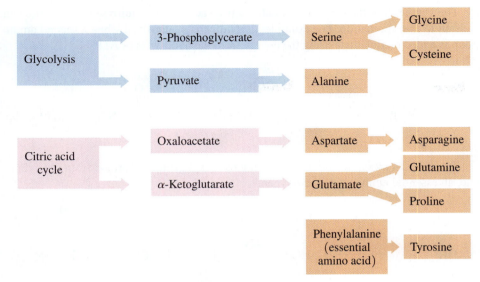

FIGURE 24.11 ▶ Nonessential amino acids are synthesized from intermediates of glycolysis and the citric acid cycle.

🅠 How is alanine formed from pyruvate?

Some of the amino acids are formed by reversing the transamination reaction that we saw in amino acid degradation. The transfer of an amino group from glutamate to pyruvate produces alanine, which is catalyzed by *alanine transaminase* (ALT).

$$\overset{+}{NH_3}$$

$$^-OOC-\overset{|}{CH}-CH_2-CH_2-COO^- + CH_3-\overset{O}{\overset{||}{C}}-COO^- \underset{\text{transaminase}}{\overset{\text{Alanine}}{\rightleftharpoons}}$$

Glutamate   Pyruvate

$$\overset{+}{NH_3}$$

$$CH_3-\overset{|}{CH}-COO^- + {}^-OOC-\overset{O}{\overset{||}{C}}-CH_2-CH_2-COO^-$$

Alanine   α-Ketoglutarate

Oxaloacetate, a keto acid from the citric acid cycle, undergoes transamination with glutamate to produce aspartate, an amino acid, and α-ketoglutarate. The transamination is catalyzed by *aspartate transaminase* (AST).

$$\overset{+}{NH_3}$$

$$^-OOC-\overset{|}{CH}-CH_2-CH_2-COO^- + {}^-OOC-CH_2-\overset{O}{\overset{||}{C}}-COO^- \underset{\text{transaminase}}{\overset{\text{Aspartate}}{\rightleftharpoons}}$$

Glutamate   Oxaloacetate

$$\overset{+}{NH_3}$$

$$^-OOC-CH_2-\overset{|}{CH}-COO^- + {}^-OOC-\overset{O}{\overset{||}{C}}-CH_2-CH_2-COO^-$$

Aspartate   α-Ketoglutarate

These two transaminases, ALT and AST, are abundant in the cells of the liver and heart, but they are present only in low levels in the bloodstream. When an injury or disease occurs, they are released from the damaged cells into the bloodstream. Elevated levels of serum ALT or AST provide a means to diagnose the extent of damage to the liver or the heart. *Alanine transaminase* is also known by the abbreviation SGPT (*serum glutamate pyruvate transaminase*) since it catalyzes the reversible transamination reaction between glutamate and pyruvate, and *aspartate transaminase* is also known by the abbreviation SGOT (*serum glutamate oxaloacetate transaminase*) since it catalyzes the reversible transamination reaction between glutamate and oxaloacetate.

⚛ **CORE CHEMISTRY SKILL**

Distinguishing Anabolic and Catabolic Pathways

The synthesis of the other nonessential amino acids may require several reactions in addition to transamination. For example, glutamine is synthesized when a second amino group is added to glutamate using the energy from the hydrolysis of ATP.

$$^-OOC-\overset{\overset{+}{N}H_3}{\underset{|}{CH}}-CH_2-CH_2-COO^- + NH_3 + \boxed{ATP} \xrightarrow{\text{Glutamine synthetase}} {}^-OOC-\overset{\overset{+}{N}H_3}{\underset{|}{CH}}-CH_2-CH_2-\overset{\overset{O}{||}}{C}-NH_2 + \boxed{ADP + P_i}$$

Glutamate · Glutamine

Tyrosine, an aromatic amino acid with a hydroxyl group, is formed from phenylalanine, an essential amino acid, and oxygen.

$$\text{Phenylalanine} + O_2 + \boxed{NADH + H^+} \xrightarrow{\text{Phenylalanine hydroxylase}} \text{Tyrosine} + H_2O + \boxed{NAD^+}$$

Chemistry Link to Health
Phenylketonuria (PKU)

In the genetic disease *phenylketonuria* (PKU), a person cannot convert phenylalanine to tyrosine because the gene for an enzyme, *phenylalanine hydroxylase*, is defective. As a result, large amounts of phenylalanine accumulate. In this situation, a *transaminase* catalyzes the transfer of the $-NH_3^+$ from phenylalanine to pyruvate to form alanine and phenylpyruvate, which is then decarboxylated to phenylacetate. Large amounts of these compounds are excreted in the urine. Phenylacetate has a characteristic odor in the urine that was used to recognize PKU in infants.

In infants, high levels of phenylpyruvate and phenylacetate cause severe mental retardation. However, the defect can be identified at birth, and all newborns are now tested for PKU. By detecting PKU early, retardation is avoided by using an infant diet with proteins that are low in phenylalanine and high in tyrosine. It is also important to avoid the use of sweeteners and soft drinks containing aspartame, which contains phenylalanine as one of the two amino acids in its structure. In adulthood, some people with PKU can eat a nearly normal diet as long as they are checked for phenylpyruvate periodically.

All newborns are tested for PKU.

Overview of Metabolism

Catabolic pathways degrade large molecules to small molecules that enter the citric acid cycle and electron transport to produce energy. Anabolic pathways use small molecules and energy to synthesize larger molecules in the cell. In the overall view of metabolism, there are several branch points from which compounds may be degraded for energy or used to synthesize larger molecules. For example, glucose can be degraded to pyruvate and then acetyl CoA for the citric acid cycle to produce energy. Glucose may also be converted to glycogen for storage. When glycogen stores are depleted, fatty acids from fats are degraded for energy. Amino acids normally used to synthesize nitrogen-containing compounds in the cells can also be used for energy after they are degraded to intermediates of the citric acid cycle. In the synthesis of nonessential amino acids, α-keto acids of the citric acid cycle enter into a variety of reactions that convert them to amino acids through transamination by glutamate (see Figure 24.12).

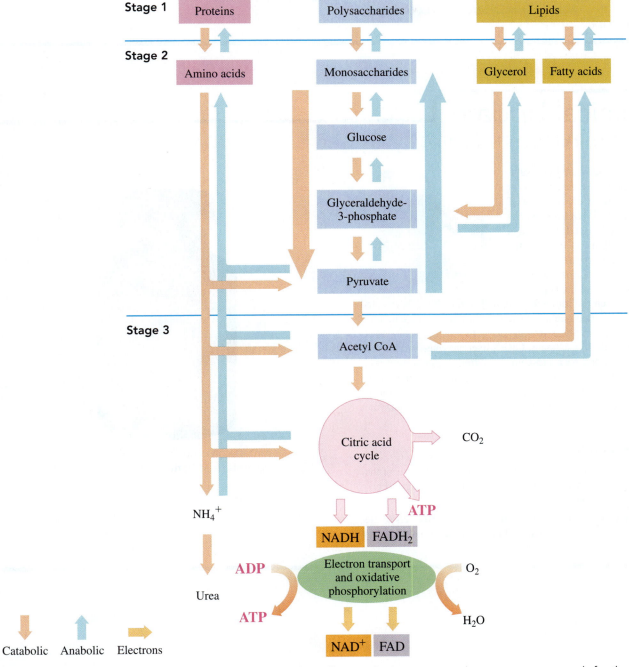

FIGURE 24.12 ▶ Catabolic and anabolic pathways in the cells provide the energy and necessary compounds for the cells.

Under what conditions in the cell are amino acids degraded for energy?

QUESTIONS AND PROBLEMS

24.9 Synthesis of Amino Acids

LEARNING GOAL Illustrate how some nonessential amino acids are synthesized from intermediates in the citric acid cycle and other metabolic pathways.

24.63 What do we call the amino acids that humans can synthesize?

24.64 How do humans obtain the amino acids that cannot be synthesized in the body?

24.65 How is glutamate converted to glutamine?

24.66 What amino acid can be converted into the amino acid tyrosine?

24.67 What do the letters PKU mean?

24.68 How is PKU treated?

 Clinical Update

Treatment of Luke's Hepatitis C

When Luke had a follow-up liver evaluation three months later, his liver enzymes were more elevated: ALT 356 Units/L and AST 418 Units/L. His doctor suggested that Luke begin interferon and ribavirin therapy for six months. Interferon and ribavirin work together as antiviral agents to inhibit the replication of the hepatitis C virus and strengthen the immune system. The interferon is injected subcutaneously or intramuscularly three times a week for nine months. The ribavarin is taken orally as 400-mg tablets twice a day.

After eight weeks of treatment, Luke's liver enzymes had lowered to ALT 85 Units/L and AST 115 Units/L. After four months of therapy, his ALT and AST enzyme levels were within the normal range. Luke will continue to have a liver profile every three months for the next year, and then every six months. Monitoring of his liver enzymes will continue throughout his life.

Clinical Applications

24.69 Draw the condensed structural formulas for the products of the reaction of alanine and α-ketoglutarate, which is catalyzed by *alanine transaminase* (ALT).

24.70 Draw the condensed structural formulas for the products of the reaction of aspartate and α-ketoglutarate, which is catalyzed by *aspartate transaminase* (AST).

Interferon is one of the antiviral agents used to treat hepatitis C.

METABOLIC PATHWAYS FOR LIPIDS AND AMINO ACIDS

Triacylglycerols

yield

Glycerol   **Fatty Acids**

to yield

undergo

β Oxidation   **Lipogenesis**

to yield

Acetyl CoA

enters

Citric Acid Cycle   that enter   **Intermediates**

to yield

NADH   **FADH$_2$**   **CO$_2$**

Proteins

yield

Amino Acids

that form α-keto acids by   to yield

Transamination

or are degraded by

Oxidative Deamination

to yield   removes an amino group as

NH$_4^+$

which enters the

Urea Cycle

that provide H$^+$ and electrons for

Electron Transport

and synthesis of

ATP   **H$_2$O**

CHAPTER REVIEW

24.1 Digestion of Triacylglycerols
LEARNING GOAL
Describe the sites and products obtained from the digestion of triacylglycerols.

- Triacylglycerols are hydrolyzed in the small intestine to yield monoacylglycerols and fatty acids, which enter the intestinal wall and form new triacylglycerols.
- Triacylglycerols bind with proteins to form chylomicrons, which transport them through the lymphatic system and bloodstream to the tissues.

24.2 Oxidation of Fatty Acids
LEARNING GOAL Describe the metabolic pathway of β oxidation.

- When used as an energy source, fatty acids link

$$CH_3-(CH_2)_6-\underset{\beta}{CH_2}-\underset{\alpha}{CH_2}-\overset{\displaystyle O}{\overset{\|}{C}}-S-CoA$$

❶

FAD

FADH$_2$

$$CH_3-(CH_2)_6-\underset{\beta}{CH}=\underset{\alpha}{CH}-\overset{\displaystyle O}{\overset{\|}{C}}-S-CoA$$

to coenzyme A to be transported into the mitochondria, where they undergo β oxidation.
- The acyl chain is oxidized to yield a shorter fatty acid, acetyl CoA, and the reduced coenzymes NADH and FADH$_2$.

24.3 ATP and Fatty Acid Oxidation
LEARNING GOAL Calculate the total ATP produced by the complete oxidation of a fatty acid.

- The activation of a fatty acid for β oxidation requires an input of two ATP.
- The energy obtained from a particular fatty acid depends on its length, with each oxidation cycle yielding four ATP and an additional 10 ATP from each acetyl CoA that enters the citric acid cycle.

24.4 Ketogenesis and Ketone Bodies

LEARNING GOAL Describe the pathway of ketogenesis.

- When high levels of acetyl CoA are present in the cell, they enter the ketogenesis pathway, forming ketone bodies such as acetoacetate, which can cause ketosis and acidosis.

24.5 Fatty Acid Synthesis

LEARNING GOAL Describe the biosynthesis of fatty acids from acetyl CoA.

- When there is an excess of acetyl CoA in the cell, the two-carbon acetyl CoA units link together to synthesize palmitate, which is converted to triacylglycerols and stored in the adipose tissue.

24.6 Degradation of Proteins and Amino Acids

LEARNING GOAL Describe the hydrolysis of dietary protein and the reactions of transamination and oxidative deamination in the degradation of amino acids.

Stomach

Proteins $\xrightarrow{\text{Pepsin}}$ Polypeptides

Small Intestine

$\xrightarrow[\text{Chymotrypsin}]{\text{Trypsin}}$

Amino acids

- The digestion of proteins, which begins in the stomach and continues in the small intestine, involves the hydrolysis of peptide bonds by proteases to yield amino acids that are absorbed through the intestinal wall and transported to the cells.

- When the amount of amino acids in the cells exceeds that needed for the synthesis of nitrogen compounds, the process of transamination converts them to α-keto acids and glutamate.
- Oxidative deamination of glutamate produces ammonium ions and α-ketoglutarate.

24.7 Urea Cycle

LEARNING GOAL Describe the formation of urea from an ammonium ion.

- Ammonium ions from oxidative deamination combine with carbon dioxide and ATP to form carbamoyl phosphate, which is converted to urea.

24.8 Fates of the Carbon Atoms from Amino Acids

LEARNING GOAL Describe where carbon atoms from amino acids enter the citric acid cycle or other pathways.

- The carbon atoms from the degradation of glucogenic amino acids enter the citric acid cycle or gluconeogenesis.
- Ketogenic amino acids produce acetyl CoA or acetoacetyl CoA for ketogenesis.

24.9 Synthesis of Amino Acids

LEARNING GOAL Illustrate how some nonessential amino acids are synthesized from intermediates in the citric acid cycle and other metabolic pathways.

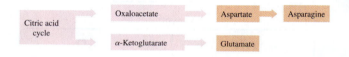

- Nonessential amino acids are synthesized when amino groups from glutamate are transferred to an α-keto acid obtained from glycolysis or the citric acid cycle.

SUMMARY OF KEY REACTIONS

The chapter sections to review are shown after the name of the reaction.

Digestion of Triacylglycerols (24.1)

Triacylglycerols $+ 2H_2O \xrightarrow{\text{Pancreatic lipase}}$ monoacylglycerols $+$ 2 fatty acids

Metabolism of Glycerol (24.1)

Glycerol $+$ ATP $+$ NAD$^+$ $\longrightarrow$ dihydroxyacetone phosphate $+$ ADP $+$ NADH $+$ H$^+$

Transamination (24.6)

Oxidative Deamination (24.6)

$$\overset{\overset{+}{NH_3}}{\underset{Glutamate}{^-OOC-CH-CH_2-CH_2-COO^-}} + H_2O + \boxed{NAD^+} \underset{\xleftarrow{\hspace{1cm}}}{\overset{\text{Glutamate}}{\underset{\text{dehydrogenase}}{\xrightarrow{\hspace{1cm}}}}}$$

$$\underset{\alpha\text{-Ketoglutarate}}{^-OOC-\overset{\overset{O}{\|}}{C}-CH_2-CH_2-COO^-} + NH_4^+ + \boxed{NADH + H^+}$$

Urea Cycle (24.7)

$$2NH_4^+ + CO_2 \longrightarrow \underset{Urea}{H_2N-\overset{\overset{O}{\|}}{C}-NH_2} + 2H^+ + H_2O$$

KEY TERMS

acidosis Low blood pH resulting from the formation of acidic ketone bodies.

beta oxidation (β oxidation) The degradation of fatty acids that removes two-carbon segments from a fatty acid chain at the oxidized β-carbon.

glucogenic amino acid An amino acid that provides carbon atoms for the synthesis of glucose.

ketogenesis The pathway that converts acetyl CoA to four-carbon acetoacetate and other ketone bodies.

ketogenic amino acid An amino acid that provides carbon atoms for the synthesis of fatty acids or ketone bodies.

ketone bodies The products of ketogenesis: acetoacetate, 3-hydroxybutyrate, and acetone.

ketosis A condition in which high levels of ketone bodies cannot be metabolized, leading to lower blood pH.

lipogenesis The synthesis of fatty acid in which two-carbon acetyl units link together to yield fatty acids, primarily palmitic acid.

oxidative deamination The loss of ammonium ion when glutamate is degraded to α-ketoglutarate.

protein turnover The amount of protein that we break down from our diet and utilize for synthesis of proteins and nitrogen-containing compounds.

transamination The transfer of an amino group from an amino acid to an α-keto acid.

urea cycle The process in which ammonium ions from the degradation of amino acids are converted to urea.

⚛ CORE CHEMISTRY SKILLS

The chapter section containing each Core Chemistry Skill is shown in parentheses at the end of each heading.

Calculating the ATP from Fatty Acid Oxidation (β Oxidation) (24.3)

- When needed as an energy source, fatty acids are linked to coenzyme A and transported into the mitochondria where they undergo β oxidation.
- The fatty acyl CoA is oxidized to yield a shorter fatty acyl CoA, acetyl CoA, and reduced coenzymes NADH and $FADH_2$.
- Although the energy from a particular fatty acid depends on its length, each oxidation cycle yields four ATP with another 10 ATP from each acetyl CoA that enters the citric acid cycle.
- When high levels of acetyl CoA are present in the cell, they enter the ketogenesis pathway, forming ketone bodies such as acetoacetate, which causes ketosis and acidosis.

Example: How many β oxidation cycles, acetyl CoA, and ATP are produced by the complete oxidation of caprylic acid, the C_8 saturated fatty acid?

Answer: An eight-carbon fatty acid will undergo three β oxidation cycles and produce four acetyl CoA. Each oxidation cycle produces four ATP (from one NADH and one $FADH_2$) for a total of 12 ATP. Each of the four acetyl CoA produces 10 ATP in the citric acid cycle or a total of 40 ATP. The 52 ATP minus two ATP for initial activation gives a total of 50 ATP from caprylic acid.

Describing How Ketone Bodies are Formed (24.4)

- Ketone bodies are formed when the body produces more acetyl CoA than it needs for energy.
- Excess acetyl CoA combines to form four-carbon and three-carbon ketone bodies.
- The ketone bodies are acetoacetate, β-hydroxybutyrate, and acetone.

Example: Acetone is a three-carbon ketone body. How is it formed from the two-carbon acetyl CoA?

Answer: Two acetyl CoA combine to form the four-carbon molecule, acetoacetate, which undergoes decarboxylation to form the three-carbon molecule acetone.

Distinguishing Anabolic and Catabolic Pathways (24.9)

- Pathways that degrade large molecules to small molecules to produce energy are catabolic.
- Those pathways that require energy for the biosynthesis of large molecules from small molecules are anabolic.

Example: Identify the following pathways as anabolic or catabolic:
  a. β oxidation of fatty acids
  b. synthesis of fatty acids
  c. degradation of amino acids
  d. synthesis of urea

Answer: **a.** catabolic
  b. anabolic
  c. catabolic
  d. anabolic

UNDERSTANDING THE CONCEPTS

The chapter sections to review are shown in parentheses at the end of each question.

24.71 Lauric acid, found in coconut oil, is a saturated C_{12} fatty acid. (24.2, 24.3)

Coconut oil contains lauric acid, a saturated C_{12} fatty acid.

a. Draw the line-angle structural formula for the activated form of lauric acid.
b. Indicate the α- and β-carbon atoms in the acyl molecule.
c. How many cycles of β oxidation are needed?
d. How many acetyl CoA units are produced?
e. Calculate the total ATP yield from the complete β oxidation of lauric acid by completing the following:

Activation	−2 ATP
_____ NADH	_____ ATP
_____ FADH$_2$	_____ ATP
_____ Acetyl CoA	_____ ATP
Total	_____ ATP

24.72 Arachidic acid is a saturated C_{20} fatty acid found in peanut and fish oils. (24.2, 24.3)

Peanuts contain arachidic acid, a saturated C_{20} fatty acid.

a. Draw the line-angle structural formula for the activated form of arachidic acid.
b. Indicate the α- and β-carbon atoms in the acyl molecule.
c. How many cycles of β oxidation are needed?
d. How many acetyl CoA units are produced?
e. Calculate the total ATP yield from the complete β oxidation of arachidic acid by completing the following:

Activation	−2 ATP
_____ NADH	_____ ATP
_____ FADH$_2$	_____ ATP
_____ Acetyl CoA	_____ ATP
Total	_____ ATP

ADDITIONAL QUESTIONS AND PROBLEMS

24.73 How are dietary triacylglycerols digested? (24.1)

24.74 What is a chylomicron? (24.1)

24.75 Why are the fats in the adipose tissues of the body considered the major form of stored energy? (24.1)

24.76 How are fatty acids obtained from stored fats? (24.1)

24.77 Why doesn't the brain utilize fatty acids for energy? (24.1)

24.78 Why don't red blood cells utilize fatty acids for energy? (24.1)

℞ Clinical Applications

24.79 A triacylglycerol is hydrolyzed in the fat cells of adipose tissues and the fatty acid is transported to the liver. (24.1, 24.2)
  a. What happens to the glycerol?
  b. Where in the liver cells is the fatty acid activated for β oxidation?
  c. What is the energy cost for activation of the fatty acid?
  d. What is the purpose of activating fatty acids?

24.80 Consider the β oxidation of a saturated fatty acid. (24.2, 24.3)
  a. What is the activated form of the fatty acid?
  b. Why is this oxidation called β oxidation?
  c. Which reactions in the fatty acid cycle require coenzymes?
  d. What is the yield in ATP for one cycle of β oxidation?

24.81 Identify each of the following as involved in β oxidation or in fatty acid synthesis: (24.2, 24.3, 24.5)
  a. NAD^+
  b. occurs in the mitochondrial matrix
  c. malonyl ACP
  d. cleavage of a two-carbon acetyl group
  e. acyl carrier protein
  f. carboxylase

24.82 Identify each of the following as involved in β oxidation or in fatty acid synthesis: (24.2, 24.3, 24.5)
  a. NADPH
  b. takes place in the cytosol
  c. FAD
  d. oxidation of a hydroxyl group
  e. coenzyme A
  f. hydration of a double bond

24.83 The metabolism of triacylglycerols and carbohydrates is influenced by the hormones insulin and glucagon. Indicate the results of each of the following as stimulating fatty acid oxidation or fatty acid synthesis: (24.2, 24.3, 24.5)
  a. high blood glucose
  b. secretion of glucagon

24.84 The metabolism of triacylglycerols and carbohydrates is influenced by the hormones insulin and glucagon. Indicate the results of each of the following as stimulating fatty acid oxidation or fatty acid synthesis: (24.2, 24.3, 24.5)
  a. low blood glucose   **b.** secretion of insulin

24.85 Why is ammonium ion that is produced in the liver converted immediately to urea? (24.7)

24.86 What compound is regenerated to repeat the urea cycle? (24.7)

24.87 Indicate the reactant in the urea cycle that reacts with each of the following compounds: (24.7)
  a. aspartate   **b.** ornithine

24.88 Indicate the products in the urea cycle that are manufactured from the reaction that uses each of the following compounds: (24.7)
  a. arginine   **b.** argininosuccinate

24.89 What component of the citric acid cycle can be produced from the carbon atoms of each of the following amino acids? (24.8)
  a. serine   **b.** lysine
  c. methionine   **d.** glutamate

24.90 What component of the citric acid cycle can be produced from the carbon atoms of each of the following amino acids? (24.8)
  a. glycine   **b.** isoleucine
  c. histidine   **d.** phenylalanine

24.91 How much ATP can be produced by the degradation of serine? (24.8)

24.92 Calculate the total ATP produced in the complete oxidation of caproic acid, $C_6H_{12}O_2$, and compare it with the total ATP produced from the oxidation of glucose, $C_6H_{12}O_6$. (24.3)

CHALLENGE QUESTIONS

The following groups of questions are related to the topics in this chapter. However, they do not all follow the chapter order, and they require you to combine concepts and skills from several sections. These questions will help you increase your critical thinking skills and prepare for your next exam.

24.93 Identify each of the following reactions in the β oxidation of palmitic acid, a C_{16} fatty acid, as activation, transport into mitochondria, first oxidation, hydration, second oxidation, or cleavage (thiolysis): (24.2)
  a. Palmitoyl CoA and FAD form α,β-unsaturated palmitoyl CoA and $FADH_2$.
  b. 3-Ketopalmitoyl CoA forms myristoyl CoA and acetyl CoA.
  c. Palmitic acid, HS—CoA, and ATP form palmitoyl CoA.

24.94 Identify each of the following reactions in the β oxidation of palmitic acid, a C_{16} fatty acid, as activation, transport into mitochondria, first oxidation, hydration, second oxidation, or cleavage (thiolysis): (24.2)
  a. α,β-Unsaturated palmitoyl CoA and H_2O form 3-hydroxypalmitoyl CoA.
  b. 3-Hydroxypalmitoyl CoA and NAD^+ form 3-ketopalmitoyl CoA and $NADH + H^+$.

  c. Palmitoyl CoA condenses with carnitine to form palmitoyl carnitine.

24.95 Draw the condensed structural formula for and give the name of the amino acid formed when the following α-keto acids undergo transamination with glutamate: (24.9)

  a. $CH_3-CH-\overset{\overset{CH_3}{|}}{C}-\overset{\overset{O}{||}}{C}-\overset{\overset{O}{||}}{C}-O^-$

  b. $CH_3-CH_2-CH-\overset{\overset{CH_3}{|}}{C}-\overset{\overset{O}{||}}{C}-\overset{\overset{O}{||}}{C}-O^-$

24.96 Draw the condensed structural formula for and give the name of the amino acid formed when the following α-keto acids undergo transamination with glutamate: (24.9)

  a. $^-O-\overset{\overset{O}{||}}{C}-CH_2-\overset{\overset{O}{||}}{C}-\overset{\overset{O}{||}}{C}-O^-$

  b. $CH_3-CH-CH_2-\overset{\overset{CH_3}{|}}{}\,\overset{\overset{O}{||}}{C}-\overset{\overset{O}{||}}{C}-O^-$

ANSWERS

Answers to Selected Questions and Problems

24.1 The bile salts emulsify fat so that it forms small fat globules for lipase hydrolysis.

24.3 Fats are released from fat stores when blood glucose and glycogen stores are depleted.

24.5 Glycerol is converted to glycerol-3-phosphate, and then to dihydroxyacetone phosphate, an intermediate of glycolysis.

24.7 The enzyme glycerol kinase would be defective.

24.9 In the cytosol at the outer mitochondrial membrane.

24.11 FAD, NAD$^+$, and HS—CoA

24.13 a.

$$CH_3-CH_2-CH_2-CH_2-CH_2-\underset{\beta}{CH_2}-CH_2-\overset{\displaystyle O}{\overset{\|}{C}}-S-CoA$$

b.

24.15 a.

b.
$$CH_3-(CH_2)_6-\overset{\displaystyle H}{\underset{}{C}}=\overset{}{\underset{\displaystyle H}{C}}-\overset{\displaystyle O}{\overset{\|}{C}}-S-CoA$$

24.17 a. and b.
$$CH_3-(CH_2)_4-CH_2-\underset{\beta}{CH_2}-\underset{\alpha}{CH_2}-\overset{\displaystyle O}{\overset{\|}{C}}-S-CoA$$

c. three β oxidation cycles

d. four acetyl CoA units

24.19 The hydrolysis of ATP to AMP involves the hydrolysis of ATP to ADP, and then ADP to AMP, which provides the same amount of energy as the hydrolysis of two ATP to two ADP.

24.21 a. 10 β oxidation cycles

b. 11 acetyl CoA units

c. 110 ATP from 11 acetyl CoA (citric acid cycle) + 25 ATP from 10 NADH + 15 ATP from 10 FADH$_2$ − 2 ATP (activation) = 148 ATP (total)

24.23 For the corresponding saturated acid stearic acid 18:0, we calculate:

a. 8 cycles of β oxidation

b. 9 acetyl CoA units

c. 90 ATP from 9 acetyl CoA (citric acid cycle) + 20 ATP from 8 NADH + 10.5 ATP from 7 FADH$_2$ − 2 ATP (activation) = 118.5 ATP (total)

24.25 Ketogenesis is the synthesis of ketone bodies from excess acetyl CoA during fatty acid oxidation, which occurs when glucose is not available for energy, particularly in starvation, low-carbohydrate diets, fasting, alcoholism, and diabetes.

24.27 Acetoacetate undergoes reduction using NADH + H$^+$ to yield 3-hydroxybutyrate.

24.29 Ketosis is a condition characterized by acidosis (a drop in blood pH values), excessive urination, and strong thirst.

24.31 Fatty acid synthesis occurs in the cytosol of cells in liver and adipose tissue.

24.33 acetyl CoA, HCO$_3^-$, and ATP

24.35 a. (3) malonyl CoA transacylase

b. (1) acetyl CoA carboxylase

c. (2) acetyl CoA transacylase

24.37 a. 4 HCO$_3^-$ **b.** 4 ATP

c. 5 acetyl CoA   **d.** 4 malonyl ACP

e. 8 NADPH   **f.** 4 CO$_2$ removed

24.39 a. Reaction 4, the reduction of the double bond to a single bond, is catalyzed by enoyl ACP reductase.

b. If fatty acid synthesis is inhibited, the bacteria cannot form cell walls and will not thrive.

24.41 The digestion of proteins begins in the stomach and is completed in the small intestine.

24.43 Hormones, heme, purines and pyrimidines for nucleotides, proteins, nonessential amino acids, amino alcohols, and neurotransmitters require nitrogen obtained from amino acids.

24.45 The reactants are an amino acid and an α-keto acid, and the products are a new amino acid and a new α-keto acid.

24.47 a.
$$H-\overset{\displaystyle O}{\overset{\|}{C}}-COO^-$$

b.
$$HS-CH_2-\overset{\displaystyle O}{\overset{\|}{C}}-COO^-$$

c.
$$CH_3-\overset{\displaystyle CH_3}{\underset{}{CH}}-\overset{\displaystyle O}{\overset{\|}{C}}-COO^-$$

24.49

24.51 $H_2N-\overset{\overset{\displaystyle O}{\|}}{C}-NH_2$

24.53 CO_2 from the citric acid cycle

24.55 NH_4^+ is toxic if allowed to accumulate in the liver.

24.57 If there is a deficiency of argininosuccinate synthetase, citrulline will accumulate.

24.59 Glucogenic amino acids are used to synthesize glucose.

24.61 a. oxaloacetate   **b.** oxaloacetate
    c. succinyl CoA   **d.** α-ketoglutarate

24.63 nonessential amino acids

24.65 Glutamine synthetase catalyzes the addition of $-NH_3^+$ to glutamate using energy from the hydrolysis of ATP.

24.67 phenylketonuria

24.69

$$CH_3-\overset{\overset{\displaystyle O}{\|}}{C}-COO^- + {}^-OOC-\overset{\overset{\displaystyle {}^+NH_3}{|}}{CH}-CH_2-CH_2-COO^-$$

Pyruvate   Glutamate

24.71 a. and b.

  c. Five cycles of β oxidation are needed.
  d. Six acetyl CoA units are produced.
  e.

Activation	−2 ATP
$5 \text{ NADH} \times \dfrac{2.5 \text{ ATP}}{\text{NADH}}$	12.5 ATP
$5 \text{ FADH}_2 \times \dfrac{1.5 \text{ ATP}}{\text{FADH}_2}$	7.5 ATP
$6 \text{ acetyl CoA} \times \dfrac{10 \text{ ATP}}{\text{acetyl CoA}}$	60 ATP
Total	78 ATP

24.73 Triacylglycerols are hydrolyzed to monoacylglycerols and fatty acids in the small intestine, which reform as triacylglycerols in the intestinal lining for transport as lipoproteins to the tissues.

24.75 Fats can be stored in unlimited amounts in adipose tissue compared to the limited storage of carbohydrates as glycogen.

24.77 The fatty acids cannot diffuse across the blood–brain barrier.

24.79 a. Glycerol is converted to glycerol-3-phosphate and then to dihydroxyacetone phosphate, which can enter glycolysis or gluconeogenesis.
  b. Activation of fatty acids occurs in the cytosol at the outer mitochondrial membrane.
  c. The energy cost is equal to two ATP.
  d. Only acyl CoA can move into the intermembrane space for transport by carnitine into the matrix.

24.81 a. β oxidation   **b.** β oxidation
  c. fatty acid synthesis   **d.** β oxidation
  e. fatty acid synthesis   **f.** fatty acid synthesis

24.83 a. fatty acid synthesis   **b.** fatty acid oxidation

24.85 Ammonium ion is toxic if allowed to accumulate in the liver.

24.87 a. citrulline   **b.** carbamoyl phosphate

24.89 a. oxaloacetate   **b.** acetyl CoA
  c. succinyl CoA   **d.** α-ketoglutarate

24.91 Serine is degraded to pyruvate, which is oxidized to acetyl CoA. The oxidation produces $NADH + H^+$, which provides 2.5 ATP. In one turn of the citric acid cycle, the acetyl CoA produces 10 ATP. Thus, serine can provide 12.5 ATP.

24.93 a. first oxidation   **b.** cleavage (thiolysis)
  c. activation

24.95 a.

$$CH_3-\overset{\overset{\displaystyle CH_3}{|}}{CH}-\overset{\overset{\displaystyle {}^+NH_3}{|}}{CH}-\overset{\overset{\displaystyle O}{\|}}{C}-O^-$$ Valine

  b.

$$CH_3-CH_2-\overset{\overset{\displaystyle CH_3}{|}}{CH}-\overset{\overset{\displaystyle {}^+NH_3}{|}}{CH}-\overset{\overset{\displaystyle O}{\|}}{C}-O^-$$ Isoleucine

CI.47 Identify each of the following as a substance that is part of the citric acid cycle, electron transport, or both: (23.1, 23.2, 23.3)

a. GTP
b. $CoQH_2$
c. $FADH_2$
d. cyt c
e. succinate dehydrogenase
f. complex I
g. isocitrate
h. NAD^+

CI.48 Use the value of 7.3 kcal per mole of ATP to determine the total kilocalories stored as ATP from each of the following: (23.4, 24.2, 24.3, 24.8)

a. the reactions of 1 mole of glucose in glycolysis
b. the oxidation of 2 moles of pyruvate to 2 moles of acetyl CoA
c. the complete oxidation of 1 mole of glucose to CO_2 and H_2O
d. the β oxidation of 1 mole of lauric acid, a saturated C_{12} fatty acid
e. the reaction of 1 mole of glutamate (from protein) in the citric acid cycle

CI.49 Acetyl CoA (HS—CoA) is the fuel for the citric acid cycle. It has the formula $C_{23}H_{38}N_7O_{17}P_3S$. (22.2, 23.1, 23.4)

a. What are the components of acetyl CoA?
b. What is the function of HS—CoA?
c. Where does the acetyl group attach to HS—CoA?
d. What is the molar mass (to three significant figures) of acetyl CoA?
e. How many moles of ATP are produced when 1.0 mg of acetyl CoA completes one turn of the citric acid cycle?

CI.50 State if each of the following produces or consumes ATP: (22.5, 22.6, 23.1, 23.4, 24.2)

a. citric acid cycle
b. glucose forms two pyruvate
c. pyruvate yields acetyl CoA
d. glucose forms glucose-6-phosphate
e. oxidation of α-ketoglutarate
f. transport of NADH across the mitochondrial membrane
g. activation of a fatty acid

CI.51 Butter is a fat that contains 80.% by mass triacylglycerols. Assume the triacylglycerol in butter is glyceryl tripalmitate. (17.4, 24.2, 24.3)

Butter is high in triacylglycerols.

a. Write an equation for the hydrolysis of glyceryl tripalmitate.
b. What is the molar mass of glyceryl tripalmitate, $C_{51}H_{98}O_6$?
c. Calculate the ATP yield from the complete oxidation of 1 mole of palmitic acid, a saturated C_{16} fatty acid.
d. How many kilocalories are released from the palmitate in 0.50 oz of butter?
e. If running for exactly 1 h uses 750 kcal, how many ounces of butter would provide the energy (kcal) for a 45-min run?

CI.52 Match these ATP yields with the given reactions: 1 ATP, 1.5 ATP, 2 ATP, 2.5 ATP, 3 ATP, 5 ATP, 10 ATP, 15 ATP, 30 ATP (22.5, 22.6, 23.1, 23.4, 24.3)

a. Glucose yields two pyruvate.
b. Pyruvate yields acetyl CoA.
c. Glucose yields two acetyl CoA.
d. Acetyl CoA goes through one turn of the citric acid cycle.
e. Succinyl CoA yield succinate.
f. Glucose is completely oxidized to CO_2 and H_2O.
g. $FADH_2$ is oxidized to FAD.

CI.53 Which of the following molecules will produce more ATP per mole when each is completely oxidized? (22.4, 22.5, 23.1, 23.4, 24.3)

a. glucose or maltose
b. myristic acid, $CH_3—(CH_2)_{10}—CH_2—CH_2—COOH$, or stearic acid, $CH_3—(CH_2)_{14}—CH_2—CH_2—COOH$
c. glucose or two acetyl CoA

CI.54 Which of the following molecules will produce more ATP per mole when each is completely oxidized? (22.4, 22.5, 23.1, 23.4, 24.3)

a. glucose or caprylic acid C_8
b. citrate or succinate in one turn of the citric acid cycle
c. glutamate or tyrosine in one turn of the citric acid cycle

ANSWERS

CI.47 a. citric acid cycle
c. both
e. citric acid cycle
g. citric acid cycle
b. electron transport
d. electron transport
f. electron transport
h. both

CI.49 a. aminoethanethiol, pantothenic acid (vitamin B_5), and phosphorylated ADP
b. Coenzyme A carries an acetyl group to the citric acid cycle for oxidation.
c. The acetyl group links to the sulfur atom (—S—) in the aminoethanethiol part of CoA.
d. 810. g/mole
e. 1.2×10^{-5} mole of ATP

CI.51 a.

$$CH_2—O—\overset{\overset{\displaystyle O}{\|}}{C}—(CH_2)_{14}—CH_3$$
$$CH—O—\overset{\overset{\displaystyle O}{\|}}{C}—(CH_2)_{14}—CH_3 + 3H_2O \longrightarrow$$
$$CH_2—O—\overset{\overset{\displaystyle O}{\|}}{C}—(CH_2)_{14}—CH_3$$

$$CH_2—OH$$
$$CH—OH + 3HO—\overset{\overset{\displaystyle O}{\|}}{C}—(CH_2)_{14}—CH_3$$
$$CH_2—OH$$

b. 807 g/mole
d. 33 kcal
c. 106 moles of ATP
e. 8.5 oz of butter

CI.53 a. maltose **b.** stearic acid **c.** glucose

Credits

Photo Credits

Chapter 1

p. 1 *bottom, left:* anyaivanova / Shutterstock
p. 1 *top, right:* whiteboxmedia limited / Alamy
p. 2 *center, left:* Andreas Reh / iStock / Getty Images
p. 2 *bottom, right:* Pearson Education
p. 3 *bottom, center:* Stephen Coburn / 123RF
p. 3 *top, right:* Eric Schrader / Pearson Education
p. 4 J.R. Eyerman / Time & Life Pictures / Getty Images
p. 5 *top, right:* Photos.com / Getty Images
p. 5 *bottom, left:* Mark III Photonics / Shutterstock
p. 5 *bottom, center:* webphotographeer / E+ / Getty Images
p. 6 Eugene Bochkarev / Getty Images
p. 7 Chris Schmidt / Getty Images
p. 8 Steve Nagy / Design Pics Inc / Alamy
p. 11 f9photos / Fotolia
p. 12 spxChrome / E+ / Getty Images
p. 13 Kevin Peschke / Alamy
p. 15 Jason Stitt / Shutterstock
p. 16 Heather Davies / Science Photo Library / Alamy
p. 19 anyaivanova / Shutterstock
p. 20 *top, left:* Pearson Education
p. 20 *top, right:* Chris Schmidt / Getty Images
p. 20 *bottom, right:* Jason Stitt / Shutterstock
p. 22 *bottom, center:* Pressmaster / Shutterstock
p. 22 *center:* ostill / Shutterstock

Chapter 2

p. 25 AVAVA / Shutterstock
p. 26 Rod Ferris / Shutterstock
p. 27 *bottom, right:* Pearson Education
p. 27 *top, center:* Scott Leigh / Getty Images
p. 28 *center, left:* Richard Megna / Fundamental Photographs
p. 28 *bottom, right:* Pearson Education
p. 28 *top, left:* National Institute of Standards and Technology
p. 28 *bottom, left:* Pearson Education
p. 29 Cheryl Casey / Shutterstock
p. 31 Nick M. Do / iStock / Getty Images
p. 33 Radu Razvan / Shutterstock
p. 34 emin kuliyev / Shutterstock
p. 37 *bottom, left:* CHASSENET / BSIP SA / Alamy
p. 37 *top, right:* legolex / Fotolia
p. 37 *center, right:* Monkey Business Images / Shutterstock.com
p. 38 Pearson Education
p. 39 Pearson Education
p. 41 *top, right:* Eric Schrader / Pearson Education
p. 41 *center, right:* Syner-Comm / Alamy
p. 41 *bottom, right:* Pearson Education
p. 42 *top, left:* CMSP / Custom Medical Stock Photo
p. 42 *center, left:* Pearson Education
p. 43 *top, right:* Julie Woodhouse f / Alamy
p. 43 *bottom, right:* Congressional Quarterly / Newscom
p. 43 *center, right:* ExQuisine / Fotolia
p. 47 WavebreakMediaMicro / Fotolia
p. 48 *top, left:* Carlos Alvarez / Getty Images
p. 48 *center, right:* Jakub Jirsák / Fotolia
p. 49 Pearson Education
p. 50 *bottom, left:* Pearson Education
p. 50 *bottom, right:* Pearson Education

p. 51

p. 51 *top, left:* Professor Pietro M. Motta / Science Source
p. 51 *center:* Professor Pietro M. Motta / Science Source
p. 51 *top, right:* VOISIN / PHANIE / Science Source
p. 52 *center, left:* Jpc-Prod / Fotolia
p. 52 *bottom, center:* Dallas Events Inc / Shutterstock
p. 53 *bottom, center:* AVAVA / Shutterstock
p. 53 *bottom, right:* Editorial Image, LLC / Alamy
p. 54 *center:* Pearson Education
p. 54 *bottom, right:* emin kuliyev / Shutterstock
p. 55 *center:* Eric Schrader / Pearson Education
p. 55 *top, right:* Jakub Jirsák / Fotolia
p. 55 *center, right:* Pearson Education
p. 57 romans14 / Fotolia
p. 59 Cristian Ciureanu / Alamy

Chapter 3

p. 63 Network Photographer / Alamy
p. 64 Norman Chan / Fotolia
p. 65 *top, right:* Bomshtein / Shutterstock
p. 65 *bottom, right:* Eric Schrader / Pearson Education
p. 65 *center:* Pearson Education / Pearson Science
p. 65 *center, left:* Pearson Science / Pearson Education
p. 66 *bottom, left:* Richard Megna / Fundamental Photographs
p. 66 *center, left:* David Murray and Jules Selmes / Dorling Kindersley
p. 66 *bottom, right:* Eric Schrader / Pearson Education
p. 66 *top, center:* Lagui / Shutterstock
p. 66 *top, right:* Pearson Education / Pearson Science
p. 66 *top, center:* Pearson Education / Pearson Science
p. 66 *top, left:* rsooll / Fotolia
p. 67 Charles Stirling (Diving) / Alamy
p. 68 *center, left:* Justinb / Fotolia
p. 68 *center, right:* Lisa Kyle Young / E+ / Getty Images
p. 68 *top, left:* Siede Preis / Photodisc / Getty Images
p. 69 *top, center:* Elena Elisseeva / Shutterstock
p. 69 *center, right:* Rafa Irusta / www.shutterstock
p. 69 *top, left:* Ray Roberts / Alamy
p. 69 *bottom, right:* Westend61 GmbH / Alamy
p. 70 Digital Vision / Alamy
p. 74 JenniferPhotographyImaging / E+ / Getty Images
p. 75 Science Photo Library / Alamy
p. 77 NASA
p. 78 Pearson Education / Pearson Science
p. 80 Stockbyte / Getty Images
p. 81 *bottom, right:* Alan Holden / Alamy
p. 81 *center, right:* Celso Pupo / Fotolia
p. 83 *center:* John A. Rizzo / Photodisc / Getty Images
p. 83 *top:* Mark Downey / Getty Images
p. 84 wsphotos / Getty Images
p. 85 *bottom, right:* Nikkytok / Fotolia
p. 85 *center, right:* Pearson Education / Pearson Science
p. 85 *center, left:* Pearson Education / Pearson Science
p. 86 *top, left:* John Scrivener / E+ / Getty Images
p. 86 *center, left:* Pearson Education / Pearson Science
p. 87 nikkytok / Fotolia

p. 88

p. 88 *center, left:* John A. Rizzo / Photodisc / Getty Images
p. 88 *top, right:* Mark Downey / Getty Images
p. 91 Network Photographer / Alamy
p. 92 *bottom, center:* Richard Megna / Fundamental Photographs
p. 92 *bottom, right:* Justinb / Fotolia
p. 93 *top, right:* Celso Pupo / Fotolia
p. 93 *center:* JenniferPhotographyImaging / E+ / Getty Images
p. 93 *center:* Pearson Education / Pearson Science
p. 95 *center:* Franz Pfluegl / Getty Images
p. 95 *bottom, left:* Pearson Education / Pearson Science
p. 95 *bottom, center:* Spencer Jones / Photodisc / Getty Images
p. 95 *bottom, right:* teleginatania / Fotolia
p. 96 Fuat Kose / E+ / Getty Images
p. 97 Khoroshunova Olga / Shutterstock
p. 100 *center, right:* Eric Schrader / Pearson Education
p. 100 *top, left:* Impala / Fotolia
p. 100 *center:* Shalom Ormsby / Photodisc / Getty Images
p. 101 *top, left:* Aleksandr Volkov / Fotolia
p. 101 Fuse / Getty Images

Chapter 4

p. 103 Martin Harvey / Alamy
p. 105 *top, right:* Pearson Science / Pearson Education
p. 105 *center, right:* Pearson Science / Pearson Education
p. 105 *center, right:* Pearson Science / Pearson Education
p. 105 *bottom, right:* Pearson Science / Pearson Education
p. 105 *bottom, right:* Pearson Science / Pearson Education
p. 106 marcel / Fotolia
p. 108 *top, left:* Pearson Science / Pearson Education
p. 108 *center, left:* Pearson Science / Pearson Education
p. 108 *bottom, left:* Pearson Science / Pearson Education
p. 109 Pearson Science / Pearson Education
p. 110 *top, left:* Pearson Science / Pearson Education
p. 110 *center, left:* Polushkin Ivan / Shutterstock
p. 113 *center, right:* IBM Research Division
p. 113 *top, right:* Russ Lappa / Pearson Education
p. 114 Pearson Science / Pearson Education
p. 116 Eric Schrader / Fundamental Photographs
p. 118 *center, right:* Atiketta Sangasaeng / Shutterstock
p. 118 *center, left:* gabyjalbert / Getty Images
p. 119 Pearson Science / Pearson Education
p. 120 *center, left:* Nancy Ross / iStock / Getty Images
p. 120 *bottom, left:* Tarasov / Shutterstock
p. 121 ANATOL ADUTSKEVICH / Getty Images
p. 124 Cindy Minear / Shutterstock
p. 125 Thorsten Rust / Shutterstock
p. 128 olly / Fotolia
p. 143 Nigel Cattlin / Alamy
p. 144 Pearson Science / Pearson Education
p. 148 craftvision / E+ / Getty Images

Chapter 5

p. 153 Monkey Business Images / Shutterstock
p. 156 *center, left:* 4x6 / Getty Images
p. 156 *bottom, left:* Josh Sher / Science Source
p. 158 Stephen Uber / E+ / Getty Images

Chapter 17

p. 608	michaeljung / Fotolia
p. 613	*center, right:* Bjorn Heller / Getty Images
p. 613	*center, left:* Charles Brutlag / Getty Images
p. 615	Jupiterimages / Getty Images
p. 617	*center, right:* blickwinkel / Jagel / Alamy
p. 617	*top, right:* Tischenko Irina / Shutterstock
p. 618	*top, left:* John Pitcher / Getty Images
p. 618	*bottom, left:* kuleczka / Shutterstock
p. 619	Pearson Education / Pearson Science
p. 621	Pearson Education / Pearson Science
p. 622	Shelby Allison / Shutterstock
p. 625	L.G. Patterson / AP Images
p. 628	Audrey Snider-Bell / Shutterstock
p. 631	Santibhavank P / Shutterstock
p. 633	*top, right:* National Heart, Lung, and Blood Institut
p. 633	*bottom:* National Heart, Lung, and Blood Institute
p. 634	Martin / Custom Medical Stock Photo
p. 636	CoverSpot / Alamy
p. 640	*top, left:* michaeljung / Fotolia
p. 640	*bottom, right:* Matt Rourke / AP Images
p. 640	*bottom, left:* Robert Clare / Alamy
p. 641	Pearson Education / Pearson Science
p. 642	Pearson Education / Pearson Science
p. 644	*top, right:* Pearson Education / Pearson Science
p. 644	*bottom, left:* rangerx / Getty Images
p. 644	*bottom, right:* sampsyseeds / Getty Images
p. 645	*center, left:* Elena Schweitzer / Getty Images
p. 645	*top, right:* Lauree Feldman / Photolibrary / Getty Images
p. 646	Pearson Education / Pearson Science

Chapter 18

p. 649	Bart Coenders / E+ / Getty Images
p. 653	*left:* blickwinkel / Alamy
p. 653	*bottom, center:* Harvey Male / Imagestate Media Partners Limited - Impact Photos / Alamy
p. 658	Pearson Education / Pearson Science
p. 659	*bottom, right:* Brasil2 / Getty Images
p. 659	*bottom, right:* David Orcea / Shutterstock
p. 659	*top, right:* Pearson Education
p. 661	Pearson Education
p. 662	*center, left:* MikhailSh / Shutterstock
p. 662	*top, center:* Pearson Education
p. 663	De Meester Johan / Arterra Picture Library / Alamy
p. 666	Rosen / Custom Medical Stock Photo / Newscom
p. 667	Eric Schrader
p. 669	*center, right:* Eric Schrader
p. 669	*top, right:* Iain Cooper / Alamy
p. 675	Pearson Education
p. 678	David Hoffman Photo Library / Alamy
p. 679	*top, right:* Iain Cooper / Alamy
p. 679	*bottom, center:* Pearson Education
p. 681	*bottom, right:* DenisNata / Shutterstock
p. 681	*bottom, right:* Eric Schrader
p. 681	*bottom, left:* Pearson Education
p. 682	Eric Schrade / Pearson Education
p. 683	Tereshchenko Dmitry / Shutterstock
p. 686	*center, right:* Analia Valeria Urani / Shutterstock
p. 686	*top, left:* David Zaitz / Alamy
p. 686	*top, right:* Pearson Education
p. 686	*bottom, left:* worldswildlifewonders / Shutterstock
p. 687	Dustin Dennis / Shutterstock

Chapter 19

p. 688	Tyler Olson / Shutterstock
p. 689	DHuss / Getty Images
p. 693	Pearson Education
p. 700	OxytocinLg / APP Pharmaceuticals
p. 703	Brasil2 / E+ / Getty image

p. 705	Laurence Mouton / PhotoAlto sas / Alamy
p. 708	janol / Getty Images
p. 710	Janice Haney Carr / Center for Disease Control
p. 712	Pearson Education
p. 714	*bottom, left:* Susan Landau and William Jagust, UC Berkeley
p. 714	*top, left:* Tyler Olson / Shutterstock
p. 715	DHuss / Getty Images
p. 717	Pearson Education
p. 718	*top, left:* Miep Van Damm / Pearson Education
p. 718	*bottom, right:* Pearson Education

Chapter 20

p. 722	Diedra Laird / The Charlotte Observer / MCT / Newscom
p. 730	Natalia Pushchina / Shutterstock
p. 740	Pearson Education
p. 743	*center, right:* Mivr / Fotolia
p. 743	*bottom, right:* Oleg Zaslavsky / Shutterstock
p. 743	*center, left:* Pearson Education
p. 744	Diedra Laird / The Charlotte Observer / MCT / Newscom
p. 745	The Photo Works / Alamy
p. 748	*top, left:* Andy Crawford / Dorling Kindersley
p. 748	*bottom, left:* arska n / Fotolia
p. 748	*top, right:* Jane norton / E+ / Getty Images
p. 748	*bottom, right:* Pearson Education
p. 751	GlaxoSmithKline

Chapter 21

p. 753	Malcom Park / RGB Ventures / SuperStock / Alamy
p. 778	John R. Kreul / khunaspix / 123RF
p. 782	Tek Image / Science Source
p. 785	Alfred Pasieka / Science Source
p. 786	Malcom Park / RGB Ventures / SuperStock / Alamy
p. 787	Mark Thomas / Alamy
p. 789	*top, right:* John R. Kreul / khunaspix / 123RF
p. 789	*center, right:* Tek Image / Science Source
p. 795	Martin M. Rotker / Science Source

Chapter 22

p. 797	KatarzynaBialasiewicz / Getty Images
p. 799	viafilms / Getty Images
p. 802	*bottom:* Koji Aoki / Getty Images
p. 802	*bottom, left:* phasinphoto / Fotolia
p. 804	Benis Arapovic / 123RF
p. 817	Andy Clark AC / TZ / Reuters
p. 818	*top, left:* Oleksii Sergieiev / Fotolia
p. 818	*center, left:* Pearson Education
p. 822	Biophoto Associates / Science Source
p. 824	Alexey Fursov / Shutterstock
p. 829	KatarzynaBialasiewicz / Getty Images
p. 830	*center, right:* Oleksii Sergieiev / Fotolia
p. 830	*bottom, right:* Alexey Fursov / Shutterstock
p. 830	*top, left:* viafilms / Getty Images
p. 832	Karen Timberlake

Chapter 23

p. 836	*bottom, left:* Javier Larrea / AGE Fotostock
p. 836	*top, right:* juanrvelasco / Fotolia
p. 838	viafilms / Getty Images
p. 839	Africa Studio / Fotolia
p. 842	yurakp / Fotolia
p. 847	Allik Camazine / Alamy
p. 849	Jill Lang / Shutterstock
p. 855	Lumi Images / Dario Secen / Getty Images

Chapter 24

p. 861	Tyler Olson / Fotolia
p. 863	Science Photo Library - STEVE GSCHMEISSNER. / Getty Images
p. 871	*center, left:* David Pruter / Getty Images
p. 871	*bottom, left:* Javier GonzA!lez / Getty Images
p. 874	Pearson Education

p. 875	*bottom, left:* Dewayne Flowers / Shutterstock
p. 875	*center:* Dmitry Lobanov / Shutterstock
p. 890	US Navy
p. 892	*center, right:* SIU BIOMED COMM Custom Medical Stock Photo / Newscom
p. 892	*center, left:* Tyler Olson / Fotolia
p. 893	Javier GonzA!lez / Getty Images
p. 894	Pearson Education
p. 896	*center, left:* Floortje / Getty Images
p. 896	*center, right:* Pearson Education
p. 900	Pearson Education

Text Credits

Chapter 1

p. 4	John Horgan, 1993. Profile: Linus C. Pauling, Stubbornly Ahead of His Time, *Scientific American*, March 1993, 36–37

Chapter 11

p. 432	Based on 2004 MedicineNet, Inc.

Chapter 17

p. 629	© Pearson Education, Inc.

Chapter 20

p. 724	Lactase image by L. Frost of 1JYN (D.H. Juers, T.D. Heightman, A. Vasella, J.D. McCarter, L. Mackenzie, S.G. Withers, B.W. Matthews (2001) *Biochemistry* 40: 14781-14794) created in Rasmol 2.7.5.2 (R. Sayle, E.J. White (1995) Trends in Biochemical Sciences (TIBS), 20(9):374.)
p. 726	Alanine transaminase Image by L. Frost of 3IHJ (M. Wisniewska, M.I. Siponen, C.H. Arrowsmith, H. Berglund, C. Bountra, R. Collins, A.M. Edwards, S. Flodin, A. Flores, S. Graslund, M. Hammarstrom, A. Johansson, I. Johansson, T. Karlberg, T. Kotenyova, A. Kotzsch, M. Moche, T.K. Nielsen, P. Nordlund, T. Nyman, C. Persson, A.K. Roos, P. Schutz, L. Svensson, A.G. Thorsell, L. Tresaugues, S. Van Den Berg, J. Weigelt, M. Welin, H. Schuler. Human alanine aminotransferase 2 in complex with PLP) created in Rasmol 2.7.5.2 (R. Sayle, E.J. White (1995) Trends in Biochemical Sciences (TIBS), 20(9):374.)
p. 732	Trypsin Image by L. Frost of 2PTN (J. Walter, W. Steigemann, T.P. Singh, H. Bartunik, W. Bode, R. Huber (1982) Acta Crystallogr. Sect.B 38: 1462-1472.) created in Rasmol 2.7.5.2 (R. Sayle, E.J. White (1995) Trends in Biochemical Sciences (TIBS), 20(9):374.)
p. 734	Alpha-chymotrypsin image by L. Frost of 3CHA (R.S. Blevins, A. Tulinsky (1985) J. Biol. Chem. 260: 4262–4275) created in Rasmol 2.7.5.2 (R. Sayle, E.J. White (1995) Trends in Biochemical Sciences (TIBS), 20(9):374.)

Chapter 21

p. 765	© Pearson Education, Inc.
p. 787	Estrogen receptor image by L. Frost of 2ERD (A.K. Shiau, D. Barstad, P.M. Loria, L. Chemg, P.J. Kushner, D.A. Agard, G.L. Greene (1998) Cell (Cambridge, MA) 95:927–937) created in Rasmol 2.7.5.2 (R. Sayle, E.J. White (1995) Trends in Biochemical Sciences (TIBS), 20(9):374.)

Glossary/Index

A

Abbreviated configuration, 129
Absolute zero, 70
Acceptor stem, 767
Accutane, 122
Acetaldehyde, 518
  from alcohol oxidation, 503, 505
  oxidization of, 509, 887
  produced in liver, 505
Acetal The product of the addition of two alcohols to an aldehyde or ketone, 527–530, 540
Acetaminophen (Tylenol), 475, 476, 650, 675
Acetate ion, 197
Acetic acid, 326, 330, 582
Acetoacetate, 873
  from amino acid degradation, 887
  ketosis and, 873–874
Acetoacetyl CoA, 887
Acetone, 521
Acetyl ACP, 878
Acetylcholine, 666
Acetylcholinesterase inhibitors, 666, 737
Acetyl CoA The compound that forms when a two-carbon acetyl unit bonds to coenzyme A, 798–799, 807
  accumulation in liver, ketone bodies and, 873
  from amino acid degradation, 887
  beta oxidation and, 865–869
  citric acid cycle and, 843
  cleavage of, 867
  ketogenesis and, 873
  ketogenic amino acid and, 887
  lipogenesis and, 876
  from pyruvate, 814, 828
Acetylene, 460
Acetylene torch, 263
Acetylsalicylic acid. See Aspirin
Achiral Molecules with mirror images that are superimposable, 531–533
Achiral compound, 532
Acid A substance that dissolves in water and produces hydrogen ions (H^+), according to the Arrhenius theory. All acids are hydrogen ion donors, according to the Brønsted–Lowry theory, 399–442, 711–713
  bases and (neutralization), 423
  Brønsted–Lowry, 403
  carboxylic. See Carboxylic acid
  characteristics of, 402, 412
  conjugate acid–base pair, 404–405
  diprotic, 408–409
  and hydroxides, 423
  naming, 401
  reaction with carbonates or bicarbonates, 423
  reactions of, 423–425
  stomach, 422
  strength of, 406–411
  strong, 406–408, 412
  weak, 406–408, 412
Acid–base titration, 425–427
Acid dissociation constant K_a The product of the concentrations of the ions from the dissociation of a weak acid divided by the concentration of the weak acid, 411–413
Acidic amino acid An amino acid that has an R group with a carboxylate group ($-COO^-$), 689, 690–692
  acidic, 690
  basic, 690
  classification of, 690–692
  polar and nonpolar, 690
  structure, 690
Acidic solution, 414, 415
  pH of, 416
  stomach acid, 422
Acidosis A condition in which the blood has a lower pH than normal, 431, 874
Acid reflux disease, 432
Acid hydrolysis The splitting of an ester molecule in the presence of a strong acid to produce a carboxylic acid and an alcohol, 596
  of amides, 676

Aconitase, 839
ACP (acyl carrier protein), 876, 878
Acquired immune deficiency syndrome (AIDS), 783–785
Actin, 803
Actinides, 106
Activation energy The energy that must be provided by a collision to break apart the bonds of the reacting molecules, 372–373
Activators, 770
Active learning, 7
  study plan for learning, 6–9
Active site A pocket in a part of the tertiary enzyme structure that binds substrate and catalyzes a reaction, 724
Active transport, 639
Activity The rate at which an enzyme catalyzes the reaction that converts a substrate to a product, 729–731
Actual yield The actual amount of product produced by a reaction, 269
Acyl carrier protein (ACP), 876, 878
Acyl CoA synthetase, 866
Addition
  negative numbers, 11
  positive numbers, 11
  significant figures, 34
Addition reaction A reaction in which atoms or groups of atoms bond to a carbon–carbon double bond. Addition reactions include the addition of hydrogen (hydrogenation) and water (hydration), 468–473
  hydration, 469–470
  hydrogenation, 468
Adenine (A), 754–755
Adenosine monophosphate (AMP), 757, 801
Adenosine triphosphate. See ATP
Adipocytes, 862
ADP Adenosine diphosphate, formed by the hydrolysis of ATP; consists of adenine, a ribose sugar, and two phosphate groups, 801, 843
Adrenal corticosteroid, 637
Adrenal gland, 637
Adrenaline (epinephrine), 536, 650
Aerobic An oxygen-containing environment in the cells, 816–817
Aerosol medications, 288
Agitation, 713
α (alpha) helix A secondary level of protein structure, in which hydrogen bonds connect the N—H of one peptide bond with the C═O of a peptide bond farther down the chain to form a coiled or corkscrew structure, 703
AIDS (acquired immune deficiency syndrome), 783–785
α-keratin, 708
Alanine, 691
  from conversion of tryptophan, 887
  converting to pyruvate, 887
Albinism, 778
Albumin, 38
Alchemists, 5
Alcohol An organic compound that contains the hydroxyl functional group ($-OH$) attached to a carbon atom, 489–495
  abuse of, 505
  ball-and-stick model, 489
  blood alcohol concentration (BAC), 505
  boiling points, 498, 499
  breathalyzer test, 505
  classifying, 489
  dehydrating to form alkene, 501–502
  disinfectant, 712
  fermentation, 818
  household products, 491
  hydroxyl groups in, 489–490
  important, 492–493
  naming, 490, 509
  oxidation, 502–504
  oxidation in body, 505
  oxidation to acetaldehyde, 503, 505
  reactions of, 501–506
  solubility in water, 498, 499
  sugar, 562, 567
Alcoholic beverages, 334

Aldehyde An organic compound with a carbonyl functional group and at least one hydrogen atom attached to the carbon in the carbonyl group, 517
  addition reactions, 541
  boiling points, 523
  naming, 518–519, 540
  oxidation and reduction, 525–527, 540
  physical properties, 523–524
  solubility in water, 523–524
  structure, 517
Alditol, 562
Aldohexose, 553, 557
Aldose A monosaccharide that contains an aldehyde group, 552
Aldosterone, 637
Alkali metal An element in Group 1A (1), except hydrogen, that is a soft, shiny metal with one electron in its outermost energy level, 106–107
Alkaline earth metal An element in Group 2A (2) that has two electrons in its outermost energy level, 107
Alkaloid An amine having physiological activity that is produced in plants, 650, 662–663
Alkalosis, 431
Alkane A hydrocarbon that contains only single bonds between carbon atoms, 447–451
  boiling points, 457–458
  combustion, 458–459
  condensed structural formulas, 448–449, 455–456
  cycloalkanes, 450–451
  density, 459
  haloalkanes, 455
  isomers, 451
  line-angle structural formulas, 448–449, 455–456
  melting points, 457–458
  naming, 453–454
  properties of, 457–460
  solubility, 459
  with substituents, 451–457
  uses of, 457
Alkene A hydrocarbon that contains one or more carbon–carbon double bonds (C=C), 460–463
  addition reactions, 468–473
  cis–trans isomers, 464–467
    modeling, 465–466
    for night vision, 467
  cycloalkenes, 462
  from dehydration of alcohol, 501–502
  identifying, 460
  naming, 461–462
Alkyl group An alkane minus one hydrogen atom. Alkyl groups are named like the alkanes except a *yl* ending replaces *ane*, 453
Alkyne A hydrocarbon that contains one or more carbon–carbon triple bonds (C≡C), 460–463
  identifying, 460
  IUPAC naming system for, 461–462
Allopurinol, 334
Allosteric enzyme An enzyme that regulates the rate of a reaction when a regulator molecule attaches to a site other than the active site, 732
Almond, 521
Alpha decay, 156–157
Alpha helix. *See* α helix
Alpha hydroxy acid (AHA), 583–584
Alpha particle A nuclear particle identical to a helium nucleus, symbol α or $^4_2$He, 153
Altitude
  high, 389
  oxygen–hemoglobin equilibrium and, 389
Aluminum, 50, 63, 107, 186, 192
  electron configuration for, 130
  specific heat for, 80
Aluminum carbonate, 199
Aluminum oxide, 192
Aluminum phosphate, 199
Aluminum sulfate, 199, 352
Alveoli, 630
Alzheimer's disease, 170, 666, 705
Americium-241, 156
Amethyst, 67
Amidation The formation of an amide from a carboxylic acid and ammonia or an amine, 671
Amide An organic compound containing the carbonyl group attached to an amino group or a substituted nitrogen atom, 650, 671–676
  in health and medicine, 674–675
  hydrolysis, 676–677, 679
  melting points, 673–674

  naming, 672–673, 679
  physical properties, 673–674
  preparation (amidation), 671–672
Amine An organic compound containing a nitrogen atom attached to one, two, or three alkyl or aromatic groups, 650–656
  aromatic, 653
  boiling points, 656
  classification, 654
  IUPAC names, 651
  line-angle structural formulas, 654
  naming, 650–652, 679
  neutralization, 658–659
  properties of, 656–661
  solubility in water, 656–657
Amine neurotransmitters, 665–670
Amine salt An ionic compound produced from an amine and an acid, 659
Amino acid The building block of proteins, consisting of an ammonium group, a carboxylate group, and a unique R group attached to a carbon, 689–694, 716
  acidic, 695–696
  acids and bases, 694–697
  basic, 695–696
  carbon atoms from, fates of, 886–888
  classification of, 887
  degradation, 882
  energy from, 881–882
  essential, 693–694, 888
  forming five-carbon compounds, 887
  forming four-carbon compounds, 887
  forming three-carbon compounds, 887
  genetic code and, 771–775
  glucogenic, 887
  ketogenic, 887
  metabolism, 880–892
  N- and C- terminal, 697
  N- and C- terminus, 697
  nonessential, 888
  oxidative deamination, 883
  protein synthesis (translation), 771
  stereoisomers, 693
  synthesis, 888–892
  transamination, 882–883
  urea cycle and, 884–886
Aminoacyl–tRNA synthetase, 771
Amino alcohols, 627–628
Amino group, protein, 882
Aminotransferase, 882
Ammonia, 38, 80, 650
Ammonium cyanate, 444
Ammonium ion, 196, 658
  amino acid degradation, 887
  oxidative deamination and, 883
  urea cycle and, 884–885
Ammonium nitrate, 243, 273
Ammonium salt An ionic compound produced from an amine and an acid, 658–660
Amount of gas (n), 291
AMP (Adenosine monophosphate), 757, 801
Amphetamine, 667
Amphiprotic. *See* Amphoteric
Amphoteric Substances that can act as either an acid or a base in water, 405, 413
Amylase, 570, 572, 809
Amylopectin A branched-chain polymer of starch composed of glucose units joined by $\alpha(1 \rightarrow 4)$- and $\alpha(1 \rightarrow 6)$-glycosidic bonds, 570, 571, 574
Amylose An unbranched polymer of starch composed of glucose units joined by $\alpha(1 \rightarrow 4)$-glycosidic bonds, 570, 571, 574
Amyotrophic Lateral Sclerosis (ALS), 743
Anabolic reaction A metabolic reaction that requires energy to build large molecules from small molecules, 798, 891
Anabolic steroid, 636–637
Anaerobic A condition in cells when there is no oxygen, 810–816
Analgesics, 615
Ancient objects, dating of, 167
Androsterone, 636
Anemia, 102, 154
Anesthesia, 496
Aniline, 474, 653
Animals
  brown fat, 849
  hibernating, 618

Anion A negatively charged ion such as Cl⁻, O²⁻, or SO₄²⁻, 186

Anomers, 559

Antabuse (disulfiram), 505

Antacids, 423, 424

Anthracene, 477

Antibiotic Substance usually produced by bacteria, mold, or yeast that inhibits the growth of bacteria, 737–738

    inhibiting electron transport, 847–848

    protein synthesis inhibition by, 774

Anticodon The triplet of bases in the center loop of tRNA that is complementary to a codon on mRNA, 767, 771

    structure of, 767

Antidiuretic hormone, 699

Antihistamine, 662

Antimatter, 153

Antimycin A, 847–848

Antioxidants, 743–744

Antipyretics, 615

Antiseptics, 499

Aqueous solutions, 330

Arachidonic acid, 614–615

    converting to prostaglandin, 614–615

Arginase, in urea cycle, 885

Arginine, 691

    degradation, 887

    in urea cycle, 885, 886

Argininosuccinate, 885, 886

Argon, 103, 105, 107

    electron configuration for, 130

Aromatic amine, 653

Aromatic compound A compound that contains the ring structure of benzene, 473–476

    benzene, 473–474

    naming, 474–475

    polycyclic aromatic hydrocarbons (PAHs), 477

    properties of, 476

Arrhenius, Svante, 400

Arrhenius theory, 401

Arsenic, 103

    function of, 109

Arthritis, 637

Artificial kidney, 359

Artificial sweeteners, 567

Asparagine, 691

    degradation, 887

    synthesis, 889

Aspartame, 566, 567, 674

Aspartate, 691, 885

    degradation, 887

    synthesis, 889

Aspirin, 48, 183, 475, 476, 591, 614–615, 675

    mechanism of action, 2

Asthma, 637

-ate, 196

Atherosclerosis, 615–616, 891

Atmosphere (atm) A unit equal to the pressure exerted by a column of mercury 760 mm high, 292

Atmospheric pressure The pressure exerted by the atmosphere, 290–291

Atom The smallest particle of an element that retains the characteristics of that element, 63, 110–113

    atomic number, 114–117

    central, 213–215

    composition of, 115

    Dalton's atomic theory, 111

    electrical charges in an atom, 111

    mass number, 114–117

    mass of, 113

    particles in, 112

    sizes of, 137–139

    structure of, 111–112

Atomic energy, 172

Atomic mass The weighted average mass of all the naturally occurring isotopes of an element, 117–121

    calculating, 119–120

Atomic mass unit (amu) A small mass unit used to describe the mass of very small particles such as atoms and subatomic particles; 1 amu is equal to one-twelfth the mass of a $^{12}_{6}C$ atom, 113

Atomic number A number that is equal to the number of protons in an atom, 114

Atomic size The distance between the outermost electrons and the nucleus, 135, 137–138

Atomic spectrum, 121

Atomic symbol An abbreviation used to indicate the mass number and atomic number of an isotope, 117

Atomic theory, 111

ATP Adenosine triphosphate; a high-energy compound that stores energy in the cells, and consists of adenine, a ribose sugar, and three phosphate groups, 801

    citric acid cycle and, 852

    electron transport and, 844–847

    energy and, 801–804

    energy from glucose, 851–854

    fatty acid oxidation and, 870–871

    formation in glycolysis, 812, 851

    hydrolysis of, 801–803

    malate–aspartate shuttle, 851

    muscle contraction and, 802

    number produced by complete oxidation of glucose, 852–853

    oxidative phosphorylation and, 848–850

    production, efficiency of, 854

    pyruvate and, 844, 852

    synthesis, electron transport and, 848–849

ATP synthase An enzyme complex (V) that links the energy released by hydrogen ions returning to the matrix with the synthesis of ATP from ADP and Pᵢ, 848

    electron transport and, 848

    heating the body, 849

    uncouplers, 849

Atropine, 663

Attraction, of unlike charges, 111

Autoclaves, 301–302

Automobile battery, 248

Automobile exhaust, 477

Avogadro, Amedeo, 251, 304

Avogadro's law A gas law stating that the volume of gas is directly related to the number of moles of gas when pressure and temperature do not change, 304–307

Avogadro's number The number of items in a mole, equal to 6.02×10^{23}, 251–252

AZT (azidothymidine), 784

B

BAC. *See* Blood alcohol concentration (BAC)

Backbone The repeating sequence of N—C—C atoms from the amino acid residues in a protein, 698, 702–704, 709

Background radiation, 164

Bacteria

    antibiotics and, 737–738

    disinfectant and, 712

Baking soda, 48, 291

Balance, electronic, 28

Balanced equation The final form of a chemical equation that shows the same number of atoms of each element in the reactants and products, 238

Ball-and-stick model, 446, 447, 450, 451, 460, 464, 489

Barbiturates, 675

    electron transport inhibition by, 847

Barium, 103, 107, 186

    light spectrum, 121

Barium chloride, 246

Barium sulfate, 199, 246

Barometer, 292

Base A substance that dissolves in water and produces hydroxide ions (OH⁻) according to the Arrhenius theory. All bases are hydrogen ion acceptors, according to the Brønsted–Lowry theory, 399–442

    acids and (neutralization), 423

    Brønsted–Lowry, 403

    characteristics of, 402, 412

    conjugate acid–base pair, 404–405

    denaturing protein, 712

    naming, 402

    reactions of, 423–425

    strength of, 406–411

    strong, 409

    weak, 409

Base dissociation constant, K_b The numerical value of the product of the ions from the dissociation of a weak base divided by the concentration of the weak base, 412

Base (nucleic acid) Nitrogen-containing compounds found in DNA and RNA: adenine (A), thymine (T), cytosine (C), guanine (G), and uracil (U), 754–755

    complementary base pairs, 761–763

Base hydrolysis (saponification) The splitting of an ester molecule by a strong base to produce a carboxylate salt and an alcohol, 597–598, 601

    of amides, 676

Basic amino acid An amino acid that contains an R group with an ammonium (—NH₃⁺) ion, 690, 695–696

Basic solution, 414, 415
  pH of, 416
β-Carotene, 467
Becquerel (Bq) A unit of activity of a radioactive sample equal to one disintegration per second, 163
Beer fermentation, 818
Beeswax, 617
Belladonna, 663
Benadryl, 659
Bends (decompression sickness), 310
Benedict's reagent, 562–563
Benedict's test A test for aldehydes with adjacent hydroxyl groups in which Cu^{2+} ($CuSO_4$) ions in Benedict's reagent are reduced to a brick-red solid of Cu_2O, 525, 563
Benzaldehyde, 521
Benzene A ring of six carbon atoms, each of which is attached to a hydrogen atom, C_6H_6, 473–474
Benzene ring, 474–475
Benzo[a]pyrene, 477
Beryllium, 105, 107, 128
Beta decay, 157–158
Beta hydroxybutyrate, 873
Beta oxidation (β oxidation) The degradation of fatty acids that removes two carbon segments from a fatty acid chain, 865–869
  compared to fatty acid synthesis, 878
  length, beta oxidation cycles and, 867–868
  number of cycles, 867–868
  pathway, 866–867
Beta particle A particle identical to an electron, symbol $_{-1}^{0}e$ or β, that forms in the nucleus when a neutron changes to a proton and an electron, 153–155
Bicarbonates, 197
Bile salt, 633–634
  cholesterol and, 634
  structure, 634
  synthesizing, 633–634
Bilirubin, 634
Biodiesel, 625
Biological effects of radiation, 154
Biological systems
  oxidation–reduction reactions in, 250
Birth control pill, 636
Bisphenol A (BPA), 493
Bisphosphate, 810
Bisulfate, 197
Bisulfite, 197
β-keratin, 708
Bleach, 236
Blood, buffers in, 430–431
Blood alcohol concentration (BAC), 505
Blood–brain barrier, 863
Blood clotting, 616, 742
Blood gases, 314
Blood glucose, 557, 875
Blood group compatibility, 568
Blood pressure
  diastolic, 294
  systolic, 294
Blood sugar. *See* Glucose
Blood types, 567, 568
Blood urea nitrogen (BUN), 884
Blood vessels, plaque in, 635
Blubber, 871–872
Body fluids
  composition of, 325
  electrolytes in, 331
  saturation in, 334
Body mass, 47–48
Body temperature, 392
  in hypothermia, 72
  variation in, 72
Body weight
  gaining weight, 78–79
  losing weight, 78–79
Boiling The formation of bubbles of gas throughout a liquid, 85
Boiling point (bp) The temperature at which a liquid changes to gas (boils) and gas changes to liquid (condenses), 84, 301
  alcohols/ethers, 498, 499
  aldehydes and ketones, 523
  alkanes, 457–458
  amines, 656
  carboxylic acids, 585–586
  change in, 355–356
  solute concentration effect, 355
Boiling point elevation, 353–354

Bombykol, 466
Bonding
  attractive forces and, 219
  variations in, 211
Bonding pairs, 204
Bonds, 64
Bone, 50
Bone density, 51
Bone pain, 164
Boric acid, 48
Boron, 103, 105, 120, 128
Boron-10, 170
Boyle's law A gas law stating that the pressure of a gas is inversely related to the volume when temperature and moles of the gas do not change, 295–297
β (beta)-pleated sheet A secondary level of protein structure that consists of hydrogen bonds between peptide links in parallel polypeptide chains, 703–704
Brachytherapy, 171
Brain tumor, 160
Branch, 451
Branched alkane, 451
Brass, 64
Breast cancer, 172
Breathalyzer test, 505
Breathing
  expiration, 296
  inspiration, 296
  pressure–volume relationship in, 296
Breathing mixtures, 66
Bromine, 103, 107, 186
Bromo group, 453
Brønsted–Lowry acids and bases An acid is a hydrogen ion donor; a base is a hydrogen ion acceptor, 403–406
Brown fat, 849
Buckminsterfullerene, 116
Buffer, 427–430
  in blood, 430–431
  calculating pH, 428–430
Buffer solution A solution of a weak acid and its conjugate base or a weak base and its conjugate acid, which maintains the pH by neutralizing added acid or base, 427–430
BUN (blood urea nitrogen), 884
Burns, steam, 86
Butanal, 518
Butane, 447, 449, 457
  structural formulas for, 450
2-Butene, 464
Butyraldehyde, 518
Butyric acid, 582
Butyryl ACP, 878

C

Cadmium, 103
Caffeine, 48, 662
Calcified cholesterol, 608
Calcium, 38, 101–102, 132, 186
  in blood, 38
  electron configuration for, 133
  food sources of, 188
  function of, 109, 188
  muscle contraction and, 803
  recommended daily amount of, 36
Calcium carbonate, 3, 199, 244
Calcium oxalate, 334
Calcium phosphate, 199, 334
Calcium sulfate, 199
Calculators
  operations with, 11
  scientific notation and, 17–18
Californium, 102, 160
Calorie (cal) The amount of heat energy that raises the temperature of exactly 1 g of water by exactly 1 °C, 73, 854
Calorimeter, 76, 854
Cancer, 785–786
  mutagens and, 776
  retinoblastoma, 786
  skin (melanoma), 786
  viruses and, 786
Cancer cells, 154
Carbamoyl group, 884, 885
Carbamoyl phosphate, 884, 885
Carbohydrate A simple or complex sugar composed of carbon, hydrogen, and oxygen, 550–579. *See* Disaccharides; Polysaccharides

blood types and, 567
   digestion of, 808–809
   as energy source, 801–803
   energy value of, 76
   metabolic pathways, 797–835
   oxidization, 810, 891
   reactions, 575
   types, 552, 574
Carbolic acid (phenol), 499
Carbon
   atomic mass, 119
   burning of, 237, 238
   description of, 64
   diamond, 116
   electron configuration for, 128
   five-carbon compounds, 887
   forms of, 116
   four-carbon compounds, 887
   function of, 109
   graphite, 116
   tetrahedral structure of, 446
   three-carbon compounds, 887
Carbon-11, 170
Carbon-14, 155, 164, 167–168
Carbonates, 197
   acids and, 423
Carbon atom
   amino acid degradation and, 882
   fates from amino acid degradation, 886–888
Carbon cycle, 551
Carbon dating, 167
Carbon dioxide
   climate change and, 75–76
   density of, 50
Carbon monoxide, 247, 310, 847
Carbon skeleton
   amino acid, 887–888
   citric acid cycle and, 887
Carbonyl group A group that has a carbon–oxygen double bond with two
   groups of atoms attached to the carbon at angles of 120°, 517
   aldehyde and ketone, 517
Carboxylate ion The anion produced when a carboxylic acid dissociates in
   water, 586, 689, 693
Carboxylate salt The product of neutralization of a carboxylic acid, which is
   a carboxylate ion and a metal ion from the base, 587–588, 600
Carboxyl group A functional group found in carboxylic acids composed of
   carbonyl and hydroxyl groups, 581
Carboxylic acid An organic compound containing the carboxyl group, 220,
   581–584
   acidity, 586–587
   boiling points, 585–586
   in metabolism, 589
   naming, 581–583, 600
   natural sources, 583–584
   neutralization, 587–588, 601
   preparing, 583–584
   properties, 585–590
   solubility in water, 586, 600
Carcinogen, 477
Career
   clinical laboratory technician, 399
   clinical lipid specialist, 608
   dental hygienist, 235
   dermatology nurse, 516
   diabetes nurse, 550
   dialysis nurse, 324
   dietitian, 62
   environmental health practitioner, 649
   exercise physiologist, 836
   farmer, 101
   firefighter/emergency medical technician, 443
   forensic scientist, 1
   hepatology nurse, 797
   histology technician, 753
   neonatal nurse, 370
   nuclear medicine technologist, 151
   nurse anesthetist, 488
   pharmacy technician, 183
   physician assistant, 722
   public health nurse, 861
   radiology technician, 688
   registered nurse, 25
   respiratory therapist, 288
   surgical technician, 580
Carnauba wax, 617

Carnitine, 866
Carnitine acyltransferase, 866
Carvone, 521
Catabolic reaction A metabolic reaction that produces energy for the cell
   by the degradation and oxidation of glucose and other molecules,
   891
Catalyst A substance that increases the rate of reaction by lowering the
   activation energy, 374–375, 723
   effect on equilibrium constant, 388, 391
   reaction rate and, 374–375
Catalytic converters, 375
Catecholamines, 666–667
Cation A positively charged ion such as Na^+, Mg^{2+}, Al^{3+}, or NH_4^+, 139,
   185
Cell
   eukaryotic *vs.* prokaryotic, 800
   structures in, 800
   uncontrolled division of (in cancer), 786
Cell membrane, 638–640, 800
   diffusion, 639
   facilitated transport, 639
   fluid mosaic model, 638
   hydrophilic and hydrophobic layers, 638
   lipid bilayer, 638
   transport through, 639
Cellophane, 359
Cellulose An unbranched polysaccharide composed of glucose units linked
   by $\beta(1 \rightarrow 4)$-glycosidic bonds that cannot be hydrolyzed by the human
   digestive system, 551, 570–572, 574
Celsius (°C) temperature scale A temperature scale on which water has a
   freezing point of 0 °C and a boiling point of 100 °C, 28, 69
   Fahrenheit scale conversion, 69–70
   Kelvin scale conversion, 70–71
Centi-, 36
Centimeter (cm) A unit of length in the metric system; there are 2.54 cm in
   1 in., 27
Central atom, 213–215
Cephalin A glycerophospholipid found in brain and nerve tissues
   that incorporates the amino alcohol serine or ethanolamine,
   627
Cesium, 105
Cesium-131, 171
Cesium-137, 163
Chain elongation, 772
Chain reaction A fission reaction that will continue once it has been
   initiated by a high-energy neutron bombarding a heavy nucleus such as
   uranium-235, 173
Chain termination, 774
Change of state The transformation of one state of matter to another; for
   example, solid to liquid, liquid to solid, liquid to gas, 81–90
   boiling, 84
   condensation, 84
   cooling curves, 87–88
   freezing, 82
   heating curves, 87
   heat of fusion, 82–83
   heat of vaporization, 85–86
   illustration of, 82
   melting, 82
   sublimation, 84–85
Chargaff's rules, 761
Charles, Jacques, 298
Charles's law A gas law stating that the volume of a gas changes directly with
   a change in Kelvin temperature when pressure and moles of the gas do
   not change, 298–299
Chemical A substance that has the same composition and properties wherever
   it is found, 2–4
Chemical change A change during which the original substance is converted
   into a new substance that has a different composition and new physical
   and chemical properties, 68
Chemical equation A shorthand way to represent a chemical reaction using
   chemical formulas to indicate the reactants and products and coefficients
   to show reacting ratios, 238
   balanced
      identifying, 238–239
      steps for creating, 239–241
   describing chemical reaction, 236–237
   mole relationships in, 260–263
      conservation of mass, 260
      mole–mole factors from an equation, 261
      mole–mole factors in calculations, 261–262
   products, 238
   reactants, 238
   symbols used in writing of, 238
   writing, 237–238

Chemical equilibrium The point at which the rate of forward and reverse reactions are equal so that no further change in concentrations of reactants and products takes place, 377–380

Chemical formula The group of symbols and subscripts that represents the atoms or ions in a compound, 189

Chemical properties The properties that indicate the ability of a substance to change into a new substance, 68

Chemical quantities, 235–287
    Avogadro's number, 251–253
    mole, 251–254
    moles of elements in a formula, 253–254

Chemical reaction The process by which a chemical change takes place, 235–287
    activation energy, 372–373
    addition reactions, 468–473
    calculations of heat in, 272–273
    chemical changes, 236
    collision theory, 372
    combination reactions, 243–244
    combustion reactions, 246
    conditions, 372
    decomposition reactions, 244
    double replacement reactions, 246
    endothermic reactions, 272
    energy in, 271–274
    energy units for, 271
    equations for, 236–242
    exothermic reactions, 271–272
    heat of reaction, 271, 272–273
    ideal gas law and, 310–311
    mass calculations for, 263–265
    molar mass, 255–259
    mole, 251
    oxidation–reduction reactions, 248–250
    rate, 372–377
    single replacement reactions, 244
    solutions in, 345–346
    types of, 243–247

Chemical symbol An abbreviation that represents the name of an element, 103

Chemiosmotic model, 848

Chemistry The study of the composition, structure, properties, and reactions of matter, 2
    problem solving, 47–49

Chemotherapy, 171

Chernobyl nuclear accident, 164

Chiral Objects or molecules that have nonsuperimposable mirror images, 531–538

Chiral carbon A carbon atom that is bonded to four different atoms or groups, 531–534

Chlorate, 197

Chloride, 186, 190
    food sources of, 188
    function of, 188

Chlorine, 102, 107, 115
    atomic mass of, 119
    function of, 109

Chlorite, 197

Chloro group, 453

Cholesterol The most prevalent of the steroid compounds; needed for cellular membranes and the synthesis of vitamin D, hormones, and bile acids, 632
    bad and good, 635
    bile salts and, 632–634
    in blood, elevated, 38, 632–633
    in body, 632–633
    cell membrane, 638
    dietary recommendations, 632–633
    excess, 633, 778
    gallstones and, 634
    HDL and LDL, 635
    high-cholesterol diet, 632–633
    plaque and, 632
    serum, 633
    structure, 632
    trans fatty acids and hydrogenation and, 622–623
    transporting, 634–636

Cholesteryl ester, 634

Choline, 627

Cholinesterase inhibitors, 666, 737

Chromatography, 65

Chromium, 64, 103
    function of, 109

Chromium-51, 167

Chylomicrons Lipoproteins formed by coating triacylglycerols with proteins for transport in the lymphatic system and bloodstream, 635, 863

Chymotrypsin, 880

Chymotrypsinogen, 734

Cinchona tree, 663

Cinnamaldehyde, 521

Cinnamon, 521

cis-11-retinal, 467

Cis isomer An isomer of an alkene in which similar groups in the double bond are on the same side, 464–465
    modeling, 465–466
    in night vision, 467

Cis–trans isomers, 464–467

Citrate, 837

Citrate synthase, 837

Citric acid, 584

Citric acid cycle A series of oxidation reactions in the mitochondria that converts acetyl CoA to CO_2 and yield NADH and $FADH_2$. It is also called the tricarboxylic cycle or the Krebs cycle, 589, 837–844
    ATP from, 852
    carbon skeletons and, 887
    dehydrogenase in, 840–842
    metabolism and, 799, 890–891
    nonessential amino acid synthesis and, 889
    overview and summary of, 838, 841
    oxidation reactions in, 841
    primary function of, 843
    product summary for, 842–843
    regulation of, 843

Citrulline, 884, 885

CK. *See* Creatine kinase

Classification of matter, 63–66. *See* Matter

Cleavage, 811
    acetyl CoA, 867
    urea cycle reaction, 886

Clindamycin, 344

Clinical laboratory technician, 399

Clinical lipid specialist, 608

Cloning, gene, 780–781

Clotting, 742

Cobalt, 103, 109

Cobalt-60, 163

Cocaine, 659, 663, 667

Codeine, 663

Codon A sequence of three bases in mRNA that specifies a certain amino acid to be placed in a protein. A few codons signal the start or stop of protein synthesis, 771
    for amino acids, 771–772
    start, stop, 772

Coefficients Whole numbers placed in front of the formulas to balance the number of atoms or moles of atoms of each element on both sides of an equation, 238

Coenzyme An organic molecule, usually a vitamin, required as a cofactor in enzyme action, 739–745
    metabolic cycle and, 799, 804–808
    reduced, citric acid cycle and, 841, 843

Coenzyme A (CoA) A coenzyme that transports acyl and acetyl groups, 807

Coenzyme Q (CoQ, Q) A mobile carrier that transfers electrons from NADH and $FADH_2$ to complex III, 846

Cofactor A metal ion or an organic molecule that is necessary for a biologically functional enzyme, 739–745

Coffee, 662

Cold pack, 273–274

Collagen The most abundant form of protein in the body, which is composed of fibrils of triple helices that are hydrogen-bonded together between the —OH groups of hydroxyproline and hydroxylysine, 704

Colligative properties, 353

Collision theory A model for a chemical reaction stating that molecules must collide with sufficient energy and proper orientation to form products, 372

Colloid A mixture having particles that are moderately large. Colloids pass through filters but cannot pass through semipermeable membranes, 352, 353
    examples of, 352

Combination reaction A chemical reaction in which reactants combine to form a single product, 243–244

Combined gas law A relationship that combines several gas laws relating pressure, volume, and temperature when the amount of gas does not change, 303–304

Combustion reaction A chemical reaction in which a fuel containing carbon and hydrogen reacts with oxygen to produce CO_2, H_2O, and energy, 246
    of alkanes, 458–459

Compact fluorescent light (CFL), 104, 123

Competitive inhibitor A molecule that has a structure similar to a substrate, and that inhibits enzyme action by competing for the active site, 736

Complementary base pairs In DNA, adenine is always paired with thymine (A—T or T—A), and guanine is always paired with cytosine (G—C or C—G). In forming RNA, adenine is always paired with uracil (A—U), 761–763

Complete proteins, 693

Compound A pure substance consisting of two or more elements, with a definite composition, that can be broken down into simpler substances only by chemical methods, 64

    attractive forces in, 218–221

    containing polyatomic ions, 197–198

    ionic. *See* Ionic compound

    organic. *See* Organic compound

Computed tomography (CT), 171

Concentration A measure of the amount of solute that is dissolved in a specified amount of solution, 339–348

    calculating at equilibrium, 385

    as conversion factors, 343–345

    dilution, 349–351

    effect of change on equilibrium, 374–375, 387–388, 391

    mass percent (m/m) concentration, 340

    mass/volume percent (m/v) concentration, 341–342

    rate of reaction affected by, 164

    volume percent (v/v) concentration, 340–341

Conclusion An explanation of an observation that has been validated by repeated experiments that support a hypothesis, 4–6

Condensation The change of state from a gas to a liquid, 84, 86–87

Condensed structural formula A structural formula that shows the arrangement of the carbon atoms in a molecule but groups each carbon atom with its bonded hydrogen atoms ($—CH_3$, $—CH_2—$, or $—CH—$), 448–449, 455–456

Conformations, 449

Coniine, 662

Conjugate acid–base pair An acid and a base that differ by one H^+. When an acid donates a hydrogen ion, the product is its conjugate base, which is capable of accepting a hydrogen ion in the reverse reaction, 404–405

Conservation of mass, 260

Conversion factor A ratio in which the numerator and denominator are quantities from an equality or given relationship, 39–49

    Avogadro's number, 252

    density as, 51–52

    dosage problems, 42

    metric–U.S. system, 40–41

    molarity, 343

    molar mass as, 257

    from percentages, 42–43

    percent concentration, 343–345

    problem solving, 44–48

    stated within a problem, 41

    temperature, 69–73

    writing, 39–44

        metric, 38, 40

        metric–U.S. system, 40–41

Cooling curve A diagram that illustrates temperature changes and changes of state for a substance as heat is removed, 87–88

Copernicium, 102

Copper, 50, 64–65, 68, 80

    atomic mass, 119

    in body, 102

    function of, 109

    isotopes of, 119

    physical properties of, 67–68

    recommended daily amount of, 36

Copper(II) nitrite, 199

Copper(II) sulfate, 249, 326

Cori cycle A cyclic process in which lactate produced in muscle is transferred to the liver to be synthesized to glucose, which can be used again by muscle, 826–827

Cork, 49–50

Corn oil, 469

Coronary heart disease, 615–616, 632–633

Corticosteroid, 637

Cortisone, 637

Cosmic radiation, 164

Cotton, 3, 167

Covalent bond A sharing of valence electrons by atoms, 292

    definition of, 185, 200

    formation of, 184

    nonpolar, 210

    polar, 210

Covalent modification Regulation of an enzyme that involves forming or breaking covalent bonds to a group on the polypeptide chain, 733–735

    definition, 733

    phosphorylation, 735

    proenzymes, 733–734

    zymogens, 733–734

"Crack cocaine", 659

Creatine kinase, 728

Crenation The shriveling of a cell because water leaves the cell when the cell is placed in a hypertonic solution, 358

Cresol, 490

Crick, Francis, 761

Critical mass, 173

C-terminus (C-terminal amino acid) The end amino acid in a peptide chain with a free carboxylate group ($—COO^-$), 697

Cubic centimeter (cm^3, cc) The volume of a cube that has 1-cm sides; 1 cm^3 is equal to 1 mL, 38

Cubic meter (m^3), 26

Curie, Marie, 102, 164

Curie, Pierre, 102

Curie (Ci) A unit of activity of a radioactive sample equal to 3.7×10^{10} disintegrations/s, 164

Curium, 102

Cyanide, 197, 847

Cyclic hemiacetal, 529–530, 558, 559

Cyclic organic compound, 661–664

Cycloalkane An alkane that is a ring or cyclic structure, 450–451

    naming, 454

    with substituents, 454

Cycloalkenes, 462

Cyclobutane, 450

Cyclohexane, 450

Cyclopentane, 450

Cyclopropane, 450

Cysteine, 691

    converting to pyruvate, 887

    synthesis, 889

Cytochrome c, 847

Cytochromes (cyt) Iron-containing proteins that transfer electrons from $CoQH_2$ to oxygen, 846, 847

Cytosine (C), 754–755

Cytosol The fluid of the cell, which is an aqueous solution of electrolytes and enzymes, 800

D

Dalton (unit of measure), 110

Dalton, John, 110, 113

    atomic theory, 111

Dalton's law A gas law stating that the total pressure exerted by a mixture of gases in a container is the sum of the partial pressures that each gas would exert alone, 312–313

Dating using half-lives, 168

    ancient objects, 167

    carbon dating, 167

d **block** The block of ten elements from Groups 3B (3) to 2B (12) in which electrons fill the five *d* orbitals in the *d* sublevels, 132

DDT, 48

Dead Sea Scrolls, 167

Dec-, 447

Decarboxylation The loss of a carbon atom in the form of CO_2, 818

    in citric acid cycle, 840

Decay curve A diagram of the decay of a radioactive element, 165–166

Deci-, 36

Deciliter (dL), 38

Decomposition reaction A reaction in which a single reactant splits into two or more simpler substances, 244

Decompression, 310

Decongestants, 659

Defibrillator, 74

Deforestation, 76

Degrees, 69

Dehydrated food, 358

Dehydration A reaction that removes water from an alcohol in the presence of an acid to form alkenes at high temperatures, 501–502

Dehydrogenases, 726

    in citric acid cycle, 840–842

Deletion mutation A mutation that deletes a base from a DNA sequence, 776

Demerol, 664, 847–848

Denaturation The loss of secondary, tertiary, and quaternary protein structure caused by heat, acids, bases, organic compounds, heavy metals, and/or agitation, 711

    enzyme, 730

    milk protein, 712

    protein, 711–713, 716, 880

Dendrites, 664

Density The relationship of the mass of an object to its volume expressed as grams per cubic centimeter (g/cm^3), grams per milliliter (g/mL), or grams per liter (g/L), 49–52

    alkanes, 459

    bone density, 51

Density (*Continued*)
   calculating, 50
     problem solving using, 51–52
     using volume displacement, 50–51
Dental hygienist, 235
Dental X-ray, 164
Deoxyribose, 755
Deposition The change of a gas directly into a solid; the reverse of
   sublimation, 84–85
Dermatitis, 122
Dermatology nurse, 516
Desalination, 356
Dextrins, 570
Dextrose. *See* Glucose
di-, 454
Diabetes
   gestational, 875
   insulin and, 875
   ketone bodies and, 875
   obesity and, 871
   Type I *vs.* Type II, 875
Diabetes nurse, 550
Dialysis A process in which water and small solute particles pass through a
   semipermeable membrane, 359–360
   by artificial kidney, 359
   hemodialysis, 359
   by kidneys, 359
   osmosis and, 359
   for renal failure, 361
Dialysis nurse, 324
Dialyzing membrane, 359
Diaphragm, 296
Diastolic pressure, 294
Dichlorvos, 48
Dicyclanil, 678
Diesel, 457
Diet
   high-cholesterol, 632–633
   high-fat, 615–616, 871
   high-protein, 884
   obesity and, 871
Dietitian, 62
Diet plan, 505
Diffusion, 639
Digestion The processes in the gastrointestinal tract that break down
   large food molecules to smaller ones that pass through the intestinal
   membrane into the bloodstream, 798, 880–885
   carbohydrate, 808–809
   dietary fats, 862–863
   lipids, 862–880
Dihydrogen phosphate, 197
Dilution A process by which water (solvent) is added to a solution to increase
   the volume and decrease (dilute) the concentration of the solute, 349–351
   concentrations and volumes of solutions, 349–350
   molarity of diluted solution, 350–351
Dimethylamine, 651
Dinitrogen oxide, 308
2,4-Dinitrophenol (DNP), 849
Dipeptide, 697
Dipole The separation of positive and negative charges in a polar bond
   indicated by an arrow that is drawn from the more positive atom to the
   more negative atom, 211
Dipole–dipole attractions Attractive forces between oppositely charged ends
   of polar molecules, 218
Diprotic acids, 408–409
Direct relationship, 15, 298
Disaccharide A carbohydrate composed of two monosaccharides joined by a
   glycosidic bond, 552, 564–570, 574
   digestion of, 809
   reactions, 575
   sweetness of, 567
Disease
   genetic, 778
   vaccine against, 783
Disinfectant, 712
Dispersion forces Weak dipole bonding that results from a momentary
   polarization of nonpolar molecules, 219
Dissociation The separation of an acid or base into ions in water, 329, 406
   constant for weak acid, 411–413
   water, 413–416
Disulfide A compound formed from thiols; disulfides contain the —S—S—
   functional group, 504
Disulfide bond Covalent —S—S— bond that forms between the
   —SH groups of two cysteines in a protein, which stabilizes tertiary and
   quaternary structures, 504–505, 707, 716

Disulfiram (Antabuse), 505
Division
   of negative numbers, 10
   of positive numbers, 10
   significant figures, 34
DNA Deoxyribonucleic acid; the genetic material of all cells, containing
   nucleotides with deoxyribose sugar, phosphate, and the four bases
   adenine, thymine, guanine, and cytosine, 754–766
   base pairs in, 761
   bases in, 754–755
   components of, 754–759
   daughter DNAs, 763
   deoxyribose in, 755
   double helix, 761–763
   genetic code and, 771
   introns and exons, 769
   mutations, 776–777
   nucleotides and nucleosides in, 755–757
   primary structure, 759–761
   recombinant, 780–782
   replication, 763–766
   synthesis, 763–764
   transcription of, 769–770
DNA fingerprinting, 782
DNA fragment, 764
DNA ligases, 764
DNA polymerase, 764
DNA viruses, 786
Docosahexaenoic acid (DHA), 615–616
Dopamine, 667–668
Double bond A sharing of two pairs of electrons by two atoms, 208
Double helix The helical shape of the double chain of DNA that is like a
   spiral staircase with a sugar–phosphate backbone on the outside and base
   pairs like stair steps on the inside, 761–763
Double replacement reaction A reaction in which parts of two different
   reactants exchange places, 246
Drug, synthesizing, 663–664
Dry ice, 84
Dubnium (Db), 160
Dyes, 477

E

E. coli (*Escherichia coli*)
   gene cloning, 780
   recombinant DNA and, 780–781
Eczema, 122
Edema, 170
EE function key, on calculators, 17
Egg whites, 713
Eicosanoids, 614
Eicosapentaenoic acid (EPA), 615–616
Einstein, Albert, 173
Electrical charges in an atom, 111
Electrolyte A substance that produces ions when dissolved in water; its
   solution conducts electricity, 329–333
   in blood, 331
   in body fluids, 331
   concentration, 331
   equivalents of, 330–331
   in intravenous solutions, 331
   strong, 329–330
   weak, 329–330
Electromagnetic radiation, 121
Electromagnetic spectrum, 121–122
Electron A negatively charged subatomic particle having a very small mass
   that is usually ignored in calculations; its symbol is e^-, 111–112
   energy levels, 121–127
   gain of, 186–187
   loss of, 185–186
   in oxidation–reduction reactions, 248–250
   sharing of, between atoms of different elements, 205
   transfer of, 184–188
   valence, 135
Electron carrier, 844–847
Electron configurations A list of the number of electrons in each sublevel
   within an atom, arranged by increasing energy, 127–135
   Period 1 (Hydrogen and Helium), 128
   Period 2 (Lithium to Neon), 128–130
   Period 3 (Sodium to Argon), 130–131
   Period 4 and above, 133–134
   and periodic table, 131
   using sublevel blocks to write electron configurations, 132–133
Electronegativity The relative ability of an element to attract electrons in a
   bond, 209–210
Electronic balance, 28

Electron transport A series of reactions in the mitochondria that transfer electrons from NADH and to electron carriers, which are arranged from higher to lower energy levels, and finally to O_2, which produces H_2O. Energy changes during these transfers provide energy for ATP synthesis, 799
ATP and, 844–854
ATP synthase and, 848–849
driving ATP synthesis (chemiosmotic model), 848
electron carriers, 844–848
energy from, 844–848
metabolism and, 890–891
regulation of, 850
toxins inhibiting, 847–848
Element A pure substance containing only one type of matter, which cannot be broken down by chemical methods, 63, 101–150
in body, 102
essential to health, 108–109
isotopes of, 117–121
Latin names for, 103
macrominerals, 108
major elements, 108
microminerals (trace elements), 108
molar mass of, 255–259
periodic table of. *See* Periodic table
periodic trends of, 122
symbols, 102–105
trace, 108–109
Emulsification, 863
Enantiomers Stereoisomers that are mirror images that cannot be superimposed, 532, 536
in biological systems, 536–537
Endorphins, 699
Endothermic reaction A reaction that requires heat; the energy of the products is higher than the energy of the reactants, 272
equilibrium shifting from temperature change, 390–391
Endpoint, 425
Energy The ability to do work, 73–76
activation, 372–373
amino acid as a source, 881–882
ATP and, 801–804
for brain and red blood cells, 863
calculations, combining, 88–89
calorie (cal) as unit of, 73
carbohydrate metabolism and, 801–804
catabolic and anabolic pathways, 798–799, 890–891
in chemical reactions, 271–274
citric acid cycle and, 837–844
collision theory, 372
electron transport and, 844–850
endothermic reactions, 272
energy-rich compounds, 812
energy values for foods, 76
exothermic reactions, 271–272
fat as a source of, 870–871
fatty acid oxidation and, 870–871
gluconeogenesis and, 826
glycolysis and, 810–816, 891
heat, 73
ionization, 139–140
joule (J) as unit of, 73
kinetic, 73
metabolism, 798–804
and nutrition, 76–79
oxidative phosphorylation and, 848–850
potential, 73
production, metabolism and, 836–860
storage as glycogen, 854
summary of metabolic pathways for, 890–891
units of, 73–74
Energy level A group of electrons with similar energy, 121–127
elements, 102–105
energy level changes, 123
Energy requirements, 80
Energy-saving fluorescent bulbs, 123
Energy units, 73–74
Energy value The kilocalories (or kilojoules) obtained per gram of the food types: carbohydrate, fat, and protein, 76–79
Enkephalins, 699
Enolase, 812
Enrofloxacin, 678
Enthalpy change. *See* Heat of reaction
Environmental health practitioner, 649
Environmental issues
climate change, 75–76
nuclear power plants, 175

Enzyme A globular protein, sometimes with a cofactor, that catalyzes a biological reaction, 723
action, 723–726
active site, 724
activity, factors affecting, 729–731
activity, regulation of, 732–735
antioxidants, 743–744
as catalyst, 723
catalyzed reactions, 724–725
classification, 726–729
cofactors and vitamins, 739–745
covalent modification, 733–735
denaturation, 730
feedback control, 733
increasing concentration, 731
induced-fit model, 725
inhibition/inhibitors, 735–739
isoenzymes, diagnosis and, 728
lock-and-key model, 725
in metabolic reactions, 807
naming, 726
pH and, 730
phosphorylation, 735
regulation and allosteric site, 732
substrate concentration and, 731
synthesizing as allosteric, 732
synthesizing as zymogen, 733–735
temperature and, 729–730
zymogens and, 733–735
Enzyme-catalyzed reaction, 724–725
Enzyme–product (EP) complex An intermediate consisting of an enzyme that binds to a product in an enzyme-catalyzed reaction, 724
Enzyme–substrate (ES) complex An intermediate consisting of an enzyme that binds to a substrate in an enzyme-catalyzed reaction, 724
Epinephrine, 668, 822
fat mobilization and, 864
Equality A relationship between two units that measure the same quantity, 36–39
Equations, solving, 12–14
Equilibrium, 370–398
calculating concentration at, 385
changing conditions/Le Châtelier's principle, 387–393
chemical, 377–380
concentration change and, 374–375, 387–388, 391
forward, reverse, and reversible reactions, 377–378
oxygen–hemoglobin equilibrium, 389
rate of reaction, 371, 372–377
shifting, 387–388
temperature change and, 374, 375, 390, 391
volume (pressure) change and, 388–389, 391
Equilibrium constant expression The ratio of the concentrations of products to the concentrations of reactants with each component raised to an exponent equal to the coefficient of that compound in the chemical equation, 380–381
Equilibrium constant, K_c The numerical value obtained by substituting the equilibrium concentrations of the components into the equilibrium constant expression, 380–383
calculating, 381–382
large, 383–384, 385
small, 384, 385
using, 383–386
Equivalent dose The measure of biological damage from an absorbed dose that has been adjusted for the type of radiation, 163
Equivalent (Eq) The amount of a positive or negative ion that supplies 1 mole of electrical charge, 330–331
of electrolytes, 330–331
Escherichia coli, 163
Essential amino acid Amino acid that must be supplied by the diet because it is not synthesized by the body, 693–694, 888
for children but not adults, 888
Essential fatty acid, 611
Ester An organic compound in which an alkyl or aromatic group replaces the hydrogen atom in a carboxylic acid, 590–593
acid hydrolysis, 596–597, 601
base hydrolysis (saponification), 597–598, 601
naming, 593–596, 600
properties, 596–599
solubility in water, 596
Ester bond, 592, 617
Esterification The formation of an ester from a carboxylic acid and an alcohol with the elimination of a molecule of water in the presence of an acid catalyst, 590–591, 601, 642
Estradiol, 636

Estrogen, 636
Ethanal, 503, 505, 518
Ethane, 457
1,2-Ethanediol (ethylene glycol), 492
Ethanoic acid, 525
Ethanol (ethyl alcohol), 48, 492
    as abused drug, 505
    density of, 50
    in hand sanitizers, 500
    lactate fermentation and, 818
    oxidation of, 503, 505
    specific heat for, 80
Ethanolamine, 627
Ether An organic compound in which an oxygen atom is bonded to two
        carbon groups that are alkyl or aromatic, 495–497
    anesthesia, 496
    boiling points, 498, 499
    naming, 495–496, 509
    solubility in water, 498, 499
Ethrane (enflurane), 497
Ethyl alcohol. *See* Ethanol
Ethylene glycol, 492, 748
Ethyne (acetylene), 460
Eukaryotic cell, 800
Evaporation The formation of a gas (vapor) by the escape of high energy
        molecules from the surface of a liquid, 84
Exact number A number obtained by counting or by definition, 31
Excess reactant, 266
Excitatory neurotransmitters, 665
Exercise, lactic acid and, 589
Exercise-induced asthma, 315
Exercise physiologist, 836
Exons The sections in a DNA template that code for proteins, 769
Exothermic reaction A reaction that releases heat; the energy of the products
        is lower than the energy of the reactants, 271–272
    equilibrium shifting from temperature change, 390–391
Expanded structural formula A type of structural formula that shows the
        arrangement of the atoms by drawing each bond in the hydrocarbon, 446
Experiment A procedure that tests the validity of a hypothesis, 4–6
EXP function key, on calculators, 17
Expiration, 296
Explosives, 475
Exposure to radiation, 164
External beam therapy, 172
Extracellular fluid, 327
Exxon Valdez oil spill (1989), 459

F

Facilitated transport, 639
FAD A coenzyme (flavin adenine dinucleotide) for dehydrogenase enzymes
        that form carbon–carbon double bonds, 806, 891
Fahrenheit (°F) temperature scale, 28, 69–73
    Celsius scale conversion, 69–70
Fainting, 294
Faraday, Michael, 473
Farmer, 101
Fat A triacylglycerol that is solid at room temperature and usually comes from
        animal sources, 619
    blubber, 872
    brown, 849
    cells, 862
    in diet, 871
    digestion of, 862–864
    energy content, 870–871
    fat and oil, 619–620
    high-fat diet, 615–616, 871
    hydrogenation, 621–623, 642
    hydrolysis, 623, 642
    leptin and, 871
    melting point, 619–620
    metabolism of, 862–880, 890–891
    obesity and, 871
    oxidation, 865–870
    saponification, 623–624, 642
    saturated, 469, 622–623, 633
    source of energy, 862–865
    stored/storage of, 871–872
    types of, 624
    unsaturated, 468, 469
Fat-soluble vitamin A vitamin that is not soluble in water and can be stored
        in the liver and body fat, 742–743
Fatty acid A long-chain carboxylic acid found in many lipids, 610–616
    activation, 865
    blood–brain barrier and, 863

degradation, 891
essential, 611
length, synthesis cycles and, 877
longer, 877
in metabolism summary, 890–891
monounsaturated, 611
omega-3, 615–616
oxidation, 865–870
oxidation, ATP and, 870–871
polyunsaturated, 611
properties of, 612–614
saturated, 611, 622–623
shorter, 877
synthesis (lipogenesis), 876–880, 878
synthesis, regulation of, 877
trans, 622–623
transporting, 866
Fatty acid synthesis, 876–880, 878
    comparing to beta oxidation, 878
f **block** The block of 14 elements in the rows at the bottom of the periodic table
        in which electrons fill the seven *f* orbitals in the 4*f* and 5*f* sublevels, 132
Feedback control A type of inhibition in which an end product inhibits the
        first enzyme in a sequence of enzyme-catalyzed reactions, 733
Fermentation The anaerobic conversion of glucose by enzymes in yeast to
        yield alcohol and CO_2, 818
Fertilizer, 196
Fever, 28, 70, 72
Fibril
    collagen, 704
    fibrous protein, 708
    hair, 708
Fibrous protein A protein that is insoluble in water; consisting of polypeptide
        chains with α helices or β-pleated sheets, and comprising the fibers of
        hair, wool, skin, nails, and silk, 708
Filament, muscle protein, 803
Filtration, 65
Fingerprinting, DNA, 782
Firefighter/emergency medical technician, 443
Fischer, Emil, 534
Fischer projection A system for drawing stereoisomers; an intersection of
        a vertical and horizontal line represents a carbon atom. A vertical line
        represents bonds that project backwards from a carbon atom and a
        horizontal line represents bonds that project forward. The most highly
        oxidized carbon is at the top, 534–535
    monosaccharides, 554–558
Fish oil, 615–616
Fission A process in which large nuclei are split into smaller pieces, releasing
        large amounts of energy, 172–175
    chain reaction, 173
Flavin adenine dinucleotide. *See* FAD
Flavor, esters and, 590
Floc, 352
Fluid mosaic model The concept that cell membranes are lipid bilayer
        structures that contain an assortment of polar lipids and proteins in a
        dynamic, fluid arrangement, 638
Fluorescent bulbs, 123
Fluoride, 186
Fluorine, 105, 107
    atomic mass, 119
Fluorine-18, 170
Fluoro group, 453
Fluoxetine hydrochloride, 669
Food
    caloric value of, 76–78
    colloids from, 353
    dehydrated, 358
    digestion of, 799, 808–809
    fatty acid composition of, 469
    freeze-dried, 85
    gout, 334
    irradiated, 163
    water in, 327
Food and Drug Administration (FDA), 104, 163
Food-borne illnesses, 163
Food intake, 78–79
Forane (isoflurane), 496
Forensic scientist, 1
Formaldehyde, 518, 521
Formalin, 521
Formic acid, 250, 582
Formula unit The group of ions represented by the formula of an ionic
        compound, 191, 252
Forward reaction, 377–378
Fossil fuels, burning of, 76
Francium, 106

Hydrocarbon An organic compound that contains only carbon and hydrogen, 446
  saturated, 446
  unsaturated, 460
Hydrochloric acid (HCl), 244, 245, 246, 422
Hydrogen, 103, 107, 197
  density of, 50
  electron configuration for, 128
  function of, 109
Hydrogenation The addition of hydrogen (H_2) to an alkene or alkyne to yield alkanes, 468, 621–623, 642
  alkenes, 468
  of unsaturated fats, 469
Hydrogen bond The attraction between a partially positive H in one molecule and a strongly electronegative atom of F, O, or N, 218–219, 221, 327, 707, 762
  acetaldehyde and acetone with water, 523–524
Hydrogen bond (protein) The interaction between water and the polar residues such as —OH, —NH_3^+, and —COO^- on the outside surface of a polypeptide chain, 707
  in triple helix, 704
Hydrogen breath test (HBT), 744–745
Hydrogen ion gradient A separation of charge across a membrane caused by the pumping of hydrogen ions from the matrix into the intermembrane space, 846
Hydrogen ions, 246
Hydrogen peroxide, 64
Hydrogen sulfate, 197
Hydrolysis The splitting of a molecule by the addition of water. Esters hydrolyze to produce a carboxylic acid and an alcohol. Amides yield the corresponding carboxylic acid and amine, or their salts.
  amides, 623, 642, 676–677
  ATP, 801–803
  esters, 596–597
  protein, 711–713
  urea cycle reaction, 886
Hydrometer, 52
Hydronium ion, H_3O^+ The ion formed by the attraction of a hydrogen ion, H^+, to a water molecule, 403
Hydrophilic
  cell membrane layer, 638
  polar amino acid, 690
Hydrophilic interaction The attraction between polar residues on the protein surface and water, 706
Hydrophobic
  cell membrane layer, 638
  nonpolar amino acid, 690
Hydrophobic interaction The attraction between nonpolar residues on the inside of a globular protein, 706
Hydroxide ion, 196
Hydroxides, 197, 402
Hydroxyl group The —OH functional group, 489
  in alcohols, 489–490
  Benedict's test and, 525
  cyclic hemiacetal, 529–530
  phenol, 489–490
Hydroxylysine, 704
Hydroxyproline, 704
Hyperbaric chambers, 310
Hyperglycemia, 557
Hyperkalemia, 104
Hypernatremia, 104
Hyperpotassemia, 104
Hyperthermia, 72
Hyperthyroidism, 150, 170
Hypertonic solution A solution that has a higher particle concentration and higher osmotic pressure than the cells of the body, 358
Hypoglycemia, 557
Hypokalemia, 104
Hyponatremia, 104
Hypopotassemia, 104
Hypothesis An unverified explanation of a natural phenomenon, 4–6
Hypothyroidism, 102
Hypotonic solution A solution that has a lower particle concentration and lower osmotic pressure than the cells of the body, 358
Hypoxia, 389

I

Ibuprofen, 475, 476, 537, 615
Ice, 50
Ideal gas constant, R A numerical value that relates the quantities P, V, n, and T in the ideal gas law equation, $PV = nRT$, 308
Ideal gas law A law that combines the four measured properties of a gas $PV = nRT$, 308–311

Imaging methods, 170–171
  computed tomography (CT), 171
  magnetic resonance imaging (MRI), 171
  positron emission tomography (PET), 170
Inches of mercury, 290, 292
Indermil, 599
Indicator A substance added to a titration sample that changes color when the pH of the solution changes, 425
Induced-fit model A model of enzyme action in which the shape of a substrate and the active site of the enzyme adjust to give an optimal fit, 725
Infant respiratory distress syndrome (IRDS), 630–631
Inflammation, 122
  NSAIDs and, 615
  in sickle cell anemia, 710
Inhibitor A substance that makes an enzyme inactive by interfering with its ability to react with a substrate, 735–739
  reversible inhibition, 736
Inhibitory neurotransmitters, 665
Inorganic compounds, 444, 445
Insecticide, 737
  electron transport inhibition by, 847
Insertion mutation A mutation that inserts a base in a DNA sequence, 776
Insoluble ionic compounds, 336–337
Inspiration, 296
Insulin, 877
  diabetes and, 875
  half-life, 881
International System of Units (SI) An international system of units that modifies the metric system, 26
Interstitial fluid, 327
Intestine
  disaccharide digestion, 809
  protein/amino acid digestion and, 881
  triacylglycerol (lipid) digestion and, 863
Intracellular fluid, 327
Introns The sections in DNA that do not code for protein, 769
Inuit people, 615–616
Inverse relationship, 295
Iodide, 186
Iodine, 36, 102
  in body, 102
  function of, 109
  radioactive iodine uptake (RAIU), 170
  tincture of, 325, 326
Iodine-125, 153
Iodine-131, 150–153, 164, 167, 170
Iodized salt, 192
Iodo group, 453
Ion An atom or group of atoms having an electrical charge because of a loss or gain of electrons, 185
  in body, 188
  equivalents, 330–331
  in ionic bonding, 185
  polyatomic, 196–199
  transfer of electrons, 184–188
Ionic bond
  definition of, 185
  formation of, 184
Ionic charge The difference between the number of protons (positive) and the number of electrons (negative), written in the upper right corner of the symbol for the element or polyatomic ion, 185
  from group numbers, 187–188
  metals with variable charge, 192–193
  writing ionic formulas from, 191
Ionic compound A compound of positive and negative ions held together by ionic bonds, 189
  chemical formulas of, 189–190
  containing two elements, naming, 192
  formulas for
    chemical, 189–190
    subscripts in, 190
    writing of, 189–191, 194
  illustration of, 185
  naming of
    description of, 192–195
    flowchart for, 203
    with polyatomic ions, 199
    summary of, 202–203
    writing formulas, 194
  with polyatomic ions, naming, 199
  properties of, 189
  subscripts in formulas, 190
  summary of naming, 202–203
  variable charge, 193

Ionic formula, 191
  variable charge
    determination of, 193–194
    metals with, 192–193
  writing, 191
Ionic solute, 328
Ionization energy The energy needed to remove the least tightly
  bound electron from the outermost energy level of an atom,
  135, 139
Ionizing radiation, 154
Iridium-192, 167, 172
Iron, 36–38, 63, 68, 80, 102
  in body, 102
  density of, 50
  function of, 109
  rusting of, 68
Iron-59, 166–167
Iron(III) sulfate, 352
Irreversible inhibitors A compound or metal ion that causes the loss of
  enzymatic activity by forming a covalent bond near or at the active site,
  737–739
Isocitrate, 839, 841
Isocitrate dehydrogenase, 840
Isoelectric point (pI) The pH at which an amino acid exists as a zwitterion
  with a net charge of zero, 690
Isoenzymes, 728
Isoleucine, 691, 887
Isomerization
  in beta oxidation cycle, 869
  in citric acid cycle, 839
  in glycolysis, 811
Isomers, 451
Isotonic solution A solution that has the same particle concentration and
  osmotic pressure as that of the cells of the body, 358
Isotope An atom that differs only in mass number from another atom of
  the same element. Isotopes have the same atomic number (number of
  protons), but different numbers of neutrons, 117–121
  identifying protons and neutrons in, 118
  magnesium, atomic symbols for, 117–118
IUPAC system A system for naming organic compounds devised by the
  International Union of Pure and Applied Chemistry, 453
  alkanes, 453–454
  alkenes, 461–462
  alkynes, 461–462
  aromatic compounds, 474–475
  description of, 447
  priority of functional groups, 520–521

J

Jaundice, neonatal, 122
Jet fuel, 457
Jojoba wax, 617
Joule (J) The SI unit of heat energy; 4.184 J = 1 cal, 73

K

Kalium, 104
Kaopectate, 352
Kaposi's sarcoma, 784
Kekulé, August, 474
Kelvin (K) temperature scale A temperature scale on which the lowest
  possible temperature is 0 K, 28, 70–71, 291
Keratin, 708
Kerosene, 457
Keto acid, 882–883
Ketogenesis The pathway that converts acetyl CoA to four-carbon
  acetoacetate and other ketone bodies, 873
Ketogenic amino acid An amino acid that provides carbon atoms for the
  synthesis of fatty acids or ketone bodies, 887
  degradation, 887
Ketohexose, 562
Ketone An organic compound in which the carbonyl functional group is
  bonded to two alkyl or aromatic groups, 517
  boiling points, 523
  important, 521
  naming, 519–520, 540
  oxidation and reduction, 525–527, 540
  physical properties, 523–524
  solubility in water, 523–524
  structure, 517
Ketone bodies The products of ketogenesis: acetoacetate, β-hydroxybutyrate,
  and acetone, 873–874
  diabetes and, 875
Ketoprofen, 615

Ketose A monosaccharide that contains a ketone group, 552
Ketosis A condition in which high levels of ketone bodies cannot be
  metabolized leading to lower blood pH, 874
Kidney
  artificial, 359
  damage from NSAIDs, 615
  malfunction of, 674
Kidney failure, 359
Kidney stones, 334
Kilo-, 36
Kilocalorie (kcal), 73
Kilogram (kg) A metric mass of 1000 g, equal to 2.20 lb. The kilogram is the
  SI standard unit of mass, 26–27, 28
Kilojoule (kJ), 73–74
Kilopascal (kPa), 290
Kinetic energy The energy of moving particles, 73
Kinetic molecular theory of gases A model used to explain the behavior of
  gases, 289, 290–292
Krebs cycle. *See* Citric acid cycle
Krypton, 133

L

Labels, units listed on, 29
Laboratory technician, 399
Lactase, 565, 566
Lactate
  accumulating in muscle, 817
  Cori cycle and, 821, 826–827
  pyruvate conversion to, 816–817
Lactate dehydrogenase
  half-life, 881
  isoenzyme, 728
Lactic acid, 584, 589
Lactose A disaccharide consisting of glucose and galactose; found in milk and
  milk products, 565–566
Lactose intolerance, 744–745
Lagging strand, 764
Lanolin, 617
Lanthanides, 106
Law of conservation
  of mass, 260
  of matter, 239
LDL (low-density lipoprotein), 635
LDL-cholesterol, 622–623
L-dopa, 536
Lead, 49–50, 103–104
Lead-206, 167
Leading strand, 764
Le Châtelier's principle When a stress is placed on a system at equilibrium,
  the equilibrium shifts to relieve that stress, 387–393, 528
Lecithin Glycerophospholipids containing choline as the amino alcohol, 627
Lecithin–sphingomyelin ratio, 631
Length measurements, 27, 37
  centimeter, 37
  millimeter, 37
Leptin, 871
Lethal dose (LD₅₀), 48
  from radiation, 164
Leucine, 691, 887
Lewis structure A representation of a molecule or ion that shows the valence
  electrons, 137, 204–209
  drawing of, 205–206
Lewis symbol The representation of an atom that shows valence electrons as
  dots around the symbol of the element, 137
Libby, Willard, 167
Lidocaine, 664
Like dissolves like, 328
Like terms, 13
Limiting reactant The reactant used up during a chemical reaction, which
  limits the amount of product that can form, 265–268
  calculating mass of product from, 267–268
  calculating moles of product from, 266–267
Line-angle structural formula A simplified structure that shows a zigzag line
  in which carbon atoms are represented as the ends of each line and as
  corners, 448–449, 455–456
Linoleic acid, 615
Lipase, 623, 726
  pancreatic, 863
Lipid bilayer A model of a cell membrane in which glycerophospholipids are
  arranged in two rows, 638
Lipids A family of compounds that is nonpolar in nature and not soluble in
  water; includes prostaglandins, waxes, triacylglycerols, phospholipids,
  and steroids, 608–648
  digestion of, 862–865

emulsification of, 863
metabolism of, 862–880, 890–891
types of, 609–610, 635
Lipogenesis The synthesis of fatty acid in which two-carbon acetyl units link together to yield fatty acids, primarily palmitic acid, 876–880, 878
Lipoprotein A polar complex composed of a combination of nonpolar lipids with glycerophospholipids and proteins that can be transported through body fluids
composition and properties, 635
HDL and LDL, 622–623
Liquid A state of matter that takes the shape of its container but has a definite volume, 67, 326
Liquid bandage, 599
Liquid solutions, 326
Lister, Joseph, 499
Listeria, 163
Liter (L) The metric unit for volume that is slightly larger than a quart, 26–27
Lithium, 103, 114, 119, 186
atomic mass, 113
electron configuration for, 128, 136
Liver
damage from NSAIDs, 615
synthesizing cholesterol, 635
synthesizing glucose, 824
urea cycle and, 885
Lock-and-key model A model of enzyme action in which the substrate is like a key that fits the specific shape of the active site (the lock), 725
Lou Gehrig's disease, 669
Low-density lipoprotein, 635
Low-pressure system (weather), 293
Luminal (phenobarbital), 675
Lungs
breathing mechanics, 296
cancer of, 157, 477
Lysine, 691, 887
Lysosome, 800

M

Macrominerals, 108–109
Magnesium, 36, 102, 119, 137, 186
electron configuration for, 136, 185
food sources of, 188
function of, 109, 188
isotopes of, 117–118
Magnesium-23, 153
Magnesium-24, 153
Magnesium-27, 153
Magnesium ion, 185
Magnetic resonance imaging (MRI), 171
Malaria, 663
Malate, 841, 842
Malate–aspartate shuttle, 851
Malate dehydrogenase, 842, 851
Malic acid, 584, 589
Malonate, 736
Malonyl ACP, 877
Malonyl CoA, 876, 878
Maltose A disaccharide consisting of two glucose units; it is obtained from the hydrolysis of starch and germinating grains, 564, 567
Manganese, function of, 109
Mannitol, 562
Mannose, 562
Manometer, 294
Margarine, 469, 621
Markovnikov, Vladimir, 469
Markovnikov's rule When adding water to alkenes with different numbers of groups attached to the double bonds, the H— adds to the carbon that has the greater number of hydrogen atoms, 469
Mass A measure of the quantity of material in an object, 28
of atom, 113
calculations for reactions, 263–265
conservation of, 260
measuring, 28, 39
molar. *See* Molar mass
Mass number The total number of protons and neutrons in the nucleus of an atom, 114–115, 144
Mass percent (m/m) The grams of solute in exactly 100 g of solution, 340
Mass/volume percent (m/v) The grams of solute in exactly 100 mL of solution, 341–342
Math skills
graphs, 14–15
negative numbers, 10–11
percentages, 12

place values, 9–10
positive numbers, 10–11
scientific notation, 15–18
solving equations, 12–14
Matrix, cellular, 866
Matter The material that makes up a substance and has mass and occupies space, 62–98
changes of state of, 81
classification of, 63–66
compound, 63–64
element, 63
gases, 82, 90
mixtures, 63–66
properties of, 67–68
pure substances, 63–64
solids, 67–68
states of matter, 67
Measured number A number obtained when a quantity is determined by using a measuring device, 30–32
exact numbers, 31
Measurements. *See* Units of measurement
conversion factors, 39–40
exact numbers, 31
length, 27
mass, 28
measured numbers, 30–32
in scientific notation, 15–16
significant figures, 30–33
temperature, 28
time, 28
volume, 26–28
Medical applications using radioactivity, 169–172
brachytherapy, 171–172
imaging methods, 170–171
radioactive iodine uptake (RAIU), 170
scans with radioisotopes, 170
Mega-, 36
Melanin, 778
Melanoma, 786
Melting The change of state from a solid to a liquid, 82
Melting point (mp) The temperature at which a solid becomes a liquid (melts). It is the same temperature as the freezing point, 82
amides, 673–674
Menaquinone (vitamin K), 743
Mendeleev, Dmitri, 105
Menstruation, 636
Mental retardation, 557
Meperidine, 664
Meprobamate, 675
Mercaptans, 493
Mercury, 50, 245
inches of, 290, 292
toxicity of, 104
Mercury(II) oxide, 244–245
Meta A method of naming that indicates two substituents at carbons 1 and 3 of a benzene ring, 474, 490, 581
Metabolic acidosis, 431
Metabolic alkalosis, 431
Metabolic reactions
enzymes and coenzymes in, 807
Metabolism All the chemical reactions in living cells that carry out molecular and energy transformations, 797–835
amino acid and protein, 880–885
ATP, energy from glucose, 851–854
ATP, oxidative phosphorylation and, 848–850
carbohydrate pathways for, 797–835, 799
catabolism and anabolism, 798, 890–891
cell structure for, 800–804
chemiosmotic model, 848
citric acid cycle and, 799
coenzymes and, 804–808
defined, 798
digesting carbohydrate, 808–809
digesting protein, 862–863, 881
energy and, 798–804
energy production and, 836–860
lipid, 862–880
obesity, 871
overview of, 890–891
oxidative phosphorylation and ATP and, 848–850
pyruvate, 816–819
stages of, 798–799, 838, 890–891

Metal An element that is shiny, malleable, ductile, and a good conductor of heat and electricity. The metals are located to the left of the heavy zigzag line on the periodic table, 107–108
  acids and, 423
  ions, as cofactors, 739–740
  with variable charge, 192–193
Metallic character A measure of how easily an element loses a valence electron, 135, 140
Metalloid Elements with properties of both metals and nonmetals, located along the heavy zigzag line on the periodic table, 107–108
Metastable, 160
Meter (m) The metric unit for length that is slightly longer than a yard. The meter is the SI standard unit of length, 26–27
Methanal, 518
Methandienone, 637
Methane, 50, 446–447, 457
Methanethiol, 494
Methanol (methyl alcohol), 328, 330, 489, 492
  poisoning, 503
  producing blindness, 492
Methionine, 691
  degradation, 887
  synthesis, 891
Methyl alcohol, 492
Methylamine, 651
Methyl salicylate, 3, 592
Metric conversion factors, 40
Metric system A system of measurement used by scientists and in most countries of the world, 26–27
Metric–U.S. system conversion factors, 40–41
MI. *See* Myocardial infarction
Micelles, 863
Micro-, 36–37
Microgram (mcg), 36
Microminerals, 109
Milk, 50
Milk of magnesia, 400
Milk protein, denaturation, 712
Milk sugar (lactose), 565, 566
Milli-, 36–37
Milliequivalents per liter (mEq/L), 331
Milligram (mg), 36–37
Milliliter (mL) A metric unit of volume equal to one-thousandth of a liter (0.001 L), 27
Millimeter (mm), 37
Millimeters of mercury (mmHg), 290
Millirem (mrem), 163
Mineral oil, 457
Mirror image, 531–535
  achiral compound, 532
Mirrors, making, 525
Mitchell, Peter, 848
Mitochondria The organelle of cells where energy-producing reactions take place, 800
Mitosis (cell division)
  uncontrolled (in cancer), 786
Mixture The physical combination of two or more substances that does not change the identities of the mixed substances, 63–66
  heterogeneous, 65
  physical processes, 64–65
  separation of, 64–65
  types of, 65
Molar. *See* Molar mass
Molarity (M) The number of moles of solute in exactly 1 L of solution, 342–343
  calculation of, 342–343
  as conversion factor, 343
  mass of solute calculated from, 340
  volume calculated from, 344–345
Molar mass The mass in grams of 1 mole of an element equal numerically to its atomic mass. The molar mass of a compound is equal to the sum of the masses of the elements multiplied by their subscripts in the formula, 255–260
  calculations using, 257–259
  of compound, 256–257
  converting to moles, 258–259
  in kitchen, 256
Molar volume A volume of 22.4 L occupied by exactly 1 mole of a gas at STP conditions of 0 °C (273 K) and 1 atm, 306–307
  conversion factors, 306
Mole A group of atoms, molecules, or formula units that contains 6.02×10^{23} of these items, 251–255
  Avogadro's number, 251–252
  calculating moles of a reactant, 262
  of elements in a formula, 253–254

relationships in chemical equations, 260–263. *See* Chemical equation
Molecular compound A combination of atoms in which stable electron configurations are attained by sharing electrons, 200
  definition of, 200
  formulas of, 200–201
  Lewis structures for, 204–205
  names of, 200–201
  prefixes used in, 201
  summary of naming, 202–203
  writing formulas from names of, 202
Molecular formula, 451
Molecule The smallest unit of two or more atoms held together by covalent bonds, 64, 372
  definition of, 200
  Lewis structures for, 204–209
  nonpolar, 216–217
  polar, 217
  polarity of, 212–213, 216–217
  shape of, 212–216
Mole–mole factor A conversion factor that relates the number of moles of two compounds derived from the coefficients in an equation, 261–262
  in calculations, 261–262
  writing of, 261
Molybdenum, 109
Molybdenum-98, 160–161
Monoacylglycerols, 863
Monomer The small organic molecule that is repeated many times in a polymer, 470
Monosaccharide A polyhydroxy compound that contains an aldehyde or ketone group, 552–553, 574
  chemical properties, 561–564
  Fischer projections, 554–558
  Haworth structures, 558–561
  important, 556–557
  metabolism and, 890–891
  oxidation, 562, 574
  reactions, 575
  reduction, 562, 574
  sweetness of, 567
  types, 553, 574
Monosodium glutamate (MSG), 588
Monounsaturated fatty acid (MUFA) A fatty acid with one double bond, 611
Morphine, 663
Mothballs, 477
Motor oil, 457
mRNA Messenger RNA; produced in the nucleus from DNA to carry the genetic information to the ribosomes for the construction of a protein, 766
  codons, 771
  pre-mRNA, 769
  processing, 769
  producing (transcription), 768–769
  protein synthesis (translation), 767–768
  synthesis of, 768
Multiple sclerosis, 629
Multiplication
  of negative numbers, 10
  of positive numbers, 10
Muscle
  anabolic steroids and, 636
  filaments, 803
  lactate accumulation in, 817
Muscle contraction, 108
Muscone, 521
Musk, 521
Mutagens, 776
Mutarotation The conversion between α and β anomers via an open chain, 559
Mutation A change in the DNA base sequence that alters the formation of a protein in the cell, 776–778
  effects of, 778
  types of, 776–777
Myelin sheath, 629
Mylar, 592
Myocardial infarction, 633, 635
Myoglobin, 708
  carrying oxygen, 689
Myosin, 803

N

Nabumetone, 615
NADH dehydrogenase, 844–847, 845

NAD⁺ The hydrogen acceptor used in oxidation reactions that form carbon–oxygen double bonds, 805–806, 891

Nandrolone, 637

Nano-, 36

Nanotubes, 116

Naphthalene, 477

Naproxen, 615

Natrium, 104

Natural gas, 76

Natural radioactivity, 150–155

Negative numbers, 10–11

Negative regulator, 732

Nembutal (pentobarbital), 675

Neon, 50, 123

    electron configuration for, 128

Neon lights, 123

Neotame, 567

Nerve gas, 665

Nervous system stimulants, 662

Neuron, 664

Neurotransmitter A chemical compound that transmits an impulse from a nerve cell (neuron) to a target cell such as another nerve cell, a muscle cell, or a gland cell, 664–670

    acetylcholine, 666

    amine, 665–670

    catecholamines, 666–667

    dopamine, 667–668

    epinephrine, 668

    excitatory, 665

    gamma-aminobutyric acid, 669–670

    glutamate, 669

    histamine, 669

    inhibitory, 665

    norepinephrine, 668

    serotonin, 668–669

    at synapse, 664

    termination of action, 665

Neutralization A reaction between an acid and a base to form a salt and water, 423

    endpoint, 425

Neutralization equations, 423–424

Neutral solution The term that describes a solution with equal concentrations of $[H_3O^+]$ and $[OH^-]$, 414, 415

Neutron A neutral subatomic particle having a mass of about 1 amu and found in the nucleus of an atom; its symbol is n or n^0, 111–112, 145

Niacin, 36

Nickel, 64, 103, 108

Nicotinamide adenine dinucleotide. *See* NAD⁺

Nicotine, 536, 662

Night blindness, 467

Night vision, cis–trans isomers for, 465

Nitrate, 196–197

Nitride, 186

Nitrite, 197

Nitrogen (N), 64, 170, 310, 326

    balance, in cells, 881

    blood urea nitrogen (BUN), 884

    compounds containing, 881

    density of, 50

    dietary, 881

    electron configuration for, 136

    excreting (urea cycle), 884, 885

    function of, 109

Nitrogen-13, 170

Nitrogen-containing compounds, 881

Nitrogen narcosis, 66

Nitrogen oxide, 669

Nitrox, 64

Noble gas An element in Group 8A (18) of the periodic table, generally unreactive and seldom found in combination with other elements, 107

Non-, 447

Noncompetitive inhibitor An inhibitor that does not resemble the substrate, and attaches to the enzyme away from the active site to prevent the binding of the substrate, 736–737

Nonelectrolyte A substance that dissolves in water as molecules; its solution does not conduct an electrical current, 329–333, 355

    solutions of, 329

Nonessential amino acid An amino acid that can be synthesized by reactions including transamination of α-keto acids in the body, 888–890

Nonmetal An element with little or no luster that is a poor conductor of heat and electricity. The nonmetals are located to the right of the heavy zigzag line on the periodic table, 107–108

    characteristics of, 108

    ionic compounds and, 189, 190

Nonpolar amino acid Amino acid with a nonpolar R group containing only C and H atoms, 690

Nonpolar covalent bond A covalent bond in which the electrons are shared equally between atoms, 210

Nonpolar lipid, 635

Nonpolar molecule A molecule that has only nonpolar bonds or in which the bond dipoles cancel, 216–217

Nonpolar solutes, 328

Nonpolar tail, 638

Nonsteroidal anti-inflammatory drugs (NSAIDs), 183, 615

Nonsuperimposable mirror images, 531

Norepinephrine, 668

Norethindrone, 636

NSAIDs. *See* Nonsteroidal anti-inflammatory drugs (NSAIDs)

N-terminus (N-terminal amino acid) The first amino acid in a peptide with a free —NH₃⁺ group, 697

Nuclear fusion, 172–175

Nuclear power plants, 175

Nuclear reactions, 156–162

    alpha decay, 156–157

    beta decay, 157–158

    gamma emission, 160

    radioactive isotopes, producing, 160–161

    radon in homes, 157

Nucleic acids Large molecules composed of nucleotides; found as a double helix in DNA and as the single strands of RNA, 753–775

    bases in, 754–755

    components of, 754–759

    nucleotide structure, 754–759

    primary structure, 759–761

Nucleoside The combination of a pentose sugar and a base, 755

    forming of di- and triphosphates, 757

    naming, 757

    producing, 755

Nucleotide Building blocks of a nucleic acid consisting of a base, a pentose sugar (ribose or deoxyribose), and a phosphate group, 754–759

    in DNA, 757

    forming, 757–758

    naming, 757

    in RNA, 757

    structure, 754

Nucleotide sequence, 776, 781

Nucleus The compact, very dense center of an atom, containing the protons and neutrons of the atom, 112

Nucleus (of cell), 800

Numbers

    negative, 10–11

    positive, 10–11

Nurse anesthetist, 488

NutraSweet, 566

Nutrition, 76–79

    daily values for nutrients, 36

    energy values for foods, 77–78

    kilocalories or kilojoules, 76

Nutritional energy, 76

Nutrition Facts label, 77

Nylon, 3

O

Obesity, 871

Observation Information determined by noting and recording a natural phenomenon, 4–6, 19

Oct-, 447

Octet A set of eight valence electrons, 184

Octet rule Elements in Groups 1A–7A (1, 2, 13–17) react with other elements by forming ionic or covalent bonds to produce a stable electron configuration, usually eight electrons in the outer shell, 184, 209

Odor, fruit, 590

Oil A triacylglycerol that is usually a liquid at room temperature and is obtained from a plant source, 619, 642

    fish, 615–616

    hydrogenation, 621–623

    melting point, 619–620

    polyunsaturated, 619

    vegetable, 622–623

Oil spill, 459

Okazaki fragment A short segment formed by DNA polymerase in the daughter DNA strand that runs in the 3′ to 5′ direction, 764

Oleic acid, 469

Olive oil, 50, 469

Omega-3 fatty acid, 615–616

Omega-6 fatty acid, 616

Oncogenic viruses, 785–786

Opium, 663

Optimum pH The pH at which an enzyme is most active, 730

Optimum temperature The temperature at which an enzyme is most active, 729

Orbital diagram A diagram that shows the distribution of electrons in the orbitals of the energy levels, 127
  drawing, 129–130

Orbital The region around the nucleus where electrons of a certain energy are more likely to be found. The *s* orbitals are spherical; the *p* orbitals have two lobes, 124
  capacity and electron spin, 126
  orbital diagram, 127
  shapes of, 124–126

Organelle, cellular, 800–801

Organic compound A compound made of carbon that typically has covalent bonds, is nonpolar, has low melting and boiling points, is insoluble in water, and is flammable, 444–447
  covalent bonds for elements in, 446
  cyclic, 661–664
  properties of, 445
  tetrahedral structure of carbon in, 446

Ornithine, 884–886

Ortho A method of naming that indicates two substituents at carbons 1 and 2 of a benzene ring, 474, 490, 581

Osmolarity, 357

Osmosis The flow of a solvent, usually water, through a semipermeable membrane into a solution of higher solute concentration, 356

Osmotic pressure The pressure that prevents the flow of water into the more concentrated solution, 356
  reverse osmosis, 356

Osteoporosis, 51

Oxaloacetate, 825
  from aspartate or asparagine degradation, 887
  in citric acid cycle, 840–841, 843
  glucogenic amino acid and, 887

Oxaloacetic acid, 589

Oxandrolone, 637

Oxidation The loss of electrons by a substance. Biological oxidation is indicated by the addition of oxygen or the loss of hydrogen. The loss of two hydrogen atoms from a reactant to give a more oxidized compound, 248, 502, 804–805
  alcohol, 502–504
  alcohol in body, 505
  aldehyde, 525–527, 540
  beta oxidation cycle, 865–870
  carbohydrate, 810, 890
  characteristics of, 841
  citric acid cycle, 841
  coenzymes, 845
  electron carriers, 845–847
  enzymes (oxidases), 726
  fatty acid, 865–870
  glucose, 810
  monosaccharide, 562, 574
  thiol, 504–505

Oxidation–reduction reaction A reaction in which the oxidation of one reactant is always accompanied by the reduction of another reactant, 248–250
  in biological systems, 250
  involving ions, 249–250

Oxidative deamination The loss of ammonium ion when glutamate is degraded to α-ketoglutarate, 883

Oxidative phosphorylation The synthesis of ATP using the energy of the hydrogen ions and electrons from the NADH and $FADH_2$ that enter electron transport to produce a hydrogen ion gradient, 844, 848–850

Oxide, 186

Oxygen
  aerobic condition, 816–817
  anaerobic condition, 810
  atomic mass of, 119
  in blood, 310
  in body, 310
  electron configuration for, 128
  function of, 109
  hydroxyl group, 489
  hyperbaric chambers, 310

Oxygen-15, 170

Oxygen–hemoglobin equilibrium, 389

Oxytocin, 699

Ozone depletion, 289

P

PABA (*p*-aminobenzoic acid), 736

PAHs. *See* Polycyclic aromatic hydrocarbons

Pain
  prostaglandins and, 615
  relievers, 591, 615, 662

Pain reliever, 475

Palmitate, synthesis, 877–879, 878

Palmitic acid, 627

Pancreatic cancer, 169

Pancreatic lipase, 863

Pancreatitis, 733

Papain, 726

Para A method of naming that indicates two substituents at carbons 1 and 4 of a benzene ring, 474, 490, 581

Paracelsus, 5, 48

Paraffins, 457

Parathion, 48

Parkinson's disease, 668

Paroxetine hydrochloride, 669

Partial pressure The pressure exerted by a single gas in a gas mixture, 312–315

Pascal (Pa), 291–292

Passive transport, 639

Patina, 249

Pauli exclusion principle, 126

Pauling, Linus, 4

p **block** The elements in Groups 3A (3) to 8A (18) in which electrons fill the *p* orbitals in the *p* sublevels, 132

PCR (polymerase chain reaction), 781

Penicillin, 650, 737

Pent-, 447

Pentane, 457
  structural formulas for, 448–449

Pentapeptide, 697

2-Pentene, 465

Pentobarbital (Nembutal), 675

Pentose, 553

Pentose phosphate pathway A metabolic pathway that oxidizes glucose to produce NADPH for biosynthesis of lipids, and five-carbon sugars required for the synthesis of nucleotides, DNA, and RNA, 815

Pentose sugars, 755

Pepper, 661

Pepsin, 422, 726, 730, 881

Peptide The combination of two or more amino acids joined by peptide bonds; dipeptide, tripeptide, and so on, 697–700, 716
  forming, 697–700
  naming, 698

Peptide bond The amide bond in peptides that joins the carboxylate group of one amino acid with the ammonium group in the next amino acid, 697
  hydrolyzing, 711–713

Peptide chain, 702

Percentage
  calculating of, 12
  conversion factor from, 42

Percent concentration
  calculation of, 340
  as conversion factor, 343–345
  mass percent, 340
  mass/volume percent, 341–342
  volume percent, 340–341

Percent yield The ratio of the actual yield for a reaction to the theoretical yield possible for the reaction, 268–270

Perchloric acid, 401

Period A horizontal row of elements in the periodic table, 105–106

Periodic properties, 135

Periodic table An arrangement of elements by increasing atomic number such that elements having similar chemical behavior are grouped in vertical columns, 105–110. *See* Electron configurations
  blocks on, 132
  classification, 106–108
    alkali metals, 106
    alkaline earth metals, 107
    halogens, 107
    metalloids, 107
    metals, 107
    noble gases, 107
    nonmetals, 107
    representative elements, 105
    transition elements, 105–106
  and electron configurations, 131
  groups, 105–106
  periods, 105–106
  trends in, 135–141
    atomic size, 135, 137–138
    group number and valence electrons, 140
    ionization energy, 135, 139

Lewis symbols, 137
  metallic character, 140
  representative elements, 105
  valence electrons, 135
Periodic trends
  atomic size, 135, 137–138
  group number and valence electrons, 140
  ionization energy, 135, 139
  Lewis symbols, 137
  metallic character, 140
  representative elements, 105
  valence electrons, 135
Permanent (hair treatment), 505
Permanent brachytherapy, 171
Perspiration, 327
Pesticides, 48, 466
PETE (polyethylene terephthalate), 592
Petrolatum jelly, 457
pH A measure of the $\left[H_3O^+\right]$ in a solution; pH $= -\log\left[H_3O^+\right]$, 416–422, 874
  calculating, 418–420
  enzyme activity and, 730
  indicators, 425
  scale, 416–422
  stomach, 730
Pharmacy technician, 183
Phenanthrene, 477
Phenobarbital (Luminal), 675
Phenol An organic compound that has a hydroxyl group ($-$OH) attached to a benzene ring, 474, 489, 493
  and antiseptics, 499
  boiling point, 499
  hydroxyl groups in, 489–490
  important, 492–493
  naming, 474, 490–492, 509
  solubility in water, 499
Phenolphthalein, 425
Phenylalanine, 476, 691, 887
  phenylketonuria and, 890
  synthesis, 890
Phenylketonuria (PKU), 566, 778, 890
Phenylpyruvate, 778
Pheromones, 466
pH meter, 416, 417
Phosphate, 197
Phosphate ester, 627–628
Phosphide, 186
Phosphite, 197
Phosphodiester linkage The phosphate link that joins the 3′ hydroxyl group in one nucleotide to the phosphate group on the 5′ carbon atom in the next nucleotide, 759
Phosphoenolpyruvate, 825
Phosphofructokinase, 811, 814, 828
Phosphoglucose isomerase, 811
Phospholipases, 628
Phospholipid A polar lipid of glycerol or sphingosine attached to fatty acids and a phosphate group connected to an amino alcohol, 627–632
  amino alcohols, 627–628
  glycerophospholipids, 627
Phospholipid bilayer, 638
Phosphopentose isomerase, 815
Phosphorus, 102, 123, 130
  function of, 109
Phosphorus-32, 164
Phosphorylation, 735, 811
Phototherapy, 122
Physical change A change in which the physical properties of a substance change but its identity stays the same, 67–68
  in appearance, 67–68
  in shape, 67–68
  in size, 67–68
  in state, 67–68
  types, 68
Physical methods of separation
  chromatography, 65
  filtration, 65
  mixtures, 64–65
Physical properties The properties that can be observed or measured without affecting the identity of a substance, 67–68
Physician assistant, 722
Pico-, 36
Piperidine, 661
PKU (phenylketonuria), 566, 778, 890
Place values, 9–10
Plaque, 632, 705

Plasma, 50, 327, 332
Plasmids, recombinant DNA and, 780–781
Platelet clotting, 616
Platinum, 103
"Plum-pudding" model, 112
Plutonium-239, 175
Pneumocystis carinii, 784
Point mutation A mutation that replaces one base in a DNA with a different base, 776
Polar amino acid An amino acid with polar R groups, 690, 695–696
Polar covalent bond A covalent bond in which the electrons are shared unequally between atoms, 210
Polar head, 638
Polarity A measure of the unequal sharing of electrons indicated by the difference in electronegativities, 210, 216
Polar molecule A molecule containing bond dipoles that do not cancel, 217
Polar solute, 328
Polar solvent, 326
Pollution, 289, 335
Polonium, 157, 163
Polyatomic ion A group of covalently bonded nonmetal atoms that has an overall electrical charge, 196–199
  compounds containing 199
  definition of, 196
  Lewis structures for, 204–209
  naming compounds containing, 199
  naming of, 199
Polycyclic aromatic hydrocarbons (PAHs), 477
Polymerase chain reaction (PCR) A procedure in which a strand of DNA is copied many times by mixing it with DNA polymerase and a mixture of deoxyribonucleotides and subjecting it to repeated cycles of heating and cooling, 781
Polymer A very large molecule that is composed of many small, repeating monomer units, 470
Polymerization, 470–472
Polypeptides, 697, 699–700
Polysaccharide A polymer of many monosaccharide units, usually glucose. Polysaccharides differ in the types of glycosidic bonds and the amount of branching in the polymer, 552, 570–573, 574, 890–891
  cellulose, 570–572
  digesting, 570, 571
Polysome, 774
Polyunsaturated fat
  dietary consumption, 615–616
  oil, 619
Polyunsaturated fatty acid (PUFA) A fatty acid that contains two or more double bonds, 611
Positive numbers, 10–11
Positive regulator, 732
Positron A particle of radiation with no mass and a positive charge, symbol β^+ or ${}_{+1}^{0}e$, produced when a proton is transformed into a neutron and a positron, 153
Positron emission, 159
Positron emission tomography (PET), 170
Potassium, 36
  in blood, 331
  electron configuration for, 133
  food sources of, 188
  function of, 109, 188
Potassium-40, 164, 167
Potential energy A type of energy related to position or composition of a substance, 73, 93
Pounds per square inch (psi), 290, 292
Powers of 10, 16
ppb, conversion factor from, 42
ppm, conversion factor from, 42
Precipitate, 337
Prednisone, 637
Prefix The part of the name of a metric unit that precedes the base unit and specifies the size of the measurement. All prefixes are related on a decimal scale, 36–39, 55
  metric and SI systems, 36
Pregnancy, gestational diabetes, 875
Pre-mRNA, 769
Preservative, 588
Pressure The force exerted by gas particles that hit the walls of a container, 290–291
  atmospheric pressure, 290–291
  of gas, 290–291
  osmotic, 356
  partial, 312–315
  units for measuring, 292
Pressure gradient, 296

Pressure–volume relationship, in breathing, 296
Primary (1°) alcohol An alcohol that has one alkyl group bonded to the alcohol's carbon atom, 497, 502–504
Primary (1°) amine, 650
Primary structure The specific sequence of the amino acid residues in a protein, 701, 716, 759–761
Principal quantum numbers, 121
Probenecid, 334
Problem solving, 44–48
  with specific gravity, 52
  using density, 51–52
  using metric factors, 46
  using two or more conversion factors, 45–46
Procaine, 664
Products The substances formed as a result of a chemical reaction, 238
Proenzyme, 733–735
Progesterone, 636
Progestin, 636
Prokaryotic cells, 800
Proline, 691, 887
Propanal, 518
Propane, 246, 457, 459
1,2,3-Propanetriol (glycerol or glycerin), 493
Properties of matter, 67–69. See Chemical change; Physical change
  physical changes of matter, 67–68
Propionaldehyde, 518
Propionic acid, 582
Propyl acetate, 254
Prostaglandins (PGs) A number of compounds derived from arachidonic acid that regulate several physiological processes, 614–615
Protein A polypeptide of 50 or more amino acid residues that has biological activity, 688–714
  definition of, 701
  denaturation, 711–713, 716, 881
  digestion of, 862, 881
  disulfide bonds, 504–505
  half-life, 881
  hydrolysis, 711–713, 716
  laboratory test values for, 38
  metabolism, 880–892
  primary structure, 701
  recommended daily amount of, 36
  secondary structure, 702–705
  sequencing, 702
  tertiary and quaternary structure, 706–711
  urea cycle and, 884–886
Protein synthesis, 767–768, 771–775
  antibiotics and, 774
  translation, 771–774
Protein turnover The amount of protein that we break down from our diet and utilize for synthesis of proteins and nitrogen containing compounds, 881
Proton A positively charged subatomic particle having a mass of about 1 amu found in the nucleus of an atom; its symbol is p or p^+, 111–112
Psoriasis, 122
Public health nurse (PHN), 861
Pure substance A type of matter that has a definite composition, 63–64
Purine, 334, 754–755
Pyridine, 661
Pyrimidine, 754–755
Pyruvate
  aerobic conditions (converting to acetyl CoA), 816
  anaerobic conditions (converting to lactate, ethanol), 817
  ATP from oxidizing, 844, 852
  digestion/metabolism and, 799, 812
  glucogenic amino acid and, 887
  in metabolism summary, 890–891
  pathways for, 816–819
Pyruvate carboxylase, 825
Pyruvate kinase, 812, 814, 826
Pyruvic acid, 589

Q

Quartz, 65
Quaternary ammonium ion An ammonium salt in which the nitrogen atom is bonded to four carbon groups, 659
Quaternary ammonium salt An ammonium salt in which the nitrogen atom is bonded to four alkyl groups, 659
Quaternary structure A protein structure in which two or more protein subunits form an active protein, 708–709, 716
Quinine, 663

R

Rad (radiation absorbed dose) A measure of an amount of radiation absorbed by the body, 163

Radiation Energy or particles released by radioactive atoms, 149–182
  alpha decay, 153
  beta decay, 153
  cosmic, 164
  definition of, 150
  exposure to, 164
  food and, 163
  gamma rays, 153
  lethal dose, 164
  measurement of, 162–165
    becquerel (Bq), 163
    curie (Ci), 164
    equivalent dose, 163
    gray (Gy), 163
    rad (radiation absorbed dose), 163
    rem (radiation equivalent in humans), 163
    sievert (Sv), 163
  medical applications of, 169–172
  natural radioactivity, 150–155. See Radioactivity
  nuclear reactions
    alpha decay, 156–157
    beta decay, 157–158
    bombardment reaction, 160–161
    gamma emission, 160
    positron emission, 159
    radioactive isotopes, producing, 160–161
  positron, 153
  radioactive decay, 156
  radioisotope half-life, 165–169
  sickness, 164–165
  types of, 153–154
Radiation protection
  beta particles, 154–155
  gamma rays, 154–155
  shielding, 154–155
Radiation sickness, 164–165
Radioactive decay The process by which an unstable nucleus breaks down with the release of high-energy radiation, 156
Radioactive iodine uptake (RAIU), 170
Radioactive waste, 175
Radioactivity, 150–155. See Radiation
  natural, 150–155
Radioisotope A radioactive atom of an element, 150
  half-life of, 165–169
  positron emission tomography (PET), 170
  scans with, 170
Radiological dating, 167
Radiology technician, 688
Radium, 155, 163
Radium-226, 157, 167
Radon-222, 157, 164, 167
Radon in homes, 157
Rate of reaction The speed at which reactants are used to form product(s), 371, 372–377
  factors affecting, 375
  formula, 373
  substrate concentration and, 731
Reactants The initial substances that undergo change in a chemical reaction, 238
  calculating mass of product from, 267–268
  calculating moles of product from, 266–267
  increasing concentration, 374, 375
Reaction
  catalysts and, 374–375, 724–725, 726
  direction of, 410
Recombinant DNA DNA combined from different organisms to form new, synthetic DNA, 780–781
Recrystallization, 333
Red blood cells, 358–359
  crenation, 358
  hemolysis, 358
Reducing sugar A carbohydrate with an aldehyde group capable of reducing the Cu^{2+} in Benedict's reagent, 562
Reduction The gain of electrons by a substance. Biological reduction is indicated by the loss of oxygen or the gain of hydrogen. A decrease in the number of carbon–oxygen bonds by the addition of hydrogen to a carbonyl bond, 248, 526
  aldehyde and ketone, 526–527, 540
  coenzymes, 804–805, 844–847
  electron carriers, 847
  fatty acid synthesis, 877
  monosaccharide, 562, 574
Refrigeration, 85
Registered nurse, 25
Relafen, 615
Release factors, 774

Rem (radiation equivalent in humans) A measure of the biological damage caused by the various kinds of radiation (rad × radiation biological factor), 163
Renal disease, 884
Rennin, 726
Replacement reactions, 244–246
  double, 246
  single, 244–245
Replication The process of duplicating DNA by pairing the bases on each parent strand with their complementary bases in the daughter strand, 763–766
  direction of, 764–766
Replication forks The open sections in unwound DNA strands where DNA polymerase begins the replication process, 764
Representative element An element in the first two columns on the left of the periodic table and the last six columns on the right that has a group number of 1A through 8A or 1, 2, and 13 through 18, 105–106
Repressor, 770
Repulsion, of like charges, 113
Respiration, 72, 551
Respiratory acidosis, 431
Respiratory alkalosis, 431
Respiratory chain, 844. *See* Electron transport
Respiratory therapist, 288
Restriction enzyme, 780
Retardation, 557
Retin-A, 122
Retinal, 467
Retinal camera, 37
Retinoblastoma, 786
Retinol (vitamin A), 743
Retrovirus A virus that contains RNA as its genetic material and that synthesizes a complementary DNA strand inside a cell, 783
Reverse osmosis, 356
Reverse reaction, 377–378
Reverse transcriptase, 783
Reverse transcription, 783
Reversible inhibition The loss of enzymatic activity by an inhibitor whose effect can be reversed, 736
Reversible reaction A reaction in which a forward reaction occurs from reactants to products, and a reverse reaction occurs from products back to reactants, 377
Rheumatoid arthritis, 637
Rhodopsin, 467
Riboflavin (vitamin B_2), 741
Ribose, 755
Ribosomal RNA (rRNA) The most prevalent type of RNA and a major component of the ribosomes, 766
Ribosome, 766, 800
  polysome, 774
  protein synthesis and, 771–772
Rigor mortis, 804
Ringer's solution, 331
Risk–benefit assessment, 47–48
RNA Ribonucleic acid; a type of nucleic acid that is a single strand of nucleotides containing adenine, cytosine, guanine, and uracil, 754–761, 766–771
  bases in, 754–755
  genetic code, 771–775
  nucleotides and nucleosides in, 754–758
  primary structure, 759–761
  protein synthesis and (translation), 767–768, 771–774
  ribose in, 755
  types of, 766–767
RNA polymerase, 768, 770
RNA viruses, 786
Rock candy, 335
Rock sample, determining age of, 167
Rotenone, 847–848
Rounding off, significant figures, 33
rRNA Ribosomal RNA; the most prevalent type of RNA and a major component of the ribosomes, 766
Rubidium, 105
Ruler, 30
Rust, 68, 237, 248
Rutherford, Ernest, 112

S

Saccharin, 567, 674
Safflower oil, 469
Salicylic acid, 591–592
Saliva, 572
Salmonella, 163
Salt An ionic compound that contains a metal ion or NH_4^+ and a nonmetal or polyatomic ion other than OH^-, 423
  definition of, 423

Salt bridge The attraction between the ionized residues of basic and acidic amino acids in the tertiary structure of a protein, 707
Saponification The hydrolysis of an ester with a strong base to produce a salt of the carboxylic acid and an alcohol, 597–598, 601, 623–624, 642
Saturated fats, 469, 622–623
  stimulating synthesis of cholesterol, 633
Saturated fatty acid (SFA) A fatty acid that has no double bonds, which has a higher melting point than unsaturated fatty acids, and is usually solid at room temperature, 611, 622–623
Saturated hydrocarbon, 446
Saturated solution A solution containing the maximum amount of solute that can dissolve at a given temperature. Any additional solute will remain undissolved in the container, 333–334
Saytzeff's rule In the dehydration of an alcohol, hydrogen is removed from the carbon that already has the smallest number of hydrogen atoms to form an alkene, 501
s **block** The elements in Groups 1A (1) and 2A (2) in which electrons fill the *s* orbitals, 132
Scan, 170–171
Scanner, 170
Scanning electron micrographs (SEMs), 51
Scanning tunneling microscope (STM), 111
Scientific method The process of making observations, proposing a hypothesis, testing the hypothesis, and making a conclusion as to the validity of the hypothesis, 4–5
Scientific notation A form of writing large and small numbers using a coefficient that is at least 1 but less than 10, followed by a power of 10, 15–18
  calculators and, 17–18
  significant zeros and, 30
  writing a number in, 15–16
SCI function key, on calculators, 17
Scuba diver, 66, 297, 310
Sea level, 75, 293, 314
Seasonal affective disorder, 122
Seawater, 104, 326
Secobarbital (Seconal), 675
Secondary (2°) alcohol An alcohol that has two alkyl groups bonded to the carbon atom with the —OH group, 497, 502–504
Secondary (2°) amine, 650, 654
Secondary structure The formation of an α helix or β-pleated sheet by hydrogen bonds, 702–705, 716
  Alzheimer's disease and, 705
Second (s) A unit of time used in both the SI and metric systems, 26, 28
Selective serotonin reuptake inhibitors (SSRIs), 669
Selenium, 36, 108–109
Semiconductor, 107
Semipermeable membrane, 352–353, 356
Sequencing, protein, 702
Serine, 691
  converting to pyruvate, 887
  synthesis, 889
Serotonin, 664, 668–669
Serum alanine aminotransferase, 889
Serum aspartate aminotransferase, 889
Serum cholesterol, 633
Sevoflurane, 497
Sex hormone, 636
Shielding, 154
Shortening, 469
Sickle cell anemia, 710
Sievert (Sv) A unit of biological damage (equivalent dose) equal to 100 rem, 163
Significant figures (SFs) The numbers recorded in a measurement, 30–32
  in calculations, 30-33, 32–35
    adding significant zeros, 34
    in addition and subtraction, 34–35
    in multiplication and division, 34
    rounding off, 33
Significant zeros, 31
Silent mutation, 776
Silicon, 103
  function of, 109
Silk, 466
Silkworm moth, 466
Silver, 50, 63, 80, 107, 236, 257, 260
Silver mirror, 525
Single bonds, 447, 448, 449, 458, 465
Single replacement reaction A reaction in which an element replaces a different element in a compound, 244–245, 249
SI units, 26–28, 40
Skin cancer, 122, 786
Skin protection plan, 539
Smoke detectors, 156
Snake venom, 628
Soap, saponification, 597–598
Soda water, 326

Sodium
electron configuration for, 130–131
food sources of, 188
formula for, 186
function of, 109, 188
recommended daily amount of, 36
Sodium bicarbonate, 199
Sodium chloride, 48, 64, 80, 190, 246, 258, 326, 328–329
Sodium hydroxide, 246
Sodium lauryl sulfate, 3
Sodium propionate, 588
Sodium sulfate, 199, 246
Solid A state of matter that has its own shape and volume, 67
changes of state of, 81–82
density of, 50–51
formation of, 337–339
properties of, 67
solid solutions, 326
Solid solutions, 326
Solubility The maximum amount of solute that can dissolve in exactly 100 g of solvent, usually water, at a given temperature, 333–339
alcohols and ethers, 498, 499
aldehydes and ketones, 523–524
alkanes, 459
amines, 656–657
phenol, 499
Solubility rules A set of guidelines that states whether an ionic compound is soluble or insoluble in water, 336
insoluble ionic compounds, 336–337
saturated solution, 333–334
soluble ionic compounds, 336–337
temperature effect on, 335
unsaturated solution, 333
Soluble ionic compounds, 336–337
Solute The component in a solution that is present in the lesser amount, 325
nonpolar, 328
polar, 328
types of, 326
Solution A homogeneous mixture in which the solute is made up of small particles (ions or molecules) that can pass through filters and semipermeable membranes, 65, 325–329. See Concentration
acidic, 414, 415
basic, 414, 415
buffer, 427–430
colloids, 352, 353
dilution of, 349–351
electrolytes, 329–333
formation of, 327–328
hydrogen bonds, 327
hypertonic, 358
hypotonic, 358
with ionic solutes, 328
isotonic solutions, 358
neutral, 414, 415
nonelectrolytes, 329–333
with nonpolar solutes, 328
osmotic pressure, 356
particles in, 354
pH, 418–420
with polar solutes, 328
polar solvent, 326
properties of, 352–361
supersaturated solution, 335
suspensions, 352, 353
types of solutes and solvents, 326
Solvent The substance in which the solute dissolves; usually the component present in greater amount, 325, 356
water as, 326–327
Solving equations, 12–14
Sorbitol, 3, 562, 567
Space-filling model, 446
Spearmint oil, 521
Specific gravity (sp gr) A relationship between the density of a substance and the density of water, 52
Specific heat (SH) A quantity of heat that changes the temperature of exactly 1 g of a substance by exactly 1 °C, 80–81
calculations using, 80–81
heat equation, 80
Spectator ions, 250
Sperm, 636
Sphingolipid A type of lipid in which glycerol is replaced by sphingosine, 627
Sphingomyelin A compound in which the amine group of sphingosine forms an amide bond to a fatty acid and the hydroxyl group forms an ester bond with phosphate, which forms another phosphoester bond to an ionized amino alcohol, 629

Sphygmomanometer, 294
Splenda, 566
Stanozolol, 637
Starch, 551, 570
animal (glycogen), 570
composition of, 570
cornstarch, 565
hydrolysis, 570
in insoluble granules, 570
plant, 570
Starches, 248
Start codon, 772
States of matter Three forms of matter: solid, liquid, and gas, 67–69. See Changes of state
gas, 67
liquid, 67
solid, 67
Steam burns, 86
Stearic acid, 469
β oxidation and, 865
Steel, 64, 76, 163, 326
Stereoisomer Isomers that have atoms bonded in the same order, but with different arrangements in space, 531
amino acid, 693
Fischer projections, 534–535
Steroid hormone, 636
Steroids Types of lipids that are composed of a multicyclic ring system, 632–637
Stimulant
caffeine, 662
central nervous system, 662
nicotine, 662
Stomach acid, 422
Stomach pH, 730
STP Standard conditions of exactly 0 °C (273 K) temperature and 1 atm pressure used for the comparison of gases, 306–307
Straight-chain polymer. See Amylose
Streetlight, sodium, 123
Stress, on equilibrium, 387–388
Stroke, 294
Strong acid An acid that completely ionizes in water, 406–408, 412
Strong base A base that completely ionizes in water, 409
Strong electrolyte A compound that ionizes completely when it dissolves in water. Its solution is a good conductor of electricity, 329–330
Strontium, 107
Strontium-90, 164, 167
Structural formula
condensed, 448–449, 455–456
expanded, 446
line-angle, 448–449, 455–456
Structural isomers Organic compounds in which identical molecular formulas have different arrangements of atoms, 451
Structure of atom, 111–112
Subatomic particle A particle within an atom; protons, neutrons, and electrons are subatomic particles, 111, 113
Sublevel A group of orbitals of equal energy within an energy level. The number of sublevels in each energy level is the same as the principal quantum number (n), 124
exceptions in sublevel block order, 134–135
number of electrons in, 126
using sublevel blocks to write electron configurations, 132–133
Sublimation The change of state in which a solid is transformed directly to a gas without forming a liquid first, 84–85
Subscript, in chemical formula, 190
Substance, 3
Substituent Groups of atoms such as an alkyl group or a halogen bonded to the main carbon chain or ring of carbon atoms, 451
alkanes with, 451–457
Substrate The molecule that reacts in the active site in an enzyme-catalyzed reaction, 724
concentration, 731
Subtraction
negative numbers, 11
positive numbers, 11
significant figures, 36
Succinate, 842
Succinate dehydrogenase, 842
Succinic acid, 589
Succinyl CoA, 840, 841, 842
from amino acid degradation, 887
Succinyl CoA synthetase, 842
Sucralose, 566, 567
Sucrose A disaccharide composed of glucose and fructose; a nonreducing sugar, commonly called table sugar or "sugar," 566, 574
Sudafed, 659

Sugar alcohols, 562, 567
Sugar cane, 566
Sugar–phosphate bond, 784
Sugar(s). *See* Sucrose
 in DNA and RNA, 755
 milk (lactose), 565
 reducing, 562
Sulfanilamide, 736
Sulfate, 196–197
Sulfide, 186
Sulfite, 197
Sulfur
 atomic mass of, 119
 electron configuration for, 130–131
 function of, 109
Sun, energy from, 786
Sunburn, 122
Superimposing, mirror image and, 531–532
Supersaturated solution, 335
Suprane (desflurane), 497
Surfactant, 630–631
Surgical technician, 580
Suspension A mixture in which the solute particles are large enough
  and heavy enough to settle out and be retained by both filters and
  semipermeable membranes, 352, 353
Sweeteners, 562, 565, 567
 sweetness of, 557, 562, 565–567
Symbols, 102–105
Synapse, 664
Synthesizing drugs, 663–664
Synthroid, 46
Système International (SI), 26
Systolic pressure, 294

T

Table salt, 48. *See* Sodium chloride
Table sugar, 48. *See* Sucrose
Tannic acid, 712
Tarnish, 236, 237, 260
Tartaric acid, 584
Technetium-99, 155, 160–161, 167
Teeth, 3, 108
Temperature An indicator of the hotness or coldness of an object, 69–73,
  290–291
 body, homeostasis in, 392
 body temperature, 72
 Celsius (°C) temperature scale, 28
 change, equilibrium and, 373, 375, 390, 391
 comparison of, 70
 conversion factors, 88
 enzyme activity and, 729–730
 equilibrium, effect on, 373, 375, 390, 391
 Fahrenheit (°F) temperature scale, 28, 69–70
 Kelvin (K) temperature scale, 28
 measurement, 28
 pressure and, 300–302
 reaction rate and, 374, 375
 solubility, 189, 335
 specific heat, 80–81
Temporary brachytherapy, 171
Temporary dipole, 219
Tertiary (3°) alcohol An alcohol that has three alkyl groups bonded to the
  carbon atom with the —OH group, 497
Tertiary (3°) amine, 650, 654
Tertiary structure The folding of the secondary structure of a protein into a
  compact structure that is stabilized by the interactions of residues such
  as ionic and disulfide bonds, 706–708, 716
Testing soil and water samples, 678
Testosterone, 636
Tetra-, 454
Tetrahedral structure, 214, 446
Tetrapeptide, 697
Tetrose, 553
Theoretical yield The maximum amount of product that a reaction can
  produce from a given amount of reactant, 269
Thermal pollution, 335
Thermometer, 28, 30
Thermotherapy, 71
Thiamine (vitamin B_1), 741
Thiol An organic compound that contains a thiol group (—SH), 489
 naming, 509
 oxidation, 504–505
Thomson, J. J., 111
Thoracic cavity, 296

Threonine, 691, 887
Thymine (T), 754–755
Thyroid cancer, 150
Time, measurement, 28
Tin, 108
Tincture of iodine, 325, 326
Titanium, 80, 102, 171
Titration The addition of base to an acid sample to determine the
  concentration of the acid, 425–427
Tobacco smoke, 477
Tocopherol, 743
Tollens' reagent, 525
Tollens' test A test for aldehydes in which the Ag^+ in Tollens' reagent is
  reduced to metallic silver, which forms a "silver mirror" on the walls of
  the container, 525–526
Toluene, 474
Toothpaste, 3
Torr (unit of measure), 290
Torricelli, Evangelista, 292
Toxicity of mercury, 104
Toxicology, 47–48
Toxins, inhibiting electron transport, 847
Trace elements, 108–109
Transacylase, 876
Transaminase, 882
Transamination The transfer of an amino group from an amino acid to an
  α-keto acid, 838, 882, 887
 amino acid synthesis and, 889
Transcription The transfer of genetic information from DNA by the
  formation of mRNA, 768
 regulation of, 769–770
 transcription bubble, 768
Transcription factor A protein that binds to DNA and controls transcription.
  It often binds with an activator, 770
Trans fatty acid, 622–623
Trans isomer An isomer of an alkene in which similar groups in the double
  bond are on opposite sides, 464
 alkenes, 464–465
Transition element An element located between Groups 2A (2) and 3A (3)
  on the periodic table, 105–106
Translation The interpretation of the codons in mRNA as amino acids in a
  peptide, 768–769, 771–775
 protein, 771–775
Translocation The shift of a ribosome along mRNA from one codon (three
  bases) to the next codon during translation, 774
Transmutation, 158–162
Transport, through cell membrane, 639
tri-, 454
Triacylglycerols A family of lipids composed of three fatty acids bonded
  through ester bonds to glycerol, a trihydroxy alcohol, 617–619, 642
  See Fat
 chemical properties, 621–626
 digestion of, 862–865
 fatty acid synthesis, 876–880
 fat utilization, 864
 hibernation and, 617–619
 hydrogenation, 621–623
 source of energy during hibernation, 618
 transporting to tissue, 866
Tricarboxylic acid cycle, 837. *See* Citric acid cycle
Triclosan, 3, 500
Trigonal planar, 213
Trimethylamine, 652
Trinitrotoluene (TNT), 475
Triose, 553
Triose phosphate isomerase, 811
Tripeptide, 697
Triple bond A sharing of three pairs of electrons by two atoms
 definition of, 208
 forming of, 208
Triple helix The protein structure found in collagen consisting of three helical
  polypeptide chains woven together like a braid, 704
Tristearin, 617
tRNA Transfer RNA; an RNA that places a specific amino acid into a peptide
  chain at the ribosome. There is one or more tRNA for each of the 20
  different amino acids, 766–767
 activation of, 771
 anticodons on, 772
 protein synthesis and, 771–776
Trypsin, 726, 734, 881
Trypsinogen, 734
Tryptophan, 691
 chemical structure of, 668
 converting to alanine, 887
Tumor, 170–172

Tylenol (acetaminophen), 650, 675
Type 2 diabetes, 573
Tyrosine, 691
  degradation, 887
  melanin formation and, 778
  synthesis, 890

U

Ultraviolet (UV) light, 122
Uncouplers, 849
Units of energy, 73–74
Units of measurement, 26–24
  International System of Units (SI), 26
  length, 27
  mass, 28
  metric system, 26
  temperature, 28
    Celsius (°C) temperature scale, 28
    Kelvin (K) temperature scale, 28
  time, 28
  volume, 26–28
Unsaturated fat
  hydrogenation, 469, 621–623, 622
  oxidation, 624, 642
  vegetable oil, 622–623
Unsaturated fatty acid A fatty acid that contains one or more carbon–carbon
  double bonds, which has a lower melting point than saturated fatty acids,
  and is usually liquid at room temperature, 611
  cis and trans isomers, 611
  oxidation, 642
Unsaturated hydrocarbon, 460. *See* Alkene; Alkyne
Unsaturated solution A solution that contains less solute than can be
  dissolved, 333
Uracil (U), 754–755
Uranium, 102, 153, 173
Uranium-235, 153, 172–173, 175
Uranium-238, 153, 156, 167
Urea, 353, 359, 444, 674, 891
  ammonium ion and, 884, 885
  amount excreted per day, 884
  formation of, 885, 886
  toxicity, 884
Urea cycle The process in which ammonium ions from the degradation of
  amino acids and CO_2 form carbamoyl phosphate, which is converted to
  urea, 884–886
  reactions, 886
Uremia, 674
Uric acid, 334
Uridine diphosphate (UDP), 820
Uridine triphosphate (UTP), 820
Urine
  density of, 50
  glucose in, 525
  pH of, 417
  specific gravity of, 52
U.S. system of measurement, metric–U.S. system conversion factors, 40–41

V

Vaccines, 783
Valence electrons Electrons in the highest energy level of an atom, 135, 136
Valence shell electron-pair repulsion (VSEPR) theory A theory that
  predicts the shape of a molecule by placing the electron pairs on a
  central atom as far apart as possible to minimize the mutual repulsion of
  the electrons, 213
Valine
  degradation, 887
  sickle cell anemia and, 710
Vanadium, 109
Vanilla, 341, 521
Vanillin, 475, 476
Vapor pressure The pressure exerted by the particles of vapor above a liquid,
  301–302
Variable charge, 192–193
Vaseline, 457
Vasopressin, 699
Vegetable oils, 445, 622–623
  hydrogenation of, 469
  partially hydrogenated, 469
Vegetables, waxy coatings of, 457
Venom, snake, 628
Vertical axis, on graph, 14
Very-low-density lipoprotein (VLDL), 635
Vinegar, 67, 291, 326, 582
Virus Small particles containing DNA or RNA in a protein coat that require a
  host cell for replication, 782–787

  attaching to host cell, 783
  oncogenic (cancer-causing), 786
  provirus, 783
  retrovirus, 783
  vaccines, 782
Vitamin An organic molecule that is essential for normal health and growth,
  and obtained in small amounts from the diet, 739–745
  fat-soluble, 742–743
  water-soluble, 740–741
Vitamin A, 467, 742, 743
Vitamin B, 740–741
Vitamin B_{12}, 36
Vitamin C, 41
Vitamin D, 742, 743
Vitamin E (tocopherol), 742, 743
VLDL. *See* Very-low-density lipoprotein
Volume The amount of space occupied by a substance, 290
  change, equilibrium and, 388–389, 391
  cubic centimeter for measuring, 38
  measuring, 26–28, 37–39
Volume displacement, density calculation from, 34–35
Volume percent (v/v) A percent concentration that relates the volume of the
  solute in exactly 100 mL of solution, 340–341
Von Gierke's disease, 797, 829

W

Water
  in body, 327
  dissociation of, 413–416
  freezing point of, 69–70, 87
  heat of fusion for, 82–83
  heat of vaporization for, 85–86
  osmosis, 356, 358
  solubility of gases in, 335
  as solvent, 326–327
  specific heat for, 80
Water dissociation constant expression, K_w The product of $[H_3O^+]$ and
  $[OH^-]$ in solution; $K_w = [H_3O^+][OH^-]$, 414, 415
Water-soluble vitamin A vitamin that is soluble in water; cannot be stored in
  the body; is easily destroyed by heat, ultraviolet light, and oxygen; and
  functions as a coenzyme, 740–742
Water-treatment plant, 352
Wavelength, 121–122
Wax The ester of a long-chain alcohol and a long-chain saturated fatty acid,
  617
Waxy coatings on fruits and vegetables, 457
Weak acid An acid that is poor donor of H^+ and dissociates only slightly in
  water, 406–408, 412
  dissociation constants for, 411–413
Weak base A base that is poor acceptor of H^+ and produces only a small
  number of ions in water, 409
Weak electrolyte A substance that produces only a few ions along with many
  molecules when it dissolves in water. Its solution is a weak conductor of
  electricity, 329–330
Wedge–dash model, 446
Weight, 28
Weight loss/gain, 78–79
Wine making, 818
Wöhler, Friedrich, 444
Wood, 164, 247, 248
Wood alcohol (methanol), 503
Work, 73

X

X-rays, 51, 122, 164, 171, 337
Xylitol, 562, 567
Xylose, 562

Y

Yeast fermentation, 818
Yogurt, 712
Yttrium-90, 158

Z

Zinc, 64–65, 193, 244, 245, 249, 250
  density of, 50
  function of, 109
  recommended daily amount of, 36
Zinc ion (cofactor), 739–740
Zwitterion The ionized form of an amino acid at its pI that has an ammonium
  group ($-NH_3^+$) and a carboxylate group ($-COO^-$), 690
Zymogen An inactive form of an enzyme that is activated by removing a
  peptide portion from one end of the protein, 733–735

Metric and SI Units and Some Useful Conversion Factors

Length	SI Unit Meter (m)	Volume	SI Unit Cubic Meter (m³)	Mass	SI Unit Kilogram (kg)
1 meter (m) = 100 centimeters (cm)		1 liter (L) = 1000 milliliters (mL)		1 kilogram (kg) = 1000 grams (g)	
1 meter (m) = 1000 millimeters (mm)		1 mL = 1 cm³		1 g = 1000 milligrams (mg)	
1 cm = 10 mm		1 L = 1.06 quart (qt)		1 kg = 2.20 lb	
1 kilometer (km) = 0.621 mile (mi)		1 qt = 946 mL		1 lb = 454 g	
1 inch (in.) = 2.54 cm (exact)				1 mole = 6.02×10^{23} particles	
				Water	
				density = 1.00 g/mL (at 4 °C)	

Temperature	SI Unit Kelvin (K)	Pressure	SI Unit Pascal (Pa)	Energy	SI Unit Joule (J)
$T_F = 1.8(T_C) + 32$		1 atm = 760 mmHg		1 calorie (cal) = 4.184 J (exact)	
$T_C = \dfrac{T_F - 32}{1.8}$		1 atm = 101.325 kPa		1 kcal = 1000 cal	
$T_K = T_C + 273$		1 atm = 760 torr			
		1 mole of gas = 22.4 L (STP)		**Water**	
		$R = 0.0821$ L·atm/mole·K		Heat of fusion = 334 J/g; 80. cal/g	
		$R = 62.4$ mmHg·atm/mole·K		Heat of vaporization = 2260 J/g; 540 cal/g	
				Specific heat (SH) = 4.184 J/g °C; 1.00 cal/g °C	

Metric and SI Prefixes

Prefix	Symbol	Scientific Notation
Prefixes That Increase the Size of the Unit		
peta	P	10^{15}
tera	T	10^{12}
giga	G	10^{9}
mega	M	10^{6}
kilo	k	10^{3}
Prefixes That Decrease the Size of the Unit		
deci	d	10^{-1}
centi	c	10^{-2}
milli	m	10^{-3}
micro	μ (mc)	10^{-6}
nano	n	10^{-9}
pico	p	10^{-12}
femto	f	10^{-15}

Formulas and Molar Masses of Some Typical Compounds

Name	Formula	Molar Mass (g/mole)	Name	Formula	Molar Mass (g/mole)
Ammonia	NH_3	17.03	Hydrogen chloride	HCl	36.46
Ammonium chloride	NH_4Cl	53.49	Iron(III) oxide	Fe_2O_3	159.70
Ammonium sulfate	$(NH_4)_2SO_4$	132.15	Magnesium oxide	MgO	40.31
Bromine	Br_2	159.80	Methane	CH_4	16.04
Butane	C_4H_{10}	58.12	Nitrogen	N_2	28.02
Calcium carbonate	$CaCO_3$	100.09	Oxygen	O_2	32.00
Calcium chloride	$CaCl_2$	110.98	Potassium carbonate	K_2CO_3	138.21
Calcium hydroxide	$Ca(OH)_2$	74.10	Potassium nitrate	KNO_3	101.11
Calcium oxide	CaO	56.08	Propane	C_3H_8	44.09
Carbon dioxide	CO_2	44.01	Sodium chloride	NaCl	58.44
Chlorine	Cl_2	70.90	Sodium hydroxide	NaOH	40.00
Copper(II) sulfide	CuS	95.62	Sulfur trioxide	SO_3	80.07
Hydrogen	H_2	2.016	Water	H_2O	18.02